FINANCIAL SERVICES LAW

FINANCIAL SERVICES LAW

THIRD EDITION

Edited by
George Walker
Robert Purves

Consultant Editor
Michael Blair QC

OXFORD
UNIVERSITY PRESS

OXFORD
UNIVERSITY PRESS

Great Clarendon Street, Oxford, OX2 6DP,
United Kingdom

Oxford University Press is a department of the University of Oxford. It furthers the University's objective of excellence in research, scholarship, and education by publishing worldwide. Oxford is a registered trade mark of Oxford University Press in the UK and in certain other countries

First Edition published in 2009
Third Edition published in 2014

Impression: 1

Published in the United States of America by Oxford University Press
198 Madison Avenue, New York, NY 10016, United States of America

British Library Cataloguing in Publication Data
Data available

Library of Congress Control Number: 2014933291

ISBN 978–0–19–968559–2

Printed and bound by
CPI Group (UK) Ltd, Croydon, CR0 4YY

CONTENTS—SUMMARY

CONTENTS

TABLE OF CASES

Note: Financial Services Authority and Financial Ombudsman Service are tabled as FSA and FOS

TABLE OF UK LEGISLATION

BILLS

OTHER NATIONAL LEGISLATION

Bahrain Legislation

Dubai Legislation

France Legislation

Malaysia Legislation

Qatar Legislation

Saudi Arabia Legislation

United Arab Emirates Legislation

US Legislation

TABLE OF EUROPEAN LEGISLATION

PRIMARY LEGISLATION

SECONDARY LEGISLATION

Decisions

Directives

Recommendations

Regulations

TABLE OF UK SECONDARY LEGISLATION

TABLE OF TREATIES AND CONVENTIONS

LIST OF ABBREVIATIONS

1MLD	First Money Laundering Directive (Directive 91/308/EEC [1991] OJ L166/77)
2MLD	Second Money Laundering Directive (Directive 2001/97/EC [2001] OJ L344/76)
3MLD	Third Money Laundering Directive (Directive 2005/60/EC [2005] OJ L309/15)
3NLD	The Three Non-life Directives/the 3rd Non-life Directive
AAOIFI	Accounting and Auditing Organisation for Islamic Financial Institutions
ABI	Association of British Insurers
ABCP	asset-backed commercial paper
ABTA	Association of British Travel Agents
ACD	authorised corporate director
ACPO	Association of Chief Police Officers of England & Wales
AFIB	Alternative Finance Investment bond
AFTA	ASEAN Free Trade Area
AICPA	American Institute of Certified Public Accountants
AIFM	Alternative Investment Fund Manager
AIFMD	Alternative Investment Fund Managers Directive
AIG	American International Group
[AIG]	[Accord Implementation Group]
AIM	Alternative Investment Market
AISG	Accountants International Study Group
AMA	advanced measurement approach
AMF	Autorité des Marchés Financiers
AML	anti-money laundering
APEC	Asia Pacific Economic Cooperation
APER	Statements of Principle and Code of Practice for Approved Persons
APF	Asset Purchase Facility
APG	Asia/Pacific Group on Money Laundering
ARA	Assets Recovery Agency
ARROW	Advanced Risk-Responsive Operating Framework
ASEAN	Association of Southeast Asian Nations
ASIC	Australian Securities and Investment Commission
AUT	Authorised Unit Trust
AUTH	Authorisation Manual
BA 2009	Banking Act 2009
BAC	Banking Advisory Committee
BACS	Banker's Automated Clearing Services
BAFTA	Baltic Free-Trade Area
BAP	Bank Administration Procedure
BANGKOK	Bangkok Agreement

BBA	British Banker's Association
BCBS	Basel Committee on Banking Supervision
BCCI	Bank of Credit and Commerce International
BCD	Directive (EC) 2006/48 relating to the taking up and pursuit of the business of credit institutions
BCOBS	Banking: Conducts of Business Sourcebook
BCRR	base capital resources requirement
BCSB	Banking Code Standards Board
BEA	Bank of England Act
BEAPFF	Bank of England Asset Purchase Facility Fund Ltd
BENCH	General Guidance on Benchmark Submission and Administration
BERR	Department for Business, Enterprise & Regulatory Reform
BIBA	British Insurance Broker's Association
BIFCOM	Banks and Investment Firms Commodity Standing Group
BIP	Bank Insolvency Procedure
BIPRU	Prudential Sourcebook for Banks, Building Societies and Investment Firms
BIS	Bank for International Settlements
BNM	Bank Negrasa Malaysia
BRAP	Better Regulation Action Plan
BRE	Better Regulation Executive
BSOC	Building Societies Regulatory Guide
BSOCS	Building Societies Sourcebook
BSOG	Building Societies Regulatory Guide
CACM	Central American Common Market
CAD I	Capital Adequacy Directive 1993
CAD II	Capital Adequacy Directive 1998
CAMEL	capital, assets, management, earnings, and liquidity
CAN	Andean Community
CAR	Capital Adequacy Ration
CARD	Consolidated Admissions and Reporting Directive
CARICOM	Caribbean Community
CASS	Client Assets Sourcebook
CBB	Central Bank of Bahrain
CBO	collaterised bond obligations
CBSG	Covered Bond Standing Group
CCB	countercyclical capital buffer
CCBS	Centre for Central Banking Studies
CCP	Central Counterparty
CDCF	Community Development Carbon Fund
CDD	customer due diligence
CDO	collateralised debt obligations
CEBS	Committee of European Banking Supervisors
CEFTA	Central European Free Trade Agreement
CEIOPS	Committee of European Insurance and Occupational Pension Supervisors
CEMAC	Economic and Monetary Community of Central Africa
CEO	Chief Executive Officer

CER	Closer Trade Relations Trade Agreement
CESL	Common European Sales Law
CESR	Committee of European Securities Regulators
CET1	Core Equity Tier 1
CFATF	Caribbean Financial Action Task Force
CFD	contract for differences
CFEB	Consumer Financial Education Body
CFS	Council for Financial Stability
CFSP	Common Foreign and Security Policy
CFTC	Commodities Futures Trading Commission
CGAP	Consultative Group to Assist the Poor
CGFS	Committee on the Global Financial System
CGIAR	Consultative Group on International Agricultural Research
CGMO	Central Gilts & Moneymarkets Office
CGSG	Capital and Groups Standing Group
CHAPS	Clearing House Automated Payment System
CICA	Canadian Institute of Chartered Accountants
CIDD	combined initial disclosure document
CIS	collective investment scheme
CIS	Commonwealth of Independent States
CIU	collective investment undertakings
CJA	Criminal Justice Act 1993
CJEU	Court of Justice of the European Union
CLC	Council for Licensed Conveyancers
CLD	Consolidated Life Directive
CLN	credit-linked note
CLS	Continuous Linked Settlement
CMA	Competition and Markets Authority
CMG	Crisis Management Group
CMR	Client Money Rules contained in the Client Money Sourcebook
CNCOM	concentration risk capital component
COAF	Complaints against the FSA
COBS	Conduct of Business Sourcebook
COLLG	Collective Investment Scheme Information Guide
COM	controls, organisation, and management
COMC	Code of Market Conduct
COMESA	Common Market for Eastern and Southern Africa
COMP	Compensation Sourcebook
COMSG	Commodity Standing Group
COND	Threshold Conditions Sourcebook
CONRED	Consumer Redress Schemes Sourcebook
COPFS	Crown Office and Procurator Fiscal Service
COREPER	Committee of Permanent Representatives
CPI	Consumer Prices Index
CPMA	Consumer Protection and Markets Authority
CPS	Crown Prosecution Service
CPSS	Committee on Payment and Settlement Systems

CR	capital resources
CRA	credit rating agency
CRAG	Credit Rating Agencies Guide
CRD	Capital Requirements Directive
CRED	Credit Unions Sourcebook
CRM	credit risk mitigation
CRMSG	Credit Risk Mitigation Standing Group
CRR	capital resources requirement
CRSG	Credit Risk Standing Group
CSD	central securities depositories
CSDR	Central Securities Depository Regulation
CSS	Securities Settlement System
CTFs	child trust funds
CTI	connected travel insurance
CTS	Council for Trade in Services
CTSA	Consumer and Trading Standards Agency
DDA	Doha Development Agenda
DEC	Decision Making Manual
DEPP	Decision Procedure and Penalties Manual
DFSA	Dubai Financial Services Authority
DGD	Deposit Guarantee Directive
DGSD	Deposit Guarantee Scheme Directive
DIFC	Dubai International Financial Centre
DISP	Dispute Resolution: Complaints Sourcebook
DMD	Distance Marketing Directive (Council Directive 02/65/EC on distance marketing of consumer financial services [2002] OJ L271/16)
DMO	Debt Management Office
DoJ	Department of Justice
DPP	Director of Public Prosecutions
DR	disclosure rules
DR–CAFTA	Dominican Republic–Central America Free Trade Agreement
DRT	Disclosure Rules and Transparency Rules
DSB	Disputes Settlement Board
DSU	Understanding on Rules and Procedures Governing the Settlement of Disputes
DTI	Department of Trade and Industry
DTR	Disclosure and Transparency Rules
DVP	delivery versus payment
DWF	Discount Window Facility
EAD	exposure at default
EAG	Eurasian Group
EBA	European Banking Authority
EBC	European Banking Committee
EC	European Commission
ECA	European Communities Act

ECAI	external credit assessment institution
ECB	European Central Bank
ECB TARGET	Trans-European Automated Real-time Gross Settlement Express Transfer system
ECBS	European Committee of Banking Supervisors
ECD	Electronic Commerce Directive (Directive 2000/31/EC [2000] OJ L178/1)
ECHR	European Convention on Human Rights
ECJ	European Court of Justice
ECO	Electronic Commerce Directive Sourcebook
ECOFIN	Economic and Financial Affairs Council (EU)
ECON	European Committee on Economic and Monetary Affairs
ECRGI	Enhanced capital requirement for general insurance
ECRLT	Enhanced Capital Requirement for long-term business
ECtHR	European Court of Human Rights
ECTR	Extended Collateral Term Repo
EEA	European Economic Area
EEC	European Economic Community
EFSF	European Financial Stability Facility
EG	Enforcement Guide
EGMONT	Egmont Group of Financial Intelligence Units
EIOPA	European Insurance and Occupational Pensions Authority
EIOPC	European Insurance and Occupational Pensions Committee
EIR	European Insolvency Regulation
ELA	Emergency Liquidity Assistance
ELAS	Equitable Life Assurance Society Limited
ELM	Electronic Money Sourcebook
EMEAP	Executive's Meeting of East Asia and Pacific Central Banks
EMIR	European Market Infrastructure Regulation
EMPS	Energy Market Participants
ENF	Enforcement Manual
EPU	European Payments Union
ESAs	European Supervisory Authorities
ESM	European Stability Mechanism
ESMA	European Securities and Markets Authority
ESAAMLG	Eastern and Southern Africa Anti-Money Laundering Group
ESC	European Securities Committee
ESME	European Securities Markets Expert Group
EU	European Union
EVRF	Enhanced Variable Rate Fund
EZPUT	Enterprise Zone Property Unit Trust
FAF	Financial Accounting Foundation
FAO	Food and Agriculture Organisation
FASAC	Financial Accounting Standards Council
FASB	Financial Accounting Standards Board
FATF	Financial Action Task Force

FBD	First Banking Directive (EEC) 77/780 on the coordination of laws, regulations and administrative provisions relating to the taking up and pursuit of the business of credit institutions
FCA	Financial Conduct Authority
FC	Financial Crime Guide
FCD	Financial Conglomerates Directive (EC) 02/87 on the supplementary supervision of credit institutions, insurance undertakings and investment firms in a financial conglomerate
FDIC	Federal Deposit Insurance Corporation
FEES	Fees Manual
FESCO	Federation of European Securities Commissions
FGD	Financial Groups Directive (EC) 02/87 on the supplementary supervision of credit institutions, insurance undertakings and investment firms in a financial conglomerate
FHC	financial holding company
FIMBRA	Financial Intermediaries and Brokers Regulatory Association
FINMAR	Financial Stability and Market Confidence Sourcebook
FLS	Funding for Lending Scheme
FPC	Financial Policy Committee
FSB	Financial Stability Board
FSC	Financial Stability Committee
FISMOU	financial information sharing agreements
FIT	fit and proper test for approved persons
FIU	financial intelligence unit
FMI	Financial Market Infrastructure
FMRF	Financial Management Reporting Framework
FOS	Financial Ombudsman Service
FPC	Financial Policy Committee
FPO	Financial Services and Markets Act 2000 (Financial Promotion) Order 2005 (SI 2005/1529)
FPRU	Friendly Societies Prudential Sourcebook
FREN	small friendly societies
FSA	Financial Services Authority
FSA 1986	Financial Services Act 1986
FSA 2010	Financial Services Act 2010
FSA 2012	Financial Services Act 2012
FSA Handbook	FSA Handbook of rules and regulations
FSAP	Financial Services Action Plan
FSAVC	free standing additional voluntary contributions
FSB	Financial Stability Board
FS(BR)	Financial Services (Banking Reform)
FSCS	Financial Services Compensation Scheme
FSF	Financial Stability Forum
FSI	Financial Stability Institute
FSMA	Financial Services and Markets Act 2000
FSMT	Financial Services and Markets Tribunal
FTAA	Free Trade Area of the Americas

FUND	Investment Funds Sourcebook
GAAP	generally accepted accounting principles
GAB	general arrangements to borrow
GABRIEL	Gathering Better Regulatory Information Electronically
GAFISUD	Financial Action Task Force on Money Laundering in South America
GASB	Government Accounting Standards Board
GATS	General Agreement on Trade in Services
GATT	General Agreement on Tariffs and Trade
GCC	Gulf Co-operation Council
GCR	group capital resources
GCRR	group capital resources requirement
GDR	Global depository receipts
GEN	General Provisions Sourcebook
GENPRU	General Prudential Sourcebook
GICR	general insurance capital requirement
GIGI	Insurance Intermediaries
GISC	General Insurance Standards Council
GSEs	Government Sponsored Entities
GSIFI	Global Systemically Important Financial Institution
HBOS	Halifax Bank of Scotland
HIPC	Heavily Indebted Poor Countries
HPP	home purchase plan
HRA	Human Rights Act
IAA	internal assessment approach
IADI	International Association of Deposit Insurers
IAIS	International Association of Insurance Supervisors
IAS	International Accounting Standards
IASB	International Accounting Standards Board
IASC	International Accounting Standards Committee
IBAs	insurance bank accounts
IBB	Islamic Bank of Britain
IBRA	Insurance Brokers (Registration) Act 1997
IBRC	Insurance Brokers Registration Council
IBRD	International Bank for Reconstruction and Development
ICA	individual capital assessment
ICA	Insurance Companies Act 1982
ICAAP	Internal Capital Adequacy Assessment Process
ICAEW	Institute of Chartered Accountants in England and Wales
ICB	Independent Commission on Banking
ICC	International Coordination Committee
ICD	Investor Compensation Directive
ICG	individual capital guidance
ICMA	International Capital Market Association
ICOB	Insurance: Conduct of Business Sourcebook

ICSID	International Centre for Settlement of Investment Disputes
ICTA	Income and Corporation Taxes Act 1988
ICVC	investment company with variable capital
IDA	International Development Association
IDD	initial disclosure document
IDD	Insider Dealing Directive (EEC) 89/592
IDO	Insider Dealing (Securities and Regulated Markets) Order 1994
IETA	International Emissions Trading Association
IFAs	independent financial advisers
IFC	International Finance Corporation
IFF	Islamic Finance Firm
IFRS	international financial reporting standards
IFSB	Islamic Financial Services Board
IFSB (CAS)	IFSB Capital Adequacy Standard for Institutions (Other than Insurance Institutions) Offering Only Islamic Financial Services, 2005
IFSB PTMDS	Disclosures to Promote Transparency and Market Discipline for Institutions Offering Islamic Financial Services, 2007
IGD	Insurance Groups Directive (Council Directive (EC) 98/78 on the supplementary supervision of insurance undertakings in an insurance group (1998) OJ L330)
IIB	Institute of Insurance Brokers
ILTR	Indexed Long-Term Repos
IMD	Insurance Mediation Directive (Council Directive (EC) 02/92 on insurance mediation (2002) OJ L9/3)
IMF	International Monetary Fund
IMFC	International Monetary and Financial Committee
IMRO	Investment Management Regulatory Organisation
INSPRU	Prudential Sourcebook for Insurers
INVPRU	Prudential Sourcebook for Investment Business
IOB	Insurance Ombudsman Bureau
IOSCO	International Organisation of Securities Commissions
IOSCO MOU	Multilateral Memorandum Concerning Consultation and Cooperation and the Exchange of Information
IPMA	International Primary Market Association (merged with ISMA on 1 July 2005 to form ICMA)
IPO	initial public offering
IPRU(BANK)	Interim Prudential Sourcebook for banks
IPRU(BSOC)	Interim Prudential Sourcebook for building societies
IPRU(FSOC)	Interim Prudential Sourcebook for friendly societies
IPRU(INS)	Interim Prudential Sourcebook for insurers
IPRU(INV)	Interim Prudential Sourcebook for investment and securities firms
IRB	internal ratings based approaches
IRHP	Interest Hedging Product
IRR	integrated regulatory reporting
IRSA	interest rate swap agreements
ISA	individual savings account

ISD	Investment Services Directive (EEC) 22/93 on investment services in the securities field
ISDA	International Swaps and Derivatives Association
ISMA	International Securities Market Association (merged with IPMA on 1 July 2005 to form ICMA)
ISPRU	Prudential Sourcebook for insurers
ISPV	insurance special purpose vehicle
ISSRO	international securities self-regulating organisation
ITC	International Trade Centre
JAC	Joint Associations Committee
JHA	Justice and Home Affairs
JMLSG	Joint Money Laundering Steering Group
KID	key information document
KII	Key investor information
KYC	know your customer
LAAC	Listing Authority Advisory Committee
LARC	Listing Authority Review Committee
LAUTRO	Life Assurance and Unit Trust Regulatory Organisation
LBG	Lloyds Banking Group
LCR	Liquidity Coverage Ration
LECB	large exposures capital base
LGD	loss given default
LIBA	London Investment Banking Association
LIBOR	London Inter-Bank Offered Rates
LLD	Lloyd's Sourcebook
Lloyd's	Lloyd's of London
LLP	limited liability partnership
LLR	lender of last resort
LM	liquidity mismatch
LMBC	London Market Insurance Broker's Committee
LR	Listing Rules
LS	sterling stock liquidity
LSF	Loi de Sécurité Financière
LTI	loan-to-income
LTICR	long-term insurance capital requirement
LTV	loan-to-value
M&GI	Mortgage and General Insurance
MAD	Market Abuse Directive (EC) 2003/6
MAR	Market Conduct Sourcebook
MARD	Making A Real Difference
MCOB	Mortgage advice and arranging: Conduct of Business Sourcebook
MCR	minimum capital requirement

MEAFs	mortgage exit administration fees
MENAFATF	Middle East and North Africa Financial Action Task Force
MGF	Minimum Guarantee Fund
MiFID	Markets in Financial Instruments Directive (Council Directive (EC) 39/2004 on markets in financial instruments)
MIG	Guide for Small Mortgage and Insurance Intermediaries
MIGA	Multilateral Investment Guarantee Agency
MIGI	Small Mortgage and Insurance Intermediaries General Rules
MIPRU	Prudential Sourcebook for Mortgage and Home Finance Firm and Insurance Intermediaries/the prudential requirements for mortgage and home finance firms and insurance intermediaries
ML	Money Laundering Sourcebook
MLD	Money Laundering Directive
MLRO	money laundering reporting officer
MMR	Mortgage Market Review
MOGI	Mortgage Intermediaries General Rules
MONEYVAL	Council of Europe Select Committee of Experts on the Evaluation of Anti-Money Laundering Measures
MOU	Memoranda/Memorandum of Understanding
MPBR	more principles-based regulation
MPC	Monetary Policy Committee
MRTSG	Market Risk and Trading Books Standing Group
MTF	multi-lateral trading facility
MTM	mark-to-market
N1	1 June 1998
N2	1 December 2001—ie the date on which FSA assumed its powers under the Financial Services and Markets Act 2000
N3	October 2004 and January 2005
NAB	new arrangements to borrow
NAFTA	North American Free Trade Agreement
NAO	National Audit Office
NATO	North Atlantic Treaty Organisation
NCCT	Non-co-operative Countries and Territories
NCIS	National Criminal Intelligence Service
NCS	Note Circulation Scheme
NEP	Note Exchange Programme
NewRO	New Regulatory Organisation
NLD	Non-Life Directive
NGI	14 January 2005—ie the date on which FSA started to regulate the sale and administration of general insurance and pure protection products
NSRF	Net Table Funding Ratio
NURSs	non-UCITS retail schemes
OBR	Office for Budget Responsibility
OECD	Organization for Economic Co-operation and Development

OEEC	Organization for European Economic Cooperation
OEIC	open-ended investment companies
OFAR	overall financial adequacy rule
OFT	Office of Fair Trading
OMO	open market operation
OMPS	Oil Market Participants
OPR	outcome performance report
ORA	Ongoing Regulatory Activities
ORCR	operational risk capital requirement
ORD	Own Funds Directive
ORSA	own risk and solvency assessment
ORSG	Operational Risk Standing Group
OSF	Operational Standing Facilities
OTC	over the counter
PBR	principles-based regulation
PCAOB	Public Companies Accounting Oversight Board
PCBS	Parliamentary Commission on Banking Standards
PD	Prospectus Directive (EC) 2003/71
PD	probability of default
PDMR	person discharging managerial responsibility
PEP	politically exposed persons
PEP	private equity plan
PERG	Perimeter Guidance Manual
PFA	Prevention of Fraud (Investments) Act 1939
PFE	potential future exposure
PIA	Personal Investment Authority
PIF	Proactive Intervention Framework
PII	Professional Indemnity Insurance
PMI	private medical insurance
PMO	Financial Services and Markets Act 2000 (Prescribed Markets and Qualifying Investments) Order 2001
PoCA	Proceeds of Crime Act 2002
POSR	The Public Offers of Securities Regulations 1995 (SI 1995/1537)
PPA	Policyholders Protection Act 1975
PPFM	principles and practices of financial management
PPI	payment protection insurance
PPS	Public Prosecution Service (Northern Ireland)
PR	prospectus rules
PRA	Prudential Regulatory Authority
PRA	(position risk addition)
PRIN	Principles for Businesses Sourcebook
PRIPS	packaged retail investment products
PROF	Professional Firms Sourcebook
PRU	Integrated Prudential Sourcebook
PSD	Payment Services Directive

PSIA profit sharing investment account
PSM professional securities market
PTSG Pillar Two Standing Group

QCS qualitative consolidated supervision
QFCRA Qatar Financial Centre Regulatory Authority
QIS qualified investor scheme/quantitative impact studies
QMV Qualified Majority Voting

RAO The Financial Services and Markets Act 2000 (Regulated Activities) Order 2001 (SI 2001/544)
RATE Risk Assessment, Tools of Supervision, Evaluation
RBA ratings-based approach
RCB regulated covered bonds
RCH Recognised Clearing House
RCR resilience capital requirement
RDC Regulatory Decisions Committee
RDIP Retail Distribution Implementation Programme
RDR Retail Distribution Review
REC Recognised Investment Exchanges and Clearing Houses Sourcebook
REMIT Regulation on Energy Market Integrity and Transparency
RID Council Directive (EC) 05/68 on reinsurance
RINGA relevant information not generally available
RIS regulatory information service
RMAR retail mediation activities return
RMM required minimum margin
RMP risk mitigation programme
ROCH Recognised Overseas Clearing House
RPB recognised professional body
RPI Retail Prices Index
RPPD responsibilities of providers and distributors for the fair treatment of customers
RRD Recovery and Resolution Directive
RRP Recovery and Resolution Plans
RTGS Real Time Gross Settlement
RTO reception and transmission of orders

SBD Second Banking Directive (EEC) 89/646 on the co-ordination of laws, regulations and administrative provisions relating to the taking up and pursuit of the business of credit institutions
SCR solvency capital requirement
SD securitised derivative
SDR special drawing rights
SE Securities Exchange
SEA Single European Act
SEC US Securities and Exchange Commission
SEP Supervisory Enhancement Programme
SEPA Single Euro Payments Area

SERV	service companies
SETS	The LSE order book for the most liquid equities
SF	supervisory formula
SFA	Securities and Futures Authority
SFO	Serious Fraud Office
SFT	securities financing transaction
SIB	Securities and Investments Board
SIFA	small IFA firms
SIFMA	Securities Industry and Financial Markets Association
SIPP	self invested personal pension scheme
SIPS	systemically important payment systems
SIV	structured investment vehicles
SLS	special liquidity scheme
SLS	special lending scheme
SME	Small and Medium-sized Enterprise
SOCA	Serious Organised Crime Authority
SOCPA	Serious Organised Crime and Police Act 2005
SPE	special purpose entity
SPP	Security and Prosperity Partnership of North America
SPU	Special Resolution Unit
SPV	special purpose vehicle
SRD	Solvency Ratio Directive
SREP	supervisory review and evaluation process
SRM	Single Resolution Mechanism
SRP	supervisory review process
SRO	self regulating organization
SROCC	SRO Consultative Committee
SRR	special resolution regime
SRU	Special Resolution Unit
SSB	*Shari'a* Supervisory Board
SSG	Securitisation Standing Group
SSM	Single Supervisory Mechanism
SSS	securities settlements systems
STR	suspicious transaction report
SUP	supervision manual
SVRF	Standard Variable Rate Fund
SWIFT	Society for Worldwide Interbank Financial Telecommunication
SYSC	Senior Management Arrangements, Systems and Controls Sourcebook
TA	Terrorism Act 2000
TAF	term auction facility
TARGET	Trans-European Automated Real-time Gross Settlement Express Transfer system
TARP	Troubled Asset Recovery Programme
TC	training and competence
TCF	treating customers fairly
TD	Transparency Directive (EC) 2004/109

TEU	Treaty on European Union
Third Parties Act	Contracts (Rights of Third Parties) Act 1999
TOBA	Terms of Business Agreement
Training & Competence	Interim Prudential Sourcebook for training and competence
TCF	Treating Customers Fairly
TPP	Trans-Pacific Partnership
TRIPS	Agreement on Trade-Related Aspects of Intellectual Property Rights
TRs	Trade Repositories
TSLF	Term Securities Lending Facility
T-TIP	Transatlantic Trade and Investment Partnership
UCITS	undertakings for collective investment in transferable securities
UCPD	Unfair Commercial Practices Directive
UCTD	Unfair Contract Terms Directive
UK	United Kingdom
UKAR	UK Asset Resolution
UKFI	UK Financial Investments
UKLA	UK Listing Authority
UNCTAD	United Nations Conference on Trade and Development
UNDP	United Nations Development Programme
UNFCOG	The Unfair Contract Terms Regulatory Guide
UNIDROIT	International Institution for the Unification of Private Law
UPRU	Prudential Sourcebook for UCITS firms
US	United States of America
UTCCR	Unfair Terms in Consumer Contacts Regulations
VAR	value at risk
WaMu	Washington Mutual
WIG	wider integrated group
WTO	World Trade Organisation
WUD	Winding-up of Credit Institutions Directive
ZIFA	Zurich IFA Ltd

EDITORS AND CONTRIBUTORS

EDITORS

Professor George Walker
Centre for Commercial Law Studies

Dr Robert Purves
3 Verulam Buildings

Michael Blair QC
Consultant Editor
3 Verulam Buildings

CONTRIBUTORS

James Darbyshire
Financial Services Compensation Scheme

Richard Everett
Lawrence Graham LLP

Simon Gleeson
Clifford Chance

Dr Andrew Henderson
Eversheds LLP

Jonathan Herbst
Norton Rose Fulbright LLP

Laura Hodgson
Norton Rose Fulbright LLP

Noleen John
Norton Rose Fulbright LLP

Matt Jones
Norton Rose Fulbright LLP

Etay Katz
Allen & Overy LLP

Paul Kennedy
Financial Reporting Council

Alex Kuczynski
Financial Services Compensation Scheme

Professor Eva Lomnicka
Four New Square and King's College London

Julia Machin
Clifford Chance

Professor Gerard McMeel
University of Manchester, Guildhall Chambers and Quadrant Chambers

Jonathan Melrose
Simmons & Simmons LLP

Peter Parker
Financial Conduct Authority

Maria Ross
Norton Rose Fulbright LLP

Deborah A Sabalot
Solicitor, Professional Associate, Outer Temple Chambers, London

Richard Sims
Simmons & Simmons LLP

Peter Snowdon
Norton Rose Fulbright LLP

Jane Welch
British Institute of International and Comparative Law

INTRODUCTION

The Second Edition of this book was published in 2008, in the immediate aftermath of the global financial crisis beginning in 2007 and escalating into 2008. This was a difficult and challenging period and we attempted to record the principal initial changes that were taking place at that time, especially the emerging proposal to construct a new regulatory landscape within the UK, as well as change at the EU and International levels. Since then, that proposal has been brought into effect, and even more fundamental changes have been brought forward in the new post-crisis climate, from 2009 to date, which are covered in this the Third Edition.

UK reform started with a series of changes specific to the risks in the banking sector itself, and to the resolution of problems caused by those risks. These include in particular the Banking Act 2009 and the Financial Services Act 2010.

Thereafter, the drive for reform has principally been institutional in shape and content following the change of Government in May 2010. This most significantly involved the replacement of the Financial Services Authority ('FSA') with the Prudential Regulation Authority ('PRA') and Financial Conduct Authority ('FCA'). The PRA is now responsible for prudential regulation of banks, insurance companies and any designated systemic securities firms while the FCA manages the prudential regulation of other, non-systemic, firms and the conduct regulation of all firms. While the FCA has been set up on a fully independent basis with effect from 1 April 2013, the PRA has been established as a subsidiary of the Bank of England to allow the Bank to be indirectly involved in the day to day oversight of banks, insurance companies and securities firms of systemic importance, as well as looking directly after payment systems and market infrastructure.

A separate Financial Policy Committee ('FPC') has been set up within the Bank of England, replacing an earlier Financial Stability Committee ('FSC'), to monitor the build-up of financial risk more generally across the financial system, with a range of new macro-prudential tools to contain these exposures. One of the first tests of this was how the FPC would respond to the build-up of UK property prices in summer and autumn 2013. The establishment of a clear macro-prudential function within the UK, with the Bank of England at its core, has been generally welcomed, although it remains to be seen how successful the FPC will be in isolating and containing systemic pressures without damaging wider recovery and growth across the economy.

Political and regulatory attention has shifted more recently once more to focus on structural reform within the industry itself. In September 2011, the Independent Commission on Banking ('ICB') recommended 'ring fencing' of retail and small and medium size enterprise banking activity within large financial groups. This was followed in June 2013 by the Parliamentary Commission on Banking Standards, whose report sought to promote higher ethical standards and standards of banking conduct. Markets and media headlines have throughout the period under review continued to be dominated by successive scandals including those on bank charges, bank bonuses, payment protection insurance ('PPI') and interest rate swaps and most recently the London Inter-bank Offered Rate ('LIBOR') abuses.

Many of these new reforms have been systemic in content and intent although there have also been political pressures as well. Significant changes having been driven by or made in response to public and media attention and calls for higher levels of customer care and protection. This has raised difficult questions of political and social balance and choice, in addition to issues of underlying market supervision and control. Financial regulation has assumed a new complexity and sophistication, as the importance of banking and financial markets has been increasingly highlighted, and as connections have been recognised between markets and social conditions, and also between earnings and wealth aspiration and the proper needs of and care for customers. Financial conduct and financial ethics have now become almost as important as the more traditional aspects of financial services, such as bank capital and liquidity regulation and control.

EU initiatives, following the crisis, were initially more selective and unconnected, although the Commission has since constructed a substantial new reform agenda. An early opportunity has been taken to create a more centralised set of EU financial institutions. The earlier EU sector committees have now been replaced with more powerful sectoral authorities (the European Banking Authority ('EBA'), European Securities and Markets Authority ('ESMA') and European Insurance and Occupational Pensions Authority ('EIOPA')). These now function within a new overarching European structure involving the System of Financial Supervisors ('ESFS') and a separate European macro-prudential body in the shape of the European Systemic Risk Board ('ESRB').

The European Commission has for some years been concerned to secure the updating of a number of earlier key measures such as the Markets in Financial Instruments Directive ('MiFID'), the Market Abuse Directive ('MAD') and the prospectus and listing provisions. In addition, however, fresh, post-crisis, initiatives have been introduced, beginning with the Alternative Investment Fund Managers Directive (principally targeted at hedge funds and private equity fund managers) and the Credit Rating Agency ('CRA') Regulation. All of this has now been built into a much more substantial post-crisis financial reform agenda with many new measures to be set out in new, increasingly detailed and comprehensive, European regulatory handbooks.

The international agenda has been dominated by the work of the substantially enhanced and extended Financial Stability Board ('FSB') under Italian and then Canadian leadership. The Canadian chairman, Mr Mark Carney, retained the chair of the FSB on becoming the Bank of England's distinguished new Governor in the summer of 2013. The FSB has issued a substantial number of new papers in such areas as enhancing market and institutional resilience, sound compensation practices, systemically important financial institutions ('SIFIs') and global SIFIs ('GSIFIs'), crisis management and resolution, macro-prudential policy, shadow banking, enhanced disclosure and financial derivatives.

Sector reform has principally been brought forward by the Basel Committee on Banking Supervision with substantial new reform programmes also being developed by such other technical agencies as the International Organisation for Securities Commissions ('IOSCO'), the International Association of Insurance Supervisors ('IAIS'), the Joint Forum on financial conglomerates and the Committee on Payment and Settlement Systems ('CPSS'). The Basel

Committee has, in particular, drafted a new and more powerful set of core banking regulatory requirements under its Basel III agenda, with significantly higher capital requirements and new liquidity and leverage controls, and has also contributed other papers on such issues as remuneration, governance, cross-border winding-up and college supervision. Parallel sets of initiatives have been introduced by each of the other sectoral bodies. All of these international and EU reforms will ultimately have to be implemented and given regulatory force and effect in the UK.

These initiatives, whether independently advanced, or more frequently connected, are designed to increase financial market stability although the price for this may turn out to be higher financial services costs, more limited choice, less innovation and higher levels of market restriction and constraint. The task of securing an appropriate balance between market and regulatory freedom and the need for stability and proper treatment of the financial consumer is never an easy one. The true function of the authorities is to focus on correcting the causes of the last financial crisis and preventing future crises, but to do so in a way that avoids unnecessary, irrelevant or distracting regulatory obligations, burdens and costs. This always raises difficult questions of judgement, balance and choice.

This Third Edition attempts to cover all of the key developments in this area and the changing nature of the regulatory environment. The book follows the same basic structure as the previous editions although much revision has been required to reflect the pace of change over the last five years. As before, the topics of Financial Markets and Exchanges are left to the companion volume, now in its second edition (2012).

The Editors wish to thank all of the authors most sincerely for their contributions, insight and expertise. We also acknowledge the formidable publishing skills of Oxford University Press and, in particular, thank Rachel Mullaly and Laura Williamson for their energy, professionalism and support. We have been very fortunate indeed to have benefitted from the expertise and experience of such a high quality writing and publishing team. This Edition could not have appeared without them. The book was prepared as of May 2013 although some further updates were included in specific chapters before final publication where this was possible. This is an area subject to rapid and continuous change and readers must be advised to confirm the latest position in each case.

Professor George Walker,
Dr Robert Purves,
Michael Blair QC
London
September 2013

Part I

REGULATORY STRUCTURE

1

UK FINANCIAL SERVICES REFORM

Financial Services Regulation

UK financial regulation has been subject to substantial revision in recent decades. The structure of financial regulation was fundamentally revised in 2000 with the creation of a single regulatory framework, and then again in 2012 with the establishment of a new macro-prudential and split prudential and conduct institutional model. Both events followed major political shifts with appointment of a Labour Government following the General Election in May 1997, followed by the election of a Coalition Conservative–Liberal Democrat Government in May 2010. Regulatory adjustment has also been driven by continued market instability, loss, and scandal, and especially following the devastating effects of the global financial crisis beginning in autumn 2007 with the contraction in inter-bank lending markets. An initial set of regulatory reforms had been adopted in the UK by the outgoing Labour Administration before the change of Government in 2010, and then again by the new Coalition Government which followed. These changes were brought into effect in response to the massive losses and damage suffered following the global financial crisis and subsequent contagious effects within the UK banking and financial system and real economy. **1.01**

A single, integrated regulatory system had been set up for all financial sectors and activities under the Financial Services and Markets Act 2000 ('FSMA') which was managed by the single Financial Services Authority ('FSA') on a unitary basis. This reflected the increasingly integrated and complex nature of modern financial markets. Following the more recent financial crises, the abolition of the FSA was announced in 2010 and its replacement by a separate Financial Conduct Authority ('FCA') and Prudential Regulatory Authority ('PRA') which was formed as a subsidiary of the Bank of England. A Financial Policy Committee ('FPC') was also created within the Bank of England to conduct macro-prudential policy. These changes were given effect under the Financial Services Act 2012 ('FSA 2012'), which amended FSMA with other substantial changes already having been made to FSMA under the Banking Act 2009 ('BA 2009') and Financial Services Act 2010 ('FSA 2010'). The fundamentally integrated nature of the underlying prudential regulation established under FSMA has been retained, in particular, with the re-application of the earlier FSA Handbook of Rules and Guidance, although this substantive body of regulatory provision is applied under the revised institutional structure. The UK has also embraced a qualified form of market or structural regulation with the proposed ring-fencing of retail and small- and medium-sized enterprise ('SME') services under the Financial Services (Banking Reform) Act 2013. Underlying substantive integration is accordingly **1.02** supplemented by institutional separation and qualified structural delineation under the new UK regime.

1.03 A complex system of financial regulation had been set up in the UK under FSMA with the FSA replacing all of the earlier sector agencies that previously operated within the UK. The FSA was not set up under FSMA directly although the Act provided for its statutory recognition and contained a number of important constitutional directions. The FSA was a private as opposed to public corporation although it carried out public duties. FSMA defined the legal powers and functions of the FSA and established an extended support or oversight regime to ensure that it exercised its statutory authority properly and discharged its assigned duties effectively. The FSA was given specific authority to issue rules and supporting guidance under FSMA whose powers have since been transferred to the FCA and PRA. The particular regulatory obligations with which financial institutions have to comply are not set out in the Act directly but in the Handbooks of Rules and Guidance issued by the FCA and PRA under the authority conferred by the Act. This has the advantages of flexibility and speed of revision in response to rapid changes in financial markets and practices, as well as of transparency and easier and cheaper access and availability. The earlier traditional advantages of industry and practitioner involvement have nevertheless been retained through the use of consultation panels, although now within a more formal statutory framework.

1.04 The statutory duties and responsibilities of the regulatory authorities have also been extended under FSMA over time beyond more traditional prudential conduct of business matters to include consumer education, public awareness, and financial crime, in addition to market confidence. These were later extended to include financial stability under the FSA 2010 with responsibility for consumer education being transferred to a new Consumer Financial Education Body ('CFEB') which subsequently became the Mortgage Advice Service. The range and type of financial institutions for which these regulatory authorities are responsible have also been increased since the enactment of FSMA to include, in particular, mortgage advice and general insurance sales as well as personal pension schemes, travel insurance, payment services, and consumer credit. This has then created a considerably more sophisticated and complex regulatory environment than could have been anticipated even before the reform process began. Further reform has been necessitated by the continuing changes in market structure, operation, and integration as well as in supporting technological advances and in national and international competition and consequent financial growth and innovation.

1.05 The system of regulation set up under FSMA has not been static or fixed and has progressed and evolved over time. Many of the changes made have been necessitated through EU implementation. A number of the other revisions have then either been internal policy-based or scandal- or crisis-driven such as with regard to pensions mis-selling, Equitable Life, split capital investment trusts, soft commissions, and the more recent forced rescue of Northern Rock. Important policy initiatives brought forward by the FSA before its dissolution included the further move to more principles-based regulation ('MPBR'), the better regulation agenda, Handbook simplification, and other initiatives on financial capability, treating customers fairly ('TCF'), and the retail distribution review ('RDR') and enforcement reviews conducted. Creating a regulatory regime that is capable of responding to continuing changes in market conditions and market practices is a dynamic process that has to be constantly adjusted and extended over time as necessary. A number of substantial further reforms have been adopted in response to the pressures created by more recent financial crises, instability, and loss.

The objective of the most recent institutional reforms has been to strengthen the role and function of the Bank of England at the centre of the UK financial system. This was considered necessary, in particular, in light of the need to monitor and manage the financial system as a whole against the build up of any exposure that could create contagious threats and consequent systemic instability. The UK has accordingly created a central bank-based macro-prudential model initially with the Financial Stability Committee ('FSC') established under the BA 2009 and then replaced by the FPC set up under the FSA 2012. A Council for Financial Stability ('CFS') was to have been set up under the FSA 2010 in place of the earlier Tripartite Committee arrangements between HM Treasury, the Bank of England, and the FSA under the FSA 2010, although these have now been replaced by the collaboration provisions incorporated under Part 4 of the FSA 2012. The PRA is responsible for the prudential regulation of banks, building societies, credit unions, insurance firms, and designated investment firms, with the FCA regulating all other investment firms, insurance brokers, and financial advisors as well as markets and exchanges. The FCA is also responsible for the conduct regulation of all financial institutions, with firms subject to PRA prudential oversight becoming 'dual regulated'. The effect of this is to 'subsidiarise' systemic prudential regulation within the Bank, with the PRA being set up as a subsidiary of the Bank of England, and with the transfer or delegation of non-systemic functions to the FCA. It is estimated that the PRA will regulate around 1,400 financial groups with the FCA being responsible for 23,000 other firms. The Bank of England will also remain responsible for monetary policy through its Monetary Policy Committee ('MPC'), market infrastructure, including payment and settlement systems, resolution, and market liquidity, as well as macro-prudential functions through the FPC. **1.06**

A substantial number of new reforms have been or are being brought into effect at the international and European levels following the global and European financial crises. Complex new agendas have been constructed, in particular, by the Financial Stability Board ('FSB'), which replaced the earlier Financial Stability Forum (FSF) in 2009, as well as by the other international financial technical committees, such as the Basel Committee on Banking Supervision, the International Organisation of Securities Commission ('IOSCO'), the International Association of Insurance Supervisors ('IAIS'), and the Committee on the Global Financial System ('CGFS'). A complex programme of directives and regulations has also been adopted or proposed by the European Commission within the EU. **1.07**

The purpose of this chapter is to consider the regulatory background to the establishment of the integrated system of financial control set up under FSMA and its amendment, in particular, under the BA 2009, FSA 2010, and FSA 2012. The original role and function of the FSA is referred to briefly with its replacement agencies, the FCA and PRA, being outlined and then examined in further detail in subsequent chapters. The principal events surrounding the financial crisis in the UK are noted and the immediate official response explained. The further institutional and structural changes brought into effect following the change of Government after the General Election in May 2010 are reviewed. The role and function of the Bank of England under the revised regulatory structure is explained including its responsibilities in connect with monetary, macro-prudential, infrastructure, resolution, and **1.08** liquidity policy. The revised inter-agency coordination arrangements adopted and arrangements for crisis management in the UK are considered and international cooperation efforts reviewed with the new Memoranda of Understanding ('MOU') entered into under the FSA 2012.

Financial Services and Markets

1.09 The FSA was set up at its formal launch on 27 October 1997.[1] The FSA's precursor was the Securities and Investments Board ('SIB') which was responsible for the regulation of securities and investment business in the UK under the Financial Services Act 1986 ('FSA 1986'). The SIB had been set up as a private limited company to which statutory functions had been delegated by the Secretary of State under the FSA 1986. Following a series of subsequent scandals and crises in the financial services area, the Labour Government, which came into power in May 1997, announced that the earlier regulatory system operating under the 1986 Act would be abolished and a new single regulatory system established. The proposed regulatory agency was initially referred to as NewRO (for New Regulatory Organisation) until it was given the formal title, the Financial Services Authority, at its launch in October 1997.[2]

Regulatory function

1.10 The FSA was originally to be responsible for the regulation of investment services and securities markets in the UK under the FSA 1986 following its establishment in 1997. It became responsible for bank supervision following transfer of this function from the Bank of England under section 21(1) of the Bank of England Act 1998 in summer 1998 ('N1'). Assumption of responsibility for banking supervision was considered necessary following the Barings crisis in February 1995 which revealed the potential difficulty of having the Bank of England continue to be responsible for both bank supervision and monetary policy. In the event of a banking crisis, the effective discharge of the central bank's monetary policy function may be undermined or otherwise adversely affected. Following the conferral of full policy and operational autonomy in connection with monetary policy on the Bank of England in May 1997, it was decided that it was necessary to remove bank supervision to a separate regulatory agency.[3] It was then confirmed through a series of subsequent Government announcements that the FSA would become responsible for the regulation of other sectors including building societies, insurance companies, friendly societies, and Lloyd's of London. The FSA assumed formal responsibility for all financial services and markets with the coming into effect of FSMA on 1 December 2001 ('N2'). The FSA also became responsible for mortgage advice and general insurance sales in October 2004 and January 2005 ('N3'), and then personal pension schemes, travel insurance, and payment services, and an extended anti-money laundering function.[4]

---

[1] GA Walker, 'United Kingdom Regulatory Reform: A New Beginning in Policy and Programme Construction' in D Arner and J Lin, *Financial Regulation—A Guide to Structural Reform* (Sweet and Maxwell 2003) ch 7.

[2] The current Memorandum of Association of the FSA is set out in n 15.

[3] HM Treasury News Release, 'The Chancellor's Statement to the House of Commons on the Bank of England', 49/97, 20 May 1997, para 13.

[4] The commencement date for the regulation of general insurance sales on 14 January 2005 was referred to as 'GI Day'. 'A Day' was the date the new pension tax simplification rules came into effect on 6 April 2006.

Financial Services and Markets Act

FSMA was enacted on 14 June 2000 after an extended consultation period. The Chancellor of the Exchequer had originally announced on 20 May 1997 that the structure of financial regulation within the UK would be revised. The then chairman of the SIB, Sir Andrew Large, was invited to take this work forward and subsequently produced a report which was presented to the Chancellor on 29 July 1997.[5] A further report was produced at the time of the FSA's launch in October 1997 with an initial plan and budget being produced in February 1998.[6] The necessary draft legislation was produced in July 1998 in the form of a package of Consultation Papers issued by HM Treasury which included an outline Bill and Explanatory Notes. Lord Burns, former Permanent Secretary to the Treasury, was asked to chair a joint committee of both Houses of Parliament to consider a number of key aspects of the Bill during the consultation and examination process. A first report was produced on 29 April 1999 and a second on 20 May 1999. The Financial Services and Markets Bill was formally introduced to the House of Commons on 17 June 1999.[7] It went into Committee stage in July 1999 and was carried over from one Parliamentary session to the next, and began its Report stage in January 2000. The number of amendments considered was 2,750, with 1,500 being adopted during over 200 hours of Parliamentary debate. The Act finally received Royal Assent on 14 June 2000. **1.11**

Regulatory transfer

Until the coming into effect of FSMA on N2, investment services regulation continued to be carried out by the Self-Regulating Organisations ('SROs') appointed under the FSA 1986 including the Securities and Futures Authority ('SFA'), the Investment Management Regulatory Organisation ('IMRO'), and the Personal Investment Authority ('PIA') (which replaced the earlier Life Assurance and Unit Trust Regulatory Organisation ('LAUTRO')), and Financial Intermediaries and Brokers Regulatory Association ('FIMBRA'). All of these bodies were formally abolished under FSMA with the Building Societies Commission and Friendly Societies Commission, and the closure of the Insurance Department of the then Department of Trade and Industry. The Bank of England staff involved with bank supervision had been relocated to the new FSA headquarters in Canary Wharf in anticipation of the coming into effect of the Bank of England Act 1998 in June 1998. The main parts of the new regulatory regime set up under FSMA came into effect on N2 at the beginning of December 2001. This represented the key date in the creation of a single integrated regulatory system in the UK although responsibility for general insurance sales and mortgage advice would only take effect in 2004 and 2005, while construction of an integrated single prudential sourcebook would have to be postponed until the coming into effect of revised European and international capital standards in 2008 and then further revised.[8] **1.12**

---

[5] Letter from the Chancellor to Sir Andrew Large, Reform of Financial Regulation, 20 May 1997; and HM Treasury News Release, 'The Chancellor's Statement to the House of Commons on Bank of England', 49/97 (20 May 1997); and SIB, 'Report to the Chancellor on the Reform of the Financial Regulatory System' (July 1997).

[6] FSA, 'Financial Services Authority: an Outline' (October 1997); and FSA, 'Plan & Budget 1998–99' (February 1998).

[7] HM Treasury, 'Financial Services and Markets Act 2000: Regulated Activities—Second Consultation Document' (October 2000).

[8] Chapters 4, 5, and 14.

Statutory framework

1.13 FSMA established the basic framework for financial regulation within the UK. This included designation of the functions and conferral of powers on the FSA and the other main supporting agencies created including the Financial Services and Markets Tribunal ('FSMT') which was replaced by the Upper Tribunal (Tax and Chancery Chamber)[9] in April 2010, the Financial Ombudsman Service ('FOS'),[10] and the Financial Services Compensation Scheme ('FSCS').[11] The FSA has since been replaced by the FCA and PRA under the FSA 2012, with the 2012 Act also creating the FPC within the Bank of England.[12]

1.14 FSMA provides for the dual authorisation and permission regime (FSMA, sections 19 and 20) and an extended definition of regulated activities (FSMA, section 22). It contains revised restrictions on financial promotion (section 21), the creation of an extended approved persons regime (section 59), and extended measures on recognised investment exchanges and clearing houses (Part 18). The introduction of a new market abuse offence (section 118) is provided for, and a prohibition imposed in connection with misleading statements and practices (section 397). The FSA was given power to issue rules and guidance (sections 132 and 157, and now sections 137A–F, G–K, O–S, and 139A–B), and significant information-gathering and enforcement powers including the issuance of penalties or public and private censure notices as well as to apply for restitution, injunction, and bankruptcy orders (Parts 24, 25, and 27), with information and disciplinary powers being strengthened under the BA 2009, FSA 2010, and FSA 2012.[13]

1.15 FSMA contains further provisions with regard to Official Listing (under Part 6 with the FSA and then the FCA being appointed the UK Listing Authority ('UKLA')), and provisions concerning banking and insurance business transfers (Part 7). There are restated statutory provisions governing collective investment schemes (Part 17), rules concerning Lloyd's of London (Part 19), the provision of financial services by the professions (Part 20) and mutual societies (Part 21). Restated measures governing auditors and actuaries (Part 22) as well as records, disclosure, and cooperation rules (Part 23), and notices (Part 26) are also included with other miscellaneous and supplemental measures (Parts 28, 29, and 30).

Rules and guidance

1.16 The detailed regulatory rules that apply to financial institutions are not set out in FSMA as such. This would have made the statute excessively long and operationally inflexible requiring costly and protracted legislative amendment in response to even minor changes in market and financial practice. The new regulatory regime is rules-based rather than exclusively statute-based, with the FCA and PRA being granted power to issue rules and guidance (sections 137A–T and 139A–B) in accordance with a simplified adoption procedure subject to public consultation, impact assessments, and Treasury oversight. As well as securing a necessary degree of flexibility in the development of the new regulatory regime, this allows the detailed provisions to be made as transparent and easy to follow as possible. This then further assists

[9] <http://www.justice.gov.uk/tribunals/tax-and-chancery-upper-tribunal>.
[10] <http://www.financial-ombudsman.org.uk/>.
[11] <http://www.fscs.org.uk/>.
[12] Paras 1.118–1.131.
[13] ss 248–250 (permission, functions and information) BA 2009, 9–13 (disciplinary powers) FSA 2010, and s 37 and Sch 9 (discipline and enforcement) FSA 2012.

accessibility and comprehensibility, with the new measures being made available on the FCA and PRA's websites, and with a Combined Handbook also being available.[14] The Handbook Online formats make all of the relevant provisions available without the need to purchase revised statutory documentation every time a relevant amendment is agreed and adopted.

The main regulatory obligations are now set out in the Handbooks of Rules and Guidance issued by the FCA and PRA under FSMA.[15] These are made up of a number of blocks consisting of initially the Glossary and then the High Level Standards Block (including the Principles for Businesses ('PRIN'), Senior Management Arrangements, Systems and Controls ('SYSC'), Threshold Conditions ('COND'), Statements of Principle and Code of Practice for Approved Persons ('APER'), Fit and Proper Test for Approved Persons ('FIT'), Financial Stability and Market Confidence Sourcebook ('FINMAR'), Training and Competence ('TC'), General Provisions ('GEN'), and FEES Manual ('Fees'). The Prudential Standards Block consists of the General Prudential Sourcebook ('GENPRU') and the Prudential Sourcebook for Banks, Building Societies and Investment Firms ('BIPRU') which replaces the earlier interim prudential sourcebooks for banks ('IPRU(BANK)'), building societies ('IPRU(BSOC)'), and securities firms ('IPRU(INV)'). The earlier interim prudential sourcebook for insurance companies ('IPRU(INS)') has been replaced by INSPRU with a new sourcebook for UCITS firms ('UPRU') and for mortgage and home finance firms and insurance intermediaries ('MIPRU').[16] The Interim Prudential Sourcebook for Friendly Societies ('IPRU(FSOC)') has been retained within the PRA Handbook. The Business Standards have now been moved from the old Block 2 to a new Block and include the revised Conduct of Business Sourcebook ('COBS'), the Client Assets Sourcebook ('CASS'), as well as the revised Insurance Conduct of Business Sourcebook ('ICOBS'), Mortgages and Home Finance: Conduct of Business Sourcebook ('MCOB'), Banking: Conduct of Business Sourcebook ('BCOBS'), and the shortened Market Conduct Sourcebook ('MAR' without the Inter-Professional Conduct in MAR3) with Money Laundering ('ML') being removed. Training and Competence ('TC') has been moved to the the High Level Standards Block. 1.17

The Regulatory Processes Block used to consist of the Authorisation Manual ('AUTH'), the Supervision Manual ('SUP'), and the Enforcement Manual ('ENF') with a revised Decision Procedure and Penalties Manual ('DEPP'), although AUTH has been removed and ENF replaced by alternative provisions including the inclusion of a new Enforcement Guide ('EG') now included in the Regulatory Guides Block.[17] The Redress Block now consists of the Dispute Resolution and Complaints Sourcebook ('DISP'), the new Consumer Redress Schemes Sourcebook ('CONRED'), and Compensation ('COMP'), with Complaints against the FSA ('COAF') having being deleted and replaced by new statutory complaints arrangements introduced under Part 6 FSA 2012.[18] The Handbook includes a Specialist 1.18

[14] <http://fshandbook.info/FS/html/handbook>.

[15] The Handbook has been extended and restructured on various occasions. On the original earlier provisions, see GA Walker, 'Financial Services Authority' in M Blair and GA Walker, *Financial Services Law* (OUP 2006), ch 1, paras 1.21–1.22. See Chapter 5.

[16] Limited provisions have been retained within the Interim Prudential Sourcebook for Building Societies (IPRU(BSOC)), Interim Prudential Sourcebook for Investment Businesses (IPRU(INV)), Interim Prudential Sourcebook for Insurers (IPRU(INS)), and Interim Prudential Sourcebook for Friendly Societies (IPRU(FSOC)), as well as IPRU(BANK).

[17] Chapter 7.

[18] Bank of England and PRA, *Complaints against the regulators*. Available at: <http://www.bankofengland.co.uk/about/Documents/complaints/complaintsscheme.pdf>. See also FSA, *Complaints against the regulators* (November 2012) CP12/30; and FSA, *Complaints against the regulators* (March 2013) PS 13/7.

Sourcebooks Block (including the new Building Societies Sourcebook ('BSOCS'), revised requirements for Collective Investment Schemes ('COLL' replacing 'CIS'), Professional firms ('PROF'), revised Recognised Investment Exchanges ('REC'), a Credit Unions New Sourcebook ('CREDS'), Regulated Covered Bonds ('RCB'), with the Electronic Commerce Directive ('ECO'), Electronic Money ('ELM'), and Lloyd's of London ('LLD') sourcebooks being deleted. The restructured Handbook also contains a Listing, Prospectus, and Disclosure Block (with Listing Rules ('LR'), Prospectus Rules ('PR'), and Disclosure Rules and Transparency Rules ('DRT')) and a revised and extended Handbook Guides Block (covering Energy Market Participants ('EMPS'), Oil Market Participants ('OMPS'), Service Companies ('SERV')), new General Guidance on Benchmark Submission and Administration ('BENCH') following the LIBOR scandal, with Small Friendly Societies ('FREN'), Overview for small IFA firms ('SIFA'), and Small Mortgage and Insurance Intermediaries ('MIGI', 'MOGI', and 'GIGI') no longer being in force. A final Regulatory Guides Block has been added (containing the Building Societies Regulatory Guide ('BSOC'), the Collective Investment Scheme Information Guide ('COLLG'), the Enforcement Guide ('EG'), a new Financial Crime: a guide for firms ('FC'), the Perimeter Guidance Manual ('PERG'), the Responsibilities of Providers and Distributors for the Fair Treatment of Customers ('RPPD'), and the Unfair Contract Terms Regulatory Guide ('UNFCOG'), with the Credit Rating Agencies Guide ('CRAG') no longer in force).

1.19 The PRA Handbook specifically now only consists of the High Level Standards (PRIN, SYSC, APER, FIT, FINMAR, GEN, and FEES), Prudential Standards (GENPRU, BIPRU, INSPRU, MIPRU, IPRU(FSOC), IPRU-INS, and IPRU-INV), Business Standards (COBS), Regulatory Processes (SUP), Redress (COMP), Specialist Sourcebooks (BSOCS and CREDS), and Regulatory Guides (BSOG).[19] The other provisions are contained in the FCA Handbook. A revised core statutory framework for the regulation of financial services and markets has accordingly been set up under FSMA with the more detailed regulatory obligations imposed on financial firms and markets being set out in the separate Handbooks of Rules and Guidance issued by the FCA and PRA under FSMA as amended under the FSA 2012.[20]

Financial Instability

1.20 The stability of banking and financial markets across the world was rocked by the events in 2007 and 2008 beginning with the tightening of credit conditions in inter-bank credit markets in autumn 2007. The financial markets, authorities, and media as well as financial institutions themselves were shocked by the events that occurred. Rather than treat this as a single event, this can be considered to have involved a series of separate overlapping crises triggered by certain common factors but with each crisis evolving in its own way, each inflicting its own specific damage, and each having different consequences. This has then led to a number of more specific national responses being adopted while attempts have been made to identify the more general common causes and construct collective reform agenda at the international, European, and national levels.

[19] Chapter 14.
[20] Chapter 6.

The crisis can be considered to have evolved in a number of separate stages.[21] **1.21**

Inter-Bank markets

London Inter-Bank Offered Rates ('LIBOR') increased sharply from August 2007, in particular, after BNP Paribas suspended payments on three investment funds connected with sub-prime lending in the US. It became increasingly difficult to obtain short-term funds on international wholesale markets although rates began to recover in summer 2008. The tightening of inter-bank rates had been triggered by growing concerns with regard to US sub-prime housing market losses which increased in early 2007. Bear Stearns had to support two of its sub-prime funds in June 2007. **1.22**

Northern Rock was forced to approach the Bank of England for support on 14 September 2007, which was declined.[22] A separate £30 billion facility to Lloyds Bank to allow it to purchase Northern Rock was also refused. Northern Rock suffered a major run on and withdrawal of funds following the announcement by the BBC that it had had to approach the Bank of England for support. Northern Rock would receive £26 billion from government lending and £30 billion in guarantees. **1.23**

Northern Rock was subsequently nationalised in February 2008 under the Banking (Special Provisions) Act 2008 after the Treasury had decided not to accept any of the private bids made to acquire the bank, including one by the Virgin Group. The Government's shares were held through UK Financial Investments ('UKFI') set up in October 2008 and UK Asset Resolution ('UKAR') established in October 2010. Northern Rock was divided into two operations with Northern Rock Plc, which took over its savings and mortgage business, and with its distressed assets being transferred to Northern Rock (Asset Management). Northern Rock Plc was sold to Virgin Money for £747 million in November 2011. **1.24**

US financial crisis

The financial crisis in the US escalated in September 2008 after the decision by the US authorities not to support Lehman Bros following a series of negotiations with major US financial institutions and the US Treasury and Federal Reserve. The Government Sponsored Entities ('GSEs'), Federal National Mortgage Association ('Fannie Mae') and Federal Home Mortgage Corporation ('Freddie Mac'), had been forced into conservatorship on 7 September 2008 and had to receive around $232 billion in total support. Concerns also arose with regard to American International Group ('AIG'), which was the largest insurance company in the world, which had to receive $85 billion on 18 September 2008. **1.25**

Discussions over a possible private 'white knight' rescue of Lehman had been conducted at the Federal Reserve Bank of New York on Friday 12 September and over the weekend 13–14 September 2008. The possible acquisition of Lehman by Bank of New York was considered, with a purchase by Bank of America considered and rejected when the chairman of Merrill Lynch persuaded the Bank to purchase the firm on Saturday 13 September 2008. Barclays offered to purchase Lehman in return for a $30 billion support facility which was not agreed. Lehman filed for bankruptcy under Chapter 11 of the US Bankruptcy Code on the morning of Monday 15 September 2008. **1.26**

[21] See GA Walker, 'Financial Markets and Exchanges Law' in M Blair, G Walker, and S Wiley, *Financial Markets and Exchanges Law* (2nd edn, OUP 2012) ch 1, paras 1.122–1.134.

[22] Chapter 14. Paras 14.23 and 14.29–14.31.

1.27 While the US authorities had anticipated that the bankruptcy of Lehman would not have systemic consequences, following the earlier purchase of Bear Stearns by JP Morgan Chase with the assistance of a $30 billion facility from the Federal Reserve in February 2008, Lehman's failure triggered an immediate run on mutual fund deposits. The US authorities had to provide an open guarantee to the $3.5 trillion US money-market fund sector by the following Friday. Over $60 billion was injected into Lehman's New York broker–dealer operations over three days before Barclays purchased its North American investment banking platform on Wednesday 17 September 2008.

1.28 The two largest investment firms, Goldman Sachs and Morgan Stanley, decided to reregister as bank holding companies to allow them access to Federal Reserve discount window support, with JP Morgan purchasing the deposit and retail branch operations of Washington Mutual ('WaMu') on 25 September 2008.

Stock market collapse

1.29 The closure of Lehman Bros triggered a collapse in banking and financial stocks in all major markets across the world. An earlier liquidity contraction was transformed into a share price collapse and then solvency and stock market crisis. The collapse in UK stock market prices was only halted by the announcement by the Prime Minister, Gordon Brown, and Chancellor of the Exchequer, Alistair Darling, of a three-point refinancing plan on the morning of Wednesday 8 October 2008 before the London stock markets opened. Up to £50 billion would be made available to the eight largest UK banks in exchange for preference shares, with the Bank of England's Special Liquidity Scheme ('SLS') being doubled to £200 billion and with guarantees being provided up to £250 billion by the Treasury to allow banks to roll over wholesale funding for up to three years.

1.30 A recapitalisation plan announced in October 2008 was adopted in other countries including in the US. The US authorities had discussed setting up a $700 billion Troubled Asset Recovery Program ('TARP') on Friday 19 September 2008 although this was rejected by Congress and only agreed on a second vote on 3 October.[23] Treasury Secretary, Hank Paulson, subsequently announced on 14 October 2008 that the first tranche of the TARP would be redirected to recapitalise major US banks and financial groups on a UK model.

1.31 The amount of the UK recapitalisation was confirmed on the following Monday 13 October 2008 following stress testing with the FSA over the weekend with RBS receiving £19 billion, HBOS £12 billion, and Lloyds TSB £5 billion, and with Barclays attempting to raise £7 billion directly from the markets. It had been agreed on 18 September 2008 that HBOS and Lloyds TSB would merge after HBOS shares fell sharply the previous day despite confirmation from the FSA as to the bank's liquidity. HBOS shares had fallen by 17 per cent earlier in March 2008 with the FSA conducting an investigation into short selling. The merger with Lloyds created the Lloyds Banking Group (LBG) with UK competition requirements having to be waived and the deal subject to European Commission conditions, which included the disposal of 632 branches. The Co-operative Bank later agreed to purchase the branches for £750 million although it was forced to withdraw in April 2013. The Chief Executive of HBOS Corporate Division, Peter Cummings, was fined £500,000 by the FSA September 2012 for breach of PRIN 3 and 6 although he questioned the selective and disproportionate

23 Emergency Economic Stabilisation Act of 2008 (Division A of Pub L 110–343 122 Stat 3765).

nature of the penalty.[24] The Parliamentary Commission on Banking Standards later attributed primary fault to former Chairman, Lord Stevenson, and former Chief Executives Sir James Crosby and Andy Hornby, with the failure having arisen as a result of an aggressive, expansionary business model and internal governance and external regulatory failure.[25]

The Government acquired a 43.4 per cent interest in LBG as part of the October 2008 support package and around 82 per cent in RBS by January 2009. RBS had produced substantial profits in 2006 and 2007 of over £9 billion in each year with a £12 billion rights issue in 2008. RBS had been the largest bank in the world at one point.[26] Its share price had risen over summer 2008 as part of a 'flight to quality' but fell 12.19 per cent after the failure of Lehman and a further 39.23 per cent by the beginning of October 2008 with rumours that it was experiencing funding difficulties. The FSA examined the losses suffered at RBS in a report in December 2011[27] and referred to six principal factors consisting of a weak capital position, over-reliance on risky short-term wholesale funding, underlying asset quality concerns, substantial credit trading losses, the ABN Amro acquisition, and its overall vulnerability to a systemic crisis which unfolded in the UK and elsewhere. The ABN Amro acquisition had only resulted in a £8.1 billion reduction in capital against a capital position of £80 billion at the end of 2007. RBS had been damaged by a wider collapse in confidence in the markets in the period following the closure of Lehman. The report was forced to accept that no regulatory action could have been taken against directors or senior managers. Areas that might justify further legislative or regulatory investigation were considered by the Treasury Committee in its response document in October 2012.[28] **1.32**

The Treasury used anti-terrorist laws to freeze £400 billion of assets of the Icelandic bank Landsbanki to cover £300 billion in UK deposits[29] after the Icelandic Government acquired 75 per cent of Glitnir on 6 October 2008, with Landsbanki being put into receivership on 7 October 2008 and Kaupthing into receivership on 9 October 2008. The UK operations of Landsbanki and Kaupthing were placed into administration.[30] **1.33**

Financial support and stimulus

The collapse in stock market prices following the closure of Lehman on 15 September led to a global recession beginning in October/November 2008 with a global depression only being averted through political intervention. The Dow Jones Industrial Average had fallen over 700 points on Monday 6 October 2008 and was below 10,000 for the first time in four years. The Dow Jones rose over 11.1 per cent (900 points) the following Monday 13 October 2008, with the FTSE rising 8 per cent following the UK rescue package. Despite this **1.34**

24 FSA, *Final Notice Peter Cummings* (12 September 2012) PCJ01301.

25 Parliamentary Commission on Banking Standards, '"An accident waiting to happen": The failure of HBOS' [HL Paper 144, HC 705] 4 April 2013.

26 'World's biggest banks 2009' *Global Finance Magazine*.

27 FSA, *The failure of the Royal Bank of Scotland* (December 2011). GA Walker, 'Royal Bank of Scotland—Reaction and Reform' *Financial Regulation International* (March 2012) Issue 12.2, 1–14.

28 Treasury Committee, *The FSA's report into the failure of RBS* [HC 640] Fifth Report of Session 2012–2013, 19 October 2012.

29 The Landsbanki Freezing Order (8 October 2008) 2008/SI 2668.

30 HM Treasury, *Events leading up to the failure of Kaupthing Singer & Friedlander Ltd* (June 2012). See also Treasury Committee, *Banking Crisis: The impact of the failure of the Icelandic banks* [HC 402] Fifth Report of Session 2008–2009 (4 April 2009).

initial recovery, markets and economies across the world had nevertheless been substantially damaged which triggered the onset of a global recession in autumn 2008.

1.35 In response to this, governments agreed to adopt a series of stimulus packages to support the markets, in particular, following the Washington G20 Summit in November 2008 and the London G20 Summit on 2 April 2009. The G20 had been formed through an extension of the earlier G7 to include all of the major emerging economies. A $789 billion (later $838 billion) stimulus package was agreed by the US Congress on 11 February 2009. Further packages were adopted within the EU, China, and elsewhere, with governments also separately financing domestic banking and financial institutional support programmes. The effect of all of this was to place increasing pressure on fiscal conditions in many countries.

Sovereign debt and Eurozone crisis

1.36 The stimulus packages adopted during 2009–2010 prevented economic recessions in countries becoming depressions, although this also exposed substantial sovereign debt vulnerabilities. The global stock market collapse was transformed into a sovereign debt crisis with potential threats of subsequent trade and currency crises. Sovereign exposures were initially revealed within the EU with Greece borrowing €45 billion from the EU and the IMF in April 2010, then €110 billion in May 2010, and a further €130 billion in February 2010. In November 2010, €85 billion was made available to Ireland, and €78 billion to Portugal in May 2011. Spain eventually agreed to ask for €100 billion to support its banks in June 2012 after an initial hesitation. A €750 billion European Financial Stability Facility ('EFSF') had been set up in May 2010 which would be replaced by a permanent European Stability Mechanism ('ESM') from 2013.

1.37 With the threat of sovereign debt and rating downgrades, most governments shifted from earlier stimulus packages to adopting domestic austerity budgets in 2010–2011 which included raising taxes, privatisations where possible, cutting government expenses, and reducing discretionary welfare costs. National and international economic conditions have continued to be dampened by low growth subsequently which reduces taxation receipts and increases welfare costs. Political attention has turned since the G20 Summit in Seoul, South Korea in November 2010 to attempting to restore global recovery, strong, sustainable, and balanced global growth and the strengthening of the international financial and regulatory system, although the austerity packages adopted in many countries have limited economic recovery and growth.

Financial Scandal

1.38 A number of other incidents involving substantial loss and damage, either to financial institutions or to their clients, have also been uncovered since the global financial crisis. These have either involved large losses being suffered by major firms or financial groups or individual rogue staff, or a number of members of staff acting in concert, engaging in criminal activity, or in breach of the civil law, or applicable regulatory provisions. This has also been connected with inappropriate sales practices involving client loss or damage. In all of these cases, firms have failed to maintain appropriate management policies or proper internal governance and oversight systems. Much of this has arisen from operational and systems failures although this has also raised difficult cultural and ethical issues including with regard to incentives and the management of conflicts of interests between firms and their customers and how firms should treat their clients more generally.

These events may not have generated wider crises and systemic threats although they have involved more specific significant instances of scandal and misconduct. This has, in turn, highlighted the need for effective parallel prudential and conduct regulation. This does not of itself justify institutional separation, as adopted in the UK with the replacement of the FSA by the FCA and PRA, although this can still be justified within a larger new financial stability model involving substantial macro-prudential as well as prudential and conduct regulation. The new UK model has also attempted to incorporate further structural and infrastructure regulatory elements in an attempt to insulate markets from further instability and loss. **1.39**

Financial losses

A number of instances of substantial losses have been recorded at various firms. Kweku Adoboli lost $2 billion at UBS having worked in its Global Synthetic Equities Trading team. He was convicted of fraud by abuse of position and false accounting in September 2011. JP Morgan Chase lost $6.2 billion in early 2012 through the activities of Bruno Michel Iksil (referred to as the 'London Whale' or 'Caveman') who was managing a $150 billion position for the bank following trades in complex synthetic credit derivatives.[31] **1.40**

A increasingly large number of convictions have also been secured against firms for such crimes as insider trading and market abuse or market manipulation, including instances in the US and UK. Raj Rajaratman, manager of the Galleon Group hedge fund, was convicted on 14 counts of conspiracy and securities fraud in May 2011, and sentenced to 11 years imprisonment and fined $150 million. Other prosecutions have followed in connection with the Galleon scandal including of Anil Kumar, formally at McKinsey & Company, and Rajat Gupta, former director at Goldman Sachs. The FSA, and FCA subsequently, have also been prosecuting an increasingly large number of parallel actions involving insider trading, market abuse, or market manipulation in the UK. **1.41**

LIBOR

Barclays was able to withstand the effects of the global and UK crisis more effectively than other major banking groups although it was the first institution to become embroiled in the LIBOR scandal in summer 2012 with the revelation that a number of major international institutions had manipulated benchmark rates. Barclays was fined £59.5 million in June 2012 by the UK FSA, and $200 million by the US Commodity Futures Trading Commission ('CFTC'), and $160 million by the US Department of Justice ('DoJ'). UBS was fined $1.5 billion by the FSA, CFTC, and DoJ on 19 December 2012 with RBS agreeing to pay £390 million ($612 million) in February 2013.[32] **1.42**

The UK Government had commissioned an inquiry into the LIBOR scandal in July 2012 to be undertaken by Martin Wheatley, Chief Executive designate of the FCA.[33] The objective was to consider whether LIBOR should be included as a regulated activity under FSMA as well as possible revisions to the LIBOR structure, governance, and possible alternative rate-setting processes as well as sanctions and transitional arrangements. An initial discussion **1.43**

---

[31] US Permanent Sub-committee on Investigations, *JPMorgan Chase Whale Trades: A Case History of Derivatives Risks and Abuses* (15 March 2013).
[32] GA Walker, 'Reference rate Manipulation and Libor' *Annual Review of Banking Law* [2013] Spring.
[33] See HM Treasury, 'The Wheatley Review' (30 July 2012) pn 68/12.

paper was issued in August 2012[34] with a final report in September 2012.[35] The Government welcomed the ten-point action plan set out in the Wheatley Review.[36] The Chancellor issued a statement on the FSA investigation into the manipulation of LIBOR and EURIBOR in June 2012 with a follow-up statement at the beginning of July 2012.[37] The Financial Services Bill was amended to bring benchmark activities within the regulatory scope of the FSMA and extended the penalties to include benchmark manipulation.[38]

Money laundering and sanctions

1.44 HSBC Holdings Plc and Standard Chartered Bank had been able to avoid the worst effects of the global financial crisis due to a more stable mix of global banking operations and without significant exposure to US sub-prime or structured finance markets. HSBC was nevertheless fined $1.921 billion by US authorities for breach of US anti-money laundering laws and US sanctions. The US authorities alleged that $881 million had been laundered through the US with $660 million transferred for banks operating in restricted countries. Standard Chartered Bank also agreed to pay $340 million in fines to the New York Department of Financial Services ('DFS') in August 2012 in connection with the alleged concealment of $250 billion of transactions involving Iranian counterparties.

Bank charges

1.45 Banks were involved in further complaints as the UK economy remained weak following the initial recession beginning in autumn 2008. There was a continuing dispute with the Office of Fair Trading ('OFT') concerning unauthorised bank charges. The OFT had commenced an investigation in March 2007 with the banks agreeing to participate in a test case to determine whether the charges were exempt from an assessment of fairness under the Unfair Terms in Consumer Contacts Regulations ('UTCCRs').[39] The OFT had noted that banks received one-third of their personal current account revenues through unarranged overdraft charges that it considered were difficult to understand, not transparent, and not subject to effective consumer control. The Supreme Court held in November 1999 that the charges were not assessable fully under the Regulations.[40] While the Supreme Court stated that the OFT could attempt to assess the charges under alternative provisions, including Regulation 5 of the Regulations, the OFT decided that it would not continue with the investigation.[41] The banks undertook to arrange a number of voluntary changes. The higher charges on unauthorised overdrafts had covered the cost of providing free banking on current accounts.

[34] See The Wheatley Review, *The Wheatley Review of LIBOR: initial discussion paper* (August 2012). See also HM Treasury, 'Independent Review into Libor publishes discussion paper' (10 August 2012) pn 73/12.

[35] See *The Wheatley Review of LIBOR: final report* (September 2012).

[36] See HM Treasury, 'Independent Review into Libor' (published 28 September 2012).

[37] See Statement by the Chancellor of the Exchequer, Rt Hon George Osborne MP, on FSA investigation into LIBOR (28 June 2012); and Statement by the Chancellor of the Exchequer, Rt Hon George Osborne MP, on LIBOR (2 July 2012).

[38] Speech by Financial Secretary to the Treasury, Rt Hon Greg Clark MP, 'Wheatley Review Final Report' (28 September 2012); and Written Ministerial Statement, 'Wheatley Review of LIBOR' (17 October 2012).

[39] OFT, *Personal current accounts in the UK* (July 2008).

[40] *Office of Fair Trading v Abbey National Plc & others* [2009] UK SC6 on appeal from the Court of Appeal (Civil Division) [2009] EWCA Civ 116. The Supreme Court considered that the charges fell within the exemption against an assessment of fairness with regard to terms relating to the adequacy of the price or remuneration against which goods or services were supplied under Regulation 6(2)(b). See also OFT, *Personal current accounts in the UK—An OFT market study* (July 2008).

[41] OFT, 'OFT announces decision and next steps on bank charges' (22 December 2009) 144/09.

The dispute raised more general policy issues with regard to the continued viability of 'free banking' services in UK under which customers were not charged for current account services where accounts were in credit.

Payment protection insurance and interest rate swaps

Banks were separately criticised for selling payment protection insurance ('PPI') attached to personal loans or mortgages to cover payments in the event that customers were unable to continue to pay, including through illness or unemployment. While these represented a legitimate and valuable product, many of the policies had been sold to customers who did not need or could not have claimed under the protection provided. The Financial Ombudsman Service ('FOS') had referred the matter to the FSA in July 2008[42] following earlier FSA enforcement action and Competition Commission review. The FSA had determined that a number of policies had been mis-sold in test samples.[43] New rules on the sale of PPI were produced by the Financial Ombudsman Service and FSA in 2010 which the banks had challenged. The British Bankers' Association ('BBA') questioned the FSA policy statement and open industry letter on PPI and FOS guidance on the handling of PPI complaints on the basis that amended provisions were being applied retrospectively to earlier sales. The judicial review brought forward by the BBA in October 2010 was rejected by the High Court in April 2011.[44] The UK banking industry had implemented the PPI sales reforms required, although it was argued that many of the PPI complaints had been based on the unfairly amended rules or were simply opportunistic. The BBA had until 10 May 2011 to appeal but elected not to do so with the banks agreeing to compensate customers where appropriate. Total provisions were estimated to be over £11 billion with complaints filing and handling deadlines being extended later. **1.46**

An equivalent set of complaints arose for business customers with regard to the sale of interest rate swap agreements ('IRSAs') and other interest rate hedging products ('IRHPs'). Banks had sold these to large numbers of business customers to help them protect against interest rate rises although these only imposed higher costs with continuing low interest rates maintained within the UK following the crisis. The FSA had conducted a review on IRHPs in 2012 following which eleven banks agreed to review sales to non-sophisticated customers. The major banks were required to appoint independent reviewers to conduct their internal **1.47**

[42] <http://www.financial-ombudsman.org.uk/publications/technical_notes/ppi/ppi-fsareferral-jul08.pdf>.

[43] Some customers were pressured into taking out PPI, it was not made clear that it was optional, they were advised to take it out when it was unsuitable, they were led to believe it was a condition for a loan or credit, exclusions were not explained, policy was added without knowledge, the costs were not disclosed or the fact that the cover would end before the loan or credit was repaid. See FSA, *The assessment and redress of Payment Protection Insurance complaints* (August 2010). The FOS followed this in its Online Resource in support of its PPI complaints handling procedure which followed the FSA policy statement.

[44] *British Bankers Association v Financial Services Authority and Financial Ombudsman Service* [2011] EWHC 999. See BBA, *Payment Protection Insurance (PPI)* (9 May 2011). The BBA challenged the FSA Statement and FOS Online Resource as making compensation available for breach of the FSA PRIN when these were not directly actionable in law. The PRIN could not be applied if these contradicted specific rules including the Insurance: Conduct of Business (ICOB) Rules. Ouseley J rejected both arguments. Section 150 (2), which provided that Principles were not actionable in law, only prevented an action for breach of statutory duty arising with regard the Principles which could still create obligations between firms and customers. The FOS could consider the Principles in determining whether action had been fair and reasonable under s 228(2) FSMA. Principles had to be complied with in all cases with rules only amounting to specific applications of general Principles. There had been no contradiction in the particular case and the FOS was entitled to award compensation where there had been a breach of the Principles without a breach of a specific rule. The ability of complaint schemes to be set up under s 404 FSMA did not provide an exclusive remedy.

investigations. The FSA published a statement on its pilot findings in March 2013.[45] Banks were expected to compensate customers for IRHPs that were mis-sold since 2001 with around £630 million being set aside for this purpose.[46]

Regulatory Response

1.48 A number of immediate regulatory actions were taken in response to the UK financial crisis during 2008–2010.[47] The Treasury, Bank of England, and FSA, as the Tripartite Authorities, issued a number of papers on regulatory reform.[48] Lord Adair Turner, FSA Chairman, issued an important report on the *Global Banking Crisis* in March 2009, with a supporting FSA Discussion Paper which provided more detailed background information on the issues raised in the *Turner Review*.[49] A number of initiatives were brought forward by the FSA, in particular, on supervision, remuneration, liquidity, enforcement, and product regulation.[50] Sir David Walker produced a report on *Corporate Governance* in July 2009.[51] The Treasury produced a White Paper on *Reforming Financial Markets* in July 2009 following an earlier paper on cross-border issues in September 2008.[52]

1.49 New resolution procedures were brought into effect under the Banking (Special Provisions) Act 2008[53] which provisions were subsequently made permanent under Part 1 of the BA 2009 and with amended bank insolvency and administration procedures in Parts 2 and 3.[54] The SRR (special resolution regime) now consists of a private sector purchaser, bridge bank, or temporary public ownership (nationalisation) mechanisms.[55] The BA 2009 sets out the special resolution objectives[56] with the Treasury issuing a Code of Practice on the use

[45] FSA, *Interest Rate Hedging Products—Pilot Findings* (March 2013). The FSA review revealed that there had been poor disclosure of exit cost, a failure to ascertain their customers' understanding of risk, advice being provided instead of non-advice sales, over-hedging and practices being driven by rewards and incentives. <http://www.fsa.gov.uk/library/communication/pr/2012/071.shtml>.

[46] FSA, *FSA agrees settlement with four banks over interest rate hedging products* (29 June 2012). Barclays, HSBC, LBG, and RBS agreed to participate in the scheme.

[47] For comment on the earlier post-crisis reforms adopted, GA Walker, 'Financial crisis—UK policy response' *The International Lawyer* (August 2011) 43 (3) [101–130]. For comment on the post-election reforms adopted, GA Walker, 'UK Regulatory Revision—A New Blueprint For Reform' *The International Lawyer* (Spring 2012) 43 (3) [101–130].

[48] The Treasury, the Bank of England, and the FSA, *Banking reform - protecting depositors: a discussion paper* (October 2007); the Treasury, the Bank of England, and the FSA, *Financial Stability and Depositor Protection: Strengthening the Framework* (January 2008) CM 7308; Tripartite Authorities, *Financial Stability and Depositor Protection* (July 2008); and Tripartite Authorities, *Financial Stability and Depositor Protection: Special Resolution Regime* (July 2008) CM 7459.

[49] FSA, *The Turner Review—A Regulatory Response to the Global Banking Crisis* (March 2009); and FSA, *A regulatory response to the global banking crisis* (March 2009) DP09/2. Para 1.53.

[50] Paras 1.54–14.56.

[51] Sir David Walker, *A Review of Corporate Governance in UK Banks and Other Financial Industry Entities* (16 July 2009).

[52] HM Treasury, *Financial Stability and Depositor Protection: Cross-Border Challenges and Responses* (September 2008).

[53] The Banking (Special Provisions) Act 2008 was used to acquire or transfer the assets or liabilities of Northern Rock in February 2008, the Bradford and Bingley in September 2008 and Heritable Bank (Landsbanki) and Kaupthing Edge (Kaupthing, Singer and Friedlander) in October 2008. Dunfermline Building Society was restructured in March 2009 using the provisions adopted under the BA 2009.

[54] Paras 1.57–1.58 and Chapter 14, paras 14.258–14.266.

[55] ss 11–13 Banking Act 2009.

[56] s 4(4)–(7) Banking Act 2009.

of stabilisation powers and the bank insolvency and administration procedures.[57] An FPC was set up within the Bank of England to consider macro-prudential matters under the BA 2009.[58]

1.50 A number of reforms were brought into effect under the Financial Services Act 2010. These included new measures on remuneration, recovery and resolution, short-selling, and consumer redress schemes. A separate CFS was to be established under the FSA 2010 to replace the earlier informal Tripartite arrangements with a new statutory basis although this had to be removed from the Bill to allow enactment.[59]

1.51 The Treasury Select Committee within the UK Parliament issued a number of reports before the General Election in May 2010. An initial report was produced on *Northern Rock* in January 2008[60] with a paper on *Financial Stability and Transparency* following in March 2008.[61] The need for further legislative and operational changes in terms of *Banking Reform* was examined in September 2008[62] with two reports on the effects of the Icelandic bank failure appearing in April 2009 and in June 2009.[63] The Committee issued a report on the action undertaken to support the *Banking Crisis* and possible options for future reform in May 2009,[64] and separate reports on *Corporate Governance and Pay*,[65] international aspects of bank regulation and supervision,[66] and *Regulation and Supervision*.[67] Two further papers were issued on EU Institutional Supervisory Reform and the problem of Too Big To Fail in 2009.[68]

1.52 All of these initiatives were brought forward in the immediate aftermath of the crisis. A number of separate institutional and structural reforms were announced by the Coalition Government following the General Election in May 2010.[69]

---

[57] s 5(1) Banking Act 2009 and HM Treasury, *Banking Act 2009 special resolution regime: code of practice* (November 2010).

[58] Para 1.59.

[59] Paras 1.60–1.61.

[60] Treasury Committee, *The Run on the Rock* [HC 56] January 2008.

[61] Treasury Committee, *Financial Stability and Transparency* [HC 371] 3 March 2008.

[62] Treasury Committee, *Banking Reform* [HC 1008] Seventeenth Report of Session 2007–08, 16 September 2008. See also Treasury Committee, *Banking Reform: Government and Financial Services Authority Responses to the Committee's Seventeenth Report of Session 2007–08* [HC 1131] Fourteenth Special Report of Session 2007–2008, 27 October 2008.

[63] Treasury Committee, *Banking Crisis: The impact of the failure of the Icelandic banks* [HC 402] Fifth Report of Session 2008–2009, 4 April 2009; Treasury Committee, *Banking Crisis: The impact of the failure of the Icelandic banks: Responses from the Government and the Financial Services Agency to the Committee's Report of Session 2008–2009* [HC 656] Fourth Special Report of Session 2008–09, 19 June 2009.

[64] Treasury Committee, *Banking Crisis: dealing with the failure of the UK banks* [HC 416] Seventh Report of Session 2008–2009, 1 May 2009; Treasury Committee, *Banking Crisis: dealing with the failure of the UK banks: Government UK Financial Investments Ltd and Financial Services Authority Responses to the Seventh Report from the Committee* [HC 956] Seventh Special Report of Session 2008–2009, 24 July 2009.

[65] Treasury Committee, *Banking Crisis: reforming corporate governance and pay in the City* [HC 519] Ninth Report of Session 2008–2009, 15 May 2009.

[66] Treasury Committee, *Banking Crisis: international dimensions* [HC 615] Eleventh Report of Session 2008–2009, 24 July 2009.

[67] Treasury Committee, *Banking Crisis: regulation and supervision* [HC 767] Fourteenth Report of Session 2008-09, 31 July 2009. See also Treasury Committee, *Banking Crisis: regulation and supervision: Responses from the Government and Financial Services Authority to the Committee's Fourteenth Report of Session 2008–09* [HC 47] First Special Report of Session 2009–2010, 27 November 2009.

[68] Treasury Committee, *Proposals for European financial supervision: further report* [HC 37] First Report of Session 2009–10, 26 November 2009; and Treasury Committee, *Too Important to Fail–Too Important to Ignore* [HC 261] Ninth Report of Session 2009–2010, 29 March 2010.

[69] Paras 1.54–1.81.

Turner review

1.53 Lord Turner produced his review of the *Global Banking Crisis* in March 2009.[70] This considered the origins of the financial crisis and assessed relevant regulatory deficiencies with recommendations for reform. The background to the crisis was examined in terms of global conditions, UK developments, international regulation, and certain theoretical issues. UK events initially focused on funding issues and then the effects of major trading book losses and subsequent emergence of wider credit problems especially in mortgages and corporate lending and commercial real estate. The review examined the need for reform in the areas of capital adequacy, accounting and liquidity, regulatory coverage, deposit insurance, bank resolution, credit rating agencies, remuneration, credit default swaps, macro-prudential analysis, supervisory approach, risk management and governance, proprietary trading, and European and international bank regulation. Additional issues were raised with regard to imposing direct controls on loan-to-value ('LTV') or loan-to-income ('LTI') ratios, wholesale product design restrictions, and macro-prudential tools although no firm conclusions were drawn at that time.

FSA reform

1.54 The FSA brought forward a number of regulatory and supervisory improvements following the crisis. These included specific initiatives on enhanced supervision, strengthened enforcement, product regulation, remuneration, and later resolution. The FSA adopted a 'Supervisory Enhancement Programme' ('SEP') following the Northern Rock scandal with the FSA's supervisory approach having been strongly criticised in an Internal Audit Report. The SEP involved higher prioritisation of supervision, direct involvement of senior management, high-impact firm oversight, increased resources, and improved coordination with the Financial Stability Directive at the Bank of England. A specific 'Heightened Supervision' model was to be developed for high-risk firms with the FSA removing its earlier 'tick-box' compliance approach. This would be further developed under the FSA's 'More Principles Based Regulatory' ('MPBR') programme.

1.55 The FSA adopted a strengthened 'credible deterrence policy' with regard to enforcement. This was referred to at the FSA Enforcement Conference in June 2009 and in other FSA speeches. Conduct of business and consumer protection was enhanced through separate initiatives including the 'Retail Distribution Review' ('RDR'), 'Mortgage Market Review' ('MMR'), and 'Treating Customers Fairly' ('TCF') work. The FSA consulted on the establishment of a new 'Product Intervention' regime with enhanced product approval procedures and requirements being imposed on firms.[71]

1.56 The FSA adopted a Remuneration Code on bonus packages following the production of a draft code in March 2009.[72] This was given effect to under SYSC 19A within the FSA and PRA and FCA Handbooks of Rules and Guidance. Firms have to establish, implement, and maintain remuneration policies, procedures, and practices that are consistent with and that promote sound and effective risk management, and must ensure that these were clearly

---

70 FSA, *The Turner Review–A Regulatory Response to the Global Banking Crisis* (n 50).

71 FSA, *Product Intervention* (January 2011) DP11/1; and FSA, *Product Intervention* (June 2011) Feedback Statement 11/3.

72 The FSA draft Code on remuneration was issued on 18 March 2009. FSA, *Reforming Remuneration Practices in Financial Services* (March 2009) CP09/10.

stated and documented.[73] Twelve remuneration principles are imposed on risk management and tolerance, supporting business strategy, objectives, and values, avoiding conflicts of interest, governance, control functions, capital, Government-supported institutions, profit-based measurement and risk adjustment, pension policy, personal investment strategies, avoidance, and structure.[74] These generally give effect in the UK to the nine FSF *Principles for Sound Compensation Practices* in April 2009[75] and nine Basel Committee Principles on the *Sound Compensation Practices*.[76]

Banking Act 2009

The Government's proposals in connection with the establishment of a set of new special resolution arrangements for banks were brought into effect under the BA 2009. These provided for the establishment of a Special Resolution Regime ('SRR') in Part 1 with amended bank insolvency and administration procedures in Parts 2 and 3. The SRR specifically consists of either a private sector purchaser, bridge bank, or temporary public ownership (nationalisation).[77] The Act sets out the special resolution objectives which seek to protect and enhance the stability of the UK financial systems, protect and enhance public confidence in the stability of the UK banking systems, protect depositors, and protect public funds.[78] The Act contains a number of general and special conditions on the exercise of powers as well as specific provisions on the transfer of securities and property, compensation, and incidental functions. **1.57**

The Treasury issued a Code of Practice on the use of stabilisation powers and the bank insolvency and administration procedures.[79] The Treasury consulted on extending the new resolution arrangements to apply to other non-bank systemically important firms in August 2012[80] with the BA 2009 being amended under the FSA 2012 to apply to groups, investment firms, and clearing houses.[81] The Banking Act 2009 contains additional provisions on amending the FSCS,[82] inter-bank payment systems,[83] and banknotes in Scotland and Northern Ireland.[84] **1.58**

Financial stability and the Financial Stability Committee

The BA 2009 amended the objectives of the Bank of England under the BEA 1998 to include contributing to protecting and enhancing the stability of the UK financial systems. This was **1.59**

---

[73] SYSC 19A 2.1R and 19A 2.4G.

[74] SYSC 19A 3.7–3.33. Additional sub-principles were imposed on scheme structure including with regard to performance assessment, no guaranteed variable remuneration, fixed and variable ratios, early termination payments, retained shares and instruments, deferral, and performance adjustment. SYSC 19A 3.33–3.53.

[75] FSF, *Principles for Sound Compensation Practices* (2 April 2009); and FSB, *Principles for Sound Compensation Practices—Implementation Standards* (25 September 2009).

[76] Basel Committee, *Compensation Principles and Standards Assessment Methodology* (January 2010).

[77] ss 11–13 Banking Act 2009. Chapter 14, paras 14.258–14.266.

[78] s 4(4)–(7) Banking Act 2009.

[79] s 5(1) Banking Act 2009, and HM Treasury, *Banking Act 2009 Special Resolution Regime: code of practice* (n 19).

[80] HM Treasury, *Financial sector resolution: broadening the regime* (August 2012) CM 8419.

[81] ss 100–102 FSA 2012. s 101 applies Parts 1 and 3 of the Banking Act 2009 to investment firms as defined in s 258A Banking Act 2009 which incorporates the definition contained in the Capital Requirements Directive 2006/49/EC.

[82] Part 4.

[83] Part 5.

[84] Part 6.

referred to as the 'Financial Stability Objective'.[85] The BA 2009 also created an FSC as a sub-committee of the Court of Directors of the Bank consisting of the Governor, the Deputy Governors, and four directors appointed by the chair of the Court.[86] The Committee was given specific functions including making recommendations to the Court on the Bank's strategy on securing its Financial Stability Objective and advising on relevant issues and the use of the Bank's stabilisation powers under the 2009 Act. The Committee would monitor the Bank's use of its stabilisation powers and functions on inter-bank payment systems and any other delegated functions.[87] The objective was to create a majority of non-executive members to provide focused financial expertise and to create the principal forum for dealing with financial stability matters within the Bank.[88] The Committee could also co-opt additional members to make the widest possible use of external experience and expertise in advising on decisions to safeguard UK financial stability.

Financial Services Act 2010

1.60 The FSA 2010 was enacted on 9 April 2010 immediately before the General Election in May 2010. The Act implemented a number of the key recommendations set out in the Treasury White Paper on *Reforming Financial Markets* in July 2009. The objectives of the FSA were amended to include a new financial stability objective which was to contribute to the protection and enhancement of the stability of the UK financial system.[89] Promoting understanding of the financial system was removed as a regulatory objective with responsibility for this being transferred to the new CFEB established under section 6A FSMA.[90]

1.61 The FSA 2010 gave the Treasury power to make provision for executive remuneration reports and imposed a duty on the FSA to make rules requiring authorised persons to implement an appropriate remuneration policy.[91] The FSA was to make rules requiring the production of Recovery and Resolution Plans ('RRPs') by authorised persons.[92] The FSA was given new power to prohibit or require disclosure of short selling.[93] The disciplinary powers of the FSA were strengthened.[94] The FSA could make rules requiring firms to establish consumer redress schemes.[95] Amendments were made to the FSCS with the FSA being given additional power to require information relevant to the stability of the financial system.[96] Technical amendments were made to the BA 2009.[97]

Council for Financial Stability

1.62 A statutory Council for Financial Stability ('CFS') was to have been created as a permanent Standing Committee of the Treasury, Bank of England, and FSA under the FSA 2010 to replace the earlier Tripartite Committee arrangements. Provision was included within the

85 s 238 BA 2009 and s 2A BEA 1998.
86 s 238 BA 2009 and s 2B BEA 1998 (1) (repealed).
87 s 2B BEA 1998 (repealed).
88 HM Treasury, *Reforming Financial Markets* (July 2009) CM 7667 Box 4A 51.
89 s 3a FSMA as amended s1 FSA 2010.
90 s 6A FSMA as inserted under s 2 FSA 2010; and continued under s 3S FSMA inserted under s 6 FSA 2012.
91 ss 4–7 FSA 2010. On the Remuneration Code, para 1.56.
92 s 7 FSA 2010. On RRPs, Chapter 14, paras 14.249–14.257.
93 s 8 FSA 2010.
94 ss 9–13 FSA 2010.
95 ss 14–15 FSA 2010.
96 ss 16–17 and 18–19 FSA 2010.
97 ss 20–21 FSA 2010.

original Financial Services Bill 2009 in this regard although this had to be removed to secure political agreement on the enactment of the rest of the Bill before the cessation of Parliament in May 2010.[98] The CFS was to consist of the Chancellor, the Governor of the Bank, and the Chairman of the FSA, and be responsible for considering emerging risks to the financial stability in the UK and taking action where appropriate. The Council was to consider international events and coordinate action to promote international financial regulation and supervision. A statement was to be prepared regarding its functions and an annual report produced. The Council was to meet, at least, quarterly.

The background to the establishment of the CFS was set out in the Treasury White Paper in July 2009.[99] The objectives were to analyse and examine emerging risks to the financial stability of the UK economy, and to meet as necessary to discuss specific risks to particular sectors or firms. Minutes were to be published to increase transparency and accountability, with reports being fed directly into effective supervisory and regulatory action. The CFS was to ensure that it communicated effectively with the markets and discuss and coordinate EU and international financial stability and regulatory positions.[100] The CFS would effectively act as a macro-prudential agent. The term macro-prudential was not commonly used at that time although it was referred to in the 2009 White Paper.[101] Responsibility for macro-prudential functions would later be transferred to the FPC created under the Financial Services Act 2012 with the earlier Tripartite and Council for Financial Stability mechanisms being discontinued and replaced by the new statutory coordination arrangements adopted under Part 4 of the FSA 2012. **1.63**

Regulatory Reform

A number of further institutional and structural reforms were adopted following the change of Government in May 2010. The new Coalition Government published three consultation papers on regulatory reform in July 2010 and February and June 2011.[102] A draft Financial Services Bill was included within the June 2011 White Paper with Explanatory Notes.[103] The Bill was subject to pre-legislative scrutiny by a Joint Parliamentary Committee and enacted on 19 December 2012.[104] The Act came into effect on 1 April 2013.[105] **1.64**

The Government had commissioned a separate report by an Independent Commission on Banking (ICB) under Sir John Vickers which produced an interim report in April 2011 and **1.65**

[98] ss 1–4 Financial Services Bill 6-EN of 19 November 2009.

[99] HM Treasury, *Reforming Financial Markets* (July 2009) Chapter 4.

[100] Paras 4.7–4.20.

[101] Para 4.4.

[102] HM Treasury, *A new approach to financial regulation: judgement, focus and stability* (July 2010) CM 7874; HM Treasury, *A new approach to financial regulation: building a stronger system* (February 2011) CM 8012; and HM Treasury, *A new approach to financial regulation: the blueprint for reform* (June 2011) CM 8083.

[103] HM Treasury, *A new approach to financial regulation: the blueprint for reform* (n 82) Chapters 3 and 4.

[104] Joint Committee of the Draft Financial Services Bill, *Draft Financial Services Bill* [HL Paper 236, HC 1447] 13 December 2011; and Joint Committee, *Bill Evidence* (16 December 2011). Available at: <http://www.parliament.uk/documents/joint-committees/Draft-Financial-Services-Bill/webwrittenevidence.pdf>. The Joint Committee was set up on a motion of the House of Commons on 18 July 2011 and the motion of the House of Lords on 20 July 2011. Para 1.72–1.75.

[105] Paras 1.82–1.89; and Chapter 2.

final report in September 2011.[106] The Government accepted all of the principal recommendations in the final ICB Report concerning the ring-fencing of retail and SMEs banking services and other recommendations on higher capital adequacy standards[107] with a White Paper and draft Banking Reform Bill being published in October 2012.[108] The Government had also to respond to the LIBOR scandal.[109]

1.66 The reconstituted Treasury Select Committee, within the new Parliamentary Session, issued a number of reports on financial reform with a separate Parliamentary Commission on Banking Standards being set up with members from both Houses of Parliament to consider professional standards and culture within the UK banking sector.[110] The Treasury has been involved with other financial initiatives including with regard to consumer credit reform and taxation.

Mansion House

1.67 The new institutional regulatory structure was announced in June 2010. The Chancellor, the Rt Hon George Osborne, referred to the need to avoid the banking crisis from becoming a sovereign debt crisis, and to measures to deal with the budgetary deficit. The independent Office for Budget Responsibility ('OBR') had been set up with other budgetary reforms and a fairer tax system to be brought into effect. Financial Secretary to the Treasury, Mark Hoban MP, launched the Government's consultation on financial regulatory reform in July 2010 with the publication of the Coalition Government's first White Paper.[111] A separate Impact Assessment was published with the White Paper which estimated the transitional costs to be around £50 million over three years.[112]

Treasury consultation

1.68 The causes of the crisis were summarised in the July 2010 Treasury document, *A new approach to financial regulation: judgement, focus and stability*, in terms of global economic imbalances, mispriced and misunderstood risk, unsustainable funding and business models, excessive build-up of debt across the financial system, and the growth of the unregulated shadow banking system.[113] The defects in terms of the earlier tripartite system were referred to in terms of failure to identify emerging risks, mitigate against them, and deal with the crisis adequately, especially in summer 2007.[114] The July 2010 paper included further detail on the reforms to be carried out with regard to the Bank of England and the FPC, the PRA,

---

[106] Independent Commission on Banking, *Interim Report* (April 2011), and Independent Commission on Banking, *Final Report* (September 2011). See also ICB, *Issues Paper–Call for Evidence* (September 2010). For discussion, Treasury Committee, *Independent Commission on Banking* [HC 1069] 20 July 2011. For comment see GA Walker, 'The Independent Commission on Banking–Interim Findings and Comment' *Law and Financial Markets Review* (April 2011); and GA Walker, 'Structural Regulation and Financial Reform–the Independent Commission on Banking' *Law and Financial Markets Review* (November 2011) 418–34. Paras 1.79–1.80.

[107] HM Treasury, 'Government publishes draft Banking Reform Bill' (12 October 2012).

[108] HM Treasury, *Sound banking: delivering reform* (October 2012) CM 8453 with draft Bill attached in Ch 3 and Explanatory Notes in Ch 4. Chapter 14, paras 14.242–14.248.

[109] Paras 1.42–1.43 and (nn 11–15).

[110] Paras 1.76–1.78 and 1.81.

[111] HM Treasury, *A new approach to financial regulation: judgement, focus and stability* (July 2010).

[112] HM Treasury, *A new approach to financial regulation—Impact Assessment* (26 July 2010) 5.

[113] HM Treasury, *A new approach to financial regulation: judgement, focus and stability* (n 82) para 1.2.

[114] Para 1.4.

Consumer Protection and Markets Authority ('CPMA', which would later be retitled the FCA), markets and infrastructure, crisis management and implementation.[115]

The Government issued a Summary of Consultation Responses document in November 2010.[116] The majority of respondents supported the establishment of the proposed framework for financial regulation with the emphasis on promoting financial stability and strengthened macro-prudential and micro-prudential regulations.[117] A number of further themes were identified, in particular with regard to ensuring an effective degree of accountability and transparency by the new regulators, balancing core statutory objectives with other key factors, ensuring effective coordination of activity between the authorities, market regulation, and the future of the UK Listing Authority ('UKLA'), and the European and international reform agenda.[118] **1.69**

The February 2011 paper, *A new approach to financial regulation: building a stronger system*, examined the role and functions of the Bank of England and FPC, PRA, and renamed FCA[119] in further detail as well as regulatory processes and coordination, compensation, dispute resolution, financial education, and relevant European and international issues.[120] The Treasury Select Committee had warned the Government that the quality of the legislation could be compromised if its timetable was pursued too rigidly, although the Government was concerned to maintain momentum and to minimise uncertainty and disruption.[121] **1.70**

The Government's policy proposals were restated in the June 2011 document with a more substantial policy overview of each of the principal issues referred to in the February 2011.[122] The Draft Bill and Explanatory Notes were also incorporated in the June 2011 document, *A new approach to financial regulation: the blueprint for reform*.[123] The Government stated that its primary objective in reforming financial regulation was to strengthen the system fundamentally by promoting 'the role of judgement and expertise' with new agencies with 'clarity of responsibility, a focused remit, appropriate tools and the flexibility to use them as they see fit' with tick-box compliance being removed.[124] The decision was taken at an early stage not to issue a new Financial Services Law but to amend FSMA 2000 under the FSA 2012. Much of the earlier substantive regulatory regime is accordingly preserved but reapplied under the new institutional structure set up. The June 2011 document noted the initiatives undertaken with the establishment of an interim FPC to begin to monitor systemic risk and advise the Government on potential macro-prudential tools, and the work undertaken within the FSA and Bank to divide the prudential and conduct of business functions in anticipation of the establishment of the PRA and FCA. **1.71**

---

115 Chapters 2–7.

116 HM Treasury, *A new approach to financial regulation: judgement, focus and stability—summary of consultation responses* (November 2010).

117 Para 2.1.

118 Para 2.4 and Ch 2.

119 HM Treasury, *A new approach to financial regulation: building a stronger system* (n 82) Figure 1.a, 5.

120 Chapters 2–7.

121 Treasury Select Committee, *Financial Regulation: a preliminary consideration of the Government's proposals* [HC 430-I] 3 February 2011, p 3.

122 HM Treasury, *A new approach to financial regulation: the blueprint for reform* (n 102) chs 1 and 2.

123 Chapters 3 and 4.

124 Para 1.13.

Joint Parliamentary Committee

1.72 The Financial Services Bill provided with the June 2011 paper was examined by a Joint Committee of both Houses of Parliament for pre-legislative scrutiny.[125] The Joint Committee was to consider and report on the Draft Bill by 1 December 2011 with an extension being granted until 16 December 2011. The report was published on 13 December 2011.[126] The Joint Committee consisted of 12 members with six from the House of Commons and six from the House of Lords. The Joint Committee was chaired by the Rt Hon Peter Lilley, MP.

1.73 The Joint Committee stated that it was vital that the legislation make proper provision for handling crises, including providing lender of last resort, and resolving bank failures.[127] It considered that successful regulation depended more on 'the regulatory culture, focus and philosophy than on structure' which was necessary to ensure that the relevant authorities 'can best ensure both financial stability and good conduct of business'.[128] There had to be a shift towards 'forward looking supervision' with staff having 'appropriate experience, approach and attitude'.[129] It was accepted that legislation could not change culture although it could influence it by setting objectives, allocating and aligning powers and responsibilities, and establishing appropriate systems of accountability.[130]

1.74 The Government issued a response paper to the Joint Committee in February 2012.[131] The Government considered that the analysis, advice, and recommendations of the Joint Committee had been invaluable in developing and bringing forward its reform programme with a number of amendments being made to the Bill based on the recommendations made. The Government commented on the specific points raised with regard to objectives, powers and responsibilities, and accountability.[132]

1.75 The amended Bill received its first reading on 26 January 2012 with its second reading on 6 February 2012.[133] The Bill received its Third Reading in the House of Commons on 22 May 2012 and was sent to the House of Lords on 26 June 2012. It received its first and second readings in the House of Lords on 23 May and 11 June 2012 and left the House on 5 December 2012. The Financial Services Act received Royal Ascent on 19 December 2012.

Treasury Select Committee

1.76 The Treasury Select Committee had produced preliminary observations on the Government's financial regulation proposals in February 2011.[134] The Committee stated that the UK financial services industry had to be regulated 'effectively but proportionately', and that it should not have to deal with 'regulation in a state of flux', with urgency possibly being

---

[125] Joint Committee of the Draft Financial Services Bill, *Draft Financial Services Bill* (n 84). The Joint Committee was set up on a motion of the House of Commons on 18 July 2011 and the motion of the House of Lords on 20 July 2011.

[126] Joint Committee (n 105).

[127] Para 10.

[128] Paras 16 and 24.

[129] Paras 24 and 188–198.

[130] Para 24.

[131] HM Treasury, *Draft Financial Services Bill–Government Response* (1 February 2012).

[132] Paras A4–81.

[133] Bill 278 with Explanatory Notes 278-EN.

[134] Treasury Committee, *Financial Regulation: a preliminary consideration of the Government's proposals* [HC 430-1] 3 February 2011 (n 101) with Oral and written evidence (Volume II) and Additional written evidence (Volume III).

'counter-productive for stability and certainty'.[135] The term 'financial stability' was hard to define in practice and the Government had to provide substantially more information on its meaning. The macro-prudential tools to be made available to the FPC had to be clarified with draft secondary legislation being made available as soon as possible. Strong accountability mechanisms had to be set up. The proposed regulatory changes had to consider the total costs to be imposed and the regulation of the non-bank sector as well. The Government responded on 5 April 2011 with the Committee issuing a follow-up report in May 2011.[136]

A separate report was published on *Accountability of the Bank of England* in November 2011.[137] It was recommended that the governance at the Bank be strengthened with the role of the Court, in particular, being substantially enhanced and with the Bank being more transparent. The Court of the Bank proposed inter alia to establish a new Oversight Committee in its response document.[138] The Treasury Committee published a report on the *Financial Conduct Authority* in January 2012 and published its consideration of the Government's response in February 2012.[139] The Committee had raised a number of specific issues with regard to the FCA's function within the new regulatory structure, including strategic and operational objectives, competition powers, and consumer responsibility, as well as accountability, wider regulatory architecture, supervisory approach, and new powers. The Committee also considered the LIBOR scandal,[140] and the FSA Report on RBS.[141] **1.77**

The Treasury Committee issued a subsequent follow-up report on the Financial Services Bill in advance of the Bill being considered by the House of Lords. While the Committee considered that the Bill had been improved it was still defective in places and, in particular, with regard to the accountability and corporate governance of the Bank, office of the Governor, the Chancellor's power of direction and macro-prudential scrutiny, as well as FCA objectives, accountability, PRA veto, and cost–benefit analysis.[142] **1.78**

Independent Commission on Banking

The Chancellor announced the establishment of the ICB on 16 June 2010 which was to report to the Cabinet Committee on Banking Reform by the end of September 2012. The ICB was chaired by Sir John Vickers with the other members consisting of Clare Spottiswoode, Martin Taylor, Bill Winters, and Martin Wolf. The ICB issued an initial *Issues Paper* in September 2010.[143] An *Interim Report* was published in April 2011 and a *Final Report* in **1.79**

---

135 p 3.

136 Treasury Committee, *Financial Regulation: a preliminary consideration of the Government's proposals*: Government Response to the Seventh Report from the Committee [HC 958] 4 May 2011. The Government Response was included as an Appendix.

137 Treasury Committee, *Accountability of the Bank of England* [HC 874] 8 November 2011.

138 Bank of England, 'Response from the Court of the Bank to the recommendations made by the Treasury Committee and Joint Committee on the Draft Financial Services Bill on the Accountability of the Bank of England' (12 January 2012). See also Treasury Committee, *Accountability of the Bank of England: Response from the Court of the Bank to the Twenty-first Report from the Committee* [HC 1769] 23 January 2012.

139 Treasury Committee, *Financial Conduct Authority* [HC 1574] 13 January 2012; and Treasury Committee, *Financial Conduct Authority: Report on the Government Response* [HC 1857] 27 February 2012. The Government Response was included within the Appendix to the February 2012 report.

140 Treasury Committee, *Fixing LIBOR: some preliminary findings* [HC 481] 18 August 2012; Treasury Committee, *Fixing LIBOR: some preliminary findings: Financial Services Authority Response to the Committee's Second report of Session 2012–2013* [HC 901] 21 February 2013.

141 Treasury Committee, *The FSA's report into the failure of RBS* [HC 640] 19 October 2012.

142 Treasury Committee, *Financial Services Bill* [HC 161] 24 May 2012.

143 ICB, *Issues Paper—Call for Evidence* (September 2010).

September 2011.[144] The ICB specifically recommended the establishment of a ring-fence around the retail and SME activities of major UK banks, with ring-fenced institutions subject to higher capital requirements with, at least, 10 per cent of risk-weighted assets and corresponding limits on leverage. Institutions would also be required to hold an additional 7–10 per cent of loss-absorbing capital through convertible debt or 'bail-in bonds', with insured depositors receiving an automatic statutory 'depositor preference' on the insolvency of a ring-fenced bank.

1.80 The Government published its response to the ICB proposals in December 2011[145] with a speech by the Chancellor,[146]and with a formal response document.[147] The Government accepted that vital banking services in the form of accepting retail deposits should only be provided by ring-fenced banks with these banks being prohibited from undertaking certain investment banking activities. The Government also supported the ICB's recommendations on loss absorbency with non-structural reforms being required to complement the ring-fencing. All banks should be subject to normal competitive market forces and be able to fail safely without government guarantee and undermining the provision of critical services. All banks should be resolvable without the need for state resources and with an appropriate resolution regime also being set up for investment firms and financial holding companies. The Government restated the principal recommendations of the ICB in a White Paper in February 2013[148] with the Chancellor discussing the reforms during a press conference at JP Morgan in Bournemouth.[149] Draft principal secondary legislation was also produced[150] with the draft Banking Reform Bill to be scrutinised by the Parliamentary Commission on Banking Standards.

Parliamentary Commission on Banking Standards

1.81 A joint Parliamentary Commission on Banking Standards ('PCBS') was set up in 2012 following the LIBOR scandal. The PCBS was to report on professional standards and culture within the UK banking sector and the lessons to be drawn on corporate governance, transparency, and conflicts of interest, and their implications for regulation and Government policy. The PCBS was asked to conduct the pre-legislative scrutiny of the draft Financial Services (Banking Reform) Bill.[151] The PCBS had identified five principal themes for possible reform by the time of its *First Report* in December 2012.[152] These were specifically concerned with how banks were structured, how they compete, run themselves, were supervised and regulated, and

---

[144] ICB, *Interim Report* (11 April 2011); and ICB, *Final Report* (12 September 2011).

[145] HM Treasury, 'Government sets out plans to reform the structure of banking in the UK' (19 December 2011) 145/11.

[146] HM Treasury, 'Banking Reform Statement by the Chancellor' (19 December 2011).

[147] HM Treasury and Department for Business Innovation & Skills, *The Government response to the Independent Commission on Banking* (December 2011) CM 8252.

[148] HM Treasury and Department for Business Innovation & Skills, *Banking Reform: a new structure for stability and growth* (February 2013) CM 8545.

[149] HM Treasury, 'Speech by the Chancellor of the Exchequer on the Reform of Banking' (4 February 2013).

[150] Financial Services and Markets Act 2000 (Excluded Activities and Prohibitions) Order 2013; Financial Services and Markets Act 2000 (Fees and Prescribed International Organisations) Regulations 2013; Financial Services and Markets Act 2000 (Ring-fenced Bodies and Core Activities) Order 2013 and alternative draft; and Financial Services and Markets Acts 2000 (Ring-fenced Bodies and Core Activities) Order 2013.

[151] Statement by the Leader of the House of Commons, the Rt Hon Sir George Young MP, HC Deb (16 July 2012) col 797 [Commons Chamber].

[152] Parliamentary Commission on Banking Standards, *First Report* [HL Paper 98, HC 848] 21 December 2012.

the law, including criminal and civil sanctions, applicable to banks and bankers.[153] The PCBS had decided to establish 11 separate panels on Financial Exclusion and Basic Bank Accounts, Mis-selling and Cross-selling, Regulatory Approach, Tax, Audit and Accounting, Scotland, Corporate Governance (board level), Operation of Wholesale Markets, Retail Competition, Corporate Governance (below board level), HBOS, and Consumer and SME Experience. The PCBS published further reports on *Banking Reform*, *Proprietary Trading*, and *The Failure of HBOS*.[154] The PCBS published its final report in June 2013.[155]

Financial Services Act 2012

The FSA 2012 received Royal Assent on 19 December 2012 and came into effect on 1 April 2013.[156] The FSA 2012 substantially amends the FSMA 2000 to create the new institutional structure to be set up in the UK. Many of the provisions are accordingly constitutional and concerned with specifying the relevant functions and powers and ensuring that all of the new agencies or entities within and outside the Bank of England work effectively together. The 2012 Act amends the BEA 1998, the BA 2009, the Consumer Credit Act 1974 and the Companies Act 1989. The 2012 Act consists of 123 sections with 21 Schedules. These generally deal with the Bank of England, amendments to FSMA, mutual societies, collaboration between the Treasury and Bank, FCA and PRA, inquiries and investigations, investigation of complaints against the regulatory bodies, offences, amendments to the BA 2009, and miscellaneous and general provisions. A consolidated copy of FSMA 2000 as amended by the Government's draft Bill had been published by the Treasury and subsequently amended.[157] **1.82**

The Government published a document setting out its general approach to the draft secondary legislation required under the FSA 2012 and amended FSMA in October 2012[158] with a consultation response document published in January 2013.[159] Specific secondary legislation was required inter alia in the areas of allocation of regulatory responsibility between the PRA and FCA (section 22A FSMA as amended),[160] threshold conditions (section 55C FSMA as amended),[161] mutual societies (Part 3 FSA 2012),[162] power of direction **1.83**

[153] Para 3. The PCBS noted that total outstanding support provided to the UK financial services sector amounted to £228 billion in March 2012 which had fallen from £456 billion in 2011 and a peak of £1.2 trillion. The £228 billion was made up of £109 billion of outstanding guarantee commitments with £119 billion being made available in cash. HM Treasury, *Annual Report and Accounts 2011—2012* [HC 2010–12] 46, 91.

[154] Parliamentary Commission on Banking Standards, *Banking reform: towards the right structure* [HL 126, HC 1012] 11 March 2013; Parliamentary Commission on Banking Standards, *Proprietary Trading* [HL 138, HC 1034] 15 March 2013; and Parliamentary Commission on Banking Standards, *An accident waiting to happen: The Failure of HBOS* [HL 144, HC 705] 4 April 2013.

[155] Parliamentary Commission on Banking Standards, *Banking reform: towards the right structure* [HL, HC] June 2013. One of the issues considered by the Commission at a late stage was whether the operations of RBS should be split to allow its non-core activities to be removed to allow it to recover and be sold back into the market more quickly.

[156] See HM Treasury, 'Financial Services Bill receives Royal Assent' (19 December 2012) 126/12.

[157] Proposed Legislation, *Financial Services and Markets Act 2000* (2000 Chapter 8). Available at: <http://www.hm-treasury.gov.uk/d/consolidated_fsma050911.pdf>.

[158] HM Treasury, *A new approach to financial regulation: draft secondary legislation* (October 2012).

[159] HM Treasury, *Financial Services Act 2012: a summary of consultation responses on draft secondary legislation and Government response* (January 2013).

[160] The Financial Services and Markets Act 2000 (PRA-Regulated Activities) Order 2013.

[161] The Financial Services and Markets Act 2000 (Threshold Conditions) Order 2013.

[162] The Financial Services Act 2012 (Mutual Societies) Order 2013.

and information gathering (section 192E-N FSMA as amended), rule-making (section 213 FSMA as amended), and designated bodies and super-complaints (section 234B FSMA as amended).

1.84 The Government had added separate provisions to the Financial Services Bill in response to the Wheatley Review on LIBOR which allowed the regulation of benchmark activities, and with the manipulation of benchmarks being made a criminal offence. A separate consultation paper was issued on *Implementing the Wheatley Review* with two proposed draft Statutory Instruments further amending the Regulated Activities Order ('RAO') issued under FSMA as amended and including new criminal offences within Part 7 of the FSA 2012 on benchmark activities.[163]

1.85 The Government decided to implement the recommendations contained in the ICB report through separate legislation rather than amendment to the Financial Services Bill. The Government published a draft Financial Services (Banking Reform) Bill in February 2013.[164] A Parliamentary *Briefing Paper on the Second Reading* of the Bill was published in February 2012.[165]

1.86 The FSA 2012 provides for the establishment of the FPC, PRA, and FCA. The FPC will be responsible for the conduct of macro-prudential policy within the Bank of England,[166] with the PRA overseeing firms that manage complex risks on their balance sheets and that create potential systemic threats.[167] The FCA will ensure that financial services business and financial services markets are conducted in a manner that advances the interests of consumers and market participants (formerly 'protecting and enhancing confidence').[168] The Act received Royal Assent on 18 December 2013.

1.87 The primary objective of the FPC is to contribute to the Bank's objective to 'protect and enhance the stability of the financial system of the United Kingdom,' in particular, by identifying, monitoring, and addressing systemic risks to protect and enhance financial system resilience. The objective is to contain systemic risks including cross-sectional risks related to structural features within financial markets (including information problems, externalities, market illiquidity, contagion, systemically important financial institutions, and inadequate market infrastructure), cross-sectional risks relating to the distribution of risk within the financial sector (principally through concentration), and cyclical risks. The drafting was amended by the Joint Committee on the draft Financial Services Bill to confirm that it was irrelevant whether the risks originated from within the UK or abroad, and that structural risks included the degree of interconnectedness between firms. The Financial Services Bill was also amended in the House of Lords to confer a secondary objective on the FPC of supporting 'the economic policies of Her Majesty's Government, including its objectives for growth and employment'.

[163] HM Treasury, *Implementing the Wheatley Review: draft secondary legislation* (November 2012). See also Draft The Financial Services and Markets Act 2000 (Regulated Activities) Order 2001; and Draft The Financial Services and Markets Act 2000 (Misleading Statements and Impressions) Order.

[164] HM Treasury, 'Government published Banking Reform Bill' (4 February 2013), Press notice 06/13, and draft Financial Services (Banking Reform) Bill 130 2012-13 with Explanatory Notes Bill 130 EN 2012–13.

[165] House of Commons, *Financial Services (Banking Reform) Bill* [Bill No. 130 of 2012–13] (28 February 2013), Research Paper 13/15.

[166] Paras 1.118–1.124.

[167] Paras 1.125–1.127, 1.129–1.131, and Ch 3.

[168] Paras 1.128–1.130 and Ch 3.

The PRA's general objective is to promote the safety and soundness of PRA-authorised persons and to seek to ensure that the business of such persons is carried on in a way that avoids any adverse effect on the stability of the UK financial system and that minimises the adverse effect that failure could have on the stability of the UK financial system.[169] The PRA is given a separate insurance objective. A number of constitutional, consultation and review provisions are imposed under FSMA as revised by FSA 2012 with a number of common provisions in respect of the PRA and FCA.[170] **1.88**

The FCA has a single strategic objective of ensuring that relevant markets function well with three operational objectives of securing an appropriate degree of consumer protection, protecting and enhancing the integrity of the UK financial system, and promoting effective competition in the interests of consumers. The FCA is given a new direct product intervention power to allow it to ban or impose restrictions on specific financial products. It will be able to disclose details of warning notices on disciplinary action and will have the authority to act against misleading financial promotions and disclose its actions in this regard. The FCA is also to assume responsibility for consumer credit regulation from the Office of Fair Trading with effect from 1 April 2014. Equivalent constitutional, consultation, and review provisions are provided for as with the PRA.[171] **1.89**

Bank of England

The regulatory changes brought into effect under the FSA 2012 have created a new central bank-based control model within the UK. This has centralised a number of market functions and strengthened the role and function of the Bank of England.[172] The Bank is now responsible for monetary policy, financial stability, the prudential regulation of depository institutions, designated investment firms and insurance companies, as well as bank resolution and market infrastructure supervision. These are in addition to its general functions as a central bank. These include note issuance, managing the Government accounts, providing advice to the Government on financial matters, managing the country's foreign exchange reserves, and providing market liquidity including emergency lender of last resort support ('LLR').[173] Debt management was transferred to the Debt Management Office ('DMO') in 1998. **1.90**

[169] Paras 1.125–1.127, 1.129–1.131, and Ch 3.

[170] ss 2A-P, 3A-S, and Sch 1ZB FSMA inserted under s 6 FSA 2012.

[171] ss 1A-T, 3A-S, and Sch 1ZA FSMA inserted under s 6 FSA 2012.

[172] See generally, G Morton and A Marsh, 'UK Central Banking and the Financial Stability' in Blair, Walker, and Wiley, *Financial Markets and Exchanges Law* (n 22) Ch 3.

[173] The Bank allowed Overend Gurney & Co Ltd to fail in 1866 although it supported Barings Bank in 1890 which marked the beginning of its assumption of responsibility to provide LLR support to banks in difficulty. Barings was supported by a consortium of major London banks set up by Governor William Lidderdale following Barings' overexposure to Argentinean debt. The nature of the Bank's responsibility in terms of providing emergency support was described by the economist Walter Bagehot in a collection of essays republished in *Lombard Street* (1873). See GA Walker, *International Banking Regulation Law Policy and Practice* (Kluwer Law 2001) Ch 1. LLR would now be provided by the Bank through Emergency Liquidity Assistance ('ELA') which operates outside its Sterling Monetary Framework ('SMF'). See paras 1.150–1.154. On the ELA provided to HBOS and RBS between October 2008 and January 2009, see report by Ian Plenderleith, *Review of the Bank of England's Provision of Emergency Liquidity Assistance in 2008–2009* (October 2012). The review had been commissioned by the Bank's Court in May 2012 with separate reports being carried out on general banking system liquidity and monetary forecasting. See report by Bill Winters, *Review of the Bank of England's Framework for Providing Liquidity to the Banking System* (October 2012); and report by David Stockton, *Review of the Monetary Policy Committee's Forecasting Capability* (October 2012).

Statutory background

1.91 The Bank of England was established in 1694 at the recommendation of the Scottish merchant William Paterson to raise funds to fund the war against the French.[174] The 1694 Act provided for the creation of The Governor and Company of the Bank of England. One and a half million pounds was to be raised with £1.2 million obtained through the sale of shares in the Bank which was lent to the Government at a perpetual interest rate of 8 per cent. The capital stock of the Bank was enlarged and restrictions introduced on forging and counterfeiting under the Bank of England Act 1696. The existence of the Bank was made conditional on the Government not redeeming the loan, with further monies being borrowed between 1709 and 1796. The Bank was declared a 'body corporate and politic forever' under an Act of 1763 subject to redemption before 1786 with the Bank's existence becoming unconditional following the Government's failure to exercise its right of redemption.

1.92 Sir John Houblon was appointed the first Governor with Michael Godfrey the Deputy Governor. An early monopoly right to issue notes was conferred under an Act of 1708 with responsibility for the management of Government securities transferred from the Exchequer in 1773. Bank of England notes were made legal tender in 1833.[175] A statutory monopoly on note issuance was created under the Bank Charter Act 1844 in England and Wales, with Scottish banks retaining their right to issue their own notes backed by Bank of England paper. The amount of notes not backed by gold, which is referred to as the fiduciary issue, was fixed at £14,535,000. Separate Issue and Banking Departments were created within the Bank. The 1844 Act was a victory for the 'Currency School' group at the time which sought to limit the total amount of banknotes in circulation, as against the 'Banking School', which argued that the currency should be allowed to adjust naturally. The Prime Minister, Robert Peel, had supported the Currency School although the fixed fiduciary issuance had to be relaxed on a number of occasions during subsequent times of crisis, in particular, in 1847 and 1857.

1.93 The 1844 Act created a statutory basis for the Gold Standard although a gold specie standard had been adopted on a de facto basis since the seventeenth century. Notes were generally convertible into gold except when this was suspended such as during the Restriction Period between 1797 and 1821. Some countries adopted a Gold Exchange Standard prior to the First World War by fixing their currencies to sterling which was, in turn, fixed to gold. The Gold Standard had to be suspended during the war period with the UK adopting a Gold Bullion Standard under the Gold Standard Act 1925 which provided for the exchange of currency for 400-ounce gold bars but without the production of any separate gold coins. The UK was forced to abandon the Gold Standard in September 1931. A separate Gold Exchange Standard would be set under the Bretton Woods Treaty agreed in 1944 which would fix the value of the US dollar to gold, and all of the other currencies to the US dollar, subject to a formal adjustment mechanism. This applied until President Richard Nixon announced the ending of dollar–gold convertibility with the closure of the 'Discount Window' in 1971 and with international currencies becoming freely floating since 1973.[176]

---

174 Bank of England Act 1694 (5 & 6 Will. & Mar. c. 20).

175 Legal tender is now determined under the Coinage Act 1971.

176 GA Walker, *International Banking Regulation Law Policy and Practice* (n 173).

The Bank of England was nationalised under the Bank of England Act 1946. This provided for the transfer of the capital stock of the Bank to the Treasury in exchange for 3 per cent Government stock.[177] The Treasury was given power to issue directions to the Bank with the Bank having power to request information or make recommendations to bankers.[178] The Bank had no statutory powers with regard to bank supervision until the Banking Act 1979 as amended under the Banking Act 1987 following the Johnson Matthey crisis in autumn 1984.[179] Banking supervision had until then been conducted on an informal and non-legal basis. This was referred to as 'moral suasion' which generally involved the exercise of individual judgement and discretion by senior bank staff subject to the implied threat of withdrawal of daily liquidity or emergency financial support.[180] The Bank's internal supervisory functions were only formalised following the Secondary or Fringe Banking Crisis in 1972–1973.[181] The earlier 'club-' based nature of this style of supervision broke down with the large number of new overseas banks entering the City of London during the early 1970s which led to the Bank supporting the introduction of statutory regulation in 1979.[182] This represented a reversal of the Bank's earlier policy which had resisted the establishment of a formal legal regime, although the Bank realised that this may assist control of the markets more effectively with the breakdown of the earlier moral suasion-based model. **1.94**

Responsibility for bank supervision was transferred from the Bank to the FSA under the Bank of England Act 1998.[183] The FSA became responsible for the regulation of all financial services and markets in the UK on an integrated basis under the FSMA 2000.[184] The constitutional position of the Bank was revised under the Bank of England Act 1998. This specifically amended the structure and operation of the Court with new provisions for the Bank's funding, accounts, and profits. The 1998 Act provided for the establishment of the MPC and a statutory basis for the Bank's functions with regard to monetary policy. **1.95**

Responsibility for bank supervision would be re-transferred to the Bank through its subsidiary PRA under the FSA 2012 with designated investment firms and insurance companies. The residual functions exercised by the FSA were transferred to the new FCA created under the FSA 2012. The Act also amended the Bank of England Act 1998 to create the FPC which replaced the FSC established under the Banking Act 2009.[185] A number of other amendments were made to the FSMA including strengthened provisions on mutual societies, coordinated crisis management, inquiries and investigations, complaints, and offences.[186] **1.96**

Operations

The Bank of England is structured in terms of its principal areas of operational activity. These consist of Monetary Analysis and Statistics, Markets, Financial Stability (and Resolution), **1.97**

[177] s 1 (1) and (2) Bank of England Act 1946 (9 & 10 Geo. 6c. 27).
[178] s 4 (1) and (3).
[179] Chapter 14, para 14.17.
[180] JJ Norton, 'The Bank of England's Lament: the Struggle to Maintain the Traditional Supervisory Practices of "Moral Suasion"' in JJ Norton (ed), *Bank Regulation and Supervision in the 1990s* (Kluwer Law 1991) ch 2.
[181] Chapter 14, para 14.15.
[182] See Walker, *International Banking Regulation Law Policy and Practice* (n 173) ch 1, s 4.
[183] s 21 Bank of England Act 1998.
[184] Paras 1.9–1.12. See also M Blair, G Walker, and R Purves, *Financial Services Law* (2nd edn, OUP 2009) ch 1.
[185] Paras 1.59 and 1.118–124.
[186] Chapters 2, 8, and 13.

Prudential Regulation, and Banking Services.[187] A range of central services are also provided with other specific Finance, Internal Audit, Communications, and Human Resources functions. The Bank also maintains a Centre for Central Banking Studies ('CCBS') which conducts collaborative research and provides teaching and technical assistance to other central banks.[188]

Monetary Analysis and Statistics

1.98 Monetary policy decisions are taken by the MPC[189] although monetary research is carried out through the Monetary Analysis Division. This includes Monetary Analysis and the Statistics and Regulatory Data Division (previously Monetary and Financial Statistics). These are responsible for carrying out the economic analysis supporting monetary policy decisions. Analytical information can be collected through the Bank's 12 regional agencies and other sources and is published through the Bank's *Inflation Report* and *Quarterly Bulletins*. This work is supported by the CCBS. Monetary Analysis includes separate teams on Structural Economic Analysis, International Economic Analysis, Monetary Assessment and Strategy, Conjunctural Assessment and Projections, and Macro Financial Analysis.

Markets

1.99 Markets is responsible for carrying out the Bank's market operations including the implementation of MPC decisions. This also includes managing foreign exchange reserves on behalf of the Treasury, delivering market analysis and intelligence, and assisting with the management of business continuity or other financial crises. The Bank maintains close contacts with other market operations including through central banks and international financial institutions and financial firms. Markets includes a separate Risk Management Division and Markets Strategy and Risk Operations Division with additional sections on Foreign Exchange and Sterling Markets.

Financial Stability

1.100 Financial Stability is responsible for monitoring the effective operations of financial markets more generally and detecting any potential sources of instability. This includes separate sections covering Markets, Sectors and Interlinkages, International Finance, Macro-prudential Strategy, the Banking System, and Prudential Policy. This also includes a separate Market Infrastructure section with Financial Stability also working with the Special Resolution Unit ('SPU') which is responsible for the exercise of the Bank's stabilisation powers under the Banking Act 2009. The unit was set up in February 2009. Information on stability matters is published through the Bank's *Financial Stability Reports*. The division works closely with other European and international organisations and committees.

Banking Services

1.101 The Bank carries out a number of transactions and functions for the Government and other financial institutions and central banks through its Customer Banking Division. This includes account services as well as managing foreign exchange or gold holdings. Some of these services were to be transferred to private institutions as part of a migration initiative.

1.102 The division also includes Notes and Market Services. Notes is responsible for UK banknote issuance under the Bank's Note Circulation Scheme ('NCS') which was introduced in 2001.

[187] See Bank of England, *Executive Team and Divisional Structure*. Available at: <http://www.bankofengland.co.uk/about/Documents/pdfs/structure.pdf>.

[188] <http://www.bankofengland.co.uk/education/Pages/ccbs/default.aspx>.

[189] Paras 1.113–1.114.

This governs the operation of the commercial cash function between NCS Members and the Bank including wholesale distribution, circulation, and replacement of banknotes.[190]

The Market Services Division is responsible for the operation of the UK Real Time Gross Settlement ('RTGS') payment system for high-value sterling transfers and for securities settlement. The RTGS provides for the continuous real-time settlement of transactions through the Clearing House Automated Payment System ('CHAPS') rather than through end-of-day net transaction settlement. This is managed through the Central Gilts & Moneymarkets Office ('CGMO'). Euro payments are made through CHAPS Euro which provides for real-time cross-border payment through the ECB TARGET (Trans-European Automated Real-time Gross Settlement Express Transfer system) and TARGET2 system which replaced TARGET in November 2007. 1.103

Central Services

Central Services consist of the Bank's Legal function as well as Security & Business Continuity and IT support. The Chief Legal Advisor reports directly to the Governor. Other general functions include Finance (with Financial Reporting and Control, Projects and Risk Oversight, and Property and Procurement), Internal Audit, Communications, and Human Resources Services. 1.104

Court of Directors

The Court of Directors is the principal decision-taking body within the Bank. The Court was retained under the BEA 1998 and consisted of the Governor, Deputy Governors for Financial Stability and Monetary Policy, and 16 directors with this number being reduced to nine under the BA 2009 and the Deputy Governor for Prudential Regulation being included under the FSA 2012.[191] 1.105

The functions of the Court are to manage the Bank's affairs, other than the formulation of monetary policy, and include determining the Bank's objectives and strategy.[192] The Court is to determine the Bank's strategy in relation to the Financial Stability Objective and to review and revise this from time to time following consultation with the FPC and Treasury.[193] The Bank is to make an annual report to the Chancellor on its activities each year.[194] The Court is to have custody of the Bank's seal with the seal only being used on authorisation of the Court or a sub-committee of the Court.[195] 1.106

All members of the Court are appointed by the Crown. Directors are appointed for four years.[196] The Governor is now appointed for a single term of eight years and the Deputy Governor for five years.[197] The Court is to meet, at least seven times a year or on notice of the Governor or Chair. The Court may delegate duties and powers to a member of the Court, any other officer, servant, or agent of the Bank or a sub-committee. The BA 1998 contains 1.107

[190] Para 1.151. See also: <http://www.bankofengland.co.uk/banknotes/Pages/about/distribution_circulation.aspx>.
[191] s 1 (1) and (2) BEA 1998; s 239 BA 2009; and s 1(1) FSA 2012.
[192] s 2 (1) and (2) BEA 1998.
[193] s 9A BEA 1998 inserted under s 4 FSA 2012.
[194] s 4 (1) BEA 1998.
[195] s 5 (1) and (2) BEA 1998.
[196] Para 2 Sch 1 BEA 1998 as amended by para 1 Sch 2 FSA 2012.
[197] Para 1 Sch 1 BEA 1998 as amended by para 1 Sch 2 FSA 2012.

additional provisions with regard to qualifications, removal, powers, meetings, proceedings, and remuneration.[198]

Oversight Committee

1.108 An Oversight Committee was created as a sub-committee of the Court under the FSA 2012.[199] The internal governance arrangements of the Bank were considered by the Treasury Committee and Joint Committee on the Financial Services Bill[200] with the Court of the Bank recommending the creation of an Oversight Committee in its response document in January 2012.[201] The objective was to extend the accountability of the Bank, in particular, to Parliament and the Treasury Committee especially with its assumption of additional responsibility in respect of financial stability under the FSA 2012. Final provisions were included within the FSA 2012 following further comment by the Treasury Committee and the Government's response.[202]

1.109 The functions of the Oversight Committee are to review the Bank's performance with regard to its objectives, the duty of the FPC to assist in achieving the Financial Stability Objective, and the Bank's strategy. It is to monitor the extent to which the objectives set by the Court have been met, to review the internal financial controls of the Bank and certain other additional matters, including FPC and MPC procedures, and member terms and conditions, and the remuneration of the Governor and Deputy Governor.[203]

1.110 The Oversight Committee is to be chaired by the chair of the Court and determine its own procedures and may delegate any functions to two or more members.[204] The Oversight Committee may arrange for reviews to be conducted in relation to any matters including performance reviews with regard to the Bank's performance and objectives.[205] Copies of performance review reports must be provided to the Treasury and published unless the Court considers that this would be against the public interest.[206] The person conducting the review may make recommendations to the Bank on the steps to be taken.[207]

Functions

1.111 The Bank can be considered to carry out five specific supervisory and regulatory functions with regard to monetary policy, financial stability, prudential regulation, resolution, and market infrastructure. The Bank also operates in sterling markets for monetary and financial stability purposes. Monetary policy was generally carried out through its Reserves Averaging Scheme

198 Sch 1 BEA 1998.

199 s 3A BEA 1998 inserted under s 3 FSA 2012.

200 See, eg, Treasury Committee, *Accountability of the Bank of England* [HC 874] Twenty-first Report of Session 2010–12, 8 November 2011.

201 Bank of England, 'Response from the Court of the Bank to the Recommendations made by the Treasury Committee and Joint Committee on the Draft Financial Services Bill on the Accountability of the Bank of England' (January 2012).

202 Treasury Committee, *Accountability of the Bank of England: Response from the Court of the Bank to the Twenty-first Report from the Committee* [HC 1769] Twenty-seventh Report of Session 2010-12, 23 January 2012 (n 112); and HM Treasury, *A new approach to financial regulation: securing stability, protecting consumers* (January 2012) CM 8268, paras 2.30–2.31.

203 s 3A BEA 1998.

204 s 3B BEA 1998.

205 s 3C BEA 1998.

206 s 3D BEA 1998.

207 s 3E BEA 1998.

although this has been suspended with the adoption of the Government's Quantitative Easing ('QE') programme and the Bank's Asset Purchase Facility ('APF'). Additional funds can be provided through the Bank's Operational Standing Facilities ('OSF') or special liquidity facilities including its Indexed Long-Term Repos ('ILTR'), Discount Window Facility ('DWF'), and Extended Collateral Term Repo ('ECTR') Facility. These supervisory, regulatory, and liquidity functions are in addition to the Bank's general central bank functions although parts of the specific policies and facilities involved may overlap from time to time.

Monetary Policy

The Court of the Bank has determined that its two Core Purposes are Monetary Stability and Financial Stability. These are to be supplemented by seven strategic priorities as set out in its *Annual Reports*.[208] These are generally concerned with meeting the 2 per cent inflation target, maintaining necessary policies, tools, and infrastructure, maintaining and improving resilience, delivery of macro-prudential policy, completing the transition to micro-prudential supervision and infrastructure oversight, implementing governance changes, and ensuring that the Bank has the correct people and processes to carry out its core purposes. **1.112**

The purpose of monetary stability is to maintain stable prices with low inflation and confidence in the currency. Inflation and rising prices reduce the value of money with monetary policy attempting to secure non-inflationary economic growth. The key monetary decisions are taken by the MPC which was set up under the BEA 1998. The objectives of the Bank are to maintain price stability in relation to monetary policy and to support the Government's policies on growth and employment. The Treasury notifies the Bank in writing through a letter from the Chancellor on price stability and economic policy.[209] The Chancellor ordered a review to be undertaken into the conduct of monetary policy in the UK in 2013 with the Bank being provided with a revised monetary mandate.[210] **1.113**

The MPC is to have responsibility for formulating monetary policy and consists of the Governor and Deputy Governors, two members appointed by the Governor, and four members appointed by the Chancellor.[211] Decisions on market intervention are to be published as soon as practicable after each MPC meeting unless this may impede or frustrate the achievement of the intervention purpose.[212] The MPC generally meets on the Wednesday and Thursday after the first Monday of each month to determine whether any monetary correction in the markets is required. Minutes from each meeting are to be published within six weeks except with regard to proceedings where this may impede or frustrate the Committee's purpose.[213] MPC procedures are to be reviewed by the Court.[214] The Bank was **1.114**

[208] See, eg, Bank of England, 'The Bank's strategic priorities in 2012/13' in *Annual Report 2012* (2012) 29.

[209] s 11 BEA 1998; and 12 (1) BEA 1998.

[210] HM Treasury, *Review of the monetary policy framework* (March 2013) CM 8588; and HM Treasury, 'Remit for Monetary Policy Committee' (20 March 2013). This generally retained the flexible 2 per cent inflation targeting policy originally adopted in 1992 although with clarified 'trade-offs' to allow higher temporary short-term inflation rates and with monetary and macro-prevention policy being properly co-ordinated. The Bank of England issued a response document which expanded on the trade-offs and the value of using explicit 'state contingent' forward guidance to support this. See Bank of England, *Monetary policy trade-offs and forward guidance* (August 2013).

[211] s 13 (1) and (2) BEA 1998.

[212] s 14 (1) and (2) BEA 1998.

[213] s 15 (1) and (2) BEA 1998.

[214] s 16 (1) BEA 1998.

given immunity from liability in damages for action or inaction in its capacity as a monetary authority under the BA 2009 unless this was in bad faith or in breach of the Human Rights Act 1998.[215]

1.115 The Government sets the inflation target of two per cent based on an annual rate of inflation calculated using the Consumer Prices Index ('CPI') rather than the the Retail Prices Index ('RPI') since December 2003. The Bank was given operational independence to secure this objective under the BEA 1998. Monetary policy is generally implemented through adjusting the Bank Rate at which banks can borrow funds from the Bank with the adjusting of interest rates affecting decisions to borrow or to spend. Increasing interest rates generally acts as a disincentive to borrow or spend, and reduces inflation, with lower interest rates increasing consumption.[216]

1.116 The framework governing the Bank's operations in the money markets is set out in its *Sterling Monetary Framework* or *'Red Book'*.[217] The Bank generally operated a Reserves Averaging Scheme until March 2009 before it adopted its Quantitative Easing policy to attempt to increase the supply of credit within the financial system following the international and UK crises. Under the Reserves Averaging Scheme, banks would announce a monthly target for their reserves balances with the Bank using its Open Market Operations ('OMOs') to secure the amount of reserves required to cover banks' aggregate demands. Banks received an interest payment at the Bank Rate where reserves remained within a range around the balance notified and were charged where they breached this range. Additional funds could be drawn down or excess monies lent through the Bank's Operational Standing Facilities ('OSF') with a 0.7 per cent lending facility and 0 per cent deposit facility.[218]

1.117 Since March 2009, the Reserves Averaging Scheme has been suspended with banks being rewarded at Bank Rate on all reserves balances. The Government set up an Asset Purchase Facility ('APF') in January 2009 to provide liquidity to the financial system through the purchase of assets from banks using Treasury bills and the DMO's cash management operations. The APF is also used by the MPC for monetary policy purposes through the purchase of assets financed by the creation of additional central bank reserves.[219] The APF has purchased around £375 billion with transactions being carried out through the Bank's subsidiary, the Bank of England Asset Purchase Facility Fund Ltd ('BEAPFF').

Financial Stability

1.118 The financial stability purpose of the Bank is carried out through the FPC. An interim FPC had been created in February 2011 which replaced the functions of the earlier FSC set up

---

[215] s 244 BA 2009.

[216] On the management of interest rates and inflation, see Bank of England, *The transmission mechanism of monetary policy*, available at: <http://www.bankofengland.co.uk/monetarypolicy/Pages/how.aspx>.

[217] See Bank of England, *The Framework for the Bank of England's Operations in the Sterling Money Markets* (June 2012) which includes both 'The Sterling Monetary Framework' (Part 1 December 2010) and 'The Bank's current operations in the sterling money markets' (Part 2 June 2012). The earlier Reserves Averaging Scheme was set out in the 2002 Red Book. The Red Book was reissued in October 2013 following the Bank's review of the provision of liquidity support within the Sterling Monetary Framework, in particular, after the Winters Report in October 2012 (n 173). The objective was to confirm the availability of liquidity to solvent banks with earlier concerns on higher risk taking, and moral hazard, being dealt with through the use of other tools such as liquidity regulation and bank resolution powers. See Bank of England, 'Liquidity insurance at the Bank of England: developments in the Sterling Monetary Framework' (October 2013). On the provision of liquidity within the Sterling Monetary Framework, see paras 1.150–155.

[218] Bank of England, 'Operational Standing Facilities' (Red Book) Ch VIII.

[219] Bank of England, 'Quantitative Easing' (Red Book) ch VIII.

under the BA 2009.[220] The FPC consists of the Governor, Deputy Governors, and Chief Executive of the FCA, one member appointed by the Governor (responsible for financial stability threat analysis), four members appointed by the Chancellor, and a Treasury representative.[221] The objectives of the FPC are to exercise its functions to contribute to achieving the Bank's Financial Stability Objective as well as support the economic policy of the Government including growth and employment. This is stated to relate primarily to the identification and monitoring of, and taking action to remove or reduce, systemic risks to protect and enhance the UK financial system.

The FPC is not to act in a way that would have a significant adverse effect on the capacity of the financial sector to contribute to the growth of the UK economy in the medium or long term. Systemic risks specifically include those attributable to structural features of financial markets, including interconnections between institutions, risk distribution and unsustainable levels of leverage, debt, or credit growth.[222] Systemic risk is only generally otherwise defined as meaning a risk to the stability of the UK financial system as a whole or a significant part of that system.[223] The Treasury is to specify the economic policy of the Government.[224] The Treasury may make written recommendations to the FPC concerning its understanding of the Bank's Financial Stability Objective, the FPC's responsibilities with regard to this objective, and the Government's economic policy and other matters to which the FPC should have regard in exercising its functions. The FPC is to notify the action taken, to be taken, or reasons for not acting.[225] The FPC is to have regard to the Bank's financial stability strategy in exercising its functions and avoid acting in a way that would prejudice the advancement of the FCA of its operational objectives or the objectives of the PRA. The FPC is to have regard to the principles of proportionality, disclosure, and UK international obligations.[226] **1.119**

The FPC functions are to monitor the stability of the UK financial system to identify and assess systemic risk, give directions, make recommendations, and prepare *Financial Stability Reports* or any other functions determined by the Court.[227] The FPC may give directions to the FCA or PRA to exercise their functions to implement a macro-prudential measure with regard to a specified class of regulated persons.[228] The FCA and PRA are to comply as soon as reasonably practicable and notify the FPC accordingly.[229] Directions may be revoked with directions, revocations, and compliance reports to be in writing.[230] A macro-prudential measure is one prescribed by the Treasury by order following consultation with the FPC or with the Governor in the event that a delay would be prejudicial to the stability of the UK financial system.[231] The FPC is to prepare written policy statements on the exercise of its **1.120**

[220] s 2B BEA 1998 inserted under s 238 BA 2009. FPC statements are published on the Bank of England website: <http://www.bankofengland.co.uk/financialstability/Pages/fpc/meetings/default.aspx>.
[221] s 9B (1) and (2) BEA 1998 inserted under s 4 FSA 2012.
[222] s 9C (1)–(3) BEA 1998.
[223] s 9C (1)–(5) BEA 1998.
[224] s 9D BEA 1998.
[225] s 9E (1) and (3) BEA 1998.
[226] s 9F (1)–(3) BEA 1998.
[227] s 9G (1) and (2).
[228] s 9H (1).
[229] s 9I (1) and (3).
[230] ss 9J and 9K BEA 1998.
[231] s 9L (1) and (2) BEA 1998.

power of direction, with Treasury orders being laid before Parliament and approved by both Houses.[232]

1.121 The FPC may make recommendations, including on the provision of financial assistance to financial institutions by the Bank or the Bank's infrastructure functions, to the Treasury, the FCA, and PRA, and any other persons.[233] The FPC is to explain the reasons for exercising its powers of direction or recommendation and to review the directions and recommendations made.[234] The Bank is to publish a record of the meetings of the FPC within six weeks subject to certain exceptions including in the public interest with delayed publication being possible where appropriate.[235]

1.122 The FPC is to continue to publish the Bank's *Financial Stability Reports*.[236] The Governor and Chancellor are to meet to discuss the reports as soon as practicable after publication with a record of the meeting being published within six weeks unless this would be against the public interest.[237] The Bank is given a separate power to give a direction to the FCA or PRA to provide specific information on documents following consultation with the relevant authority and publication unless this would be against the public interest.[238]

1.123 The Bank of England and FSA issued a discussion paper on macro-prudential tools in December 2011.[239] This distinguishes between time-varying and cross-sectional systemic risk and between balance-sheet, lending, and market structure macro-prudential tools. Balance-sheet tools include countercyclical capital buffers, restrictions on distributions, leverage ratio limits, sectoral capital requirements, and time-varying provisioning or liquidity buffers. Transaction tools include loan-to-value ('LTV') or loan-to-income ('LTI') restrictions, and margining requirements. Market tools include requiring the use of central counterparties ('CCPs') and trading venue conditions, such as using 'circuit breakers'.[240]

1.124 The Treasury issued a consultation document on the FPC's powers of direction in September 2012[241] with the FPC issuing a draft policy statement on countercyclical capital buffers ('CCB') and sectoral capital requirements in January 2013.[242] The Government published its response to the responses received in January 2013.[243] The Government confirmed that the FPC would set the rate of the CCB with the Bank publishing further guidance on the use of sectoral capital requirements and relevant indicators used.[244] The FPC would also be given a time-varying leverage ratio but only from 2018 and subject to review in 2017. A first Macro-prudential Measures Order in respect of maintaining additional own funds to cover

---

232 s 9M and 9N BEA 1998.

233 ss 9O, 9P, 9Q, and 9R BEA 1998.

234 s 9S and 9T BEA 1998.

235 s 9U and 9V BEA 1998.

236 s 9W BEA 1998.

237 s 9X BEA 1998.

238 s 9Y and 9Z BEA 1998.

239 Bank of England and FSA, *Instruments of Macroprudential Policy* (December 2011).

240 Tables 3.A and 3.B, Bank of England (n 239), 17 and 19.

241 HM Treasury, *The Financial Services Bill: The Financial Policy Committee's macro-prudential tools* (September 2012) CM 8434.

242 Bank of England, *The Financial Policy Committee's powers to supplement capital requirements—A Draft Policy Statement* (January 2013).

243 HM Treasury, *The Financial Services Act 2012: summary of consultation responses on draft secondary legislation and Government response* (January 2013), ch 3.

244 Paras 3.18 and 3.24.

residential and commercial property exposures or financial sector exposures was issued in March 2013 and came into effect on 1 April 2013.[245]

Prudential Regulation

Prudential regulation is carried out by the PRA which was set up as a subsidiary of the Bank. The PRA is responsible for the prudential regulation of approximately 900 deposit-taking institutions, including banks, building societies, and credit unions, as well as 500 insurances companies, including general insurers, life insurance companies, London Market wholesale firms, and mutual insurers including friendly societies.[246] **1.125**

The PRA is created under the FSA 2012.[247] The PRA is required to act in a way that advances its general objective insofar as is reasonably possible with the general objective being to promote the safety and soundness of PRA-authorised persons.[248] The PRA has a separate insurance objective to contribute to securing an appropriate degree of protection for policy holders.[249] The Treasury may specify additional objectives by order.[250] **1.126**

The PRA is to determine and review its strategy in relation to its objectives, and give and review guidance in discharging its general functions with regard to different categories of PRA-authorised persons or regulated activities.[251] The PRA must maintain arrangements for supervising PRA-authorised persons and is subject to a general duty to consult with PRA-authorised persons or interested parties including the PRA Practitioner Panel.[252] The PRA is subject to independent review on behalf of the Treasury with regard to the economy, efficiency, and effectiveness with which it uses its resources to discharge its functions.[253] **1.127**

The FCA is responsible for the regulation of the conduct of PRA-authorised firms and the prudential regulation of all other financial services firms not regulated by the PRA. The general duties, objectives, supervision, monitoring and enforcement requirements, and consultation obligations of the FCA are set out in Chapter 1 of Part 1A FSMA as amended. Its general functions are to act in a way that is compatible with its strategic objective and advances one or more of its operational objectives so far as is reasonably possible. Its strategic **1.128**

245 The Bank of England Act 1998 (Macro-prudential Measures) Order 2013. Relevant CCB and SCR core indicators are published on the Bank's website: <http://www.bankofengland.co.uk/financialstabilty/Pages/fpc/coreindicators.aspx>.

246 Firms subject to prudential regulation by the PRA are to be specified by order of the Treasury under s 22A FSMA with the Treasury producing The Financial Services and Markets Act 2000 (PRA-regulated Activities) Order (SI 2013/556). Deposit taking and insurance are included under art 2(a), (b), and (c) and Lloyd's of London related activities by art 2(e), (f), and (g) of the PRA RAO. Under arts 2(d) and 3(1), the PRA may designate a person dealing in investments as principal to be subject to PRA regulation which brings securities and investment firms within its potential scope of authority. Arts 4, 5, 6, and 7 deal with the exercise of the power, review of designations, withdrawal and cessation with the PRA to produce a statement of policy under art 9. The Bank of England and FSA produced a draft policy statement in October 2012. See Bank of England and FSA, *Designation of investment firms for prudential supervision by the PRA: consultation on a draft policy statement* (October 2012). See also E Murphy, 'Changes to the Bank of England' *Quarterly Bulletin* [2013] Q1, 20–28, 22. See also Chapter 5.

247 The PRA was originally set up as the Prudential Regulation Authority Limited and was renamed under the FSMA as amended. s 2A(1) FSMA inserted under s 5 FSA 2012.

248 s 2B FSMA.

249 s 2C (2).

250 s 2D (1).

251 s 2E and 2I.

252 ss 2K, 2L, and 2M.

253 s 2O FSMA.

objective is ensuring that relevant markets function well with three operational objectives defined in terms of consumer protection, integrity, and competition.[254] The FCA is to maintain arrangements for supervising authorised firms and to determine and to enforce compliance.[255] The FCA is subject to a general duty to consult which includes with the FCA Practitioner Panel, Smaller Business Practitioner Panel, Markets Practitioner Panel, and Consumer Panel all set up under the revised provisions in FSMA.[256] The activities of the FCA are also subject to Treasury review.[257]

1.129 The FCA and PRA are to have regard to the revised regulatory principles imposed under FSMA with the FCA also considering financial crime and the PRA considering the adverse effect of its activities on competition in relevant markets.[258] The regulatory principles relate to efficiency, proportionality, sustainable growth, consumer responsibility, senior management responsibility, regulatory coordination, disclosure, and transparency.[259] The FCA and PRA are required to follow generally accepted principles of good corporate governance.[260] The FCA and PRA are subject to a statutory duty to coordinate the exercise of their functions and enter into a general Memorandum of Understanding and specific Memorandum on with-profits insurance policies.[261] The Treasury may by order specify the boundaries of the respective functions of the FCA and PRA subject to Parliamentary approval.[262]

1.130 The PRA is given the power to require the FCA to refrain from taking specified action or to issue directions with regard to with-profits policies subject to prior consultation and Treasury and Parliamentary notice.[263] Directions may be issued by either regulator to the other in respect of the consolidated supervision of relevant groups.[264] The FCA and PRA are subject to a statutory duty to cooperate with the Bank of England including the sharing of information.[265] The regulators may enter into separate arrangements with regard to the provision of services between themselves.[266] The FCA and PRA are required to establish complaints arrangements with a new Complaints Commissioner to be established.[267] The investigation of complaints against the regulators is provided for under Part 6 FSMA.[268]

1.131 The regulatory approach of the PRA was set out in two policy statements with regard to banks and insurance companies.[269] The PRA has issued separate policy statements on enforcement and investigations as well as power of direction over qualifying parent undertakings

[254] ss 1B(1)–(3) and 1C, 1D, and 1E FSMA inserted under s 6 FSA 2012. See chs 2 and 3.
[255] s 1L FSMA.
[256] ss 1M, 1N, 1O, 1P, 1Q, and 1R FSMA.
[257] ss 1S and 1T FSMA.
[258] ss 1B(5)(A) and 2H(1)(A) FSMA.
[259] s 3B(1) FSMA.
[260] s 3C FSMA.
[261] ss 3D, 3E, and 3F FSMA.
[262] ss 3G and 3H FSMA.
[263] ss 3I, 3J, and 3L FSMA.
[264] s 3M FSMA.
[265] s 3Q FSMA.
[266] s 3R FSMA.
[267] <http://www.fscc.gov.uk/>.
[268] ss 84–88 FSA 2012. See also Bank of England and FSA, *Complaints against the regulators* (November 2012) CP12/30; and Bank of England and FSA, *Complaints against the regulators* (March 2013) PS 13/7.
[269] Bank of England, *The Prudential Regulation Authority's approach to banking supervision* (April 2013); and Bank of England, *The Prudential Regulation Authority's approach to insurance supervision* (April 2013). See also Bank of England and FSA, *The PRA's approach to banking supervision* (October 2012); and 'The Prudential Regulation Authority' Bank of England *Quarterly Bulletin* [2012] 1–9.

under FSA 2012.[270] Separate statements were issued on the designation of investment firms for PRA supervision, the PRA's Handbook, and compensation.[271] The PRA has also consulted on regulatory fees and levies for 2013–2014, and credit risk internal ratings-based approaches which consolidates relevant earlier FSA material.[272]

Resolution

Resolution is managed through the Bank's Special Resolution Unit ('SRU'). A statutory Special Resolution Regime ('SRR') was created under the Banking (Special Provisions) Act 2008 to provide for the nationalisation of Northern Rock. This was replaced by permanent provisions under the BA 2009 which came into effect on 21 February 2009. These are referred to as the stabilisation powers.[273] This provides for three specific resolution options including transfer of a bank's property or shares to a private sector purchaser, temporary transfer to a bridge bank (set up as a subsidiary of the Bank of England), and public ownership (nationalisation). The BA 2009 also established a special Bank Insolvency Procedure ('BIP'), which specifically assists timely payments to insured depositors, and a Bank Administration Procedure ('BAP') which allows any part of a failed institution to be placed into administration.[274] **1.132**

The BA 2009 specifies the statutory objectives of the SRR. These consist of protecting and enhancing the stability of the UK financial system, protecting and enhancing public confidence in the stability of the UK banking systems, depositor protection, public funds protection, and avoiding interference with property rights against the Human Rights Act 1998.[275] A Code of Practice was to be issued by the Treasury on the exercise of stabilisation powers and the BIP and BAP.[276] The Code was issued by the Treasury in November 2010.[277] The resolution options generally operate, with the PRA determining whether a bank should be placed into the SRR following consultation with the Bank and the Treasury.[278] The Bank is responsible for the exercise of the private sector purchaser and bridge bank stabilisation options.[279] The Treasury is to determine whether an institution is to be taken into temporary public ownership.[280] The BA 2009 contains specific provisions governing the transfer of securities and property as well as compensation and incidental functions.[281] The BA 2009 amends Part 15 FSMA with regard to the operation of the Financial Services Compensation **1.133**

[270] Bank of England, *The Prudential Regulation Authority's approach to enforcement: statutory statements of policy and procedure* (1 April 2013); Bank of England, *Conducting statutory investigations: policy statement* (18 April 2013); and Bank of England, *The power of direction over qualifying parent undertakings: statement of policy* (1 April 2013).

[271] Bank of England, *Designation of investment firms for prudential supervision by the Prudential Regulation Authority: statement of policy* (25 March 2013); Bank of England, *Regulatory Reform: amendments to the Prudential Regulation Authority Handbook* (March 2013) Policy Statement 1/13; and Bank of England, *Financial Services Compensation Scheme—management expenses levy limit 2013/14* (25 March 2013) Policy Statement 2/13.

[272] Bank of England, *Prudential Regulation Authority Regulated fees and levies: rates proposals 2013/14* (9 April 2013) Consultation Paper 3/13; and Bank of England, *Credit risk: internal ratings based approaches* (28 March 2013) Consultation Paper 4/13.

[273] s 4 (2) (a) BA 2009. See also Bank of England, HM Treasury and FSA, *Financial stability and depositor protection: special resolution regime* (July 2008).

[274] Chapter 13, paras 13.260–13.266.

[275] s 4(4)–(8) BA 2009.

[276] s 4(1) BA 2009.

[277] HM Treasury, *Banking Act 2009—Special resolution regime: Code of Practice* (November 2010).

[278] s 7 BA 2009.

[279] ss 11 and 12 BA 2009.

[280] s 13 BA 2009.

[281] ss 14–32, 33–48, 49–62, and 63–75 BA 2009.

Scheme including with regard to contingency funding, contribution to special resolution costs, and borrowing from the National Loans Fund.[282]

1.134 The SRR was used with regard to the Dunfermline Building Society and Southsea Mortgage and Investment Company Limited. Core parts of the Dunfermline were transferred to the Nationwide Building Society in March 2009, including its retail and wholesale deposits, branches, head office, and originated residential mortgages, with social housing loans being transferred to DBS Bridge Bank Ltd temporarily, and subsequently transferred to the Nationwide in July 2009.[283] The Southsea bank was placed into BIP with DBO LLP being appointed liquidator in June 2011. The firm only had 250 depositors with retail deposits of around £7.4 million. Bradford & Bingley was nationalised under the powers available with the Banking (Special Provisions) Act 2008.

1.135 The Bank's SRU works with the PRA in developing RRPs required under the amendments made to the FSMA under the FSA 2010.[284] This requires that the PRA issue general rules concerning the preparation of Recovery plans and Resolution plans.[285] The FSA had issued a Consultation Paper and Discussion Paper on RRPs in August 2011.[286] Amended draft core rules and an RRP Information Pack were produced in May 2012.[287]

1.136 The Treasury consulted on the possible extension of the scope of the SRR in August 2012 to include investment firms and parent undertakings, central counterparties ('CCPs'), non-CCP financial market infrastructures, and insurers.[288] Draft legislation was produced to extend resolution to cover investment firms, investment firm and bank parent undertakings, and CCPs. Amendments to the BA 2009 were incorporated in Part 8 of the FSA 2012 covering groups, investment firms, and UK clearing houses.[289]

1.137 Separate initiatives have been undertaken to extend domestic resolution procedures to apply in cross-border situations. Specific difficulties arose with regard to the cross-border liquidation of Lehman Brothers which filed for Chapter 11 bankruptcy protection in the US on 15 September 2008. Lehman Brothers International (Europe) was placed in administration in the UK on the same day with Tony Lomas, Steven Pearson, Dan Schwarzmann, and Mike Jervis, Pricewaterhouse Coopers LLP, being appointed joint administrators.[290] The closure of Lehman led to 75 separate sets of bankruptcy proceedings being conducted across

---

[282] Part 4 BA 2009.

[283] Dunfermline Building Society Property Transfer Instrument 2009 (30 March 2009); and DBS Bridge Bank Limited Supplemental and Onward Property Transfer Instrument 2009 (1 July 2009). See also Bank of England, *Report under Section 80 (1) of the Banking Act 2009 on the Dunfermline Building Society (DBS) Bridge Bank* (July 2010).

[284] ss 139B–F FSMA inserted under s 7 FSA 2010.

[285] ss 139B and 139C FSMA as amended.

[286] FSA, *Recovery and Resolution Plans* (August 2011) CP11/16 including 'Draft Handbook Text'; and FSA, 'RRP Guidance pack for firms' (August 2011).

[287] FSA, *Recovery and Resolution Plans* (May 2012) FS12/1; FSA, *RRP Information Pack* (May 2012); and FSA, *Draft Amendments to FINMAR* (May 2012).

[288] HM Treasury, *Financial sector resolution: broadening the regime* (August 2012) CM 8419; and HM Treasury, *Financial sector resolution: summary of responses* (October 2012).

[289] ss 100–102 FSA 2012.

[290] See PWC, *Lehman Brothers International (Europe)—In Administration. Joint Administrators' ninth progress report for the period from 15 September 2012 to 14 March 2013* (12 April 2013). See also: <http://www.pwc.co.uk/business-recovery/administrations/lehman/index.jhtml>.

the world.[291] Lehman had $639 billion in assets and $613 billion in liabilities with LBIE owing £35 billion ($53.8 billion) to European creditors. LBIE creditors may be paid in full, although this may take a number of years.[292] The Federal Deposit Insurance Corporation ('FDIC') and the Bank of England had entered into an MOU on cross-border resolution in January 2010[293] with a joint paper on resolution strategies for large and complex firms being issued in December 2012.[294] This sets out a 'top-down' approach using the appointment of a single resolution authority acting at the holding-company or parent-company level within each complex group, with two parallel strategies operating in the US and UK.

The FSB has been examining the issues that arise with regard to the risks created by global systemically important financial institutions ('GSIFIs') including on resolution and RRPs. The FSB produced a set of twelve *Key Attributes* for the design and operation of effective resolution regimes in October 2011[295] with additional guidance on RRPs for GSIFIs being produced in November 2012.[296] The November 2012 paper included specific guidance for Crisis Management Groups ('CMGs') on recovery triggers and stress scenarios, developing resolution strategies and operational resolution plans, and identification of critical functions and critical shared services.[297] The FSB had identified an initial group of 29 GSIFIs in November 2011 using a Basel Committee on Banking Supervision template with this list subsequently being reduced to 28 in November 2012.[298] The FSB issued subsequent reports on SIFI supervision and on SIFI resolution.[299] **1.138**

The European Commission issued a Consultative Communication on the establishment of an EU Framework for Cross-Border Crisis Management in October 2009 which contained specific measures on Early Intervention (including restoration of stability and financial soundness), Resolution (crisis management using resolution tools), and Insolvency (reorganisation and winding-up).[300] This was followed by a Communication on Bank Resolution funds in May 2010[301] and a formal Crisis Management Communication in October 2010.[302] The Commission subsequently produced a full draft Directive for Recovery and Resolution for credit institutions and investment firms in June 2012 (referred to as the BRR) with a **1.139**

[291] Pricewaterhouse Coopers, *Lehman Brothers' Bankruptcy. Lessons learned from the survivors* (August 2009).

[292] 'Lehman Europe creditors may be repaid in full' *Reuters* (15 April 2013). Available at: <http://www.reuters.com/article/2013/04/15/europe-lehman-idusl2nod20am20130415>.

[293] FDIC and Bank of England, *Memorandum of Understanding concerning consultation, cooperation and the exchange of information related to the resolution of insured depository institutions with cross-border operations in the United States and the United Kingdom* (10 January 2010) final.

[294] FDIC and Bank of England, *Resolving Globally Active, Systemically Important, Financial Institutions* (10 December 2012). See also M Gruenberg and P Tucker, 'Global banks need global solution when they fail' *Financial Times* (10 December 2012).

[295] FSB, *Key Attributes of Effective Resolution Regimes for Financial Institutions* (October 2011).

[296] FSB, *Recover and Resolution Planning: Making the Key Attributes Requirements Operational* (November 2012).

[297] FSB (n 296) Annexes 1, 2, and 3.

[298] FSB, 'Policy Measures to Address Systemically Important Financial Institutions' (4 November 2011); and FSB, 'Update of group of global systemically important banks (G-SIBs)' (1 November 2012). See also Basel Committee, *Global Systemically Important Banks: Assessment methodology and the additional loss absorbency requirement* (November 2011).

[299] FSB, *Increasing the Intensity and Effectiveness of SIFI Supervision* (1 November 2012); and FSB, *Resolution of Systemically Important Financial Institutions* (November 2012).

[300] European Commission, *Building a Crisis Management Framework for the Internal Market* (19 March 2010).

[301] European Commission, *Bank Resolution Funds* (25 May 2010) COM (2010) 254 final.

[302] European Commission, *An EU Framework for Crisis Management in the Financial Sector* (October 2010) COM (2010) 579 final.

substantial Staff Working Document.[303] The Staff Working Document examined the relevant procedural issues and consultation, policy content, definitional problems and subsidiarity, policy options, analysis, and impact, with an assessment of the overall impact of the preferred options identified, and continuing monitoring and evaluation.

1.140 The Draft BRR includes specific provisions on resolution authorities, recovery and resolution plans, removal of impediments to resolvability, intra-group financial support, early intervention and special management, resolution conditions, general principles, valuation, resolution tools and powers (including sale of business, bridge institution, asset separation, and bail-in), restrictions on termination and counterparty safeguards, restriction on judicial proceedings, cross-border resolution, relations with third countries, and resolution funding with further amending and consequential provisions.

Market Infrastructure

1.141 The Bank is responsible for a number of aspects of Financial Market Infrastructure ('FMI') Supervision. While the Bank has traditionally monitored payment systems, this has been extended more recently to include securities settlement systems ('CSSs') and central counterparties ('CCPs'). CCPs are central agencies that stand behind financial transactions (including OTC derivatives and commodity contracts) which confirm settlement. The Bank estimated that UK payment systems transactions were worth around £184 trillion or 127 times UK gross domestic product ('GDP'). The provisions on inter-bank payment systems were brought into effect under Part 5 of the BA 2009. Seven systems were recognised with the BACS (originally Bankers' Automated Clearing Services), CHAPS (Clearing House Automated Payment System), CLS (originally Continuous Linked Settlement), Faster Payments Service, Euroclear UK and Ireland Limited, ICE Clear Europe Limited, and LCH.Clearnet Limited.

1.142 Securities settlement systems facilitate the sale and purchase of bonds, shares, and other securities. This generally involves clearing, which determines net cash and security commitments, and settlement, with the actual delivery of cash and securities. The principal Recognised Clearing Houses ('RCH') in the UK are CME Clearing Europe Limited, Euroclear UK and Ireland Limited, European Central Counterparty Limited, ICE Clear Europe Limited, LCH.Clearnet Limited, LIFFE Administration and Management, and the London Metal Exchange. A number of Recognised Overseas Clearing Houses ('ROCH') have been recognised which are regulated under FSMA.[304] Euroclear UK and Ireland Limited is separately approved as an operator under the Uncertificated Securities Regulations 2001.[305]

1.143 The Bank deals with FMI supervision under its Financial Stability functions. The Bank works with the FCA on trading infrastructure and market conduct subject to the terms of the MOU entered into between the Bank, FCA, and the PRA on the supervision of markets and market infrastructure at the international level.[306] FMI supervision is generally conducted

---

303 European Commission, 'Proposal for a Directive establishing a framework for the recovery and resolution of credit institutions and investment firms and amending Council Directives' (6 June 2012) COM/2012/0286 final; and European Commission Staff Working Document, *Proposal for a Directive establishing a framework for the recovery and resolution of credit institutions and investment firms* (6 June 2012) SWD(2012)166 final.

304 s 292 FSMA. These include Cassa di Compensazione e Garanzia SpA, Eurex Clearing ag, European Multilateral Clearing Facility NV, ICE Clear U.S. Inc, LCH.Clearnet SA, Six x-Clear Ltd and the Chicago Mercantile Exchange.

305 The Uncertificated Securities Regulations SI 2001/3755 as amended SI 2003/1398, 2006/3221, 2010/2628 and 2012/917 with further Uncertificated Securities (Amendment) Regulations to come into effect 2013.

306 Para 1.169.

in accordance with the Principles for FMIs agreed by the Committee on Payment and Settlement Systems ('CPSS') and the Technical Committee of the International Organisation of Securities Commissions ('IOSCO') in April 2012.[307] These strengthened and harmonised existing standards on systemically important payment systems ('SIPS'), central securities depositories ('CSDs'), securities settlements systems ('SSSs'), and central counterparties ('CCPs'), with additional guidance on OTC derivative CCPs and trade repositories ('TRs').

The CPSS and IOSCO paper consists of 24 principles structured in terms of general organisation (legal basis, governance, and comprehensive risk management framework), credit and liquidity risk management (credit risk, collateral, margin, and liquidity risk), settlement (settlement finality, money settlements, and physical deliveries), central securities depositories and exchange-of-value settlement systems, default management (participant-default rules and procedures and segregation and portability), general business and operational risk management (including custody and investment risks), access (access and participation, tiered participation arrangements, and FMI links), efficiency (efficiency and effectiveness, and communication procedures and standards) and transparency (disclosure of rules, key procedures, and market data and disclosure by trade repositories). Five further specific sets of responsibility are identified for central banks, market regulators, and other relevant authorities involved with FMIs covering regulation, supervision and oversight, disclosure adoption, and cooperation. UK requirements and Bank practice comply with the principles and responsibilities. **1.144**

The Bank's policy with regard to payment systems oversight was published in September 2009.[308] A new regime for the oversight of inter-bank payment systems was created under Part 5 of the BA 2009. This allows for the Treasury to recognise systems that are arrangements designed to facilitate or control the transfer of money between banks or building societies participating in the relevant arrangements where they comply with criteria set.[309] The Treasury may issue recognition orders in respect of relevant systems if it is satisfied that any deficiencies in the design of the system or disruption to its operation would threaten the stability of or confidence in the UK financial system or have serious consequences for business or other interests throughout the UK.[310] The Bank may publish principles and a code of practice on inter-bank payment systems.[311] No separate code of conduct was initially published although fourteen principles were set out in the Bank's September 2009 document. Payment systems generally include pure payment systems which provide for the transfer of money, and 'embedded' systems that are linked to the settlement of some other obligation such as securities within an SSSs or CCPs, or a margin payment under a CCPs. Separate recommendations have been issued by the CPSS and IOSCO on SSSs and CCPs.[312] The Bank publishes update reports on *Payment Systems Oversight* on an annual basis.[313] **1.145**

307 CPSS and IOSCO, *Principles for financial market infrastructures* (April 2012).

308 Bank of England, *The Bank of England's oversight of interbank payment systems under the Banking Act 2009* (September 2009).

309 s 182 (1) and (3) BA 2009. Provision for the establishment of a new retail Payment Systems Regulator as a subsidiary of the FCA was included in Part 5 of the Financial Services (Banking Reform) Bill 62 2013-14. This followed an earlier Treasury consultation paper on Opening up UK Payments (March 2013) and response document in October 2013.

310 ss 184 (1) and 185 (1) BA 2009.

311 ss 188 and 189 BA 2009.

312 CPSS-IOSCO, *Recommendations for securities settlement systems* (2001); and CPSS-IOSCO, *Recommendations for central counterparties* (2004).

313 See, eg, Bank of England, *Payment Systems Oversight Report 2012* (March 2013).

1.146 SSSs and CCPs are regulated under Part 18 FSMA as RCHs. Applications are made for recognition either by investment exchanges or clearing houses with the Treasury issuing regulations setting out the qualifications for recognition.[314] Regulations were issued in 2001.[315] Part 18 FSMA is amended under FSA 2012 to assign responsibility for clearing houses to the Bank and investment exchanges to the FCA. A separate specialist Sourcebook for Recognised Investment Exchanges ('REC') is incorporated within the FCA Handbook. Securities settlement regulation was to be amended following the coming into effect of the proposed EU Central Securities Depository Regulation ('CSDR').[316]

1.147 CCPs are regulated under the European Market Infrastructure Regulation ('EMIR') which came into effect in August 2012.[317] The EMIR imposes reporting and risk management obligations on financial derivative transactions. All counterparties with outstanding contracts have to report contracts and any new contracts entered into to an authorised trade repository ('TR'). The European Securities and Markets Authority ('ESMA') can require counterparties to clear specific types of OTC derivative contracts through authorised CCPs. Bilateral collateral obligations are imposed on contracts not cleared through a relevant CCP. Twenty sets of technical standards are to be adopted under EMIR. Nine sets of technical standards were adopted by the Commission in December 2012 on OTC Derivatives, Reporting to Trade Repositories and Requirements for Trade Repositories and Central Counterparties which came into effect in March 2013.[318] Applications for authorisation under EMIR are made to the Bank which determines whether the application is complete within 30 days and whether it will recommend authorisation to a supervisory college within a further four months. Notifications and applications for exemptions are to be made to the FCA in the UK.[319] Supervisory Colleges are to be established for each CCP and include authorities from other Member States involved with the home competent authority acting as the chair body.

1.148 Payment and settlement systems may separately apply for protections as 'designated systems' under the European Settlement Finality Regulations.[320] The Settlement Finality Directive was originally adopted in May 1998[321] and amended in June 2009.[322] The objective of the 1998 Directive was to reduce systemic risks associated with participation in payment and securities settlement systems, in particular, in the event of the insolvency of another participant in the system. It contains specific provisions on the legal enforceability of transfer orders and netting, the commencement of insolvency with no retroactive effects ('zero hour rules') and with collateral security being protected against insolvency. The 2009 Directive

---

[314] ss 286–288 FSMA.

[315] Financial Services and Markets Act 2000 (Recognition Requirements for Investment Exchanges and Clearing Houses) Regulations 2001. See also Bank of England, *Proposed rules for recognised clearing houses and approved operators* (February 2013) Consultation Paper.

[316] European Commission, *Proposal for a Regulation on improving securities settlement in the European Union and on central securities depositories (CSDs)* and amending Directive 98/26/EC (7 3 2012) COM (2012) 73 final.

[317] Regulation no 648/2012 of the European Parliament and of the Council of 4 July 2012 on OTC derivatives, central counterparties and trade repositories.

[318] <http://eur-lex.europa.eu/johtml/do?uri=oj:l:2013:052:som:en:html>.

[319] <http://www.fca.org.uk/firms/markets/international-markets/emir>.

[320] The Financial Markets and Insolvency (Settlement Finality) Regulations 1999 no 2979.

[321] Directive 98/26/EC of the European Parliament and of the Council of 19 May 1998 on settlement finality in payment securities settlement systems.

[322] Directive 2009/44/EC of the European Parliament and of the Council of 6 May 2009 amending Directive 98/26/EC on settlement finality in payment and securities settlement systems and Directive 2002/47/EC on financial collateral arrangements as regards linked systems and credit claims.

introduced minor changes to the Settlement Finality Directive and Financial Collateral Directive[323] following a Commission review in 2005 and 2006. This included protecting night-time settlement and linked systems with credit claims-eligible systems having to apply to the Bank for designation to benefit from the protections provided.

1.149 The Bank set out its approach to the supervision of FMIs in a paper in April 2013.[324] The Bank will apply its general supervisory risk assessment model to FMIs based on risk (potential systemic impact and risk context) and mitigating factors (including operational mitigants, financial mitigants, and structural mitigation). The Bank will oversee the design of FMI rules and management practice in applying them. It will also attempt to determine whether a particular FMI's governance, operational design, policies, or actions generate any unacceptable risks to financial stability with appropriate corrective action being taken as required. FMIs are to complete self-assessments against the CPSS–IOSCO *Principles* and review these annually. The Bank conducts an assessment of the risks created to financial system stability by the FMIs design or service interruption. The FMI will be expected to undertake any mitigating action required with spot checks or on-site examinations being conducted. Prioritised issues may be identified with any material risks being dealt with early and pre-emptively. The Bank will cooperate with overseas authorities including through relevant Colleges. The Bank will exercise its information-gathering and direction powers as necessary with sanctions being applied where appropriate.

Liquidity Management

1.150 One of the key responsibilities of a central bank is to provide liquidity support to the financial system. The purpose of the Bank's operations in the sterling money markets is to implement MPC policy and to reduce the cost of disruption to the liquidity and payment services provided to the UK economy. Financial liquidity is principally managed through the reserves accounts held by the main commercial banks with the Bank, and with banks being able to adjust their balances using Operational Standing Facilities ('OSFs'). Additional liquidity may be available using one of three other facilities with the Banks Indexed Long-Term Repo ('ILTR'), Extended Collateral Term Repo Facility ('ECTR'), and Discount Window Facility ('DWF').[325] Central banks generally use repurchase facilities which operate as secured loans. These provide for the immediate sale of securities subject to a forward obligation to repurchase them at a specific period. The Bank's sterling monetary operations are set out in its Red Book.[326]

1.151 Liquidity facilities are managed through commercial bank reserves accounts with the Bank of England. This is distinct from banknote issuance which is also managed by the Bank. Total UK banknotes in circulation are around £58 billion,[327] with Scottish banks issuing £4 billion notes and Northern Irish banks £2.1 billion notes. Three banks are entitled to continue to issues their own notes in Scotland, the Bank of Scotland, Royal Bank of Scotland, and Clydesdale Bank, and four banks in Northern Ireland, the Bank of Ireland, First Trust Bank,

[323] Directive 2002/47/EC of the European Parliament and of the Council of 6 June 2002 on financial collateral arrangements.

[324] Bank of England, *The Bank of England's approach to the supervision of financial market infrastructures* (April 2013).

[325] See Bank of England, *A summary of the current Bank of England operations in the sterling money markets* (May 2013). Available at: <http://www.bankofengland.co.uk/markets/Documents/sterlingoperations/summaryops130502.pdf>.

[326] Bank of England (n 217) including the revised 2013 edition.

[327] <http://www.bankofengland.co.uk/banknotes/Pages/about/stats.aspx#1>.

Danske Bank, and Ulster Bank. Scottish and Northern Irish banknotes have to be backed by Bank of England notes under the revised provisions contained in Part 6 of the BA 2009.[328] This allows for an exchange of Bank of England notes under a Note Exchange Programme ('NEP') in the event of the insolvency of an issuing bank. Bank of England banknote circulation is managed under the Note Circulation Scheme ('NCS') which allows member commercial banks, cash-in-transit companies, and the Post Office to hold Bank of England notes.[329] Banknotes are published by De La Rue plc, Basingstoke, Hampshire. The production of UK coinage is managed through the Royal Mint with around 28 billion pieces of coin in circulation worth around £3.75 billion.

1.152 The Bank's LTRO is used to provide additional liquidity to the banking system on a regular basis.[330] LTROs are conducted monthly and usually offered on the mid-month Tuesday with a three month and six month maturity. Funds are provided in sterling to eligible liability reporters providing either narrow or wider collateral. Narrow collateral is generally made up of Government gilts (including gilt strips), sterling Treasury bills, Government non-sterling marketable debt, Bank of England securities, and other sovereign and central bank debts, with wider collateral including other government, institutional, and bank securities.[331] Minimum bid-offer amounts are for £5 million with a £1 million minimum bid-offer increment. Settlement is trade day (T) plus two (T+2).

1.153 The Bank's ECTR facility provides contingency liquidity support on a discretionary basis used in the event of anticipated or actual market stress.[332] Funds are again in sterling and made available to eligible liability reporters registered with the Bank's DWF. Narrow and wider collateral will be accepted as well as DWF Collateral Securities and DWF Loan Collateral. Funds are made available for up to six months with minimum bid-offer amounts of £5 million and increments of £1 million. Settlement is T+1.

1.154 The DWF is another discretionary facility which can either be made available in the event of individual bank (idiosyncratic) or more general market disturbances. The objective is to provide short-term liquidity without increasing moral hazard and reducing the institution's prudent liquidity risk management.[333] The facility operates by allowing eligible banks and building societies to borrow Government gilts for 30 or 364 days against collateral. This can

---

[328] Part 6 BA 2009; and Scottish and Northern Ireland Banknote Regulations 2009 SI 2009/3056. See also Bank of England, *The Scottish and Northern Ireland Banknotes Rules 2011 and Statement of Penalty Policy* (24 June 2011).

[329] Members of the NCS in 2010 were G4S Cash Centres (UK) Ltd, Bank of Scotland, Post Office Ltd, Royal Bank of Scotland Plc and Vaultex UK Ltd. Para 1.102.

[330] Bank of England, *Red Book* (n 217) Chapter VIII.

[331] Wider collateral includes: sovereign and central bank debt not accepted within narrow collateral; international institution bonds; G10 Government guaranteed agency bonds; UK Government guaranteed bank debts; US housing corporation securities; UK and Dutch prime residential mortgage-backed securities (RMBS); UK, French, German, and Spanish regulated covered bonds; UK, US, and EEA ABS backed by auto loans and equipment leases; US ABS backed by student and consumer loans; specific non-UK Government guaranteed bank debts; and portfolios of senior corporate bonds and commercial paper issued by non-financial companies in the UK, US, and EEA. A third level of collateral would be permitted from 2014 made up of less liquid securitisations, own name securitisations and loan portfolios. See Bank of Engand, 'Liquidity insurance and the Bank of England: developments in the Sterling Monetary Framework' (n 217).

[332] Bank of England, *Red Book* (n 217) Chapter VIII.

[333] See Bank of England, *Red Book* (n 217) Chapter VIII. DWF fees were lowered unded the revised 2013 Red Book with delayed disclosure to avoid stigma and roll-overs permitted after 30 days. See Bank of Engand, 'Liquidity insurance and the Bank of England: developments in the Sterling Monetary Framework' (n 217).

then be used to draw down under other repo facilities. DWF collateral generally corresponds with wider collateral with the Bank also accepting other loan collateral subject to specific conditions. The DWF can be used in exceptional circumstances to obtain sterling funds directly rather than gilts.

The Bank set up a separate Special Liquidity Scheme ('SLS') following the financial crisis to allow institutions to exchange high-quality mortgage-backed and other securities for Treasury Bills for up to three years. This was established in April 2008 to assist banks in borrowing during the tightening of credit conditions immediately before the global financial crisis beginning in September 2008. Under the scheme, £185 billion of bills was provided. Drawdown closed in January 2009 with the SLS ending three years later in January 2012. A separate US-dollar repo operation was also set up in September 2008 to make available dollars on an exchange basis.[334] **1.155**

The Bank also manages other schemes principally to increase liquidity and corporate credit as well as to support lending to households and non-financial companies. The Asset Purchase Facility ('APF') was established by the Chancellor of the Exchequer in January 2009 to purchase high-quality assets through the issuance of Treasury bills. This was set up to increase liquidity within the markets and to support the Bank's Quantitative Easing policy.[335] £375 billion of assets had been purchased by early 2013.[336] The APF included separate gilts, corporate bond, commercial paper, and secured commercial paper facilities. Assets are purchased through the Bank of England Asset Purchase Facility Fund Limited ('BEAPFF') which is a subsidiary of the Bank. **1.156**

A separate Funding for Lending Scheme ('FLS') was set up by the Bank and Treasury in July 2012.[337] The purpose was to allow banks and building societies to increase lending to households and SMEs. Banks were able to borrow Treasury Bills for up to four years. The original scheme was to run until 2014 although this was extended in April 2013 to January 2015. **1.157**

Agency Coordination and Crisis Management

A complex regulatory structure has been set up following the recent crises in financial markets and, in particular, with the institutional changes brought into effect under the FSA 2012. The Bank is responsible for monetary policy through the MPC, macro-prudential policy through the FPC, prudential regulation through the PRA, resolution through the SRU, and financial market infrastructure through its FMI operations, with market support being provided through its Markets division. Conduct and market regulation is dealt with separately by the FCA with compensation managed by the FSCS, consumer complaints by the FSO, and regulatory complaints by the new Complaints Commissioner. A number of statutory mechanisms and internal governance revisions within the Bank have been made with a series of MOU being entered into to attempt to ensure that all of the separate parts of the system work effectively together. **1.158**

334 Bank of England, 'Coordinated Central Bank Action to Improve US dollar Liquidity' (18 September 2008).

335 See HM Treasury, 'statement on financial intervention to support lending to the economy' (19 January 2009). See also Bank of England, 'Quantitative Easing' in *Red Book* (n 217) Chapter VIII.

336 See M Joyce, M Tong, and R Woods, 'The United Kingdom's quantitative easing policy: design, operation and impact' *Quarterly Bulletin* [2011] Q3, 200–12.

337 HM Treasury, 'Funding for Lending Scheme' (13 July 2012).

1.159 PRA and FCA coordination is dealt with under Chapter 3 of Part 1 FSMA. The FCA and PRA are subject to the common revised regulatory principles set out in FSMA as well as general principles of good corporate governance.[338] They are also under a statutory duty to coordinate the exercise of their respective functions especially with regard to consultation, exchange of information and advice, and complying with their respective duties.[339] Two MOU were to be entered into between FCA and PRA governing general coordination of activity[340] and specifically with regard to with-profits insurance policies.[341] The Treasury may also specify the respective functions of the regulators by order.[342] The PRA has entered into a separate MOU with the FSCS.[343] The FCA has entered into a number of separate MOU including with the FOS[344] and the Financial Reporting Council ('FRC').[345] Other MOU have been entered into by the FCA inter alia with the Department of Enterprise, Trade and Investment in Northern Ireland,[346] and the Council for Licensed Conveyancers ('CLC').[347]

1.160 Collaboration between the Treasury and the Bank of England, FCA, and PRA is dealt with under Part 4 FSA 2012. This contains specific provision on the duty of the Bank to notify the Treasury of the need for public funds with the Treasury being able to issue a power of direction in certain circumstances.[348] The Treasury, Bank, and PRA are subject to a separate statutory duty to coordinate the discharge of their respective functions.[349] Two separate MOU are to be entered into on Crisis Management and International Organisations.[350]

FCA and PRA

1.161 The FCA and PRA have entered into a 68-point MOU governing their relationship as required under FSMA as amended.[351] The MOU refers to their distinct mandates and separate roles and responsibilities.[352] The MOU deals with information sharing and confidentiality.[353] Each regulator will make its own rules and policies in light of its separate objectives

---

338 ss 3B and 3C FSMA.

339 s 3D (1) FSMA.

340 ss 3E and F FSMA. Bank of England, 'Memorandum of Understanding (MOU) between the Financial Conduct Authority (FCA) and the Prudential Regulation Authority (PRA)'. Available at: <http://www.bankofengland.co.uk/about/Documents/mous/moufcapra.pdf>.

341 Bank of England, 'With-Profits, Memorandum of Understanding'. Available at: <http://www.bankofengland.co.uk/about/Documents/mous/mouwithprofits.pdf>.

342 s 3G FSMA.

343 Bank of England, 'Memorandum of Understanding between the Prudential Regulation Authority and the Financial Services Compensation Scheme Ltd.' (27 June 2012). Available at: <http://www.bankofengland.co.uk/about/Documents/mous/moufscspra.pdf>.

344 FCA and FOS, 'Memorandum of Understanding between the Financial Conduct Authority (the FCA) and the scheme operator, the Financial Ombudsman Service Limited'.

345 FCA and FRC, 'Memorandum of Understanding between the Financial Reporting Council (FRC) and the Financial Conduct Authority (FCA)' (April 2013).

346 FCA and DETINI, 'Memorandum of Understanding between the Financial Conduct Authority and the Department of Enterprise, Trade and Investment in Northern Ireland' (7 March 2013).

347 FCA and CLC, 'Memorandum of Understanding between the Financial Conduct Authority (FCA) and the Council for Licensed Conveyancers' (17 April 2013).

348 ss 58–63 FSA 2012.

349 s 64 FSA 2012.

350 ss 65–66 FSA 2012.

351 Bank of England, 'Memorandum of Understanding (MOU) between the Financial Conduct Authority (FCA) and the Prudential Regulation Authority (PRA)' (n 340) para 1.

352 Paras 1 and 3–5.

353 Paras 6–9 and 10–12. Specific arrangements governing the collection of regulatory data and avoidance of duplication is dealt with under Annex 2.

although they will consult and will avoid the imposition of incompatible requirements, will meet regularly, and will ensure routine coordination on rule-making.[354] The MOU contains specific provisions on authorisation,[355] supervision of dual regulation firms,[356] Lloyds' supervision,[357] with-profits policies,[358] overseas firms,[359] and UKLA coordination.[360] It also deals with formal regulatory processes and enforcement,[361] including the PRA's right to veto FCA regulatory actions,[362] reporting regulatory failure,[363] financial crime and fraud,[364] and coordination with other authorities.[365] The MOU includes additional provisions on fees,[366] cross-border positions,[367] and maintaining and reviewing the MOU.[368]

Crisis management

A statutory framework for crisis management has been set up under Part 4 FSA 2012. The Bank of England is required to provide the Treasury with an immediate 'public funds notification' in three cases under the new coordination procedures.[369] These apply where the Treasury or Secretary of State may reasonably be expected to provide financial systems in respect of a financial institution, the stabilisation options, BIP or BAP under the BA 2009 may have to be exercised, or the FSCS may have to request a loan from the National Loans Fund or financial assistance from the Treasury to fund expenses under the scheme.[370] Any substantial changes must be notified where the risk continues.[371] The Treasury is given a statutory power of direction and may require the Bank to provide financial assistance, other than in ordinary market conditions, or exercise any of its stabilisation powers or BAP powers.[372] These may be exercised where either a public funds notification has been given or qualifying financial assistance has been provided which has not been recovered.[373] Copies of any directions are to be laid before Parliament as soon as reasonably practicable.[374] **1.162**

The Treasury, Bank, and PRA are subject to a statutory duty to coordinate in the discharge of their functions and to prepare and maintain an MOU to determine how this will be achieved.[375] A 39-point MOU has been entered into for this purpose.[376] This sets out the framework of coordination for financial crisis management which is defined as managing the risk of instability or **1.163**

[354] Paras 13–16.
[355] Paras 17–21.
[356] Paras 22–27.
[357] Paras 28–32.
[358] Paras 33–34.
[359] Paras 35–36.
[360] Paras 37–40.
[361] Paras 41–49.
[362] Paras 50–52.
[363] Paras 54–55.
[364] Paras 56–57.
[365] Paras 58–61.
[366] Paras 62–64.
[367] Para 65.
[368] Paras 66–68.
[369] s 58(1) and (2) FSA 2012.
[370] s 58(3)–(5) FSA 2012.
[371] s 59 FSA 2012.
[372] s 61(2) FSA 2012.
[373] s 60(2) and (3) FSA 2012.
[374] s 63.
[375] ss 64–65 FSA 2012.
[376] HM Treasury, Bank of England and PRA, 'Memorandum of Understanding on financial crisis management'. Available at: <http://www.bankofengland.co.uk/about/Documents/mous/moufincrisis.pdf>.

failure and preventing crystallisation.[377] The MOU states that the key principle of financial crisis management is to make clear who is in charge of what and when, with the separate responsibilities of each of the parties being specified.[378] This replaces the earlier MOU that was adopted in 1998 and revised in 2006 between the Treasury, the Bank, and FSA as the Tripartite authorities.

1.164 The Bank is given general primary operational responsibility for financial crisis management, with the Chancellor and Treasury having sole responsibility for any decision on the use of public funds, and for keeping Parliament and the public informed and ensuring compliance with UK international obligations.[379] The Bank has operational responsibility for mitigating and managing risk to financial stability with the circumstances in which the Bank is to notify the Treasury being restated.[380] The Bank must also approach the Treasury for approval if it proposes to make any Emergency Liquidity Assistance ('ELA') available to one or more financial institutions.[381] Assessments will generally be conducted on the basis of the generic risk stages set out in the PRA's Proactive Intervention Framework ('PIF').[382] The MOU contains additional specific provisions on assessment, timing, and updates.[383]

1.165 The Bank is to act on an autonomous basis if it can manage the risk to financial stability without public funds.[384] Where public funds may be involved, the Bank is to lead the operational response working closely with the Treasury to develop options to mitigate the risks concerned. Ad hoc or standing committees may be set up to support coordination with the Treasury providing the Bank with information on particular issues of interest or concerns.[385] The MOU expands on the procedures applicable with regard to the exercise by the Chancellor of the power of direction over the Bank.[386] The Bank is to act as the Treasury's agent in conducting a support operation.[387] Any special purpose vehicle ('SPV') used may be funded through the issuance of Government securities, Bank loans using share capital provided by the Treasury, or another mechanism as determined by the Treasury.[388]

1.166 The Bank may not exercise a stabilisation power without Treasury consent where this would affect public funds.[389] The Bank is to be indemnified by the Treasury where it is required to implement any specific SRR.[390] The power of direction is disapplied with regard to PRA supervisory decisions, the Bank's regulation of systemic post-trade infrastructure, MPC and FPC policy decisions, and the Bank's published framework for the provision of liquidity support to the financial system.[391] Specific additional provisions are included with regard

[377] Paras 1–3.
[378] Paras 4–7.
[379] Paras 4–7.
[380] Paras 8–11.
[381] Para 12.
[382] Para 13. Bank of England, *The PRA's approach to banking supervision* (April 2013) Table A p 32. This sets out five stages of: low risk to viability of firm (stage 1); moderate risk to viability of firm (stage 2); risk to viability absent action by the firm (stage 3); imminent risk to viability of firm (stage 4); and firm in resolution or being actively wound up (stage 5).
[383] Paras 14–18.
[384] Para 19.
[385] Paras 21–4.
[386] s 61 FSA 2012; and paras 25–33.
[387] Para 26.
[388] Para 27.
[389] Para 28.
[390] Para 30.
[391] Para 33.

to coordination with other organisations, compliance with international obligations, and communicating with Parliament and the public.[392]

International organisations

The Bank, PRA, and FCA are separately required under the FSA 2012 to enter into an MOU on the coordination of their relevant functions with regard to membership of the European Supervisory Authorities ('ESAs'), EU institutions, and other international organisations,[393] with 17 sets of bodies being referred to in the MOU.[394] The MOU sets out 13 points of coordination. The MOU stresses the need for the UK to secure a coherent and consistent position internationally despite separate representation on different bodies.[395] The MOU creates a framework for consultation and cooperation among the relevant authorities to secure this despite their different individual responsibilities and competences.[396] The Treasury is to be responsible for the overall institutional structure of financial regulation at the domestic and international levels and for domestic legislation.[397] UK authorities are to consult and coordinate their positions on international groups and negotiations with equivalent principles applying at the domestic level.[398] The MOU refers to the International Coordination Committee ('ICC') set up under the FSA 2012[399] which is chaired by the Treasury and is to meet at least quarterly, and to be accountable to the Chancellor.[400] **1.167**

The MOU sets out seven basic principles governing coordination. These are generally based on reporting, consultation, information and documentation exchange, attendance facilitation where possible, consideration of opinions, consistent objectives, and compliance with relevant international laws and regulations.[401] Authorities are to attempt to take into consideration the interest and objectives of each other where issues are raised at international meetings and there is no agreed UK position with other authorities being advised appropriately as soon as possible afterwards.[402] The MOU is to be reviewed and revised appropriately at least annually.[403] **1.168**

Market infrastructure

The Bank of England, including the PRA, have entered into a separate forty-two point MOU with the FCA on market infrastructure.[404] This establishes a high-level framework for cooperation in connection with the supervision of markets and market infrastructure under FSMA and BA 2009.[405] The MOU outlines the separate responsibilities of the FCA in **1.169**

---

392 Paras 34, 35–6, and 37–9.
393 s 66 (1) FSA 2012.
394 Bank of England, PRA, and FCA, 'MoU between the FCA and the Bank of England, including the PRA'. Available at: <http://www.bankofengland.co.uk/about/Documents/mous/mouintorg.pdf>.
395 Para 1.
396 Para 2.
397 Para 3.
398 Paras 4–6.
399 s 66 FSA 2012.
400 Paras 7–10.
401 Para 11.
402 Para 12.
403 Para 13.
404 Bank of England, PRA, and FCA, 'Memorandum of Understanding between the Financial Conduct Authority and the Bank of England, including the Prudential Regulation Authority'. Available at: <http://www.bankofengland.co.uk/about/Documents/mous/moumarket.pdf>.
405 Para 1.

respect of organised financial markets and the Bank with regard to post-trade systems.[406] The MOU contains specific provisions on information exchange,[407] consultation with regard to entities supervised by the FCA or the Bank,[408] group and dual regulated entities,[409] supervisory cooperation,[410] policy and rule making,[411] financial crime,[412] recognised payment systems,[413] emergency action,[414] cooperation on international representation,[415] confidentiality,[416] maintenance,[417] and FCA, Bank, and PRA relationships.[418]

Overseas authorities

1.170 The Bank and regulators have entered into a number of other separate MOU with other overseas authorities and agencies. Many of these were intended to replicate the earlier MOU entered into with the FSA although these required updating and amendment. Transitional provisions were incorporated within the FSA 2012[419] although the FSA contacted each of its MOU counterparties separately to explain the transfer of responsibilities and amend the MOU accordingly. The changes proposed specifically related to the use of information for the functions covered, permitting the exchange information between UK authorities, confirming which MOU would be transferred to which agency, and providing that the new separate MOU would operate independently. Overseas authorities were invited to enter into a new MOU where this was considered appropriate.[420]

406 Paras 2–7.
407 Paras 8–9.
408 Paras 10–12.
409 Paras 13–15.
410 Paras 16–24.
411 Paras 25–27.
412 Paras 28–29.
413 Paras 30–31.
414 Paras 32.
415 Paras 33–34.
416 Paras 35–37.
417 Paras 38–40.
418 Paras 41–42.
419 s 119 and Schs 20 and 21 FSA 2012.
420 A list of the current MOU entered into between the Bank, the PRA and overseas authorities is provided on the Bank of England website: <http://www.bankofengland.co.uk/about/Documents/mous/mouexampleletter.pdf>.

2

STATUTORY FRAMEWORK FOR UK FINANCIAL SERVICES REGULATION

Introduction: From Consolidation to Collaboration

The regulatory reforms culminating in the Financial Services Act 2012 ('FSA 2012') and the break-up of the Financial Services Authority ('FSA') have complicated but in many ways reinforced the original vision of a consolidated statutory framework for all financial services regulation under the Financial Services and Markets Act 2000 ('FSMA'). Apart from the emergency legislation required to address the banking crisis of 2007–2008,[1] there has been no attempt to re-establish separate statutory regimes for banking, insurance, markets, or other sectors. Indeed, the planned extension of FSMA to cover consumer credit regulation from 1 April 2014 has led the Government to claim that it will, 'for the first time, bring conduct of business regulation under a single financial services regulator, ending confusion for consumers, duplication for many firms, and ensuring a single strategic regulatory view across retail financial services'.[2] While the Government has created a new regulation of financial conduct regime, the integrated model of prudential regulation set up under FSMA has essentially been kept intact except that responsibility for prudential supervision of systemic and non-systemic firms has been divided. 2.01

FSMA is undoubtedly more complicated because of the need to accommodate collaboration between the two new 'twin peaks' regulators—the Financial Conduct Authority ('FCA') and the Prudential Regulation Authority ('PRA')—and the new accountability mechanisms involving the Bank of England. However, it has largely survived the demise of the single regulator because of its sheer size, which makes unpicking impractical, and because it is framework legislation, capable of developing a variety of regulatory approaches and solutions through secondary legislation and other non-legislative mechanisms. 2.02

Structure

FSMA currently consists of 35 Parts, covering topics as diverse as the chapter headings in this book. Of the 30 Parts at Royal Assent on 14 June 2000, three have been replaced: Part 1A (The Regulators) replacing Part 1, Part 4A (Permission to Carry on Regulated Activities) replacing Part 4, and Part 9A (Rules and Guidance) replacing Part 10. There are five new Parts: 8A (Short Selling), 12A (Powers Exercisable in Relation to Parent Undertakings), 2.03

[1] See the Banking (Special Provisions) Act 2008.

[2] Statement of the Minister of Consumer Affairs to the House of Commons, 6 March 2013.

Table 2.1 The Financial Services and Markets Act 2000 (FSMA)

Part[3]	Coverage
1A. The Regulators	The general duties, statutory objectives, constitution, funding, and accountability of the FCA and the PRA (replacing the previous Part 1)
2. Regulated and Prohibited Activities	The Treasury's powers to set the scope of regulation by order, including the regulation of financial promotions, with prohibitions for persons who are not authorised or exempt
3. Authorisation and Exemption	Setting out which persons are to be authorised, either through a permission given by the FCA or the PRA, or under European legislation
4A. Permission to Carry on Regulated Activities	Applications for permission to carry on regulated activities, and the powers of the FCA and the PRA to give, vary, or revoke permissions (replacing the previous Part 4)
5. Performance of Regulated Activities[4]	Approval of persons to perform controlled functions, specified by the FCA and the PRA, and their powers to make principles and codes of conduct for approved persons, and impose censure, financial penalties, and prohibitions
6. Official Listing	Powers of the FCA as UK listing authority (reflecting the Market Abuse and Prospectus Directives)[5]
7. Control of Business Transfers	Mechanisms for the transfer of banking and insurance business, with court sanction
8. Penalties for Market Abuse	The market abuse provision and the FCA's power to make a code and censure or impose penalties (reflecting the Market Abuse Directive)[6]
8A. Short Selling	The FCA's investigation and disciplinary powers in support of its functions under the Short Selling Regulation[7]
9. Hearings and Appeals	The Tribunal and its procedure; financial assistance
9A. Rules and Guidance	Powers of the FCA and the PRA to impose rules and give guidance, procedure, and competition scrutiny for their regulating provisions and practices (replacing the previous Part 10)
9B. Ring-Fencing[8]	The Treasury's powers to impose restrictions on ring-fenced bodies; ring-fencing rules and group restructuring powers of the FCA and the PRA
11. Information Gathering and Investigations	Powers of the FCA, the PRA, and the BIS[9] to require the production of information and documents, to require reports, and to conduct investigations

[3] Many users still follow the Roman numbering system used at the time of Royal Assent; however, the conventional Arabic numbering system now used to draft statutory legislation is adopted here.

[4] The FS(BR) Bill is expected to make significant changes to Part 5. See the Government's Response to the Parliamentary Commission on Banking Standards, July 2013, Chapter 2, which announced that the Government would introduce a new senior persons and licensing regime to replace the approved persons regime, and make other changes to ensure accountability.

[5] Directives 2003/6/EC on insider dealing and market manipulation (Market Abuse Directive) and 2003/71/EC on the prospectus to be published when securities are offered to the public or admitted to trading on a regulated market (Prospectus Directive) as amended—FSMA was amended by SI 2005/381 and SI 2005/1433 and subsequently by 2012/1538.

[6] Amended by SI 2005/381.

[7] Regulation (EU) No 236/2012 of the European Parliament and of the Council of 14 March 2012 on short selling and certain aspects of credit default swaps. See the Financial Services and Markets Act 2000 (Short Selling) Regulations 2012 (SI 2012/2554).

[8] To be inserted under the FS(BR) Bill, introduced on 4 February 2013.

[9] Department for Business, Innovation and Skills.

Table 2.1 *Continued*

Part	Coverage
12. Control over Authorised Persons	Approval by the FCA and the PRA of persons who acquire control over authorised persons
12A. Powers Exercisable in Relation to Parent Undertakings	Powers of the FCA and the PRA to give directions to parent undertakings of qualifying authorised persons
13. Incoming Firms: Intervention by FCA or PRA	Powers of the FCA and the PRA to intervene in the activities of authorised persons based in other EEA States who are exercising passporting rights
14. Disciplinary Measures	Powers of the FCA and the PRA to censure, impose financial penalties, or suspend permissions for breaches of requirements imposed under FSMA
15. The Financial Services Compensation Scheme	The compensation scheme and the scheme manager ('FSCS')
15A. Power to Require FSCS Manager to Act in Relation to Other Schemes	The Treasury's power to require the scheme manager to exercise functions in relation to a relevant compensation scheme, and powers of the FCA and the PRA to make rules
16. The Ombudsman Scheme	The ombudsman scheme and the functions of the scheme operator, the Financial Ombudsman Service ('FOS')
16A. Consumer Protection and Competition	Super-complaints and references to the FCA, competition powers of the FCA
17. Collective Investment Schemes	The regulation of collective investment schemes, including authorised unit trusts, open-ended investment companies, recognised overseas schemes, master–feeder structures, and unregulated schemes
18. Recognised Investment Exchanges and Clearing Houses	The regulation of investment exchanges by the FCA and of clearing houses by the Bank of England
18A. Suspension and Removal of Financial Instruments from Trading	The FCA's powers to suspend and remove financial instruments from trading
19. Lloyd's	Making the Society of Lloyd's an authorised person, and giving the FCA and the PRA certain powers to direct its affairs and those of its members, and managing and members' agents
20. Provision of Financial Services by Members of the Professions	An exemption for members of the professions providing financial services to clients under the supervision of designated professional bodies, subject to FCA oversight
21. Mutual Societies	Former Treasury powers to transfer certain functions under mutuals legislation, now contained in Part 3 of FSA 2012
22. Auditors and Actuaries	The appointment of auditors and actuaries on behalf of authorised persons; their rights and duties
23. Public Record, Disclosure of Information and Cooperation	The FCA's public record (or Register) of regulated persons, and restrictions on disclosure of confidential information, duties of the FCA and the PRA to cooperate with others

Table 2.1 *Continued*

Part	Coverage
24. Insolvency	Powers for the FCA and the PRA to bring insolvency proceedings, and rights to receive information and be heard by the court
25. Injunctions and Restitution	Powers of the FCA, the PRA, and BIS to seek injunctions and restitution for regulatory contraventions and offences
26. Notices	Procedures to be followed by the FCA and the PRA in issuing notices
27. Offences	Offences for misleading statements and supplying false information to the FCA and the PRA; prosecution of insider dealing, terrorist financing, and money-laundering offences
28. Miscellaneous	FCA powers to establish consumer redress schemes, Treasury powers to enforce international obligations, and other miscellaneous provisions
29. Interpretation	Definitions, interpretation
30. Supplemental	Commencement; scope and control of statutory instruments

15A (Powers to Require FSCS Manager to Act in Relation to Other Schemes), 16A (Consumer Protection and Competition), and 18A (Suspension and Removal of Financial Instruments from Trading). The Financial Services (Banking Reform) Bill ('FS(BR) Bill') introduced on 4 February 2013 will add a 36th Part 9B (Ring-Fencing) and make significant changes to Part 5 (Performance of Regulated Activities) and to the FCA's new competition functions under Part 16A.

2.04 At Royal Assent in June 2000, FSMA contained 433 sections and 22 Schedules. Following implementation of FSA 2012 on 1 April 2013 and the FS(BR) Bill, FSMA will have doubled in length to more than 800 sections. More than 200 statutory instruments have been made under or in connection with FSMA.

2.05 FSMA will now be supplemented by provisions of and under the following primary legislation:

a. FSA 2012: which mostly contained amendments to FSMA (Part 2), but also includes continuing provisions on mutual societies (Part 3), collaboration between the Treasury and the Bank of England, the FCA, or the PRA (Part 4), Treasury powers to order inquiries and investigations (Part 5), investigation of complaints against the regulators (Part 6), offences relating to financial services (Part 7—substituting and supplementing Part 27 of FSMA), amendments to the Banking Act 2009 ('BA 2009') (Part 8),[10] miscellaneous provisions enabling the Treasury to transfer consumer credit regulation from the OFT to the FCA[11] and payment of penalties to the Treasury (Part 9), and general powers including transitional provisions relating to commencement of FSA 2012 and amendments to FSMA (Part 10).
b. The Bank of England Act 1998 ('BEA 1998'): Part 1A of which concerns the functions of the Bank and the Financial Policy Committee ('FPC') in relation to financial stability, including powers to direct the FCA or the PRA to take macro-prudential measures and to make recommendations, as well as Treasury powers.

[10] See para 2.05(c) following.
[11] See paras 2.01, 2.33, 2.80.

c. BA 2009: which provides for a special resolution scheme for banks (Part 1), for bank insolvency (Part 2), and bank administration (Part 3), inter-bank payment systems (Part 5), and miscellaneous powers (Part 6).
d. The Financial Services Act 2010 ('FSA 2010'): which mostly contained amendments to FSMA, but also provides savings and transitional provisions, and powers under sections 4–5 for the Treasury to make regulations requiring reports on executives' remuneration.
e. The FS(BR) Bill: which mostly contains amendments to FSMA, but also provides for establishment of the Payments Systems Regulator overseen by the FCA and a special administration regime for infrastructure systems (Parts 5 and 6).

This statutory framework is supplemented by the regulators' Handbooks of rules and guidance,[12] memoranda of understanding, and reports and findings of the regulators, Parliamentary committees and independent reviews, as well as materials produced by the FPC, the recognised investment exchanges and clearing houses, Lloyd's, and the designated professional bodies, and an increasing body of rules, directions, and case law from the Upper Tribunal and the FOS.[13] There is also an expanding body of European directives, regulations, and guidelines, which is increasingly substituting for domestic UK provisions, including through the activities of the three new European supervisory authorities: the European Banking Authority ('EBA'), the European Insurance and Occupational Pensions Authority ('EIOPA'), and the European Securities and Markets Authority ('ESMA').[14] **2.06**

Framework

The basic statutory framework for financial regulation under FSMA has been retained and is essentially the same except for the division of FSA functions between the FCA and the PRA. FSMA creates offences for carrying on certain specified activities without authorisation. By seeking and obtaining authorisation, firms submit to the jurisdiction of the FCA for conduct matters, and systemic firms submit to prudential regulation by the PRA. FSMA sets out the functions of the FCA and the PRA in relation to that jurisdiction and the purposes for which they are exercised, and the associated checks and balances. FSMA specifies who must join the 'club' of regulated firms, and authorises the FCA and the PRA to make and administer the 'club rules'. **2.07**

Sources of complexity

The move to a 'twin peaks' framework, also involving the Bank of England, has made FSMA significantly more complicated. Almost every Part includes a section defining the circumstances in which the FCA or the PRA is to be regarded as the 'appropriate regulator'—generally the PRA for PRA-authorised persons or PRA-regulated activities, and the FCA in other cases, although circumstances vary. In addition, there are often provisions defining the powers of each regulator separately, and obligations to consult each other, and sometimes powers for one regulator, including the PRA under section 3I, to direct or restrain action by the other. Part 1A gives each regulator separate objectives, but requires them each to have regard to the other's and to consult and coordinate their activities, including in particular **2.08**

12 Chapter 5.
13 See para 2.24(iv) following and Chapter 7.
14 See Chapter 3.

memoranda of understanding and provisions enabling them to share resources and services under section 3R. The new powers of the Bank of England in relation to financial stability and macro-prudential regulation under Part 1A of BOE 1998 and the Treasury's powers of direction under Part 4 of FSA 2012 also replace the previous tripartite arrangements for crisis management.

2.09 The framework was already complex because FSMA itself specifies only a small part of the substantive regulatory requirements which apply. The scope of the perimeter offences which force firms into regulation is specified in secondary legislation made by the Treasury. FSMA contains more than 100 separate powers to make statutory instruments, many of which have been exercised. The detailed procedures for most of the applications and other processes administered by the FCA and the PRA are determined by them in accordance with the requirements of FSMA. Regulated persons need to look to the regulators' own Handbooks for their rules.

2.10 FSMA is then essentially a statutory rulebook for the FCA, the PRA, and the other bodies exercising functions under FSMA, which means that its main interest for other readers is in understanding their rights when dealing with those bodies. To put these rights into context readers need to understand the substantive regulatory framework.

2.11 The diversity of the regulators' functions provides additional complexity. Creating a consolidated regulatory framework for financial services is not as simple as giving the regulators licensing, standard-setting, and enforcement functions. For example, the FCA's powers to make clients' money rules under section 137B9, and the regulators' powers to impose assets requirements under section 55L or 55M on authorised persons, are extended to impact on third parties through the creation of a trust or enforceable protections over assets held.

2.12 Furthermore, the creation of a consolidated regulatory framework and subsequent reforms have provided an opportunity to solve problems that eluded earlier regulatory systems. Previous regulators' enforcement functions were extended to include investigation and prosecution powers for insider dealing and money-laundering offences,[15] and powers to deal with market abuse through penalties, public censure, or restitution.[16] Following FSA 2012, FSMA confers enhanced powers to ban misleading advertisements which breach FCA rules,[17] make remuneration rules,[18] tackle mis-selling,[19] and regulate benchmarks such as LIBOR.[20] Further planned changes include ring-fencing powers and a tough, new, senior persons and licensing regime for banks and potentially other financial services firms.[21] Equally, there has been an accretion effect with the regulators seen as recipients of functions without an obvious separate authority, or in respect of firms and bodies which they already

[15] See ss 401, 402 (proceedings for offences), which refer to Part 5 of the Criminal Justice Act 1993 (insider dealing) and prescribed regulations relating to money laundering (the Money Laundering Regulations 2007, SI 2007/2057, and the Transfer of Funds (Information on the Payer) Regulations 2007, SI 2007/3298), as well as Sch 7 to the Counter-Terrorism Act 2008.

[16] See s 123 (penalties and censure) and ss 383, 384 (restitution).

[17] See s 137S.

[18] See s 137H.

[19] See ss 55N(5) (remedial requirements), 137D (product intervention rules), 404-404G (consumer redress schemes).

[20] See s 137F.

[21] See the FS(BR) Bill.

regulate. When the London Stock Exchange decided to seek a listing, the role of listing authority was transferred to the new FSA (now FCA) in May 2000.[22]

This accretion effect has continued, mainly through extensions to the scope of regulation, to include funeral plans, e-money, credit unions, mortgages, insurance mediation, and home finance,[23] and even after the demise of the FSA. The FCA is the supervisory authority under the Money Laundering Regulations 2007 for certain categories of authorised and other firms providing money lending services and certain other firms.[24] Experience of the banking crisis in 2007–2008 has led the Government to conclude that the regulators—as well as the Treasury and the Bank—need significantly greater powers to deal with a crisis.[25] In addition, the creation of the FCA has provided an opportunity to give it an explicit competition objective—with a new focus on value for money for consumers—under section 1E, and transfer responsibility for consumer credit regulation from the OFT. **2.13**

A third reason is the extent of the checks and balances on the regulators in discharging their functions. One of FSMA's original aims was to create a regulatory system which was more effective in protecting consumers and maintaining confidence in the financial system. There were worries that more powerful regulators could be over-powerful, and practitioners in particular were concerned to avoid a position in which regulatory action became too easy. Furthermore, the obligation under the Human Rights Act 1998 for Ministers to certify that FSMA was compatible with the Convention rights focused attention on the fairness of the regulators' procedures. **2.14**

A key objective of the Coalition Government has been to enhance these accountabilities further. The Joint Committee which considered the draft Financial Services Bill observed that 'Successful regulation depends more on the regulatory culture, focus and philosophy than on structure', and a key aspect of cultural change needed would be a shift toward forward-looking supervision: 'A change in culture is not something that legislation can guarantee, but legislation can influence the culture of a regulator by: (1) setting objectives; (2) allocating and aligning powers and responsibilities; and (3) establishing appropriate systems of accountability'.[26] Consequently, the accountability mechanisms established under Part 1A of FSMA, and under Part 1A of BOE 1998 and Parts 4–6 of FSA 2012, are considerably more elaborate than previously, and include significantly enhanced powers for the Treasury.[27] **2.15**

Finally, there is the effect of Europe. The Government has established a consolidated regulatory framework in the UK against a background of separate single market directives for credit institutions, life and general insurance, and investment services and collective investment schemes. The Government and the regulators need to be able to implement these directives either directly through FSMA or through secondary legislation under it. When a directive requires duties to be imposed on the FCA or the PRA as competent authority, FSMA or regulations made under it need to be capable of implementing that requirement. Equally, when a directive requires authorised persons to be subject to certain requirements, the regulators need to be able to implement those requirements through their rules. **2.16**

[22] Official Listing of Securities (Change of Competent Authority) Regulations 2000, SI 2000/1968.
[23] Through provisions and amendments in the RAO (see para 2.39).
[24] See Part 4 of SI 2007/2157, with regulation 3(3)(a) and Sch 1.
[25] See the Banking (Special Provisions) Act 2008 and the FS(BR) Bill.
[26] Report by the Draft Financial Services Bill Joint Committee, 19 December 2011, paras 24, 367.
[27] See para 2.27.

2.17 As far as possible FSMA was designed to accommodate existing and expected obligations from Europe, either through general or consolidated provisions incorporating European law such as provisions in Schedule 3 (EEA passport rights), Schedule 6 (threshold conditions), or Part 13 (incoming firms), or through powers to make secondary legislation. However, there have been concerns both to demonstrate substantive and precise implementation in new provisions and to avoid 'gold-plating'.[28] In practice, Government draftsmen have not been satisfied with the powers in FSMA, and there has been frequent recourse to the European Communities Act 1972 ('ECA 1972').

2.18 The establishment of the three European Supervisory Authorities (EBA, EIOPA, and ESMA) has accelerated the impact of European legislation, which has to-date been a complicating factor. However, European legislation increasingly has direct effect or imposes maximum harmonisation restrictions, which are more likely to substitute for existing UK materials. In the longer term, this could lead to a reduction in substantive UK law, with regulatory obligations set out instead in directly applicable EU measures.[29]

The regulators' functions

2.19 The functions of the FCA and the PRA are discussed in detail in later chapters. They may be conferred directly by FSMA or through secondary legislation under it. FSMA gives special significance to these functions and accordingly consideration needs to be given to the implications of conferring new functions on the regulators through external legislation, as many provisions of FSMA will not otherwise automatically apply. Sections 1A (for the FCA) and 2A (for the PRA) of FSMA provide that functions conferred on the regulators under the Insolvency Act 1986, BA 2009, FSA 2012, and qualifying EU provisions specified by Treasury order, are to be treated as functions conferred by or under FSMA.[30]

2.20 Features which apply only to functions conferred by or under FSMA include:

(i) aspects of the regulators' governance and accountability which are set out in Schedules 1ZA (for the FCA) and 1ZB (for the PRA) to FSMA and in Part 6 of FSA 2012—delegation, reporting, scope of the complaints scheme and the independent investigator, records, non-Crown status of the regulators' functions, and their qualified exemptions from liability in damages;

(ii) the regulators' main fee-raising powers[31] may be exercised only to enable them to meet expenses incurred for a purpose which is incidental to carrying out their functions conferred by or as a result of (not just under) FSMA;

(iii) the regulators' information-gathering powers under section 165, which apply only to information and documents reasonably required in connection with the exercise by the regulators of functions conferred on them by or under FSMA; and

(iv) the scope of the confidentiality restriction in section 348, which protects information received for the purposes of, or in the discharge of, any functions of the FCA or the PRA (or BIS) under any provision made by or under FSMA.

[28] See, eg, 'Implementation of EU legislation', an independent study for the Foreign and Commonwealth Office by R Bellis, November 2003; and 'Lost in Translation? Responding to the challenges of European law', National Audit Office, May 2005.

[29] See Chapter 3.

[30] See the Financial Services and Markets Act 2000 (Qualifying EU Provisions) Order 2013, SI 2013/419.

[31] See para 23 of Sch 1ZA (FCA), and para 31 of Sch 1ZB (PRA).

2.21 Several functions under FSMA similarly relate to the monitoring and enforcement of requirements imposed (or treated as imposed) under FSMA, including disciplinary powers, powers to prosecute offences under Part 27, and powers under Part 25 (Injunctions and Restitution). The FSA had a duty to establish arrangements for monitoring and enforcing compliance with requirements by or under FSMA. Following the recommendations of the Joint Committee, the FCA's and the PRA's functions were broadened to include 'supervising' authorised persons, in addition to the FCA's duty to monitor and enforce compliance with FSMA requirements by persons other than authorised persons.[32]

2.22 Other aspects of the regulators' functions are also not so restricted. For example, the regulators' general duties, including their statutory objectives and common regulatory principles under section 3B, apply to the way they determine their general policy and principles for exercising any functions, not simply those conferred by or under FSMA.

2.23 A previous exception to the application of the general duties was the FSA's (now FCA's) functions as UK listing authority under Part 6, which could be transferred by Treasury order to another body and were treated as separate from the FSA's other functions for many purposes. This distinction was removed under FSA's 2012, and the definition of 'consumer' under section 1G, which determines the scope of two of the FCA's objectives, extended to include investors in financial instruments. However, the general duties do not apply to the FCA's functions under mutuals legislation, which have separate provisions for fees and penalties, or to its prospective concurrent functions under competition legislation or to the regulators' functions in relation to payments systems regulation.[33]

Other bodies and their functions

2.24 FSMA confers or provides for functions to be performed by several bodies apart from the FCA and the PRA:

(i) Ministers—the Treasury, the Secretary of State, and the Lord Chancellor, generally in making statutory instruments, or making or approving appointments, although the Treasury in particular has acquired significant new powers of approval and direction under FSA 2012;[34]
(ii) the Bank of England and the FPC—most of the Bank's powers and accountabilities in relation to financial services regulation are conferred under BEA 1998, FSA 2012, and BA 2009, but the Bank is the appropriate regulator for recognised clearing houses under Part 18 of FSMA, to which many of the rule-making, investigation and enforcement, and accountability provisions under FSMA attach by virtue of Schedule 17A.

[32] See s 1L for the FCA; s 2K for the PRA. Paras 104 and 109 of the Explanatory Notes to FSA 2012 provide that:

'The concept of "supervision" encompasses matters such as monitoring the activities of authorised persons in the light of the FCA's objectives [or "monitoring the safety and soundness of PRA-authorised persons"], forming a view on the person's long-term strategy for doing business, providing advice and, where appropriate, warnings, monitoring compliance with regulatory requirements and taking disciplinary action where appropriate'.

[33] See para 2.76(i) following in respect of mutuals legislation, and provisions of the FS(BR) Bill including amendments to the FCA's competition functions under Part 16A.

[34] See para 2.25 following. See also the proposed ring-fencing powers under the FS(BR) Bill.

(iii) other public bodies and officials—the Competition and Markets Authority (CMA), the Director of Public Prosecutions (and the Director of Public Prosecutions for Northern Ireland), and Government-appointed investigators and reviewers;
(iv) the courts and the Upper Tribunal (Tax and Chancery Chamber), before which appeals of the former Financial Services and Markets Tribunal are now heard;[35]
(v) recognised investment exchanges and clearing houses, Lloyd's, and designated professional bodies (Parts 18–20);
(vi) the Money Advice Service—described in section 3S of FSMA as the consumer financial education body, with twin functions of enhancing the public's understanding and awareness of financial matters and its ability to manage its own financial affairs, which is overseen and funded by the FCA under Schedule 1A;
(vii) the scheme manager for the Financial Services Compensation Scheme ('FSCS') (Part 15), which has an enhanced role under BA 2009;
(viii) the scheme operator for the Financial Ombudsman Service ('FOS') and its panel of ombudsmen (Part 16); and
(ix) various FCA and PRA officials and appointments—their governing bodies, chairmen, chief executives, and members,[36] the various statutory panels,[37] and the independent investigator,[38] as well as persons not directly contemplated in FSMA such as non-statutory panels[39] and the FCA's Regulatory Decisions Committee.[40]

2.25 The functions of most of these bodies will be discussed in later chapters. However, several general features are worth considering. First, although FSMA creates checks and balances on the regulators in discharging their functions, none of these is permitted to undermine their accountability to the Treasury.

2.26 FSMA requires the regulators themselves to create many of their own checks and balances, in particular applying appropriate principles of corporate governance, interpreting their own objectives, and publishing their own strategies, memoranda of understanding, and reports, and appointing their own panels and independent investigator, rather than have these entities imposed upon them.[41] Where this does not provide sufficient independence, so that an external body is needed as in competition scrutiny, the final decision is usually reserved for the Treasury.

2.27 The role and accountability of the Treasury have been significantly enhanced as a result of FSA 2012.

(i) The regulators' constitutions must provide for their governing bodies and Chairman to be appointed and subject to removal by the Treasury, and FSMA provides for the

---

[35] See Part 9 (hearings and appeals), together with the Tribunal Procedure (Upper Tribunal) (Amendment) Rules (SI 2010/747) made also under s 36 of the Tribunals, Courts and Enforcement Act 2007, and financial assistance regulations (SI 2001/3632) and costs regulations (SI 2001/3633).

[36] See Sch 1ZA (FCA), paras 2–8, and Sch 1ZB (PRA), paras 2–16.

[37] Established under ss 1M–1R (FCA) and 2L–2N (PRA) (arrangements for consulting practitioners and consumers).

[38] Described in the joint complaints scheme as the Complaints Commissioner.

[39] As an informal part of the regulators' arrangements for consulting practitioners or consumers established under ss 1M and 2L.

[40] As a decision-maker under the FCA's procedures determined under s 395—see the Decision Procedures and Penalties Manual ('DEPP') in the FCA Handbook.

[41] Obligations under Part 1A of FSMA, Part 6 of FSA 2012.

Treasury to approve other key appointments, namely the independent investigator, and the chairmen of the statutory consultative panels, the FSCS, and the FOS.[42]

(ii) The Treasury makes the most of the statutory instruments under FSMA, including crucially those which determine the scope of regulation, as well as the designation of regulated activities requiring prudential regulation by the PRA under section 22A and scope of the proposed ring-fencing regime under Part 9B.[43] There are more powers relating to the regulators' objectives and accountability which enable the Treasury to 'fine-tune' the statutory framework without the need for further primary legislation. The main statutory instruments made by other Ministers are the Tribunal rules and the Financial Assistance regulations, made by the Lord Chancellor, and provisions relating to insolvency, some of which are made by the Secretary of State.[44] Most of these require only the negative resolution procedure, and don't come into force unless a contrary resolution is passed in either House. However, the key instruments now require the prior approval of each House (under the advance affirmative procedure), unless the Treasury states that in its opinion, by reason of urgency, the instrument needs to be made immediately.[45]

(iii) The Treasury may order a review of the economy, efficiency, and effectiveness with which the FCA (under section 1S) or the PRA (under section 2O) have used their resources in discharging all or any of their statutory functions, or under Part 5 of FSA 2012 order an inquiry into a serious failure in the system established by FSMA or BA 2009 or in their operation.[46]

(iv) The Treasury has the final decision in competition scrutiny of the FCA's and the PRA's regulating provisions and practices, as well as the recognition and scrutiny of investment exchanges and clearing houses, and its approval is required for incorporation of the Takeover Code into the FCA's code of market conduct.[47]

(v) The Treasury receives the regulators' strategies and annual reports on the discharge of their functions and numerous other matters including the extent to which their objectives have been met, their consideration of the regulatory principles in section 3B, and coordination of their functions. The Treasury can impose additional reporting requirements.[48]

(vi) The Treasury may direct the FCA, the PRA, and other bodies in relation to requirements under international obligations, such as compliance with single market directives and treaty obligations, under section 410.[49] Proposed new sections 410A–B will also authorise the Treasury to make regulations requiring the regulators to collect fees to meet the expenses of Treasury participation in prescribed international organisations.[50]

42 s 84 of FSA 2012; ss 1N(3), 1O(4), 1P(3), 1Q(3), 2M(3), and 212(4), and Sch 17, para 3(2).

43 To be inserted under the FS(BR) Bill.

44 See Parts 9 (hearings and appeals) and 24 (insolvency) respectively.

45 See s 3H and the list at s 429.

46 The first review (originally of the FSA under former s 10) was undertaken by the Auditor and Comptroller General who reported on 30 April 2007: <http://www.nao.org.uk/pn/06-07/0607500.htm>.

47 Chapter 4 of Part 9A—the CMA determines whether provisions or practices may cause or contribute to the prevention, restriction or distortion of competition and makes recommendations to the relevant regulator; under s 140H if the CMA is dissatisfied with the regulator's response it may refer the matter to the Treasury to determine whether, and if so what, action should be taken; s 120 (references to the City Code).

48 Sch 1ZA, para 11 for the FCA; Sch 1ZB, para 19 for the PRA, which is also required to consult the public about its report under paras 20–21.

49 See also s 405 on implementing third country decisions.

50 To be inserted by the FS(BR) Bill.

2.28 Finally, FSMA avoids direct formal accountability of the regulators to Parliament. The Treasury would order any inquiry or review under FSA 2012. Similarly, the regulators' annual reports are made to the Treasury, which in turn must lay them before Parliament. However, the Treasury is accountable to Parliament for its functions under FSMA and its oversight of the regulators, and in practice the Treasury Select Committee and other parliamentary committees often seek evidence and ask questions directly from the regulators and their officials, and make recommendations directly to them.

Scope

2.29 The scope of regulation under FSMA is determined primarily through the specification of regulated activities under Part 2 of FSMA, which, in turn, forces firms carrying on those activities into regulation. However, the scope of regulation is not as simple as that. FSMA also impacts on:

(i) controllers, qualifying parent undertakings, directors, officers, and persons who perform functions on behalf of regulated firms in respect of regulated activities (under Parts 5, 11, 12, 22, and 27);[51]

(ii) persons who communicate financial promotions of specified activities (under Parts 2 and 27 of FSMA as well as Part 7 of FSA 2012);

(iii) persons who engage in market activities covered by listing, prospectus, disclosure, takeover, market abuse, investment exchanges and clearing houses, misleading practices, and insider dealing regimes (under Parts 6, 9, 18, and 27 of FSMA as well as Part 7 of FSA 2012);

(iv) persons who may be recipients or the subject of regulatory or other guidance (whether as part of supervision or under section 139A);

(v) third parties who may be concerned in the activities of regulated firms (including assets requirements under Part 4A, business transfers under Part 7, client money and money-laundering rules under Part 9A, operators and participants in collective investment schemes under Part 17); and

(vi) mutual societies (in respect of registration and other functions transferred to the FCA or the PRA under Part 21 of FSMA or under Part 3 of FSA 2012).

2.30 FSMA itself specifies the potential scope of regulation, primarily through the main purpose described in its long title ('the regulation of financial services and markets') and the variety of matters covered by FSMA and particularly in section 22 (regulated activities) and Schedule 2 to FSMA. The actual scope of regulation under FSMA is specified by or as a result of secondary legislation made by the Treasury. Even the regulators' functions in relation to mutuals may be transferred to another body under Part 21 of FSMA and Part 3 of FSA 2012.

2.31 Schedule 2 is one of FSMA's more confusing features. It contains an indicative list of the activities and investments in respect of such activities which may be specified for the purpose of:

(i) the general prohibition under section 19 and the definition of regulated activities under section 22, including PRA-regulated activities under section 22A;[52]

---

[51] See also the proposed Part 9B powers against qualifying parent undertakings of ring-fenced bodies, and new senior persons and licensing regimes to be inserted under the FS(BR) Bill.

[52] See also the definitions of 'core activity' and 'core services' in the proposed ss 142B–C of FSMA to be introduced under the FS(BR) Bill.

(ii) the financial promotion restriction as a result of section 21(11) and consequently the FCA's financial promotion rules under section 137R(1);
(iii) the jurisdiction of the FOS as a result of sections 226(4) and 227(4) (now supplemented by the consumer credit jurisdiction under section 226A);
(iv) the investments subject to exemption from gaming restrictions as a result of section 412(3); and
(v) the scope of the misleading statements offence which the FCA may prosecute as a result of section 89(1) of FSA 2012.

The original explanatory notes to FSMA suggest that Schedule 2 has a limiting effect.[53] However, strictly speaking, the list in Schedule 2 supplements section 22 and does not limit the Treasury's powers in specifying activities, as section 22(2) and (3) and corresponding provisions in other sections make clear. Furthermore, section 22(4) defines an investment widely as any 'asset, right or interest', and activities may in any event be specified more generally in relation to property of any kind. However, because of doubts about whether even these wide provisions could accommodate activities relating to credit rating agencies and benchmarks, FSA 2012 introduced section 22(1A) as well as Part 1A of Schedule 2 to include them specifically. **2.32**

In practice, several activities have already been specified by the Treasury which are not strictly included in Schedule 2, such as those relating to funeral plan contracts and e-money.[54] However, the Government has trodden warily in departing from the activities and investments specified in Schedule 2, even where there have been obvious similarities with some of the investments already specified. The Government legislated to amend Schedule 2 before specifying the relevant scope orders in respect of home reversion plans and certain Islamic arrangements, reclaim funds, and loans and other forms of credit as well as contracts for hire of goods (hire purchase) in order to accommodate the transfer of consumer credit functions to the FCA.[55] **2.33**

The FCA and the FOS have gone beyond the list in Schedule 2 by specifying certain unsecured types of lending in the FOS's compulsory and voluntary jurisdictions respectively, even before the introduction of a specific consumer credit jurisdiction under section 226A by the Consumer Credit Act 2006, as well as specifying other ancillary activities carried on in respect of regulated activities and lending.[56] **2.34**

---

[53] Explanatory notes for Sch 2:

'777. This Schedule does not define what activities are regulated under the Act. The regulated activities will be those activities which are prescribed using the power conferred by section 22. The Schedule sets out a list of "activities" and "investments" which, together, indicate the broad scope of activities which are potentially regulated under the Act. The scope of the Act is not strictly limited by the Schedule, but rather by the overall object and purpose of the Act. However, the general nature of the activities set out in the Schedule serves to inform and therefore indirectly limit the extent of the Treasury's power to bring further activities within the scope of the Act.

778. It is within this overall object and purpose that the power under section 22 to prescribe the regulated activities operates. Orders made under that section will be an exhaustive statement of the regulated activities'.

[54] See arts 9B, 59, 74A, and 87 of the consolidated RAO.

[55] Through the Regulation of Financial Services (Land Transactions) Act 2005, the Dormant Bank and Building Society Accounts Act 2008, and FSA 2012 respectively.

[56] See the rules in DISP 2.3–2.5 in the FCA Handbook.

Regulated activities

2.35 The concept of regulated activities is central to the scope of regulation under FSMA. By the 'general prohibition' under section 19, persons carrying on or purporting to carry on regulated activities in the UK must either be authorised under FSMA, or exempt, although as we shall see later in this chapter, further exclusions apply. Breach of section 19 is an offence under section 23, although subsection (3) provides a defence if an accused person can show he took all reasonable precautions and exercised all due diligence to avoid committing the offence. Transactions are also potentially unenforceable, and there may be a liability to pay compensation.[57]

2.36 The FCA's functions may generally be exercised to advance its objectives, which in turn relate to 'regulated financial services' provided in carrying on regulated activities,[58] even where the FCA is exercising these functions in respect of other, non-regulated, activities of a regulated firm.[59] The FCA's consumer protection objective under section 1C and its competition objective under section 1E apply by virtue of section 1G to regulated activities even when carried on under an exemption.[60] The definition of the UK financial system in section 1I, which specifies the scope of the integrity objective in section 1D, also includes regulated activities. The FCA's proposed new continuity objective will protect the continuity in the UK of specified core services provided in the course of carrying on core regulated activities.[61] The definition of regulated activities is equally central to the accountability of the PRA, since the scope of its responsibilities and its general objective under section 2B to promote the safety and soundness of PRA-authorised persons, are determined by the designation of PRA-regulated activities under section 22A of FSMA.

2.37 A regulated activity is defined by section 22(1) as:

> an activity of a specified kind which is carried on by way of business and—
>
> (a) relates to an investment of a specified kind; or
>
> (b) in the case of an activity of a kind which is also specified for the purposes of this paragraph, is carried on in relation to property of any kind.[62]

As discussed earlier,[63] subsection (1A) adds credit rating and benchmark activities to this list.

2.38 Schedule 2 supplements this section by setting out an indicative list of activities and investments which may be specified, although nothing in Schedule 2 limits the Treasury's power.[64]

---

[57] FSMA, ss 26–29.

[58] See definition in s 1H.

[59] For example, through the link between each regulator's objectives and their powers to make general rules under ss 137A and 137G, and the power to take steps to advance their objectives in granting or varying a permission under s 55B(4).

[60] See s 1G(3); ss 425A–B extend the definition of 'consumer' for other purposes to include users of services provided by appointed representatives and by investment firms in providing relevant ancillary services under the Markets in Financial Services Directive ('MiFID'), as well as by persons other than authorised persons; the various definitions of 'consumer' used in FSMA have also been extended to include users of financial services which were regulated under predecessor legislation before FSMA and subsequent scope extensions—see SI 2001/1821 art 3 and SI 2002/1501 art 4.

[61] See the FS(BR) Bill which amends s 2B of FSMA and introduces Part 9B.

[62] Activities specified under this head include operating a collective investment scheme, a stakeholder or personal pension scheme, or a reclaim fund. See arts 4(2), 51-52, 63N of the RAO (and para 2.39 following).

[63] See para 2.32.

[64] ibid.

The range of activities which may be specified is very wide but covers in effect three broad categories:

(i) dealing as principal in investments, including through contracts or services which firms issue and perform themselves, such as deposits, insurance contracts, securities, regulated mortgages, and funeral plan contracts;
(ii) advice and intermediation in respect of dealing in investments, including markets themselves as well as credit rating agencies and benchmarks; and
(iii) holding or administering investments and other property on behalf of customers.

The consolidated order made under section 22 (the 'Regulated Activities Order' or 'RAO') has a number of important features. First, the RAO specifies not regulated activities themselves but activities and investments 'of a specified kind'.[65] In giving or varying permissions for authorised persons to carry on a regulated activity under Part 4A, the FCA or the PRA (under section 55E) specifies its own description of the activities covered by the permission within the specified kinds of activity. The same applies to descriptions of regulated activities in other instruments, whether made by the regulators or by other bodies. **2.39**

Secondly, the RAO excludes a number of activities when carried on with an exempt or authorised person with the appropriate permission. There is scope for an element of circularity in specifying activities, and activities falling inadvertently outside regulation, which needs to be guarded against. Many of these exclusions are not therefore available to authorised persons.[66] **2.40**

Thirdly, and related to this, the Treasury needs to ensure that the RAO extends to all activities required to be covered by single market directives. The text of various directives is included as Schedules to the RAO. Article 4(4) provides for exclusions to be disregarded for an investment firm or credit institution in providing investment services and activities on a professional basis,[67] and Article 4(4A) makes similar provision for insurance or reinsurance in relation to a risk or commitment in an EEA State. **2.41**

Fourthly, paragraph 25 of Schedule 2 gives the Treasury power in specifying activities and investments to make exemptions, confer functions and jurisdiction, and make changes to other legislation including amending primary legislation. This power has been used to make supplemental or consequential changes to other legislation relating to those activities, and to FSMA itself in a number of cases, including transitional provisions such as interim permissions when introducing new regulated activities.[68] **2.42**

Finally, the RAO is not the only determinant of whether an activity is a regulated activity. Section 22(1) requires that the activity should be carried on by way of business, and section **2.43**

65 See s 22(1) and art 4 of the RAO; also n 112, following.

66 See, eg, exclusions which are not available to authorised persons under arts 16, 22, 29, 29A, 54A, 62, 63, 63C, 63D, 63G, 63H, 63K, and 63L.

67 Any service provided to a third party listed in s A of Annex I to the markets in financial instruments directive (the text of which is set out in Sch 2 to the RAO), read with art 52 of Commission Directive 2006/73/EC (the text of which is set out in Part 4 of Sch 2); and activity listed in Section A of Sch I to that directive.

68 See, eg, the supplemental certification regime established for excluded e-money issuers under SI 2001/544, arts 9C–9G, and the offence established for false claims to be certified under art 9I, together with provision for rules under art 9H and exclusion from the FSCS under art 9J, and the register provisions for unauthorised persons carrying on insurance mediation activities in arts 92–96. Other examples of direct amendments to FSMA such as that inserted by SI 2001/544, art 97 are spent by virtue of the substitution of Part 4A for the previous Part 4.

419 provides for a further order specifying circumstances in which activities are and are not to be treated as carried on by way of business.[69]

2.44 The effect of this order is that activities in relation to deposits are not treated as carried on by way of business if they are not held out as accepted on a day-to-day basis and are accepted only on particular occasions.[70] By contrast, investment business activities are carried on by way of business only by persons who carry on the business of engaging in one or more such activities, and similar provision applies to arranging and advice on regulated mortgage contracts, regulated home reversion and purchase plans, and regulated sale and rent back agreements; insurance mediation activities are carried on by way of business only if taken up or pursued for remuneration.[71] Meanwhile trustees of occupational pension schemes (other than relevant small or insured schemes) may be treated as carrying on the regulated activity of managing investments unless all day-to-day decisions are delegated to a person who is authorised or exempt in relation to that activity, or involve pooled investments on the advice of an authorised or exempt person.[72]

2.45 The regulation of collective investment schemes under Part 17 also impacts on regulated activities. Units in a collective investment scheme are a specified kind of investment in the RAO, and establishing and operating a collective investment scheme are specified kinds of activity.[73] However, the definition of a collective investment scheme can itself be amended. Exclusions can be and are specified through separate orders made under section 235(5).[74]

2.46 As discussed earlier,[75] the Treasury has exercised its power under section 22A to specify those regulated activities which are PRA-regulated activities: accepting deposits (Article 5 of the RAO), effecting and carrying out contracts of insurance (Article 10), and the activities of Lloyd's and managing agents (Articles 57–58).[76] Dealing in investments as principal may also be included when carried on by an authorised investment firm designated by the PRA under Article 3 having regard to its assets and its impact on the PRA's ability to advance its objectives in relation to other PRA-authorised persons in its group, having consulted the FCA.

Exemptions

2.47 FSMA provides for various types of exemption. Some of these arise directly under FSMA, although again their scope is in practice determined by secondary legislation or recognitions under FSMA:

(i) an exemption under section 285 for recognised investment exchanges and clearing houses as respects any regulated activity which is carried on as part of its business as an investment exchange, or which is carried on for the purposes of or in connection with the provision of clearing services by it or another person; and a similar exemption for

[69] The Financial Services and Markets Act 2000 (Carrying on Regulated Activities by Way of Business) Order 2001, SI 2001/1177, as amended.

[70] ibid, art 2 (reflecting the earlier test in the Banking Act 1987).

[71] ibid, arts 3 (reflecting the test in Directive 2002/92/EC on insurance mediation) and 3A–3D.

[72] ibid, art 4, as amended by SI 2005/922 to include inter alia insurance contracts as well as units in collective investment schemes and investment trusts.

[73] See the RAO, arts 51 and 81.

[74] See the Financial Services and Markets Act 2000 (Collective Investment Schemes) Order 2001, SI 2001/1062 as amended.

[75] See paras 2.27(ii), 231(i), 2.36.

[76] The Financial Services and Markets Act 2000 (PRA-Regulated Activities) Order 2013, SI 2013/556

recognised, EEA or third party central counterparties in respect of activities carried on for the purposes of or in connection with services specified in their recognition;

(ii) an exemption for appointed representatives under section 39 in respect of prescribed regulated activities for which an authorised person has taken responsibility, provided that in the case of investment services business, their name has been entered in the applicable register maintained by the FCA or the equivalent register in the relevant EEA Member State of an incoming principal; and

(iii) specification in an exemption order under section 38.[77]

The exemptions for appointed representatives and for persons specified in an exemption order are not available to authorised persons, who must instead have these activities covered by their permission.[78] This latter restriction applies to incoming firms which rely on a single market or Treaty passport under Schedule 3 or 4; and to so-called 'exempt investment firms' under the Financial Services and Markets Act 2000 (Markets in Financial Instruments) Regulations 2007 which are in fact authorised persons.[79] However, there is no such restriction for recognised bodies under section 285. **2.48**

Paragraph 25 of Schedule 2 provides for exemptions to be specified in the RAO and other scope orders. As set out earlier, the RAO provides for exclusions from the main types of activity specified in it. Unlike other exemptions, excluded activities are not themselves regulated activities, which means that they fall outside the regulators' scope and responsibilities for many purposes. Exemptions from the definition of collective investment scheme also in effect create exclusions from regulated activities.[80] **2.49**

In addition to formal exemptions, certain regulated activities are not treated as carried on in breach of the general prohibition when: **2.50**

(i) they are underwriting activities carried on by a member of Lloyd's (provided the FCA or the PRA has not directed that the general prohibition applies)—see section 316(1);

(ii) they are exempt regulated activities, carried on under rules made by a designated professional body and approved by the FCA under section 332;[81] or

(iii) they are not carried on in the UK.[82]

There is no explicit provision for this, but it has generally been assumed that the general and financial promotion prohibitions in FSMA do not apply to the Crown, or to the FCA, the PRA, and the other creatures of FSMA in performing their statutory functions under it.[83] **2.51**

---

[77] See the Financial Services and Markets Act 2000 (Exemptions) Order 2001, SI 2007/1201, as amended.

[78] See s 38(2) and the chapeau to s 39(1).

[79] SI 2007/126 (as amended) at regulations 4A–4C. The exemption relates to certain requirements of the Markets in Financial Instruments Directive and other directives. It is limited to firms which have a relevant office in the UK and do not seek to exercise passporting rights; may not hold client money; and whose permitted activities are limited to the provision of investment advice, or the reception and transmission (to certain types of firm) of orders in certain types of investment.

[80] s 235(5)—see the Financial Services and Markets Act 2000 (Collective Investment Schemes) Order 2001, SI 2001/1062, as amended.

[81] The 'exemption' is created by s 327.

[82] See paras 2.62–2.67.

[83] The FCA might otherwise need to authorise itself; some doubt has been cast on this assumption by art 63Q of the RAO, which provides a specific exclusion for the FCA from the activity of administering a specified benchmark when it administers the benchmark itself. However, this is in conjunction with a provision that the FCA is to be treated as having permission to carry on that activity for the purposes of interpreting the activity of 'providing information' in art 63O(2)(a)(i).

Financial promotions and misleading statements

2.52 As discussed earlier,[84] the scope of financial services regulation is not confined to the carrying on of regulated activities, and a separate restriction and other criminal offences apply to the promotion of financial services.

2.53 The financial promotion restriction in section 21 was one of the major innovations under FSMA. Under predecessor legislation, such as the Financial Services Act 1986 ('FSA 1986'), the definitions of many of the activities comprising investment business included offering to carry on those activities. These were supplemented by separate prohibitions on cold-calling and investment advertising, for persons without exemption or authorisation, or approval by an authorised person.

2.54 Under FSMA, offering is not specified as a type of regulated activity in the RAO.[85] There is instead a single prohibition in section 21(1), which applies, subject to exemptions, to any communication which is not made or approved by an authorised person:

> A person (A) must not, in the course of business, communicate an invitation or inducement to engage in investment activity.

2.55 'Engaging in investment activity' is defined by section 21(8) as entering or offering to enter into an agreement the making or performance of which constitutes a controlled activity, or exercising rights conferred by a controlled investment to acquire, dispose of, underwrite, or convert a controlled investment. Controlled activities and investments are specified by the Treasury by order, and Schedule 2 is treated as providing an indicative list of activities and investments which may be specified, but does not limit the powers conferred on the Treasury.

2.56 However, the bulk of the consolidated Financial Promotion Order ('FPO')[86] concerns the various exemptions which specify circumstances in which the restriction does not apply. This is because the scope of the restriction is very wide:

(i) it applies to any communication of an invitation or inducement, as well as causing such a communication to be made (section 21(13));

(ii) most of the exclusions for regulated activities in the RAO are not replicated in the corresponding 'controlled activities' specified in the FPO—this level of detail is not always apparent in a communication so that enforcement particularly against unauthorised persons would be difficult;

(iii) there is no automatic exemption in section 21 for exempt persons and other persons to whom the general prohibition in section 19 does not apply; and

(iv) the business test 'in the course of business' is wider than the 'by way of business' test for regulated activities, potentially applying to any business, even one which does not involve financial services, and the Treasury has not exercised its power to specify circumstances in which this does not apply under section 21(4).

---

[84] See para 2.29.

[85] 'Offering' is nevertheless still specified in much of Sch 2, and has in effect been specified as a component of 'ancillary activities' for the purposes of the FOS's jurisdiction. See DISP 2.6.4G.

[86] Remade as the Financial Services and Markets Act 2000 (Financial Promotions) Order 2005, SI 2005/1529 under s 21 and Sch 2. Like the RAO, the FPO continues to be amended frequently, as the scope of regulation changes.

The exemptions generally apply to the circumstances of the communication rather than to the circumstances of the underlying controlled activity, and these circumstances often need to be widely framed in order to avoid catching legitimate communications of non-financial services inadvertently. On the other hand, the Treasury needs to be wary of making exemptions too wide,[87] and has in effect continued the distinction between different types of communication such as advertisements and cold-calling through a new classification of communications[88] as: **2.57**

(i) 'real time'—in the course of a personal visit, telephone conversation, or other interactive dialogue—or 'non-real time', such as communications made by letter or e-mail or contained in a publication;
(ii) where the communication is real time, 'solicited'—that is, where the personal visit, telephone call, or other interactive dialogue is initiated by the recipient of the communication—or 'unsolicited'.

FCA rules do not permit authorised persons to approve a real time communication by an unauthorised person, because of the practical difficulties of doing so in advance and the consequences of an unapproved communication in terms of unenforceability of contracts.[89] Accordingly, particular care is required with real-time communications. Exemptions for real time communications by appointed representatives, for example, require them to comply with financial promotion rules which means that breach of FCA rules may involve an offence.[90] **2.58**

The main exemptions in the FPO are specified by reference to one or more of the following features:[91] **2.59**

(i) communications to particular types of recipient—suppliers, existing customers, shareholders, employees, creditors, trustees and beneficiaries, sophisticated investors, high net worth individuals, investment professionals, overseas persons;
(ii) communications by particular types of person—advice centres, employers, exempt persons, appointed representatives, issuers, journalists, directors, members of a profession, trustees, persons acting as a mere conduit, clients of an authorised person;
(iii) communications in particular circumstances or through a particular medium—one-off, follow-up and solicited communications, introductions and generic promotions, electronic commerce communications, interviews and broadcasts, communications relating to a takeover or subject to other safeguards or rules, communications which contain a specified message or warning; and
(iv) communications relating to particular types of investment activity or investment—deposits, insurance, dealing, securities.

These differences mean that it is usually quite difficult to reconcile the regulated activities and the financial promotion regimes, and it is often the financial promotion restriction **2.60**

[87] Not least because s 137R(3) restricts the FCA's powers to make financial promotion rules for authorised persons in respect of communications which would not contravene the restriction.
[88] See arts 7 and 8 of the FPO, as amended.
[89] See COBS 4.10.4R in the FCA Handbook.
[90] See art 16(2) of the FPO.
[91] See the consolidated FPO generally.

which has the wider scope. Consequently, the FPO has been amended several times, and was one of the main aspects of FSMA considered as part of the two-year review of FSMA in 2003–2004.[92]

2.61 Further determinants of the scope of regulation under FSMA are the misleading statements and misleading impression offences now in sections 89–90 of the 2012 Act (supplemented by section 91 for benchmarks following the LIBOR scandal), the scope of which is specified in terms of types of activities and types of investments by the Treasury under section 93. The effect of the section is to give the FCA jurisdiction to prosecute misleading statements, so that exclusions are generally inappropriate. The existence of the offence also gives the FCA jurisdiction to seek an injunction, including a remedial injunction, or restitution under Part 25.

Territorial scope

2.62 The territorial scope of regulation is determined partly in FSMA and partly in secondary legislation. Again territorial scope can differ according to the aspect being considered. It is worth bearing in mind, however, that there is a practical limit on the territorial application of any national law, since in general only national courts can be expected to uphold it. It is of course possible that in some cases foreign courts will be authorised or required by their own national law to take account of whether a person is acting in breach of UK law, for example where an international treaty applies. This applies to some extent with the single market directives. However, such questions are outside the scope of this chapter.

2.63 The definition of regulated activity in section 22 contains no territorial restriction, although the RAO contains several exclusions for activities carried on by, through, or to overseas persons.[93] The definition of regulated mortgage contract for example applies only if the loan is secured on property in the UK.[94]

2.64 However, the main territorial restriction lies in the general prohibition in section 19, which applies the prohibition to regulated activities carried on in the UK. This is supplemented by section 418, which provides that any regulated activity is treated as carried on in the UK if it is carried on from an establishment maintained in the UK, or by a firm with its registered office in the UK if day-to-day management is in the UK or it is exercising passporting rights as a UK firm.

2.65 There is no such territorial limit on the corresponding restriction in section 20 which applies to authorised persons, so that their permissions might need to extend to regulated activities carried on by them worldwide. Similarly, there is no restriction on the scope of most of the regulators' rule-making powers, although in practice they often impose a restriction or distinction through the application provisions in their rules.

2.66 There is equally no territorial limit on references to regulated activities in the regulatory objectives, although the UK financial system is defined for the purposes of the FCA's integrity objective in terms of 'the financial system operating in the United Kingdom'.[95] The

92 See para 2.81. A similar order is made under s 238 for communications by authorised persons in relation to unregulated collective investment schemes.

93 See art 72 of the RAO.

94 See art 61(3)(a)(ii).

95 See s 1I.

regulators' general duties and section 3B(1)(b) require them in discharging their general policy or rule-making functions to have regard to the desirability of sustainable growth of the UK in the medium or long term, and there are numerous provisions requiring the regulators to coordinate and report on their dealings with overseas regulators.

Finally, the FPO specifies exemptions by references to certain incoming and outward communications, whereas the misleading statements offences in section 89 of FSA 2012 require the statement, the intended person to be induced, or the agreement, to take place in the UK. The move to home State supervision means that exemptions will increasingly apply to incoming communications, as they already do for electronic-commerce communications, while the FCA will be responsible for policing outward communications by UK firms.[96] **2.67**

Markets

FSMA provides for regulation of markets through the specification of dealing and of markets themselves as regulated activities,[97] and through Part 6 provisions relating to listing and prospectuses, recognition of investment exchanges and clearing houses under Part 18, market abuse under Part 8, and powers to prosecute for insider dealing under Part 27. The scope of the market abuse regime is specified in terms of an order under section 118. These provisions have been substantially amended following implementation of the Market Abuse Directive and the Prospectus Directive.[98] **2.68**

Miscellaneous

Confidentiality and disclosure

Section 348 protects the confidentiality of information obtained by the FCA and the PRA in the discharge of their functions, as well as information obtained by other 'primary recipients', namely investigators, the BIS, their employees, and other persons appointed as skilled persons, auditors, and experts on their behalf, by restricting their disclosure without permission. **2.69**

Section 349 gives the Treasury power to prescribe exemptions or 'gateways' from the restriction on disclosing confidential information without permission, subject to restrictions on its use. These regulations,[99] which have been frequently amended, aim to provide the FCA, the PRA, and other recipients of confidential information with sufficiently wide gateways either to enable or assist them to perform any of their public functions, or to enable or assist other public bodies to perform their functions. **2.70**

In practice, the main restriction here is the duty of professional secrecy imposed under the various single market directives, and the regulations distinguish between directive information (which has narrower gateways) and non-directive information (which enjoys wider gateways). **2.71**

---

[96] See Chapter 3.

[97] RAO, arts 14 and 25.

[98] The Financial Services and Markets Act 2000 (Market Abuse) Regulations 2005, SI 2005/381, which also specify the markets covered by s 118, and the Prospectus Regulations 2005, SI 2005/1433.

[99] SI 2001/2188 as amended; s 352 makes breach of restrictions on the use of information imposed under these regulations, and of ss 348 and 350(5) (Revenue information) an offence, subject to defences.

2.72 The section 348 restriction provides an absolute exemption under section 44 of the Freedom of Information Act 2000, but the self-help gateways might in theory permit the FCA to disclose information to enable or assist it to give guidance under section 139A or as part of the public record it must maintain under section 347. The function of giving guidance applies to such information and advice as it 'considers appropriate', and the contents of the Register are similarly governed, while both regulators are now required in exercising their general policy and rule-making functions to have regard to the desirability of publishing information about regulated persons, or requiring regulated persons themselves to publish information which advances their objectives, and the principle that they should exercise their functions as transparently as possible.[100] The FCA would take into account the restriction, its general policy on transparency, and any single market provisions, in deciding whether publication was appropriate or not.

2.73 Section 348 is not the only restriction on disclosure. The procedural provisions of FSMA require the regulators to issue warning and decision notices before publishing statements of censure.[101] Before FSA 2012, section 391 prohibited either the regulator or any recipient of a notice (including a third party) from publishing details of any warning or decision notice until the regulator had issued a final notice, or (with the recipient's consent) after the regulator had withdrawn it. As a matter of policy, the FSA was reluctant to publish details of supervisory or enforcement action until it took effect.[102] However, in line with the new regulatory principle on maximising transparency under section 3B(1)(h), section 391 now provides that regulators must publish such information about a decision notice (or a supervisory notice which has taken effect) as they consider appropriate. Regulators may also publish such information about certain warning notices (including as to statements of censure) as they consider appropriate, having first consulted the recipients, and subject to safeguards of fairness to the recipients, avoiding prejudice to the interests of consumers, the stability of the financial system, and other matters relevant to their objectives.[103] Section 413 protects communications with legal advisers in connection with legal advice or legal proceedings from any requirement of production, disclosure, or inspection under FSMA. This applies both to regulated firms and to the regulators themselves.

2.74 Finally, section 353 provides for the Treasury to make regulations permitting the disclosure of information to the regulators to enable or assist them to discharge their functions or to any person to enable or assist the discloser without contravening any duty to which the discloser may be subject. The regulations made under this section permit disclosures by the FOS and the FSCS, as well as by skilled persons and other experts appointed in respect of regulated firms.[104] This and the duties for the FCA and the PRA to cooperate with the Bank of England and other regulators (including overseas regulators) under section 354, 354A, and 354B are subject to the confidentiality restriction in section 348 (and in practice to the gateways

---

[100] See s 3B(1)(g)–(h).

[101] See ss 66 (misconduct by approved persons); 88A (sponsors); 91 (issuers and applicants); 123 (market abuse); 131G (short selling regulation); 192K (qualifying parent undertakings); 205 (contraventions by authorised persons); 249, 345–345A (auditors and actuaries); 312E (recognised bodies).

[102] By contrast, the Tribunal Procedure (Upper Tribunal) Rules 2008, SI 2008/2698 as amended, contain a presumption of publicity—see rule 37(1).

[103] Subs (6) for the FCA; subs (7) for the PRA.

[104] The Financial Services and Markets Act 2000 (Disclosure of Information by Prescribed Persons) Regulations 2001, SI 2001/1857 as amended.

established through regulations under section 349). There is a similar, but unrestricted, provision under section 351A permitting disclosures by or on behalf of auditors and trustees of authorised unit trusts for the purpose of compliance with FCA or PRA rules implementing the UCITS directive.[105]

Relationship to external legislation

2.75 The implementation of FSMA impacted a large volume of legislation which referred to predecessor legislation,[106] and FSMA is referred to in many other statutes and secondary instruments. Some of this legislation confers functions directly on the FCA or the PRA, in which case there is usually provision for some or all of those functions to be treated as conferred by or under FSMA.[107] For example:

(i) functions in relation to mutual societies, which are treated as conferred by or under FSMA for some but not all purposes, since mutuals legislation makes specific provision for these;[108]
(ii) functions as investigating authority under the Proceeds of Crime Act 2002, which are treated as conferred under FSMA by virtue of paragraph 26 of Schedule 1ZA to FSMA;
(iii) functions as a qualifying body under the Unfair Terms in Consumer Contracts Regulations 1999, and as a designated enforcer under Part 8 of the Enterprise Act 2002, which are treated as conferred by or under FSMA;[109]
(iv) functions in relation to insolvency legislation, which are treated as conferred by or under FSMA.[110]

2.76 However, certain functions conferred on the regulators, for example the Treasury's functions delegated to the Bank of England under the Uncertificated Securities Regulations 2001, are not treated as conferred by or under FSMA. In this case the legislation itself provides for fee-raising powers.[111] Similarly, the FCA's prospective functions under Part 5 (Regulation of Payment Services) of the FS(BR) Bill will be treated as conferred under FSMA only for the purposes of its statutory exemption from liability.

2.77 Most of the other references to FSMA in external legislation are to:

(i) definitions of bank, insurer, and other authorised persons—care may be needed here to ensure that authorisation under FSMA is not taken to imply FCA or PRA approval or

---

[105] Inserted by SI 2011/1613.

[106] See, eg, the Financial Services and Markets Act 2000 (Consequential Amendments and Repeals) Order 2001, SI 2001/3649, as well as further orders SI 2001/3629, SI 2001/3801, SI 2001/3647; and more recently in relation to FSA 2012, the Financial Services Act 2012 (Consequential Amendments) Order 2013, SI 2013/636, as well as SI 2013/642.

[107] See paras 2.19–2.21.

[108] See Sch 2 to the Financial Services and Markets Act 2000 (Mutual Societies) Order 2001, SI 2001/2617, as amended in particular by SI 2013/496; the regulators' supervisory, monitoring and enforcement duties and general duties are expressly disapplied.

[109] See reg 16 of SI 1999/2083 as amended, and art 3 of the Designation Order SI 2004/935. The FCA's prospective functions under competition legislation by virtue of the FS(BR) Bill will also be treated as conferred as a result of FSMA, although its general duties will be disapplied.

[110] See the Insolvency Act 2000 Schs 1, 2. Now replaced by ss 1A(6)(a) (for the FCA) and 2A(6)(a) (for the PRA).

[111] SI 2001/3755—see regulation 6.

supervision of the firm in respect of the right, activity, or other privilege referred to in the legislation;[112]

(ii) the regulators and their functions conferred by or under FSMA, usually for the purpose of conferring gateways from confidentiality provisions applying to other regulators. In the absence of contrary provision, the FCA is the successor to the FSA in all external legislation since it is the same body.[113]

2.78 Increasingly, new functions have been conferred on the regulators through regulations implementing single market directives under ECA 1972. Initially, the regulations themselves provided for the regulator's functions—including functions as a competent authority—to be treated as conferred under FSMA.[114] However, the functions conferred or required may sometimes fall already within an existing regulatory function under FSMA, for example the regulators' 'supervision' functions, or the FCA's function of giving guidance under section 139A; or by virtue of requirements on other regulated persons being treated as conferred under FSMA, which activates the FCA's monitoring and enforcement functions.

2.79 As discussed earlier,[115] sections 1A (for the FCA) and 2A (for the PRA) now provide for functions under certain legislation (the Insolvency Act 1986, BA 2009, FSA 2012) to be treated as functions conferred by or under FSMA. The Treasury may also specify qualifying EU provisions in respect of which functions are to be treated as conferred under FSMA, or requirements may be enforced under FSMA.[116]

Future Development

2.80 In anticipating future development, it is useful to consider the mechanisms through which the regulatory framework has evolved to date. As discussed earlier,[117] FSMA built a substantial degree of flexibility into the regulatory regime so that it could evolve without the need for further primary legislation, and this has been enhanced further through a broad extension of the powers and diversity of the regulators, and of the Treasury's powers to 'fine-tune' their responsibilities. So far FSMA has been able to accommodate major domestic changes such as depolarisation and its extension to mortgage and general insurance intermediaries. FSA 2012 made specific provision for the transfer of responsibility for consumer credit regulation

---

112 Because the activities that such entities have permission or exemption to carry on are defined in secondary legislation and generally need to be kept up-to-date or 'ambulatory' (ie reflecting the latest version of the RAO as amended from time to time), provision is generally made for the definition to be 'read' with reference to s 22, Sch 2, and any relevant order made under s 22.

113 See s 1A.

114 For example, regulation 23 of the Financial Services (Distance Marketing) Regulations 2004, SI 2004/2095; regulation 27 of the Capital Requirements Regulations 2006, SI 2006/3221; and reg 5 of the Transfer of Funds (Information on the Payer) Regulations 2007, SI 2007/3298 and regulation 24 of the Money Laundering Regulations 2007, SI 2007/2157.

115 See para 2.19.

116 The Financial Services and Markets Act 2000 (Qualifying EU Provisions) Order 2013, SI 2013/419. Provisions specified include: any directly applicable regulation made under the markets in financial instruments directive or the UCITS directive; the emission allowance auctioning regulation; the European market infrastructure regulation and any directly applicable regulation made under it; the short selling regulation and any directly applicable regulation made under it.

117 See paras 2.2, 2.9.

from the OFT to the FCA, and the Government has announced that this will commence from 1 April 2014.[118]

Secondly, there has been use of deregulatory mechanisms. For example, the two-year review of FSMA in 2003–2004 considered various aspects of the operation of FSMA shortly after implementation. Progress and outcomes of the review were announced on 2 December 2004.[119] Broadly, the review concluded that FSMA was working well and recommendations could be incorporated either in changes to secondary legislation or in changes to the FSA's (and where appropriate the FOS's) own rules and procedures. However, the Treasury identified a number of deregulatory amendments to FSMA itself through an order under the then Regulatory Reform Act 2006.[120] **2.81**

Thirdly, the development of further European directives, regulations, and guidance, including from the European Supervisory Authorities, will need to be accommodated, either through the mechanisms established under FSMA, or using powers under ECA 1972. As discussed earlier,[121] it is possible that some of these will have a simplifying effect on the UK framework, substituting directly for UK materials, given the Government's commitment to avoid gold-plating. Full European harmonisation might see the UK regulators acting primarily as competent authorities implementing a European regulatory framework, albeit subject to UK accountability mechanisms. **2.82**

Finally, as we have seen, the possibility exists for further changes arising from primary legislation—either as a result of some further unanticipated crisis or regulatory failure, or as a result of a change in Government policy. The recently announced replacement of the 'failed' approved persons regime in Part 5 by a new senior persons and licensing regime, and a proposed new secondary competition objective for the PRA, signal an increased willingness to intervene through legislation,[122] although FSMA's ability to absorb the most recent institutional changes (albeit with increased complexity) suggests that its basic structure will remain fairly stable. Further potential areas for development include the FCA's role as a competition regulator, consolidation of financial services and pensions regulation, and changes in response to global initiatives.[123] The twin peaks model is still untested in the UK and much will therefore depend on the performance of the new regulators. **2.83**

[118] ibid.

[119] Statement by the then Financial Secretary, Stephen Timms MP, and FSMA Bulletin 43.

[120] The Regulatory Reform (Financial Services and Markets Act 2000) Order 2007.

[121] See para 2.18.

[122] Through the FS(BR) Bill. See the Government's Response to the Parliamentary Commission on Banking Standards, July 2013, Chapter 2, and para 4.17.

[123] See Chapter 3.

3

EUROPEAN FINANCIAL SERVICES

Introduction

The purpose of this chapter is to describe the evolution of European Union ('EU') financial services law and its impact on the development of financial services law in the United Kingdom. The chapter is in two parts: the first describes the evolving role and functions of the EU institutions, the sources of Community Law, the effects of the various Treaty changes, the establishment of the single market in financial services and the moves to establish a banking union. The second part covers the substantive financial services measures which have been adopted since the 1970s. **3.01**

The EU Institutions

Since the establishment of the European Economic Community ('EEC') in 1957, Member States have been committed to the creation of a single integrated market, free of restrictions on the movement of services, capital, goods, and persons. Four institutions were charged by the Treaty Of Rome (EC) with delivering these objectives: the Council, the Commission, the Court of Justice ('ECJ'), and the European Parliament ('EP'). **3.02**

The Commission

The Commission is composed of members nominated by Member States, who are chosen 'on the grounds of their general competence and whose independence is beyond doubt'. The Commission was given the right of legislative initiative—a right which it still enjoys today. It alone had the power to propose legislation, which had to be agreed by the Council before it could become legally binding on Member States. The Commission is commonly described as the guardian of the Treaty, since one of its main functions was to ensure that the provisions of the Treaties and the measures taken by the Community institutions are applied. It is required to monitor the application of EU law by the Member States and has the power to bring an action against a Member State or against the Council before the ECJ on the grounds that the Member State or Council has failed to comply with its obligations under the EC Treaty. **3.03**

The Council

The Council of Ministers consists of representatives of Member States, who are normally the Government Ministers within whose competence a particular proposal lies. The Economic and Financial Affairs Council ('ECOFIN') generally handles financial services matters, **3.04** although it is not unknown for a financial services proposal to be included in the agenda for a meeting of Agriculture Ministers. The Council's agreement is required before a legislative proposal which has been put forward by the Commission can be adopted, but the details of any proposal have to be first negotiated in a Council working party, composed of representatives of Member States and the Commission, and chaired by the Council. The presidency of the Council rotates every six months, and the Member State holding the presidency has the right to decide which of the various proposals under negotiation to prioritise.

3.05 The Council relies heavily on the support of the Committee of Permanent Representatives ('COREPER'), which was set up initially under Article 151 EC. COREPER is staffed by senior officials from Member States and headed by Permanent Representatives of ambassadorial rank. Its function is to consider and analyse draft legislative proposals from the Commission and to set the agenda for Council meetings. That agenda is divided into Parts A and B: Part A consists of matters that can be adopted by the Council without further discussion (so-called 'A' points), because the text has been agreed by COREPER; Part B consists of matters on which the Council working party and then COREPER have failed to reach agreement (so-called 'B' points). Although COREPER has no power to take substantive decisions, it has been aptly described as a 'veritable decision-making factory'.[1]

European Parliament ('EP')

3.06 The EP was initially confined to a consultative role in respect of those matters laid down by the EC Treaty. It was not until the Single European Act ('SEA') of 1986 that the EP was given some real power in the legislative process. From then on, the EP could propose amendments to legislation and even block proposals in limited cases. The Maastricht Treaty of 1992 extended the influence of the EP by introducing the co-decision procedure which required the consent of both the Council and the EP before a measure could be adopted. The EP thus became a major player in the passage of EU legislation. Although the EP has no right of legislative initiative, it can ask the Commission to bring forward a proposal for new legislation. It can also bring proceedings against another EU institution in the ECJ, on the grounds of violation of the Treaty.

European Court of Justice ('ECJ')

3.07 The principal function of the ECJ is to ensure that, in the words of Article 164 EEC,[2] 'in the interpretation and application of this Treaty the law is observed'. It can hear inter-institutional disputes, as well as actions brought by the Commission against a Member State or one Member State against another for failure to comply with an obligation under the Treaty. It can also hear references from national courts for a preliminary ruling on the interpretation of the Treaties and the validity and interpretation of acts of the EC institutions. Through preliminary rulings, which are binding on the referring courts and, indirectly, on other national courts faced with similar questions, the ECJ has built up a formidable body of case law, which has had a major impact on European integration.

[1] See J Lewis, 'National Interests, COREPER' in *The Institutions of the European Union*, J Peterson and M Shackleton (eds) (OUP 2006), Chapter 14.

[2] Latterly art 220 EC; see now art 19(1.1) TEU.

Sources of EU Law

The primary sources of EU law are found in the Treaties, other international agreements to which the EU is party, and the general principles of law developed by the ECJ in its case law. **3.08**

The Treaties

The European Economic Community (EEC) was established by the Treaty of Rome in 1957 with six Member States. The UK acceded to the EEC in January 1973 and it has now become a European Union of 28 Member States.[3] In 1986, the Single European Act ('SEA') removed the requirement for unanimity in the Council for the adoption of legislation and introduced the principle of Qualified Majority Voting ('QMV').[4] It also brought in a new 'legal base' in Article 100a, which was to form the basis for all future internal market measures and allowed the adoption of regulations and decisions, as well as directives. The EP was given more powers in the legislative process. The Treaty of Maastricht of 1992, also known as the Treaty on European Union ('TEU') created the European Union and renamed the EEC as the 'European Community' ('EC'). It established a 'three pillars' structure, consisting of the EC, Common Foreign and Security Policy ('CFSP'), and Justice and Home Affairs ('JHA').[5] The Agreement on the European Economic Area ('EEA') of 1992 extended the application of European law to Norway, Iceland, and Liechtenstein. The Treaty of Lisbon introduced major changes to the TEU and the EC Treaty, renaming the latter 'Treaty on the Functioning of the European Union' ('TFEU'). Under the TEU, the European Council was formally recognised as an EU institution, charged with providing the EU with the 'necessary impetus for its development' and 'defining the general political guidelines thereof'.[6] The legislative procedure was divided into 'ordinary' and 'special' procedures and changes were made to voting procedures in the Council of Ministers.[7] **3.09**

EU Legislation

A secondary source of EU law is the legislation made under the Treaties, in the form of regulations, directives, and decisions. Regulations are directly applicable and binding in each Member State. Directives are binding on Member States as to the result to be achieved, while leaving Member States to decide on the form and method of implementation in national law. Regulations are applied from the date on which they come into force and directives from the date in which domestic implementing measures take effect. It would be wrong, however, to assume that directives can be ignored by the practitioner until they have been implemented in UK law. Even where a directive has not yet been implemented by a Member State, the ECJ has held that a state may be liable in damages for failure to implement by the directive deadline.[8] In some cases, an individual may also be able to rely on the provisions of a directive against a government which has not implemented by the due implementation date.[9] **3.10**

---

[3] Croatia became the 28th Member State in July 2013.
[4] See para 3.13.
[5] JHA was later renamed 'Police and Judicial Cooperation in Criminal Matters' ('PJCC')
[6] Art 15(1) TEU.
[7] See n 10.
[8] Cases C-6 and 9/90 *Frankovich and Bonafaci v Italy* [1991] ECR 1–5357.
[9] Case 8/81 *Becker* [1982] ECR 53.

3.11 The EC Treaty envisaged a system of progressive harmonisation of national laws to the extent necessary for the proper functioning of the Common Market and in the financial services area the directive was initially employed as the legislative instrument to achieve that harmonisation. More recently, much greater use has been made of regulations, which leave no discretion to Member States since they are automatically binding on Member States and their nationals.

Legislative Process

3.12 The Treaties provide for the adoption of legislation and other legal acts in pursuit of the objectives set out in the Treaties. Each legislative proposal must be based on one or more Treaty articles, referred to as the 'legal base', which determines the legislative procedure to be used, and the types of laws that may be adopted. The ordinary legislative procedure introduced under the TEU was previously known as 'co-decision' and requires the Council and the EP to adopt legislation jointly. Under the special legislative procedures, the Council or, in very limited cases, the EP, may adopt legislation alone.

3.13 When a new policy proposal is put forward by the Commission in the form of a draft directive or draft regulation, it is sent to the Council and the EP. The Council will refer the proposal to a working group of representatives of Member States, who will endeavour to reach agreement on the text including any amendments. Any outstanding disagreement may be referred to COREPER, who will seek to resolve the issue. The proposal will also be considered by the EP, which assigns it to a lead committee, which appoints a 'rapporteur' to write a first draft opinion on the proposal. The Committee on Economic and Monetary Affairs ('ECON') is the main committee dealing with financial services matters. The rapporteur's draft opinion is debated in a plenary session of the EP which accepts or rejects the proposed amendments. There are normally two readings of a measure. After the first reading the EP communicates its position to the Council. If the EP's amendments are not all accepted by the Council, or if the Council has further amendments of its own, the proposal is sent back for second reading in the EP. If agreement cannot be reached, the matter goes to the Conciliation Committee to agree a compromise. A jointly approved text must be formally adopted by the Council and the EP to become law. The Council decides most financial services proposals (except fiscal measures) by Qualified Majority Voting ('QMV'). QMV requires a majority of 260 votes out of 352, representing a numerical majority of the Member States, in favour of a measure. Thus successful opposition to a proposal depends on garnering a 'blocking minority' of votes in the Council, currently 93 votes. Member States are allocated votes in the Council in proportion to the size of their population.[10]

Case law of the ECJ

3.14 The importance of the ECJ and its impact on the development of the EU should not be underestimated. Through a series of landmark decisions, the ECJ did much to further European integration in the 1970s and early 1980s, when legislative initiatives were stalled in the Council. At the time, the adoption of harmonisation directives required unanimity in the Council and since they contained an excessive amount of detail, it often took years to reach agreement, by which time the directive might well be out of date. The ECJ demonstrated that it was willing to use the principles of 'direct effect' and 'supremacy' of

[10] The TEU introduced a double majority rule for Council decisions: from November 2014 a qualified majority will require 55% of Member States, representing 65% of the EU population.

Community Law to enforce certain Treaty provisions, despite the fact that the Council had failed to adopt the implementing legislation envisaged by the Treaty.

Direct Effect and Supremacy of Community Law

The principle of the supremacy of Community Law over any conflicting provision in national law was established by the ECJ in the *Costa v ENEL* decision of 1964.[11] The ECJ had earlier in the *Van Gend en Loos* case[12] laid down the principle that certain Treaty provisions could have direct effect within the legal order of the Member State. In the *Reyners* case[13] the Court held that Article 52 of the EEC Treaty, which provided for freedom of establishment, had direct effect, notwithstanding the absence of detailed implementing legislation. In the same year, Article 59 of the EEC Treaty on the freedom to provide services in other Member States was also held to have direct effect.[14] The effect of these decisions was to make those directives redundant which were designed solely to abolish discrimination on the grounds of nationality. The underlying message to the Council was that, if it continued to hold up the adoption of implementing directives, it ran the risk that the Court might fill in the detail of the Treaty provisions in a way that was not necessarily to the liking of the Member States. **3.15**

The principle of direct effect was later applied by the Court to directives where the wording of the provision in question could be said to be precise and unconditional. The ECJ has held that both Treaty provisions and directive provisions can have 'vertical direct effect'—in other words, that they can be relied on by EU nationals against the state or a public authority, but it has refused to accept that directives may have 'horizontal direct effect' in relations between private parties. On the other hand, the ECJ has ruled that some articles of the EC Treaty are capable of conferring rights on private individuals or undertakings which may be relied on against other private undertakings. In the *Viking*[15] and *Laval*[16] cases, the ECJ rejected the argument that the horizontal direct effect of the Treaty fundamental freedoms could only apply as against public and quasi-public authorities. The significance of these cases for financial services practitioners is that discriminatory conduct by private market operators may be open to challenge on the grounds that it restricts fundamental Treaty freedoms. The ECJ had indicated in an earlier case that the then Article 49 which prohibits discrimination on grounds of nationality in relation to establishment could apply to premiums charged by an insurance company if they were found to be discriminatory.[17] **3.16**

Another seminal judgment was handed down in the *Cassis de Dijon* case.[18] Although this concerned Article 30 of the EEC Treaty dealing with the free movement of goods, the implications of the judgment were wide-ranging. The Court held that goods which had been produced and lawfully marketed in one Member State (the 'home State'), should be allowed to be marketed in other Member States, unless the importing state, (the 'host State') could invoke a mandatory requirement such as public health and safety or consumer protection, **3.17**

---

[11] Case 6/64 *Costa v ENEL* [1964]ECR 585.

[12] Case 26/62 *NV Algemene Transport en Expeditie Onderneming Van Gend en Loos v Nederlandsche administratie der belastingen* [1963] ECR 1.

[13] Case 2/74 *Reyners v Belgium* [1974] ECR 631.

[14] Case 33/74 *Van Binsbergen v Bestuur van de Bedrijfsvereniging voor de Metaalnijverheid* [1974] ECR 1299.

[15] Case C-438/05 [2007] ECR I-10779.

[16] Case C-341 [2007] ECR I-11767.

[17] Case 251/83 *Eberhard Haug-Adrion v Frankfurter Versicherungs AG* [1984] ECR 4277.

[18] Case 120/78 *Rewe-Zentral AG v Bundesmonopolverwaltung für Branntwein* [1979]ECR 649.

in order to exclude it. This was the origin of the principle of mutual recognition, which was later to form the basis for the programme of harmonisation of financial services legislation.

General Good Test

3.18 Having outlawed discrimination on grounds of nationality, the Court turned its attention to those national rules which applied equally to nationals and other EU nationals, but which nevertheless could constitute indirect discrimination, because they differed from those of the home State. In the financial services area, the so-called 'general good' or 'public interest' test has been applied to assess the validity of rules applying to firms seeking to carry out business in a Member State on a branch or services business. The ECJ has developed the 'general good' test as a measure of whether a Member State is allowed to impose its own rules (mainly but not necessarily consisting of conduct of business rules) on EEA firms where those rules have the effect of restricting the firm's exercise of its freedoms under the EC Treaty. The test is not defined in EU legislation but originates in the case law of the ECJ. It is essentially a negative test in that Member States are only allowed to impose their domestic rules on firms if those rules meet certain conditions. Those conditions are that the rule in question:

(i) must be non-discriminatory;
(ii) must not duplicate equivalent home State rules to which the firm is already subject;
(iii) must be objectively necessary to achieve an 'imperative' general good objective (such as consumer protection);
(iv) must be proportionate; that is, it must be the least restrictive method of attaining a general good objective; and
(v) must not cover a matter which has already been harmonised at Community level.[19]

3.19 The *Alpine Investments* case[20] provides an example of a challenge to a financial services rule on the grounds that it interfered with a firm's right to provide investment services from its home State into other Member States. The case concerned a Dutch law effectively banning cold calls made from the Netherlands to other Member States to try to persuade potential investors to buy commodity futures. The ECJ upheld the Dutch restrictions on the basis that, although they amounted to a restriction on the right to provide services, they nevertheless met the conditions necessary to satisfy the general good test and consequently could be applied.

3.20 Another example of a firm challenging a domestic restriction that applied equally to national and incoming EEA firms can be found in the *Caixa Bank* case.[21] Here the French banking subsidiary of a Spanish bank challenged the prohibition under the French Monetary and Financial Code on the provision of interest-bearing current accounts. The case was referred by the Conseil d'Etat to the ECJ for a preliminary ruling on the question whether the prohibition constituted an obstacle to freedom of establishment under the Treaty. The ECJ upheld the challenge in a preliminary ruling in October 2004, concluding that the prohibition did constitute a restriction on freedom of establishment in that it was a serious obstacle for companies from other Member States carrying on business in France via a subsidiary and seeking to raise funds from the public. Although the prohibition was alleged to be justified

---

[19] See *Gebhard v Consiglio dell'Ordine degli Avvocati e Procuratori di Milano* [1995] ECR 4165; and Case 205/84 *Commission v Germany* [1986] ECR 3755.
[20] Case 384/93 *Alpine Investments v Minister van Financien* [1995] ECR I–1141.
[21] Case C-442/02 *Caixa Bank France v Ministry for Economy, Finance and Industry* (2005) 1 CMLR 39.

on consumer protection grounds and as a means of encouraging long-term savings, the ECJ found that the prohibition was disproportionate in that there were other less restrictive means of securing those objectives.

These cases illustrate the fact that EC law can be used successfully to challenge national laws that may have been accepted without question by financial institutions. They demonstrate that the general good test is available not only to firms passporting into a Member State under a Single Market Directive, but also to other EEA firms engaged in cross-border services or branch business, and to nationals of that Member State, if they are in a position to invoke any of the Treaty freedoms. **3.21**

Impact on UK Law

It is easy to lose sight of the many ways in which UK law has had to adjust to meet the demands of EU law. Some effects are more visible than others; for example, the major legislative changes required to accommodate the single market directives conferring the so-called 'single passport' on banks, investment firms, and insurance companies.[22] For EU purposes, the United Kingdom ('UK') comprises Great Britain and Northern Ireland, thus excluding the Channel Islands and the Isle of Man, although the UK does include Gibraltar in relation to EU financial services law. The UK Government is in the awkward position of being responsible under Community law for ensuring that the Government of Gibraltar implements all EU financial services legislation, despite having no powers to enforce compliance. **3.22**

Other changes have been more subtle. The increasing constraints on the UK's legislative discretion prevent it, for example, from pursuing a policy of deregulation in areas where this would conflict with Community obligations to regulate in accordance with agreed EU minimum standards. Conversely, it may be more difficult for the UK to raise standards unilaterally if those standards can only apply to UK firms who have to compete in EU markets with firms from other Member States operating under the minimum Community standards. On the other hand, the UK would not be permitted to impose more stringent requirements than those in a directive which is based on maximum harmonisation. Thus, one of the negotiating priorities for the UK in the revised Capital Requirements Directive ('CRD IV')[23] was the freedom to impose higher capital requirements on UK banks than those specified in the Commission's original proposal. **3.23**

The relationship between EU law and UK law, particularly in the area of securities law, is very much one of cross-fertilisation. The UK was one of the few Member States to have established a sophisticated system of securities regulation and had a thriving international financial market by the time the EC launched its programme on investment services. Consequently, the UK was in a position to inject ideas based on practical experience into the Community process. Whatever the inspiration for a particular directive, the final product can never simply replicate the regime in one Member State. The result has to be a compromise between Member States with widely differing traditions, markets, and ambitions. The directive will inevitably require a number of changes to existing law and it will often only cover a small proportion of the matters already dealt with under domestic law. The 1992 **3.24**

[22] See FSMA, Sch 3.
[23] See para 3.67.

Investment Services Directive ('ISD'), for example, did not impose licensing requirements on investment advisers and commodity futures traders, although they had been required to be licensed in the UK since the Financial Services Act 1986 ('FSA 1986'). It was not until November 2007 with the implementation of MiFID[24] that all Member States were required to license investment advisers and commodity derivatives firms, who were then able to benefit from the single passport.

3.25 While it is straightforward to identify those EU requirements which are adopted as Regulations, it is becoming increasingly more difficult to identify those provisions of UK law which implement directives, and so the EU origins of much of UK law are becoming increasingly invisible as a growing number of these measures are absorbed into the general body of law. It still remains vital to be able to trace the origins of an EU derived provision, since its EU derivation will affect its continuing interpretation and application and constrain the ability of the UK to change it. Financial services directives typically require Member States to provide a transposition table when notifying implementation to the Commission so that the Commission is better able to verify implementation.[25]

Implementation: Copy-out v gold-plating

3.26 When implementing any directive which applies only to a subset of FCA or PRA regulated firms, the UK is almost invariably faced with the dilemma of whether to extend the directive requirements to all UK-regulated firms, where relevant, or to leave the rules for other firms unaltered. The latter option can rapidly result in a confusing and incoherent rulebook and create competitive distortions. For example, the Insurance Mediation Directive ('IMD') conduct requirements apply only to insurance intermediaries and not to the direct sale forces of insurance companies.[26] The option of extending the directive's provisions to all firms can equally be unattractive in policy terms, given the widespread resistance to 'gold-plating' and implementing even more onerous measures. To avoid accusations of gold-plating, the Treasury and the former FSA increasingly resorted to 'copying out' the relevant directive provisions in statutory instruments and FSA rules.

3.27 On the other hand, where it is a question of tidying up the statute book following EU legislation, it may not be possible to make the desired changes by means of secondary legislation under the European Communities Act ('ECA') 1972. Although this has the great advantage of speed and convenience, there are severe constraints on the amendments to primary legislation that can be made under the ECA. Under section 2(2) of the ECA regulations may be made:

(a) for the purpose of implementing any Community obligation of the UK, or enabling any such obligation to be implemented, or of enabling any rights enjoyed or to be enjoyed by the UK under or by virtue of the Treaties to be exercised; or
(b) for the purpose of dealing with matters arising out of or related to any such obligation or right.

---

24 Directive 2004/39/EC [2004] OJ L145/1.

25 For Commission policy see its Communication of 14 November 2006, 'A Strategic Review of Better Regulation in the EU', Brussels, COM(2006) 689 final.

26 See para 3.96.

It is apparent that section 2(2) cannot therefore be used to tidy up UK primary legislation if this is not required by the provisions of the directive itself,[27] even where this would be highly desirable in the interests of a more coherent statute or rule book. This is the consequence for pioneering a system of financial services regulation, rather than starting from the beginning with the directive.[28] **3.28**

The trend towards maximum harmonisation and the use of regulations rather than directives seems likely to have a considerable impact on UK law.[29] In many areas of financial services law such as capital requirements and investment services, domestic law is progressively being replaced by EU regulations. **3.29**

Establishing the Single Market in Financial Services

Commission White Paper on Completing the Internal Market

The Commission White Paper of 1985 'Completing the Internal Market' called for a new approach to financial services legislation, arguing that the principle of mutual recognition established by the ECJ in the *Cassis de Dijon* case[30] could be adapted to allow the free movement of financial services within the EU.[31] The Commission proposed that banks and other financial institutions should be able to provide financial services in any Member State, provided that they were authorised by their home State, in accordance with harmonised prudential standards. Other Member States would be required to recognise their home State authorisation and would be unable to impose additional licensing requirements. This established the foundations for the passporting system for banks, insurance companies, and investment firms. **3.30**

The Commission White Paper was followed by the Single European Act of 1986, which introduced qualified majority voting for almost all internal market measures. The momentum generated by these initiatives continued until the Maastricht Treaty in 1992, which included a new objective of economic and monetary union, with the creation of a single currency. The enlargement of the Community from 12 to 15 Member States in 1995 and renewed concentration on the preparations for the introduction of the single currency in 1999 and 2002 deflected attention from the goal of the single market in financial services. However, the European Commission seized the initiative in 1998 with the launch of the Financial Services Action Plan ('FSAP'),[32] designed to capitalise on the future introduction of the euro. **3.31**

Financial Services Action Plan

The FSAP was an ambitious programme of legislative activity designed to achieve a 'single deep and liquid capital market' in Europe. A target date of 2005 was eventually set, by which time some 42 separate regulatory measures (not all of them legislative) were due to **3.32**

[27] See n 89.

[28] This problem does not arise where the PRA or FCA has power to implement a directive through their own rules under FSMA.

[29] See, eg, the conclusions of the June 2009 European Council; available at: <http://www.consilium.europa.eu/uedocs/cms%20data/docs/pressdata/en/ec/108622>.

[30] Case 120/78 *Rewe-Zentral AG v Bundesmonopolverwaltung für Branntwein* [1979] ECR 649.

[31] COM (85) 310.

[32] COM (1998) 625.

be adopted, covering the wholesale and retail markets, 'state of the art' prudential rules, and supervision and tax harmonisation. The Commission saw an urgent need for reform, following the coming into force of the ISD in 1996 and the consequent shift of emphasis from regulation of banking to regulation of securities business, coupled with growing interest in market regulation. In the Commission's view, this necessitated action on two fronts to enable EU legislation to be amended more quickly to adapt to fast-moving securities markets and to introduce a streamlined approach to drafting legislation. The Commission pressed for framework legislation in place of detailed directives, which could be supplemented by guidance, a plea which was to be later endorsed by the Lamfalussy Report in 2001.

Lamfalussy Report

3.33 In February 2001, the so-called Committee of Wise Men, chaired by Baron Lamfalussy, delivered a Report[33] to the Council, which was fiercely critical of the structures then in place for agreeing, implementing, and enforcing EU securities legislation. The Report concluded that the chances of delivering the FSAP commitments on time were 'close to zero'. Legislative procedures were too slow, the average time for agreeing a directive under co-decision was about two years and the Council continued to introduce what was seen as unnecessary complexity into draft legislation during negotiations. Member States were criticised for incorrect and uneven implementation of directives. The legislative process was unable to respond quickly to changing market conditions. It produced badly drafted and ambiguous texts and no clear distinction was drawn between essential framework principles and detailed implementing rules. These were essentially the same criticisms that had been voiced by the Commission in the 1985 White Paper and again when drawing up the FSAP.

3.34 The Lamfalussy Report recommended the adoption of a new four-level structure of regulatory measures for use in the securities markets in the first instance:[34]

- Level 1: principle-based legislation, adopted as before in accordance with the co-decision procedure by the Council and the European Parliament. Level 1 legislation should define the implementing powers for the Commission under Level 2.
- Level 2: detailed implementing measures, consisting either of Commission directives or regulations, made under powers conferred by the Level 1 directive, under a new streamlined accelerated legislative procedure, in which the Commission was assisted by two institutional committees. Technical advice was prepared by the Committee of European Securities Regulators ('CESR'),[35] following a request from the Commission and after consultation with market users. A vote was taken by qualified majority of the Member States represented in the European Securities Committee ('ESC').[36] The European Parliament had power to pass a resolution within three months on the draft implementing measures and within one month of the vote by the ESC if the Level 2 measures go beyond implementing powers.

[33] Final Report of the Committee of Wise Men on the Regulation of European Securities Markets (February 2001).

[34] The system was extended to the banking and insurance sectors in 2003: see para 3.35.

[35] CESR replaced the former FESCO (the Federation of European Securities Commissions). See Commission Decision 2001/527 [2001] OJ L191/43 and was in turn replaced by ESMA; see para 3.40.

[36] Set up by Commission Decision of 6 June 2001.

- Level 3: enhanced cooperation between the members of CESR to ensure proper implementation of Level 1 and Level 2 measures. CESR could issue guidance and common, non-binding standards. It would also review national regulatory practice.
- Level 4: The Commission, which is responsible for policing the implementation of EU legislation, concentrated on more effective enforcement of compliance, if necessary, bringing infringement proceedings under Article 226 of the Treaty against a Member State before the ECJ for non-implementation or incorrect implementation of EU legislation.

Lamfalussy: banking and insurance

Although the Lamfalussy Report was concerned only with the securities markets, its recommendations were subsequently adopted in relation to banking and insurance. The Level 3 Committee of European Banking Supervisors ('CEBS') was set up by Commission Decision on 5 November 2003,[37] with a separate Committee of European Insurance and Occupational Pension Supervisors ('CEIOPS'). The former Banking Advisory Committee ('BAC') created under the First Banking Directive in 1977,[38] which had acted both as an advisory and as a comitology committee, was divided into two, becoming at Level 2 the European Banking Committee ('EBC') and CEBS at Level 3, while the European Insurance and Occupational Pensions Committee ('EIOPC') replaced the former Insurance Committee under a 2005 Directive which established a new organisational structure for the financial services committees.[39] **3.35**

After the FSAP

The Lamfalussy recommendations came too late to have any major influence on the shape of the legislation coming out of the FSAP. Four FSAP directives were adopted under the Lamfalussy procedures: the Market Abuse and Prospectus Directives, MiFID and the Transparency Directive. While all four made use of the Level 2 facility, the Level 1 directives hardly measured up to the Lamfalussy model of framework principles. MiFID, in particular, contained an excessive amount of detail and prescription at Level 1, which was supplemented by further detail at Level 2.[40] With the adoption of virtually all the measures envisaged in the FSAP, the Commission turned its attention away from new legislation and focused on other priorities including making the Lamfalussy process work, implementing 'Better Regulation' through consultation, impact assessments, simplification and codification of existing legislation and strengthening the enforcement of Member State implementation.[41] **3.36**

From Single Market to Banking Union

The prospect of entrenching better regulation disciplines in Commission policy processes was shattered by the financial crisis that began in 2007 and which battered financial markets after the failure of Lehman Brothers in 2008 and then triggered a Eurozone crisis beginning **3.37**

[37] Commission Decision 2004/5/EC.

[38] First Council Directive 77/780/EEC relating to the taking up and pursuit of the business of credit institutions [1977] OJ L322/ 30.

[39] Directive 2005/1/EC [2005] OJ L79/9.

[40] See Commission Decision 2006/73/EC [2006] OJ L241/26; Commission Regulation 1287/2006 [2006] OJ L241/1.

[41] Commission White Paper on Financial Services Policy 2005–2010.

in 2010. A common feature of this period, of what the Commission described as regulatory and supervisory 'repair', was the marked reduction in the influence of the financial services industry and of the UK in EU fora.[42]

International standards

3.38 The financial crisis led to three broad policy responses in terms of international standards implementation and institutional and fiscal reform. The first was international and has two aspects. The membership of the principal international standard setting bodies were widened specifically to include the G20 countries.[43] Measures were also designed to address the problem of banks which were 'too big to fail' or 'too big to rescue', and to reduce the probability of future system-wide financial crises and lessen their impact. The Financial Stability Forum ('FSF'), which was renamed the Financial Stability Board ('FSB') to mark its expanded membership, agreed to a regulatory agenda of 67 recommendations in 2008,[44] which would be taken forward by the sectoral international standard setters.[45] Over the following years, new standards on the quantity and quality of capital, liquidity, and leverage, the clearing of OTC derivatives, credit rating agencies ('CRAs'), remuneration, supervisory colleges, deposit insurance, and cross-border bank insolvency and resolution were agreed.

EU initiatives

3.39 Since the standards agreed by the FSB and other international bodies are not legally binding, they cannot be applied in the EU without amending EU law, which led to a raft of legislative proposals emerging from the Commission.[46] The Commission proposals, however, did not simply copy out international standards. In some areas there was sub-implementation, such as on the definition of regulatory capital in CRD IV to accommodate the interests of Germany and France, and over-implementation in others, such as on remuneration. Where the FSF's focus was on mitigating risks arising from remuneration policies,[47] the EU brought in rules to prevent credit institutions paying a bonus larger than 100 per cent of a salary, or 200 per cent with shareholder approval.

EU institutional structures

3.40 The second response was institutional. Following the collapse of Lehman Brothers in September 2008, the Commission appointed a committee of experts, chaired by Jacques de Larosière, a former managing director of the IMF and Governor of the Bank of France, to review financial supervision within the EU.[48] The report and subsequent legislation led to the creation of four new bodies: a European Systemic Risk Board (an EU Committee) to undertake macro-prudential analysis, issue risk warnings, and make recommendations,

42 The UK remained highly influential in international fora, and played an instrumental role in policy making on liquidity and revised capital standards at Basel and on recovery and resolution policy at the FSB.

43 For details see Chapter 4.

44 See Report of the Financial Stability Forum on Enhancing Market and Institutional Resilience, 7 April 2008, <http://www.financialstabilityboard.org/publications/r_0804.pdf>.

45 See Chapter 4.

46 The Commission estimated that, in 2010–2011, financial services accounted for approximately 40 per cent of its legislative activity.

47 See Recommendation II 19.

48 See the report for the Commission of the High Level Group on Financial Supervision in the EU, 25 February 2009. The recommendations in the report were agreed by the committee, although the content of the report as a whole was not.

and the reconstitution of the three Lamfalussy Committees as EU agencies with powers over national competent authorities and, in limited circumstances, directly over firms. These three agencies are the European Securities and Markets Authority ('ESMA' replacing CESR), the European Banking Authority ('EBA' replacing CEBS), and the European Insurance and Occupational Pensions Authority ('EIOPA' replacing CEIOPS),[49] which are collectively referred to as the European Supervisory Authorities or ESAs.

Functions of the ESAs

The principal responsibilities of the ESAs are those of a system manager, not a day-to-day supervisor, and may be summarised as deepening the single market, raising supervisory standards, and helping to mitigate crises. Their main functions are to: **3.41**

- Identify EU-wide risks (which is a role shared with the ESRB);
- Develop regulatory standards and the single rule-book for firms by:
  1) Drafting regulatory technical standards and regulatory implementing standards for the Commission to adopt, and
  2) Adopting guidelines with national competent authorities making every effort to comply with these or explain within two months why they will not be complying;
- Assess the implementation of standards (including the investigation of alleged breaches of EU law and organising and conducting peer reviews of competent authorities);
- Promote effective collaboration and coordination by national supervisors (including through the establishment of consistent and effective colleges of supervisors for financial groups, and offering to mediate with binding or non-binding effect between supervisory authorities in disagreement);
- Coordinate in crises (including banning financial activities and adopting decisions requiring supervisors to take specific remedial action when the Council has declared an emergency); and
- Play a limited role in direct supervision in specific cases (currently restricted to credit rating agencies and trade repositories).

Powers of the ESAs

To discharge these functions, the ESAs have been given specific powers over national competent authorities and, in defined circumstances, over firms. The ESAs' powers over firms apply only in respect of those rules that are directly applicable and (other than in respect of the direct supervision of credit rating agencies and trade repositories), where the relevant competent authority has not complied with an ESA binding decision. The ESAs have the power to make binding decisions in the following areas: **3.42**

- A power to obtain information from competent authorities and, where this information is not supplied, from firms;[50]
- A power to investigate alleged breaches of EU law, with the ESA being able to request the Commission to take infraction proceedings where there has been a breach of EU law. In

[49] See Regulation (EU) No 1093/2010 (EBA),[2010] OJ 331/12; Regulation (EU) No 1094/2010 (EIOPA), [2010] OJ L331/48; Regulation (EU) No 1095/2010 (ESMA), [2010] OJ L331/84 (collectively referred to below as the 'ESA Regulations'); Regulation (EU) No 1092/2010 establishing the ERSB, [2010] OJ L331/1; and Council Regulation (EU) No 1096/2010 conferring specific tasks on the ECB in respect of the ERSB, [2010] OJ L331/162.

[50] Art 35 of each of the ESA Regulations.

addition, the ESA may take an individual decision directed at a financial market participant requiring it to comply with EU law, where the following conditions are met:

— the competent authority has not complied with the recommendation of the ESA;
— that recommendation has been confirmed in a formal opinion by the Commission, with opinions being non-binding, requiring the competent authority to comply with EU law;
— the competent authority has not complied with the formal opinion;
— the breach of law concerns a directly applicable requirement, (such as a regulation); and
— it is necessary to take action to maintain or restore neutral conditions of competition or to ensure the orderly functioning and integrity of the financial system.[51]

• A power to settle disagreements between supervisory authorities with binding effect in order to ensure compliance with EU law. This applies only where a provision in a sectoral directive so provides.[52] Recital 32 makes clear that, where EU law confers discretion on a competent authority, decisions taken by the ESA cannot replace the valid exercise of that discretion in accordance with EU law. In addition, a binding mediation decision may not impinge in any way on the fiscal responsibilities of Member States (which is referred to as the 'fiscal safeguard' clause).[53]
• A power to take a decision binding on supervisory authorities when:
  1) the Council has declared an emergency;[54]
  2) coordinated action is necessary to address a serious risk to orderly markets and the stability of the financial system; and
  3) the decision will address these risks by ensuring that financial market participants and competent authorities satisfy the requirements laid down in EU law,[55] with the scope of this decision-making power also being subject to the fiscal safeguard clause.[56]
• A power to impose a temporary ban or restriction on financial activities, where the Council has declared an emergency or where a provision in a sectoral directive so provides.[57] Such provisions currently exist in the Alternative Investment Fund Managers Directive ('AIFMD'),[58] and the Short-Selling Regulation,[59] whose legality the UK has challenged, primarily on the basis that it is in breach of the principle established in the ECJ's decision in *Meroni*.[60]

---

[51] Art 17 of each of the ESA Regulations.
[52] Art 19 of each of the ESA Regulations.
[53] Art 38 of each of the ESA Regulations.
[54] It is for the Council to determine the existence of an emergency, following a request by any ESA, the Commission or the ESRB. An emergency is defined as 'adverse developments which may seriously jeopardise the orderly functioning and integrity of financial markets or the stability of the whole or part of the financial system in the Union'. See art 18(1) of each of the ESA Regulations.
[55] Art 18 of each of the ESA Regulations.
[56] Art 38 of each of the ESA Regulations.
[57] Art 9(5) of each of the ESA Regulations. A ban on an activity, eg buying or selling, necessarily includes the object of the ban, eg, an equity or a derivative.
[58] See Directive 2011/61/EU,[2011] OJ L147/1, art 47(4) of which purports to dilute the ESA's power under Art 9(5) of the ESMA Regulation to prohibit or restrict a financial activity for a limited period, to a power to request a competent authority to do so.
[59] Regulation (EU) No 236/2012 on short selling and certain aspects of Credit Default Swaps, [2012] OJ L86/1. See para 3.167.
[60] Cases 9 and 10/56, *Meroni v High Authority* [1958] ECR 133.

Any decision of an ESA may be reviewed and set aside by the ESA Appeal Board, and on a point of law by the ECJ.[61]

Delegated Legislation

The creation of the ESAs coincided with the entry into force of the Treaty of Lisbon, which provided a formal Treaty base for subordinate legislation that had previously been agreed under co-decision by Comitology Committees under the Comitology Procedure. Delegated legislation may now be adopted in one of three ways. Delegated legislation made under a pre-Lisbon directive or regulation, and which has not been amended to bring it into line with the Lisbon Treaty, will continue to be made by comitology committees. Secondly, where legislation has been adopted under the Lisbon Treaty, legislative powers may be delegated directly to the Commission to adopt Delegated Acts or Implementing Acts. Thirdly, power may be delegated to the ESAs to draft rules for the Commission to adopt under Article 290 or 291 of the TFEU. Such rules are known as 'binding technical standards', and take the form of 'regulatory technical standards'[62] or 'implementing technical standards'.[63] **3.43**

Delegated and Implementing Acts

Delegated Acts under Article 290 of the TFEU are rules of general application that supplement or amend certain non-essential elements of the provision in the relevant directive or regulation. Although Delegated Acts are described as non-legislative acts of general application, they will, nevertheless, often be legislative in nature, although the legislative act must define the objectives, scope, content, and duration of the delegation.[64] They may be characterised as answering the question, 'what'. Thus a provision setting out what further tests an advertisement has to meet to be clear, fair, and not misleading would be a Delegated Act. Implementing Acts under Article 291 of the TFEU amplify 'how' a requirement should be given effect within Member States, such as more detailed rules specifying how supervisors should ensure that firms at all times have sufficient capital. Implementing Acts need not be legislative in character; they may also be individual administrative decisions such as those taken by the Commission or the ESAs. **3.44**

There are two significant differences in procedure between Articles 290 and 291. The first is that the European Parliament may veto a Delegated Act but its role in respect of Implementing Acts is limited to determining whether the Commission's rules are intra vires. The second is that, if the Council wishes to prevent the Commission adopting a Delegated Act, it can only do so by qualified majority. The voting arrangements that applied under the pre-existing comitology procedures have been entrenched in the TFEU. An amended, Comitology Regulation sets out the procedure for the involvement of the Council and Parliament in implementing acts.[65] **3.45**

---

[61] Arts 60–61 of each of the ESA Regulations.

[62] Arts10–14 of each of the ESA Regulations set out the required procedures: these include consultation and cost–benefit analysis.

[63] Art 15 of each of the ESA Regulations sets out the required procedure which includes consultation and cost–benefit analysis.

[64] The distinction between legislative and non-legislative acts hinges on the procedures for enacting the relevant measures; legislative acts are enacted by legislative procedures, while non-legislative acts are not. For implementing acts as administrative decisions, see the opinion of the AG in Case C-270/12, paras 17–81.

[65] Regulation (EU) No 182/2011, [2011] OJ L55/13.

Regulatory and Implementing Technical Standards

3.46 Articles 290 and 291 of the TFEU provide the basis for EU legislation to require the relevant ESA to draft rules for the Commission to adopt, in whole or in part, with or without amendment. Recital 22 of each ESA Regulation provides that the ESA drafted rules should apply only to areas 'which do not involve policy choices'.[66] The Council and Parliament have a right to object to Regulatory Technical Standards, but no equivalent procedure for controlling Implementing Technical Standards was included in the ESA Regulations.

Towards a banking union

3.47 By 2010 it had become clear that more needed to be done to restore financial stability. The establishment of the ESAs and their role in monitoring the national competent authorities was a useful step towards achieving greater consistency in the development and application of EU rules, while the creation of the ESRB helped to identify macro-prudential risks, but these measures by themselves were not sufficient to prevent another crisis in the Eurozone. By this time it had emerged that the balance sheets of a significant proportion of the banking industry in the Eurozone were impaired. Funding both for sovereigns in peripheral Eurozone states and their banks had dried up. New capital could come only from the Eurozone as a whole. Aligning fiscal responsibility with responsibility for supervision and resolution of banks had always been one of the main design constraints on European regulatory architecture. In a currency union where stressed sovereigns have to look to the Eurozone for support, the risk of any misalignment would create moral hazard and could result in national supervisors transferring the cost of bank failure to other members of the Eurozone or, conversely, the costs of a failure of supervision by an EU level supervisor having to be met by tax-payers in the country of the bank's incorporation. The remorseless logic of a single currency led to the Commission's proposals for the establishment of a Eurozone banking union, involving three key elements:

- a single banking supervisor;
- a single resolution authority and resolution fund; and
- a common system for deposit protection.

3.48 The Commission has issued proposals on all three pillars; a Single Supervisory Mechanism ('SSM') has been adopted, giving the European Central Bank ('ECB') the responsibility for prudential supervision. In July 2013, the Commission published its proposal for a Single Resolution Mechanism ('SRM') which is designed to complement the SSM.[67] The Commission had already proposed amendments to the Deposit Guarantee Scheme Directive ('DGSD')[68] to establish a common system for deposit protection. Without substantial amendment, the prospects for adoption of the revised draft directive do not look encouraging at present, given the opposition to its provisions and to those of the proposal to amend the Investors Compensation Scheme Directive ('ICD')[69] providing for mandatory lending between national compensation schemes.

66 The implication of a technical standard excluding policy choices is that a delegated act may include them. A delegated act, however, is limited to 'supplement[ing] or amend[ing] certain non-essential elements' of the empowering legislation. It is not clear what kind of policy choices could avoid this limitation.

67 See para 3.86.

68 Directive 94/19/EEC on Deposit Guarantee Schemes, [1994]OJ L135/5, see para 3.130.

69 Directive 97/9/EC on Investor Compensation Schemes, [1997] OJ L84/22, see para 3.131.

Single Supervisory Mechanism

The Regulation on the Single Supervisory Mechanism[70] confers the task of prudential supervision of credit institutions incorporated or established in the Eurozone on the ECB.[71] The main features of the Regulation are the following: **3.49**

1) The Banking Union encompasses all Member States who are members of the Eurozone, and other Member States that wish to participate.
2) The ECB is responsible for the authorisation and prudential supervision of all banks incorporated in participating Member States, but will only directly supervise 'significant' banks. It will have a power of direction over those smaller banks which it does not directly supervise.
3) Where the ECB supervises a bank, it does so as a competent authority in each participating Member State operating through a combination of directly applicable regulations (including Capital Requirements Regulation ('CRR')) and national laws implementing EU directives (which means that the ECB will have to respect any relevant national discretions in a directive, including CRD IV; the ECB also has a power of direction over national competent authorities requiring them to use their domestic powers where it does not possess equivalent powers).
4) The ECB is given significant powers of investigation and enforcement and may direct national competent authorities to provide all necessary assistance to facilitate the exercise of these powers. Where the exercise of its right to undertake an on-site inspection requires authorisation by a judicial authority under national law, the proportionality of the order being sought may be reviewed, but the judicial authority may not review the necessity for the inspection nor call for any information on the ECB's file. The ECB's power to require information to be provided and to conduct on-site inspections applies not only to banks and their employees within the banking union, but also to providers of outsourced services outside the banking union.
5) The decision-making, review, and accountability arrangements have had to be devised within a Treaty framework which allocates most decision-making exclusively to the Governing Council of the ECB (a body that is composed solely of Governors of central banks in the Eurozone) and whose decisions cannot be reviewed other than on a point of law and then only by the ECJ. Complex arrangements have had to be devised to reconcile the existing Treaty framework with the fact that national supervisors take a large number of decisions, many of which affect the rights of individuals.[72] The ECB Regulation accordingly establishes a Supervisory Board which makes recommendations that are deemed to have been adopted by the Governing Council, unless the latter objects within 10 working days. A person to whom the decision is directed (or any other person with a direct and individual concern) may request that the decision be reviewed and for that purpose the ECB Regulation establishes an independent internal Administrative Board of Review of five people, excluding employees of the ECB. The opinion of this

[70] Council Regulation 1024/2013 conferring specific tasks on the ECB, [2013]OJ L287/63, and Regulation 1022/2013 amending Regulation 1093/2010 establishing the EBA, [2013]OJ L287/5.

[71] Art 127(6) TFEU. This requires unanimity in the Council and expressly precludes the ECB having a role in the supervision of insurance undertakings.

[72] The matters on which the ECB is able to take decisions in its supervisory capacity, include capital and liquidity ratios, banks' business activities, and levels of risk, their remuneration policies and distributions to shareholders, and a power to levy a fine of up to 10 per cent of annual turnover of the consolidated group.

Board is then taken into account by the Supervisory Board in a revised decision which is deemed adopted by the Governing Council unless it objects within 10 working days. Finally, the EBA Regulation is amended to address the risk of a Eurozone bloc vote.[73]

Emerging Trends

3.50 Certain trends can be observed in EU financial services regulation over the last few decades. The first wave of legislation required each Member State to set up an authorisation and prudential supervision regime for credit institutions (mainly banks and building societies in the UK) and insurance undertakings in the first instance. National licensing was then replaced by a system of mutual recognition of home State authorisation and prudential supervision. Subsequently, there was a move away from institutional supervision to functional supervision, with the imposition of similar requirements on institutions carrying on the same type of business. This coincided with the emergence of a system of securities and markets regulation, which also brought in regulation of conduct of business for the first time. More sophisticated risk-based capital requirements have also been developed with further changes being brought into effect following the recent financial crisis in Europe and elsewhere.

Legislative convergence

3.51 Legislation initially took the form of directives, which laid down minimum standards for prudential supervision and conduct of business. The early focus on capital requirements only switched to conduct of business with the adoption of the ISD when bank investment firms became subject to conduct of business rules for the first time. The fact that conduct of business rules varied considerably across the Community detracted from the benefits of the single passport for financial institutions. A bank was subject only to the prudential supervision regime of its home State, but if it provided investment services in other Member States, it could find itself subject to different conduct of business rules in each state. These problems were more acute in the case of services business, where there was additional uncertainty and friction between Member States as to whose rules should apply. Maximum harmonisation was seen by the Commission as the answer to some of these problems with the adoption of regulations rather than directives, as the legislative instrument of choice. Legislating by directly applicable regulations relieved the Commission of the task of monitoring Member State implementation of directives, although it did not remove the pressure to ensure more consistent interpretation and enforcement of EU legislation by Member States.

3.52 Maximum harmonisation by itself could have had a paralysing effect on the ability of EU legislation to keep up with developments in the financial markets. This problem has been addressed to some extent by the introduction of a system of delegated legislation, which now has a formal Treaty base under the Lisbon Treaty. The disadvantage of subordinate legislation is that it can cause tension between the Council and European Parliament, on the one hand, and the Commission, on the other, as the former seek to preserve their legislative discretion in sensitive policy areas and the latter seeks to extend its discretion. Inevitably, there will be

[73] This represents a significant change from the Commission's proposal, art 4(1)(l) of which conferred on the ECB the task of coordinating and expressing a common position of banking union members at the Board of Supervisors and the Management Board of the EBA, while art 5(2) required national competent authorities to 'assist the ECB on its request with the preparation and implementation of any acts relating to the tasks referred to in article 4'.

question marks in some cases as to whether the Level 2 measures are in line with the Level 1 instrument.[74] Following the financial crisis, the focus has now switched away from removing barriers to the single market and strengthening consumer protection and back to prudential supervision and financial stability. As the EU rule book becomes ever more detailed and opaque, there is a high risk that the lack of any rigorous economic analysis of the likely effect of the rules on market participants, coupled with the absence of any post hoc evaluation, will result in a regulatory environment characterised by high costs of compliance, barriers to entry, and market and regulatory failures.

Supervisory convergence

Since the adoption of the principle of home State authorisation and prudential supervision, variations in national supervisory competence and culture have emerged as a growing problem. In the securities area, FESCO and its successor CESR attempted to achieve a common approach on supervisory standards, but they lacked the necessary authority to force recalcitrant Member States to comply. The establishment of the ESAs has marked a significant change in this regard. The ESAs now have the power to adopt Supervisory Guidelines, assess the application of standards, and promote effective collaboration through colleges of supervisors and binding mediation. ESMA also directly supervises credit rating agencies and trade repositories. The ESAs have enhanced powers to obtain information from competent authorities and, in some cases, directly from firms. The establishment of the ESAs, however, may tempt the Commission to transfer, or attempt to transfer, more powers to them than is permissible under EU law. The UK has challenged the legality of Article 28 of the Commission's Regulation on Short-Selling primarily on this basis.[75] As with legislative convergence, moves to achieve supervisory convergence in all Member States now have to adjust to the introduction of the Single Supervisory Mechanism allocating jurisdiction for prudential supervision of credit institutions within the Eurozone to the ECB.[76] The ECB will almost certainly exert a powerful influence on EU policy making, on the application of EU rules and on supervision. This is likely to show itself in the following ways: **3.53**

1. The views of the ECB will carry more weight with the EU legislature, because of its direct supervisory responsibilities.
2. The ECB's interpretation of any EU rule is likely to be supported subsequently by members of the Banking Union in the EBA, if only to preserve a level playing field between participating and non-participating Member States.
3. The ECB will drive the harmonisation of supervisory practices in the Banking Union in order to ensure the consistent application of its directives to the supervisory authorities; it may use its power to adopt regulations for this purpose.
4. Supervisory harmonisation withing the Banking Union will set the agenda for the creation of the single supervisory manual being drawn up by the EBA to apply to all 28 Member States. The EBA manual will be non-binding and should respect the diversity of the banking industry, and the importance of judgment in the supervisory process.

[74] See paras 3.115–3.118.
[75] See para 3.167.
[76] See para 3.49.

Convergence in enforcement

3.54 Despite the steps that have been taken to achieve greater convergence in legislation and supervision, enforcement had received little legislative attention until 2010 and the publication of the Commission's Consultative Communication on Reinforcing Sanctioning Regimes in the Financial Services Sector,[77] although the ECJ had earlier built up a body of case law designed to secure the effectiveness and uniform application of Community Law. The principles of equivalence and effectiveness laid down by the ECJ mean, first, that the domestic rules applying to Treaty-based actions cannot be less favourable than those applying to similar domestic actions, and secondly, that those rules cannot make it impossible in practice to exercise rights derived from Community Law. Traditionally, EU financial services legislation did not interfere with the enforcement regime in force within Member States, although directives were principally concerned with the public, rather than private, enforcement of securities regulation and generally contained a few provisions stating that sanctions should be effective, proportionate, and dissuasive. It was generally left to Member States to decide whether civil or criminal sanctions should be introduced for breach of an EU requirement. Consequently, there were wide variations in the sanctions regimes operating in diifferent Member States which was highlighted by studies prepared by the three Lamfalussy Committees.[78] Article 19(1) of the TEU merely states that Member States shall provide remedies sufficient to ensure effective legal protection in the fields covered by EU law but Article 83(2) of the TFEU expressly provides for the EU's competence to impose criminal sanctions in harmonised areas. The Commission has since decided to take forward proposals for minimum common sanctions in the sectoral directives. So far, broadly similar provisions have been proposed in the financial directives currently under revision including CRD IV, MiFID II, IMD II, MAR, and UCITS V which are considered further below. The common features are:

- A list of breaches to which specific sanctions must apply;
- A list of sanctions which competent authorities must be empowered to impose in respect of specified breaches. These range from public censure and the issuance of cease and desist orders to fines of up to 10 per cent of turnover for legal persons (or €5 million for natural persons) and revocation of the firm's authorisation and banning of individuals from holding a management or other similar position;
- A non-exhaustive list of seven criteria to be taken into account when imposing sanctions; and
- A requirement to facilitate and protect whistle-blowers.

Common approach to third country institutions

3.55 The financial crisis confirmed that the EU could not isolate itself from global financial shocks. Events such as the sub-prime mortgage crisis in the USA and the collapse of Lehman Brothers appeared to reawaken the latent hostility in some Member States towards third country financial institutions, who were seen as exploiting the benefits of the single market without necessarily subjecting themselves to the same disciplines as EU institutions. Even when a third country firm wanted to set up a subsidiary in the EU, which would be an EU national and therefore subject to the same rules, it could come up against the 'reciprocity'

[77] COM (2010) 716.

[78] See CEBS Report, March 2009/47; CESR Report 2009, 08/220; CEIOPS Report 2009, 21/09.

doctrine established in the ISD (and carried over to MiFID), which could ultimately require the suspension of authorisation decisions by the relevant Member State in cases where the third country in question did not grant reciprocal access to EU nationals. Where third country firms were headquartered outside the EU and did not have any form of establishment within the EU, it was more difficult to assert jurisdiction, although this has not prevented the Commission from proposing that third country investment firms should be required in some cases to establish a branch in a Member State if the firm wishes to do business with a retail client in that state.[79] Member States could adopt different approaches to branches of third country firms and opportunities for regulatory arbitrage certainly arose. While the somewhat awkward reliance on the equivalence of home-country standards has continued in many areas as the price for doing business in the EU, the Commission has also increased its efforts to assert jurisdiction over third country institutions, such as hedge funds and credit rating agencies,[80] and to require Member States to treat branches of third country institutions no more favourably than branches of EU institutions.[81] A markedly different approach was, however, adopted in relation to third country issuers, where the equivalence principle has been abandoned in favour of allowing non-EU issuers to select the EU Member State of their choice as their 'home State' under the Prospectus Directive ('PD'), thereby entitling them to be treated in the same way as EU nationals, and to benefit from the rights conferred by the PD.

Single Market Legislation—Banking

Much of the UK law on the regulation of banks, securities business, and insurance companies is derived from EU law. A UK statutory system[82] for the licensing of banks or deposit-taking institutions was introduced in 1979 following the adoption of the First Banking Directive in 1977. The Directive laid down the basic requirements for obtaining a licence to operate as a credit institution—separate and adequate own funds, effective management by at least two persons of sufficiently good repute, and experience—requirements which continue to apply, as supplemented by the later Banking Directives. **3.56**

Second Banking Directive

The Second Banking Directive ('2BCD') was adopted in 1989[83] and introduced the principle of home-State authorisation and prudential supervision for credit institutions established in Member States. This meant that a bank, once authorised as a credit institution in its home Member State, could provide a wide range of banking and investment services throughout the EC by opening branches or by supplying services in other Member States, without being subjected to any local licensing requirements. The 2BCD retained the definition of 'credit institution' which had been adopted in the First Banking Directive, as an institution 'whose **3.57**

[79] See the proposals for MiFID II, para 3.121.
[80] See paras 3.73 and 3.102.
[81] A requirement which first appeared in art 9 of the First Banking Directive, Directive 77/780/EEC. See now the proposals in MiFID II, para 3.122.
[82] Banking Act 1979.
[83] Directive 89/646/EEC [1989] OJ L386/1. The Second Banking Directive was consolidated in 2000 under the Banking Consolidation Directive 2000/12/EEC of 20 March 2000 and then amended and reissued as the Directive relating to the taking up and pursuit of the business of credit institutions (recast), Directive 2006/48/EC. This was in turn repealed and replaced by Directive 2013/36/EU; see n 101.

business is to receive deposits or other repayable funds from the public and to grant credits for its own account'.[84] Banks and other financial institutions already benefited from the directly effective right under the Treaty to set up branches or provide services in other Member States, but until the 2BCD, the host State of the branch would insist on the bank applying for local authorisation and could impose a requirement to have separate endowment capital.[85]

3.58 The licensing conditions were expanded under the 2BCD to include minimum initial capital and own funds requirements, [86] together with provisions allowing home State regulators to vet the suitability of controlling shareholders of banks.[87]

3.59 The UK implementing provisions dealing with controlling or qualifying shareholders are contained in Part XII FSMA. These illustrate the difficulties involved in disentangling provisions designed to implement EU obligations from other provisions where the UK has decided to extend their application. In line with EU law, Part XII applies only in respect of UK incorporated entities and not to branches of firms incorporated in other Member States. Nor does it apply to branches of firms incorporated in third countries. The FSMA provisions do, however, apply to UK-authorised firms other than those operating under a passport, and therefore go beyond the minimum requirements imposed under the banking and other financial services directives. The significance of this is that the UK could decide at any time to reduce the regulatory obligations imposed in this area to the minimum directive requirements. The super-equivalent provisions do not have to be interpreted in line with the directives, but they would have to be compatible with EC law generally where relevant.

Post-BCCI Directive

3.60 Following the collapse of the Bank of Credit and Commerce International ('BCCI') in 1991, the prudential requirements in the banking and other financial services directives were tightened in Directive 95/26/EC[88] on prudential supervision to deal with the type of abuse that had emerged in that case. In particular, where a bank or financial institution formed part of a group, the group structure had to be sufficiently transparent to enable the effective prudential supervision of the authorised firm. Banks and insurance companies were required to locate their head offices in the same Member States as their registered offices requirement which already applied to investment firms under the ISD.[89] More controversially, external auditors of banks and other financial institutions were required to report to the 'competent' or supervisory authorities any irregularities which might suggest a material breach of the law applying to financial institutions or which might affect the continuation of the business.

3.61 The first two requirements are now implemented in the threshold conditions in Schedule 6 to FSMA, but again extend beyond the requirements of Directive 95/26/EC to apply to

---

[84] Art 4, Directive 2006/48/EC.

[85] The MiFID II proposal reintroduces a requirement for branch capital for third country firms; see para. 3.119.

[86] These implemented the Basel provisions at the time, see Chapter 4.

[87] See the Communication from the Commission on Intra-EU Investment in the Financial Services Sector, C/2005/4080, 21 October 2005, reminding Member States of the relevant Treaty freedoms and their application to supervisory decisions in relation to cross-border consolidation.

[88] Directive 95/26/EC on reinforcing prudential supervision, now consolidated in Directive 2006/48/EC, [2006] OJ L177/1.

[89] The 2BCD did not impose a substantive obligation to this effect, but contained only a recital reference. This was not sufficient to allow the European Communities Act 1972 to be used to introduce an amendment to primary legislation.

authorised firms which do not benefit from a passport. Moreover, the group structure or 'close links' provisions apply in the case of a non-EU firm seeking to carry on regulated activities in the UK though a branch. Similarly, the auditors' reporting obligations, contained in Part XXII FSMA and the Communication by Auditors Regulations 2001,[90] extend beyond UK and passporting firms.

Capital Directives

Considerable efforts were devoted to harmonising capital requirements as a key part of the licensing and prudential supervision requirements for banks. The Own Funds Directive[91] was the first attempt in EC law to harmonise definitions and standards relating to bank capital ('own funds'). This was followed by the Solvency Ratio Directive[92] and the Large Exposures Directive[93] on the monitoring and control of large exposures. The Capital Adequacy Directive ('CAD'), adopted in 1993,[94] set out for the first time ongoing capital requirements to cover risks inherent in the trading book business of banks, such as market or position risk, interest rate risk, settlement and counterparty risk, and large exposures. The amending CAD II Directive, adopted in 1998 on the capital adequacy of investment firms and credit institutions,[95] allowed the use of internal risk management models for calculating capital requirements in relation to market risk. **3.62**

Capital Requirements Directives

The CRD[96] was designed to bring EU legislation into line with the 2004 Basel II Accord on capital adequacy. Basel II was designed to address the large areas for capital arbitrage embedded in the structure of Basel I which was originally adopted in 1988.[97] The Basel Accords are not legally binding and although the EU has traditionally followed Basel in setting capital requirements, this is not necessarily a straightforward process. There is inevitably a delay in translating Basel requirements into EU law, since adjustments have to be made to provisions originally designed for large international banks to cater for the wide range of banks and investment firms in the EU. There is also a natural reluctance on the part of those EU Member States who are not members of the Basel Committee to adopt without question requirements which they did not participate in negotiating. This awkward interface between the two regimes has caused difficulties in the past, especially when EU banks have been unable to take advantage of a relaxation of the Basel requirements, because they were still bound by tighter EU requirements until necessary revisions have been made. **3.63**

The CRD consists of three pillars: **3.64**

- Pillar 1 sets out the minimum capital requirements for credit market, and operational risk.

[90] The Financial Services and Markets Act 2000 (Communications by Auditors) Regulations 2001 (SI 2001/2587.

[91] Directive 89/299/EEC, now consolidated, as amended, in Directive 2006/48/EC [2006]OJ L177/1.

[92] Directive 89/647/EEC, now consolidated, as amended, in Directive 2006/48/EC.

[93] Directive 92/121/EEC, now consolidated, as amended, in Directive 2006/48/EC.

[94] Directive 93/6/EEC, now consolidated, as amended, in Directive 2006/48/EC.

[95] Directive 98/31/EC, now consolidated, as amended, in Directive 2006/48/EC.

[96] Directive 2006 /49 relating to the Capital Adequacy of investment firms and credit institutions (recast) [2006] OJ L177/201/49.

[97] For a summary of these, see P Jackson (1999), 'Capital Requirements and Bank Behaviour: The Impact of the Basle Accord', Basle Committee on Banking Supervision Working Papers, No 1, April.

- Pillar 2 establishes a supervisory review mechanism and requires banks and supervisor authorities to determine whether additional capital should be held against risks not covered in Pillar 1, and to take action where necessary.
- Pillar 3 creates a parallel market disclosure regime and requires banks to publish details of their risks, capital, and risk management.

3.65 The CRD framework was more sensitive to the risks that banks face than CAD although the financial crisis would subsequently confirm that banks had failed to maintain sufficient capital. The new framework included an explicit measure for operational risk and more sensitive risk weightings against credit risk. The internal ratings-based ('IRB') approach allowed banks to rely to some extent on their own estimates of credit risk. The CRD also provided incentives for banks to improve their risk management, with more sensitive risk weights as firms adopted more sophisticated approaches to risk management. Overall, the quantum of capital held by banks collectively remained broadly unchanged as a result of the CRD, although in preparation for the operation of CRD/Basel II, banks had expanded their balance sheets considerably, so that the ratio of regulatory capital to total non-risk weighted assets in a number of internationally active banks fell to very thin levels of 2 per cent or less.

3.66 Following the financial crisis, the CRD was revised a number of times. The CRD II amendments[98] reflected the recommendations of the FSF and covered: (i) large exposures, (ii) hybrid capital instruments, (iii) supervisory colleges, (iv) liquidity risk management, (v) securitisations, (vi) waivers for banks organised in networks, and (vii) adjustments to various technical provisions. CRD III[99] followed the work being undertaken in parallel by the Basel Committee and contained amendments covering capital requirements for the trading book and for resecuritisations (and structured financial instruments) and the supervisory review of remuneration.[100]

CRD IV/CRR

3.67 The Basel III revisions represented the most substantial response to the crisis; these have been adopted in an amended form in the EU in CRD IV,[101] which requires Member State implementation as a directive, and the Capital Requirements Regulation[102] ('CRR') which is directly applicable. The main features of CRD IV/CRR are: (i) the imposition of new liquidity standards for the first time; (ii) a revised definition of capital; (iii) a new leverage ratio; (iv) additional capital buffers; (v) enhanced counterparty credit risk; and (vi) the removal of many of the earlier national options and discretions, and the imposition of maximum harmonisation in many areas. The difference between CRD IV and CRR is that the former includes additional requirements on authorisation, governance, remuneration, supervisory cooperation and information sharing, enhanced Pillar 2 and Pillar 3, Basel capital buffers, as well as home/host relationships, under which host states lose their shared responsibility for branch liquidity. The CRR contains further detailed provisions harmonising the definition of capital, the quantum of capital and liquidity. Both CRD IV and CRR contain legislative

[98] Directive 2009/111/EC, [2009] OJ 302/97.
[99] Directive 2010/76/ EU, [2009] OJ 329/3.
[100] See further Chapter 4.
[101] Directive 2013/36/EU on access to the activity of credit institutions and the prudential supervision of credit institutions and investment firms [2013] L176/338 (This repealed and replaced the recast Banking Directive, Directive 2006/48/EC).
[102] Regulation 575/2013, [2013] OJ L176/1.

delegations for delegated acts as well as for over 100 regulatory technical standards and regulatory implementing standards. These will all be adopted by the Commission as directly applicable regulations and will form a major part of the single rule book for banks.

Consolidated supervision

The principle of consolidated supervision was adopted by the Basel Committee early on in relation to banking groups, following the Banco Ambrosiano crisis in 1982. The First Consolidated Supervision Directive in 1983 required Member States to take into account the risks to the solvency of an authorised bank posed by other group companies. The 1983 Directive was replaced by the Second Consolidated Supervision Directive[103] which expanded the scope of consolidated supervision to cover a wider range of banking groups although the focus remained on the risks posed by other group companies to the bank. In particular, the responsibilities of the 'solo' supervisor of other companies in the group remained unaffected although the Directive introduced the requirement that the various banking, insurance and securities supervisors must cooperate closely and exchange relevant information in respect of group companies covered by the Directive. CAD I extended the provisions of the Second Consolidated Supervision Directive to those non-banking groups which contained an investment firm covered by the ISD. **3.68**

Financial Conglomerates Directive

The Financial Conglomerates Directive ('FCD'),[104] adopted in 2002 and implemented in the UK in January 2005, made significant changes to the former regimes for the supervision of banking/investment groups and insurance groups. The FCD is aimed at the supervision of those conglomerates with group companies in both the banking or investment sectors and in the insurance sector and with a significant volume of business in each. The banking/investment sector is widely defined and has been expanded by MiFID to include activities such as investment research and financial analysis as well as including activities that are not regulated in the UK by the PRA or FCA, such as finance leasing and the financing of commercial transactions. Such conglomerates pose significant regulatory challenges to ensure that there are no regulatory gaps in the assessment of relevant business risks, controls, and financial resources in groups, whose business spans different financial sectors and is likely to be located in different jurisdictions, both inside and outside the EU. This makes cooperation between home and host State authorities essential. The Directive builds on the concept of the Coordinating Supervisor in the CRD instead of attempting to introduce a single European regulator for the group. CEBS produced guidelines on how the home/host supervisory arrangements should work in practice. **3.69**

The FCD must be applied to financial conglomerates that are only sub-groups within a wider financial group. There are special provisions for non-EEA conglomerates. Different arrangements apply depending on whether the supervision of the conglomerate in the third country is considered to be equivalent to the EU regime. The UK rules implementing the FCD apply only to those conglomerates for which the UK regulator is the Coordinating Supervisor. Either the insurance or banking/investment capital rules apply, depending on **3.70**

[103] Directive 92/30/EEC on the supervision of credit institutions on a consolidated basis [1992] OJ L110/52.

[104] Directive 2002/87/EC [2002] OJ L35/1.

the dominant business of the group. Until the insurance solvency requirements are updated under Solvency II, this is likely to produce very different results.[105]

3.71 The FCD was amended in November 2011[106] with the amending Directive also revising the sectoral directives to permit supervisors to perform consolidated banking supervision and insurance group supervision at the level of the ultimate parent entity, even where that entity was a mixed financial holding company. Directive 2011/89/EU also revised the rules for the identification of conglomerates, introduced a transparency requirement for the legal and operational structures of groups and brought alternative investment fund managers within the scope of supplementary supervision in the same way as asset management companies.[107]

Single Market Legislation—Credit Rating Agencies

3.72 Credit rating agencies ('CRAs') have played an increasingly important role in global banking and securities markets with ratings being used by investors, issuers, and governments in making investment and financing decisions. The financial crisis led to a fundamental reappraisal of the role of the CRAs, particularly as a result of their ratings of structured financial products backed by sub-prime mortgages, such as collaterised bond obligations ('CBOs') or collaterised debt obligations ('CDOs'). There was widespread criticism of the over-reliance placed by both regulators and financial institutions on ratings, which had been to a significant extent encouraged by the incorporation of ratings in the EU sectoral directives, thereby enabling financial institutions to benefit from lower capital requirements, while giving the agencies a quasi-institutional status. The agencies were criticised for conflicts of interest, since they were paid by issuers or banks, for the quality of their ratings and a lack of accountability. Rating methodologies were judged to be insufficiently rigorous and incapable of validation.

3.73 Regulation 1060/2009[108] was adopted to seek to address some of the perceived problems that had arisen with CRAs. It established a registration system for credit rating agencies, based on registration in, and supervision by, the home Member State of the agency. Most agencies had their headquarters outside the EU and the Regulation therefore had to follow a somewhat circuitous route when seeking to subject such CRAs to EU supervision. Instead of following the normal pattern of requiring the CRA to register as a condition of providing its services in the EU, the Regulation prevented EU credit institutions, insurance undertakings, investment firms, UCITS, and issuers from using credit ratings for regulatory purposes, unless the rating had been issued by an agency established in the EU and registered in accordance with the Regulation. To register and to maintain its registration status, a CRA had to comply with requirements on independence and avoidance of conflicts of interest, the competence of ratings analysts, use of methodologies, and transparency. CRAs frequently operated through groups of companies. This, coupled with the inherently transnational nature of their operations led initially to a complex system of registration and supervision,

105 ibid.

106 Directive 2011/89/EU, [2011] OJ L323/113.

107 Art 5 of the directive required the Commission to report by 31 December 2012 on whether to expand the scope of the directive and mandate stress tests. The Commission report COM (2012) 785 concluded that it was not an opportune time to propose legislation but that it would keep the situation under review.

108 OJ [2009] L302/1.

involving not only the agency's home State, but also CESR and a College of Supervisors. The Regulation also provided for the certification of third country CRAs and the endorsement of third country ratings by EU registered agencies.

In 2011, an amending Regulation ('CRA 2')[109] was adopted, transferring supervision from the Member States and CESR to ESMA. This was to be the first example of direct supervision of individual financial institutions at EU level. A further regulation ('CRA 3') amending CRA 2 was agreed in May 2013[110] to address some of the unresolved substantive issues that had arisen. By this stage sovereign debt ratings had become contentious due to the immediate impact of a downgrade of sovereign debt on the stability of financial markets. Lack of accountability of the CRAs was still seen as a problem, while conflicts of interest continued to threaten the independence of the CRAs. **3.74**

CRA 3 establishes a limit on the frequency of unsolicited sovereign debt ratings and imposes a cap on agencies' shareholdings in rated firms to reduce conflicts of interest. The Regulation also gives investors, who relied on a rating, a right of action for damages for breach of the regulatory requirements, although amendments introduced during the legislative process restrict liability to cases where that reliance is reasonable and allow agencies to limit liability under certain conditions. The reversal of the burden of proof, which was a feature of the Commission's original draft regulation, has been removed. CRA 3 also provides for publication of all available ratings on a European rating platform to be available from June 2015. On the regulatory side, the accompanying Directive 2013/14/EU [111] amends the UCITS and AIFMD directives to reduce these funds' reliance on external credit ratings when assessing the creditworthiness of their assets. **3.75**

Single Market Legislation—Payment Services

The objectives of the 2007 Payment Services Directive ('PSD')[112] were to remove legal barriers to the creation of a single payments area within the EU; to make cross-border payments as easy, cheap, and secure as national payments; to increase competition by providing for open access to payments markets; and to harmonise consumer protection standards. The Commission estimated that the creation of a single euro payments area in the EU would save the EU economy €50 billion–€100 billion a year. The main provisions of the PSD, most of which are maximum harmonising, are:[113] **3.76**

- The creation of a new category of firm, referred to as a 'payment institution', for businesses providing payment services and which are not credit institutions or e-money institutions, post office giro institutions, EU central banks, or other public authorities. A payment institution must be authorised in its home State and it must have initial capital of between €20,000 and €125,000 depending on the activities it undertakes and hold additional capital on the basis of one of three specified methodologies.[114]

---

[109] Regulation 513/2011, [2011] OJ L145/30.

[110] Regulation 462/2013, [2013] OJ L146/1.

[111] Directive 2013/14/EU, [2013] OJ L145/1.

[112] Directive 2007/64/EC, [2007] OJ L319/1. An amended Payment Services Directive was published in July 2013, COM (2013) 547, together with a draft Regulation on Multilateral Interchange Fees COM (2013) 550.

[113] Art 86.

[114] See arts 5–10 of Directive 2007/64/EC for authorisation requirements for payment institutions, including methodologies for determining regulatory capital.

- The establishment of a passporting regime to give effect to the right of establishment and the right to provide services. Where the payment institution proposes to provide services in a host state through an agent, the passporting procedures apply to that agent. The home State may refuse to register the agent, if the host State has reasonable grounds for suspecting that the engagement of the agent could increase the risk of money laundering or terrorist financing.[115]
- A waiver from the authorisation requirement and associated capital and prudential rules for small providers. Firms with a waiver are entitled to be listed on the register of payment institutions but are not permitted to passport into other Member States under the PSD. They are also subject to the conduct of business rules imposed under the PSD.[116]
- Payment systems are largely unaffected by the provisions of the PSD, since its main focus is on the relationship between the provider of a service and the customer.[117] However, to increase competition, Member States are required to ensure that rules on access to payment systems are objective, non-discriminatory, and proportionate, and do not inhibit access unnecessarily. There is also a requirement on payment systems not to impose on providers or users of payment services restrictive rules on effective participation in other payment systems, nor to apply a rule that discriminates between authorised payment service providers or between registered payment service providers, nor to apply any restriction on the basis of institutional status.[118]
- The services that fall within the scope of the PSD are set out in the Annex and include debit and credit card payments; direct debits and credits; standing orders; issuing/acquiring payment instruments; and money transfers. Cheques and cash back (but not all cash transactions) are explicitly excluded from its scope.[119]
- Extensive conduct of business requirements are applied to all providers of payment services, including credit institutions, e-money institutions, and payment institutions benefitting from a waiver. These requirements include pre-contractual disclosure, information about charges and currency conversion, maximum time limits for the crediting of a payment, and a right to a refund (if payment is not transferred, or if the payment service provider cannot prove that it has been properly authorised).[120]

3.77 There are two other instruments that are relevant to the provision of payment services. These are the Cross-border Payments Regulation[121] and the Regulation on Information on the Payer Accompanying Transfers of Funds Regulation.[122] The Cross-border Payments Regulation, which replaces Regulation 2560/2001, provides that a payment service provider may not charge more for a cross-border payment denominated in euro than for a corresponding domestic payment in euro. The Regulation also seeks to promote the Single Euro Payments Area ('SEPA') by requiring accounts which are accessible ('reachable') for domestic euro-denominated direct debits also to be reachable by the SEPA Direct Debit Scheme. The

[115] Arts 27 and 17 of Directive 2007/64/EC.

[116] Art 26 of Directive 2007/64/EC.

[117] See the definition of payment systems in art 4(6) and the exemptions in art 3(h) and (i) of Directive 2007/64/EC.

[118] Art 28(1) of Directive 2007/64/EC, but see art 28(2) for the exemptions from these access provisions.

[119] See Annex to Directive 2007/64/EC and art 3 for services that are specifically excluded from the scope of the Directive.

[120] The Payment Services Directive is supplemented by the SEPA project. This is designed to create the technical infrastructure permitting a single euro payments area to be created.

[121] Regulation EC 924/2009, [2009] OJ L266/11.

[122] Regulation EC 1781/2006, [2006] OJ L345/1.

Regulation on Information on the Payer Accompanying Transfers of Funds[123] gives effect to the Financial Action Task Force ('FATF') Special Recommendation on Terrorist Financing VII (FATF SRVII). It requires complete information (name, address, and account number) about the payer to be sent with a transfer of funds. Information and record keeping requirements under the PSD are consistent with the Regulation.

Single Market Legislation—Electronic Money

The Commission has sought to create a level playing field between bank and non-bank issuers of e-money, despite the opposition of a number of Member States. The E-Money Directive was adopted in 2000 and amended in 2009.[124] The main provisions of the E-Money Directive are: **3.78**

- The creation of a new category of authorised non-bank 'E-money Institution' subject to initial and regulatory capital requirements. The funds received in exchange for e-money may be invested only in high quality liquid assets such as cash, government securities, debt issued by the multilateral development banks and sight deposits with Zone A credit institutions.[125]
- A prohibition on e-money institutions making loans.[126]
- An option for Member States to waive some or all of the Directive's provisions for small E-money issuers, whose outstanding e-money liabilities do not normally exceed €5 million or ever exceed €6 million.[127] Businesses operating under the waiver have no passporting rights and may not permit the amount of money on a customer's electronic storage device to exceed €150.

The Commission subsequently provided guidance in January 2005 on when the purchase of services through pre-paid mobile phones constituted the issuance of e-money. It considered that there would be such a payment relationship where either: (a) there is a direct transfer of e-value; or (b) the mobile operator acts as a facilitator (or intermediary) in the payment mechanism in such a way that the customer and merchant would also have a direct debtor-creditor relationship.[128] **3.79**

A revised E-Money Directive[129] repealing the first E-Money Directive, was adopted in September 2009. It is a maximum harmonisation directive. It lowers the barriers to entry and its prudential provisions, unless otherwise stated, incorporate those of the Payment Services Directive ('PSD').[130] The main changes are: **3.80**

- A reduction in the initial level of regulatory capital;

---

[123] Regulation EC 1781/2006; an amending draft Regulation has now been issued; see para 3.173.

[124] E-Money Directive 2000/46/EC, [2000] OJ L275/39, now repealed by Directive 2009/110/EU, [2009] OJ L267/7.

[125] Arts 4–5 of the E-Money Directive 2000/46/EC.

[126] Art 1(5) of Directive 2000/46/EC.

[127] Art 8(1) of Directive 2000/46/EC.

[128] Application of the E-Money Directive to mobile operators, Guidance Note from the Commission services, 18 January 2005.

[129] Electronic Money Directive 2009/110/EC, [2009] OJ L267/7.

[130] See art 3(1) of Directive 2009/110/EC. 'Without prejudice to this Directive, Articles 5 and 10–15, Article 17(7) and Articles 18 to 25 of Directive 2007/64/EC shall apply to electronic money institutions *mutatis mutandis*.'

- The incorporation by reference of the PSD's requirements on authorisation, registration, accounting and statutory audit, outsourcing, liability, record keeping, professional secrecy, right to apply to the courts, exchange of information, and passporting;[131]
- A widening of the range of permitted activities, thereby making the activity more attractive to operators of mobile phones and transport systems;[132]
- Amendment of the waiver criteria with firms not having average outstanding amount of e-money that exceeds €5m and with firms not having a conviction for any offence relating to money laundering, terrorist financing or other financial crime;[133]
- A ban on the payment of interest and restrictions on the imposition of time limits on the redemption of e-money.[134]

Single Market Legislation—Mortgage Credit

3.81 In 2011, after years of consultation, the Commission finally published its proposal for a directive on mortgage credit. The Commission opted for a mininimum harmonisation directive, rather than seeking to impose uniformity on a very diverse market, thereby leaving a substantial degree of discretion to Member States. The proposal focuses on the provision of mortgage credit to consumers by non-credit institutions and on the activities of credit intermediaries. The main problems identified in the mortgage credit market involved inadequate and unclear advertising and pre-contractual information, the lack of competent advice, failure to carry out proper credit screening, and inconsistent regulation of credit intermediaries.

3.82 The draft directive sought to address these problems by requiring all mortgage credit institutions and credit intermediaries to be subject to adequate authorisation, registration, and supervision. It stipulates minimum competence requirements for both mortgage credit providers and credit intermediaries and imposes new conduct of business requirements such as an obligation to act in the best interests of the consumer. Much of the proposal concentrates on advertising and marketing and the provision of pre-contractual information. The creditworthiness of the borrower must be properly assessed, but there is also an obligation on the borrower to provide the necessary information to enable an assessment to be made. The scope of the directive remains controversial and it is still unclear whether buy-to-let mortgages will be included. On the provision of pre-contractual information, there is some opposition to the requirement for a European standardised information sheet, given the diversity of the mortgage market in Member States.

Single Market Legislation—Insolvency

3.83 Cross-border insolvency has proved to be one of the most intractable issues facing the EU and has assumed greater political importance after the financial crisis and the collapse of

[131] Title II of Directive 2009/110/EC.

[132] They may also provide operational and ancillary activities related to the issuance of e-money; and operate payment systems and undertake all the activities listed in the annex of the PSD including the provision of credit in line with points 4, 5, or 7 of that annex, though not from funds received in exchange for e-money. Deposit-taking continues to be prohibited. See art 6 of Directive 2009/110/EC.

[133] Art 9 of Directive 2009/110/EC.

[134] Arts 12 and 11 of Directive 2009/110/EC.

several global financial institutions. The European Insolvency Regulation ('EIR')[135] provided for a choice of law in insolvency proceedings without attempting to harmonise substantive insolvency. It expressly excluded credit institutions, insurance undertakings, investment firms and collective investment undertakings from its scope. Credit institutions and insurance undertakings were, however, subject to their own sectoral directives the Winding-up of Credit Institutions Directive ('WUD')[136] and the Winding-up of Insurance Undertakings Directive,[137] and the Commission brought forward a proposal in 2012 to include investment firms (but not collective investment undertakings) within the scope of the WUD. There are no proposals as yet to deal with group insolvency. It has proved extremely difficult to reach any EU consensus on insolvency law because of the lack of any burden-sharing fiscal arrangements. Attention has turned instead to resolution and recovery procedures with the launch of the EU Framework for Bank Recovery and Resolution in June 2012, in the hope that its proposals for prevention, early intervention, and resolution will mean that future recourse to taxpayers can be avoided.

Bank recovery and resolution

The financial crisis highlighted a key weakness of the policy framework: the impossibility of imposing losses on the creditors of a large bank without first placing it into insolvency. Insolvency of a large or a highly interconnected bank, however, could result in dramatically greater losses to the wider economy than the cost of a publicly financed bail-out. The challenge for the EU and others was to find the means of rescuing an insufficiently solvent bank with minimal recourse to public funds. Achieving this objective requires banks to structure themselves in such a way that, if they cease to be viable, they can be restructured, split-up, and parts sold off without the economic disruption of insolvency, and with the costs of resolution (including the losses the bank has incurred) falling as far as possible on creditors. This implies that existing shareholders would be 'wiped out' and creditors (bond-holders, non-insured depositors, and others) would be converted into equity holders, whose stakes would then, if necessary, be written down or written off. These decisions would be taken when a bank was held to have reached the point of non-viability which would not require a bank to have entered insolvency. **3.84**

The EU's proposed Recovery and Resolution Directive ('RRD')[138] is the legal instrument for giving effect to the policy set out at international level by the FSB as part of the G20 package of reforms.[139] The main provisions of the draft RRD are as follows: **3.85**

- A requirement on banks to draw up Recovery Plans (to address a deteriorating financial situation) and resolution plans (to prepare options when a bank is no longer viable and to ensure that critical functions, such as computer systems, are maintained);

[135] Regulation (EC) 1346/2000 on Insolvency Proceedings [2000]OJ L160/1.

[136] Directive 2001/24/EC on the Winding-up of Credit Institutions, [2001]OJ L125/15.

[137] Directive 2001/17/EC on the Winding-up of Insurance Undertakings [2001] OJ L110/28.

[138] See Commission proposal of 6 June 2012 for a Recovery and Resolution Directive COM (2012) 280; and European Commission Staff Working Document, *Proposal for a Directive establishing a framework for the recovery and resolution of credit institutions and investment firms* (Brussels, 6 June 2012) SWD (2012)166 final. See also *An EU Framework for Cross-Border Crisis Management in the Banking Sector* COM (2009) 561; and Commission Staff Working Document, *An EU Framework for Cross-Border Crisis Management in the Banking Sector* SEC (2009) 1407.

[139] See, eg, FSB, *Consultative Document—Effective Resolution of Systemically Important Financial Institutions* (July 2011); FSB, *Key Attributes of Effective Resolution Regimes for Financial Institutions* (October 2011); FSB, *Resolution of Systemically Important Financial Institutions* (November 2012); and FSB, *Recovery and Resolution Planning: Making the Key Attributes Requirements Operational* (November 2012). See further Chapter 4.

- A power for authorities to require banks to remove any obstacles to resolution, including legal or operational structures that might otherwise compromise critical functions, threaten financial stability, or involve costs to the taxpayer;
- A provision permitting financial groups, with the approval of the relevant supervisors and shareholders, to enter into intra-group support agreements providing loans, guarantees, or assets for use as collateral;
- An early intervention power requiring banks to implement their Recovery Plans and a power to appoint a special manager where such plans proved insufficient to restore a bank to health;
- A common resolution tool-kit for authorities to use where a bank has reached the point of non-viability and is failing or likely to fail. The main tools include: (a) the sale of all or part of the business; (b) separating the viable (good) assets of a bank and its essential functions into a new bridge bank which would then be sold to another entity, with the non-viable (bad) assets remaining with the old bank and being liquidated; (c) separating the bad assets into an asset management vehicle to clean the bank's balance sheet (subject to compliance with the EU rules on state aid); and (d) recapitalising a bank by converting creditors into shareholders, referred to as the 'bail-in' tool. This requires banks to have a minimum percentage of their total liabilities in instruments eligible for bail-in with the instruments being written down in a pre-defined order in terms of seniority of claims;
- The establishment of resolution colleges to facilitate cooperation on recovery and resolution planning and, more contentiously, on resolution actions. The EBA would undertake binding mediation under Article 19 of the EBA Regulation, where disagreements could not otherwise be settled;[140] and
- A requirement on Member States to establish pre-funded resolution funds and for these to be required to lend to each other. Member States will be allowed to use their deposit guarantee schemes as resolution funds, provided that they are still able to pay insured depositors in the event of failure.

Single resolution mechanism

3.86 The timing of the publication of the RRD proposal was somewhat unfortunate as the RRD was followed almost immediately by the European Council's endorsement of the proposed Banking Union, which included proposals for a common resolution mechanism. It would create unacceptable political tensions if the ECB, when exercising its powers under the SSM to de-authorise a bank that had reached the point of non-viability, passed the responsibility for resolution, including the costs of resolution to the Member State. It is therefore difficult to see how the SSM could operate effectively if recovery and resolution were to remain in the hands of national authorities. The Commission's proposal for a Single Resolution Mechanism[141] was published in July 2013 and tries to addess any misalignment of responsibilities by applying the rules in the RRD, but giving oversight of the subsequent resolution

[140] The exercise of this power would be constrained by art 38 of the EBA Regulation which prevents the EBA taking a decision under arts 18 or 19 which impinge in any way on the fiscal responsibilities of Member States, and by the *Meroni* jurisprudence which prevents agencies from taking decisions with a wide margin of discretion. See *Meroni & Co., Industrie Metallurgiche, società in accomandita semplice v High Authority*, Cases 9 & 10/56 [1958] ECR 133; n 60.

[141] COM (2013) 520 establishing uniform rules and unform procedure for the resolution of credit institutions and certain investment firms in the framework of a Single Resolution Mechanism and a Single Bank Resolution Fund.

process to a combination of the Commission and a Single Resolution Board, which would be an EU agency, whose members would be the executive and deputy executive directors, the Commission, the ECB, and participating Member States.

Single Market Legislation—Insurance

The pattern of EC legislation in the last 15 years has been to legislate for banks, in the first instance, and then to apply the same rules with minor modifications to investment firms. Insurance regulation has followed a slightly different path and there have been few attempts to integrate insurance regulation with the regulation of banking and investment business at European level, principally due to the different nature of the underlying risks and business models involved. EU law specifically prohibits an insurance company from carrying on any business other than insurance business. The FSA in the UK was accordingly limited in the extent to which it could establish a fully integrated Prudential Sourcebook for all financial institutions to a large extent due to the constraints imposed by EU legislation.[142] **3.87**

EC insurance regulation did, however, adopt the same system of home State authorisation and prudential supervision, but with separate regimes applying to life and non-life business. The concept of a single market for insurance has taken rather longer to establish and some of the early generation insurance directives seemed to be drafted with little respect for the principles of the Treaty, as interpreted by the ECJ. Some insurance regulators found it difficult, for example, to accept the right of insurance companies to provide insurance for a policyholder in another Member State if they had not established a branch in that Member State. **3.88**

Life assurance

Although the Second Life Assurance Directive of 1990[143] purported to facilitate cross-border services business, it nevertheless allowed the Member State where the policyholder was based to impose a highly restrictive regime on the insurance company, regulating matters such as premium scales, policy terms and conditions and imposing requirements such as on the localisation of assets. Fortunately, the Third Life Directive, adopted in 1992[144] limited the powers of host States to restrict services business. The Third Directive laid down a system of home State authorisation and prudential supervision for life assurance companies, replicating to a large extent the banking regime. **3.89**

Non-life assurance

The same pattern was followed in relation to non-life assurance. A licensing system was established under the First Non-Life Directive in 1973,[145] followed by a Directive on Services,[146] and the Third Non-Life Directive in 1992.[147] **3.90**

[142] See Chapter 13.

[143] Directive 90/619/EEC, now consolidated in Directive 2002/83/EC on Life Assurance [2002] OJ L345/1.

[144] Directive 92/96/EEC, now consolidated in Directive 2002/83/EC on Life Assurance.

[145] Directive 73/239/EEC [1973] OJ L228/19.

[146] Directive 88/357/EEC [1988] OJ L172/1.

[147] Directive 92/49/EEC [1992] OJ L228/1.

3.91 The insurance directives were initially implemented in the UK under the Insurance Companies Act 1982. They are now implemented in FSMA and rules made under that Act. Although an attempt was made to harmonise the provisions covering the exercise of passporting rights by UK and EEA firms under Schedule 3 to the Act, the variations in the relevant sectoral directives made this impossible. The different notification procedures,where an institution is passporting into or out of the UK, must therefore be retained until the directives themselves are changed.

Consolidated supervision of insurance groups

3.92 The EU provisions on consolidated supervision of insurance companies followed the same model adopted for banks and investment firms. The 1998 Directive on Supervision of Insurance Undertakings in a Group[148] focused on the solo supervision of the insurance company in the group and the risks posed by other group companies to policyholder security. There was no attempt to supervise non-insurance companies within the group. The FCD now remedies this omission, at least, in relation to those financial conglomerates with a significant amount of banking or investment business.[149]

Reinsurance

3.93 Most Member States already regulated reinsurance, although it was not until 2005 that an EU Directive setting up a home State licensing system for EU reinsurers was agreed.[150]

Solvency II

3.94 The capital requirements for insurers date back in some cases to the 1970s. The Solvency II Directive adopted in 2009[151] represents an ambitious attempt to introduce an EU risk-based approach to the solvency requirements of life and non-life insurers and reinsurers, replacing the existing Solvency I Directives. The Directive, like the CRD, consists of three pillars:

- Pillar 1 sets out a valuation standard for liabilities to policyholders and the capital requirements for insurers in relation to insurance, credit, market and operational risk. Firms may use their own capital models if they obtain the approval of their supervisor;
- Pillar 2 establishes the supervisory review process, which focuses on evaluating the adequacy of capital and risk management systems and processes. Supervisors may require a firm to hold additional capital against risks not adequately covered in Pillar 1;
- Pillar 3 requires firms to publish details of their risks, capital and risk management processes.

3.95 Solvency II gives supervisors considerable discretion and flexibility in the operation of group supervision to sub-groups within a larger insurance group, a discretion which is not available to supervisors under the FCD. The Commission proposed a new group capital regime that could allow insurance groups meeting the criteria to maintain their solvency capital requirement at group level rather than at solo level, in return for guarantees of group support. This proved highly controversial and was not in the event agreed. Solvency II was

[148] Directive 98/78/EC [1998] OJ L330/1.

[149] See paras 3.69–3.70.

[150] Directive 2005/68/EC on Reinsurance and amending Council Directives 73/239/EEC, 98/78/EC, and 2002/83/EC [2005] OJ L323/1; see Chapter 14.

[151] Directive 2009/138/EC [2009] OJ L335/1. Directive 2013/58/EU, [2013] OJ L341/1 postpones implementation until 1 January 2016.

finally adopted on 25 November 2009 with the key operational details contained in the Omnibus II Directive.[152] This Directive contained legislative delegations permitting the Commission to adopt more detailed rules calibrating, for example, the capital requirements set out in framework form in Solvency II.

Insurance Mediation Directive

The objective of the 2002 Insurance Mediation Directive ('IMD')[153] was to remove obstacles preventing insurance and reinsurance intermediaries from operating freely throughout the EU. Its main provisions consisted of the imposition of a new registration requirement although this is a misnomer and is, in reality, an authorisation requirement. The conditions attaching to registration are the requirement to possess appropriate knowledge and ability and to be of good repute. In addition, insurance and reinsurance intermediaries are required to have professional negligence insurance in respect of a single claim of €1 million and annual claims totalling €1.5 million. The IMD requires Member States to choose one or more of four prescribed methods to ensure that monies paid to a broker for onward transmission to the insurer or the insured are paid to the intended person.[154] The IMD is minimum harmonising and exempts general insurance intermediaries if five conditions are met. The IMD contains limited conduct of business requirements. These cover basic disclosure of information about the firm, whether it is acting as a tied agent, whether advice is being given, and the complaint procedures.[155] **3.96**

The IMD may have benefitted a limited number of intermediaries in the wholesale and reinsurance sectors. In the retail sector, by contrast, the cost of introducing the directive's requirements is unlikely to have been offset by any material benefits in opening up the Single Market, since the market is typically highly localised. Nonetheless, on 3 July 2012 the Commission proposed extensive revisions to the IMD (referred to as IMD 2)[156] and sought to align the disclosure regime for insurance investment products with that for investment products proposed under the packaged retail investment products ('PRIPS') initiative, which was announced on the same day.[157] The main changes proposed cover: **3.97**

- Scope, with the revised directive extending to sales of insurance and reinsurance contracts by the sales forces of insurers and re-insurers and not merely by independent intermediaries as now. A 'light touch' notification obligation would be imposed on those providing claims management activities and loss adjusting, and on those providing insurance on an ancillary basis, such as travel agents selling travel insurance, and, depending on the activities undertaken, aggregator websites;
- Passporting and host State rights, which are aligned with the provisions of other sectoral directives, particularly MiFID;[158]

[152] COM (2011) 8. The Council and Parliament agreed amendments in November 2013.

[153] Directive 2002/92/EC [2002] OJ L9/3.

[154] Art 4 of the IMD.

[155] For exemptions see art 1(2) of the IMD; for the conduct requirements see art 12 of the IMD. The conduct provisions do not apply to intermediaries arranging cover for large risks or reinsurance.

[156] Commission proposal for a directive on insurance mediation (recast) COM (2012) 360.

[157] Commission proposal for a directive on Packaged Retail Investment Products, COM (2012) 352, see para 3.144.

[158] It is notable that the Commission proposes giving host states far greater powers to protect their policy holders in an area of limited impact, than it is in an area such as banking where the potential impact on depositors is far greater.

- Delegated acts permitting the Commission to adopt harmonised definitions of adequate knowledge and ability and criteria for determining professional qualifications, experience, and skill, together with requirements for continuing professional education;
- Disclosure of remuneration, the size of any commission, the sales targets, and the basis for any variable remuneration; and
- A ban on tied services, except for 'bundling', provided that the bundled services can be obtained separately and information is disclosed on the costs and charges of each component of the package.[159]

Single Market Legislation—Collective Investment Schemes

UCITS

3.98 The first example of a home State licensing system for financial services arose as early as 1985 with the first UCITS Directive,[160] which provided a passport for certain types of securities collective investment schemes that could be marketed to the public in any Member State once they had been authorised by their home State. The 1985 UCITS Directive is also notable in that it introduced the division of responsibilities between the home State, responsible for licensing and prudential supervision of the UCITS, and the host State, responsible for regulation of marketing of the product and other conduct of business rules. This was a distinction which was to be endorsed in later directives, such as the 2BCD, the Insurance Directives, the ISD, and MiFID. The precise dividing lines are, however, unclear in practice and continue to generate considerable controversy and debate between financial institutions and Member States.[161] The UCITS Directive, as amended by two later directives in 2001[162] is unique in that it is the only example of product regulation found in EU financial services law. As such, it has proved difficult to reconcile and develop in line with mainstream EU financial services regulation, which focuses on regulation of the product or service provider.

UCITS IV

3.99 A further amending directive, known as 'UCITS IV', was adopted in July 2009. Together with four Level 2 implementing measures, the directive provided for a management company passport, with the management company being subject to prudential and conduct of business rules, broadly similar to those in MiFID. UCITS IV also established a procedure for national and cross-border mergers of UCITS and introduced master-feeder structures to permit asset pooling. The simplified prospectus was replaced by a key information document ('KID') setting out the required information in plain language and in investor-friendly terms. New notification procedures were introduced, allowing marketing of the fund in another Member State immediately following notification by the home State regulator of the fund to the host State competent authority. Finally, the directive provided for measures to improve supervisory cooperation.

---

[159] See para 3.54 on sanctions and para 3.144 on the requirements for insurance investment products.

[160] Directive 85/611/EEC on undertakings for collective investment in transferable securities [1987] OJ L375/10.

[161] See para 3.108.

[162] Directive 2001/107/EC on management companies and simplified prospectuses [2002] OJ L41/20; Directive 2001/108/EC on investments of UCITS [2002] OJ L41/35.

UCITS V

A further revision of UCITS was proposed by the Commission in July 2012[163] as one of three elements of its consumer policy response to the financial crisis. The amendments were designed to clarify the duties and obligations of UCITS depositaries to establish rules on the remuneration of UCITS managers and to provide for a common approach by Member States to sanctions for breach of UCITS requirements.[164] **3.100**

Alternative Investment Fund Managers Directive ('AIFMD')

Hedge funds and private equity funds were singled out for criticism after the financial crisis, perhaps unfairly, since it was accepted that they were not responsible for triggering the crisis. Hedge funds were seen as a source of risk because of their contribution to the growth of structured credit markets and to asset price inflation. Moreover, the unwinding of large leveraged positions had a pro-cyclical effect on declining markets and contributed to the reduction in market liquidity. Private equity funds, on the other hand, did not exacerbate the macro-prudential risks, but were nevertheless included in the scope of the directive, together with all those collective investment undertakings that were not subject to the UCITS directives. **3.101**

The difficulty facing the EU in attempting to regulate hedge funds was that most funds were based in third countries, although many managers were established in the EU and particularly in the UK. In addition, hedge funds were traditionally sold to professional investors, who were normally considered to be able to look after their own interests, without additional protection from EU legislation. The view that prevailed, however, was that during the financial crisis, many professional investors, including pension funds, had shown themselves incapable of carrying out their own due diligence, with the result that the interests of individual investors, such as pensioners, were adversely affected. There was therefore a need for greater regulation. **3.102**

The Alternative Investment Fund Managers Directive ('AIFMD') was adopted in 2011[165] ostensibly targeting AIF managers rather than the funds due to the impossibility of asserting jurisdiction over third country funds, although it should be noted that some provisions apply to an EU manager managing a non-EU AIF, even where the fund is not marketed in the EU. Many provisions of the AIFMD focus on the fund itself, such as rules on asset valuation and on the use of leverage while other provisions require the appointment of an independent depositary. Moreover, compliance with the provisions of the AIFMD gives the fund itself a passport throughout the EU. **3.103**

The AIFMD, together with the Commission delegated Regulation,[166] imposes comprehensive authorisation, capital and operating requirements on AIFMs. They are subject to rules on remuneration, conflicts of interest, risk management and liquidity management, organisational requirements, and rules on valuation. AIFMs are also required to comply with extensive disclosure requirements, covering reporting both to investors and to the competent authorities. The net result is that alternative investment funds, such as hedge funds, **3.104**

---

163 COM(2012) 350.

164 The Commission issued a further consultation paper in July 2012, entitled 'UCITS: Product Rules, Liquidity Management, Depositary, Money Market Funds, Long-Term Investments'. If formally adopted, this would be known as 'UCITS VI'.

165 Directive 2011/61/EU [2011] OJ L174/1.

166 Commission Delegated Regulation (EU) 231/2013 [2013] OJ L83/1.

targeting professional investors are more strictly regulated in some respects than UCITS which are aimed at retail investors.

Venture Capital Regulation

3.105 The Regulation on European Venture Capital Funds[167] is designed to make it easier for venture capitalists to raise capital across the EU for the benefit of SME start-ups. The Regulation provides for a single rule book to apply to those venture capital funds, which meet three conditions: (a) the fund invests 70 per cent of its capital in SMEs; (b) the capital is provided in the form of equity or quasi-equity finance; and (c) the fund does not use leverage. All venture capital funds that qualify for designation as 'European Venture Capital Funds' must comply with a single set of rules governing matters such as disclosure to investors and operational requirements. Qualifying funds will be provided with a European marketing passport giving them access to eligible investors throughout the EU. Eligible investors will be professional investors, high net worth individuals, or business angels.

Single Market Legislation—Investment Services

Investment Services Directive ('ISD')

3.106 The regulation of investment services was closely modelled on the regime which had already been established for banks, although it departed from the banking model with the introduction of conduct of business rules and market rules, both of which proved controversial. The ISD[168] introduced a licensing system for a range of investment services, together with the introduction of home State authorisation and prudential supervision, thus achieving in one directive what had taken two or three separate measures for banking and insurance firms. The ISD adopted a functional approach to securities regulation by requiring Member States to set up a prior licensing system for any firm whose business was to provide one or more of the investment services listed in Section A of the Annex to the ISD. This approach can be contrasted with the previous institutional approach of the 2BCD, under which a bank, once authorised as a credit institution, could provide any of the services listed in the Annex to the 2BCD, provided that such services were covered by its authorisation as a credit institution in the home State.

3.107 The Annexes to the ISD and 2BCD had different purposes. In the case of the 2BCD, the Annex listed a range of activities that could be carried out by a bank throughout the EU without being subjected to any local licensing requirements. In the case of the ISD, Section A of the Annex contained a list of investment services, each of which was subject to a prior licensing requirement. The early enthusiasm for an ISD passport and consequent pressure from some trade associations in the UK to have identical provisions in the two Annexes soon evaporated when it was realised that this would mean setting up a licensing system for activities such as 'advice to undertakings on capital structure, industrial strategy and related matters and advice and services relating to mergers and the purchase of undertakings'. The awkward interplay between the two Annexes is carried over in MiFID where Annex 1 serves

[167] Regulation (EU) 345/2013 on European venture capital funds [2013] OJ L115/1.
[168] Directive 93/22/EEC [1993] OJ L194/27, now replaced by MiFID.

the same purpose as the ISD Annex. MiFID has, however, resolved many of the problems that emerged after implementation of the ISD.

Home/host conflict

The conduct of business regime and the division of responsibilities between home and host States proved to be one of the more intractable issues requiring resolution. The ISD required Member States to establish rules of conduct to be observed by authorised ISD firms. These were to be applied and enforced by the Member State 'in which a service was provided'. Unfortunately, Member States could take diametrically opposite views about where services were provided and hence whose rules should apply to services business. **3.108**

Both banks and investment firms suffered as a result of this difference of opinion as banks providing investment services were subject to the same conduct of business rules as investment firms under the ISD and both were required to notify the relevant competent authorities of their intention to provide services 'within the territory of another Member State' for the first time. Firms could find themselves subject, not only to home State rules, but also to rules in one or more Member States, if they had clients in those States. Efforts by the Commission to resolve the impasse proved unsuccessful. The Commission attempted to provide guidance in its Interpretative Communication on 'Freedom to Provide Services and the Interest of the General Good in the Second Banking Directive'[169] on the question of where services were provided. Although the Communication was expressly restricted to 'problems specifically related to the Second Directive', it was equally relevant to the ISD, because of the similar provisions in both directives and because of the application of the ISD to bank investment firms. The 'characteristic performance' test advocated in the Communication was nevertheless rejected by many Member States, though supported by the UK, and the battle over jurisdiction continued to generate tension between Member States. It was left to MiFID to resolve the issue.[170] **3.109**

Professional/retail business

Another obstacle facing investment firms seeking to carry on business in another Member State under the ISD was the failure of many Member States to observe the requirement in Article 11(1) of the ISD that conduct of business rules should be 'applied in such a way as to take account of the professional nature of the person for whom the service is provided'. Not only did the conduct of business regime vary widely from one Member State to another, but many States did not distinguish between wholesale institutional clients and retail clients of an investment firm. The ISD did not contain any agreed definition of professional investor. Nor did it attempt any meaningful harmonisation of conduct of business rules. Any harmonisation that was in place took the form of minimum harmonisation, allowing Member States to impose more rigorous requirements on domestic and incoming firms alike, subject only to the constraints of Community law and the general good test developed by the ECJ. **3.110**

Markets in Financial Instruments Directive ('MiFID')

MiFID was a major piece of legislation and possibly the most ambitious directive to have come out of the FSAP. It was adopted under the Lamfalussy procedures. Like its predecessor, the ISD, it applies to bank and non-bank investment firms providing investment services. MiFID introduced significant changes to the ISD in relation to scope, organisation, and internal controls, harmonisation of conduct of business rules and regulatory responsibilities. **3.111**

[169] [1997] OJ C209/6.

[170] Even now, the problem awaits full resolution; see para 3.114.

A large part of MiFID deals with the regulation of markets and alternative trading systems, referred to as 'Multilateral trading facilities' ('MTFs').[171]

3.112 The main changes introduced by MiFID were the following:

- MiFID extended the definition of investment services to include investment advice and commodity derivatives business;
- MiFID provided for detailed harmonisation of conduct of business rules;
- MiFID introduced a definition of professional client; and
- MiFID largely clarified the responsibilities of home and host regulators.

Agreed definition of professional client

3.113 By introducing a definition of 'professional client'in Annex II and by requiring Member States to distinguish between professional investors and retail investors when applying their conduct of business rules, MiFID paved the way for more proportionate regulation of conduct of business in all Member States.

Resolving the home/host conflict

3.114 MiFID dealt with the conflict of regulatory jurisdiction over services business that had emerged under the ISD by allocating sole jurisdiction over the application of MiFID conduct of business rules in relation to services business carried on by a MiFID firm to the home State of that firm.[172] Services provided by a branch 'within its territory' would be the responsibility of the state of the branch. This did not answer the question of when are services provided within the territory of a Member State, which was the issue that had strained regulatory relations since the implementation of the 2BCD and the ISD.[173] The Electronic Commerce Directive ('ECD') had earlier avoided the issue by allocating jurisdiction over services provided via the Internet ('information society services') to the country of origin, which was the country from which they were provided, irrespective of the country of destination, and irrespective of whether they were provided from the home State or from a branch in another Member State.[174] CESR issued a consultation paper in December 2006 dealing with services jurisdiction and other MiFID issues. It was nevertheless clear that it considered itself unable to impose a common interpretation on CESR members. In guidance issued in May 2007[175] CESR summarised the views of consultees and indicated that it was seeking a definitive interpretation from the Commission on Article 32(7).

MiFID and maximum harmonisation

3.115 The changes introduced by MiFID purporting to provide for maximum harmonisation of conduct of business rules are also open to different interpretations. It is debatable whether MiFID clearly provides for maximum harmonisation. Article 19(10) of MiFID authorises the Commission to adopt Level 2 measures in 'order to ensure the necessary protection of investors and the uniform application of paragraphs 1 to 8. Is the reference

[171] For a detailed account of the market aspects of MiFID, see *Financial Markets and Exchanges Law* (OUP 2007) Ch 11.

[172] Art 31(1).

[173] See para 3.109.

[174] See para 3.140.

[175] CESR, 'The Passport under MiFID: Recommendations for the Implementation of the Directive 2004/39/EC' (May 2007). The Commission response of 18 June 2007 was disappointing: it did not come up with a definitive view.

to 'uniform application' sufficient to convert the harmonisation provisions into maximum harmonisation?

The wording of the Level 2 Directive, Directive 2006/73, is much clearer with Article 4(2) stating that: **3.116**

> Member States may retain or impose requirements additional to those in this directive only in those exceptional cases where such requirements are objectively justified and proportionate so as to address specific risks to investor protection or to market integrity that are not adequately addressed by this Directive and provided that one of the following conditions is met....

Although the Level 2 Directive spells out that Member States cannot go further than the directive, except in certain circumstances, this is wording that one would expect to find in MiFID itself if Member States genuinely intended it to be a maximum harmonisation directive. Moreover, the proposition that MiFID is a maximum harmonisation measure is based on the premise that it and the Level 2 implementing measures deal adequately at EU level with investor protection. It seems odd, to say the least, to allow the Level 2 Directive, rather than MiFID, to provide for exceptions on the grounds that it does not address specific risks. If the MiFID Level 1 provisions constitute maximum harmonisation, they ought also to authorise any exceptions. A Level 2 measure should not be able to provide for exceptions to a Level 1 measure except where expressly authorised by the Level 1 measure, nor can a Level 2 measure convert Level 1 provisions into maximum harmonisation provisions, if the wording of the Level 1 measure does not clearly and unambiguously support that interpretation. **3.117**

Against this, it can be argued that MiFID is a Lamfalussy directive and maximum harmonisation was one of the main recommendations in the Lamfalussy Report.[176] Moreover, Member States appear to have accepted the provisions of the Level 2 Directive at face value, at least for the time being. The UK has sought Commission approval for certain additional provisions[177] and has taken the view that other domestic provisions that might be judged inconsistent with Article 4(2) fall outside the scope of MiFID. **3.118**

MiFID II

The Commission published its proposed revisions to MiFID on 20 October 2011. As with CRD IV, this comprises both a directive, MiFID II,[178] and a regulation, MiFIR.[179] The proposals were the result of an extended consultation process involving market participants, national regulators, and CESR (now ESMA). The draft directive amends the MiFID exemption for dealing on own account, strengthens the corporate governance requirements for investment firms, introduces an authorisation requirement for so-called 'Data Reporting Services Providers', establishes a framework for product intervention rules, both at national and at EU level, and attempts to harmonise the treatment of third country firms by requiring them to establish a branch within the EU if they wished to provide services to retail clients. A branch established by a third country firm would be required to have 'sufficient initial capital' at its 'free disposal'. **3.119**

176 Although neither the Market Abuse Directive nor the Transparency Directive purports to be a maximum harmonisation measure.

177 See the art 4 Notification made by HM Treasury on 18 September 2007 covering inter alia dealing commissions and packaged products. Available at <http://www.hm-treasury.gov.uk>.

178 COM (2011) 656.

179 COM (2011) 652.

3.120 Many of these proposals are controversial. The product intervention rules purport to give ESMA the power to prohibit or restrict, on a temporary basis, relevant financial activities or the marketing and sale of financial instruments in the EU where it is satisfied that its action will address a threat to investor protection or to the integrity of financial markets or financial stability that existing EU regulatory requirements are ineffective and any measures taken by national competent authorities do not adequately address the threat. It is not clear how providing ESMA with such a power would be compatible with the principle established by the ECJ in *Meroni*,[180] according to which it is not possible to delegate power to an agency involving a wide degree of discretion, since it thereby transfers responsibility by replacing the choices of the delegator with those of the agency to whom the power is delegated.

3.121 The provisions of the draft MiFID II dealing with third country firms represent another attempt by the Commission to assert jurisdiction over those global financial institutions which do business with retail clients in the EU. The draft seeks to impose an obligation on Member States to require third country firms providing investment services to a retail client within their territory to establish a branch in the relevant Member State. There is an exemption for those third country firms where the investment services are provided at the 'own exclusive initiative' of the client. Again, the issue of where services are provided has raised difficulties, since the draft is based on the supposition that the existence of a client within the EU means that the third country firm is providing an investment service within the territory of the EU. The Commission has again proposed the 'own initiative' test as a means of exempting firms from authorisation. This test had been rejected by the UK, among others, as having no support under Community law generally or in the text of the Banking Directives, when it was put forward by the Commission as an appropriate criterion for determining whether or not a banking service was provided within the territory of a Member State. While it may be relevant to the way in which a Member State chooses to regulate a service being provided within its territory, it does not seem relevant to determining whether in fact that service is being provided within its territory. It can therefore be described as arbitrary in its application and wholly impractical to operate.

3.122 Other provisions in the proposal impose additional requirements on portfolio managers, investment advisors, and on the marketing of complex financial products such as structured products. Independent advisors and portfolio managers will be prohibited from making or receiving third party payments. Member States are also required to treat branches of third country firms no more favourably than branches of EU firms.

Single Market Legislation—Compensation

Deposit insurance and investor compensation

3.123 The impact of EU law extends to investor compensation and depositor protection, but not as yet to the protection of insurance policyholders, although a proposal on insurance guarantee schemes is being prepared. The 1994 Deposit Guarantee Scheme Directive ('DGSD')[181] and the 1997 Investor Compensation Directive ('ICD')[182] generally provide for small depositors

[180] Cases C-9/56 and 10/56, *Meroni v High Authority* [1958] ECR 133 (see para 3.42).
[181] Directive 94/19/EEC on deposit guarantee schemes [1994] OJ L135/5.
[182] Directive 97/9/EC on investor compensation schemes [1997] OJ L22.

and investors to be compensated by the protection scheme established under the relevant directives in the home State of the authorised bank or investment firm, even where the claim arises in respect of business done with a branch in another Member State.

It is therefore important to be aware of the requirements of the DGSD and ICD and the way in which they have been implemented, not only in the UK but also in other Member States. UCITS Management Companies which benefit from a passport under the UCITS Management Companies Directive[183] are now also covered by the ICD. **3.124**

It proved easier to integrate the DGSD with UK law than the later ICD. The difficulty in implementing the ICD was mainly due to the fact that the UK had already established a comprehensive system of investor compensation under the Financial Services Act 1986, which applied to a far wider range of investment firms and investment business than those covered by the ICD and provided a higher level of compensation. Compensation was, however, restricted under the previous UK scheme to claims in respect of investment business carried on in the UK. **3.125**

Reconciling the two regimes has resulted in a complicated set of provisions in the Compensation Sourcebook in the former FSA Handbook.[184] Any claim for compensation needs to be analysed in terms of whether it falls within the scope of either of the two Directives in the first instance. The level of compensation available will depend on which scheme is responsible for compensating investors, whether the claim arose in respect of branch business outside the home State, the level of compensation provided by the branch State and the level of compensation provided by the home State. **3.126**

The reason why both home and host State compensation schemes may need to be considered in relation to a directive claim is because under the DGSD and the ICD, investment firms are entitled, but not required, to seek 'top-up' cover for their branch business in other Member States, where the host State's scheme is more generous than the home State scheme.[185] **3.127**

Member States must ensure that, if they raise the level of compensation under their domestic schemes, the same amount of compensation is available to depositors, or investors, who have done business with domestic firms through branches established in other Member States. Any discrimination against EEA depositors, investors, or policyholders will be in breach of the Treaty provisions on non-discrimination, whether or not the matter is covered by a directive. The FSA changed the rules of the Financial Services Compensation Scheme ('FSCS') to cover contracts of insurance issued by UK insurance undertakings through establishments in other Member States in relation to EEA risks with effect from 25 July 2008.[186] Previously, only contracts of insurance issued by UK insurers through an establishment in another Member State in relation to UK risks were covered. **3.128**

The financial crisis highlighted that compensation schemes were not, as then constituted, capable of preventing a collapse in consumer confidence. The Commission's initial response following the crisis was to propose increasing the amount of protection accorded to **3.129**

[183] Directive 2001/107/EC on management companies and simplified prospectuses [2002] OJ L41/20.
[184] Chapter 7.
[185] The export ban in the DGSD and the ICD lapsed in 1999.
[186] Policy Statement 08/8, Financial Services Compensation Scheme: EEA branches of UK insurers.

consumer deposits, to reduce the time permitted to meet claims and to end co-insurance.[187] The DGSD was amended to require Member States to ensure that their deposit guarantee schemes would meet claims of up to €50,000 per insured depositor, a limit that would automatically increase to €100,000 by 31 December 2010, unless a Commission report concluded that such an increase would be inappropriate and not financially viable. The deadline for meeting claims was also reduced to 20 working days.[188]

3.130 The Commission sought a further revision of the DGSD to address what it saw as obstacles to maintaining a level playing field and to ensure that a scheme would be able to pay covered depositors even if the relevant Member State was too fiscally stretched to do so. The proposed revisions, published in 2010,[189] included:

- a target level of pre-funding schemes of, at least, 1.5 per cent of protected deposits by 2020;
- the application of risk-based levies to determine the contributions of credit institutions;
- the introduction of mandatory lending between schemes, where a particular national scheme has insufficient funds;
- the removal of Member States' discretion to exclude certain depositors or deposits from coverage with the effect that generally only the deposits of financial institutions and 'authorities' would be uninsured;
- the extension of coverage to deposits in non-EU currencies; and
- a requirement for compensation to be paid within seven calendar days of a bank failing.

3.131 The Commission's 2010 proposal to amend the ICD contained similar features.[190] Key provisions included:

- increasing the compensation limit in each Member State to a maximum of €50,000 with a three-year transitional period for schemes that pay more than this from the date for transposition;
- requiring compensation schemes to make a partial payment of one-third of the likely claim, if final payment has not been made within nine months of a firm going into default;
- pre-funding the compensation scheme of 0.5 per cent of the value of the insured monies and financial instruments held, administered, or managed by the investment firms or UCITS, with Member States having 10 years to ensure that schemes reached this level;
- the introduction of mandatory lending between schemes, where a particular national scheme has insufficient funds with each scheme being ready to lend 10 per cent of its pre-fund but with no fund being able to borrow more than 20 per cent of the total amount available for lending;
- expanding the scope of the ICD to include losses due to the failure of third party custodians, UCITS depositaries, and UCITS sub-custodians; and
- aligning the ICD with the definitions contained in MiFID, with the ICD having used the definitions contained in its predecessor ISD.

[187] Commission proposal of 15 October 2008, COM (2008) 661 which proposed a €50,000 limit to be increased within a year to €100,000; payouts to be made within three working days, and an end to 10 per cent co-insurance.

[188] Directive 2009/14/EC, [2009] OJ L68/3. The higher limit was duly applied.

[189] Commission Proposal COM (2010) 368/2. The Commission has now proposed the establishment of a common deposit guarantee scheme as one of the pillars underpinning the proposed banking union: see paras 3.47–3.48.

[190] Commission proposal COM (2010) 371 amending Directive 97/9/EC.

In December 2013, agreement was reached on the DGSD, following substantial amendments to the contentious provisions on mandatory lending.

Insurance Guarantee Schemes

Plans have been underway for over a decade to close the gap at EU level for compensation to be made available in the event of the insolvency of an insurance company. These have as yet been unsuccessful. The European Commission set up a working group in February 2002 to examine the need for insurance guarantee schemes. A Commission Consultation Paper on Insurance Guarantee Schemes was produced in May 2008[191] which analysed the problems and evaluated the options available with a consultative White Paper on the harmonisation of insurance guarantee schemes being published on 12 July 2010.[192] The main elements put forward by the Commission in a minimum harmonisation draft directive accompanying the White Paper were: **3.132**

- establishing an IGS as a last resort mechanism which comes into effect when other national protection mechanisms have failed;
- cover for life and non-life insurance policies, but not for pension funds and reinsurance;
- cover limited to natural persons and those legal persons who meet specific criteria such as micro and small businesses;
- the establishment of individual schemes at national level and not a single pan-EU guarantee scheme;
- adoption of the home State principle, so that a scheme covers all an insurer's business including business written on a branch or services basis; and
- schemes to be pre-funded with risk based levies and a target level of 1.2 per cent of gross written premia over a 10 year period.

No formal Commission proposal has been published at the time of publication.

Compensation and group supervision

Home State compensation based on the default of a single entity, whether a bank, investment firm or insurance company, may prove increasingly difficult to reconcile with the principle of group or consolidated supervision under the FCD and Solvency II and with any move to introduce the concept of group insolvency into EU legislation.[193] **3.133**

Consumer Protection

EU harmonisation of conduct of business rules is principally designed to harmonise those rules aimed at protecting the retail investor or retail policyholder, on the basis that differences in national laws in this area constitute a barrier to the free movement of services while Community measures can facilitate the integration of the internal market. In the financial services area, most EU harmonisation legislation is devised on a sectoral basis and aimed at specific types of financial institution such as banks, insurance companies and investment **3.134**

[191] Markt 2008/08.
[192] Commission White Paper on Insurance Guarantee Schemes COM(2010) 370.
[193] See, eg, the Commission Report on Responses to the Public Consultation on Reorganisation and Winding up of Credit Institutions.

firms. In general, however, attempts to harmonise conduct of business rules have applied only to investment business and the marketing of insurance.[194]

Horizontal Directives

3.135 UK financial institutions have to contend not only with specific 'vertical' sectoral directives, such as MiFID and the Life Assurance Directive, but also with 'horizontal' consumer protection directives, which apply to all businesses dealing with consumers. Directives, such as the Unfair Contract Terms Directive ('UCTD')[195] and the Distance Marketing Directive ('DMD'),[196] have had a significant impact on the domestic law governing the marketing of financial services, together with the Electronic Commerce Directive ('ECD'),[197] which is not, however, limited to consumer business.

Definition of consumer

3.136 EU consumer protection law protects all consumers, usually defined as 'any natural person who is acting for purposes which are outside his trade, business or profession',[198] regardless of the consumer's level of sophistication. EU sectoral directives on the other hand, such as MiFID, aim to tailor regulation more appropriately to the needs of the end user by requiring conduct of business rules to take into account the nature of the investor as a retail or professional client or potential client. The result, at the UK level, may be that the FCA is obliged to require firms to provide unnecessary and unwanted protections for sophisticated individual customers, due to the obligation to implement a particular consumer protection directive. Conversely, small- and medium-sized companies are unprotected under EU consumer laws, although they are treated in the same way as consumers under financial services directives, such as the ICD and DGSD.

Distance Marketing Directive

3.137 The DMD requires Member States to distinguish between the information to be given to investors, policyholders, and other consumers before they enter into a distance contract for the provision of financial services and non-distance contracts. The DMD is based on the premise that distance selling creates additional risks for investors, although some Member States, including the UK, take the view that high pressure sales techniques carried out face-to-face could be equally, if not more, damaging. The DMD requires information to be provided to the consumer about the firm, the service being provided, including any risks attached, the contract and the applicable law, the price payable, cancellation rights, and redress mechanisms. The effect of the DMD provisions on cancellation has been to add substantially to the complexity of the cancellation provisions contained in the FCA Handbook. The DMD presented the former FSA with the dilemma of whether to apply the new requirements to all products and services or whether to create a new distinction in the rulebook between distance and non-distance selling. The FSA decided to create two regimes, ostensibly to avoid imposing additional costs on firms, and while the resulting complexity has avoided accusations of gold-plating, it does little to improve the coherence of the Rulebook.

---

194 Insurance Mediation Directive, Directive 2002/92/EC [2002] OJ L9/3.

195 Directive 93/13/ EEC on unfair terms in consumer contracts [1995] OJ L95/29. See para 3.142.

196 Directive 2002/65/EC on the distance marketing of consumer financial services [2002] OJ L271/16, paras 3.137–3.139.

197 See para 3.140.

198 Art 2 of the DMD.

The DMD also raises difficult questions about regulatory jurisdiction in relation to cross-border distance selling. The DMD began as an attempt to impose maximum harmonisation rules to be applied by the 'country of origin'. Had this been successful, it would have meant that Member States would no longer be able to impose higher standards than the Community level, even on their own nationals. This would have allowed financial institutions to market their products and services throughout the EU on the basis of a single set of Community standards. It would also have had the advantage of defusing the arguments over jurisdiction since, if all Member State rules are the same, the question of whose rules apply becomes much less important. **3.138**

Unfortunately, the agreed text of the DMD did not adopt the maximum harmonisation approach throughout, nor did it opt unambiguously for country of origin control. The final version contains some maximum harmonisation provisions but also allows Member States, for example, to continue to apply the additional information requirements of the Life Assurance Directive, requirements which are based on minimum harmonisation and which are the responsibility of the host State. The result is uncertainty, not only with regard to whose rules apply in relation to a particular issue but also whether those rules are maximum or minimum requirements. The UK has taken the view that it is implicit on the basis of the transitional provisions, in Article 16 of the DMD, that it should be implemented on a country of origin basis. Whether this succeeds in defusing any potential regulatory conflicts will depend on whether other Member States have adopted the same approach. **3.139**

Electronic Commerce Directive

The 'country of origin' test for jurisdiction first appeared in the ECD[199] and should be distinguished from both the home State and host State approaches. The ECD was designed to liberalise the provision of 'information society services', which are essentially services provided via the web, email, or mobile phones. The Member State where the service provider is established is responsible for ensuring compliance with the ECD in respect of services provided from that State. The State of establishment, or the country of origin as it has come to be known, is the State where the service provider pursues an economic activity through a fixed establishment for an indefinite period. Where Internet services are provided from a branch of a financial institution in another Member State, the branch State, as opposed to the home State, will therefore be responsible for ensuring compliance with the ECD. The State into which the services are provided, the country of destination, is not allowed to impose restrictions on the inward provision of information society services. **3.140**

The ECD applies to all undertakings providing information society services, including financial institutions, but its provisions have created particular problems on implementation in the financial services area due to its territorial scope which differs from that of the DMD and many of the sectoral directives.[200] **3.141**

Unfair Contract Terms Directive

The UCTD[201] aims to protect consumers against unfair contract terms by requiring terms in consumer contracts to be drafted in plain and intelligible language, with any ambiguities **3.142**

[199] Directive 2000/31/EC [2000] OJ L178/1. For a detailed analysis of the ECD, see M Blair and G Walker (eds), *Financial Markets and Exchanges Law* (OUP 2007) Chapter 12.
[200] See para 3.138–3.139.
[201] Directive 93/13/EEC on Unfair Terms in Consumer Contracts [1995] OJ L95/29.

being interpreted in the consumer's favour. The FSA, and now the FCA, are among the authorities in the UK designated to enforce the provisions of the UCTD. The FCA's powers under the Unfair Terms in Consumer Contracts Regulations[202] enable it to challenge unfair contract terms used by regulated firms in standard form contracts. Ultimately, it can force firms to stop using such terms.

Unfair Commercial Practices Directive ('UCPD')

3.143 The Unfair Commercial Practices Directive ('UCPD') was adopted in 2005.[203] It was a horizontal measure intended to prohibit unfair and misleading business to consumer commercial practices, whether they take the form of acts or omissions. A practice is unfair if it is contrary to the requirements of professional diligence (which would include under FCA rules) and if the practice is likely to distort materially the economic behaviour of the average relevant consumer.[204] Obtaining proof for the second test may have made it more difficult to take preventative enforcement action. While the UCPD is generally a maximum harmonising measure, it is minimum harmonising for immovable property and financial services[205] and therefore required few changes to be made in the FSA (FCA) Handbook in the UK. It is enforced in the UK under the Enterprise Act,with the FCA listed as a designated enforcer under Part 8 of the Act.[206]

Packaged Retail Investment Products ('PRIPs')

3.144 This proposal on packaged retail investment products was launched in 2012[207] in an effort to standardise the disclosure requirements across a range of retail investment products, including investment funds, issues of securities, retail structured products, and investments packaged as insurance policies. The draft proposed the introduction of a key information document ('KID') containing standardised information. The PRIPs KID is based on the UCITS KID and the product provider is responsible for producing the document. This task may be delegated although the provider retains responsibility. While the original objective of the PRIPS was commendable in that it sought to rationalise and streamline the existing disclosure requirements in EU legislation, the proposal continues the previous piecemeal approach which leaves much to MiFID II and IMD 2 to resolve.

Single Market Legislation—Issuer Disclosure

3.145 EU law has had a significant impact on issuer disclosure requirements. The first step was taken in 1979 with the Admissions Directive[208] which harmonised the conditions applicable to official listing. This was followed by the Listing Particulars Directive,[209] the Regular

[202] Unfair Terms in Consumer Contracts Regulations 1994 (SI 1994/3159); and Unfair Terms in Consumer Contracts Regulations 1999 (SI 1999/2083).

[203] Directive 2005/29/EC, OJ L149/22.

[204] Art 5 of Directive 2005/29/EC.

[205] Art 3(9) of Directive 2005/29/EC. The definition of 'financial services' is that used in the DMD.

[206] See The Enterprise Act 2002 (Part 8) (Designation of the Financial Conduct Authority as a Designated Enforcer) Order 2013.

[207] COM (2012) 352.

[208] Directive 79/279/EEC on admission of securities to Official Stock Exchange Listing [1979] OJ L66/21, now consolidated in Directive 2001/34/EC [2001] OJ L184/1.

[209] Directive 80/390/EEC [1980] OJ L100/1 now consolidated in Directive 2001/34/EC.

Information Directive,[210] the Directive on Acquisition of Major Shareholdings,[211] and the Directive on Mutual Recognition of Listing Particulars.[212] Together these have a created a comprehensive disclosure regime for securities admitted to official listing.

It was not until 1989 that disclosure requirements for unlisted securities were addressed. The Public Offers Directive[213] laid down a similar disclosure regime to apply to unlisted securities offered to the public for the first time in a Member State. The harmonisation of disclosure requirements was seen as an essential step in the integration of capital markets in the EU, by providing equivalent protection for investors throughout the EU. This, it was hoped, would encourage issuers to seek official listing on a number of stock exchanges or to engage in multiple issues by reducing the costs involved in complying with widely differing requirements. Common disclosure standards were also designed to foster investor confidence, thereby leading to greater interpenetration of the national securities markets. **3.146**

Unfortunately, these ambitions were not realised. During the 1990s, it became clear that the EU was still a long way from achieving the benefits of a single capital market. One of the more visible failures was the lack of any significant number of cross-border issues, due largely to the ability of host Member States to impose additional requirements on the issuer and to require the translation of the prospectus into the local language. Another defect of the former EU regime was its concentration on officially listed securities while ignoring the requirements applying to admission to trading on a regulated market. **3.147**

Prospectus Directive

As a result of these shortcomings, two major directives were adopted in 2003 and 2004 under the Lamfalusssy procedures: the Prospectus Directive ('PD')[214] and the Transparency Directive.[215] The PD has been implemented in the UK in the Prospectus Regulations 2005 and the FCA's Prospectus Rules. **3.148**

The main significance of the PD is that it introduces a passporting system for issuers so that a prospectus approved by the competent authorities of one Member State must be accepted by any other Member State as valid for an offer of securities to the public in that Member State or for admission of securities to trading on a regulated market operating in the Member State. The PD also contains a definition of 'offer to the public' which was conspicuously lacking in the old Prospectus Directive. The definition is, however, very wide and may be interpreted differently by Member States.[216] The host Member State has no power to approve the prospectus or to impose additional requirements. Nor can a host Member State require a translation of the whole of the listing particulars, if the original is drawn up in English. Only a translation of the summary note prepared by the issuer can be required in this case. If the issuer seeks admission to trading on a regulated market in the host State, it may be required **3.149**

[210] Directive 82/121/EEC [1982] OJ L48/26. The directive has been replaced by the Transparency Directive whose provisions are now consolidated in Directive 2001/34/EC.

[211] Directive 88/627/EEC, now consolidated in Directive 2001/34/EC.

[212] Directive 90/211/EEC [1990] OJ L112/24.

[213] Directive 89/298/EEC [1989] OJ L124/8, replaced by the Prospectus Directive, Directive 2003/71/EC.

[214] Directive 2003/71/EC [2003] OJ L345/64.

[215] Directive 2004/109/EC [2004] OJ L390/38.

[216] See Chapter 8.

to comply with additional admission requirements, provided that these meet the general good test laid down by the ECJ.[217]

3.150 The PD is significant in that it is a 'maximum harmonisation' directive. Member States are not permitted to impose requirements on issuers, even domestic issuers, beyond those laid down in the PD in respect of matters covered by the directive. This raises questions about the continuing ability of the FCA, as the UK competent authority, to impose rules on issuers which go beyond the requirements of the PD. The validity of FCA requirements going beyond those in the PD will depend on an analysis of the scope of the directive, as determined by the provisions of the PD itself, the legal base for the PD and any clarification provided by the recitals to the PD.

3.151 The PD is also significant in that non-EU issuers can take advantage of rights under the directive by selecting the EU home State of their choice, rights which were previously only available to EU issuers and EU nationals. This new open market policy was dictated largely by economic and political considerations, with the EU seeking to encourage the increasing number of third country issuers seeking access to EU capital markets,[218] in line with the FSAP aspiration of creating a 'single deep liquid EU market'.

3.152 In 2010, the Commission adopted an amending Directive[219] which relaxed the requirements of the PD in relation to the number of investors and the size of the offer that could be made without triggering the prospectus requirements. The thresholds were raised to €5 million and 150 investors. The concept of 'key information' was introduced in the prospectus summary, which became more detailed in form and content. An exemption was created for offers by way of retail cascade, subject to certain conditions.

3.153 The treatment of certain third country issuers for the purposes of the PD was clarified by Commission delegated Regulation 311/ 2012.[220] This provided that certain third country Generally Accepted Accounting Principles ('GAAP') could be treated as equivalent to International Financial Reporting Standards ('IFRS') and be accepted within the EU. Other amendments have been made to the PD in the form of two Commission delegated Regulations. The first of these, Commission delegated Regulation (EU) 486/2012,[221] covers the form and content of final terms to a base prospectus and prospectus summaries, which are required to be included in retail debt and equity prospectuses. The second Regulation 862/2012[222] amends the PD Regulation in relation to the consent to use of a prospectus in a retail cascade, together with other provisions relating to indices compiled by an issuer and related parties and profit forecasts.

Transparency Directive

3.154 The Transparency Directive ('TD')[223] was adopted in 2004 under the Lamfalussy procedures. Although the TD is a Lamfalussy directive, unlike the PD, it is not a maximum harmonisation directive. It was designed to improve the quality, quantity, and timeliness of the

[217] See paras 3.18–3.21.
[218] Contrast the approach taken in the E-Commerce Directive whose benefits are available only to EU nationals.
[219] Directive 2010/73/EEC, [2010] OJ L327/1.
[220] Commission Delegated Regulation 311/2012, [2012] OJ L103/13
[221] Commission Delegated Regulation 486/2012, [2012] L150/1.
[222] Commission Delegated Regulation 862/2012, [2012] OJ L256/4.
[223] Directive 2004/109/EC [2004] OJ L390/38.

periodic information provided to investors in securities admitted to trading on a regulated market and is a key measure in improving corporate governance. Responsibility for ensuring compliance by issuers rests with the regulator in the home State of the issuer, ie the state of incorporation for EU issuers. Third country issuers can choose a 'home State' within the EU, as under the PD. The home State of the issuer can impose more stringent requirements than those contained in the TD, whereas the host State of the regulated market is prohibited from going further than under the TD.

The TD requirements build on the provisions of Regulation 1606/2002 on the application of international accounting standards and introduce requirements on the content and timing of annual and half-yearly financial reports, together with interim management statements for issuers of shares who did not already produce quarterly reports. The provisions on disclosure of major shareholdings, which originally applied only to officially listed companies under the Major Shareholdings Directive, are amended and now extend to companies admitted to trading on a regulated market. **3.155**

In 2013 an amending directive was adopted,[224] providing inter alia for the abolition of the requirement to publish quarterly financial information and interim management statements and extending the definition of 'financial instrument' to include cash derivatives. **3.156**

Single Market Legislation—Insider Dealing and Market Abuse

One of the other significant aspects of capital market regulation that has received attention at EU level has been with regard to insider dealing. The 1989 Insider Dealing Directive ('IDD')[225] was the first attempt to prohibit insider dealing in all EC Member States. This contained a definition of inside information and required Member States to prohibit persons from taking advantage of or disclosing such information. **3.157**

The IDD emphasised the importance of equality of access to information. The obligation imposed on issuers in the Admissions Directive to inform the public as soon as possible of any major developments which were likely to affect the price of the issuers' shares was extended by the IDD to all companies whose securities were admitted to trading on an official market. **3.158**

Market Abuse Directive

The EU provisions on insider dealing were to remain unchanged until the adoption of the Market Abuse Directive ('MAD') in 2003.[226] The Directive was intended to enhance the integrity of EU financial markets by establishing a common EU-wide framework for preventing and detecting market abuse and for ensuring a proper flow of information to the market. MAD not only updated the insider dealing provisions in the IDD but also introduced the concept of market manipulation, the opportunities for which had grown considerably due to the increase in cross-border trading, the development of common trading platforms by investment exchanges, the variety of new investment products and trading **3.159**

[224] Directive 2013/50/EU [2013] OJ L294/13.

[225] Directive 89/592/EEC [1989] OJ L334/30. See Chapter 10.

[226] Directive 2003/6/EC [2003] OJ L96/16. Several implementing measures have been adopted, including Commission Directive 2003/124/EC on the definition and public disclosure of inside information and Commission Regulation (EC) 2273/2003 on exemptions for buy-back programmes and stabilisation. See further Chapter 9.

venues and the growing number of market participants. 'Market manipulation' was designed to cover the case where a person seeks to distort the price of financial instruments, or effect transactions or orders to trade, or disseminates information in a manner which gives or is likely to give false or misleading signals about financial instruments.

3.160 On insider dealing, MAD prohibits anyone in possession of inside information from dealing (or attempting to deal) in relevant 'securities', a term which, for the purposes of MAD, includes financial and commodity derivatives. MAD sets out three categories of inside information to cover:

- financial instruments which are not commodity derivatives;
- commodity derivatives; and
- intermediaries executing client orders.

3.161 MAD specifies four ways in which financial markets can be manipulated: through the dissemination of false or misleading rumours; using some form of deception when trading; or where transactions or orders to trade could give false or misleading signals as to the demand for, or supply of, or price of financial instruments, or where the price was deliberately fixed at an abnormal or artificial level, unless this was for a legitimate reason and it conformed to accepted market practice.

3.162 As well as prohibiting market abuse, MAD aims to improve the flow of information to the market by requiring prompt disclosure of inside information by all issuers whose securities are admitted to trading on a regulated market. Share dealings by insiders, as defined under MAD, have to be disclosed and anyone producing investment research has to ensure that the information is presented fairly and any interests or conflicts of interest are disclosed. MAD also requires that those arranging financial transactions notify the competent authority of any suspicious transactions which might constitute market abuse.

3.163 The trigger for application of MAD is the admission to trading (or an application for admission to trading) of any financial instrument on any EU regulated market. MAD then applies to all transactions in the EU in that instrument, whether the transaction is undertaken on or off a regulated market. MAD is the first directive to stipulate that each Member State should designate a single competent authority with ultimate responsibility for ensuring compliance with the directive. MAD went further than other directives at the time in requiring that competent authorities are given a range of powers to enforce the provisions of the directive. Although MAD requires Member State competent authorities to cooperate in dealing with market abuse in recognition of the fact that securities trading has increasingly become international in nature, the MAD provisions on jurisdiction are not always clear. For example, Article 10 of MAD envisages that the authorities in the Member State where the conduct took place will have jurisidiction to take action as well as the authorities in the Member State on whose market the securities are admitted to trading.

MAD II

3.164 Following a public consultation in 2010, the Commission adopted proposals at the end of 2011 for a regulation and a directive on market abuse and criminal sanctions.[227] The

[227] COM (2011) 651, Proposal for a Regulation on insider dealing and market abuse; COM (2011) 654, Proposal for a Directive on criminal sanctions for insider dealing and market manipulation.

proposals were criticised inter alia for not addressing the uncertainty which had arisen as a result of the ECJ's decision in the Spector case.[228] The draft regulation extends the scope of MAD to financial instruments traded on Multilateral Trading Facilities, other organised trading facilities and over-the-counter ('OTC') dealings, so that trading on all platforms is covered. The scope is also extended to cover market abuse in the commodity and related derivatives markets. The proposal seeks to reinforce regulators' investigation and enforcement powers and introduces a new offence of 'attempted market manipulation'. The parallel draft Directive requires Member States to introduce criminal sanctions for insider dealing and market manipulation, where these are committed intentionally. The Justice Ministers approved the Commission's proposals on criminal sanctions in December 2012.[229]

In the light of the inter-bank lending rate scandals in the UK and other Member States, the Commission adopted amendments in 2012 to the proposals for a Directive and Regulation on insider dealing and market manipulation, to prohibit the manipulation of benchmarks, including LIBOR and EURIBOR, and to make such manipulation a criminal offence.[230] **3.165**

Regulation on Energy Market Integrity and Transparency ('REMIT')

MAD did not deal adequately with market integrity in the electricity and gas markets, and accordingly Regulation 1227/2011[231] was introduced to impose EU-wide rules on insider dealing and market manipulation in the wholesale energy markets. **3.166**

Regulation on Short Selling and Credit Default Swaps

At the height of the financial crisis, several Member States introduced bans or restrictions on short selling. Regulation (EU) 236/2012[232] was subsequently adopted by the Commission to establish a common EU regulatory framework in this area. It imposes transparency and reporting requirements on those engaged in short selling and treats the buying of credit default swaps in some circumstances as equivalent to taking a short position. ESMA is required by Article 28 of the Regulation to prohibit, or impose conditions on the entry into short sales, where there is a threat to the orderly functioning and integrity of the financial markets or to financial stability and action by national competent authorities has been ineffective. The UK has challenged[233] the legality of Article 28 on the grounds: (a) that it is contrary to the principle established in *Meroni*; (b) it purports to empower ESMA to impose measures of general application, contrary to the ECJ decision in *Romano*;[234] and (c) it purports to confer a power on ESMA to adopt non-legislative acts of general application, contrary to Articles 290 and 291 TFEU. **3.167**

[228] *Spector Photo NV v CBFA*, Case C-45/08, where the ECJ held that a person would be regarded as using information if he dealt while in possession of that information, even if the information had no influence on the decision to deal.

[229] The Council agreed a compromise with the European Parliament on the draft regulation in June 2013, thereby enabling negotiations to start on the draft directive.

[230] COM (2012) 420 (amended proposal for a directive); COM (92012) 421 (amended proposal for a regulation).

[231] Regulation 1227/2011 [2011] OJ L326/1.

[232] Regulation 236/2012 [2012] OJ L86/1.

[233] Case C-270/12, *UK v Council and Parliament* [2012] OJ C273/3.

[234] Case C-98/80 *Romano v Institut National d'Assurance Maladie Invalidite* [1981] ECR 1241.

Single Market Legislation—Money Laundering

3.168 The origins of EU money laundering legislation can be found in the Recommendations issued by the Financial Action Task Force on Money Laundering ('FATF') which was set up by the G7 in 1989. The First EU Directive ('1MLD'), which was adopted in 1991[235] implemented in EU law the original 40 FATF recommendations on money laundering which had been agreed in 1990. 1MLD concentrated on the laundering of drugs money through banks (credit institutions) and other financial institutions.

3.169 The Second Money Laundering Directive ('2MLD')[236] extended the definition of money laundering to cover the laundering of the proceeds of 'serious crime' while a range of non-financial institutions were brought within the scope for the first time, including lawyers, notaries, accountants, estate agents, art dealers, jewellers, auctioneers, and casinos. The customer identification requirements were tightened up and a prohibition on 'tipping off' was introduced.

Third Money Laundering Directive

3.170 The Third Money Laundering Directive[237] ('3MLD') was adopted in 2005 and should have been implemented by all Member States by December 2007. 3MLD implements the June 2003 FATF revised recommendations and replaces 1 and 2MLD. It extends the definition of money laundering to cover, not only concealing or disguising the proceeds of serious crime, but also the financing of terrorism. This is caught irrespective of whether the funds involved have been lawfully or criminally acquired.

3.171 The other major changes introduced by 3MLD include the adoption of new definitions of 'politically exposed person', 'beneficial owner', and 'trust or company service provider'. The provisions dealing with beneficial owners and trusts have presented problems for the UK in implementation.[238] The Directive also incorporates the FATF recommendations on the adoption of a risk-based approach to identification and verification of customer identity, introducing a simplified due diligence procedure for some cases and enhanced due diligence in others. 3MLD widens the possibility of relying on third parties for identification and verification purposes although ultimate responsibility remains with the firm itself. Reliance can also be placed on third parties in other jurisdictions where those jurisdictions are deemed to have regimes equivalent to the EU. Assessing third country equivalence remains a Member State competence although, somewhat reluctantly, the Commission has agreed to publish on its website a list of those third countries considered by Member States to be equivalent, while stressing that it has no power under 3MLD to establish a binding positive list.

Draft Fourth Money Laundering Directive

3.172 In 2013 the Commission issued legislative proposals aimed at giving effect to the revised FATF standards published in February 2012. The proposals take the form of a draft fourth

---

[235] Directive 91/308/EEC [1991] OJ L166/77, replaced by 3MLD.

[236] Directive 2001/97/EC [2001] OJ L344/76, subsequently replaced by 3MLD.

[237] Directive 2005/60/EC of 26 October 2005 on the prevention of the use of the financial system for the purpose of money laundering and terrorist financing [2005] OJ L309/15.

[238] See Chapter 11.

Money Laundering Directive[239]('4MLD') and a draft Regulation on wire transfers.[240] The main changes introduced by the draft 4MLD relate to the risk-based approach and third country equivalence, extend the definition of 'politically exposed person', impose new requirements on identification of beneficial owners, and tighten the simplified due diligence procedures brought in under 3MLD. Tax evasion and other serious fiscal offences are added to the list of predicate offences. The draft regulation on wire transfers amends the 2006 Regulation on transfers of funds[241] and aims to increase the traceability of payments by requiring the inclusion of information on payees. It will impose a requirement on payment service providers to verify the identity of beneficiaries for payments originating outside the EU for amounts over €1000.

[239] Draft Directive on the prevention of the use of the financial system for the purpose of money laundering and terrorist financing, COM (2013) 45.

[240] Draft Regulation on information accompanying transfers of funds COM (2013) 44.

[241] Regulation EC 1781/2006; see para 3.77.

4

INTERNATIONAL AGREEMENTS AND SUPRANATIONAL BODIES

> Issues of extra-territoriality or disputes of jurisdictional authority inevitably come to the fore as spaces and the rules which govern them are contested. Spaces and rule-making authority may come to be shared, but the ways in which they are shared and the outcomes of such sharing depend upon the institutional mechanisms which are established to deal with jurisdictional disputes.[1]

Global Markets, Local Regulation

Much has been written and said about globalisation and whether it is, in fact, now an irresistible force, particularly in the global economy.[2] The financial markets have shown themselves increasingly to be a global process 'not hindered or prevented by territorial or jurisdictional boundaries'[3] but they are, nonetheless, markets which continue to operate within the bounds of both economic activity and national political and legal regulation[4] or a system of 'international cooperation based on home country control'.[5] **4.01**

'All legislation is prima facie territorial'[6] but in the past 75 years, national legal and regulatory systems have had to deal increasingly with the impact of trans-national effects in relation to competition and anti-trust issues (the US Uranium anti-trust cases of the 1970s as well as the Hartford Fire and Boeing/McDonnell Douglas investigations), environmental issues (Chernobyl and other environmental and pollution cases), human rights issues, the 'war on terrorism' (intelligence sharing and stopping terrorist financing), and more recently the global financial crisis and the impact of the Eurozone debt crisis.[7] Numerous agreements **4.02**

[1] A Hudson, 'Beyond the Borders: Globalisation, Sovereignty and Extra-territoriality' (1998) *Geopolitics* 3(1), 89–105.

[2] 'With global flows of capital and the internationalisation of production, we live in a world in which the complexity of spatial relations is more obvious than the simple legalistic maps of state sovereignty' RBJ Walker, *Inside/Outside: International Relations as Political Theory* (1993).

[3] J Rosenau, 'The dynamics of globalisation: toward an operational framework', (1996) *International Studies Association*.

[4] AC Hudson, 'Reshaping the regulatory landscape: border skirmishes around the Bahamas and Cayman offshore centres', (1998) *Review of International Political Economy*, 5:3.

[5] EB Kapstein, 'Shockproof, the end of the Financial Crisis', (1996) *Foreign Affairs*, Jan/Feb.

[6] *American Banana Co v United Fruit Co* 213 US 347, 357 (1909) ('The foregoing considerations would lead, in case of doubt, to a construction of any statute as intended to be confined in its operation and effect to the territorial limits over which the lawmaker has general and legitimate power. 'All legislation is prima facie territorial', quoting *Ex parte Blain*, LR 12 Ch Div 522, 528).

[7] See J Almunia, 'Building and Sustaining Solid Financial Markets: challenges for international cooperation', Economic and Social Council of the United Nations (Speech 08/192) 14 April 2008; also PR Lane, 'Financial Globalisation and the Crisis', BIS Working Papers, No 397, December 2012, JEL.

have been negotiated and international or supranational bodies have been established in order to foster cooperation between governments, between regulators, and between industry participants to overcome the obstacles to the continued development of the financial markets and to maximise the benefits of a global financial market.[8]

4.03 However, the growth of globalisation can also lead to political problems resulting from the loss of national sovereignty and the diminution of governmental autonomy; and the economic and social problems resulting from the impact of trade internationalisation.[9] Supranational bodies have tended to be composed of the powerful, for example the Group of 10 ('G-10'),[10] who have the greatest interest and the most to gain by a global, collaborative approach. This does not mean that regional multilateral bodies and cooperation are ineffective, only that their impact is generally less than those comprising and representing the interests of the more developed countries. Nor does it mean that the developed countries will always take a cooperative approach especially if they perceive their national or economic interests would be damaged thereby. However, all of these bodies depend upon the give and take of discussion, negotiation, and collaboration to reach their objectives, and some have been more successful than others in achieving those goals.

4.04 This chapter sets out some of the international agreements and supranational bodies in the banking and financial services sector that carry out a wide range of functions including collating collective research and the compilation of statistics, acting as a forum for discussion and debate, providing a framework for standard setting, establishing compliance and monitoring standards or rules, and mediating disputes between national interests.

International Bodies and International Agreements

4.05 International bodies and international agreements in the banking and financial services sector have tended to follow the trend in capital flows and generally have served to expand cross-border competition or to promote financial stability or to facilitate cross-border financial transactions.[11]

4.06 Broadly speaking, international bodies and agreements can be broken down into several broad categories: inter-governmental trade and services agreements, inter-regulator agreements, international technical agreements and trade and professional body agreements, and industry codes of conduct.[12]

4.07 There are a number of inter-governmental trade and services agreements that have an impact on the financial sector. The World Trade Organisation ('WTO') is probably the most

[8] See Chapter 1. For a useful overview, also see EB Kapstein, BIS Working Papers, No 199, *Architects of stability? International cooperation among financial supervisors*, BIS Monetary and Economic Department, February 2006; <http://www.bis.org/publ/work199.pdf>. See also GA Walker, 'Financial Markets and Exchanges' in M Blair, G Walker, and S Wiley, *Financial Markets and Exchanges Law* (2nd edn, OUP 2012) paras 1.119–156.

[9] VA Schmidt, 'The New World Order, Incorporated: The Rise of Business and the Decline of the Nation State', (1995) *Daedalus*, Vol 124, No 2 spring.

[10] See n 86.

[11] WR White, 'International agreements in the area of banking and finance: accomplishments and outstanding issues', BIS Working Paper No 38, October 1996. See also GA Walker, *International Banking Regulation Law, Policy and Practice* (Kluwer Law 2001) ch 5.

[12] White (n 11) at p 4.

notable and its role and structure will be dealt with later in this chapter. However, there are other organisations such as the United Nations Conference on Trade and Development ('UNCTAD') that have had a significant impact on the development of banking and capital markets around the world.

UNCTAD, established in 1964 to promote the development-friendly integration of developing countries into the world economy, provides a forum for inter-governmental deliberations supported by discussions with experts and exchanges of experience. It also undertakes research, policy analysis, and data collection for the debates of government representatives and experts. It also provides technical assistance to developing countries with special attention to the needs of the least developed countries and of economies in transition. UNCTAD also jointly sponsors with the WTO the International Trade Centre ('ITC') that deals with the operational aspects of trade development with an emphasis on trade promotion including the Millennium Development Goals[13] and the Aid for Trade agenda. The ITC is industry facing in contrast to UNCTAD's primarily government facing role and ITC's technical assistance focuses on assisting businesses in developing countries. UNCTAD also cooperates with UN regional commissions to support international projects in various developing countries.[14] **4.08**

The second category of international agreement is that of inter-regulator agreements and memoranda of understanding ('MOU') particularly in the areas of international cooperation and information sharing. Bodies such as the International Organisation of Securities Commissions ('IOSCO') have led the way in promoting the use of MOUs as an effective regulatory device. In 1991, the Technical Committee of IOSCO released its 'Principles for Memoranda of Understanding'[15] which provided a blueprint for securities and futures regulators to use when developing MOUs with their counterparts. These Principles covered the subject matter of the MOU, confidentiality, implementation procedures, the rights of persons subject to an MOU request, consultation, public policy exception, types of assistance, permitted uses, participation by the requesting authority, and cost-sharing. In 2012, IOSCO revised its general principles for countries wishing to enter into such MOUs with its paper on Multilateral Memorandum of Understanding concerning Consultation and Cooperation and the Exchange of Information.[16] **4.09**

[13] The Millennium Declaration, signed by 189 countries in 2000, established the Millenium Development Goals with with the purpose to improve conditions for the world's poorest people. See the UN Millenium Development Goals Report 2013; <http://www.un.org/millenniumgoals/pdf/report-2013/mdg-report-2013-english.pdf>. The UN is also developing policy plans for a post-2015 sustainability and development agenda through the Development Cooperation Forum (DCF) on the future of a renewed global partnership for development, and characteristics of a monitoring and accountability framework between public and private sectors. See UN Task Force Report, Realising the Future We Want for All, May 2012; available at: <http://www.un.org/en/development/desa/policy/untaskteam_undf/untt_report.pdf>.

[14] <http://www.unctad.org>. See also Report of the Panel of Eminent Persons: *Enhancing the Development Role and Impact of UNCTAD* (June 2006); <http://www.unctad.org/sections/edm_dir/docs/osg20061_en.pdf>. The Panel of Eminent Persons was revived in 2011 to advise the Secretary-General of UNCTAD in their personal capacities on the key and emerging economic development challenges and to provide concrete ideas for international initiatives on how to deal with them, and how to position UNCTAD strategically in this context. See UNCTAD Secretary-General's Panel of Eminent Persons, Second Report 'Addressing key economic issues to advance sustainable development: Ideas for actions, 2013; available at: <http://unctad.org/en/PublicationsLibrary/osg2013d3_en.pdf>.

[15] <http://www.iosco.org/library/pubdocs/pdf/IOSCOPD17.pdf>. For comment, see GA Walker, 'International Supervisory Co-operation', in W Blair, A Allison, G Morton, P Richards-Carpenter, GA Walker, and N Walmsley, *Banking and Financial Services Regulation*, (3rd edn, Butterworths 2002) ch 1.

[16] <http://www.iosco.org/library/pubdocs/pdf/IOSCOPD386.pdf>.

4.10 In many cases, MOUs have enabled regulators to agree the basis on which they will be able to share information on a bilateral basis between the relevant requesting and requested market authorities. Although not legally enforceable, these MOUs are usually trigger-based agreements where information is shared once certain triggering events have occurred. Pre-agreed exposure levels are part of this triggering mechanism because they permit an integrated multilateral assessment of market risks. So a significant decrease in a member's capital position, or large cash flows in proprietary or customer accounts, or a concentration of positions in any futures or options contract may all trigger the need for information sharing between regulatory authorities. All information shared is generally kept confidential, even if the MOU is terminated.

4.11 Whilst home supervisors have organisation-wide supervisory oversight responsibility, cooperation with host supervisors on issues related to the operation of firms in host markets is essential. In May 1996, the Basel Committee[17] and IOSCO agreed to promote additional cooperative and collaborative arrangements to improve their supervision of diversified financial groups.[18] The principal focus of their initiative is the types of groups or institutions for which such arrangements would be useful and appropriate, the types of information that may need to be exchanged, ways to facilitate the resolution of possible legal, confidentiality, policy, or practical issues that may arise, and any additional arrangements that may be appropriate to coordinate the activities of the relevant supervisors.[19] Other initiatives between regulatory bodies have included 'A Report from the Regulators Participating in the Windsor Meeting'[20] that detailed the progress domestic regulators[21] had made towards sharing information with their peers from other countries.

4.12 However, instances have arisen where regulatory cooperation may not always be the case. The Technical Committee of IOSCO addressed the issue in its 'Report on Issues Raised for Securities and Futures Regulators by Under-Regulated and Uncooperative Jurisdictions'[22] and the consequent resolution committing IOSCO members to provide cooperation and assistance in regulatory matters.[23] Similarly, following the *Sumitomo* case, supervisors of commodity futures markets from 17 countries met in London to discuss the oversight of commodity futures markets. The 'London Communiqué on the Supervision of Commodity Futures Markets'[24] was subsequently released by the Japanese Ministry of International Trade and Industry in conjunction with the Japanese Ministry of Agriculture, Forestry

---

[17] See para 4.121.

[18] IOSCO, 'A Resolution Concerning Cross-Border Transactions'; available at: <http://www.iosco.org/library/resolutions/pdf/IOSCORES12.pdf)>.

[19] See Committee on Payment and Settlement Systems Technical Committee of the International Organisation of Securities Commissions, 'Principles for financial market infrastructures', April 2012; available at: <http://www.bis.org/publ/cpss101a.pdf>.

[20] The Windsor Declaration arose out of a meeting in May 1995 of representatives of the regulatory authorities of 16 countries responsible for supervising the activities of the world's major futures and options markets. The Windsor Declaration sought to address the areas of cooperation between market authorities, protection of customer positions, funds and assets, default procedures, and regulatory cooperation in emergencies. The President's Committee of IOSCO adopted a resolution supporting further work by the IOSCO Technical Committee as discussed in the Windsor Declaration.

[21] The following countries participated in the Windsor meeting: Australia, Brazil, Canada, France, Germany, Hong Kong, Italy, Japan, the Netherlands, Singapore, South Africa, Spain, Sweden, Switzerland, the United Kingdom, and the United States of America.

[22] <http://riskinstitute.ch/140190.htm>.

[23] <http://www.iosco.org/library/resolutions/pdf/IOSCORES11.pdf>.

[24] <http://www.cftc.gov/opa/press96/opaderiv2.htm>.

and Fisheries, the US Commodity Futures Trading Commission, and the UK Securities and Investments Board. Such communiqués are, however, statements of intent rather than enforceable agreements but they form an important part of the regulator's armoury.

Similar agreements have arisen in the funds industry[25] where the insolvency or threatened insolvency of a fund manager, trustee, custodian, or affiliated companies of any of these entities can often trigger a crisis of confidence. The IOSCO Discussion paper, 'Regulatory Cooperation in Emergencies',[26] identified the main scenarios of emergencies in the funds industry and considered the relevant regulatory cooperation policies and, in particular, the policies for determining suspension of redemption of units in collective investment schemes. **4.13**

Cooperation between home and host country supervisors also needed addressing in relation to Year 2000 cross-border issues. In a paper titled, 'Supervisory Cooperation on Year 2000 Cross-Border Issues',[27] the Basel Committee put forward five recommendations to ensure that banking supervisors were prepared. The issue of global financial conglomerates has also given rise to a number of other regulatory responses and the Principles for the Supervision of Financial Conglomerates[28] prepared by the tripartite group of bank, securities, and insurance regulators, and the Joint Forum's Framework for Supervisory Information Sharing[29] built upon the Tripartite Committee's recommendations that supervisory cooperation should be one of the eight major principles of financial supervision.[30] **4.14**

In banking, regulatory cooperation began with the bank supervisors' Concordat of 1975.[31] A revised version of the Concordat was issued in 1983, a supplement in 1990, and a normative version in 1992 ('Minimum Standards for the Supervision of International Banking Groups and Their Cross-Border Establishments')[32] that addressed the respective roles of the home and host supervisor, the need for effective consolidated supervision by the home supervisor, and the mechanics of supervisory information exchanges. Other regulatory responses have been directed to improving the global supervision of banks' international activities and BIS's 'The Supervision of Cross-Border Banking',[33] making it clear that the financial activities of international banks must be subject to effective home and host supervision. Regulators are keen to ensure that all cross-border banking operations are subject to effective home and host supervision and the BIS's 'Minimum Standards for the Supervision of International Banking Groups and their Cross-Border Establishment'[34] provided a detailed summary of the requirements and the principles for supervision. **4.15**

---

[25] See 'Discussion Paper on International Cooperation in Relation to Cross-Border Activity of Collective Investment Schemes' (1996) that included a template of a mutual recognition agreement and a declaration on Co-operation and Supervision of Cross-Border Investment Management Activity that provides a framework for providing regular information about relevant cross-border activity.

[26] IOSCO, Technical Committee, Working Group 5.

[27] Basel Committee on Banking Supervision, Publication 38.

[28] Basel Committee on Banking Supervision, Publication 47, updated as Joint Forum on the Principles for the Supervision of Financial Conglomerates, September, 2012; available at: <http://www.bis.org/publ/joint29.pdf>.

[29] Basel Committee on Banking Supervision, Publication 45.

[30] Basel Committee on Banking Supervision, Paper 20.

[31] Committee on Banking Regulations and Supervisory Practices, Report to the Governors on the supervision of banks' foreign establishments, BS/75/44e.

[32] Basel Committee on Banking Supervision, Publication 314.

[33] Basel Committee on Banking Supervision, Publication 27.

[34] See n 29.

4.16 These concepts were further elaborated in 10 key principles of information sharing issued by the G-7 finance ministers in May 1998.[35] Given the goal of improving cooperation through information-sharing, the objective of this agreement was to provide supervisors with guidance for the possible identification of a coordinator or coordinators, and identify the mechanisms from which supervisors can select in emergency and non-emergency situations. The need for regulatory cooperation across banking and financial services industry groups is also taken up by the Group of Thirty ('G-30')[36] in their report on reducing systemic risk. 'Global Institutions, National Supervision and Systemic Risk'[37] examined the potential for systemic risk arising from the gap between the global operations of financial institutions and markets and nationally based systems of accounting, reporting, law, and supervision. This G-30 report concluded that regulatory cooperation across borders and functions will come about only 'if supervisors recognise their mutual interdependence and adopt common supervisory techniques'.[38]

4.17 Since the financial crisis the G-30 has been focusing on governance issues, both within the regulators[39] and regulated firms.[40] Another area of development in international agreements has been in what White calls the 'plumbing' of global banking and finance,[41] which are those technical agreements between countries, regulators, or industry participants which simply allow the system to work on a global basis. Examples of this type of agreement are the International Standards Organisation's SWIFT (Society for Worldwide Interbank Financial Telecommunication)[42] agreements. SWIFT's primary function is to establish standards and agreements between industry members and to lay down the standards for inter-bank communications and messaging. The ISO has also developed other new standards such as UNIFI

[35] The Coordinator Paper, Bank for International Settlement, 1999.

[36] The Group of Thirty was established in 1978 as a private, non-profit, international body composed of senior representatives of the private and public sectors and academia. Its objectives are to deepen understanding of international economic and financial issues, to explore the international repercussions of decisions taken in the public and private sectors, and to examine the choices available to market practitioners and policymakers.

[37] The Group of Thirty, A Study Group Report, 1997. See also: Financial Reform: a Framework for Financial Stability, January 2009; available at: <http://www.group30.org/images/PDF/Financial_Reform-A_Framework_for_Financial_Stability.pdf>.

[38] Quoted in G30 Working Group, Global Institutions, National Supervision and Systemic Risk, 1997. The G-30 has also established a working group on Financial Regulatory Systems. The purpose of this Financial Regulatory Systems Working Group is to assess the strengths and weaknesses of different types of regulatory systems, including looking at the three main regulatory structures adopted: integrated single financial regulator, the functional approach, and the institutional or sector-by-sector approach in the key markets including: Australia, Brazil, Canada, China, France, Germany, Hong Kong, India, Italy, Japan, Mexico, the Netherlands, Singapore, Spain, South Africa, Switzerland, the United Kingdom, and the United States. The Working Group will report in 2008.

[39] The G-30 work programme currently includes a Working Group on Corporate Governance Banking Supervisors to look to provide recommendations designed to enhance the overall effectiveness of supervision by identifying specific initiatives and processes both to assist supervisors directly in discharge of their responsibilities and to promote alignment of boardroom expectations and responses to such initiatives and processes. The report will address the role of supervision within the regulatory framework, while assessing the ability of supervisors to draw on substantial internal support, effectively use channels of communication within an institution, and evaluate the performance of their boards and aim to provide clarity on the responsibilities between supervisors and boards.

[40] 'Toward Effective Governance of Financial Institutions', (G30 Working Group Special Report) 2012.

[41] White (n 11) at p 8.

[42] SWIFT is a cooperative society under Belgian law, which its member-shareholders own and control. With 7,600 members and participants in 200 countries whose daily messaging through the system regularly exceed 9 million, SWIFT has a Board of 25 independent directors, appointed by the shareholders which is responsible for overseeing and governing the company.

to achieve standards of convergence among all organisations that develop messages to support financial business transactions.[43] Other such architectural agreements include those global standards in private law promulgated by UNIDROIT (the International Institute for the Unification of Private Law) whose basic statutory objective is to modernise and, where appropriate, harmonise uniform rules of private law.[44] The uniform rules prepared by UNIDROIT are concerned with substantive law rules but they address legal issues arising from new technologies and changing commercial practices where transactions are trans-national by their nature.

The final category of international cooperation is the multitude of trade body and professional organisations that establish standards, agree protocols, and adopt standard forms in the interests of their sector of the banking and financial services industry. Organisations such as International Swaps and Derivatives Inc,[45] the International Capital Markets Association,[46] and G-30 have all been instrumental in obtaining industry cooperation in a wide range of areas and developing standardised documentation and articulating industry best practice. **4.18**

The World Trade Organisation and Financial Services

The World Trade Organisation ('WTO') was established in 1995 as the successor body to the General Agreement on Tariffs and Trade ('GATT') whose origins as a forum for global trade date back to the post-Second World War period. Originally a system developed through a series of trade negotiations, or rounds, held under GATT, the first GATT rounds dealt mainly with tariff reductions as between member countries, but later negotiations included other areas such as anti-dumping and non-tariff measures and the 1986–94 Uruguay Round led to the WTO's creation. **4.19**

Still fundamentally a negotiating forum, the WTO has 159 member countries accounting for over 97 per cent of world trade and another 25 countries have observer status. **4.20**

Decisions are made by the entire membership of the WTO. This is typically by consensus, and although a majority vote is also possible, it has never been used in the WTO. The WTO's **4.21**

[43] ISO 20022-UNIversal Financial Industry Message scheme ('UNIFI') is the international standard that defines the ISO platform for the development of financial message standards.

[44] See, eg, UNIDROIT Convention on Substantive Rules for Intermediated Securities, 2009; available at: <http://www.unidroit.org/english/conventions/2009intermediatedsecurities/convention.pdf>.

[45] The International Swaps and Derivatives Association Inc was founded in 1985 and is the global trade association representing participants in the privately negotiated derivatives markets such as swaps and options in all asset classes (including interest rate, currency, commodity and energy, credit and equity derivatives). ISDA has over 800 member institutions from 60 countries and has developed standard master agreements (the ISDA Master Agreement) as well as publishing a wide range of other related market documentation materials and instruments covering a variety of transaction types. It has also produced legal opinions on the enforceability of netting and collateral arrangements and acts to secure recognition of the risk-reducing effects of netting in determining capital requirements.

[46] The International Capital Market Association, which came into being on 1 July 2005 as a result of a merger between the International Securities Market Association ('ISMA') and the International Primary Market Association ('IPMA'), is the self-regulatory organisation and trade association representing the investment banks and securities firms issuing, trading, and dealing in the international capital markets worldwide. ICMA's 430 members represent all of the major participants in the global capital markets and are located in 52 countries around the world.

agreements must be ratified by all members in accordance with their local requirements in order to be effective.

4.22 The WTO's decision-making body is the Ministerial Conference that meets at least once every two years. The WTO General Council comprises ambassadors to the WTO and heads of delegation who meet at the WTO's headquarters in Geneva several times a year. The General Council also meets as the Trade Policy Review Body and the Dispute Settlement Body. More specialised councils such as the Goods Council, Services Council, and Intellectual Property ('TRIPS') Council report to the General Council as well as a number of other specialised committees, working groups and working parties deal with the individual agreements and other areas such as the environment, development, membership applications, and regional trade agreements.

WTO Agreements

4.23 The WTO agreements, negotiated and signed by the member nations, provide the legal ground-rules for international commerce. The WTO system's overriding purpose is to help trade flow as freely as possible and to remove obstacles by ensuring that individuals, companies, and governments comply with the both transparent and predictable trade rules. There are three major areas of trade which are covered by the WTO: the General Agreement on Tariffs and Trade ('GATT'), which governs trade in goods, the General Agreement on Trade in Services ('GATS'), and the Agreement on Trade-Related Aspects of Intellectual Property Rights ('TRIPS'). GATS provides for four methods of supply of services: cross-border supply, consumption abroad, commercial presence, and presence/movement of natural persons.

4.24 Under the WTO agreements, countries cannot normally discriminate between their trading partners. Obligations contained in GATS can be separated into two categories: general obligations which apply directly and automatically to all member countries of the WTO, regardless of the existence of commitments made for each sector; and conditional obligations which apply to sectors where the WTO member country has assumed market access and national treatment obligations.

4.25 Granting more favourable access to one member (for example, a lower customs duty rate for one of their products) requires that State to extend the same treatment to all other WTO members. This principle is known as most-favoured-nation treatment. This 'most-favoured-nation' principle is the backbone of the three major areas of trade: GATT, GATS, and TRIPS. Other general obligations include transparency by which WTO member countries are required to publish all measures of general application relevant to the WTO's functions and to establish national enquiry points to respond to other members' information requests.

4.26 The granting of market access is another commitment undertaken by individual WTO members in specified sectors after negotiations that may be made subject to one or more limitations. The other general obligation of WTO members is that of 'national treatment' which means treating one's own nationals and foreigners equally. In services, it means that once a foreign company has been allowed to supply a service in one's country there should be no discrimination between the foreign and local companies. Under GATS, a country only has to apply this principle when it has made a specific commitment to provide foreigners access to its services market. It does not have to apply national treatment in sectors where it has not made any commitment even though the service is permitted under a liberalised regime. Even in the sectors where it has made commitment for market access, GATS does allow limitations on national treatment to be taken fully or partially.

Dispute Resolution under WTO Proceedings

The WTO also provides a dispute resolution role in interpreting agreements and resolving conflicts between member countries. Disputes in the WTO may arise where one country adopts a trade policy measure or takes some action that one or more fellow WTO members considers to be breaking the WTO agreements or to be a failure to comply with its obligations under the agreements. **4.27**

The Uruguay Round agreement introduced a more structured process with more clearly defined stages in the procedure, and imposed greater discipline for the length of time a case should take to be settled. The Uruguay Round agreement emphasised that prompt settlement is essential if the WTO is to function effectively, and it set out in considerable detail the procedures and the timetable to be followed in resolving disputes. Cases referred under the WTO's dispute resolution procedures usually take about one year to reach resolution, or up to 15 months if the case is appealed. The Uruguay Round agreement also strengthened the enforcement mechanisms, and rulings are automatically adopted unless there is a consensus to reject a ruling. Although WTO procedures do resemble a court or tribunal, the preferred solution is for the WTO member countries to negotiate and settle the dispute between them. The first stage is therefore consultations between the governments concerned, and even when the case has progressed to other stages, consultation and mediation are still the objective of the enforcement process. **4.28**

Such a dispute was the request made on 13 March 2003 by Antigua and Barbuda pursuant to Article 4 of the Understanding on Rules and Procedures Governing the Settlement of Disputes ('DSU')[47] and Article XXIII of GATS regarding certain legal and regulatory measures applied by authorities in the USA that affected the cross-border supply of gambling and betting services whose cumulative impact resulted, according to Antigua, in making unlawful the supply of gambling and betting services on a cross-border basis. Antigua and the USA held consultations in April 2003, but these consultations did not resolve the dispute. Antigua therefore requested the WTO Disputes Settlement Board ('DSB') to establish a Panel to examine, in the light of the relevant provisions of the covered agreements and to make such findings as will assist the DSB in making the recommendations or in giving the rulings provided for in those agreements. Antigua and Barbuda requested the Panel to find that the USA's prohibition on the cross-border supply of gambling and betting services and its measures restricting international money transfers and payments relating to gambling and betting services are inconsistent with the USA's Schedule of specific commitments under the GATS and Articles XVI:1, XVI:2, XVII:1, XVII:2, XVII:3, VI:1, VI:3, and XI:1 of the GATS. **4.29**

Antigua argued that a vast array of gambling and betting games and services were being offered on a commercial basis in the USA and elsewhere, and since the mid-1990s Antigua had built up a primarily Internet-based, 'remote-access' gaming industry as part of its economic development strategy. Antigua submitted that US federal and state laws were preventing Antigua's online gaming industry from competing with US-based gambling firms. **4.30**

[47] WTO, Dispute Resolution Panel, DS285.

4.31 The initial WTO panel decision had found that these services were outside the WTO rules for trade in services on the basis that the USA could use federal gaming laws to protect public morals or maintain public order. However, on appeal it was held that the USA had to clarify its laws that were deemed to be over-broad in certain areas and therefore limited the cross-border trade in these services. The parties, both of whom claimed victory, referred the implementation of this ruling to arbitration.

4.32 Since this decision, Antigua referred the matter to a WTO Compliance Panel which found that the US had not taken measures to bring its federal gambling laws into line with its commitments and in June 2007, Antigua filed a request to suspend its trade concessions and the matter has been referred to a WTO arbitrator. The US has also taken steps to remove gambling and betting from its schedule of Article XXI WTO commitments in an effort to frustrate the outcome of the dispute resolution process in this case.[48]

Financial Services under the WTO

4.33 In 1997, 70 WTO members concluded a financial services agreement (the Financial Services Annex)[49] covering more than 95 per cent of trade in banking, insurance, securities, and financial information. The WTO's work programme, the Doha Development Agenda ('DDA'), added negotiations and other work on non-agricultural tariffs, trade, and environment, WTO rules such as anti-dumping and subsidies, investment, competition policy, trade facilitation, transparency in government procurement, intellectual property, and a range of issues raised by developing countries as difficulties they face in implementing the present WTO agreements.[50]

4.34 The Financial Services Annex to the GATS Agreement applies to measures affecting the supply of financial services in WTO Member States. A financial service is defined as any service of a financial nature offered by a financial service supplier of a member country. Financial services includes all insurance and insurance-related services, and all banking and other financial services (excluding insurance) and includes the following activities:

Insurance and insurance-related services including:

(i) direct insurance (including co-insurance):
   (A) life,
   (B) non-life;
(ii) reinsurance and retrocession;
(iii) insurance intermediation, such as brokerage and agency;
(iv) services auxiliary to insurance, such as consultancy, actuarial, risk assessment, and claim settlement services. Banking and other financial services (excluding insurance) including:
(v) acceptance of deposits and other repayable funds from the public;

[48] See summary of this dispute at <http://www.wto.org/english/tratop_e/dispu_e/cases_e/ds285_e.htm>.

[49] Fifth Protocol to the General Agreement on Trade in Services, S/L/45; available at: <http://www.wto.org/english/tratop_e/serv_e/10-anfin_e.htm>.

[50] The Doha Round of negotiations broke down in July 2008 as a result of a failure to agree various agricultural reforms and protections for agriculture in developing and emerging member countries. The status of the remainder of the commitments, including those relating to access to financial services (see Testimony of Dr SJ Key to the US House of Representatives, 15 November 2005; available at: <http://financialservices.house.gov/media/pdf/111505sk.pdf>) remains unclear.

(vi) lending of all types, including consumer credit, mortgage credit, factoring and financing of commercial transaction;
(vii) financial leasing;
(viii) all payment and money transmission services, including credit, charge and debit cards, travellers cheques, and bankers drafts;
(ix) guarantees and commitments;
(x) trading for own account or for account of customers, whether on an exchange, in an over-the-counter market or otherwise, the following:
(A) money market instruments (including cheques, bills, certificates of deposit);
(B) foreign exchange;
(C) derivative products including, but not limited to, futures and options;
(D) exchange rate and interest rate instruments, including products such as swaps, forward rate agreements;
(E) transferable securities;
(F) other negotiable instruments and financial assets, including bullion;
(xi) participation in issues of all kinds of securities, including underwriting and placement as agent (whether publicly or privately) and provision of services related to such issues;
(xii) money broking;
(xiii) asset management, such as cash or portfolio management, all forms of collective investment management, pension fund management, custodial, depository, and trust services;
(xiv) settlement and clearing services for financial assets, including securities, derivative products, and other negotiable instruments;
(xv) provision and transfer of financial information, and financial data processing and related software by suppliers of other financial services;
(xvi) advisory, intermediation, and other auxiliary financial services on all these activities listed, including credit reference and analysis, investment and portfolio research and advice, advice on acquisitions and on corporate restructuring, and strategy.

For the purposes of Article I of the GATS Agreement, 'services supplied in the exercise of governmental authority' means activities conducted by a central bank or monetary authority or by any other public entity in pursuit of monetary or exchange rate policies, activities forming part of a statutory system of social security or public retirement plans, and other activities conducted by a public entity for the account or with the guarantee or using the financial resources of the Government. **4.35**

WTO members have agreed, however, that they will not be prevented from taking measures for prudential reasons, including for the protection of investors, depositors, policyholders, or persons to whom a fiduciary duty is owed by a financial service supplier, or to ensure the integrity and stability of the financial system. Where such measures do not conform to the provisions of the Agreement, they will not be used as a means of avoiding the member's commitments or obligations under the Agreement. Furthermore, nothing in the Agreement requires a member to disclose information relating to the affairs and accounts of individual customers or any confidential or proprietary information in the possession of public entities. **4.36**

A WTO member may also recognise prudential measures of any other country in determining how the member's measures relating to financial services are to be applied. Such recognition, which may be achieved through harmonisation or otherwise, may be based upon an agreement or arrangement with the country concerned or may be accorded autonomously. **4.37**

A WTO member that is a party to such an agreement or arrangement is required to afford adequate opportunity for other interested WTO members to negotiate their accession to such agreements or arrangements, or to negotiate comparable ones with it, under circumstances in which there would be equivalent regulation, oversight, implementation of such regulation, and, if appropriate, procedures concerning the sharing of information between the parties to the agreement or arrangement. Where a WTO member accords recognition autonomously, it must afford adequate opportunity for any other WTO member to demonstrate that such circumstances exist.

4.38 Participants in the Uruguay Round, which came into force on 1 January 1995, have also taken on specific commitments with respect to financial services under GATS on the basis of an alternative approach to that covered by the provisions of Part III of that Agreement.[51] It was agreed that this approach could be applied subject to the understanding that it does not conflict with the provisions of the Agreement, it does not prejudice the right of any member to schedule its specific commitments in accordance with the approach under Part III of the Agreement, the resulting specific commitments apply on a most-favoured-nation basis, and no presumption has been created as to the degree of liberalisation to which a member is committing itself under the Agreement.

4.39 Interested WTO members have also subscribed to the following specific commitments in relation to financial services.[52]

4.40 In addition to Article VIII of the Agreement, each member has agreed to provide a list of provisions in its schedule pertaining to financial services that contain existing monopoly rights and will endeavour to eliminate them or reduce their scope.

4.41 Notwithstanding Article XIII of the Agreement, each member will ensure that financial service suppliers of any other member established in its territory are accorded most-favoured-nation treatment and national treatment as regards the purchase or acquisition of financial services by public entities of the member in its territory.

4.42 Each member will permit non-resident suppliers of financial services to supply, as a principal, through an intermediary, or as an intermediary, and under terms and conditions that accord national treatment, the following services:

- insurance of risks relating to maritime shipping and commercial aviation and space launching and freight (including satellites), with such insurance to cover any or all of the following: the goods being transported, the vehicle transporting the goods and any liability arising as a result, and goods in international transit, as well as reinsurance and retrocession, and the services auxiliary to insurance as referred to in sub-paragraph 5(a)(iv) of the Annex;
- the provision and transfer of financial information and financial data processing as referred to in sub-paragraph 5(a)(xv) of the Annex and advisory and other auxiliary services, excluding intermediation, relating to banking and other financial services as referred to in sub-paragraph 5(a)(xvi) of the Annex.

[51] Uruguay Round Agreement, Decision on Financial Services.

[52] WTO, Understanding on Commitments in Financial Services; available at: <http://www.wto.org/english/tratop_e/serv_e/21-fin_e.htm>.

Each member will also permit its residents to purchase in the territory of any other member the financial services indicated in sub-paragraph 3(a), sub-paragraph 3(b), and sub-paragraphs 5(a)(v) to (xvi) of the Annex. **4.43**

Each member will grant financial service suppliers of any other member the right to establish or expand within its territory, including through the acquisition of existing enterprises, a commercial presence. **4.44**

A WTO member may, however, impose terms, conditions, and procedures for authorisation of the establishment and expansion of a commercial presence insofar as they do not circumvent the member's obligation and they are consistent with the other obligations of the Agreement. **4.45**

A member will permit financial service suppliers of any other member established in its territory to offer in its territory any new financial service. A new financial service is a service of a financial nature, including services related to existing and new products, or the manner in which a product is delivered, that is not supplied by any financial service supplier in the territory of a particular member but which is supplied in the territory of another member. **4.46**

No WTO member will take measures that prevent transfers of information or the processing of financial information, including transfers of data by electronic means, or that, subject to importation rules consistent with international agreements, prevent transfers of equipment, where such transfers of information, processing of financial information, or transfers of equipment are necessary for the conduct of the ordinary business of a financial service supplier. Nothing in this paragraph, however, restricts the right of a WTO member to protect personal data, personal privacy, and the confidentiality of individual records and accounts so long as such right is not used to circumvent the provisions of the Agreement. **4.47**

Each WTO member will permit temporary entry into its territory of the following personnel of a financial service supplier of any other member that is establishing or has established a commercial presence in the territory of the member: **4.48**

(a) senior managerial personnel possessing proprietary information essential to the establishment, control, and operation of the services of the financial service supplier; and
(b) specialists in the operation of the financial service supplier.

Each WTO member will also permit, subject to the availability of qualified personnel in its territory, temporary entry into its territory of the following personnel associated with a commercial presence of a financial service supplier of any other member: **4.49**

(a) specialists in computer services, telecommunication services, and accounts of the financial service supplier; and
(b) actuarial and legal specialists.

Each member will endeavour to remove or to limit any significant adverse effects on financial service suppliers of any other member of: **4.50**

(a) non-discriminatory measures that prevent financial service suppliers from offering in the member's territory, in the form determined by the member, all the financial services permitted by the member;
(b) non-discriminatory measures that limit the expansion of the activities of financial service suppliers into the entire territory of the member;

(c) measures of a member, when such a member applies the same measures to the supply of both banking and securities services, and a financial service supplier of any other member concentrates its activities in the provision of securities services; and

(d) other measures that, although respecting the provisions of the Agreement, affect adversely the ability of financial service suppliers of any other member to operate, compete, or enter the member's market, provided that any action taken under this paragraph would not unfairly discriminate against financial service suppliers of the member taking such action.

4.51 WTO members are also required to endeavour not to limit or restrict the present degree of market opportunities nor the benefits already enjoyed by financial service suppliers of all other members as a class in the territory of the member, provided that this commitment does not result in unfair discrimination against financial service suppliers of the member applying such measures.

4.52 Under terms and conditions that accord national treatment, each WTO member also commits to grant to financial service suppliers of any other member established in its territory access to payment and clearing systems operated by public entities, and to official funding and refinancing facilities available in the normal course of ordinary business.

4.53 In addition to the existing WTO agreements, the WTO Financial Leaders Group that comprises private sector representatives from Canada, the European Union, Hong Kong, Japan, Switzerland, and the USA have also commented on the various negotiating proposals relating to financial services that have been tabled in the WTO Council for Trade in Services ('CTS').[53] In particular, this group found that in the future the WTO financial services negotiations should reflect the following goals.

- Foreign investors should have the right to establish through a wholly-owned presence or other form of business ownership, and to operate competitively through established vehicles available to national businesses. Thus, limits to investment in joint ventures and domestic financial institutions should be lifted and fully-owned subsidiaries, branches, and representative offices should be allowed for foreign financial services providers. In addition, arbitrary 'economic needs tests' and restrictions on regional and product-specific activity should be abolished.
- Foreign direct investors should have the same access to domestic and international markets as domestic companies. They should be treated for regulatory and other purposes on the same basis as domestic companies.
- Unnecessary restrictions on cross-border financial services business and consumption of services abroad should be removed, to encourage trade without requiring establishment, particularly taking account of technological advancement, including electronic commerce.
- The temporary posting of key business personnel should be facilitated by the creation of a system of easily obtained and renewable permits.
- Existing investments should be grandfathered by WTO member countries that did not commit to do so in the 1997 Agreement.

[53] Financial Leaders Group, Commentary on Proposals for Liberalisation in Financial Services, 21 September 2001.

- Countries wishing to accede to membership in the WTO should do so on the basis of commitments to substantial financial liberalisation consistent with the 1997 Financial Services Agreement and the goals set forth above, resulting in commercially meaningful access.
- In order to ensure that market access and national treatment commitments achieve their promised objectives, there is a pressing need to supplement them with new commitments on improved transparency and, in addition, domestic regulatory reform as necessary and appropriate for each specific sector.
- Transparent domestic rules and administrative procedures are an essential part of liberalising financial services. Clear and reliable information about a country's financial services laws and practices promotes equitable trade and competition. Regulatory regimes, even restrictive ones, should be made more transparent. This is an obligation on all WTO members, whether they make specific commitments or not.
- To encourage private savings for retirement, in recognition of worldwide ageing populations, WTO members should commit to lock in and improve market access in the provision of pension and asset management products and services.
- The dissemination and processing of financial information to provide clients with competitive services necessary for the conduct of ordinary business should be permitted.

The WTO does and will continue to fulfil an important role in the international arena of financial services but it depends heavily upon the goodwill and good faith of all of its members to negotiate, adopt, and fulfil the commitments to create a global financial services market.[54] **4.54**

Regional Trade Agreements

Trade liberalisation is also increasingly important in other areas of financial services and there are a number of regional trade agreements that affect financial services. **4.55**

The largest of the regional trade organisations is that established under the North American Free Trade Agreement ('NAFTA'),[55] a regional agreement between the Government of Canada, the Government of the United Mexican States, and the Government of the United States of America to implement a free trade area. **4.56**

The objectives of this Agreement, which includes national treatment, most-favoured-nation treatment, and transparency, are to eliminate barriers to trade in, and facilitate the cross-border movement of, goods and services between the territories of the parties, promote conditions of fair competition in the free trade area, increase substantially investment opportunities in the territories of the parties, provide adequate and effective protection and enforcement of intellectual property rights in each party's territory, create effective procedures for the implementation and application of this agreement, for its joint administration, and for the resolution of disputes, and establish a framework for further trilateral, regional, and multilateral cooperation to expand and enhance the benefits of NAFTA. **4.57**

---

54 See n 45.

55 North American Free Trade Agreement; available at: <http://www.nafta-sec-alena.org>. The enlarged European Union (see Chapter 3) represents a market which is about 10 per cent larger than the USA.

4.58 NAFTA is operated through the NAFTA Secretariat, a unique organisation established pursuant to Article 2002 of the Agreement to administer the mechanisms specified under NAFTA to resolve trade disputes between national industries and/or governments in a timely and impartial manner. Under NAFTA each of the participating governments has established permanent, national section offices in each country.

4.59 The financial sector provisions of NAFTA (Chapter Fourteen) set out a declaration of principles with respect to openness of the financial sector, together with safeguards to permit participating parties to maintain distinct approaches to the regulation of their financial sectors, including safeguards that protect each party's approach to regulation,[56] the supply of financial services from outside a country,[57] the terms and conditions under which financial institutions from one country can operate in another country,[58] and the settlement of disputes in the financial sector.[59]

4.60 NAFTA was intended to open the participants' financial sectors to the supply of services through cross-border trade or establishment by financial suppliers from the other countries without interfering with national approaches to financial sector regulation.[60] The Agreement declares the general principle that freedom of cross-border trade requires each party to permit its residents and nationals to purchase financial services from suppliers of other parties located anywhere in the free trade area. On the other hand, the cross-border provision states explicitly that it does not entail any obligation on the parties to permit providers either to do business or to solicit in their territory.

4.61 Another key provision of the Agreement was in relation to the right of establishment in other participant countries. While Article 1404 states that 'financial services providers of a Party should be permitted to establish financial institutions in the territory of another Party in the juridical form determined by the provider', it continues to specify that the participation of the external providers be 'through separate financial institutions as may be required by that Party'.[61] Establishment alone does not ensure that foreign firms are able to serve another country's needs for financial services. They must also be free to supply their services once they become established. The 'National Treatment' provisions[62] determine the operating conditions for those institutions that have been permitted to operate under the Establishment Article. NAFTA clearly takes the broader concept of competitive national treatment and while defining national treatment as 'treatment no less favourable than that accorded by a party'[63] to its own nationals; the Agreement nonetheless requires that policies, whether providing different or identical treatment, must offer 'equal competitive opportunities',[64] the condition that foreign providers not be disadvantaged relative to domestic suppliers.

4.62 The application of many of the principles of the financial sector portion of NAFTA must rely on interpretation and enforcement, and even the results of most careful negotiations may fail

---

[56] NAFTA Agreement, art 1403, Regulatory Measures.
[57] ibid, art 1405, Cross-border Trade.
[58] ibid, art 1404, Establishment and art 1407, National Treatment.
[59] ibid, art 1413, Consultations; art 1414, Financial Services Committee; art 1415, Dispute Settlement and art 1416, Investment Disputes in Financial Services.
[60] NAFTA Agreement, art 1403.
[61] ibid, art 1403(2).
[62] ibid, Chapter Three.
[63] ibid, art 1405(2).
[64] ibid, art 1405(5).

to meet their expectations in practice. On the whole, the dispute settlement provisions follow the general provisions in Chapter Eleven of the Agreement with allowance for the needs of the financial sector. The Agreement also provides for a Financial Services Committee[65] to supervise implementation, to consider issues referred to it, and to participate in dispute settlement. Under the procedure laid down by NAFTA, disputes will be referred to a Tribunal consisting of panelists drawn from a roster of individuals with expertise in the financial sector. If the complaint is upheld by the Tribunal, the complaining party may suspend benefits in the financial services sector.

In addition, the Agreement contains a number of reservations in the area of financial services. As NAFTA is a multilateral agreement, the participants, rather than making specific commitments, have agreed on a set of general principles. Schedule A of the Agreement sets out the reservations to the Agreement of both federal and provincial or State governments, and Schedule B contains the areas where the parties reserve the right to derogate (or reverse) provisions of the agreement in the future. Canada, at one extreme, presented a single reservation of the national government, whereas the USA presented 18, and Mexico, 26. **4.63**

Of the three parties, Canada appears to have fared the best in the short run as a result of NAFTA but the USA would probably gain the most benefits in the long run with the opening up of two major markets to its financial institutions under the Agreement. Access to Mexican financial markets will be more valuable to US banks than to Canadian ones, but Mexico has undoubtedly benefited from the opening up of its financial sector while being able to shelter its financial system from substantial foreign competition during the period of its transition from State to private ownership. **4.64**

The Security and Prosperity Partnership of North America

In addition to NAFTA, the US, Canada, and Mexico launched their joint Security and Prosperity Partnership of North America ('SPP') in March of 2005 as part of a trilateral effort to increase security and enhance prosperity among the participating countries through greater cooperation and information sharing. SPP was neither an agreement nor a treaty but was intended to complement, rather than replace, existing bilateral and trilateral fora and working groups and it is intended to establish agreed priorities for ongoing and new trilateral and bilateral initiatives, give existing efforts additional momentum, and create new programmes and initiatives where necessary and appropriate. **4.65**

In the post-9/11 world, the SPP was designed to establish a cooperative approach to advance common security and prosperity and identified five priorities for cooperative approaches to common challenges and opportunities including: **4.66**

- Competitiveness
- Safe food and products
- Energy and environment
- Smart and secure borders
- Emergency management and preparedness

65 ibid, art 1412, Annex 2001(2).

4.67 SPP Prosperity working groups included a financial services group intended to work towards the freer flow of capital and the efficient provision of financial services throughout North America including facilitating cross-border electronic access to stock exchanges without compromising investor protection, promoting further collaboration on training programmes for bank, insurance, and securities regulators and supervisors, and seeking ways to improve convenience and cost of insurance coverage for carriers engaged in cross-border commerce. However, in 2009 it appears that this SPP initiative went into abeyance although there has been some discussion on revising some of these proposals as a bi-lateral regulatory cooperation initiative between the US and Canada.[66]

4.68 Latin America has a number of other regional trade agreements in place including the Dominican Republic–Central America Free Trade Agreement ('DR–CAFTA')[67] whose objective is to open new opportunities and to help those regional economies to expand their opportunities for growth in the USA.

4.69 In particular, DR–CAFTA seeks to level the playing field for US financial services. While the US finance and insurance markets are largely open to imports from all countries, including Costa Rica, El Salvador, Guatemala, Honduras, Nicaragua, and the Dominican Republic, the same is not true for current US access to those countries' finance and insurance markets. DR–CAFTA gives US companies the opportunity to export financial services and products to the region. Costa Rica, which has the most developed insurance sector in the region, committed for the first time to liberalise its insurance market. In addition, DR–CAFTA contains provisions allowing the establishment of foreign insurance providers through branches or subsidiaries and new rules permitting cross-border provision of marine, aviation, and transportation insurance.

4.70 DR–CAFTA also liberalises the region's banking and securities sectors. Parties must provide market access for financial institutions without limits on the value of transactions, number of operations, or number of persons employed. Central American parties must permit cross-border trade in financial services and allow other parties' financial institutions to provide any new financial services that it would permit its own institutions to provide. DR–CAFTA contains specific binding commitments affecting asset management services and El Salvador, Guatemala, Honduras, and Nicaragua have committed to allow branch banking and generally opened up other areas of financial services to US financial product providers.

4.71 Other regional trade agreements that include provisions on banking and financial services include the Free Trade Area of the Americas ('FTAA'), the Caribbean Community ('CARICOM'), the Asia Pacific Economic Cooperation ('APEC'), the Gulf Co-operation Council ('GCC'), the Association of Southeast Asian Nations ('ASEAN'), the African Union, the East African Community, the Japan/Singapore Economic Partnership Agreement, the

[66] On 4 February 2011, the US and Canada announced the formation of a 'Regulatory Cooperation Council' to improve regulatory cooperation on a cross-border basis (available at: <http://actionplan.gc.ca/en/page/bbg-tpf/beyond-border-action-plan>) but its work programme is currently limited and does not include financial services issues such as the extraterritorial application of the US Dodd-Frank Act to Canadian financial services institutions; available at: <http://www.whitehouse.gov/sites/default/files/omb/oira/irc/us-canada_rcc_joint_action_plan.pdf>.

[67] The US Congress approved the Central American–Dominican Republic Free Trade Agreement (CAFTA–DR) in July 2005 and the President signed it into law on 2 August 2005. As at the date of publication, El Salvador, Honduras, Nicaragua, Guatamala, the Dominican Republic, and Costa Rica have taken the legislative steps required to ratify the DR-CAFTA Agreement.

South Asian Association for Regional Cooperation, and the Southern Africa Development Community.[68]

[68] The regional trade associations are:

AFTA	ASEAN Free Trade Area	Brunei, Darussalam, Cambodia, Indonesia, Laos, Malaysia, Myanmar, Philippines, Singapore, Thailand, Vietnam
APTA	Asia Pacific Trade Agreement	Bangladesh, China, India, Korea, Laos, Sri Lanka
ASEAN	Association of South East Asian Nations	Brunei, Darussalam, Cambodia, Indonesia, Laos, Malaysia, Myanmar, Philippines, Singapore, Thailand, Vietnam, New Zealand
CAN	Andean Community	Bolivia, Colombia, Ecuador, Peru
CARICOM	Caribbean Community and Common Market	Antigua & Barbuda, Bahamas, Barbados, Belize, Dominica, Grenada, Guyana, Haiti, Jamaica, Monserrat, Trinidad & Tobago, St. Kitts & Nevis, St. Lucia, St. Vincent & the Grenadines, Surinam
CACM	Central American Common Market	Costa Rica, El Salvador, Guatemala, Honduras, Nicaragua
CEFTA	Central European Free Trade Agreement	Albania, Bosnia and Herzegovina, Kosova, Macedonia, Moldova, Montenegro, Serbia
CEMAC	Economic and Monetary Community of Central Africa	Cameroon, Central African Republic, Chad, Congo, Equatorial Guinea, Gabon
ANZCERTA	Closer Trade Relations Trade Agreement	Australia, New Zealand
CIS	Commonwealth of Independent States	Armenia, Belarus, Kazakhstan, Kyrgyz Republic, Moldova, Russian Federation, Tajikistan, Ukraine
CEZ	Common Economic Zone	Belarus, Kazakhstan, Russian Federation, Ukraine
COMESA	Common Market for Eastern and Southern Africa	Angola, Burundi, Comoros, Democratic Republic of Congo, Djibouti, Egypt, Eritrea, Ethiopia, Kenya, Madagascar, Malawi, Mauritius, Namibia, Rwanda, Seychelles, Sudan, Swaziland, Uganda, Zambia, Zimbabwe
DR-CAFTA	Dominican Republic–Central American Free Trade Association	Costa Rica, Dominican Republic, El Salvador, Guatamala, Honduras, Nicaragua, United States
EAC	East African Cooperation	Burundi, Kenya, Rwanda, Tanzania, Uganda
EAEC	Eurasian Economic Community	Belarus, Kazakhstan, Kyrgyz Republic, Russian Federation, Tajikistan
EC	European Union	Austria, Belgium, Bulgaria, Croatia, Cyprus, Czech Republic, Denmark, Estonia, Finland, France, Germany, Greece, Hungary, Ireland, Italy Latvia, Lithuania, Luxembourg, Malta, Netherlands, Poland, Portugal, Romania, Slovak Republic, Slovenia, Spain, Sweden, United Kingdom
ECOWAS	Economic Cooperation Organisation	Benin, Burkina Faso, Cape Verde, Cote Ivoire, Gambia, Ghana, Guinea, Guinea-Bissau, Liberia, Mali, Niger, Nigeria, Senegal, Sierra Leone, Togo
EEA	European Economic Area	EU, Iceland, Liechtenstein, Norway
EFTA	European Free Trade Association	Iceland, Liechtenstein, Norway, Switzerland
GCC	Gulf Cooperation Council	Bahrain, Kuwait, Oman, Qatar, Saudi Arabia, United Arab Emirates

Trans-Pacific Partnership

4.72 In November 2009 the United States stated its intention to participate in the Trans-Pacific Partnership ('TPP') negotiations to conclude an Asia–Pacific trade agreement. On 12 November 2011, the governments of Australia, Brunei Darussalam, Chile, Malaysia, New

GSTP	General System of Trade Preferences among Developing Countries	Algeria, Argentina, Bangladesh, Benin, Bolivia, Brazil, Cameroon, Chile, Colombia, Cuba, Democratic People's Republic of Korea, Ecuador, Egypt, Ghana, Guinea, Guyana, India, Indonesia, Islamic Republic of Iran, Iraq, Libya, Malaysia, Mexico, Morocco, Mozambique, Myanmar, Nicaragua, Nigeria, Pakistan, Peru, Philippines, Republic of Korea, Romania, Singapore, Sri Lanka, Sudan, Thailand, Trinidad and Tobago, Tunisia, United Republic of Tanzania, Venezuela, Vietnam, Yugoslavia, Zimbabwe
LAIA	Latin American Integration Association	Argentina, Bolivia, Brazil, Chile, Colombia, Cuba, Ecuador, Mexico, Panama, Paraguay, Peru, Uruguay, Venezuela
MERCOSUR	Southern Common Market	Argentina, Brazil, Paraguay, Uruguay
MSG	Melanesian Spearhead Group	Fiji, Papua New Guinea, Solomon Islands, Vanuatu
NAFTA	North American Free Trade Agreement	Canada, Mexico, United States
OCT	Overseas Countries and Territories	Anguilla, Antilles, Aruba, Ascension Island, British Antarctic Territory, British Indian Ocean Territory, British Virgin Islands, Cayman Islands, Falkland Islands, French Polynesia, French Southern and Antarctic Territories Wallis and Futuna Islands, Greenland, Mayotte, Miquelon, Montserrat, Netherlands, New Caledonia, Pitcairn, Saint Helena, Saint Pierre and South Georgia and South Sandwich Islands, Tristan da Cunha, Turks and Caicos Islands
PICTFA	Pacific Island Countries Trade Agreement	Cook Islands, Fiji, Kiribati, Micronesia, Nauru, Niue, Papua New Guinea, Samoa, Solomon Islands Tonga, Tuvalu, Vanuatu
PAN-ARAB	Pan-Arab Free Trade Area	Bahrain, Egypt, Iraq, Jordan, Kuwait, Lebanon, Libya, Morocco, Oman, Qatar, Saudi Arabia, Sudan, Syria, Tunisia, United Arab Emirates, Yemen
PATCRA	Agreement on Trade and Commercial Relations between the Government of Australia and the Government of Papua New Guinea	Australia, Papua New Guinea
PTN	Protocol relating to Trade Negotiations among Developing Countries	Bangladesh, Brazil, Chile, Egypt, Israel, Mexico, Pakistan, Paraguay, Peru, Philippines, Republic of Korea, Romania, Tunisia, Turkey, Uruguay, Yugoslavia
SACU	Southern African Customs Union	Botswana, Lesotho, Namibia, South Africa, Swaziland
SADC	Southern African Development Community	Angola, Botswana, Lesotho, Malawi, Mauritius, Mozambique, Namibia, South Africa, Swaziland, Tanzania, Zambia, Zimbabwe

Zealand, Peru, Singapore, Vietnam, and the United States announced the broad outlines of an ambitious agreement to improve trade and investment among the TPP partner countries as well as promoting innovation, economic growth and development, and supporting the creation and retention of jobs. Other Asia–Pacific countries including Japan have also now entered the negotiations which cover manufactured goods, agricultural products, and services suppliers as well as seeking to deepen trade and investment in the region. Progress on an agreement is expected in 2013/14.

Transatlantic Trade and Investment Partnership

Another initiative is the Transatlantic Trade and Investment Partnership ('T-TIP') which was announced on 14 June 2013 by President Obama, together with European Commission President Barroso and European Council President Van Rompuy. **4.73**

T-TIP arose out of the establishment of the Transatlantic Economic Council in 2007 as an EU–US high level forum for the discussion of economic issues and strategic global economic questions. Three advisory groups were set up - the Transatlantic Legislators' Dialogue, the Transatlantic Consumer Dialogue and the Transatlantic Business Dialogue - to assist the work of the Council. In November 2011 the Transatlantic Economic Council was directed to establish a High-Level Working Group on Jobs and Growth to identify policies and measures to increase EU-US trade and investment to support mutually beneficial job creation, economic growth, and international competitiveness. **4.74**

The T-TIP is intended to be an 'ambitious, comprehensive, and high-standard trade and investment agreement'[69] that will offer significant benefits and boost economic growth in the United States and the EU. The T-TIP will specifically seek to open markets and strengthen **4.75**

SAPTA	South Asian Preferential Trade Arrangement	Bangladesh, Bhutan, India, Maldives, Nepal, Pakistan, Sri Lanka
SPARTECA	South Pacific Regional Trade and Economic Cooperation Agreement	Australia, Cook Islands, Fiji, Kiribati, Marshall Islands, Micronesia, Nauru, New Zealand, Niue, Papua New Guinea, Solomon Islands, Tonga, Tuvalu, Vanuatu, Western Samoa
Trans-Pacific SEP	Tripartite Agreement Trans-Pacific Strategic Economic Partnership	Brunei, Chile, Darussalam, New Zealand, Singapore
UEMOA	West African	Benin, Burkina Faso, Côte d'Ivoire, Guinea Bissau, Mali
WAEMU	Economic and Monetary Union	Niger, Senegal, Togo

Reproduced with the kind permission of the World Trade Organisation, Regional Trade Agreement; available at: <http://rtais.wto.org/UI/PublicMaintainRTAHome.aspx>.

PAN-ARAB currently only covers goods and commodities but in 2007 the Union of Arab Banks held a conference to consider the social legal and practical issues underpinning cooperation between Arab banks and financial institutions with a view to strengthening regional economic cooperation on both trade and investment levels between the Arab countries in line with the establishment of the Arab Customs Union following on from PAN-ARAB.

69 See <http://europa.eu/rapid/press-release_SPEECH-13-544_en.htm>.

rules-based investment, eliminate all tariffs on trade and costly 'behind the border' non-tariff barriers that impede the flow of goods, including agricultural goods, improve market access on trade in services and reduce the cost of differences in regulations and standards by promoting greater compatibility, transparency, and cooperation and develop rules, principles, and new modes of cooperation on issues of global concern, including intellectual property and market-based disciplines addressing state-owned enterprises and discriminatory localisation barriers to trade. However, the US has taken the initial position that financial services are not to be included in the first rounds of any agreement after months of criticism and complaints from the European leaders about the implementation of the US Dodd-Frank Act and the regulation of over-the-counter derivatives.[70]

Global Bankers—the World Bank and the International Monetary Fund

4.76 The International Monetary Fund ('IMF') and the World Bank Group[71] are the world's bankers and yet they carry out a unique joint role as a flywheel to the global economy. They play an important, if sometimes controversial, role in global banking and financial services although recent years have seen the increasing politicisation of these economic institutions—from all sides of the political spectrum. As a result, the IMF and the World Bank have become at once more critical to global economic stability but also have generated considerable political resistance to their global economic policies.

4.77 The two organisations are intended to complement each other's work. While the IMF's focus is chiefly on macroeconomic performance and on macroeconomic and financial sector policies, the World Bank is concerned mainly with funding project-based economic measures and longer term development and poverty reduction issues. The World Bank's activities include lending to developing countries and countries in transition to finance infrastructure projects, the reform of particular sectors of the economy, and broader structural reforms. The IMF provides financing not for particular sectors or projects but for general support of a country's balance of payments and international reserves while the country takes policy action to address its difficulties.

4.78 Established in 1945[72] both the World Bank and the IMF were founded to help promote the health of the world economy and they are still the central institutions of the international monetary system. The IMF and the International Bank for Reconstruction and Development ('IBRD'), now more commonly known as the World Bank, were set up to promote long-term economic development, including through the financing of infrastructure

---

[70] See: <http://www.nasdaq.com/article/lew-nixes-including-financial-rules-in-eu-trade-talks-20130715-00789>.

[71] The World Bank is not a bank but a specialised agency which has become a group of five closely associated development institutions: the International Bank for Reconstruction and Development ('IBRD'), the International Development Association ('IDA'), the International Finance Corporation ('IFC'), the Multilateral Investment Guarantee Agency ('MIGA'), and the International Centre for Settlement of Investment Disputes ('ICSID').

[72] The IMF was conceived in July 1944 at the Bretton Woods Conference (see n 79) where a charter (or Articles of Agreement) of an international institution to oversee the international monetary system and to promote both the elimination of exchange restrictions relating to trade in goods and services, and the stability of exchange rates was drawn up. The IMF came into existence in December 1945, when the first 29 countries signed its Articles of Agreement; see <http://www.imf.org/external/pubs/ft/aa/index.htm>.

projects, such as road-building and improving water supply. Together these institutions provide a wide variety of low-interest loans, interest-free credit, and grants to developing countries. The World Bank also works with countries in their anti-corruption efforts and has as well a number of mechanisms[73] in place to prevent corruption and fraud in bank-financed projects.

The World Bank is operated as a cooperative, with its member countries as shareholders.[74] A Board of Governors that is composed of the finance ministers or development ministers of their respective countries represents the World Bank's shareholders. The governors, who meet once a year at the Bank's annual meetings, are the ultimate policymakers. The Board of Governors to the President and the Executive Directors delegates day-to-day decision-making at the Bank. The Bank's President is, by tradition, a national of the largest shareholder, the USA.[75] Elected for a five-year renewable term, the President of the World Bank chairs meetings of the Board of Directors and is responsible for overall management of the Bank. Every member government of the World Bank Group is represented by an Executive Director. The five largest shareholders—France, Germany, Japan, the UK, and the USA—each appoint an Executive Director, while other member countries are represented by 19 Executive Directors. Approximately 9,000 economists, educators, environmental scientists, financial analysts, anthropologists, engineers, and many others who come from over 160 different countries and many of whom work in local country offices carry out the work of the Bank. **4.79**

The IMF is also accountable to its member countries and operates through its Board of Governors. Key policy issues relating to the international monetary system are considered twice-yearly in a committee of the governors called the International Monetary and Financial Committee ('IMFC'). A joint committee of the Boards of Governors of the IMF and World Bank called the Development Committee also advises and reports to the governors on development policy and other matters of concern to developing countries. **4.80**

However, the day-to-day work of the IMF is carried out by an Executive Board whose powers to conduct the business of the IMF are delegated to it by the Board of Governors. The Executive Board has 24 Executive Directors, with the Managing Director as chairman. In addition, a First Deputy Managing Director and two other Deputy Managing Directors assist the Managing Director. **4.81**

The Executive Board of the IMF usually meets three times a week, in full-day sessions at the IMF's headquarters in Washington, DC. The IMF's five largest shareholders[76]—the USA, **4.82**

[73] The World Bank has established a Department of Institutional Integrity for whistleblowing and reporting in relation to projects funded by it.

[74] The number of shares a country has in the World Bank is based roughly on the size of its economy. The USA is the largest single shareholder, with 16.41 per cent of votes, followed by Japan (7.87 per cent), Germany (4.49 per cent), the UK (4.31 per cent), and France (4.31 per cent). The rest of the shares are divided among the other member countries.

[75] Dr Jim Yong Kim, became the 12th President of the World Bank Group on July 1, 2012. Born in South Korea, Dr Kim is a naturalised US citizen.

[76] Unlike some international organisations that operate under a one-country-one-vote principle, the IMF has a weighted voting system such that the larger a country's quota in the IMF—determined broadly by its economic size—the more votes it has. The IMF's resources come mainly from the quota (or capital) subscriptions that countries pay when they join the IMF, or following periodic reviews in which quotas are increased. Countries pay 25 per cent of their quota subscriptions in Special Drawing Rights ('SDRs') or the major

Japan, Germany, France, and the UK—along with China, Russia, and Saudi Arabia, have their own seats on the Board. The other 16 Executive Directors are elected for two-year terms by groups of countries, known as constituencies.

4.83 The IMF's aims include promoting the balanced expansion of world trade, the stability of exchange rates, the avoidance of competitive devaluations of currencies, and the orderly correction of balance of payment problems. It serves to prevent economic crises in the system by providing technical assistance and training to Member States and encouraging countries to adopt sound economic policies, and it provides a global funding system that allows members needing temporary financing to address balance of payments problems to borrow but also to implement adjustment and reform economic policies. The IMF has, therefore, become the principal forum for discussion of the stability of the international monetary and financial system, but also of national economic policies in a global context.

4.84 In September 2000 at the annual meetings of the IMF and World Bank, the IMF set out some new major priorities including striving to promote sustained non-inflationary economic growth that benefits all people of the world and to be the centre of competence for the stability of the international financial system.[77] It also made commitments that it would focus more clearly on its core macroeconomic and financial areas of responsibility and work with other institutions established to safeguard global public goods and be an open institution, learning from experience and dialogue, and adapting continuously to changing circumstances.

4.85 The IMF's financing comes from quotas that are intended broadly to reflect the individual members' relative size in the world economy: the larger a country's economy in terms of output, and the larger and more variable its trade, the higher its quota tends to be. The USA therefore contributes the most to the IMF,[78] whereas Palau, the world's smallest, only contributes 0.001 per cent. The most recent (14th) quota review came into effect in December 2010 and raised IMF quotas to over $715 billion.[79] In addition, the IMF may borrow to supplement the resources available from its quotas. The IMF has two sets of standing arrangements

currencies; the IMF can call on the remainder, payable in the member's own currency, to be made available for lending as needed. Quotas determine not only a country's subscription payments, but also the amount of financing that it can receive from the IMF, and its share in SDR allocations. Quotas also are the main determinant of countries' voting power in the IMF. See <http://www.imf.org/external/np/sec/memdir/members.htm>.

[77] The Heavily Indebted Poor Countries ('HIPC') Initiative grew out of the United Nation's Millennium Declaration and the World Bank has adopted its 'Millennium Development Goals' as part of its commitment to 'an expanded vision of development, one that vigorously promotes human development as the key to sustaining social and economic progress in all countries, and recognises the importance of creating a global partnership for development'. In the spring of 2005, the World Bank and IMF implemented a new Debt Sustainability Framework in Low-Income Countries, which is seeking to reduce the challenge to low income countries by providing guidance on new lending to those countries whose main source of financing is official loans. The framework has been developed with the intention to provide better monitoring and prevent the accumulation of unsustainable debt; see <http://www.worldbank.org>.

[78] US contributions are 17.69 per cent of total quotas.

[79] The 14th General Review of Quotas resulted in:

- doubling quotas from approximately SDR 238.5 billion to approximately SDR 477 billion, (about $715 billion);
- shifting more than 6 per cent of quota shares from over-represented to under-represented member countries;
- shifting more than 6 per cent of quota shares to dynamic emerging market and developing countries ('EMDCs');

to borrow if needed to cope with any threat to the international monetary system. These are the General Arrangements to Borrow ('GAB') established in 1962 between the G-10 governments and Switzerland, and the New Arrangements to Borrow ('NAB') introduced in 1997 with 25 participating lender countries and institutions. Under the two arrangements, the IMF currently has up to SDR 370 billion (about $554 billion) available to lend.[80]

The IMF's Articles of Agreement call for it to oversee the international monetary system, including by exercising firm 'surveillance'—that is, oversight—over its member countries' exchange rate policies.[81] Under the Articles, each member country undertakes to collaborate with the IMF in its efforts to ensure orderly exchange arrangements and to promote a stable system of exchange rates. More specifically, member countries agree to direct policies toward the goals of orderly economic growth with reasonable price stability, together with orderly underlying economic and financial conditions, and to avoid manipulating exchange rates for unfair competitive advantage. In addition, each country undertakes to provide the IMF with the information necessary for its effective surveillance. The membership has agreed that the IMF's surveillance of each member's exchange rate policies has to be carried out within the framework of a comprehensive analysis of the general economic situation and economic policy strategy of the member. **4.86**

The regular monitoring of economies, and associated provision of policy advice, that IMF surveillance involves can help signal dangers ahead and enable members to act in a timely way to avoid trouble. **4.87**

The IMF conducts its oversight in three ways: country surveillance, which takes the form of regular (usually yearly) comprehensive consultations with individual member countries about their economic policies, with interim discussions as needed; global surveillance, which entails reviews by the IMF's Executive Board of global economic trends and developments; and regional surveillance, under which the IMF examines policies pursued under regional arrangements. This includes IMF Board discussions of developments in the European Union, the euro area, the West African Economic and Monetary Union, the Central African Economic and Monetary Community, and the Eastern Caribbean Currency Union. IMF also participates in surveillance discussions of such groups of countries as the G-7 and Asia Pacific Economic Community. **4.88**

Any IMF member country can request IMF support if it has a balance of payments need. The IMF is not, however, an aid agency or a development bank. It lends to help its members tackle balance of payments problems and restore sustainable economic growth.[82] Once IMF **4.89**

- significantly realigning quota shares. As a result, China became the 3rd largest member country in the IMF, and there are four EMDCs (Brazil, China, India, and Russia) among the 10 largest shareholders in the Fund; and
- preserving the quota and voting share of the poorest member countries; see <http://www.imf.org/external/np/exr/facts/quotas.htm>.

80 <http://www.imf.org/external/np/exr/facts/gabnab.htm>.

81 IMF, Articles of Agreement, S 3(b).

82 In March 2009, the IMF announced a major overhaul of its lending framework, including modernising conditionality, introducing a new flexible credit line, enhancing the flexibility of the Fund's regular stand-by lending arrangement, doubling access limits on loans, adapting its cost structures for high-access and precautionary lending, and streamlining instruments that were seldom used. It also introduced speeded up lending procedures and redesigned its Exogenous Shocks Facility to make it easier to access for low-income countries; see

assistance has been agreed, limits on which are set in relation to a member's quota in the IMF, foreign exchange funds are deposited with the country's central bank to supplement its international reserves and thus to give general balance of payments support.

4.90 When a country approaches the IMF for financing, either in the form of standby arrangements or by extended fund facilities,[83] it may be in a state of economic crisis or near-crisis and the IMF provides the country's authorities with advice on the economic policies that may be expected to address the problems most effectively. For the IMF also to provide financing, it must agree with the country's authorities on a programme of policies aimed at meeting specific, quantified goals regarding external viability, monetary and financial stability, and sustainable growth. Details of the programme are spelled out in a 'letter of intent' from the government concerned to the Managing Director of the IMF.[84] IMF lending is conditional upon the acceptance of this IMF programme of policies to correct the borrower country's balance of payments problem and both the borrower country and the IMF must agree on specific economic policies that are required; the IMF disburses funds in phases linked to the borrowing country's actually meeting its scheduled policy commitments.

4.91 IMF funding is also intended to be temporary and repayment periods are relatively short[85] and the IMF expects borrower countries to give priority to the repayment of their loans. IMF borrowers are generally developing countries, countries in transition from central planning to market-based systems, or emerging market countries recovering from financial crises whose access to the international capital markets is limited.

4.92 The IMF is also known for its policy advice and its policy-based lending to countries in times of economic crisis. The objective of this advice is to help strengthen the design and implementation of members' economic policies, including by strengthening skills in the

<http://www.imf.org/external/np/exr/facts/howlend.htm>) More reforms have been in place since November 2011. Lending criteria are set out in the IMF's Standby Lending Arrangements; see <http://www.imf.org/external/np/exr/facts/sba.htm>.

83 As the credit crunch began to affect developing country economies in October 2008, the IMF announced that it had received requests from Belarus, Pakistan, and Hungary to provide financial assistance. The IMF also operates a Poverty Reduction and Growth Facility for certain countries and a supplemental reserve facility to provide short-term financing.

84 The Managing Director of the IMF is Christine Lagarde who was appointed on 5 July 2011.

85 The IMF now has a range of lending facilities available. These include:

- The Extended Credit Facility ('ECF') succeeds the Poverty Reduction and Growth Facility ('PRGF') as the Fund's main tool for providing medium-term support to LICs with protracted balance of payments problems. Financing under the ECF currently carries a zero interest rate, with a grace period of 5½ years, and a final maturity of 10 years.
- The Standby Credit Facility ('SCF') provides financial assistance to LICs with short-term balance of payments needs. The SCF replaces the High-Access Component of the Exogenous Shocks Facility ('ESF'), and can be used in a wide range of circumstances, including on a precautionary basis. Financing under the SCF currently carries a zero interest rate, with a grace period of four years, and a final maturity of eight years.
- The Rapid Credit Facility ('RCF') provides rapid financial assistance with limited conditionality to LICs facing an urgent balance of payments need. The RCF streamlines the Fund's emergency assistance for LICs, and can be used flexibly in a wide range of circumstances. Financing under the RCF currently carries a zero interest rate, has a grace period of 5½ years, and a final maturity of 10 years.
- Stand-By Arrangements ('SBA'). The bulk of non-concessional IMF assistance is provided through SBAs. The SBA is designed to help countries address short-term balance of payments problems. Program targets are designed to address these problems and disbursements are

institutions responsible, such as finance ministries and central banks.[86] The IMF began providing technical assistance in the mid-1960s when many newly independent countries sought help in setting up their central banks and finance ministries. The IMF also provided technical assistance in the early 1990s, when countries in central and eastern Europe and the former Soviet Union began their shift from centrally-planned to market-based economic systems. The IMF offers training courses for government and central bank officials of member countries at its headquarters in Washington and at regional training centres, and through visits by IMF staff, supplemented by hired consultants and experts. The IMF also played an important role in managing the Eurozone sovereign debt crisis in 2012.

made conditional on achieving these targets ('conditionality'). The length of a SBA is typically 12–24 months, and repayment is due within 3¼–5 years of disbursement. SBAs may be provided on a precautionary basis—where countries choose not to draw upon approved amounts but retain the option to do so if conditions deteriorate—both within the normal access limits and in cases of exceptional access. The SBA provides for flexibility with respect to phasing, with front-loaded access where appropriate.

- Flexible Credit Line ('FCL'). The FCL is for countries with very strong fundamentals, policies, and track records of policy implementation and is useful for both crisis prevention and crisis resolution. FCL arrangements are approved, at the member country's request, for countries meeting pre-set qualification criteria. The length of the FCL is one or two years (with an interim review of continued qualification after one year) and the repayment period the same as for the SBA. Access is determined on a case-by-case basis, is not subject to the normal access limits, and is available in a single up-front disbursement rather than phased. Disbursements under the FCL are not conditional on implementation of specific policy understandings as is the case under the SBA because FCL-eligible countries are trusted to be able to implement appropriate macroeconomic policies. There is flexibility to either draw on the credit line at the time it is approved or treat it as precautionary. In case a member country draws, the repayment term is the same as that under the SBA.
- Precautionary and Liquidity Line ('PLL'). The PLL replaced the Precautionary Credit Line ('PCL'), building on its strengths and enhancing its flexibility. The PLL can be used for both crisis prevention and crisis resolution purposes by countries with sound fundamentals and policies, and a track record of implementing such policies.

  Duration of PLL arrangements can be either six months or 1–2 years. Access under the six-month PLL is limited to 250 per cent of quota in normal times, but this limit can be raised to 500 per cent of quota in exceptional circumstances where the balance of payments need is due to exogenous shocks, including heightened regional or global stress. 1–2 year PLL arrangements are subject to an annual access limit of 500 per cent of quota and a cumulative limit of 1000 per cent of quota. The repayment term of the PLL is the same as for the SBA.
- Extended Fund Facility ('EFF'). This facility was established in 1974 to help countries address medium- and longer-term balance of payments problems reflecting extensive distortions that require fundamental economic reforms. Arrangements under the EFF are thus longer than SBAs—normally not exceeding three years at approval, with a maximum extension of up to one year where appropriate. However, a maximum duration of up to four years at approval is also allowed, predicated on the existence of a balance of payments need beyond the three-year period, the prolonged nature of the adjustment required to restore macroeconomic stability, and the presence of adequate assurances about the member's ability and willingness to implement deep and sustained structural reforms. Repayment is due within 4½–10 years from the date of disbursement.
- Rapid Financing Instrument ('RFI'). The RFI was introduced to replace and broaden the scope of the earlier emergency assistance policies. The RFI provides rapid financial assistance with limited conditionality to all members facing an urgent balance of payments need. Access under the RFI is subject to an annual limit of 50 per cent of quota and a cumulative limit of 100 per cent of quota. Emergency loans are subject to the same terms as the FCL, PLL and SBA, with repayment within 3¼–5 years; see <http://www.imf.org/external/np/exr/facts/howlend.htm>.

[86] In 2013 the IMF announced its intention to set up an 'IMF University' to provide online access to policy, economics and other courses to improve understanding of economic policy issues by governments and individuals around the world; see <http://www.imf.org/external/np/sec/pr/2013/pr13221.htm>.

4.93 The IMF also works with national governments and other international institutions to:

- strengthen the legal, regulatory, and supervisory frameworks for banks;
- review minimum capital requirements for banks and financial institutions;
- develop a core set of international accounting standards;
- finalise a set of core principles for good corporate governance;
- avoid exchange rate regimes that are vulnerable to attack; and
- ensure a freer flow of timely financial data to markets.[87]

4.94 The IMF has also been working with the Basel Committee on Banking Supervision to improve regulatory standards.

4.95 Although the financing capacity of the IMF itself is considerable, the greater part of international financial flows comprises private flows. The IMF therefore works with the private sector to manage and resolve financial crises and to reduce the impact of economic turmoil by improving risk assessment and encouraging closer and more frequent discussion between countries and private investors. In September 2000, the IMF has established a Capital Markets Consultative Group to provide a basis for regular communication between international capital market participants and the IMF on matters including global economic and market developments and the development of measures to strengthen the global financial system.

4.96 When economic or financial crises do occur, IMF-supported programmes are expected to be able to restore stability through their mix of official financing, policy adjustments, and associated gains in confidence among private investors. In certain cases, however, such actions as coordinated debt restructuring by private creditors may be needed. IMF members have agreed on some principles to guide the involvement of the private sector in crisis resolution.

4.97 The IMF collaborates actively with the World Bank, the regional development banks, the World Trade Organisation, the United Nations agencies, and other international bodies. The IMF is also a member of the Financial Stability Board, which brings together the national authorities responsible for financial stability in significant international financial centres, international regulatory and supervisory bodies, committees of central bank experts, and international financial institutions.[88]

4.98 The World Bank Group, on the other hand, provides funding to many of the world's low-income countries who are generally excluded from the international money markets or who cannot afford to do so at high interest rates. Direct contributions and loans from developed countries are made by the World Bank Group to these countries who receive grants, interest-free loans, and technical assistance from the World Bank to enable them to provide basic services including education and medical programmes (including HIV/AIDS). In the case of the World Bank loans, countries have 35 to 40 years to repay, with a 10-year grace period.

4.99 Interest-free credit and grant financing from the International Development Association ('IDA') is funded by some 50 of the developed countries that provide the money for this

87 See para 4.213.

88 The Financial Stability Board is the successor of the Financial Stability Forum. See 'IMF Membership in the Financial Stability Board', Legal and Monetary and Capital Markets Departments of the IMF, 22 February 2013: see <http://www.imf.org/external/np/pp/eng/2013/022213.pdf>.

funding by making contributions every four years.[89] IDA credits make up about one quarter of the Bank's financial assistance but aside from IDA funds, very little of the Bank's income is provided by its member countries.

In 1996, with the IMF, the World Bank launched the Heavily Indebted Poor Countries ('HIPC') Initiative in an effort to cut the debts of the world's poorest, most indebted countries. The HIPC Initiative, combined with other types of debt relief, will cut by two-thirds the external debt in these countries, lowering their debt levels to below the overall average for developing countries.[90] **4.100**

Higher-income developing countries can receive loans from the IBRD. Countries that borrow from the IBRD can repay over longer time periods than if they had borrowed from a commercial bank.[91] Developing country governments borrow money for specific programmes, including poverty reduction efforts, delivery of social services, protection of the environment, and promotion of economic growth that will improve living standards.[92] The IBRD raises almost all its money in the world's financial markets—$35 billion in fiscal 2012.[93] With an AAA credit rating, the IBRD issues bonds to raise money and then passes on the low interest rates to its borrowers. **4.101**

The World Bank Group also acts in collaboration with other institutions in fighting international poverty. For example, it has worked with governments and the private sector to launch the new BioCarbon Fund and with the International Emissions Trading Association ('IETA') to launch the Community Development Carbon Fund ('CDCF'). It has also joined with the Food and Agriculture Organisation ('FAO') and the United Nations Development Programme ('UNDP') to sponsor the Consultative Group on International Agricultural Research ('CGIAR') to reduce hunger and poverty, improve human nutrition and health, and protect the environment. Through the Consultative Group to Assist the Poor ('CGAP'), the World Bank has worked with these and other donor organisations[94] to provide access to financial services (such as loans and savings) for the poor, including microfinance. **4.102**

---

89 The US, UK, and Japan are the largest contributors to IDA funding. See: <http://www.worldbank.org/ida/papers/IDA16_Donor_Contributions_Table_1.pdf>.

90 See World Bank, 'Heavily Indebted Poor Countries (HIPC) Initiative and Multilateral Debt Relief Initiative (MDRI)—Status of Implementation and Proposals for the Future of the HIPC Initiative', 8 November 2011.

91 IBRD loans are relatively flexible and can be repaid by borrowers in periods up to 30 years including grace period, as long as the weighted average maturity does not exceed 18 years. See: <http://treasury.worldbank.org/bdm/pdf/IFL_MajorTermsConditions_en.pdf>.

92 In fiscal 2012 IBRD provided loans totaling more than US$35 billion supporting 11,728 projects in 172 countries; see <http://www.worldbank.org/projects>.

93 See World Bank website: <http://www.go.worldbank.org/LAG4BZ1VD1>.

94 For example, the Bill and Melinda Gates Foundation to establish the Global Financial Inclusion (Global Findex) Database to measure how people in 148 countries save, borrow, make payments, and manage risk. See A Demirguc-Kunt and L Klapper, World Bank Policy Research Working Paper 6025, 'Measuring Financial Inclusion–The Global Findex Database', April 2012; available at: <http://www-wds.worldbank.org/external/default/WDSContentServer/IW3P/IB/2012/04/19/000158349_20120419083611/Rendered/PDF/WPS6025.pdf>.

The Bank for International Settlements

4.103 The Bank for International Settlements ('BIS') was established in 1930,[95] making it the oldest international financial institution and the principal centre for international central bank cooperation.

4.104 In the aftermath of the First World War, the BIS was established as part of the Young Plan (1930)[96] to deal with the issue of the reparation payments imposed on Germany by the Treaty of Versailles. The BIS quickly outgrew this role and the Bank's activities focused on cooperation among central banks and other agencies with a special function in promoting monetary and financial stability.

4.105 Central bank cooperation through the BIS has taken place through the regular meetings in Basel, the Bank's headquarters,[97] of central bank governors and other experts. The Bank has its own secretariat and has developed its own research facilities in financial and monetary economics. It also performs an international function in collating and disseminating global economic and financial statistics.

4.106 International cooperation came to the fore again in the aftermath of World War II, and until the early 1970s BIS focused on implementing and defending the Bretton Woods system.[98] In the 1970s and 1980s, the BIS's focus was on managing cross-border capital flows during the oil crises and the international debt crisis. The 1970's banking crisis also brought the issue of regulatory supervision of internationally active banks to the fore, resulting in the 1988 Basel Capital Accord and its 'Basel II' revision of 2001 to 2006. More recently, as a result of the

---

[95] Hague Convention respecting the Bank for International Settlements of 20 January 1930, 104 League of Nations Treaty Series 441.

[96] The Young Plan was adopted by the Allied Powers in 1930 and set the total war reparations at $26,350,000,000 to be paid by Germany to the Allies over a period of 58½ years. Global economic depression of the 1930s was already deepening and a payment moratorium was called for the fiscal year 1931–32. When the Nazi party took over Germany, Germany defaulted on the unpaid reparations debt. After Germany's defeat in the Second World War, an international conference decided in 1953 that Germany would pay the remaining debt only after the country was reunified. Nonetheless, West Germany paid off the principal by 1980; then in 1995, after reunification, the new German Government announced it would resume payments of the remaining interest.

[97] BIS has recognised international status through the Agreement between the Swiss Federal Council and the Bank for International Settlements to determine the Bank's legal status in Switzerland of 1 February 1987 as amended, Compendium of Swiss Laws (0.192.122.971.3) such that the property and assets of the BIS—along with assets of third parties entrusted to the BIS— have immunity in Switzerland and certain other jurisdictions from such measures as expropriation, seizure, or confiscation. The BIS has also been granted various immunities in the People's Republic of China, where the BIS has a representative office in Hong Kong, SAR, and in Mexico.

[98] The Bretton Woods system of international economic management was established in 1944 to set out the rules for commercial and financial relations among the world's major industrial states. In July 1944, delegates from all 44 Allied nations gathered at the Mount Washington Hotel, situated in the New Hampshire resort town of Bretton Woods, for the United Nations Monetary and Financial Conference and the resulting Bretton Woods Agreement set up a system of rules, institutions, and procedures to regulate the international political economy. The Agreement established the framework for the International Bank for Reconstruction and Development (later the World Bank) and the International Monetary Fund. The chief features of the Bretton Woods system were an obligation for each country to adopt a monetary policy that maintained the exchange rate of its currency within a fixed value—plus or minus 1 per cent—in terms of gold; and the provision by the International Monetary Fund of finance to bridge temporary payments imbalances. The system eventually collapsed in 1971 following the United States' suspension of convertibility from dollars to gold.

1997 Asian economic crisis, the issue of financial stability in the wake of economic integration and globalisation has been at the BIS's centre of attention.

The Bank operates within the terms of its Statutes[99] and its three most important decision-making bodies are: **4.107**

- the General Meeting of member central banks;
- its Board of Directors; and
- the Management of the Bank.

The BIS has 60 member central banks,[100] all of which are entitled to be represented and vote in the General Meetings. Voting power is determined by the number of BIS shares issued in the country of each member represented at the meeting. **4.108**

The BIS Board of Directors has 19 members and six ex officio directors, comprising the governors of the central banks of Belgium, France, Germany, Italy, and the UK, and the Chairman of the Board of Governors of the US Federal Reserve System.[101] Each ex officio member appoints another member of the same nationality. The BIS Statutes also provide for the election to the Board of not more than nine governors of other member central banks.[102] The Board of Directors elects a chairman and vice-chairman from among its members for a three-year term. **4.109**

The Board, which meets at least six times per year, is responsible for determining the strategic and policy direction of the BIS, supervising the management, and fulfilling the specific tasks given to it by the Bank's Statutes. The Consultative Committee and the Audit Committee, made up of selected Board members, also assist the Board in its work. **4.110**

Apart from providing the forum for monetary policy cooperation, the BIS also carries out certain banking functions for the central bank community (eg gold and foreign exchange transactions), as well as trustee and agency functions. The BIS's statutes require it 'to serve as a prime counterparty for central banks in their financial transactions, by providing an appropriate range of banking services and maintaining its reputation for absolute confidentiality and security'. **4.111**

The BIS has, therefore, developed a range of banking services specifically designed to assist central banks and monetary authorities in the management of their foreign exchange and gold reserves. It also acts as a banker to, and manages funds for, international financial institutions. The BIS does not accept deposits from, or generally provide financial services to, private individuals or corporate entities, nor is it permitted to make advances to governments or open current accounts in their name. The BIS was the agent for the European Payments Union,[103] **4.112**

---

99 <http://www.bis.org/about/statutes-en.pdf>.

100 Members are the central banks or monetary authorities of:

Algeria, Argentina, Australia, Austria, Belgium, Bosnia and Herzegovina, Brazil, Bulgaria, Canada, Chile, China, Colombia, Croatia, the Czech Republic, Denmark, Estonia, Finland, France, Germany, Greece, Hong Kong SAR, Hungary, Iceland, India, Indonesia, Ireland, Israel, Italy, Japan, Korea, Latvia, Lithuania, Luxembourg, Macedonia (FYR), Malaysia, Mexico, the Netherlands, New Zealand, Norway, Peru, the Philippines, Poland, Portugal, Romania, Russia, Saudi Arabia, Serbia, Singapore, Slovakia, Slovenia, South Africa, Spain, Sweden, Switzerland, Thailand, Turkey, the United Arab Emirates, the United Kingdom, and the United States, plus the European Central Bank; see <http://www.bis.org/about/orggov.htm>.

101 <http://www.bis.org/about/board.htm>.

102 The governors of the central banks of Canada, Japan, the Netherlands, Sweden, and Switzerland are currently the elected members of the Board.

103 The European Payments Union ('EPU') was established on 1 July 1950 by the country members of the Organisation for European Economic Cooperation ('OEEC') as an organisation of European recipients of US

helping the European currencies restore convertibility after the Second World War. Similarly, the BIS has acted as the agent for various European exchange rate arrangements, including the European Monetary System[104] which preceded the move to a single currency.

4.113 The BIS has also provided or organised emergency financing to support the international monetary system when required.[105] During the Great Depression, the BIS organised support credits for both the Austrian and German central banks and, in the 1960s, the BIS arranged special support credits for the Italian lira and the French franc and the Group Arrangements to support sterling.[106] More recently, the BIS has provided finance for Mexico in 1982 and Brazil in 1998 in the context of IMF-led stabilisation programmes and worked with the IMF to provide funding during the Eurozone sovereign debt crisis.

4.114 In addition to the BIS's secretariat, a number of other international committees and organisations focusing on financial stability and the international financial system have their headquarters at the BIS. These include the Group of Ten[107] which comprises of the governors of the central banks of Belgium, Canada, France, Germany, Italy, Japan, the Netherlands, Sweden, Switzerland, the UK, and the USA which has established a number of standing committees to study the functioning and architecture of international financial markets. The most important of these standing committees are the Markets Committee,[108] the Committee on the Global Financial System,[109] the Central Bank Governance Forum,[110]

economic assistance. The EPU was intended to be a temporary system, designed to assist European countries 'until they are fully able to take their place in a world-wide system'. The EPU was a multilateral settlement scheme set up to achieve the ideal of trade equilibrium among members and removal of trade discriminations.

[104] The European Monetary System was organised in 1979 to stabilise foreign exchange and counter inflation among its members. After 1986, changes in national interest rates were used to keep the currencies within a narrow range (the Exchange Rate Mechanism) but in the early 1990s the EMS was strained by the differing economic policies and conditions between its members, and in September 1992 Britain permanently withdrew from the system.

[105] The BIS extends short-term credits to central banks, usually on a collateralised basis. From time to time, the BIS also coordinates emergency short-term lending to countries in financial crisis. In these circumstances, the BIS advances funds on behalf of, and with the backing and guarantee of, a group of supporting central banks. It does not lend to governments or to individual financial institutions; see <http://www.bis.org/banking/>.

[106] See FJ Garvin, *Gold, Dollars and Power: the politics of monetary relations 1958–1971* (2003).

[107] The Group of Ten (G-10) refers to the group of countries (Belgium, Canada, France, Germany, Italy, Japan, the Netherlands, Sweden, Switzerland, the UK, and the USA) that have agreed to participate in the General Agreements to Borrow, a supplementary borrowing arrangement that can be invoked if the IMF's resources are estimated to be below its members' needs. The General Agreements to Borrow was established in 1962 when the governments of eight IMF members—Belgium, Canada, France, Italy, Japan, the Netherlands, the UK, and the USA—and the central banks of two others, Germany and Sweden, agreed to make resources available to the IMF for drawings by participants, and, under certain circumstances, for drawings by non-participants. The Group was strengthened in 1964 by the association of Switzerland, then a non-member of the IMF, but the name of the G-10 remained the same, hence there are actually 11 members. The Bank for International Settlements (BIS), European Commission, IMF, and OECD are also official observers of the activities of the G-10. Source: IMF, Factsheet: a Guide to Committees, Groups and Clubs, September 2005.

[108] The Markets Committee (formerly known as the Committee on Gold and Foreign Exchange) was established in 1962 and when the Gold Pool arrangements collapsed in 1968, members continued to meet at the BIS for open and informal exchanges of views focusing on recent developments in foreign exchange and related financial markets, an exchange of views on possible future trends, and consideration of the short-run implications of particular current events for the functioning of these markets.

[109] The Committee on the Global Financial System monitors and examines broad issues relating to the financial markets and systems with a view to elaborating appropriate policy recommendations and assisting the governors of the G-10 central banks in recognising, analysing, and responding to threats to the stability of financial markets and the global financial system.

[110] The Central Bank Governance Forum compiles, analyses, and disseminates a wide variety of information on governance and organisational arrangements among central banks. The group also serves as a venue for the exchange of views among governors on matters relating to the design and operation of their institutions. The

the Basel Committee on Banking Supervision,[111] and the Committee on Payment and Settlement Systems[112] and the Irving Fisher Committee on Central Bank Statistics.[113]

These standing committees promote cooperation through the exchange of information and expertise. Committees are usually chaired by senior officials of member central banks and are composed of experts from the central banks. In the case of the Basel Committee, members also include non-central bank supervisory authorities. Committee members are mainly (but not exclusively) from G-10 countries. Some committees also develop and propose common international standards that are implemented through national legislation. **4.115**

The BIS headquarters also hosts the secretariats of a number of independent organisations that do not have any direct reporting links to the BIS or its member central banks. These are the Financial Stability Board ('FSB'), the International Association of Insurance Supervisors ('IAIS'), and the International Association of Deposit Insurers ('IADI').[114] **4.116**

Established in 1994, the IAIS represents insurance supervisory authorities of some 200 jurisdictions in 140 countries. The IAIS was formed to promote cooperation among insurance supervisory authorities, to set international standards for insurance supervision and regulation, to provide training to members, and to coordinate work with regulators in the other financial sectors and international financial institutions, and its secretariat is hosted by the BIS. **4.117**

The IAIS issues global insurance principles, standards, and guidance papers for the industry and provides its members with training and support on issues related to insurance supervision. It also organises meetings and seminars for insurance supervisors and holds an annual conference for supervisory and industry representatives. The IAIS works closely with other standard setting bodies such as the International Insurance Foundation and the International Insurance Society. The day-to-day operations of the IAIS are carried out by its Executive Committee, whose members represent different geographical regions. It is supported by three main committees—the Technical Committee which oversees global insurance regulatory and supervisory standards; the Emerging Markets Committee which **4.118**

focus is on the institutional and organisational setting in which central banks pursue monetary and financial policies, not the policies themselves; see <http://www.bis.org/about/cbgov.htm>.

111 The Basel Committee is the primary global standard-setter for the prudential regulation of banks and provides a forum for cooperation on banking supervisory matters. Its mandate is to strengthen the regulation, supervision and practices of banks worldwide with the purpose of enhancing financial stability. The Committee reports to the Group of Governors and Heads of Supervision ('GHOS'). The Committee seeks the endorsement of GHOS for its major decisions and its work programme; see <http://www.bis.org/bcbs/about.htm>.

112 See para 4.141; The Committee on Payment and Settlement Systems ('CPSS') was originally established in 1980 to address issues concerning the development of electronic funds transfer systems and the question of competition and cooperation in payment systems. In 1989 the G-10 Governors set up an ad hoc Committee on Interbank Netting Schemes to study in more detail the policy issues relating to cross-border and multicurrency inter-bank netting schemes, including a set of minimum standards for the operation of bilateral and multilateral netting schemes and an agreed approach for the joint oversight of such systems.

113 The Irving Fisher Committee on Central Bank Statistics is a forum of central bank economists and statisticians, as well as others who want to participate in discussing statistical issues of interest to central banks. It is associated with the International Statistical Institute (ISI); see <http://www.bis.org/ifc/index.htm>.

114 The IADI's objectives are to contribute to the stability of financial systems by promoting international cooperation in the field of deposit insurance and to encourage wide international contact among deposit insurers and other interested parties. The Association seeks to enhance the understanding of common interests and issues related to deposit insurance, set out guidance to enhance the effectiveness of deposit insurance systems, with such guidance taking into account different circumstances, settings, and structures, and facilitate the sharing and exchange of expertise on deposit insurance issues through training, development, and educational programmes as well as providing advice on the establishment or enhancement of effective deposit insurance systems.

assists emerging insurance markets to establish sound insurance supervisory systems; and the Budget Committee which controls the finances of the IAIS. These committees organise a number of working groups to accomplish their objectives including the Financial Conglomerates Subcommittee which coordinates the work of IAIS members for the Joint Forum, the Insurance Fraud Subcommittee which analyses fraudulent activities by or on insurance companies and seeks to help prevent and detect insurance fraud in the industry, and the Insurance Laws, Regulations, Practices and Standards Subcommittee which collects and analyses information through a global insurance laws database.

4.119 The IAIS has issued a number of documents relating to the regulation and supervision of insurance including its insurance core principles and methodology,[115] the Insurance Concordat regarding the supervision of cross-border insurance activities,[116] principles for the conduct of insurance business,[117] and principles for carrying on insurance business over the Internet.[118] IAIS has also been active in establishing detailed standards relating to capital adequacy and solvency for insurers and reinsurers.[119]

4.120 IAIS has also been very involved in the establishment of certain standards for the industry and the development of best or most prudent practices. In some cases, these standards set out best practices for a supervisory authority; in others, they describe the practices a well managed insurer would be expected to follow and thereby assist supervisors in assessing the practices that companies in their jurisdictions should have in place.

The Basel Committee

4.121 The Committee on Banking Regulations and Supervisory Practices or the Basel Committee was established at the end of 1974 and comprises members from Argentina, Australia, Belgium, Brazil, Canada, China, France, Germany, Hong Kong, India, Indonesia, Italy, Japan, Korea, Luxembourg, Mexico, Netherlands, Russia, Saudi Arabia, Singapore, South Africa, Spain, Sweden, Switzerland, Turkey, United Kingdom, United States, and observers from the European Commission, European Central Bank, European Banking Authority, International Monetary Fund, and Financial Stability Institute.[120]

These countries are represented by their respective central banks and also by the authority with formal responsibility for the prudential supervision of banking business where this is not the central bank, such as the UK Prudential Regulation Authority. The Basel Committee meets regularly four times a year and it has five main expert sub-committees:

- The Supervision and Implementation Group
- The Policy Development Group
- The Macroprudential Supervision Group
- The Accounting Task Force
- The Basel Consultative Group

115 Insurance core principles and methodology, October 2003.

116 Principles applicable to the supervision of international insurers and insurance groups and their cross-border business operations, December 1999.

117 Principles for conduct of insurance business, December 1999.

118 Principles for the supervision of insurance activities on the Internet, October 2004.

119 Principles on capital adequacy and solvency, January 2002.

120 <http://www.bis.org/bcbs/membership.htm>.

and a number of technical working groups[121] and task forces on specific topics that also meet regularly.

The Basel Committee's role is to provide a forum for banking supervisors and to formulate broad supervisory standards and guidelines and to recommend statements of best practice for the banking industry. It has no power to make or enforce those standards and individual national authorities must take the necessary steps—statutory or otherwise—to implement them. The Committee does not, therefore, have any formal supranational supervisory authority, and its conclusions do not, and were never intended to, have legal force. The role of the Committee is therefore to encourage convergence among its members and other countries to adopt common approaches and common standards without harmonisation of the detail of member countries' supervisory techniques. **4.122**

The Basel Committee reports to the central bank governors of the G-10 countries and seeks the G-10 governors' endorsement for its major initiatives. The Committee's Secretariat is provided by the BIS. The Secretariat is staffed mainly by professional supervisors on temporary secondment from member institutions and in addition to its secretarial work for the Committee and its many expert sub-committees, the Secretariat also provides advice to supervisory authorities in both member and non-member countries. **4.123**

In 1983 the Committee finalised an agreement (the Concordat) that set out the principles for sharing supervisory responsibility for foreign banks and their branches (Principles for the Supervision of Bank's Foreign Establishments) on the basis that no foreign banking establishment should be able to avoid supervision and that supervision should be adequate. Further amendments of this Concordat have added to it further minimum standards for the supervision of banks and mechanisms for the sharing of information, the consolidated supervision of banking groups, and the exchange of prudential information between banking supervisors in different countries. **4.124**

The Basel Accord

In 1988, the Committee introduced a capital measurement system commonly referred to as the Basel Capital Accord which sought to introduce a credit risk measurement framework with a minimum capital standard of 8 per cent by 1992 for all banking institutions in the Member States. This framework has been progressively introduced not only in member countries but also in virtually all other countries with active international banks. This document set out the agreement among the G-10 central banks to apply common minimum capital standards to their banking industries, to be achieved by end-year 1992. The standards adopted are almost entirely addressed to credit risk, the main risk incurred by banks and the agreement contains two main sections, (a) the definition of capital, and (b) the structure of risk weights. **4.125**

The agreement also defines the target standard ratio and the transitional and implementing arrangements and four technical annexes covering the definition of capital, the counterparty **4.126**

[121] These working groups include the Accord Implementation Group, the Capital Task Force, International Liaison Group (with 16 non-G-10 countries), Working Group on Corporate Governance, Cross-Border Banking Group, Electronic Banking Group, Joint Forum (with IAIS and IOSCO), Joint IOSCO–BCBS Working Group on Trading Book, and the Research Task Force.

risk weights, the credit conversion factors for off-balance-sheet items and the transitional arrangements as also included. Since 1988, five amendments to the Accord have been made to the agreement.

Basel II

4.127 In June 1999, the Committee issued a new proposal for a New Capital Adequacy Framework (Basel II)[122] to replace the 1988 Accord that was finally adopted in June 2004 and implemented from 1 January 2007, although certain provisions were deferred to year-end 2007. This text is intended to serve as the basis for national rule-making and approval processes to continue, and for banking organisations to complete their preparations for Basel II's implementation.

4.128 Basel II represents a major revision of the international standard on bank capital adequacy that was introduced in 1988. It aligns the capital measurement framework with sound contemporary practices in banking, promotes improvements in risk management, and is intended to enhance financial stability.

4.129 The Basel II capital framework consists of three pillars: minimum capital requirements, which seek to refine the standardised rules set forth in the 1988 Accord; supervisory review of an institution's internal assessment process and capital adequacy; and effective use of disclosure to strengthen market discipline as a complement to supervisory efforts.

4.130 The Basel II framework represents the work of the Committee to secure international convergence on supervisory regulations governing the capital adequacy of internationally active banks.

4.131 Following the publication of the first round of proposals for revising the capital adequacy framework in June 1999,[123] a consultation process was carried out by all of the Committee's member countries as well as quantitative impact studies, and the proposals were circulated to supervisory authorities worldwide.

4.132 The result of that process, which was endorsed by the Central Bank Governors and Heads of Banking Supervision of the G-10 countries, is an agreed framework for measuring capital adequacy and the minimum standards to be achieved which the national supervisory authorities represented on the Committee proposed for adoption in their respective countries.

4.133 The Basel II framework is designed to establish minimum levels of capital for internationally active banks. As under the 1988 Accord, national authorities are free to adopt arrangements that set higher levels of minimum capital and may put in place supplementary measures of capital adequacy for the banking organisations they authorise or license. More generally, under the second pillar, supervisors should expect banks to operate above minimum regulatory capital levels.

---

122 Basel Committee on Banking Supervision: 'Basel II, International Convergence of Capital Measurement and Capital Standards: a Revised Framework', Publication 107 (June 2004).

123 Basel Committee on Banking Supervision: 'A New Capital Adequacy Framework', Publication 50 (June 1999).

National authorities may use a supplementary capital measure as a way to address, for example, the potential uncertainties in the accuracy of the measure of risk exposures inherent in any capital rule or to constrain the extent to which an organisation may fund itself with debt. Where a national authority uses a supplementary capital measure (such as a leverage ratio or a large exposure limit) in conjunction with the measure set forth in this framework, in some instances the capital required under the supplementary measure may be more binding. This framework is intended to promote stronger risk management practices within the banking industry based on the three pillars of minimum capital requirements, supervisory review, and disclosure for market discipline. The Committee specifically sought to establish more risk-sensitive capital requirements that are conceptually sound, and paid due regard to particular features of the present supervisory and accounting systems in individual member countries. **4.134**

One significant innovation of the Basel II framework is the greater use of risk assessments provided by banks' internal systems as inputs to regulatory capital calculations. Basel II also sets out a detailed set of minimum requirements designed to ensure the integrity of these internal risk assessments, and each supervisor must develop their own set of review procedures for ensuring that banks' systems and controls are adequate to serve as the basis for the capital calculations. **4.135**

The Basel II framework provides a range of options for determining the capital requirements for credit risk and operational risk in order to allow banks and supervisors to select approaches that are most appropriate for their operations and their financial market infrastructure, and it allows for a limited degree of national discretion in the way in which each of these options may be applied, to adapt the standards to different conditions of national markets. Monitoring and review of the Basel II framework will be carried out by the Accord Implementation Group ('AIG') to promote consistency in the framework's application by encouraging supervisors to exchange information with each other on their implementation approaches. Based on the work of the AIG, the Committee has issued general principles for the cross-border implementation of the Basel II framework, and more focused principles for the recognition of operational risk capital charges under advanced measurement approaches for home and host supervisors.[124] **4.136**

The Basel II framework also highlights the need for banks and supervisors to give attention to the second (supervisory review) and third (market discipline) pillars. The Basel Committee has also stated its awareness of the need for interaction between regulatory and accounting approaches at both the national and international level and the impact that the comparability of the resulting measures of capital adequacy and for the costs associated with the implementation of these approaches has on the industry.[125] **4.137**

The Basel Committee is continuing to look at evolving issues for the industry such as combating terrorist financing, supervisory practices for dealing with weak banks, risk management in electronic banking, the management and supervision of operational risk, transparency and disclosure by banks, accounting and auditing issues, and the cooperation between banking supervisors including discussion and information sharing. **4.138**

---

[124] Basel Committee on Banking Supervision: 'Implementation of Basel II: Practical Considerations', Publication 109 (July 2004).

[125] Basel II: International Convergence of Capital Measurement and Capital Standards: A Revised Framework, June 2004; available at: <http://www.bis.org/publ/bcbs107.htm>.

4.139 More recently, the Committee has moved more aggressively to promote other supervisory standards worldwide. In collaboration with many non-G-10 supervisory authorities, the Committee in 1997 developed 'Core Principles for Effective Banking Supervision',[126] that provides a comprehensive blueprint for an effective supervisory system and to facilitate implementation and assessment for supervisory purposes, the Committee developed the 'Core Principles Methodology'[127] in 1999.

4.140 The Committee has encouraged contacts and cooperation between its members and other banking supervisory authorities and other supervisors in financial services, in particular the International Organisation of Securities Commissions ('IOSCO') in areas of mutual concern such as the management of derivatives activities in banks and securities houses, and it has worked closely with IOSCO and the IAIS to consider the risk and prudential requirements for diversified financial conglomerates.

4.141 The Basel Committee also circulates to supervisors throughout the world research papers and statistical information, and it holds an International Conference of Banking Supervisors that takes place every two years.

Basel III

4.142 Basel III is part of the Committee's continuing efforts to enhance the banking regulatory framework and builds on the Basel II framework. Basel III is a comprehensive set of reform measures,[128] developed by the Basel Committee to strengthen the regulation, supervision and risk management of the banking sector. These measures aim to improve the banking sector's ability to absorb shocks arising from financial and economic stress whatever the source, improve risk management and governance, and strengthen banks' transparency and disclosures. Basel III principally consists of enhanced Core Equity Tier 1 ('CET1') capital requirements, with a 4.5 per cent minimum ration, 2.5 per cent conservation buffer, 0–2.5 per cent counter-cyclical buffer, and 1–3 per cent systemic risk buffer, as well as a short 30-day Liquidity Coverage Ration ('LCR') and 1-year Net Table Funding Ratio ('NSRF') and a minimum leverage ratio of 3 per cent own funds.

4.143 Reforms have included bank-level, or micro-prudential, regulation, which will help raise the resilience of individual banking institutions during periods of stress, as well as macro-prudential system wide risks that can build up across the banking sector and the procyclical amplification of these risks over time.[129] These two approaches to supervision are intended to be complementary as greater resilience at the individual bank level reduces the risk of system wide shocks. The Committee has also adopted other reform papers in areas such as bank

[126] Basel Committee on Banking Supervision: 'Core Principles for Effective Banking Supervision', Publication 30 (September 1997).

[127] Basel Committee on Banking Supervision: 'Core Principles Methodology', Publication 61 (October 1999).

[128] See Basel III: A global regulatory framework for more resilient banks and banking systems, December 2010 (rev June 2011): see <http://www.bis.org/publ/bcbs189.pdf>, and Basel III: The Liquidity Coverage Ratio and liquidity risk monitoring tools, January 2013; see <http://www.bis.org/publ/bcbs238.pdf>.

[129] See Basel III: A global regulatory framework for more resilient banks and banking systems, December 2010 (rev June 2011); see <http://www.bis.org/publ/bcbs189.pdf>, and Basel III: The Liquidity Coverage Ratio and liquidity risk monitoring tools. January 2013; see <http://www.bis.org/publ/bcbs238.pdf>.

remuneration,[130] cross-border insolvency and resolution[131] and the operation of the supervisory colleges.[132]

Financial Stability Institute

In 1999, the BIS and the Basel Committee created the Financial Stability Institute ('FSI') to assist supervisors around the world in improving and strengthening their financial systems. The objectives of the FSI are to promote sound supervisory standards and practices globally, and to support full implementation of these standards in all countries, to provide supervisors with the latest information on market products, practices, and techniques to help them adapt to rapid innovations in the financial sector, to help supervisors develop solutions to their multiple challenges by sharing experiences in focused seminars and regional workshops, and to assist supervisors in employing the practices and tools that will allow them to meet everyday demands and tackle more ambitious goals. **4.144**

The aim of FSI is to produce skilled supervisors who are key to the effective supervision of the financial sector. Supervisors need to understand the risks inherent in financial activities and establish an adequate framework of supervision and regulation. The FSI therefore provides banking supervisors with information and technical support including organising topical seminars and special meetings for banking supervisors, holding regional workshops and seminars for banking supervisors, and providing both document and Internet-based information through its FSI Connect and FSI Information programme. **4.145**

The Committee on Payment and Settlement Systems

In 1980, the governors of the central banks of the G-10 countries established a Group of Experts on Payment Systems whose purpose was to take forward work on payment system issues including addressing concerns about the development of electronic funds transfer systems. The Group of Experts on Payment Systems also studied the characteristics of new types of inter-bank netting schemes, on which the Bank for International Settlements published a report in 1989.[133] In 1989, the G-10 Governors set up an ad hoc Committee on Inter-bank Netting Schemes to study the policy issues relating to cross-border and multicurrency inter-bank netting schemes. **4.146**

As a follow-up to the work of the Committee on Interbank Netting Schemes, and more generally to take over and extend the activities of the Group of Experts on Payment Systems, the G-10 Governors established in 1990 the Committee on Payment and Settlement Systems ('CPSS'). The CPSS is one of the permanent G-10 central bank committees reporting to the G-10 Governors whose secretariat is provided by the BIS in Switzerland. **4.147**

130 Basel Committee on Banking Supervision, Compensation Principles and Standards Assessment Methodology, January 2010; see <http://www.bis.org/publ/bcbs166.pdf>.

131 Basel Committee on Banking Supervision, Report and Recommendations of the Cross-border Bank Resolution Group, March 2010; see <http://www.bis.org/publ/bcbs169.pdf>.

132 Basel Committee on Banking Supervision, Good practice principles on supervisory colleges, October 2010; see <http://www.bis.org/publ/bcbs177.pdf>.

133 Bank for International Settlements: 'Report on Netting Schemes' (February 1989).

4.148 The principal purpose of the CPSS is to analyse and promote awareness of risks and to develop minimum standards or best practices, and the CPSS and its member central banks have played a leading role in promoting efficient and robust payment and settlement arrangements. The CPSS therefore serves as a forum to monitor and analyse developments in domestic payment, settlement, and clearing systems as well as in cross-border and multicurrency settlement schemes, and also developments in domestic payment, settlement, and clearing systems and in cross-border and multicurrency settlement schemes.

4.149 The CPSS also provides a means of coordinating the oversight functions exercised by the central banks with respect to payment systems. In addition to addressing general concerns regarding the efficiency and stability of payment, clearing, settlement, and related arrangements, the CPSS also considers the relationships between payment and settlement arrangements, central bank payment and settlement services, and the major financial markets that are relevant for the conduct of monetary policy.

4.150 Since its creation, the CPSS has published various reports covering large-value funds transfer systems, securities settlement systems, settlement mechanisms for foreign exchange transactions, clearing arrangements for exchange-traded derivatives and retail payment instruments, including electronic money. The CPSS's 'Red Book' on payment systems also provides extensive information on the most important payment and settlement systems in the CPSS countries.

4.151 CPSS also has a role as a standard setter and through the publication of the Core principles for systemically important payment systems, the CPSS/IOSCO Recommendations for Securities Settlement Systems,[134] and the CPSS/IOSCO Recommendations for Central Counterparties,[135] the CPSS has contributed to the establishment of best practice. The CPSS has cooperated with other bodies, including the IOSCO, the Basel Committee, and the G-10 Deputies, to address issues of common concern as well as maintaining contact with many global payment system providers, industry associations, and other regulatory authorities. The Committee has undertaken an active work programme concerning the arrangements for the settlement of securities transactions, and has worked jointly with the Technical Committee of IOSCO to improve the efficiency and security of securities settlement systems worldwide, including cross-border securities settlement arrangements.[136] CPSS also works with other regional payment and settlement bodies in emerging regional central bank groups focusing on payment systems, for instance in eastern and central Europe, in Asian EMEAP countries, and in Latin America.

4.152 The CPSS has also contributed to the discussions surrounding the need for sound risk management in large-value funds transfer systems.[137] The work of the CPSS, such as the Core Principles, has emphasised the importance of payment systems that are 'systemically important', rather than drawing a line exclusively between 'large-value' and 'retail', and looked at

---

[134] Bank for International Settlements: 'Committee on Payment and Settlement Systems, Recommendations for Securities Settlement Systems', Publication 46 (November 2001).

[135] Bank for International Settlements: 'Committee on Payment and Settlement Systems, Recommendations for Central Counterparties', Publication 64 (November 2004).

[136] Both Committees published the final report on the Recommendations for Securities Settlement Systems, see n 103.

[137] Estimates compiled by the CPSS indicate that these systems transfer the equivalent of several trillion dollars per day in CPSS countries, a large portion of which is related to the settlement of financial market transactions.

the introduction of real-time gross settlement systems.[138] The CPSS has recently started new work in the area of large-value payment systems.[139]

Another key aspect of the Committee's work remains the implementation of a strategy to mitigate foreign exchange settlement risk. In 1996, the G-10 Governors endorsed a report prepared by the CPSS entitled 'Settlement risk in foreign exchange transactions'[140] which provided a clear definition of settlement risk in foreign exchange transactions and a corresponding method to measure it properly. The G-10 central banks decided to reaffirm and strengthen the strategy as set out in the July 1998 follow-up report 'Reducing foreign exchange settlement risk: a progress report'. **4.153**

In August 2003, the CPSS published a report on 'The role of central bank money in payment systems'[141] which looked at the issue of competition and cooperation between central banks, and commercial banks and practical issues such as which institutions may have accounts at the central bank, the range of services provided by central banks to meet the needs of account holders, and ways to mitigate credit and liquidity risks. **4.154**

The CPSS has also undertaken substantial work in the area of retail payment instruments and systems, to identify current market trends, and to explore policy issues that may arise for central banks in this context, and it has published three reports[142] analysing the characteristics of systems used in these countries to effect, clear, and settle payments initiated with particular retail payment instruments. The CPSS has also been involved in developing the legal and regulatory framework for 'electronic money'[143] and the G-10 Governors have asked the BIS, in cooperation with the CPSS, to closely monitor global developments of electronic money products and their potential impact on policy issues. **4.155**

Following the failure of Barings in the early 1990s, the CPSS undertook a systematic review and analysis of risks in clearing arrangements for derivatives in the G-10 countries. It published a report in March 1997[144] which describes the structure of the clearing arrangements for exchange-traded derivatives, and which identifies possible weaknesses in such arrangements. The CPSS has also been involved in the development of new payment system services by various providers, both domestic and international, and in this connection, the CPSS, together with the Group of Computer Experts, has undertaken various surveys on the development of e-money[145] and an internal survey on certification authorities and public key infrastructure. **4.156**

---

138 See CPSS report: 'Real-time gross settlement systems', Publication 22 (March 1997).

139 Bank for International Settlements: 'Committee on Payment and Settlement Systems, New Developments in Large Value Payment Systems', Publication 67 (May 2005).

140 CPSS report: 'Settlement risk in foreign exchange transactions', Publication 17 (March 1996).

141 Bank of International Settlements: 'Committee on Payment and Settlement Systems, The role of central bank money in payment systems', Publication 55 (August 2003).

142 See 'Retail payments in selected countries: a comparative study', published in September 1999, describing and comparing the retail payment instruments in use in G-10 countries and Australia; 'Clearing and settlement arrangements for retail payments in selected countries', September 2000; and 'Policy issues for central banks in retail payments', March 2003.

143 Bank of International Settlements: 'Committee on Payment and Settlement Systems, Survey of developments in electronic money and internet and mobile phone payments', Publication 62 (March 2004).

144 Bank of International Settlements: 'Committee on Payment and Settlement Systems, Clearing arrangements for exchange-traded derivatives', Publication 23 (March 1997).

145 Bank of International Settlements: 'Committee on Payment and Settlement Systems, Survey of electronic money developments', Publication 48 (November 2001).

4.157 In 2005, the CPSS set up a new working group on oversight, whose task is to map and compare the objectives that central banks have for their oversight of payment and securities settlement systems[146] and the methods they use to achieve these objectives, and other recent projects include work on international remittance systems in considering and comparing the remittance markets in different countries to identify general principles for international money transfers.

4.158 Finally, in 2011, the CPSS has also published in collaboration with IOSCO three documents designed to promote global efforts to strengthen financial market infrastructures ('FMIs'):

- a report entitled 'Principles for financial market infrastructures';[147]
- a consultation paper on an assessment methodology for these new standards;[148] and
- a consultation paper on a disclosure framework for the standards.[149]

The new principles are also designed to ensure that the infrastructure supporting global financial markets is robust to withstand financial shocks. They apply to all systemically important payment systems, central securities depositories, securities settlement systems, central counterparties and trade repositories. These FMIs provide the 'plumbing' of the financial markets in that they conduct the clearing, settlement and transaction reporting for the markets. These standards will provide important support for the G20 strategy to make the financial system more resilient by making central clearing of standardised OTC derivatives mandatory.[150]

4.159 The new standards (called 'principles') replace the three existing sets of international standards set out in the Core principles for systemically important payment systems (CPSS, 2001); the Recommendations for securities settlement systems (CPSS-IOSCO, 2001); and the Recommendations for central counterparties (CPSS-IOSCO, 2004). These three sets of standards have been strengthened and harmonised by raising minimum requirements, providing more detailed guidance and broadening the scope of the standards to cover new risk-management areas and new types of financial market infrastructure.

4.160 The new principles introduce new or more demanding requirements in many important areas including:

- the financial resources and risk management procedures an FMI uses to cope with the default of participants;
- the mitigation of operational risk;
- the links and other interdependencies between FMIs through which operational and financial risks can spread;
- achieving the segregation and portability of customer positions and collateral;
- tiered participation; and
- general business risk.

---

146 Bank of International Settlements: 'Committee on Payment and Settlement Systems, Central Bank Oversight of payment and settlement systems', Publication 68 (May 2005).

147 CPSS/IOSCO, 'Principles for financial market infrastructures', April 2012; see <http://www.bis.org/publ/cpss101a.pdf>.

148 CPSS/IOSCO, 'Assessment methodology for the principles for FMIs and the responsibilities of authorities', Consultative report, April 2012; see <http://www.bis.org/publ/cpss101b.pdf>.

149 CPSS/IOSCO, 'Disclosure framework for financial market infrastructures' Consultative report, April 2012; see <http://www.bis.org/publ/cpss101c.pdf>.

150 In September 2009, G20 Leaders agreed at their Pittsburgh summit that:

Securities and the International Organisation of Securities Commissions

The International Organisation of Securities Commissions ('IOSCO') is an international organisation of securities exchange regulators who cooperate in setting guiding principles for the world's capital markets. IOSCO was formed in 1983, when an inter-American regional association was transformed into an international cooperative body. IOSCO is the most important cooperative forum for securities regulatory agencies and is now one of the key global standard setting bodies whose members regulate over 90 per cent of the world's security markets.[151] The decision to form the IOSCO was taken by 11 regulatory agencies from North and South America at a gathering in Ecuador in April 1983. In 1984 securities regulators from France, Indonesia, Korea, and the UK joined the Organisation. **4.161**

The member bodies of the IOSCO have resolved: **4.162**

- to cooperate together to promote high standards of regulation in order to maintain just, efficient, and sound markets;
- to exchange information on their respective experiences in order to promote the development of domestic markets;
- to unite their efforts to establish standards and an effective surveillance of international securities transactions; and
- to provide mutual assistance to promote the integrity of the markets by a rigorous application of the standards and by effective enforcement against offences.

IOSCO has three categories of members, Ordinary, Associate, and Affiliate. There are currently over 200 IOSCO members with 117 ordinary members, 12 associate members, and 74 affiliate members. Ordinary members include government bodies such as a securities commission or a self-regulatory body such as a stock exchange, where there are no governmental regulatory bodies in a particular country. Associate members are national regulatory bodies of a country which is already an ordinary member or any other eligible body with an appropriate responsibility for securities regulation.[152] Affiliate members are other regulatory bodies where the national regulatory body is already an ordinary member of IOSCO[153] and are therefore **4.163**

'All standardised OTC derivative contracts should be traded on exchanges or electronic trading platforms, where appropriate, and cleared through central counterparties by end-2012 at the latest. OTC derivative contracts should be reported to trade repositories. Non-centrally cleared contracts should be subject to higher capital requirements. We ask the FSB and its relevant members to assess regularly implementation and whether it is sufficient to improve transparency in the derivatives markets, mitigate systemic risk, and protect against market abuse'.

See Financial Stability Board, OTC Derivatives Market Reforms. Fifth Progress Report on Implementation, 15 April 2013; see <http://www.financialstabilityboard.org/publications/r_130415.pdf>.

151 <http://www.iosco.org>.

152 ibid.

153 Affiliate members include the Alberta Securities Commission, the British Columbia Securities Commission, the Dubai Financial Services Authority, the Indian Forward Markets Commission, the Japanese Ministries of Agriculture, Forestries, and Fisheries and International Trade and Industry, the Japanese Securities and Exchange Surveillance Commission, the Korea Insurance Deposit Corporation, the Lubuan Offshore Financial Services Authority, the North American Securities Administrators Association, and the US Commodities and Futures Commission.

members of the SRO Consultative Committee. An SRO or international body is eligible for affiliate membership provided it has an appropriate interest in securities regulation.

4.164 IOSCO and its General Secretariat are based in Madrid, Spain but most of its work has been carried out by its members through a number of committees. In 2012, the board of ISOCO was reconstituted and the Board absorbed the functions of the Executive Committee, the Technical Committee and Emerging Markets Committee Advisory Board. By commissioning a single integrated body to take on the governance, standard-setting and development functions of the Organisation, it was felt that IOSCO will be more effective and efficient in conveying its messages in one voice.

4.165 In March 2013, Greg Medcraft, the Chairman of the Australian Securities & Investment Commission ('ASIC') became the chairman of IOSCO's board. The Board is composed of 32 members who will serve a two-year term to 2014. Members include all former Technical Committee members, representatives from each of IOSCO's four regional Committees and the Chair and Vice-Chair of the Emerging Markets Committee. The Emerging Markets Committee remains as a separate committee of the board for the time being. The criteria for membership of the Board will be reviewed with a view to ensuring a permanent structure is in place by IOSCO's Annual Meeting in Rio de Janeiro in September 2014.

4.166 IOSCO also has merged the policy and standard-setting work of the Technical Committee Standing Committees and Emerging Markets Committee Working Groups, in each area of securities market regulation. An initiative of its Strategic Direction review, the new structure is intended to improve the effectiveness of the committees, making them more robust and inclusive. The meeting approved the membership of these Committees, drawing members from both emerging and developed markets, and full-fledged Self-Regulatory Organisations ('SROs').

4.167 IOSCO's SRO Consultative Committee ('SROCC') also contributes to IOSCO's work programme by exchanging views and information among its members on a number of emerging regulatory issues facing SROs, including matters related to corporate governance, high frequency trading, risks when intermediary firms outsource back office functions, and cooperation among regulatory bodies. The SROCC has also carried out an evaluation of the training programs co-organised by the SROCC and EMC for SRO officials and emerging market regulators. The SROCC has also discussed possible ways for SROs to contribute more effectively to the IOSCO's core work utilising experiences and expertise as frontline regulators.

4.168 To enhance the overall effectiveness of the Organisation's new strategic direction, the IOSCO Secretary General proposed the creation of an IOSCO Foundation as a vehicle to raise funding from a range of sources to finance IOSCO activities in selected areas. New funding would go towards expanding the services offered to members, including technical assistance, education and training, and research on global securities market issues. Members voiced support for the initiative and agreed the next steps to be taken with regard to the setting up of the Foundation.

4.169 The Regional Standing Committees, of which there are four, meet to discuss specific regional problems and issues of the members of the Organisation that constitute them. The four Regional Standing Committees include the Africa/Middle East Regional Committee, the Asia-Pacific Regional Committee, the European Region.

4.170 The IOSCO meets on an annual basis in order to discuss any important issues that relate to world securities and future markets. The Annual Conference is staged in a different city every year in a member country. The various Committees and members of the IOSCO also meet, but according to their own agendas and requirements.

IOSCO does not have the power to make any rules or legally enforceable standards, but its members (the national securities authorities) resolve to cooperate with each other to ensure better regulation of the markets, on a domestic and international level, in order to maintain just, efficient, and sound markets. **4.171**

These authorities agree to implement certain principles of securities regulation that are based upon the Organisation's three principal objectives: **4.172**

- the protection of investors;
- ensuring that markets are fair, efficient, and transparent; and
- the reduction of systematic risk in the markets.[154]

Implementation may therefore require implementation through a variety of methods depending upon the jurisdiction in question. It may be necessary to implement a change in legislation or regulation, a change in policy or practice by the regulatory body, or a bilateral or multilateral agreement. **4.173**

To achieve these objectives, the principles need to be implemented under the relevant national legal framework. The principles are grouped into eight categories including Principles relating to the Regulator, Principles for Self Regulation, Principles for the Enforcement of Securities Regulation, Principles for Cooperation in Regulation, Principles for Issuers, Principles for Collective Investment Schemes, Principles for Market Intermediaries, and Principles for the Secondary Market. **4.174**

IOSCO publishes a variety of reports which are a valuable source of information on the principles that underlie effective securities regulation and the tools and techniques necessary to give effect to those principles and changing trends in securities markets. **4.175**

Part of IOSCO's role is to allow national securities regulators to share information on a domestic and international level, and to remove impediments to international cooperation. **4.176**

In recent years, IOSCO has been putting greater emphasis on the Multilateral Memorandum Concerning Consultation and Cooperation and the Exchange of Information ('IOSCO MOU'). To date, 95 members have signed the IOSCO MOU and a further 24 have expressed their commitment to doing so in accordance with the document's Appendix B.[155] The IOSCO MOU is now proving to be an effective tool, particularly in combating cross-border financial crime. **4.177**

In broad terms, IOSCO's priorities are to maintain and enhance its programmes for setting new standards and principles in specific areas, to continue with implementation of the IOSCO Principles, and to strengthen and extend cross-border cooperation between regulators, especially for enforcement purposes. IOSCO's achievements over the past year are many and varied. They include promulgation of the Code of Conduct Fundamentals for Credit Rating Agencies;[156] new Principles on Client Identification and Beneficial Ownership for **4.178**

[154] IOSCO, 'Objectives and Principles of Securities Regulation', p 5; see <http://www.iosco.org/library/pubdocs/pdf/IOSCOPD323.pdf>.

[155] IOSCO, Annual Report 2011; available at: <http://www.iosco.org/library/index.cfm?section=mou_siglist#AnnexB>.

[156] IOSCO, 'Code of Conduct Fundamentals for Credit Rating Agencies' (December 2004).

the Securities Industry;[157] key reports on Strengthening Capital Markets Against Financial Fraud[158] and on Islamic Capital Markets; a survey on the implementation of the IOSCO Principles as they relate to auditor oversight and productive cooperation with global banking and insurance regulators through the Joint Forum.[159]

4.179 It is undoubtedly the world's leading standards setter for securities regulation. Its high profile is now widely acknowledged by members and by other bodies in the international financial community who recognise IOSCO's achievements over recent years. The IOSCO Objectives and Principles of Securities Regulation have become the fundamental reference for benchmarking and assessing securities regulation in any jurisdiction worldwide, and a powerful basis for setting standards in specific areas of regulation and for addressing new issues as they emerge.[160]

Joint Forum

4.180 The IOSCO shares a relationship with the Basel Committee and the IAIS through the Joint Forum.[161] The Joint Forum traces its origins from the Tripartite Group, which was formed in early 1993 to address a range of issues relating to the supervision of financial conglomerates. The Tripartite Group was created at the initiative of the Basel Committee and composed of bank, securities, and insurance supervisors, acting in a personal capacity but drawing on their experience of supervising different types of financial institutions. The Tripartite Group recognised the trend towards cross-sector financial conglomerates and issued a report in July 1995 raising issues of concern in the prudential supervision of financial conglomerates.[162] The purpose of this report, published as a discussion document, was to identify challenges that financial conglomerates pose for supervisors and to consider ways in which these problems may be overcome. To carry this work forward, the Joint Forum was established in 1996 as a cooperative cross-sectoral forum whose parent bodies are IOSCO, the Basel Committee, and the IAIS. Fifteen countries are currently represented in the Joint Forum: Australia, Belgium, Canada, France, Germany, India, Italy, Japan, Netherlands, South Africa, South Korea, Spain, Switzerland, the UK, and the USA. The EU Commission attends in an observer capacity[163]. The chairmanship of the Joint Forum rotates between the three sector committees and is named for a two-year term.

4.181 These three parent bodies, IOSCO, Basel Committee, and IAIS, approve the Joint Forum's mandates and reports. The Joint Forum has a specific mandate to undertake work on risk assessments and capital and, if appropriate, to develop further guidance and principles and/or identify best practices, with special focus on risk aggregation, operational risk management, credit risk management and transfer, business continuity, outsourcing and the disclosure of financial risks.[164]

---

[157] IOSCO, 'Principles on Client Identification and Beneficial Ownership for the Securities Industry' (May 2004).

[158] IOSCO, 'Strengthening Capital Markets Against Financial Fraud' (February 2005).

[159] 30th IOSCO Annual Conference Opening Ceremony—speech by Jane Diplock, AO Chairman of the IOSCO Executive Committee and New Zealand Securities Commission: <http://www.iosco.org>, p 2.

[160] ibid, p 3.

[161] The Joint Forum was original referred to as the 'Joint Forum on Financial Conglomerates'.

[162] Basel Committee: 'The supervision of financial conglomerates' (A report by the tripartite group of bank, securities and insurance regulators) (July 1995).

[163] <http://www.bis.org/bcbs/jointforum.htm>.

[164] <http://www.bis.org>.

Comprised of an equal number of senior bank, insurance, and securities supervisors representing each supervisory constituency, the Joint Forum usually meets three times per year, and has three main subgroups, which are the risk assessment and capital, the business continuity, and the regulatory and market differences subgroups. The growing emergence of financial conglomerates and the blurring of distinctions between the activities of firms in each financial sector have heightened the need for cooperative efforts to improve the effectiveness of supervisory methods and approaches. **4.182**

The Joint Forum has studied issues of common interest to the three financial sectors and developed guidance and principles to identify best practices, as appropriate, for: **4.183**

- risk assessments and management, internal controls, and capital;
- the use of the audit and actuarial functions in the supervision of regulated entities and corporate groups containing regulated entities;
- corporate governance, including fit and proper tests;
- outsourcing by regulated firms of functions and activities; and
- different definitions of banking, insurance, and securities activities, and the potential that they may lead to regulatory arbitrage.

In order to achieve this objective, the Joint Forum's mandate[165] requires it to: **4.184**

- address and promote understanding of issues common to the banking, securities and insurance sectors, including the supervision of financial conglomerates;
- analyse cross-sectoral market and regulatory developments;
- examine cross-sectoral gaps and conflicts in regulation and supervision;
- develop guidance and principles and/or identifies best practices on cross-sectoral technical, regulatory and/or policy issues to encourage cross-sectoral consistency and alignment where appropriate, and reduce opportunities for regulatory arbitrage; and facilitate cooperation, coordination and information sharing among banking, insurance and securities supervisors (or representatives of the Parent Committees) and further supports the Parent Committees by identifying synergies or duplication in their work efforts.

The Joint Forum therefore provides the framework to permit different sectoral regulators to address these issues.[166]

The Organisation for Economic Co-operation and Development

The Organisation for Economic Co-operation and Development ('the OECD') developed out of the Organisation for European Economic Co-operation ('OEEC') that was established in 1947 to coordinate the Marshall Plan[167] for the reconstruction of Europe following the Second World War. **4.185**

165 <http://www.bis.org/bcbs/jfmandate.htm>.

166 Basel Committee on Banking Supervision: 'The Joint Forum, Core Principles: Cross sectoral comparison' (November 2001).

167 The Marshall Plan grew out of a speech by then US Secretary of State George C Marshall on 5 June 1947 that outlined a proposal for the economic regeneration of Europe post-Second World War. The USA offered up to $20 billion for relief provided the European nations could agree a plan on how they would use the aid, thus cooperating and acting as a single economic unit for the first time.

4.186 An economic counterpart to the North Atlantic Treaty Organisation ('NATO'), the OECD took over from the OEEC in 1961 with a mandate to be an effective means of international coordination and to assist sound economic expansion in member countries and other countries in the process of economic development, and to contribute to growth in world trade on a multilateral, non-discriminatory basis.

4.187 There are 30 member countries of the OECD whose members produce 60 per cent of the world's goods and services, but increasingly the OECD has been expanding its remit to include work on issues such as sustainable development, bringing together environmental, economic, and social concerns across national frontiers for a better understanding of the problems, and the means to tackle them together.

4.188 Decision-making power is vested in the OECD's Council. The Council comprises one representative per member country and the European Commission. The Council meets regularly at the level of ambassadors to the OECD, and decisions are taken by consensus. The Council meets at ministerial level once a year to discuss key issues and set priorities for OECD work. The OECD Secretariat's various directorates carry out the work mandated by the Council.

4.189 The OECD Secretariat is based in Paris and has a staff of 2,500 to support the activities of its committees.[168] A Secretary-General, assisted by four Deputy Secretaries-General, heads the OECD Secretariat. The Secretary-General also chairs the Council. As well as running the day-to-day operations of the OECD, the OECD Secretariat collects data, monitors trends, and analyses and forecasts economic developments, and carries out and publishes research on social changes or evolving patterns in trade, environment, agriculture, technology, taxation, and more.

4.190 Representatives of the OECD member countries meet in specialised committees to discuss ideas and to review progress in specific policy areas, such as economics, trade, science, employment, education, or financial markets. There are approximately 200 OECD committees, working groups, and expert groups.[169]

4.191 The OECD, unlike the World Bank or the International Monetary Fund, is not a financial institution and it does not act as a bank or financial institution. The OECD's focus is on the determination of key issues through the collection of data and its analysis, and then moving on to collective discussion of policy and decision-making, and finally implementation.[170] Discussions at the OECD sometimes evolve into negotiations where OECD countries agree on the 'rules of the game' for international cooperation, and they may culminate in formal agreements, for example agreements on combating bribery, on export credits, or on capital movements; or they may produce standards and models for international taxation, or recommendations and guidelines covering corporate governance or environmental practices.

[168] The OECD Secretariat is organised in departments or directorates and these include the Executive Directorate, the Economics Department, the Development Co-operation Directorate, the Directorate for Financial and Enterprise Affairs, the Directorate for Employment, Labour and Social Affairs, Public Affairs and Communications Directorate, Statistics Directorate, Public Governance and Territorial Development Directorate, Centre for Tax Policy and Administration, Directorate for Education, the Environment Directorate, the Trade Directorate, the Directorate for Science, Technology and Industry, the Directorate for Food, Agriculture and Fisheries, and the Centre for Co-operation with Non-members.

[169] See Directory of Bodies of the OECD, 2012: <http://www.oecd-ilibrary.org/docserver/download/0112021e.pdf?expires=1375780558&id=id&accname=guest&checksum=7AADD0CBA428F977A69E6548E129C9AF>.

[170] See OECD, International Regulatory Co-operation: Addressing Global Challenges, 2013; see <http://www.oecd-ilibrary.org/governance/international-regulatory-co-operation_9789264200463-en>.

The Financial Action Task Force

In 1989, in response to mounting concern over money laundering, the Financial Action Task Force on Money Laundering ('FATF') was established by the G-7 Summit that was held that year in Paris. The G-7 Heads of State or Government and the President of the European Commission, recognising the threat posed to the banking system and to financial institutions, convened the Task Force from the G-7 Member States, the European Commission, and eight other countries.[171] **4.192**

FATF was given the responsibility of examining money laundering techniques and trends and reviewing the action that had already been taken at a national or international level. In April 1990, FATF issued a report containing a set of Forty Recommendations, which provide a comprehensive plan of action needed to fight against money laundering. Since then FATF has continued to examine the methods used to launder criminal proceeds and has completed two rounds of mutual evaluations of its member countries and jurisdictions. It has also updated the Forty Recommendations to reflect the changes that have occurred in the fight against money laundering, and has sought to encourage other countries around the world to adopt anti-money laundering measures. FATF also conducts research into anti-money laundering measures and the typologies employed by money launderers and FATF publishes reports and other information on the schemes being employed by both money launderers and terrorists to infiltrate the global banking and financial system. **4.193**

In 2001, the development of standards in the fight against terrorist financing was added to the mission of the FATF and FATF has promulgated nine special recommendations regarding terrorist financing including putting in place agreements to ratify and implement UN instruments on terrorist financing, criminalising the financing of terrorism and money laundering associated with it, freezing and confiscating terrorist assets, requiring reporting of suspicious transactions relating to terrorist financing, providing international cooperation in relation to stopping terrorist financing, the licensing and registration of money transmission activities to prevent informal or 'hawala' networks from being used to finance terrorism, recording basic information regarding wire transfers of money to prevent its use for money laundering, and reviewing the adequacy of national laws to prevent non-profit and charitable organisations from being exploited for terrorist financing. In October 2004, the FATF published a Ninth Special Recommendations, further strengthening the agreed international standards for combating money laundering and terrorist financing. **4.194**

In February 2012, the FATF completed a review of its standards and published the revised FATF Recommendations.[172] This revision of the Recommendations and Special Recommendations is intended to strengthen global safeguards and further protect the integrity of the financial system by providing governments with stronger tools to take action **4.195**

---

[171] During 1991 and 1992, the FATF expanded its membership from the original 16 to 28 members which are Argentina, Australia, Austria, Belgium, Brazil, Canada, Denmark, the European Commission, Finland, France, Germany, Greece, Gulf Co-operation Council—whose members include Bahrain, Kuwait, Oman, Qatar, Saudi Arabia, and the United Arab Emirates—Hong Kong (China SAR), Iceland, Ireland, Italy, Japan, Luxembourg, Mexico, Kingdom of the Netherlands, New Zealand, Norway, Portugal, Russian Federation, Singapore, South Africa, Spain, Sweden, Switzerland, Turkey, the UK, and the USA.

[172] <http://www.fatf-gafi.org/media/fatf/documents/recommendations/pdfs/FATF_Recommendations.pdf>.

against financial crime. They have been expanded to deal with new threats such as the financing of proliferation of weapons of mass destruction, and to be clearer on transparency and tougher on corruption. The nine Special Recommendations on terrorist financing have been fully integrated with the measures against money laundering. This has resulted in a stronger and clearer set of standards.

4.196 FATF member countries[173] are committed to the discipline of multilateral monitoring and peer review and regularly carry out monitoring programmes in relation to their implementation of the FATF Recommendations. In the self-assessment programme, each member country provides information on the status of its implementation of the Forty Recommendations and Nine Special Recommendations by responding each year to a standard questionnaire. This information is then compiled and analysed, and provides the basis for assessing the extent to which both individual countries and the group as a whole have implemented the Recommendations. The second element for monitoring the implementation of the Forty Recommendations is the mutual evaluation process whereby each member country receives an on-site visit conducted by a team of three or four selected experts in the legal, financial, and law enforcement fields from other member governments. Following the monitoring visit the team draws up a report assessing the extent to which the evaluated country has moved forward in implementing an effective system to counter money laundering and to highlight areas in which further progress may still be required. Countries that are found to be non-complying with the Forty Recommendations may have other members tighten their anti-money policies in relation to those countries, and FATF may apply various types of moral pressure to secure compliance. Ultimately, FATF can also apply Recommendation 21 to that non-cooperative country which would result in FATF issuing a statement to its members and their financial institutions to give 'special attention' to business relations and transactions with persons, companies, and financial institutions domiciled in the non-cooperative country. Such measures can have a very substantial effect on the financial and banking systems of a country that has failed to comply with FATF standards and, as a final measure, the FATF membership of the non-cooperative country can be suspended.[174]

4.197 FATF also has a number of associate regional bodies including the Asia/Pacific Group on Money Laundering ('APG'), the Caribbean Financial Action Task Force ('CFATF'), the Council of Europe Select Committee of Experts on the Evaluation of Anti-Money Laundering Measures ('MONEYVAL'), the Eurasian Group ('EAG'), the Eastern and Southern Africa Anti-Money Laundering Group ('ESAAMLG'), the Financial Action Task Force on Money Laundering in South America ('GAFISUD'), the Middle East and North Africa Financial Action Task Force ('MENAFATF'), and the Egmont Group of Financial Intelligence Units ('EGMONT') that cooperate on the exchange of information relating to money laundering activities.

4.198 The private sector also has an interest in preventing the use of financial institutions for money laundering activities and the Wolfsberg Group of international private banks[175] has adopted

---

[173] There are 36 members of FATF and two regional bodies, the European Commission and the Gulf Co-operation Council; see <http://www.fatf-gafi.org/pages/aboutus/membersandobservers/>.

[174] As at the date of publication, no countries were on the list of non-cooperative countries: <http://www.fatf-gafi.org/document/4/0,3343,en_32250379_32236992_33916420_1_1_1_1,00.html>.

[175] Banco Santander, Bank of Tokyo-Mitsubishi UFJ, Barclays Bank PLC, Citigroup, Credit Suisse, Deutsche Bank, Goldman Sachs, HSBC, JP Morgan Chase, Société Générale, UBS.

the Wolfsberg AML Principles that include guidelines for client acceptance and client identification as a means of establishing best practice in anti-money laundering procedures.[176]

IASB and International Accounting Standards

The history of international accounting standards which began in 1966 with the proposal to establish an International Study Group whose members included the Institute of Chartered Accountants in England and Wales ('ICAEW'), the American Institute of Certified Public Accountants ('AICPA'), and the Canadian Institute of Chartered Accountants ('CICA') has been fundamental to the development of the global capital markets. The working group that was formed (the Accountants International Study Group ('AISG')) published a number of papers and in June 1973 the International Accounting Standards Committee ('IASC') was established[177] to agree and set out international standards. However, agreement on these fundamental issues has been neither easy nor straightforward and there are still substantive differences that the successors of these bodies are still trying to reconcile. **4.199**

The IASC was disbanded in 2001 and its successor, the International Accounting Standards Board ('IASB'), is an independent, privately funded accounting standard setter located in London. The IASB has 14 members who report to an oversight body (the Trustees of the International Accounting Standards Committee Foundation) that was formed as a Delaware not-for-profit corporation in 2000/2001. The objectives of the IASC Foundation are to develop, in the public interest, a single set of high quality, understandable, and enforceable global accounting standards that require high quality, transparent, and comparable information in financial statements and other financial reporting to help participants in the world's capital markets and other users make economic decisions, to promote the use and rigorous application of those standards, to take account of, as appropriate, the special needs of small and medium-sized entities and emerging economies, and to bring about convergence of national accounting standards and International Accounting Standards ('IAS')[178] and International Financial Reporting Standards ('IFRS'). **4.200**

The IASB also has a Standards Advisory Council that acts as a standards advisory body and it provides a forum for organisations and individuals with an interest in international financial reporting to take part in standard setting. The Council has approximately 50 members and individual members are appointed for a renewable term of three years and have diverse geographical and professional backgrounds. The Council is responsible for giving advice to the IASB on agenda decisions and priorities in the IASB's work, and for informing the IASB **4.201**

[176] See: <http://www.wolfsberg-principles.com/standards.html>.

[177] The IASC was founded in June 1973 as a result of an agreement between the accountancy bodies in Australia, Canada, France, Germany, Japan, Mexico, the Netherlands, the UK and Ireland, and the USA, and these countries constituted the Board of IASC at that time. The international professional activities of the accountancy bodies were organised under the auspices of the International Federation of Accountants (IFAC) in 1977 but in 1981, IASC and IFAC agreed that IASC would have full and complete autonomy in setting international accounting standards and in publishing discussion documents on international accounting issues. At the same time, all members of IFAC became members of IASC but this membership link was discontinued in May 2000 when IASC's constitution was changed as part of the reorganisation of IASC.

[178] Statements of International Accounting Standards issued by the Board of the International Accounting Standards Committee ('IASC') between 1973 and 2001 are designated 'International Accounting Standards' ('IAS').

of the views of the organisations and individuals on the Council on major standard setting projects, and giving other advice to the IASB or the Trustees.

4.202 The IASB has a separate interpretative body (the International Financial Reporting Interpretations Committee—formerly the Standing Interpretations Committee) which comprises 15 members representing the wider accounting and financial community. The Committee reviews various accounting issues that are likely to receive divergent or unacceptable treatment in the absence of authoritative guidance, with a view to reaching consensus on the appropriate accounting treatment. In developing interpretations, the Committee meets approximately every six weeks to address issues including newly identified financial reporting issues not specifically dealt with in International Financial Reporting Standards, or issues where unsatisfactory or conflicting interpretations have developed, or seem likely to develop in the absence of authoritative guidance, with a view to reaching a consensus on the appropriate treatment.

4.203 The IASB announced in April 2001 that its accounting standards would be designated 'International Financial Reporting Standards' ('IFRS') and that it would adopt all of the International Accounting Standards issued by the IASC. The Interpretations of International Accounting Standards issued by the International Financial Reporting Interpretations Committee do not have the same status as IASs, although financial statements should not be described as complying with International Accounting Standards unless they comply with all the requirements of each applicable Standard and each applicable interpretation of the Standing Interpretations Committee. The IASB has adopted a conceptual framework underlying its financial reporting standards and interpretations, the Framework for the Preparation and Presentation of Financial Statements (the Framework)[179] that sets out the concepts that underlie the preparation and presentation of financial statements for external users as well as publishing the IFRSs, and the interpretations of International Accounting Standards developed by the International Financial Reporting Interpretations Committee.

The Financial Accounting Standards Board

4.204 The US-backed Financial Accounting Standards Board ('FASB') was established in 1973[180] as the designated organisation in the private sector for establishing standards of financial accounting and reporting. Those standards govern the preparation of financial reports and have been officially recognised as authoritative by the Securities and Exchange Commission (Financial Reporting Release No 1, Section 101 and reaffirmed in its April 2003 Policy Statement) and the American Institute of Certified Public Accountants (Rule 203, Rules of Professional Conduct, as amended May 1973 and May 1979).

4.205 The FASB was established to improve standards of financial accounting and reporting for the guidance and education of the public, including issuers, auditors, and users of financial information, and the FASB seeks to improve the usefulness of financial reporting by focusing on the primary characteristics of relevance and reliability and on the qualities of comparability

179 Available from the IASB.

180 Prior to the current structure being put in place, financial accounting and reporting standards in the US were established by the Committee on Accounting Procedure of the American Institute of Certified Public Accountants (1936–59) and then by the Accounting Principles Board, also a part of the AICPA (1959–73). The pronouncements of those predecessor bodies remain in force unless amended or superseded by the FASB.

and consistency, to keep standards current to reflect changes in methods of doing business and changes in the economic environment, to consider promptly any significant areas of deficiency in financial reporting that might be improved through the standard-setting process, to promote the international convergence of accounting standards concurrent with improving the quality of financial reporting, and to improve the common understanding of the nature and purposes of information contained in financial reports. The FASB also develops broad accounting concepts as well as standards for financial reporting and provides guidance on implementation of standards. Research is conducted by the FASB staff and others, including foreign national and international accounting standard setting bodies, on various accounting matters.

Like the IASB, the FSAB reports to an independent Financial Accounting Foundation ('FAF') that is separate from all other constituent organisations. However, its Board of Trustees is made up of members from these constituent organisations[181] having interest in financial reporting and approved by the FAF Trustees. There also are a number of Trustees-at-large who are not nominated by those organisations, but are chosen by the sitting Trustees and who are responsible for selecting the members of the FASB and its advisory council as well as ensuring adequate funding of their activities and for exercising general oversight with the exception of the FASB's resolution of technical issues. **4.206**

Financial Accounting Standards Advisory Council ('FASAC') has responsibility for consulting with the FASB on technical issues on the Board's agenda including project priorities, matters likely to require the attention of the FASB, selection and organisation of task forces, and such other matters as may be requested by the FASB or its chairman. The Council has more than 30 members who are broadly representative of preparers, auditors, and users of financial information. **4.207**

Finally, in 1984, the FAF established the Governmental Accounting Standards Board ('GASB') to set standards of financial accounting and reporting for State and local governmental authorities such as State bodies and municipal or city governments. As with the FASB, the FAF is responsible for selecting its members, ensuring adequate funding, and exercising general oversight. **4.208**

Sarbanes-Oxley and its Impact on Non-US Entities

Although not a supranational body, one of the most far-reaching pieces of legislation in the global financial services and particularly the capital markets and banking sector in recent years is the US's Sarbanes-Oxley Act of 2002.[182] This law, passed in the wake of the Enron and WorldCom financial scandals, was designed to strengthen corporate governance and to restore investor confidence in the US markets. However, the legislation is extremely wide ranging and establishes new or enhanced standards for all US public company[183] boards, **4.209**

[181] FAF Constituent Organisations are: the American Accounting Association, American Institute of Certified Public Accountants, the CFA Institute, the Financial Executives International, the Government Finance Officers Association, the Institute of Management Accountants, the National Association of State Auditors, Comptrollers, and Treasurers, and the Securities Industry Association.

[182] Pub L No 107–204, 116 Stat 745 (2002).

[183] Public companies include all companies required to file reports under the Securities and Exchange Act of 1934 or to file registration statements under the Securities Act of 1933. Certain other 'listed companies'—ie those having listings on one or more US exchanges—and small business issuers are also required to comply with some of its provisions.

management, and public accounting firms, and its impact both within and outside the US has been seismic in terms of corporate reporting.

4.210 The impact of Sarbanes-Oxley has been far wider—wider even than the extraterritorial reach of the US legislation—in that it has driven many of the major developed markets to consider and implement similar corporate governance legislation and has resulted in a step change in the approach of regulators to many issues including public company reporting, senior management responsibility, and auditor independence.

4.211 The Act was intended 'to protect investors by improving the accuracy and reliability of corporate disclosures made pursuant to the securities laws, and for other purposes'. One of these 'other purposes' has been to extend the reach of US law and the regulatory authority of the US Securities and Exchange Commission ('SEC') to foreign corporations registered on US stock exchanges. European companies, their directors and officers, as well as their independent auditors and legal advisors have therefore had to address the many issues arising from this legislation.

4.212 The key feature of the law was to expand greatly the responsibilities of audit committees and to impose stringent independence requirements, effectively prohibiting international accounting firms from providing certain non-audit services including legal services, management consultancy services, and other professional services to any of their audit clients listed or registered on US exchanges. The law also required sweeping new certification requirements for directors and officers of US registrant corporations that financial reports contain 'no untrue statement or omissions of material facts' and required accountants to attest to some new representations as to a company's compliance with financial reporting requirements.

4.213 The Sarbanes-Oxley Act requires companies to establish mandates for directors and officers, regarding 'corporate responsibility' certifications and assessments, in connection with each and every quarterly or annual financial report, including representations by the company's chief executive officer and chief financial officer that they have reviewed the quarterly and annual reports, assertions by these officers that they are responsible for the company's system of internal control, certification, based on evaluations made within 90 days of the respective financial reports, that such internal controls are adequate and effective, and certification that these officers have disclosed, both to the company's audit committee of the board of directors and to the company's independent auditors any significant deficiencies in controls, and all instances of possible fraud (whether or not material) involving management or any employees with significant control responsibilities. The law also contains provisions for the protection of corporate whistleblowers in some circumstances.[184] Finally, the law imposes very wide criminal and civil penalties and sanctions for companies and their officers that violate US securities laws and regulations with criminal penalties of up to 20 years' imprisonment for the destruction, alteration, or falsification of any documents, corporate records, or audit records subject to any investigation of any agency or department of the US Government.

[184] The US First Circuit Court held in *Carnero v Boston Scientific Corp*, 433 F.3d 1 (1st Cir. 2006) that Congress did not intend the whistleblowing provisions of Sarbanes-Oxley to apply extraterritorially. However, the US Federal Courts for the Southern District of New York have recently held that these provisions may still apply to US company's conduct overseas. See *O'Mahony v Accenture*, 07 Civ. 7916, 2008 U.S. Dist. LEXIS 10600 (S.D.N.Y. 5 February 2008).

The Sarbanes-Oxley Act also established a new Public Companies Accounting Oversight Board ('PCAOB'), under ultimate oversight of the SEC, with authority over registered public accounting firms (whether domestic or foreign) regarding auditing and audit standards, audit quality control, and auditor independence standards and rules, inspections of accounting firms registered with the Board, and the ability to carry out investigations and disciplinary proceedings against auditors of US registered public companies. The board is not a US government agency but is made up of five individuals who are selected by the chairman of the Board of Governors of the Federal Reserve System and the Secretary of State of the Department of the Treasury, and who report to the Securities and Exchange Commission. The law also proposed mandatory rotation of registered public accounting firms. **4.214**

The Act also acknowledged the role of the Financial Accounting Standards Board ('FASB'), under the oversight of the SEC, to promulgate and define US generally accepted accounting principles ('GAAP'). **4.215**

The company's auditors are required to attest to management's assessment of the adequacy and effectiveness of internal controls, and new financial reporting disclosure requirements have been adopted including a mandatory financial reports feature whereby all material correcting adjustments required by the company's independent auditors are disclosed, that all material off-balance sheet transactions, arrangements, obligations (including contingent obligations) have been disclosed, the requirement of pro forma financial information, provided in any public filings or press releases or other public disclosures, and the confirmation that these contain no untrue statements, or any omissions, of material facts. The law has also established new conflicts of interest standards and rules of conduct for securities analysts. **4.216**

Non-US companies whose securities are not registered on US stock exchanges will not be directly affected by Sarbanes-Oxley, but for those companies that are registrants with the SEC and on US stock exchanges, the effects are far-reaching. The Act expressly applies to any non-US company registered on US exchanges under either the Securities Act or the Exchange Act, regardless of such company's country of incorporation or corporate domicile. The Act requires that auditors of such registrants, regardless of their nationality or place of business, be subject to the oversight of the PCAOB and to the statutory requirements of Sarbanes-Oxley. Directors and officers of registrants, namely chief executive officers and chief financial officers (or finance directors) and regardless of nationality, are required by Sarbanes-Oxley to provide the enumerated certifications and to conduct the internal controls assessments set forth in the Act.[185] Penalties and sanctions—both criminal and civil—under Sarbanes-Oxley apply equally to US and non-US corporate registrants,[186] and their directors and officers, and their independent auditors and legal advisors. **4.217**

[185] See PricewaterhouseCoopers Securities Litigation Review 2007; <http://10b5.pwc.com/PDF/2007%20SECURITY%20LIT%20STUDY%20W-LT.PDF>.

[186] These powers have already been exercised by the SEC Department of Enforcement and other US enforcement agencies including the Department of Justice against a number of non-US firms including: A.C.L.N. (Belgium); Adelphia; Allied Irish Bank (Ireland); AOL Time Warner; Cendant; Elan (Ireland); Enron; Global Crossings; ImClone; Learnout & Hauspie (Belgium); Livent (Canada); McKesson HBOC; Microsoft; Microstrategies; Montedison (Italy); National Steel; Paracelsus (Germany); Rite-Aid; Sensormatic; Sunbeam; Tyco (Bermuda); UBS PaineWebber (Switzerland); Waste Management; WorldCom; and Xerox. See D Dooley, *Sarbanes-Oxley: A Guide for Europeans, Part I*, European Business Forum, Vol 12, Winter 2002.

4.218 The application of Sarbanes-Oxley to US registered companies and its wider impact abroad had not, however, been without criticism or comment.[187] However, several European countries have also adopted legislation comparable in scope to the Sarbanes-Oxley Act. The French Financial Security Act (Loi de Sécurité Financière—LSF) of August 2003 introduced new requirements on disclosures to shareholders and the market for the purposes of corporate governance and internal control. The Autorité des Marchés Financiers ('AMF') has also indicated that it will be requiring non-EU issuers listed or offering their securities in France to comply with their requirements that are, in some respects, more stringent than the Sarbanes-Oxley requirements.

4.219 The UK has similar provisions in that in July 2003, the revised non-statutory Combined Code on Corporate Governance promulgated by the Financial Reporting Council was issued which supersedes the Combined Code issued by the Hampel Committee in 1998 and includes the Turnbull guidance on internal control, the Smith guidance on audit committees, and various items of good practice guidance from the Higgs Report. The Code, although non-statutory, is referred to in the UK Listing Rules, which are published by the Financial Services Authority as the UK Listing Authority ('UKLA'), and all UK listed companies subject to the Listing Rules must include in their annual report a statement of their compliance with their Combined Code or explain matters of non-compliance. The Financial Reporting Council has instigated a review of the Turnbull guidance, and the Companies Act 2006 now provides a statutory statement of directors' duties and the extension of criminal sanctions for breaches of directors' duties. The Companies Act 2006 also allows auditors to limit their liability subject to shareholder approval and the UK has implemented the various provisions of the EU Transparency Directive[188] on shareholder reporting.[189]

Global Regulatory Convergence—The Credit Crunch and the Role of Supranational Bodies in Creating Financial Stability in the Global Market

4.220 In the second half of 2007 and 2008, the increasingly difficult economic and market conditions arising (in part but not wholly) from the collapse of the US sub-prime mortgage market and the accompanying reluctance of global banks to lend to one another at inter-bank rates approximating central bank policy rates (the 'credit crunch') triggered a number of international reactions to try to bring financial stability back into the markets.

4.221 The traditional role of the national central banks in dealing with the effects of global financial instability was called into question by the credit crunch. Foreshadowing the coming

[187] 'Political blindness to the international relations viewpoint was evident from the US failure to consult regulatory counterparts abroad and from the heated political rhetoric accompanying SOX, advertised as the most sweeping reform of American business practices since the 1930s. By US standards, SOX is a codification, fitting easily if clumsily into the US corporate template, more nearly incremental tinkering than substantive reform. This rhetoric–reality gap reflects uncertainty about how bad things were on the one hand and public perceptions that they are certainly awful on the other. Sweeping rhetoric lets the public think Congress is doing something; limited substance enables regulators to hold back in case less is wrong than many think'. Lawrence A Cunningham (Professor of Law and Business, Boston College), speech to the FESE Convention at the Guildhall, London on Thursday, 12 June 2003.

[188] Directive 2004/109/EC.

[189] FSA: Transparency Obligations Directive (Disclosure and Transparency Rules) Instrument 2006 amending the Disclosure and Transparency Rules.

storm, former US Treasury Secretary Robert Rubin put the sentiments bluntly when he wrote in 2003: 'Our politics may not be well suited to coping with the new risks of the global economy'.[190]

Financial Stability Board and the Global Financial Crisis

In October 2007, the G-7 Ministers and Central Bank Governors asked the Financial Stability Forum ('FSF') (now the Financial Stability Board ('FSB')) to undertake an analysis of the causes and weaknesses that produced the credit crunch and to set out recommendations for increasing the resilience of markets and institutions. The FSF, whose work drew on a number of supranational bodies including the Basel Committee on Banking Supervision ('BCBS'), the International Organisation of Securities Commissions ('IOSCO'), the International Association of Insurance Supervisors ('IAIS'), the Joint Forum, the International Accounting Standards Board ('IASB'), the Committee on Payment and Settlement Systems ('CPSS'), the Committee on the Global Financial System ('CGFS'), the International Monetary Fund ('IMF'), the Bank for International Settlements ('BIS'), reported to the G-7 Ministers and Governors at their meeting in Washington in April 2008.[191] **4.222**

In order to re-establish confidence in the soundness of markets and financial institutions, national authorities including central banks took exceptional steps including monetary and fiscal stimulus, central bank liquidity operations, policies to promote asset market liquidity, and actions to resolve problems at specific institutions with a view to facilitating adjustment and dampening the impact on the real economy. The financial system has, however, remained under stress and the FSF proposed concrete actions in the five specific areas: **4.223**

- Strengthened prudential oversight of capital, liquidity, and risk management;
- Enhancing transparency and valuation;
- Changes in the role and uses of credit ratings;
- Strengthening the authorities' responsiveness to risks;
- Robust arrangements for dealing with stress in the financial system,

the goal being to strengthen the efficiency and resilience of the system without hindering the processes of market discipline and innovation that are essential to the financial system's contribution to economic growth.

The report set out a number of specific recommendations including: **4.224**

- The Basel II capital framework should be implemented on a timely basis.
- National supervisors would strengthen the Basel II capital treatment of structured credit and securitisation activities.
- Capital requirements for certain complex structured credit products such as collateralised debt obligations of asset-backed securities would be studied and raised.
- Proposals would be put forward to strengthen the capital treatment for banks' liquidity facilities to off-balance sheet asset-backed commercial paper conduits.

---

190 RE Rubin, *In an Uncertain World* (Random House 2003).

191 Report of the Financial Stability Forum on Enhancing Market and Institutional Resilience, <http://www.fsforum.org/publications/r_0804.pdf> and its October 2008 follow up report on implementation, <http://www.fsforum.org/press/pr_081009f.pdf>.

- Authorities should ensure that the capital buffers for monoline insurers and financial guarantors are commensurate with their role in the financial system.
- Banking supervisors would issue for consultation sound practice guidance on the management and supervision of liquidity.
- Banking supervisors would use Basel Pillar 2 to strengthen banks' risk management practices, to sharpen banks' control of tail risks and mitigate the build-up of excessive exposures and risk concentrations.
- Banking supervisors would strengthen guidance relating to the management of firm-wide risks, including concentration risks.
- The IASB would improve the accounting and disclosure standards for off-balance-sheet vehicles on an accelerated basis and work with other standard setters toward international convergence.
- The International Auditing and Assurance Standards Board, as well as the major national audit standard setters and relevant regulators should consider the lessons learned during the market turmoil and, where necessary, enhance the guidance for audits of valuations of complex or illiquid financial products and related disclosures.
- Credit rating agencies should improve the quality of the rating process and manage conflicts of interest in rating structured products and IOSCO has reissued its Code of Conduct Fundamentals for Credit Rating Agencies.
- Supervisors, regulators, and central banks—individually and collectively—would take additional steps to more effectively translate their risk analysis into actions that mitigate those risks.
- At the international level, the FSF would give more force to its own risk analysis and recommendations, both directly and through the actions of its members, by initiating and following up action to investigate and mitigate risk.
- Authorities' exchange of information and cooperation in the development of good practices will be improved at national and international levels so that, by end-2008, a college exists for each of the largest global financial institutions.
- Banking supervisors and central banks should improve cooperation and the exchange of information including in the assessment of financial stability risks. The exchange of information should be rapid during periods of market strain.
- International bodies should enhance the speed, prioritisation, and coordination of their policy development work including encouraging joint strategic reviews by standard setting committees to better ensure policy development is coordinated and focused on priorities.
- Central bank operational frameworks should be sufficiently flexible in terms of potential frequency and maturity of operations, available instruments, and the range of counterparties and collateral, to deal with extraordinary situations.
- Banking authorities should clarify and strengthen national and cross-border arrangements for dealing with weak banks and review, and where necessary, strengthen deposit insurance arrangements.
- For the largest cross-border financial firms, the most directly involved supervisors and central banks should establish a small group to address specific cross-border crisis management planning issues and this group should hold its first meeting before the end of 2008.

4.225 In November 2008, the G20 countries called for a larger membership of the FSF and a broad consensus emerged in the following months towards placing the FSF on stronger institutional ground with an expanded membership - to strengthen its effectiveness as a mechanism for national authorities, standard setting bodies and international financial institutions to address vulnerabilities and to develop and implement strong regulatory, supervisory and other policies in the interest of financial stability. As announced at the G20 Summit of April 2009, an expanded FSF would be re-established as the Financial Stability Board ('FSB') with a broadened mandate to promote financial stability.

The mandate of the FSB is to: **4.226**

- assess vulnerabilities affecting the financial system and identify and oversee action needed to address them;
- promote coordination and information exchange among authorities responsible for financial stability;
- monitor and advise on market developments and their implications for regulatory policy;
- advise on and monitor best practice in meeting regulatory standards;
- undertake joint strategic reviews of the policy development work of the international standard setting bodies to ensure their work is timely, coordinated, focused on priorities, and addressing gaps;
- set guidelines for and support the establishment of supervisory colleges;
- manage contingency planning for cross-border crisis management, particularly with respect to systemically important firms; and
- collaborate with the IMF to conduct Early Warning Exercises.

Members of the FSB are committed to pursuing the maintenance of financial stability, maintaining the openness and transparency of the financial sector, implementing established international financial standards (including the 12 key International Standards and Codes),[192] and agreeing to undergo periodic peer reviews, using among other evidence IMF/World Bank Public Financial Sector Assessment Program ('FSAP') reports. **4.227**

The FSB meets in plenary sessions two times per year and to broaden the circle of countries engaged in work to promote international financial stability, the FSB also has regional consultative groups[193] which holds regional meetings which includes non-member financial authorities. **4.228**

The IMF as the Lender of Last Resort

In the first half of 2008 as the impact of the credit crunch deepened, several banking institutions found themselves in financial difficulties which required national central banks to step in to maintain financial stability and avoid contagion in the banking sector. In the UK, Northern Rock plc, was finally taken into public ownership by the UK Government in February 2008[194] and US investment bank, Bear Stearns, was 'rescued' by JP Morgan Chase at the behest of the US Federal Reserve. The Danish Central Bank (Danmarks Nationalbank) was also called upon to take over the assets of Roskilde Bank A/S[195] and questions began to arise regarding the role of the IMF as the lender of last resort. **4.229**

[192] See <http://www.financialstabilityboard.org/cos/key_standards.htm>.

[193] See <http://www.financialstabilityboard.org/about/rcg.pdf> for composition of Regional Consultative Groups.

[194] See: The Northern Rock PLC Transfer Order 2008, SI 2008/432.

[195] See: Press release dated 24 August 2008, Danish Central Bank: <http://www.nationalbanken.dk/DNUK/PressRoom.nsf/side/PressDNN20087204/$file/DNN20087204.pdf>.

4.230 From Bretton Woods onwards, the IMF had stepped in to help resolve currency crises such as those that afflicted developing economies such as Mexico, Asian countries, and Argentina in the 1990s.[196] The situation in 2008 is, however, arguably different because the IMF was now being asked to help the central banks of the major developed economies, in particular the US and the UK. Previously, there had always been an assumption that the US would bail out whoever needed to be bailed out because it is the main contributor of funds to the IMF;[197] however, when the US economy was experiencing major economic problems leading to global contagion in the markets then the supranational regulatory authorities were in largely uncharted territory.[198]

4.231 The question then arose of whether the IMF should become the international lender of last resort to the national lenders of last resort or even whether the IMF should become a global supervisor with an 'early warning system' for bank failures.[199] The IMF lacks the fundamental requirement for such a role, however, in that it has no power to print money in order to create liquidity in the system.[200] In addition, the IMF acts by consensus and as we have seen national regulators have needed to take decisive action to shore up the markets and do not have the luxury of time to consider, debate, and consult a wide range of interests.

4.232 It has also been suggested that the IMF might become a super-regulator for banks given the global reach of the major investment banking institutions but it would appear that the IMF is too far away from the day-to-day supervision of institutions to do so effectively. However, the IMF continues to play an important role in ensuring multilateralism because the challenges facing the world economy are of a global nature, requiring strong action and close cooperation.[201]

The Global Economy and the Future of Supranational Bodies

4.233 In a response to a 2006 BIS Working paper on financial stability, Peter Praet of the National Bank of Belgium had said: 'Contrary to monetary policy, the responsibility for financial stability is shared with other authorities; in particular, supervisors and treasuries. The governance of the process is—unavoidably—complex, and the potential for frictions, both domestic and international, is high, especially given that public money is at stake'.[202] This

[196] There was, of course, the sterling crisis in the mid 1970s but that was a UK-specific problem rather than a global one. For a historical analysis of the history of the lender of last resort theory, see WR Cline, 'The Case for a Lender-of-Last-Resort Role for the IMF', Center for Global Development and Institute for International Economics, 23 September 2005; see <http://www.petersoninstitute.org/publications/papers/cline0905imf.pdf>.

[197] See 'An International Lender of Last Resort, the IMF and the Federal Reserve', Representative Jim Saxton, Vice Chairman, US House of Representatives, Joint Economic Committee, February 1999; see <http://www.house.gov/jec/imf/lolr.pdf>.

[198] See EB Kapstein, BIS Working Papers No 199, *Architects of stability? International cooperation among financial supervisors, BIS Monetary and Economic Department*, February 2006, p 15.

[199] See JD Sachs, *The International Lender of Last Report: What are the Alternatives?* See <http://www.bos.frb.org/economic/conf/conf43/181p.pdf>.

[200] S Fischer, *On the Need for an International Lender of Last Resort*, New York, 3 January 1999. See <http://www.imf.org/external/np/speeches/1999/010399.htm>.

[201] IMF, Communiqué of the International Monetary and Financial Committee of the Board of Governors of the International Monetary Fund, Press Release No 08/78, 12 April 2008.

[202] BIS Working Paper 199, 'Observations on the paper by E Kapstein' (P Praet, National Bank of Belgium) at 22. See <http://www.bis.org/publ/work199.pdf>.

was now being borne out by the credit crunch and governments have increasingly turned to the supranational bodies for a solution.

In considering the role of the IMF, Alistair Darling, the UK Chancellor of the Exchequer, has called for reform of both the IMF and World Bank, institutions he says that were set up over 60 years ago and designed for another age.[203] These bodies, the Chancellor argued, needed to be reformed and refocused to deal with the challenges of which financial stability was perhaps the most pressing but not the only example of where the various member nations need to act together. **4.234**

In a speech at the Washington think tank, the Brookings Institute, Darling urged that urgent action was required on the big challenges facing the global economy—financial stability and how to deal with rising food and commodity prices that are already impacting developing and developed countries alike.[204] **4.235**

Although both governments and central banks around the world have already taken action in response to these developments and made coordinated efforts to improve liquidity in money markets, the issue remains as to how to inject and maintain confidence in the financial markets in the face of the ongoing uncertainty in the financial markets. Darling did recognise that some of the instability has arisen through investors and institutions chasing 'the search for yield' during a period where the markets have experienced historically low interest rates. He said: **4.236**

> Financial innovation has brought considerable benefits. It has allowed increased access to finance, with the easier and more efficient allocation of capital with, and between, economies. It has also increased the scope for risk to be diversified. That is all to the good. But recent events have also highlighted that the increased complexity and sophistication of markets carry risks that need to be better managed and understood. Innovation brings huge benefits provided institutions and regulators can understand what they are doing. The problem is that too many institutions, too many boards who have primary responsibility for what their firms are doing, failed to understand the risks to which they became exposed. There must therefore be greater transparency in the financial markets, providing greater certainty and confidence. That is why today, in the present context, the sooner institutions disclose their positions the better. This is not just a matter for individual banks. It matters to us all. I see that in the past few days some banks have pleaded mea culpa. Indeed, but we are all feeling the consequences.

The Chancellor indicated that international coordination is necessary and cooperation between supervisors is important—so that problems can be identified before they take hold and spread. However, he warned that: **4.237**

> [o]ur response needs to be measured and proportionate—we must not repeat what I might call the 'Enron mistake', where in an attempt to deal with an undoubted problem, there were unintended and undesirable consequences. It is not a question of more regulation—often it is a question of regulators and management doing their job effectively.

Darling said that there were two key lessons that can be drawn from the current crisis: first, that national economies are inextricably linked and that events in one country can impact on others around the world and second that there is a need for governments and regulators to

[203] A Darling MP, '*The Response to Global Economy Issues*', Brookings Institution, 11 April 2008; see <http://www.brookings.edu/~/media/events/2008/4/11%20global%20economy/0411_global_economics_darling.pdf>. See also A Darling, Back from the Brink: 1000 days at No 11 (Atlantic 2011).

[204] ibid.

take action in response to the risks that have been identified. He called for the IMF to work with the Financial Stability Forum to develop an early warning system, focusing its surveillance more closely on financial sector issues and on the links between developments in the financial sector and the wider economy and to strengthen its analysis of 'spillovers' between national economies.[205] However, this new role would require reform of these institutions in order to make the IMF more representative of its members' roles in the global economy and that these long-standing and established organisations needed to be ready to change otherwise they risk becoming marginalised and ineffective in supporting the cooperation needed to deal with global events and issues.

4.238 However, the debate continues and a global regulatory solution remains at some distance. The supranational bodies must, therefore, continue to fulfil their role in providing forums for cooperation and discussion and in keeping the lines of communication between the regulators and between the regulators and market participants open.[206]

[205] The Financial Stability Forum published its paper on *Credit Risk Transfer: Developments from 2005–2007* in July 2008 but its recommendations to regulators and supervisors including that 'Supervisory authorities need to ensure that they have the requisite resources and expertise to oversee CRT activities at the firms they supervise, and should ensure that these firms in turn have the capacity to understand and manage all of the risks in their CRT positions' is, in the case of the credit crunch, definitely a case of shutting the stable door after the horse has bolted.

[206] As Benjamin Franklin told the US Continental Congress, 'We must all hang together or assuredly we shall all hang separately'. An admonition that has resonances for the global markets today just as it did in 1776.

Part II

FINANCIAL SERVICES REGULATION

5

THE PRA AND FCA AND THE HANDBOOKS OF RULES AND GUIDANCE[1]

The Prudential Regulation Authority and the Financial Conduct Authority

Constitutional provisions

FSMA as amended by the Financial Services Act 2012 ('FSA 2012') establishes the FCA and the PRA as the statutory regulators of UK financial services business, in succession to the FSA, with effect from 1 April 2013, a date which the FSA called 'Legal Cutover' or 'LCO'. 5.01

FSMA, section 1A renames the body corporate previously known as the Financial Services Authority as the Financial Conduct Authority. Section 2A renames the body corporate first incorporated by the Bank of England as the Prudential Regulation Authority Limited as the Prudential Regulation Authority. FSMA, sections 1A and 2A specify that the FCA and the PRA respectively have the functions conferred on each of them by or under FSMA, or under other enactments,[2] or under qualifying EU provisions.[3] FSMA, Schedule 1ZA imposes requirements as to the FCA's constitution and makes additional provision concerning the status of the FCA, the discharge of the FCA's functions, and FCA penalties and fees.[4] FSMA, Schedule 1ZB makes parallel provision as to the constitution, functions, status, penalties, and fees of the PRA.[5] In particular, each regulator is given statutory immunity from liability in damages for anything[6] done or omitted to be done (by it, or its employees or contractors) in good faith and in discharge or purported discharge of its functions.[7] 5.02

---

[1] The author records with thanks the able assistance of Teniola Onabanjo, Barrister at 3 Verulam Buildings, Gray's Inn, in the preparation of this chapter.

[2] Including the Insolvency Act 1986, the Banking Act 2009, and the Financial Services Act 2012.

[3] FSMA, s 1A(3) and (6). 'Qualifying EU provisions' means directly applicable provisions of EU law that confer functions on the FCA, as specified in the Financial Services and Markets Act 2000 (Qualifying EU Provisions) Order 2013 (SI 2013/419).

[4] These include, eg, (under Sch 1ZA, para 8) that the FCA may in general discharge its functions through subcommittees or members of staff, but reserving some functions (in particular the legislative function of making rules, issuing codes, issuing statements, or giving directions), to the FCA's governing body.

[5] These include the requirement (under para 2) that the Governor of the Bank of England must be the chairman of the PRA and that the Bank of England's Deputy Governor for prudential regulation must be the Chief Executive of the PRA. As with the FCA, para 16 provides that while the PRA may generally make arrangements for any of its functions to be discharged by subcommittees or members of staff, its legislative functions are reserved to its governing body.

[6] Except acts that are incompatible with rights under the Convention for the Protection of Human Rights and Fundamental Freedoms (see the Human Rights Act 1998, s 6(1)).

[7] FSMA, Sch 1ZA, para 25 (FCA); FSMA, Sch 1ZB, para 33 (PRA).

The remit of the FCA and the PRA

5.03 The 'general prohibition' in FSMA, section 19 (read with section 21) provides that no person may lawfully carry on a 'regulated activity' by way of business in the UK unless he is an authorised person or an exempt person. Much of the rest of this book is devoted to a detailed discussion of different regulated activities, but for present purposes, FSMA, section 55A explains how the necessary authorisation is obtained and, in doing so, explains the different remits of the FCA and the PRA. Authorisation under FSMA is obtained indirectly, by applying for 'permission' to carry on specific regulated activities.[8] Section 55(1) provides that an application for permission may be made to the appropriate regulator. Section 55(2) elaborates on this (in part) by providing that 'the appropriate regulator' means the PRA, in a case where the regulated activities to which the application relates 'consist of or include a PRA-regulated activity'; or the FCA, in any other case.

5.04 However, a regulated activity is a 'PRA-regulated activity' only if it is designated as such in subordinate legislation[9] made by HM Treasury under FSMA, section 22A. FSMA, sections 417 and 2B(5) then define a 'PRA-authorised person' as a person that has permission to carry on a regulated activity that is designated as a PRA-regulated activity. Authorisation by the PRA subjects a firm to regulation by the PRA in respect of matters relevant to the PRA's statutory objectives, but does not relieve the firm of regulation by the FCA in respect of matters relevant to the FCA's separate statutory objectives. Accordingly, FSMA uses the term 'authorised person' to refer to all persons with permission under FSMA and the term 'PRA-authorised person' as shorthand for a firm that is *dual-regulated* by both the PRA and the FCA.

5.05 At the time of writing, only the regulated activity of accepting deposits, the regulated activities of effecting or carrying out contracts of insurance, and the regulated activities specific to the operation of the insurance market at Lloyd's of London have been designated as PRA-regulated activities.[10] Provision has also been made[11] for the PRA to designate the regulated activity of dealing in investments as principal as PRA-regulated activity, when that activity is carried on by a specific investment firm, thereby bringing systemically important investment firms within the PRA's remit. However, that power has not yet been exercised. At present, therefore, the PRA's regulatory remit extends only to deposit taking businesses (that is, banks and building societies) and to insurance businesses operating in the Lloyd's of London insurance market and in the wider UK insurance market. One consequence is that both the FCA and the PRA are inaptly named: the PRA is in fact a prudential regulator, but only for the (dual-regulated) subset of the FSMA-authorised firms operating in the UK; the FCA is the conduct regulator for all FSMA-authorised firms, but *also* the single prudential regulator for all FSMA-authorised firms that do not fall within the PRA's carefully circumscribed remit.[12]

---

8 See, eg, FSMA, s 417, read with s 31, which provides in part that an 'authorised person' under FSMA includes 'a person who has . . . permission to carry on one or more regulated activities'.

9 The Financial Services and Markets Act 2000 (PRA-regulated Activities) Order 2013 (SI 556/2013).

10 ibid, art 2.

11 ibid, art 3.

12 This explains the (otherwise perplexing) appearance of a full suite of prudential requirements in the FCA's Handbook of Rules and Guidance.

General Functions, Statutory Objectives, Regulatory Principles, and General Duties

The FCA

FSMA, section 1B(6) defines the FCA's 'general functions' as its function of making rules under the Act; its function of preparing and issuing codes under the Act; its function in relation to the giving of general guidance under the Act; and its function of determining the general policy and principles by reference to which the FCA performs its particular functions under the Act. The FCA's general functions are, therefore, the principal mechanisms by or through which, directly or indirectly, it discharges the myriad of particular functions given to it under FSMA and other legislation. **5.06**

FSMA, section 1B(2) gives the FCA the 'strategic objective' of ensuring that relevant markets function well. 'Relevant markets' are extensively defined to include the financial markets, the markets for 'regulated financial services'[13] and the markets for regulated activity services lawfully provided by persons who are not authorised under FSMA.[14] Section 1B(3) gives the FCA 'operational objectives' of (a) securing an appropriate degree of protection for consumers;[15] (b) protecting and enhancing the integrity[16] of the UK financial system;[17] and (c) promoting effective competition in the interests of consumers in the markets for regulated financial services or services provided by certain recognised investment exchanges.[18] The FCA is required (having first consulted with the PRA) to give guidance about how it intends to advance its operational objectives in discharging its general functions in relation to different categories of authorised person or regulated activity.[19] **5.07**

As compared with the statutory objectives of the FSA under the previous regime, perhaps the most notable features of the FCA's statutory objectives are first, the inclusion of an overt (albeit subordinated) competition objective,[20] and secondly, the strong emphasis on the protection of consumers, which to some degree reflects the genesis of the present regulatory regime in the financial crisis of 2007 and the various financial scandals which followed. For example, in considering what degree of protection for consumers may be appropriate in order to achieve the consumer protection objective, the FCA must[21] have regard to 'the general principle that those providing regulated financial services should be expected to **5.08**

[13] Also extensively defined in FSMA, s 1H(2) to mean services provided (a) by authorised persons in carrying on regulated activities; (b) by authorised persons in carrying on a consumer credit business in connection with the accepting of deposits; (c) by authorised persons in communicating, or approving the communication by others of, invitations to engage in investment activity; (d) by authorised persons who are investment firms, or credit institutions, in providing relevant ancillary services under the Markets in Financial Instruments Directive; (e) by persons acting as appointed representatives; (f) by payment service providers in providing payment services; (g) by electronic money issuers in issuing electronic money; (h) by sponsors to issuers of securities; and (i) by primary information providers to persons who issue financial instruments.

[14] FSMA, s 1F.

[15] FSMA, s 1C.

[16] Widely defined in FSMA, s 1D to include soundness, stability, and resilience; the absence financial crime; the absence of market abuse; orderly operation; and transparency of price formation.

[17] FSMA, s 1D.

[18] FSMA, s 1E.

[19] FSMA, s 1K. At the time of writing, the current guidance (dated July 2013) can be found at <http://www.fca.org.uk/your-fca/documents/approach-to-advancing-its-objectives>.

[20] See para 5.113 *et seq.*

[21] Under FSMA, s 1C(2)(e).

provide consumers with the level of care that is appropriate having regard to the degree of risk involved in relation to the investment or other transaction and the capabilities of the consumers in question'.

5.09 Having defined the FCA's general functions, strategic objective, and operational objectives, FSMA then defines, in section 3B, eight 'regulatory principles'. These are wide-ranging and include the need to use resources in the most efficient and economic way; the principle of proportionality; the desirability of sustainable growth in the economy of the United Kingdom; the general principle that consumers should take responsibility for their decisions; and the responsibility of the senior management of financial services for compliance with regulatory requirements. These 'regulatory principles' are analogous to, although more extensive than, the 'principles of good regulation' or 'supervisory principles' which applied to the FSA under the previous regime.[22]

5.10 FSMA then imposes a complex hierarchy of 'general duties' on the FCA. First, in discharging its general functions, the FCA must, so far as reasonably possible, act in a way which is compatible with its strategic objective and advances one or more of its operational objectives.[23] Second, the FCA must, so far as is compatible with acting in a way which advances the consumer protection objective or the integrity objective, discharge its general functions in a way which promotes effective competition in the interests of consumers[24]—effectively subordinating the competition objective to the consumer protection and integrity objectives. Third, in discharging its general functions the FCA must have regard to the regulatory principles and to the importance of taking action intended to minimise the extent to which it is possible for financial services business to be used for a purpose connected with financial crime.[25] Finally, and most generally, the FCA is required in managing its affairs to 'have regard to such generally accepted principles of good corporate governance as it is reasonable to regard as applicable to it'.[26]

The PRA

5.11 FSMA, section 2J defines the PRA's general functions as its function of making rules; its function of preparing and issuing codes; and its function of determining the general policy and principles by reference to which it performs particular functions under this Act. As for the FCA, therefore, the PRA's general functions are the principal mechanisms by or through which, directly or indirectly, it discharges the particular functions given to it under FSMA and other legislation.

5.12 One notable difference between the functions of the PRA and the functions of the FCA is that, unlike the FCA, the PRA has no general function of giving general guidance under FSMA.[27] Correspondingly, although the PRA is enjoined by FSMA, section 2I(1) to give guidance 'about how it intends to advance its objectives in discharging its general functions in relation to different categories of PRA-authorised person or PRA-regulated activity', it has no other FSMA power to give guidance. In particular, the PRA has no FSMA power

---

22 See FSMA, s 2(3), before amendment by the FSA 2012.
23 FSMA, s 1B(1).
24 FSMA, s 1B(4).
25 FSMA, s 1B(5).
26 FSMA, s 3C.
27 See FSMA, s 1B(6)(c) for the FCA general function of 'giving general guidance under FSMA'.

equivalent to the FCA's power in FSMA, section 139A(3) to give 'general guidance' to FCA-regulated persons[28] generally, or to a class of such persons. A glance at the PRA Handbook shows that it is nevertheless replete with guidance of all kinds. The result appears to be that although the guidance now in the PRA handbook has no formal status under FSMA, that guidance will nevertheless bind the PRA to the extent that, for example, it establishes a legitimate expectation in public law. As to the future, the PRA will no doubt continue to give guidance in various forms,[29] but untrammelled by the consultation requirements that attach to 'general guidance' given by the FCA under FSMA.[30]

The PRA's general objective[31] is to promote the safety and soundness of PRA-authorised persons.[32] The PRA is to advance that objective primarily by seeking to ensure that the business of PRA-authorised persons is carried on in a way which avoids any adverse effect on the stability of the UK financial system;[33] and seeking to minimise the adverse effect (in particular, disruption of the continuity of financial services) that the failure of a PRA-authorised person could be expected to have on the stability of the UK financial system.[34] In addition, for as long as the effecting or carrying out of contracts of insurance as principal (that is, insurance business) is to any extent a PRA-regulated activity,[35] the PRA has the additional 'insurance objective' of 'contributing to the securing of an appropriate degree of protection for those who are or may become policyholders'.[36] The insurance objective applies alongside the general objective when a PRA function is exercisable in relation to insurance business.[37] It is notable, therefore, that the PRA's objectives are much more narrowly focused than the FCA's multi-layered objectives, and that except in relation to with-profits insurance, the PRA has no overt consumer protection objective. The PRA is required to determine, publish and keep under review (at least annually) its strategy in relation to its objectives.[38] The PRA's objectives do not, however, require it to operate a 'zero-failure regime' in which no PRA-authorised firm is permitted to fail.[39] **5.13**

Like the FCA, the PRA is required to have regard to the regulatory principles in FSMA, section 3B when discharging its general functions. In addition, the PRA is required to consider how the discharge of its general functions may impact on 'competition in the markets for services provided by PRA-authorised persons in carrying on regulated activities', and to minimise any adverse effect on that competition.[40] Finally, like the FCA, the PRA is required, in managing its affairs, to 'have regard to such generally accepted principles of good corporate governance as it is reasonable to regard as applicable to it'.[41] **5.14**

---

[28] Defined in this FSMA, s 139A(9) to mean 'an authorised person, or any person who is otherwise subject to rules made by the FCA'.
[29] See generally para 5.82 *et seq.*
[30] See FSMA, s 139A(5).
[31] FSMA, s 2B(3)(a).
[32] FSMA, s 2B(2).
[33] Widely defined in FSMA, s 1T.
[34] FSMA, s 2B(3)(b) read with s 2B(4).
[35] FSMA, s 2C(3).
[36] FSMA, s 2C(2).
[37] FSMA, s 2F.
[38] FSMA, s 2E.
[39] FSMA, s 2G. For this purpose, 'failure' is defined in FSMA, s 2J(3) to include entry into insolvency (itself widely defined in FSMA, s 2J(4)); the application of stabilisation options under the Banking Act 2009, Part 1; or inability to meet claims such that the Financial Services Compensation Scheme may be engaged.
[40] FSMA, s 2H.
[41] FSMA, s 3C.

The boundary between FCA and PRA responsibilities

5.15 FSMA gives HM Treasury the power to specify in subordinate legislation matters that, in relation to the exercise by either regulator of its functions relating to PRA-authorised persons, are to be, or are to be primarily, the responsibility of one regulator rather than the other.[42] The order may provide that one regulator is or is not to have regard to specified matters when exercising specified functions, or require one regulator to consult the other. Except in cases of urgency, no such order may be made without an affirmative resolution of Parliament.[43] If an order is urgent, it may be made without Parliamentary approval,[44] but in that case it ceases to have effect after 28 days unless Parliament approves it in the meantime.[45] At the time of writing, no such orders have yet been made.

Arrangements for the supervision of regulated firms and for enforcement

5.16 Both the FCA and the PRA are required to make arrangements to supervise the authorised persons, or PRA-authorised persons, within their respective remits.[46] Each regulator's supervisory arrangements are underpinned by the availability of disciplinary measures, including public censure, financial penalties, and the suspension or restriction of permission to carry on regulated activities. FSMA Part 14 provides[47] that the power to impose disciplinary measures rests with 'the appropriate regulator'. That is the PRA in respect of (a) requirements imposed by the PRA under FSMA; (b) PRA decisions or orders[48] approving or prohibiting persons who perform (or intend to perform) controlled functions for PRA-authorised persons; and (c) requirements imposed under directly effective 'qualifying EU provisions' when the PRA is designated as the appropriate regulator in subordinate legislation.[49] The FCA is the appropriate regulator in the case of a contravention of any other requirement imposed by or under FSMA.[50]

5.17 FSMA, section 1L requires the FCA to maintain arrangements designed to enable it to monitor (and enforce) compliance by persons other than authorised persons with requirements (under FSMA or qualifying EU measures) in respect of which the FCA is the appropriate regulator under FSMA, Part 14. FSMA, section 401 allocates the power to prosecute breach of requirements, the contravention of which constitutes an offence.[51] Important examples of such requirements include FSMA, section 23(1) which makes a contravention of the general prohibition[52] an offence, and FSMA, section 25(1), which makes a breach of the financial promotion restriction[53] an offence. Investigation and prosecution of these offences underpins the enforcement of the 'regulatory perimeter'. As prefigured by FSMA, section 1L, section 401 allocates the prosecution power in respect of authorisation offences to the FCA.[54]

42 FSMA, s 3G.
43 FSMA, s 3H(1).
44 FSMA, s 3H(2).
45 FSMA, s 3H(3).
46 FSMA, s 1L (FCA) and s 2K (PRA).
47 See FSMA, s 204A.
48 Under FSMA, ss 56(6), 59(1), and 59(2).
49 The Financial Services and Markets Act 2000 (Qualifying EU Provisions) Order 2013 (SI 2013/419).
50 FSMA, s 204A(6).
51 FSMA, s 204(5).
52 FSMA, s 19.
53 FSMA, s 21.
54 FSMA, s 401(3A) (listing the offences in respect of which the PRA is the appropriate regulator), read with s 401(3B), which provides that 'the FCA is the "appropriate regulator" in respect of any other offence'.

Requirements to consult

Like the FSA before it, the FCA is required, under FSMA, section 1M, to make and maintain effective arrangements for consulting practitioners and consumers on the extent to which the FCA's general policies and practices are consistent with its general duties under FSMA, section 1B. Those arrangements must[55] include the establishment of a practitioner panel, a smaller business practitioner panel, a markets practitioner panel, and a consumer panel. The FCA has a statutory duty to consider the representations made to it under the arrangements and to publish its responses to those representations.[56] The PRA has a similar duty to consult PRA-authorised persons (or persons appearing to the PRA to represent the interests of such persons) on the extent to which the PRA's general policies and practices are consistent with its general duties.[57] That is underpinned by a requirement[58] to establish a PRA-practitioner panel and by a statutory duty to consider and publish its responses to the representations made.[59] 5.18

Coordination between the regulators

An obvious consequence of splitting the functions of the former FSA between the FCA and the PRA is that there will be areas and issues in respect of which the functions of the new regulators will overlap and potentially conflict. FSMA, section 3D(3) therefore introduces the concept of 'matters of common regulatory interest' to both regulators: a function conferred on either regulator relates to matters of common regulatory interest if (a) the other regulator exercises similar or related functions in relation to the same persons; (b) the other regulator exercises functions which relate to different persons but relate to similar subject matter; or (c) its exercise could affect the advancement by the other regulator of any of its objectives (which, in the case of the FCA and for the purpose of the provisions about coordination, means its operational objectives and not its strategic objective). 5.19

FSMA, section 3D(1) then requires the FCA and the PRA to ensure the coordinated exercise of their functions. Coordination is expressed to be 'with a view to ensuring' (a) that each regulator consults the other in connection with any proposed exercise of a function that may have a material adverse effect on the advancement by the other regulator of any of its objectives; (b) that where appropriate each regulator obtains information and advice from the other regulator in connection with the exercise of its functions in relation to matters of common regulatory interest in cases where the other regulator may be expected to have relevant information or relevant expertise; and (c) that where either regulator exercises functions in relation to matters of common regulatory interest, both regulators have regard,[60] in particular, to the regulatory principles of efficiency[61] and proportionality.[62] The duty to coordinate is not absolute: it applies only to the extent that compliance is compatible with 5.20

55 FSMA, ss 1N to 1Q.
56 FSMA, s 1R.
57 FSMA, s 2L.
58 FSMA, s 2M.
59 FSMA, s 2N.
60 FSMA, s 1B(5)(a) (FCA) and s 2H(1)(a) (PRA).
61 FSMA, s 3B(1)(a): the need to use the resources of each regulator in the most efficient and economic way.
62 FSMA, s 3B(1)(b): the principle that a burden or restriction which is imposed on a person, or on the carrying on of an activity, should be proportionate to the benefits, considered in general terms, which are expected to result from the imposition of that burden or restriction.

the advancement by each regulator of any of its objectives,[63] and does not impose a burden on the regulators that is disproportionate to the benefits of compliance.[64]

5.21 The duty to coordinate is underpinned by a statutory requirement[65] for the FCA and the PRA to prepare, maintain, regularly review,[66] and publish[67] a memorandum which describes in general terms (a) the role of each regulator in relation to the exercise of functions conferred by or under FSMA which relate to matters of common regulatory interest;[68] and (b) how the regulators intend to comply with the duty to coordinate in relation to the exercise of those functions. FSMA is permissive about the range of issues that the memorandum may cover,[69] but requires[70] that the memorandum must address the coordination by the regulators of (i) the exercise of their functions relating to membership of, and their relations with, the European Supervisory Authorities;[71] (ii) their relations with regulatory bodies outside the United Kingdom; and (iii) the exercise of their functions in relation to the Financial Services Compensation Scheme.

5.22 In fulfilment of their obligation, the FCA and the PRA have entered into a 68-point Memorandum of Understanding[72] ('MOU'). The MOU refers to the distinct mandates and separate roles and responsibilities of each regulator.[73] Each regulator will make its own rules and policies in light of its separate objectives, although they will consult and avoid the imposition of incompatible requirements, meet regularly, and ensure routine coordination on rule making.[74] The MOU contains specific provisions on information sharing and confidentiality,[75] authorisation,[76] supervision of dual-regulated firms,[77] Lloyds' supervision,[78] with-profits policies,[79] overseas firms,[80] and UKLA coordination.[81] The MOU also deals with formal regulatory processes and enforcement,[82] including the PRA's right to veto FCA regulatory actions,[83] reporting regulatory failure,[84] financial crime and fraud,[85] and

[63] Although not, in the case of the FCA, its strategic objective; see FSMA, s 3D(4).
[64] FSMA, s 3D(2).
[65] FSMA, s 3E(1).
[66] FSMA, s 3E(4).
[67] FSMA, s 3E(7), subject to s 3E(8).
[68] As defined in FSMA, s 3D(3), earlier: see s 3E(9).
[69] FSMA, s 3E(2)(a)–(o).
[70] FSMA, s 3E(3).
[71] ie the European Banking Authority, the European Insurance and Occupational Pensions Authority, and the European Securities and Markets Authority.
[72] FCA and PRA, 'Memorandum of Understanding (MoU) between the Financial Conduct Authority (FCA) and the Prudential Regulation Authority (PRA)', 1 April 2013, at <http://www.fca.org.uk/your-fca/documents/mou-between-the-fca-and-the-pracoordination>.
[73] Paras 1 and 3–5.
[74] Paras 13–16.
[75] Paras 6–9 and 10–12. Specific arrangements governing the collection of regulatory data and avoidance of duplication are dealt with under Annex 2.
[76] Paras 17–21.
[77] Paras 22–27.
[78] Paras 28–32.
[79] Paras 33–34.
[80] Paras 35–36.
[81] Paras 37–40.
[82] Paras 41–49.
[83] Paras 50–52.
[84] Paras 54–55.
[85] Paras 56–57.

coordination with other authorities.[86] The MOU includes additional provisions on fees,[87] cross-border positions,[88] and the maintenance and review of the MOU.[89]

The regulators have a separate duty (under FSMA, section 3F), to prepare and maintain a memorandum[90] which describes in general terms (a) the role of each regulator in relation to the exercise of functions conferred by or under FSMA so far as they relate to with-profits insurers, and (b) how the regulators intend to comply with the duty to coordinate in relation to the exercise of those functions so far as they relate to the effecting or carrying out of with-profits policies by with-profits insurers.[91] **5.23**

The PRA's power of direction

As noted earlier, the PRA's general objective[92] is to promote the safety and soundness of PRA-authorised persons.[93] It is to advance that objective primarily by seeking to ensure that the business of PRA-authorised persons is carried on in a way which avoids any adverse effect on the stability of the UK financial system,[94] and by seeking to minimise the adverse effect (in particular, disruption of the continuity of financial services) that the failure of a PRA-authorised person could be expected to have on the stability of the UK financial system.[95] It is a possible consequence of the dual-regulation of PRA-authorised persons under FSMA that regulatory action proposed by the FCA as conduct regulator may result in the failure of a PRA-authorised firm. Conceptually, for example, an FCA requirement that a dual-regulated firm must pay substantial compensation to its customers in respect of the mis-selling of a financial product might threaten the financial viability of that firm. If the firm concerned is of particular significance, that failure may in turn threaten the achievement of the PRA's statutory objectives. **5.24**

FSMA reconciles this tension between the FCA's powers and the PRA's objectives by giving the PRA a power of direction, by which it can require the FCA not to exercise a power, or require the FCA to exercise a power in a specified manner.[96] The PRA may give a direction if, in the PRA's opinion, (a) the exercise of the FCA's power in the manner proposed may threaten the stability of the UK financial system, or result in the failure[97] of a PRA-authorised person in a way that would adversely affect the UK financial system;[98] and (b) a direction is necessary to avoid that possible consequence.[99] **5.25**

86 Paras 58–61.
87 Paras 62–64.
88 Para 65.
89 Paras 66–68.
90 At the time of writing the Bank of England website includes an undated With-Profits MoU, at <http://www.bankofengland.co.uk/about/Documents/mous/mouwithprofits.pdf>.
91 Defined in FSMA, ss 3F(5)(a) and (b).
92 FSMA, s 2B(3)(a).
93 FSMA, s 2B(2).
94 Widely defined in FSMA, s 1T.
95 FSMA, s 2B(3)(b) read with s 2B(4).
96 FSMA, s 3I(6).
97 For this purpose, 'failure' is defined in FSMA, s 2J(3) to include entry into insolvency (itself widely defined in FSMA, s 2J(4)); the application of stabilisation options under the Banking Act 2009, Part 1; or inability to meet claims such that the Financial Services Compensation Scheme may be engaged. See FSMA, s 3I(9).
98 FSMA, s 3I(4).
99 FSMA, s 3I(5).

5.26 The PRA may give a direction[100] in respect of (a) the exercise of FCA's regulatory powers in relation to PRA-authorised persons generally, a class of PRA-authorised persons, or a particular PRA-authorised person; or (b) the exercise of the FCA's insolvency powers in relation to a PRA-authorised person; an appointed representative whose principal is a PRA-authorised person; or a person who is carrying on a PRA-regulated activity in contravention of the general prohibition. For this purpose, the FCA's 'insolvency powers' are[101] its powers under FSMA Part 24 (Insolvency) and its 'regulatory powers' are (subject to two limitations) widely defined to mean its powers in relation to the regulation of authorised persons. The two limitations[102] are, first, that the PRA may not direct the exercise of the FCA's power to consent (or not) to the PRA's decision to grant an application for permission to carry on a PRA-regulated activity. Secondly, the PRA may not direct the exercise of the FCA's power to consent (or not) to the PRA's proposed variation of the permission of a PRA-authorised person. In short, therefore, the FCA retains its autonomy as to who may be authorised under FSMA and as to the scope of permission of an authorised person. More generally, the FCA is not required to comply with a direction if or to the extent that in the opinion of the FCA, compliance would be incompatible with any EU obligation or any other international obligation of the United Kingdom.[103]

5.27 FSMA, section 3J gives the PRA a similar power of direction where the FCA's proposed exercise of powers relates to the provision of financial benefits under with-profits policies at the discretion of the insurer, or may affect the amount, timing or distribution of financial benefits, or the entitlement to future benefits under with-profits policies.[104] The power of direction is available if PRA is of the opinion that the giving of the direction is desirable in order to advance the PRA's general objective or its insurance objective.[105]

5.28 FSMA, sections 3K and 3L set out administrative and procedural requirements in relation to the giving, revocation and publication of PRA-directions under sections 3I and 3J. The regulatory arrangements under FSMA as ameneded by FSA 2012 therefore reflect the financial crisis from which they originated because, notwithstanding the policy concern that the FCA should be more overtly consumer-focused than the FSA, the arrangements partially subordinate the FCA to the PRA, in pursuit of financial stability.

Directions relating to consolidated supervision

5.29 A range of EU directives impose a requirement for, or are relevant to, the consolidated supervision of financial groups and conglomerates. Such a group may comprise both FCA-authorised persons and PRA-authorised persons (that is, single and dual regulated firms). FSMA, section 3M accordingly facilitates consolidated supervision by allowing either the FCA or the PRA, where it is the 'supervising regulator' (that is, the EU competent authority for the purpose of consolidated supervision of some or all members of a group of companies), to give a direction requiring the other regulator to exercise, or not to exercise, a relevant function in a specified manner in relation to authorised persons who are members of the relevant

100 FSMA, s 3I(2).
101 FSMA, s 3I(3)(b).
102 FSMA, s 3I(3)(a).
103 FSMA, s 3I(8).
104 FSMA, s 3J(4).
105 FSMA, s 3J(5).

group.[106] The direction may be given if the supervising regulator (probably in most cases the PRA, since consolidated supervision is generally a prudential issue) considers that it is necessary for the effective consolidated supervision of the relevant group.[107] The regulators' 'relevant functions' in respect of which a direction may be given are relatively widely defined,[108] but do not include the functions of making rules or codes, giving guidance, or (in the case of the FCA) the function of consenting (or not) to the PRA's decision to grant an application for permission to carry on a PRA-regulated activity, or the function of consenting (or not) to the PRA's proposed variation of the permission of a PRA-authorised person. As with PRA-directions under FSMA, sections 3I and 3J, the directed regulator is not required to comply with a direction under section 3M if or to the extent that in its opinion compliance would be incompatible with any EU obligation or any other international obligation of the United Kingdom.[109] FSMA, sections 3N and 3O set out administrative and procedural requirements in relation to the giving, revocation, and publication of directions under section 3M.

Government and Parliamentary oversight

Central government and Parliamentary oversight of the regulators is facilitated by FSMA, Schedules 1ZA (FCA) and 1ZB (PRA). Each regulator is required at least once a year to make a report to HM Treasury on, amongst other things: (a) the discharge of that regulator's functions;[110] (b) the extent to which in its opinion its objectives have been advanced;[111] (c) its consideration of the regulatory principles that both regulators must apply under FSMA, section 3B;[112] (d) how it has complied with its FSMA, section 3D duty to coordinate the exercise of its functions with the other regulator;[113] and (e) any directions given by the PRA to the FCA either (i) under FSMA, section 3I requiring the FCA to refrain from specified actions; or (ii) under FSMA, section 3J, in relation to with-profits policies.[114] Each regulator is also required to report on additional matters that are specific to it.[115] HM Treasury is required to lay each such report before Parliament.[116] Separately, the PRA is required to give the Treasury a copy of any PRA direction under FSMA, section 3I,[117] and regulators are required to give the Treasury a copy of the memorandum that they prepare in compliance with their duty to coordinate the exercise of regulatory functions.[118] The Treasury must lay those directions[119] and the memorandum before Parliament.[120] **5.30**

In support of oversight by central government, HM Treasury has the power to appoint an independent person to conduct a review of the economy, efficiency, and effectiveness with **5.31**

106 FSMA, s 3M(5).
107 FSMA, s 3M(4).
108 FSMA, s 3M(7).
109 FSMA, s 3M(10).
110 FSMA, Sch 1ZA, para 11(1)(a) (FCA); FSMA, Sch 1ZB, para 19(1)(a) (PRA).
111 FSMA, Sch 1ZA, para 11(1)(b) (FCA); FSMA, Sch 1ZB, para 19(1)(b) (PRA).
112 FSMA, Sch 1ZA, para 11(1)(f) (FCA); FSMA, Sch 1ZB, para 19(1)(f) (PRA).
113 FSMA, Sch 1ZA, para 11(1)(g) (FCA); FSMA, Sch 1ZB, para 19(1)(d) (PRA).
114 FSMA, Sch 1ZA, para 11(1)(h) (FCA); FSMA, Sch 1ZB, para 19(1)(e) (PRA).
115 For example, FSMA, Sch 1ZA paras 11(1)(b) and (c) requires the FCA to report separately on the extent to which in its opinion it has acted compatibly with or advanced its strategic and operational objectives.
116 FSMA, Sch 1ZA, para 11(1)(4) (FCA); FSMA, Sch 1ZB, para 19(1)(4) (PRA).
117 FSMA, s 3L(5).
118 FSMA, s 3E(5).
119 FSMA, s 3L(5).
120 FSMA, s 3E(6).

which the FCA[121] or the PRA[122] has used its resources in discharging its functions. The appointed investigator has a statutory right to obtain documents and information for the purposes of that review.[123]

The FCA and PRA Handbooks

5.32 The FCA and the PRA exist to perform functions connected with the regulation of financial services. FSMA distinguishes the regulators' particular functions from their general functions.[124] The FCA's and PRA's particular functions are not defined as such. They include all the myriad tasks that each regulator is required to perform under FSMA, other primary legislation, subordinate legislation, and European legislation. These include the enforcement of the regulatory perimeter; the authorisation, supervision, and discipline of financial services firms and their employees; cooperation with other regulators at local, European, and international level; the prevention of financial crime; providing public information about financial services; and reporting to Parliament and the public.

5.33 The FCA's Handbook of Rules and Guidance ('the FCA Handbook') and the PRA's Handbook of Rules and Guidance ('the PRA Handbook') (together 'the Handbooks') and now also the PRA Rulebook (on which see paragraph 5.38 below) are some of the most important products or physical expressions of the regulators' general functions: each Handbook is the primary restatement of the rules, codes, and guidance through which that regulator performs its particular functions. The Handbooks are, therefore also the most obvious physical expression of the FCA's and PRA's policy.

5.34 FSA 2012 provided for the transfer of the functions of the FSA to the FCA and the PRA. In order to aid smooth transition between regulation by the FSA and regulation by the FCA and PRA, it was necessary to ensure that the FCA and PRA had in place rule-books which would come into effect on 1 April 2013,[125] the day they acquired their powers. In order to assist the transition, FSA 2012, section 119(3) provided that:

> The Treasury may by order make such provision as they consider necessary or expedient for transitory, transitional or saving purposes in connection with the commencement of any provision made by or under this Act.

5.35 FSA 2012, section 119(4)(b) specifically provided that an order under section 119(3) may:

> make provision treating any relevant instrument which was made, issued or given by the Financial Services Authority under any enactment . . . and is designated by the FCA, the PRA or the Bank of England (or any two or more of them) in accordance with the order—
>
> (i) as having been made, issued or given by the designating body or bodies;
> (ii) as having been made, issued or given (or also made, issued or given) under a corresponding provision of this Act or of an enactment as amended by or under this Act.

5.36 Pursuant to FSA 2012, section 119, the Treasury made the Financial Services Act 2012 (Transitional Provisions) (Rules and Miscellaneous Provisions) Order 2013 (SI 2013/161) ('the Transitional Order') which enabled the FCA and PRA to 'designate a relevant instrument,

121 FSMA, s 1S.
122 FSMA, s 2O.
123 FSMA, s 2T (FCA) and s 2P (PRA).
124 FSMA, ss 1B(6) and 2J(1).
125 See para 5.01.

or part of a relevant instrument'.[126] The Transitional Order also enabled the regulators to make modifications to the designated instruments.[127] Thus, the Transitional Order enabled the regulators to create the separate FCA and PRA Handbooks, by a combination of designation and modification of the instruments underlying the FSA Handbook. In practice, the FCA and the PRA undertook the task of designation by considering the provisions in the modules and sourcebooks of the FSA Handbook by reference to their powers and statutory objectives to decide whether it was desirable to designate particular provisions. In some cases the designation covered an entire sourcebook or module (for example, the FCA designated the whole of the Insurance Conduct of Business Sourcebook ('ICOB')), and in other cases the designation applied only to a particular provision (or part of a provision) in a sourcebook or module. The modifications made to designated provisions were mostly minor, for example changing references to 'FSA' to 'FCA' and correcting statutory references.[128] Other modifications were more significant, for example, deleting the part of a provision that extended beyond the designating regulator's powers and regulatory responsibilities.

In addition to designation and modification, more substantial changes to the FSA Handbook were required in order to align the new rule-books with the future objectives and functions of the FCA and PRA. The provisions giving effect to these substantial changes were consulted on by the FSA on behalf of the FCA and the PRA and made by the regulators in exercise of their new powers under FSMA as amended. An example are the provisions in Chapters 10A (FCA) and 10B (PRA) of the Supervision Manual which give effect to a revised approved persons regime. **5.37**

As well as the designated provisions and the provisions giving effect to substantive changes which came into effect on 1 April 2013, both regulators have continued to make new provisions and create sourcebooks and modules. An example is the new Investment Funds Sourcebook ('FUND') in the FCA Handbook. The PRA has indicated its intention to replace the material carried forward from the FSA Handbook with a PRA Rulebook. Accordingly, new instruments will be implemented into the current online PRA Handbook in PDF format so as to distinguish them from the 'legacy material' in the present PRA Handbook.[129] Thus, the form of the PRA Handbook is set to change in years to come. The PRA Rulebook is already significant: as of 1 January 2014, it contains the PRA rules implementing the EU Capital Requirements Directive. **5.38**

What material goes into the Handbooks?

Although it is accurate to describe the Handbooks as the primary re-statement of the rules, codes, and general guidance, through which the regulators perform their particular functions (see paragraph 5.33), that description needs explanation and elaboration. The FCA and the PRA have each published a Reader's Guide to their Handbook (in the form of a joint Reader's Guide), from which some of what follows is extracted and which readers are recommended to review: **5.39**

(a) The FCA and PRA are under statutory obligation to make some of their written output public. For example, FSMA, section 138G requires the regulators to exercise their rule-making powers in writing, in a document that FSMA identifies as a 'rule-making

[126] Financial Services Act 2012 (Transitional Provisions) (Rules and Miscellaneous Provisions) Order 2013 (SI 2013/161), art 2(1).

[127] Idem.

[128] The main designation instrument is FCA 2013/8 and PRA 2013/3. The main modification instruments are FCA 2013/9, PRA 2013/4, and FCA 2013/10, and PRA 2013/5.

[129] PRA, Consultation Paper CP5/13: Strengthening capital standards: Implementing CRD IV (August 2013), paras 1.23 – 1.25.

instrument'.[130] FSMA also requires the regulators to publish all their rule-making instruments.[131] Most other legislative provisions made by the regulators (such as codes and, in the case of the FCA, general guidance) are also in practice made by instrument. Each regulator publishes the instruments it makes on its website. That fulfils the regulators' obligations to publish their rules. The definitive version of each regulators rules at any time is the version contained in the legal instruments.[132] What appears in the Handbooks are not the instruments themselves, but a consolidated re-statement of the instruments in force at a given time.

(b) In fact, there are a number of versions of the Handbooks. At the time of writing, the online consolidated Handbooks are available via the Handbook Online website[133] which is jointly operated by the FCA and the PRA. The website allows the user to access the FCA Handbook (displaying provisions applying to FCA-regulated firms), the PRA Handbook (displaying provisions applying to PRA-regulated firms), and a 'combined view' which show the provisions of both Handbooks. Each of the provisions of the online Handbooks is labelled to show which regulator is applying a particular provision to firms. The website also offers the functionality for users to 'time travel' (that is, to view versions of the Handbooks that were in force on a specified date in the past). The FSA website enabled users to create 'tailored handbooks' containing only the provisions of the FSA Handbook that was relevant to their business. However, the FCA and the PRA withdrew the facility to produce tailored handbooks on 1 April 2013.[134] The consolidated Handbooks may contain typographical improvements, with no legal effect (such as cross-referencing and spelling corrections), which do not appear in the underlying legal instruments. At the time of writing, users may also subscribe for printed versions of the 'combined view' or individual modules or sourcebooks of the Handbooks. The printed versions are updated monthly.

(c) What goes into the Handbooks is essentially a matter of choice by the regulators. That has several consequences. First, the FSA published a great deal of general guidance that was closely connected with the FSA Handbook, but which did not form part of it. The FCA and/or the PRA have designated or adopted much of this guidance and as with the status quo ante, this guidance does not form part of the Handbooks. 'Handbook guides' are guides to a regulator's Handbook as a whole. They indicate which material in the Handbook is likely to be relevant to firms of a particular type. At the time of writing, there are three Handbook Guides in the FCA Handbook and none in the PRA Handbook. 'Regulatory guides' address particular topics in a regulator's Handbook. They include the FCA Perimeter Guidance Manual ('PERG') which address the perennial issue of which activities are regulated and which are not, the FCA and PRA Building Societies Regulatory Guide ('BSOG') and the FCA Enforcement Guide ('EG'). Although the Regulatory Guides contain guidance (on which see paragraph 5.82), they are not part of the Handbooks as such.[135] Second, the regulators operate (increasingly web-based) systems to deal with applications for authorisation and regulatory reporting. Each of those systems reflects policy choices and imposes

130 FSMA, s 138G(2).
131 ibid, s 138G(4).
132 ibid, s 138H.
133 <http://fshandbook.info/FS/index.jsp>.
134 Reader's Guide, 18.
135 See, eg, EG 1.8.

requirements (for example, as to the form of application or reporting) that are the product of the performance of the regulators' functions and the exercise of regulators' powers,[136] but they do not form part of the Handbooks. Third and finally, the FCA Handbook includes some requirements not made by FCA. The powers to make rules relating to the Financial Ombudsman scheme are shared between the FCA and the Financial Ombudsman Service ('FOS'). FOS rules are subject to FCA consent or approval and appear in the FCA Handbook.

(d) The Handbooks do not generally include statutory instruments such as orders, regulations, and the rules of the Upper Tribunal (Tax and Chancery Chamber);[137] or insolvency or winding-up rules; or rules made by self-regulatory bodies such as designated investment exchanges or recognised professional bodies. However, provisions of the FCA Handbook or PRA Handbook may include extracts from or cross-references to directly applicable non-FCA/PRA legislative materials. These are labelled 'UK' or indicated with a Union Jack icon alongside the text. European legislation affecting financial services is ever more voluminous, detailed, and prescriptive. In response, the FSA where possible adopted a policy of implementing European requirements by 'intelligent copy-out'. The provisions of COBS that implement MiFID are a good example. These provisions form part of the Handbooks and it is likely that the FCA and PRA will in future adopt a similar approach to implementing European Requirements. Allied to that, provisions of the Handbooks often include a note indicating precisely which European requirement they are intended to implement. In addition, the Handbooks may include extracts from and cross-references to non-FCA/PRA, European legislative material, such as directives and directly applicable regulations. This material is labelled 'EU' in the Handbooks, or indicated with an EU flag icon alongside the text.

An overview of the structure and content of the Handbook

The present structure of the Handbooks closely follows that of the FSA Handbook from which the content of the Handbooks was largely derived. In particular, the seven-block structure has been retained. The following table sets out the structure of the Handbooks as they stand at the time of writing, both to provide an overview of the Handbooks at large and also introduce the FCA/PRA abbreviations for each sourcebook or module of the Handbooks, which are used throughout the rest of this chapter. **5.40**

In order to provide a comparison to the FSA Handbook, the second column contains a list of all sourcebooks and modules that comprised the FSA Handbook as at 31 March 2013, that is, just before the Handbooks came into force on 1 April 2013. The fourth column then states, with respect to each sourcebook or module, whether the FCA and/or PRA has included a version of the sourcebook or module in its Handbook. The composition of each Handbook reflects, in part, the choice made by each regulator in designating the provisions of the FSA Handbook. Modules or sourcebooks added by the FCA and/or PRA since 1 April 2013 are shown in italics in the table. **5.41**

[136] For example, the power to give directions as to the form of applications for the variation of a firm's permission, in FSMA, s 55U(4).

[137] Which replaced the Financial Services and Markets Tribunal.

Table 5.1

High-Level Standards (Block 1)	PRIN	Principles for Businesses (the fundamental obligations of all firms under the regulatory system)	FCA Handbook PRA Handbook
	SYSC	Senior management arrangements, systems, and controls (the responsibilities of directors and senior management)	FCA Handbook PRA Handbook
	COND	Threshold conditions (the minimum standards for becoming and remaining authorised)	FCA Handbook
	APER	Statements of principle and code of practice for approved persons (the fundamental obligations of approved persons)	FCA Handbook PRA Handbook
	FIT	The fit and proper test for approved persons (the minimum standards for becoming and remaining an approved person)	FCA Handbook PRA Handbook
	FINMAR	Financial stability and market confidence sourcebook (provisions relating to financial stability, market confidence, and short selling)	FCA Handbook PRA Handbook
	TC	Training and competence (the commitments and requirements concerning staff competence)	FCA Handbook
	GEN	General provisions (interpreting the Handbook, fees, approval by the FCA and PRA, emergencies, status disclosure, the FCA logo, and insurance against fines)	FCA Handbook PRA Handbook
	FEES	Fees manual (the fees provisions for funding the FCA and PRA, FOS, and FSCS)	FCA Handbook PRA Handbook
Prudential Standards (Block 2)	GENPRU	General Prudential Sourcebook (General Prudential Sourcebook for Banks, Building Societies, Insurers and Investment Firms)	FCA Handbook PRA Handbook
	BIPRU	Prudential Sourcebook for Banks, Building Societies and Investment Firms	FCA Handbook PRA Handbook
	INSPRU	Prudential Sourcebook for Insurers	PRA Handbook FCA Handbook
	MIPRU	Prudential Sourcebook for Mortgage and Home Finance Firms and Insurance Intermediaries	FCA Handbook PRA Handbook
	UPRU	Prudential Sourcebook for UCITS firms	FCA Handbook
	IPRU (FSOC)	Interim Prudential Sourcebook for Friendly Societies (residual prudential and notification requirements)	FCA Handbook PRA Handbook
	IPRU(INS)	Interim Prudential Sourcebook for Insurers (residual prudential and notification requirements)	FCA Handbook PRA Handbook
	IPRU(INV)	Interim Prudential Sourcebook for Investment Business (residual prudential and notification requirements)	FCA Handbook PRA Handbook
Business Standards (Block 3)	COBS	New Conduct of Business Sourcebook (the conduct of business requirements applying to firms with effect from 1 November 2007)	FCA Handbook PRA Handbook

Table 5.1 *Continued*

	ICOBS	Insurance: New Conduct of Business Sourcebook (the non-investment insurance conduct of business requirements)	FCA Handbook
	MCOB	Mortgages and Home Finance: Conduct of Business Sourcebook (the requirements applying to firms with mortgage business and other home finance customers)	FCA Handbook
	BCOBS	Banking: Conduct of Business Sourcebook	FCA Handbook
	CASS	Client assets (the requirements relating to holding client asset and client money)	FCA Handbook
	MAR	Market conduct (Code of Market Conduct, Price stabilising rules, Support of the Takeover Panel's Functions, Alternative Trading Systems, what is acceptable market conduct and what is market abuse)	FCA Handbook
Regulatory Processes (Block 4)	SUP	Supervision (supervisory provisions including those relating to auditors, waivers, individual guidance, notifications and reporting)	FCA Handbook PRA Handbook
	DEPP	Decision Procedures and Penalties Manual	FCA Handbook
Redress (Block 5)	DISP	Dispute Resolution (the detailed requirements for handling complaints and the Financial Ombudsman Service arrangements)	FCA Handbook
	CONRED	Consumer Redress Schemes Sourcebook (the requirements for all firms that advised, arranged or managed investments in an Arch cru fund). Came into force on 1 April 2013	FCA Handbook
	COMP	Compensation (the rules governing the eligibility under, and levies for, the Financial Services Compensation Scheme)	FCA Handbook PRA Handbook
	COAF	Complaints against the FSA (details of the scheme handling complaints against the FSA)	Deleted
Specialist Sourcebooks (Block 6)	BSOCS	Building Societies Sourcebook	PRA Handbook
	COLL	Collective Investment Schemes	FCA Handbook
	CREDS	Credit Unions New Sourcebook	FCA Handbook PRA Handbook
	FUND	Investment funds sourcebook (requirements for firms covered by AIFMD). Came into force 22 July 2013	FCA Handbook
	PROF	Professional firms (requirements applying to professional firms whether exempt or authorised)	FCA Handbook
	RCB	Regulated Covered Bonds	FCA Handbook
	REC	Recognised investment exchanges[138]	FCA Handbook
Listing, Prospectus and Disclosure (Block 7)	LR	Listing Rules	FCA Handbook
	PR	Prospectus Rules	FCA Handbook
	DTR	Disclosure Rules and Transparency Rules	FCA Handbook

[138] Pursuant to FSMA, s 285A, the Bank of England is responsible for supervising recognised clearing houses. Accordingly, provisions in the FCA Handbook which related to clearing houses were not designated and REC is an FCA-only sourcebook.

High-level standards and the rise and fall of principles-based regulation

5.42 The Financial Services Act 1986 ('FSA 1986') created the Securities and Investments Board ('SIB') as the regulator of the various self-regulating organisations ('SROs') operating in the financial services industry. The SIB rulebook grew rapidly in its complexity and density.

5.43 As a reaction to this complexity, the then chairman of the SIB, Sir David Walker, secured the passage of a series of amendments to FSA 1986, by way of the Companies Act 1989. In particular, the 1989 Act inserted FSA 1986, section 47A, which conferred the power to 'issue statements of principle with respect to the conduct and financial standing expected of persons authorised to carry on investment business'.

5.44 FSA 1986, section 47A(2) provided that failure to comply with a statement of principle was a ground for taking disciplinary action or exercising powers of intervention, but did not of itself give rise to any right of action by investors, or affect the validity of any transaction. The SIB then promulgated 10 Principles for Businesses and 40 'designated rules', which were directly applicable to members of the SROs and formed the backbone of SIB's regulatory rulebook.

High-level standards in the Handbook

5.45 Following the SIB model, the FSA Handbook included several high-level standards. Insofar as the relevant provisions have been designated by the FCA and/or PRA, these standards are now to be found in the Handbooks. There are high level standards that apply generally (GEN, FEES); to authorised persons (PRIN and COND); to approved persons (APER and FIT); and to senior management (SYSC, and to an extent APER and FIT). Apart from GEN, FEES, and parts of SYSC (for example, guidance on the Public Interest Disclosure Act 1998 and whistleblowing in SYSC 18), these high-level standards are essentially principles-based:

(a) principles for authorised persons (rules and guidance in PRIN);
(b) principles by reference to which the regulators will determine whether a firm meets the threshold conditions in order to be given and retain authorisation (the threshold conditions in FSMA, Schedule 6 and FCA guidance in COND);
(c) principles for senior management (rules and guidance in SYSC);
(d) principles for approved persons (statements of principle breach of which constitutes misconduct, and the code and guidance in APER);
(e) principles by reference to which the regulators will assess whether a person is fit and proper to perform a controlled function (guidance in FIT).

5.46 Central to all of these are the Principles for Businesses (PRIN). The FCA's approach to the suitability and other threshold conditions in Schedule 6 (COND), for example, will depend on whether the firm is ready, willing, and organised to abide by the Principles. Senior management are responsible for ensuring that they have appropriate arrangements (SYSC) to assure compliance with the Principles. Whether a person is fit and proper to perform a controlled function for an authorised person (FIT), and the standards which will be expected of him or her in performing those functions (APER), will be assessed ultimately by reference to whether their employer will be able to comply with the Principles.

5.47 These high-level rules are enforceable by the regulator, but breach of them is not actionable by consumers or other persons affected by that breach (see paragraph 5.73).

High-level rules in European financial services legislation

Some European financial services legislation, for example MiFID[139] has included high-level principles in its architecture. There is, however, a tension between the policy aim of better regulation and the policy aim of the deeper integration of European financial markets. The latter aim tends to have priority in Europe and to compel the production of ever more detailed, prescriptive legislation. **5.48**

The rise, fall, and rise of principles-based regulation

In the previous edition of this work, it was noted that the FSA was committed to the objective of 'better regulation', an idea which was taking hold both domestically and in Europe. A key early strategy for better regulation enunciated by the Better Regulation Task Force, and accepted (in principle at least) by the Government of the day, was 'one in, one out'. In a speech to the FSA in June 2005, Sir David Arculus (then head of the Better Regulation Task Force) explained that strategy as follows: **5.49**

> its much too easy for . . . regulators to react to events . . . by producing yet another equivalent of the Dangerous Dogs Act. Most times there is already a law in place which is perfectly adequate but which is not being followed properly. Sometimes of course there does need to be a change in the law, and when that is the case, [the BRTF proposes] . . . that a compensatory simplification measure be brought in.
>
> Simplification might mean deregulation or it might mean consolidation of an existing regulation or it might mean rationalisation—using horizontal regulation (such as a general duty not to trade unfairly) to replace a variety of sector specific regulations. Alternatively, it might mean a targeted sectoral guide.[140]

The idea of better regulation was courted in Europe as well: **5.50**

> To my mind better regulation should mean not only fewer, and where they do exist, better targeted rules, but also that the design of these rules is based on open consultation and detailed economic impact analysis. This is vital. We must change our mindset in the EU from a presumption of rule making to deal with problems to a presumption of no rule making unless a vigorous set of tests are passed. Starting with: is there a market failure? Indeed the success, or failure, of any measure—be it legislative or non-legislative—largely depends on the input received from regulators, supervisors and market participants.[141]

It is that rationalisation, making the most of existing general duties, as a deliberate substitute for making additional specific rules, driven by the political, commercial, and common-sense desire for better regulation, that underlay the FSA's focus on 'principles-based regulation'. **5.51**

In Consultation Paper 05/10 published in July 2005, the FSA outlined its strategy for reviewing its Handbook. The FSA commented that a key reason for undertaking a review of its Handbook was that it wanted the Handbook to reflect its vision and values, which included: **5.52**

> an approach to rule-making based as far as possible on principles rather than prescription; a focus on senior management responsibility; and acting in a proportionate and risk-based way.[142]

---

[139] See in particular MiFID, Art 19.

[140] The speech can be found at <http://www.fsa.gov.uk/Pages/Library/Communication/Speeches/2005/0705_sda.shtm>.

[141] C McCreevy, *The Blueprint for the Development of European Financial Services—The Legislative and Regulatory Programme*, Speech to the Association of Compliance Officers in Ireland Conference, Dublin, 26 November 2007.

[142] FSA, 'Consultation Paper 05/10: Reviewing the FSA Handbook' (July 2005).

5.53 The FSA also sought to expand the notion of principle-based regulation beyond its role as a device to guide and reduce the content of the FSA Handbook and towards a new relationship with the firms it regulated. The following is an extract from the FSA's flagship statement on principles-based regulation in 2007:

> Principles-based regulation . . . means a different approach to how we deal with regulated entities whether in the context of day to day supervisory contact, the information we request, or when necessary, the way we use our enforcement powers. It also means different expectations of firms and how they engage with the regulatory issues they face. Our aim is to focus more clearly on the outcomes we as regulators want to achieve, leaving more of the judgement calls on how to achieve those outcomes to the senior management of firms.[143]

5.54 Several years on, it is clear, first, that the FSA's focus on principles-based regulation did not have the desired effect of reducing the size or complexity of the FSA Handbook. The Handbooks inherited by the FCA and the PRA contain numerous detailed prescriptive rules and run to thousands of pages.[144] Secondly, following the international banking crisis that emerged during 2008, the new regulators (following a pattern set by the FSA) are much less willing to rely on the judgement of the firms they regulate.

5.55 As to the failure to simplify and reduce the FSA Handbook:

(a) It was noted in the previous edition of this work that there were a number of practical limitations on principles-based regulation, some of which implied that a substantial reduction in detailed rules would be difficult to achieve: principles-based regulation was never a 'one size fits all' solution. There are areas of financial services regulation where detailed prescriptive rules are necessary and desirable. Areas in which detailed rules are likely to predominate include prudential regulation (for example detailed rules specifying the basis for the valuation of assets and liabilities, the quality of capital firms are required to hold, and the level or amount of capital that firms must hold).

(b) The FSA operated and its successors the FCA and the PRA, operate in a wider arena than just the United Kingdom. The impetus for financial services regulation comes from a variety of sources, for example from international bodies such as the BIS, the IAIS, and international initiatives on accounting standards;

(c) More locally, the European Community has significant legislative competence in the financial services field. Notwithstanding its rhetoric in favour of principles-based regulation, its legislation, which the UK is required to implement, is often prescriptive or maximum-harmonising. That drives the kind of 'copy-out' implementation strategies outlined in paragraph 5.39(d). The result may be principles-based, if that is the character of the underlying rules, but that is often not the case.

5.56 As to the relationship with regulated firms, both the FCA and the PRA have moved away from the conception that 'principles-based regulation' should facilitate a more flexible relationship between the regulators and regulated firms, in which reliance is placed on the judgment of senior management. In May 2011 the FSA's Chief Executive[145] explained that

---

143 FSA, 'Principles-based Regulation: Focusing on the outcomes that matter' (April 2007) p 6.

144 Although it is of course difficult to say how much more complex the FSA's Handbook might have become, had the FSA not aspired to principles-based regulation.

145 Speech by Hector Sants, PRA Banking Conference, 19 May 2011.

the 'judgment-based supervisory model' that he expected the new regulators to adopt was based on:

> the presumption that regulators cannot rely on the judgement of the management of the firms they supervise, and must take their own view formed from their own analysis about the significant issues which affect the safety and soundness of the firm. Furthermore, where that judgement differs from the firm's management, the regulator must act.

Consistent with that analysis, the FCA describes itself as a 'judgment-based' regulator which will intervene early in respect of products and selling processes so as 'to tackle potential risks to consumers before they take shape'.[146] The PRA similarly describes itself as 'judgment-based'.[147] Perhaps paradoxically, however, principles continue to play an essential role in this new regulatory relationship. That is not least because high-level principles provide an essential platform for early intervention by the regulators (whether by way of supervision or enforcement), perhaps in advance of the point at which the regulator can establish that a firm has breached a specific rule. 'Principles-based regulation' therefore facilitates the new regulatory relationship, just as it did the old, and 'principles' retain their importance as a component of the regulatory regime. **5.57**

What are 'principles'?

Principles are rules (made using the regulators' legislative powers) that are expressed at a high level of generality. The most obvious examples are the FCA and PRA Principles for Businesses in the PRIN Module of each Handbook, set out in the table following. **5.58**

FCA and PRA Principles for Business	FCA	PRA
Principle 1: Integrity—A firm must conduct its business with integrity.	Yes	Yes
Principle 2: Skill, care, and diligence—A firm must conduct its business with due skill, care and diligence.	Yes	Yes
Principle 3: Management and control—A firm must take reasonable care to organise and control its affairs responsibly and effectively, with adequate risk management systems.	Yes	Yes
Principle 4: Financial prudence—A firm must maintain adequate financial resources.	Yes	Yes
Principle 5: Market conduct—A firm must observe proper standards of market conduct.	Yes	No
Principle 6: Customers' interests—A firm must pay due regard to the interests of its customers and treat them fairly.	Yes	No
Principle 7: Communications with clients—A firm must pay due regard to the information needs of its clients, and communicate information to them in a way which is clear, fair, and not misleading.	Yes	No
Principle 8: Conflicts of interest—A firm must manage conflicts of interest fairly, both between itself and its customers, and between a customer and another client.	Yes	Yes
Principle 9: Customers: relationships of trust—A firm must take reasonable care to ensure the suitability of its advice and discretionary decisions for any customer who is entitled to rely upon its judgment.	Yes	No
Principle 10: Clients' assets—A firm must arrange adequate protection for clients' assets when it is responsible for them.	Yes	No
Principle 11: Relations with regulators—A firm must deal with its regulators in an open and cooperative way, and must disclose to the appropriate regulator appropriately anything relating to the firm of which that regulator would reasonably expect notice.	Yes	Yes

[146] FCA, *The FCA's approach to advancing its objectives (July 2013)* 12. See also Martin Wheatley's speech at the ABI Biennial Conference: '100 days of FCA', 9 July 2013.

[147] PRA, The Prudential Regulation Authority's approach to insurance supervision (April 2013) 3 and 8.

As the table shows, the FCA has 11 Principles for Business while the PRA has six.[148] The PRA's reduced suite of principles broadly reflects the fact that it does not (except in relation to with-profits insurance) have any overt consumer protection objective. The following practical points should be noted in relation to the Principles for Business and other high-level rules in the Handbooks:

(d) principles cannot be invented 'on the hoof'. They are the product of the regulators' formal legislative processes (including where necessary, consultation, CBA, feedback, making by the governing body—see paragraphs 5.95 *et seq.*);
(e) principles are aimed at outcomes or behaviours that are required from a number of (or indeed, all) regulated firms, no matter how diverse their business, structure, or governance. For example, under PRIN firms must 'act with integrity', 'treat their customers fairly', 'maintain adequate financial resources';
(f) principles are specific as to outcome, but not as to the method by which each firm is to achieve that outcome;
(g) deciding whether (or not) a firm has achieved the outcome required by a principle almost always requires judgement by the regulator. The central role of that judgement is reflected in the language in which principles (including those in PRIN) are drafted: for example, capital must be adequate, behaviour must be reasonable or fair;
(h) because principles are rules, they are capable of being breached. Breach can be the basis for the exercise of supervisory or enforcement powers by the regulators, as a public body (see paragraph 5.69 *et seq.*);
(i) there is a well-established body of public law that sets out the standards against which the courts will test the adequacy of the exercise of powers by a public body on the basis of judgements by its officials.

The relationship between principles and other rules

5.59 Because principles are rules of general application, they will apply in areas where the regulators have made other, more detailed rules, and guidance.

5.60 Sometimes the more detailed rules will be expressed as an expansion or explanation of what a particular principle means. An example is COBS 20 (With-profits) which expands on Principle for Businesses 6 as it applies to with-profits policyholders. But this will not always be the case. Often, detailed rules will simply occupy space that is also occupied by a principle. Detailed prudential rules, for example, occupy the same space as Principle for Businesses 4 (adequate resources).

5.61 If both a principle and a detailed rule apply to the same situation, a court will construe the detailed rule and the principle together, based on the ordinary meaning of the words in which both are expressed (if there is no defined meaning—on which see paragraph 5.126 *et seq.*). If the defined or ordinary meaning of the words is unclear or ambiguous, the court will look to the purpose of both the rule and the principle. In *R (on the application of British Bankers Association) v Financial Services Authority* [149] Ousley J rejected the argument of the British Bankers Association that Principles could not be used to augment specific rules, holding that:

---

[148] FCA Handbook, PRA Handbook PRIN 2.1.1R.
[149] [2011] EWHC 999 (Admin), [2011] All ER (D) 222 (April).

> ...Principles are best understood as the ever present substrata to which specific rules are added. The Principles always have to be complied with. The specific rules do not supplant them and cannot be used to contradict them. They are but specific applications of them to the particular requirements they cover. The general notion that the specific rules can exhaust the application of the Principles is inappropriate.[150]

Thus, principles have a role to play in determining the scope of a firm's obligations even when detailed rules clearly apply. This plainly lends support to the regulators' 'judgment based' approach to early intervention, outlined earlier.

The regulators may dispense with the application of their rules only: **5.62**

(a) on application by a firm for a waiver or modification of the detailed rule, where the regulator is satisfied that the rule may be waived or modified and that the criteria in FSMA 2000, section 138A are met (see paragraph 5.75); or
(b) by consulting on and then making rules that substitute principles for more detailed rules.

Other than by these means, a regulator has no power to dispense with the application of the detailed rules it has made. **5.63**

As a corollary, principles will be directly relevant when detailed rules do not apply, do not cover the situation under consideration, or are ambiguous as to the outcome that is required in the particular circumstances. **5.64**

The powers exercised to make the Handbooks

By far the largest component of the material that is re-stated in the Handbooks is the product of the regulators' legislative functions (see paragraph 5.95). But by no means all the material in the Handbooks is the product of those functions. A rule-making instrument (see paragraph 5.111) must specify the statutory or other provision under which it is made.[151] The FSA's practice was to include, in Schedule 4 to each sourcebook or module of the FSA Handbook, a list of powers exercised in making the instruments consolidated into the particular sourcebook or module. The FCA and the PRA have discontinued this practice.[152] However, the FCA has continued the FSA's practice of setting out the full range of powers exercised to make the material in its Handbook as a whole, in Schedule 4 to the General Provisions Sourcebook ('GEN').[153] The PRA has chosen not to retain Schedule 4 to its version of GEN. **5.65**

Rules

The regulators' most obvious legislative function (see paragraph 5.95) is their function of making rules. For example, the FCA's and PRA's main high-level standards, its Principles for Businesses ('PRIN'), are rules. Through rules, the regulators may impose binding and enforceable requirements on the persons they regulate, and these may impact on third **5.66**

150 [2011] EWHC 999 (Admin), [2011] All ER (D) 222 (April) at [162].
151 FSMA, s 138G(2).
152 Reader's Guide, 22 and 32.
153 But note that the instruments by which Handbook provisions are made must still include an indication of the specific powers on which the relevant regulator relies to make the provisions in question.

parties.[154] Most rules (other than evidential provisions, on which see paragraph 5.70) are labelled 'R' in the Handbooks.

5.67 Although the regulators have many rule-making powers, foremost is the general rule-making power in FSMA, sections 137A (for the PRA) and 137G (for the FCA). The regulators have the power to make general rules applying to both regulated and some unregulated activities of authorised persons.[155]

5.68 Certain rules may apply to persons who are not authorised, but are nevertheless within the FCA's and/or PRA's regulatory scope, or may impact on third parties:[156]

(a) rules made by the FCA under FSMA, Part 6 (listing, disclosure, prospectus, transparency, and corporate governance rules) apply (i) to issuers, offerors, and applicants; (ii) in effect to directors, sponsors, employees; and (iii) to the FCA itself, as listing authority;
(b) client money rules made by the FCA under FSMA, Part 9A impact on the rights of third parties;
(c) rules made by the FCA and the FOS for the Financial Services Compensation Scheme ('FSCS') and Ombudsman schemes, under FSMA, Parts 15 and 16, bind the FSCS scheme manager, the FOS, and individual Ombudsmen, and affect claimants, former authorised persons, voluntary jurisdiction participants, and parties to a complaint generally;
(d) rules under FSMA, Part 17 affect trustees, depositaries, auditors, and other operators of regulated and unregulated collective investment schemes—some but not all of which are required to be authorised;
(e) notification rules under FSMA Part 18 affect recognised investment exchanges;
(f) directions under FSMA, Part 19 affect former underwriting members of Lloyd's, and current members to the extent that the FCA and/or the PRA applies a FSMA 'core provision' to the Lloyd's market;
(g) rules under FSMA, Part 20 affect exempt professional firms, for example for the purpose of ensuring that their clients are aware they are not authorised;
(h) under FSMA, Part 22, the FCA and/or the PRA may impose duties on auditors and actuaries;
(i) persons may be liable to pay fees in connection with the discharge of FCA or PRA functions, pursuant to fees rules made under FSMA, Schedule 1ZA, paragraph 23 and Schedule 1ZB, paragraph 31 respectively.[157]

Breach of rules

5.69 Breach of rules does not itself constitute an offence,[158] although breach may result in, or be a component of, an offence. For example, (a) certain exemptions under the Financial Services and Markets Act 2000 (Financial Promotions) Order[159] are available only in respect

154 For example, breach of rules may confer rights of action under s 138D; rules made by the FCA under s 137B may provide for client money to be held on trust.
155 However, GEN 2.2.17R makes clear that general rules are to be interpreted in the Handbooks as applying only to regulated activities, unless the contrary intention appears.
156 Most of these are considered in more detail in other chapters.
157 Such as persons making applications or seeking FCA or PRA approvals.
158 FSMA, s 138E(1).
159 SI 2005/1529.

of communications that comply with FCA rules;[160] (b) it is a defence to the 'misleading statements' offence under FSA 2012, section 89 to show that a statement was made in conformity with price-stabilising rules or control of information rules.[161] However, the primary significance of rules for authorised persons is that breach triggers a regulator's investigation, disciplinary, and other enforcement powers, including public censure, financial penalties, injunctions, and restitution.[162]

Evidential provisions

Rules made by either regulator under FSMA, section 138C may provide for breaches to give rise to no consequences under FSMA except that breach may be relied on as tending to establish breach of another specified rule, and conversely that compliance may be relied on as tending to establish compliance with the other specified rule. Such 'evidential provisions' are labelled 'E' in the Handbooks. **5.70**

Effect of breach on non-authorised persons and transactions

Most rules and other requirements apply only while firms remain authorised, so that a regulator may in some instances keep a firm's Part 4A permission in place even if there are no activities that it is able to carry on.[163] Breaches of requirements imposed through rules generally only expose non-authorised persons to the risk of injunctions or restitution orders imposed by the courts under FSMA, sections 380 and 382. The FCA or PRA may, however, take action to remove or restrict the status or rights of non-authorised persons who are concerned in a breach of rules. For example, approved persons may be found unfit to perform controlled functions, or indeed any functions, on behalf of an authorised person, or disciplined for misconduct if they are knowingly concerned in a breach by the authorised person for whom they perform a controlled function.[164] **5.71**

Breach of rules, save for rules made by the FCA under FSMA, sections 137C and 137D, does not make a transaction void or unenforceable.[165] However, private contractual terms between parties may have that effect. **5.72**

Private rights of action for contravention of a rule

The general position is that contravention by an authorised person of a rule made by the FCA is actionable at the suit of a private person who suffers loss as a result of the contravention, subject to defences and other incidents applying to actions for breach of statutory duty.[166] The FCA has the power to prevent private actions by making rules specifying that particular provisions do not give rise to private rights of action if breached.[167] The FCA has exercised that power to remove private rights of action for certain high-level rules such as PRIN, SYSC, and financial resources rules.[168] By contrast, contravention by an authorised person **5.73**

[160] See art 16(2)(b) of the Financial Promotion Order 2005, SI 2005/1529.
[161] FSA 2012, s 89(3).
[162] Breaches of rules including the Principles for Businesses are relevant to each regulator's consideration of whether an authorised person continues to meet the threshold conditions so that breaches may trigger variation, including imposition of limitations or requirements, or cancellation of the firm's permission.
[163] As envisaged under FSMA, ss 55H(6), 55I(6), and 55J(8).
[164] See FSMA, ss 56 (prohibition orders), 63 (withdrawal of approval), and 66 (disciplinary powers).
[165] See ibid, s 138E(2).
[166] ibid, s 138D(2).
[167] FSMA, s 138D(3).
[168] ibid, s 138D(2) is not disapplied for the rules in GEN.

of a rule made by the PRA is only actionable at the suit of a private person if the PRA so provides.[169] The Treasury may make (and has made) regulations providing that in specified cases, breach of a rule is actionable not only at the suit of a private person, but also at the suit of other persons.[170]

Incidental and supplementary powers

5.74 FSMA, section 137T provides that rules made by either regulator may contain incidental, supplemental, consequential, and transitional provisions, and make different provision for different cases. Either regulator may also make provisions by reference to rules made by the other regulator. The general rule-making power and powers to make most other rules do not normally authorise the regulators to sub-delegate. However, there are exceptions such as FSMA, section 214 which permits the regulators to authorise the FSCS to determine certain matters for the purposes of the compensation scheme, and FSMA, Schedule 17 paragraph 13, which provides for individual ombudsmen to be able to waive time limits for referral of complaints.

Waiver and modification of rules

5.75 Both the FCA and the PRA have a general power to waive or modify the majority of their rules,[171] with the consent of, or on the application of, the person who is subject to the relevant rules.[172] The regulator concerned may direct that a rule does not apply to the applicant (a waiver), or that the rule applies subject to the modifications specified in the direction (a modification), if the regulator is satisfied that:

(a) compliance with the unmodified rule would be unduly burdensome or would not achieve the purpose for which the rule was made; and
(b) the direction would not adversely affect the advancement of any of its objectives.[173]

5.76 The direction may be subject to conditions[174] which generally take effect as limits on the scope of extent of the direction (for example a time limit), or conditions precedent to the continued validity of the direction (for example, a requirement that a firm should hold additional capital or take some other step while the direction is in force). Either regulator may revoke a direction of its own accord or vary it with the consent of or on the application of the firm concerned.[175]

5.77 The regulators are required to publish directions waiving or modifying rules unless the regulator concerned is satisfied that it is unnecessary or inappropriate to do so, and if necessary to consider publishing in an anonymised form.[176] Publication serves a number of

[169] ibid, s 138D(1).
[170] ibid, s 138D(4). See the Financial Services and Markets Act 2000 (Rights of Action) Regulations 2001, SI 2001/2256, and the Financial Services and Markets Act 2000 (Fourth Motor Insurance Directive) Regulations 2002, SI 2002/2706.
[171] Rules made by either regulator under FSMA, s 137O (threshold condition code) are excluded. In addition, Trust scheme rules, Scheme particulars rules, Contractual scheme rules, and Contractual scheme particulars rules made by the FCA under FSMA, ss 247, 248, 261I, and 261J are excluded, but there is a parallel waiver power for those rules in FSMA, ss 250 and 261L.
[172] FSMA, s 138A(1). There are other waiver powers associated with particular rule-making powers, elsewhere in FSMA.
[173] FSMA, s 138A(1) and (4).
[174] ibid, s 138A(6).
[175] ibid, s 138A(7).
[176] ibid, s 138B(1)–(3) and (5).

interests, including maintaining consistency of decision-making, ensuring that all firms of a similar kind are aware of what concessions might be available and ensuring that private rights of action are not unnecessarily undermined.

Statements of principle, codes, directions, and requirements

FSMA, section 64 provides for statements of principle and a code[177] describing the conduct expected of approved persons.[178] Statements of principle are labelled with the letter 'P' in the Handbooks. The classification of these statements of principle is difficult.[179] FSMA, section 64(11) provides that the power to issue statements of practice is to be treated as part of the regulators' rule-making function and in many respects statements of principle are treated as rules. The Reader's Guide says that the principles are binding on approved persons.[180] However, many of the statutory provisions that apply to rules do not apply to statements of principle, or have to be replicated.[181] There is no power to waive or modify statements of principle, and misconduct does not itself give rise to private rights of action. **5.78**

FSMA, section 119 provides that the FCA must issue a code (known as the Code of Market Conduct)[182] giving guidance to those determining whether or not behaviour amounts to market abuse. The Code is supplemented by guidance. Making codes is a general function subject to the FCA's general duties in FSMA,[183] section 1B (see paragraph 5.6) and one of the FCA's legislative functions (see paragraph 5.95). Although similar in many ways to general guidance (on which see paragraph 5.82), the Code of Market Conduct is distinct in that breach of its provisions may be indicative of misconduct or market abuse. In this respect the provisions of the Code are similar to evidential provisions and are labelled 'E' in the FCA Handbook. **5.79**

The Code of Market Conduct also has another distinctive feature. Because of concerns about the breadth of the definition of market abuse, FSMA, section 122(1) provides a formal safe harbour for those who behave in a way that is described in the code applicable at the time as behaviour that, in the opinion of the FCA, does not amount to market abuse. These conclusive provisions are labelled 'C' in the FCA Handbook. **5.80**

Directions

Certain directions and requirements imposed by the FCA or the PRA under FSMA are treated as made in the exercise of legislative functions.[184] All such provisions are labelled 'D' in the Handbooks. **5.81**

[177] Set out in APER.

[178] Persons approved by the FCA or PRA under FSMA, s 59 to perform controlled functions on behalf of an authorised person in respect of regulated activities.

[179] They are not to be confused with the Principles for Businesses in PRIN, which apply to authorised persons. However, several of the principles for approved persons in APER are the same as or derived from those in PRIN.

[180] Reader's Guide, 25 and 32.

[181] See, eg, FSMA, s 64(11) which replicates for statements of principle the power in FSMA, s 137T to make different provision for different circumstances or cases.

[182] Set out in MAR.

[183] The PRA also has a function of issuing codes; FSMA, s 2J(1).

[184] Directions by the FCA or PRA under FSMA, ss 316, 318, and by the FCA under FSMA, s 328.

General guidance and individual guidance

5.82 The FCA has a function of giving general guidance, under FSMA, section 139A. The function is very wide and includes the giving of guidance consisting of such information and advice as the FCA considers appropriate:

(a) with respect to the operation of specified parts of FSMA and of any rules made by the FCA under it;
(b) with respect to any matters relating to functions of the FCA; and
(c) with respect to any other matters about which it appears to the FCA to be desirable to give information or advice.

5.83 FSMA, section 139A(7) provides that references to guidance given by the FCA include references to any recommendation made by the FCA to FCA-regulated persons generally, or to any class of FCA-regulated person.[185] By far the largest component of the FCA Handbook is 'general' guidance in that sense, labelled 'G' in the FCA Handbook. The majority of the guidance re-stated in the FCA Handbook, or associated with the Handbook (for example in the Handbook Guides and Regulatory Guides—on which see paragraph 5.39(c)) is also 'general guidance' within the formal definition in FSMA, section 139B(5): guidance which is 'general' in the sense outlined earlier, but also 'intended to have continuing effect and given in writing or other legible form'. FSMA, section 1K provides that general guidance given by the FCA under section 139A must include guidance about how it intends to advance its operational objectives in discharging its general functions in relation to different categories of authorised person or regulated activity.

5.84 The PRA does not have a statutory power to give guidance equivalent to the FCA's power under section 139A. However, as with the FCA, the PRA must[186] give guidance about how it intends to advance its objectives in discharging its general functions in relation to different categories of PRA-authorised person or PRA-regulated activity. Notwithstanding that it does not have a power equivalent to the FCA's section 139A guidance power, the PRA considers that it can give guidance on matters relating to rules made by the PRA under FSMA and to matters relating to its functions. Indeed the PRA has carried forward into its own Handbook many of the provisions in the FSA Handbook labelled 'G'. These provisions are, however, not adopted or made pursuant to a statutory power. The PRA has indicated that it intends to move away from the FSA's practice of publishing a diverse array of normative material outside of its formal rules. In particular, the PRA does not intend to issue significant detailed guidance to clarify its policy, whether in the form of guidance issued publicly or advice given by supervisors to individual firms. If, in the PRA's judgment, guidance material is required, the material will be issued in the form of 'Supervisory Statements'.[187] The PRA's expectation is that such statements will be 'focused on the PRA's expectations, aimed

[185] FCA-regulated person' is defined in FSMA, s 139A(9) as (a) an authorised person; or (b) any person who is otherwise subject to rules made by the FCA, so arguably does not apply to approved persons, even though the need for approval is triggered by the FCA's controlled functions rules made under FSMA, s 59. Advice to consumers is not regarded as given to 'persons generally', and is not included in the FCA Handbook, except in relation to Block 5 of the FCA Handbook covering dispute resolution: complaints ('DISP') and compensation ('COMP').

[186] Under FSMA, s 2I(1). See generally, para 5.12.

[187] See, eg, March 2013 Letter to firms and *The PRA's approach to banking supervision* (April 2013), para 209.

at facilitating firms' judgement in determining whether they meet these expectations, and will not be overly detailed'.

In addition to 'general guidance', there are other forms of guidance that may be equally significant to the performance of the regulators' functions. In particular the FCA Handbook, anticipates that the FCA may (like the FSA before it), give 'individual guidance', to authorised firms at their request or at the FCA's own initiative, addressing issues of individual relevance or concern to the firm. The distinction between general guidance and individual guidance has procedural consequences because specific requirements attach to the issue of general guidance on rules (considered in paragraph 5.112). As already noted, the PRA does not have the power to give guidance under FSMA. However, the indication is that the PRA will continue to give individual guidance to PRA-regulated firms. **5.85**

Other public material published by the regulators, and confirmed industry guidance

In the previous edition of this work, it was noted that the FSA published a mass of general public material, which sat outside the FSA Handbook. This included everything from market bulletins, through regulatory updates to speeches, case studies, 'Dear CEO letters', and FAQs. The FSA's usual approach was to append a statement to that material indicating that it was not general guidance under FSMA. The FSA resolved the resulting difficulty for firms in deciding exactly what weight to give to such material when deciding what was required to comply with FSA rules by putting other public material relevant to compliance with rules explicitly on the same footing as general guidance in the FSA Handbook and individual guidance: **5.86**

> If a firm has complied with the Principles, high-level rules and other rules then it is irrelevant whether they have complied with any other material we have issued. But firms can rely on all the material we publish. This is fundamental to our approach. So if a firm takes a reasonable course of action which we have indicated, in general public material or in a specific individual exchange (such as a supervisory letter), as being in compliance with a rule, then we will not take action against the firm for not having complied with the rule. The status of the general public material—the process it has been through, the format in which it has been published—does not affect that. For example it does not matter whether it is a specific rule or formal guidance in the Handbook, or a case study or 'Dear CEO' letter on our website.[188]

Some of the general public material published by the FSA has been adopted by the FCA.[189] The FCA is also likely to publish more material of its own. The indication from DEPP 6.2.1G(4) (see paragraph 5.92(a)) is that the FCA will follow the FSA's approach to such material. It has already been noted earlier that the PRA intends to limit the amount of material it publishes, and where it considers it necessary to issue guidance, this will be in the form of Supervisory Statements. **5.87**

In the previous edition of this work, it was also noted that the FSA published a Discussion Paper in November 2006[190] in which it opened a debate on whether and in what circumstances it should rely on industry guidance instead of publishing public material of its own. From a regulator's perspective, industry guidance has the dual benefit of directly engaging **5.88**

[188] FSA, 'Principles-based regulation: focusing on the outcomes that matter' (April 2007) 10.
[189] See, eg, FCA 2013/32: Legal Cutover (FCA (Non-Handbook Guidance)) Instrument 2013.
[190] FSA, 'Discussion Paper 06/5: FSA Confirmation of Industry Guidance' (November 2006).

industry associations and practitioners in constructive debate about what is required to comply with particular rules, and of distributing responsibility for the volume and complexity of regulatory guidance. But, as with the FSA's general public material, a critical question for firms was whether, and to what extent, the FSA would have regard to industry guidance and a firm's compliance with it, in deciding whether the firm had complied with or breached a relevant FSA rule. In the Policy Statement of September 2007[191] which followed the Discussion Paper, the FSA confirmed that subject to the conditions and processes set out in the Policy Statement, it would confirm appropriate industry guidance.

5.89 In April 2007, the FSA, following its approach to guidance generally, explained its approach to confirmed industry guidance as follows:

> Firms are not required to adhere to any guidance, whether given directly by us or confirmed by us. However, case studies and other useful examples of how to meet our principles and rules, particularly when tailored to specific groups of firms, can clearly be helpful. . . . If a firm takes a reasonable course of action that is indicated by FSA-confirmed industry guidance to be in compliance with a specific rule or principle (or part of it), we will treat them as having complied with that rule or principle providing that guidance was appropriate to them.[192]

5.90 The FSA's conclusions following feedback on its discussion paper on industry guidance were set out in its Policy Statement of September 2007.[193] The conclusions followed the same general approach. As has been noted, the FSA confirmed that, subject to the conditions and processes set out in the Policy Statement, it would confirm appropriate industry guidance. Perhaps the most significant conditions were that the wording of the FSA's confirmation did not offer firms a safe harbour for compliance with industry guidance,[194] that the obligation was on the producer of the guidance to keep it up to date and to notify the FSA of material changes, and that FSA confirmation would last for three years, after which it would lapse, unless there was a review in the interim.

5.91 Once again, the indication from the FCA's designation of DEPP 6.2.1G(4) (see paragraph 5.92(a)) is that the FCA will confirm appropriate industry guidance and that it will follow the FSA's approach to such guidance.

The effect of guidance

5.92 The general position in relation to FCA guidance, therefore, is as follows:

(a) Compliance with guidance does not provide a formal 'safe-harbour', but the FCA indicates in DEPP 6.2.1G(4) that:

> the FCA will not take action against a person for behaviour that it considers to be in line with guidance, other materials published by the FCA in support of the Handbook, or FCA-confirmed industry guidance which were current at the time of the behaviour in question.

[191] FSA, 'Policy Statement 07/16: FSA Confirmation of Industry Guidance' (September 2007).
[192] FSA, 'Principles-based regulation: focusing on the outcomes that matter' (April 2007) 11.
[193] FSA, 'Policy Statement 07/16: FSA Confirmation of Industry Guidance' (September 2007).
[194] The wording of the confirmation is that 'the FSA has reviewed this [industry guidance] and has confirmed that it will take account of it when exercising its regulatory functions. This [industry guidance] is not mandatory and is not FSA guidance. This FSA view cannot affect the rights of third parties'. See PS 07/16, para 2.32.

(b) SUP 9.4 sets out the effect of individual guidance given by the FCA: If a person acts in accordance with current individual written guidance given to him by the FCA in the circumstances contemplated by that guidance, then the FCA will proceed on the footing that the person has complied with the aspects of the rule or other requirement to which the guidance relates (SUP 9.4.1G). Chapter 6 of the FCA's Reader's Guide similarly states that if a person acts in accordance with general guidance in the circumstances contemplated by that guidance, the FCA would proceed on the footing that the person had complied with the aspects of the rule or other requirement to which the guidance related.

(c) Guidance is not binding on those to whom the FCA's rules apply. Nor are the variety of other public materials that the FCA publishes to support the rules and guidance in the FCA Handbook. Such materials are intended to illustrate the ways, but not the only ways in which a person can comply with the relevant rules.[195]

(d) Guidance does not set the minimum standard required to comply with a rule, nor is there any presumption that a failure to comply with guidance is indicative of a failure to comply with the rule to which it relates: there may be a number of different ways of complying with a rule. The FCA Enforcement Guide indicates that the FCA will take care to ensure that a firm's ability to choose how best to comply with particular rules is recognised, so that industry guidance does not become 'a prescriptive regime in place of FCA rules'.[196]

(e) The absence of guidance or other public material on a particular issue does not prevent the FCA from taking supervisory or enforcement action.[197]

(f) Guidance and supporting materials are, however, potentially relevant to an enforcement case[198] (and so also to the exercise of the FCA's supervisory and other powers short of enforcement). A decision-taker may take guidance and supporting materials into account:

    (i) to help assess whether it could reasonably have been understood or predicted at the time that the conduct in question fell below the standards required by PRIN;[199]
    (ii) to explain the regulatory context;
    (iii) to inform a view of the overall seriousness of the breaches;
    (iv) to inform consideration of a firm's defence that the FCA was judging the firm on the basis of retrospective standards; or
    (v) as part of expert or supervisory evidence about the standards that applied at the time of the breach.[200]

(g) It will be for the FCA (or the relevant decision-taker in an enforcement context) to determine whether and to what extent the supporting material is relevant to compliance with the particular rule. That will depend, for example, on the type and accessibility of the supporting material and (in an enforcement context) on the nature of the firm's defence.[201]

---

195 FCA Handbook, EG 2.23.
196 FCA Handbook, EG 2.30.
197 FCA Handbook, EG 2.27.
198 FCA Handbook, EG 2.25.
199 FCA Handbook, EG 2.25(1).
200 FCA Handbook, EG 2.25(2) to (5).
201 FCA Handbook, EG 2.26.

(h) Guidance on rules, FSMA, or any other matter represents the FCA's view, and does not bind the courts, for example in relation to action by or on behalf of a third party. Nevertheless, FCA guidance may be persuasive, and its existence may in some circumstances affect the factual matrix within which a claim is determined. FCA guidance will also be taken into account by the Ombudsman in considering what is fair and reasonable in all the circumstances.[202]

5.93 The position in relation to the PRA's guidance material cannot be stated as fully. The PRA has neither designated nor adopted an equivalent to the FCA Decision Procedure and Penalties Manual ('DEPP') or the FCA Enforcement Guide ('EG'). The PRA's Reader's Guide does not explain the effect of the mass of former FSA guidance now contained in the PRA Handbook, or related to the PRA Handbook (for example, BSOG). However, firms may have a legitimate expectation that (as with the approach taken by the FSA), where a firm has acted in accordance with guidance in circumstances contemplated by that guidance, the PRA will proceed on the footing that the person had complied with the aspects of the rule or other requirement to which the guidance relates.

5.94 The PRA has not followed the FCA's approach to individual guidance.[203] Accordingly, the PRA has not designated or adopted Chapter 9 of the FSA's Supervision Manual (Individual Guidance). Thus, the status of individual guidance given by the PRA is not entirely clear at present. It should be noted that whilst the PRA chose not automatically to confirm all individual guidance given to firms by the FCA (on the basis that the PRA has a different regulatory and supervisory focus than the FSA), some individual guidance (including Individual Capital Requirements Guidance and Individual Liquidity Guidance) have been automatically confirmed.[204] In respect of individual guidance confirmed by the PRA, firms may have a legitimate expectation that the PRA's approach will be similar to that taken by the FCA.

Handbook Processes

The regulators' legislative functions

5.95 The Delegated Powers and Deregulation Committee of the House of Lords reviewed the powers of the FSA to make secondary legislation under FSMA and accepted in principle that the delegation of powers to the FSA was appropriate, subject to safeguards, for example that the Treasury rather than the FSA should prescribe the definition of 'private person' eligible to seek damages for breaches of FSA rules, on which see paragraph 5.73 *et seq.*

5.96 The FCA's legislative functions are a subset of its general functions (see paragraph 5.6). The legislative functions are defined in FSMA, Schedule 1ZA paragraph 8 as:

(a) making rules;
(b) issuing codes;
(c) issuing statements; and
(d) giving directions.

202 See FCA Handbook, DISP 3.6.4R(1).

203 FSA, 'Consultation Paper 12/24: Regulatory Reform: PRA and FCA regimes relating to aspects of authorisation and supervision' (September 2012).

204 FSA, 'Latest update as we transition to the Prudential Regulation Authority (PRA))' (February 2013 letter to firms). The letter is available at: <http://www.bankofengland.co.uk/pra/Documents/about/pratransitionupdate1302.pdf>.

The PRA's legislative functions are set out in FSMA, Schedule 1ZB, paragraph 16 and are identical to the FCA legislative functions listed earlier. In addition, the PRA has the legislative function of issuing guidance about its objectives, under FSMA, section 2I. **5.97**

The general position is that the FCA or PRA may make arrangements for any of its functions to be discharged by a committee, sub-committee, officer, or member of staff. However, in exercising its legislative functions, each regulator must act through its governing body.[205] The FCA's function of issuing general guidance may not be discharged by an officer or member of staff of the FCA,[206] but as it is not a legislative function, it need not be discharged by the FCA's governing body, the FCA Board. Thus, it may be given by an appropriate committee or sub-committee of the FCA Board. **5.98**

FSA 2012, section 85 provides that the arrangements that the FCA and PRA must make for the investigation of complaints arising in connection with the exercise of (or failure to exercise) its functions need not extend to complaints arising in connection with their legislative functions.[207] Instead, most of the regulators' legislative functions as well as other functions which are exercised to make the materials restated in the Handbooks are subject to other provisions in FSMA such as requirements for consultation, notification, publication, and competition scrutiny. These are considered in paragraphs 5.100 *et seq.* The 'Handbook processes' are the internal mechanisms and procedures by which the regulators' comply with these requirements. **5.99**

Consultation

Prior to the enactment of FSMA, a statutory requirement for consultation was something of an innovation in financial services legislation. The Financial Services Act 1986 required the Securities and Investments Board to have regard to the costs of compliance.[208] Consultation was simply a good way of informing and improving its decision-making by offering firms and consumer bodies the opportunity to make observations on its proposals and on the associated costs and benefits. The practice of consulting has developed across the public sector, driven by work and guidance by the Cabinet Office. However, the requirements under FSMA (as it applied to the FSA and now applies to the FCA and PRA) are more prescriptive and, because they are binding on the regulators there is little flexibility to dispense with the requirements. **5.100**

The main consultation requirement in relation to the Handbooks, namely that for rules, is set out in FSMA, section 138I for the FCA and 138J for the PRA. Before making any rules, each regulator is required to consult with the other[209] and after doing so, the regulator proposing to make rules must publish its draft rules in the way appearing to it to be best calculated to bring them to the attention of the public.[210] The draft rules must be accompanied by: **5.101**

(a) a cost–benefit analysis;
(b) an explanation of the purpose of the proposed rules;

---

[205] FSMA, Sch 1ZA, para 8(2); Sch 1ZB, para 16(2).
[206] FSMA, Sch 1ZA, para 8(4).
[207] For this purpose, the FCA's legislative functions includes the function of giving general guidance, as defined in FSMA, s 139B(5) (see Financial Services Act 2012, s 85(4)).
[208] Under Financial Services Act 1986, Sch 7, para 2A.
[209] Save that the FCA need not consult with the PRA when it proposes to make rules in relation to recognised investment exchanges under FSMA, Part 18 (FSMA, s 138I(10)).
[210] See ss 138I(1) and 138J(1) for rules.

(c) (where a regulator proposes to make a rule which would apply to both authorised persons which are mutual societies and other authorised persons) a statement setting out its opinion whether or not the impact of the proposed rule on mutual societies will be significantly different from its impact on other authorised persons and if so, details of the difference;[211]
(d) an explanation of the its reasons for believing that making the proposed rules is compatible with its general duties under FSMA, section 1B(1) and 5(a) (for the FCA) and section 2B(1) or, as the case requires, section 2C(1) or 2D(3), and section 2H (for the PRA) (commonly known as a 'compatibility statement'); and
(e) notice that representations about the proposals may be made to the regulator within a specified time.

5.102 FSMA, section 138L allows the FCA to dispense with public consultation[212] on proposed rules if it considers that the delay in consultation would be prejudicial to the interests of consumers. FSMA, section 138M provides a specific exemption from consultation on FCA temporary product intervention rules, if the FCA considers that it is necessary or expedient not to consult on such rules in order to advance its consumer protection objective or its competition objective.[213]

5.103 The PRA may dispense with public consultation[214] on its proposed rules if it considers that the delay in consultation would be prejudicial to the safety and soundness of PRA-authorised persons, or in a case where FSMA, section 2C (the PRA's insurance objective) applies, be prejudicial to securing the appropriate degree of protection for policyholders. However, there is no discretion to dispense with consultation requirements if, for example, the regulator considers that delay would prejudice someone other than a consumer (in the case of the FCA) or a policyholder (in the case of the PRA), or that no useful purpose would be served by consultation, for example because the proposed amendments are minor in nature. That is difficult enough, but in fact the majority of the regulators' legislative functions require consultation in all cases, with no discretion not to consult.[215]

Cost–benefit analysis

5.104 The requirement for a cost–benefit analysis applies to most rules made by the regulators, with the exception of the rules and other provisions specified in FSMA, section 138I(6) (FCA) and section 138J(6) (PRA). The draft Financial Services and Markets Bill defined cost–benefit analysis as an estimate of the costs of complying with the rules[216] together with an analysis of the benefits. However, this was amended following the interim Cruickshank Report on competition in UK banking[217] to make clear that costs should include all economic costs,

[211] See FSMA, s 138K(2).
[212] The requirement to consult the PRA remains.
[213] FSMA, s 138M(1).
[214] The PRA is still required to consult the FCA.
[215] For example, where the FCA issues a statement of policy under FSMA, s 124 as to the imposition of penalties in cases of market abuse; and issuing statements of policy on the imposition of disciplinary measures on authorised firms under FSMA, s 211. By contrast, the FCA may dispense with consultation in respect of the code of market conduct if it considers that there is an 'urgent need' to publish the code (FSMA, s 121(6)). See FSMA, s 121(9) in relation to alterations or replacements of the code.
[216] Along the lines of the provision in the Financial Services Act 1986, Sch 7 para 2A.
[217] Banking Review Competition and Regulation in Financial Services: Striking the Right Balance (July 1999); Final Report (March 2000); Government response (August 2000).

and not just compliance costs. This has been carried forward into FSMA as amended by FSA 2012. The obligation to publish a cost–benefit analysis need not deter the regulators from making deregulatory changes. The regulators are not required to publish a cost–benefit analysis if they consider that their proposals, if complied with, will result in no increase in costs or that any increase will be of minimal significance.[218]

Purpose

The explanation of the purpose of the proposed rules is given in the regulator's consultation on the proposed rules. The FSA's practice was to include a high-level 'purpose' statement at the beginning of each section of the FSA Handbook, to facilitate a purposive interpretation of the chapter. The regulators have retained the 'purpose' statement in the modules and sourcebooks that they have designated as part of their Handbooks.[219] Many legislative functions have a purpose test: for example, general rules made by the FCA under FSMA, 137A or by the PRA under FSMA, section 137G are made for the purpose of advancing the statutory objectives of the regulator concerned, and the explanation provided clearly needs to reflect that test. Finally, the tests for giving a waiver or modification of rules under FSMA, section 138A (see paragraph 5.75) may be informed by the explanations given in the Handbooks and the consultation paper. **5.105**

Compatibility with the general duties

The so-called 'compatibility statement'[220] in respect of the general duties (see paragraph 5.101) is required only in respect of consultation on rules. The statement is not required for other general functions such as the making of codes or the making of principles for approved persons, even though, like rules, they too are expressly subject to the general duties. **5.106**

Compatibility with general duties requires the FCA to act, so far as is reasonably practicable, in a way which is compatible with its strategic objective and advances one or more of its operational objectives.[221] The PRA is required to act, so far as reasonably possible, in a way which advances its general objective.[222] Where the PRA's insurance objective (or any additional objective specified pursuant FSMA, section 2D) is engaged, the PRA must act in a way which is compatible with its general objective and insurance objective (or specified objective, as the case may be) and which advances those objectives.[223] In addition, both regulators must have regard to the regulatory principles in FSMA, section 3B. In one sense, having to give their reasons should be no hardship, and consultation on those reasons should help the regulators improve their decision-making, since they must already comply with the general duties in making the rules and the FCA must comply with the duties in giving general guidance. Nevertheless, a full statement of compatibility with the general duties, on top of a cost–benefit analysis, can add considerably to the length of a consultation document. **5.107**

Furthermore, this obligation overlaps substantially with both regulators' general duty to consult practitioners (which in the case of the FCA includes two statutory panels and an **5.108**

218 FSMA, s 138L(3)–(5), and equivalent provisions in other consultation requirements.

219 Every provision in the Handbooks must be interpreted in the light of its purpose: FCA Handbook, PRA Handbook GEN 2.2.1R.

220 Required by FSMA, s 138I(2)(d) and s 138J(2)(d).

221 FSMA, s 1B(1).

222 FSMA, s 2B(1).

223 FSMA, ss 2C(1) and 2D(3).

additional panel for smaller businesses), and the FCA's duty to consult consumers on the extent to which their policies and practices are consistent with their general duties.[224]

Consultation periods and implementation

5.109 Finally, the regulators must include in their consultation a statement that representations about the proposals may be made to the regulator concerned within a specified period, and must pay regard to these representations before taking the proposed action.[225] Following consultation, the regulators must publish a feedback statement, and if the proposals have changed significantly (which implies that they may change their proposals), a revised cost–benefit analysis.[226]

5.110 Nevertheless, FSMA does not expressly provide that an inappropriate failure to consult would automatically invalidate the rules made; nor does it expressly require the regulators to consult when they amend or revoke rules,[227] although an amendment would arguably involve the insertion of new rules. Nor would a failure to publish a feedback statement with a revised cost–benefit analysis or a failure to notify the Treasury and the Bank of England as required[228] necessarily invalidate the making, amendment, or revocation of an instrument.

Publication

5.111 FSMA requires that the function of making rules is executed in writing[229] and that a rule-making instrument must be published. A failure to publish a rule-making instrument will invalidate that instrument at least in the case of the rules that it contains. The definitive version of a rule is that contained in the rule-making instrument and there are provisions for a copy of the instrument to be verified by a regulator for the purposes of legal proceedings.[230] There can be no breach of a rule if the relevant rule-making instrument has not been published in accordance with FSMA, section 138G, and a rule-making instrument will be void to the extent that it does not specify the provisions of FSMA under which the rules are made.[231]

Reduced consultation on guidance

5.112 When FSMA originally came into force, the consultation provisions applicable to the FSA's general guidance were a close match of the consultation provisions applicable to rules. Following consultation in 2005 and 2006, a Regulatory Reform Order came in to force on 12 July 2007. One effect of that Order was to reduce the consultation requirements applicable to general guidance on FSA rules. The reduced consultation requirements have been carried forward into FSMA as amended by FSA 2012 so that the position in relation to consultation on FCA general guidance is as follows:[232]

(a) the FCA is required to consult the PRA and to publish a draft of the proposed general guidance in the way best calculated to bring it to the attention of the public;
(b) publication must indicate that the FCA is open to representations about the proposed general guidance;

224 FSMA, ss 1M–IQ, 2L, and 2M. See generally, para 5.18.
225 ibid, s 138I(2)(e) and 3, and s 138J(2)(e) and 3, in the case of consultation on proposed rules.
226 ibid, s 138I(4) and (5) and s 138J(4) and (5), in the case of consultation on proposed rules.
227 Compare the reference to altering or revoking rules in FSMA, s 138F.
228 FSMA, ss 138F and 139B.
229 ibid, s 138G(1).
230 ibid, s 138H.
231 ibid, ss 138G(3) and (6).
232 ibid, s 139A(5).

(c) the FCA must have regard to any representations received before making the proposed general guidance;
(d) the FCA may dispense with these consultation requirements if it considers that the delay in complying with them would be prejudicial to the interests of consumers; and
(e) if the FCA gives general guidance that it intends to have continuing effect and that is in written or other legible form, it must give the Treasury a copy of that guidance without delay. It must also notify the Treasury if that guidance is later altered or revoked.[233]

Competition scrutiny

Unlike the FSA which did not have a competition objective, the FCA has a competition objective of promoting effective competition in the interests of consumers in the markets for regulated financial services, or services provided by a recognised investment exchange in carrying on regulated activities in respect of which it is by virtue of section 285(2) exempt from the general prohibition.[234] The competition objective is an operational objective and as such falls to be considered when the FCA is discharging its general functions (which include making rules and codes and giving general guidance as well as general policy-making). As has been noted earlier, in discharging its general functions, the FCA is required to act in a way which advances one or more of its operational objectives. Whilst the PRA does not have a competition objective, in discharging its general functions, it is required, under FSMA, section 2H(1)(b) to have regard to the need to minimise any adverse effect on competition in the relevant markets that may result from the manner in which the PRA discharges those functions. Accordingly, when making rules, the FCA has a positive obligation to promote competition whilst the PRA must, at the very least, minimise the risk that those rules would have a negative effect on competition. **5.113**

Under FSMA, Part 10 (as it had effect before the coming into force of FSA 2012), the FSA was subject to 'scrutiny' by the Office of Fair Trading ('OFT') and the Competition Commission ('the competition authorities'). In particular, the OFT was required to keep under review the FSA's regulating provisions[235] and practices, and to make a report if it considered that they or any combination of them were having an adverse effect on competition, in which case the Competition Commission was required to investigate.[236] **5.114**

The 'competition scrutiny' provisions under FSMA, as amended by FSA 2012, have been relaxed. Significantly, there is no longer an obligation to the OFT (which, at the time of writing is shortly to be merged with the Competition Commission), to keep regulating provisions and practices under review. The relaxation of the requirements is justifiable, especially in the case of the FCA which has a positive duty to promote competition. Instead, FSMA includes provision for both competition authorities to give 'section 140B' advice to the regulators. **5.115**

The OFT gives section 140B advice[237] to a regulator if it gives advice to the regulator under section 7 of the Enterprise Act 2002 and the advice states that in the opinion of the OFT, one or more of the following would have the effect of preventing, restricting, or distorting **5.116**

[233] ibid, s 139B.
[234] FSMA, s 1E(1).
[235] Defined in FSMA, s 159(1) (as it has effect before the Financial Services Act 2012 came into force) to mean 'practices adopted by the FSA in the exercise of functions under FSMA'.
[236] FSMA, s 160 (as it has effect before the Financial Services Act 2012 came into force).
[237] FSMA, s 140B(2).

competition in connection with the supply or acquisition of any goods or services in the United Kingdom or a part of the United Kingdom:

(a) a regulating provision[238] or practice of the regulator;
(b) two or more regulating provisions or practices (of that regulator or of both regulators) taken together;
(c) a particular combination of regulating provision or practices (of that regulator or of both regulators); or
(d) a feature, or combination of features, of a market in the United Kingdom that could be dealt with by regulating provision or practices (of that regulator or of both regulators).

5.117 The Competition Commission gives 'section 140B advice'[239] to a regulator if a report published by it under section 136 of the Enterprise Act 2002 (investigations and reports on market investigation reference) contains: (a) a decision that one or more of the matters listed in paragraph 5116(a)–(d) may cause or contribute to the prevention, restriction or distortion of competition in connection with the supply or acquisition of any goods or services in the United Kingdom or a part of the United Kingdom, and (b) a recommendation that any action should be taken by that regulator.

5.118 The competition authorities are required to consult with a regulator before giving section 140B advice.[240] If either competition authority gives section 140B advice to a regulator, the regulator concerned must, within 90 days of receiving the advice, publish a response stating how it proposes to deal with the advice and in particular, whether it has decided to take any action, or to take no action, in response to the advice, if it has decided to take action, what action it proposes to take, and its reasons for its proposals.[241] If, after the regulator publishes its opinion, the competition authority remains concerned, it may refer the matter to the Treasury who has the power to direct the regulator concerned to take such action as may be specified in the direction.[242]

Interpretation of the Handbooks

5.119 It is important to remember that each of the Handbooks is for the most part a re-statement of separate rule-making instruments of the regulator concerned, each containing legislative provisions. The definitive version of the Handbooks is contained in these instruments, and the provisions of the Handbooks are verified for court proceedings by reference to these.[243]

5.120 As secondary legislation, rules are already subject in principle to the provisions of the Interpretation Act 1978. However, both the FCA and the PRA Handbooks include a General Provisions Sourcebook ('GEN') which establishes specific rules of interpretation for the Handbooks, some of which displace the more general requirements of the Interpretation Act.

5.121 Of particular importance to the interpretation of the Handbooks in their current form are the provisions appearing in both Handbooks at GEN 2.2.13AR and GEN 2.2.23R

[238] Defined in FSMA, s 140. For the FCA: any rules, general guidance, statement, or code issued by the FCA; for the PRA: any rules, statement, or code issued by the PRA.
[239] FSMA, s 140B(3).
[240] FSMA, s 140C.
[241] FSMA, s 140G.
[242] FSMA, s 140H.
[243] FSMA, s 138H.

to 2.2.25G. Given that the substantial part of the Handbooks were created by designating provisions in the FSA Handbook, the regulators considered that it was necessary to include these provisions in order to ensure that the two newly independent Handbooks continued to work as effectively as possible.

GEN 2.2.13AR provides that: **5.122**

> unless a contrary intention appears, to the extent that a provision made by the appropriate regulator ('the referring provision') contains a cross-reference to another provision that is not made by that regulator ('the referred provision'), the referred provision is to be taken to have been made by the appropriate regulator to the extent necessary to make the referring provision function with the full effect indicated by the reference.

The obvious intention here is to deal with the situation where a provision of the FSA Handbook designated by a regulator refers to another provision which has not been designated so that the 'referred provision' is not in fact contained in the regulator's Handbook. **5.123**

GEN 2.2.23R provides that where a provision made by both the FCA and the PRA goes beyond the FCA's or PRA's powers or regulatory responsibilities, that provision is to be interpreted as applied by that regulator to the extent of that regulator's powers and regulatory responsibilities only. The stated purpose of this rule is to deal with a provision which appears identically in each regulator's Handbook but is only relevant in part to each regulator's powers and regulatory responsibilities. GEN 2.2.25G(2) explains the intended effect of this provision using the example SYSC 6.1.1R, which requires a firm to maintain adequate policies and procedures to ensure compliance with its obligations under the regulatory system. The guidance explains that SYSC 6.1.1R should be interpreted: **5.124**

(a) as applied by the FCA in respect of a PRA-authorised person's compliance with regulatory obligations that are the responsibility of the FCA (for example, in respect of a bank maintaining policies and procedures to ensure compliance with banking conduct requirements in BCOBS); and
(b) as applied by the PRA in respect of a PRA-authorised person's compliance with those regulatory obligations that are the responsibility of the PRA (for example, in respect of a bank maintaining policies and procedures to ensure compliance with financial resources requirements in BIPRU).

SYSC 6.1.1R further requires a firm to maintain adequate policies and procedures for countering the risk that the firm may be used to further financial crime. Given that the prevention of financial crime falls within the FCA's regulatory scope only,[244] it should follow from GEN 2.2.23R that the part of SYSC 6.1.1R which relates to financial crime is read as being applied by the FCA only. It remains to be seen whether GEN 2.2.23R will achieve its intended interpretative effect in practice. **5.125**

In addition to the above, the General Provisions module ('GEN') of each of the Handbooks contains the following interpretative provisions: **5.126**

(a) Every provision in the Handbooks must be interpreted in the light of its purpose[245] (on which see paragraph 5.105). GEN 2.2.2G goes on to explain:

244 FSMA, s 1B(5).
245 FCA Handbook, PRA Handbook GEN 2.2.1R.

The purpose of any provision in the Handbook is to be gathered first and foremost from the text of the provision in question and its context among other relevant provisions. The guidance given on the purpose of a provision is intended as an explanation to assist readers of the Handbook. As such, guidance may assist the reader in assessing the purpose of the provision, but it should not be taken as a complete or definitive explanation of a provision's purpose.

(b) Evidential provisions indicated by the use of the letter 'E' (see paragraph 5.70) are to be taken to provide that contravention of the rule does not give rise to any of the consequences provided for by provisions of the Act other than FSMA, section 138C.[246]

(c) In the Handbook (except IPRU, unless otherwise indicated) an expression in italics which is defined in the Glossary has the meaning given there. An expression in italics which relates to an expression defined in the Glossary must be interpreted accordingly.[247] When italics have not been used, then (unless the context otherwise requires) an expression bears its natural meaning subject to the provisions of the Interpretation Act 1978.[248]

(d) GEN 2.2.11R applies the Interpretation Act to the entire Handbook, and in particular, unless the contrary intention appears:

(i) expressions in the Handbook have the same meanings as in FSMA;
(ii) references to an enactment are references to that enactment as amended;
(iii) words importing the masculine gender include the feminine gender, and words importing the singular include the plural, and vice versa;
(iv) GEN 2.2.13R goes further and provides that references to other provisions of the Handbook are references to those provisions as amended from time to time (rather than at the time they were made); in other words, references to other provisions in the Handbook are ambulatory and do not have to be updated when those provisions are amended;
(v) References to step-children and step-siblings (for example, in controllers and close link provisions) include children and siblings whose parents are in civil partnership under the Civil Partnership Act 2004;[249]
(vi) A requirement for a communication or notice or similar to be 'in writing' means that (unless contrary intention appears), the communication, etc. must be in legible form and capable of being reproduced on paper, irrespective of the medium used. References to 'writing' are interpreted accordingly;[250]
(vii) A document includes information recorded in any form, including electronic form;[251]

---

[246] FCA Handbook, PRA Handbook GEN 2.2.3R. But see GEN 2.2.4G(2): Other provisions in the Handbook, although also identified by the status letter 'E' in the margin or heading, are actually not rules but provisions in codes and GEN 2.2.3R does not apply to them. These code provisions are those provisions in the Code of Practice for Approved Persons (APER 3 and APER 4) and the Code of Market Conduct (MAR 1) with the status letter 'E'.

[247] GEN 2.2.7R.

[248] GEN 2.2.9G.

[249] GEN 2.2.12AR.

[250] GEN 2.2.14R.

[251] GEN 2.2.16G.

(viii) General rules (made under FSMA, section 137A for FCA and section 137G for PRA) are to be treated as applying to a firm with respect to the carrying on of all regulated activities, and not the carrying on of other activities, unless and to the extent that a contrary intention appears.[252]

(ix) If a partnership or unincorporated association is dissolved, but its authorisation is preserved under FSMA, section 32, any partnership or unincorporated association which succeeds to the business is to be regarded as the same firm for the purposes of the Handbook unless the context otherwise requires.[253]

[252] GEN 2.2.17R.
[253] GEN 2.2.18R.

6

REGULATORY PROCESSES—AUTHORISATION, SUPERVISION, AND ENFORCEMENT

There are four ways in which a person can conduct regulated activities in the UK without contravening the Financial Services and Markets Act 2000 ('the FSMA'):[1] they can be either exempt, passported, unauthorised but exempted from the general prohibition,[2] or hold a relevant permission under Part 4A of the FSMA.[3] **6.01**

In general, exempt persons are exempt either because they are quasi-public bodies (such as the central banks) or because their functions are otherwise deemed to be of public value (for example, trade unions are exempt from insurance regulation in the provision of strike benefits for members).[4] **6.02**

Passported firms are firms established in other EEA Member States who have a right under EEA law to carry on business in the UK through a branch (or more than 90 per cent owned financial institution subsidiary) under their home state regulatory status,[5] either under a specific directive passport,[6] or under the EEA Treaties as a 'Treaty Firm'.[7] It should be noted at this point that derivative clearing houses authorised under the European Markets Infrastructure Regulation[8] ('EMIR') will not be passported, but are, like UK clearing houses, exempted under section 285.[9] **6.03**

An EU passported firm is entitled to conduct only those activities which are specified as passported activities in the relevant directive and covered by its domestic authorisation. It is therefore not uncommon for passported firms to apply for additional permissions in the UK in respect of activities which they wish to conduct but are outside the scope of the passport. The UK Regulators are prepared to give what are known as 'top up' permissions to **6.04**

---

[1] All section references in this chapter are to FSMA unless otherwise stated.
[2] This is the slightly odd status of Lloyds of London, s 316 of the FSMA.
[3] s 19(1) and 31(1) FSMA.
[4] ss 38–39A of the FSMA.
[5] See Chapter 3.
[6] The relevant directives are listed in para 1 of Sch 3 to the FSMA. They are the Banking Directive, the Insurance Directives, the Reinsurance Directive, the Markets in Financial Instruments Directive ('MiFID'), the Insurance Mediation Directive, and the UCITS Directives and the Emissions Allowance Auctioning Regulation, and will in due course include management companies under the Alternative Investment Management Fund Directive (see Chapter 3).
[7] Comprising the ConsolidateTreaty on the Functioning of the European Union and the separate Agreement on the Eurpean Economic Area.
[8] 648/2012/EU (see Chapter 3).
[9] For EEA rights, see s 31 of, and Schs 3 and 4 to, the FSMA.

such applicants. These firms are accordingly both passported and have one or more Part 4A permissions in the UK.

6.05 Brief mention should also be made of the 'Treaty firm' regime. In addition to the specific EEA directives creating passports, EEA firms also have the benefit of the EU Treaty commitment to free movement of capital. It is therefore theoretically possible for a firm to demonstrate that it is entitled to conduct its business in the UK by reason of its rights under that Treaty regardless of its authorisation status. The Treaty firm regime exists in order to accommodate any such right.

6.06 The vast majority of financial firms, however, fall into the fourth category of being permitted to engage in regulated activities by reason of being authorised to do so under Part 4A of the FSMA.

6.07 It is worth noting at this point that the terminology of 'authorisation' under the FSMA is non-intuitive. Under the predecessor to the FSMA, the Financial Services Act 1986 (the 'FSA 1986'), a firm became an authorised person when it received authorisation from the appropriate regulator. When the FSA 1986 was replaced by the FSMA, this structure was changed. An applicant now applies only for one or more permissions to do one or more activities; therefore there are separate permissions for dealing as principal, dealing as agent, taking deposits, and so on. There is therefore technically no such thing as an application for authorisation *per se*. However, the decision was taken to retain the term 'authorised person' in the FSMA. This explains the somewhat odd section 31, which provides that a person who has one or more permissions is automatically an 'authorised person'.

Exemption and Exempt Persons

6.08 An exempt person is not an authorised person and references in the FSMA to 'authorised persons' do not include exempt persons. Thus, for example, for the purposes of section 21 (financial promotions), an exempt person cannot approve a financial promotion. Exempt persons can be exempt either because the FSMA itself grants exemption, or because they are identified as exempt in the Exemption Order.[10] The FSMA itself provides that certain entities are exempt; for example, recognised investment exchanges and recognised clearing houses are exempt persons under section 285 of the FSMA. Appointed representatives are exempt persons by virtue of section 39. Persons can also be exempt under the Exemption Order: under this a number of named entities (and types of entity) are exempt in relation to certain types of specified regulated activity. So, for instance, the Bank of England is exempt in respect of any regulated activity (with the exception of effecting or carrying out insurance business). By contrast, a local authority is exempt in respect of deposit-taking, but not otherwise.

6.09 The difference between being directly exempted under the FSMA and being exempted by the Order is that by virtue of section 38 a person cannot be an exempt person as a result of

[10] Financial Services and Markets Act 2000 (Exemption) Order 2001 (SI 2001/1201) as amended; see also the Financial Services and Markets Act 2000 (PRA-Regulated Activities) Order 2013 (SI 2013/556).

the Order if he is authorised under Part IV. The effect of this is that a person who becomes authorised loses the benefit of his exemption under the Order. So, even if an authorised person is explicitly named in the Order or is of a type covered by the Order, if he intends to carry on any regulated activity he will need to obtain specific Part IV permission for that activity as part of his authorisation. In a similar vein, under section 39 of the FSMA an authorised person can also never be exempt from the general prohibition as an appointed representative. However, if a person is exempt because of activities as a recognised investment exchange or recognised clearing house, then he may be authorised for another regulated activity, since these entities are exempted under the FSMA and not under the Order.

Authorisation

Is authorisation required?

The question of whether a person requires authorisation is a matter of law and the answer depends on the facts when construed in the light of sections 22 and 418 and the Regulated Activities Order.[11] It is regularly noted that for firms whose business is on the borders of regulated activity, the compliance burden of ensuring that they stay on the right side of the regulatory boundary may exceed the compliance burden involved in becoming authorised. **6.10**

Who can be authorised?

Individuals, bodies corporate, partnerships, and unincorporated associations are eligible to apply for authorisation (although certain activities may only be carried on by persons with a particular legal status).[12] Particular provision is made in the FSMA for partnerships and unincorporated associations under section 32. Where these entities carry on a business, the authorisation is granted to the business and not the entity; therefore, where a partnership is dissolved and a successor partnership takes on the old partnership business, the business retains its authorised status. **6.11**

Non-EU Firms which are incorporated overseas may apply for authorisation if their activities are such that authorisation is required. This is necessary if they establish a subsidiary or a branch in the UK. In such cases, it is the entity which is authorised, and in principle, the UK regulator's regulatory jurisdiction extends over the entire firm. However, much of the scope of the relevant UK regulators rule-books is confined to UK activities. **6.12**

Consequences of authorisation

Position under the FSMA

Section 19 provides that a person is prohibited from engaging in regulated activity in the UK unless he is authorised or exempt, and commits a criminal offence if he does so otherwise. This leaves open the question of what happens where a person who is authorised by reason of having a permission to do one type of regulated activity engages in a different regulated **6.13**

[11] ibid.
[12] See para 6.23(e).

activity for which he does not have permission. This is dealt with by section 20, which provides that if an authorised person does this 'he will be taken to have contravened a requirement imposed on him by the UK Regulator'. This slightly odd formulation is there because the regulator can only bring enforcement action in respect of a rule, and this wording means that a breach of this provision of the statute is justiciable before the regulatory tribunal as a breach of a rule. It also brings into effect section 138D of the FSMA, which confers upon private persons (but not others) a right to sue an authorised person for damages in the tort of breach of statutory duty.

6.14 A contravention of section 20 of the FSMA by an authorised person does not make him guilty of an offence or make any transaction void or unenforceable (in contrast to a breach of section 19 of the FSMA by an unauthorised person). There is one exception to this: a person who carries on a consumer credit business without permission does commit a criminal offence even if they have other permissions (section 23(1A)), and any resulting credit agreements will be void.

The UK Regulators

6.15 Part of the UK response to the financial crisis was to break up the old financial regulator, the Financial Services Authority (the 'FSA'), into two new regulators, the Prudential Regulation Authority (the 'PRA') and the Financial Conduct Authority (the 'FCA'). The PRA is primarily responsible for capital regulation of certain entities (banks, insurers, and broad-scope investment firms), whereas the FCA is responsible for issues relating to conduct of business, market integrity, and product disclosure. The vast majority of firms are regulated only by the FCA, but almost all larger firms are regulated by both the FCA and the PRA.[13] The PRA is technically the senior regulator, in that it has a statutory power to give directions to the FCA (section 3I) as regards the regulation of firms which are subject to both regulators.

6.16 The FCA's jurisdiction extends to every activity covered by the Regulated Activities Order.[14] The PRA's jurisdiction, by contrast, is limited to those activities specified in the PRA Order.[15] That order specifies four broad heads of activity which require PRA authorisation:

(1) accepting deposits;
(2) effecting and carrying out contracts of insurance;
(3) Lloyds underwriting, syndicate management, and other activity; and
(4) Certain types of dealing in investments as principal.

The last requires a word of explanation. Paragraph 3(4) of the PRA Order provides that the PRA may designate certain types of firm (broadly, full-service investment firms) as PRA regulated where the firm's assets (or the assets of the group of which it is a member) exceed a threshold to be determined. Paragraph 8 of the PRA Order requires the PRA to publish a statement of policy setting out that threshold. The current statement of policy[16] indicates that this power will be exercised where the firm (or the investment business of the group of which it is a part) has assets exceeding £15 billion.

---

[13] The FCA estimate that they regulate 26,000 firms in total, and are the sole supervisor for 23,000.

[14] The Financial Services and Markets Act (Regulated Activities) Order 2001, SI 2001/544.

[15] The Financial Services and Markets Act 2000 (PRA-Regulated Activites) Order 2013, 2013/556, made under s 22A of the FSMA.

[16] 'Designation of investment firms for prudential supervision by the Prudential Regulation Authority' (March 2013).

The application for authorisation varies according to the identity of the relevant regulator. For firms who wish to engage in both PRA- and FCA-authorised activities, the application for authorisation is made to the PRA; in other cases to the FCA. However, where the applicant is dual regulated, the PRA may only grant permission where the FCA has consented to the grant of the permission, and the FCA may impose conditions on the grant of the permission. The effect of this in practice is that where a firm wishes to undertake both PRA- and FCA-regulated business, the grant of permission is a single grant from the PRA; it is not the case that the firm has both a PRA permission to undertake PRA activities and an FCA permission to undertake FCA activities (section 55F). **6.17**

Once a firm has become authorised it cannot make an application for another authorisation. A firm which wishes to change the scope of its authorisation, either by expanding or reducing that scope, must do so by requesting a variation of permission from the relevant regulator. Where the firm is regulated solely by the FCA this is straightforward. However, where the firm is both PRA and FCA regulated, then it must apply to the PRA for variation of that permission, and the PRA may vary the permission only with the consent of the FCA. **6.18**

Consequences of authorisation

The obvious consequence of authorisation is that the authorised person is subject to the rules of the UK regulators. Although these rules are currently divided into an FCA Handbook and a PRA Handbook, a combined version is published so that firms which are both PRA and FCA regulated can operate according to a single set of rules. **6.19**

An authorised person has certain privileges as regards financial advertising, and is able both to communicate and to approve financial promotions (subject to specific financial promotion rules and a statutory regime which restricts promotion of unregulated collective investment schemes by authorised firms—see Chapter 18 as regards Collective Investment Schemes). The authorised person will also be subject to the disciplinary regime, and certain individuals employed by the firm will be separately registered with the relevant UK Regulator under the Approved Persons regime, also leaving them subject to discipline by the relevant regulator. **6.20**

The authorisation process

The threshold conditions

Section 55B requires that in giving or varying permission, or imposing or varying any requirement, the FCA or the PRA must ensure that the applicant will satisfy and continue to satisfy the threshold conditions in relation to all of the regulated activities for which he has or will have permission. The threshold conditions are set out in Schedule 6 of the Act. Both the PRA and the FCA produce a 'Threshold Conditions Code' which supplements the Schedule 6 requirements—the FCA's version is in the COND section of the FCA Handbook, and the PRA's version is set out in its documents 'Approach to Banking Supervision' and 'Approach to Insurance Supervision' of April 2013. **6.21**

Schedule 6 contains four sets of conditions: **6.22**

(i) Conditions for firms authorised and regulated by the FCA only (paragraphs 2B–2F);
(ii) FCA specific conditions for firms authorised by the PRA and subject to dual regulation (paragraphs 3B–3E);
(iii) PRA-specific conditions for insurers (paragraphs 4A–4F); and
(iv) PRA-specific conditions for other PRA-authorised persons (paragraphs 5A–5F).

6.23 The primary features of the new threshold conditions are as follows:

(a) both the FCA and the PRA are required to satisfy themselves that the firm is structured in a fashion which enables it to be effectively supervised. This involves consideration of the firms involvement with other persons, and in particular its reliance on other members of any group of which it itself is a member;

(b) in addition to the requirement to have appropriate financial resources, an applicant is now required to have appropriate non-financial resources. This relates to the resources available to the firm, ranging from the expertise of its managers to the sophistication and robustness of its IT systems;

(c) for FCA applications the applicant must be able to show that its business model is appropriate and is capable of being conducted in a sound and prudent manner;

(d) the PRA is required to be satisfied that any firm which applies to it for approval must be administered in a 'prudent' manner;

(e) there are no limitations on the legal status of FCA applications, but an applicant to the PRA for deposit-taking permission must be either a partnership or a body corporate, and an applicant for permission to engage in insurance business must be either a body corporate (but not an LLP), a registered friendly society or a member of Lloyds;

(f) there are some restrictions in relation to the location of offices. If the person is a body corporate constituted under the law of any part of the UK, then both its head office and any registered office must be in the UK. This does not apply if the only regulated activity concerned is insurance mediation, in which case there are specific rules. If the person concerned has his head office in the UK but is not a body corporate, then it must carry on business in the UK.

Part 4A Permissions

6.24 As explained earlier, authorised persons attain their authorised status by being granted a permission under Part IV of the FSMA.

6.25 Permissions are given in respect of regulated activities—that is, the final permission granted will relate to one or more activities which are regulated activities by virtue of the Regulated Activities Order.

6.26 Both the FCA and the PRA have the power[17] to:

(i) impose limits on the carrying on of any particular regulated activity, for example, as to circumstances in which the activity may or may not be carried on. This power is frequently used;

(ii) grant a narrower or wider scope of permission for a particular regulated activity than that for which application is made;

(iii) give permission for an activity which has not been included in the application itself.

6.27 Both the FCA and the PRA may impose conditions on the permissions of a person who is authorised by both of them, although they are encouraged to consult in advance of such action.

6.28 Both the PRA and the FCA have the power to impose requirements on any permission which they have granted at any stage. The FCA is also required to consult the PRA where it proposes to impose a requirement on the permission of an FCA-authorised entity which

[17] s 42(7).

is part of a group which includes a PRA-authorised person (section 55L(7)). In principle, requirements may only be imposed if the relevant regulator is satisfied that the firm concerned is failing, or is likely to fail, to satisfy the threshold conditions, or that the firm has not conducted the relevant regulated activity for the last 12 months, or that restriction is 'desirable' in order to advance one of its statutory objectives. However, precautionary restrictions can be imposed on firms which are taken over, even if there is no immediate justification for using the power (section 55O).

Requirements may cover activities which are not regulated activities and can be imposed by reference to membership of a group. They may also be time limited. **6.29**

Requirements and limitations are published on the PRA and FCA register as they are an essential part of a firm's permission. **6.30**

Either UK regulator may exercise its own-initiative powers to impose restrictions on the permission of a firm at the request of certain types of overseas regulators (section 55Q(1)).[18] **6.31**

Some firms have extremely complicated permissions. In many cases this is not a reflection of their business but is a result of the complex transition process by which firms which were authorised under the pre-FSMA legislation (mainly the Financial Services Act 1986) were automatically granted authorisation and Part IV permissions under the FSMA when it came into force on 1 December 2001. In some cases this resulted in firms with substantially similar businesses having different permissions—particularly in relation to limitations and requirements imposed. Indeed the regulators' approach to limitations and requirements has developed over time. This needs to be borne in mind when looking at any existing permission for purposes of information or comparison where the firm was authorised before 1 December 2001 under the FSA 1986. **6.32**

Variations and cancellations

Once a person is authorised, he may apply to have his permission varied by adding or removing regulated activities, varying descriptions, and varying or cancelling requirements and limitations (section 55H for the FCA, section 55I for the PRA). Both the FCA and the PRA have certain powers to vary and cancel permissions on its own initiative (section 55J). **6.33**

Application procedure

General

The basis for the authorisation application procedure is provided for in section 55U. This requires the application to contain a statement of the regulated activities proposed, to provide an address in the UK for service. Both the PRA and the FCA have the power to specify the mode of application, and have done so. For both regulators, a considerable amount of material regarding application is available on their websites. **6.34**

Time limits

Section 55V of the FSMA requires either regulator to determine an application before the end of the period of six months beginning with the date on which it received the completed application. However, in reality regulators have considerable scope for finding an application **6.35**

[18] See also the Financial Services and Markets Act 2000 (Own-Initiative Power)(Overseas Regulators) Regulations 2001 (SI 2001/2639).

to be incomplete, and in general it takes a considerable amount of time after the submission of the initial application for the regulator to agree that it is now complete and that the six-month period has commenced. It is also notable that the more complex the applicant's business, the more likely it is that there will be an extended interim period before the regulator is satisfied that the application is indeed complete.

Approved persons

6.36 An individual who is approved by either of the UK regulators to perform a controlled function within an authorised firm is called an 'approved person'. Approved persons are not the same as 'authorised persons'. The status of approved person is given to certain persons who carry out certain functions in relation to an authorised person. Their status is dependent on their position with the authorised firm—it is not transferable, they are not authorised in their own right. This is an important point which is often misunderstood, particularly by the individuals concerned. Section 59 provides for certain functions within an authorised firm to be performed only by approved persons. The principal consequences for an individual of being an approved person is that they are subject to the disciplinary regime of the relevant regulator—in particular its powers to impose unlimited fines and make public statements about the approved person.

6.37 The Handbook provisions relating to the approved persons regime are not all to be found in the same place, which can cause confusion. The Senior Management Arrangements, Systems and Controls Sourcebook ('SYSC') contains the rule as to who must be registered for the required function known as the 'apportionment and oversight function' (see Chapter 5). SYSC also requires firms that carry on designated investment business to allocate the compliance oversight function to a director or senior manager. However, for further detail on what each of the controlled functions comprises one has to look at the Supervision Manual ('SUP') Chapter 10—SUP 10A is the chapter which applies to FCA approved persons, and SUP 10B for PRA approved persons, and the Statements of Principle and Code of Practice for Approved Persons ('APER') contains the Principles applicable to approved persons and the Code of Practice that applies to those Principles. There are special rules as to the functions which apply for overseas firms and incoming firms. However, for most firms the position is that they must:

(a) register each director or partner and non-executive director in respect of the relevant 'Governing Function' (one of CF1 to CF6 as appropriate);
(b) appoint someone to each of the 'Required Functions' (CF8 to CF12B)—the Required Functions include the apportionment and oversight function (CF8), the compliance oversight function (CF10), and the money laundering reporting function (CF11), and these will be relevant in all cases. Other Required Functions (such as the EEA investment business oversight function (CF9) or the actuarial function (CF12) are applicable only to certain types of business;
(c) consider if they need to register one or more individuals for each of the systems and controls function (CF28), the significant management function (CF29), and/or the customer function (CF30).

6.38 As a practical matter therefore at an early stage in the application a firm needs to decide which controlled functions are relevant to it and who will fulfil them. It is likely that most firms carrying on designated investment business will need to register one or more persons with a customer function (CF30). This is because these persons will be involved in advising, managing, or trading on behalf of customers. In many cases, where a firm has retail clients or deals with consumers, there is an associated examination requirement for the customer functions. It is important to identify whether there are any qualification requirements which need to be satisfied and whether or not the persons who will be registered already meet the necessary requirement. If not, arrangements need to be made for them to take the appropriate examinations—they will not be registered for the customer functions until they can satisfy the relevant regulator that they meet the necessary criteria. This can in turn delay the granting of an authorisation. In some cases it is possible to apply for a waiver of particular training requirements—such an application is made at the same time as the authorisation application. In any event the applicant needs to be satisfied that all of the persons who will be registered as approved persons are competent for the roles which they are to carry on and that it can substantiate its belief in that competence.

It should be noted that specifying the names of potential approved persons in a firm's approval for authorisation does not amount to an application for approval of that person: separate application forms must be completed in relation to each of those individuals who will perform controlled functions under the approved persons regime. **6.39**

The approved persons regime has also been divided between the two regulators. In broad terms there are two classes of roles within a firm which may only be filled by persons who have been approved by the regulator to perform those roles. These are 'customer-dealing functions' and 'significant influence functions'. For PRA regulated firms, significant influence functions require approval from the PRA while customer-dealing functions require approval from the FCA (for non-PRA regulated firms, both significant influence and customer dealing functions require approval from the FCA). There is nothing in the architecture of the system which prohibits dual approval—it is always theoretically possible that a function could fall within both the FCA and the PRA definitions. However, the FCA is required by section 59A of the FSMA to exercise its power to specify controlled functions in a way that will minimise the likelihood that approvals fall to be given by both the FCA and the PRA in respect of the performance by a person of significant influence functions in relation to the activity of the same firm. The FCA is also permitted to 'delegate' its approval of certain function to the PRA, although this has not been done (section 59B). **6.40**

		PRA	FCA
CF 1	Director function	X	X
CF 2	Non-executive director function	X	X
CF 3	Chief executive function	X	X
CF 4	Partner function	X	X
CF 5	Director of unincorporated association function	X	X
CF 6	Small friendly society function	X	X
CF 8	Apportionment and Oversight function		X
10 A	CASS operational oversight function		X
CF 11	Money laundering reporting function		X
CF 28	Systems and controls function	X	X
CF 29	Significant management function		X
CF 30	Customer function		X
CF 40	Benchmark submission function		X
CF 50	Benchmark administration function		X

6.41 Any application for permission must show that the relevant functions to be performed once the firm is authorised must be filled by authorised persons. It is not necessary to identify individuals at the time of the initial application, but the regulator must be satisfied that credible arrangements have been put in place to recruit approved persons before business commences.

Determining applications

6.42 In the normal course the application is handled by staff within the authorisations department of the relevant regulator who have the power to grant applications on the terms applied for. During discussions on the application that the relevant regulator may have with the applicant it may become apparent that the firm should apply for a further or different limitation or requirement or permission, and in such circumstances it may revise its application. The internal staff then have the power to grant the application. Within the FCA, where a decision concerns the refusal or proposed refusal of an application or the grant of an application subject to a limitation or requirement not applied for by the applicant, the decision will be made under executive procedures (as specified in the Decision Procedure and Penalties manual ('DEPP')) unless the applicant makes representations to the regulator, in which case the decision will be made by the Regulatory Decisions Committee ('RDC'). For the PRA, a decision to decline authorisation may only be challenged before the Tribunal.

6.43 During the authorisation process there may, in very limited cases, be a warning notice issued. This can happen where an applicant is applying in respect of an existing business and it is discovered that the existing business was being carried on without the necessary authorisation or permission. Where staff members consider that an application should be refused or should be granted subject to a limit or requirement which was not applied for, or for a narrower description of regulated activity than that to which the application relates, they will recommend to the RDC that a warning notice be given. The warning notice procedure is a matter for decision by the RDC and enables the person concerned to make representations to the RDC before any decision notice is issued. After considering representations the RDC may decide to grant the application and, if appropriate, issue a decision notice. The concept of warning notices and decision notices is described in more detail in paragraphs 6.88 to 6.92.

Supervision Process

A risk-based approach

6.44 Both the PRA (section 2K) and the FCA (section 1L) are required to maintain arrangements for supervising the firms which they have authorised. These arrangements are set out in the supervision chapter of the relevant handbooks (SUP). Although technically both PRA and FCA have their own separate SUP, the majority of the text is common to both.

6.45 Both the FCA and the PRA have restated their approach to the supervision of the firm which they regulate in the recent past. The FCA has moved away from the old 'firm-by-firm' methodology (known as the 'Arrow' review process), and is committed to structured supervision work looking at market structures, business models, and product types as well as individual firm performance.

The basis of the new FCA approach is a division of firms into four categories. These are: **6.46**

C1 banking and insurance groups with a very large number of retail customers, and universal/investment banks with very large client asset balances and trading operations.
C2 firms across all sectors with a substantial number of retail customers and/or large wholesale firms.
C3 firms across all sectors with retail customers and/or a significant wholesale presence.
C4 smaller firms, including almost all intermediaries.

Firms which fall into the C1 and C2 categories are classified as 'fixed portfolio', which means that they have a single nominated supervisor. Firms which fall into the C3 and C4 categories will be supervised on a pooled basis, with supervisory contact being intermittent and (usually) rare.

FCA supervision is implemented through three key techniques: **6.47**

- Firm Systematic Framework ('FSF') structured conduct assessments of firms (these replace the old Arrow assessments).
- Event-driven work—this will involve a responsive approach either to discovered problems or to emerging market-wide risks, and will be aimed at securing customer redress or other remedies.
- Issues and products—this is intended to be a fast, intensive campaign aimed at specific sectors or products that put—or may put—customers at risk.

The Firm Systematic Framework

The basis of the FSF is a business model and strategy analysis. This is based on the business model assessment conducted when the firm applied for authorisation, and considers whether the firm's business model is conducive to the interests of customers and market integrity. This is then supported by an assessment of how the firm embeds fair treatment of customers and ensures market integrity. This assessment has four modules: **6.48**

- governance and culture
- product design
- sales or transaction processes
- post sales/services and transaction handling

The FSF approach is a higher-level approach than the Arrow approach—assessment will be conducted through interviews between supervisors and the firm to look at processes in relevant areas. Detailed testing will only be used where it appears to be the only practical way to assess a particular risk. The aim is to move the process away from a formulaic systems exercise and towards a more dynamic business-based approach. **6.49**

For C1 firms, the FCA carries out a firm-by-firm business model and strategy analysis, in the context of the market they operate in. This analysis is likely to be conducted on a two-year cycle. For C2 firms, the FCA will take a group of similar firms in the same industry sector to identify common risks. For C3s the FCA will look at a sample of firm's business models across the sector, but will in general be looking for outliers—that is, firms whose business model is significantly different from those of their peers. It remains to be seen how this will interact with FCAs public commitment not to lean against innovation in the industry. FSF assessments of C3 firms are likely to happen on a four-year cycle. C4 firms will be assessed **6.50** on an FSF basis intermittently. The FCA's Revised Approach to Small Firms Supervision ('RASFS') process is based on a 'touch point' with every firm at least once every four years (this will not necessarily be an inspection visit; it could be a telephone call, an online assessment, or an invitation to a roadshow). However, the basis of RASFS is a collection of information from a variety of sources (including complaints data) which seeks to identify firm risk levels, with focused intervention on all firms classified as high risk, and a randomly selected 25 per cent of those classified as medium risk.

Wholesale supervision

6.51 Although the FCA is primarily focused on retail and consumer sales, it retains responsibility for supervision of the wholesale markets. The primary role for the FCA in this regard is policing market abuse, and FCA is committed to disregard the ordinary wholesale market principle of caveat emptor and to intervene more assertively in the wholesale markets. Two justifications are provided for this; first, that wholesale market conduct may have an impact on retail investors, and second, that wholesale market conduct which damages confidence in markets or financial products has a negative impact on trust in the integrity of markets as a whole.

6.52 There are therefore wholesale conduct modules in the FSF for some insurance, banking, and investment firms in the C1 and C2 categories. These modules relate to product design and pre-sales/transaction behaviour, sales and trading, and post-sales/transaction and ongoing provision of services. These modules will not be applied to wholesale firms in the C3 or C4 categories.

FCA prudential supervision

6.53 The FCA is also a prudential supervisor for those firms which it regulates which are not subject to PRA supervision. For the vast majority of FCA firms prudential supervision will be simple, involving nothing more than ensuring that the equity of the firm concerned exceeds the prescribed minimum. However, some FCA-only firms may be complex or sophisticated.

6.54 There is an important difference between the FCA approach to prudential supervision and the PRA approach. Whereas the focus of the PRA is on the impact of failure of the firm concerned on the stability of the financial system, the focus of the FCA is on the impact of the failure of the firm concerned on customers, and of the integrity of the financial system. Interestingly, this latter may be a more present concern for the FCA, in that in some of the areas which it regulates, a relatively small number of providers could mean that the failure of any one of them could have a negative impact on the market for that product. As regards the protection of customers, the FCA's primary focus will be on the protection of customer assets.

6.55 The FCA approach to prudential supervision again involves a classification of firms. The classes are:

CP1 firms whose disorderly failure would have a significant impact on the market in which they operate, and whose businesses involve large client asset or money balances.

CP2 firms whose disorderly failure would have a significant impact on the functioning of the market in which they operate, but where there is a small client asset or money balances involved.

CP3 firms whose disorderly failure is unlikely to have any significant impact.

CP1 firms will be subject to a full Internal Capital Adequacy Assessment process ('ICAAP') and Individual Liquidity Adequacy Assessment ('ILAA'). Such firms are also likely to be full service firms under the current European Capital Adequacy Directive (the 'CAD')[19] and under the new Capital Requirements Regulation and Directive (the 'CRD/CRR')[20], and therefore subject to the full range of bank capital adequacy requirements under European law. Some CP2 firms are also likely to be full service firms, but these will only be subject to ICAAP or ILAA if they are within the CAD/CRD. For CP3 firms, baseline monitoring to capital against minimum levels is likely to be the only technique employed. **6.56**

PRA supervision

The PRA emphasises that its approach to supervision differs from that of the FCA in that it is primarily based on judgment.[21] The PRA focuses primarily on threats to the stability of the UK financial system, and therefore looks at individual firms in the light of this mandate rather than as separate entities. This means that the primary focus is on those activities which a firm engages in which are regarded as 'critical economic functions'—notably payment, settlement and clearing; retail banking; corporate banking; intra-financial system borrowing and lending; investment banking; and custody services. **6.57**

The PRA divides the firms which it supervises into five categories:[22] **6.58**

Category 1 is the most significant firms whose size, interconnectedness, complexity, and business type means that their failure would cause very significant disruption to the UK financial system. This class includes insurers whose failure would cause disruption to the interests of a substantial number of policy holders.

Category 2 consists of significant firms whose failure would cause some disruption to the UK financial system, and insurers whose failure would cause disruption to the interests of substantial numbers of policyholders.

Category 3 consists of firms whose individual failure would cause minor disruption to the UK financial system, but where difficulties across the whole sector or sub-sector have the potential to generate disruption, along with insurers whose failure would have some chance of causing disruption to some policyholders.

Category 4 consists of firms whose failure would result in minor disruption to the UK financial system, but where difficulties across the whole sector would have the potential to cause disruption.

Category 5 consists of firms whose failure would cause almost no disruption, and whose failure as a sector or sub-sector could cause some disruption.

In assessing the degree of disruption that a failure of a firm will cause, the PRA will take into account the substitutability of the services concerned—this is if users of a firm can obtain equivalent services very easily from other suppliers with minimal substitution costs, the firm is unlikely to be viewed as capable of causing major disruption even if it is very large.

As part of its review of its regulated firms, PRA will consider business risk, and in particular, when considering a firm's business model, will review whether the way in which one firm **6.59**

[19] 2006/49 EC (see Chapters 3 and 14).

[20] 2013/36/EU and Regulation 575/2013 respectively (see Chapters 3 and 14).

[21] See the PRA document entitled 'The Prudential Regulation Authority's approach to banking supervision' of April 2013, available on the PRA website.

[22] See paras 50 *et seq.* of the PRA 'approach' document referenced in fn 21.

carries on its business could have adverse effects on other participants in the system. It will also consider whether, for example, unsustainable expectations of growth, could build incentives towards excessive risk-taking into the risk profile of the firm concerned. For firms which are classed as Category 1 this analysis will be more detailed, and will include reviews of the drivers of profitability, risk appetite, performance targets, and underlying assumptions, and a firm's own forecasts and their plausibility. It should be noted that if PRA is not satisfied that it has full information about these factors, it is open to it to find that the firm does not satisfy the 'supervisability' criterion for continuing to remain authorised. Other issues that may feed into this determination include the organisational structure of the group and its ability to provide sufficient information to the PRA. Peer review also forms an important part of this process.

6.60 In considering an individual firm, the PRA focuses heavily on the management of that firm, and in particular on its board. This goes well beyond the requirement for the individuals concerned to satisfy the formal requirements for approved person status. In particular, the PRA focuses on the following key factors.

Culture and behaviour The PRA expects firms to have a culture that supports prudent management, by minimising incentives for excessive risk-taking, prioritising the safety and soundness of the institution itself, and ensuring that all levels of management are held to account for acting in accordance with the culture of safety.

Competence All those involved in management—including the board—are expected to have (or to develop, if they do not have it when appointed) understanding of the different areas of the business and the main prudential risks and controls. This requirement applies to at least some (but not all) of the independent directors.

Structure Firms are expected to have in place clear structures of accountability and delegation of responsibilities for individual committees, including checks and balances to prevent dominance by an individual. In particular, where there are unregulated entities in a group containing a PRA-supervised entity, the PRA will expect the boards of those entities to have regard to the PRA's objectives. This is particularly the case where a UK bank has an unregulated holding company, or is owned by an overseas entity. If the boards of such unregulated companies fail to satisfy the PRA that they are committed to ensuring compliance with the PRAs objectives, it is open to the PRA to find that the corporate structure does not satisfy the requirement that the PRA-regulated entity is supervisable.

6.61 The PRA also requires firms to have robust frameworks for risk management and financial and operational control, commensurate with the nature, scale, and complexity of their business, and consistent with their safety and soundness. This requires a robust risk-management framework and its effective and consistent implementation throughout the organisation.

6.62 Prudential supervision is also conducted at a group level, and this creates the potential for conflict where a group contains both FCA- and PRA-authorised firms. In general, if a group contains a PRA firm, the PRA will be the lead supervisor of the group, and will deal with consolidated supervision. However, where the group is headed by an FCA-regulated entity, group supervision is a joint responsibility of the PRA and the FCA.

Supervisory tools

6.63 For many firms their principal contact with their regulator is through the completion of the various reports which are required by SUP. Failures to supply such reports on time or the supply of incomplete reports may provoke action from the relevant regulator. These include the annual controllers and annual close links reports, both of which must be submitted within four months of the firm's accounting reference date. Certain types of firm have to make annual compliance reports. All firms have to make financial reports—the timing and content of these reports is specific to the type of firm concerned. Regulators impose automatic penalties for late filing of returns. The preparation of all these reports (but particularly the financial report) is a serious matter and incomplete, incorrect, or late reports are taken seriously by the regulators.

Firms are also required to inform their regulator of a wide range of matters. These are detailed in SUP and include: **6.64**

(i) any matters which could have a significant adverse impact on the firm's reputation;
(ii) any matter which could affect the firm's ability to continue to provide adequate services to its customers;
(iii) civil proceedings where the amount of the claim is significant in relation to the firm's financial resources or its reputation;
(iv) the fact that the firm is prosecuted for or convicted of any offence involving fraud or dishonesty or that penalties are imposed on it for tax evasion;
(v) the fact that it becomes aware that an employee may have committed a fraud against one of its customers;
(vi) the fact that it becomes aware of a significant breach of an applicable regulatory rule or principle.

The above sets out only a few examples from the list of notification requirements—all authorised firms need to make sure that they are aware (see SUP 15) of the notification requirements applicable to them. Firms should also be aware of the need to give their regulator advance notice of changes in name, business name, principal place of address, or if they become subject to or cease to be subject to the supervision of an overseas regulator. SUP sets out the basis on which notifications may be made to the regulators. **6.65**

Many firms which enter into reportable transactions must also comply with the transaction reporting requirements of SUP 17. These reports enable the FCA to monitor both the activities of firms and oversee the markets in transferable securities. **6.66**

Auditors have a key role to play in assisting the regulators in their supervisory functions. All authorised firms are required to appoint an auditor (regardless of whether they would otherwise be obliged to do so) and an auditor must be qualified in a way which satisfies the requirements of SUP. Firms are required by regulatory rules to cooperate with their auditors and auditors are required to cooperate with the appropriate regulator in the discharge of their statutory functions. Auditors are obliged to report certain matters to the relevant regulator and the auditors of certain types of business are required to make annual reports to the regulators on specific matters.[23] In particular the auditors' report to the regulator covers the firm's financial statements and regulatory reporting—and the auditor must submit a letter annually commenting on the firm's internal controls—however this letter need only cover matters which have come to the auditor's attention while undertaking the work required to **6.67**

[23] By the Financial Services and Markets Act 2000 (Communications by Auditors) Regulations 2001 (SI 2001/2587).

produce the reports on the financial statements and accounting records. Auditors of firms are also required to provide client assets reports to the FCA which contain an opinion on the firm's systems for the custody, identification, and control of custody assets and compliance with client money rules. Auditors are independent and have no privilege against disclosure of this information to the regulators.

6.68 The regulators identify sectoral issues which they considers may raise particular regulatory concerns—for example the adequacy of financial promotions to retail customers—and may then conduct theme visits or desk-based theme reviews designed to enable them to gather information on a particular industry sector (for example, hedge funds) or on a particular type of matter (for example, financial crime). Thematic work can help the regulator to form a view as to whether its risk assessments of sectors or activities is likely to be sound. The selection of firms for visitation is more likely to be determined by the position of that firm in the sector concerned than by any suspicion on the part of the regulator that the firm itself has been engaged in inappropriate conduct.

6.69 Principle 11 requires a firm to cooperate with its regulator, and from time to time regulators will, through visits or desk-based reviews, ask firms to provide information, documentation, or to attend meetings in order to enable them to gather information for supervisory purposes.[24] In addition, the FCA carries out mystery shopping where persons appointed by it may pose as potential retail customers to enable them to assess the selling of financial products to consumers.

Information gathering and investigations

6.70 Sections 165 to 169A and section 284 confer wide-ranging information gathering and investigation powers on the PRA and the FCA to require information from regulated firms. As part of such investigations FCA may also require information from other persons connected with the authorised firm which is the subject of the investigation. It should also be noted that FCA is able to commence an investigations into the affairs of an unauthorised person where that person is a listed company and there is reason to suspect a breach of the listing rules (section 97). Failure to comply with requirements imposed in the exercise of these powers can give rise to the commission of criminal offences punishable by imprisonment and/or a fine.

6.71 Through the use of these information gathering and investigation powers the regulators are able to acquire information from authorised firms, persons who work in such firms, and, in certain circumstances, third parties. This enables each of them to investigate the wide range of matters for which it is the enforcement authority, including contraventions of regulatory rules, the commission of insider dealing offences, and of market abuse and breaches of anti-money laundering requirements.

6.72 The PRA has a separate investigatory power under section 165A to investigate the activities of certain persons where it believes that the activities of those persons may be detrimental to the stability of the UK financial system. This power applies to:

(a) a person who has a legal or beneficial interest in any of the assets of a relevant investment fund;
(b) a person who is responsible for the management of certain investment funds (this includes any fund which holds UK assets—section 165A(8));

[24] For further details, please see Chapter 5, para 5.42 and following.

(c) any service provider to any authorised person;
(d) any other person who is designated in an order made by the treasury as a person whose activities pose a threat to the UK financial system; and
(e) any person who is connected with any of the above.

Skilled person reports

Section 166 confers power on both the PRA and the FCA to require a firm to appoint a third party (usually a firm of solicitors or accountants) to provide them with a report on any matter about which they could require the provision of information or production of documents from that firm (section 165). A skilled person's report can also be required where a firm is alleged to have maintained incomplete records if matters required to be recorded under the regulations. In such a case the regulator can require the firm to appoint a skilled person to update the records (section 166A). The imposition of this requirement (known as a 'skilled persons report') can be applied both to an authorised person and any other member of the authorised person's group. A skilled person acts independently of the authorised firm, but the authorised firm is required to pay its fees. The skilled person report exercise can be a source of considerable disruption to a firm—requiring it to commit significant resources to providing information and assistance to the skilled person—and also involves significant expense. **6.73**

SUP 5 sets out guidance on the approach to the use of skilled person reports which makes it clear that the reports may be required in connection with monitoring, remedial, and preventative purposes. There is a perception that skilled person reports lead to enforcement action: in practice, only a tiny proportion of the skilled reports that are commissioned actually result in enforcement action in the form of a Final Notice. **6.74**

If a skilled person is appointed, SUP 5 imposes particular duties on the firm. It sets out the terms which must be included in a contract between the firm and the skilled person. In particular the firm is required to waive any duty of confidentiality owed by the skilled person to the firm which might limit the provision of information or opinion by the skilled person to the relevant regulator. The contract must be governed by the laws of a part of the UK and provide that the relevant regulator will have a right to enforce the provisions which are included in the contract in order to comply with the SUP requirements. The rules require the firm to provide all reasonable assistance to any skilled person. This includes providing access at all reasonable business hours to the firm's accounting and other records in whatever form, providing such information and explanations as the skilled person reasonably considers necessary or desirable, and permitting the skilled person to obtain information directly from the firm's auditor to the extent the skilled person reasonably considers he needs such information or it is desirable for the proper performance of his duties. **6.75**

Enforcement Processes

The development of multiple regulators leads necessarily to multiple enforcement procedures. This is less problematic than it may seem, in that the PRA's public position is that it would not expect to rely on its enforcement powers, preferring to intervene *ex ante* to remedy problems. However, the FSMA and FSA 2012 do vest the PRA with a full range of enforcement powers. **6.76**

6.77 Both the FCA and the PRA are obliged to publish statements of policy as regards various aspects of their enforcement policy. Both the FCA and the PRA have published statements under section 63C, on financial penalties for persons performing controlled functions without approval, sections 69 and 210 on penalties to be imposed for breaches of rules, and section 395 relating to procedures, including the giving of supervisory notices, warning notices, decision notices, and the giving of consent by one regulator to another.[25] It should be noted that the act enables the regulators to impose penalties on certain unregulated persons—notably, section 404C permits the regulators to impose penalties on persons who were but are no longer authorised, section 192K on qualifying parent undertakings (defined in section 192B as parent companies of authorised persons incorporated in the UK), section 345 on auditors of authorised persons, and section 249 on auditors of authorised unit trusts. The FCA also has a variety of other penalty powers, including section 88C (imposition of penalties on sponsors in respect of listing particulars), section 89S (imposition of financial penalties on primary information providers), section 93 (penalties on listed companies for breaches of listing rules), section 124 (penalties for market abuse), section 131G (penalties for breach of the short selling rule). Section 312J requires the publication of a statement of policy on the exercise of the power under section 312F to impose a penalty on recognised entities (exchanges and clearing houses).

6.78 Both EG (which is technically not part of the FCA Handbook, since it is merely a 'regulatory guide') and DEPP[26] (which is part of the Handbook) contain significant provisions which expand on the FCA's enforcement policy and set out applicable rules and guidance which apply when the FCA exercises its statutory powers. EG 2 sets out the FCA's approach to enforcement generally when considering whether to exercise its enforcement powers: it includes descriptions of the case selection criteria it uses in different types of cases. EG 3 sets out the FCA's policy on using its powers to require information and reports, and on carrying out investigations. Annex 2 to EG sets out guidelines on investigation where a case may concern both the FCA and other prosecuting and investigating agencies. The guidelines set out some broad principles which the various agencies have agreed should be applied in order to assist in determining which of them should investigate cases to avoid duplication and similar matters. Any firm which is facing a serious enforcement matter may find that other agencies are or could be involved, in which case these guidelines may be relevant.

Disciplinary measures

6.79 As noted earlier, in general, PRA is not expected to resort to formal enforcement except in unusual circumstances, whereas formal enforcement remains the focus of FCA's activities. Thus the following discussion is couched in terms of the FCA alone. However, the PRA has the full range of enforcement powers available to it.

6.80 Part XIV of the FSMA specifies the main disciplinary measures in relation to firms available to the regulators. However, there are additional powers elsewhere within the FSMA and, as regards private censures, the FCA operates its own, non-statutory procedure. Section 415B requires the FCA to consult with the PRA before it takes certain enforcement action against

[25] The PRA's statements are published together in a document entitled 'The Prudential Regulation Authority's approach to enforcement: statutory statements of policy and procedure' of April 2013 available on the PRA website. The equivalent FCA material comprises Chapter 6 of DEPP.

[26] On DEPP, see paras 6.96 *et seq.*

a person who has a permission from the PRA, or who is in a qualifying relationship (per section 415B(4)) with a PRA person or is PRA authorised.

Public censure

If the FCA considers that an authorised person has contravened a requirement of the FSMA, the FCA may publish a statement to that effect.[27] Requirements imposed under the FSMA include FCA rules. **6.81**

Private warnings

The FCA operates a private warning procedure as described in EG 7. The FSMA makes no specific reference to any such procedure, and its scope and its use therefore falls to be governed only by the EG provisions. According to EG 7, the private warning procedure may be used in a wide range of circumstances—and indeed private warnings may be given not only to approved persons and authorised persons but also to unauthorised persons—for example, in the context of potential market abuse. Private warnings may be given in a wide range of cases—both where the FCA has power to bring formal disciplinary action but, for whatever reason, has determined that it is not appropriate to do so, and more generally. **6.82**

Private warnings do not constitute formal disciplinary action, nor do they amount to a determination that there has been a contravention of a requirement or that there has been misconduct. Nevertheless, the private warning forms part of an authorised firm's or approved person's compliance history. They may therefore be relevant in the future if the FCA is deciding whether to commence disciplinary action in relation to a future breach—but they cannot be relied on to determine whether or not that future breach has taken place or in determining the level of the sanction for it. **6.83**

Whilst private warnings are a useful tool, and may be welcomed by firms and approved persons for the reason that they avoid the publicity of a public censure or fine, there are nevertheless some concerns associated with the private warning process. For example, a person who receives a private warning is not able to raise the matter with the RDC. A private warning may be given in circumstances where no action could be brought against that individual in respect of a rule breach; nevertheless, the private warning will be on his regulatory record. The fact that the warning is private does not affect the fact that it is a fairly serious matter for anyone who receives it. Recipients of such a warning should ensure that any comments they have on the matter are recorded by them in writing to the FCA for placing on their file. **6.84**

Financial penalties

If the regulator considers that an authorised person has contravened a requirement imposed by or under the FSMA, it may impose on him a penalty of such amount as it considers appropriate.[28] There is no statutory limit on the size of the penalty which may be imposed, and is payable to the relevant regulator. A person cannot be required both to pay a penalty and have his authorisation withdrawn. The FSMA requires the regulators to issue a statement of policy with respect to the imposition of penalties and in particular for determining what the amount of a penalty may be. In practice this policy statement is fulfilled through the provisions of EG and DEPP. As explained in the following, a financial penalty is accompanied by the publication of a public notice which contains a fair amount of detail—a financial penalty **6.85**

[27] s 205.
[28] ibid, s 206.

might therefore be distinguished from a public censure/statement in a legal sense, but in practice the imposition of a financial penalty also results in a public statement which can be written in a censorious manner.

Other disciplinary measures

6.86 In addition to the disciplinary measures of public statements and financial penalties the FCA has other measures available to it where it considers it necessary to take protective or remedial action. These include varying and cancelling permissions and withdrawing a firm's authorisation or an individual's status as an approved person, or prohibiting an individual from performing specified functions.[29] There is also a power to suspend a permission to engage in a particular activity for a specified period (section 206A)—therefore it would be possible to permit a brokerage firm to continue to deal in securities, but to suspend its permission to hold client money. The UK regulators also have powers to intervene against a firm which is exercising passport rights, and EG Chapter 8 sets out the grounds for exercising these powers.[30]

6.87 Both regulators have the powers to apply to the court for injunctions[31] to restrain breaches of their rules, and the FCA has a separate power (section 381) to apply in respect of market abuse. EG Chapter 10 provides guidance on the use of the FCA's powers to apply for such orders. In practice this power tends to be used in situations where firms are not authorised but should be, or in other very serious cases. If the average authorised firm encounters the FCA's enforcement powers, it is most likely to be in the context of an action for breach of FCA rules resulting in the imposition of a financial penalty or the issuing of a public censure. Thus, while the other powers available to the FCA are noted, the following paragraphs deal principally with the disciplinary powers and processes available to the FCA for breach of the FCA's requirements by authorised firms and approved persons.

Warning notice

6.88 If either regulator proposes to publish a statement or impose a penalty it must give the authorised person a warning notice which sets out the terms of the statement or the amount of the penalty. Section 387 provides that a warning notice must both state the action which the regulator proposes to take and give reasons for it. When the regulator proposes to impose a financial penalty or issue a public censure (and in most other cases where a warning notice or decision notice is given),[32] it will be subject to section 394. This means that it must allow the authorised person access to the material on which it relied in taking the decision which gave rise to the notice and allow him access to any secondary material which, in the opinion of the regulator, might undermine that decision. Secondary material is material on which the regulator did not rely but which it considered in reaching its decision, or which was obtained by it in connection with the matter to which the notice relates. There has been and still is considerable controversy over the scope of section 394 since it does not require the regulator to give a person access to all the material which it has. It remains for the regulator to decide whether it has 'secondary material' which might undermine its decision. Section 394 limits

29 ibid, ss 45, 46, and 54.
30 ibid, ss 194 to 201.
31 ibid, s 380; market abuse: s 381; incoming firms: s 198.
32 See s 392 of the FSMA.

the material that may need to be provided, such that certain excluded material, including material which is subject to legal advice privilege, does not have to be disclosed.

The warning notice must give at least a 28-day period during which representations may be made. After the expiry of that period the FCA must then decide 'within a reasonable period' whether to issue a decision notice. **6.89**

Decision notice

If the FCA decides to publish a statement or impose a penalty, it must give the authorised person concerned a decision notice which sets out the terms of the statement or the amount of the penalty. If the regulator publishes a statement or imposes a penalty then the authorised person has the right to refer the matter to the Tribunal. **6.90**

A decision notice must state the regulator's reasons and other matters, as required for the warning notice. It must also indicate the recipient's right to have the matter referred to the Tribunal. **6.91**

Final notices

Once a decision notice has been issued, if the authorised person does not refer the matter to the Tribunal the FCA must, on taking the action to which the decision notice relates, give the person concerned a Final Notice. The Final Notice sets out the terms of the statement/the amount of the penalty and, unlike the warning notice and decision notice, it is made public. Copies of all the Final Notices which have been issued in enforcement proceedings are available on the FCA's website. It can be extremely valuable to review these notices, as the FCA uses them to report more than just the very basic details of the matter concerned. Final Notices can be quite lengthy. They set out the facts on which the FCA relies, the opinions of the FCA on the issues raised, and details of its reasoning for the action taken. In practice the FCA uses the Final Notice (and the accompanying press release) to send messages to the industry generally as part of its 'credible deterrence' strategy. **6.92**

Enforcement procedures

Section 395 requires both regulators to determine the procedures which they will follow for the giving of supervisory, warning, and decision notices. The section provides a considerable degree of flexibility for the regulator in determining these procedures. Once the regulator has stated its procedure the FSMA requires it to follow that procedure and, if it changes it in a material way, to publish a revised statement. A failure in a particular case to follow a procedure does not affect the validity of a notice given, but may affect any consideration of the matter by the Tribunal. **6.93**

The Tribunal

During the course of development of the FSMA there was considerable concern expressed about the breadth of the regulator's powers to impose penalties on authorised firms and the fact that, under the FSMA, the regulator will in many cases be investigator, jury, and judge. As a result, the FSMA provided for the establishment of the Financial Services and Markets Tribunal, which heard appeals from the decision of the FSA to impose decision notices. The FSMT has now been abolished, and its functions transferred to the Tax and Chancery Chamber of the Upper Tribunal, created under the Tribunals, Courts and Enforcement Act 2007 ('the 2007 Act'). Part 1 of the 2007 Act creates a new two tier tribunal structure; the **6.94**

First-tier Tribunal and the Upper Tribunal are established under section 3 of the 2007 Act. Provisions relating to procedure before the tribunal in respect of appeals relating to financial services can be found in sections 133 to 133B of the Act. The Upper Tribunal generally sits as a three-man panel; a high court judge sitting with two lay members who have experience in financial services.

6.95 A hearing before the Tribunal is not an appeal but a review from the beginning of the facts and matters concerned. The Tribunal may consider any evidence relating to the subject matter of the reference whether or not it was available to the relevant regulator at the material time. The parties are permitted to raise matters not directly brought before the Regulatory Decisions Committee—but save in exceptional cases the Tribunal will expect the regulator to confine its position to the charges already set out in its statement of case.

When is disciplinary action involving a penalty or censure likely?

6.96 DEPP 6.2 sets out a non-exhaustive list of factors that will be considered by the FCA in determining whether to take disciplinary action involving a financial penalty or censure. These include:

(i) the nature and seriousness of the suspected breach. This can include consideration of whether the breach was deliberate or reckless, its duration and frequency, whether it reveals serious or systemic weaknesses in the firm, and whether it caused a loss or risk of loss to consumers or other market users. It is also expressly noted that in judging nature and seriousness the FCA may also consider whether there are a number of smaller issues, which individually may not justify disciplinary action, but which do so when taken collectively. This could arise for example where the FCA identifies a number of relatively small rule breaches, which taken together indicate a general concern with the firm's approach to systems and controls on compliance matters;

(ii) the conduct after the breach. This particularly takes into account whether the breach was brought to the attention of the FCA by the firm or approved person concerned and the degree of cooperation shown during investigation of the breach. It will also be relevant to have regard to remedial steps that have been taken—in particular whether consumers have suffered loss and been compensated and whether disciplinary action has been taken against staff involved (where appropriate);

(iii) the previous regulatory record of the firm or approved person (and this might take into account previous private warnings);

(iv) whether the behaviour contravenes guidance published by the FCA;

(v) action taken by the FCA in previous similar cases and action taken by other regulatory authorities. In particular, where action may be taken by another regulatory authority, the FCA will consider whether that action would be adequate to address the FCA's concerns. Nevertheless, the involvement of an overseas regulator will not necessarily prevent the FCA from taking its own action. In the case of Credit Suisse First Boston International (and certain of its employees)[33] the FSA imposed penalties and other disciplinary measures as a result of conduct that took place in Japan in relation to Japanese business activities, which included attempts to mislead the Japanese authorities.

[33] Final Notice against Credit Suisse First Boston International dated 11 December 2002; <http://www.fsa.gov.uk/pubs/final/creditsuisse-fb_11dec02.pdf>; Final Notice against Christopher Allan Goekjian dated 22 September 2003; <http://www.fsa.gov.uk/pubs/final/goekjian_22sept03.pdf>; Final Notice against Anthony Blunden dated 10 November 2003; <http://www.fsa.gov.uk/pubs/final/blunden_10nov03.pdf>.

DEPP 6.4 sets out the criteria that the FCA will use in deciding whether it is appropriate to issue a public censure rather than impose a financial penalty, while DEPP 6.3 sets out the specific factors that the FCA will take into account when deciding whether to impose a penalty for market abuse. 6.97

Action against approved persons

DEPP 6.2.4G to DEPP 6.2.9G set out further particular guidance on the circumstances in which an approved person might face disciplinary action. The FCA has made it clear that it will only take disciplinary action where there is evidence of personal culpability on the part of the approved person. In practice this means that his behaviour must either have been deliberate or below the standard which would be reasonable in all the circumstances. The FCA has issued Statements of Principle which apply to approved persons and a Code of Practice for Approved Persons which is relevant in helping to determine whether conduct amounts to a breach of a Principle.[34] The issues referred to in paragraphs 6.96, 6.97, and 6.101 are relevant in determining the type of action taken. 6.98

The FCA's statutory powers to take disciplinary action against approved persons are based on section 66 of the FSMA. This provides that action may be taken against an approved person where it appears to the FCA that he is guilty of misconduct. He will be guilty of misconduct if, while an approved person: 6.99

(i) he has failed to comply with a Statement of Principle (being the principles applicable to approved persons); or
(ii) he has been knowingly concerned in a contravention by the firm of a requirement imposed on it by or under the FSMA.

Thus there are two separate bases on which action may be brought against an approved person. The concept of 'being knowingly concerned' in a contravention is potentially quite wide—a person may be knowingly concerned by knowing the facts involved, he does not necessarily need to know that that amounts to a contravention by the firm of a requirement.

Discipline for breaches of the Principles for Businesses

The FCA Principles are, as a matter of law, rules. They are rules which are drafted in general rather than specific terms. Nevertheless, it is possible for the FCA to discipline a firm for breach of a Principle alone—the FCA has done so in the past and intends to do so in the future. It should be noted that although in the past, FSA justified bringing enforcement action based on principles alone as part of 'principles-based regulation', the post-2007 retreat from principle-based regulation towards a more formalised approach is unlikely to result in a reduction in enforcement action based on a breach of the Principles alone. 6.100

When might there be a public censure or public statements?

Public censures may be issued under section 205, public statements may be made about approved persons under section 66, and public statements may be made under section 123 and section 91 respectively in cases of market abuse and contravention of listing rules. As already noted the warning notice procedure applies to any decision to issue such a public censure or statement. In determining whether it is appropriate to issue a public statement 6.101

34 See s 64.

rather than impose a financial penalty the FCA states (in DEPP 6.4) that it considers all relevant circumstances including the following:

(i) where a profit has been made or loss avoided as a result of the breach or misconduct this may be a factor in favour of a financial penalty;
(ii) the more serious the breach or misconduct whether in nature or degree, the more likely it is that a financial penalty will be considered appropriate;
(iii) a poor disciplinary record or compliance history may be a factor in favour of a financial penalty as it may act as a deterrent to future cases;
(iv) whether the person has inadequate means to pay an appropriate financial penalty.

What factors influence the level of financial penalties?

6.102 DEPP 6.2 sets out some of the factors involved in a decision as to whether to impose a financial penalty on a firm or an approved person. Where the FCA has decided to impose a financial penalty, some of the factors it will have regard to in determining the level of that penalty are set out in DEPP 6.5 and include:

(i) the seriousness of the misconduct or contravention (which can include its duration and frequency and the loss or risk of loss caused to consumers and market users);
(ii) the extent to which the contravention or misconduct was deliberate or reckless. This can include having regard to whether there has been a failure to comply with the firm's procedures and whether there has been no apparent consideration given to the consequences of the behaviour that constitutes the contravention. Deliberate or reckless behaviour is likely to result in a higher penalty than would otherwise be the case;
(iii) regard will be had as to whether the penalty is to be imposed on an individual and as to the size, financial resources, and other circumstances of the firm or individual. The FCA will not impose a financial penalty that could cause serious financial hardship or financial difficulties. However, this has not prevented it from imposing significant penalties on individuals where it has thought it appropriate to do so. For example, a CSFB employee was subject to a penalty of £150,000 for his involvement in the matter referred to earlier[35] and the Head of Trading at Evolution Beeson Gregory was ordered to pay £75,000 for his part in a matter which led to a breach of market conduct rules by his firm;[36]
(iv) the amount of profits accrued or loss avoided;
(v) conduct following the contravention;
(vi) disciplinary record and compliance history;
(vii) previous action taken by the FSA, the FCA, or the PRA;
(viii) action taken by other regulators.

6.103 The FSA always operated a practice of taking into account a firm's cooperation in determining the level of any financial penalty, and the FCA will continue to take account of a

[35] Final Notice against Christopher Allan Goekjian dated 22 September 2003; <http://www.fsa.gov.uk/pubs/final/goekjian_22sept03.pdf>.

[36] Final Notice against Evolution Beeson Gregory Limited and Christopher Potts dated 12 November 2004; <http://www.fsa.gov.uk/pubs/final/evolution_12nov04.pdf>.

firm's overall cooperation in setting the level of a penalty.[37] However, in addition the FCA operates a formal discount scheme specifically for early settlement. This scheme is clearly designed to do two things: to encourage the earliest possible settlement—there is a sliding scale of discount percentages depending upon how early in the enforcement process settlement is reached—and to distinguish early settlement from other types of cooperation with the Regulator. The purpose is to give a clear encouragement to early settlement.

Enforcement procedures

The decision-making process

The existing FSA Enforcement Division has been retained within the FCA. A referral to the Enforcement Division can be made by a number of different FCA divisions. Consequently, the question of whether a firm may be referred to enforcement may not always be because of a matter that has arisen in the course of its normal supervisory relationship. **6.104**

Once a case has been accepted by the Enforcement Division a case team is established which will usually hold an initial scope meeting with the person/firm concerned as part of the planning process. The purpose of these meetings is to give an indication of the scope of the investigation, the type of documents to which access will be required, and similar matters. These discussions should be a matter of course and should include the supervisor of relationship managed firms. As a minimum the FCA case team should set out the nature of and reasons for its concerns and a clear explanation of why the matter has been referred to enforcement. If, as the investigation progresses, the nature of the FCA's concerns change significantly then it should reassess them so as to satisfy itself that the investigation remains appropriate. **6.105**

As the case progresses the FCA prepares a draft preliminary investigation report. The draft investigation report should clearly set out the facts found by the investigation and the rule breaches alleged so that those who are the subject of the investigation can comment properly, with a full understanding of the rule breaches which form the basis of the proposed action. **6.106**

EG 4.30 to 4.33 provide that the FCA will usually send a preliminary findings letter to any person under investigation before considering whether to recommend to the RDC that enforcement action be initiated. That letter will set out the facts which the FCA considers relevant, will usually annex the investigator's preliminary investigation report (referred to earlier), and will invite the person concerned to comment on whether those facts are complete and accurate. It is important for a firm to deal with the preliminary findings letter and preliminary investigation report seriously and devote sufficient resources to dealing with them fully, since they will form the basis of subsequent decisions and actions taken by the FCA. The firm should use its response to correct any errors of fact, explaining why it believes the FCA's assertions of fact are deficient, and/or to provide further information where it feels that the FCA has not obtained a complete picture. It should ensure that the response includes any mitigating factors or other comments which it wishes to advance. A reasonable period (normally 28 days) is allowed for a response—responses received outside any deadline set by the regulator are not likely to be taken into account. **6.107**

[37] There are different calculation mechanisms for setting penalties for market abuse (DEPP 6.5C) than for other types of breach (DEPP 6.5B).

The decision-maker—the Regulatory Decisions Committee

6.108 The FSMA's requirements for decision-making procedures in relation to the issue of warning and decision notices are broadly expressed:

> the procedure must be designed to secure, among other things, that the decision which gives rise to the obligation to give any such notice is taken by a person not directly involved in establishing the evidence on which that decision is based.[38]

6.109 It must be noted therefore that this is deliberately constituted as an administrative and not a judicial procedure. The warning notice procedure must set out not only the proposed action but the reasons for it—it is not the same as a charge sheet in criminal proceedings. The decision must be taken by the FCA, not by an independent body—in the FCA's view the FSMA requires any decision-making body to be part of the FCA and not entirely independent of it.

6.110 Thus the system for decision-making established by the FCA is an internal process. In practice the function is generally carried out by the Regulatory Decisions Committee ('RDC') which is a committee of the FCA's Board whose members are appointed by the Board. However, apart from the chairman, none of the members of the RDC is an FCA employee. In addition, the RDC has its own dedicated legal advisers and support staff—all RDC staff are separate from the FCA staff involved in conducting investigations and making recommendations to the RDC. So while the RDC is determinedly part of the FCA as regards its decision-making, there is independence between it and between the Enforcement team prosecuting the relevant case. This is designed to ensure that there is a degree of objectivity on the part of the RDC when it comes to hearing the Enforcement team's submissions.

6.111 Where FCA enforcement staff consider that there is a case, they will make a recommendation to the RDC that a warning notice or supervisory notice be given. The RDC considers whether the material on which the case is founded is sufficient to support the action. Where it decides to issue the warning notice or first supervisory notice the notice will specify that the recipient has at least 28 days to make representations—and will also stipulate a timeframe within which the recipient is allowed to indicate that he wishes to make oral representations.

6.112 As an additional measure of independence and objectivity, when the FCA has given the relevant notice, the RDC will not meet with or discuss the matter with FCA enforcement staff without the recipient being present or otherwise able to respond. Where the recipient so indicates, a meeting will be convened to allow the recipient of the notice the opportunity to make oral representations and to allow relevant FCA staff to respond to those representations. The recipient may be legally represented if he wishes.

Settlement of enforcement cases

6.113 The FCA is keen that, wherever possible, enforcement cases settle early. This is largely because enforcement investigations are resource-intensive and time consuming and settlement can result in consumers obtaining compensation earlier than would otherwise be the case. There is a formal discount scheme for early settlement of cases, with discounts of 30 per cent, 20 per cent, or 10 per cent depending on how early in the enforcement process settlement is reached, from the initial stages up until the issuance of the decision notice.

38 s 395.

Settlements of enforcement cases are not the same as settlements of commercial litigation—in particular they are not confidential. They result in the publication of a Final Notice which sets out the terms of the agreed settlement (usually a financial penalty and, where it has been considered appropriate, the payment of compensation to consumers). Importantly, the firm concerned is generally prohibited from making any public statement beyond an agreed press release, so once a firm has agreed a final notice it loses its opportunity to put its case to the wider world. **6.114**

Settlement of a case can take place at any time. Settlement decisions are taken by the FCA Executive (by two members of FCA senior management, one of whom will be from the Enforcement division). The RDC is not involved in taking any decisions on statutory notices that result from settlement leaving it as an FCA body with the responsibility of taking enforcement decisions in the absence of agreed settlement—this ensures that there is a proper separation and transparency between the Enforcement Division and the RDC. However, despite this separation and as already noted, it is not until disputes reach the Tribunal that there is a process which can be said to be entirely independent of the FCA. **6.115**

Where a settlement is agreed this will not obviate the need for a decision notice, which will be in agreed form. The vast majority of disciplinary cases that result in a financial penalty have, in the past, been 'settled' and this is likely to continue in the future.[39] The effect of this is that the Final Notice is likely to have been negotiated with the FCA—both as to its content and indeed as to the final decision, for example on the rules or Principles which are held to have been breached. Therefore, while Final Notices can be extremely educational to read, it must be borne in mind that they are often the result of a negotiation and may well therefore not give as complete a picture as if the matter had proceeded to a full and unnegotiated decision. **6.116**

---

[39] In the FSA's financial year 2012/13, 76 cases were closed, of which 39 were resolved through executive settlement.

7

FINANCIAL REDRESS—COMPLAINTS, DISPUTES, AND COMPENSATION

Introduction: Regulatory Objectives

The Financial Services Act 2012 ('FSA 2012') implemented 'a new approach to financial regulation', on which HM Treasury had commenced consultation in July 2010.[1] FSA 2012 carried out reform of the 'tripartite model' operated under the Financial Services and Markets Act 2000 ('FSMA'). FSA 2012 established two new regulatory bodies—the Prudential Regulation Authority ('PRA') and the Financial Conduct Authority ('FCA'). The move to a 'twin peaks' model of financial regulation with the establishment of two regulators, has impacted on both the Financial Ombudsman Service ('FOS') and the Financial Services Compensation Scheme ('FSCS'), but both remain independent, market-integrated bodies. 7.01

The scope of reform considered FOS and FSCS, as well as the Money Advice Service ('MAS') (previously the Consumer Financial Education Body). MAS, and the continuing Consumer Panel have a keen interest in consumer complaints, disputes, and compensation, but are not examined further in this chapter. 7.02

Following FSA 2012, the FCA has an express consumer protection objective—'securing an appropriate degree of protection for consumers',[2] subject to its strategic objective of 'protecting and enhancing confidence in the UK financial system',[3] and alongside its other operational objectives of integrity and efficiency and choice.[4] 7.03

The PRA's general objective is 'promoting the safety and soundness of PRA authorised firms',[5] which is to be met 'primarily by (a) seeking to ensure that the business of PRA authorised firms is carried on in a way which avoids any adverse effect on the stability of the UK financial system and (b) seeking to minimise the adverse effect that the failure of a PRA authorised person could be expected to have on the stability of the UK financial system'.[6] In addition, the PRA has an insurance objective—'contributing to the securing of an appropriate degree of protection for those who are or may become policyholders'.[7] 7.04

---

[1] HM Treasury: A New Approach to Financial Regulation: Judgement, Focus and Stability (July 2010). See Chapter 1.
[2] s 1C(i). Chapter 5.
[3] s 1B(ii).
[4] s 1B(iii).
[5] s 2B(ii). Chapter 5.
[6] s 2B(iii).
[7] s 2C(ii).

7.05 As part of the regulatory system, the Government recognised the roles of FOS and FSCS to 'provide consumers—particularly retail customers—with appropriate mechanisms to protect them if things go wrong'.[8] The Government noted the 'important functions that underpin consumer and market confidence in financial services, and which thereby helped to secure better consumer outcomes'. In respect of FOS, the Government noted: 'access to swift and impartial resolution of disputes between firms and consumers is an important element of the Government's vision for enhanced consumer protection in financial services. Therefore... the Government intends for the FOS to remain an operationally independent alternative dispute resolution service and for the FCA to take on the Financial Service Authority (FSA)'s existing functions in relation to the FOS'.[9] In respect of FSCS, the Government stated: 'compensation plays an important role in supporting consumer confidence in any financial regulatory framework. In the UK system, the FSCS also has a specific and important part to play in financial stability by supporting the swift and orderly resolution of failed firms. Given that the FSCS will play a key role in supporting the objectives of both the PRA and FCA, it is important that both regulators should have direct input into the Scheme'.[10]

7.06 While remaining single entities, integrated for the full scope of protection, both FOS and FSCS are subject to the new governance arrangements put in place under FSA 2012. Memoranda of Understanding (MOU) must be in place between FOS and the FCA, and between FSCS and both the PRA and FCA. The MOUs will state how the FOS and FSCS will work with the regulators. Those MOUs are now published on the respective regulators' websites. Further, both FOS and FSCS will be subject to audit by the National Audit Office, and a requirement for consultation on a published Annual Plan and Budget.[11]

7.07 FSMA's provisions relating to FSCS had, in any event, under the Banking Act 2009 (BA 2009), been amended to reflect the introduction of the resolution regime, and under the Financial Services Act 2010 (FSA 2010) to include the power to require FSCS to act in relation to other schemes.[12] Further changes to both FOS and FSCS in primary or secondary legislation can be expected, in particular, to reflect changes in European law. The European Commission consulted on alternative dispute resolution in the area of financial services to encourage the creation of alternative dispute resolution schemes and ensure that financial services providers adhere to them.[13] On 22 April 2013, the Council of the European Union adopted a Directive on Alternative Dispute Resolution and Online Dispute Resolution[14] to 'provide for simple, fast and low-cost out of court settlement procedures designed to resolve disputes between consumers and traders arising from the sales of goods and services'. The Council expected that 'Existing national ADR schemes should be able to continue to operate within the new framework'.[15] FOS works with FIN-NET—a network of European financial

---

[8] HM Treasury: A New Approach to Financial Regulation: Building a Stronger System (February 2011). Chapter 5.

[9] Para 6.17.

[10] Para 6.8.

[11] See Chapter 1, para 1.159.

[12] Part 15A.

[13] EC Consultation Document—Alternative Dispute Resolution in the Area of Financial Services (11 December 2008). Chapter 18.

[14] Council of the European Union: PE CONS 79/12 and PE CONS 80/12.

[15] Presse 162, 22 April 2013.

dispute resolution services—which the Directive recommends should be 'strengthened'.[16] In its draft 'Effective Approaches' document,[17] the Organisation for Economic Co-operation and Development (OECD) recommended that 'consumers have access to adequate complaints handling and redress mechanisms that are accessible, affordable, independent, fair, accountable, timely and efficient'—for which schemes may be put in place by regulators or governments. Financial services providers 'should have in place mechanisms for complaint handling and redress' and 'an independent redress process should be available'. The OECD also recommended that complaints data should be made public. As the UK's guarantee and protection scheme, FSCS will be subject to any new directives. In July 2010, the European Commission published proposals in connection with deposit guarantee schemes, investor compensation schemes, and a possible insurance guarantee schemes directive, which would have some impact on FSCS. These proposals are at varying stages of progress. Further, the role of FSCS in bank resolution may be affected by the Directive on Bank Recovery and Resolution, a draft which was published by the European Commission on 6 June 2011.[18]

With the protections offered by FOS and FSCS, the FCA inherited powers from the FSA to direct financial redress for the benefit of consumers. Further, FSA 2012 introduces new processes for regulatory action in cases of 'mass detriment'—'action by firms operating in the financial sector resulting in detriment for a large number of consumers'.[19] The FCA has powers to address widespread issues of consumer detriment such as issuing new rules or guidance or using its powers at Section 404 FSMA to deliver an industry wide redress scheme or the adoption of a single firm redress scheme. The consumer redress scheme's provisions were updated by FSA 2010, at Part XXVIII of FSMA.[20] **7.08**

The concept of 'super-complaints' in the financial services sector has been introduced under FSA 2012. FOS must disclose information to the FCA which might assist the FCA to advance 'one or more of the FCA's operational objectives'[21] or may notify the FCA of areas where mass detriment may arise. The framework provides for designated 'super complainants'. This allows consumer bodies to raise with the FCA issues where large numbers of consumers are suffering detriment. HM Treasury consulted on draft criteria[22] including, for example, that such consumer bodies must 'demonstrate that they are able to deal with any competition and economic issues involved in super-complaint cases, whether through in-house experience or using external advice'. A super-complaint may be made by such consumer body, duly designated by HM Treasury[23] or by FOS or a regulated person[24] to which the FCA must publish its response (stating what if any action it will take) within 90 days.[25] **7.09**

16 Recital 53.

17 Draft Effective Approaches to Support the Implementation of the G20 High-level Principles of Financial Consumer Protection for Informal Consultation, dated 16 May 2013.

18 See Chapter 3.

19 A New Approach to Financial Regulation: Securing Stability, Protecting Consumers (January 2012).

20 ss 404–404G. Chapter 3.

21 s 232A.

22 A New Approach to Financial Regulation: Draft Secondary Legislation (2013); 'Guidance for bodies seeking designation as super-complainants to the Financial Conduct Authority'.

23 s 234C.

24 s 234D.

25 s 234E.

The FCA has published guidance on the making of a super-complaint.[26] It expects to be consulted before a super-complaint is made or publicised.

Routes to Financial Redress

Claims for financial redress outside FSMA

7.10 Although consumers have enhanced protection and alternative routes to financial redress under FSMA, it is worth noting some of the remedies existing outside the scope of this legislation. In the investment sector, this has developed alongside conduct of business regulation, as discussed later in this chapter. In other sectors, for example insurance broking, there is a long and substantial body of case law (not considered in this chapter).

7.11 Investors seeking redress may have received advice from an individual or firm acting in a professional capacity or bought an investment (or other regulated) product directly from a provider. The advisory relationship is likely to give rise to a duty of care, concurrent in contract and tort.[27] The consumer would be owed a duty of skill and care to the standard expected from the reasonably competent professional adviser at the time. The key principle is that, if the parties have contractually defined the way in which they will conduct their business, then that will determine the scope of responsibility assumed (and may therefore exclude any assumption of a wider tortious duty).[28] In the case of *Redmayne Bentley Stockbrokers v Isaacs* (June 2010), the court held that regulatory requirements are not implied into the contractual relationship unless the parties choose to do so, but that a firm does always have a duty to exercise reasonable skill and care in carrying out its services.

7.12 The duty of care in the investment context was considered in *Seymour and others v Christine Ockwell & Co and others*.[29] *Seymour* confirmed that the advisory duty was not delegated by the firm, so that insofar as the adviser lacked the necessary expertise, the customers should have been referred to an expert. When determining the duty of care, the court will have regard to the level of advice which might have been expected by a consumer. If the facts of a case do not fall within an established category of duty of care, then the test used to establish whether a duty of care exists is that set out by the House of Lords in *Her Majesty's Commissioners of Customs and Excise v Barclays Bank Plc*,[30] namely (i) whether the defendant has assumed responsibility to the claimant; (ii) the threefold test: (a) whether the claimant's loss was reasonably foreseeable; (b) there was sufficient proximity between the parties; and (c) it is fair, just, and reasonable to impose a duty of care; and (iii) that the duty should be incremental to an established category of duty. Where the investor is highly experienced and sophisticated, and so more likely to have been prepared to accept the risk of trading losses, in the absence of an express contractual duty, an advisory duty, in contract or in tort, is unlikely.[31] The *Springwell* judgment was not challenged on appeal[32] and has been followed

[26] FCA GC 13/1 'Consultation on guidance under Section 234F relating to super-complaints and section 234D references' (February 2013).

[27] *Henderson v Merrit Syndicates Limited* [1993] 2 AC 145.

[28] ibid.

[29] [2005] PNLR 39.

[30] [2006] UKHL 28 (21 June 2006).

[31] These factors were material in *Springwell Navigation Corp v J P Morgan Chase* [2008] EWHC 1186 (Comm).

[32] [2010] EWCA Civ 1221.

in a number of cases, notably *Titan Steel Wheels Ltd v The Royal Bank of Scotland plc*[33] and *Standard Chartered Bank v Ceylon Petroleum Corporation*[34] (confirmed in the Court of Appeal decision).[35] In both the latter cases, the court considered whether a common law duty of care would have arisen notwithstanding that, on their facts, the bank in question was able to rely on various non-reliance and entire agreement clauses in the contractual documentation, but concluded that such a duty did not arise. Another recent case in which no duty of care was found is that of *Michael Wilson and another v MF Global UK Ltd*[36] in which the court held that the terms of the parties' legal relationship did not change as a result of the defendants providing their clients with market information and opinions. Similarly, the recent case of *Bank Leumi (UK) plc v Wachner*,[37] in which the court held that the type of 'advice' provided was at the lower end of the spectrum (amounting to 'trading floor' opinion), supported a lower-level duty of care.

There are two recent decisions which show that, in certain circumstances, the courts will find a duty of care owed by the financial institution in question. The Court of Appeal in *Zaki v Credit Suisse (UK) Limited*[38] held that, on the balance of probabilities, Credit Suisse had made recommendations to Ms Zaki on the 'advantages and disadvantages of purchasing the product' in breach of the suitability rule at COB 5 (now at COBS 9 in the FCA Handbook), as opposed to 'the mere giving of information',[39] which serves to highlight the often fine line evidentially between the provision of information and the provision of advice). The Court of Appeal held that 'it was unrealistic to suppose that he [the Credit Suisse salesman] did not, at least from time to time, cross from the territory of information into the territory of recommendation or advice, at least in the sense of either pointing out that a product was advantageous in the then current market conditions or in agreeing with such an observation [by the customer]'. Even though Ms Zaki was not successful on the issue of causation, the Court of Appeal's decision supports the view that the sales process will generally involve giving advice and making recommendations. This 'substance over form' approach to the proper application of the conduct of business rules was followed in the more recent case of *Basma Al Sulaiman v (i) Credit Suisse Securities (Europe) Limited; and (ii) Plurimi Capital LLP*.[40] **7.13**

The second notable recent decision where a duty of care was found to have arisen is that of the Court of Appeal in *Rubenstein v HSBC Bank plc*[41] where it was held that HSBC had provided negligent advice in breach of its duty of care, and (in overturning the first instance judgment that a customer's loss on his investment was too remote to be recoverable) that the loss was caused by the collapse in the value of the assets held within the unsuitable investment (not by the 'unthinkable' market turmoil in September 2008) and that the loss was not only foreseeable but had also been foreseen, and so recoverable in damages. In terms of when 'advice' will be given, the first instance judge (whose comments on the issue of when a duty of care arises were not challenged on appeal) had concluded that the key to the giving of advice is that the information is either accompanied by a comment or value judgment on the relevance **7.14**

33 [2010] EWHC 211.
34 [2011] EWHC 1785.
35 [2012] EWCA Civ 1049.
36 [2011] EWHC 138.
37 [2011] EWHC 656 (Comm).
38 [2011] EWHC 2422.
39 [2011] EWHC 2652 (Ch) (cf the outcome in *City Index Ltd v Balducci*).
40 [2013] EWHC 400 (Comm).
41 [2011] EWHC 2304 (QB).

of that information to their client's investment decision, or is itself the product of a process of selection involving a value judgment, so that the information will tend to influence the decision of the recipient. In both of these scenarios, the judge at first instance found that such information acquired the character of a recommendation. This approach was followed in the recent case of *Green and Rowley v RBS*.[42]

7.15 The consumer might also have a claim against the product provider for misrepresentation (giving rise to a claim for damages under the Misrepresentation Act 1967) or for negligent misstatement. The circumstances of the investor will be relevant to determining whether he is owed any liability by a firm. In the financial services sector, (overturning the judgment at first instance) the Court of Appeal, in the case of *Peekay Intermark Ltd and another v Australia and New Zealand Banking Group Ltd*,[43] found that the experienced and sophisticated investor did not rely on pre-contractual representations, which were displaced by subsequent documentation making clear the nature and risks of the investment, but on 'his own assumption that the investment product... corresponded to the description he had previously been given'. Following the principles in *Hedley Byrne v Heller*,[44] if a product provider has disseminated information to an identified category of person such as the consumer for an identified purpose and on which the consumer relied, a duty of care may also arise on which the claim for negligent misstatement (although not for suitability) would be based. The recent case of *Green & Rowley v RBS* considered the issue of whether the *Hedley Byrne* duty included the content of COB 2.1.3 (duty to take reasonable steps to ensure communications are clear, fair and not misleading) and COB 5.4.3 (duty to take reasonable steps to ensure claimants understand the nature of the risks involved in entering the interest rate swap). The court concluded in that case that the *Hedley Byrne* duty does not go further than a duty to take reasonable care not to make false statements and does not, in effect through the back door, import any of the regulatory standards in relation to 'advice'. However, the claimants have obtained permission to appeal the decision on this issue (among others) on grounds of public interest.

7.16 There have also been some recent notable cases dealing with the exclusion of a duty of care in the financial services context. Following the Court of Appeal decision in *Springwell*, the case of *Cassa di Risparmio della Republica di San Marino S.p.A. v Barclays Bank Ltd*[45] further demonstrated the courts' willingness to uphold arranging banks' no representation and no duty of care disclaimers, where they are properly drafted and incorporated, against sophisticated claimants so that they are contractually estopped from pursuing a claim for negligent misrepresentation. The first instance decision of the Court of Session in Scotland in *Grant Estates Limited v Royal Bank of Scotland plc*[46] further added to the established line of cases in this regard, confirming that these disclaimers will generally also be effective as against retail clients (which had been open to doubt following the decision of the High Court in *Raiffeisen Zentral Bank Osterreich AG v The Royal Bank of Scotland*,[47] which had concluded that the question of whether a contractual provision is a basis clause or an exclusion clause should be one of substance not form). However, it remains unclear from these cases whether

42 [2012] EWHC 3661.
43 [2006] EWCA Civ 386.
44 [1964] AC 465.
45 [2011] EWHC 484 (Comm).
46 [2012] CSOH 133.
47 [2010] EWHC 1392.

contractual estoppel also applies to claims made under section 138D FSMA (which replaces the previous section 150 right of action), in particular because COBS 2.1.2R specifically prohibits exclusion clauses.

Whether for negligence or negligent misstatement, in common with claims for professional negligence generally, the consumer would be entitled to expect to recover his economic loss in accordance with usual principles. The Court of Appeal confirmed that in claims for negligent financial advice, the conventional, negligence, approach to causation should apply (*Beary v Pall Mall Investments*),[48] so that there was no scope for following 'exceptional departures' from the established principles.[49] **7.17**

Although claims in negligence or misrepresentation are likely to provide the most obvious causes of action for consumers seeking financial redress in this sector, deceit would also be available as the basis for a claim, not just for fraud or theft but in the event of deliberate misrepresentations of facts or opinions. Further, a relationship of trust and confidence is likely to exist or be built up between a client and his financial adviser, giving rise to fiduciary duties on the firm. In the context of fiduciary duties, the Law Commission has been recently asked to review the legal obligations that arise from these duties upon parties who invest other parties' money, including pension scheme trustees and investment managers, and, in particular, whether these duties are being interpreted too narrowly as simply being to maximise short-term financial returns.[50] The Commission expects to consult on the issues by October 2013 and provide its recommendations to Government by June 2014. **7.18**

Under the FSMA structure, *Seymour* confirmed that, generally, a product provider, rather than an adviser, does not owe an advisory duty of care to investors, absent negligent misstatement. In that case, the individual adviser remained the party solely liable to the customers, but was entitled to a contribution from the provider. The court was influenced in part by the view that any duty of care on the provider would be a duty 'which by-passed the regulatory regime and side-stepped the contractual remedy',[51] that is, that the FSMA structure does not impose a general advisory duty on the provider, although there may be exceptions. A provider may assume a responsibility to the investor by its conduct—for example, in meetings with the investor—and be found to have provided investment advice to which conduct of business rules apply.[52] Previously a duty of care owed to investors has been extended to lenders found to have operated in close collaboration with offices of authorised intermediaries.[53] Although generally not responsible for investment advice given by firms of authorised independent financial advisers, or the risks of borrowing, a lending building society was held to be responsible for torts committed by the advisers on the basis of a 'joint enterprise'. The judge was satisfied that there had been a sufficient degree of cooperation between the advisers and the lender to develop and market the lender's product—in this case, equity release mortgages—to consumers such that the lender owed a liability to investors arising from the conduct of the advisers. **7.19**

---

48 [2005] EWCA Civ 415.

49 Such as developed by the House of Lords in *Chester v Afshar* [2005] 1 AC 134.

50 The Law Commission: Fiduciary Duties of Investment Intermediaries Terms of Reference dated 26 March 2013.

51 His Honour Judge Havelock-Allan QC, p 59.

52 *Walker v Inter-Alliance Group plc and Scottish Equitable plc* [2007] EWHC 1858.

53 *Investors Compensation Scheme v West Bromwich Building Society* [1999] Lloyd's Rep PN 496.

7.20 The potential mis-selling of interest rate hedging products ('IRHPs') to small and medium-sized businesses has become an area of significant interest in 2013. Following a review carried out by the FSA in 2012, eleven banks agreed to review the sale of IRHPs made since December 2001 to certain categories of 'non-sophisticated' customers. Where it is considered appropriate, these banks will be required to provide redress on the basis of what is fair and reasonable in the circumstances.[54] At the same time, customers will be likely to seek redress from FOS or through the courts (or both). FOS has already issued two provisional decisions in relation to the sale of IRHPs, upholding the customers' complaints in both cases.[55] On the other hand, the first two IRHP court decisions[56] came down in favour of the defendant banks. It is difficult to know whether the differences in these outcomes are as a result of the different factual circumstances in play in these cases or because of a more 'consumer-friendly' approach on the FOS's part. A claim currently pending in the High Court has also raised the possibility of IRHP claims being overlaid with claims in respect of LIBOR (London inter-Bank Offered Rate). The claimants in that action have brought a claim in relation to loans made to them with an associated interest rate swap and interest rate collar agreement, payments under which were set by reference to three-month Sterling LIBOR. The court has allowed the claimants in this case to amend their pleadings to add claims based on alleged implied representations by the defendant bank and/or implied contract terms as to the integrity of the LIBOR rates.[57] The allegations in this regard rely heavily on regulatory findings against Barclays in respect of LIBOR: *Graiseley Properties Limited & ors v Barclays Bank plc*,[58] although Barclays has appealed in respect of this particular allegation.[59]

7.21 The FCA has published guidance on the responsibilities of providers and distributors under section 139A FSMA.[60] This follows the same approach taken by the FSA in their guidance issued under (the old) section 157 FSMA.

Claims for financial redress under FSMA

Unauthorised persons

7.22 FSMA provides for consumers to make claims for losses sustained as a result of parting with money or property pursuant to agreements made by or through unauthorised persons carrying on regulated activities. Such agreements are both unenforceable and give rise to rights to recover both money paid and compensation for any loss sustained as a result.[61] This enforces the 'perimeter' of regulation and protects the consumer. The amount of compensation may be agreed by the parties or awarded by the court. The court has the power, if it 'is satisfied that

[54] The FSA set out the principles in line with which each of the banks must conduct the review of its sales in its publication 'Interest Rate Hedging Products Pilot Findings'; issued in January 2013 and amended in March 2013: <http://www.fca.org.uk/static/pubs/other/interest-rate-swaps-2013.pdf>. On IRHP, see Chapter 1 para 1.47.

[55] FOS's provisional decisions in the complaint of W family against Bank E (October 2012) and in the complaint of Business H against Bank S (October 2012).

[56] In *Grant Estates* and *Green & Rowley*.

[57] [2013] EWHC 471 (Comm) (cf the decision in relation to amending the pleadings in *Deutsche Bank AG & Ors v Unitech Global Ltd & Anor*). On LIBOR, see Chapter 1, para 1.43.

[58] [2012] EWHC 3093.

[59] The appeal is being heard together with the appeal in relation to this issue in *Deutsche Bank AG & Ors v Unitech Global Ltd & Anor*.

[60] *The Responsibilities of Providers and Distributors for the Fair Treatment of Customers'* Guide which is part of the FCA Handbook.

[61] FSMA, ss 26 and 27. See also, *Broderick and others v Centaur Tipping Services Ltd* (27 July 2006).

it is just and equitable in the circumstances of the case', to allow the agreement to be enforced and money or property to be retained.[62] In exercising this discretion the court is directed to 'whether the person carrying on the regulated activity concerned reasonably believed that he was not contravening the general prohibition by making the agreement'[63] or whether (if applicable) 'the provider knew that the third party was (in carrying on the regulated activity) contravening the general prohibition'.[64] If deposits have been taken, in breach of the general prohibition, the 'depositor' has the statutory right to apply for an order returning the money, if he is not entitled under the agreement with the deposit taker to recover his money without delay.[65]

In addition, if a consumer deals with an authorised person who carries out a regulated activity otherwise than in accordance with a permission under FSMA, the contravention is actionable at the suit of a person who suffers loss as a result.[66] **7.23**

These statutory remedies were considered on a liquidators' application for directions (*Re Whiteley Insurance Consultants (also known as Kingfisher Travel Insurance Services) (a firm)*).[67] As the firm traded first as unauthorised and then as authorised, both sections 26 and 28 and section 20 applied. On the facts, the court declined to exercise the discretion under section 28, so that agreements were unenforceable, but in respect of (what the court described as) the 'later period', the court considered whether policyholders had suffered any loss and could make a claim under section 20(3) for damages or otherwise. Other more recent decisions involving section 26 FSMA include *Helden v Strathmore Ltd*[68] and *Charles Cleland Helden v Strathmore Ltd*,[69] in which the Court of Appeal dismissed an appeal against a first instance decision that a charge was enforceable despite the fact that it was entered into in breach of the general prohibition (section 19 FSMA). **7.24**

Breach of statutory duty—Conduct of Business Rules

Consumers have the right to bring actions for breach of statutory duty. On 1 April 2013, following amendments to FSMA made by FSA 2012, the majority of the functions of the FSA were transferred to the FCA and/or the PRA. The key change for the actions for damages regime under FSMA was that section 150 itself was deleted and replaced by a new section 138D. Section 138D(2) provides that 'a contravention by an authorised person of a rule made by the FCA is actionable at the suit of a private person who suffers loss as a result of the contravention, subject to the defences and other incidents applying to actions for breach of the statutory duty'. The interpretation of the word 'actionable' in this context (as used in section 150 FSMA) was considered in *R (British Bankers' Association) v Financial Services Authority*[70] in April 2011, in which it was held that 'actionable' meant 'giving rise to a cause of action in a court of law' and dismissed the argument that it should be given the broader meaning of 'capable of giving rise to obligations for compensation'. Rights of action under **7.25**

---

62 ibid, s 28(3).
63 ibid, s 28(5).
64 ibid, s 28(6).
65 ibid.
66 FSMA, s 20.
67 [2008] EWHC 1782.
68 [2010] EWHC 2012 (Ch) (30 July 2010).
69 [2011] EWCA Civ 542.
70 [2011] EWHC 999 (Admin).

section 138D(2) FSMA are only available in relation to contraventions of rules made by the FCA (and the PRA) under FSMA. These rights are not available in respect of contraventions of evidential provisions or guidance in the FCA Handbook. However, the FCA is permitted under section 138D(3) to specify that rights of action are not available for certain of its rules. Rules that FCA has specified under this section include the Principles for Businesses ('PRIN') and the Senior Management Arrangements, Systems and Controls sourcebook ('SYSC'). There must have been a contravention by an authorised person as defined in section 31 FSMA, for a right of action to exist. This approach was supported in the case of *Hall and others v Cable and Wireless plc*.[71]

7.26 The default position is that a rule made by the PRA will not be actionable by a private person, although the PRA may provide that individual rules are actionable under section 138D(1). In Policy Statement PS13/5,[72] published in March 2013, the PRA stated that the only rules in the PRA Handbook that would give rise to a right of action are those set out in SUP 10B, which relate to rights of action for a person who has suffered loss as a result of contravention of rules relating to approved persons.

7.27 Subject to the exceptions specified in Regulation 6 of the Rights of Action Regulations,[73] rights of action under section 138D are only available to 'private persons'. Under regulation 3(1)(a) of the Rights of Action Regulations, any individual (ie a non-corporate person) will be a 'private person' unless he suffers loss in the course of carrying on: (i) a regulated activity; or (ii) an activity that would be a regulated activity if it did not fall within one of the exclusions in Article 72 (overseas persons) or Article 72A (information society services) of the Financial Services and Markets Act 2000 (Regulated Activities) Order 2001 (SI 2001/544) (the 'RAO'). Regulation 3(1)(b) allows for a person that is not an individual to be a 'private person' provided he does not suffer the loss in the course of 'carrying out business of any kind'. The interpretation of this exclusion was considered in the case of *Titan Steel Wheels*,[74] in which it was held that it should be given a wide meaning; in other words, in most cases, only individuals (and not businesses) will be able to benefit from this statutory right of action.

7.28 For consumers who have received investment advice and are able to bring a claim in common law, the claim for breach of statutory duty under (the old) section 150 strengthens the position. Further, when determining the standard and duty of skill and care of the reasonably competent professional adviser, courts are likely to have regard to the Conduct of Business Rules a firm would have been expected to follow. For example, in *Loosemore v Financial Concepts*[75] the investor's claim raised the obligation to ascertain sufficient information regarding the investor's personal and financial circumstances, and give suitable advice on the client's investments, on the basis such advice would reflect the risks inherent in the recommended financial products. The court was satisfied that the relevant test applied to a firm would 'ordinarily include compliance with the rules'.[76] Similarly, in *Seymour*, the court

71 [2009] EWHC 1793 (Comm).
72 See <http://www.fca.org.uk/your-fca/documents/policy-statements/fsa-ps-13-05>.
73 The Financial Services and Markets Act 2000 (Rights of Action) Regulations 2001 (SI 2001/2256).
74 [2010] EWHC 211.
75 [2001] 1 Lloyd's Rep 235.
76 HHJ Raymond Jack QC, at 241.

found that 'the regulations afford strong evidence as to what is expected of a competent adviser in most situations'.[77] The position is further supported by the comments of Mr Justice Beatson in *Shore v Sedgwick*[78] in which the judge opined that the starting point for determining the extent of an advisor's duty of care both under statute and at common law is the relevant regulatory regime.

Although the application of conduct of business rules may bolster the duty of care owed by a firm, it does not delineate the scope of such duty. In *Seymour*, the judge accepted that they were not 'necessarily co-extensive'.[79] In *Gorham and others v British Telecommunications plc and others*[80] it was seen as part of the giving and receiving of advice on pension provision and life assurance that the interests of the policyholder customer's dependent family should have been considered. Accordingly, the adviser owed a duty to the family dependents not to give negligent advice to the policyholder which adversely affected their interests. In this case, the investor had been advised not to be a member of his employer's pension scheme but to contribute to a personal pension plan. The investor did not join the occupational pension scheme and, following his death, the family dependents did not qualify for the lump sum death benefit payable. Operating under the Conduct of Business Rules by its then regulator, LAUTRO, the pension provider suggested those rules defined the scope of any duty of care, and the omission of any obligation under the rules to take into account interests of third parties, such as family members, indicated there was no duty owed to family members in those circumstances. This view was rejected by the Court of Appeal.[81] Accordingly, although generally firms might expect the duty of care not to exceed widely the scope of conduct of business rules, it is clear from the *Gorham* case that a duty of care may exist at common law which is broader than the duty under conduct of business rules and that statutory remedies do not exclude common law remedies.[82] 7.29

The normal legal principles of causation apply so that the breach must have caused the loss both as a matter of fact and at law. The loss must also not be too remote and must be of a type that is recoverable through the court in damages. In *Rubenstein*, the judge at first instance took the view that the measure of damages under (the then) section 150 FSMA was no different from that which could be recovered for breach of contract or in tort and that the same approach to causation, foreseeability, and remoteness would apply. *Camerata Property Inc v Credit Suisse Securities (Europe) Ltd*[83] applied the same legal principles, but the court concluded on the facts of that case that the losses incurred on a Lehman Brothers' note were unrecoverable as the collapse of Lehman Brothers was held to be unforeseeable. 7.30

[77] At 34.

[78] [2007] EWCH 3054.

[79] ibid. See also *Shore v Sedgwick Financial Services Ltd and others* [2007] EWHC 2509.

[80] [2000] 1 WLR 2129.

[81] It is summarised in *Seymour*: 'the Court was not impressed by an argument that because of the statutory and regulatory duties superimposed by the Financial Services Act on the common law duty of care owed... it was unnecessary and inappropriate to widen that common law duty so as to include a duty to Mrs Gorham as well'.

[82] In *Seymour*: 'the existence of a regulatory regime is not preclusive of a common law liability not duplicated by that regime'; see also *Re Whiteley Insurance Consultants (also known as Kingfisher Travel Insurance Services) (a firm)* [2008] EWHC 1782.

[83] [2012] EWHC 7 (Comm).

7.31 In the investment and insurance broking sectors, the FCA has inherited conduct of business standards (in part required by European Directives), previously implemented by the FSA. The Conduct of Business Rules for investment business are contained in the COBS Sourcebook of the FCA Handbook. A firm must act 'honestly, fairly and professionally' in accordance with the best interests of the client.[84] A firm must take reasonable steps to ensure that a 'personal recommendation is suitable'[85] and has an obligation to obtain necessary information[86] without which a firm must not make a 'personal recommendation'.[87] There are detailed rules for specific areas of business, and separate rules for general insurance mediation ('ICOBS') and home finance advice and arranging ('MCOB').[88] In addition to general standards, conduct of business rules may include particular requirements for certain products, generally those with higher risks for consumers.[89] On 1 November 2009, the FSA introduced a new framework for regulating retail banking conduct of business (BCOBS). This responsibility has similarly been inherited by the FCA from 1 April 2013.

7.32 The proper interpretation of ICOBS (and its predecessor, ICOB) has been considered by the courts in the context of Payment Protection Insurance ('PPI') mis-selling claims, one of the hot topics in the financial services arena in recent years. The line of cases considered by the courts to date has confirmed the view that section 150 (now section 138D) FSMA requires a claimant to establish that loss has been suffered as a result of a breach of duty. Causation was not established in the cases heard to date on the primary basis that non-compliance with procedural regulatory rules had no causative effect on loss.[90]

Agents and appointed representatives

7.33 A provider may be liable to an investor if the investor dealt via its agent, such as an appointed representative. FSMA provides that 'the principal of an appointed representative is responsible, to the same extent as if he had expressly permitted it, for anything done or omitted by the representative in the carrying on of business for which he has accepted responsibility'.[91] In *Martin v Britannia Life Ltd*,[92] the court looked at both ostensible and apparent authority of the agent to determine whether the principal was liable. Where the appointed representative acts with ostensible authority to advise beyond the terms of the written appointment, the principal may be liable for the financial advice given by its appointed representative, even if it is outside the terms of appointment.

7.34 However, it would be wrong to expect that the appointed representative's conduct will always fix the principal with liability. Albeit considered under section 44 of the Financial Services Act 1986, in *Emmanuel & Emmanuel v DBS Financial Management plc*,[93] the court identified the relevant transactions as completed directly between the appointed representative

84 COBS 2.1.1R.
85 COBS 9.2.1R.
86 COBS 9.2.2R.
87 COBS 9.2.6R.
88 For example, at ICOBS 5.3 and MCOB 4.7.4.
89 For example, payment protection insurance (ICOBS 5.3.2R) or pensions (COBS 19).
90 For ICOB: *Harrison and another v Black Horse Ltd* [2011] EWCA Civ 1128; followed for ICOBS in *Mark Williams and Karen Williams v Black Horse Ltd* [2011] EW Misc 21 (CC) (7 December 2011). Chapter 1, para 1.46.
91 s 39(3).
92 [2000] Lloyd's Law Reports PN 412.
93 Unreported, 16 March 1994.

and the investors outside the scope of the appointed representative's agreement to act as agent for the principal, and so could not be seen to have been as agent for the principal. The mere fact that dealings with the investor were in the course of the appointed representative's business did not establish that the principal was responsible or had accepted responsibility. Further, recent case law suggests that, notwithstanding the existence of a principal, the appointed representative may be held by the court, depending on the particular facts of the case, to be (along with the investor) one of the ultimate parties to the contract for the provision of financial advice. That was the decision of Mr Justice Hodge in the recent High Court decision of *Goldstone & Anor v Becque Wayman Investments Limited & Ors*.[94]

Clients' assets

Consumers are also protected by the detailed rules contained in the Client Assets Sourcebook ('CASS') of the FCA Handbook, developing Principle 10 of the FCA's Principles for Businesses (Clients' assets), for the holding and segregation of client money and assets.[95] The rules provide for the segregation of investors' assets and funds, imposing obligations on firms to ensure funds are properly held and to report any breaches of client money requirements. **7.35**

There are obligations of 'safe custody' on firms for the 'safeguarding and administration of assets' (as a regulated activity). The rules 'are designed primarily to restrict the commingling of client and firm's assets and minimise the risk of the client's safe custody assets being used by the firm without the client's agreement or contrary to the client's wishes, or being treated as the firm's assets in the event of its insolvency'.[96] The segregation of clients' money and assets should therefore put the investor in a better position to recover his property in the event of a dispute or the failure of a firm. **7.36**

Following its consultation paper issued in September 2012,[97] the FSA subsequently made changes to its client assets regime to bring it in line with the segregation and portability requirements under the European Market Infrastructure Regime ('EMIR').[98] In the same consultation paper, the FSA also (i) consulted on a proposal to allow investment firms to operate 'multiple client money pools' (which the FSA considered would, if implemented, be the 'most radical change that has been made to the client money regime in over 20 years', and (ii) issued a discussion paper that provided an overview of the fundamental review of the client money and custody assets regime. The fundamental review is focused at improving the regime to lead to better results if a firm that holds client money and/or custody assets becomes insolvent. As stated by the FSA,[99] the objectives of the review are to: (a) 'improve the speed of return of client assets following the insolvency of an investment firm'; (b) 'reduce the market impact of an insolvency of an investment firm that holds client assets'; and (c) 'achieve a greater return of client assets to clients following the insolvency of an investment firm'. It was expected that the FCA will publish its feedback to the consultation and final rules in relation to the 'multiple client money pools' proposal in June 2013. At the same **7.37**

94 [2012] EWHC 3549 (Ch).
95 A firm must arrange adequate protection for clients' assets where it is responsible for these.
96 CASS 6.1.22 and CASS 6.1.23G.
97 CP12/22.
98 See Chapter 4.
99 Para 1.13 of CP12/22.

time, the FCA was expected to publish its feedback to the discussion paper and consult on proposed rule changes.

FCA's product intervention powers

7.38 In its October 2012 'Journey to the FCA' paper, the FSA made clear that the FCA's focus would be on early intervention to enable it to discharge its statutory objective of consumer protection. In particular, at page 44, it wrote:

> In practice, we will be more concerned about consumers—especially more vulnerable consumers—who might lose money or become further indebted, than about firms being able to continue in business (where the FSCS provides a safety net), except where the integrity of markets is threatened, or the firm represents a prudential risk. This will require us to develop a new, more sophisticated approach to monitoring emerging risks that could harm consumers, and capturing issues that affect consumers of basic products, as well as those buying more sophisticated products and services'.

In that context, the FCA has a new power, set out at Part 9A FSMA, to make temporary product intervention rules with immediate effect, where it considers it expedient to meet its consumer protection objective or its competition objective. This power allows the FCA to block the launch of a product or service or to prohibit an existing product or service.

Promotions and public statements

7.39 In addition to conduct of business rules, there are the restrictions imposed on financial promotions, breach of which gives rise to actions by consumers. Under FSMA,[100] in order to communicate an invitation or inducement to engage in investment activity a person must be authorised or the content of the communication approved by an authorised firm. An agreement entered into in consequence of an unlawful communication is unenforceable.[101] The investor is entitled to recover money or property paid and compensation for 'any loss sustained by him as a result of having parted with [any money or other property]'.[102] The detailed implementation of the financial promotions regime is to be found in regulations[103] and the COBS rules: 'a firm must ensure that a communication or financial promotion is fair, clear, and not misleading',[104] although it is a defence to an action for damages under s 138D if a firm took 'reasonable steps'.[105] The 'general rule' when communicating with retail clients is that 'a firm must ensure that information: (1) includes the name of the firm; (2) is accurate and in particular does not emphasise the potential benefits of relevant business or relevant investment without also giving a fair and prominent indication of any relevant risks; (3) is sufficient for, and presented in a way that is likely to be understood by, the average member of the group to whom it is directed, or by whom it is likely to be received; and (4) does not disguise, diminish or obscure important items, statements or warnings'.[106] Additional requirements apply to different products, or to 'direct offers' promotions that include a form by which any response may be made (for example letters with tear-off application forms attached)[107] so that the potential investor is able to make an 'informed assessment'.[108]

---

[100] s 21.
[101] s 30.
[102] s 30(2).
[103] SI 2001/1335 (as amended).
[104] COBS 4.2.1R.
[105] COBS 4.2.6R.
[106] COBS 4.5.2R.
[107] COBS 4.7.
[108] COBS 4.7.4G.

Section 24 FSA 2012 gives the FCA a new power, set out at section 137R FSMA, to require firms to withdraw or amend a misleading financial promotion with immediate effect, and to announce that it has taken disciplinary action. The FCA will be permitted to take this action if it considers that the financial promotion has breached, or is likely to breach, its financial promotion rules. 7.40

Under section 89 FSA 2012 it is a criminal offence for a person to make a statement which he knows to be false or misleading in a material respect (or is reckless as to whether it is) or dishonestly conceals any material facts with the intention of (or recklessly) inducing another person to enter into or offer to enter into, or refrain from entering into or offering to enter into, a relevant agreement or to exercise, or refrain from exercising any rights conferred by a relevant investment. 7.41

There is a further right of redress for investors in collective investment schemes. Part XVII FSMA includes an action for damages. This part of FSMA has undergone only minor changes as a result of the FSA 2012 other than to clarify that the FCA has responsibility for the regulation of collective investment schemes under the new regime. The definition of 'collective investment scheme'[109] remains unchanged.[110] In the event of a contravention by an authorised firm of section 238 or section 240, which apply where an authorised firm communicates invitations or inducements to participate in a collective investment scheme, an investor has the right to claim damages.[111] 7.42

Redress by the FCA

Section 11 FSA 2012 replaces Part 4 FSMA with a new Part 4A dealing with the application, granting, limitation, variation, and cancellation of permission to carry on regulated activities (as defined in section 22 FSMA). As part of the regulators' armoury to vary or cancel a firm's permission, section 55N replicates the power in the old section 43 of FSMA, but with the additional power at section 55N(5) which allows the FCA or PRA to require a firm to take remedial action in respect of past conduct. This places on a statutory footing the FSA's practice of requiring firms to carry out 'root cause analysis'.[112] 7.43

In addition to the powers that the regulators have to impose regulatory sanctions against firms and individuals (including, issuing public censures, imposing potentially unlimited financial penalties, varying or cancelling a firm's Part 4A permission, intervening against an incoming EEA or Treaty firms, suspending or restricting the approval given to an approved person, prohibiting an individual from performing regulated functions, withdrawing the approval of an approved person, or imposing a penalty on a person who has performed a controlled function without approval), the FCA also has the power to seek restitution and redress for consumers. The FCA has been very clear that one of the key elements of its regulatory approach will be securing redress when things go wrong. Supervision of firms will be based around three pillars: firm-specific; products and issues; and 'events'. 'Events' are described as 'situations in firms where there is heightened risk to consumers or where consumers have experienced some loss and we need to act quickly to stop the situation from 7.44

[109] s 235 of FSMA. See Chapter 18.

[110] The High Court decision in *The Secretary of State for Business, Innovation and Skills v Sky Land Consultants PLC* [2010] EWHC 399 (Ch) has provided some helpful clarification on the application of s 235 of FSMA.

[111] ibid, s 241.

[112] See DISP 1.3.5R and the example of the Bank of Scotland Final Notice issued on 23 May 2011.

worsening'.[113] 'Event-driven work— dealing faster and more decisively with problems that are emerging or have happened, and securing customer redress or other remedial work where necessary'.[114] Enforcement will be focused among other things on 'continuing to prioritise getting compensation for consumers'.[115] 'We will also place more emphasis at an earlier stage on securing redress where consumers have suffered harm'.[116]

7.45 It has also emphasised the importance that it will place on the role of senior management to manage firms so that they have the interests of consumers at heart. The record of a senior manager in relation to fair treatment of customers will be one of the factors that the FCA will take into account when deciding whether an application for approval for that senior manager should be granted. These factors taken together show the emphasis that the FCA will have on focusing senior managers on the delivery of redress in appropriate cases. The FCA will focus on the conduct at the senior level and, in particular, on whether this delivers good outcomes for consumers. 'Firms senior management teams set the culture of their organisation so we must ensure that the targets and aspirations set out at the top turn into good outcomes for consumers'.[117] In considering whether to approve a person for a significant influence function FCA will 'look at the individuals personal integrity, financial soundness, honesty and record of treating customers fairly'.[118] Where issues or products across firms give cause for concern and the need for remedial action, the FCA will place the onus on firms and senior management to deliver that redress—'Where appropriate, we will require the whole sector to consider the need for remedial action. We will place the onus on firms and their significant influence function holders to complete remediation without on-going regulatory intervention'.[119]

7.46 The focus on redress has also been emphasised in recent FSA speeches.[120]

---

[113] p 29, Journey to FCA ('Journey to the Financial Conduct Authority' (October 2012)), which can be accessed at: <http://www.fsa.gov.uk/static/pubs/other/journey-to-the-fca-standard.pdf>.

[114] p 27, Journey to FCA (n 117).

[115] p 37, Journey to FCA (n117).

[116] p 38, Journey to FCA (n117).

[117] p 8, Journey to FCA (n 117).

[118] p 21, Journey to FCA (n 117).

[119] p 30, Journey to FCA (n 117).

[120] 1. Clive Adamson, 25 January 2012

The FCA Conduct Strategy will emphasise five main elements

'…*Fourthly, it's to secure redress for consumers if failures do occur—and so we're asking those firms that are moving customers into risky investments, or mis-handling their complaints to put customers right*'.

2. Clive Adamson, 5 March 2013

'*When thing do go wrong, the FCA will have the appetite to act faster and more decisively and robustly to seek redress for consumers where it is due*'.

And on senior management to set the right tone : '*What the FCA will be looking for is senior management to set the right tone from the top and ensure that this is being embedded across all levels of their firms. We also want senior management to be open and honest in their dealings with the regulator—and I am pleased to see cases where that is happening effectively. But let me be clear—where we find cases of individuals or firms misleading or providing us assurances that they cannot meet, we will take tough action, including enforcement action, where appropriate*'.

3. Martin Wheatley, 12 March 2013

'*These are important changes. They will make a difference. But they also demand a change in attitude among firms. The FCA will increasingly look at where business or products are going and be having an early conversation if we suspect the wrong outcomes are likely….And when we do have those conversations, I expect CEOs and Boards to react; not to send in a troupe of lawyers like a scene from*

A consumer's complaint may also be pursued by action taken by the FCA under Part XXV of FSMA (Injunctions and Restitution). Restitution orders may be made[121] in circumstances where 'a person has contravened a relevant requirement', and that person has derived profits as a result or others have suffered loss. Payment may be made to those affected of the profits and/or to the extent of the loss.[122] The FCA is under an obligation to distribute any such receipts to those affected persons.[123] **7.47**

Broadly, the power to require restitution, or to apply to the court for an order of restitution, exists where a firm or person (i) has breached a relevant requirement or has been knowingly concerned in such a breach (sections 382 and 384(1) FSMA): this power can be exercised by either the FCA or the PRA; or (ii) has engaged in, or required or encouraged others to engage in, market abuse (sections 383 and 384(2) FSMA)—this power is only available to the FCA. In considering whether to exercise its powers to seek or obtain restitution under sections 382 and 384 FSMA, the FCA will consider the relevant circumstances of each case, which may include a number of factors listed in its Enforcement Guide ('EG') 11.3. In an example from the time when the FSA was the regulator, the FSA imposed a penalty on Lloyds TSB in 2003 of £1.9 million for the mis-selling of precipice bonds but the firm also agreed to provide compensation of around £98 million in respect of 22,500 sales.[124] In connection with the FSA's investigations into split capital investment trusts, the settlement agreed with over 20 firms led to the creation of Fund Distribution Limited, a company set up to receive and distribute settlement payments from firms to individual investors who lost funds as a result of investing in 'zeros'.[125] **7.48**

FSMA confers wide powers upon the FCA and PRA to apply to court for an injunction against anyone, whether authorised or not. Under FSMA, the FCA or the PRA may apply to the court for an injunction (i) in connection with the contravention of a 'relevant requirement' (section 380 FSMA); (ii) in a case of market abuse (section 381 FSMA); and (iii) in **7.49**

"A Few Good Men" to tell us that we need to do more file reviews, or to justify what the management know is ethically wrong'.

The FCS will, like the FSA before it, take a firm's approach to remediation into account when determining whether to take enforcement action against the firms.

DEPP 6.2.1G sets out factors what will be considered:

'The conduct of the person after the breach, including the following:

...(c) any remedial steps the person has taken in respect of the breach'.

Remediation will also be taken into account when deciding whether to issue a public censure or impose a financial penalty.

DEPP 6.4.2G:

'...(5) If the person has admitted the breach and provides full and immediate cooperation to the FCA and takes steps to ensure that those who have suffered loss due to the breach are fully compensated for those losses, this may be a factor in favour of a public censure rather and a financial penalty'.

The approach to proactive remediation can also be a mitigating or aggravating factor in relation to the level of a financial penalty:

DEPP 6.5.A.3:

'...(d) any remedial steps taken since the breach was identified, including whether those were taken on the firm's own initiative or that of the FCA...for example identifying whether consumers...suffered loss and compensating them where they have'.

[121] ibid, s 382.
[122] ibid, s 382(2).
[123] ibid, s 382(3).
[124] Final Notice, dated 24 September 2003.
[125] FSA Press Release, dated 24 December 2004.

relation to certain incoming EEA insurance companies, at the request of a home state regulator of an incoming EEA firm (section 198 FSMA). The FCA's EG sets out the FCA's policy in relation to applications for injunctions. Broadly, the FCA will apply to the court when such an application would be the most effective way of dealing with the FCA's concerns, taking into account the factors set out in EG 10.

7.50 Other action to secure financial redress for consumers may include an industry-wide review into mis-selling. Under the previous regime of the Financial Services Act 1986, The Securities and Investments Board ('SIB') established the 'Pension Review', followed by the 'FSAVC [Free Standing Additional Voluntary Contributions] Review'. The Pension Review imposed a large, wide scale proactive obligation on firms to identify investors who may have been mis-sold personal pension plans between 1988 and 1994; and where such sales were not compliant, and caused the investor loss, to calculate, offer, and pay redress. The SIB issued detailed guidance (supplemented by the Personal Investment Authority) on determining both the eligibility of claims (ie the 'liability' of firms to investors) and quantifying investors' losses. Over the course of the Pension Review, it is estimated that £13 billion–£14 billion was paid by way of redress to investors.

7.51 Under FSMA,[126] in October 2010, new rule-making powers came into force enabling the (then) FSA to require firms to establish and operate compensation schemes for consumers who suffer loss as a result of firms' widespread and regular failure to comply with their regulatory obligations.[127] During 2011, the FSA invoked its power under section 404F(7) FSMA several times to impose consumer redress schemes on individual firms.[128] In April 2012, the FSA published a consultation paper[129] on a consumer redress scheme relating to the unsuitable advice given to certain consumers to invest in two non-UCITS retail schemes, known as the Arch cru funds.[130] This was the first time the FSA used its power under section 404 FSMA to propose a consumer redress scheme. In December 2012, the FSA published a policy statement[131] on the Arch cru consumer redress scheme, in which it decided to proceed with the scheme but has given consumers the opportunity to opt in to having their sales reviewed rather than requiring firms to review all sales proactively. The scheme commenced on 1 April 2013.

7.52 From that date, the FCA took over the consumer redress powers from the FSA. The types of redress the FCA can secure under a consumer redress scheme are those which it considers to be just in relation to a case. For example, it may require firms to top up pensions or offer to vary the terms of a contract rather than provide direct financial compensation. However, the FCA must have regard to the nature and extent of the losses or damage in question[132] and will therefore take into account the kind of relief which a court would grant.

7.53 Sections 192A–N Part 12A FSMA give the FCA and the PRA power to direct a 'qualifying parent undertaking' to take action if the appropriate regulator considers (under the

---

126 ss 404 and 404A-G.
127 FSA's Guidance Note No.10 (2010).
128 For example, Welcome Financial Services Limited.
129 CP12/9.
130 cf Arch cru Investment Funds and cf Arch cru Diversified Funds.
131 PS12/24.
132 s 404A(5) of FSMA.

general condition in section 192C(2) FSMA) that it is desirable to give direction in order to advance: (a) in the case of the FCA, one or more of its operational objectives; (b) in the case of the PRA, any of its objectives. In the FSA's draft statement of policy issued as Appendix 7 to CP12/34 in November 2012, Paragraph 21 refers to the fact that a requirement may refer to the past conduct of the parent undertaking (section 192D(3)). The FCA is interpreting this provision to enable it to require a parent undertaking to pay redress to consumers for claims against its subsidiaries arising from professional negligence or firms providing unsuitable advice.

Claims against the FCA

In addition to making claims or complaints on its own behalf or for the benefit of investors, the FCA might also be on the receiving end of claims from consumers or authorised firms. Part IV of Schedule 1 to FSMA provides the FCA with an exemption from liability to damages for 'anything done or omitted in the discharge or purported discharge of the FCA's functions',[133] although this is not available in the event of bad faith or an unlawful act or omission under section 6(1) of the Human Rights Act 1998. In the case of *Tee v Lautro Ltd*,[134] the claimant proceeded against LAUTRO for negligence and misfeasance in public office following enforcement action taken against the individual's company. While the claim was struck out following the defendant's reliance upon a similar immunity from damages provided by the Financial Services Act 1986,[135] the court was also satisfied that there was no duty of care owed by LAUTRO in negligence, and misfeasance required proof of malice, not mere recklessness. **7.54**

Investigation of Complaints Against Regulators

Under FSA 2012, Part 6 requires arrangements for the investigation of complaints against the regulator. This complaints scheme succeeds the Office of the FSA Complaints Commissioner, and is contained in a standalone document published by the regulators, and no longer in the Rule Book (previously in the COAF Sourcebook).[136] Following consultation,[137] the Government decided to provide for an independent complaints system with a single Complaints Commissioner and system operating across both the FCA and PRA, which will also cover the Bank of England's regulatory functions in relation to recognised clearing houses and payment systems.[138] **7.55**

The regulators must publish the draft of the proposed complaints scheme.[139] The proposed scheme was published in the Bank of England and FSA Consultation Paper CP12/30 (November 2012). The final complaints scheme was published in Policy Statement 13/7 (March 2013). Although the complaints scheme covers the relevant functions of the FCA, PRA, and the Bank of England, it does not cover FOS or FSCS (or the MAS). **7.56**

133 Para 19(1).
134 Unreported, 16 July 1996.
135 FSA 1986, s 187.
136 Complaints against the regulators (The Bank of England, the Financial Conduct Authority and the Prudential Regulation Authority (1 April 2013)).
137 A New Approach to Financial Regulation: Securing Stability, Protecting Consumers (January 2012).
138 Para 3.32.
139 s 86.

7.57 The independent 'investigator' is appointed by the regulators with approval of HM Treasury and is to be 'free at all times to act independently of the regulators', and investigate 'without favouring the regulators'.[140]

7.58 The Scheme is to cover complaints about the way in which the regulators have acted or omitted to act, including complaints alleging (a) mistakes and lack of care, (b) unreasonable delay, (c) unprofessional behaviour, (d) bias, and (e) lack of integrity. Complaints may be made by anyone directly affected by the way in which the regulators have carried out their functions, and should be made within 12 months. Excluded from the Scheme are complaints about the regulators' relationships with employees, contractual commercial disputes, as well as complaints which are no more than dissatisfaction with the regulators' general policies, or the exercise or failure to exercise a discretion where no unreasonable, unprofessional, or other misconduct is alleged.[141]

7.59 As under the previous COAF scheme, there are two stages: investigation by the relevant regulator and, if the complainant remains dissatisfied with the outcome of a complaint, investigation by the Complaints Commissioner. Stage 1 requires an 'efficient and fair investigation'. 'Low impact' complaints may be resolved by the area responsible at the regulator. Communications to the investigator may be confidential. The Complaints Commissioner will produce a final report which, subject to confidentiality, may be published. The regulators have published guidance on the complaints process.[142] Under the complaints scheme, the Investigator may recommend a compensatory payment be made to the complainant (on an ex gratia basis) or other steps to remedy the matter complained of. FSA 2012 provides the Investigator with the powers to administer and manage the complaints scheme and the handling of complaints. As with other bodies under FSA 2012, the Investigator has retained statutory exemption from liability and damages.[143]

7.60 Sir Anthony Holland, appointed as the Financial Services Complaints Commissioner on 3 September 2004, will continue as the Complaints Commissioner. In the year 2011–2012, the Office of the FSA Complaints Commissioner concluded 161 cases, of which 78 per cent were from individual complainants. Of these 161 cases, 70 were determined to be outside the scope of the scheme, 45 were not investigated, 16 were excluded from the scheme, and 30 Stage 2 investigations were completed.[144] Of the 30 Stage 2 investigations completed, 25 complaints were published.

Complaint Handling by Firms

DISP

7.61 For authorised firms (and others including consumer credit licensees and other FOS voluntary jurisdiction participants), the FCA Handbook prescribes a complaints handling process. Generally, this is fully applicable to all authorised firms, with some exceptions, such as

[140] s 84.

[141] Policy Statement 13/7.

[142] 'Complaints against the regulators: Making a complaint against Bank of England, Financial Conduct Authority or Prudential Regulatory Authority'.

[143] s 88.

[144] Annual Report 2011/12.

authorised professional firms for non mainstream regulated entities or for auction regulation bidding,[145] with a professional body to handle complaints,[146] or credit unions.[147] Credit unions may take a distinct and proportionate approach.[148] Separate requirements (including reporting) apply to The Society of Lloyd's. For members of Lloyd's, complaint procedures at Lloyd's must first be completed.[149] Although complaint handling may be outsourced,[150] firms are responsible for the acts and omissions of an outsourcer.

The complaint handling requirements for firms are contained in the DISP Rules.[151] These Rules are to ensure that complaints are dealt with promptly, fairly, and that firms take action to rectify the cause of complaints. An action may arise under section 138D (formerly section 150 FSMA) for breach of these Rules.[152] DISP Chapter 1 deals with complaint handling procedures for firms ('Treating Complainants Fairly'); Chapters 2 to 4 (and Chapter 5 of FEES) deal with FOS. Since their introduction in 2001,[153] the DISP Rules have been reviewed and updated over the last decade to reflect regulatory policy and to implement changes to the law both in the UK and EU (eg the Markets in Financial Investment Directive ('MiFID'),[154] in November 2007,[155] or the Insurance Mediation Directive).[156] Subject to certain exemptions for records, and reporting, DISP has been extended to payment service providers,[157] electronic money issuers,[158] and UCITS management companies.[159] **7.62**

DISP 1 sets out the general requirements for firms to have internal complaint handling procedures. The procedures must be 'effective and transparent for the reasonable and prompt handling of complaints', and deal with 'any expression of dissatisfaction whether oral or written, and whether justified or not', relating (if not MiFID business) to the provision of financial services or products, which alleges financial loss, material distress, or material inconvenience.[160] Complainants must be able to make complaints free of charge.[161] Complaints should be used by firms to identify any 'root causes' affecting other processes or products which should be remedied.[162] For PPI, this is expressly addressed in DISP.[163] For MiFID business, the information from complaints should be used to assess compliance procedures.[164] The complaints procedures should provide for receiving complaints, **7.63**

---

145 DISP 1.1.5R.
146 DISP 2.3.4R.
147 DISP 1.1.5.A.R.
148 DISP 1.1.6.A.R.
149 DISP 1.11.
150 DISP 1.1.19G.
151 And in CRED for credit unions.
152 DISP Sch 5.
153 For example, Consultation Paper 49: 'Complaints Handling Arrangements: Feedback Statement on CP33 and Draft Rules' (May 2000).
154 2004/39/EC. See Chapter 3.
155 FSA Consultation Paper 06/19: 'Reforming Conduct of Business Regulation'; FSA Policy Statement 07/9: 'Treating Complainants Fairly' (July 2007).
156 DISP 1.1.8.R.
157 DISP 1.1.10A.
158 DISP 1.1.10C.
159 DISP 1.1.10E.
160 DISP 1.3.1R. and Glossary definition of 'complaint'.
161 DISP 1.3.1.A.
162 DISP 1.3.3R.
163 Appendix 3.4.
164 DISP 1.3.4G; SYSC 6.1.

responding to complaints, referring complaints to other firms, the appropriate investigation of complaints, and notifying complainants of their right to go to FOS where relevant. Firms must appoint an individual with responsibility for compliance.[165]

7.64 Firms must publish summary details (in writing) of their internal complaints process, refer customers to the availability of these details 'at, or immediately after, the point of sale' (or in payment services procedures), on request or on receipt of a complaint.[166] Firms may display in branches and offices a notice indicating that the firm is covered by FOS.[167]

7.65 A complaint must be investigated 'competently, diligently and impartially' and the subject matter, outcome, and any remedial action or redress must be assessed 'fairly, consistently and promptly'.[168] If upheld, redress or remedial action must be offered, and promptly complied with if accepted, and the review and decision explained in a way that is 'fair, clear and not misleading'.[169] Relevant factors in the assessment of a complaint by a firm include any FSA guidance and FOS decisions concerning similar complaints against that firm.[170] Providers should in any event learn lessons from past FOS determinations or FSA/FCA and FOS guidance.[171]

7.66 With some exceptions, complaints must be dealt with within prescribed time limits at DISP 1.6 (and at the earliest possible opportunity).[172] The time limits require firms to send a prompt acknowledgement of a complaint and to keep the complainant informed of progress.[173] Time-barred complaints may be rejected without considering the merits.[174]

7.67 A 'final response' must be sent by the end of eight weeks.[175] The FSA expected firms to have dealt with 'almost all' complaints within eight weeks.[176] If unhappy with the outcome, or if a firm is not in a position to give a final response within eight weeks, the complainant is entitled to refer the matter to FOS (and must be advised of this).[177] The FSA expected firms to set out 'prominently' the information regarding FOS.

7.68 The previous option for firms of a 'two-stage' complaints process, including a local office and then head office review if the complainant remained unsatisfied was deleted from DISP (from 1 July 2012). This avoids the possibility of what FSA regarded as 'iterative' responses.

7.69 DISP also deals with the possibility that the recipient of the complaint may not be solely responsible for the matter complained of, in which case it may refer the complaint to the other firm provided that it does so promptly, confirms the complaint by 'final response', and complies with its own obligations if jointly responsible for the complaint.[178]

---

165 DISP 1.3.7.R.
166 DISP 1.2.1R.
167 DISP 1.2.5G.
168 DISP 1.4.1R.
169 DISP 1.4.1R.
170 DISP 1.4.2G.
171 DISP 1.3.2.A.
172 DISP 1.4.3.G.
173 DISP 1.6.1R.
174 DISP 1.8.1R.
175 DISP 1.6.2R.
176 DISP 1.6.7G.
177 DISP 1.6.2.R; see also DISP 1.6.4R.
178 DISP 1.7.1R.

In addition to the handling of a complaint, DISP requires record keeping and reporting (with some exceptions for complaints resolved by close of business on the business day following receipt).[179] Complaint records must be retained for at least three years from the date of receipt of the complaint,[180] and five years for MiFID or UCITS business and complaints must be reported to the FSA twice a year in the prescribed format (at Annex 1R to DISP 1).[181] Reporting includes not only the total number of complaints, to be broken down by categories and generic product types, but also the time taken for dealing with complaints and total redress paid.[182] A complaint is 'closed' when the final response has been sent, or where an earlier response has been accepted in writing by the complainant.[183] Complaint reports relating to certain investment activities are to also identify the individual investment adviser.[184] The report to the FSA is to confirm the details of a single contact at the firm for complainants.[185] In any event, adequate management information about complaints is important as part of a firm's 'TCF' obligations. Where the number of complaints exceed 500, firms must publish a 'complaints data summary'.[186] **7.70**

Following Principle 6, customers must be treated fairly in the complaints process. This has been reflected in industry guidance.[187] A firm is expected to adopt a helpful attitude towards a customer making a legitimate complaint and make reasonable enquiry, rather than adjudicating a complaint purely on the words and evidence of the customer alone. The FSA's interpretation of the DISP obligations is apparent from various publications, such as the 'Dear CEO letters'. Firms are under an express obligation to cooperate with FOS and meet any awards made against them by FOS—prompt compliance is required.[188] The FSA took enforcement action where firms have failed to comply with FOS awards. In the case of *Heather Moor & Edgecomb Ltd*, the Financial Services and Markets Tribunal[189] ordered the firm's permission be cancelled unless an award was paid. The FSA also acted where firms have failed to ensure effective complaints handling procedures and adequate resources for handling complaints or personnel trained to carry out fair investigations.[190] Firms should offer a proactive redress or remediation exercise if there is evidence of a wider consumer detriment.[191] **7.71**

The DISP Sourcebook identifies particular categories of complaint to which prescriptive or different treatment applies. First, complaints which are subject to the FSAVC Review are not subject to the time limit requirements for dealing with complaints, or the reporting requirements to the FSA.[192] The FSAVC Review commenced before the implementation **7.72**

179 DISP 1.5.1R.
180 DISP 1.9.1R.
181 DISP 1.10.1R.
182 DISP 1.10.2.R.
183 DISP 1.10.7.R.
184 DISP 1.10.2A.
185 DISP 1.10.9.R.
186 DISP 1.10.A.
187 Joint paper by the Association of IFAs and ABI: 'Working Together to Deliver Good Customer Experiences—Responsibilities of Providers and Advisers' (October 2006).
188 DISP 1.4.4R; DISP 3.7.12R.
189 19 May 2008.
190 For example, the FSA's final notice to Mandrake Associates Limited dated 17 July 2008.
191 DISP 1.3.6G.
192 DISP 1.1.11.R.

of the FSMA regime and the time limits might not be achievable due to the complicated nature of dealing with such complaints, in particular assessing and quantifying any loss and redress. Consumer redress schemes were added[193] to bind firms and FOS to the prescribed methodology. Particular areas of mortgage endowment and payment protection insurance complaints are subject to detailed evidential and redress guidance.[194]

Major sources of complaints

7.73 The numbers of complaints to the industry, which are then referred to FOS, have identified a number of major themes: mortgage endowments, bank charges, and payment protection insurance (PPI). PPI has been expensive for the industry. As at January 2013, £8.9 billion was paid to consumers with complaints about PPI from January 2011.[195]

7.74 To set consistent standards, the DISP Sourcebook includes detailed guidance for 'Handling Payment Protection Insurance Complaints'.[196] The guidance addresses how a complaint should be assessed to determine whether there was a 'breach or failing' by the firm, how to determine the way the complainant would have acted if 'the breach or failing' had not occurred, and what redress to offer. A firm should assess the complaint fairly, giving appropriate weight and balanced consideration to all available evidence.[197] DISP Appendix 3.3 contains detail on how to ascertain and test evidence and what inferences may or may not be drawn, for example, from oral evidence or reliance on contemporaneous documentation. Where the sale was 'substantially flawed', subject to evidence to the contrary, the firm should presume that the complainant would not have bought PPI. Examples are provided.[198] Redress should put the complainant 'in the position he would have been if he had not bought any [PPI]'.[199]

7.75 In 2011–2012, PPI complaints accounted for 60 per cent of new cases to FOS (amounting to 157,716 cases). In view of its concerns regarding the sales of PPI and firms assessment of complaints, FSA had published proposals for guidance on the fair assessment and redress of complaints relating to PPI, and rules requiring firms to reassess complaints about PPI sales.[200] FSA also published an 'open letter' to the industry detailing common failings in PPI sales practices: failings in the conduct of the sale, failings around eligibility and exclusions and limitations, failings around suitability, failings around price disclosure, additional failings specific to single premium policy sales, and additional failings specific to regular premium policies. In 2010, FSA entered into further consultation,[201] followed by a policy statement.[202] FSA's purpose was to ensure consistent and fair handling of complaints and 'fairer outcomes' to consumers. FSA also announced that it would be 'monitoring the implementation of our guidance closely to ensure real change is delivered'.[203]

---

[193] DISP 1.1.11.AR.

[194] DISP Appendix 1 and Appendix 3.

[195] FCA, 29 March 2013.

[196] DISP Appendix 3.

[197] DISP Appendix 3.3.1G.

[198] DISP Appendix 3.6.2.

[199] DISP Appendix 3.7.2.

[200] Consultation Paper 09/23 'The Assessment and Redress of Payment Protection Insurance Complaints'.

[201] CP10/6 'The Assessment and Redress of Payment Protection Insurance Complaints; Feedback on CP09/23 and further consultation'.

[202] PS10/12 'The Assessment and Redress of Payment Protection Insurance Complaints; Feedback on the further Consultation in CP10/6 and final handbook text'.

[203] FSA press release, August 2010.

FSA has taken enforcement action in relation to the handling of PPI complaints. In February 2013, FSA announced it had fined three Lloyds Banking Group firms a total of £4.3 million for delayed PPI redress payments. While the guidance in PS10/12 was subject to challenge by judicial review, in proceedings brought by the British Bankers Association and Nemo Personal Finance Limited commenced on 8 October 2010, FSA had issued guidance to firms by a letter to trade associations dated 21 January 2011 on how to handle complaints in the meantime. In January 2013, the Cooperative Bank Plc was fined £113,300 for failing to pay due regard to the interests of its customers and treat them fairly, under Principle 6 of PRIN, when dealing with PPI complaints (while FSA's guidance was being challenged) in an inadequate manner likely to lead to the failure to identify complaints capable of being progressed during that period. 7.76

Before PPI, the largest source of complaints to FOS had been in respect of mortgage endowments, that is, the sales of endowment policies as repayment vehicles for mortgages taken out to buy the investor's home.[204] The DISP Rules set out both the approach and standards firms should use when investigating such complaints, and how any financial loss should be assessed and what redress should be offered as 'fair and appropriate compensation'.[205] As for PPI, the complaint handling process requires the gathering of all relevant facts and information, making a fair and objective assessment of whether the firm has failed to comply with the relevant duty owed to the complainant, and assessing whether any failure of duty by it was in the circumstances a material failure, in the sense that if it had not occurred the complainant would have been likely to have acted differently.[206] It also directs that certain assumptions should be made in favour of the complainant 'unless the contrary is demonstrated' (for example, that the complainant could have afforded a repayment mortgage).[207] 7.77

The FSA took action to enforce the proper handling of endowment mis-selling complaints, which illustrated its view of firms' complaint handling obligations. The FSA wrote to large firms dealing with mortgage endowment claims raising concerns about, and providing 'urgent guidance' for, the handling of those complaints[208] and followed up to remind firms 'of the importance of handling complaints in a way that is consistent with the principle of treating customers fairly' and to warn of enforcement action.[209] 7.78

---

[204] The history of these complaints was examined for FOS by David Severn.
[205] DISP App 1.
[206] DISP App 1.1.6G.
[207] DISP App 1.2.2G.
[208] 'The Tiner letter'.
[209] The Annex to the 'Tiner letter' listed nine specific action points to assist firms to deal with complaints fairly:

(1) recognise in the assessment of the complaint that the key risk for the consumer is that the endowment may not repay the mortgage loan;
(2) avoid too narrow a view of the scope of the advisory duty in the context of mortgage advice;
(3) recognise that oral evidence can be good and sufficient evidence, avoiding too ready a dismissal of evidence from the consumer which is not supported by documentary proof;
(4) investigate the issue diligently in particular so as to take into account the selling practices at the time, the training, instruction, sales scripts, and incentives given to advisers at the time, and the track record of the particular adviser;
(5) go the extra mile to clarify ambiguous issues or conflicts of evidence before finding against the consumer;
(6) avoid making a conclusive assumption that a pre-existing endowment held at time of sale, whether for purposes of savings or mortgage repayment, is sufficient evidence of understanding and acceptance of the key risk;

7.79 The action taken by the FSA against firms at that time demonstrated its attitude to complaint handling. In December 2003, the FSA imposed a penalty on Friends Provident Life and Pensions Limited for the mishandling of endowment mortgage complaints.[210] The FSA found that the complaints handling procedures were unfair towards the customers. In particular, the FSA concluded that the firm's complaints handling procedures meant that the firm dismissed a consumer's case where the complainant's evidence was not supported by contemporaneous documentation, the firm had made assumptions that customers understood risks associated with the endowment policy if the customer had had a pre-existing endowment policy, and the firm had assumed that the customers were satisfied with the advice if they did not exercise cancellation rights. The FSA did not consider that the firm had put in place effective and appropriate complaints procedures.[211]

7.80 In March 2004, the FSA imposed a penalty on Allied Dunbar Assurance plc for flaws in its procedures for handling mortgage endowment complaints.[212] The FSA identified that its complaint handlers had conducted poor-quality investigations and there was a failure to collect sufficient evidence to make a fair assessment to both the consumer's attitude to risk and the suitability of sale. In particular, the firm did not give clear instructions to its complaints-handling staff about the types of evidence it should consider (including the customer's version of events), did not give clear instructions about the weight to be attached to the different types of evidence when coming to a decision, unfairly restricted (by the written procedures) the ability of a complaint handler to uphold a complaint where a sale was plainly unsuitable if, for example, the customer did not complain specifically that the sales advice failed to explain the risks of an endowment policy, and tended to give disproportionate weight to the views of the sale adviser when assessing the facts. Unfair assumptions were made that customers had accepted the risks associated with an endowment mortgage; for example if the customer had held a pre-existing endowment. The FSA concluded investigations were of poor quality, did not gather sufficient evidence, or make a fair assessment, so that unsound decisions were made to reject complaints.[213]

7.81 In May 2005, the FSA imposed a penalty on Abbey National plc for mishandling mortgage endowment complaints.[214] The FSA found that '[b]y putting its own interests ahead of those of its customers with a mortgage endowment complaint, Abbey had singularly failed to treat its customers fairly'.[215] In particular, the FSA found that insufficient steps had been taken

(7) avoid making too literal and narrow an interpretation of the issue of the complaint as expressed by the consumer;
(8) avoid rejecting complaints solely on the basis that the consumer signed a proposal form or failed to exercise the cancellation right and so must be presumed to have been satisfied with the advice and the product at time of sale; and
(9) avoid claiming as evidence of risk warning at time of sale (so as to justify rejection of the complaint) either:
(a) the absence of a statement in product literature that repayment of the mortgage was guaranteed; or
(b) a statement in product particulars that the firm will monitor the plan and advise the consumer if the level of contribution is insufficient for the target amount to be repaid.

210 Final Notice dated 15 December 2003.
211 FSA Press Release dated 17 December 2005.
212 Final Notice dated 18 March 2004.
213 FSA Press Release dated 19 March 2004.
214 Final Notice dated 25 May 2005.
215 FSA Press Release dated 25 May 2005.

to establish the customer's attitude to risk at the point of sale, and the subject matter of the complaint had not been fully investigated. The firm had an obligation to carry out an objective investigation to make a genuine enquiry and assessment, and in the FSA's view the firm had breached Principle 2 in failing to conduct its business with due skill, care, and diligence in relation to its handling of mortgage endowment complaints, and Principle 6 in failing to pay due regard to the interests of its customers or to treat them fairly.

The mortgage and PPI guidance at DISP Appendices 1 and 3 address such issues in directing the approach to complaint handling by firms. Further, in April 2010, FSA published a 'Review of complaint handling in banking groups'. FSA emphasised the importance it attached to handling complaints as part of treating customers fairly. **7.82**

FSA found poor complaint-handling standards within most banks it assessed. FSA identified four areas which had the most significant impact on the quality of complaint handling: **7.83**

> Culture: most of the banks assessed had not embedded a culture that focused on delivering fair outcomes for complainants. . .;
>
> Root cause analysis: the extent and quality of root cause analysis undertaken varied between banks and this affected the extent to which they were able to identify recurrent or systemic problems and take appropriate action. . .;
>
> Quality of front-line complaint handling: in most banks assessed, the quality of complaint handling undertaken by front-line staff (where complaint handling was not the main function of their role) was poor, with inadequate investigations and poor decision-making. . .;
>
> Quality assurance of complaints: most of the quality assurance arrangements. . . were focused on checking adherence to process. . . rather than assessing the quality of responses to customers and whether the outcome was fair.

To assist firms, FSA published a 'template' which it stated it would use to review complaint files. It was following the review that FSA proposed to remove the two-stage complaint-handling process which it found 'can act as a barrier to fair complaint handling', and which is now no longer available. **7.84**

Complaint history

Firms are to ensure lessons learnt from FOS determinations are effectively applied in future complaint handling.[216] This has included published information (in FOS's Newsletters) and now extends to determinations on a searchable database.[217] The making and outcome of a complaint might also be relevant to an individual's employment and status. The SUP reporting rules require identification of retail investment advisers,[218] and the FCA Supervision regime includes 'The Retail Investment Adviser Complaints Alert Form',[219] where redress exceeds £50,000 or more than three complaints are upheld in a year. **7.85**

The FCA, when considering the fitness and propriety of an individual, will have regard to that individual's complaint history.[220] For these reasons, as well as general principles, in the **7.86**

[216] DISP 1.3.2.AG.
[217] s 230A.
[218] SUP 10A.14.24.R.
[219] SUP 10. Annex 9R Form G.
[220] FIT 2.1.3(6)R.

event a complaint is made against an individual, the firm should, if possible, seek to obtain that individual's response to the substance of the complaint.

7.87 In 2008, the FSA issued proposals for publishing complaints data about firms.[221] The Hunt Report (discussed at para 7.179) recommended that FOS 'should work with the FSA, industry and consumer stakeholders to define a common complaints dataset to enable joint publication of performance data on a firm-specific basis in the medium term'. Tables of the numbers of complaints and how they are handled by firms are now compiled. Firms report complaints data to FCA and FCA publishes six-monthly complaints data by firm showing (by product groups) numbers of complaints opened, closed, closed within eight weeks and upheld. Firms' reports must also include the amount of redress paid. This covers firms that report 500 or more complaints in a six-month period. For the second half of 2012, this covered 95 per cent of reported complaints, totalling 3,422,384, of which 63 per cent were about PPI.

Financial Ombudsman Service

Introduction

7.88 Part XVI FSMA establishes FOS, described as 'a scheme under which certain disputes may be resolved quickly and with minimum formality by an independent person'.[222] FSA 2012 did not change this part of the architecture. FOS describes itself 'as part of the statutory arrangements designed to help underpin consumer confidence in financial services. But unlike a regulator, we don't fine or dispute financial businesses. And unlike a regulator our role is to resolve *individual* disputes—as a quicker and more informed alternative to the courts'.[223] In July 1998, as part of the consultation on the Financial Services and Markets Bill, HM Treasury had identified that 'it is important that consumers should have access to cheap, quick, informal and effective dispute resolution arrangements'.[224] For this purpose, a single ombudsman scheme was proposed. This single scheme replaced the 'patchwork quilt'[225] of eight pre-existing dispute resolution schemes: the Banking Ombudsman; the Building Societies Ombudsman; the FSA Complaints Services; the Insurance Ombudsman; the Investment Ombudsman; the Personal Insurance Arbitration Services; the PIA Ombudsman; and the SFA Complaints and Arbitration Services.

7.89 According to HM Treasury's consultation, the new scheme was intended to operate 'if a consumer fails to obtain satisfaction from a firm's internal complaints handling arrangements', and firms were to be required 'to cooperate with the Scheme's investigation of a case'. It was not to be for or against firms or customers. A decision in favour of the consumer was to be binding on the firm, but not consumers.

[221] FSA Discussion Paper 08/3: 'Transparency as a Regulatory Tool' (May 2008).
[222] FSMA, s 225(1).
[223] Ombudsman News Issue 109 April/May 2013.
[224] Financial Services and Markets Bill: A Consultation Document, Part 1, Overview of Financial Regulatory Reform.
[225] As described in the FSA's Consultation Paper 4: 'Consumer Complaints' (December 1997).

As well as under FSA 2012, FOS has been subject to review and revision—firstly at the request of HM Treasury, as part of the review of implementation of the FSMA with the benefit of two years' experience (the 'N2 plus 2' review), although HM Treasury limited the scope of the review. HM Treasury noted key, non-negotiable safeguards for FOS, in particular that it remained independent, decisions are dealt with on the merits, and the service remained free to consumers (even those with unsuccessful complaints).[226] The informality of procedure and protection for consumers from adverse costs consequences are important features of FOS and were later supported by Lord Hunt in his report 'Opening up, reaching out, and aiming high—an agenda for accessibility and excellence in the Financial Ombudsman Scheme' ('the Hunt Report') published in April 2008. These fundamental characteristics have been preserved under FSA 2012. **7.90**

The scheme operator

The Financial Ombudsman Service Limited is the 'scheme operator' (as defined by FSMA) of the Financial Ombudsman Service. The company was established by the FSA to carry out the statutory functions of the scheme operator under Part XVI FSMA. The 'body corporate' is a company limited by guarantee, set up under Part II of Schedule 17 to FSMA and amended by FSA 2012. It is the FCA as the successor to the FSA, to whom FOS is accountable. FCA must ensure FOS is capable of exercising its functions.[227] The FCA and FOS must publish a memorandum of understanding on how they will cooperate with each other.[228] The published MOU dated 1 April 2013, deals with issues of governance, cooperation, and information sharing. It notes that the FCA and FOS may be dealing with the same issues from their respective perspectives,[229] or FOS may wish to notify the FCA of any concerns about the fitness and priority of firms or approved persons.[230] **7.91**

As required by Schedule 17, the scheme operator has a chairman and a Board who are responsible for the operation of the scheme but who have no involvement in considering individual complaints. The chairman and Board members are subject to appointment, and removal, by the FCA. The chairman's appointment must be approved by HM Treasury. Although Board members are appointed by the FCA, 'the terms of their appointment (and in particular those governing removal from office) must be such as to secure their independence from the FCA in the operation of the scheme'.[231] The Board comprises public-interest appointments. Issues decided by the Board include the appointment of the Ombudsmen, the making of rules in respect of the scheme's voluntary jurisdiction (subject to the approval of the FCA), the making of rules relating to the levying of case fees (subject to the approval of the FCA), and the approval and recommendation to the FCA of the annual budget. **7.92**

Subject to having regard to the parties' rights of privacy, the Ombudsman may disclose information to the FCA and other regulatory or statutory bodies to assist those bodies to discharge those functions.[232] FOS and the FCA may share information for the discharge of **7.93**

[226] The Financial Secretary to the Treasury's Statement on the Two Year Review of the Financial Services and Markets Act (dated 4 November 2003).
[227] Sch 17, para 2.
[228] Sch 17, para 3A. See Chapter 1, para 1.159.
[229] Para 4.
[230] Para 18.
[231] FSMA, Sch 17, Part II, Clause 3(3).
[232] DISP 3.8.3.R.

their respective statutory functions under FSMA regulations, (now updated),[233] and FOS may make similar disclosure to the OFT. FSA 2012 also added (as Section 232A) a duty on FOS to provide information to FCA to assist FCA's operational objectives.

7.94 FOS may also refer regular, widespread failings to the FCA[234] where consumers have suffered loss and FOS would be likely to uphold complaints and make money awards. FCA has 90 days to publish its response.

7.95 Part II of Schedule 17 requires an annual report from FOS and the Chief Ombudsman,[235] and an annual budget to be approved by the FCA.[236] The budget must be approved before each financial year and must 'include an indication of (a) a distribution of resources deployed in the operation of the scheme, and (b) the amounts of income of the scheme operator arising or expected to arise from the operation of the scheme'. Under the 2012 Act, the annual accounts must be sent to the Comptroller and Auditor General to be certified,[237] and the annual plan must be consulted on each financial year.[238]

7.96 FOS, with FCA and OFT, collaborate further as members of the 'Coordination Committee', which contributes 'to the identification and consideration of emerging risks'.[239] FSCS is an observer at the Committee.

7.97 FOS also has MOUs with the Office of Fair Trading ('OFT') (as consumer credit regulator), the Information Commissioner's Office ('ICO') (dealing with Data Protection Act breaches), and the Claims Management Regulator ('CMR'). With OFT, FOS shares information and issues with regulatory implications for the OFT, as well as routine information sharing. The ICO MOU addresses concerns about firms' compliance with data protection laws. With CMR, FOS will provide information about complaints relating to CMCs and trends in CMCs' conduct.

7.98 Part II of Schedule 17 provides for 'a panel of persons, appearing to [the scheme operator] to have appropriate qualifications and experience, to act as Ombudsmen for the purposes of the scheme'[240] and for one member of the panel to act as Chief Ombudsman.[241] All Ombudsman appointments, by the scheme operator, are to ensure the independence of the individuals. As at the end of 2011–2012, FOS had a Chief Ombudsman, two Principal Ombudsmen, three Lead Ombudsmen, seven Managing Ombudsmen, and 104 other Ombudsmen. The bulk of cases are dealt with by teams of case workers and adjudicators.[242] In practice, although the determination of complaints is reserved to an Ombudsman,[243] investigations may be delegated to staff and complaints determined by designated staff so cases may only be seen

[233] The Financial Services and Markets Act 2000 (Disclosure of Information and Prescribed Pensions) Regulations 2001, SI 2001/1857; The Financial Services and Markets Act 2000 (Disclosure of Confidential Information) Regulations 2001, SI 2001/2188.

[234] Under s 234D.

[235] Para 7.

[236] Para 9.

[237] Sch 17, para 7A.

[238] Sch 17, para 9A.

[239] FOS/FCA MOU, para 15.

[240] Para 4.

[241] Para 5.

[242] DISP 3.9.1A.R.

[243] Sch 17, para 14(2)(f).

by an Ombudsman if they are unusual, difficult, or contentious. FOS will first offer guidance to assist resolution of the complaint, failing which the matter proceeds to an adjudication assessment or mediation, and if not settled, to the Ombudsman. The Court of Appeal has upheld the delegation by the Ombudsman under DISP 3.3, in particular for summary dismissal.[244] In 2011–2012, of 222,333 cases resolved, 201,793 were by adjudicators and 20,540 by Ombudsmen.

Part XVI FSMA and Schedule 17 provide some particular powers, and protection, to FOS. The Ombudsman has the power to compel production of documents or information from 'a party to a complaint'. This is limited to 'information and documents, the production of which the Ombudsman considers necessary for the determination of the complaint'.[245] Failure to comply may lead to sanctions[246] including that the 'defaulter' to be treated as if in contempt of court.[247] However, FOS has no such powers to obtain information from third parties who might hold relevant material. It is for the parties to the complaint to seek to obtain and present such evidence. **7.99**

FOS has immunity from liability for damages for acts or omissions 'in the discharge, or purported discharge, of any functions under this Act in relation to the compulsory jurisdiction'.[248] This does not apply in the event of bad faith or in respect of an award of damages under section 6(1) of the Human Rights Act 1998.[249] Complaints subject to the compulsory or consumer credit jurisdictions are treated as court proceedings for defamation laws.[250] Personal data may also be exempt from subject access provisions where processed in the discharge of the statutory function and it would be prejudicial to that function.[251] **7.100**

The operation of FOS

Part XVI FSMA, and Schedule 17, set out the keystones for the operation of FOS: compulsory jurisdiction (including determination under the compulsory jurisdiction and awards),[252] consumer credit jurisdiction,[253] voluntary jurisdiction,[254] costs,[255] and funding.[256] The 2012 Act confirmed the liability of successor firms for past business.[257] This framework is built upon by the DISP Rules contained in the FCA Handbook (in the Redress Module). **7.101**

FSA 2012 added the obligation on FOS to publish its determinations.[258] FOS has been consulting on how it expects to meet this duty and published responses to its proposals.[259] Decisions will be published on the website on a searchable database, and include the name **7.102**

244 *FOS v Heather, Moor & Edgecomb Ltd* [2008] EWCA 643.
245 ibid, s 231(3).
246 s 232(2).
247 ibid, s 231(4).
248 ibid, Sch 17, para 10.
249 ibid, para 10(2).
250 Sch 17, para 11.
251 s 233.
252 s 226.
253 s 226A.
254 s 227.
255 s 230.
256 ss 234 and 234A.
257 s 234B.
258 s 230A.
259 Transparency and the FOS—publishing ombudsman decisions: meaning of requests (January 2012).

of the business but not the name of or information which identifies consumer (and may not be published at all if such redaction is significant).

Compulsory jurisdiction—framework

7.103 Under section 226, compulsory jurisdiction applies to any firm, against which a complaint is made, being authorised at the time of the act or omission to which the complaint relates, and the complaint relates to an activity regulated under the Act and subject to the compulsory jurisdiction rules.[260] The Ombudsman can consider all disputes arising from the carrying on of such regulated activity. FOS's compulsory scope has extended since N2, adding credit unions, mortgage and general insurance brokers consumer credit,[261] payment services,[262] and the issuance of electronic money.[263] The 'Thornton Review' recommended combining the functions of FOS and the Pensions Ombudsman but this has not been carried out.[264] HM Treasury is now preparing for consumer credit regulation to pass to the FCA with effect from 2016.

7.104 The FCA is responsible for making the DISP Rules dealing with the compulsory jurisdiction. These rules determine the scope of compulsory jurisdiction, those eligible to claim, and in what circumstances a claim may be made. FSMA also identifies, in particular, the application of relevant time limits and a requirement on consumers to communicate first the 'substance' of a complaint to the firm giving it a 'reasonable opportunity to deal with it'.[265]

7.105 FSMA provides for the determination of complaints under the compulsory jurisdiction to be 'by reference to what is, in the opinion of the Ombudsman, fair and reasonable in all the circumstances of the case'[266] for which relevant factors may be specified.[267]

7.106 FSMA also requires a written statement of a decision, with reasons, signed by the Ombudsman, which 'determination' the complainant must accept or reject.[268] The complainant's notification no longer need be in writing.[269] If accepted by the consumer, the Ombudsman's decision is binding on the consumer and the firm, and is 'final'.[270] Once accepted, FOS will not review the award such as the amount of redress, unless there may be material, new evidence.[271] FOS's decision may include an award against the firm for the payment of 'fair compensation for loss or damage', not to exceed a monetary limit (fixed by the FSA), although recommendation of a higher amount may be made, or a direction to take 'just and appropriate' steps, and is enforceable by the consumer.[272] It is possible to make both a money award and a direction to take steps.[273] Although 'prompt compliance' is required, Schedule 17 identifies that money

[260] ibid, s 226(2) and (4).
[261] ibid, s 226A (added by the Consumer Credit Act 2006).
[262] From 1 November 2009, FOS has provided the 'out of court' redress mechanism under the Payment Services Directive.
[263] From 30 April 2011.
[264] P Thornton: *A Review of Pensions Institutions* (June 2007).
[265] FSMA, Sch 17, para 13.
[266] ibid, s 228(2).
[267] ibid, Sch 17, para 14.
[268] ibid, s 228(3) and (4).
[269] The 2012 Act, Sch 11 para 4(2).
[270] ibid, s 228(5).
[271] *R (Cook) v FOS* [2009] EWHC 426 (Admin).
[272] ibid, s 229(2)(b), and (9).
[273] *Bunney v Burns Anderson plc* [2007] EWHC 1740 (Ch).

awards 'registered in accordance with scheme rules' may be enforced by the County Court in England and Wales, and by similar procedures in Scotland and Northern Ireland.[274] FOS is required to maintain 'a register of each money award'.[275] This was satisfied by an internal database at FOS,[276] although the Court of Appeal suggested that the register, as an official list or record, should be open to public inspection.[277]

FSA 2012 clarified that 'late' acceptance of a determination is not treated as a rejection,[278] and further that FOS's rules may allow for correction of clerical mistakes in a written statement of determination, and that procedural irregularity does not render a determination void.[279] **7.107**

The maximum monetary award is capped at £150,000 (from 1 January 2012) and was previously £100,000. The High Court has decided that even if the FOS award is accepted, the complainant may claim additional damages from the firm.[280] In *Clark,* the claimants accepted the FOS award and a payment of £100,000 (the then limit) but brought proceedings for additional losses to £500,000, giving credit for the £100,000 award. On appeal to the High Court it, was held that the doctrine of 'merger' did not apply due to a distinction between the cause of action being considered by the court and the matter determined by FOS. The court decided it did not need to rely on the fact that the complainants had made an express statement seeking to reserve the right to pursue the matter through the courts. **7.108**

The decision in *Clark* contradicted an earlier decision in the High Court holding that complainants who accepted an award were bound by the full and final settlement and could not bring a civil claim in relation to the same matter.[281] In *Andrews*, the court found that FOS was a 'tribunal' for the purpose of the doctrine of 'merger', and the complainant could not bring two claims arising out of the same facts. **7.109**

FOS does make some of the DISP Rules,[282] such as the procedures for reference of complaints and for their investigation, consideration, and determination by an Ombudsman.[283] **7.110**

274 Para 16.
275 DISP 3.7.7.R.
276 See the judgment of the Financial Services and Markets Tribunal in *Heather, Moor & Edgecomb Ltd v FSA* (sitting on 19 May 2008).
277 *R (Heather, Moor & Edgecomb Ltd) v FOS* [2008] ECWA Civ 642.
278 Section 228(6)A.
279 Sch 17 para 14(fa), (fb), and para 16B.
280 *Clark and Clark v In Focus Asset Management & Tax Solutions* [2012] EWHC 3669 (QB).
281 *Andrews v SBJ Benefit Consultants* [2010] EWHC 2875 (Ch).
282 Sch 17, para 14.
283 Sch 17, para 14(2) contains a non-exhaustive list of issues which may be dealt with by these rules, which may: '(a) specify matters which are to be taken into account when determining whether an act or omission was fair and reasonable; (b) provide that a complaint may in specified circumstances be dismissed without consideration of its merits; (c) provide for the reference of a complaint, in specified circumstances and with the consent of a complainant, to another body with a view to its being determined by that body instead of by an ombudsman; (d) make provision as to the evidence which may be required or admitted, the extent to which it should be oral or written and the consequences of a person's failure to produce any information or document which he has been required (under Section 231 or otherwise) to produce; (e) allow an Ombudsman to fix time limits for any aspect of the proceedings and to extend a time limit; (f) provide for certain things in relation to the reference, investigation, or consideration (but not determination) of a complaint to be done by the member of the scheme operator staff instead of by an ombudsman; (g) make different provision in relation to different kinds of complaint'. Paragraph 14(3) allows for the dismissal of complaints 'without consideration of its merits' to include complaints which are frivolous or vexatious, complaints best dealt with in legal proceedings, or if there are 'other compelling reasons'.

FOS must publish any such rules in draft for consultation, inviting representations, which rules then may only be made with the consent of the FCA.[284] The similar procedure for consumer credit complaints is dealt with at Schedule 17.[285]

Voluntary jurisdiction—framework

7.111 Section 227 adds the 'voluntary jurisdiction'. This relates to activities which are or would be made subject to the compulsory jurisdiction. With the approval of the FCA, FOS makes rules for the operation of its voluntary jurisdiction. Such rules may determine who is an eligible claimant, and make different provisions for complaints arising from different activities.[286] These FOS rules are described as 'standard terms'.[287] The standard terms may require funding to FOS 'by participants' of the voluntary jurisdiction scheme, and make 'provision as to the ordering of costs'.[288] FSMA also provides for the 'standard terms' to include an immunity from damages for FOS, on the same basis as for the compulsory jurisdiction.[289]

7.112 Any part of the voluntary jurisdiction may also be delegated by FOS to a body responsible 'for the operation of broadly comparable scheme ... for the resolution of disputes'.[290]

7.113 The FCA is to receive from FOS a copy of the voluntary jurisdiction rules once made 'without delay' and written notice of the revocation of any such rules.[291] These rules must be printed and available to the public immediately after being made. As with the compulsory jurisdiction, any proposed voluntary jurisdiction rules must be published in draft for consultation and representations invited within a specified time; a 'statement of the difference' must be published if significant changes follow the consultation period.[292]

Costs

7.114 As already noted, costs awards may not be made by FOS against a complainant in respect of the firm's costs.[293] However, FOS may make costs orders, including an award against a complainant 'for the purpose of providing a contribution to resources deployed in dealing with the complaint' under the compulsory jurisdiction if the consumer's conduct was improper or unreasonable or responsible for an unreasonable delay.[294] Costs awards due to FOS are recoverable as a debt,[295] and costs awards against the respondent firm are to be treated as a money award for the purposes of enforcement.[296]

Funding

7.115 FOS is funded by the financial services industry under rules made by the FCA (see paragraphs 7.90 and 7.179).[297] Complainants are not to be charged. Fees are to be paid to FOS

284 Sch 17, para 14(4)–(7).
285 Part 3A.
286 Sch 17, Part IV.
287 Sch 17, para 18.
288 Para 18(3).
289 Para 18(5).
290 Para 19.
291 ibid.
292 Para 22.
293 FSMA, s 230(3).
294 ibid, s 230(4).
295 ibid, s 230(6).
296 ibid, s 230(7).
297 ibid, ss 234, 234A.

by firms (or via the OFT for consumer credit jurisdiction) but FSMA allows for the rules to include a reduction or waiver of fees, different fees for different stages of a complaint, a refund of fees, and different arrangements for different complaints.[298]

DISP—jurisdiction of FOS

DISP Chapter 2 deals with FOS's jurisdiction. The essential requirements for a complaint to FOS[299] are that the complainant is an 'eligible complainant'; the complaint is subject to the compulsory or voluntary jurisdiction, both in terms of the firm and the activity (and the place) giving rise to the complaint; for compulsory jurisdiction, the act or omission complained of occurred after N2 (otherwise the complaint has to be dealt with on the terms of the relevant predecessor scheme, if any);[300] and the firm must have failed to resolve the complaint (to the complainant's satisfaction) within eight weeks. **7.116**

There are transitional arrangements dealing with complaints which were, or would otherwise have been, made to one of the pre-existing dispute resolution services (which are part of the compulsory jurisdiction for former members).[301] The procedures for such claims may be modified by DISP to follow the rules of the relevant predecessor scheme. **7.117**

Time limits

There are time limits for making complaints to FOS.[302] A complaint cannot be made to FOS less than eight weeks after receipt of the complaint by the firm, unless the firm has already sent its 'final response'. After the final response has been sent, properly advising the complainant of the possibility of referring the matter to FOS (including contact details), a complaint cannot be made to FOS more than six months later. FOS's application of the six-month time limit[303] was upheld when challenged in the High Court in *Bankole*.[304] Complaints cannot be first made (to the firm or FOS) more than six years from the event complained about or, if later, more than three years from the date on which the complainant became aware or ought reasonably to have become aware of the cause for complaint, in the absence of any prior (and acknowledged or recorded) referral within that period of the complaint to the firm or FOS.[305] This reflects the law on limitation in England and Wales, that is, the standard six-year limitation period for claims in contract and tort, subject to the three-year extension applicable in negligence claims, save that a 15-year 'long stop' is not applied under DISP. The time limits do not apply in exceptional circumstances or where the firm does not object, but otherwise the firm can reject such complaints without considering the merits.[306] **7.118**

The position on limitation is modified for mortgage endowment 'risk' complaints.[307] For these complaints, the firm must have written to the complainant warning of a high risk that the endowment policy will not produce a sum large enough to repay the target amount **7.119**

---

298 ibid, Sch 17, para 15.
299 DISP 2.2.1R.
300 DISP 2.1.1.G.
301 Financial Services and Markets Act 2000 (Transitional Provisions) (Ombudsman Scheme and Complaints Scheme) Order 2001.
302 DISP 2.8.
303 DISP 2.8.2(1)R.
304 *R (Bankole) v FOS* [2012] EWHC 3555 (Admin).
305 DISP 2.8.2.R.
306 DISP 1.8.1.R.
307 DISP 2.8.7.R.

(known as a 'red letter') which triggers the three-year period of knowledge for the complaint, together with a warning (of at least six months) of the expiry of the time limit. Failure to give such warning will mean that time for making the complaint will not start to run for the purpose of a complaint to the FOS. The time limits also do not apply to claims in respect of past business reviews, under the Pension Review and the FSAVC Review,[308] and also for any future review of past business approved by HM Treasury.

Eligible complainant

7.120 FOS is to protect consumers, ie, private individuals and small businesses and organisations. The service is available to those consumers who need it most—defined as 'eligible complainants'.[309] Businesses are eligible only if they are 'micro-enterprises'. A charity, or trust, is 'eligible' subject to group annual turnover, annual income, or net asset value respectively being less than £1 million.[310] Following implementation of MiFID, a 'professional client' or an 'eligible counterparty' is excluded,[311] as well as firms complaining in respect of an activity for which they hold a permission.[312] For consumer credit business, further exclusions apply, eg, a body corporate or a partnership of more than three persons.[313] A complainant must have had one of the specified relationships with the firm: a complaint is generally only accepted by FOS if it arises out of a customer or potential customer relationship.[314] There are specific categories of eligible 'indirect complaints' which allow complaints where the complainant may have a legitimate ground for dispute with the regulated firm but is not the identified customer.[315] FOS's interpretation of 'eligible complainant', in particular whether the complainant had a customer relationship with the firm, was upheld by the court in the case of *Goff*.[316] FOS did not accept jurisdiction on the basis that the claim was from an 'alleged customer'.

7.121 Complaints may be made by a representative of a complainant, where authorised by the complainant or by law.[317] The complainant does not need to live or be based in the UK.

Firms and activities—the compulsory jurisdiction

7.122 With some limited exceptions, all authorised firms are subject to the compulsory jurisdiction.[318] Compulsory jurisdiction applies to acts or omissions by an authorised firm carrying out a regulated activity, and firms are responsible for complaints against their appointed

308 DISP 2.8.5R.
309 DISP 2.7.1R.
310 DISP 2.7.3R.
311 DISP 2.7.9(2)R.
312 DISP 2.7.9(1)R.
313 DISP 2.7.9(3)R.
314 DISP 2.7.6.R.
315 The examples are beneficiaries of personal or shareholder pension schemes, beneficiaries or intended beneficiaries of insurance contracts (eg employees covered by a group permanent health policy taken out and arranged by the employer but which provides benefits for the employee); those who have given a firm a guarantee or security for a mortgage or loan; those who have relied upon a cheque guarantee card issued by a firm; the true owner of a cheque or bill of exchange collected by a firm for someone else's account; the recipient of a banker's reference given by a firm; or the holder of units in a collective investment firm or a holder of units in a collective investment scheme where the firm is the 'operator' or 'depository', as defined by the FSA Handbook Glossary, providers of guarantees or securities for mortgages or loans, various complaints under the Consumer Credit Act, as well as complaints by a beneficiary against a trust or estate of which the respondent firm is trustee or personal representative.
316 *R (Goff) v FOS* [2011] EWHC 1112 (Admin).
317 DISP 2.7.1–2R.
318 DISP 2.3.

representatives.[319] Since N2 compulsory jurisdiction has been extended to credit unions (from 2 July 2002), to mortgage business on (31 October 2004) and to general insurance broking (from 14 January 2005)—the Insurance Mediation Directive ('IMD')[320] requires adequate complaints handling processes. MiFID also refers to an 'extra-judicial mechanism for investors' complaints'.[321] In addition to the FSA regulated firms, covering about 21,000 firms, consumer credit (regulated by the Office of Fair Trading) was added from April 2007 and includes 'licensees' under the Consumer Credit Act 1974, not just FSMA-authorised firms.[322] Compulsory jurisdiction also includes some banking services—lending money secured by a charge on land (ie mortgages), lending money other than 'restricted credit', paying money by a 'plastic card' (ie, credit cards), and 'ancillary banking services' which services include the operation of cash machines and of safe deposit boxes, and issuance of 'electronic money'.[323] Compulsory jurisdiction also catches any connected ancillary activities.[324] With effect from 1 January 2009, 'connected travel insurance' became a regulated activity and part of FOS's compulsory jurisdiction; 'Payment services' was added in November 2009.[325]

The scope of voluntary jurisdiction is offered for activities which were not, but are now, regulated or would be regulated activities (or consumer credit activities) usually required to be carried on from an establishment in the UK, the banking activities noted earlier, or general and long-term insurance mediation.[326] National Savings & Investments and The Post Office have joined the voluntary jurisdiction. Voluntary jurisdiction also includes 'ancillary activities' provided in connection with these identified activities. **7.123**

The territorial scope of FOS jurisdiction is limited to activities carried on from an establishment in the UK (save that collective portfolio management services may be protected if carried out cross-border from another EEA State).[327] There is some extension under voluntary jurisdiction for insurance and banking, if the activity is elsewhere in the EEA and directed wholly or partly at the UK, is governed by contracts made under the law of England and Wales, Scotland, or Northern Ireland, and the home State EEA regulator has been notified by the firm that it intends to participate in the FOS voluntary jurisdiction.[328] **7.124**

FOS procedures

DISP 3 sets out the procedures for assessing complaints and grounds for rejection, including evidence and time limits, how FOS will determine what is 'fair and reasonable', the types of loss and damage for which awards may be made, the limits on awards, and what awards may be made for costs.[329] Further, following the consumer redress scheme provisions of section 404B(11), failure to apply or follow a redress scheme may also be subject of a complaint.[330] **7.125**

[319] DISP 2.3.3G.
[320] 2002/92/EC, art 10. On IMD, see Chapter 4.
[321] Art 53.
[322] DISP 2.4.1R.
[323] DISP 2.3.2.B.
[324] DISP 2.3.1R.
[325] DISP 2.3.2A.
[326] DISP 2.5.1R.
[327] DISP 2.6.1.R, 2.6.3R.
[328] DISP 2.6.4R.
[329] DISP 3.1.1.G.
[330] DISP 2.3.2.C.G.

Dismissal of a complaint

7.126 Before assessing the merits of a complaint, the Ombudsman may make a decision that the complaint (or complainant) is ineligible, or that the complaint should otherwise be dismissed without consideration of its merits.[331] Before a complaint is dismissed as 'out of jurisdiction', the parties must have the opportunity to comment and, when making the decision, FOS must give reasons to the complainant.[332]

7.127 Before complaints are dismissed 'without consideration of the merits',[333] the complainant will be given an opportunity to make representations and receive a reasoned decision.[334] Grounds for dismissal include where the Ombudsman is satisfied the complainant has not suffered real loss or harm, the complaint is 'frivolous or vexatious', or has no 'reasonable prospect of success'.[335] One per cent of cases were dismissed as 'frivolous and vexatious' in 2011–2012. The list of grounds expressly provides that a complaint may be dismissed if it is about 'the legitimate exercise of a firm's commercial judgement'. Complaints about investment performance (not involving negligence or maladministration) or the exercise of discretion under a rule, or the failure to consult beneficiaries before exercising such discretion where there is no legal obligation to do so, or where not all potential complainants have consented to the referral of the complaint, may also be dismissed. Other grounds to reject a complaint at this stage include if the matter has been subject to scrutiny either under and in accordance with standards of a past business review or consumer redress scheme, or by FOS (unless new evidence is available)[336] or a former scheme or a comparable dispute resolution process or by the court, or is more suitable for such scrutiny. Employee disputes are to be dismissed, and also excluded is a 'pure landlord and tenant issue arising out of a regulated sale and rent back agreement'. DISP includes, as a catch-all, 'other compelling reasons'.[337] If the complainant consents, complaints may also be referred to another more suitable complaints scheme.[338]

7.128 In addition, a complaint may be dismissed where a firm has made an offer which is 'fair and reasonable in relation to the circumstances alleged by the complainant and which is still open for acceptance'.[339] FOS might seek to negotiate a settlement between the parties, and it is expressly contemplated FOS will seek to resolve complaints between the parties by mediation or other means, such as an investigation and provisional assessment.[340]

Test cases

7.129 A test case procedure was introduced after the 'N2 plus 2' review of FOS. If satisfied that a complaint raises an 'important or novel point of law, which has important consequences', the complaint may be dismissed, to be considered by a court as a test case.[341] If at the request of the firm, the firm must undertake to meet the complaint's costs.

[331] FSMA, Sch 17, para 14(2)(b).
[332] DISP 3.2.3R.
[333] DISP 3.3.1R.
[334] DISP 3.3.2R.
[335] DISP 3.3.4.
[336] See *Cook*.
[337] DISP 3.3.4(17)R.
[338] DISP 3.4.1R.
[339] DISP 3.3.4(4)R.
[340] DISP 3.5.1R.
[341] DISP 3.3.5R.

Complaint investigation procedures

FOS's processes are designed to comply with requirements of the Human Rights Act 1998, and in particular Article 6 of the European Convention on Human Rights ('ECHR'). FOS's procedures were upheld before the European Court of Human Rights in *Heather Moor & Edgecomb Ltd v United Kingdom* 1550/09 (2011) ECHR 1019. Under Article 6, parties are entitled to 'a fair and public hearing within a reasonable time by an independent and impartial tribunal established by law' in the determination of any civil rights and obligations. FOS makes awards binding on firms. Complainants and firms have the opportunity of making representations to FOS, and commenting on a 'provisional assessment'.[342] This provisional determination summarises the complaint and relevant facts and indicate a proposed decision, on which the 'losing' party (or sometimes both sides) can comment. If disputed, the matter is reconsidered. Alternatively, an 'adjudication' may be issued to both parties, which is referred to an Ombudsman if disputed by any party (in effect, an 'appeal'). Generally, complaints are decided on the basis of paperwork but parties may seek to make oral representations at a hearing, before the complaint is finally determined, subject to satisfying the Ombudsman that the issues are material and that a hearing will help.[343] The Ombudsman will decide whether a hearing should be held (usually after an adjudication and before any final decision) and, if so, whether by telephone, in public or in private,[344] having regard to the ECHR.[345] In practice, hearings are rare and if a firm requests a hearing, the complainant has the opportunity of attending, if necessary with representation—neither side has a 'private' hearing. The hearing is not a 'trial' on an adversarial basis at which there is a cross-examination of the complainant or witnesses at the end of which 'judgment' is delivered, but part of FOS's investigation into the issues which allows the parties to address the Ombudsman directly. The Ombudsman is likely to reserve the matter for further consideration. 20 oral hearings took place in 2011–2012.[346] **7.130**

The flexibility and informality of the complaint process allows the Ombudsman to consider what evidence is required and how that should be presented.[347] Firms are to cooperate fully with FOS in the handling of complaints.[348] Normally a written complaint form is submitted, and further issues are dealt with in correspondence or by telephone, not usually by face-to-face meetings. A firm may be asked to submit witness statements. A respondent firm would be expected to be able to produce contemporaneous letters and notes from its file. Complaints may be decided on the basis of evidence available or dismissed in the absence of information.[349] Evidence of third parties, including the FSA and experts, may be taken into account.[350] Evidence may be excluded if it would be inadmissible before a court, but the Ombudsman is not bound by rules of admissibility. Evidence may also be received by FOS in confidence[351] so that the other party only sees an edited version. Facts are determined on the balance of probabilities. **7.131**

342 DISP 3.5.4R.
343 DISP 3.5.5R.
344 DISP 3.5.6.R.
345 DISP 3.5.7G.
346 FOS Annual Review 2011/12.
347 DISP 3.5.8R.
348 DISP 1.4.4R.
349 DISP 3.5.9R.
350 DISP 3.5.12G.
351 DISP 3.5.10G.

7.132 When considering or investigating a complaint, FOS is entitled to disclose information to parties to the complaint or as part of his determination process. For compulsory jurisdiction, a party's dealings with the Ombudsman attract the privilege from defamation allowed for court proceedings.[352] The Ombudsman must have regard to the parties' rights to privacy,[353] and does not have to disclose information under the Data Protection Act 1998 if that would prejudice performance of its function.[354] As noted earlier, the Ombudsman has the power to require parties to the complaint to provide specified information which it considers necessary for the fair determination of the complaint.[355] Failure to comply with a requirement allows the court to deal with the person as if they were in contempt.[356]

7.133 The Ombudsman has the discretion to fix, and extend, any time limits during the determination process.[357] A failure by a firm to comply with time limits might lead to an award for any material distress or material inconvenience caused to the complainant.[358] If a time limit is not met by either party, the Ombudsman may proceed regardless or dismiss the complaint.[359]

The decision

7.134 An important feature of FSMA is that complaints are determined by what is 'fair and reasonable in all the circumstances of the case'[360] and in DISP.[361] This includes, but is not limited to, legal liability. The Ombudsman is to 'take into account the relevant law, and regulations, Regulator's rules, guidance and standards, codes of practice and, where appropriate, what he considers to have been good industry practice at the relevant time'.[362] In the PPI judicial review,[363] the Court found FOS could make awards for breach of principles, even if contradicted or exhausted by an FSA rule. The Court confirmed 'it would be a breach of statutory duty for [FOS] to reach a view on a case without taking the Principles into account in deciding what would be fair and reasonable and what redress to afford'. Previously, FOS welcomed the ABI guidance on handling health insurance complaints, which set standards for the industry.[364] The FSA may also approve Industry Guidance—although that cannot affect the rights of third parties, such as consumers, it may help FOS to establish what was thought a good practice at the time or explain that a firm's approach was not unique.[365] Under s 404B, FOS will follow any relevant consumer redress scheme,[366] in addition to the particular guidance for Mortgage Endowment and PPI complaints which firms should (and FOS will) follow. To be consistent in its interpretation of the law, and its approach to complaints of a similar type, FOS identify 'lead cases'. The outcome of a lead case is then applied to 'follow

352 FSMA, Sch 17, para 11.
353 DISP 3.8.1R.
354 FSMA, s 233.
355 ibid, s 231.
356 ibid, s 232.
357 DISP 3.5.13R.
358 DISP 3.5.14R.
359 DISP 3.5.14(1)R, 3.5.15R.
360 FSMA, s 228(2).
361 DISP 3.6.1.
362 DISP 3.6.4R.
363 *R (British Bankers Association) v FSA and FOS* [2011] EWHC 999 (Admin). On PPI, see Chapter 1 para 1.46.
364 FOS Corporate Plan & 2008/09 Budget (January 2008).
365 FSA: 'Policy Statement 07/16 on Industry Guidance' (September 2007).
366 DISP 3.6.5A.

on' cases, ie, those which turn on the same findings required to determine the lead case. The Court of Appeal, in *R (Heather Moor & Edgecomb Ltd) v FOS*, approved FOS's approach to a complaint based on legal analysis of the relevant standard of care, and noted the need for FOS to be consistent in its decisions.

The determination of an Ombudsman must be made in writing, signed with reasons.[367] Any clerical mistakes may be corrected.[368] If accepted by the complainant, it is binding on the complainant and the firm—if rejected by the complainant it is not binding on either the complainant or the firm. Determinations may be accepted late if there are exceptional circumstances.[369] Following the 'N2 plus 2' review, the FSA confirmed there was not to be any right of appeal from an Ombudsman decision, which the Hunt Report supported and which remains the position. **7.135**

A decision may include a money award of 'fair compensation', an interest award, a costs award, or a direction.[370] The money award may include both financial loss and pain and suffering or damage to reputation or distress and inconvenience (including distress and inconvenience suffered during the course of the complaint).[371] The maximum money award is now £150,000[372] plus any interest and costs, although more may be recommended, including under a consumer redress scheme.[373] Where the complaint involves more than one firm, the Ombudsman may direct how the award is allocated[374] after investigating such connected complaints together.[375] **7.136**

After consultation, the FSA withdrew a proposal to cap amounts awarded for distress and inconvenience, but the usual amount is £150–£500. Awards of £1,000 or more are exceptional. FOS has published details of how such awards are usually approached.[376] The award may be for costs 'reasonably incurred by the complainant', and is not subject to the £150,000 cap,[377] but complainants usually do not require professional advice, and costs awards are uncommon.[378] A firm must comply promptly with an award accepted by the complainant[379] which is binding (or any earlier agreed settlement) and FOS must maintain a register of money awards and directions made[380]—as noted, a money award can be recovered or enforced with the courts,[381] and a direction can be enforced by injunction.[382] Reports of Ombudsmans' determinations will now be published.[383] **7.137**

367 DISP 3.6.6.R.
368 DISP 3.6.7R(1).
369 DISP 3.6.6.R (4A).
370 DISP 3.7.1R.
371 DISP 3.7.2R.
372 DISP 3.7.4R.
373 DISP 3.7.6G.
374 DISP 3.6.3G.
375 DISP 3.5.3G.
376 Technical Note: 'Compensation for distress, inconvenience or other non-financial loss' (July 2008).
377 DISP 3.7.9R.
378 DISP 3.7.10G.
379 DISP 3.7.12R.
380 DISP 3.7.7R.
381 FSMA, Sch 17, para 16.
382 ibid, s 229(9).
383 DISP 3.6.8G.

7.138 FOS is not able to direct a firm to pay redress, the cost of which exceeds the monetary limit. Before *Clark*, any such direction was understood to be subject to an 'implicit limitation that it will not be enforced' against the firm.[384]

7.139 In December 2003, the Board of FOS commissioned the Personal Finance Research Centre at the University of Bristol 'to carry out an independent assessment of the work of FOS'. The report, dated July 2004,[385] concluded that the 'case handling process' was 'both robust and fit for purpose. It complies with principles of due and fair process, and ensures that cases are considered on their merits'.

Voluntary jurisdiction

7.140 Unlike the DISP Rules made by the FSA prescribing the scope of compulsory jurisdiction, voluntary jurisdiction is subject to the 'standard terms' made by FOS, with the approval of the FSA, and set out at DISP Chapter 4, to which firms commit on a contractual basis.[386] In short, the DISP Rules otherwise applicable are generally extended for voluntary jurisdiction participants, including the complaint handling procedures of the firms themselves (at DISP 1), the rules and guidance (at DISP 2), and the complaints handling procedures (at DISP 3).

7.141 The exemption from liability in damages in Schedule 17 to the Act is included in DISP for the voluntary jurisdiction function,[387] and the provisions for the making of awards and their enforcement are similarly extended by the Rules.[388]

7.142 Firms may withdraw from voluntary jurisdiction, subject to satisfying FOS's conditions.[389] In particular, a firm must provide to FOS a written plan explaining how customers will be notified to offer withdrawal from voluntary jurisdiction and the continuing of handling complaints prior to this withdrawal, which plan must be approved by FOS. The firm must also be up to date in meeting levies and fees.

Funding

7.143 FOS's funding regime for its compulsory jurisdiction, consumer credit, and voluntary jurisdiction is in Chapter 5 of the FEES Module of the Handbook. Firms (including those under the consumer credit and voluntary jurisdictions) are to pay annual fees of a general levy and case fees, unless a firm is exempt (ie has no reasonable likelihood of conducting business with eligible claimants).[390] As such, large institutional firms, market counterparties, and the like do not contribute to the funding of FOS.

7.144 The raising of future levies will follow the approval by the FCA of FOS's annual budget.[391] FOS now notifies the OFT of the contribution for the consumer credit jurisdiction.[392] FOS publishes its plan and budget.[393] The approved budget for 2012–2013 was £191.1 million.[394]

384 *Bunney v Burns Anderson plc* [2007] EWHC 1240 (Ch).
385 'Fair and reasonable. An assessment of the Financial Ombudsman Service'.
386 DISP 4.2.1.
387 DISP 4.2.8R.
388 DISP 4.2.4–5R.
389 DISP 4.2.7R.
390 FEES 5.1.4R.
391 FSMA, Sch 17, para 9.
392 s 234 A(1).
393 Our plans and budget for 2013–2014, January 2013.
394 FEES 5 Annex 1R.1.

For 2013–2014, the FCA has approved a budget of £283.6 million.[395] Generally, firms pay both a general levy and case fees (but for consumer credit, different rules apply). FOS is about 80 per cent funded by case fees and 20 per cent by the general levy. Firms must contribute to the general levy.[396] It is consulted on by the FCA and FOS. The general levy is apportioned between firms according to the relevant 'tariff basis' and the extent of 'relevant business' of the firm, by reference to 18 industry blocks.[397] Firms with higher levels of relevant business generally pay a higher levy, although the methodology varies between industry blocks—some blocks pay a flat fee, others pay a variable fee calculated by reference to size and levels of business. The calculation of the general levy was based on information submitted by firms each year to the FSA (and was collected for FOS by the FSA).[398] The general levy for 2012–2013 was £17.7 million, net of £1.5 million from consumer credit firms[399] and will be increased to £23 million for 2013–2014, net of £2.3 million from consumer credit firms. In addition, under FSMA, there is a 'standard case fee' which is payable in respect of complaints closed by FOS including consumer credit complaints[400] and voluntary jurisdiction[401] and in FEES[402] This is to ensure that firms which generate complaints contribute proportionately higher amounts to FOS's costs, although small credit unions, cash plan heath providers, and small friendly societies are exempt.[403] The standard case fee[404] is consulted on each year,[405] and for 2013–2014 is £550,[406] and firms are only charged for the 26th (increased from the third) and subsequent cases in each year.[407] As a result FOS expect only 1 per cent of firms will pay any case fees,[408] but this is not for earlier financial years.[409] For PPI, a supplementary case fee[410] of £350 also applies, and for major banking groups (who provide 75 per cent of the caseload) an 'on account' system of special case fees[411] is charged.[412]

The voluntary jurisdiction firms pay under the 'standard terms'.[413] Consequential modifications are made to the FEES Rules.[414] There are nine voluntary jurisdiction 'blocks' applying a range of general tariff measures (eg for National Savings & Investments a £10,000 flat fee applies).[415] The case fee of £550 is the same. For the consumer credit jurisdiction, the contribution under section 234A may comprise the costs of establishing FOS for this purpose, **7.145**

395 FCA Consultation Paper CP13/1 (April 2013).
396 FEES 5.3.6R.
397 FEES 5 Annex 1R.
398 FEES 5.4.1R.
399 FEES 5 Annex 1R.2.
400 Sch 17 para 16c.
401 Sch 17 para 18.
402 FSMA, Sch 17, para 15; FEES 5.5.1R.
403 FEES 5.5.3–4R.
404 FEES 5.5.B.12.
405 FEES 5.5.B.11.G.
406 FEES 5 Annex 1.
407 FEES Annex 3R.
408 FOS Annual Review 2011/12.
409 FEES 5.5.15R.
410 FEES 5.5B.17.
411 FEES 5.5B.20.
412 FEES Annex 3R.
413 FSMA, Sch 17, para 18.
414 DISP 4.2.6R.
415 FEES Annex 2R.

FOS's operation of this jurisdiction, and 'collection costs'. The OFT imposes and collects the contributions from each relevant firm.

7.146 Whether the general levy, or a case fee, payment is to be made by a firm within 30 calendar days of the date of the invoice[416]—issued and collected by the FCA for the general levy or by FOS directly for case fees.[417] A fee and interest are charged for late payment.[418]

7.147 FOS may take steps to recover payment and refer non-paying firms to the FSA.[419] Both the FSA and FOS have the discretion to reduce or refund a fee if it is inequitable due to exceptional circumstances of a particular case but firms may not seek to recover any overpayment due to mistake after two years.[420]

7.148 New joiners to FOS receive a discounted general levy depending on which quarter of the financial year the firm joins. The fee is reduced by 25 per cent per quarter.[421] Departing firms remain liable to pay both standard and special case fees, and do not receive a refund of any general levy, except in exceptional circumstances.[422]

7.149 In its report, the Personal Finance Research Centre identified alternative methods of raising fees, including a tiered structure by reference to 'detriment' or charges linked to time spent on a case, but preferred the current system. In order to address the costs risks of resourcing FOS to handle PPI cases, the 'supplementary case fee' was introduced.

7.150 The Court of Appeal considered FOS's funding in the case of *FOS v Heather, Moor & Edgecomb Ltd*.[423] The Trowbridge County Court had found FOS's case fees to be 'unreasonable' and dismissed FOS's claim to enforce payment against a firm. On appeal, it was found that the rule requiring payment of the standard case fee was not unreasonable and not unlawful, so that if a complaint is investigated the case fee is properly payable. Stanley Burnton LJ commented that 'a system under which firms make a payment of a fee in respect of the services of the Ombudsman in investigating and deciding complaints against them is, in my judgement, a perfectly rational response to the need to fund the scheme'.[424]

FOS's experience

7.151 FOS's Annual Review for 2011–2012 confirmed the huge growth in the number of complaints to FOS. From 28,400 complaints, 340 staff, and a budget of £21 million reported for 2000–2002, FOS received 264,375 new cases (including 150,000 PPI cases) in recent years and 1,268,798 'frontline' enquiries, had 1,700 staff, and a cost base of £180 million in 2011–2012. It resolved 222,333 cases, making offers of redress in 64 per cent.

---

416 FEES 5.7.
417 FEES 5.7.2R.
418 FEES 5.5B.25R.
419 FEES 2.2.3–4G.
420 FEES 2.3.
421 FEES 5.8.1R.
422 FEES 5.1.6A.G.
423 [2008] EWCA Civ 643.
424 Stanley Burnton LJ also noted that the 'FSA rules require firms to deal with complaints fairly and effectively and a complaint to FOS is likely to be made only when a firm's response to a complaint is regarded by the complainant as unsatisfactory'.

FOS—past case management examples

The surge of cases in recent years has highlighted the role of Claims Management Companies ('CMCs') acting on a 'no win no fee' basis but receiving a sizable cut of any redress. CMCs accounted for 69 per cent of PPI cases in 2011–2012.[425] FOS has a MOU with the CMR, and has sought to agree processes with CMCs to facilitate case handling. 7.152

FOS has been faced with significant and difficult cases to resolve. Of the early caseload, the decisions regarding dual rate mortgages received much attention. FOS received complaints from borrowers whose lender was operating two 'standard' variable borrowing rates, and pre-existing borrowers were being placed on the higher of the two rates upon the expiry of fixed term mortgage deals. The lower standard rate was not being made available to such pre-existing customers. FOS dealt with these complaints by using the 'lead case' procedure. The decision against the use of dual standard variable rates led to mortgage lenders changing their practice. FOS determined the complaint by reference to what was 'fair in the circumstances of the case taking into account the law, the principles of the mortgage code, and good industry practice'.[426] 7.153

The uncertainties surrounding the Equitable Life Assurance Society Limited ('ELAS') also included a large number of complaints against that firm. By its 'lead' case procedure, FOS upheld a complaint from a guaranteed annuity rate policyholder (decision dated March 2005), clearing the way for 'follow-on' cases. In contrast, by a decision dated 22 March 2005, the Chief Ombudsman dismissed a batch of complaints regarding alleged 'over bonusing' by ELAS, as referred to by Lord Penrose.[427] Because of the number of complaints, and level of both policyholders' and public interest, FOS published the reasons for its decision to dismiss the complaints in this case. FOS noted that the issue had already been considered in detail by the FSA, that the complaints by policyholders would be better dealt with by the court, and that if successful, the outcome of complaints could have wider implications in terms of the company's policyholders and would have added to the 'turbulence affecting this aspect of the affairs of [ELAS] and its members'. The Chief Ombudsman exercised the discretion to dismiss the complaints without consideration of their merits. 7.154

Prior to PPI, Mortgage Endowment cases became the largest single source of complaints for FOS, totalling over 265,000 complaints. FOS published David Severn's report on the history of these complaints.[428] 7.155

In the light of the waiver from DISP granted to banks for complaints about unauthorised overdraft charges, in July 2007, FOS decided to put individual complaints on hold until the outcome of the OFT test case was known (except for hardship cases) as 'the law is one of the things that the ombudsman has to take into account when [FOS] decide cases. So [FOS has] decided not to continue our work on unauthorised overdraft charges until the legal position has been clarified'.[429] The decision of the Supreme Court in the bank charges litigation[430] meant that the FOS did not need to handle these claims in the same numbers. 7.156

[425] FOS Annual Review 2011–2012.

[426] FOS briefing note dated 12 September 2002.

[427] Report of the Equitable Life Inquiry by Lord Penrose printed on 8 March 2004.

[428] The Financial Ombudsman Service and mortgage endowment complaints, published by FOS on 29 May 2008.

[429] FOS FAQ on complaints about bank charges (updated 23 May 2008).

[430] *Abbey National Plc and others v The Office of Fair Trading* (2009) UKSC6.

7.157 FOS decisions on cases are also influential more widely. Firms are required to pay attention to FOS decisions by way of guidance, although FOS's approach to non-disclosure issues was adopted in the reforms of retail insurance law[431] and FOS's views on recoverable losses were referred to by the Court of Appeal in the case of *Rubenstein v HSBC Bank Plc*.[432]

Challenges to FOS

7.158 The statutory footing and responsibilities of FOS, its place in the regulatory architecture, and its dispute resolution function have been considered and upheld by the Court of Appeal and by the European Court of Human Rights—in litigation bought by a firm, Heather, Moor and Edgecomb Limited. In the Court of Appeal,[433] the firm challenged the decision of FOS on the following grounds:

a) on its true construction, Section 288(1) of [FSMA] requires FOS to determine complaints in accordance with the rules of English law;
b) 'that construction of [FSMA] is required in order to avoid an infringement of the [firm's] Convention rights under Article 6 and Article 1 of the First Protocol';
c) in the present case, the Ombudsman failed to apply the rules of English law, or to take them into account, but instead made a decision by reference to what he considered to be fair and reasonable. It follows that his decision falls to be quashed for error of law. For this reason, his decision was one that no reasonable Ombudsman could have made;
d) in any event, the Ombudsman should have held an oral hearing in public and he should have given his decision in public, but he wrongfully refused to do so.

7.159 The Court of Appeal dismissed the challenge. The reasons may be summarised as follows:

a) 'by use of the formula in Section 228, Parliament excluded that possibility';
b) the rules applied by the Ombudsman are sufficiently predictable... arbitrariness on the part of the Ombudsman including an unreasoned and unjustified failure to treat like cases alike would be a ground for judicial review;
c) 'the Ombudsman was entitled to reach this conclusion on the evidence before him' and had applied the appropriate test; and
d) 'in the present case, the court is concerned with a scheme under which disputes may be resolved quickly and with minimum formality, a consideration that justifies holding a public oral hearing only when that is necessary fairly to determine the dispute in question... So far as the requirement under Article 6 of a public hearing is concerned, there has been a public hearing before this court and a public hearing in judicial review proceedings is available to any complainant or respondent who considers that the Ombudsman has made an unlawful decision. More generally, where, as in the present case, a complaint can fairly be determined on written evidence and without oral submissions... given the nature of the jurisdiction and desirability of speedy decision and minimum cost with minimum formality, it is normally not necessary for the Ombudsman to hold a public hearing... the purpose of ensuring public scrutiny of the decisions of FOS is satisfied by the availability of judicial review proceedings in which any decision alleged to have been unfair or arbitrary or otherwise unlawful will be published. It follows that no breach of Article 6 has been established'.

---

431 Consumer Insurance (Disclosure and Responsibilities) Act 2012.
432 [2012] EWCA Civ 1184.
433 *R (Heather, Moor and Edgecomb Limited) v FOS* [2008] EWCA Civ 642.

Following the firm's unsuccessful judicial review of FOS, and having been refused permission to appeal to the House of Lords, the firm made an application to the European Court of Human Rights arguing that Article 6 had been violated, that FOS had wrongly refused to hold an oral hearing and had failed to deliver its decision publicly. It also complained that FOS was not independent or impartial and that the complaint system was not compatible with the rule of law. The complaints were rejected as 'manifestly ill-founded by the European Court on 14 June 2011.[434] 7.160

The European Court agreed with the conclusion of the Ombudsman and the Court of Appeal that an oral hearing was not necessary, and that decisions may be made on written submissions. The Court recognised that 'the holding of the hearing is not an absolute obligation' and in light of the statutory function of FOS to resolve 'disputes quickly and with minimum formality', in the light of the key consideration of the overarching principle of fairness, those requirements were complied with, by a process of written submissions, so the complaint did not necessitate an oral hearing before the Ombudsman. The Court of Appeal's hearing in judicial review reinforced 'the Court's conclusion that the absence of an oral hearing before the Ombudsman was not contrary to Article 6'. The Court also agreed that domestic proceedings and the Court of Appeal's judgment achieved the purpose of Article 6 in publicising the proceedings. Noting the 'fair and reasonable' approach of the FOS, the Court considered 'that the scope of the Ombudsman's discretion is not so broad as to automatically contravene the principle of foreseeability that is an integral part of the rule of law'. Further, the Court found 'no sign of any arbitrariness in the decision of the Ombudsman. It... found that the procedure conducted by the Ombudsman provided sufficient opportunity to the applicant to know the details of [the complaint] and to respond to it'. The European Court accepted that a legislative policy of providing a mechanism such as FOS to resolve disputes quickly and with minimum formality is not inappropriate to protect consumers in financial services. 7.161

On 21 May 2013, judgment was given following a separate challenge to FOS, by judicial review, on three grounds: 'the time taken by [FOS] to determine the claimant's rights at common law and under Article 6...'; 'the decision was taken without convening an oral hearing...'; and 'unfairness'.[435] The Court considered the roles of the Adjudicator, the Ombudsman, the service review manager, and the Independent Assessor. Taking the process as 'a whole', the judge did not find a breach of Article 6 rights, decided that 'it was extremely unlikely that an oral hearing would have assisted', and that the 'fairness' of the Ombudsman's approach was apparent. 7.162

The right to an oral hearing had been considered by the Court of Appeal in 2005.[436] The Court noted the Ombudsman had explained to the complainant there was 'ample material' to deal with the issue and that there was 'no entitlement as of right to an oral hearing'. The Court of Appeal accepted this position could not justify a judicial review. 7.163

An allegation of lack of independence or bias had also been made in proceedings on the basis that 'the legislative structure of FSMA indicated that the FOS lacked independence from the FSA'.[437] The Court noted the 'statutory provisions specifically provide for independence', did 7.164

[434] *Heather, Moor and Edgecomb Limited v United Kingdom* 1550/09 [2011] ECHR 1019.

[435] *The Queen on the application of Calland v Financial Ombudsman Service Ltd* [2013] EWHC 1327 (Admin).

[436] *R (Seoirse Treabhar Ropaigealach) v FOS* [2005] EWCA Civ 269.

[437] *R (Bamber and BP Financial) v FOS* [2009] EWCA CIV 593.

not find any 'unconscious bias by those who comprise the panel of Ombudsmen appointed', and further noted the availability of 'judicial review, independent and judicial scrutiny'.

7.165 As noted in the *Rubenstein* case,[438] the Court recognises the expertise of FOS in settling financial services disputes, and its statutory function in doing so. As FOS exercises a public function, and makes decisions based on a 'fair and reasonable' jurisdiction, a firm wishing to challenge a decision needs to overcome the threshold and test of judicial review proceedings. An applicant must show that the decision was illegal, procedurally improper, or irrational. A firm may fail to do so even if the Court accepts that the firm does not owe any legal liability to the complainant or that the Ombudsman has interpreted any relevant contracts and applicable code of practice.[439] The High Court in Northern Ireland noted that 'a Court should treat a decision of the [FOS] with respect and give it a reasonably generous margin of appreciation in order to reflect the particular expertise which the [FOS] has and which [FOS] will make use of in reaching any conclusion'.[440]

7.166 In the *Norwich & Peterborough Building Society* case the Court found that the decision of FOS had failed to take a material consideration into account but that the Ombudsman was entitled to exercise his own judgement as to fairness and in doing so had not acted irrationally. The Court did not impose its own view of fairness and the decision was upheld.

7.167 This test and outcome was confirmed in the case of *Green*.[441] The Court noted that the FOS's discretion 'is wide but must be exercised reasonably. The decision can be challenged by judicial review but in most cases (assuming no procedural unfairness or failure to follow particular law) will require any challenger to a decision to establish that it was irrational…'. In *Green,* the judge found that 'on the material before him, I do not think it is possible to determine that the Ombudsman's decision on causation was irrational'.

7.168 In *Cook*, a challenge to FOS on whether it reasonably refused a complainant's request to review an amount of redress previously awarded and accepted was also dismissed. The Court concluded that FOS could reasonably refuse the request on the basis the report did not constitute material new evidence.[442] It was clear that FOS could reasonably reach the conclusion it had not to review a determination in the light of further evidence.

7.169 The Court also referred to 'the width of the Ombudsman's duty to decide what is fair and reasonable, and the width of the materials he is entitled to call to mind for that purpose' in the PPI judicial review.[443]

7.170 It is clear that the Ombudsman's discretion allows an award of redress beyond damages a Court would have awarded. In *IFG*,[444] the Court confirmed that 'the Ombudsman is free to make an award which differs from that which a court applying the law would make, providing he concludes that the award he wishes to make is one which is fair and reasonable in all the circumstances of the case and provided he has taken into account matters identified in

438 [2012] EWCA Civ 1184.
439 *R v FOS ex parte Norwich & Peterborough Building Society* [2002] EWCA 2379.
440 *Walker's Application* (2013) NIQB 12.
441 *R (Green) v FOS and Others* [2012] EWHC 1253 (Admin).
442 *R (Cook) v FOS* [2009] EWHC 426 (Admin).
443 *R (BBA) v FSA and FOS* [2011] EWHC 999 (Admin).
444 *R (IFG Financial Services Limited) v FOS and Others* [2005] EWHC 1153.

Rule 3.8.1 paragraph (2)'. An award of redress was quashed by the Court in *Garrison*.[445] The Court found that, in that case, there was 'no logical connection between the redress ordered and the error found'. In short, the redress does not fulfil the aim set by the Ombudsman himself and is, therefore, on its face, irrational. FOS had applied a standard benchmark for the calculation of the award in that case, not suited to its particular circumstances.

The Ombudsman is entitled to rely on his own expertise in considering investment risks.[446] However, the Court noted that this may not be appropriate where the financial products were complex or their practical application was unknown, in which circumstances the Ombudsman would be expected to call on additional expertise. Following the failure of Lehman Brothers, the Ombudsman did demonstrate it may not need to adhere to the law of causation in determining complaints. The Ombudsman noted the possibility of significant financial institutions failing and 'the fact that there were (relatively) extreme market conditions in this case does not appear to me to justify a change in that approach'—this was then referred to in the *Rubenstein* case. **7.171**

As noted earlier, FOS has also successfully resisted challenges to its decision making on more procedural issues including the six-month time limit in which to make a complaint to FOS (in *Bankole*), and the test of 'eligible complainant' (in *Goff*). In *Bruce*,[447] the court upheld FOS's approach to dealings with partners of a dissolved partnership, where FOS had written to all partners but received comments from only one. The judge found that the partners were 'clearly on notice and clearly had plenty of opportunity to put its submissions'. This approach to dealing with one partner who communicates with others is now in DISP.[448] **7.172**

The two-year review, the Hunt Report, and the NAO Report

Although unchanged in essence since N2, the basis of FOS's role as the adjudicator of disputes has been reviewed and revised from time to time. Two issues were raised by the two-year review of FSMA in a joint consultation paper issued by the FSA and FOS.[449] **7.173**

The first issue was whether the decisions of FOS should be subject to an appeal, and the second was whether regulatory action by the FSA should replace decisions on individual cases by FOS. FOS already referred to the FSA issues with regulatory implications under the existing MOU, but this was considered further. The outcome of the consultation, reported in a joint FSA and FOS policy statement,[450] rejected the prospect of appeals but agreed there would be benefit in greater involvement of the FSA in cases with 'wider implications' and an improved process for test cases. **7.174**

This 'N2 plus 2' review took into account industry concerns that firms had no effective method of challenging decisions of FOS.[451] Firms expressed concern as to the binding **7.175**

[445] *R v FOS ex parte Garrison* [2006] EWHC 2466 (Admin).
[446] *R (Williams) v FOS* [2008] All ER(D) 35 (Jul).
[447] *R v FOS ex parte Bruce* [2007] EWHC 1646 (Admin).
[448] DISP 3.1.3R.
[449] Consultation Paper 04/12: 'FSMA 2 Year Review: Financial Ombudsman Service' (July 2004).
[450] FSMA 2 Year Review: 'Financial Ombudsman Service, Feedback on CP04/12 and supplementary FOS consultation on procedural rules' (March 2005).
[451] In HM Treasury's statement dated 4 November 2003, it was considered 'appropriate to examine whether Ombudsman decisions should be subject to some form of appeal in specific circumstances. It is vital that firms and consumers alike have confidence in the Ombudsman's decisions even when they do not like them' (para 36).

nature of FOS's decisions and the use of decisions as precedents which impacted on firms' future conduct. Further, challenge was accepted as being more difficult due to FOS's 'fair and reasonable' scope. The FSA concluded that not only would amendment to primary legislation be required to provide for an external appeals procedure but the current decision-making process of an adjudicator and Ombudsman, and the availability of judicial review, was adequate. Further, an appeal mechanism would increase FOS's costs and impede speed and informality. This was upheld by the courts and was unaltered by the 2012 Act.

7.176 This review identified that communications could be improved for cases with 'wider implications'. FOS and the FSA agreed to liaise to identify and understand such cases having regard to factors such as a large number of customers, a large number of firms, the financial integrity of a firm, interpretation of the FSA's rules or guidance, or common industry practice. The FSA would consider whether to comment on the interpretation or application of rules, whether the case raised material issues about existing FSA policy, whether to take action either to obtain (more advantageous) redress for consumers or for enforcement, whether the FSA's investigation was likely to be more effective and timely than FOS's process, and whether HM Treasury should be asked to authorise an industry-wide review (under section 404 and 404B of FSMA). Under FSA 2012, FOS may now refer larger-scale complaints to the FCA under Section 234D.

7.177 Under the 'wider implications' procedure, FOS wrote to FSA regarding the sales of PPI. By letter dated 1 July 2008, the Chairman of the FOS wrote to the Chairman of the FSA to alert FSA to its complaint-handling experience:

> Under the wider implications process we agreed to draw to each other's attention complaint issues that appear to us to have wider implications and where there may be a need for you to consider regulatory action to ensure that consumers who have suffered widespread detriment do not lose out. My Board considers it is appropriate now to draw formally to your attention under the wider implications process the issues arising from past payment protection sales.
>
> FSA's own thematic work and that of the Competition Commission suggests that large numbers of consumers who have (or have had) PPI policies may have been mis-sold. There is evidence of widespread and regular failure on the part of many firms to comply with FSA's rules and insurance law. In order for these consumers to receive redress it is inappropriate for them to have to make complaints individually to firms or ultimately to the [FOS]. Complaints may not be pursued by less confident customers, whilst large numbers of other complaints may be raised by customers who in practice have little prospects of success. Significant issues for customers and firms would need to be determined by the Ombudsman dealing with large volumes of disputes and acting in a manner some might perceive as quasi-regulatory. While the number of consumers who have made complaints about PPI to the [FOS] constitutes a substantial part of our caseload, it is apparent to us that this number constitutes a tiny fraction of those who would be entitled to redress. We are presently assessing the need for wider regulatory action in the light of the latest information about present practices.
>
> We intend to provide you with further information about our experience so that regulatory action can be designed to ensure that firms take appropriate and proportionate remedial action. It is of course for FSA, together if appropriate with HM Treasury, to decide exactly what regulatory tools should be used to bring about the required outcome. But my Board is in no doubt that simply allowing consumers individually to bring complaints is not the right way to tackle what is a systemic problem.

The FSA has stated that FOS's decisions are not about enforcing FSA Rules; they are 'about protecting the rights of consumers'.[452] For an issue with wider implications in which the FSA does not become involved, FOS may seek industry and consumer input. This might cover the wider context such as how widespread and longstanding the commercial practice in the market has been, why it was adopted, those affected (both firms and consumers), and their legitimate expectations, the relevant rules and codes of practice and generally accepted industry practice at the material time, consequences for the industry and consumers if the Ombudsman upholds or rejects a practice in an individual case, and the potential effect and practicability of different redress options. **7.178**

In 2008, Lord Hunt carried out, at the invitation of FOS, a review of FOS's relationship with consumers, the financial services industry, and other stakeholders. The Hunt Report made 73 recommendations. The core foundation of a 'fair and reasonable' decision, file-based reviews, no appeals, and no charge for complainants, were all approved by Lord Hunt. Lord Hunt called on FOS to refocus on its founding principles of speed, informality, and independence, and noted 'if my conclusions are accepted and my recommendations implemented, I believe that the demographic profile of those using the FOS should, must, and will broaden . . .'. The Court of Appeal in *Edgecomb* acknowledged that FOS should not be stifled by the imposition of legal doctrine, and that the recommendations of the Hunt Report 'can do much to allay any concerns, in any important area of consumer dispute resolution, about the values and principles of what we know by the expression 'the rule of law'. **7.179**

FOS welcomed the 'detailed and thought provoking report' noting that some of the recommendations 'involved innovative—and sometimes radical—departures from current practice'.[453] FOS published policy statements on accessibility and transparency setting out its **7.180**

---

452 FSA Policy Statement 07/16 (September 2007).

453 FOS press release dated 9 April 2008. The press release summarised the report as follows:

In his review, Lord Hunt concludes that:

the ombudsman's approach to settling disputes on the basis of 'what is fair and reasonable' is essential—to underpin the ombudsman's credibility as an informal non-legalistic alternative to the courts;

charging consumers to access the ombudsman—as some have proposed—would comprehensively damage accessibility;

there is no convincing case for an external appeals mechanism—on top of the ombudsman service's current internal appeals procedure;

there should be no change to the ombudsman's current approach to formal hearings (holding them only where absolutely necessary—as most disputes can be decided on the basis of paper evidence);

there is no requirement for a small firms' division—as long as the ombudsman's Small Businesses Taskforce continues to focus on the particular needs of small firms;

there should be closer monitoring and regulation of the activities of claims management companies;

there should be greater openness—in relation to the ombudsman's approach, the relationship between the ombudsman and the regulatory system, and the performance of individual financial services businesses in handling customer complaints.

Lord Hunt's review includes 73 specific recommendations for the ombudsman service, including:

significantly increasing investment in pro-active communications—including TV advertising, consumer campaigns and strategic partnerships with government and others;

commissioning a new consumer-friendly brand name instead of 'Ombudsman';

offering a freephone service (instead of the current subsidised 0845 number) and extended opening hours;

appointing 'case advisers'—working alongside adjudicators and ombudsmen —to guide the most vulnerable consumers through the complaints-handing process;

launching an awards scheme to identify and reward businesses who handle complaints well—matched by a 'wooden spoon' for the worst performers;

'decisions of principle' on these issues.[454] Responding to recommendations of the Hunt Report on accessibility, the policy statement reported, for example, that the FOS did not plan a name change, would consider the 'overall budgetary impact of providing calculations in compensation awards that involve a formula', and did not 'propose any changes to the status of ombudsman decisions—or to the current system involved in delivering ombudsman decisions'. The Policy Statement also considered numerous awareness and consumer proposals. On transparency, FOS decided that its 'published material will continue to focus on how we approached the kinds of complaints that we have actually received...' and 'so do not propose to publish what our approach might be to hypothetical future cases'; and that 'case reports that focus on key principles' will be published, to be integrated with an 'evolving online digest of [FOS] processes and approach'. Alongside the FSA's proposal to publish firms' complaints data, the FOS planned to publish 'information about individual businesses—both the numbers of cases and the proportion upheld'—but these measures have now been overtaken by the publication of decisions by FOS under FSA 2012.

7.181 Most recently, on 12 July 2012, the National Audit Office published its FOS report—'Efficient handling of financial services complaints'. The review did not address the legal and regulatory framework (under Parliamentary scrutiny in any event), but concentrated on complaint handling and efficiency measures—making five specific recommendations[455] and identifying volatility of demand as a key challenge.

Financial Services Compensation Scheme

Introduction

7.182 One of the aims of FSMA was to 'rationalise the existing arrangements through the creation of a single ombudsman scheme and a single compensation scheme'.[456] Part 15 of FSMA provides for the Financial Services Compensation Scheme ('FSCS'). In recent years, Part 15 has been amended by Part 4 BA 2009, a new Part 15A has been inserted into FSMA by FSA 2010, and there have been subsequent amendments to both Part 15 and 15A by section 38 and Schedule 10 of FSA 2012. As a result of the latter, from 1 April 2013, the FCA and the PRA have inherited the responsibility for setting the rules of the FSCS from the FSA.

7.183 The FSCS's role has been enhanced significantly in recent years, particularly as regards its role in the effective resolution of deposit-takers that get into difficulties. The provisions of the BA 2009 (notably Parts 2 and 4), together with supporting changes made to FSMA and the FSCS COMP Rules, are to enable FSCS to deliver a faster payout of deposit compensation, in particular to seek to pay the majority of depositors within seven days of failure.

---

publishing comprehensive information on all aspects of ombudsman policy and methodology (but not decisions on all cases)—as well as benchmarked data on how individual financial services businesses handle complaints;

placing all the ombudsman service's formal communication with the regulators on the public record.

[454] Policy statement: 'Improving service to our users: Our strategic approach to accessibility' (July 2008); Policy Statement: 'Our strategic approach to transparency' (July 2008).

[455] p 10.

[456] HM Treasury: 'Financial Services and Markets Bill: a consultation document—Part 1, overview of financial regulatory reform' (July 1998).

This follows the consultation by the authorities, commenced in 2007, following the run on Northern Rock. These changes to the FSCS are discussed further later in this chapter.

The FSCS replaced eight pre-existing compensation schemes or arrangements: the Deposit Protection Scheme;[457] the Building Societies Investor Protection Scheme;[458] the Policyholders Protection Scheme;[459] the Friendly Societies Protection Scheme;[460] the Investors Compensation Scheme ('ICS');[461] the PIA Indemnity Scheme;[462] the FSA's scheme covering 'Section 43 firms';[463] and the ABI Spouses and Dependants Scheme.[464] From 1 December 2001 to the summer of 2008, the FSCS had paid total compensation of over £1 billion, of which about £500 million was in the insurance sector, and £400 million for investment claims (including Pension Review).[465] In the banking crisis, from the autumn of 2008, FSCS then paid £23 billion to fund the transfers of deposit accounts. After events at Northern Rock in 2007, the nature and purpose of the FSCS had come under close scrutiny, which led in particular to FSCS's enhanced role from a financial stability perspective as implemented by the Banking Act 2009. **7.184**

As noted in HM Treasury's 1998 consultation, the regulatory system does not guarantee the solvency or survival of authorised firms, as repeated by the Tripartite Authorities in 2008.[466] In its early consultation,[467] the FSA noted that 'effective compensation arrangements for customers where individual firms authorised by the FSA are no longer able to meet their liabilities [to consumers of financial services' firms] will have a key role to play in achieving [the protection of consumers]'.[468] In addition to the consumer protection objective, the existence of a compensation scheme also supported the FSA's 'market confidence' objective. The CP noted that 'as well as providing protection in the last resort for consumers, the existence of compensation also helps to reduce the systemic risk that a single failure of a financial firm may trigger a wider loss of confidence in the rest of the financial sector concerned (eg through a run on deposit-taking institutions)'.[469] In the light of Northern Rock and the financial crisis of 2008, significant reforms were proposed to improve the compensation scheme from both consumer protection and market confidence perspectives, which are addressed below. From 1 April 2013, the compensation scheme is one of the means by which the FCA will meet its statutory objectives of securing an appropriate degree of protection for consumers and protecting and enhancing the integrity of the UK financial system. The compensation scheme is also one of the means by which the PRA will meet its statutory objectives of promoting the safety and soundness of PRA-authorised firms (by seeking to minimise the adverse effect that the failure of a PRA-authorised person could be expected to have on the **7.185**

457 Banking Act 1987.
458 Building Societies Acts 1986 and 1997.
459 Policyholders Protection Act 1975.
460 Friendly Societies Act 1992.
461 Financial Services Act 1986.
462 ibid.
463 ibid.
464 A voluntary industry scheme.
465 FSCS Annual Report 2007/08.
466 'Financial stability and depositor protection: strengthening the framework' (January 2008).
467 FSA Consultation Paper 5: 'Consumer Compensation' (December 1997) (CP5).
468 Para 1.
469 Para 11.

stability of the UK financial system) and its insurance objective of contributing to the securing of an appropriate degree of protection for those who are or may be policyholders.

The Scheme Manager

7.186 The structure of compensation arrangements under the Act is similar to that put in place for the scheme operator of FOS. The FSA originally established the Financial Services Compensation Scheme Limited, a company limited by guarantee, as the Scheme Manager. The Scheme Manager is to have a chairman and a Board, and its members are the Scheme Manager's directors.[470] The chairman and other members of the Board are appointed and removed by the FCA and/or the PRA (collectively, 'the Regulators'), with the approval of HM Treasury in the case of the chairman.[471] As previously explained by the FSA,[472] directors are recruited and sit as 'public interest members, not as representatives of a particular group or industry sector'.[473]

7.187 The FSCS is to be accountable to, but operationally independent from, the Regulators. The Regulators must ensure that the FSCS is 'at all times capable of exercising' its functions under FSMA,[474] but the appointment of directors is to be on terms 'such as to secure their independence from [the Regulators] in the operation of the compensation scheme'.[475] In CP5, the FSA previously explained: 'where the compensation arrangements are separate but still closely related to the regulator … this has the advantage of separating policy-making for the compensation arrangements, allowing the Board of the Scheme to concentrate on management of the claims process'.[476] Each of the PRA, the FCA, and the FSCS is required to take such steps as they consider appropriate to cooperate with each other.[477] Each regulator must consult the other before making the scheme rules. A new section 3E(3)(c) FSMA, inserted by section 6 of FSA 2012, requires the Regulators to set out in their MOU how they will exercise their functions in relation to the FSCS. As previously with the FSA, an MOU has been agreed (and published in April 2013) between the PRA and the FSCS and between the FCA and the FSCS respectively.[478] Before 1 April 2013, the FSCS published its annual plan on a voluntary basis, in addition to producing an annual report, publication of which is a statutory requirement under section 218 FSMA. Section 218 has been amended by FSA 2012 to allow HM Treasury to direct the scheme manager to comply with provision of the Companies Act 2006 dealing with accounts and audit which would otherwise not apply to it. A new section 217B FSMA requires the scheme manager to prepare and publish an annual plan, and requires it to consult on the plan as necessary. A new section 218ZA FSMA provides for the accounts of the FSCS to be audited by the National Audit Office. The National Audit Office carries out the audit functions of the Comptroller and Auditor General. The Treasury must lay before Parliament the certified accounts of the FSCS and the report of the

470 s 212(3) FSMA.
471 s 212(5) FSMA.
472 FSA Consultation Paper 24: 'FSA—Consumer Compensation: Further Consultation' (June 1999).
473 Para 7.3.
474 s 212(2) FSMA.
475 s 212(5) FSMA.
476 Para 64 of the FSA Consultation Paper 24.
477 A new s 217A FSMA.
478 See <http://www.fca.org.uk/your-fca/documents/mou/mou-between-the-fscs-and-the-fca>.

Comptroller and Auditor General. The Regulators exercise further oversight by fixing the amount of 'management expenses' which may be levied by the FSCS.[479]

The Scheme

Section 38 and Schedule 10 of FSA 2012 amended FSMA to provide for the Regulators to make rules to 'establish a scheme for compensating persons in cases where (a) relevant persons are unable, or are likely to be unable, to satisfy claims against them, or (b) persons who have assumed responsibility for liabilities arising from acts or omissions of relevant persons ("successors") are unable, or likely to be unable, to satisfy claims against the successors that are based on those acts or omissions'.[480] This set of rules, the Compensation ('COMP') Sourcebook in both the FCA and PRA Handbooks, is the 'Financial Services Compensation Scheme'. The PRA is responsible for rules relating to deposits and insurance provision, and the FCA is responsible for all other types of regulated activity covered by the FSCS (which is dealt with later in this chapter). The amendments to section 213 FSMA made by FSA 2012 provide for the Treasury to make an order specifying the cases in which the FCA may, or may not, make rules, and the cases in which the PRA may, or may not, make rules. The relevant order has been approved in draft by each House of Parliament.[481] **7.188**

'Relevant person' includes 'an authorised person at the time the act or omission giving rise to the claim against him took place' and 'an appointed representative at that time'.[482] 'Claims' is not defined by FSMA, but in the FCA/PRA Glossary (as 'a valid claim made in respect of a civil liability'). The Scheme is to deal both with the assessment and payment of compensation 'in respect of claims made in connection with regulated activities', and its funding with 'power to impose levies on authorised persons, or any class of authorised person'.[483] The further provisions in Part XV are not to limit the Regulators' general power to establish the Scheme.[484] **7.189**

Section 218A FSMA (as introduced by Section 176 BA 2009, and amended by FSA 2012) confers a power on the Regulators to make rules allowing them to obtain information that will assist the FSCS in carrying out its work, or in preparing for a possible need to pay compensation (even when no default is imminent). Section 219 FSMA provides the FSCS with certain powers to obtain information from authorised firms or certain other firms from the time the authorised firm could be declared in default for the purposes of the scheme. **7.190**

The FSCS may seek from a 'relevant person', in respect of whom a claim is made under the Scheme, 'specified information' or 'specified documents' where these are considered to be 'necessary for the fair determination of the claim' or alternatively 'to be necessary (or likely to be necessary) for the fair determination of other claims made (or which the FSCS expects may be made) in respect of the relevant person concerned'.[485] These powers may be enforced by contempt proceedings.[486] In addition, information may also be obtained from a person **7.191**

[479] s 223(1) FSMA.
[480] s 213(1) FSMA.
[481] s 429 FSMA; The Financial Services and Markets Act 2000 (Financial Services Compensation Scheme) Order 2013 (SI 2013/598).
[482] s 213(9) FSMA.
[483] s 213(3)(a) and (b) FSMA.
[484] s 213(7) FSMA.
[485] FSMA, s 219.
[486] ibid, s 221.

'knowingly involved in the act or omission giving rise to the claim' (but not generally from third parties holding information). It also allows the FSCS to obtain information from a bank which is subject to the special resolution regime (which is discussed later in this chapter), or from the Bank of England, to enable the maximum amount the FSCS would be able to contribute to the costs of the special resolution regime to be calculated. The FSCS has the right to inspect relevant documents held by insolvency practitioners[487] and by the Official Receiver.[488] In the context of insurance, the FSCS has an additional power. The administrator of an insurer which effects or carries out contracts of insurance shall, at the FSCS's request, provide any assistance identified by the FSCS as being necessary to enable it (a) to administer the compensation scheme in relation to contracts of insurance, and (b) to secure continuity of insurance in relation to contracts of long-term insurance.[489] More generally, the regulators and the FSCS may also disclose information to each other for the discharge of their respective functions.[490]

7.192 As with the regulators and FOS, the FSCS has statutory immunity under FSMA.[491] Subject to the same exceptions for acts or omissions in bad faith or unlawful as a result of section 6(1) Human Rights Act 1998, statutory immunity is provided for damages 'for anything done or omitted in the discharge, or purported discharge, of the Scheme Manager's functions'. The FSCS must, however, establish ECHR-compliant procedures 'for the handling of any complaints of maladministration relating to any aspect of the operation of the compensation scheme'.[492]

Provisions of the Scheme

7.193 FSMA allows for the COMP Rules to provide for the circumstances in which a relevant person may trigger the scheme; the type of eligible claimant and eligible claim; the procedure to be followed in making a claim; the making of interim payments; limits on the compensation amounts; and for payment to be made to persons other than the claimant, as well as for its funding by levy on authorised firms.[493] This is a non-exhaustive list. FSMA notes that 'different provision may be made with respect to different kinds of claim'.[494]

7.194 In contrast to FOS's regime under the DISP Rules, the FSCS operates five different 'sub-schemes', some of which are markedly different to the others. This reflects the different policy approaches towards different sectors of the financial services market. It is also a legacy of the pre-existing compensation arrangements; there are transitional arrangements for claims against firms which failed, or claims which arise in respect of acts or omissions which occurred, before FSMA took effect.[495]

487 ibid, s 220.

488 ss 220 and 224 FSMA.

489 The Financial Services and Markets Act 2000 (Administration Orders Relating to Insurers) Order 2010 (SI 2010/3023).

490 The Financial Services and Markets Act 2000 (Disclosure of Information by Prescribed Persons) Regulations 2001 (SI 2001/1857), as amended by The Financial Services Act 2012 (Consequential Amendments and Transitional Provisions) Order 2013 (SI 2013/472).

491 s 222 FSMA.

492 COMP 2.2.8R.

493 s 214(1) FSMA.

494 s 214(2) FSMA.

495 Financial Services and Markets Act 2000 (Transitional Provisions, Repeals and Savings) (Financial Services Compensation Scheme) Order 2001 (SI 2001/2967) as amended.

At 1 December 2001, the Scheme comprised three sub-schemes—accepting deposits, insurance business, and designated investment business. In these three sectors, the most active, pre-existing, compensation bodies were the Deposit Protection Board, the Policyholders Protection Board ('PPB'), and the ICS respectively. Each was set up independently from the other, in response to particular events or policy needs, and reflected the types of business protected by each, with differences in scope, the approach to claims, and levels of protection. Many of those differences are preserved within the FSCS. A further two sub-schemes have since been added, reflecting the increased regulatory responsibilities of the FSA previously, and now the FCA—the home finance mediation sub-scheme, with effect from 31 October 2004 (and now including home finance) and the general insurance mediation sub-scheme, with effect from 14 January 2005. For the same reason, the scope of the accepting deposit sub-scheme was also extended to include credit unions with effect from 2 July 2002 (and to include Northern Ireland credit unions from 31 March 2012), and the general insurance mediation sub-scheme was extended to cover 'combined travel insurance' from 1 January 2009.[496] **7.195**

When considering the application of the Scheme's rules, it is important to identify the relevant sub-scheme. **7.196**

The accepting deposits and designated investment business sub-schemes also serve to implement two European Directives—the Deposit Guarantee Schemes Directives ('DGSD'),[497] and the Investor Compensation Directive ('ICD').[498] The ICD notes that 'whereas the protection of investors and maintenance of confidence in the financial system are an important aspect of the completion and proper functioning of the internal market in this area; whereas to that end it is therefore essential that each Member State should have an investor compensation scheme'.[499] The Directives were initially implemented by the amendment to the Deposit Protection Scheme and the ICS. On 12 July 2010, the Commission adopted a legislative proposal for a thorough revision of the Directive on Deposit Guarantee Schemes and Investor Compensation Schemes. **7.197**

The review of the DGSD mainly dealt with a harmonisation and simplification of protected deposits, a faster payout, and an improved financing of deposit protection schemes. These proposed amendments follow urgent legislative changes that the Commission proposed in 2008 and that came into force in early 2009, which included a maximum harmonisation limit of €100,000 or non-Eurozone currency equivalent (the UK has set this at £85,000), and a requirement to pay depositors compensation within 20 working days.[500] The changes to the compensation limit and payout timescales were implemented on 31 December 2010. **7.198**

The review of the ICD is also concerned with the compensation limit, currently a minimum requirement of €20,000 (the UK has set this at £50,000), proposed faster payout, financing of investor compensation schemes, and possible extension of the scope of the ICD. **7.199**

---

496 FSA Policy Statement 08/4: 'Regulating connected travel insurance—feedback on CP07/22 and final rules' (May 2008).
497 1994/19/EC. See Chapter 3.
498 1997/9/EC. On the DGSD and ICD, see Chapter 4.
499 Recital 4.
500 Directive 2009/14/EC.

7.200 The review of the DGSD and ICD remains ongoing. As a result, when exercising its policy-making responsibility, the Regulators cannot put in place arrangements which do not satisfy the requirements of the directives, although in fact the FSCS offers greater levels of protection in the investment context. In July 2010, the Commission also issued a White Paper on insurance guarantee schemes ('IGS') which seeks to set out a coherent framework for EU action on IGS protection for policyholders and beneficiaries. In particular, it proposes introducing a Directive to ensure that all Member States have an IGS that complies with a minimum set of design requirements. The consultation period for the proposals closed on 30 November 2010. Subject to the terms of any such directive, if implemented, the FSCS insurance business sub-scheme may require amendment in order to comply.

The COMP Rules

7.201 There are 17 Chapters to the COMP Rules. The following paragraphs consider, in particular, the implementation in COMP of those possible provisions identified at section 214 of FSMA.

'The circumstances in which a relevant person is taken (for the purposes of the Scheme) to be unable, or likely to be unable, to satisfy claims made against him' (section 214(1)(a))

7.202 The purpose of the scheme is to be effective on the insolvency, or other inability (but not unwillingness) of an authorised firm to meet claims against it. Compensation may only be paid in respect of a claim against 'a relevant person who is in default'.[501] The 'default' process is set out at COMP Chapter 6.

7.203 Only a 'relevant person' may be declared in default. 'Relevant person' as defined by FSMA[502] is modified for the FSCS to 'a participant firm' (or an appointed representative),[503] which excludes incoming EEA firms which are credit institutions, ISD investment firms, or UCITS management companies, although the latter two may 'top up' into the FSCS (discussed further in this chapter). 'Participant firm' also excludes firms subject to the rules of the Law Society (England and Wales) or the Law Society of Scotland, which operate their own compensation arrangements, but other 'professional' firms (such as accountants and actuaries), authorised to carry on regulated activities under FSMA, are participants in the Scheme.

7.204 The COMP Rules transpose the 'unable or likely to be unable' test from FSMA, enabling the FSCS to declare firms 'in default' if so satisfied.[504] Further, if a 'protected claim' exists, the FSCS may determine a default following an insolvency event (eg a winding up, a court order appointing a liquidator, administrator, or provisional liquidator, or a company voluntary arrangement), or a determination by a 'home State regulator' of an inability of the firm to pay claims with no early prospect of being able to do so.[505]

7.205 For the designated investment business, home finance mediation and general insurance mediation sub-schemes, where the FSCS may receive claims against smaller 'high street firms', the FSCS has power to declare the firm in default if it is satisfied that the firm 'cannot be contacted at its last place of business and that reasonable steps have been taken to establish

501 COMP 3.2.1(2)R.
502 s 213(9) FSMA.
503 COMP 6.2.1R.
504 COMP 6.3.2R.
505 COMP 6.3.3R.

a forwarding or current address, but without success; and there appears to the FSCS to be no evidence that the relevant person will be able to meet claims against it'.[506] For example, where a sole trader has disappeared, and no evidence is available on which to be satisfied that the individual is unable, or likely to be unable, to meet claims, the FSCS may still declare the firm in default.

The COMP Rules also reflect the requirement of the DGSD and ICD that, for claims covered by these Directives, the default decision is by the competent authority (ie the appropriate regulator) or follows a judicial ruling that has the 'effect of suspending the ability of eligible claimants to bring claims against the participant firm'.[507] In practice, for larger firms, such as banks and insurers, the FSCS is likely to be triggered by a judicial ruling or other appointment of an insolvency practitioner. However, for smaller firms, such as credit unions and many IFAs, the FSCS carries out its own 'solvency' investigation before being able to declare a firm in default. **7.206**

If necessary, the FSCS has the power to fund insolvency proceedings by a claimant against a firm where it would help the FSCS 'to discharge its functions'.[508] **7.207**

Following a declaration of default of a firm, the FSCS 'must take appropriate steps to ensure that potential claimants are informed of how they can make a claim for compensation as soon as possible',[509] although there is no time limit on making applications to the FSCS. The FSCS is to publish information generally on the operation of the scheme.[510] **7.208**

'For a claim to be entertained only if it is made by a specified kind of claimant' (section 214(1)(f))

The FSA's (as the previous Regulator) view was that 'in general cover should focus primarily on private individuals and smaller commercial entities' to be available to those least able to sustain loss.[511] COMP Chapter 4 defines 'eligible claimant' by listing a table of exclusions.[512] These exclusions are directed to professional and governmental parties and reflect those permitted under the DGSD and ICD[513] including a size test for companies with a higher threshold than under DISP (in particular, a turnover limit of £6.5 million).[514] Individuals and small businesses are generally protected, although there are exclusions for those deemed to be connected to a firm which has failed, eg directors (as defined in the Glossary), or those 'who in the opinion of the FSCS are responsible for, or who have contributed to, the relevant person's default', although both these categories of claimant can be treated as eligible in specified circumstances (such as to achieve the efficient performance of FSCS's functions or if it would be, in FSCS's opinion, beneficial to the generality of eligible claimants).[515] Those with claims connected to money laundering transactions are also excluded. Claimants need not be UK residents. Other than if the specified circumstances set out at COMP 4.3.8R **7.209**

506 COMP 6.3.4R.
507 COMP 6.3.1(2)R.
508 COMP 2.2.4R.
509 COMP 2.2.7R.
510 COMP 2.2.3R.
511 CP5, para 83.
512 COMP 4.2.2R.
513 Annex 1.
514 Adopted from the Companies Act 2006 (Amendment) (Accounts and Reports) Regulations 2008 (SI 2008/395).
515 COMP 4.3.8R.

exist, there are no exceptions to the list of exclusions for claims under the designated investment sub-scheme or the home finance mediation sub-scheme. There are limited exceptions to the exclusions in the accepting deposits sub-scheme, in particular 'large partnerships'.[516] Following the financial crisis, for claims in relation to protected deposits, and for other protected claims from 1 October 2012, the FSCS's eligibility rules in respect of claimants have been simplified to ensure that the FSCS can pay compensation quickly and effectively.

7.210 Although there are no exceptions to the exclusions for the designated investment sub-scheme (unless the specified circumstances at COMP 4.3.8R exist), the COMP rules do permit in some circumstances a claim of this type to be made on behalf of an individual by an individual's pension fund, or by small employers' pension schemes.[517] Where a claimant may be a bare trustee or 'nominee company', the FSCS is to treat the underlying beneficiaries as having the claim.[518]

7.211 The position for the insurance business and general insurance mediation sub-schemes is more complicated. First, a 'small business' test[519] applies, as opposed to the 'large companies'[520] or 'large partnerships' exclusions. Further, to preserve protected status available under the Policyholders Protection Act 1975 ('PPA') for insurance contracts, all partnerships are eligible in respect of contracts entered into before 1 December 2001.[521]

7.212 All types (and sizes) of policyholder may be an 'eligible claimant' in the insurance business and general insurance mediation sub-schemes for claims 'in respect of a liability subject to compulsory insurance'. The defined compulsory insurances are under the Road Traffic Act 1988, the Employer's Liability (Compulsory Insurance) Act 1969, the Nuclear Installations Act 1965, and the Riding Establishments Act 1964, and their Northern Ireland equivalents. Accordingly, a company of any size with compulsory employer's liability insurance from a failed insurer may be eligible for protection from the FSCS. Albeit under the terms of the Policyholders Protection Act 1975 ('PPA'), the Court of Appeal considered the scope of 'in respect of' compulsory insurance in the context of a claim for defence costs under employers' liability insurance and concluded that those costs were included.[522]

7.213 The 'eligible claimant' exclusions generally apply to persons whose claims arise under the Third Parties (Rights Against Insurers) Act 1930[523] but this is modified for claims under general insurance contracts: if the policyholder himself would otherwise be eligible, so the third party will be;[524] the exclusion does not apply to claims under contracts of employer's liability insurance where the liability is or would have been the subject of compulsory employer's liability cover;[525] finally, if the liability to the third party had been agreed or established before the insurer's default, the third party will be eligible.[526] The adjustment for third parties'

516 COMP 4.3.1(1)R.
517 COMP 12.6.2AR.
518 COMP 12.6.2R.
519 Turnover of less than £1 million.
520 As above. Defined by reference to s 382 of the Companies Act 2006.
521 COMP 4.3.4R.
522 *R v FSCS, ex parte Geologistics Ltd* [2005] EWCA Civ 1905.
523 COMP 4.2.2(16)R.
524 COMP 4.3.5(1)R.
525 COMP 4.3.5(2)R.
526 COMP 4.3.5(3)R.

employer's liability claims provides a significant extension for these types of claims which are often for latent disease and therefore predate compulsory employer's liability insurance. The particular role of the FSCS in the handling of mesothelioma claims was addressed by HM Treasury and the FSA following the House of Lords decision in *Barker v Corus*.[527] Following consultation[528] the Transitional Order and COMP rules[529] were amended to allow the FSCS to contribute to employers' and 'live' insurers' settlements of such claims.

The insurance business sub-scheme is also divided between general insurance contracts and long-term insurance business. For long-term insurance business, the exclusions to eligible claimants are disapplied save for those connected to the firm in default, or its failure, or those whose claim arises from a money laundering transaction.[530] **7.214**

'A claim to be entertained only if it falls within a specified kind of claim' (section 214(1)(g))

The scope of 'protected claims',[531] reflects the five different sub-schemes. Generally a 'claim' requires the firm to owe the claimant a 'civil liability' (unlike FOS's 'fair and reasonable' approach). Although the Scheme is limited to certain activities under the scope of FSMA, compensation is not restricted to claims against firms for activities for which a firm had a permission. **7.215**

A claim may be 'for' a deposit,[532] or 'in connection with' investment business, mortgage business, or non-investment insurance mediation,[533] and the insurance business sub-scheme protects claims 'under a protected contract of insurance'.[534] **7.216**

A 'protected deposit' is a 'deposit', as defined under the Financial Services and Markets Act 2000 (Regulated Activities Order) 2001 (as amended) ('RAO'),[535] but extended for credit unions, made with the relevant person in the UK and, in certain circumstances, with an EEA branch of a UK firm.[536] Deposits in all currencies are protected. A bond issued by a credit institution as part of its capital, a secured deposit, a deferred share issued by a building society, and a non-nominative deposit are all excluded from protection.[537] **7.217**

For protected deposits, the FSCS was set up as a 'pay box' facility. It protects the balances of transactional and savings accounts. It does not protect claims concerning advice on deposit accounts or the arranging of deposit accounts. Nor does the FSCS have any role to intervene in the case of a failing deposit taker. However, as discussed later in this chapter, the nature of depositor protection and the FSCS's role has changed following the financial crisis of 2008. **7.218**

The designated investment business sub-scheme, the home finance mediation sub-scheme, and the general insurance mediation sub-scheme all protect claims for bad advice, including **7.219**

527 [2006] UKHL 20.

528 'Mesothelioma compensation: amending the Financial Services Compensation Scheme', September 2006.

529 COMP 4.4R.

530 COMP 4.3.2R.

531 COMP Chapter 5.

532 COMP 5.2.1(1)R.

533 COMP 5.2.1(3)–(5)R.

534 COMP 5.2.1(2)R.

535 SI 2001/544 (as amended).

536 COMP 5.3.1R.

537 COMP 5.3.1(2)R.

breach of Conduct of Business Rules (giving rise to a liability under section 138D of FSMA), as well as loss of funds.

7.220 'Protected investment business' comprises 'designated investment business'[538] which includes a range of regulated activities, such as advising, managing, arranging, agreeing to arrange (contained in the RAO), and investments (also defined in the RAO). 'Protected investment business' includes, for example, claims by investors against advisers for misappropriation of investments or funds, bad advice on the buying or selling of investments, or mismanagement of investments. The FSCS's scope exceeds the requirements of the ICD, which states only that 'each scheme must cover money and investments held by an investment firm in connection with an investor's investment operations which, where an investment firm is unable to meet its obligations to its investor clients, cannot be returned to the investor'[539] and applies to a limited list of 'investments',[540] and does not include, for example, long-term insurance products such as personal pension plans or endowment policies.

7.221 'Protected investment business' also covers the activity of a manager or trustee of an authorised unit trust and of an authorised corporate director or depositary of an open ended investment company, providing the claim is made by the holder of underlying units.[541]

7.222 The FSCS's role in the context of investments has the potential to change depending on the outcome of the independent review of the special administration regime for investment banks ('SAR') being conducted by Peter Bloxham. BA 2009[542] required the Treasury to review the 'Investment Bank Special Administration Regulations 2011' by February 2013, and required the review to be carried out by a person with expertise in the law of insolvency or financial services. The first phase of Mr Bloxham's review was completed in April 2013, taking into account in particular the experiences encountered in relation to the three firms to have been placed in special administration up to that date.[543] The interim report recommends further work to explore the issues identified. Mr Bloxham is coordinating closely with the FCA's own review of its client assets regime. A final report is expected to be made to the Treasury in the summer of 2013.

7.223 'Protected home finance mediation' follows the scope of the RAO and includes 'home finance transactions' such as advising, arranging, or making arrangements with a view to 'regulated mortgage contracts'.[544] In so far as 'arranging' is conducted by a 'mortgage lender', that is also protected. However, mortgage lending and mortgage administration are not protected, despite being regulated activities. After consultation, the FSA concluded it would 'not be proportionate or cost effective to include mortgage lending or administration within the scope of the Scheme'.[545]

---

538 COMP 5.5.1R.

539 Recital 8.

540 Previously defined at Art 1 by reference to the Investment Services Directive (93/22/EC) and now by the Markets in Financial Instruments Directive (2004/39/EC).

541 COMP 5.5.1(2) and (3)R.

542 s 236.

543 MF Global UK Limited, Worldspreads Limited and Pritchard Stockbrokers Limited.

544 COMP 5.6.1R.

545 FSA Consultation Paper 146: 'The FSA's approach to regulating mortgage sales' (August 2002).

The scope of 'protected non-investment [ie general] insurance mediation' refers to 'insurance mediation activities', defined by the RAO, in connection with 'relevant general insurance contracts' or 'pure protection contracts'.[546] These defined terms exclude reinsurance and aviation, marine, and credit insurance, for which individuals and small businesses are unlikely to need protection. Mediation of long-term care insurance contracts is dealt with as an 'investment' under the designated investment sub-scheme. 7.224

For insurance business, different rules apply depending on whether the contract of insurance under which a claim is made was issued before or after 1 December 2001. This is to preserve protection for claimants under contracts issued before FSMA came into force, who would have had an expectation of protection. There are also the particular arrangements in place for third party claims under employers' liability policies written before this insurance became compulsory. 7.225

The definition of 'relevant general insurance contract'[547] excludes certain classes such as aviation, marine, goods in transit, and credit insurance (although credit insurance was a protected class under the PPA). Reinsurance contracts are not protected.[548] With effect from 1 January 2004, insurance contracts issued after that date at the Society of Lloyd's are protected, although only in the event that the Lloyd's Central Fund is unable to meet claims to the FSCS level of protection.[549] Long-term insurance contracts are protected[550] whether issued before or after commencement. 7.226

For contracts of insurance issued before commencement, a claim is protected if made under a 'United Kingdom policy', as defined for the purposes of the PPA,[551] or certain employer's liability contracts. A policy is a 'United Kingdom policy' 'if, had any of the obligations under the contract evidenced by the policy been performed at the relevant time, such performance would have formed part of an insurance business which the insurer was authorised to carry on in the United Kingdom, whether or not such obligation(s) would have been performed in the United Kingdom'.[552] 7.227

The COMP Rules also require certain claims to be treated as liabilities 'under a protected contract of insurance', in particular claims for premiums paid to insurers for policies which have not commenced or the unexpired portion, third party claims under section 151 of the Road Traffic Act 1988 (where the insurer would otherwise be entitled not to meet a claim from the policyholder), and claims for the proceeds of long-term insurance contracts which have matured or been surrendered but which proceeds have not been paid to the claimant.[553] 7.228

'The procedure to be followed in making a claim' (section 214(1)(h) FSMA)

'Rules by virtue of subsection (1)(h) may, in particular, allow the scheme manager to treat persons who are or may be entitled to claim under the scheme as if they had done so' (section 214(1A) FSMA)

---

546 COMP 5.7.1R.
547 See definition in the Glossary to the FCA/PRA Handbook; COMP 5.4.2(3)R.
548 COMP 5.4.2(4)R.
549 COMP 5.2.4(5)R and 6.3.6R.
550 COMP 5.4.2(3)R.
551 COMP 5.4.5(1)(a)R.
552 *Ackman and Scher v Policyholders Protection Board* [1994] 2 AC 57, Lord Goff of Chieveley at 103–4.
553 COMP 5.4.7R.

'A reference in any enactment or instrument to a claim or claimant under this Part includes a reference to a deemed claim or claimant in accordance with subsection (1A)' (section 214(1B) FSMA)

7.229 The COMP Rules are largely silent as to the procedure to be followed by the FSCS when determining claims for compensation. The FSCS's process must be 'procedurally fair and in accordance with the ECHR'.[554] Following the FSA's Policy Statement PS12/15 in September 2012, claimants are no longer required to make an application for compensation if FSCS chooses to treat them as having done so.[555] This has been the position for deposits since the integral role the FSCS played in the financial crisis.[556] As well as facilitating the faster payment of compensation in circumstances such as a deposit-taker failure, this is additionally relevant to FSCS's role in relation to any of the stabilisation tools available for deposit takers under BA 2009. For example, the FSCS may be required by HM Treasury to contribute to the costs of any resolution tool,[557] such as the transfer of accounts of FSCS-eligible depositors to another bank. However, in practice, there will still be certain types of claim in respect of which the FSCS would require completion of a written application form (see further following).

7.230 Where, for example, the claim is for breach of conduct of business rules, the FSCS usually requires completion of a written application form from claimants, setting out the details of their personal and financial circumstances, the history of dealings with the firm and the basis of the claim for compensation and, in particular, a detailed description of the facts of the advice given by the firm to the claimant. In the event of an application containing 'any material inaccuracy or omission, the FSCS may reject the application unless this is considered by the FSCS to be wholly unintentional'.[558]

7.231 Payments of compensation may be conditional upon an assignment to the FSCS of a claimant's rights against the relevant person or third parties, and must be so in the context of deposits.[559] The FSCS's usual practice is to take a written assignment of rights. Following the rules introduced first only for deposit claims on 29 October 2008[560] and then for all protected claims on 1 October 2012, the FSCS has the option of taking an automatic assignment of, and/or be automatically subrogated to, all or any of the claimant's rights against the failed firm and against any third parties for all sectors other than insurance.[561] An offer of compensation may be withdrawn if it 'is not accepted or if it is not disputed within 90 days of the date on which the offer is made',[562] although any such offers may be repeated.[563] In the event that offers were made when they should not have been, the FSCS 'must withdraw any offer'.[564]

554 COMP 2.2.1R.
555 COMP 3.2.1AR.
556 Originally introduced in this context on 6 December 2009 in COMP 15.1.11R (since replaced by COMP 3.2.1AR).
557 s 214B FSMA.
558 COMP 8.2.1R.
559 COMP 7.2.1R.
560 COMP Chapter 15.
561 COMP 3.2.1A and COMP 7.3R.
562 COMP 8.3.1R.
563 COMP 8.3.3R.
564 COMP 8.3.4R.

For the designated investment, home finance mediation, and general insurance mediation sub-schemes, there are modifications to the 'civil liability' test. Where it is reasonable to do so, the FSCS may disregard a defence of limitation.[565] This also extends to claims under a consumer redress scheme.[566] Save for protected home finance mediation, the FSCS is also to ignore the fact a claim is extinguished by operation of law if solely as a result of the dissolution of the company against which the claim is made.[567] Claims which have already been dealt with by a firm under an industry review (eg the Pension Review or the FSAVC review) may also not be reopened.[568] 7.232

'The making of interim payments before a claim is finally determined' (section 214(1)(i) FSMA)

Payment of a claim is generally to be made 'as soon as reasonably possible' after the FSCS has calculated the amount of compensation due, which would follow the FSCS's determination of eligibility, and in any event (i) 'within 20 working days' in relation to a claim for a protected deposit unless the PRA has granted FSCS an extension, in which case payment must be made no later than 30 working days from that date;[569] or (ii) 'within three months' in relation to any other claim, although the PRA may grant a six-month extension.[570] This reflects the time for payment of compensation under the DGSD and ICD respectively, although the rule applies to all the sub-schemes. The rule does not require payments within a certain period of a firm's failure—the time period commences from the FSCS's calculation of the compensation amount. Other than for claims covered by the DGSD and ICD, the FSCS may pay a lesser sum in final settlement, if the amount of the claim is uncertain and it would be prudent to do so.[571] For all types of claims, a payment may be made 'on account' in similar circumstances.[572] 7.233

In the event that the claimant may have 'any reasonable prospect of recovery in respect of the claim from any third party or by applying for compensation to any other party', the FSCS may make a payment on account or pay a lesser sum in final settlement,[573] save for DGSD and ICD claims. Alternatively, for protected investment business or home finance mediation, instead of a payment on account or payment of a lesser sum, as the FSCS is the fund of 'last resort', payment may be postponed by the FSCS in these circumstances (again, with the exception of an ICD claim)[574] or where recovery may be made from the principal of an appointed representative.[575] 7.234

The FSCS may postpone payment of insurance business compensation where the liability is covered 'by another contract of insurance with a solvent insurance undertaking or where it appears that a person other than the liquidator may make payments or take such action to secure the continuity of cover as the FSCS would undertake'.[576] The payment of 7.235

565 COMP 8.2.4R.
566 COMP 8.2.4AR.
567 COMP 8.2.5R.
568 COMP 8.2.7R.
569 COMP 9.2.1(3)R.
570 COMP 9.2.1(4)R.
571 COMP 11.2.4R and 11.2.5R.
572 COMP 11.2.4R.
573 COMP 11.2.5R.
574 COMP 9.2.2(2)R.
575 COMP 9.2.2(1)R.
576 COMP 9.2.2(3)R.

compensation in respect of certain bonuses under long-term insurance contracts may also be postponed where uncertain but otherwise this compensation, and compensation in respect of liabilities subject to compulsory insurance, is to be paid as 'soon as reasonably practicable' (after the benefit has fallen due or the insurer was declared in default).[577]

7.236 Time for payment of compensation is also extended for claims subject to the Pension Review (ie subject to the Specification of Standards and Procedures issued by the FSA in October 1994, as supplemented and modified by subsequent guidance issued by the FSA), or subject to the FSAVC Review Model Guidance (issued by the FSA in May 2000).[578] This reflects the particular redress processes applicable to these two classes of claim for which the regulator has prescribed particular methods of quantification and payment of redress, which might not be achievable within a three-month timescale.

7.237 Reflecting the exclusion to 'eligible claimant',[579] claimants subject to pending money laundering proceedings may have payment of compensation postponed.[580]

'Limiting the amount payable on a claim to a specified maximum amount or a maximum amount calculated in a specified manner' (section 214(1)(j) FSMA)

'Rules by virtue of subsection (1)(j) may, in particular, allow, or be subject to rules which allow, the scheme manager to settle a class of claim by payment of sums fixed without reference to, or by modification of, the normal rules for calculation of maximum entitled for individual claims' (section 214(1C) FSMA)

7.238 Compensation for protected deposits, protected investment business, and protected home finance mediation is subject to a maximum sum, per claimant, per firm.[581] For protected deposits the limit is now £85,000.[582] A maximum payment of £50,000 is provided for the other two sub-schemes.[583] Interest may be paid, which is not taken into account when applying these limits.[584]

7.239 For insurance business and general insurance mediation claims, compensation is generally payable to 90 per cent of the claim, without limit, but compensation in respect of a liability subject to the compulsory insurances is in full (although third party claims for pre-compulsory employer's liability are protected to 90 per cent). The absence of a limit reflects the exposure of an individual or small business to the type of loss for which insurance might have been purchased. The amount of a claim under an insurance policy may be disproportionate to the premiums paid and exceed the means of the policyholder, for example the cost of rebuild and repair to a house. The unlimited level of compensation is available for claims against both insurers and brokers, as the failure of a broker to arrange suitable (or any), say, home insurance, can have consequences for the client equally drastic as the failure of the insurer to meet the claim. Further, 'enhanced' protection to 100 per cent is provided by the FSCS

[577] COMP 9.2.2(6)R, COMP 12.4.11AR and COMP 12.4.9R.
[578] COMP 9.2.2(4)R.
[579] COMP 4.2.2R.
[580] COMP 9.2.2(5)R.
[581] COMP 10.2.3R.
[582] From 31 December 2010.
[583] From 1 January 2010.
[584] COMP 11.2.7R and 11.2.8R.

for an insurer's periodical payments, under section 101 of the Courts Act 2003 (extending section 4 of the Damages Act 1996).

7.240 The absence of a cap for insurance claims means that compensation from the FSCS may exceed the award which FOS might make (which is limited to £150,000).

7.241 Each claimant is entitled to his own compensation limit. Unless a bare trust, a trust is a single claimant irrespective of the number of beneficiaries and the compensation payable to a trust may be adjusted if not all the beneficiaries would be 'eligible claimants'.[585] Clients with funds in a client account are entitled to make compensation claims for their own share.[586] Each person sharing a joint claim is entitled to his or her own maximum compensation limit, and joint claims are presumed to be equal in the absence of evidence to the contrary,[587] although claims by a business trading in partnership are treated as one claim and therefore only one limit is available.

7.242 Initially introduced only in respect of claims for protected deposits on 31 December 2010, but then extended to all types of claim, the FSCS has the ability to pay compensation without investigating one (or all) of: the eligibility of the claimant; the validity of the claim; and the amount of the claim, if the costs of the investigation are disproportionate to the benefits.[588] This rule is likely (although not exclusively) to be most often deployed in cases where the claims presented to the FSCS are of a 'high volume/low value' nature.

Quantification

7.243 The quantification of claims for compensation is dealt with at COMP Chapter 12. Compensation, other than in respect of a claim for a protected deposit, is paid in respect of an 'overall net claim', ie after taking account of any other payments the claimant might have received from the firm, the FSCS, or any third party, and after application of 'set off'.[589] Such amounts are deducted from the total claim, not the amount of compensation. For claims in relation to protected deposits, compensation payments are made on an 'overall gross basis', as one of the suite of measures introduced following the financial crisis to ensure a more streamlined claims' process and so enable a faster pay-out.[590] Once satisfied the conditions for a claim have been met, the FSCS is to calculate the amount of compensation 'as soon as reasonably possible'.[591]

7.244 Claims for protected deposits are quantified at the date of default.[592] Following the financial crisis, one of the suite of measures introduced by the FSA as a result of Policy Statement PS09/11: 'Banking and compensation reform' dated July 2009, implemented from 31 December 2010, included the regulatory obligation upon deposit-takers to be able to provide a 'Single Customer View'. This, in turn, enables the FSCS to have ready access to, and within 72 hours of a default, a reliable and consistent view of aggregate deposits for each eligible depositor per authorised deposit-taker and thereby ensure a fast payout and at least

585 COMP 12.6.5R.
586 COMP 12.6.7R.
587 COMP 12.6.10R.
588 COMP 12.2.10R.
589 COMP 12.2.1 and 12.2.4R.
590 COMP 12.2.1(2)R and 12.2.6AR.
591 COMP 12.2.8R.
592 COMP 12.3.1R.

within the DGD's requirement of 20 business days.[593] Other changes implemented by the FSA at the same time, and as discussed earlier in this chapter, included: simplifying the eligibility criteria for FSCS payments; allowing gross payment to be made; providing liquidity to the FSCS; streamlining the claims' process; and raising consumer awareness of the FSCS (in particular, by requiring deposit-takers to advertise information about FSCS and its role).[594]

7.245 For protected investment business, home finance mediation, and general insurance mediation, the FSCS has discretion as to the date at which claims are quantified[595] (save that the category of an 'ICD claim' must be quantified as at the date of the firm's default).[596] To avoid uncertainty and detriment to claimants affected by defaults where the underlying value of their investment remains uncertain, the FSCS has additional flexibility to pay full compensation and disregard the residual value of the investment for defaults on or after 1 October 2012. The rule at COMP 11.2.9R means that the FSCS still first tries to pay compensation in the normal way for the loss the investor has suffered. However, if this is not possible because there are problems establishing the underlying value of the investment, the FSCS must conclude that it would not be appropriate to pay the investor less than the full compensation in a final settlement or make a payment on account. It is only then that it can pay compensation, in return for an assignment of rights against the firm in default and/or any third party, without taking the residual value of the investment into account.

7.246 Claims for return of property or in respect of uncompleted transactions are compensated to the extent of the investor's loss. For other claims in these three sub-schemes (eg claims for bad advice), the FSCS 'may pay compensation for any claim... only to the extent that the FSCS considers that the payment of compensation is essential in order to provide the claimant with fair compensation'.[597] This rule gives the FSCS discretion to develop and apply its own methods or bases of quantification. The FSCS is not obliged to follow the assessment of damages which a court would undertake.

7.247 The wording of this rule reflects a previous rule applicable to claims to ICS. In *R v Investors Compensation Scheme, ex parte Bowden*,[598] the House of Lords considered the interpretation of that ICS Rule. In short, when quantifying the relevant investors' claims, ICS had deducted the amount of the 'benefit' (or income) investors had received as a result of the authorised firm's advice and limited the recovery of professional fees. Whether or not such deductions would have been followed by a court when assessing damages for those claims, the House of Lords was satisfied that ICS had the discretion to determine its own basis of compensation which did not need to match the damages a court would award. Lord Lloyd of Berwick found 'a broad discretion to include within the definition of a compensatable claim either the claim as a whole, or those elements of the claim which the management company considers essential in order to provide fair compensation and to exclude those elements which do not meet that requirement'.[599] Accordingly, for 'advice' claims, the FSCS's approach is to determine what it considers to be a reasonable basis to provide 'fair

593 COMP Chapter 17.
594 COMP Chapter 16.
595 COMP 12.3.5R, 12.3.7R, and 12.3.8R.
596 COMP 12.3.6R.
597 COMP 12.4.2R, 12.4.17R, and 12.4.20R.
598 [1995] 3 All ER 605.
599 At 611.

compensation'. The House of Lords also confirmed that it was legitimate to develop policies for the quantification of classes of claim of a similar type. Notwithstanding the broad discretion afforded to FSCS, Mr Justice Haddon-Cave, in the Judicial Review case of *Emptage*, concluded that there had been a 'package' of advice, by linking the investment advice with the mortgage advice in that case, resulting in the FSCS, in the judge's view, not awarding the claimant 'fair compensation'.[600] The FSCS appealed this decision. Although the Court of Appeal recognised the FSCS's broad discretion to decide how fair compensation is to be assessed and to develop policies in that regard, it dismissed the appeal on the basis that the FSCS had departed from its own policy in determining what constituted 'fair compensation' in the circumstances of that case.

Certain losses are excluded from compensation in the investment sub-scheme if they relate to or depend on: [1] a failure of investment performance to match a guarantee given or representation made; or [2] a contractual obligation to pay or promise to pay which the FSCS considers to have been undertaken without full consideration passing to the relevant person or in anticipation of possible insolvency; or [3] the mere fluctuation in the value of an investment.[601] Similar (appropriately adjusted) exclusions apply to claims for protected home finance mediation.[602] **7.248**

Compensation for investment business claims may also be reduced if the FSCS is satisfied of contributory negligence on the part of the claimant or where 'payment of the full amount would provide a greater benefit than the claimant might reasonably have expected or than the benefit available on similar investments with other relevant persons', which it would be inequitable for the FSCS to ignore.[603] Because these provisos are not in the ICD, they cannot be applied to that class of claim. Further, neither this nor the general discretion on the method of quantification is available to claims covered by either the Pension Review or FSAVC Review, for which redress is to be calculated in accordance with the regulatory guidance[604] nor in the context of claims which fall to be dealt with (or have properly been dealt with) under a consumer redress scheme.[605] In contrast to DISP, which appends the methodology for the quantification of claims for endowment mis-selling, the FSA guidance for the quantification of those claims is not referred to in the COMP Rules. **7.249**

As well as the 'essential in order to provide the claimant with fair compensation' discretion, compensation for mortgage advice and arranging or general insurance mediation may also be reduced for contributory negligence and in general insurance mediation for 'excessive benefits'.[606] **7.250**

Reflecting the predecessor scheme, the nature of payments by the FSCS in the insurance business sub-scheme is as much about 'protection' as 'compensation'. In addition to the compensation function, there is the objective of continuity of insurance, both for long-term and general insurers. Compensation 'may not necessarily be enough to enable [long term] **7.251**

[600] *R (on the application of Charmaine Emptage) v The Financial Services Compensation Scheme Limited* (Case no CO/3196/2011).
[601] COMP 12.4.3R.
[602] COMP 12.4.18R.
[603] COMP 12.4.8R.
[604] COMP 12.4.6R, 12.4.7R.
[605] COMP 12.4.22R.
[606] COMP 12.4.19R and 12.4.21R.

policyholders to find alternative cover' and general insurance claims can have a long tail resulting in costs and delays for policyholders. Compensation is payable if continuity is not achieved.[607]

7.252 The provisions for continuity are derived from sections 216 and 217.[608] For long-term insurance, the FSCS 'must make arrangements to secure continuity of insurance',[609] which may comprise the transfer of business or the issue of substitute policies.[610] Continuity for long-term insurance policyholders is only to be provided where it is 'reasonably practicable' and if, in the opinion of the FSCS at the time it proposes to make the arrangements, the cost is justified by the benefits.[611] The obligation to consider continuity for a long-term insurer is triggered by insolvency proceedings,[612] not by the FSCS exercising any discretion or making any assessment of 'unable or likely to be unable' to pay claims. The level of protection is limited to 90 per cent of benefits under the contracts, with future premiums to be adjusted accordingly.[613]

7.253 Whether the FSCS can arrange continuity will depend on a number of factors including the state of the insurer itself and identifying a willing transferee for the business. Whilst investigating or pursuing continuity, the FSCS is to meet 90 per cent of the benefits falling due under the insurer's long term contracts.[614] Recognising the involvement of an insolvency practitioner, and the possibility that continuity may be required to meet short-term cash flow needs, claims falling due may in fact be funded by the insolvency practitioner with the benefit of an indemnity from the FSCS (which option is also available for a compensation payout).[615] Benefits falling due do not include bonuses unless 'declared and vested' before the date of trigger for the FSCS.[616] Further, benefits which the FSCS considers are 'excessive' are also not protected.[617] However, continuity must be provided for benefits not yet determined to be excessive, even if under investigation by the FSCS, unless the claim for protection (ie the benefit falling due) 'arises out of the exercise of any option under the policy'.[618]

7.254 Although expressed as a power ('may') rather than an obligation ('must'), for an insurance undertaking 'in financial difficulties', the COMP Rules make similar provision for continuity, for both general and long-term insurance.[619] In addition to transfers of the business, or the issue of substitute policies, the additional measure of 'assistance to the relevant person to enable it to continue to effect contracts of insurance or carrying out contracts of insurance' is included.[620] The FSCS may therefore fund payments by the insurer. This might be implemented under the terms of a scheme of arrangement. Again, a 'costs test' applies.[621]

---

607 COMP 3.2.1(4)R.
608 COMP 3.3R.
609 COMP 3.3.1R.
610 COMP 3.3.2R.
611 COMP 3.3.1(3)R.
612 COMP 3.3.1(1)R.
613 COMP 3.3.2A and 3.3.2B.
614 COMP 3.3.2C.
615 COMP 3.3.2C(4)R.
616 COMP 3.3.2D(1)R.
617 COMP 3.3.2D(2)R.
618 COMP 3.3.2E.
619 COMP 3.3.3R and 3.3.6R.
620 COMP 3.3.4(2)R.
621 COMP 3.3.3(1)R and 3.3.7R.

This continuity regime reflects section 216 FSMA, which provides for continuity of long-term insurance policies, and section 217, which deals with insurers in financial difficulties. These two sections, in turn, followed the approach of the PPA.[622] 7.255

In the event that continuity of insurance cannot be achieved, the FSCS may pay compensation. As for all sub-schemes (other than in respect of protected deposits), compensation is payable on the 'overall net claim',[623] allowing deduction of liabilities owed by policyholders to the insurer. The FSCS must determine a specific quantification date for a claim.[624] 7.256

Compensation for claims under general insurance contracts are to be calculated in respect of a liability subject to compulsory insurance or 'in accordance with the terms of the contract',[625] and for long-term insurance contracts 'in accordance with the terms of the contract as valued in the liquidation' (to which the Insurers (Winding Up) Rules 2001 currently apply), or in the absence of a liquidation valuation, 'in accordance with such reasonable valuation techniques as the FSCS considers appropriate' to include benefits fallen due and bonuses to which a value has been or is likely to be attributed.[626] Long-term insurance contract compensation may be adjusted by the FSCS for any 'excessive benefit', defined as a benefit 'no reasonable and prudent insurer in the position of the relevant person would have so decided given the premiums payable and other contractual terms'.[627] 7.257

Such reduction to or disregard of a claim may only be made following an actuary's written recommendation.[628]

'For payment to be made, in specified circumstances, to a person other than the claimant' (section 214(1)(k) FSMA)

Generally, payment is to be made to the claimant 'or as directed by the claimant'.[629] Pension Review compensation must usually be paid to the trustee of an occupational pension scheme or to a personal pension scheme or other product provider (or both).[630] The COMP Rules expressly allow for payments to be made other than to the eligible claimant, for example to personal representatives or beneficiaries of a trust.[631] Similarly, those entitled to funds held on client account are regarded as the claimant, rather than the firm in whose name the account is held.[632] The COMP Rules make clear that claims by personal representatives, agents, or trustees, are distinct from the individual acting in that capacity.[633] The FSCS may pay compensation in any form and by any method (or any combination of them) that it determines is appropriate, including (without limitation) directly to an authorised deposit-taker or, in cases involving a client money shortfall, directly to a firm taking over the business rather than to the individual clients.[634] 7.258

622 PPA, ss 11 and 16.
623 COMP 12.2.1R and COMP 12.2.4R.
624 COMP 12.3.2R.
625 COMP 12.4.9R and 12.4.10R.
626 COMP 12.4.11R, 12.4.11AR, and 12.4.12R.
627 COMP 12.4.13R.
628 COMP 12.4.14R.
629 COMP 11.2.1AR.
630 COMP 11.2.2R.
631 COMP 3.2.2R.
632 COMP 12.6.7R.
633 COMP 12.6.1R.
634 COMP 11.2.3AR.

'The scheme may provide for the determination and regulation of matters relating to the scheme by the scheme manager' (section 214(3) FSMA)

7.259 Claimants are not required to be legally represented and the FSCS does not meet the costs of representation. In assessing claims, the FSCS will have regard to all available evidence, such as contemporaneous client files and information provided by the firm in default, as well as the claimant's evidence. The FSCS has specific power to deal with claims under an insurance policy where it is not 'evidenced by a policy'.[635]

7.260 The FSCS is to be procedurally fair and act in accordance with the ECHR. The recourse for discontented claimants, once the FSCS's internal review procedure has been exhausted, is by judicial review. This meets the requirement of the ICD that 'Member States shall ensure that an investor's right to compensation may be the subject of an action by the investor against the compensation scheme' (Article 13). There is no external 'appeal' procedure.

7.261 Recent cases have confirmed that judicial review is the appropriate method of challenge and highlights the deference which the courts will show to expert decision makers in difficult technical or policy matters. Beatson J commented that: 'the primary decision maker is likely to have developed an expertise' and that the courts would be reluctant to interfere with a decision unless it is 'so aberrant that it cannot be classed as rational'.[636]

'Specified territories, areas, or localities' (section 214(4) FSMA)

7.262 Dealings in the UK with an authorised firm are generally protected. Deposit, investment, and general insurance mediation protection is extended to 'passporting' firms under the home State principle, ie claims against a UK-authorised firm, exercising an EEA right to trade in another EEA State, will be protected by the FSCS to the extent that the claim is covered by the scope of the DGSD or ICD or IMD respectively.[637] Protected home finance mediation depends on the customer being a UK resident, or the firm's establishment being in the UK,[638] as well as the relevant property being in the UK (under the Glossary definition of 'regulated mortgage contract').

7.263 The ICD also provides for incoming EEA firms to be able to 'top up' the level of compensation offered by their home States by joining the FSCS. The minimum level of compensation under the ICD is €20,000. As a result, for example, investment firms from those Member States opening branches in the UK may elect to top up the level of protection available to investors with the UK branches by joining the FSCS, so that their customers will receive the same limit of protection as customers of UK investment firms, albeit the first €20,000 would be met by the home State scheme, and the remainder by the FSCS. Incoming EEA firms may elect to participate in the FSCS,[639] and under the Electing Participants Regulations,[640] topping up is available to MiFID investment firms, UCITS management companies, or IMD insurance intermediaries who establish UK branches in the exercise of an EEA right.[641] When subsequently quantifying compensation, the FSCS must 'take account of the liability

635 COMP 5.4.6R.

636 *R v FSCS, ex parte ABS Financial Planning Ltd and others* [2011] EWHC 18 (Admin).

637 COMP 5.3R, 5.5R, and 5.7R.

638 COMP 5.6.2R.

639 s 213(10) FSMA.

640 Financial Services and Markets Act 2000 (Compensation Scheme: Electing Participants) Regulations 2001, SI 2001/1783.

641 COMP 14.2R.

of' the home State scheme.[642] If preferred, for reasons of expediency or otherwise, FSMA allows for rules to enable the FSCS to make the full payment of compensation, including that portion due from an overseas scheme, facilitating a single payment to claimants, and then recover that cost from the overseas scheme (although this section could apply to other governmental schemes).[643]

For the insurance business sub-scheme, the geographical location of risk is relevant to whether a claim is protected. The COMP Rules implemented the changes in the Policyholders Protection Act 1997, so that if the contract was issued (i) in the UK, risks in the UK, the EEA, and the Channel Islands and the Isle of Man are protected; (ii) in another EEA State, only risks in the UK are protected; and (iii) in the Channel Islands or Isle of Man, risks in the UK, the Channel Islands, or the Isle of Man are protected.[644] How to determine the situation of a risk is addressed by the COMP Rules.[645] Policies issued by EEA branches of UK insurers are also covered. **7.264**

Recovery/funding of cost of compensation

The FSCS is funded by a levy on regulated firms. To mitigate the cost of compensation, the FSCS seeks to recover from firms in default and third parties in respect of claims paid.[646] **7.265**

Many firms declared in default are subject to formal insolvency proceedings. Having taken an assignment of, or been automatically subrogated to, claimants' legal rights following the payment of compensation, the FSCS has rights to participate in insolvency proceedings of authorised firms. This recognises the FSCS's position as a likely creditor of such firms, often becoming the largest single creditor once compensatable claims have been paid. **7.266**

The rights to participate in insolvency proceedings no longer include those provided to the Deposit Protection Board,[647] which had preferred rights to receive dividends on all the claims of compensated depositors, not just the compensated claim. However, the FSCS does have the benefit of the priority afforded to policyholders or direct insurance creditors of insolvent insurers.[648] **7.267**

The Independent Commission on Banking, chaired by Sir John Vickers, published its final report in September 2011.[649] As part of this report it recommended 'In insolvency (and so also in resolution), all insured depositors should rank ahead of other creditors to the extent that those creditors are either unsecured or only secured with a floating charge'. On 19 December 2011 the Government published its response to the report by the Independent Commission of Banking, including to the recommendations around depositor preference: 'On balance, the Government supports depositor preference. However, the Government believes that further analysis and consultation is needed on the scope—in particular on the relative merits **7.268**

[642] COMP 12.4.1R and 12.4.4R.
[643] s 214(6) FSMA and COMP 15R.
[644] COMP 5.4.3R.
[645] COMP 5.4.4R.
[646] s 215 FSMA.
[647] Banking Act 1987, s 58.
[648] Under reg 32 of the Insurers (Reorganisation and Winding Up) Regs 2004, SI 2004/353, implementing the EC Directive on the reorganisation and winding up of insurance undertakings (2001/17/EC).
[649] On the ICB report, see Chapter 1, paras 1.65 and 1.79 and Chapter 14, paras 14.242–14.248.

of limiting depositor preference to insured deposits, as opposed to extending it to either all deposits, or a different subset'.

7.269 In June 2012, HM Treasury published 'Banking reform: delivering stability and supporting a sustainable economy', in which it considered further the issue of depositor preference and recommended the adoption of depositor preference on the following basis: 'Having considered extending the coverage of depositor preference beyond insured deposits, on balance the Government considers that limiting preference to insured deposits, as the ICB recommended, would be the optimal level of coverage—this is because:

- it would best meet the Government's financial stability objectives;
- analysis and evidence submitted by banks and other stakeholders suggests that the expected costs of funding and pro-cyclical effects increase as coverage of preferred deposits increases;
- it should not have a significant impact—if any—in creating a perception that overseas creditors will be disadvantaged, as a substantial majority of insured deposits are expected to be in ring-fenced banks, which will not be able to branch outside of the EEA—only non-ring-fenced banks can do this; and
- it is the simplest form of depositor preference, both for markets and for regulators, as FSCS-coverage is easily definable and transparent. It also does not carry the same risk of arbitrage that, for example, extending coverage to include corporate deposits might (as investors may seek to re-characterise their exposures to banks as deposits)'.

7.270 Currently, proposals around UK depositor preference are awaiting the outcome of the European Commission's discussions in relation to the proposed 'Directive establishing a framework for the recovery and resolution of credit institutions and investment firms and amending Council Directives 77/91/EEC and 82/891/EC, Directives 2001/24/EC, 2002/47/EC, 2004/25/EC, 2005/56/EC, 2007/36/EC, and 2011/35/EC, and Regulation (EU) No 1093/2010'.[650] The proposed directive has raised questions about the use of depositor preference in EU Member States and the UK Government is awaiting the outcome of these discussions.

7.271 As part of the claim process, the FSCS seeks an assignment of the claimant's rights against the firm in default, but also third parties.

7.272 Where the FSCS takes an assignment of rights from a claimant, or has determined that it shall be immediately and automatically subrogated pursuant to COMP 7.3R, 'it must pursue all and only such recoveries as it considers are likely to be both reasonably possible and cost effective to pursue'.[651] The FSCS retains amounts recovered to set against future levy needs, but where an amount exceeds the compensation paid to the claimant (whose assigned rights have given rise to the recovery) the surplus (less reasonable costs) are forwarded to the claimant in relation to claims other than deposits.[652] Recoveries in relation to claims for protected deposits are dealt with on a pro-rata basis relative to the respective share of the overall loss as between the FSCS and the depositor.[653]

---

650 See Chapter 3. On recovery and resolution, see Chapter 14, paras 14.249–14.257 and 14.258–14.270.
651 COMP 7.4.1R.
652 COMP 7.6.2R.
653 COMP 7.5R.

In addition, to avoid claimants (in relation to claims other than for deposits) with large losses awaiting a dividend distribution from an insolvency practitioner before accepting any offer of compensation (and assigning their rights to dividends to the FSCS), the FSCS is to 'ensure that the claimant will not suffer disadvantage' in such circumstances by, after the event, reconciling the position had the investor awaited receipt of the dividend before applying for compensation.[654] 7.273

The construction and effect of a form of assignment of rights previously relied on by ICS under a similar regime was considered by the courts[655] and in *FSCS v Abbey National Treasury Services plc*,[656] the power of the FSCS to take assignments of investors' claims was disputed. This challenge was rejected on the basis that the FSA had power under FSMA to include provision in the COMP Rules for assignment to the FSCS of investors' claims against third parties. The court found such provision to be 'obvious' and an 'integral' component of a compensation scheme, such that the power falls within section 213(1), or as an incidental or supplemental matter within (the old) section 156(2) (now at section 137T FSMA). Further, the court rejected the defence that compensation paid by the FSCS to investors is to be taken into account in the calculation of loss recoverable by the FSCS as assignee of the investors' claims, finding 'no reason in principle... why assigned claims should be restricted to the net loss'. Accordingly, FSCS may pursue recoveries where a claimant's losses do not exceed the compensation paid. The position has subsequently been clarified following the amendment to section 215 FSMA by section 175 of the Banking Act 2009. 7.274

Funding: Section 214(1):(b) 'the establishment of different funds for meeting different kinds of claim'; (c) 'the imposition of different levies in different cases'; (d) limiting the 'levy payable by a person in respect of a specified period'

The principle is that the 'good' subsidise the 'bad', ie those firms still trading fund the costs of the FSCS for those firms which have failed.[657] The funding rules are in the FEES Module of the FCA and PRA Handbooks. The FSCS has three types of cost—compensation costs, management expenses, and a MERS levy,[658] and may levy for what it has incurred or for what it expects to incur. Compensation costs are costs incurred in paying compensation, ie the amounts paid to claimants (or for their benefit). Management expenses are the costs of establishing, maintaining, and operating the FSCS. Management expenses are split between 'base costs' and 'specific costs'. 'Base costs' are those costs which are incurred irrespective of the level of activity of the scheme (eg the salary of board members, rent incurred on the premises from which the FSCS operates, etc.), and are charged to all firms liable for the FSCS levy (by reference to regulatory fees).[659] Compensation costs and specific costs reflect the level of claims activity and are charged to a class or sub-class by reference to the activity giving rise to the claim (and not a firm's permissions).[660] 'Establishment costs', recoverable for the first three years of the FSCS, have now been collected. A MERS levy is a levy that FSCS can impose on participant firms to meet the management expenses incurred by it in connection 7.275

654 COMP 7.6.2R and 7.6.4R.
655 *ICS v West Bromwich Building Society* [1998] 1 All ER 98.
656 [2008] EWHC 1897.
657 s 213(3)(b) FSMA.
658 FEES 6.1.5G.
659 FEES 6.4.5R.
660 FEES 6.5.2R.

with acting on behalf of the manager of the relevant scheme in accordance with Part 15A FSMA (which is discussed later in this chapter).

7.276 After detailed consultation,[661] the FSA adopted an ICS-style funding model and a 'pay-as-you-go' model for the FSCS. The approach is that the costs of claims are allocated to sectors or sub-sectors with responsibility for the business giving rise to claims reflecting the obligation 'to take account of [this] desirability'.[662]

7.277 With effect from 1 April 2008, a revised funding system was put in place, following a detailed review.[663] There were five funding classes: deposit, life and pensions, investment, home finance, and general insurance. Save for deposit, each class is split into two sub-classes: providers and intermediaries. Costs were borne by the relevant sub-class, to an annual limit, then by the connected sub-class to its limit, and if further funds were required, the remaining classes could have been levied as part of this 'general retail pool' (with the exception of the home finance provider sub-class which does not contribute to the general retail pool). A 'clean break' was implemented from the previous system, with firms receiving debits or credits for amounts owed to or by the previous contribution groups. Firms which did not carry out business which could give rise to potential claims (and had no reasonable likelihood of doing so) were exempt from the levy (except for base costs).[664]

7.278 The total levy capacity was £4.03 billion (or £4.73 billion including home finance providers).

7.279 On 1 April 2013, the FSCS's new funding arrangements were introduced following an extensive FSA consultation.[665] Under the new arrangements, there are separate funding classes for PRA-authorised firms and for FCA-authorised firms. Similarly to the previous regime, although there is no limit on the compensation which the FSCS may pay in each year, there are limits on the levies which may be raised on each class or sub-class.[666] Further, following a subsequent FSA consultation,[667] in addition to the five FCA FSCS funding classes already included in the FCA pool by CP12/16, all authorised deposit takers, general insurers, life insurers, and home finance providers will now contribute to the retail pool, in relation to their FCA regulatory fees, when it is triggered by costs arising from the intermediation classes.

7.280 The FSCS raises a levy for costs expected for each financial year (for management expenses) or the following 12 months (for compensation costs).[668] Further levies may be raised during a year. There is no 'joining fee' but firms leaving regulation may be subject to an exit levy.[669] Topped up EEA firms receive a discount for the level of their home State cover.[670] From 1 April 2014, the FSCS will have the ability to, when setting the annual compensation costs

[661] Concluding with FSA Consultation Paper 86: 'Financial Services Compensation Scheme Draft Funding Rules' (March 2001).

[662] FSMA, s 213(5).

[663] FSA Consultation Paper 07/5: 'FSCS Funding Review and FSA Policy Statement 07/19' (November 2007).

[664] FEES 6.2.1R.

[665] CP12/16: 'FSCS Funding Model Review' (July 2012).

[666] FEES 6 Annex 2.

[667] CP13/1: 'FSCS Funding Model Review'.

[668] COMP 6.3.1R.

[669] FEES 6.4.8R and 6.7.6R.

[670] FEES 6.6.1R.

levy, take into consideration the compensation costs expected in the 36 months following the levy (with the exception of the deposit class) instead of the current 12-month period.

Funds are raised against and held for the benefit of individual classes and sub-classes. The FSCS is to use its resources 'in the most efficient and economic way' and in managing funds the FSCS is to act 'prudently'.[671] Although the FSCS may levy for the cost of claims paid in error but in good faith,[672] it must also try to recover those amounts unless unreasonable or uneconomic to do so.[673] **7.281**

In the event of a short-term lack of funds for claims, the FSCS may raise a further levy or arrange borrowing between classes, the cost of which (at the Bank of England's repo rate) will be added to a future levy raised on the borrowing class.[674] The FSCS has also arranged external commercial borrowing facilities in the event of short-term cash flow need. Following the amendments made by Section 173 of the Banking Act 2009, the Treasury may make loans from the National Loans Fund to the FSCS. If the FSCS has more funds than required, it may pay a refund to the relevant class or sub-class 'on any reasonable basis'.[675] **7.282**

Recoveries are allocated to the relevant sub-class, but if another sub-class contributed to the relevant compensation costs, recoveries are paid first in that order.[676] **7.283**

Current practice is for the FCA to raise its fees, FOS's fees, and the FSCS's levy at the same time, on a single invoice. Firms must notify the FSCS of relevant sub-classes and tariff data, but the FSCS may rely on the information supplied to the regulators. Failure to submit information leads to an administrative fee of £250 and the default option for calculating the tariff.[677] The levy raised on behalf of the FSCS is enforceable as a debt.[678] Levies are to be paid within 30 days[679] (or quarterly by direct debit with the FSCS's agreement) failing which 'additional administrative fees' of £250 are payable to the FSCS, together with interest at a rate of 5 per cent over the Bank of England repo rate.[680] As for the FCA and FOS, if the FSCS levy is calculated on mistaken data, a firm is to have two years in which to seek an adjustment.[681] Adjustments may be made to a levy on a number of grounds, including 'on any reasonable basis'.[682] **7.284**

Each year, the Regulators consult on the FSCS's proposed expenditure for the following year. Under section 223 FSMA, the FSCS cannot levy for 'management expenses' an amount in excess of a limit fixed by the Rules as applicable to that period. The Regulators consult on that limit each year based on the FSCS's budget. The limit is then incorporated in the FEES Rules.[683] **7.285**

---

671 FEES 6.3.12R.
672 s 223C FSMA; FEES 6.3.10R.
673 COMP 8.3.5R.
674 FEES 6.3.2AG and 6.3.17R.
675 FEES 6.3.21R.
676 FEES 6.3.19-20R.
677 FEES 6.5.16R.
678 s 213(6) FSMA; FEES 2.2.3G.
679 FEES 6.7.3R.
680 FEES 2.2.1R.
681 FEES 2.3R.
682 FEES 6.3.22R.
683 FEES 6 Annex 1.

Financial Stability and Depositor Protection

7.286 Following the financial turmoil that commenced in late 2007, the (then) Tripartite Authorities (being, HM Treasury, the Bank of England, and the FSA) undertook a programme of work to reform UK regulation of the banking industry, and particularly to improve the tools available to resolve the situation when a deposit taker gets into difficulties.[684] The Tripartite Authorities outlined their commitment to a target of seven days for providing the depositors of a failed bank with access to at least a proportion of their funds, and the balance within the following few days (and at least within the DGSD's requirement of 20 business days). The Tripartite consultation documents published in January[685] and July 2008[686] and 2009[687] outlined a comprehensive package of reforms that would be needed to achieve this. The critical nature of the role played by the FSCS was demonstrated during the financial crisis. It played a key role in compensating retail depositors of a number of deposit takers which required resolution during 2008 and 2009.

7.287 In particular, in September and October 2008, the first banks were declared in default by the FSA under the COMP Rules. The FSA made declarations of default for Bradford & Bingley Plc, Heritable Bank Plc, Kaupthing Singer & Friedlander Limited, and the UK branch of Landsbanki Islands hf. In respect of the first three, exercising its powers under the Banking (Special Provisions) Act 2008 (the 'BSPA'), HM Treasury made Orders for the transfer of deposit business to a third party.[688] These Orders provided for the transferee bank (rather than individual depositors) to receive payment from FSCS in the amount which FSCS would otherwise have paid in respect of claims for protected deposits following the default of the banks. If and to the extent that those deposits were not FSCS protected, HM Treasury met the cost. Any protected deposits not so transferred, and remaining with the banks in default, were dealt with by the FSCS under the COMP Sourcebook.

7.288 In order to fund its contribution to the cost of transfer of the protected deposits, which exceeded the maximum amount FSCS was able to raise by levy, FSCS borrowed from the Bank of England, on a short-term basis, which was then refinanced with HM Treasury. To protect the levy payers, for reasons of financial stability, FSCS was not to make repayments of the borrowing other than from recoveries (received from the banks in default) or in respect of interest accrued on the borrowing, together with other management costs, subject to an annual (aggregate) cap of £1 billion.

684 See Chapter 1, paras 1.20–1.89 and Chapter 14, paras 14.23–14.41.

685 Financial stability and depositor protection: strengthening the framework—HM Treasury, Bank of England, and FSA.

686 Financial stability and depositor protection: special resolution regime—HM Treasury, Bank of England, and FSA.

687 Special resolution regime: safeguards for partial property transfers; Special resolution regime: The FSMA (Contribution to Costs of Special Resolution Regime) Regulations 2009 (SI 2009/807) and Special resolution regime: The Building Societies (Insolvency and Special Administration) Order 2009 (SI 2009/805) and related insolvency rules, and financial assistance to building societies.

688 The Bradford & Bingley Plc Transfers of Securities and Properties etc Order 2008 (SI 2008/2546), the Kaupthing Singer & Friedlander Limited Transfer of Certain Rights and Liabilities Order 2008 (SI 2008/2674), the Heritable Bank Plc Transfer of Certain Rights and Liabilities Order 2008 (SI 2008/2644), and the Transfer of Rights and Liabilities to ING Order 2008 (SI 2008/2666).

In addition to the Orders, the FSA made various rule changes to COMP, including increasing the maximum compensation limit for protected deposits. The FSA also amended the 'exit levy' rules[689] to enable the FSCS to raise exit levies, on firms which cease to be 'participant firms', in respect of prospective compensation costs for past defaults, although this was later amended. **7.289**

In respect of Landsbanki Islands hf, the UK branch had elected to 'top up' (under the then version of COMP 14) so that depositors entitled to the first tranche of compensation from the home State compensation scheme were protected for the 'top up' payment by the FSCS. In advance of the reforms under the Banking Act, and in the absence of powers under the BSPA, it was recognised that the provisions in the COMP Sourcebook did not adequately address the handling of claims in respect of over 300,000 accounts with the UK branch. By the Compensation Sourcebook (Accelerated Compensation for Depositors) Instrument 2008, made on 29 October 2008, the FSA added COMP 15 to the Compensation Sourcebook 'to facilitate an accelerated payment of compensation' for depositors under which FSCS may modify the general claims handling and payment process. In particular, COMP 15[690] provided the FSCS with a variety of powers in respect of the payment of compensation without an application, early compensation for term or notice accounts, the form and method of paying compensation, the payment of compensation to which a claimant is entitled from another scheme, and the rights and obligations of the relevant person and third parties. Relying on such powers, on 4 November 2008, the FSCS made a determination under COMP 15 in respect of Landsbanki. **7.290**

These events confirmed the FSCS's role as a participant in the 'safety net' for authorised firms. For deposit takers in particular, this experience supported the reform programme 'to provide for a new, permanent framework for dealing with banks before and after they experience financial stress'[691] and the resolution measures taken confirmed that 'in the light of recent events in the financial markets, it has become apparent that preserving the flexibility of the Authorities is crucial'.[692] **7.291**

The Government introduced BA 2009 which came into force on 21 February 2009 following the expiry of the emergency legislation in the BSPA.[693] BA 2009 introduced a Special Resolution Regime ('SRR') which comprises a set of tools for resolving a deposit taker, including transfer to a private sector purchaser, transfer temporarily to a bridge bank owned and controlled by the Bank of England, and the Bank Insolvency Procedure (the 'BIP') which is designed to allow for rapid payments to FSCS-eligible depositors. Each stage of the SRR process requires the Bank of England, HM Treasury, the PRA, and the FCA to coordinate their activities. The PRA is responsible for triggering the SRR in respect of all firms subject to the SRR. The PRA is also responsible for the authorisation of a bridge bank and ongoing supervision of institutions in the SRR. The Bank of England is responsible for the operation of the SRR, including the decision in relation to which of the SRR tools to use and its implementation, apart from the temporary public ownership tool. HM Treasury is **7.292**

[689] FEES 6.7.6R.
[690] Many of these powers have now been moved to other parts of the COMP sourcebook following changes made to the rules by the FSA effective on 1 October 2012.
[691] Consultation Paper (November 2008), para 1.8.
[692] ibid, para 1.46.
[693] See Chapter 14, paras 14.260–14.266.

responsible for decisions with implications for public funds and, in particular, is responsible for the decision to place a bank into temporary public ownership. The FCA must be consulted by the other authorities at specified stages of the SRR. It is also envisaged that it will take on a leading role in respect of deposit takers not regulated by the PRA if such a category of firms ever emerges.

7.293 The FSCS is also expected to work closely with the authorities in the operation of the SRR. The FSCS has a potential role both in respect of the stabilisation resolutions, and specifically in the event of a payout to FSCS-eligible depositors. Part 4 of BA 2009 amended FSMA to ensure FSCS is able to fulfill this enhanced role. In particular, it introduced new sections 214(1A), 214(1B) and section 214(1C) to facilitate the speedy payment of compensation to depositors or to facilitate the speedy transfer of their accounts to another bank under Part 2 BA 2009. Part 4 also made possible three more substantial changes, including powers for the Treasury to make detailed provision by regulations in relation to: (i) the introduction of pre-funding,[694] (ii) the use of the FSCS to contribute to the costs of the use of the SRR,[695] and (iii) the use of the National Loans Fund to make loans to the FSCS.[696]

7.294 The provisions of BA 2009 at Part 2 dealing with the BIP, together with the changes made to FSMA and the COMP Rules referred to variously earlier (such as the introduction of the SCV, dispensing with the requirement for an application for compensation by claimants, and the payment of compensation on a gross basis), enabled the FSCS to deliver the faster payout of deposit compensation and, in particular, to seek to pay the majority of depositors within seven days of a failure. Under Part 2 BA 2009, a bank liquidator has two objectives: Objective 1 is 'to work with the FSCS so as to ensure that as soon as reasonably practicable each depositor (a) has the relevant account transferred to another financial institution, or (b) receives payment from (or on behalf of) the FSCS'; Objective 2 is to wind up the affairs of the bank so as to achieve the best results for the bank's creditors as a whole.[697] Importantly, Objective 1 takes precedence over Objective 2. In addition to the precedence of Objective 1, the FSCS has additional powers that it can deploy in this context: for example, to inspect information held by a liquidator under Section 220 FSMA; and under Section 221A FSMA, to arrange for its functions to be discharged on its behalf by another person, such as the bank liquidator. The Liquidation Committee (comprising the Bank of England, the PRA, and the FSCS) will recommend to the liquidator either an account transfer (facilitated by FSCS funds) or FSCS payout, or both. In doing so, the Liquidation Committee must consider the desirability of achieving Objective 1 as quickly as possible.[698] FSCS is responsible for the payout of depositors, but would work with the Authorities in connection with any transfer to another financial institution. As explained earlier, with effect from 1 January 2011, all deposit takers are required to maintain a SCV: 'a single consistent view of an eligible claimant's aggregate protected deposits with the relevant firm which contains the information required by COMP 17.2.4R but excluded from that view those accounts where the eligible claimant is a beneficiary rather than the account holder or if the account is not active as defined in COMP 17.2.3R(2)'. Firms with more than 5,000 accounts are required

694 s 214A FSMA.

695 See Part 1 of the Banking Act; s 214B FSMA; The Financial Services and Markets Act 2000 (Contribution to Costs of Special Resolution Regime) Regulations 2010, SI 2000/2220.

696 s 223B FSMA.

697 s 99 of the Banking Act.

698 s 102 of the Banking Act 2009.

to maintain the SCV in electronic form; firms with less than 5,000 accounts may hold the SCV file in paper based format. The SCV is to be provided by a deposit taking firm within 72 hours of request. It is expected to be up to date and accurate. Its reliability is critical to faster payout. The SCV file is to be submitted to FSCS and its agent for testing and verification. The file is then converted into a payment file from which FSCS will make the payments to individual depositors. The SCV is intended to capture the vast majority of deposit accounts, in particular most individual depositors. Those accounts in the SCV are intended to be paid within the seven-day target. Following simplification of the COMP eligibility rules, nearly all depositors are eligible for compensation. The SCV will exclude certain accounts such as dormant accounts, accounts subject to legal dispute, and trust/beneficiary accounts where further information is required to identify the beneficiaries (and their eligibility for compensation). Further, the SCV will 'flag', using keys and codes applied by each individual deposit taker, accounts that need further consideration before compensation can be paid, eg 'gone aways' or where there is lack of clarity as to the status of the depositor. Where depositors/accounts are not fit to be paid without further review, or are excluded from the SCV, further information will be required from the depositor or from the liquidator.

In discharging its recoveries' obligation, following the depositor payout (which FSCS is obliged to do on a 'gross' basis under COMP 12.2.1 and 12.2.6A), the FSCS will take the place of the depositors as a creditor in the estate of the failed deposit taker. The FSCS expects to remain on the Liquidation Committee after payout, to work with the liquidator in relation to the realisation and distribution of the bank's assets. The FSCS expects to be admitted as a creditor for the amounts paid through the SCV (but to include balances above the FSCS compensation limit) and in respect of accounts paid that are not in the SCV. **7.295**

The FSCS's role has been extended still further in recent times in recognition of the key part it played during the financial crisis. The FSA 2010 inserted a new Part 15A into FSMA to enable the Treasury to require the Scheme Manager to make payments on behalf of another compensation scheme (or a government or other authority) that pays compensation in respect of institutions that provide financial services, including institutions that are not authorised financial services firms under FSMA.[699] The amended legislation gives the FSCS certain grounds for declining to act, such as it not being satisfied it will be able to obtain the necessary information and/or an amount to cover its expected expenses.[700] **7.296**

---

699 s 224B–F.
700 s 224E FSMA.

8

LISTING AND PUBLIC OFFERS

Introduction

Listing and public offers in the UK

In November 2003, the European Union[1] adopted its new Prospectus Directive,[2] the 'centrepiece' of its drive to create a 'large, liquid and integrated'[3] European securities market. The Prospectus Directive regime, implemented in the UK from 1 July 2005 (through local implementation in the Financial Services and Markets Act 2000 or via 'direct effect' EU Regulation),[4] forms the basis of the regulatory framework for listing and public offers in the UK. **8.01**

As its name suggests, the Prospectus Directive regime regulates the information to be disclosed in connection with a public offer or admission to listing (referred to as 'admission to trading' in the Prospectus Directive)[5] on a regulated market[6] in the EU. It governs the circumstances when an offering document (a prospectus) is necessary. It also regulates prospectus content and layout, as well as determining when a prospectus may be used for offers to the public in other jurisdictions or for admission to listing (or trading) elsewhere in Europe. **8.02**

The first part of this chapter outlines the background to, and the structure of, the regime and its implementation in the UK. It describes when a prospectus is required and what it must contain. In addition, it describes the listing regime in the UK, which combines admission to the 'Official List' with admission to trading on one of the markets of the London Stock Exchange.[7] **8.03**

---

[1] The Prospectus Directive regime also applies to the additional EEA jurisdictions of Iceland, Liechtenstein and Norway. Throughout this chapter, where references are made to the European Union and EU, they should be deemed to include the additional EEA jurisdictions. Later in the chapter, in references to UK legislation and the FCA Handbook, the phrase EEA is used, reflecting the language used in the relevant sections and rules.

[2] Directive 2003/71/EC of the European Parliament and of the Council of 4 November 2003 on the prospectus to be published when securities are offered to the public or admitted to trading and amending Directive 2001/34/EC.

[3] Recital 5 of Directive 2003/71/EC. See n 2.

[4] See 'UK implementation'.

[5] The terms listing, admission to listing and admission to trading tend to be used interchangeably by practitioners.

[6] Determined pursuant to Directive (EC) 2004/39 of the European Parliament and of the Council of 21 April 2004 on markets in financial instruments amending Council Directives 85/611/EEC and 93/6/EEC and Directive 2000/12/EC of the European Parliament and of the Council and repealing Council Directive 93/22/EEC.

[7] In the context of the Prospectus Directive regime, the relevant market of the London Stock Exchange is the Main Market. Other London Stock Exchange markets include the Professional Securities Market (or PSM) and AIM. On the principal UK markets and exchanges, see GA Walker, 'Financial Markets and Exchanges' and 'Exchange Review, Regulation and Evolution' in M Blair, G Walker, and S Wiley, *Financial Markets and Exchanges Law* (OUP 2012) Chapters 1 and 2.

Additional listing obligations and continuing obligations

8.04 The second part of this chapter considers the UK listing requirements and the ongoing obligations faced by issuers admitted to listing and trading in the UK. These obligations are derived from other European legislation (as implemented in the UK), in addition to the Prospectus Directive regime. The Market Abuse Directive[8] (regulating behaviour) was implemented in 2005. The Transparency Directive[9] (regulating ongoing disclosure of information once securities are admitted to trading on an EU-regulated market) was implemented in 2007. Other European legislation includes the (self-explanatory) Statutory Audit Directive[10] and Company Reporting Directive,[11] implemented in 2008. There are also some UK-specific requirements, such as sponsor obligations, derived from UK legislation[12] and imposed by the UK Listing Rules.[13]

Evolution—legislative change

8.05 Over the last 10 years, the listing and public offer regime has evolved, although the majority of changes have occurred since the previous edition of this book was published in 2009. This chapter highlights key recent developments.

8.06 At a European level, these include changes to the overall Prospectus Directive regime itself as well as the impact of more general European changes (such as the 'Omnibus 1 Directive'[14] amendments, reflecting the powers given to the new European supervisory authorities from 1 January 2011).[15] As regards changes specific to the Prospectus Directive regime, an amending Directive,[16] which made revisions to the Prospectus Directive and Transparency Directive, was published in December 2010 and had to be implemented by Member States

[8] Directive 2003/6/EC of the European Parliament and of the Council of 28 January 2003 on insider dealing and market manipulation (market abuse).

[9] Directive 2004/109/EC of the European Parliament and of the Council of 15 December 2004 on the harmonisation of transparency requirements in relation to information about issuers whose securities are admitted to trading on a regulated market and amending Directive 2001/34/EC.

[10] Directive 2006/43/EC of the European Parliament and of the Council of 17 May 2006 on statutory audits of annual accounts and consolidated accounts, amending Council Directives 78/ 660/EEC and 83/349/ EEC and repealing Council Directive 84/253/EEC.

[11] Directive 2006/46/EC of the European Parliament and of the Council of 14 June 2006 amending Council Directives 78/660/EEC on the annual accounts of certain types of companies, 83/349/EEC on consolidated accounts, 86/635/EEC on the annual accounts and consolidated accounts of banks and other financial institutions and 91/674/EEC on the annual accounts and consolidated accounts of insurance undertakings.

[12] s 88 of the Financial Services and Markets Act 2000.

[13] FCA Handbook. Listing Rules, Chapter 8.

[14] Directive 2010/78/EU of the European Parliament and of the Council of 24 November 2010 amending Directives 98/26/EC, 2002/87/EC, 2003/6/EC, 2003/41/EC, 2003/71/EC, 2004/39/EC, 2004/109/ EC, 2005/60/EC, 2006/48/EC, 2006/49/EC, and 2009/65/EC in respect of the powers of the European Supervisory Authority (European Banking Authority), the European Supervisory Authority (European Insurance and Occupational Pensions Authority) and the European Supervisory Authority (European Securities and Markets Authority).

[15] Three new European supervisory authorities were created on 1 January 2011. The European Securities and Markets Authority ('ESMA') replaced the Committee of European Securities Regulators ('CESR'). The European Banking Authority ('EBA') replaced the Committee of European Banking Supervisors ('CEBS'). The European Insurance and Occupational Pensions Authority ('EIOPA') replaced the Committee of European Insurance and Occupational Pensions Supervisors ('CEIOPS').

[16] Directive 2010/73/EU of the European Parliament and of the Council of 24 November 2010 amending Directives 2003/71/EC on the prospectus to be published when securities are offered to the public or admitted to trading and 2004/109/EC on the harmonisation of transparency requirements in relation to information about issuers whose securities are admitted to trading on a regulated market.

by 1 July 2012. There were also some consequential (and direct effect) EU Regulations in March[17] and June 2012[18] and in April 2013.[19] At a UK level, these changes were implemented through amending secondary legislation (in July 2011,[20] July 2012,[21] and July 2013).[22]

Developments unique to the UK in recent years include changes to listing categories on the Official List, in April 2010.[23] In addition, more recently, the Financial Conduct Authority ('FCA') assumed responsibility[24] for listing as part of revisions to Part 6 of the Financial Services and Markets Act 2000 ('FSMA') brought in by the Financial Services Act 2012 ('FSA 2012') made on 1 April 2013. In discharging its functions as competent authority for Part 6 of FSMA, the UK competent authority has commonly used an alternative name of UK Listing Authority ('UKLA'). The FCA is continuing this practice.[25] **8.07**

The impact of the financial crisis on listing and public offers

Viewed against the backdrop of a 'tidal wave' of new legislation in the last few years, following the October 2008 financial crisis and Eurozone crisis, it is, perhaps, no surprise that the UK public offer and listing regime should be affected by regulatory developments. Many of the recent changes to the public offer and listing regime derive, however, from routine five-year 'health-checks' of the Prospectus and Transparency Directives. These reviews were scheduled 'pre-crisis', as part of the implementation of the Directives, designed, merely, to iron out any initial teething problems. **8.08**

Having said that, a key theme of the Prospectus Directive regime has always been the need to balance two potentially conflicting aims: on the one hand, enabling companies and sovereigns to have access to alternative and more diverse sources of capital and to gain access to broader retail markets in Europe: on the other, ensuring appropriate investor protection through adequate disclosure and information. **8.09**

This theme was emphasised when the Prospective Directive was introduced in 2003 and was reflected, too, in the most recent piece of Prospectus Directive regime legislation, on 30 April 2013,[26] when the European Commission justified changes on the basis that it will 'reduce administrative burdens for issuers' whilst 'maintaining an adequate level of investor protection'. **8.10**

Striving for an appropriate balance between these two factors is a theme which will continue to resonate in the current economic climate. Access to bank funding still remains a challenge **8.11**

[17] Commission Delegated Regulation (EU) No 486/2012 of 30 March 2012 amending Regulation (EC) No 809/2004 as regards the format and the content of the prospectus, the base prospectus, the summary and the final terms and as regards the disclosure requirements.

[18] Commission Delegated Regulation (EU) No 862/2012 of 4 June 2012 amending Regulation (EC) No 809/2004 as regards information on the consent to use of the prospectus, information on underlying indexes and the requirement for a report prepared by independent accountants or auditors.

[19] Commission Delegated Regulation (EU) No 759/2013 of 30 April 2013 amending Regulation (EC) No 809/2004 as regards the disclosure requirements for convertible and exchangeable debt securities.

[20] The Prospectus Regulations 2011 (SI 2011/1668).

[21] The Prospectus Regulations 2012 (SI 2012/1538).

[22] The Prospectus Regulations 2013 (SI 2013/1125).

[23] These are discussed in more detail under 'The UK Listing Regime'. Premium and standard listing categories were created in April 2010, replacing the previous primary and secondary listing categories.

[24] From the Financial Services Authority ('FSA').

[25] FCA Handbook. Prospectus Rule ('PR') 1.1.2G.

[26] Commission Delegated Regulation (EU) No 759/2013 of 30 April 2013. See n 19.

for many issuers, who are looking increasingly to the capital markets as a source of funds. Investors, meanwhile, continue to search for yield, leading them to consider more complex products and lower credits, which can lead to them taking on higher levels of risk.

8.12 When considering the most recent changes to the public offer and listing regime, perhaps the biggest impact of the financial crisis has been in the way in which regulators seem acutely conscious of the need to balance ease of issuance against perceived investor risk. In practice, regulators are tending to err on the side of caution and to interpret the Prospectus Directive regime legislation extremely restrictively, particularly in the case of any securities targeted to retail, rather than professional, investors.

8.13 This is manifesting itself in a number of ways. At a European level, examples include some stringent recommendations for market practice which the European Securities and Markets Authority (or 'ESMA'), the body composed of European competent authorities, proposed to the European Commission as part of its technical advice[27] during the 'five-year review' process. There have also been some recent cautious changes of approach reflected in the ESMA Q&A on the Prospectus Directive regime.[28] In the case of the UK, this tension can be seen most starkly in the nascent retail bond market, for bonds admitted to trading on the Main Market of the London Stock Exchange[29] but which opt for the London Stock Exchange ORB (or Order book for Retail Bonds) platform, designed to enable issuers to target retail investors more easily. The FCA is interpreting[30] the concept of 'easily analysable' very strictly in disclosure for any prospectuses for bonds using the ORB platform and targeted at retail investors, requiring additional drafting changes to make prospectuses easier for retail investors to understand.

8.14 Finally, in this context, it is worth emphasising that the Prospectus Directive regime was only intended to regulate information disclosure. Recital 18 to the Directive stated that 'The provision of full information concerning securities and issuers of those securities promotes, together with rules on the conduct of business, the protection of investors'. That has not changed.

8.15 The regime is not intended to control the types or range of products which might be offered[31] to the public or admitted to trading, nor to control the types of investors to whom such products might be sold.

8.16 Accordingly, this chapter does not cover existing or proposed legislation attempting to control appropriate placement of securities or products, such as the Markets in Financial Instruments Directive ('MiFID')[32] and associated legislation. Similarly, it does not address prospective changes targeting sales of specific products, such as the Packaged Retail Investment Products ('PRIPs') initiative and the current proposals on key information documents for investment products.[33] Finally, it does not consider the European Directive amending certain financial

---

27 ESMA, Final Report to the European Commission, July 2011.

28 ESMA Q&A on prospectuses, 20th updated version, October 2013.

29 See n 7.

30 Since July 2013. This approach has been relayed via recent FCA comments on draft prospectuses submitted for review. The FCA also issued a consultation (UKLA/TN/632.1) in October 2013 about expanding this approach to all retail non-equity prospectuses.

31 ESMA, Final Report to the European Commission, July 2011.

32 Directive (EC) 2004/39. See n 6.

33 3 July 2012: Proposal for a regulation of the European Parliament and of the Council on key information documents for investment products.

and disclosure obligations in the Transparency Directive, which, although coming into force on 26 November 2013, will not need to be implemented by Member States until November 2015.[34]

The Prospectus Directive Regime

This section considers the background to the listing and public offer regime in the UK. It looks at the aim of the Prospectus Directive regime, the concept of passporting, the role of competent authorities and home Member States, and the Lamfalussy process. It also discusses the route through which such measures were implemented in the UK in 2005 and recent UK changes to the regime. **8.17**

Background

Aim

The Prospectus Directive was one of the Directives which formed part of the European 'Financial Services Action Plan' ('FSAP').[35] The aim of the Directive was to make it easier and cheaper for issuers to raise capital throughout the EU. The way in which it sought to achieve this was by creating a uniform offering and disclosure regime across EU Member States. This would enable issuers to offer their securities to the public in any EU Member State, or to seek admission to trading on any regulated market of an EU Member State, using a single prospectus, approved by a single regulator. This concept is known as a 'passport'. **8.18**

Before the Prospectus Directive, in order to make an offer of securities to retail investors in a Member State, it was necessary to have a prospectus which satisfied the requirements of that Member State. But a prospectus which satisfied the requirements of one Member State would not necessarily satisfy the requirements of another. This was despite the fact that Member States' legislation in this area was all based on an earlier European Directive.[36] As the Prospectus Directive acknowledges,[37] the mechanism which existed for the Member States to recognise each other's prospectuses (a 'mutual recognition mechanism'), effectively did not work. In practice, regulators tended to add their own, specific requirements. This resulted in a system which was 'partial and complex'.[38] **8.19**

The passporting mechanism

In its opening Recitals, the Prospectus Directive states that it is essential to the achievement of the (European) internal market that there is granted 'a single passport to the issuer [of securities]'. The Prospectus Directive expressly prohibits any competent authority undertaking **8.20**

[34] Directive 2013/50/EU of the European Parliament and of the Council of 22 October 2013 amending Directive 2004/109/EC of the European Parliament and of the Council on the harmonisation of transparency requirements in relation to information about issuers whose securities are admitted to trading on a regulated market, Directive 2003/71/EC of the European Parliament and of the Council on the prospectus to be published when securities are offered to the public or admitted to trading and Commission Directive 2007/14/EC laying down detailed rules for the implementation of certain provisions of Directive 2004/109/EC.

[35] In May 1999, the Financial Services Action Plan was adopted by the European Commission. COM (1999) 232.

[36] Directive 2001/34/EC of the European Parliament and of the Council of 28 May 2001 on the admission of securities to official stock exchange listing and on information to be published on those securities.

[37] Directive 2003/71/EC, Recital 1. See n 2.

[38] Directive 2003/71/EC, Recital 1. See n 2.

any approval or administrative procedures in relation to a prospectus for which another competent authority has given a certificate of approval. All that is required is that the competent authority of the issuer's home Member State[39] delivers to the competent authority of the host Member State: i) a certificate of approval of the prospectus; ii) a copy of the prospectus; and iii) if required by the host Member State, a translation of the summary of the prospectus.

8.21 The competent authority of the issuer's home Member State is required to arrange for an approved prospectus to be 'passported' (in other words, forwarded on under a single passport mechanism) to any requested jurisdictions (known as host Member States) upon a request being made by the issuer (or other person responsible for drawing up the prospectus). The authority must do so within either one working day or a maximum of three working days following the request, depending upon whether the request is made before or after the prospectus has been approved.

8.22 The passporting mechanism enables the approved prospectus to be used either to make an offer to the public in other selected EU jurisdictions or, alternatively, to seek admission to listing and trading on the regulated market of a stock exchange elsewhere in the EU. This enables issuers to access greater numbers of investors using one single approved prospectus, including investors who, for example, might be restricted to investing only in securities admitted to trading on a domestic market.

8.23 When the Prospectus Directive was introduced, some commentators felt that a measure of its success would be the extent to which passporting was successful. It is interesting to note that, in the period from January to December 2012, 4,113 prospectuses (not including supplements) were approved across the EU. Of these, competent authorities received requests to passport less than a quarter (only 23.5 per cent) to one or more jurisdictions. The UK accounted for the bulk of these EU prospectus approvals (approving 658 prospectuses out of the overall EU total of 4,113), but the UK received requests to passport only 84 (12.8 per cent) of those 658 prospectuses elsewhere in the EU. (Other jurisdictions, such as Germany, passported over 70 per cent of approved prospectuses).[40]

8.24 It would, of course, be possible to undertake a comparative year-by-year analysis of the growth (or decline) of passporting since 2005, to try to draw conclusions about whether or not the 'level playing field' achieved its aims. When reviewing the figures, though, the most striking fact relates to the overall number of prospectus approvals. The number of prospectus approvals has fallen considerably since 2006 and 2007, reflective, no doubt, of the financial and economic crises. By way of comparison, roughly twice as many prospectuses overall (8,481) were approved across the EU in 2006 than were approved in 2012. Perhaps unsurprisingly, numbers peaked in 2007, with 10,389 prospectuses approved, overall, across the EU (with the UK approving 1,515 prospectuses). Since 2007, there has been a fairly steady decline in approval numbers.[41]

Competent authorities

8.25 The Prospectus Directive requires each Member State to designate an authority, which must be independent from market participants, as competent to approve prospectuses. It sets out

[39] See 'Competent authorities', para 8.25.

[40] 13 June 2013. ESMA '*Report—Data on Prospectuses Approved and Passported—January 2012 to December 2012*'.

[41] CESR data, as reported in the ESMA June 2013 report.

complicated provisions for determining in the case of any prospectus which authority is, or may be, competent to approve it.[42] That jurisdiction is known as the home Member State. Any other jurisdiction (into which the prospectus may be passported) is known as the host Member State. The rules for determining the home Member State are summarised, briefly, later in this chapter. For EU issuers, the rules mean that there is, effectively, no choice of home Member State in respect of shares or debt with a denomination of less than €1,000. The relevant competent authority will be the competent authority in the Member State where the company has its registered office. For other types of products, though, there is a choice. Provided that the denomination is at least €1,000 (or near equivalent in other currencies), the person offering the securities or seeking their admission to trading on an EU regulated market may choose the competent authority to approve the prospectus, on an issue by issue basis. For 'third-country' issuers (not incorporated in a Member State) planning to issue shares, convertible bonds, or other securities giving the right to acquire shares or to issue low denomination (less than €1,000) debt, the rules are more complex. Even today, those rules still refer to the date of entry into force of the Directive (approximately 10 years ago) and provide that the competent authority will be that of the Member State where the first offer to the public or application for admission to trading on a regulated market is made after that date. A similar case-by-case choice exists for 'third-country' issuers of securities with denominations of €1,000 or above (or equivalent in another currency).

Uniform approach: Lamfalussy and creating a level playing field

In order to enable the use of a passport mechanism in this way, it was necessary to have a uniform disclosure regime across Europe. The Lamfalussy legislative structure played a part in this. **8.26**

The aim of the Lamfalussy[43] legislative structure was to simplify and speed up the EU legislative process in the arena of financial services as part of the FSAP. The so-called 'Lamfalussy process' is based on a four-level approach to legislation 'framework principles, implementing measures, cooperation and enforcement'.[44] The key stages are Levels 1 and 2. **8.27**

In the case of the Prospectus Directive regime, Level 1 is the Directive, requiring implementation into local legislation in Member States. The Directive sets high level political objectives and 'framework principles'. It is therefore restricted to matters such as when a prospectus is required, which authority is or may be competent to approve it, which language(s) it must be written in, and how and when it must be published and supplemented. The Prospectus Directive says little about the detailed contents of prospectuses. It merely contains a general statement of principle that a prospectus must contain 'all information which, according to the particular nature of the issuer and of the securities, is necessary to enable investors to make an informed assessment of the assets and liabilities, financial position, profits and losses and prospects of the issuer and of the rights attaching to the securities'.[45] **8.28**

Under Lamfalussy, Level 2 deals with substantive content of the legislation and technical requirements. In the context of the Prospectus Directive regime, the detailed content **8.29**

[42] Directive 2003/71/EC, art 2(1)(m) and (n). See n 2.
[43] Named after the chair of a 'Committee of Wise Men' set up by the ECOFIN Council in July 2000 and which reported in February 2001.
[44] Directive 2003/71/EC, Recital 6. See n 2.
[45] Directive 2003/71/EC, art 5(1). See n 2.

specifications for prospectuses are contained in a Level 2 EU regulation which also came into force on 1 July 2005 (the Prospectus Directive Regulation).

8.30 The Prospectus Directive Regulation, by virtue of being an EU[46] Regulation, has direct effect in each Member State. That means that the content requirements for prospectuses are identical throughout the EU, which creates uniformity and a level playing field across Europe.

8.31 In addition, the Prospectus Directive is a 'maximum harmonisation' directive, meaning that competent authorities are not entitled to add additional provisions when implementing. This has achieved a level 'baseline' for disclosure—although, to-date, there are still slight anomalies in interpretation between competent authorities. There is an exception under the Prospectus Directive which provides[47] that competent authorities or exchanges may impose additional requirements in the context of admission to trading of securities on a regulated market (notably, with regard to corporate governance), but those requirements may not, directly or indirectly, restrict the drawing up, the content, and the dissemination of a prospectus approved by a competent authority.

Levels 3 and 4

8.32 For completeness, Level 3 relates to coordination of Member States' implementation. In the case of the Prospective Directive regime, the Committee of European Securities Regulators ('CESR') developed standards and (non-binding) guidelines[48] for harmonising supervisory practices in the European market for financial services.[49] CESR has since been replaced by ESMA,[50] which adopted and updated the CESR guidelines in March 2013. Finally, under the Lamfalussy process, Level 4 relates to supervising the application of measures laid down at Levels 1 and 2—essentially, enforcement. The European Commission is to take steps to ensure compliance, should there be an infringement.[51]

ESMA Q&A

8.33 In addition, although they are also not binding, ESMA[52] publishes regular 'Q&A' papers, addressing how certain provisions of the Prospectus Directive should be interpreted. As at November 2013, 20 versions of the prospectus Q&A have been published, with the latest version in October 2013.

UK implementation

8.34 The next section of this chapter considers how the Prospectus Directive regime was implemented in the UK. It looks at the way in which the Directive was implemented in July 2005, as well as recent changes.

---

46 The Regulation also has effect in the additional three EEA jurisdictions of Norway, Liechtenstein, and Iceland.

47 Directive 2003/71/EC, Recital 15. See n 2.

48 CESR's recommendations for the consistent implementation of the European Commission's Regulation on Prospectuses No 809/2004, January 2005.

49 ESMA/2013/319. ESMA update of the CESR recommendations—The consistent implementation of Commission Regulation (EC) No 809/2004 implementing the Prospectus Directive.

50 Since 1 January 2011.

51 For example, in April 2006, the European Commission formally requested Italy and Belgium to complete implementation of the Prospectus Directive into national law in the form of a 'reasoned opinion', as part of action against 19 different Member States in respect of eight different Directives.(Press release IP/06/503, 19 April 2006.)

52 Formerly CESR published FAQs, but this was assumed by ESMA from 1 January 2011.

In summary, various pieces of legislation and guidance need to be considered together,[53] notably: **8.35**

i) Part 6 of the Financial Services and Markets Act 2000 (FSMA);
ii) the Prospectus Directive Regulation; and
iii) the FCA's Prospectus Rules in the FCA Handbook.

These are described in more detail later in this chapter.

In addition, although not directly relevant to UK implementation, the CESR (now ESMA) Level 3 recommendations[54] may be relevant. These are non-binding guidance[55] regarding consistent implementation, but, in determining whether the rules have been complied with, the FCA will take into account whether an issuer has complied with the recommendations.[56] Moreover, although not directly relevant to the Lamfalussy Levels 1–4, the FCA maintains a Knowledge Base[57] on its website, with a series of Guidance Notes (comprising Procedural Notes and Technical Notes) about the FCA's policy approach to certain items. Some relate to internal listing policy, but others give guidance[58] on the FCA's current approach to certain Prospectus Directive regime provisions. The UKLA has recently issued consultations[59] on some of these items to seek market input. The FCA also publishes Primary Market Bulletins ('PMBs') to the market, from time to time, outlining policy approaches. **8.36**

UK implementation—original implementation in 2005

The Prospectus Directive had to be implemented in each Member State by 1 July 2005. In the UK, the Prospectus Directive was implemented through the Prospectus Regulations 2005.[60] The Regulations revoked the previous UK legislation[61] and made the legislative changes necessary to implement the Prospectus Directive and its supporting Prospectus Directive Regulation. These changes were made to the FSMA. Part 6 of the FSMA was amended to include relevant sections to implement provisions from the Directive. For example, a new section 87A of FSMA was added which included the general disclosure obligation (that is, 'all information which, according to the particular nature of the issuer and of the securities, is necessary to enable investors to make an informed assessment'), implemented from the Prospectus Directive. In addition, Part 6 of FSMA authorised the Financial Services Authority (FSA), as the 'competent authority', to make and publish the Prospectus Rules (as well other rules). The Prospectus Rules set out the prospectus requirements for issuers wishing to comply with the regime, including the form and content of a prospectus, the period of validity of a prospectus, and the ways in which a prospectus may be published. **8.37**

53 FCA Handbook. Prospectus Rule 1.1.6G.
54 CESR's recommendations for the consistent implementation of the European Commission's Regulation on Prospectuses No 809/2004, January 2005.
55 Para 9. CESR's recommendations for the consistent implementation of the European Commission's Regulation on Prospectuses No 809/2004, January 2005.
56 FCA Handbook. Prospectus Rule 1.1.6G.
57 <http://www.fca.org.uk/firms/markets/ukla/knowledge-base>.
58 <http://www.fca.org.uk/your-fca/documents/handbook/handbook-readers-guide>.
59 Consultation on the UKLA's Primary Market Bulletin No 2, July 2012 and Consultation on the UKLA's Primary Market Bulletin No 5, February 2013.
60 The Prospectus Regulations 2005 (SI 2005/1433).
61 The Public Offers of Securities Regulations 1995 (SI 1995/1537) were repealed. The Financial Services and Markets Act 2000 (Offers of Securities) Order 2001 (SI 2001/2958) was repealed. Part of the Financial Services and Markets Act 2000 (Official Listing of Securities) Regulations 2001 (SI 2001/2956) were repealed.

8.38 The Prospectus Directive Regulation (Level 2—containing detailed content requirements for prospectuses) did not need to be implemented in the UK. Accordingly, although the FSA's (now FCA's) Prospectus Rules set out extracts from the Regulation and copy out segments from various Annexes of the Prospectus Directive Regulation, they have merely been 'extracted' and replicated, for ease of reference, within the Prospectus Rules.[62]

8.39 The Prospectus Rules ('PRs') apply to prospectuses to be produced in relation to an offer to the public in the UK or to admission to trading on the Main Market of the London Stock Exchange (the 'regulated market' in the UK for the purposes of the Prospectus Directive regime).

8.40 The Prospectus Rules do not apply to 'listing particulars' which are prepared in order to obtain listing and admission to trading on the Professional Securities Market ('PSM') of the London Stock Exchange, as the PSM is not a regulated market.

8.41 There are some disclosure similarities, however, as the rules which apply to the listing particulars for securities to be admitted to the PSM cross-refer to some of the PR disclosure requirements.

UK implementation—recent changes in the UK

8.42 As mentioned in the Introduction section, there have been changes to the Prospectus Directive regime since 2005. The amending Directive,[63] published in December 2010, which came into force on 1 January 2011 had to be implemented by Member States by 1 July 2012. This was implemented in full in the UK by The Prospectus Regulations 2012,[64] with effect from 1 July 2012. Some of these changes have a direct impact on public offers and listing in the UK. The changes, such as increased so-called wholesale denominations and broader exemptions from offers to the public, are described later in this chapter.[65]

8.43 Interestingly, the UK also chose to implement two (only) of the provisions from the 2010 amending Directive slightly early. These took effect from 31 July 2011 (almost one year ahead of the implementation deadline). The UK's approach was to select and enact two changes which it felt might help small businesses in the UK to access capital markets funding. The two changes (made to Part 6 of FSMA and to Schedule 11A to FSMA, via the Prospectus Regulations 2011)[66] were: to remove the need to produce a prospectus if the offer was less than €5 million (or equivalent); and to raise the minimum number of investors for which a prospectus is required from 100 to 150 investors per EEA state. The exemptions from the need to produce a prospectus for an offering are described in more detail later in this chapter,[67] but the reason that the UK approach is of interest is because the few other Member States who chose to implement changes early, ahead of the 1 July 2012 deadline, typically implemented changes at the opposite end of the spectrum; that is, those relating to high denomination securities (which are, typically, sold to professional investors). The UK,

[62] The PRs and content requirements are discussed in more detail under the heading 'Drawing up the Prospectus'.

[63] Directive 2010/73/EU. See n 16.

[64] The Prospectus Regulations 2012. See n 21.

[65] See the 'Public offers and admission to listing and trading in the UK' heading.

[66] The Prospectus Regulations 2011. See n 20.

[67] Under the 'Public offers and exemptions' heading.

in contrast, saw the changes as an opportunity to try to improve liquidity for small businesses and small- and medium-sized enterprises ('SMEs') in the economy.[68]

For completeness, there were also minor changes made by the Prospectus Regulations in 2013,[69] but these were more of a tidying-up drafting measure to amend a sub-paragraph in FSMA, rather than being of any consequence. **8.44**

Public Offers and Admission to Listing and Trading in the UK

Having looked at the background to the Prospectus Directive regime and how it was implemented in the UK, this section brings us to the main focus of this chapter: what are the legal requirements in relation to listing and public offers in the UK? Given the nature of the regime and its focus on disclosure, it is of no surprise that the question really becomes 'When is an approved prospectus required?' **8.45**

Basic premise

The basic premise of the Prospectus Directive regime is that before any offer of transferable securities can either be made to the public in any Member State or admitted to trading (listing) on a regulated market in any Member State a prospectus must have been vetted and approved by a regulatory authority and 'published'.[70] **8.46**

In the UK, this requirement is implemented in section 85 in Part 6 of FSMA. Section 85(1) of FSMA makes it unlawful to make an offer of transferable securities to the public in the UK without such a prospectus having been approved and published. Section 85(2) makes it unlawful to request admission of transferable securities to trading on a regulated market in the UK in the absence of such a prospectus. **8.47**

This basic premise has sometimes caused some confusion. It is therefore important to stress that a prospectus is required in either circumstance: that is, either when an offer to the public is to be made or, alternatively, if admission is being made to a regulated market. This means that, even where an offer might fall within a possible 'offer' exemption,[71] the fact that securities are being admitted to trading will mean that a prospectus will be required. **8.48**

That is because Article 3(3) of the Prospectus Directive provides that any admission of securities to trading on a regulated market situated or operating in a Member State is subject to publication of a prospectus. **8.49**

The meaning of 'transferable securities', 'making an offer to the public', 'admission to trading' and 'regulated market' are discussed later in this chapter. **8.50**

Scope—exemptions

Before discussing offers and admission to trading and various exemptions, though, it is important to mention that some issuers and some products fall outside the scope of the Prospectus Directive regime altogether. **8.51**

---

[68] HM Treasury, Consultation on early implementation of amendments to the Prospectus Directive, March 2011.

[69] The Prospectus Regulations 2013. See n 22.

[70] Directive 2003/71/EC. See n 2.

[71] Discussed below under the 'Public offers and exemptions' heading.

8.52 As regards issuers, principally, these are debt securities issued by a Member State or by a Member State's regional or local authorities, by a public international body of which at least one Member State is a member, by the European Central Bank or by the central bank of any Member State; any securities guaranteed by a Member State or by a Member State's regional or local authorities; units issued by certain collective investment undertakings; and certain debt securities issued by credit institutions and covered by a deposit guarantee scheme.[72] However, most (although not all) of these issuers do have the option to draw up a prospectus in accordance with the Directive if they wish—presumably to take advantage of the passporting facility under the Directive. It is worth double-checking whether a particular issuer is able to opt in, rather than making any assumptions. One oddity, for example, is that charities (non-profit organisations) are exempt from scope, but, unusually, are not given the option to opt in.[73]

Scope—transferable securities and exempt transferable securities

8.53 The Prospectus Directive only applies to 'transferable securities', so anything which does not fall within that definition will not be caught.

8.54 Section 102A(3) of FSMA defines a 'transferable security' by reference to the definition in MiFID,[74] using the same definition, but excluding 'money-market instruments' with a maturity of less than 12 months.

8.55 Article 4(18) of MiFID defines transferable securities broadly: 'those classes of securities which are negotiable on the capital market, with the exception of instruments of payment, such as: a) shares in companies and other securities equivalent to shares in companies, partnerships or other entities, and depositary receipts in respect of shares; b) bonds or other forms of securitised debt, including depositary receipts in respect of such securities; and c) any other securities giving the right to acquire or sell any such transferable securities or giving rise to a cash settlement determined by reference to transferable securities, currencies, interest rates or yields, commodities or other indices or measures.'

8.56 The MiFID definition applies to classes of securities which are negotiable on a capital market. A common question is whether commercial paper (or CP) having a maturity of less than 12 months will be classed as a money-market instrument and therefore fall outside the scope of the Directive. Standard CP with a maturity of less than one year is generally considered to be exempt.

8.57 In addition to securities which do not fall within the transferable securities definition in section 102A of FSMA, some other 'transferable securities' are exempted.

8.58 Section 85(5) of FSMA provides that certain of the transferable securities listed in Schedule 11A to FSMA are not caught by section 85. It also provides that any other transferable securities listed in the FCA's Prospectus Rules are not caught by either section 85(1) of FSMA[75] or 85(2) UK of FSMA.[76] These exemptions and other exemptions are discussed later in this chapter. A word of caution: there are slight differences between the exemptions in the

[72] Directive 2003/71/EC, Art 1(2). See n 2.
[73] Directive 2003/71/EC, Art 2. See n 2.
[74] Directive (EC) 2004/39. See n 6.
[75] Offers to the public in the UK.
[76] Admission to listing and trading in the UK.

Prospectus Rules for offers and admission to trading, so these are set out separately in what follows.

Moreover, in relation to public offers, section 86 of FSMA also lists some types of offers where a prospectus will not be required. **8.59**

Public offers and exemptions

First, in relation to public offers, Section 85(5) of FSMA makes it clear that the prohibition contained in section 85(1) of FSMA (that is, the prohibition on offering transferable securities 'to the public' without an approved prospectus in the UK) does not apply to any of the transferable securities listed in Schedule 11A to FSMA or to other transferable securities specified in the Prospectus Rules. **8.60**

Schedule 11A to FSMA sets out the types of issuers exempted from the public offer regime under the Prospectus Directive (including, for example, EEA State issuers). It also implements Article 1(2)(h) of the Prospectus Directive which states that the Prospectus Directive shall not apply to offers of less than €5,000,000 (increased recently from €2,500,000 and implemented[77] as part of the 31 July 2011 changes in the UK).[78] **8.61**

PR 1.2.2 also sets out the forms of transferable securities to which the prohibition in section 85(1) of FSMA does not apply. PR 1.2.2 states that the prohibition contained within section 85(1) of FSMA does not apply to offers of transferable securities of the following types: a) shares issued in substitution for shares of the same class provided the issue does not increase the issued share capital; b) transferable securities offered in connection with a takeover or merger if an equivalent document is made available; c) shares allotted free of charge to existing shareholders and dividends paid out in the form of shares of the same class as the shares in respect of which the dividend is paid. This exemption is available so long as a document containing information on the number and nature of the shares and the reasons for and details of the offer are made available; d) securities offered allotted or to be allotted to existing or former directors or employees by their employer or an affiliated undertaking which has securities admitted to trading on a regulated market. This exemption is only available where a document containing information on the number and nature of the securities and the reasons for and details of the offer are made available. **8.62**

As mentioned, those exemptions in Schedule 11A to FSMA and PR 1.2.2 relate to certain types of transferable security. There are also certain types of offer which will be exempt from the requirement to produce a prospectus. **8.63**

Offer of securities to the public

First, though, what is an 'offer of securities to the public' in the context of the Prospectus Directive regime? **8.64**

The term 'offer of securities to the public' is defined extremely widely in the Prospectus Directive as 'a communication to persons in any form and by any means, presenting sufficient information on the terms of the offer and the securities to be offered, so as to enable an **8.65**

77 FSMA, Sch 11A, Part 2, para 9.
78 Prospectus Regulation 2011. See n 20.

investor to decide to purchase or subscribe these securities'. The definition can be construed to apply to any communication which enables an investor to subscribe or buy securities.

8.66 This was implemented in the UK under section 102B of FSMA (offer of transferable securities to the public). The UK legislation clarified that the definition of offer, particularly the communication aspect of the definition, does not apply to communications in connection with trading on a regulated market, a multilateral trading facility, or a prescribed market under section 130A of FSMA (any market which is prescribed for the purposes of the offence of market abuse under Part 8 of FSMA).[79] The clear policy aim here is to provide clarification to ensure that genuine market transactions and the offer of prices through screens are not caught through the wide definition agreed in the Prospectus Directive.

8.67 Moreover, the domestic implementation clarifies that the definition of offer is limited to the UK:[80] an offer of securities to overseas persons will not amount to an offer under FSMA, although, clearly, the domestic law in the jurisdiction in question will be relevant.

Exempt offers to the public

8.68 Certain types of offers are exempt from the requirement to produce an approved prospectus. These offer exemptions are set out in section 86 of FSMA and implement Article 3(2) of the Prospectus Directive. The various exemptions are discussed later in this chapter.

8.69 There are also four points to highlight in relation to section 86 FSMA and the exemptions. First, they are still 'offers to the public', but are exempt from the requirement to prepare an approved prospectus. In practice, this subtle distinction is rarely significant, but it is relevant in relation to withdrawal rights under Article 16 of the Prospectus Directive, as implemented in section 87G and section 87Q of FSMA.[81] Secondly, many of these exemptions were affected by the 1 July 2012 revisions. Amendments include changes to the definition of 'qualified investors', higher thresholds (for example, increasing one threshold from €50,000 to €100,000 and another threshold from 100 people to 150 people) and the addition of a new section 86(1A) and (1B), to tally with the new consent regime introduced from September 2012. Thirdly, the general view is that various exemptions can be combined and are not mutually exclusive, so, for example, the qualified investor exemption may be combined with other exemptions. Fourthly, as mentioned earlier, even where an offer may be exempt (and would thus not require a prospectus), this would be 'trumped' by a request for admission to trading on a regulated market.

Exempt offers—Offers to qualified investors

8.70 The first offer exemption in section 86 of FSMA is where 'the offer is made to or directed at qualified investors only' (section 86(1)(a)). The definition of qualified investor is set out in section 86(7) of FSMA which implements Article 2(1)(e) of the Prospectus Directive.

8.71 This is one area which has been considerably simplified under recent changes. Historically, there was a strong overlap (but some slight discrepancies) between the definition of 'qualified investor' in the Prospectus Directive and 'professional investor' in MiFID.[82] A sensible step, as part of the 2010 amending Directive changes, was to bring the definition of 'qualified

---

79 FSMA, s 102B(5). See Chapter 9, Market Abuse.
80 FSMA, s 102B(2).
81 See 'Supplementary prospectuses and withdrawal rights'.
82 Directive (EC) 2004/39. See n 6.

investor' in the Prospectus Directive regime in line with the MiFID definition, by cross-referring directly to the investor classifications in MiFID.

As a consequence, the requirement for the FSA to maintain a special 'qualified investors register' (which had been required under section 87R of FSMA) was discontinued on 1 July 2012. 8.72

Exempt offers—Offers to fewer than 150 persons

A further offer exemption in section 86(1)(b) is where 'the offer is made to or directed at fewer than 150 persons, other than qualified investors, per EEA State'. As explained earlier,[83] this was increased (from 100 persons) as part of the mandated 1 July 2012 changes, but, in the UK, was implemented slightly earlier, on 31 July 2011. 8.73

On a pan-European basis, the definition also makes it clear that the 150 persons exemption applies per Member State. On this basis it should be possible to offer to fewer than 150 persons in any number of EEA jurisdictions without requiring a prospectus to be approved. 8.74

This exemption may also be clearly combined with the qualified investors exemption, ensuring that issuers can offer in the UK to any number of qualified investors and up to another 150 persons (not being qualified investors). 8.75

Offers to trustees of a trust, members of a partnership in a capacity as such, or two or more persons jointly should be treated as an offer to a single person.[84] 8.76

Exempt offers with a minimum consideration or minimum denomination

Where the minimum denomination is set at €100,000 (referred to, informally, but fairly widely, as a wholesale denomination), it is anticipated that investors who are likely to be buying at such high denominations have sufficient experience and 'financial awareness' so as not to require the same level of disclosure information and protections as a pure retail investor. 8.77

The same view is taken about a minimum consideration of €100,000 for a security (or bundle of one or more products). 8.78

Accordingly, offers where the minimum threshold or minimum consideration is €100,000 or equivalent in another currency do not require the disclosure and protections afforded by a prospectus (although a prospectus will still be required in order to admit securities to trading on an EU-regulated market). These exemptions are contained in section 86(1)(c) and (d) of FSMA. 8.79

Exempt offers—total consideration less than €100,000

Under section 86(1)(e) of FSMA, to mirror the provisions of article 3(2) of the Prospectus Directive, no prospectus is needed where 'the total consideration for the transferable securities being offered [in the EEA States] cannot exceed 100,000 euros (or an equivalent amount)'. 8.80

In line with the clarification made in the Prospectus Directive of 'in the Union' by the 2010 amending Directive, the phrase 'in the EEA States' was added into section 86(1)(e) of FSMA from 1 July 2012. 8.81

83 See 'UK implementation—recent changes in the UK', at para 8.42.
84 FSMA, s 86(3).

8.82 In a UK context, some commentators have queried why this provision is necessary, given the exemption contained in Schedule 11A of FSMA which takes offers of transferable securities included in an offer where the total consideration for the offer in the European Union is less than €5,000,000 out of scope.[85]

Exempt offers—consent

8.83 An additional provision was added to section 86 of FSMA as part of the July 2012 changes. Under section 86(1A) of FSMA, a new approved prospectus will not be required for an offer of securities provided that the issuer has consented to the use of the prospectus. Section 86(1A) of FSMA applies if the transferable securities are being sold or placed through a financial intermediary where the transferable securities have previously been the subject of one or more offers to the public falling within paragraphs (a) to (e) of subsection 86(1) of FSMA (ie, one of the exempt offers discussed in the paragraphs earlier) and the issuer or other person who was responsible for drawing up the prospectus has given written consent to the use of the prospectus for the purpose of the current offer.

8.84 There is a further condition. There must be a 'current' prospectus. This means a prospectus which has been approved by the FCA and which is within the 12-month validity period and which has been supplemented, if necessary, in accordance with section 87G of FSMA. Alternatively, in the case of non-equity transferable securities falling within Article 5(4)(b) of the Prospectus Directive, the securities concerned must not have ceased to be issued in a continuous or repeated manner.

8.85 This addition of issuer consent to use of the prospectus was an attempt to address issuer worries about prospectus liability, deriving from the so-called 'retail cascade' concerns which arose after 2005. This was as a result of the drafting of a sub-paragraph in Article 3(2) of the Prospectus Directive. The problem was that Article 3(2) stated that, even if an initial placement fell within one of the offer exemptions, a 'subsequent resale' of those securities might be classed as a separate offer. Moreover, if securities were placed through a financial intermediary, it would be necessary to look through to the 'final placement' to determine whether the offer fell within one of the offer exemptions. This caused some concerns for issuers. First, a placement of any retail denomination securities—that is, with a denomination of less than €50,000 or equivalent (from 1 July 2005) or less than €100,000 or equivalent (from 1 July 2012)—might be sold on in such a way as, unwittingly, to trigger a public offer by the issuer (or, at least, one which regulators might try to argue was instigated on behalf of the issuer). Second, issuers were also concerned that, notwithstanding any appropriate legending or disclaimer language in a prospectus, an issuer might be deemed to be responsible for prospectus content for offers made after the intended 'life' of the prospectus (that is, beyond the period for which the issuer intended the prospectus to be used for its offer, as opposed to the standard 12-month validity for an approved prospectus under the Prospectus Directive regime). The addition of a requirement for an issuer's written consent to the use of the prospectus means that an issuer may take some comfort from the fact that it now has ultimate control about who may use the prospectus for authorised sales and the time frame for any offer and any use of the prospectus.

[85] Sch 11A to FSMA, para 9(1).

Annex XXX of the Prospectus Directive Regulation[86] also specifies that an issuer may give either general consent to financial intermediaries who meet 'clear and objective conditions' or may give consent to one or more specified intermediaries. **8.86**

Admission to listing and trading in the UK

The second prohibition contained within section 85 of FSMA relates to admission to trading. Section 85(2) of FSMA provides that it is unlawful to request the admission of transferable securities to a regulated market in the UK unless an approved prospectus has been made available. **8.87**

There are two things to note. As described in the Introduction section to this chapter, the regime refers to 'admission to trading', rather than 'listing'. In general parlance, practitioners tend to refer to these two terms interchangeably. In the UK, admission to the Official List, administered by the FCA, is combined with admission to trading on one of the markets the London Stock Exchange.[87] **8.88**

Secondly, it refers to a 'regulated market'. The Main Market of the London Stock Exchange is a 'regulated market'. For Prospectus Directive regime purposes, it is important to note that only those securities admitting to trading on the Main Market fall within section 85(2) of FSMA. (Neither the PSM nor AIM are regulated markets for this purpose.) **8.89**

As with the public offers prohibition in section 85(1) of FSMA, there are certain exemptions from section 85(2). Section 85(6) of FSMA makes it clear that the prohibition contained in section 85(2) of FSMA does not apply to transferable securities listed in Part I of Schedule 11A to FSMA. It also provides that other transferable securities specified in the Prospectus Rules will fall outside the scope of section 85(2). **8.90**

There are a couple of nuances to highlight in relation to admission to trading. **8.91**

First, in the case of admission to trading, section 85(6)(a) only exempts those transferable securities listed in Part I of Schedule 11A (such as, for example, those issued by EEA State issuers), whereas Schedule 11A to FSMA contains two parts. Section 85(6)(a) does not exempt transferable securities listed in Part II of Schedule 11A to FSMA (for example, the sub €5,000,000 exemption). In contrast, in relation to public offers, section 85(5)(a) refers to the whole of Schedule 11A to FSMA. **8.92**

Secondly, in the case of exemptions set out in the Prospectus Rules, the exemptions from the requirement to publish a prospectus in relation to the admission to trading limb are different from the public offer exemptions. **8.93**

The relevant PR rule is PR 1.2.3 which states that the prohibition contained within section 85(2) FSMA does not apply to admission to trading of transferable securities of the following types: **8.94**

a) shares representing, over a 12-month period, less than 10 per cent of the number of shares of the same class already admitted to trading;
b) shares issued in substitution for shares of the same class provided the issue does not increase the issued share capital;

86 See 'General contents of a prospectus', at para 8.100.
87 See 'The UK Listing Regime' section.

c) transferable securities offered in connection with a takeover or merger if an equivalent document is made available;
d) shares allotted free of charge to existing shareholders and dividends paid out in the form of shares of the same class as the shares in respect of which the dividend is paid if a document containing information on the number and nature of the shares and the reasons for and details of the offer are made available;
e) securities offered, allotted, or to be allotted to existing or former directors or employees by their employer or an affiliated undertaking which has securities of the same class admitted to trading on a regulated market if a document containing information on the number and nature of the securities and the reasons for and details of the offer are made available;
f) shares resulting from the conversion or exchange of other transferable securities; or
g) transferable securities already admitted to trading on another regulated market.

Drawing up the Prospectus

8.95 Having described when a prospectus is required—either for a public offer or admission to trading on a regulated market in the UK—the next section outlines the legislative provisions governing what the prospectus needs to look like.

Format of prospectus—single document or tripartite

8.96 The Prospectus Directive provides that a prospectus can be drawn up as a single document or as separate documents comprising: a) a registration document (which contains information relating to the issuer (essentially, a business description)); b) a securities note (which provides details of the securities to be offered or admitted (essentially, terms and conditions)); and c) if applicable, a summary (which conveys the essential characteristics and risks associated with the issuer and securities). The registration document, accompanied by the securities note (updated, if applicable) and the summary (if applicable), together, constitute a valid prospectus. Issuers are able to file a registration document, which is valid for up to 12 months. They can then, subject to the obligation to update the registration note in PR 2.2.5, file a securities note and summary when they plan to offer or issue the securities.

8.97 In early drafts of the Prospectus Directive, the registration document concept reflected the current US approach, and the intention was to require such a document to be filed annually. Indeed, one radical approach which was mooted during the drafting process for the Prospectus Directive was to require the registration document (which would contain all material information in respect of the issuer) to be a 'live' document, kept up-to-date on a relatively continuous basis, in a manner similar to the ongoing disclosure requirements triggered by the filing of a registration statement with the United States Securities and Exchange Commission ('SEC') pursuant to the United States Securities Act of 1933. The securities note would then contain all additional information relating to the securities being offered or admitted to trading on a regulated market and the summary note would, in a brief, non-technical manner, convey the essential characteristics and risks associated with the issuer and the securities.

8.98 This approach was sensibly abandoned before the Directive was finalised. The concept of a tripartite prospectus remains, but only as an option. Issuers have the choice to draw up a prospectus as a single document or, alternatively, as two or three separate documents. In practice, the majority of issuers opt for a single document.

For certain non-equity transferable securities, an issuer can choose to produce a prospectus which contains all the information concerning the issuer, but, rather than relating to a particular issue, it contains a menu of general terms and conditions for a possible range of different transferable securities which may be issued over the next 12 months. These are commonly referred to as base prospectuses. For any particular issue, the particular criteria for the deal (such as whether the notes have a fixed interest rate or a floating interest rate, the maturity date, and the interest coupon) can then be selected and indicated in a short pro forma document known as final terms ('Final Terms') which completes the base prospectus for the issue. Even in the case of prospectuses for programmes (such as base prospectuses for Medium Term Note ('MTN') programmes), issuers tend to prepare their prospectuses as single documents, updating their disclosure only when necessary in connection with a proposed offering or admission to trading, to comply with obligations under PR 2.2.8 to publish a supplementary prospectus, if necessary. **8.99**

General contents of a prospectus

Section 87A(2), (3), and (4) of FSMA provide for the general contents of prospectuses. As described earlier,[88] a prospectus is required to contain the necessary information to enable investors to make an informed assessment of the assets and liabilities, financial position, profits and losses, and prospects of the issuer of the transferable securities and of any guarantor; and the rights attaching to the transferable securities. In addition, the necessary information must be presented in a form which is comprehensible and easy to analyse. **8.100**

Specific contents of a prospectus

In relation to detailed content, though, as already described, the content is mandated by the directly applicable EU Prospectus Directive Regulation. **8.101**

The Prospectus Directive Regulation contains detailed Annexes setting out, by product, what each prospectus for each product must contain. In 2005, there were 19 separate disclosure Annexes. Additional Annexes were added by two of the recent amending Regulations to the Prospectus Directive Regulation (in March[89] and June[90] 2012). There are now 30 Annexes, in total. **8.102**

The nature of the prospectus disclosure required will depend on whether the securities fall within the Prospectus Directive definition of equity securities or non-equity securities and the applicability of the various disclosure schedules and 'building blocks' in the Prospectus Directive Regulation. **8.103**

Annexes I, II, and III in the Prospectus Directive Regulation outline information generally required for share prospectus disclosure. The other Annexes range across different types of debt and derivative products, such as asset-backed securities, convertible and exchangeable bonds, securities issued by banks, third-country states and regional authorities, as well as special provision for rights issues. **8.104**

One Annex (Annex XVIII) is simply a table or chart, indicating, in the form of a shaded grid, how the different disclosure Annexes should be used together. A Delegated Regulation **8.105**

[88] See 'UK implementation—original implementation in 2005', at para 8.37.
[89] Commission Delegated Regulation (EU) No 486/2012 of 30 March 2012. See n 17.
[90] Commission Delegated Regulation (EU) No 862/2012 of 4 June 2012. See n 18.

dated 30 April 2013,[91] which was published in the Official Journal of the European Union on 8 August 2013, makes further changes to the Prospectus Directive Regulation, including making changes to Annex XVIII.

8.106 The premise of the Annexes and the building blocks is fairly straightforward. As an example, for an issue of unsecured debt securities having a small denomination of, say, €1,000, a corporate issuer would look to fulfil the disclosure requirements set out in Annexes IV and V of the Prospectus Directive Regulation. One Annex relates to the registration statement (essentially, business description disclosure) requirements. The other specifies the particular disclosure which is required for the 'securities note' (essentially, terms and conditions). In addition, a prospectus summary will be required and will need to comply with new requirements for prospectus summaries, discussed later in the chapter. Where securities are asset-backed, the disclosure requirements for the underlying pool of securities or assets are contained in a separate disclosure Annex and, similarly, for derivative securities (in Prospectus Directive regime terms, meaning anything where more or less than 100 per cent of principal may be returned) details of any underlying criteria must be disclosed.

8.107 The new Annexes added in 2012 include Annexes permitting more limited disclosure requirements for certain issuers, such as for rights issues or for SMEs and companies with reduced market capitalisation. Finally, as well as amending Annex XVIII, the latest Delegated Regulation[92] also applies the proportionate disclosure regime to certain convertible or exchangeable securities.

8.108 However, certain of the additional Annexes do not relate to specific issuers or products, but, rather, impose some new, more prescriptive requirements which apply to a number of specific products.

8.109 First, detailed rules have been laid down, in Annex XXII, for the format and content for the summary for any prospectus. In addition, in cases where a summary is not strictly required (for example, in the case of debt securities with a denomination of €100,000 or above, where the prospectus is being prepared for listing purposes), but an issuer opts to include a summary (and chooses to call it a 'summary'), the document must follow the prescribed format.

8.110 Separately, in the case of a prospectus which has been compiled as a base prospectus for a programme (rather than for a 'stand-alone' deal), new Annex XX classifies disclosure information in relevant Annexes into 'Categories' (Category or 'Cat' A, B, or C). It mandates which information must be contained 'up-front' and disclosed only in the base prospectus (Cat A) and which, more limited, deal-specific information may be left to be completed at a later stage, and filled in as part of the Final Terms for a particular issue (Cat C).

8.111 This is, arguably, one area in which the tendency towards investor protection can be seen. For example, any formulae must be contained in a prospectus and must be checked by competent authorities, rather than being left to be added in to any separate, shorter accompanying Final Terms at the time of issue. Similarly, where products contain variables and permutations, worked examples and illustrations are now required to be included in prospectuses.

[91] Commission Delegated Regulation (EU) No 759/2013 of 30 April 2013. See n 19.
[92] Delegated Regulation (EU) No 759/2013 of 30 April 2013. See n 19.

As mentioned in connection with offers to the public and the new provision in section 86 of FSMA,[93] new Annex XXX of the Prospectus Directive Regulation sets out detailed requirements relating to issuers giving consent to financial intermediaries using its prospectus. Consent to use of the prospectus may be given on either a general basis (to any financial intermediary meeting certain criteria and conditions) or on a specific basis (to particular, named entities). 8.112

Prospectus summaries

All prospectuses (whether or not in the form of one document) need to contain a summary. The only exception to the requirement to include a summary is a prospectus relating to debt securities having a minimum denomination of at least €100,000. However, the Prospectus Directive regime expressly provides that no civil liability attaches to those persons responsible for the summary (including any translation) unless it is misleading, inaccurate, or inconsistent when read together with the other parts of the prospectus. 8.113

Historically, there was no particular guidance regarding the content of summaries, subject to an overall word limit of no more than 2,500 words and a requirement that it convey, 'briefly and in non-technical language the essential characteristics and risks associated with the issuer and transferable securities to which the prospectus relates'. There are slight wording changes to summary requirements in the amendments to the Prospectus Directive Regulation made in July 2012, such that the summary must now be drafted in 'clear language' and present 'key information in an easily accessible and understandable way', but this drafting change is not significant. Since 1 July 2012, there have been two other key changes to summaries. 8.114

As regards length, the word limit has now been removed. Instead, the limit is set in relation to the length of the rest of the prospectus: either 7 per cent of the length of the prospectus or 15 pages, whichever is longer. The second change is more significant. As mentioned,[94] a new Annex (Annex XXII), introduced with effect from 1 July 2012, now prescribes exactly what must be included in a summary (including a requirement for negative statements where something is not applicable). 8.115

In the case of base prospectuses and Final Terms, there is a further change. An 'issue-specific summary', significantly in the form of the main base prospectus summary, must now be completed and annexed to the Final Terms for each issue. As at the date of writing, some competent authorities were requiring this to be annexed to Final Terms even if the particular tranche was of denominations of €100,000 or above (when a summary would not ordinarily be required). This is being requested where the issue is being done as a 'drawdown' off a retail base prospectus (that is, a prospectus permitting issuance in smaller denominations of less than €100,000, as well as in higher wholesale denominations). It is, though, possible that this approach may change. 8.116

Risk factors

Continuing the theme and the original premise of investor protection through disclosure, the Prospectus Directive regime requires all issuers to include disclosure on risk factors. 8.117

[93] See 'Exempt offers—consent', at para 8.83.
[94] See 'Specific contents of a prospectus', at para 8.101.

Recital 19 to the Prospectus Directive stated that 'Investment in securities, like any form of investment, involves risk. Safeguards for the protection of the interests of actual and potential investors are required in all Member States in order to enable them to make an informed assessment of such risks and thus to take investment decisions in full knowledge of the facts…'.

8.118 The risk factors must also be summarised in any summary section. That, in itself, is not new, although, one of the areas of concern, recently, has been the requirement, as specified in new Annex XXII of the Prospectus Directive Regulation, to summarise only 'key information on the key risks' to the issuer, its industry, and its securities. In the UK, this is reflected at Section D, Annex 22 of PR Appendix 3. The FCA recently revised its guidance on risk factors[95] (as at July 2013, following a market consultation) to reflect market concerns that such a requirement to select only 'key' risks to summarise, rather than being able to summarise all risk factors, might expose issuers to liability. The FCA will therefore allow issuers to include disclaimer text, alerting investors to the fact that the summary section may not contain all key risks.

8.119 In addition, the UK regulator is keen to stress that any risk factors should be specific to an issuer and/or any industry, rather than being generic.

Incorporation by reference

8.120 Information may be incorporated in the prospectus by reference to one or more previously or simultaneously published documents that have been approved by the FCA or filed with or notified to it in accordance with the Transparency Directive. Information incorporated by reference must be the latest available to the issuer, offeror, or person requesting admission.

8.121 The summary must not incorporate information by reference.

Languages

8.122 The Prospectus Directive contains complicated provisions for determining which language(s) the prospectus must be written in and it makes much use of the phrase 'a language customary in the sphere of international finance'. If a prospectus is drawn up only in 'a language customary in the sphere of international finance', the only translation that is likely to be required is that in some circumstances a competent authority may require the summary to be translated into 'its official language(s)'. In particular, even where a summary is not otherwise required (because the prospectus relates to the admission to trading on a regulated market of debt securities having a minimum denomination of at least €100,000), Member States may choose to require in their national legislation that a summary be drawn up in their official language(s).

8.123 In the Prospectus Rules, PR 4.1 requires that, if an offer to the public and admission to trading is sought only in the UK, the prospectus must be prepared in English.

8.124 Where the United Kingdom is the home Member State, for the purpose of the scrutiny of a prospectus by the FCA, PR 4.1.3 states that the prospectus must be drawn up either in English or in another language customary in the sphere of international finance, with the FCA deeming a language to be 'customary in the sphere of international finance' if accepted

---

[95] UKLA/TN/621.2.

for scrutiny and filing of documents in at least three international capital markets in each of the following: Europe, Asia, and the Americas.

Responsibility for a prospectus

The rules in PR 5.5 specify the persons responsible for a prospectus.[96] **8.125**

The Prospectus Directive does not specifically state who should take statutory responsibility for prospectuses, but Article 6 of the Prospectus Directive imposed an obligation on Member States to ensure that statutory responsibility applies to at least 'the issuer or its administrative, management or supervisory bodies, the offeror, the person asking for admission to trading on a regulated market or the guarantor, as the case may be'. Within these parameters, Member States were given the ability to determine who should take statutory responsibility for prospectuses. **8.126**

The UKLA, following a consultation in 2005,[97] used the previous (pre-2005) regime as the basis for the new rules and the policy approach was, generally, to replicate the previous regime as closely as possible. In the UK, therefore, the rules only require the directors or proposed directors of an issuer to accept responsibility if the securities are equity shares. In the case of non-equity securities or convertible or exchangeable securities, it is optional for individuals to choose to take responsibility for the prospectus in addition to the issuer. **8.127**

In relation to equity shares, PR 5.5.3 states that the following are responsible: a) the issuer of the transferable securities; b) if the issuer is a body corporate: i) each person who is a director of that body corporate when the prospectus is published; and ii) each person who has authorised himself to be named, and is named, in the prospectus as a director or as having agreed to become a director of that body corporate either immediately or at a future time; iii) each person who is a senior executive of any external management company of the issuer; c) each person who accepts, and is stated in the prospectus as accepting, responsibility for the prospectus; d) in relation to an offer: i) the offeror, if this is not the issuer; and ii) if the offeror is a body corporate and is not the issuer, each person who is a director of the body corporate when the prospectus is published; e) in relation to a request for the admission to trading of transferable securities: i) the person requesting admission, if this is not the issuer; and ii) if the person requesting admission is a body corporate and is not the issuer, each person who is a director of the body corporate when the prospectus is published; and f) each person not falling within any of the previous paragraphs who has authorised the contents of the prospectus. **8.128**

For all other securities, PR 5.5.4 specifies the following as being responsible: a) the issuer of the transferable securities; b) each person who accepts, and is stated in the prospectus as accepting, responsibility for the prospectus; c) in relation to an offer, the offeror of the transferable securities, if this is not the issuer; d) in relation to a request for an admission to trading of transferable securities, the person requesting admission, if this is not the issuer; e) if there is a guarantor for the issue, the guarantor in relation to information in the prospectus that relates to the guarantor and the guarantee; and f) each person not falling within any of the previous paragraphs who has authorised the contents of the prospectus. **8.129**

[96] In accordance with s 84(1)(d) of FSMA and for the purposes of Part 6 of FSMA.
[97] Consultation Paper CP05/7. April 2005.

Supplementary prospectuses and withdrawal rights

8.130 In addition to determining when a prospectus must be produced, the Prospectus Directive regime also imposes a specific obligation to produce a supplement to a prospectus in certain circumstances. It also awards statutory 'walk away rights' or investor 'withdrawal rights' in certain circumstances when a supplement is published.

8.131 Article 16 of the Prospectus Directive provides that a supplementary prospectus is required if a significant new factor, material mistake, or inaccuracy relating to the information contained in the prospectus arises or is noted during the relevant period. In the UK, the provision is implemented in section 87G of FSMA.

8.132 Section 87G(3) of FSMA sets out the relevant period when a supplementary prospectus may be required. It has recently been clarified. Originally, the relevant period was defined as beginning when the prospectus is approved and ending with the closure of the offer or when trading begins. There was some uncertainty over which of the two dates would take precedence as the Prospectus Directive and FSMA were silent as to whether it should be the earlier, or later, of the closure of the offer or admission. The favoured interpretation was that it should be the later of the closure of the offer or admission. Article 16 of the Prospectus Directive was amended by the 2010 amending Directive to clarify this interpretation[98] and implemented in the UK, via The Prospectus Regulations 2012.[99]

8.133 One other common debate is what is meant by 'significant'. It is defined in section 87(G) of FSMA as 'significant for the purposes of making an informed assessment of the kind mentioned in section 87A(2)'. That is the general disclosure obligation, deriving from the Prospectus Directive, to tell investors everything they need to know to make their investment decision.

8.134 The debate has often been from two different angles. On the one hand, issuers often fear triggering investor withdrawal rights if a supplement is published. On the other, there can sometimes be a reluctance from competent authorities to permit issuers to prepare a supplement if, in their view, the change which an issuer wishes to make is not significant. For example, in October 2013, the UK Listing Authority, in a Technical Note on supplementary prospectuses[100] stated that 'We believe that Article 16 requires us to consider whether the matter presented in a supplementary prospectus is indeed a significant new factor, material mistake or inaccuracy [...] capable of affecting the assessment of the securities, and also whether the matter relates to the information included in the [original] prospectus...'.

8.135 In addition, the European Commission (through ESMA) is currently consulting on whether to specify pre-determined 'trigger events' which might require a supplement to be published. ESMA issued a consultation paper on 15 March 2013,[101] which closed in summer 2013, setting out 10 suggested scenarios or 'triggers'. The sample scenarios proposed in the ESMA consultation were: a) publication of new annual audited financial statements; b) profit forecast for equity securities and depositary receipts; c) profit estimate for an annual financial period; d) change in control of the issuer for equity securities and depositary receipts;

[98] By adding the phrase 'whichever occurs later' into art 16(1) of the Prospectus Directive.

[99] The Prospectus Regulations 2012. See n 21.

[100] UKLA/TN/605.2—Supplementary prospectuses.

[101] Consultation Paper ESMA/2013/316. Draft Regulatory Technical Standards on specific situations that require the publication of a supplement to the prospectus.

e) public takeover bids for equity securities and depositary receipts; f) Working Capital Statements for certain equity securities; g) admission to trading or offer to the public in an additional EU Member State; h) new significant financial commitment for equity securities; i) any decision of governmental, legal or arbitration proceedings already disclosed in the prospectus; and j) increase in aggregate amount of the programme.

The FCA reported in its latest Primary Market Bulletin ('PMB') publication, published in October 2013, that ESMA is currently considering the comments received on the ESMA consultation and will submit draft regulatory technical standards to the European Commission by 1 January 2014. **8.136**

In the meantime, the determination of 'significant' remains something for an issuer to determine. Separately, for minor amendments and corrections, the option remains for an issuer to publish a correction notice to the market (as outlined in the ESMA Q&A—question 23: 'in case the prospectus contains a mistake or inaccuracy that is not material or significant pursuant to Article 16 of the Directive, the issuer should be entitled to make an announcement to the market explaining the mistake or inaccuracy…').[102] **8.137**

Withdrawal rights

Following a change in July 2012, a slightly uncertain issue also exists with regard to investor withdrawal rights and when they apply following publication of a supplement. **8.138**

Article 16(2) of the Prospectus Directive FSMA contains withdrawal rights for investors in certain circumstances. As mentioned, this is implemented in the UK in section 87Q of FSMA. Section 87Q(4) and (5) of FSMA states, with emphasis added in bold: '…(4) A person ('P') may withdraw P's acceptance of an offer of transferable securities to the public before the specified time where the conditions in subsection (5) are satisfied. (5) The conditions are that: a) a prospectus **which relates to an offer of transferable securities** to the public has been published; b) a supplementary prospectus has been published; [continues]…'. **8.139**

The phrase 'which relates to an offer of transferable securities to the public' was added in July 2012. The problem is that it is not wholly clear what the phrase is intended to mean. A commonly debated view during the evolution of the amendments to the Prospectus Directive in 2010 was that it would mean that a supplement to a wholesale prospectus would not be caught by the statutory investor walk away right. Technically, though, as implemented in the UK, an offer of wholesale securities with a denomination of €100,000, in section 86 of FSMA, still counts as an 'offer of securities to the public', albeit an offer (an 'exempt offer') for which a prospectus is not required, unless the securities will be admitted to trading on a regulated market. **8.140**

Conversely, the inclusion of the new text in Article 16(2) of the Prospectus Directive seems unusual if nothing were intended by it. One question is whether special emphasis should be given to the phrase 'relates to', thereby meaning that a prospectus which 'relates to' admission to trading (as in the case of a wholesale prospectus) would not be caught. Recital 23 to the 2010 amending Directive[103] lends some weight to this argument: **8.141**

> …In order to improve legal certainty, it should be clarified when the requirement to publish a supplement to the prospectus and the right of withdrawal end. Those provisions should be

[102] Updated as at December 2012, but appearing in the October 2013, version 20 of the ESMA Q&A.
[103] Directive 2010/73/EU. See n 16.

> looked at separately. The obligation to supplement a prospectus should be terminated at the final closing of the offering period or the time when trading of such securities on a regulated market begins, whichever occurs later. On the other hand, the right to withdraw an acceptance should be applicable only where the prospectus relates to an offer of securities to the public and the new factor, mistake or inaccuracy arose before the final closing of the offer and the delivery of the securities....

As at August 2013, in light of the uncertainty in the underlying legislation, as well as the fact that there may be differing interpretations in different jurisdictions, many issuers are adopting a cautious approach with regard to withdrawal rights for wholesale prospectuses.

The UK Listing Regime

8.142 As described earlier,[104] in the UK, the listing process comprises two aspects: admission to the Official List administered by the FCA, combined with admission to trading on one of the markets of the London Stock Exchange.

8.143 As well as being given powers under Part 6 of FSMA[105] to make rules in relation to those who are seeking admission of securities to trading on a regulated market or offering securities to the public in the UK (namely, the Prospectus Rules), the UK Listing Authority was also given powers to make other rules. In relation to the listing regime in the UK, these include other rules which are contained in its FCA Handbook alongside the Prospectus Rules. That segment of the FCA Handbook also contains rules in relation to:

(i) issuers who are listed on (or are seeking admission to) the Official List (the Listing Rules or LRs); and
(ii) issuers who have financial instruments admitted to trading on a regulated market in the UK (the Disclosure and Transparency Rules or DTRs).

Listing—general

8.144 As competent authority, the FCA is responsible for maintaining the Official List and for admitting to listing the securities covered by Part 6 of FSMA. The FCA is empowered by section 73A of FSMA to make rules governing the admission to listing, the enforcement of those obligations, and suspension and cancellation of listing. These rules, which also contain the over-arching Listing Principles, are collectively known as the Listing Rules.

8.145 As described in an FSA publication in March 2010,[106] there are a number of reasons why issuers might chose to be admitted to the Official List. These were described as including 'access to additional equity and debt capital; greater visibility in the market; and growth not limited by cash resources'. The benefits are balanced by some consequential obligations, such as additional responsibilities of directors, requirements for greater disclosure of information, and compliance with corporate governance requirements.

---

104 See 'Introduction', at para 8.01.
105 FSMA, s 73A.
106 FSA. Listing Regime FAQs. March 2010.

Listing categories—premium and standard

Following changes on 6 April 2010 (with some limited transitional relief until 2011), there are now two categories of listing: 'premium' and 'standard'.[107] Premium listing is only available for equity shares of commercial companies, closed-ended investment funds, and open-ended investment companies. A standard listing is also a possible option for equity. All other listings (such as, for preferred shares, convertible bonds, ordinary debt securities, depositary receipts, warrants, and other securitised derivatives) are a standard listing only. **8.146**

These replaced the previous categories of 'primary' and 'secondary' listing, following FSA consultations in 2009 on changes to the UK listing regime,[108] and were intended to bring greater clarity and transparency to the Official List and, also, to the obligations that apply to different categories of listing. **8.147**

A standard listing sets requirements that are based on the minimum EU directive standards.[109] A listing that is described as a premium listing will include requirements that exceed those required under relevant EU directives, including the need to comply with Listing Principles and sponsor requirements. **8.148**

Listing obligations—premium equity listing—Listing Principles

The Listing Principles apply to every listed company with a premium listing of equity shares. The Listing Principles are designed to assist listed companies in identifying their obligations and responsibilities under the Listing Rules and the DTRs, as opposed to imposing additional obligations. Their purpose is to ensure that listed companies pay due regard to the fundamental role they play in maintaining market confidence and ensuring fair and orderly markets. There are six Listing Principles, set out below, which are contained in LR 7. **8.149**

The Listing Principles are: **8.150**

Principle 1—A listed company must take reasonable steps to enable its directors to understand their responsibilities and obligations as directors.

Principle 2—A listed company must take reasonable steps to establish and maintain adequate procedures, systems, and controls to enable it to comply with its obligations.

Principle 3—A listed company must act with integrity towards holders and potential holders of its listed equity securities.

Principle 4—A listed company must communicate information to holders and potential holders of its listed equity securities in such a way as to avoid the creation or continuation of a false market in such listed equity securities.

Principle 5—A listed company must ensure that it treats all holders of the same class of its listed equity securities that are in the same position equally in respect of the rights attaching to such listed equity securities.

Principle 6—A listed company must deal with the FCA in an open and cooperative manner.

Historically, much of the debate on Listing Principles centred on Listing Principles 2 and 4, with additional guidance being provided on both rules. Recently, though, there has also **8.151**

[107] LR 1.5.1.

[108] CP09/24 and CP09/28.

[109] LR 1.5.1.

been some debate on Listing Principle 6 and, in July 2013, the FCA revised its guidance[110] in relation to Listing Principle 6:

> . . . LP6 requires premium listed issuers to deal with the FCA in an open and co-operative manner. This obligation is broader than simply requiring issuers to ensure that they deal with the FCA in an open and co-operative manner on on-going matters. In particular, LP6 also requires issuers to approach the FCA in relation to significant transactions. However, it is not necessary for issuers to contact the FCA in relation to all transactions. . . .

The guidance then lists some 'rules of thumb' for issuers to use in determining when to contact the FCA.

Listing obligations—premium equity listing—sponsors

8.152 The sponsor regime is a 'super-equivalent' regime imposed on the premium listing segment only. The statutory basis for the regime is set out in section 88 of FSMA and sponsor rules are set out in the FCA Handbook at LR 8. There have been some recent changes to the sponsor regime. FSMA was amended, on 1 April 2013, to extend the FCA's powers in relation to the approval, supervision, and discipline of sponsors. The FCA was granted new powers to impose limitations or other restrictions on the services to which a sponsor's approval relates at the time of granting a sponsor's approval or in relation to existing sponsors. Powers also include the power to suspend a sponsor or to fine sponsors. To reflect the changes brought in by the Financial Services Act 2012, LR 8 was also amended.

Listing obligations—premium equity listing—other obligations

8.153 In addition to having to adhere to Listing Principles and sponsor requirements, a corporate issuer of equity securities with a premium listing will have to comply with other listing obligations in the Listing Rules, as well as the Prospectus Rules and DTRs. In the Listing Rules, these other obligations include eligibility requirements, continuing obligations, and other general obligations. Briefly, these are: a) eligibility requirements—an issuer will be required to comply with the relevant requirements of LR 2 and LR 6 (three-year revenue earning record, control of an independent business, unqualified working capital statement); b) continuing obligations—an issuer will be required to comply with the DTRs and the continuing aspects of the Prospectus Rules, as well as LR 9 (Pre-emption rights, Combined Code disclosure, Model Code), LR 10 (Significant transaction rules), LR 11 (Related party rules), LR 12 (Repurchases of securities), and LR 13 (Contents of circulars); and c) general obligations—an issuer will also be subject to LR 1, LR 2, LR 3, and LR 5. Issuers that are closed-ended investment funds and open-ended investment companies that have premium listed equity shares must comply with either LR 15 or LR 16 of the Listing Rules, as applicable, as well as complying with many of the requirements in Listing Rules 6 to 13 of the Listing Rules.

8.154 One change brought in as part of the introduction of the premium and standard regime (although subject to transitional arrangements) was in relation to overseas incorporated companies. Under the previous primary and secondary listing regime, there were some slight differences in the way in which overseas and UK incorporated companies were required to adhere to super-equivalent provisions. For example, historically, LR 9 set different standards for

[110] UKLA/ TN/209.1—Guidance consultation.

overseas and UK incorporated companies. One example is the 'Comply or Explain' requirement (stating in the annual report whether the company complies with the UK Combined Code and providing an explanation). Overseas companies were not subject to this obligation and were subject to slightly different requirements instead. Another example is the requirement to offer pre-emption rights to existing shareholders (which did not apply to companies incorporated outside the United Kingdom). The revised regime in April 2010 removed many of the differences. For example, the new regime requires overseas companies with a premium listing of equity shares to comply with the pre-emption requirements (although there were some transitional provisions to 5 April 2011). However, a number of differences still remain. For example, DTR 7.1 (relating to the requirement to have an audit committee (pursuant to the Statutory Audit Directive requirements)) only applies to UK incorporated issuers and not to overseas issuers.

Listing obligations—standard listing—other securities

In contrast, securities with a standard listing will have to comply with more limited Listing Rules. These depend on the type of product. For example: equity shares and non-equity shares will need to comply with LR 14 (Standard listing—shares); debt securities will need to comply with LR 17 (Debt and debt-like securities: standard listing); certificates representing certain securities (GDRs) will need to comply with LR 18; securities derivatives will need to comply with LR 19; and, finally, miscellaneous securities will need to refer to LR 20. In addition, all securities will need to comply with LR 2 and LR 3, which apply to all securities. **8.155**

Listing obligations—listing particulars for professional securities market and certain other securities

In addition, primarily in relation to debt securities, where securities are to be admitted to trading on the Professional Securities Market ('PSM') of the London Stock Exchange, as opposed to the Main Market, the content requirements for the listing particulars are set out in the Listing Rules at LR 4. The PSM is not a regulated market and therefore the Prospectus Rules and the requirements of section 85(2) of FSMA do not apply. The 'general duty of disclosure in listing particulars' obligation is set out at section 80 of FSMA and LR 4 sets out the content requirements for listing particulars—although, in fact, cross-referring to certain of the debt disclosure Annexes outlined in the Prospectus Rules. **8.156**

The following minimum information from the Prospectus Directive Regulation must be included in listing particulars: a) for an issue of bonds including bonds convertible into the issuer's shares or exchangeable into a third-party issuer's shares or derivative securities, irrespective of the denomination of the issue, the minimum information required by the schedules applicable to debt and derivative securities with a denomination per unit of at least €100,000 (that is, the 'wholesale' debt disclosure requirements); b) the additional information required by the underlying share building block, where relevant; c) for an issue of asset-backed securities, irrespective of the denomination per unit of the issue, the minimum information required by the schedules and building blocks applicable to asset-backed securities with a denomination per unit of at least €100,000; d) for an issue of certificates representing shares, irrespective of the denomination per unit of the issue, the schedule applicable to depositary receipts over shares with a denomination per unit of at least €100,000 (except that item 13.2 (relating to profit forecasts) in Annex 10 and Annex 28 is not to apply); e) for an issue of securities by the government of a non-EEA State or a local or regional authority of a non-EEA State, the schedule applicable to securities issued by third countries and their **8.157** regional and local authorities; and f) for all issues that are guaranteed, the information in the guarantee building block. For all other issues, the FCA would expect issuers to follow the most appropriate schedules and building blocks in the Prospectus Directive Regulation, in order to determine the minimum information to be included in listing particulars.

8.158 There are three key points to highlight in relation to listing particulars and the PSM. First, the less onerous wholesale disclosure obligations apply irrespective of the denomination of the securities. However, where securities have a denomination which is less than €100,000 (or its equivalent in other currencies), issuers need to beware of making an 'offer to the public' in the UK. That is because, in order to do so, they would need to have an approved prospectus for the purpose of section 85(1) of FSMA. Listing particulars prepared in compliance with LR 4 will not satisfy the requirements for retail denomination securities under the Prospectus Directive regime, nor will they fall within the offer exemption in section 86(1)(d) of FSMA. Similarly, for the same reason (namely, that there is no 'approved prospectus' complying with the Prospectus Directive regime), it will not be possible to make use of the Prospectus Directive regime 'passport' option within the EU for denominations of less than €100,000 or equivalent, either for an offer or for admitting to trading elsewhere.

8.159 Separately, for the avoidance of doubt, securities admitted to trading on the PSM do not trigger Transparency Directive compliance obligations or requirements to comply with the DTRs. In fact, for many issuers, one of the reasons to admit to trading on the PSM (rather than on a regulated market) is in order to avoid the DTRs, which, for denominations of less than €100,000, will require ongoing accounts to be prepared in accordance with IFRS (subject to certain, limited exceptions). Instead, for securities admitted to trading on the PSM, continuing obligations are derived from LR 17.

The Disclosure and Transparency Rules ('DTRs')

8.160 As a consequence of having securities admitted to trading on a regulated market in the UK, an issuer will be subject to on-going obligations. These are contained in detailed rules set out in seven chapters in the FCA Handbook.

8.161 The final section of this chapter considers these rules—that is, the Disclosure and Transparency Rules ('DTRs').

8.162 These chapters of the FCA Handbook were mentioned, briefly, earlier in the chapter and include: the Disclosure Rules (DTR 1, DTR 2, and DTR 3), derived from the Market Abuse Directive; the Transparency Rules (DTR 1, DTR 4, DTR 5, and DTR 6), which implement the Transparency Directive requirements, and the Corporate Governance rules (DTR 1 and DTR 7) which implement the Statutory Audit Directive and Company Law Directive requirements. Some rules apply to shares only. Some rules to debt securities only. Some rules apply to both.

Disclosure rules

8.163 The disclosure rules apply to issuers who have requested or approved admission of their securities to a regulated market based in the UK and to persons discharging managerial responsibility in those issuers and their associates. This extends the application of the rules beyond listed issuers. However, it is worth noting that the regime set out in DTR 2 does not extend to financial instruments (including derivatives) which are issued by another party.

Given the purpose of the Disclosure Rules, it is not surprising that the bulk of this segment regulates disclosure of inside information and, also, sets out penalties for failure to comply. **8.164**

Disclosure of inside information

There are a number of key issues under the disclosure regime in DTR 2. The starting point is to establish whether an issuer is in possession of inside information. If so, the question is whether the disclosure can be delayed. If disclosure can be delayed, issuers can consider selective disclosure. **8.165**

DTR 2.2.1 requires inside information to be disclosed as soon as possible. Inside information is defined in section 118C of FSMA and is information of a precise nature which: a) is not generally available; b) relates to one or more issuers of qualifying investments; and c) would be likely to have a significant impact on the price of the qualifying investments or on the price of related investments. **8.166**

DTR 2.2.3G to DTR 2.2.8G provide detailed guidance to assist issuers in identifying inside information, based on a 'likely to be used by reasonable investor' and a 'price sensitivity' (likely to have a significant effect on the price) test. **8.167**

In particular, DTR 2.2.6G specifies the types of information which are likely to be relevant in making this assessment. In establishing whether a piece of information amounts to inside information issuers should, in particular, carefully consider the limits of the test which require the information to be both precise (see section 118C(5) of FSMA) and price-sensitive (including the reasonable investor test aspects). **8.168**

Information may be commercially sensitive but this does not mean it meets the test for inside information. If an issuer has inside information, it should consider whether an immediate announcement is required or whether the issuer can delay disclosure. DTR 2.2.9G(2) provides guidance on the use of a holding announcement when an issuer is faced with an unexpected and significant event which requires a short delay to clarify the situation prior to making a regular disclosure to the market. If the information does not amount to inside information, the Disclosure and Transparency Rules are not relevant and the issuer is not constrained under the Disclosure and Transparency Rules in how it deals with that information. **8.169**

DTR 2.7 provides guidance on dealing with rumours. There is a possibility that the knowledge which an issuer has that a particular piece of information or story is false could, in very limited circumstances, amount to inside information. The guidance given in DTR 2.7.3(G) makes it clear that the knowledge that a rumour is false is unlikely to amount to inside information and, even if it did, the issuer would usually be able to delay disclosure, often indefinitely. The more accurate a rumour, the more likely it is that there has been a breach of confidentiality and that disclosure is required as soon as possible. DTR 2.7.2(G) gives additional guidance on this point and reinforces the importance of maintaining the confidentiality of inside information. **8.170**

Delaying disclosure

An issuer may delay disclosure of inside information in the limited circumstances set out in DTR 2.5. The market understands that the disclosure of inside information can be delayed in appropriate circumstances and that such delay in disclosure will normally be limited to impending developments or matters in the course of negotiation. Issuers should be careful to distinguish between an event which gives rise to inside information (such as, the loss of **8.171** an important contract) that requires disclosure as soon as possible under DTR 2.2.1R and subsequent events (such as, attempts to renegotiate the contract) that may benefit from the delay provisions (DTR 2.5.4G (1)).

8.172 The question of the meaning of 'as soon as possible' recently came into focus again in the context of another new piece of EU legislation, the Credit Rating Agency Regulation ('CRA3'),[111] which came into force on 20 June 2013. One of the changes in CRA3 is that rating agencies must now give issuers 24- (as opposed to 12-) hours' notice of an impending change in rating or outlook. This triggered discussions, albeit on a 'hypothetical' basis, about whether the additional 12-hours' notice might mean that an issuer would have an obligation to consider making a disclosure ahead of the proposed announcement of the change by the agency in order to comply with the 'as soon as possible' test.

8.173 An issuer must disclose the inside information as soon as possible if it is not able to ensure the confidentiality of the information (DTR 2.6.2R).

Selective disclosure

8.174 Where an issuer is delaying disclosure of inside information in accordance with the DTRs, it can selectively disclose the information to persons who owe the issuer a duty of confidentiality and have a valid reason to receive the information. The list of persons who fall into this category set out in DTR 2.5.7G is not exhaustive, but includes advisers, lenders, major shareholders, and credit rating agencies.

Insider lists and senior managers

8.175 The basic requirement is for an issuer to draw up a list of employees and persons acting on its behalf who have access to inside information. The list is not a list of persons who actually have inside information, but, rather, those who have access to the information. This is an important matter for issuers to consider in deciding who should be on the list.

8.176 Guidance provides a practical approach for issuers who are responsible for ensuring that insider lists cover not only their own employees but also persons acting on the issuer's behalf or account, namely advisers. The guidance is designed to provide a practical solution for issuers and clarifies that it is not necessary for an issuer to maintain a list of all the individuals working for another firm or company acting on its behalf or account where it has: a) recorded the name of the principal contact(s) at that firm or company; b) made effective arrangements, which are likely to be based in contract, for that firm or company to maintain its own list of employees, both working on behalf of the issuer and with access to inside information on it; and c) made effective arrangements for that firm or company to provide a copy to the issuer of its list as soon as possible upon request.

8.177 For advisers, a person needs to meet a two-stage test to be included on the insider list in DTR 2.8.8G. Persons need both to be acting for the issuer and have access to inside information to be included on the list.

8.178 DTR 3.1.2R requires persons discharging managerial responsibility and persons connected to such persons (as defined in section 96B(1) of FSMA) to disclose all transactions conducted on their own account in the shares or derivatives or financial instruments relating to

[111] Regulation (EU) No 462/2013.

shares, to the issuer within four days of the transaction. This information must then, in turn, be notified to a Regulatory Information Service (DTR 3.1.4 R(1)).

DTR3 does not clarify what is meant by 'own account' in relation to director dealings. **8.179**

Penalties

Issuers should be aware that non-compliance with certain elements of the DTR rules may also have the following legal consequences over and above the punishment for regulatory breach. **8.180**

First, it is a criminal offence to make an intentionally misleading or reckless statement, promise or forecast or dishonestly conceal any material facts for the purpose of inducing another person to buy or sell or exercise any rights conferred by a relevant investment. From 1 April 2013, this offence is contained in section 89 and 90 FSA 2012. The offence was formerly contained in section 397 of FSMA, which was repealed by the FSA 2012. Secondly, under sections 2 and 3 of the Fraud Act 2006, it is a criminal offence either to make false representations or to fail to disclose information when there is a legal duty to do so. Thirdly, there may be offences under the market abuse regime set out in Part 8 of FSMA.[112] Market abuse offences include: insider dealing, improper disclosure, misuse of information, manipulating transactions, manipulating devices, dissemination; distortion and misleading behaviour—each of which may have application to elements of the DTR rules. There may also be implications under Part V of the Criminal Justice Act 1993 relating to inside information. (It is a criminal offence to transact in securities that are price-sensitive to that information; encourage another person to deal in securities that are price-sensitive to that information; or improperly disclose inside information.) **8.181**

Transparency rules

Whilst the Prospectus Directive deals with disclosure in relation to offers and admission to trading on a regulated market, the Transparency Directive harmonises the requirements to disclose information about issuers whose securities are already admitting to trading on a regulated market. One of the main features is to require periodic financial reports, but it also obliges shareholders in such companies to disclose major shareholdings. In addition, the Transparency Directive deals with the mechanisms for disseminating and storing such information. The FSA's approach to implementing this 'minimum harmonisation' directive in 2006 was to implement the directive minimum provisions, and to retain super-equivalent provisions only if they could be clearly justified in terms of cost to benefit, and where they were strongly supported by both issuers and investors. **8.182**

Amendments to Part 6 of FSMA (made by Part 43 of the Companies Act 2006) together with the FSA's Transparency Obligations Directive (Disclosure and Transparency Rules) Instrument 2006 served to implement the Transparency Directive in the United Kingdom. Three new chapters were added to the DTRs: periodic financial reporting (DTR 4), vote holder and issuer notifications (DTR 5), and continuing obligations and access to information (DTR 6). **8.183**

Periodic financial reporting

A copy-out approach was taken to implement the requirements of the Transparency Directive, resulting in the creation of DTR 4. **8.184**

112 See Chapter 9—Market Abuse.

8.185 DTR 4 requires listed companies to produce an Annual Financial Report, Half-yearly Report, and Interim Management Statements. It also sets out the responsibility statements, content requirements, and publication deadlines for each report, together with the partial exemptions available to issuers of debt, convertible securities, GDRs, and non-EEA issuers.

8.186 In order to implement Article 7 of the Transparency Directive, a statutory civil liability regime has been imposed for periodic financial information published under the provisions made implementing the Transparency Directive.

8.187 The regime is set out in section 90A of FSMA and Schedule 10A to FSMA,[113] and applies to all companies with securities admitted to trading on a regulated market in the UK. The regime also applies to companies admitted to trading on an overseas regulated market if the UK is that company's home Member State.

8.188 The liability regime applies to information required to be produced under DTR 4 (such as, contained in the Annual Financial Report, Half-yearly Report, and Interim Management Statements) as well as to some additional information described later in this chapter.

8.189 Section 90A of FSMA and Schedule 10A to FSMA provide that an issuer will be liable to pay compensation to a person who acquires, continues to hold, or disposes of, the securities in reliance on published information to which section Schedule 10A applies or suffers a loss in respect of the securities as a result of any untrue or misleading statement in or omission from that published information.

8.190 A company will only be liable if a director knew that the statement was untrue or misleading, was reckless as to whether it was reckless or misleading, or knew the omission to be dishonest concealment of material fact. The regime restricts liability to third parties to the company itself, although the directors involved in the misstatement/omissions may be held liable to the company.

8.191 The scope of the regime has been expanded since the previous edition of this book. Having previously been restricted to periodic disclosures under the Transparency Directive, it was expanded on 1 October 2010, following a Government-sponsored review,[114] to apply to other announcements, such as those made to the market by way of a Regulated Information Service ('RIS'). Schedule 10A does not, however, extend to cover liability for mis-statements in prospectuses, which remains governed by section 90 of FSMA.

Vote holder and issuer notification

8.192 The Transparency Directive provisions relating to the disclosure of major shareholdings were implemented in the UK through sections 89A to 89L of FSMA and DTR 5.

8.193 The new DTR 5 regime applies to all companies whose shares are admitted to trading on a regulated market for whom the UK is the home Member State. The regime also applies to UK companies incorporated under section 4(2) of the Companies Act 2006[115] with shares admitted to trading on a prescribed market.

113 Inserted by The FSMA (Liability of Issuers) Regulations 2010 (SI 2010/1192) on 1 October 2010.
114 March 2007, 'The Davies Review of Issuer Liability: Liability for misstatements to the market'.
115 Amended from s 1(3) of the Companies Act 1985 in the FCA Handbook by the Companies Act 2006 (Consequential Handbook Amendments No 3) Instrument 2009 (FSA 2009/50), with effect from 1 October 2009.

DTR 5.1.2 states that a person must notify the issuer of the percentage of its voting rights he holds as shareholder or through his direct or indirect holding of qualifying financial instruments if, as a result of an acquisition, disposal, or change in the breakdown if the voting rights, percentage of those voting rights: i) reaches, exceeds, or falls below 3 per cent, 4 per cent, 5 per cent, 6 per cent, 7 per cent, 8 per cent, 9 per cent, 10 per cent, and each 1 per cent threshold thereafter (in the case of a UK issuer); or ii) reaches, exceeds or falls below 5 per cent, 10 per cent, 15 per cent, 20 per cent, 25 per cent, 30 per cent, 50 per cent, and 75 per cent (in the case of a non-UK issuer), as a result of an acquisition, disposal, or events changing the breakdown of voting rights in the issuer. DTR 5 follows the provisions and definitions of the TD, and is therefore referenced to direct and indirect control of voting rights attaching to a share. **8.194**

DTR 5.1.3 provides exemptions from the general notification requirements potentially available to custodians and nominees, market makers, credit institutions, and shares acquired for settlement purposes or held as collateral. **8.195**

Continuing obligations and access to information

DTR 6 contains detailed provisions relating to the dissemination of regulated information. This chapter also includes a number of continuing obligations to work alongside those set out in LR 9 and applies to issuers admitted to trading on a regulated market. **8.196**

DTR 6.1 sets out detailed information requirements aimed at ensuring that all shareholders are treated equally in terms of access to information, and the exercise of their voting rights. These provisions are aimed at existing shareholders, the FSA, and the market and are set out as follows: a) provision of information relating to proposed amendments to constitution (DTR 6.1.2); b) equality of treatment (DTR 6.1.3); c) exercise of rights by holders (DTR 6.1.4); d) exercise of rights by proxy (DTR 6.1.5); e)appointment of a financial agent (DTR 6.1.6); f) electronic communications (DTR 6.1.7); g) information about changes in rights attaching to securities (DTR 6.1.9); h) information about meetings, issue of new shares and payment of dividends—share issuers (DTR 6.1.12); i) information about meetings and payment of interest—debt security issuers (DTR 6.1.14); j) non-EEA states exemption (DTR 6.1.16); k) regional and local authority exemption (DTR 6.1.18); l) exemption for issuers of convertible securities, preference shares, and depository receipts (DTR 6.1.19). **8.197**

The rules make it clear that all regulated information disclosed under this chapter must be filed simultaneously with the FCA (DTR 6.2.2 R). The rules also detail the language requirements for issuers with securities admitted to trading in more than one EEA State. **8.198**

DTR 6 operates alongside the Companies Act 2006 provisions[116] relating to issuers using 'electronic means' to communicate with equity and debt holders, but the Companies Act 2006 is to take precedence over DTR 6 in situations where both apply.[117] Under DTR 6, the consent obtained must be in writing, and identification arrangements must be put in place so that those persons entitled to exercise voting rights are effectively informed. The decision to use electronic means to communicate with shareholders or debt securities holders must be taken in general meeting, and the use of electronic means must not depend on the location of the seat of residence of the recipient.[118] **8.199**

[116] Sch 5 to the Companies Act 2006.
[117] DTR 6.1.8.
[118] DTR 6.1.8.

Corporate governance

8.200 Finally, DTR 7 was introduced in order to implement the corporate governance statement requirement of the Company Reporting Directive and the audit committee requirement of the Statutory Audit Directive.

Audit committees

8.201 DTR 7.1 contains the requirement for companies whose securities have been admitted to trading on a regulated market to have an audit committee which contains at least one member who is independent and at least one member who is competent in accounting and/or auditing. Such companies are also required to base any proposal to appoint a statutory auditor on a recommendation from the audit committee. In addition, these companies should make a statement available to the public disclosing which body carries out the functions required by DTR 7.1.3 R (audit committee in most cases) and how it is composed.

8.202 It is important to note that much of DTR 7.1 overlaps with requirements laid down in the Combined Code. The FSA have therefore added DTR 7.1.7 to make it clear that in their view, compliance with provisions A.1.2, C.3.1, C.3.2, and C.3.3 of the Combined Code will result in compliance with DTR 7.1.1 R to DTR 7.1.5 R.

8.203 As mentioned earlier,[119] Chapter 7.1 of the Disclosure and Transparency Rules (relating to the requirement to have an audit committee (pursuant to the Statutory Audit Directive requirements) only applies to UK incorporated issuers and not to overseas issuers.

Corporate governance

8.204 DTR 7.2 applies to an issuer whose securities are admitted to trading and which is a company within the meaning of section 1(1) of the Companies Act 2006 (DTR 1B.1.5 R). DTR 7.2 requires issuers to which this section applies to include a corporate governance statement as a specific statement in its directors' report, and goes on to list content requirements for this statement.

8.205 Several parts of this rule overlap with the pre-existing governance rules in place for UK companies with a premium equity listing, specifically the LR 9.8.6 requirements to 'comply or explain' against the UK Combined Code on Corporate Governance. DTR 7.2.8 clarifies the FSA's view that compliance with provisions A.1.1, A.1.2, A.4.6, B.2.1, and C.3.3 of the Combined Code satisfy the requirements of DTR 7.2.7.

8.206 Finally, DTR 1B.1.5A G clarifies that LR 9.8.7A, LR 14.3.24, and LR 18.4.3 extend the application of DTR 7.2 for certain overseas companies which have securities admitted to the Official List maintained by the FCA.

119 See para 8.154.

9

MARKET ABUSE

Background to the Introduction of the Market Abuse Regime

Introduction

9.01 This chapter looks at the civil market abuse regime introduced under the Financial Services and Markets Act 2000 ('FSMA'), as subsequently amended following the implementation of the EU directive on insider dealing and market manipulation (market abuse) ('MAD').[1] The chapter looks in turn at:

- the background to the introduction of the market abuse regime;
- the nature of the market abuse regime and underlying processes;
- an outline of the market abuse offences;
- market abuse offences concerning the use of information;
- market abuse offences that concern market manipulation and false or misleading behaviours;
- discovering and punishing market abuse; and finally
- European developments.

9.02 Part VIII of FSMA introduced a broad new power to tackle suspected wrongful behaviour on financial markets, namely the 'civil offence' of market abuse under section 118 of FSMA. These market abuse provisions sit alongside other powers, most importantly, the criminal offences of misleading statements and impressions[2] and insider dealing,[3] as well as the regulatory regime applying to regulated firms and individuals, and listed companies. The details of the market abuse regime are considered further in paragraph 9.17 *et seq.*, but firstly this section will consider the background to the introduction of the market abuse provisions and, in particular, will focus on the practitioner and academic criticisms levelled against the pre-FSMA criminal law powers and the failure of certain high-profile prosecutions relating to wrongdoing on financial markets. This section also considers the impact of MAD which forms part of the market abuse regime. The scope and status of the new proposed EU market abuse regulation ('Market Abuse Regulation')[4] and the proposed directive relating to

[1] Directive 2003/6/EC on insider dealing and market manipulation (market abuse) and related directives.

[2] ss 89 and 90 of the Financial Services Act 2012. Earlier measures relating to misleading statements and practices were contained in s 47 of the Financial Services Act 1985, which were then replaced by s 397 of FSMA (see discussion in M Blair, G Walker, and R Purves, *Financial Services Law*, 2nd edn, OUP 2009, Ch 10, para 10.46 *et seq.*) before in turn being replaced by ss 89 and 90 of the 2012 Act. See also the new offence relating to misleading statements in relation to benchmarks introduced under s 91 of the 2012 Act. On Insider Dealing and Misleading Statements and Impressions, see Chapter 10.

[3] Part V of the Criminal Justice Act 1993.

[4] European Commission Proposal for a Regulation of the European Parliament and of the Council on insider dealing and market manipulation (market abuse) 2011/0295 (COD).

criminal sanctions in relation to market abuse ('CSD')[5] are discussed later in this chapter at paragraph 9.22 *et seq*.

9.03 Since the introduction of the new UK regulatory architecture, the FCA has taken over from the FSA enforcement powers with respect to the market abuse regime.

Market abuse provisions in FSMA intended to fill a legislative 'gap'

9.04 The intended role of the FSMA market abuse regime was made clear in a statement made by the Economic Secretary to the Treasury during parliamentary consideration of FSMA:

> We protect the financial markets in two ways. First, there are the criminal regimes for market manipulation and insider dealing. Those are both serious criminal offences, which carry a maximum sentence of seven years in jail and an unlimited fine. Secondly, there is the regulatory regime under which various regulatory bodies can take action against regulated persons for market abuse. However, there is a gap in the protections.[6]

The market abuse offences were intended by the government of the time to fill this 'gap'.[7] This was seen as supporting the FSA's regulatory objectives at the time, namely market confidence, the protection of consumers, and the reduction of financial crime.[8] As the then Economic Secretary stated, 'We are perceived to have fair and clean markets. We need to ensure that we keep it that way'.[9]

The failure of legislation adequately to protect against market misconduct

9.05 Before the introduction of the civil offence of market abuse in Part VIII FSMA, the main provisions to combat market misconduct were the statutory criminal offences of insider dealing,[10] and the earlier misleading statements and practices offence[11] and common law criminal offence of conspiracy to defraud. The first of the pre-FSMA legislative weapons against market misconduct, the criminal insider dealing offence, was considered by commentators and practitioners at the time to be unsatisfactory at targeting market abuse not

[5] European Commission Proposal for a Directive of the European Parliament and of the Council on criminal sanctions for insider dealing and market manipulation 2011/0297 (COD).

[6] Melanie Johnson, Economic Secretary to the Treasury, Standing Committee A, 2 November 1999, HMSO.

[7] See also the First Report (29 April 1999) and Second Report (2 June 1999) of the House of Lords and House of Commons Joint Committee on Financial Services and Markets (the 'Burns Reports'). The First Report commented that: 'The market abuse regime is intended to supplement, but not replace, the existing criminal sanctions for insider dealing, misleading the market and market manipulation. It is designed to allow the FSA to deal with any conduct that is damaging to the markets and in particular it is intended to enable the FSA to deal with market-abusive behaviour by non-authorised persons which is not caught by the existing criminal offences'. The two Burns Reports and the Governmental responses provide illuminating background on the drafting history of the pre-MAD version of FSMA.

[8] FSMA, s 2(2). Section 2(2) has now been repealed. The FCA now has one 'strategic objective'—'to ensure that the relevant markets function well' (s 1B(2), FSMA) and three 'operational objectives', namely: (i) 'to secure an appropriate degree of protection for consumers (the consumer protection objective)' (s 1C, FSMA); (ii) 'to protect and enhance the integrity of the UK financial system' (the integrity objective) (s 1D(1), FSMA); and (iii) 'to promote effective competition in the interests of consumers in the markets for regulated financial services and services provided by recognised investment exchanges (RIEs)' (the competition objective) (s 1E, FSMA). See Chapter 2.

[9] Melanie Johnson, n 7. See for further practitioner commentary on this point, Freshfields Bruckhaus Deringer, *Financial Services: Investigation & Enforcement* at para 13.9 (2nd edn, Bloomsbury 2005), and J Bagge, C Evans, G Wade, and M Lewis, 'Market Abuse: Proposals for the new regime', (2000) PLC 11(9), 35–42, at 36.

[10] CJA, Part V.

[11] Financial Services Act 1986, s 47, subsequently replaced by FSMA, s 397 and since replaced by ss 89 and 90 FSA 2012 relating to misleading statements and impressions (see Chapter 10).

least as a result of the perception that a criminal offence was not a suitable means of regulating complicated market behaviour, due to the structural restrictions of prosecuting a criminal offence (for example, the need to comply with criminal procedure, including a trial by a lay jury, with the presumption of innocence, the required standard of proof that the offence has to be proved beyond reasonable doubt, and the fact that the legislation should always be construed in the defendant's favour where there is ambiguity). In practice, very few successful prosecutions had been brought under the offence. In the 12-year period up to 1997 just 30 prosecutions resulted in only 13 successful convictions.[12] As with insider dealing, the lack of prosecutions resulting in successful convictions was also perceived as a flaw in the 'misleading statements and practices' regime, with one practitioner citing 'a widespread perception that the current legislation has failed to deter or punish abuses effectively'.[13]

How the new regime has fared, 12 years on, and the ongoing role of the criminal offences, is discussed further in paragraph 9.275 *et seq*. Interestingly, experience over the past few years has seen a resurgence of the use of criminal insider dealing prosecutions because of the deterrent effect of criminal sanctions and the perceived public and media need for more stringent penalties.[14] **9.06**

The failure of high-profile prosecutions to bring to justice those suspected of market misconduct offences

The debate leading up to the eventual introduction of the market abuse regime was fuelled by the failure of a number of landmark prosecutions during the 1980s and 1990s, most notably, the *Blue Arrow* and *Guinness/Saunders* cases, which attracted considerable media and public attention, and were perceived as having failed in their attempts to bring to justice those suspected of market misconduct. **9.07**

The Blue Arrow case and the failure of the 'conspiracy to defraud' offence to catch market misconduct

The *Blue Arrow* case[15] concerned behaviour during a rights issue in Blue Arrow plc which was intended to raise capital for the takeover by Blue Arrow of Manpower Inc. It was alleged that the market was misled by Blue Arrow's directors and financial advisers overstating how many of the shares in the Blue Arrow rights issue had been taken up at the close of the issue. This resulted in the prosecution of 14 parties involved with the rights issue for conspiracy to defraud, including the directors of Blue Arrow, and its financial advisers County NatWest. Ultimately, just four of the initial defendants were convicted by the jury, with these convictions being overturned by the Court of Appeal due to procedural difficulties experienced by the defendants. In the opinion of Mann LJ, giving the judgment of the court, their conviction was flawed for the following reasons. **9.08**

- The trial judge had directed the jury to consider only a limited number of the offences alleged by the indictment, in an attempt to make the trial more manageable. However, this meant that the judge summed up on different matters than that on which counsel had addressed the jury, which was a material irregularity in the course of the trial. The judge should instead have used his severance powers at the start of the trial to cut down the unmanageably large indictment.

[12] Statistics cited by Mr Paul Boateng, MP, in Hansard written answers, 1 February 1999, Column 430.
[13] A Sykes, 'Market Abuse: A Civil Revolution?' (1999) *JIFM* 1(2) 59–67, at 67.
[14] The FCA have stated this would be their preferred approach where possible for insider dealing offences see Chapter 10.
[15] *R v Cohen* [1992] 142 NLJ 1267.

- The trial lasted for 184 days, of which the jury was absent from court on a total of 126 days. Mann LJ held that there was a basic assumption that juries should determine guilt or innocence on evidence it could comprehend, remember, and that had been given at such a time as to make an impression on the jury's deliberation. This was not the case on these facts, and so the conviction could not stand.

Criticisms of the failure of the prosecution in the Blue Arrow case

9.09 The failure of the prosecution of the *Blue Arrow* case to provide a (lasting) conviction for market misconduct generated considerable criticism, with commentators again questioning the role of criminal prosecutions in essentially regulatory domains, particularly where there is no element of direct personal gain.[16] The difficulties faced by a criminal prosecution were primarily in finding a manageable indictment, and presenting the case in an understandable manner to a lay jury.

The Saunders saga and the involvement of human rights to frustrate successful prosecutions for market misconduct

9.10 In the *Saunders* case,[17] Ernest Saunders, a former director of Guinness plc, was compelled by Department of Trade and Industry Inspectors to provide evidence relating to their investigation of suspected wrongdoing connected with Guinness plc's takeover of Distillers Company plc. Evidence obtained in these investigations was subsequently used in criminal proceedings against Saunders, in which he was found guilty of a number of fraud offences. The European Court of Human Rights ('ECtHR') held that the use in a criminal trial of evidence obtained under compulsory powers, 'was oppressive and substantially impaired his ability to defend himself against the criminal charges facing him'. The ECtHR concluded that Saunders was therefore: 'deprived of a fair hearing within the meaning of article 6(1) . . .'.[18] This judgment, the basic effect of which was to limit greatly the authorities' powers to use self-incriminating evidence in proceedings for market misconduct, was again greeted with considerable criticism. One commentator highlighted a lack of proportionality in the decision, criticising the ECtHR's unwillingness to accept 'that the complexity of corporate fraud and the vital public interest in the investigation of such fraud and the punishment of those responsible should be taken into account in assessing whether statements made before the inspector . . . properly violated the right to a fair hearing'.[19]

The Market Abuse Directive

9.11 The detail of the market abuse regime under section 118 introduced under FSMA, discussed further later in this chapter, was subsequently underpinned by the EU-wide harmonised requirements relating to insider dealing and market manipulation under MAD,[20]

[16] See, eg, D Kirk, 'Blue Arrow: The SFO on trial', (1992) *ICCLR*, 3(1), 331–3.

[17] *Saunders v United Kingdom* [1996] 23 EHRR 313.

[18] ibid, para 76 of the Judgment. Art 6(1) of the European Convention on Human Rights grants the right to a fair trial: 'a fair and public hearing within a reasonable time by an independent and impartial tribunal established by law'.

[19] J Andrews, 'Hiding behind the veil: financial delinquency and the law', (1997) *EL Rev*, 22(4), 369–73. See also M Stallworthy, 'Company investigations and the prosecution of fraud in the United Kingdom: conflicting public interests', (1997) *ICCLR*, 8(4), 115–19, for a similar discussion.

[20] MAD was the first directive introduced under the so-called Lamfalussy process—for a further discussion see Chapter 3. MAD was followed by Regulation 2273/2003 on buy-backs and stabilisation, Directive 2003/125/EC on investment research, 2003/124/EC on public disclosure of inside information, and 2004/72/EC which considered insider lists and suspicious transaction reporting.

implemented in the UK on 1 July 2005. The philosophical approach of MAD, embedded in its recitals, is derived from the premise that the smooth functioning of securities markets and public confidence in markets are considered by the EU to be prerequisites for economic growth and wealth, and that market abuse harms the integrity of markets. At the same time, it was noted that the effectiveness of legislation against market abuse varied considerably throughout the EU, as did the consistency in national enforcement of such legislation. Therefore, MAD may be understood to have been an attempt both to tackle the problem of market abuse and to harmonise across the EU national governments' approach to market abuse through effective laws consistently applied in all EU Member States.[21] In the intervening years MAD has been subject to various reviews, culminating in the proposed new Market Abuse Regulation and CSD, both of which are discussed later in this chapter (see paragraph 9.284 *et seq*).

Access to and fairness of information

The focus of European initiatives has not merely related to detection and punishment—it has also addressed the need to enhance the timely and equal distribution of information and the fairness of that information.[22] **9.12**

For example, MAD[23] introduced across the EEA requirements that investment research be fairly presented and conflicts properly disclosed. The obligations on listed companies to announce price-sensitive information previously contained in Chapter 8 of the United Kingdom Listing Authority ('UKLA') Listing Rules were also modified as a result of MAD.[24] The Disclosure Rules (which comprise three chapters of the Disclosure Rules and Transparency Rules ('DTR')) issued by the FCA[25] contain an obligation[26] on issuers to announce inside information as soon as possible (subject to a right in certain circumstances to delay announcement so as not to prejudice the issuer's 'legitimate interests'), as well as clarifying the circumstances and manner in which announcements should be made. This replaced the obligation under the former listing rules regime to make an announcement of 'major new developments', or changes in its 'financial condition', the 'performance of its business', or its 'expectation as to its performance', where such information was price-sensitive.[27] At the same time, issuers are subject to an obligation in the Listing Rules ('LR') to comply with 'listing principles'. Principle 2 (at LR 7.2.1R) requires that listed companies **9.13**

[21] MAD, Recitals 11–13.

[22] In the UK the importance of this issue from the regulatory perspective can be seen from the number of enforcement actions under the Listing Rules for late or misleading announcements by listed companies. See, eg, FSA Final Notices to Marconi plc (11 April 2003); SFI Group plc (11 December 2003); Universal Salvage plc and Martin Christopher Hynes (19 May 2004); Sportsworld Media Group plc and Geoffrey John Brown (29 March 2004); the 'Shell' Transport and Trading Company plc and the Royal Dutch Petroleum company NV (24 August 2004) (also a market abuse decision); Pace Micro Technology plc (26 January 2005), Woolworths Group plc (11 June 2008) Wolfson Microelectronics (19 January 2009), Photo-Me (21 June 2010), JJB Sports (25 January 2011), and Lamprell (18 March 2013).

[23] Art 6(5), MAD, implemented further by the Commission Directive 2003/125/EC of the European Parliament and of the Council as regards the fair presentation of investment recommendations and the disclosure of conflicts of interest and implemented in the UK by amending the then FSA Conduct of Business Rules.

[24] For a discussion of the Listing Rules, Prospectus Rules, and the Disclosure and Transparency Rules, see Chapter 10 at para 10.79 *et seq.*

[25] Note that under FSMA, s 91, the FCA in its capacity as competent authority for the purposes of official listing can impose sanctions for breaches of the Listing Rules, Prospectus Rules, and Disclosure and Transparency Rules.

[26] DTR 2.2.9G.

[27] UKLA Listing Rules 9.1–9.2 (no longer in force).

take reasonable steps to establish and maintain adequate procedures, systems, and controls to enable them to comply with their obligations. The concern is not so much the substance of the disclosures that issuers will have to make regarding inside information, but rather the adequacy of the systems in place for identifying and disclosing such information.

9.14 In addition to the basic disclosure rule and exceptions to that rule and the listing principles, the DTRs also impose rules on issuers relating to the control of insiders and inside information. For example, issuers are required to establish effective arrangements to deny access to inside information to persons other than those who require it for the exercise of their functions within the issuer,[28] and to have in place measures which enable public disclosure to be made via a regulatory information service ('RIS') as soon as possible in case the issuer is not able to ensure the confidentiality of the relevant inside information.[29]

9.15 Further, in a move criticised for its lack of clarity and the administrative burden it imposes, issuers are required to draw up and maintain lists of persons who have access to inside information.[30]

9.16 Finally, in a broadening of the previous obligations, persons discharging managerial responsibilities and 'their connected persons' are required to notify the issuer in writing of the occurrence of all transactions conducted on their own account in the shares of the issuer, or derivatives or any other financial instruments relating to those shares within four business days of the day on which the transaction occurred. The issuer must in turn inform the RIS of any disclosure by such a person.[31] This is in addition to the Model Code which has been carried through into the Listing Rules in substantially similar form.

The Nature of the Market Abuse Regime and Underlying Processes

Introduction

9.17 As discussed at paragraph 9.04, the FSMA market abuse regime was introduced as a civil offence to fill the 'gap in the protections' between existing criminal offences on the one hand and the regulatory enforcement powers on the other.[32] This section will outline the significance of the distinction between civil and criminal offences with particular emphasis placed on procedural rules. It will also look at human rights issues and how these affect the market abuse regime.

The nature of the offences—European Court of Human Rights

9.18 In the *Saunders* case,[33] as noted at paragraph 9.10 earlier, the ECtHR passed judgment on the use of statements that a person has been compelled to make in a civil investigation for market misconduct being used in a subsequent criminal trial. Under Art 6(1) of the European Convention on Human Rights ('ECHR'),[34] it is a breach of the right to a fair trial where

---

[28] DTR 2.6.1R.
[29] ibid, 2.6.2R.
[30] ibid, 2.8.1R, implementing art 6(3) of MAD.
[31] The Rules are set out in full at DTR 3.1 and implement art 6(4) of MAD.
[32] Melanie Johnson, n 7, and see generally para 9.04 *et seq.* of this chapter.
[33] *Saunders v United Kingdom*, n 15 above.
[34] Convention for the Protection of Human Rights and Fundamental Freedoms, agreed by the Council of Europe at Rome on 4 November 1950, as it has effect for the time being in relation to the UK through the

evidence that has been obtained by compulsion in the course of an investigation into market misconduct is used in a subsequent criminal trial. One might ask, then, why this impacts on the market abuse regime under Part VIII of FSMA, which is stated to be a civil regime. Although the UK Government has classified the market abuse regime as civil in nature, the ECtHR has indicated that it is prepared to look beyond the classification of an offence by a national government, and reclassify it as a criminal offence for the purposes of the ECHR, if appropriate.[35]

The significance of the distinction between criminal and civil offences

The question as to whether or not the market abuse regime is in reality a criminal regime rather than a civil regime has sparked a considerable amount of debate and indeed was discussed at the time the regime was introduced.[36] The discussion is clearly one of significance for a number of reasons: the standard of proof in a criminal matter is such that the tribunal of fact must be satisfied 'beyond all reasonable doubt' that the accused is guilty of the offence; by contrast, in a civil matter, the standard of proof is a belief that 'on the balance of probabilities' a matter has been proved; in serious criminal matters, the prosecution ordinarily needs to prove that the defendant had the requisite *mens rea* (mental element) to commit the offence (such as intention to commit the crime, subjective recklessness as to its commission, dishonesty or a specific level of knowledge); there is no *mens rea* for a civil matter; certain protections are granted to the defendant in a criminal matter, for example, the right not to be compelled to answer questions;[37] such rights are not available in a civil matter; and as a general principle, in criminal matters, legislation is construed in the defendant's favour where there is any ambiguity. Finally, the ECHR grants defendants in a criminal trial the right to a fair trial; these rights are not guaranteed to the same extent for civil matters **9.19**

In order to address this concern, a number of procedures were factored into the FSMA regime, which in effect seek to preserve the right against self-incrimination in respect of statements made under compulsion.[38] These are described at paragraph 9.42 *et seq.*[39] **9.20**

Human Rights Act 1998 ('HRA'), s 1(2): 'Those Articles (i.e., the Articles of the ECHR) are to have effect for the purposes of this Act…'.

[35] See, eg, *Bendenoun v France* [1994] 18 EHRR 54.

[36] Note also that the classification of the offence for the purposes of the ECHR was discussed in the First Burns Report (see the notes at para 9.04 for further discussion of the Burns Reports). In the section of the Report considering the proposed market abuse regime, it was observed that, 'although the draft Bill classifies the market abuse regime as civil, such classification under the domestic law is not conclusive for the ECHR and that, for that purpose, is likely to be regarded as criminal' (para 278).

[37] It is a central principle of English criminal procedure that a defendant may not be compelled to testify against himself when he is charged with a criminal matter. Criminal Evidence Act 1898 (as amended), s 1(1) provides as follows: 'A person charged in criminal proceedings shall not be called as a witness in pursuance of this Act in the proceedings except upon his own application'. In practice, this means that during the course of an investigation, a person should not be compelled (through the use of sanctions for non cooperation) to give evidence that may be used against him in a subsequent prosecution.

[38] Melanie Johnson, n 7, discussing the criticism that an early draft of the Financial Services and Markets Bill was not compatible with the ECHR: 'We recognised that there was a possibility that it would be classified as criminal for convention purposes and to avoid any risk of a finding that the Bill does not fully comply with the convention requirements, we decided to introduce the relevant protections. The first protection is against the use of compelled statements in proceedings to impose a market abuse penalty on the person who gave those statements'. It has been pointed out that the privilege against self-incrimination, in the context of the market abuse regime, only applies to *statements* made under *compulsion*. The privilege does not extend to documents (whether given under compulsion or not), or statements voluntarily made to FSA investigators. See *Financial Services* (n 10), at para 4.224.

[39] In response to the concerns of and the recommendation in the First Burns Report that the Government 'could incorporate criminal justice safeguards…into the enforcement regimes' (para 281), the Government

9.21 The question of whether the market abuse regime offences are criminal for the purposes of Article 6 of the ECHR has been considered in a number of cases.

9.22 In the *Davidson and Tatham* case[40] what was then the Financial Services and Markets Tribunal ('FSMT')[41] considered as a preliminary matter whether market abuse was a criminal or civil charge, and concluded that, whilst not being criminal charges for the purposes of domestic law, the penalties for market abuse were criminal charges for the purposes of the ECHR. In reaching a decision in the *Davidson and Tatham* case, the FSMT referred to the judgment of the Court of Appeal in *Han v Customs and Excise Commissioners* [2001] EWCA Civ 1048 which concerned a civil penalty for dishonest evasion of tax. The issue was whether such a civil penalty was a criminal charge for the purposes of Article 6 of the ECHR. In that case the court summarised the relevant jurisprudence of the ECtHR and identified three criteria routinely applied by that court for the purpose of determining whether an applicant was the subject of a criminal charge.

9.23 The first criterion is the categorisation of the allegation in domestic law. In the case of the market abuse regime, the FSMT concluded that the market abuse offences were not categorised as criminal offences in domestic law. However, as was stated in the *Han* case, that was no more than a starting point and was not decisive of the nature of the allegation and it would therefore be necessary to look at the second and third criteria, namely the nature of the offence and the severity of the penalty.

9.24 It was concluded in the *Han* case that, under the second criterion, the court considers whether or not, under the law concerned, the 'offence' is one which applies generally to the public at large or is restricted to a specific group. In the case of market abuse, the FSMT in the *Davidson and Tatham* case noted that sections 118 and 123 of FSMA apply generally to the public at large and the penalty was not imposed as a disciplinary matter. As to the third criterion (the severity of the penalty), the sizes of the penalties imposed were clearly of a substantial, punitive, and deterrent nature rather than of a compensatory nature. As discussed earlier, the first criterion was considered to be no more than a starting point and was not in itself decisive, and accordingly in the decision, consideration of the second and third criteria prevailed.

9.25 The issue was again considered in the *Parker* case.[42] In that case, the FSA contested the proposition that an allegation of market abuse would give rise to a criminal charge within the meaning of Article 6, ECHR, the significance being relevant to a potential argument which would have been unfavourable to the FSA, on the standard of proof (as to which, see paragraph 9.29).

9.26 The FSMT then analysed a number of the underlying cases (which did not appear to have been cited to the FSMT in the *Davidson and Tatham* decision) including the *Fleurose* Court of Appeal case.[43] That case related to a 'registered person' subject to the jurisdiction of the

introduced the procedural safeguards into FSMA discussed at para 9.42. In response to these changes, the Second Burns Report acknowledged that the changes would 'increase certainty and reduce the chance of successful legal challenge on ECHR grounds' (para 19).

[40] *Paul Davidson and Ashley Tatham v FSA*, FSMT Case 031, 16 May 2006.

[41] In April 2010, the Financial Services and Markers Tribunal was abolished and its functions transferred to the Upper Tribunal (Tax and Chancery Chamber) under the Transfer of Tribunal Functions Order 2010.

[42] *James Parker v FSA*, FSMT Case 037, 18 August 2006.

[43] *Fleurose v Disciplinary Appeal Tribunal of the Securities and Futures Authority Limited* [2001] EWCA Civ 2015.

Disciplinary Tribunal and Disciplinary Appeals Tribunal of the Securities and Futures Authority ('SFA'), a self-regulatory organisation under the pre-FSMA regime. The function of those bodies found their broad equivalence in the FSA's Regulatory Decisions Committee ('RDC') and the FSMT, although the analogy was not exact. Fleurose had been suspended from acting as a registered person for two years and ordered to contribute £175,000 towards the SFA's costs because of his improper conduct as a trader in manipulating the FTSE 100 Index. Schiemann LJ, giving the judgment of the court, quoted extensively from the judgment of Potter LJ in *Han and others*,[44] mentioning in particular the three criteria already referred to and it would seem concluded that the fact that only a registered person was subject to the disciplinary authority of the tribunals, and that no punitive or deterrent penalty was imposed, meant that the offence in *Fleurose* was not criminal in character. A similar view had prevailed in other cases relating to disciplinary tribunals, (see *Pine v Law Society* [2001] EWCA Civ 1574, (where it was accepted without argument that the solicitors' disciplinary tribunal exercised a civil jurisdiction), and for example, *Rayner* and *Townsend v FSA*, [FSMT] Case 009, 6 August 2004).

The FSMT in the *Parker* case came to the conclusion that in its view the analogy with the disciplinary tribunal cases was weak, and that Parker's position was much closer to that of the appellants in *Han* and therefore agreed with the FSMT in the *Davidson and Tatham* decision that an allegation of market abuse, even when punished in accordance with section 123 of FSMA, and therefore by a route which is classed as civil for domestic law purposes, had to be treated for ECHR purposes as a criminal charge. In reaching this view, the FSMT considered that the conduct in the *Parker* case, if proved, could lead to the imposition not only of the civil penalty but could also expose the person to criminal prosecution (in the instant case, by reason of FSMA, section 402(1)(a) under the Criminal Justice Act 1993, section 52) and it was not necessary to be a member of a closed group (for example, an 'approved person' for FCA purposes) to be subject to a penalty. The FSMT also concluded that the penalty imposed on Parker was both punitive and deterrent in character and was intended so to be. **9.27**

Burden of proof and the standard of proof applicable to the market abuse offence

Burden of proof

The FSMT in the *Davidson and Tatham* case addressed the question of what consequences would follow from its finding as to the categorisation of the market abuse offences.[45] As an initial point, the FSMT found that it was clear from Article 6(2) of the ECHR that the first consequence would be that the burden of proof would indeed lie on the FSA to prove their case.[46] Of the other five minimum rights mentioned in Article 6(3) the most relevant, **9.28**

---

[44] ibid, para 9.22.

[45] Art 6 of the ECHR gives the right to a fair trial. Art 6(1) relates to civil rights and obligations and provides that everyone is entitled to a fair and public hearing within a reasonable time by an independent and impartial tribunal. Art 6(2) relates to criminal offences and provides that everyone charged with a criminal offence shall be presumed innocent until proved guilty according to law. Art 6(3) defines five minimum rights which apply to everyone charged with a criminal offence. These five minimum rights are: the right to be informed promptly of the nature and cause of the accusation; the right to have adequate time and facilities for the preparation of the defence; the right to defend himself in person or through legal assistance of his own choosing, or, if he has not sufficient means to pay for legal assistance, to be given it free when the interests of justice so require; the right to examine witnesses against him and to obtain the attendance and examination of witnesses on his behalf; and the right to an interpreter.

[46] The point was also discussed by the FSMT in *Parker*, where the FSMT, commenting on the fact that the FSA accepted that the burden of proof would lay on it, expressed the view that this would be the case in any case

according to the FSMT, was the right to legal assistance and this was addressed in statutory provisions in FSMA (sections 134 to 136).[47]

Standard of proof

9.29 The standard of proof in a criminal matter is that the tribunal of fact must be satisfied 'beyond all reasonable doubt' that the accused is guilty of the offence; by contrast, in a civil matter, the standard of proof is a belief that 'on the balance of probabilities' a disputed matter has been proved, a less arduous standard. Under the market abuse provisions in section 123(1), the required standard of proof for market abuse is not specifically stated as either civil or criminal. Rather, it is stated that the FCA only needs to be 'satisfied' (subject to the defences that may apply under section 123(2)) that market abuse or 'requiring or encouraging' took place to impose a penalty on the guilty party. The question is therefore: on what basis will the FCA be 'satisfied' that market abuse has taken place? Clear guidance on this question was provided by the FSA at the introduction of the FSMA regime: 'In such proceedings, the burden will be on the FSA and the FSA will plainly have to prove its case on a balance of probabilities'.[48]

Application of the balance of probabilities test

9.30 What the standard of proof should be, and how this should be applied, has been considered in a number of cases determined by what was the Financial Services and Markets Tribunal ('FSMT') before its function transferred to the Upper Tribunal (Tax and Chancery Chamber) ('Upper Tribunal') in April 2010 under the Transfer of Tribunal Functions Order 2010.[49] In *Arif Mohammed*,[50] the applicant, Arif Mohammed, submitted that a market abuse case was akin to a criminal offence, and that the burden of proof would therefore be on the FSA to prove its case beyond reasonable doubt. The FSA, conversely, submitted that the burden should be a 'balance of probabilities', albeit subject to the principle adopted by the FSMT in previous decisions[51] that the more serious the allegation, the more cogent the evidence needs to be to prove it (the so-called 'sliding scale principle'). Whilst recognising that the previous decisions referred to were not market abuse cases, and that specific considerations arise in such cases (including the fact that enforcement action may be taken against persons who are not regulated by the FSA) the FSMT agreed with the FSA that the sliding scale principle would apply.

9.31 The point was also considered in subsequent FSMT cases and the more recent Upper Tribunal *Swift Trade* case.[52] In the *Davidson and Tatham* case, the FSMT considered at length the various authorities cited to it. As part of this, the FSMT referred to the Court of Appeal judgment in *R v Mental Health Review Tribunal*[53] and in particular the comments in the

in which a penalty has been imposed, apart perhaps from a minor penalty occasioned by a technical regulatory breach and with no suggestion of moral turpitude, regardless of Art 6(2) of the ECHR (which provides that anyone charged with a criminal offence is to be presumed innocent until proved guilty).

[47] In *Davidson v FSA*, FSMT Case 010, 9 August 2004, Davidson was indeed granted the right to apply for legal assistance (although in the event it was refused).

[48] FSA Policy Statement 59 (April 2001)—Code of Market Conduct Feedback on CP59 and CP76, para 4.11.

[49] ibid, n 43.

[50] *Arif Mohammed v FSA*, FSMT Case 012, 29 March 2005.

[51] *Geoffrey Alan Hoodless and Sean Michael Blackwell v FSA*, FSMT Case 007, 3 October 2003, at 21, *Legal & General Assurance Soc Ltd v FSA*, FSMT Case 011, 18 January 2005, at 19.

[52] *Canada Inc and Beck v Financial Services Authority*, Upper Tribunal, (FS/2011/0017; FS/2011/0018), 2 August 2011. The Swift Trade decision is currently on appeal to the Court of Appeal.

[53] *R (On the Application of AN) v Mental Health Review Tribunal* [2005] EWCA Civ 1605.

judgment that 'the essential point that runs through the authorities is that the civil standard of proof is flexible in its application and enables proper account to be taken of the seriousness of the allegations to be proved and of the consequences of proving them'. According to the judgment, the more serious the allegation, or the more serious the consequences if the allegation is proved, the stronger the evidence would have to be for the allegation to be proved on the balance of probabilities. Although there remained a distinction in principle between the civil standard and the criminal standard, the practical application of the flexible approach, according to the judgment, was that they were likely in certain contexts to produce the same or similar results.

In the light of the authorities reviewed, the FSMT formed the view that[54] although the market abuse offences were criminal charges for the purposes of Article 6 of the ECHR, there was no provision in Article 6 that the appropriate standard of proof is the criminal standard. The FSMT concluded that the civil standard of proof was sufficiently strong to establish what has to be established. **9.32**

The position was also considered in the *Parker* case and the FSMT agreed with the FSMT in *Davidson and Tatham*, for the same reason. In the *Parker* case, the FSMT referred in particular to the judgment of Lord Nicholls in *Re H* [1996] 1 All ER 1 at pages 16–17: **9.33**

> The balance of probability standard means that a court is satisfied an event occurred if the court considers that, on the evidence, the occurrence of the event was more likely than not. When assessing the probabilities the court will have in mind as a factor, to whatever extent is appropriate in the particular case, that the more serious the allegation the less likely it is that the event occurred and, hence the stronger should be the evidence before the court concludes that the allegation is established on the balance of probability. Fraud is usually less likely than negligence... Built into the preponderance of probability standard is a general degree of flexibility in respect of the seriousness of the allegation.
>
> Although the result is much the same, this does not mean that where a serious allegation is in issue the standard of proof required is higher. It means only that the inherent probability or improbability of an event is itself a matter to be taken into account when weighing the probabilities and deciding whether, on balance, the event occurred. The more improbable the event, the stronger must be the evidence that it did occur before, on the balance of probability, its occurrence will be established.

Lord Nicholls also referred to the comments of Ungoed-Thomas J in *Re Dellow's Will Trusts*:[55]

> The more serious the allegation, the more cogent is the evidence required to overcome the unlikelihood of what is alleged and thus to prove it.

In the *Parker* case, the FSMT concluded there could be no doubt that an allegation that a person had been guilty of conduct for which he should be punished by a penalty of £300,000 was a very grave charge and compelling evidence had to be adduced if it was to be established. In other words, if one applies the 'sliding scale', the slide must be very close to the upper end of the scale. Importantly, the FSMT found that in a practical sense, even if not semantically, it was difficult to draw a meaningful distinction between the standard it had to apply and the criminal standard. **9.34**

[54] Following *B v Chief Constable of Avon and Somerset Constabulary* [2001] 1 WLR 340.

[55] *Re Dellow's Will Trusts, Lloyds Bank Ltd v Institute of Cancer Research* [1964] 1 All ER 771 at 773, [1964] 1 WLR 451 at 455.

9.35 This point was again raised in the *Swift Trade* case (subject to appeal)[56] where the Upper Tribunal dismissed Swift Trade's contention that the standard of proof should be 'a heightened civil standard of proof which is virtually indistinguishable from the criminal standard of proof'. The Upper Tribunal confirmed that the correct standard of proof was the balance of probabilities, agreeing with findings in *Davidson and Tatham* that there is nothing in Article 6 ECHR which demanded proof to any particular standard.

9.36 The Upper Tribunal also referred back to the judgment of Lord Nicholls in *Re H*,[57] and noted that although the observations of Lord Nicholls were, in the Upper Tribunal's view, admirably clear, they nevertheless led in some quarters to the view that there was a third standard, lying somewhere between the ordinary civil and the criminal standards, and varying in a somewhat undefined way broadly in line with the gravity of an allegation. This matter had been put beyond argument by Lord Hoffman in *Re B (Children)* [2008] UKHL 35 at [13]: 'the time has come to say, once and for all, that there is only one civil standard of proof and that is proof that the fact in issue more probably occurred than not'.

9.37 Swift Trade also argued that the FSA bore the burden of showing that the section 123(2) defence (which applies to a person who believes on reasonable grounds that his conduct does not amount to market abuse—(see paragraph 9.91) was not satisfied. However, the Upper Tribunal concluded that this argument was not consistent with the wording of that subsection (which provides that no penalty may be imposed 'if there are reasonable grounds for the FSA to be satisfied' that the defence is made out) and that the burden of establishing the defence must therefore rest on the person who advanced it.

How the test has been applied in practice

9.38 Looking at some examples of how this has been applied in practice, in the *Baldwin* case[58] (a case of alleged market abuse: misuse of information) the FSMT concluded in favour of Baldwin and another party, WRT, that there was no evidence that a disputed telephone call had taken place. The FSMT also rejected the FSA submission of the expert evidence provided as it did not establish that an expert investor would not have acted in the way that Baldwin did in the absence of inside information.

9.39 Notwithstanding the requirements as to cogency of evidence, circumstantial evidence can be sufficient.[59] In the *Shevlin* case (an RDC decision),[60] Shevlin argued that the FSA, in the absence of clear evidence that Shevlin had access to inside information, did in fact access that information and based his decision to trade upon it, had failed to prove their case. He argued they were relying exclusively on circumstantial evidence. Those circumstances included the FSA's admission that they were unable to confirm with any precision when Shevlin was alleged to have logged into the email accounts of senior executives and accessed the relevant information. Whilst acknowledging that it was unable to demonstrate conclusively Shevlin's access to inside

[56] *Canada Inc and Beck v Financial Services Authority*, Upper Tribunal, (FS/2011/0017; FS/2011/0018), 2 August 2011, currently on appeal (see n 57).

[57] *Re H* [1996], ibid, para 9.33.

[58] *Timothy Edward Baldwin and WRT Investments Ltd v FSA*, FSMT Case 026, 24 January 2006.

[59] In her speech on 22 May 2007 (*Market Abuse Policy & Enforcement in the UK*), Sally Dewar, Market Abuse Policy & Enforcement in the UK, commented that 'it is rare to find a "smoking gun"; and often cases hinge on circumstantial evidence. It is quite common for insider traders to come up with alternative rationales for their trading strategies that can be difficult to disprove'.

[60] FSA Final Notice to John Shevlin, dated 1 July 2008 (RDC).

information, the FSA stated it was able to draw inferences from the weight of the circumstantial evidence in the case when it was considered as a whole and draw conclusions from the material.

In the *Harrison* decision (an FSA decision settled at stage 1)[61] the FSA found that inside information had passed to Harrison, even though it had not been possible to determine the precise circumstances and terms in which the information had passed to Harrison as the relevant telephone calls had not been taped.[62] **9.40**

Spector Photo: rebuttable presumption

In the *Spector Photo* case[63] (relating to how Belgium had implemented MAD into local law), the European Court of Justice ('ECJ') considered the MAD insider dealing offence discussed later in this chapter, and in particular the meaning to be given to 'use' of information (that is to say whether the 'use' contained in MAD should be given a broad meaning so as to catch any actions taken by a person who was also in receipt of inside information, irrespective of the causal connection). In the event, the ECJ concluded that the fact that a person in possession of inside information acquires or disposes of, or tries to acquire or dispose of, for his own account or for the account of a third party, either directly or indirectly, the relevant financial instruments gave rise to a rebuttable presumption that that person has 'used that information' within the meaning of MAD. However, this rebuttable presumption is to be considered in the light of the purposes of the directive, and is subject to the defences in the directive.[64] This is discussed later in this chapter at paragraph 9.132. **9.41**

The privilege against self-incrimination as it relates to the market abuse offence

As mentioned earlier, a number of procedures have been factored into the FSMA regime which have the effect of seeking to preserve the right against self-incrimination in respect of statements made under compulsion.[65] An FCA investigator may require any person who is or may be able to give information relevant to an investigation, to attend an interview with the investigator and answer questions, or otherwise provide such information as the investigator may require.[66] However, there is a specific limitation on the use to which this information can be put in the context of market abuse. According to section 174(2) of FSMA, no evidence relating to such a statement may be adduced and no question relating to it may be asked by the prosecution or the FCA unless evidence relating to the statement is first raised by or on behalf of the person who made the statement. **9.42**

European Convention on Human Rights—obligations on public authorities

The FCA's obligation to act compatibly with the ECHR, which underlies the market abuse offence

In addition to the issue of the privilege against self incrimination, there is a broader obligation on the FCA for its acts to be compatible with human rights. The Human Rights Act **9.43**

[61] FSA Final Notice to Steven Harrison, dated 8 September 2008 (SDM).

[62] The finding also concluded that the conduct in question had not been deliberate.

[63] (C-45/08) *Spector Photo Group NV, Chris Van Raemdonck v Commissie voor het Bank-, Financie-en Assurantiewezen* (*CBFA*).

[64] For further discussion, see para 9.132.

[65] ibid, n 42. In response to the concerns of and the recommendation in the First Burns Report that the Government 'could incorporate criminal justice safeguards . . . into the enforcement regimes' (para 281), the Government introduced the procedural safeguards into FSMA. In response to these changes, the Second Burns Report acknowledged that the changes would 'increase certainty and reduce the chance of successful legal challenge on ECHR grounds' (para 19).

[66] FSMA, s 173(1) and (2).

('HRA') states that it is unlawful for a 'public authority' to act in a way which is 'incompatible' with an ECHR right.[67] For these purposes, a 'public authority' is defined as any person who exercises functions of a public nature, which would seemingly include the FCA in its role as the regulator of the financial services industry in the UK.[68] On this basis, the FCA must comply with the ECHR rights and, in particular, must not act in a way that is incompatible with a person's right to a fair trial. The view expressed by HM Treasury is that the structural safeguards built into the system in terms of the structure and process of the FSMT/ Upper Tribunal, as well as the rules relating to the use of statements obtained under compulsion, are such as to be compatible with the FCA's human rights obligations when policing the market abuse provisions (as well as when carrying out its public functions generally).[69]

Fair process

9.44 A couple of FSMT decisions illustrate the significance of fair process considerations. The first of these involves the *Davidson and Tatham* case[70] discussed at paragraph 9.22 *et seq.* earlier, where the first FSMT hearing was aborted on the application of the FSA, after it emerged that the chairman of the FSA's RDC had discussed the proceedings privately with one of the members of the FSMT panel.[71] A subsequent hearing took place with a reconstituted panel.

9.45 The FSMT has also considered on a couple of occasions the position of parties 'identified' in Decision Notices.

9.46 The first relates to Sir Phillip Watts, the former chairman of Shell, who took action against the FSA before the FSMT in relation to the FSA's Final Notice against Shell[72] for market abuse. Watts alleged that the Final Notice improperly and unfairly implicated him in Shell's wrongdoing (although he was not mentioned by name, he argued that there are implicit references to him). Watts argued that the unfairness stemmed from the fact that ordinarily where an FSA notice would be prejudicial to an identified third party, that third party should be given a copy of the notice before a final decision is made, with the right to refer the decision to the FSMT.[73] The FSMT held[74] that the purpose of the warning procedure is to provide rights to third parties, but it limited the availability of such rights to persons who are 'identified in the decision notice' and not, as Watts argued, to a person who is identified only through the matter to which the reasons in the decision notice relates.[75] The FSMT further decided that where a market abuse allegation is directed against a company, this does not necessarily impute criticism to individuals associated with the running or management of the company, although it tempered this by adding that whether it is fair to take separate

[67] HRA, s 6(1).

[68] See, eg, the statement in *Canada Inc & Peter Beck v FSA*, Upper Tribunal, Case FS0017 & 0018, 2 August 2011, at para 22.

[69] In *Rayner & Townsend v FSA*, FSMT Case 009, 6 August 2004, it was noted that the FSMT had been set up to ensure that the regulatory decision making process as a whole was compatible with the ECHR by providing an independent, impartial FSMT. The FSMT also has 'original jurisdiction' ie hearings before it are full rehearings—see, eg, the discussion in *Davidson and Tatham*. The role and powers of the FSMT have since been transferred to the Upper Tribunal.

[70] *Paul Davidson and Ashley Tatham v FSA*, FSMT Case 031, 16 May 2006.

[71] The original market abuse Final Notice from the FSA to Davidson is not available to the public.

[72] FSA Final Notice to Shell Transport and Trading Company plc and The Royal Dutch Petroleum Company NV dated 24 August 2004.

[73] FSMA, s 393.

[74] *Sir Philip Watts v FSA*, FSMT Case 020, 7 September 2005.

[75] ibid, para 49.

action against companies and the individuals running that company would depend on the facts of the case.[76]

A similar point arose in the FSMT decision relating to *Jan Laury*.[77] Laury was the compliance officer at an FSA regulated firm. Laury took objection to the Final Notice relating to the firm on the basis that it contained implied criticism of him, which was unjustified, and which he had no opportunity to contest or correct. **9.47**

The FSMT considered the two potentially conflicting propositions that, on the one hand (as argued by Laury) identification need not be expressed and may be implicit, and on the other (as argued by the FSA) that reference to external sources is not permissible, and concluded that there was in reality no true inconsistency, citing as an example that if a managing director was the subject of criticism in the notice, the description 'managing director' was itself a sufficient identification and there was no need to go to outside sources to discover his or her name. According to the FSMT, what one was not allowed to do was to add material from external sources to the material in the notice in order to identify an individual impliedly the subject of the criticism. On the facts of the *Jan Laury* case, the FSMT did not consider that the argument that a reader might possibly take loosely expressed criticisms as referring to Laury was sufficient—only a positive identification could satisfy the terms of section 393 of FSMA ('identifies a person'). Accordingly to the FSMT, where a particular function or particular department of a firm was referred to as having failings, it did not necessarily follow that a particular individual could be inferred to have been at fault, even if that individual was held by the head of department or the person responsible for that function. **9.48**

Finally, it is also relevant to consider the procedural changes introduced by the FSA, as it then was, to its processes following criticism relating to the fairness and transparency of the FSA's enforcement approach raised in the *Legal & General* case[78] and addressed in the so-called Strachan report.[79] **9.49**

Unreasonable behaviour and costs

A number of cases have addressed the question of whether the FSA's conduct has been unreasonable. This has occurred in the context of applications to recover costs. **9.50**

The legislation in place at the time governing the award of costs by the FSMT was found in paragraph 13 of Schedule 13 to FSMA and in Rule 21 of the Financial Services and Markets Tribunal Rules 2001 (SI 2001/2476).[80] **9.51**

[76] ibid, paras 50 and 54. Note also that the FSMT stated that where an individual is identified by sources external to the Final Notice (as Watts was identified by the media), s 393 would not require that individual to be given a right of response (para 52). As it transpired, on 9 November 2005, the FSA announced that they had decided to close their investigation against Watts. FSA: 'FSA closes enquiries into Shell individuals', FSA/PN/118/2005, 9 November 2005; see <http://www.fsa.gov.uk/Pages/Library/Communication/PR/2005/118.shtml>.

[77] *Jan Laury v FSA*, FSMT Case 046, 2007.

[78] In *Legal & General Assurance Society v FSA*, FSMT Case 015, 18 January 2005, the FSMT commented (at para 191) that: 'it was for FSA not L&G to control the process so that it was fair, effective and reasonably prompt. If L&G was not cooperating in securing a review which could be used effectively for enforcement, it was for FSA to impose a suitable exercise'.

[79] FSA, 'Enforcement process review—Report and recommendations' (July 2005), available at <http://www.fsa.gov.uk/pubs/other/enf_process_review_report.pdf>. See in particular paras 3.2–3.8 which explain the criticisms of the lack of fairness and transparency in the enforcement process.

[80] The legislation that relates to the award of costs by the Upper Tribunal is now found in rule 10 of the Tribunal Procedure (Upper Tribunal) Rules 2008. This provides the Upper Tribunal may only make an order in

9.52 Paragraph 13 of Schedule 13 to FSMA permitted the FSMT to order a party to pay the whole or part of the costs or expenses incurred by the other party to proceedings in connection with the proceedings where it considered the first party had acted vexatiously, frivolously or unreasonably. The FSMT also had power, where it considered that a decision of the FSA was unreasonable, to order the FSA to pay the whole or part of the costs or expenses incurred by the other party in connection with the proceedings. This legislation has been replaced, but the current legislation also gives powers to the Upper Tribunal to award costs where, amongst other things, the decision made by the FCA was unreasonable.[81] Rule 21(3) provided that where the FSMT makes a costs order it may either (a) fix the amount or (b) direct that the costs should be assessed on such basis as it should specify by a costs official (of the court).[82]

9.53 In the Cost Decision of *Davidson and Tatham*,[83] an application made to the FSMT following the *Davidson and Tatham* decision, the FSMT sought to address whether the FSA's decision had been unreasonable. The approach adopted by the FSMT was to look at this, given the facts and circumstances which were known or ought to have been known to the FSA at the time when the decision was made. In taking this approach, the FSMT took note of the fact that the process leading to the FSA's decision was not a full judicial hearing of the kind conducted by the FSMT.[84]

9.54 From the arguments of the parties, the FSMT identified three elements of the disputed decision which they claimed to be unreasonable, and which the FSMT considered relevant, namely the approach to the evidence and the facts; the approach to the law; and the approach to the penalties. As to the first, the FSMT found on the facts that it was unreasonable that the evidence of one particular party had been preferred to the evidence of another (Davidson). The FSMT also noted that the decision-making process at the time of the disputed decision had the defects identified in the enforcement process review which had taken place in the light of the *Legal & General* decision (see paragraph 9.49). Finally, the FSMT concluded that in its view it was not reasonable to decide against criminal proceedings on the ground that a higher penalty could be imposed by a civil penalty. It was also unreasonable to proceed to ignore the same mitigating factors as would have applied in criminal proceedings to reduce the level of the penalties. The FSMT found that in its view the amount of the final differential between the penalties imposed on two of the parties was not reasonable. It also found that after hearing Tatham's representations, it was unreasonable for the RDC not to form the view that Tatham reasonably believed that his behaviour did not amount to market abuse and that consequently they did not have the legal power to impose the penalty. In terms of the level of the penalty on Davidson, appearing in the Decision Notice, the FSMT found that although the notice took account of some mitigating factors it did not take account of all the factors

respect of costs or expenses if the Upper Tribunal considers that a party or its representative has acted unreasonably in bringing, defending, or conducting the proceedings, or, in a financial services case, the Upper Tribunal considers that the decision in respect of which the reference was made was unreasonable.

[81] Rule 10(3)(e) of the Tribunal Procedure (Upper Tribunal) Rules 2008 (SI 2008/2698).

[82] The provisions dealing with costs awards are now found in rule 10 of the Tribunal Procedure (Upper Tribunal) Rules 2008 (SI 2008/2698).

[83] *Paul Davidson and Ashley Tatham v FSA*, FSMT Case 040, 16 May 2006.

[84] See also *Legal and General Assurance Society Ltd v FSA*, FSMT Case 015, 18 January 2005: 'when dealing with a large volume of regulatory matters informally and speedily, FSA should not be expected to follow procedures, or express its conclusions, as required of a court'.

that should have been borne in mind and was of the view that it was unreasonable of the RDC not to mitigate the levels of the penalties more than they did.[85]

A costs application was also made in the *Baldwin* case[86] (Costs Decision). The applicants had been accused of market abuse but the FSMT had found that they were not guilty and that no penalty should be imposed. In determining the costs question, the FSMT found it was required to look at the decision itself. Arguments were raised in the proceedings that the 'Wednesbury' test should be applied (a decision is 'Wednesbury unreasonable' if it is 'so unreasonable that no reasonable authority could ever have come to it') but the FSMT did not consider this test would be appropriate, helpful, or conducive to clarity and the FSMT considered paragraph 13 (as it then was) required it to make its own judgement as to what was reasonable. On the facts, the FSMT did not find itself able to conclude that the FSA's decision was unreasonable. **9.55**

The Market Abuse Offences

Market abuse in Part VIII FSMA and the impact of MAD on the market abuse regime

This section discusses the definition of behaviour that constitutes market abuse under section 118 of FSMA, as amended to implement MAD. Paragraph 9.93 *et seq.* will consider the prescribed behaviour types that constitute abusive behaviour and the 'safe harbours' which are available, together with a discussion of the guidance and evidential provisions issued by the FCA in the Code of Market Conduct ('COMC') and other exceptions and defences. This section will begin, however, by considering briefly the impact of the introduction of MAD on the market abuse regime. A revised version of the MAD (to take the form of a regulation, and a directive relating to criminal sanctions) is, at the time of writing, under discussion and an overview of the status and scope is set out in paragraph 9.284. **9.56**

The 'regular user' test at the heart of the pre-MAD market abuse regime

The types of behaviour covered by the pre-MAD market abuse regime related to three basic types of behaviour, namely: **9.57**

(i) misuse of information—behaviour based on information not generally available to market users;
(ii) false or misleading impressions—behaviour giving a false or misleading impression as to the price of investments; and
(iii) distortion—behaviour distorting the market.

The cornerstone of the regime was the 'regular user test', that is to say, that behaviour which would be likely to be regarded by a 'regular user' of the market as a failure on the part of the person or persons concerned to observe the standard of behaviour reasonably expected of a person in his or their positions in relation to the market. 'Regular user' was defined, in relation to a particular market, as 'a reasonable person who regularly deals on that market in investments of the kind in question'.[87] The FCA's guidance indicates that the regular user test

[85] The FSMT added that matters identified as being unreasonable were unlikely to recur in the future as the decision notice in these references was issued before the many changes in the decision-making process recommended by the enforcement process review of 2005, were implemented.
[86] *Timothy Edward Baldwin and WRT Investments Ltd*, FSMT Case 028, 5 April 2006.
[87] Definition now contained in FSMA, s 130A(3).

was designed to import an objective element into the judgement of market behaviour, while retaining some subjective elements related to the markets in question.[88]

The FSMA market abuse regime following the implementation of the provisions of MAD

9.58 A number of key changes were introduced into the UK market abuse system as a result of the implementation of MAD in the UK on 1 July 2005.[89] In considering the introduction of MAD, HM Treasury and the FSA formulated the view that although the new MAD offences and the offences under the pre-MAD regime (the so-called 'legacy offences') conceptually covered very similar ground, their terms were not co-extensive (and indeed the general approach taken was different), and accordingly the MAD offences relating to insider dealing and market manipulation were in effect superimposed onto the legacy offences. The pre-MAD 'legacy' offences therefore still exist, but will only apply where a person's conduct does not fall within any of the MAD behaviour types. The regular user test remains in place for the legacy offences, but not the post-MAD offences (the view was taken that the 'regular user' test would be inconsistent with the approach taken by MAD). The post-MAD offences instead are assessed solely by consideration of the behaviour types set out and the specific safe harbours, exceptions, and defences, and guidance and evidential provisions set out in the legislation and the COMC.[90]

Sunset clause for the legacy offences

9.59 The legacy offences were subject to a sunset date of 30 June 2008—in other words, they were to cease to have effect on 30 June 2008 unless positive action was taken to retain them. The Treasury committed to review the efficacy of the super-equivalent provisions to determine whether or not their retention as part of the UK market abuse regime was justified. The Treasury released a consultation paper in February 2008,[91] which recommended an extension of the sunset date of the super-equivalent provisions to 31 December 2009, pending the outcome of the 2008 European Commission ('EC') review of MAD. This deadline has subsequently been further extended to 31 December 2014[92] in light of the continued review and discussions relating to the proposed new Market Abuse Regulation and the proposed CSD.

9.60 In its review of the sunset clauses the Treasury considered that the evidence supporting the retention of the super-equivalences was finely balanced. According to the Treasury, the costs did not appear to be significant and, while the proven benefits were hard to quantify, proposed changes in the FSA's approach to enforcement might increase the use of and hence the demonstrable benefit of the super equivalences. The Treasury, however, considered that by having an extension, this would enable a wider consideration of the benefits of the super-equivalent provisions in the context of the forthcoming EC review and would minimise transition costs for industry.

9.61 As part of the consultation, the Treasury gave an overview of the areas where the legacy regime was wider in its coverage than the post-MAD offences, citing for example that the concept of 'relevant information not generally available' ('RINGA') used in the legacy offence of misuse

---

[88] MAR 1.2.21G.
[89] For a general discussion regarding the background to the introduction of MAD, see para 9.11.
[90] See discussion at para 9.93.
[91] HM Treasury: 'FSMA market abuse regime: a review of the sunset clauses, a consultation' (February 2008).
[92] Added as per the Financial Services and Markets Act 2000 (Market Abuse) Regulations 2011 (SI 2011/2928).

of information is wider in scope than 'inside information' used in the post-MAD offences of market abuse (insider dealing) and market abuse (improper disclosure); that the post-MAD provisions required some specified positive action (eg dealing, effecting trade, disseminating information, etc.) whereas the super-equivalent provisions focus on 'behaviour' that might capture inaction; the post-MAD insider dealing provisions required the existence of an 'insider', as defined, but the legacy offence of misuse of information did not require an 'insider'; and differences in the definitions of investments to which the provisions apply. The paper also set out a number of specific examples, but criticism of some of these was subsequently expressed.[93]

At the time, no cases had been brought under the super-equivalent provisions since the introduction of the MAD offences, but there have since been a number (see paragraphs 9.180 and 9.226). **9.62**

The Code of Market Conduct

Under section 119(1) of FSMA, the FCA is required to prepare and issue a code containing such provisions as it considers will give appropriate guidance to those determining whether or not behaviour amounts to market abuse. This requirement has been satisfied in the form of the COMC, which is contained in Chapter 1 of the FCA's Market Conduct handbook ('MAR'). The structure of the COMC is based around each of the behaviour types now in section 118. It considers each type of behaviour and sets out descriptions of behaviour that, in the opinion of the FCA, do or do not amount to market abuse. In addition, the COMC sets out factors that, in the opinion of the FCA, are to be taken into account in determining whether or not behaviour amounts to market abuse.[94] It also sets out certain safe harbours which will apply.[95] In addition to those safe harbours set out in the COMC, there are a number of statutory exceptions in FSMA discussed further at paragraph 9.234.[96] The COMC does not, however, exhaustively describe all types of behaviour that may or may not amount to market abuse. In particular, the FCA has stressed that the descriptions of behaviour which amount to market abuse should be read in the light of the elements specified by FSMA as making up the relevant type of market abuse and any relevant descriptions of behaviour which, in the opinion of the FCA, do not amount to market abuse.[97] The provisions of the COMC are designated with letter codes. Those relevant to the following discussion of the COMC are 'E' (which indicates an evidential provision), 'G' (which represents FCA guidance), and 'C' (which indicates a safe harbour). The status of the provision is a reflection of the weight attributed to it. An evidential statement (E) specifies descriptions of behaviour that, in the opinion of the FCA, amount to market abuse; and factors that, in the opinion of the FCA, are to be taken into account in determining whether or not behaviour amounts to market abuse. Evidential provisions are indicative in nature: they create rebuttable presumptions of compliance with or contravention of the binding rules to which they refer. By contrast, guidance (G) is used only to explain the implications of other provisions or to indicate **9.63**

93 See HM Treasury: 'FSMA Market Abuse Regime: Final Impact Assessment on the Sunset Clauses' (June 2008).

94 MAR 1.1.5G.

95 This derives from s 119(2).

96 FSMA, ss 118(5)(a) and (b) and 120(1)(a) as explained at MAR 1.10. See para 9.234 for a further discussion of these provisions.

97 MAR 1.1.6G.

possible means of compliance, but it is not binding on those to whom FSMA applies and nor does it have 'evidential' effect. Guidance is generally designed to throw light on a particular aspect of regulatory requirements. The existence of a safe harbour (C) is of particular importance to market participants as this is conclusive evidence that conduct falling within the safe harbour does not amount to market abuse.[98] For further discussions as to the construction of the COMC considered in the Winterflood Court of Appeal judgment, see paragraph 9.86.[99]

9.64 The COMC which existed under the pre-MAD regime underwent significant changes at the time of the introduction of MAD, partly to accommodate the new MAD offences and defences as discussed earlier, but also in part as a result of an exercise being undertaken by the FSA to simplify its rulebooks and related material. The FSA indicated at the time that the removal of material as part of this latter exercise was therefore not an indication that the former wording and guidance was incorrect, but simply that it did not need to be stated.[100] The effect, therefore, is that, other than to the extent inconsistent with MAD, guidance in the former COMC may still be indicative of the FCA's views and approach, although of course the relevance of this as a reference source will diminish over time.

Other source material

9.65 There are a number of other sources of information on the market abuse regime. The FCA publishes an online periodical called *MarketWatch* which provides updates on the market conduct issues into which the FCA is looking.[101] This is by no means exclusively related to market abuse nor is it official guidance. It is stated to be primarily a news source—updating practitioners on recent or planned developments through brief summaries or highlighting successful instances of enforcement action—although it does appear to function as an informal channel for the communication of the FCA's views. In addition, the FSA has in the past sporadically issued guidance or policy on a particular topic, for example the guidance that pre-hedging convertible bond issues would likely amount to market abuse.[102] So-called Level 3 guidance[103] is also produced by what is now the European Securities and Markets Authority ('ESMA'), which replaced the Committee of European Securities Regulators ('CESR') as part of the process of assimilating practices among national regulators.

'Precedent Value'

9.66 It is also worth looking at the question of what value the decided cases under the market abuse regime to-date have. In simple terms, this will depend on the type of decision, and, in the case of FSA/FCA decisions, the process adopted. These can be of various broad types. The first category is decisions made by the FCA itself following FCA processes and procedures. These can either result from full hearings of the Regulatory Decisions Committee

[98] See Chapter 6 of the FCA's, *Reader's guide: an introduction to the Handbook*; available at <http://www.fca.org.uk/static/documents/handbook/readers-guide.pdf>, for the full explanation of codes used in the FCA Handbook.

[99] *Winterflood Securities Ltd & Others v Financial Services Authority* [2010] EWCA.

[100] Joint Treasury/FSA Consultation Paper: 'UK implementation of the EU Market Abuse Directive' (June 2004) paras 4.2–4.12.

[101] The FSA also at one stage separately issued answers to Frequently Asked Questions on the market abuse regime. Following PS124 (July 2002), the FAQs were added as an Annex to MAR1 and post-MAD they have been moved from MAR to an Appendix in *MarketWatch* issue 12. At the time of writing, 44 issues of *MarketWatch* have been published.

[102] PS149: 'Market Abuse: Pre-Hedging convertible and exchangeable bond issues'.

[103] See Chapter 3.

('RDC'), or, in reality could be the result of a settlement reached with the FCA. Before changes were introduced on 28 August 2007, the way in which a particular decision had been reached was not made clear in the Final Notices, although it could often be gleaned from textual references or time frames referred to in the Final Notices. Moreover, not only could the scope and effect of settled decisions be the result of negotiation and compromise (where commercial considerations no doubt come into play), but also the wording of Final Notices itself, and this needs to be borne in mind when considering 'precedent value' of these decisions. After changes to the FSA enforcement procedure in 2007, decisions reached by settlement are concluded by the Settlement Decision Makers ('SDM') rather than the RDC, and Final Notices refer to this specifically as well as the stage at which the particular matter was settled (reflected in the percentage of discount on penalties for early settlement). The same process also applies to decisions made outside the context of the section 118 market abuse regime, for example, decisions reached by the FCA under FCA rules or principles.

The FCA may also invoke the jurisdiction of the High Court in market abuse cases. This, for example, happened in the *Alexander* case,[104] discussed further at paragraph 9.230, where (in addition to a prohibition order issued by the FSA) the jurisdiction of the High Court was invoked to grant a restraining order, a freezing injunction, and a restitution order. The Court (as opposed to the FCA's own RDC) was also asked by the FSA as part of this process (which the FCA is entitled to do under section 129 FSMA) to set the penalty for market abuse. **9.67**

Decisions and certain other matters may also be referred to the Upper Tribunal (formerly the FSMT). As discussed further in Chapter 1, the Upper Tribunal operates independently from the FSA/FCA and its decisions are undertaken by way of a full rehearing. Following on comments made in the *Legal & General* decision, FSMT/Upper Tribunal decisions, and also FSA /FCA Notices, reported decisions now also reflect the submissions made in order to reflect the fuller debate and conclusions drawn. **9.68**

In this chapter, decisions are marked as being either FSA or FCA decisions or FSMT/Upper Tribunal cases. FSA decisions post-28 August 2007 and FCA decisions are shown as either having been made by the SDM or RDC so the relative weight of the decisions can be gauged. **9.69**

There are also now a number of Court of Appeal decisions where actions or decisions of the Upper Tribunal have been appealed. See, for example, *FSA v Hobbs* [2013] EWCA Civ 918 and *Winterflood Securities Ltd & Ors v FSA* [2010] EWCA Civ 423, which are discussed later in this chapter. **9.70**

Finally, there are a number of cases referred to the ECJ by national courts relating to the interpretation of MAD.[105] **9.71**

Scope of the definition of market abuse in section 118

The definition of behaviour that constitutes market abuse is contained in section 118 of FSMA. For conduct to be market abuse, it must relate to specified types of investments (described at paragraph 9.73 *et seq.*), fall within the stipulated territorial scope (described at paragraph 9.79 *et seq.*), and also fall within one of the stipulated types of behaviour **9.72**

[104] FSA Final Notice to Barnett Michael Alexander, dated 14 June 2011 (SDM).

[105] See references in respect of (C-445/09) *IMC Securities BV v Stichting Autoriteit Financiële Markten*, 07 July 2011 and (C-19/11) *Markus Geltl v Daimler AG*, 28 June 2012; (C-45/08) *Spector Photo Group NV, Chris Van Raemdonck v Commissie voor het Bank-, Financie- en Assurantiewezen CBFA* (C-45/08).

(described at paragraph 9.93 *et seq.*). Section 123(1) goes on to provide that the FCA cannot impose a fine or, in effect, publish a censure where, having considered any representation made to it in response to a warning notice, there are reasonable grounds for it to be satisfied that the person in question believed on reasonable grounds that this behaviour was not market abuse or he took all reasonable precautions and exercised all due diligence to avoid behaving in a way that would be.[106] This is commonly referred to as the 'statutory defence' (see paragraph 9.91).

The 'qualifying investments' element

9.73 The first element of the market abuse definition is that the behaviour must occur in relation to qualifying investments,[107] admitted to trading on a prescribed market,[108] or in respect of which a request for admission to trading on such a market has been made. In the case of market abuse falling within the first two types described later in this chapter (market abuse (insider dealing) and market abuse (improper disclosure)) the scope is extended to investments which are related investments in relation to qualifying investments. A 'related investment', in relation to a qualifying investment, means an investment whose price or value depends on the price or value of the qualifying investment.[109] 'Qualifying investments' means transferable securities; units in collective investment undertakings; money-market instruments; financial futures contracts, including equivalent cash settled instruments; forward interest rate agreements; interest rate, currency, and equity swaps; options to acquire any of these, including equivalent cash settled instruments, and in particular options on currency and on interest rates; derivatives on commodities; and any other instrument admitted for trading on a regulated market in an EEA jurisdiction or for which a request for admission to trading on such a market has been made.[110]

9.74 It should also be noted that the scope of coverage is in effect extended in the case of the legacy offences. For these offences, behaviour that occurs in relation to anything that is the subject matter, or whose price or value is expressed by reference to the price or value of the qualifying investments, or occurs in relation to investments (whether or not they are qualifying investments) whose subject matter is the qualifying investments, is to be regarded as 'occurring in relation to qualifying investments'.

9.75 According to the FCA, behaviour occurring prior to a request for admission to trading may potentially also be covered (relevant/indicative factors being where a person acts in relation to qualifying investments in respect of which a request for admission to trading is subsequently made, and where that behaviour continues to have an effect after the application has been made, or after admission to trading).[111]

9.76 The range of markets included within the definition of 'prescribed market', and therefore the scope of the market abuse regime, has also been modified post-MAD. Under the previous regime, market abuse was limited to behaviour occurring in relation to investments traded

[106] This is discussed further at para 9.84.

[107] FSMA, s 118A. See para 9.100 *et seq.* with respect to qualifying investments in the context of auctions of relevant EU emissions allowances.

[108] Discussed at para 9.76. Also see para 9.100 *et seq.* with respect to prescribed auction platforms.

[109] FSMA, s 130A(3). At its most obvious, therefore, this would include derivatives referable to qualifying investments.

[110] Art 1(3) of MAD.

[111] MAR 1.2.5E.

only on markets established under the rules of the UK recognised investment exchanges[112] (currently the LSE, LIFFE Administration and Management, ICE Futures Europe, the LME, BATS Trading Limited, and ICAP Securities and Derivatives Exchange Limited).[113] The MAD offences on the other hand apply additionally to all 'regulated markets' throughout the EEA.[114]

The scope of qualifying investments was considered by the Upper Tribunal in the *Swift Trade* reference[115] in the context of the market abuse (manipulating transactions) offence (see paragraph 9. 182 *et seq*). That particular offence relates to 'effecting transactions or orders' in certain circumstances and which have, or are likely to have, certain stipulated effects. The Upper Tribunal agreed with the argument raised by the FSA, that the wording of section 118, which refers to 'behaviour which occurs... *in relation to*' qualifying investments and includes, in the context of the market abuse (manipulating transactions) offence, 'effecting transactions or orders to trade' meant that it was not necessary that there be trading *directly* in a qualifying investment. In outline, the case had involved trading by Swift Trade in contracts for differences ('CFDs') in relation to shares traded on the LSE through direct market access arrangements ('DMA'). Under those arrangements, the DMA providers would automatically hedge the CFD transactions with matching transactions in the underlying securities on the LSE. The Upper Tribunal was satisfied on the facts that Swift Trade's orders were placed in the knowledge and with the expectation that the DMA providers would immediately and automatically match them with hedging orders and with the intention that they should do so. **9.77**

As part of their case, Swift Trade had argued that CFDs themselves were not qualifying investments for these purposes, and were not capable of falling within the definition of 'equity swaps' deriving from MAD, but given the finding previously cited, the Upper Tribunal did not address this particular point. Note, however, that in the *Shevlin* case (see footnote 60) in 2008, the RDC proceeded on the basis that CFDs constituted 'related investments' for the purposes of the market abuse (insider dealing) offence.[116] **9.78**

Territorial scope—where behaviour takes place

Under the territoriality provisions in FSMA,[117] the post-MAD market abuse regime applies to behaviour only if it occurs in the UK, or if the behaviour, wherever it takes place, occurs in relation to qualifying investments which are admitted (or requested to be admitted) to trading on a prescribed market situated in, or operating in, the UK.[118] In the case of market abuse **9.79**

[112] This will therefore include AIM which is a market established under the rules of an RIE, namely the LSE.

[113] The FCA's list of recognised investment exchanges is available at <http://www.fsa.gov.uk/register/exchanges.do>. See the pre-MAD amendment versions of FSMA, s 118(3)(a) and Financial Services and Markets Act 2000 (Prescribed Markets and Qualifying Investments) Order 2001 (SI 2001/996) ('the PMO'), art 4.

[114] Regulated markets are those markets listed by EEA jurisdiction regulators in accordance with art 4(14) of the Markets in Financial Instruments Directive 2004/39/EC of 21 April 2004. The FCA presently lists BATS Europe Regulated Market, ICAP Securities & Derivatives Exchange–Main Board, ICE Futures Europe, LSE–Regulated Market, NYSE Euronext London, LIFFE, and the London Metal Exchange. For further details please see <http://www.fsa.gov.uk/register/exchanges.do>.

[115] *Canada Inc and Beck v Financial Services Authority*, Upper Tribunal, (FS/2011/0017; FS/2011/0018), 2 August 2011, currently on appeal (see n 57).

[116] FSA Final Notice to John Shevlin 2008 (n 60).

[117] FSMA, s 118A(1)(a) and (b). Modified provisions apply with respect to auctions of relevant EU emissions allowances discussed at para 9.100 *et seq*.

[118] See, eg, FCA Final Notice to Michael Coscia, dated 3 July 2013 (SDM); (settled at early stage) where the relevant trading activities originated in the US, but orders were submitted to a UK prescribed market (ICE Futures).

(insider dealing) and market abuse (improper disclosure), this extends to related investments.[119] Under the arrangements set out in MAD, behaviour could therefore potentially be covered by the market abuse provisions operating in more than one EEA jurisdiction. For example, conduct undertaken in, say, Germany relating to shares admitted to trading on the LSE would constitute relevant behaviour for the purposes of the UK market abuse regime (as it occurs in relation to shares admitted to trading on a regulated market in the UK), as well as being relevant behaviour for the purposes of the German market abuse regime (as it is behaviour occurring within Germany relating to securities listed on an EEA regulated market). For a discussion of the coordination and cooperation which would apply between the UK and German authorities in such circumstances, see Chapter 10 at paragraph 10.108.

9.80 The question of the territorial effect of the market abuse regime was discussed in a preliminary hearing of the FSMT in the *Jabre* case.[120] The decision related to an earlier section 118(1) which referred to behaviour occurring 'in relation to qualifying investments "traded" (as opposed to "admitted to trading") on a prescribed market', and so the detailed arguments are not directly in point. However, it was found that transactions undertaken on the Tokyo market in respect of shares which were also listed on the LSE did occur in relation to qualifying investments 'traded' on a prescribed market and the decision did contain the observation:

> The vice of insider dealing, and the reason why it was prohibited, was that it reduced confidence in the integrity and transparency of the market in the particular security which was being abused. The FSA had an interest in preventing market abuse that impacted on the market and its institutions because the abuse related to shares traded within the territory of its authority.

Vicarious liability

9.81 The extent to which a firm should be vicariously liable for market abuse offences was also considered in the *Jabre* decision. In that case, the hedge fund management firm on whose behalf Mr Jabre was trading argued that it could not be held responsible for market abuse on the basis of vicarious liability or the principles of 'attribution'. The FSA were satisfied that on the facts and having regards to the language and purpose of the market abuse provisions in FSMA, the firm could be liable for market abuse on the basis that Jabre's acts amounted to market abuse and were attributable to the firm. The FSA reached this conclusion having regard to, amongst other matters: Jabre's seniority and status within the firm (at the relevant time Jabre held the title of 'Managing Director'; was a member of the firm's Management Committee (albeit that this was an informal committee); was one of three individuals on the firm's Investment Management Committee; and was responsible for managing six of the firm's funds including the fund to which the events in the case related, the fact that he clearly had authority to enter into the relevant transactions; the fact that within an agreed overall strategy his dealings were largely unsupervised and he exercised a large degree of autonomy).

9.82 The issue was also considered in the *Cattles* case,[121] discussed later in this chapter at paragraph 9.223 *et seq*. In that case, the FSA confirmed that the principle in *Re Hampshire Land Co* [1896] 2 Ch 743 (broadly speaking, that the conduct and knowledge of a company

[119] As to the extended scope for the legacy offences, see para 9.74.
[120] *Philippe Jabre v FSA*, FSMT Case 036, 2006—Decision on Market Abuse.
[121] Final Notice to Cattles Limited, dated 28 March 2012 (RDC).

director in breach of his duties should not generally be attributed to the company) would not apply in the market abuse context to the extent that, as discussed in *Meridian Global Funds Management Asia Ltd v Securities Commission* [1995] 2 AC 500, attribution is itself the intention of a relevant provision. In that case Lord Hoffman's concern had been that the purposive approach should not be defeated:

> In such a case, the court must fashion a special rule of attribution for that particular substantive rule. This is always a matter of interpretation: given that it was intended to apply to a company, how was it intended to apply? Whose act (or knowledge, or state of mind) was for this purpose intended to count as the act etc of the company?

According to the FSA, as neither intent, knowledge, nor governance were necessary elements in the offence, it could not be the case that a company could only be liable for the acts of its directors when it was complicit (notwithstanding that the absence of complicity may be a mitigating factor with respect to penalties). The FSA observed that the market abuse provisions 'are effect based and do not depend on knowledge', and the FSA gave strong policy reasons for the attribution of acts in relation to such offences.

The mental element

It is often said that market abuse is 'effects-based' and indeed that the absence of having to prove intention or recklessness will result in a more responsive and effective system of offences. It is true that there is no requirement in section 123 that the person who committed market abuse did so 'intentionally' or 'recklessly'. **9.83**

That is not to say, however, that the market abuse regime is without reference to the mental state of the person who is accused of market abuse. The mental state of such persons is referenced in four distinct ways:

(i) the availability of what is in effect a defence under section 123(2)(a) relating to the defendant's state of mind;
(ii) definitions of conduct that constitutes market abuse which refer (either directly or by implication) to a person's motive or knowledge;
(iii) statements made in the COMC which presuppose that a person's motive or knowledge may be relevant in certain circumstances; and
(iv) the FCA's policy on sanctioning market abuse.

Looking at these in turn, according to section 123, the FCA may not impose a penalty on a person where, amongst other things, the FCA has reasonable grounds to be satisfied that 'he believed on reasonable grounds' that his behaviour did not constitute market abuse or 'requiring or encouraging'.[122] It has been argued that this is a 'specified mental element to the offence'.[123] In addition, the state of mind of the defendant may also in certain circumstances be considered when determining whether or not he committed one of the behaviour types under section 118 that constitute market abuse. Certain (but not all) of the behaviour types contain an explicit reference to the mental state of the defendant. For example, **9.84**

[122] FSMA, s 123(2)(a). Jain, 'Significance of mens rea in insider trading', (2004) *Comp Law* 25(5), 132–40, 'despite there being no express intent requirement, if the defendant can prove the required state of mind of either reasonable belief or due diligence being exercised by him, he will not be subjected to a penalty by the Financial Services Authority'. As to requiring and encouraging, see para 9.98.

[123] Alcock, 'Market abuse—the new witchcraft?' (2001) *NLJ* 151/1398, Issue, 7001 (Sept).

'dissemination' under section 118(7) requires that the person disseminating false information 'knew or could reasonably be expected to have known' that the information was false or misleading.

9.85 More colour is given in the COMC.[124] The COMC begins by confirming the basic proposition that the definition of market abuse in section 118 'does not require the person engaging in the behaviour in question to have *intended* to commit market abuse'.[125] However, there are a number of situations in which the state of mind of the accused does come into play in the COMC. For example, in the context of market abuse (manipulating transactions), the fact that a person has an 'actuating purpose' to induce others to trade in a qualifying investment, or to position or move the price of a qualifying investment will, in the FCA's opinion, be indicative of an absence of 'legitimate reasons' for the transaction itself.[126] Conversely, the absence of such a purpose will be a relevant factor to consider, but is not in itself indicative of legitimate reasons. Similarly, the fact that a transaction was executed with the purpose of creating a false or misleading impression will be indicative of a lack of 'legitimate reasons' and the absence of such a purpose will be one of a number of relevant factors. The final way in which the state of mind of the defendant is relevant to the market abuse regime is that the FCA will consider the guilty party's state of mind when considering the sanction to impose. Under the FCA's enforcement policies, the FCA will take into account whether or not the breach was 'deliberate or reckless' when deciding whether or not to proceed against market abuse.[127]

9.86 The mental element, and construction of the COMC, were considered in the Winterflood Court of Appeal judgment.[128] As will be discussed later in this chapter, the *Winterflood* case involved the execution of a share ramping scheme by a Mr Simon Eagle of the brokerage firm SP Bell with respect to the shares in an AIM-listed company, Fundamental-E Investments Plc. In that judgement, Moore-Bick LJ firstly clarified that the definition of 'abuse' at s 118 FSMA 'does not require any particular state of mind on the part of the person whose behaviour is under consideration'.

9.87 The court also considered the construction of the COMC. The particular point referred asked the court to decide whether the relevant provisions of the COMC required an examination of whether establishing 'purpose' was relevant to the question of whether behaviour will amount to market abuse for the purposes of the pre-MAD market abuse (distortion) offence. The appellants (the defendants in the Upper Tribunal) argued that the evidential provisions of the COMC (MAR 1.5.8E) stated positively that where an actuating purpose exists with respect to interfering with the proper operation of the market, such behaviour will be market abuse—and that therefore where no actuating purpose is present, there can be no market abuse. The Court of Appeal disagreed, finding that MAR 1.5.8E contained no such implicit reverse logic—ie that showing one particular evidential provision could not be met was evidence that no market abuse had been committed. Moore-Bick LJ did not rule out that implicit reverse logic might apply in cases where the COMC presented a true dichotomy between behaviour definitively and singly constituting market abuse so that

124 See para 9.63 for further discussion on the COMC.
125 MAR 1.2.3G (emphasis added).
126 See MAR 1.6.5E.
127 DEPP 6.2.1G (1)(a). See also Chapter 6 at para 6.96.
128 *Winterflood Securities Ltd & Ors v Financial Services Authority* [2010] EWCA Civ 423.

absence of such behaviour would necessarily and inevitably amount to a statement that there was no market abuse, but MAR 1.5.8E was not one of them.

The court also drew attention to the classification of the material in MAR by reference to the FSA's power to make guidelines supplementing the statutory offences in FSMA—in particular, noting that for evidential provisions their purpose is: **9.88**

> …to provide those who use the market and those who are responsible for maintaining market discipline with principles that, although not definitive, can be regarded as having persuasive authority. To that extent, they can be relied upon, but that does not touch the question of whether they are to be read as permitting by implication any conduct not specifically identified in that way.

The point was noted in the subsequent *Geddis* case (see paragraph 9.212), in the context of the market abuse (manipulating transactions) offence. The Upper Tribunal noted that Mr Geddis's failure consisted in not taking sufficient care, while holding a dominant position, to avoid creating a disorderly market. This was negligent, not deliberate, market abuse. That accords with the Court of Appeal's ruling in Winterflood that there is no requirement for intention within the market abuse regime—a want of care, rather than an intention to commit market abuse, is sufficient if the behaviour is in fact abusive.[129] **9.89**

Spector Photo

As mentioned in paragraph 9.41, the ECJ *Spector Photo* case considered the construction of the expression 'use of' in the context of MAD and concluded that the fact that a person in possession of inside information acquires or disposes of, or tries to acquire or dispose of, for his own account or for the account of a third party, either directly or indirectly, the relevant financial instruments gave rise to a rebuttable presumption that that person has 'used that information' within the meaning of MAD, irrespective of the causation. However, this rebuttable presumption is to be considered in the light of the purposes of the directive, and is subject to the defences in the directive. This is discussed further at paragraph 9.132. **9.90**

The statutory defence

As discussed earlier in this chapter, Section 123(1) provides that the FCA cannot impose a fine or, in effect, publish a censure where, having considered any representation made to it in response to a warning notice, there are reasonable grounds for it to be satisfied that the person in question believed on reasonable grounds that this behaviour was not market abuse or he took all reasonable precautions and exercised all due diligence to avoid behaving in a way that would be construed to comprise such behaviour.[130] **9.91**

The s 123(1) defence has been discussed in a couple of cases (see also, for example, the *Hannam* case discussed at paragraph 9.165). In the *Davidson and Tatham* case, for example, although it was found that no market abuse had taken place, the FSMT observed that, on the facts of that case, there were reasonable grounds for being satisfied that the applicants took all reasonable precautions and exercised all reasonable due diligence to avoid behaving in a way which **9.92**

[129] See also, eg, *Greenlight* decision (n 176), where the FSA acknowledged that behaviour may constitute market abuse even where not deliberate or reckless. There, the FSA agreed that Mr Einhorn did not believe that the information that he had received was inside information, and he did not intend to commit market abuse.

[130] This is discussed further at para 9.84.

amounted to market abuse or requiring or encouraging another to engage in market abuse. More generally, the adjudicating bodies have been slower to find that the statutory defence has been satisfied. In the *Jabre* case, for example, the RDC considered that although the compliance procedures operated by the firm in question may have been sufficient by the standards prevailing and expected in 2003 to protect the firm from a general finding that its systems and controls were in breach of Principle 3 of the FSA's Principles for Businesses ('a firm must take reasonable care to organise and control its affairs responsibly and effectively, with adequate risk management systems'), in a context where market abuse has occurred, FSMA required a higher standard (that the firm should 'take all reasonable precautions and exercise all due diligence to avoid' engaging in market abuse). It was found that there were other steps which the firm could have taken and which were in place in some major firms at the material time.

The types of behaviour constituting market abuse

9.93 Once it is established that behaviour falling within the appropriate territorial scope has occurred in relation to relevant qualifying investments (or, where appropriate, related investments), it is necessary to ascertain whether the behaviour falls within one of prescribed types of behaviour.[131] These behaviour types fall into two broad categories, namely:

- behaviour which relates to the use of information, and
- behaviour which manipulates the market or creates a false or misleading impression.[132]

9.94 The provisions of Part VIII FSMA do not require the person engaging in the relevant behaviour to have intended to carry out market abuse—it is sufficient that one of the behaviour types is present[133] (although for a discussion of the mental element built into the regime, see paragraph 9.83). For all of the behaviour types, market abuse may be committed either by one person acting alone or by two or more persons acting jointly or in concert.[134]

9.95 Behaviour is stated to extend to both action and inaction.[135] That said, it would appear on closer analysis that this would apply only to the legacy offences. This would also seem to be supported by comments made in the Treasury review of the sunset clauses, (for example the Treasury view was that a failure to correct information giving a false or misleading impression would fall within scope of Type 7 behaviour).[136] Section 118(1) states that market abuse is behaviour which occurs in relation to qualifying investments (etc.) (see paragraph 9.73) and which falls within any one or more of the behaviour types described at paragraph 9.93 *et seq*. However, when these specific definitions of behaviour types are considered, it becomes apparent that there are real divergences in the drafting between the post-MAD offences and the legacy offences. The MAD offences prescribe certain very narrowly defined types of action ('an insider deals or attempts to deal', 'an insider discloses inside information', 'effecting transactions or orders to trade', 'the dissemination of information', etc.) rather than the broader concept of 'behaviour', capable of accommodating inaction, retained by the legacy

[131] FSMA, s 118(1)(b).

[132] Note that the legacy offences are due to expire on 31 December 2014. See para 9.59 *et seq*.

[133] MAR 1.2.3G.

[134] FSMA, s 118(1).

[135] FSMA, s 130A(3). This is elaborated on in an evidential provision in the COMC (MAR 1.2.6E) which explains that, in the FCA's view, failure through inaction to discharge a legal or regulatory obligation would be indicative of relevant behaviour. Similar considerations will apply where a person who has created a reasonable expectation that he will act in a particular manner has failed to satisfy any duty or obligation which has arisen to inform persons that their expectations are not correct.

[136] HM Treasury: 'FSMA market abuse regime: a review of the sunset clauses, a consultation' (February 2008).

offences.[137] It should be noted that the requiring and encouraging element discussed at paragraph 9.78 may be committed by failing, or refraining from taking, any action. By contrast, under the criminal law insider dealing provisions, there is no scope for inaction to constitute the criminal offence at all (see discussion in Chapter 10, paragraph 10.03).

Behaviour relating to the use of information

9.96 The first three behaviour types that constitute market abuse relate, broadly speaking, to the use of information.[138] These are as follows:

- Type 1—market abuse (insider dealing)

This applies where an insider deals, or attempts to deal, in a relevant qualifying investment or related investment on the basis of inside information relating to the investment in question.[139] The meaning of insider and inside information is discussed at paragraphs 9.105 and 9.106 *et seq.*

- Type 2—market abuse (improper disclosure)

This applies where an insider discloses inside information to another person otherwise than in the proper course of the exercise of his employment, profession, or duties.[140]

- Type 3—market abuse (misuse of information) (legacy offence)[141]

This applies to behaviour which is neither market abuse (insider dealing) nor market abuse (improper disclosure) but rather based on information which is not generally available to those using the market (known as 'RINGA') but which, if available to a regular user of the market, would be, or would be likely to be, regarded by him as relevant when deciding the terms on which transactions in qualifying investments should be effected. The behaviour must also be likely to be regarded by a regular user of the market as a failure on the part of the person concerned to observe the standard of behaviour reasonably expected of a person in his position in relation to the market.

Behaviour relating to false or misleading impressions

9.97 Behaviour types 4 to 7 relate, broadly speaking, to transactions which are market abuse as a result of a false or misleading impression being created or manipulation of the market occurring. These are as follows:

- Type 4—market abuse (manipulating transactions)

This applies to effecting transactions or orders to trade (otherwise than for legitimate reasons and in conformity with accepted market practices[142] on the relevant market) which either

[137] HM Treasury's discussion of the regulatory impact of the various models for implementation of MAD (UK Implementation of the EU Market Abuse Directive, Annex B, Regulatory Impact Assessment) cites this as a key advantage for the retention of the legacy offences alongside MAD offences. The Treasury make it clear that in their opinion the MAD offences are drafted in such a way that inaction would not (in their example) constitute market manipulation under any of types 4–6 referred to at para 9.97, but it would be behaviour likely to give a regular user a false or misleading impression under legacy offence type 7.

[138] This regime is co-existent with the insider dealing regime in the CJA. See Chapter 10 for a discussion of this.

[139] FSMA, s 118(2), as discussed at para 9.125 *et seq.*

[140] ibid, s 118(3), as discussed at para 9.159.

[141] ibid, s 118(4), as discussed at para 9.173 *et seq.*

[142] 'Accepted market practices' means practices that are reasonably expected in the financial market in question and are accepted by the FCA (or other competent EEA authority)—FSMA, s 130A(3). In other words,

give, or are likely to give, a false or misleading impression as to the supply of, or demand for, or as to the price of, one or more qualifying investments ('false or misleading impressions'), or alternatively secure the price of one or more such investments at an abnormal or artificial level ('price positioning').[143]

- Type 5—market abuse (manipulating devices)

This applies to effecting transactions or orders to trade which employ fictitious devices or any other form of deception or contrivance.[144]

- Type 6—market abuse (dissemination)

This type of behaviour applies to the dissemination of information by any means which gives, or is likely to give, a false or misleading impression as to a qualifying investment by a person who knew or could reasonably be expected to have known that the information was false or misleading.[145]

- Type 7—market abuse (misleading behaviour and distortion) (legacy offence)

This applies to conduct which does not constitute market abuse (manipulating transactions), market abuse (manipulating devices), or market abuse (dissemination), but which is either likely to give a regular user of the market a false or misleading impression as to the supply of, demand for, or price or value of, qualifying investments, or alternatively would be, or would be likely to be, regarded by a regular user of the market as behaviour that would distort, or would be likely to distort, the market in such an investment. In either case, the behaviour must be likely to be regarded by a regular user of the market as a failure on the part of the person concerned to observe the standard of behaviour reasonably expected of a person in his position in relation to the market.[146]

Requiring and encouraging

9.98 According to section 123(1)(b) of FSMA, a person may also be subject to a penalty where the FCA is satisfied that that person, by taking or refraining from taking any action, has required or encouraged any other person or persons to engage in behaviour which, if engaged in by the first person, would amount to market abuse. The pre-MAD COMC contained extensive guidance on when behaviour would or would not be regarded as 'requiring or encouraging'. This guidance has not been replaced in the post-MAD COMC which contains only two examples of conduct that may constitute requiring or encouraging,[147] namely where (a) a director of a company, while in possession of inside information, instructs an employee of that company to deal in qualifying investments or related investments in respect of which

---

there is a formal 'acceptance' requirement and market practices will therefore not automatically be 'accepted' for these purposes simply because they are commonplace or generally accepted within the market. Commission Directive 2004/72/EC implements sections of MAD as regards accepted market practices and sets out guidance in Arts 2 and 3 for the competent authorities of Member States to follow in evaluating market practices. ESMA (formerly CESR) also publishes a 'master list' of the practices that are accepted by various EEA competent authorities: <http://www.esma.europa.eu/page/accepted-markets-practices>.

[143] FSMA, s 118(5), as discussed at para 9.183 *et seq*.

[144] ibid, s 118(6), as discussed at para 9.216.

[145] ibid, s 118(7), as discussed at para 9.220 *et seq*.

[146] ibid, s 118(8) as discussed at para 9.225. This provision is equivalent to s 118(2)(b) and (c) of FSMA under the pre-MAD regime.

[147] As to which, see MAR 1.2.23G.

the information is inside information; and (b) a person recommends or advises a friend to engage in behaviour which, if he himself engaged in it, would amount to market abuse.

There have been various cases involving 'requiring and encouraging', for example, in the *Harrison* case, which is discussed at paragraph 9.155. Also, in the *Darwin Clifton* case,[148] Darwin Clifton was fined for 'requiring' the company of which he was a director to engage in market abuse. See also the *Erik Boyen* case,[149] where Erik Boyen was fined, partly for 'encouraging' an inexperienced third party to purchase shares when he was in possession of inside information relating to the company in question; the *Jeremy Burley* case,[150] where Jeremy Burley was fined partly for 'encouraging' a third party to sell his shares on the basis of inside information by telling him of his intention to sell his own shares; and the *Jay Rutland* case,[151] in which the FSA fined Jay Rutland partly for 'encouraging' his fellow brokers to disclose inside information when selling shares, as well as encouraging them to pitch the stock to as many customers as possible. **9.99**

Auctions of EU Emissions Allowances

Changes to the market abuse regime were introduced in July 2012 by the UK Recognised Auction Platform Regulations ('RAP Regulations')[152] to reflect the EU Emission Allowance Auctioning Regulation[153] (which regulates, amongst other things, bidding on auction platforms for relevant transactions in emissions allowances). The effect of the RAP Regulations is that key provisions relating to the market abuse offences are modified to reflect the specific circumstances of auction platform bidding.[154] The Emission Allowance Auctioning Regulation (Articles 38 to 41) also introduces a parallel regime relating insider dealing and market manipulation with respect to transactions not otherwise covered (such as two-day spot transactions). To reflect this, the RAP Regulation provides that section 118 FSMA is to have effect as if a new, eighth offence were added (as section 118(8A)), to capture behaviour which contravenes Articles 38 to 41. **9.100**

In terms of implementation, the concept of 'qualifying market' (see paragraph 9.76) is replaced by the concept of 'prescribed auction platforms'. Under the Prescribed Markets and Qualifying Investments Order,[155] both the MAD offences and the legacy offences (as modified by the RAP Regulations) apply in relation to 'recognised auction platforms' (namely UK-recognised investment exchanges which have also been recognised for the purposes of the RAP Regulations). The (modified) MAD offences apply additionally to all other auction platforms which have been appointed under the Emission Allowance Auctioning Regulation. 'Qualifying investments' for the purposes of the MAD and legacy offences are auctioned products which are MiFID financial instruments. **9.101**

148 FSA Final Notice to Darwin Lewis Clifton OBE and Byron Holdings Limited, dated 27 January 2009 (SDM).

149 FSA Final Notice to Erik Boyen, dated 12 January 2009 (SDM).

150 FSA Final Notice to Jeremy Burley, dated 19 July 2010 (SDM).

151 FSA Final Notice to Jay Rutland, dated 9 July 2012 (SDM).

152 SI 2011 No 2699.

153 Commission Regulation (EU) No 1031/2010 of 12 November 2010 on the timing, administration and other aspects of auctioning of greenhouse gas emission allowances pursuant to the emission allowance trading directive.

154 See regulation 6 and Sch 1, RAP Regulations.

155 Financial Services and Markets Act 2000 (Prescribed Markets and Qualifying Investments) Order 2001 (SI 2001/996) as amended.

9.102 For the purposes of section 118(8A) (as inserted by the modifications made by the RAP Regulations), qualifying investments are all auctioned products which are not MiFID financial instruments, and the prescribed auction platforms are all auction platforms which have been appointed under the Emission Allowance Auctioning regulation.

9.103 This chapter focuses on the market abuse regime other than in the context of auctions of emission allowances, although passing reference is made to certain COMC provisions relating to auction platforms.

Market Abuse Offences that Concern the Use of Information—Definitions

9.104 The first two types of behaviour described earlier both relate to acts undertaken by an 'insider' with respect to 'inside information'.

Insider

9.105 For the purposes of the market abuse provisions, the term 'insider' has a specific meaning and is determined by the capacity or circumstances in which information is received (for example where information is received as part of a person's employment, profession, or duties).[156] Being an insider is not in itself necessarily offensive—it is simply a way of separating those to whom, from a policy perspective, the market abuse (insider dealing) and market abuse (improper disclosure) offences potentially apply, from those to whom it should not (such as individuals acting in a private capacity innocently obtaining information which they do not know, or could not reasonably be expected to know, was inside information).

'Inside information'

9.106 The definition of 'inside information' differs according to whether or not the qualifying investments (or related investments) to which the behaviour relates are commodity derivatives.[157] In both cases, the information must be of a 'precise' nature,[158] and not generally available.[159] In the case of qualifying investments (or related investments) which are *not*

---

[156] According to FSMA, s 118B, an 'insider' is any person who has 'inside information' as a result of membership of an administrative, management, or supervisory body of an issuer of qualifying investments; holding capital of an issuer of qualifying investments; having access to the information through the exercise of his employment, profession or duties, or criminal activities. An insider also extends to any person obtaining information by other means and which he knows, or could reasonably be expected to know, is inside information. According to MAR 1.2.8E, for these purposes, a person could be 'reasonably expected to know' that information in his possession is inside information where a normal and reasonable person in the position of that person would both (a) know that the person from whom he received it is an 'insider', and (b) know that it is inside information. Note that it is only in the latter category of insider that knowledge is relevant—for the other categories, the person concerned does not need to know that the information is inside information (MAR 1.2.9) (cf the position under the CJA offence discussed in Chapter 10 which requires knowledge).

[157] According to MAR 1.2.17G, this is explained by the differences in the nature of information which is important to commodity derivatives markets.

[158] Information is to be regarded as being of a 'precise' nature for the purposes of the market abuse rules if it (a) indicates circumstances that exist or may reasonably be expected to come into existence or an event that has occurred or may reasonably be expected to occur, and (b) is specific enough to enable a conclusion to be drawn as to the possible effect of those circumstances or that event on the price of the qualifying investments or related investments—FSMA, s 118C(5).

[159] See the explanation at paras 9.110–9.111, as to when information is to be considered as 'generally available' for the market abuse rules.

commodity derivatives,[160] inside information is information which in addition relates to one or more issuers of the qualifying investments or to one or more of the qualifying investments; and would, if generally available, be likely to have a 'significant effect' on the price of the qualifying or related investments. This will be the case if and only if it is information of a kind which a reasonable investor would be likely to use as part of the basis of his investment decision.[161]

Where the qualifying investments (or related investments) are commodity derivatives, inside information is information relating directly or indirectly to one or more commodity derivatives which,[162] in addition to being of a 'precise' nature and not being generally available, users of markets on which the derivatives are traded would expect to receive in accordance with any accepted practices on those markets (ie information which is routinely made available to users of those markets or which is required to be disclosed by a statutory provision, market rules, or contracts, or customs on the relevant underlying commodity market or commodity derivatives market).[163] **9.107**

Pending orders

An important change introduced into the post-MAD market abuse regime was the proposition that 'in relation to a person charged with the execution of orders concerning qualifying investments or related investments' information relating to inside information will include information which has stipulated characteristics conveyed by a client relating to the client's pending orders.[164] This differs from the approach taken in the pre-MAD regime where (in the context of what is now the market abuse (misuse of information) offence) dealing or arranging activities undertaken on the basis of so-called 'trading information'[165] benefited from safe harbour treatment. In place of the trading information safe harbour, two new safe harbours relating to the 'dutiful execution of client orders' and the 'legitimate carrying on of the business of market makers etc' have been introduced. The practical implications of this change are discussed at paragraph 9.145 *et seq*. **9.108**

Section 118C(4) goes on to provide that inside information relating to a client's pending orders must satisfy the criteria which apply to non-commodity derivatives (even though the definition applies to all qualifying investments, ie including commodity derivatives). In other words, in addition to being precise and not generally available, to fall within this section the information must relate to one or more issuers or one or more qualifying investments, and be likely to have a significant effect on the price of those qualifying investments.[166] In this **9.109**

[160] FSMA, s 118C(2).

[161] ibid, s 118C(6). Note also that the question of whether information is likely to have a significant effect on the price of issuers' shares, financial instruments, and related investments is dealt with in the context of the Disclosure Rules. Please see para 10.82 *et seq.* generally.

[162] ibid, s 118C(3). It would not appear to be relevant for the purposes of this definition whether or not the information would have a 'significant effect' on the price of qualifying or related investments.

[163] ibid, s 118C(7).

[164] ibid, s 118C(4). A 'pending order' is where a person is approached by another in relation to a transaction and (a) the transaction is not immediately executed on an arm's length basis in response to a price quoted by that person; and (b) the person concerned has taken on a legal or regulatory obligation relating to the manner or timing of the execution of the transaction—MAR 1.2.16E.

[165] For the definition of trading information, in the pre-MAD regime, see para 9.145.

[166] According to s 118C(6), information would be likely to have a significant effect on price if and only if it is information of a kind which a reasonable investor would be likely to use as part of the basis of his investment decisions.

context, therefore (as distinct from the general definition of inside information as it applies to commodity derivatives), it would seem the requirement relating to significant effect on the market will be relevant.

FSA guidance and evidential provisions as to information that is not 'inside information' on the basis of whether information is 'generally available'

9.110 The FCA has identified a number of factors which are to be taken into account in determining whether or not information is 'generally available'. The presence of such factors would be indicative that the information would be regarded as being generally available.

9.111 The factors set out in the COMC are whether the information has been disclosed to a prescribed market or a prescribed auction platform[167] through an RIS or has otherwise been disclosed in accordance with the rules of that market; whether the information is contained in records which are open to inspection by the public; whether the information is otherwise generally available, including through the Internet, or some other publication (including if it is only available on payment of a fee), or is derived from information which has been made public; whether the information can be obtained by observation by members of the public without infringing rights or obligations of privacy, property, or confidentiality;[168] or the extent to which the information can be obtained by analysing or developing other information which is generally available.[169] For the purpose of considering what constitutes generally available information, FCA guidance[170] indicates that it is not relevant that the information in question is only generally available *outside* of the UK.[171]

Rumours

9.112 The issue of what constitutes 'generally available' information was discussed in the *Arif Mohammed* case (a misuse of information case under the pre-MAD market abuse regime).[172] In that case, Mohammed argued that he had not traded on the basis of inside information because the sale of the particular division of the company in question was subject to widespread rumours. The FSMT held, however, that in order to hold that 'information' was available to the public, something 'precise in nature' is required. Rumours would not be sufficient for this. The interrelation between rumours and information was also considered in the *Jabre* case discussed at paragraph 9.114.

Precise Information

9.113 As mentioned in paragraph 9.106, inside information is required to be 'of a precise nature'. Information is precise if it indicates circumstances that exist or may reasonably be expected

[167] An 'auction platform' in this context means a platform on which auctions of emissions allowances are held in accordance with Commission Regulation (EU) No 1031/2010 of 12 November 2010 on the timing, administration, and other aspects of auctioning of greenhouse gas emission allowances pursuant to the emission allowance trading directive.

[168] The example given in MAR is where a passenger on a train passes a burning factory and calls his broker and tells him to sell shares in the factory's owner. In that instance, the passenger will be acting on information which is generally available, since it is information which has been obtained by legitimate means through observation of a public event. MAR 1.2.14.

[169] MAR 1.2.12E. Whilst not identical, these factors follow fairly closely the non-exhaustive list of circumstances set out in the CJA where information is, or, in some cases, may be considered to be, made public—see s 58 of the CJA.

[170] MAR 1.2.13E.

[171] This again mirrors the guidance for the criminal regime which states that information may be treated as made public even though it is published only outside the UK. See s 58(3)(e) of the CJA.

[172] *Arif Mohammed v FSA*, FSMT Case 012, 29 March 2005.

to come into existence or an event that has occurred (or may reasonably be expected to occur), and is specific enough to enable a conclusion to be drawn as to the possible effect of those circumstances or that event on the price of qualifying investments or related investments.[173]

In terms of the former, to take an example, in the *Jabre* case[174] the FSA also found that even though Jabre may not have been told in terms that the investment bank in question had the mandate, and may not have been told that the issue of securities by the Japanese bank in question would definitely be launched, or told when it would be launched, the information he was given did provide, 'with reasonable certainty, grounds to conclude' that 'possible future developments' would occur. As to the likely timing of the prospective issue, it was widespread in the market that the Central Bank of Japan had set a particular deadline for the improvement of the Tier 1 Ratios of the four major Japanese banks, which would have led any market participants to conclude that an issue of fresh capital of the kind canvassed could not be long delayed. **9.114**

In what has become a series of cases looking at the information flows between corporate brokers and buy side institutions, the question of when inside information is passed has been given further consideration. The *Greenlight* and *Einhorn* cases[175] provide an interesting example. In outline, David Einhorn, principal at a hedge fund manager, Greenlight Capital, declined to be brought over an information barrier and receive inside information as part of market soundings being undertaken by the corporate broker of an issuer, Punch Taverns. A conversation subsequently took place on that basis during which it was subsequently held that inside information was indeed given to Mr Einhorn. Three separate pieces of information were given to Mr Einhorn, namely (i) that the issuance was intended to repay in total Punch Taverns' existing convertible bond, and therefore the issue size would be considerable relative to its market capitalisation; and (ii) that the issuance process was at an advanced stage, being likely to take place within a week; and (iii) that all major shareholders were being consulted and were supportive of the issuance. **9.115**

The FSA stated that:

> In isolation, none of the previously cited points would (in the context of the Punch Call) amount to inside information. However, taken together these points did constitute inside information particularly because they disclosed to Mr Einhorn the purpose and anticipated size and timing of the issuance.

The decision makes it clear that the information imparted on the call met the statutory definition of inside information because it was precise (whether or not it was generally available and likely to have a significant price effect was less contentious here on the facts) notwithstanding that the transaction was not a certainty at the time—it was not necessary for Mr Einhorn to be told the issuance was definitely going to proceed. The information indicated an event that may reasonably have been expected to occur.

The issue has also been considered in the debt markets in cases censuring two traders at Dresdner Kleinwort,[176] Mr Morton, a director within Dresdner Kleinwort and co-head of **9.116**

---

173 s 118C(5). In terms of the requirement relating to possible effect on price, see also the 'significant effect on price' requirement discussed at para 9.120.

174 *Philippe Jabre v FSA*, FSMT Case 036, 10 July 2006.

175 FSA Final Notices to David Einhorn and Greenlight Capital Inc., dated 15 February 2012 (RDC).

176 FSA Final Notices to Darren Morton and Christopher Parry, dated 7 October 2009 (RDC).

the Structured Investment Unit, was contacted by Barclays Capital concerning a new issue of Barclays floating rate notes ('FRNs'). Barclays Capital wanted to ascertain the appetite for participating in the issue. In essence, Mr Morton argued that he did not believe his actions amounted to market abuse because what he had done was, he believed, in accordance with acceptable market practice around debt issues, and did not in fact entail receipt by him of inside information since the information he received was imprecise as the issue might not in fact materialise, and was in any event not price sensitive. This, however, was not accepted by the FSA. Whilst the FSA accepted that neither Mr Morton nor Mr Parry (a Vice President in the same unit as Mr Morton who had effected the relevant trades in the market and was also found to have engaged in market abuse) believed he had received inside information, it concluded that this belief was not reasonable, regardless of the market practice.

9.117 The second limb of the test, ie whether information is sufficiently 'specific' to enable a conclusion to be drawn on the possible effect or price, was considered by the Upper Tribunal in the *Massey* case.[177] The Upper Tribunal noted that the wording did not contain any requirement for a conclusion as to the actual or probable effect on the price, nor whether or not the occurrence of an alteration was more probable than not, but only as to the 'possible' effect, but expressed doubts over whether it could be right to read the wording so literally—to do so would arguably render the phrase 'specific enough to enable a conclusion to be drawn', which had a 'strong note of definiteness' almost empty of effect. The Upper Tribunal did not on the facts find it necessary to decide the point since, on the facts, they found an effect was possible and, if it occurred, it would be to reduce the price.

Significant effect on price

9.118 The question of what would have a significant effect on price was discussed in the Woolworths decision,[178] albeit in the context of the Disclosure Rules and Listing Principles. This is discussed further at Chapter 10, paragraph 9.116.The point was also subsequently considered in the *Massey* case[179] in the context of the market abuse regime where the Upper Tribunal formed the view that the phrase 'likely to have a significant effect on the price' was not used in FSMA in its ordinary sense; rather, meaning the expression had a specially extended meaning as a result of s118C(6) FSMA (namely that information would be likely to have a significant effect on price if and only if it is information of a kind which a reasonable investor would be likely to use as part of the basis of his investment decisions). The Upper Tribunal accordingly found on the facts that, whether or not the information in question was (in the ordinary sense) likely to have a significant effect on the price, it was clear that it was information 'of a kind which a reasonable investor would be likely to use in this way'.

Analysis using expertise and resources

9.119 As is the case under CJA insider dealing, a key question to address is whether a professional investor in the market who is able to apply expertise and resources to investment analysis will be treated as having information which is not generally available to the market. The answer to this, according to guidance issued under the COMC,[180] is 'no'. According to that guidance, it is not relevant that the observation or analysis is only achievable by a person with above-average financial resources, expertise, or competence. Thus, for example,

[177] Upper Tribunal *FSA v Massey* [2011] UKUT 49 (TCC), ref FIN/2009/0024, 2 February 2011.
[178] FSA: Final Notice to Woolworths Group plc dated 11 June 2008. RDC hearing.
[179] Upper Tribunal *FSA v Massey* [2011] UKUT 49 (TCC), ref FIN/2009/0024, 2 February 2011.
[180] MAR 1.2.13E(2).

a professional investor who employs expert analysts, buys in investment research, or commissions external market research would still in principle be using information which was generally available, even though a private investor without such expertise or resources would not have the same level of information access or analysis. This was confirmed by an FSA discussion paper on investment analysis, where the FSA conclude that: 'information which can be obtained by research and analysis conducted by, or on behalf of, users of a market is to be regarded for the purposes of this section as being generally available to them'[181] and thus would not be inside information. This is in line with the philosophy of the MAD, which states that research and estimates developed from publicly available data should not be regarded as inside information.[182]

Star analysts' reports

In the financial markets, there are a number of 'star analysts' whose reports on the prospects of particular issuers or their securities are sufficiently highly rated that the existence of a recommendation from such an analyst is enough in itself to cause a significant movement in the price of the securities in question. This therefore gives rise to the question whether knowledge of such a recommendation, prior to it becoming generally available, can be inside information. **9.120**

The position relating to the distribution of research by analysts/investment firms was considered in the FSA Decision relating to Roberto Casoni[183] although that decision related to Principle 3 of the FSA's Statement of Principles for Approved Persons. Casoni was a research analyst for an investment bank in London, and was involved in the approval process for the bank to initiate coverage on a particular Italian company. Casoni had prepared the research report, which contained a buy recommendation with a medium risk and a target price. Before the publication of the report, it was found that Casoni had selectively disclosed details of his valuation methodology, final recommendation, and the target price to certain clients and was found to have breached Principle 3. **9.121**

Guidance in the FSA's Conduct of Business Rules at the time (at COB 7.16.13G)[184] made it clear that it was inappropriate for an employee (whether or not an investment analyst) to communicate the substance of any relevant investment research. The FSA stated that the rules relating to the fair distribution of research were fundamental to maintaining orderly markets and it was imperative that analysts were fully aware of the restrictions and acted in accordance with them. The FSA considered that, by selectively disseminating such information to clients ahead of publication, Casoni allowed those clients the opportunity to pre-empt the conclusions of the published research and thereby potentially influenced their investment decisions ahead of the rest of the market. **9.122**

Shareholder activism

The question has also arisen in practice as to whether the fact that certain shareholders in a company form a collective shareholder activism group, or information on steps that group intends to take, might constitute inside information. The question of whether an intention **9.123**

---

[181] FSA DP15: 'Investment research—Conflicts and other issues', at para 5.21.

[182] MAD Recital 31.

[183] FSA Final Notice to Roberto Chiarion Casoni dated 20 March 2007. Note that the case was settled at an early stage (Stage 1–30 per cent discount under the FSA's Executive Settlement procedures).

[184] The current equivalent is COBS 12.2.11G.

to create a shareholder activist group constitutes inside information may depend on the facts—for example, if an entity is contacted to sound its interest in joining, it would fall to be considered whether that information is, for example, sufficiently precise. In principle, however, it would have seemed likely that the creation of a group intending to aggregate their shareholdings to bring pressure on a company could satisfy the tests, as would decisions or impending actions of the group, and appropriate safeguards would therefore need to be put in place in such circumstances (see generally FSA *MarketWatch*, Issue 20, May 2007).

Market Abuse Offences that Concern the Use of Information—the Offences

9.124 The following paragraphs address the detailed provisions of the market abuse offences relating to the use of information.[185]

Market abuse (insider dealing)—Type 1

9.125 The key elements of the definition of 'insider dealing' are first, that the insider must deal or attempt to deal, in qualifying or related investments, and secondly, that the dealing, or attempt to deal, must be made *on the basis of* inside information.[186] The meaning of inside information in this context is discussed in paragraph 9.106.

Types of conduct that fall within 'insider dealing'

9.126 The FCA has given a number of examples of situations that, in its opinion, fall within the definition of insider dealing and accordingly constitute market abuse.[187] The first of these is dealing on the basis of inside information which is not trading information. 'Trading information' means, broadly speaking, information concerning potential or executed transactions in investments.[188] It is to be noted that the converse is not necessarily the case, that is to say dealing on the basis of trading information will not automatically be outside the scope of market abuse.

9.127 The second example is so-called 'front-running', that is to say where an insider enters into a transaction for his own benefit, taking advantage of the anticipated impact on the market or auction clearing price of an order which he is to carry out with or for another person. This proposition was introduced to the market abuse regime as a result of MAD, although this needs to be read in the context of the safe harbours relating to the 'dutiful execution of client

[185] For the purposes of the following discussion, it is assumed that the behaviour relates to qualifying investments on prescribed markets, and that the requirements as to territorial scope are satisfied, as are the definitions of insider and inside information.

[186] Note that the reference to 'dealing', required by MAD, is narrower than the 'behaviour' provided for in the pre-MAD 'misuse of information'. This was one of the reasons for the retention of the legacy offence of misuse of information. For a general discussion see para 9.58.

[187] MAR 1.3.2E.

[188] 'Trading information' is defined in MAR as information that investments of a particular kind have been or are to be acquired or disposed of, or that their disposal is under consideration, or the subject of negotiation; that investments of a particular kind have been or are not to be acquired or disposed of; the quantity of investments acquired or disposed of, or to be acquired or disposed of, or whose acquisition or disposal is under consideration or the subject of negotiations; the price (or range of prices) at which investments have been or are to be acquired or disposed of or the price (or range of prices) at which investments whose acquisition or disposal is under consideration, or the subject of negotiation, may be acquired or disposed of; or the identity of the persons involved or likely to be involved in any capacity in an acquisition or disposal.

orders' and the 'legitimate business of market makers etc' discussed at paragraph 9.145 *et seq.* Prior to that, front running was not an offence per se under the pre-MAD regime (as a result of the pre-MAD 'trading information' safe harbour) although it would of course potentially give rise to a breach of FCA rules, principles, or statements of principle on the part of FCA authorised firms or approved persons. The difference in the post-MAD regime is that an analysis needs to be undertaken as to whether the behaviour in question is 'legitimate' or 'dutiful'.

The final example relates to an offeror or potential offeror, or a person acting for the offeror in the context of a takeover entering into a transaction in a qualifying investment, on the basis of inside information concerning the proposed bid that provides merely an economic exposure to movements in the price of the target company's shares (for example, a spread bet on the target company's share price). **9.128**

Types of conduct that are not 'on the basis of' inside information

The COMC provides various guidance relating to circumstances which, in the FCA's opinion, should be taken into account in determining whether or not a person's behaviour is 'on the basis of' inside information.[189] If the criteria set out in these factors are met this would be an indication that the behaviour in question has not been undertaken 'on the basis of' inside information. Certain safe harbours are also set out in the COMC. **9.129**

Safe harbour—implementing own intention to deal. The COMC provides a safe harbour clarifying the fairly self-evident proposition that a person's carrying out his own intention to deal will not in itself constitute market abuse.[190] This issue has come up in particular in the context of shareholder activism. In general terms, knowledge of a person's own activist intentions should not preclude that person from dealing, although knowledge of the intention of a number of shareholders could potentially do so, depending on the facts (see paragraph 9.123).[191] **9.130**

Material influence. The FSA had previously indicated that, in its opinion, a person's behaviour would be 'on the basis of' inside information where information is the reason for, or a material influence on, a decision to deal or attempt to deal. The relevant section of the COMC (MAR 1.3.4) has, however, since been removed as a result of the *Spector Photo* case[192] discussed at paragraph 9.90, and it is worth looking at this more closely. **9.131**

In the *Spector Photo* case, the ECJ considered the question of whether or not MAD should be interpreted to cover steps taken 'on the 'basis of' inside information, or could extend to any relevant 'use' made of a person who is at the same time in possession of inside information (whether or not the steps taken were on the basis of that information). The UK, as intervener in *Spector*, had argued against an interpretation which would put any primary insider in possession of inside information, who entered into a market transaction, automatically within the prohibition on insider dealing, on the basis that it would entail extending the scope of the prohibition beyond what was appropriate and necessary to attain the goals pursued by MAD. In the event, the ECJ concluded that the fact that a person in possession of inside information takes certain steps with respect to the relevant financial instruments gives rise **9.132**

[189] MAR 1.3.3E.
[190] MAR 1.3.6.C.
[191] For further discussion, see *MarketWatch* 20.
[192] *Spector Photo Group NV, Chris Van Raemdonck v Commissie voor het Bank, Financie-en Assurantiewezen (CBFA)* (Case C-45/08).

to a rebuttable presumption that that person has 'used that information' within the meaning of MAD but that presumption needed to be considered in the light of the purposes of the directive, and is subject to the defences in the directive.

9.133 In terms of the impact on the UK implementation, the FSA concluded that only a minor change was needed to the COMC and that FSMA did not require amendment as it remained consistent with the *Spector* case, so much of the COMC remains as it had been previously, and no change was made to the 'on the basis of' wording used in FSMA. The FSA did, however, delete MAR 1.3.4, which had previously stated:

> 1.3.4 E In the opinion of the *FSA*, if the *inside information* is the reason for, or a material influence on, the decision to *deal* or attempt to *deal*, that indicates that the *person's behaviour* is 'on the basis of' *inside information*.

According to the relevant consultation paper issued at the time,[193] the FSA felt this evidential provision suggested the FSA would need evidence of a person's intention, as a separate element, to prove insider dealing, and that in the light of the *Spector* case, their view was that this was not necessary. In practical terms, it is suggested that, given the effect of the *Spector* case was to create a rebuttable presumption to be considered in the light of the purposes of MAD, and subject to the defences of the directive, that the question of material influence would still be relevant.

9.134 Coming back, then, to the question of material influence, the approach had been previously underlined in the *Bracken* finding (a finding under the misuse of information offence in the pre-MAD regime)[194] where Bracken's behaviour was deemed to be 'on the basis of' inside information because of the timeliness of his trading and the fact that he did not seek permission to trade under his employer's policy. The FSA concluded that this meant his decision to trade was 'materially influenced' by the inside information. In the *Arif Mohammed* case (a case relating to the pre-MAD misuse of information offence), the FSMT reiterated the message that for conduct to be *based on* inside information it must be one of the reasons for the dealing, but went further to say it need not be the only reason for the dealing.[195]

Mosaic theory

9.135 Although it does not necessarily follow from the above that a decision to deal or attempt to deal will not be taken to be 'on the basis of' information if it is immaterial, that would seem to be a common sense approach. Thus, if a professional investor were to thoroughly research a potential investment using myriad sources of publicly available information, and be inadvertently given a piece of incidental inside information which would in itself not have a material impact on its decision to deal, it would appear that this should not itself, in the context of wider research, constitute market abuse (insider dealing). This is sometimes referred to as the 'mosaic' or 'jigsaw' factor.

9.136 The mosaic theory also needs to be considered in the light of the *Greenlight/Einhorn* case.[196] This is one of a number which have looked closely at conversations between corporate brokers and buy side institutions as part of market soundings ahead of a corporate event, such as a debt issue. Mr Einhorn had been approached by the corporate broker acting for

193 FSA Quarterly consultation (No 26), Consultation Paper 10/22, October 2010.
194 FSA Final Notice to Peter Bracken, dated 7 July 2004.
195 *Arif Mohammed v FSA*, FSMT Case 012, 29 March 2005.
196 FSA Final Notices to David Einhorn and Greenlight Capital Inc., dated 15 February 2012 (RDC).

Punch Taverns, but had asked not to be 'wall crossed', and a conversation which subsequently took place was to have taken place on that basis. However, Mr Einhorn was given three pieces of information, none of which, according to the FSA, constituted inside information, but the FSA concluded that the information should be read together and as such was sufficient to be inside information.

This gives rise to the question as to how this decision, relating to the aggregation of information, affects the mosaic theory. Ultimately, the application with respect to particular information, or pieces of information, will be fact specific. It is worth noting however that in the *Einhorn* case, all the information came from the same source (the corporate broker), and also came within a short period of time. The circumstances were therefore closely aligned, To follow the mosaic analogy, the tiles in the Einhorn case were also fairly large. It may therefore well be that the same approach would not necessarily be taken where multiple pieces of, in themselves, imprecise information are aggregated. **9.137**

As a general proposition, it seems unlikely that contra-directional dealing (ie selling an investment where the inside information held by a person indicates that the price of the investment will rise (or vice versa)) would be dealing 'on the basis of' that information. **9.138**

Wall crossing

As mentioned earlier in this chapter, the FCA has been giving considerable attention to conversations between corporate brokers and buy side institutions in the context of market soundings, in part resulting from their statistical analysis of price movements ahead of certain events (such as a new issue of shares). Market soundings are calls intended to gauge the interest of the buy side in the particular event (such as buying into a new issue) and the indicative price at which they may be prepared to do this. It is now common for firms to have measures in place to clarify ahead of a conversation whether the person called is to be made an insider, or 'wall crossed' (that is to say, brought over the Chinese Wall, or information barrier, so that the person wall crossed becomes privy to information held by the corporate broker on the other side of the wall). It is clear from the *Greenlight/Einhorn* cases that the FCA's (and RDC's) view is that reliance on an understanding that a person will not be wall crossed is not in itself sufficient—it will nonetheless be necessary to make an evaluation of the information actually imparted. **9.139**

Prior decisions to deal and pre-existing strategies

The question of whether particular transactions were entered into on the basis of prior decisions, or pre-existing strategies, has been discussed in a number of cases. **9.140**

In the *Parker* case,[197] Parker contended the transactions in question were hedging (in relation to share options, or shares, owned by Parker in the relevant company) and delta neutral strategies (straddles) (in relation to which the direction of movement in price of the shares was of less relevance, the greater relevance being that there was sufficient movement in the shares one way or another). Having looked at the evidence (which in broad terms showed a number of transactions and a change of direction occurring immediately prior to the announcements in question) it was concluded that Parker deliberately set out to profit from relevant information and could not bring himself within the then safe harbour which applied where a decision to deal was not influenced by the relevant information. **9.141**

[197] *James Parker v FSA*, FSMT Case 037, 18 August 2006.

9.142 The RDC also considered the question of pre-existing trading patterns in the *Jabre* decision.[198] That decision related to the misuse of information legacy offence as well as, in the case of Jabre personally, breaches of FSA Principle 2 (Due Skill, Care and Diligence) and 3 (Market Conduct) of the FSA's Statements of Principles for Approved Persons and, in the case of GLG, breach of Principle 5 (Market Conduct) of the FSA's Principles for Businesses. Jabre had been brought across a Chinese Wall (information barrier) by an investment bank as part of pre-marketing of a convertibles issue by a Japanese bank, SMFG, and had subsequently, prior to the announcement of the issue, shorted SMFG shares. It was again contended that the transactions in question were part of a pre-existing trading strategy. On the facts, Jabre believed, based on public information, that major Japanese banks were under pressure from the Bank of Japan to bring their Tier 1 Ratios back up towards internationally required standards. Accordingly, Jabre had started to borrow shares in the major Japanese banks and had subsequently started to short sell shares in SMFG.[199]

9.143 The FSA, however, considered stock borrowing of the kind in question to be a preparation for a possible selling pattern, but not itself evidence that such selling had necessarily been decided on or would necessarily have occurred. It did not consider such stock borrowing to be evidence of a 'trading pattern', or that a single short trade convincingly provided a basis for a 'trading pattern'. Nor, in the absence of any definite orders to execute sales or trades at pre-determined market price levels which, it had also been contended, was a continuing strategy, did the FSA consider that the *ex post facto* assertion of an intention to sell or trade at a particular price level was in those circumstances sufficient evidence of a 'pre-existing trading pattern' to justify the short selling which occurred between Jabre's having been brought over the Chinese Wall and the public announcement by SMFG of whose intentions he had been given confidential and privileged advance information and which the FSA concluded was a material influence on the trades which followed. The FSA noted in particular the scale and repetitive pattern of the trades in question and the fact that immediately following the public announcement, one of the funds managed by Jabre executed further short sales.

9.144 The question of the basis for decisions was also considered in the FSA decision in the *Shevlin* case.[200] In that case, Shevlin had also asserted that whilst he had made the contract for differences ('CFDs') trade to which the case related, he had traded on the basis of his own research, not inside information. Shevlin argued that the FSA had applied the wrong test in reaching its conclusions—he stated that the FSA had directly assessed his trading on the assumption that he was a sophisticated investor by looking at expert evidence as to how trading should have been undertaken on the basis of the claimed trading philosophy and parameters, whereas he was merely an amateur trading on his own account on the basis of his own research. In the event, the FSA did not accept Shevlin's assertions that he based his trading on information obtained by research or analysis and that it was therefore based on information generally available. The FSA found, rather, from the weight of the circumstantial evidence surrounding this matter when it was considered as a whole, that it was based on inside information.

198 FSA Final Notice to Philippe Jabre and GLG Partners LP, dated 1 August 2006.

199 There was contested evidence as to whether or not Jabre had been told by the broker in a pre-marketing call relating to a proposed issue of convertible preference shares that he could 'maintain his existing trading pattern'.

200 *John Shevlin v FSA*, FSMT Case 060, 12 June 2008 (RDC).

Market makers, dealers, and intermediaries

The trading information safe harbour under the pre-MAD regime. A theme that is common to the CJA insider dealing offence, and indeed both the pre- and post-MAD market abuse regimes, is the need to protect, through appropriate safeguards, the normal functioning of the professional marketplace. This applies particularly with respect to market makers, dealers and intermediaries, and those involved in the corporate finance sector where there is a risk that strictures relating to inside knowledge could be contrary to what is generally understood to be legitimate and common market practice. In the context of market makers, dealers, and intermediaries, as discussed at paragraph 9.108, the 'trading information' safe harbour that existed under the pre-MAD market abuse regime[201] was not been carried forward to the post-MAD regime, but was replaced by two safe harbours, the first relating to the 'dutiful execution of clients' orders', and the second relating to the 'legitimate carrying on of the business of market makers, etc'. These safe harbours are not co-extensive with the former trading information safe harbour under the pre-MAD regime; the trading information safe harbour was fairly clear in its application. Under the post-MAD regime it is instead necessary to consider whether particular behaviour would fall within the dutiful execution and legitimate market making etc safe harbours; that is to say, whether that behaviour can properly be said to be 'dutiful' or 'legitimate'. **9.145**

The dutiful execution of client orders

According to MAR 1.3.12C, the dutiful carrying out of, or arranging for the dutiful carrying out of, an order on behalf of another will not in itself amount to market abuse by the person carrying out that order.[202] This also applies where the person acts as portfolio manager. This safe harbour is amplified by guidance[203] which suggests that the dutiful execution carve-out will apply whether or not the person carrying out the order or the person for whom he is acting in fact possesses inside information. In other words, knowledge will not necessarily prevent execution from being dutiful, although a distinction is made between information which is trading information and that which is not—in the FSA's opinion, the fact that inside information is not limited to trading information would indicate that the behaviour is not the dutiful carrying out of an order on behalf of a client. It does not, however, necessarily follow that the converse is the case, that is, it does not necessarily follow that inside information limited to trading information will mean that behaviour will fall within the dutiful execution safe harbour, but it would seem to be the corollary that this would be the starting point. The key issue, therefore, is whether an intermediary's execution will in these circumstances be dutiful and the COMC sets out a number of factors which are, in the FCA's opinion, relevant in determining this question (the presence of these factors being indicative of dutiful execution). These in effect relate to what are either proper or acceptable standards in the market place, standards which can be enhanced through disclosure, pragmatic need (ie the need to facilitate effective execution), or what is *de minimis* (ie where the behaviour in question has no impact on price). **9.146**

[201] Dealing or arranging deals did not amount to a 'misuse of information' solely because it was based on information as to that person's intention, or any other person's intention, to deal or arrange deals in relation to any qualifying investment, or information concerning transactions that had taken place (subject to certain carve-outs relating to takeover bids and certain primary market activity).

[202] This carve-out derives from wording found in Recital 18 to MAD.

[203] MAR 1.3.13G.

Legitimate business of market makers, etc.

9.147 The second safe harbour applies to market makers and other persons lawfully dealing in qualifying investments or related investments on their own account ('market makers/dealers').[204] According to the safe harbour, the carrying on of the legitimate business of own account dealing by market makers/dealers (including entering into an agreement for the underwriting of an issue of financial instruments) will not in itself amount to market abuse (insider dealing).[205] The effect of this safe harbour should be to protect the business of market makers/dealers who have knowledge of client orders/executed transactions, and will take this information into account when, for example, making markets. There is, of course, a subtle but important distinction between the proper conduct of such business and abuse, say, through front running. The safe harbour accordingly tries to establish, by setting out relevant factors,[206] what would be legitimate in such circumstances and, in the same way as the 'dutiful execution' safe harbour,[207] does so by reference to matters such as what are proper or acceptable standards in the marketplace, standards which can be enhanced through disclosure, or what is *de minimis*. There is, of course, in practice likely to be an overlap between the 'dutiful execution' safe harbour and the 'legitimate business of market makers, etc.' safe harbour, particularly in the dual capacity markets. As with the 'dutiful execution' safe harbour, the fact that inside information is not limited to trading information will, in the FCA's opinion, be an indication that behaviour is not in pursuit of legitimate business.[208]

Corporate finance and takeovers

9.148 The market abuse regime creates a safe harbour for certain types of takeover or merger activities. The need for this is fairly self-explanatory as corporate finance houses undertaking activities on behalf of, say, an offeror for a listed target will by definition have information relating to the proposed offer. The safe harbour provides that in the context of a public takeover bid or merger, behaviour based on inside information relating to another company[209] for the purpose of gaining control of that company or proposing a merger with that company, does not in itself amount to market abuse.[210] The activities benefiting from the safe harbour include seeking irrevocable undertakings or expressions of support from the holders of securities in the target in relation to an offer or making arrangements in relation to an issue of securities which will be used as consideration or will be issued in order to fund the takeover or merger offer. This in turn includes arrangements for the underwriting or placing of those securities and any associated hedging arrangements by underwriters or places which are

[204] MAD Recital 18 states that: 'the mere fact that market-makers, bodies authorised to act as counterparties, or persons authorised to execute orders on behalf of third parties with inside information confine themselves... to pursuing their legitimate business... should not in itself be deemed to constitute use of such information'.

[205] According to guidance in MAR 1.3.7C, this safe harbour will apply even if the person concerned in fact possesses trading information which is inside information.

[206] MAR 1.3.10E.

[207] Although note that, whilst some of these factors are the same or similar, there are differences between the two sets of factors.

[208] MAR 1.3.9E.

[209] Guidance issued in the COMC clarifies that the information in question can be twofold: first information relating to the offer or potential offer; and secondly information discovered during due diligence (MAR 1.3.18G). But note that as the CJA safe harbour is limited to market information (ie the equivalent of the first limb), stakebuilding on the basis of information in the second limb is effectively precluded.

[210] MAR 1.3.17C.

proportionate to the risks assumed. Making arrangements for any cash alternative to the offer is also included in the enumerated activities.

The COMC also goes on to indicate that, in the FCA's opinion, relevant factors in determining whether a person's behaviour is for the purpose of his gaining control of the target or proposing a merger (and indicating that it is) are whether the transactions concerned are in the target company's shares (presumably as opposed to, say, CFDs referable to the company's shares) or whether the transactions concerned are for the sole purposes of gaining control or affecting that merger. **9.149**

Review of cases and emerging themes

The following looks at some of the decisions which illustrate the FSA's/FCA's approach to insider dealing in cases pursued under the market abuse regime, and the sort of fact patterns that the FSA/FCA believes amount to insider dealing, as well as themes emerging. **9.150**

A number of the earlier cases dealt with under the pre-MAD misuse of information offence, but which would now most likely fall within the market abuse (insider dealing) offence related to reasonably senior employees of listed companies who have received information as part of their employment (see, for example, the *Bracken*[211] case (former Group Head of Communications at an LSE-listed company) and the *Malins* case,[212] (finance director)), or other professionals with access to information. **9.151**

Corporate executives This theme has continued with more recent cases. For example, in the cases relating to Mehmet Sepil, Murat Ozgul, and Levent Akca,[213] CEO, chief commercial officer, and exploration manager of the Turkish oil company, Genel Enerji. In 2009, Genel acquired a 25 per cent interest in a licence granted to Heritage Oil plc (Heritage), a company quoted on the LSE, to explore for oil at Miran in Iraq. Heritage and Genel also entered into merger discussions and agreed to share confidential information. Genel were subsequently informed of the positive conclusion of tests on oil extracted at Miran. The three Genel executives placed orders to purchase Heritage shares and, on Heritage announcing the positive results from Miran, each of the three Genel executives sold their shares realising substantial profits. The FSA issued decisions against the executives finding they had engaged in insider dealing—each of them having been shown to have possessed the inside information regarding positive results of the oil tests and as a result purchased sizeable holdings, and having sold them immediately following the public announcement of those results. **9.152**

In the *Darwin Clifton* and *Byron Holdings* case,[214] Darwin Clifton by virtue of his non-executive position with an AIM-listed company came into possession of inside information as to an oil exploration contract being negotiated by that company, and directed Byron Holdings, a company of which he was a director, to purchase shares in the company. Byron was found to have committed market abuse (insider dealing). Mr Clifton was fined for 'requiring' Byron to engage in this activity. **9.153**

A number of interrelated decisions arose emanating from information concerning Monterrico Metals plc. Richard Ralph was the executive chairman of Monterrico, a mining **9.154**

[211] FSA Final Notice to Peter Bracken, dated 7 July 2004.
[212] FSA Final Notice to Jonathan Malins, dated 20 December 2005.
[213] FSA Final Notices to Mehmet Sepil, Murat Ozgul and Levent Akca, dated 12 February 2010 (SDM).
[214] FSA Final Notice to Darwin Lewis Clifton OBE and Byron Holdings Limited, dated 27 January 2009 (SDM).

company listed on AIM, in which he bought shares during a takeover period (while takeover discussions were taking place with a Chinese mining consortium). Both Ralph and Filip Boyen, who both executed Ralph's trade and separately dealt on his own account, were found to have engaged in insider dealing and improper disclosure. Filip Boyen subsequently disclosed Ralph's dealing to Erik Boyen, who dealt further for his brother's account, and his own account, and then himself was also found to have encouraged insider dealing by a third party under section 123(1)(b) FSMA.

9.155 **Market Professionals** In 2007, Margaret Cole, then director of FSA enforcement, announced a focus on city or business professionals.[215]Prior to that announcement, the FSA had already fined a hedge-fund manager, GLG, and Philippe Jabre, a former managing director of the firm, £750,000 each for market abuse and breaching FSA principles. This case[216] is discussed further at paragraph 10.154. The subsequent *Harrison* case[217] also involved an investment manager at a hedge fund. The case (which was settled at stage 1) was a 'requiring and encouraging' case relating to the post-MAD insider dealing offence and focused on the issue of recognition of inside information. Mr Harrison had been contacted by the investment bank arranging a refinancing of a French company in order to help ascertain the correct pricing and obtain other feedback on the specifics of the proposed refinancing (which involved the tender for certain of its existing bonds and the issue of new notes) which necessitated giving Harrison inside information. Subsequent to the call, Harrison arranged for a colleague to purchase existing bonds in the knowledge, according to the decision, that there was to be an imminent refinancing which would involve the company tendering for those bonds at a premium. The FSA accepted that Harrison did not consider at the time that the information was inside information, and that his behaviour was not deliberate, but failed to consider what should have been a clear and obvious risk that purchasing further bonds before the information was generally available would result in engaging in conduct that would amount to market abuse.

9.156 This theme has since been developed in a number of decisions, and notably has extended to cover a broader array of professionals. For example, in the context of the *Greenlight/Einhorn* cases (see paragraph 9.115) related actions were also taken in respect of Andrew Osborne[218] the corporate broker involved in the relevant conversations, and Alexander Edward Ten Holter,[219] who undertook trade execution and other services at Greenlight's UK affiliate, as well as being its compliance officer.

9.157 Other cases involving professionals such as brokers effecting trades and corporate brokers importing information, as well as the 'buy side' clients involved in particular incidents, are discussed further at paragraph 9.165 *et seq.* in the context of market abuse (improper disclosure).

9.158 **Debt Markets** The FSA publicly censured two Dresdner Kleinwort traders for market abuse in relation to a debt issue in a case perceived by many as laying down a marker to participants in debt issues in which it was argued the position was unclear. This is discussed further at paragraph 9.116.

---

[215] The FSA's approach to insider dealing, speech made by Margaret Cole, 4 October 2007.
[216] FSA Final Notice to Philippe Jabre and GLG Partners LP, dated 1 August 2006.
[217] FSA Final Notice to Steven Harrison, dated 8 September 2008.
[218] FSA Final Notice to Andrew Osborne, dated 15 February 2012 (RDC).
[219] FSA Final Notice to alexander Edward Ten Holter, dated 26 January 2012 (RDC).

Market abuse (improper disclosure)—Type 2

The second behaviour type that constitutes market abuse is where an insider discloses inside information to another person otherwise than in the 'proper course' of the exercise of his employment, profession, or duties, irrespective of whether or not that information is used by someone else as the basis for dealing.[220] This definition of improper disclosure under the FSMA market abuse provisions is similar to the definition of the 'disclosure offence' under the CJA provisions, where it is a criminal offence for an insider to disclose inside information 'otherwise than in the *proper* performance of the functions of his employment, office or profession'.[221] In both cases, the definition of the wrongful conduct hinges on the propriety of a disclosure by a professional, etc., of inside information. **9.159**

The FSA has indicated that it will take into account a range of factors to determine if disclosure was made in the 'proper course' of the exercise of his employment, profession, or duties. These factors, the presence of which are indicative that disclosure is made in the 'proper course', include whether the rules of a prescribed market or a prescribed auction platform, the FCA, or the Takeover Code, permit the disclosure or whether the disclosure is accompanied by the imposition of confidentiality requirements upon the person to whom disclosure was made and is otherwise reasonable and for one of a number of stipulated purposes or in fulfilment of a legal obligation.[222] Although not specifically stated in the factors, an example of proper disclosure might be the disclosure of information to potential counterparties to a transaction solely for the purpose of broking a transaction where it would be normal market practice to do so, and to do so with those counterparties. **9.160**

Safe harbours

The COMC sets out a number of safe harbours from the market abuse (improper disclosure) offence. These apply in respect of disclosures made to a government department, the Bank of England, the Competition Commission, the Takeover Panel, or any other regulatory body or authority for the purposes of fulfilling a legal or regulatory obligation,[223] or otherwise to such a body in connection with the performance of the functions of that body.[224] **9.161**

There is also a safe harbour relating to the fulfilment of obligations under the Listing Rules, Prospectus Rules, and Disclosure and Transparency Rules or any similar regulatory obligation.[225] **9.162**

As a separate exercise the FSA amended the COMC after consultation[226] relating to the circumstances in which brokers could, when selling shares owned by persons discharging managerial responsibilities ('PDMR'), disclose to the purchaser the fact that the seller fell within that category. The need to clarify this had arisen as a result of discussions the FSA had since it set out its position in *MarketWatch* 35 in June 2010, which in turn had been prompted by concern within the industry, as a result of differing market practices, to clarify **9.163**

[220] FSMA, s 118(3).

[221] CJA, s 52(2)(b) discussed in Chapter 10, para 10.13 *et seq.*

[222] According to MAR 1.4.5E(2), these purposes include enabling the proper performance of employment and to facilitate giving advice or a commercial transaction.

[223] MAR 1.4.3C(1).

[224] MAR 1.4.3C(2).

[225] MAR 1.4.4C.

[226] FSA quarterly consultation paper (CP11/27).

the point (in some quarters, for example, it was felt that such disclosure should, at least as a commercial point, be made).

9.164 The result of the consultation was to add a new safe harbour in MAR 1.4.4AC to the effect that disclosure of inside information by a broker to a potential buyer regarding the fact that the seller of qualifying investments is a PDMR, or the identity of the PDMR or the purpose of the sale by the PDMR where the disclosure is made *only* to the extent necessary, and *solely* in order to dispose of the investment (emphasis added); the illiquidity of the stock is such that the transaction could not otherwise be completed; and the transaction could not be otherwise completed without creating a disorderly market.

Examples of 'improper disclosure'

9.165 As discussed at paragraph 9.156, there has been in recent years increasing focus on professionals in the market, including brokers effecting trades, and corporate brokers involved in market soundings or offering corporate transactions for their clients.

9.166 **Broker Cases** Examples can be found in the decisions relating to William Coppin and Perry Bliss.[227] Mr Coppin and Mr Bliss were brokers employed by Pacific Continental Securities (UK) Limited. They obtained inside information that a company traded on an AIM, Provexis plc, had entered into a collaboration agreement with Unilever, which would be announced shortly to the market. They each disclosed inside information to retail customers of PCS and encouraged them to purchase the shares in relation to which Mr Coppin and Mr Bliss had the inside information. As well as receiving fines, Mr Coppin and Mr Bliss were both prohibited from performing any function in relation to any regulated activity carried on by any authorised or exempt person. A similar finding of improper disclosure, and also 'requiring or encouraging' pursuant to s 123(1)(b) was also made in respect of Alexei Krilov-Harrison in a case resulting from similar facts.[228]

9.167 **Corporate brokers** In a case related to the *Greenlight/Einhorn* cases the FSA decided that Andrew Osborne,[229] who arranged the conference call between Greenlight and the management of Punch Taverns, (prior to which Mr Einhorn had stated that he did not wish to be wall crossed) was found to have engaged in market abuse by improperly disclosing inside information as to the transaction.

9.168 The question of disclosure of information by corporate brokers was again considered in the Hannam decision[230] (since referred to the Upper Tribunal by Mr Hannam, which had not issued its decision at the time of writing). Mr Hannan was Chairman of Capital Markets at JP Morgan Cazenove and corporate adviser to Heritage Oil. Although Mr Hannam had implicit authority from Heritage to make the disclosure of the information contained in the key emails in question, and was acting in his client's interests, the FSA's case was that he did not consider whether he was disclosing inside information, or whether it was necessary to disclose the information in order properly to discharge his responsibilities to his client.

9.169 Mr Hannam in turn made a number of arguments which are interesting to consider. Part of Mr Hannam's case was that the contents of one of the key emails was neither sufficiently

[227] FSA Final Notice to William James Coppin, dated 7 December 2010 (SDM); FSA Final Notice to Perry John Bliss, dated 13 December 2010 (SDM).

[228] FSA Final Notice to Alexei Krilov-Harrison, dated 03 November 2009 (SDM).

[229] FSA Final Notice to Andrew Osborne, dated 15 February 2012 (RDC).

[230] FSA Decision Notice, Ian Charles Hannam, 27 February 2012 (RDC).

precise nor price-sensitive to constitute inside information, although this was not accepted by the RDC. This does, however, point to the difficulties that can arise as a practical matter in adjudging when information exchanged, in Mr Hannam's view, as part of his normal activities, overstepped the mark and became inside information.

The RDC also found that, although on the facts the argument was not directly in point, inside information can be improperly disclosed even where the recipient is already aware of the information from a different source. In the RDC's view, information could be disclosed to an individual to whom that information has already been revealed. Even if the information is the same, the mere fact that another person has stated it might lend credence to its veracity. Further, according to the RDC, it might carry more weight depending on by whom it is disclosed. **9.170**

Mr Hannam also argued, amongst other things, that if the relevant emails were sent in the proper course of the exercise of his employment, profession, and duties (on the basis that his professional duty, and his specific mandate, as strategic and financial adviser to Heritage, was proactively to advance Heritage's negotiations with the relevant parties and the emails in question were intended to facilitate such negotiations) and, as such, in accordance with the provisions of section 118(3) FSMA, his behaviour could not constitute market abuse. He also argued that he would in any event have a defence under section 123(2) FSMA as he had acted in accordance with the mandate given to him by Heritage, believing this to be in the proper course of the exercise of his employment, profession and duties, and therefore believed on reasonable grounds that he had not committed market abuse. These arguments were not however accepted by that FSA—their view was that Mr Hannam had disclosed inside information where this was unnecessary, unwarranted, and purely in furtherance of his client's commercial interests, and doing so was not reasonable, nor was it in fulfilment of a legal obligation. On that basis, the FSA found that Mr Hannam had no reasonable grounds to believe that he had not committed market abuse, so could not avail himself of the statutory defence. As mentioned at paragraph 9.164, the decision has since referred to the Upper Tribunal by Mr Hannam, which had not issued its decision at the time of writing. **9.171**

Corporate executives An example, linking insider dealing, improper disclosure and the encouraging offence under section 123 (1)(b), can be found in the FSA decisions relating to Jeremy Burley[231] and Jeffery Burley.[232] Jeremy Burley was managing director of a Ugandan company which provided vehicles and equipment to oil and gas exploration companies in Uganda. His father, Jeffery, managed a share-trading account in the UK which he used to trade shares on behalf of his son. In June 2009 Jeremy Burley acquired inside information as to Tower Resources, traded on AIM, namely that drilling in Uganda looked unlikely to produce oil. Before Tower Resources announced this news, Jeremy Burley passed the inside information to his father and instructed him to sell his Tower Resources shares, thereby avoiding a loss of £21,700. Jeffery Burley was found to have committed market abuse by virtue of insider dealing. **9.172**

Market abuse (misuse of information)—Type 3 (legacy offence)

The third behaviour type that constitutes market abuse (and the final type falling within the scope of conduct connected to the use of information) is 'misuse of information'. This **9.173**

[231] FSA Final Notice to Jeremy Burely, dated 19 July 2010 (SDM).
[232] FSA Final Notice to Jeffrey Burley, dated 19 July 2010 (SDM).

is a legacy offence and as such only applies to behaviour not falling within the market abuse (insider dealing) or (improper disclosure) behaviour types, but which otherwise involves the misuse of information as judged by the standard of a 'regular user'.[233] The two requirements for the 'misuse of information' are first that the behaviour must be based on information which is not generally available to those using the market but which, if available to a regular user of the market, would be, or would be likely to be, regarded by him as relevant when deciding the terms on which transactions in qualifying investments should be effected. The second requirement is that the behaviour must be likely to be regarded by a regular user of the market as a failure on the part of the person concerned to observe the standard of behaviour reasonably expected of a person in his position in relation to the market.[234]

9.174 According to evidential provisions in the COMC, relevant factors in determining whether information is to be considered as 'relevant information' (and which are indicative that it is) are: the extent to which the information is reliable; if the information is new or fresh information; whether the information provides grounds to conclude that a future event (which would trigger a disclosure requirement) will occur; or if there is no other material information available to inform users of the market.[235] The factors set out in paragraph 9.110 *et seq.* relating to whether or not information is generally available, and when behaviour is 'based on' inside information, will also be relevant in the context of market abuse (misuse of information).

'Types of conduct that do not constitute the "misuse of information"'

9.175 The safe harbours applying to a person's own intention to deal, legitimate business of market making, etc., dutiful execution of clients' orders, and relevant behaviour in the context of a public takeover bid or merger would apply equally in the case of market abuse (misuse of information).

The 'regular user' test

9.176 As discussed at paragraph 9.58, market abuse (misuse of information) is a legacy offence and as such remains subject to the regular user test. The standards expected by a regular user have been considered in a number of market abuse decisions where the FSA has held that the defendant had failed to meet the regular user standard partly on the grounds that it had not complied with appropriate professional standards[236] (for example, in *Bracken* and *Middlemiss*,[237] a failure to comply with share-dealing codes imposed on the senior staff of listed companies). In *Arif Mohammed*, the FSMT held that Mohammed's failure to comply with the dealing rules applicable to auditors, while not amounting to market abuse per se, could reasonably be taken to indicate a failure to observe expected market standards.[238] In the *Parker* case[239] the FSMT also found that Parker's behaviour fell below the standard to be expected. He was professionally qualified and was employed by a listed company in a senior position of trust.

9.177 The FCA has also set out in the COMC a number of relevant (and, where present, indicative) factors when considering whether a regular user would reasonably expect relevant

---

233 See discussion at para 9.57.

234 FSMA, s 118(4).

235 MAR 1.5.6E.

236 The COMC previously explicitly provided (MAR 1.2.3E(4)) that the regular user was likely to consider the position of the person in question and the standards reasonably to be expected of that person at the time of the behaviour in the light of that person's experience, level of skill, and standard of knowledge.

237 FSA Final Notice to Robert Middlemiss, dated 10 February 2004.

238 *Arif Mohammed v FSA*, FSMT Case 012, 29 March 2005, para 43.

239 *James Parker v FSA*, FSMT Case 037, 18 August 2006.

information to be disclosed to users of the market or to be announced, and as such whether the behaviour is likely to fall below the requisite standard. These factors refer to various disclosure requirements required by any legal or regulatory requirement[240] as well as information routinely made the subject of a public announcement even if not subject to any formal requirement (for example, changes to published credit ratings, changes to the constituents of an index, or information to be the subject of official announcements by government, central monetary, or fiscal authorities, or regulatory bodies/exchanges). This in fact represents somewhat of a watering down of the 'disclosable' and 'announceable' requirements of earlier versions of the COMC, but still underlines the importance of these issues.

Examples of conduct which constitutes the 'misuse of information'

There are subtle distinctions between the coverage of market abuse (insider dealing) and (improper disclosure) on the one hand, and market abuse (misuse of information) on the other. The Treasury Consultation of the Sunset Clauses[241] referred, for example, to various circumstances in which it believed that the legacy offence of misuse of information could be wider than the post-MAD offences and pointed to the wider definition of 'relevant information', the lack of a price sensitivity test, and the lack of definition of 'insider'. **9.178**

The FCA has also provided a number of examples of situations where the conduct concerned constitutes the 'misuse of information',[242] including, for example, informal, non-contractual icing (that is 'reserving') of qualifying investments by the manager of a proposed issue of convertible or exchangeable bonds, which are to be the subject of a public marketing effort, where this has the effect of withdrawing the qualifying investments from the lending market in such a way that other market participants are disadvantaged. This is predicated on the fact that market abuse (inside information) will only apply to dealings or attempts to deal, whereas market abuse (misuse of information) may in principle apply to behaviour (in this case, icing), falling short of dealing or attempts to deal.[243] **9.179**

Review of cases

The *Henry Cameron* case,[244] relating to company announcements by Sibir Energy plc (Sibir), an AIM-listed company of which he was at the relevant time CEO, provided an interesting example of MAD and legacy offences being used in conjunction. The FSA found that Mr Cameron caused Sibir to make two related party transaction announcements which gave or were likely to give a false or misleading impression as to the price or value of Sibir shares for the purposes of the market abuse (dissemination) offence. These announcements understated the amount of payments authorised to be advanced to the related party by $198 million. The FSA at the same time found that Mr Cameron had committed market abuse for the purposes of the legacy offence of market abuse (misleading behaviour and distortion offence). With respect to the misleading behaviour offence, the FSA subtly differentiated the *failure* to inform the market of the true size and additional amounts of certain loans to the majority **9.180**

[240] These include information required to be disseminated under the Listing Rules, Prospectus Rules, and Disclosure and Transparency Rules (or equivalents in the relevant jurisdiction), information required to be disseminated by the Takeover Code or SARs (or their equivalents) and information required to be disclosed by an issuer under the laws, rules, or regulations applying to the relevant market. MAR 1.5.7E.

[241] See para 9. 59 *et seq.*

[242] MAR 1.5.10E.

[243] MAR 1.5.10E(2).

[244] FSA Final Notice to Henry Ogilvy Cameron, dated 6 July 2010 (SDM).

shareholder from that act of making an incorrect announcement. In addition, the FSA noted that Cameron also failed to disclose that the loans were effectively unsecured—the loans amounted to some $328.5 million—and therefore the market would have been misled as to the nature and value of Sibir's assets, its true risk and therefore the value of its shares.

Flow chart—offences relating to the use and disclosure of information

9.181 The basic components involved in the offences relating to the use and disclosure of information (applicable to the non-commodity derivatives definition of inside information) are set out in Figure 9.1 by way of illustration.

Market Abuse that Concerns Market Manipulation, Misleading Behaviour, or Distortion

9.182 Having looked at the behaviour types relating to the use of information, the following considers conduct falling within the four behaviour types that relate to manipulation or misleading behaviour.[245]

Market abuse (manipulating transactions)—Type 4

9.183 The fourth type of behaviour that constitutes market abuse consists of effecting transactions or orders to trade (otherwise than for legitimate reasons and in conformity with accepted market practices on the relevant market) which give, or are likely to give, a false or misleading impression as to the supply of, or demand for, or as to the price of, one or more qualifying investments ('false or misleading impressions'), or which secure the price of one or more such investments at an abnormal or artificial level ('price positioning').[246] Both of these categories are considered further later in this chapter. However, a key factor is that both relate to 'effecting transactions or orders'. Behaviour falling short of this will therefore not fall within market abuse (manipulating transactions), but could fall within market abuse (misleading behaviour and distortion). This is considered further at paragraph 9.225. This offence does not in itself presuppose any intention or purpose although this is not to say that the mental state of the person undertaking the behaviour will be irrelevant—see, for example, the discussion at paragraph 9.93 *et seq*.

Indications that behaviour is not for a legitimate reason

9.184 The following factors are, in the FCA's opinion, relevant in considering whether a person's behaviour in entering into a manipulating transaction is for a legitimate reason (and, if present, are indicative that it is not),[247] namely if the person has an actuating purpose behind the transaction to induce others to trade in, bid for, or to position or move the price of, a qualifying investment; if the person has another, illegitimate, reason behind the transactions, bid, or order to trade; or if the transaction was executed in a particular way with the purpose of creating a false or misleading impression.

Indications that behaviour is for a legitimate reason

9.185 The COMC also sets out a number of relevant factors which, conversely, if present, would be indicative that a person's reasons for entering into a manipulating transaction are

[245] For the purposes of the following discussion, it is again assumed that the other requirements relating to the market abuse definition (ie that behaviour relates to relevant qualifying investments on prescribed markets and geographical scope) are satisfied.

[246] FSMA, s 118(5).

[247] MAR 1.6.5E.

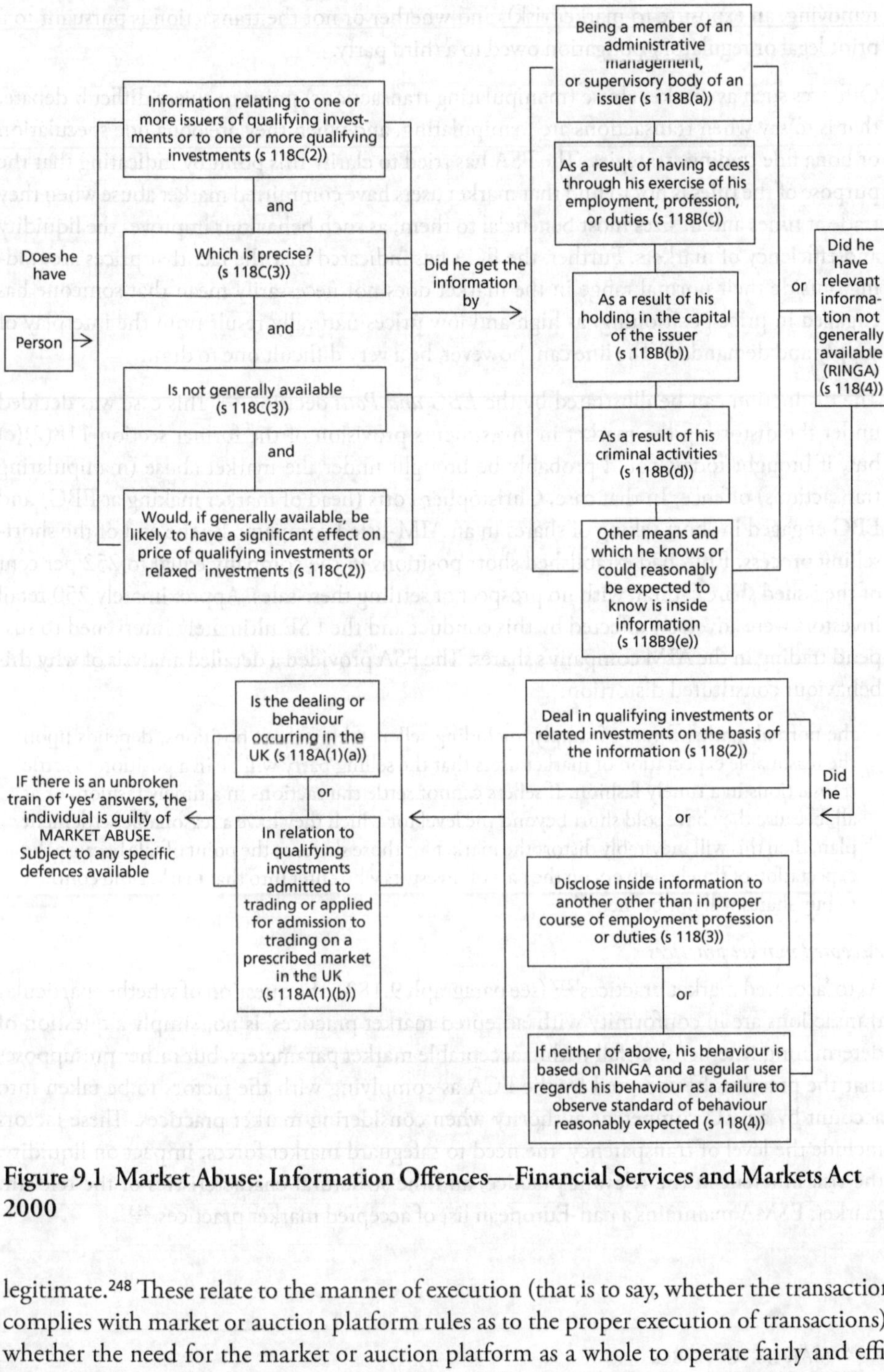

Figure 9.1 Market Abuse: Information Offences—Financial Services and Markets Act 2000

legitimate.[248] These relate to the manner of execution (that is to say, whether the transaction complies with market or auction platform rules as to the proper execution of transactions), whether the need for the market or auction platform as a whole to operate fairly and efficiently has been taken into account, the nature of the transactions themselves (that is to say, the extent to which the transaction generally opens a new position, so creating, rather than

[248] MAR 1.6.6E.

removing, an exposure to market risk), and whether or not the transaction is pursuant to a prior legal or regulatory obligation owed to a third party.

9.186 Offences such as market abuse (manipulating transactions) point to a very difficult debate, that is to say when transactions are manipulating, and when they are bona fide speculation or bona fide trading strategies. The FSA has tried to clarify this point by indicating that the purpose of the rules is not to find that market users have committed market abuse when they trade at times and in sizes most beneficial to them, as such behaviour improves the liquidity and efficiency of markets. Further, the FCA has indicated that the fact that prices are trading outside their normal range in the market does not necessarily mean that someone has engaged in price positioning, as high and low prices naturally result from the interplay of supply and demand.[249] The line can, however, be a very difficult one to draw.

9.187 The distinction can be illustrated by the *EBG and Potts* decision.[250] This case was decided under the distorting the market in investments provision of the former section 118(2)(c) but, if brought today, could probably be brought under the market abuse (manipulating transactions) offence. In that case, Christopher Potts (head of market making at EBG) and EBG engaged in short selling of shares in an AIM-listed company. By the end of the short-selling process, EBG had established short positions in the company equal to 252 per cent of the issued share capital, with no prospect of settling these sales. Approximately 250 retail investors were adversely affected by this conduct and the LSE ultimately intervened to suspend trading in the AIM company's shares. The FSA provided a detailed analysis of why this behaviour constituted distortion:

> the normal market forces of supply, including sellers taking short positions, depends upon the reasonable expectation of market users that the selling party will be in a position to settle transactions in a timely fashion. If sellers cannot settle transactions in a timely fashion, or at all, because they have sold short beyond the level for which they have a reasonable settlement plan, then this will inevitably distort the market for those shares at the point of sale because the expectation of timely delivery on the part of investors who enter into that market and contract to buy shares will not be met.[251]

Accepted market practices

9.188 As to 'accepted market practices'[252] (see paragraph 9.183), the question of whether particular transactions are in conformity with 'accepted market practices' is not simply a question of determining whether they fall within acceptable market parameters, but rather presupposes that the practices be accepted by the FCA as complying with the factors to be taken into account by an EU competent authority when considering market practices. These factors include the level of transparency, the need to safeguard market forces, impact on liquidity, the risk inherent in the relevant practice, and the structural characteristics of the relevant market. ESMA maintains a pan-European list of accepted market practices.[253]

---

249 MAR 1.6.7G–1.6.8G.

250 FSA Final Notice to Evolution Beeson Gregory Limited and Christopher Potts dated 12 November 2004.

251 ibid, para 37.

252 Commission Directive 2004/72/EC implements sections of the MAD as regards accepted market practices and sets out guidance in arts 2 and 3 for the competent authorities of Member States to follow in evaluating market practices.

253 Available at <http://www.esma.europa.eu/page/accepted-markets-practices>.

Types of conduct that fall within the definition of 'manipulating transactions' relating to false or misleading impressions

MAR sets out a number of examples of what, in the FCA's opinion, would constitute 'manipulating transactions' involving false or misleading impressions as to the supply of, demand for, or price of, qualifying investments, absent a legitimate reason.[254] These examples include transactions such as so-called 'wash trades' (ie transactions effected where there is no real assumption of market risk or change of beneficial ownership). Typically, this could be by way of a party (or parties acting in collusion or concert) simultaneously entering into purchase and sale transactions for the same security using different brokers in order to give the impression of liquidity, or increasing interest, in that security.[255] Another example cited is entering orders into an electronic trading system, at prices which are higher than the previous bid or lower than the previous offer, and withdrawing them before they are executed, in order to give a misleading impression that there is demand for or supply of the qualifying investment at that price. **9.189**

Types of conduct that fall within the definition of 'manipulating transactions' relating to price positioning

As to price positioning, again the COMC sets out a number of examples illustrating what, in the FCA's opinion, would constitute 'manipulating transactions', absent a legitimate reason.[256] These include, for example, what is in effect cornering the market through a dominant position over the supply of or demand for a qualifying investment and 'abusive squeezes'[257] (which presupposes amongst other things that behaviour is entered into with the purpose of positioning at a distorted level the price at which others have to deliver, take delivery, or defer delivery to satisfy their obligations in relation to a qualifying investment). Another example cited is entering small orders into an electronic trading system, at prices which are higher than the previous bid or lower than the previous offer, in order to move the price of the qualifying investment.[258] **9.190**

---

[254] MAR 1.6.2E. According to MAR 1.6.9E, the FCA will take into account a number of factors in determining whether a person's behaviour creates false or misleading impressions, including, broadly speaking, the extent to which orders to trade/transactions: (a) represent a significant proportion of the daily volume of transactions in the qualifying investment on the market concerned; (b) lead to a significant change in the price of an investment; (c) include position reversals in a short period; (d) are concentrated within a short time period and lead to a price change which is subsequently reversed; (e) change the representation of the order book available to market participants and are then removed before being executed; and (f) are effected around the time at which reference prices are calculated and affect such calculations.

[255] MAR 1.6.3G states that a stock lending/borrowing or repo/reverse repo transaction, or another transaction involving the provision of collateral, does not constitute a wash trade under this provision.

[256] MAR 1.6.4E. According to MAR 1.6.10E, the FCA will take into account the following factors when considering whether conduct amounts to price positioning, including the extent to which: (a) the person had an interest in the price of the investment; (b) the extent to which price volatility movements are outside the normal ranges; and (c) a person has successively and consistently increased or decreased his bid or offer for an investment.

[257] The FCA has specified a number of factors to be taken into account when deciding if a person has engaged in an abusive squeeze—MAR 1.6.11E. These factors are the extent to which: (a) a person is willing to relax his control or influence for the sake of an orderly market; (b) a person's activity risks causing settlement default by market users on a multilateral basis; (c) prices under the delivery mechanisms of the market diverge from the prices outside of those mechanisms; and (d) the immediate market compared to the forward market is unusually expensive or inexpensive.

[258] An example given by the FCA in MAR 1.6.15E is where a trader trades with himself by simultaneously buying and selling the same qualifying investment to give the appearance of a legitimate transfer of title or risk at a price outside the normal trading range for the qualifying investment. The price of the qualifying investment

Review of cases relating to market abuse (manipulating transactions)

9.191 The following looks at some of the cases relating to this offence, and certain themes which have emerged.

9.192 **'Layering' and arguments as to 'legitimate reasons'** A number of cases have addressed the practice of so-called 'layering'. In the *Swift Trade* case[259] the Upper Tribunal upheld the FSA's decision to fine Swift Trade £8 million for breach of the market abuse (manipulating transactions) offence.

9.193 The FSA's case was that Swift Trade 'systematically and deliberately engaged in a form of manipulative trading activity known as "layering" in relation to shares traded on the LSE'. 'Layering' involves entering a series of orders on one side of the LSE's order book (amounting to a large volume) without a genuine intention that the orders would be executed. The orders were placed at prices which were far from the normal 'bid' or 'touch' price which meant that they were unlikely to attract counterparties, whilst still achieving the objective of moving the price of the relevant shares as the market adjusted to the apparent shift in the balance of supply and demand. The movement in price was followed by the execution of a trade on the opposite side of the book, which profited from that price movement. This trade was then followed by the rapid deletion of the original (unexecuted) orders and by repetition of the behaviour in reverse on the other side of the order book. In other words, the aim of the trading was to move the price up in order to benefit from sale at a high price and then move the price down again in order to buy at a lower price.

9.194 Swift Trade claimed, amongst other things, that the activity about which the FSA complained was not manipulative, but was legitimate high-volume day trading by which traders bet on intra-day price changes in the equity markets, and that the trades were transparent to the market and were in accordance with market practice. It also sought to rely on the fact that it was not Swift Trade itself which was initiating the trades, but the independent dealers over whose activities Swift Trade had no control. Finally, Swift Trade argued that, even if the trading was manipulative, Swift Trade had no reason to think that what was being done was improper and was therefore entitled to the benefit of the defence set out in section 123(2) of FSMA. The evidence of the FSA's expert and other witnesses, however, showed 'the unusual nature of Swift Trade's conduct, compared with that of other users' and concluded that 'Swift Trade could have had no real desire to trade the large orders it placed'.

9.195 The Upper Tribunal concluded on the evidence that the 'layering' carried out by Swift Trade was 'deliberate, manipulative, designed to deceive other market users, successful in that aim, and undertaken for motives of profit'. It said that 'the repetition was too frequent, and the patterns too similar… to be attributable to coincidence or some other chance event'. The FSA also produced a number of emails which made it clear that Swift Trade was well aware of the

is relevant to the calculation of the settlement value of an option. He does this while holding a position in the option. His purpose is to position the price of the qualifying investment at a false, misleading, abnormal, or artificial level, making him a profit or avoiding a loss from the option. It is also interesting to consider whether an action could be brought under the ss 89–91 FSA 2012 misleading statements and impressions offences (or their predecessor in s 397 FSMA) in these circumstances. The acts in question would appear to have created a false or misleading market in the investment in question, but query whether any other party would have been 'induced' to enter into a transaction in such circumstances.

[259] *Canada Inc and Beck v Financial Services Authority*, Upper Tribunal, (FS/2011/0017; FS/2011/0018), 2 August 2011, currently on appeal (see n 57).

manipulative practices which were being used and that those alerts and communications that were issued by Swift Trade to the dealers to try and prevent these manipulative practices were 'no more than cosmetic, produced with an eye to their possible examination by regulators'. As mentioned at paragraph 9.35, the matter was at the time of writing subject to appeal.

'Layering' was considered further in the recent enforcement action taken against Michael Coscia,[260] who had traded through his company Panther Energy Trading LLC, using a DMA provider to execute an algorithmic trading strategy that, the FCA claimed was a 'layering' scheme. Coscia executed the trades against commodity futures on ICE Futures Europe ('ICE'), specifically targeting Brent, Gas Oil, and WTI. **9.196**

Coscia had designed an algorithm that achieved precisely such an effect—small orders around the best price were immediately followed by several large orders on the other side of the order book at progressively improving price levels, prompting other market participants to place orders in the same direction, while Coscia's algorithmic orders had already been cancelled, save one which would be partially executed before the pattern was repeated in reverse. The large orders, being placed for a short period of time (that is, the entire sequence would take place within 300 milliseconds, or 0.3 seconds) and being inevitably cancelled following execution of the small orders, created a false impression of liquidity and represented a significant proportion of the total supply and demand on the order book. **9.197**

Further to the *Coscia* case, and in response to 'technological development leading to an increased reliance on algorithmic and automated trading and HFT', the FCA issued a summary of findings in *MarketWatch* (Issue 44) to highlight its renewed interest in and scrutiny over algorithmic trading, stating that notwithstanding the market liquidity it provides, the FCA anticipates a rise in disciplinary action correlating with its increased prevalence.[261] The FSA had previously highlighted its concerns relating to layering or 'spoofing' in its *MarketWatch* Issue 33 in 2009. **9.198**

Share ramping The FSA also considered a number of cases relating to what was found to be 'share ramping'. **9.199**

For example, in the *Eagle* case,[262] Mr Eagle was found to have instigated and effected a share ramping scheme involving Fundamental E-Investments ('FEI'), a company traded on AIM. Mr Eagle had used stockbroking company SP Bell, of which he was controller and Chief Executive, to embark on a course of market abuse in relation to FEI through the use of rollovers, delayed rollovers, and the manipulation of share prices, thereby intentionally misleading the market and positioned the share price of FEI at an artificially high level so that the market in FEI shares was distorted. **9.200**

The penalty imposed by the FSA comprised the disgorgement of £1.3 million by way of profit made by Mr Eagle through commissions earned personally (£1.2 million) and notional interest thereon, plus £1.5 million by way of punitive sanction. Mr Eagle has also been prohibited. **9.201**

In a related case under the market abuse (manipulating transactions) offence, Graham Betton was fined £25,000 and a prohibition order made against him. Mr Betton had instructed SP **9.202**

260 FCA Final Notice to Michael Coscia, dated 3 July 2013 (SDM).
261 *MarketWatch*, Financial Conduct Authority, August 2013/No 44.
262 FSA Final Notice to Simon Eagle, dated 18 May 2010 (RDC).

Bell staff to sell FEI shares to clients, many of whom were unaware that the shares were being bought and sold on their behalf. In order to defer clients having to pay for the shares, many of the trades were rolled over from client to client without being settled. Mr Betton was found to have been aware that the purpose of the scheme was to defer payment for the shares indefinitely and he personally executed at least 75 rollover trades in excess of 340 million shares in FEI. Mr Betton therefore assisted in the share ramping scheme in relation to FEI.

9.203 **Manipulation of Net Asset Value** A number of cases have looked at what was found to be the manipulation of net asset value ('NAV') by fund managers.

9.204 In the *Chaligné*, *Sejean*, and *Dallio* Upper Tribunal reference[263] Chaligné, like Winterflood/Eagle, focused on underlying motive, or, as it was referred to in Eagle, actuating purpose, in relation to the fourth type of section 118 behaviour. Mr Chaligné had, through an executing broker, Cantor Fitzgerald Europe, shored up the price of securities (through repeated purchasing) in which the fund he managed through a management company (Cambos) had established a long position. He did so, repeatedly and on a short-term basis, at times when such prices were critical to the calculation of the fund's NAV. The Upper Tribunal found that Mr Chaligné, as well as Mr Sejean (Chaligné's primary contact at CFE) and Mr Dallio, a 'relatively inexperienced' trader at CFE, and who had executed a number of the orders in question, had all committed market abuse (manipulating transactions).

9.205 Manipulation of NAV was also considered in the *Visser* and *Fagbulu* decisions.[264] It was found that Mr Visser (CEO of Mercurius Capital Management Limited (Mercurius) had, amongst other things, actively manipulated the NAV of the Mercurius international hedge fund, by repeatedly engaging in, and twice instructing Mr Fagbulu (Mercurius' compliance officer) to commit market abuse in illiquid securities held by the fund, and by causing the fund to enter into ostensibly highly profitable but ultimately fictitious transactions. The FSA found that Mr Fagbulu assisted Mr Visser in manipulating the NAV of the fund and false transactions. Both were fined and prohibited.

9.206 **Orders at the close** There have been a number of cases relating to the placing of orders at the close in order to affect the closing price of the financial instruments in question.

9.207 By way of illustration, in the *Goenka* case,[265] Mr Goenka, a Dubai-based private investor, placed a series of orders of Reliance Industries Global Depositary Receipts in the final seconds of the LSE's closing auction. The FSA found that the orders were placed and the trades were executed with the intention of artificially increasing the closing price of the Reliance GDRs above a certain level and that Mr Goenka avoided a loss of $3,193,640 which he would have suffered under the terms of an OTC structured product which matured on 18 October 2010, and for which pay out depended on the closing price of Reliance GDRs. Mr Goenka was fined $9,621,240 comprising a penalty of $6,517,600 plus a restitution element of $3,103,640 to be paid to the counterparty bank.

9.208 **Commodity Markets** The FSA had for some time expressed the intention to look more closely at conduct in the commodities markets, an area where it had not previously ventured,

263 *Chaligné, Sejean and Dallio v FSA*, Upper Tribunal, Cases FS 2001/0001, 0002, and 0003.
264 *Visser and Fagbulu v FSA*, Upper Tribunal, Cases FS/2010/0001 and 0006, 9 August 2011.
265 FSA Final Notice to Rameshkumar Satyanarayan Goenka, dated 17 October 2011 (SDM).

and there have now been a number of cases in this sector, commencing with the *Perkins* case,[266] a case relating to trading on ICE Futures Europe.

The *Andrew Kerr* case[267] and the related *Hobbs* case[268] related to trading coffee futures and related coffee futures options on the London International Financial Futures and Options (LIFFE) market, as with the Goenka case, involved orders at the close. Mr Kerr, who was employed by a broker, was found to have been a participant in a plan instigated by a client to manipulate the price of coffee futures. Mr Kerr placed an order on the client's behalf during the one-minute period in which the monthly coffee options reference price was determined which the FSA found had the effect of positioning the price at an artificial or abnormal level. The FSA accepted that Mr Kerr had not instigated the abusive scheme on the part of his client, but found he had willingly participated in it. **9.209**

The client in the Kerr case (Mr Hobbs, a proprietary trader at Mizuho), however, referred his case to the Upper Tribunal and, on the same facts, was found not to have committed market abuse. Mr Hobbs had instructed Mr Kerr to place a buy order outside the narrow range in which the options had traded, resulting in a last-minute increase in the reference price, such that the default positions of those holding expiring options were reversed (from 'in the money' to 'out of the money' for each 'put' and 'call' option respectively). However, on examination of the delta trading strategy pursued by Mr Hobbs and the overall size of his start position, the fact that it was reasonable to expect that Mr Hobbs might achieve greater liquidity for this long (buy) order nearer the close, and the fact that the relevant closing price was not a particularly relevant factor for trading in the underlying futures (or for that matter determining whether an option holder would choose to exercise his options), the Upper Tribunal, whilst critical of much of Mr Hobbs' evidence, found there to be no market abuse and that the trade was, in fact, carried out for legitimate reasons and was in conformity with accepted relevant market practices. **9.210**

The FSA subsequently sought to appeal on the basis that the Upper Tribunal had wrongfully failed to consider whether Mr Hobbs was not a fit and proper person by reason of his conduct towards Mr Kerr and his lying during the investigation of his trading. The FSA did not seek to challenge the Upper Tribunal's finding that Mr Hobbs had not been guilty of market abuse. The Upper Tribunal accepted that the FSA had raised an arguable point of law, but, because of statements to this effect made on the FSA's website, found that it had discontinued its proceedings against Mr Hobbs. This was appealed and the appeal was upheld.[269] The Court of Appeal was invited to decide to make a prohibition order, but declined to do so, **9.211**

[266] Final Notice re Stephen Perkins, 24 June 2010. Stephen Perkins was fined £72,000 (reduced from £90,000 for early settlement) and prohibited for five years for market abuse (false or misleading impressions and securing an abnormal or artificial price) in connection with Brent Crude Futures contracts traded on the ICE Futures Europe exchange (ICE). Mr Perkins was a broker with an execution only oil brokerage firm whose job was to execute orders placed with him by clients. The firm conducted no discretionary or proprietary trading. On 30 June 2009, Mr Perkins traded high volumes of Brent on ICE via its online trading platform in the early hours of the morning, despite not having client authorisation to do so. His trading gave a false and misleading impression as to the supply, demand and price of Brent and increased the price of Brent to an abnormal or artificial level. Mr Perkins' explanation for his behaviour was that he was drunk, which the FSA accepted on the basis of medical evidence; there was no identifiable overall motive for his trading.

[267] FSA Final Notice to Andrew Charles Kerr, dated 1 June 2010 (SDM).

[268] *Hobbs v FSA*, Upper Tribunal, ref no FS/2010/0024, 22 November 2012.

[269] Court of Appeal: *FCA v Hobbs* [2013] EWCA Civ 918.

and remitted the question back to the Upper Tribunal to consider, noting that Mr Hobbs was as a practical matter no longer performing a function in relation to a regulated activity.

9.212 The Geddis case[270] attracted much attention, primarily because the Upper Tribunal took a very different view of the facts from the FSA, and refused to endorse the FSA's attempt to fine and prohibit Mr Geddis and instead decided that a public censure alone was appropriate for what was in the circumstances 'careless' market abuse.

9.213 The case related to trading on the London Metal Exchange ('LME'). The relevant contracts traded on the LME are based on warrants, instruments that entitle the holder to take delivery of a number of lots of the specified metal. If a market participant controls the supply of the underlying—ie it has a dominant position—it can position the price at which those with a short position would have to borrow metal under LME contracts (in order to deliver under their short contracts) at a level above the true market price: a so-called 'abusive squeeze'. Abusive squeezes are identified by the FCA in the Code of Market Conduct as a form of market abuse by way of manipulating transactions. The LME has a set of rules—the Lending Guidance—designed to prevent the potential for abuse of a dominant position, including by way of an abusive squeeze. On 21 November 2008, Mr Geddis, a trader of long standing employed by Dresdner Kleinwort, built a position in lead futures contracts on the LME which rapidly amounted to a dominant position. This required Mr Geddis under the Lending Guidance to lend to other market participants at a specified level. However, Mr Geddis did not follow the Lending Guidance and instead continued to trade at significantly higher levels, causing other market participants to have to borrow at an inflated level. The position he built would have produced a profit for the firm of $1.4 million if it had not subsequently been unwound. Following the end of trading in the relevant lead contracts for delivery that day, Mr Geddis immediately sent for his desk head and the firm's compliance officer. The LME rang up while they were meeting and instructed the firm to unwind its position and to compensate market participants who had borrowed at excessive levels. This the firm immediately did, paying compensation of over £30,000. The firm was subsequently fined £150,000 by the LME for breaching LME rules.

9.214 The FSA's case was that this was an instance of premeditated market abuse for which Mr Geddis should be both fined £100,000 (although reduced due to his straitened financial circumstances having been made redundant by the firm and unable to find other suitable employment due to the FSA investigation) and prohibited. Mr Geddis's motive, according to the FSA, was to make a profit for his employer. However, the Upper Tribunal accepted Mr Geddis's evidence that his trading was unpremeditated and was what he described as a 'moment of madness'. According to the Tribunal's ruling Mr Geddis was unable to explain his course of trading, saying he had 'lost focus' and been 'caught up in the moment'. What seems to have swayed the Upper Tribunal in particular, in addition to Mr Geddis's live evidence, and his immediate steps to remedy the situation once he realised his mistake, was the pattern of trading itself. The Upper Tribunal gave its view that the events of 21 November 2008 were inconsistent with a premeditated attempt to profit from an abusive squeeze, since the dramatic rise in price occasioned by Mr Geddis's trading could not fail to be noticed: which is exactly what happened, prompting the LME to telephone the firm. The Upper Tribunal therefore concluded that the appropriate penalty in Mr Geddis's case was a

[270] [2011] UKUT 344 (TCC).

public censure. It also rejected the FSA's finding that Mr Geddis was not fit and proper and so should be prohibited. On the contrary, the Upper Tribunal found him to be a person of integrity.

The parties proceeded on the basis that it was agreed that Mr Geddis's trading amounted to market abuse—it was not disputed that the conduct 'secured the price of [relevant contracts] at an abnormal level'. The Upper Tribunal did not therefore have to analyse the statutory provisions or consider the FSA guidance on abusive squeezes in the COMC. What the Tribunal did note was that Mr Geddis's failure 'consisted in not taking sufficient care, while holding a dominant position, to avoid creating a disorderly market'. This was negligent, not deliberate, market abuse. That accords with the Court of Appeal's ruling in Winterflood[271] that there is no requirement for intention within the market abuse regime—a want of care, rather than an intention to commit market abuse, is sufficient if the behaviour is in fact abusive. **9.215**

Market abuse (manipulating devices)—Type 5

The fifth behaviour type that constitutes market abuse is where a person's conduct consists of effecting transactions or orders to trade which employ fictitious devices or any other form of deception or contrivance.[272] This would seem to presuppose some kind of deliberate act. The COMC again sets out a number of examples of conduct which, in the FCA's view, will constitute 'manipulating devices'.[273] The use of the word 'employed' would suggest there needs to be an interaction or link between the transaction or orders on the one hand, and the device, deception, or contrivance on the other, although the nature and extent of that relationship, whether in timing terms or otherwise, is not clear from the examples given. The examples include publicly voicing an opinion about a qualifying investment (or its issuer) and profiting subsequently from the impact of the opinion on positions held, without having simultaneously disclosed that conflict of interest to the public in a proper and effective way.[274] Other examples given include disseminating misleading positive information with a view to increasing the price of the investment in question ('pump and dump')[275] or, if the person disseminating the information has a short position, disseminating misleading negative information with a view to decreasing the price of the investment in question ('trash and cash'). **9.216**

Trash and cash schemes gained significant media coverage in March 2008 when HBOS plc (HBOS) was thought to have become a victim of false rumours spread by short-sellers.[276] The FSA launched an investigation into the HBOS rumours, but was unable to uncover evidence that the rumours were spread as part of a concerted attempt by individuals to profit by manipulating the share price. **9.217**

[271] *Winterflood Securities Ltd v FSA* [2010] EWCA Civ 423.

[272] FSMA, s 118(6). The FSA will take the following factors into account in determining whether a fictitious device or other form of contrivance has been used (and, if present, are indicative that it has) (a) if orders to trade are preceded or followed by the dissemination of false or misleading information by the person trading; or (b) if orders to trade are undertaken before or after the dissemination of research or recommendations which are erroneous, biased, or demonstrably influenced by the personal interest of the person trading. MAR 1.7.3E.

[273] MAR 1.7.2E.

[274] MAR 1.7.2E (1).

[275] MAR 1.7.2E(3).

[276] Various rumours had circulated to the effect that a British bank faced funding difficulties. Some identified HBOS by name. FSA, FSA concludes HBOS rumours investigation, 1 August 2008, FSA/PN/086/2008; see <http://www.fsa.gov.uk/pages/Library/Communication/PR/2008/086.shtml>.

9.218 The press release of 1 August 2008, 'FSA concludes HBOS rumours investigation' FSA/PN/086/2008, also indicates the FSA's willingness to take a strong stance, and to pursue criminal prosecutions where possible:

> Market participants should, however, expect that our surveillance and investigation activity will continue at a high level of intensity. Where individuals or firms appear to have benefited following false or misleading rumours, we will require individuals and/or firms to provide immediate access to traders, information and trading strategies as well as to make available email, messaging and telephone records. Where there is evidence of market abuse then we will take enforcement—including criminal—action.

9.219 The FSA conducted a thematic review into market rumours,[277] and recommended as a result various measures that firms should have in place—including a clear and transparent policy on handling rumours, a procedure for handling unverified information, regular and/or formalised training appropriate to the organisation, surveillance, and monitoring of trading activities, and greater visibility of compliance officers within the organisation for those with a higher risk of exposure to rumours.

Market abuse (dissemination)—Type 6

9.220 The sixth type of conduct that constitutes market abuse is behaviour which consists of the dissemination of information by any means which gives, or is likely to give, a false or misleading impression as to a qualifying investment by a person who knew or could reasonably be expected to have known that the information was false or misleading.[278] As discussed at paragraph 9.84, this offence carries both a subjective element (that is to say, the knowledge of the person in question) and an objective element (whether he could reasonably be expected to have that knowledge). According to the COMC,[279] knowingly or recklessly spreading false or misleading information about a qualifying investment through the media, including in particular through an RIS or similar information channel, would, in the FCA's opinion, fall under this heading, as would undertaking a course of conduct in order to give a false or misleading impression about a qualifying investment. Cited examples of behaviour which may constitute market abuse (dissemination) are posting false or misleading information about the takeover of a company whose shares are qualifying investments on an Internet chat room knowing that information to be false or misleading, or where a person responsible for the content of information provided to an RIS is reckless as to whether the information submitted is false or misleading.[280] For the purposes of this provision, the dissemination of information by a journalist is to be assessed by taking into account the codes governing the journalism profession, unless he derives any advantage or profits from the dissemination of the information.[281] The suspected behaviour relating to the HBOS rumours reported in

[277] Published in *MarketWatch* Issue No 30, November 2008: <http://www.fsa.gov.uk/pubs/newsletters/mw_newsletter30.pdf>.

[278] FSMA, s 118(7). According to MAR 1.8.4E, in the FSA's opinion, if a normal and reasonable person would know or should have known that information was false or misleading, that indicates that the person disseminating the information could reasonably be expected to have known the same. However, if a person disseminating the false or misleading information could only know it was false or misleading through access to information that was properly behind a Chinese Wall, then, in the FCA's opinion, he is not taken to know that the information was so false or misleading. MAR 1.8.5E.

[279] MAR 1.8.3E.

[280] Example provided at MAR 1.8.6E(2).

[281] FSMA, s 118A(4).

media coverage[282] could potentially have fallen under this category of market abuse, as well as under the manipulating devices category.

Questions relating to the nature of dissemination and knowledge were discussed in the *James Corr* final notice[283] (see paragraph 9.224). In that case, the FSA stated that dissemination can be 'by any means' and that, by approving and signing with a view to publication the accounts of Cattles Limited (which were found to have contained information that gave a false or misleading impression to the market as to the value of its shares), Mr Corr (the finance director of Cattles) accepted responsibility for the content of the financial statements. **9.221**

Review of cases

It is likely that the *Shell* case, if brought today, would be brought under the market abuse (dissemination) offence.[284] In that case, the FSA concluded that certain Shell entities were guilty of market abuse through a dissemination of false or misleading information concerning announcements of their levels of hydrocarbon reserves. During the period 1998 to 2004, it was found that Shell regularly overstated its hydrocarbon levels in statements to the market, which the FSA held would be likely to give a false or misleading impression as to the price of UK-listed Shell shares (as reserve levels are a key performance indicator for companies in the oil and gas industries).[285] In the judgment of the FSA, an average investor in listed shares on the FTSE-100 would not expect the information disclosed to the market concerning reserve levels to be false or misleading and Shell was therefore guilty of market abuse.[286] The evidential provision at MAR 1.8.4E indicates that if a normal and reasonable person would know or should have known that information was false or misleading, that indicates that the person disseminating the information could reasonably be expected to have known the same. Evidence in the *Shell* case suggested that it was known internally (or at least suspected) that the disclosed information was inaccurate. A number of decisions relating to inaccurate or misleading announcements have also been made under the Disclosure Rules—see discussion at paragraph 9.269. **9.222**

There have been a number of market abuse (dissemination) cases since then, including a series of cases relating to Cattles Limited ('Cattles') and its subsidiary Welcome Financial Services Limited ('Welcome') touched on earlier in this chapter, Cattles was found to have disseminated information that gave a false or misleading impression to the market as to the value of its shares in circumstances where it could reasonably be expected to have knowledge that the information was false or misleading. **9.223**

The FSA publicly censured Cattles and its subsidiary, Welcome, for market abuse (dissemination). It was also found that Cattles had committed breaches of the Listing Rules. The FSA also fined and banned two former directors, James Corr[287] and Peter Miller (the finance director of Welcome),[288] for publishing misleading information and for being knowingly concerned in the other breaches. John Blake, director and CEO of Welcome, was also found **9.224**

---

[282] See further discussion at para 9.217 *et seq*.
[283] FSA Final Notice to James Joseph Corr, dated 28 March 2012 (RDC).
[284] FSA Final Notice to Shell Transport and Trading Company, plc and The Royal Dutch Petroleum Company NV, dated 24 August 2004.
[285] ibid, paras 61 and 69.
[286] ibid, para 64.
[287] FSA Final Notice to James Joseph Corr, dated 28 March 2012 (RDC).
[288] See FSA Final Notice to Peter Miller, dated 28 March 2012 (RDC).

to have committed market abuse (dissemination) and to have been knowingly concerned in a breach of FSA Principle 3 (Management and Control) by Welcome. Mr Blake had approved the accounts which were incorporated into the parent, Cattles', correspondingly inaccurate documents. The FSA deemed Blake to have disseminated the information as ultimate responsibility for oversight of financial figures lay with him, and on the basis of the objective test Blake could reasonably have been expected to know that the relevant information was false or misleading. As managing director with responsibility for operations, and being also in particular approved to perform the apportionment and oversight function, Blake had a duty to take all necessary steps to satisfy himself with respect to that information. Without finding that Blake did in fact have actual knowledge of the misstatement at the time, the FSA noted Blake's experience and apparent expertise in the issues underlying and surrounding the cause of the misstatement (calculations in respect of deferments on Welcome's loan book).

Market abuse (misleading behaviour and distortion)—Type 7 (legacy offence)

9.225 The seventh type of conduct that constitutes market abuse, as described at paragraph 9.97 relates to both 'misleading behaviour' and 'distortion'. This is a legacy offence and as such catches behaviour only to the extent it does not fall within the other types of conduct relating to manipulation. To fall within this offence, the behaviour must be such as is likely to give a regular user of the market a false or misleading impression as to the supply of, demand for, or price or value of, qualifying investments. In terms of distortion, the behaviour must be such as would be, or would be likely to be, regarded by a regular user of the market as behaviour that would distort, or would be likely to distort, the market in such an investment. In both cases the behaviour must be likely to be regarded by a regular user of the market as a failure on the part of the person concerned to observe the 'standard of behaviour' reasonably expected of a person in his position in relation to the market.[289] The offence is based on behaviour generally rather than specifically behaviour relating to transactions, and is therefore wider than the equivalent MAD offences, given that the MAD covers simply 'transactions' and 'orders'. An example of behaviour which would, in the FCA's view, be market abuse under this heading is the movement of physical commodity stocks or empty cargo ships where such movement creates the specified impression.[290]

Review of cases relating to market abuse (misleading behaviour and distortion)

9.226 As mentioned earlier in this chapter at paragraph 9.180, the *Henry Cameron* case involved both a finding of market abuse (dissemination) and misleading behaviour and distortion.

9.227 According to the COMC, factors to take into account when determining if behaviour is likely to give a regular user a 'false or misleading impression' regarding qualifying investments[291] are the experience and knowledge of the users of the market or auction platform in question; the structure of the market or auction platform, including its reporting, notification, and transparency requirements; the legal and regulatory requirements of the market

---

289 FSMA, s 118(8). The regular user concept is explained at para 9.57.

290 MAR 1.9.2E. Note, however, 'Market Abuse Directives: Level 3—First Set of CESR (the predecessor to ESMA) guidance and information on the common operation of the Directive', which sets out various examples of types of practice which in the view of CESR members could potentially contravene the prohibition on market manipulation, cites as an example of dissemination of false and misleading information (a post-MAD offence) the movement of physical commodity stocks to create a misleading impression as to the supply or demand for a commodity or the deliverable into a commodity futures contract.

291 MAR 1.9.4E.

or auction platform concerned; the identity and position of the person responsible for the behaviour which has been observed (if known); and the extent and nature of the visibility or disclosure of the person's activity. MAR sets out a number of factors relevant in determining whether behaviour creating a false or misleading impression or distorting the market has failed to meet the standard expected by a regular user.[292] These relate to the manner of execution (that is to say, whether the transaction complies with market or auction platform rules as to the proper execution of transactions), whether or not the need for the market or auction platform as a whole to operate fairly and efficiently has been taken into account, and whether or not the transaction is pursuant to a prior legal or regulatory obligation owed to a third party. These reiterate factors which, in the context of market abuse (manipulating transactions), are indicative of there being 'legitimate reasons',[293] but in the current context are stated to be factors which are relevant, rather than necessarily being indicative. Additional factors in the context of the 'regular user test' are the characteristics of the market or auction platform in question, including the users and applicable rules and codes of conduct; the position of the person in question; and the standards reasonably to be expected of him in light of his experience, skill, and knowledge. Where an organisation has created a false or misleading impression, a relevant factor will also be whether the individuals responsible could only know they were likely to create a false or misleading impression if they had access to other information that was being held behind a Chinese Wall or similarly effective arrangements.

Short Selling Rules In June and September 2008 two Instruments amending the COMC relating to short sales were introduced by the FSA. The first required disclosure of 'significant' short positions created or increased while the issuer was pursuing a rights issue. Thus, provisions were added into the COMC the effect of which was that failure to give adequate disclosure that the holder has reached or exceeded a 'disclosable short position'[294] where: (1) that position relates, directly or indirectly, to securities which are the subject of a rights issue; and (2) the 'disclosable short position' is reached or exceeded during a rights issue period, constituted behaviour which, in the opinion of the FSA, was market abuse (misleading behaviour).[295] The June 2008 Short Selling Instrument was introduced at short notice, and without consultation (and indeed some practitioners questioned how appropriate it was to fit these provisions into the existing market abuse framework), but according to the FSA the provisions were justified by the circumstances at the time: **9.228**

> In current market conditions, there is increased potential for market abuse through short selling during rights issues. As a result, there has been severe volatility in the shares of companies conducting rights issues. This is potentially damaging not only to the issuers in question but also to confidence in the overall fairness and quality of the UK market. It can be particularly prejudicial to the interests of small investors. The problem is compounded by the length of time taken to complete rights issues.[296]

[292] MAR 1.9.5E.

[293] See para 9.184.

[294] A disclosable short position is a short position which represents an economic interest of 0.25 per cent of the issued capital of a company.

[295] For the purposes of MAR 1.9.2AE, as then was 'adequate disclosure' meant disclosure made on an RIS by 3.30 pm the following business day (MAR 1.9.2BR).

[296] Generally, also see FSA: 'Financial Services Authority introduces disclosure regime for significant short positions in companies undertaking rights issues', 13 June 2008, FSA/PN/057/2008; <http://www.fsa.gov.uk/pages/Library/Communication/PR/2008/057.shtml>, and 'Short Selling Instrument 2008—Frequently Asked Questions 20 June 2008 Update'; <http://www.fsa.gov.uk/pubs/other/Shortselling_faqs.pdf>.

9.229 Subsequently, in September 2008, in the turmoil following the demise of Lehman Brothers, and the proposed takeover of HBOS by Lloyds TSB following the collapse in HBOS shares, further evidential provisions were introduced into the COMC again at short notice and without consultation.[297] These provisions in effect prohibited until 16 January 2009, the active creation or increase of net short positions in publicly quoted UK banks, UK insurers, or their parents by providing that such activity would, in the opinion of the FSA, be engaging in market abuse (misleading behaviour). The only exception to this related to market makers.

9.230 The September 2008 Short Selling Instrument also required public disclosure of net short positions in UK financial sector companies when these reached, exceeded or fed below certain specified thresholds (namely 0.25 per cent, 0.35 per cent, 0.45 per cent, and 0.55 per cent of the company's issued share capital and every 0.1 per cent threshold thereafter). According to Hector Sants, the then Chief Executive of the FSA:

> While we still regard short selling as a legitimate investment technique in normal market conditions, the current extreme circumstances have given rise to disorderly markets. As a result, we have taken this decisive action, after careful consideration, to protect the fundamental integrity and quality of markets and to guard against further instability in the financial sector.

9.231 With effect from 6 August 2010 the FSA made further changes to the rules, designed to implement the short selling powers granted to it in section 8 of the Financial Services Act 2010 and in order to effect further interim changes pending the finalisation of the pan European short selling disclosure regime. This involved moving the relevant provisions from the COMC to Chapter 2 of a new Handbook module, known as the Financial Information and Market Confidence Sourcebook ('FINMAR'), and including much of the material previously contained in a series of FAQs on the short selling requirements (thus placing it on an official footing).

9.232 Since that time, the EU Short Selling Regulation[298] (the 'SSR') has come into force (on 25 March 2012), and represents a pan-European disclosure regime for net short positions in EEA-listed shares and sovereign debt. It also introduced a ban on naked physical short sales of EEA-listed shares and sovereign debt, and a ban on naked credit default swap positions in EEA sovereign debt. The regime applies to short positions relating to the issued share capital of companies that are admitted to trading on a regulated market or MTF in the EEA and debt instruments issued by a sovereign issuer, whether or not the trading takes place on a regulated market or MTF, and whether or not such trading takes place outside of the EEA. For net short trades that are permitted pursuant to the SSR, a two-tier disclosure regime applies, requiring disclosure to the relevant regulator at a threshold of 0.2 per cent and each successive 0.1 per cent thereafter, and a public disclosure to the market at a threshold of 0.5 per cent and each successive 0.1 per cent thereafter. In addition to the disclosure regime, a person holding a disclosable net short position is required to keep a record of the gross positions which make a net short position for a period of five years.

9.233 In enforcing the SSR the FCA has powers to issue information requests and conduct investigations, and if a person then knowingly or recklessly provides information to the FCA

[297] By the Short Selling (No 2) Instrument 2008 (FSA 2008/50) in MAR 1.9.2 C, D, & E (19 September 2008).

[298] Regulation (EU) No 236/2012.

in such context which is false or misleading in a material particular, this will constitute an offence under the revised provisions of the Act.[299] The FCA also has emergency powers which enable it to prohibit, restrict, or limit short selling transactions where there is a disorderly fall in the price of a security during a single trading day.[300]

Statutory exceptions

As mentioned at paragraph 9.63, FSMA provides a number of statutory exceptions which state that particular behaviour does not amount to market abuse. These exceptions operate in addition to the safe harbours which apply in the COMC to particular types of market abuse. The first of these exceptions concerns behaviour which conforms with a rule which itself provides that conforming with the rule does not amount to market abuse.[301] For example, where a person complies with the control of information rule concerning the establishment of Chinese Walls[302] for the purposes of withholding information from one part of a firm to another, or complies with those parts of the DTRs[303] relating to disclosures of information, such a person will not have committed market abuse. The second of the statutory exceptions[304] states that compliance with the relevant provisions of the EC buy-back programmes and Stabilisation Regulation will not amount to market abuse.[305] **9.234**

Takeover Code

Finally, a safe harbour is set out in the COMC so that behaviour conforming with a relevant rule of the Takeover Code[306] concerning the disclosure announcement, communication, or release of information will of itself not amount to market abuse provided certain conditions are met.[307] The third FSMA exception relates to behaviour where it is done by a person acting on behalf of a public authority in pursuit of monetary policies or policies with respect to exchange rates or the management of public debt or foreign exchange reserves. **9.235**

FCA Principles

The FCA also has the ability to take action against FCA authorised firms for breaches of FCA rules, (including the Principles for Businesses) or against FCA approved persons for breaches of the FCA's Statements of Principle and Code of Practice for Approved Persons. **9.236**

---

299 See s 131L, FSMA. See Chapters 5, 6, 7, and 12.

300 FINMAR 2.5.

301 FSMA, s 118A(5)(a).

302 SYSC 10.2.2R(1).

303 DTR 2, as discussed at para 9.13. The guidance at MAR 1.10.2G(2) refers to those part of the Part 6 rules (namely the Disclosure Rules and Prospectus Rules) which relate to the timing, dissemination, or availability, content, and standard of care applicable to a disclosure, announcements, communication, or release of information.

304 FSMA, s 118A(5)(b).

305 MAR 1.10.1G(1) confirms that conforming with arts 3–6 of the EC Regulation and MAR 2 will not amount to market abuse.

306 The rules governing the substantial acquisition of shares issued by the Takeover Panel.

307 MAR 1.10.4C (a safe harbour) which implements FSMA, s 120(1). The relevant rule must relate to the timing, dissemination, or availability of, content, and standard of care applicable to a disclosure, announcement, communication, or release of information, and be one listed in the table set out at MAR 1.10.5C. The behaviour must also be expressly required or expressly permitted by the rules in question (the associated notes being treated as part of the relevant rule for these purposes) and conform to any General Principles set out in the stipulated part of the Takeover Code relevant to that rule.

With reference to the Principles for Businesses, principles relating to acting with integrity (Principle 1), with due skill, care, and diligence (Principle 2), and observing proper standards of market conduct (Principle 5) are particularly relevant in the context of market abuse, although note also that there have been a number of decisions where systems and controls issues have been brought into play by finding a breach of Principle 3 ('a firm must take reasonable care to organise and control its affairs responsibly and effectively, with adequate risk management systems'), an aspect on which increasing emphasis is being placed. Principles-based enforcement can be used in its own right (including in circumstances where behaviour does not necessarily fall within the market abuse offences) and in certain cases have featured in combination with market abuse offences.[308]

9.237 A number of high profile principles-based cases have emerged. In the *Citigroup* case, Citigroup Global Markets Limited ('CGML') executed a trading strategy on the European government bond markets which very broadly involved the firm building up and then rapidly exiting from very substantial long positions in European government bonds over a period of an hour, using specially configured technology. The trade caused a temporary disruption to the volumes of bonds quoted and traded on the MTS platform, a sharp drop in bond prices, and a temporary withdrawal by some participants from quoting on that platform. The FSA imposed a financial penalty consisting of the relinquishment of profits of £9,960,860 and an additional penalty of £4 million for breaching FSA Principles 2 and 3 by failing to conduct its business with due skill, care, and diligence and failing to control its business effectively.[309]

9.238 In terms of Principle 2 it was found in that in planning and authorising the strategy, CGML did not have due regard to the inherent risks including the likely consequences the execution of the trading strategy could have for the efficient and orderly operation of the MTS platform and did not ensure that clear parameters for the size of the trade were understood, communicated, and reviewed. As to Principle 3, it was found that there was a failure within CGML to escalate the detailed trading strategy adequately and in advance to senior management, and a failure to consult with applicable control functions. Accordingly, insufficient weight and attention were given to the franchise risk to which the trading gave rise; the execution risk arising from, amongst other things, the use of a spreadsheet that was not fully testable; the market impact risk, (ie that the trade might have an adverse effect on price and on quotation levels on MTS and the effect that this might have on market confidence); and legal and regulatory risk resulting from the above. Secondly, it was found there were inadequate systems for the supervision of traders.

9.239 Another key example of the FSA's principles-based approach is the *Deutsche*[310] case and the related decision concerning David Maslen, the bank's former Head of European Cash Trading. The *Deutsche* case arose from two separate transactions conducted by Deutsche Bank AG in 2004. The first transaction (the 'Scania' transaction) was in relation to a book build which involved Maslen. The Scania shares were listed on the Swedish Stock Exchange, which at the time was not a prescribed market. The provisions of MAR therefore did not apply to the Scania transaction. While being actively involved in the book build, the FSA found that Maslen gave instructions for proprietary trading which occurred at a sensitive

[308] See, eg, FSA Final Notice to Philippe Jabre, dated 1 August 2005.
[309] FSA Final Notice to Citigroup Global Markets Limited, dated 28 June 2005.
[310] FSA Final Notice to Deutsche Bank AG, dated 10 April 2006 (SDM).

time during the build, without notifying or seeking clearance from the Bank's compliance or senior management or checking the Bank's restricted list.

In addition, Deutsche had made a series of announcements to its Equity Sales Force in London by means of an internal messaging system and various of the announcements were found to be incomplete, and/or inaccurate and/or failed to make appropriate disclosures or adequately consider all relevant issues. Further, the internal announcements stated that Deutsche would be reporting its holding to the Stockholm Stock Exchange prior to it actually doing so. As a result the contents of the announcements were disclosed by Equity Sales to some of the Deutsche's clients who had participated in the book build prior to it being disclosed by the Stockholm Exchange. **9.240**

The second transaction related to a Swiss company, Cytos, listed on the Swiss Exchange, whose share price was stabilised by a Zurich-based trader under instruction from Deutsche's London staff. The FSA's price stabilising rules did not apply to the Cytos transaction, but Deutsche decided that its internal procedures in relation to price stabilisation, based on the FSA's stabilisation regime, should apply to the Cytos transactions. The FSA found that Deutsche did not ensure that the trader who conducted the stabilisation trades in Zurich understood and followed the internal procedures regarding stabilisation that Deutsche had intended to apply to the Cytos transaction nor escalate issues arising from the stabilisation exercise to compliance in a timely manner. **9.241**

The FSA imposed a fine of £3,500,000 on Deutsche for breaching FSA Principle 5 (failing to observe proper standards of market conduct) and Principle 2 (failing to conduct its business with due skill, care, and diligence) in relation to the Scania transaction, a penalty of £500,000 in respect of breaches of Principle 2 in relation to the Cytos transaction and an additional amount of £2,363,643 in respect of the loss avoided by Deutsche in relation to the Scania transaction. The FSA also imposed a financial penalty of £350,000 on David Maslen, for being knowingly concerned in the failure to observe proper standards of market conduct in the Scania transaction.[311] **9.242**

A further example of principles-based enforcement was the *Pignatelli* case relating, as it was subsequently described, to 'outside information'. In that case, the FSA fined Sean Pignatelli £20,000 for breaches of Principles 2 (Due Skill, Care and Diligence) and 3 (Market Conduct) of the FSA's Statements of Principle for Approved Persons, for conduct relating to information which, as it turned out, was not in fact 'inside information'. Pignatelli, US equity salesman at an investment bank, had received an analyst's email concerning a particular company. The email was worded in such a way as to appear that it might have contained inside information about the company's prospects but it did not in fact contain inside information. The FSA found Pignatelli to be in breach of Principle 2 of the FSA's Statements of Principle for Approved Persons for failing to consider whether or not the email might have contained inside information and as a result, failing to escalate the matter as required by internal procedures. The FSA found Pignatelli to be in breach of Principle 3 of the FSA's Statements of Principle for Approved Persons, for subsequently relaying the information to the clients in a way that in the FSA's view gave the impression that it was inside information. **9.243**

[311] FSA Final Notice to David John Maslen, dated 10 April 2006 (SDM).

9.244 A couple of more recent cases have also considered behaviour relating to information which did not, for various reasons, turn out to be inside information.

9.245 In March 2012, the FSA fined Nicholas Kyprios £210,000 (reduced by 30 per cent from £300,000 under the FSA's executive settlement procedures) for breach of Principle 2 and Principle 3 of the FSA's Statement of Principles for Approved Persons. Mr Kyprios, who was Head of Credit Sales at Credit Suisse Securities (Europe) Limited, relayed information to two fund manager clients concerning a €2.5-billion bond issue by its client, Liberty Global, Inc., by inviting them to participate in a game of charades. This information was treated internally by Credit Suisse as 'inside information' but was not in fact 'inside information' for the purposes of FSMA and the FSA found that Mr Kyprios breached Principle 3 by disclosing the information to a potential investor without the permission of Credit Suisse, and also in breach of Credit Suisse's wall crossing procedures. The FSA also found that Mr Kyprios breached Principle 2 by disclosing client confidential information without the permission of Liberty. In the *Christopher Gower* decision[312] Mr Gower, a research analyst employed by MF Global and an FSA approved person (CF30) sent a Bloomberg instant message to 14 clients of MF Global, a Bloomberg reporter, and MF Global equity salesmen following a meeting he had had with the Chief Executive Officer of Punch Taverns plc, a listed company traded on the LSE. The FSA found that Mr Gower's instant message gave the impression that inside information had been disclosed to Mr Gower (where there was none—the discussion concerned solely information which was in the public domain) and his disclosures were misleading as they did not accurately reflect the discussion between himself and the CEO of Punch Taverns. The FSA considered that Mr Gower breached Principle 3 of the FSA's Statements of Principle for Approved Persons and imposed a fine of £50,000.

Discovering and Punishing Market Abuse

Suspicious transaction reporting

9.246 As part of the measures introduced by MAD aimed at combating insider dealing and market manipulation, a new, wide-ranging requirement was introduced, namely the requirement to report suspicious transactions.[313] This sits alongside, but is different from, the reporting requirements under the Proceeds of Crime Act 2002 ('PoCA'). The requirement set out in MAD is that, broadly speaking, any professional arranging transactions in financial instruments,[314] who reasonably suspects that a transaction constitutes market abuse, must notify the competent authority.[315] An EU Directive implementing aspects of MAD elaborated on this requirement, stating that investment firms and credit institutions:

> shall decide on a case-by-case basis whether there are reasonable grounds for suspecting that a transaction involves insider dealing or market manipulation ... [and] shall be subject to the rules of notification.[316]

312 Final Notice, Christopher William Gower, 12 January 2011 (RDC).

313 Note that the obligation to report relates to transactions, not orders; see FSA *MarketWatch* Issue 12, June 2005.

314 Note that the definition of financial instruments includes commodity derivatives.

315 Art 6(9) of MAD.

316 Art 7 of Commission Directive 2004/72/EC.

These EU requirements have been implemented in the UK via provisions in the FCA's Supervision Manual (SUP). The basic reporting rule is very similar to the wording in the EU directives, stating that: **9.247**

> A firm which arranges or executes a transaction with or for a client in a qualifying investment admitted to trading on a prescribed market and which has reasonable grounds to suspect that the transaction might constitute market abuse must notify the FCA without delay.[317]

A similar elaboration to that described earlier applies to investment firms/credit institutions.[318] Further rules in SUP 15.10 describe the content and means of making the notification to the FCA and SUP 15 Annex 5 sets out a number of indicative examples of whether a transaction is suspicious.[319] Essentially, suspicious transaction reporting deputises to the market the requirement to monitor itself for abusive behaviour. **9.248**

Appropriate reporting—practical issues

On a practical level, to enhance effective supervision, and indeed to avoid what could otherwise be considerable logistical problems, the FSA originally made it clear that it would not expect to receive purely defensive reports. In numerical terms, the FSA initially indicated that what it had in mind was, across the market, about 200 reports a year. By way of comparison the National Criminal Intelligence Service, the body to which reports were at the time made under PoCA, received over 30,000 in the first year, over double that in the second year, and was at over 100,000 reports per year in the third year. The practical dilemma faced by firms has been how to manage their suspicious transaction reporting obligations. At the same time as wanting what would appear to be qualitative filtering of potentially reportable suspicious transactions, the FSA indicated that the reporting requirement should be triggered by actual suspicion, and therefore would not need sophisticated systems and controls to administer, or dedicated resources. However, as mentioned earlier, the test set out in SUP 15.10.2 is having 'reasonable grounds to suspect' (an objective test), elaborated by guidance in SUP 15.10.4 (which suggests that there will need to be sufficient indications that an activity might constitute market abuse, which will include taking into account the perspective of other transactions or behaviour) which would suggest something more than this. As it transpired, the FSA found that they were receiving too few STRs and have since undertaken a series of reviews and consultation to increase awareness and the need for appropriate systems and controls and training. For example, in 2006, the FSA carried out a thematic review of the suspicious transaction reporting regime, the STR Review 2006. In FSA *MarketWatch* 18,[320] the FSA stated that it regarded suspicious transaction reports ('STRs') as a 'key intelligence asset', and emphasised that market practitioners need to be 'proactive in working' with the **9.249**

[317] SUP 15.10.2R.

[318] SUP 15.10.3R, based on the requirement of art 7 of Commission Directive 2004/72/EC.

[319] These include the following examples that may indicate insider dealing: a client opens an account and immediately gives an order to conduct a significant transaction; a transaction is significantly out of line with the client's previous investment behaviour; a client specifically requests immediate execution of an order regardless of the price at which the order would be executed; there is unusual trading in the shares of a company before the announcement of price sensitive information relating to the company; or an employee's own account transaction is timed just before clients' transactions and related orders in the same financial instrument. The following are stated as examples of market manipulation: an order will, because of its size in relation to the market in that security, clearly have a significant impact on the supply of or demand for or the price or value of the security; a transaction appears to be seeking to modify the valuation of a position while not decreasing/increasing the size of that position; or a transaction appears to be seeking to bypass the trading safeguards of the market.

[320] FSA *MarketWatch*, Issue 18, December 2006.

FSA in preventing market abuse. The FSA warned that they 'will identify firms which fail to submit STRs over time'. Importantly, the FSA detailed the core policies and processes which they hope to see at all firms, namely: initial/induction training on STRs and market abuse more generally; regular emails/newsletters/refresher training updating all relevant staff on key regulatory changes; extra detailed and continuous education of compliance staff; and some level of compliance checking of key staff's understanding of their obligations.

9.250 The FSA have also looked at particular market sectors. In FSA *MarketWatch* 28,[321] the FSA reported that it had made visits to a number of small firms that trade or facilitate trading in the UK exchange-traded commodities markets, with a threefold purpose: to review the market abuse controls in place; to increase dialogue to improve understanding of the areas of greatest market abuse risk in commodity markets; and to raise the profile of the need to submit STRs in the commodity markets.

9.251 More recently, there has been a significant increase in the FCA's focus on the STR regime as a key tool in enabling, protecting, and enhancing, the integrity of the UK financial system. This focus has included supervisory visits to firms to more closely review the systems and controls in place to identify suspicious transactions. According to the FCA,[322] this has resulted in substantial improvements in the quality of STR submission from most of the firms visited, and a substantial increase in the number of submissions received (these increased from a total of 584 in 2011 to 1018 in 2012). The FCA has also indicated that it has also increasingly made contact with firms to discuss instances where suspicious transactions have not been reported, and it will continue to look for patterns of consistent under-submission, or defensive reporting.

9.252 There have also now been cases in this area, from which the FCA's expectations of the role of individuals in relation to suspicious transactions have become underlined. For example, in the *Agnew* decision[323] arising out of the Greenlight/Punch Taverns matter discussed at paragraph 9.115, the FSA concluded that Mr Agnew, a broker at JP Morgan Cazenove who received from Greenlight an order to execute orders in significant amounts, should have recognised in the light of the circumstances that there were reasonable grounds to suspect that the transactions constituted market abuse and that he should have internally reported the suspicions. Mr Agnew was found to have failed to act with the due skill, care, and diligence required of an approved person in accordance with the Statement of Principle 2.

9.253 In the *Lockwood* decision,[324] Mr Lockwood, an investment adviser at a retail stockbroking firm was found to have breached Principle 3 of the FSA's Statements of Principle and Code of Practice for Approved Persons by failing to observe proper standards of market conduct by failing to identify that a transaction was being conducted on the basis of inside information, despite being in receipt of clear warning signals. The FSA emphasised that STRs are one of the FSA's primary intelligence assets which allow the FSA to benefit from participants' proximity to the market and assist the FSA in identifying possible market abuse and that it expected market participants to be alert to indications that customers are seeking to use regulated firms to facilitate financial crime, including insider dealing. According to the FSA,

[321] FSA *MarketWatch*, Issue 28, June 2008.
[322] FCA *MarketWatch*, Issue 44, August 2013.
[323] Final Notice, Caspar Jonathan William Agnew, dated 3 October 2011 (RDC).
[324] Final Notice, Mark Lockwood, dated 1 September 2009 (RDC).

where there is a clear risk that a trade is in breach of relevant legal or regulatory requirements, a market participant should refuse to execute the trade and where it is not apparent to a broker whether or not the trade is in breach or the suspicion only becomes apparent once a trade has been executed, the trader should report the trade internally in order to facilitate the appropriate filing of a STR.

Protected disclosures

FSMA contains an interpretative provision[325] that shields persons who have made 'protected disclosures' from breaching any market abuse provision concerning the disclosure of information. A disclosure of information must satisfy three conditions in order to be protected in this manner: **9.254**

(i) the information must cause the person making the disclosure to know, suspect, or have reasonable grounds for suspecting that another person has engaged in market abuse;
(ii) the information came to the person making the disclosure in the course of his profession, trade, business, or employment; and
(iii) the disclosure is made to the FCA as soon as is practicable after the information comes to the attention of that person.

The condition in (iii) will also be satisfied where an employee makes a disclosure to the nominated officer of his employer for receiving such disclosures. The practical impact of this provision is that where a person has made a disclosure either to the FCA or to his employer's nominated officer to report his suspicions that another person has engaged in market abuse, the person making the disclosure will not himself have committed market abuse, and so this provision is effectively a defence to market abuse.

Interrelation with reports to SOCA

As noted at paragraph 9.246, the system of suspicious transaction reporting introduced by MAD is in addition to, and to a degree overlaps with, the PoCA reporting requirements. By way of illustration, insider dealing could constitute both a criminal offence under CJA insider dealing,[326] as well as being market abuse. Similarly, certain misleading statements and impressions could constitute a criminal offence under sections 89 and 90 FS Act 2012,[327] whilst at the same time constituting an offence under the market abuse regime. In circumstances involving both a suspicion of market abuse and a suspicion of the laundering of the proceeds of insider dealing, two reports would be required, one to the Serious Organised Crime Agency ('SOCA') and one to the FCA.[328] **9.255**

Other than the reporting requirement itself, there are important differences between the two reporting regimes. Under the market abuse regime there is no process for obtaining clearance for participating in market abuse, and the restriction on tipping off simply requires that the fact that a report has been made should not be revealed to any person (particularly not the person that is the subject of the report or related persons).[329] Under PoCA, a person asked to participate in what is suspected to be money laundering, is required to make a disclosure,[330] **9.256**

325 FSMA, s 131A.
326 The CJA insider dealing offence is discussed further in Chapter 10.
327 The offences under ss 89 and 90 FS Act 2012 are discussed further in Chapter 10.
328 FSA *Market Watch*, Issue 12 (special edition) June 2005.
329 SUP 15.10.9R.
330 PoCA, s 330.

can proceed with the transaction only with consent (which is deemed given by SOCA after certain statutory conditions are met if not express)[331] and is under a requirement not to tip off the clients in such a way as might prejudice an investigation.[332] The FSA also clarified that the market abuse reporting requirement applies to actual transactions, not orders to trade, although it has also said that if any firm voluntarily wishes to bring a suspicious order to the regulator's attention, it is welcome to do so.[333]

Sanctions and enforcement policy—decision to enforce sanctions under the market abuse regime rather than prosecute a criminal offence

9.257 As will be apparent from the preceding sections, in certain situations, suspicious market misconduct may in principle constitute both market abuse and a breach of one of the criminal law offences (for example, misleading statements or impressions, or insider dealing).[334] In the Enforcement Guide ('EG'), the FCA has issued guidelines on the factors that it will take into account in such situations when deciding whether to pursue a criminal prosecution rather than impose a sanction for market abuse.[335] These include the seriousness of the misconduct; whether there are victims who have suffered loss; the effect of the misconduct on the market; whether the person suspected of misconduct has been cooperative; and whether the misconduct involves dishonesty or an abuse of a position of authority or trust.[336] The FSA has commented that in the past, it has focused on the civil route, but now believes that the effective use of both the civil and criminal routes is critical to achieving its aims. According to the FSA[337]

> the civil route will continue to be used, [but] we are now, in recognition of the significant deterrent effect of custodial sentences, making more use of the criminal options available to us in appropriate... cases. We have also made it clear that we will be imposing increased financial penalties in cases we pursue through the civil route.

This was reinforced in a speech by Philip Robinson, the FSA's then Director of Financial Crime, at the end of 2008:

> We've made a conscious decision that if people have to go to prison for us to achieve our objective of cleaning up the market—that's what will have to happen.

9.258 The large increase in the number of prosecutions since then, as discussed further in Chapter 10, shows that the criminal route is increasingly preferred although a couple of factors in the cases have apparently tended the FSA towards leniency via the civil route. The first is cooperation. When the FSA prosecuted Malcolm Calvert for insider dealing in 2010, it took only civil action against Bertie Hatcher,[338] in return for his evidence in the prosecution. The fine levied on Mr Hatcher amounted only to his profit of the market abuse, after tax. This cooperation now has a basis in the rules whereby the FCA will take into consideration

331 ibid, s 335.
332 ibid, s 333.
333 FSA *Market Watch*, Issue 12 (special edition), June 2005.
334 And indeed could potentially fall within certain other regulatory enforcement powers in certain circumstances—see discussion in Chapter 10.
335 EG, paras 12.8(1)–(13).
336 In the conviction of Asif Butt for insider dealing (see Chapter 10, para 10.39) Judge Elwen's sentencing drew attention to a breach of trust that was 'breathtaking in audacity'—indicating a criminal prosecution was appropriate under these guidelines.
337 *Market Watch* No 26 (April 2008).
338 FSA Final Notice to Bertie Hatcher, dated 12 May 2008 (SDM).

cooperation in the prosecution of a coconspirator as one of the factors in its decision of whether to prosecute (see paragraph 12.8(12A) of the Enforcement Guide).

Another factor tending towards leniency has been shown to be a willingness to self report to the FCA in the first place. The case against the three senior executives of Turkish oil company, Genel Enerji AS, in 2010 is the clearest instance of this (see paragraph 9.148). The final notices for all three state that the FSA was contacted by the executives' solicitors with details of their share transactions, that they admitted their conduct and that otherwise the FSA might have prosecuted them. **9.259**

FCA's power to impose penalties in cases of market abuse

According to section 123(1) of FSMA, if the FCA is satisfied that a person has either engaged in market abuse, or by taking or refraining from taking any action, has required or encouraged another person or persons to engage in behaviour which, if engaged in by the first person would amount to market abuse (generally referred to as 'requiring and encouraging'), it may impose one of two sanctions on the first person: either punish the first person with a penalty of such an amount that it considers appropriate,[339] or alternatively, it may publish a statement to the effect that that person has engaged in market abuse.[340] However, the FCA may not impose such a sanction on a person if there are 'reasonable grounds' for it to be satisfied that the person in question believed his behaviour did not fall within the scope of requiring and encouraging, or that he took all reasonable precautions and exercised all due diligence to avoid behaving in a way which fell within that scope.[341] **9.260**

The FCA has provided guidance as to when it will publicise a breach rather than imposing a penalty. Broadly speaking, a penalty is seen as a more serious sanction and so a financial penalty will be favoured in cases where, for example, the firm has profited from its breach, the misconduct is of a serious nature, or the firm has a poor disciplinary record.[342] Where the FCA decides to impose a penalty, the level of that penalty is determined by the FCA on the basis of a number of factors set out in the FCA's policy with respect to penalties.[343] **9.261**

In March 2010, the FSA amended the rules in the Decision Procedure and Penalties chapter of the FSA Handbook to introduce a formula for calculating the financial penalty to be paid to the FSA in enforcement cases. The aims behind this were to promote transparency and consistency in penalty setting and to increase the levels of penalties. The formula for calculating penalties consists of a five step approach, having as its objectives disgorgement, discipline and credible deterrence. It is pursuit of this last aim that led the FSA (now FCA) to adopt an approach which it has calculated will lead to a tripling of the current level of fines. **9.262**

In summary, the five steps are as follows: **9.263**

- **Disgorgement**: The FSA will seek to deprive the firm or individual of the financial benefit derived directly from the breach by calculating the profit gained or the loss avoided.
- **The seriousness of the breach**: The FCA will then calculate a (punitive) figure that reflects the nature, impact and seriousness of the breach. For firms, this will be up to 20 per cent

[339] FSMA, s 123(1).
[340] ibid, s 123(3).
[341] ibid, s 123(2). See also discussion at para 9.84.
[342] DEPP 6.4.2G.
[343] The FCA is required by FSMA, s 124 to issue a statement of its policy with respect to the imposition of penalties for market abuse and the amount of those penalties. See generally Chapter 6.

of the firm's relevant revenue over the period of the breach and from the product or business area to which the breach relates. For individuals (other than in market abuse cases), this will be up to 40 per cent of the individual's relevant income, which will be the gross amount of all benefits received by that individual from the employment in connection with which the breach occurred.

- **Aggravating and mitigating factors:** The FCA can then make an adjustment (up or down) to the figure arrived at in Step 2 to reflect any mitigating or aggravating factors.
- **Adjustment for deterrence:** The FCA can increase the figure arrived at under Step 3 if it considers it too low to have a credible deterrent effect.
- **Settlement discount:** Finally, the FCA will apply any discount for settlement in accordance with the current scheme.

9.264 Earlier consultation also proposed setting a minimum level of £100,000 for market abuse fines. However, following industry comments the FSA amended this to apply only to market abuse cases which the FSA considers to be serious (as described in the Policy Statement issued by the FSA after the consultation). Market abuse committed deliberately should usually be expected to be assessed as serious.

9.265 The FSA has stated that it has adopted the new approach in spite of industry opposition. The main criticism was that the proposed five-step process would not achieve the objectives of transparency and consistency as they allowed the FSA too much discretion in too many of the stages. The FSA's response to this was that this discretion was appropriate due to the scope of cases it deals with. It felt that the new formula would be an improvement on the previous approach as it would make penalty setting more transparent and easier to predict. Most importantly it will ensure that the penalties imposed are 'fair, proportionate and appropriate'. Other industry criticism centred around the potentially dramatic increase in the levels of penalties, especially for larger firms. It was felt that this would damage firms' current open and cooperative approach to the FSA, and deter individuals from becoming approved persons. It was also felt that the higher penalties would mean an increase in challenges to FSA decisions. The FSA responded at the time that it believed firms were now accustomed to its more intrusive supervisory approach and higher penalties were unlikely to damage the relationship. The FSA has said that it had accounted for an increase in challenges to its decisions, but felt that any impact on resources would be outweighed by the savings made through increased compliance.

FCA's power to apply for restitution orders as a sanction for market abuse

9.266 In addition to the power to impose penalties for market abuse under section 123, the FCA may apply to the court for a restitution order (in cases of market abuse (or requiring and encouraging) where either profits accrued to a person as a result of the abuse, or one or more persons suffered loss or have been adversely affected as a result of the abuse).[344] The amount of the

[344] It is noted that the powers in ss 381 and 383 to apply to court for an injunction or restitution order in cases of market abuse sit alongside the FCA's power to apply to court for an injunction or restitution order where a person has breached a 'relevant requirement' under FSMA (ss 380 and 382). It must be considered whether the powers in ss 380 and 381 (injunctions) and ss 382 and 383 are mutually exclusive. The answer to this will turn on the meaning of the phrase 'relevant requirement'. This is defined as a requirement which is imposed by or under FSMA or a requirement imposed by another Act the contravention of which would constitute a criminal offence mentioned in s 402(1) (s 380(6)(a) and s 382(9)(a)) (see further discussion in Chapter 10.55). The better view is therefore that 'requirement' means (a) any positive step that FSMA requires a person to take;

restitution order will be such sum as appears to the court to be just having regard to the profits made or loss or adverse effect suffered (or both).[345] However, according to section 383(3) of FSMA (which mirrors the provisions of section 123(2) of FSMA, discussed at paragraph 9.98) the court should not make a restitution order if it is satisfied that the person believed (on reasonable grounds) that his behaviour did not constitute market abuse or took reasonable precautions to avoid behaving in a way that constitutes market abuse (or requiring and encouraging).[346] In addition to this, the FCA has a separate power to require FCA authorised persons to make restitution in cases of market abuse (or requiring and encouraging)—a power that it is able to exercise without going to court.[347]

Injunctions in the cases of market abuse

The FCA may also apply to the court for an injunction where there is a reasonable likelihood that any person will engage in market abuse or where there is a reasonable likelihood that any market abuse that has occurred will continue or be repeated.[348] The court may also make an order requiring a person who is or has engaged in market abuse to take steps to remedy the abuse (or mitigate its effect), or to restrain a person who may be (or may have been) engaged in market abuse from disposing of or otherwise dealing with any of its assets which the court is satisfied he is reasonably likely to dispose of or otherwise deal with. **9.267**

The *Barnett Alexander* case[349] marked the first use of that power by the FSA. The FSA obtained both a restraining order prohibiting the market abuse (subsequently made permanent) and a freezing injunction against Mr Alexander, freezing £1 million of his assets in May 2010. In addition, section 129 of FSMA provides that where the FSA has applied to the court for an order under sections 381 or 383 of FSMA, it may request the court to order the person concerned to pay a penalty to the FCA. In other words, the FCA can ask the court to set the penalty for market abuse rather than the FSA's own Regulatory Decisions Committee. That is what occurred in this case. The court ordered Mr Alexander to pay £700,000 to the FSA by way of penalty and £322,818 by way of restitution. **9.268**

Interrelation between different enforcement powers

As discussed at paragraph 9.222, the FCA may also take action against authorised persons for breach of rules or principles for business under its general enforcement powers, as well as taking action against individuals under the approved persons regime. The FCA's general **9.269**

or (b) any prohibition the contravention of which leads to criminal prosecution for an offence mentioned in s 402(1) (in the sense that when one is prohibited from doing something there is a requirement not to do it). The requirement not to commit market abuse is a requirement, but it is not a requirement the contravention of which leads to criminal prosecution. Thus, a breach of the market abuse provisions would not be a breach of a relevant requirement, and so the injunction or restitution order in ss 380 and 382 would not be available—only the alternatives in ss 381 and 383 would be. The existence of the two sets of parallel provisions would seem to support this approach. For further discussion, see E Lomnicka, *The Financial Services and Markets Act : An Annotated Guide* (Sweet & Maxwell 2002) at para 1-009.

345 FSMA, s 383(4)–(5).

346 ibid, s 383(3).

347 ibid, s 384(5).

348 ibid, s 381.

349 FSA Final Notice to Barnett Michael Alexander, dated 14 June 2011 (SDM). Mr Alexander was a self-employed trader dealing in shares, contacts for differences (CFDs) and spread bets from his home address. He was found by the FSA (and the court) to have implemented an abusive scheme to influence the price of CFDs and spread bets offered by retail providers of those products in his favour.

enforcement powers also include prohibition orders, frequently used in market abuse cases,[350] as well as enforcement powers in relation to the Listing Rules.

Misleading announcement by issuers

9.270 A number of cases, all of which broadly concern 'misleading announcements' by listed issuers,[351] illustrate the different approaches that the FCA may take with regard to enforcement action. At one end of the scale is the *AIT* decision,[352] in which two directors of AIT were found guilty of the criminal offence of what was then under section 397(1)(c) of FSMA of recklessly making false or misleading statements relating to a profit forecast, which relied on the existence of non-existent lucrative contracts.[353] In the Final Notice against Shell,[354] on the other hand, the FSA concluded that Shell was guilty of civil market abuse through the dissemination of false or misleading information concerning announcements of its levels of hydrocarbon reserves. By contrast, cases of misleading announcements have been pursued as breaches of Listing Rule Requirements—see, for example, the *SFI* decision[355] where the FSA censured an issuer for breach of the rules relating to the accuracy of information announced to the market. The *Woolworths* decision[356] dealt with the position where information which the RDC decided should have been announced was not in fact announced. In that decision, the FSA fined Woolworths £350,000 for breaches of Disclosure Rule 2.2.1 and Listing Principle 4 (see also footnote 22).

Enforcement policy

Approach

9.271 As to the FCA's overall approach to enforcement, Margaret Cole, as the then new director of FSA enforcement, adopted the theme of 'Bold and Resolute' for FSA enforcement in 2006. The theme has evolved into the current theme of 'Credible Deterrence'. By 'Credible Deterrence', the FSA means 'using enforcement strategically as a tool to change behaviour in the industry' so that wrongdoers 'realise that they face a real and tangible risk of being held to account and expect a significant penalty'.[357] In addressing the aim of the FSA, Margaret Cole commented as follows:

> I should make clear that our aim is to clean up the market, to change behaviour by making best use of all the powers—criminal, civil and administrative—that are available to us. If people have to go to prison for us to achieve that aim then that's what we are prepared to do. But sending people to prison isn't the aim in itself. [...] we intend to be bolder and more resolute about proceeding with market abuse and insider dealing cases so that we can actually bring about a change in the culture in the City. We've got to get all the market players to take this subject seriously.[358]

---

350 For further discussion of the FCA's general enforcement powers, see Chapter 6.
351 Note also the liability regime under s 90A, FSMA.
352 *R v Bailey and Rigby* [2005] EWCA Crim 3487.
353 As discussed further at Chapter 10, para 10.66.
354 FSA Final Notice to Shell Transport and Trading Company plc and The Royal Dutch Petroleum Company NV dated 24 August 2004, as discussed at para 9.222. Note that the Final Notice also acknowledges that two Shell entities were in breach of the listing rules (they failed to take all reasonable care to ensure that announcements were not misleading, false, or deceptive and did not omit anything likely to affect the import of that information—para 70 of the Final Notice). However, the FSA chose not to penalise separately for this contravention on the basis that it was based on substantially the same facts as the market abuse findings.
355 FSA Final Notice to SFI Group plc, dated 11 December 2003.
356 FSA Final Notice to Woolworths Group plc, dated 11 June 2008.
357 FSA, 'Enforcement annual performance account 2007/08' at 4.
358 'How Enforcement makes a difference', speech by Margaret Cole, 18 June 2008.

Margaret Cole also highlighted that the FSA's key priorities were: insider dealing by City or business professionals who abuse positions of trust by misusing information legitimately passed to them for them to perform their jobs (for example, lawyers, accountants, brokers, and so on); repeat offenders—where the FSA suspected systematic trading on inside information; and cases where there is significant profit made or loss avoided. Since then, regulatory focus has now diversified from the equities markets, which used to count for a preponderance of cases, with cases now also covering commodities markets, and there have also been cases in relation to the debt markets as well as a recent focus on high frequency trading and manipulative schemes such as 'layering' (see 9.192 *et seq.*). In a speech in June 2013 Tracey McDermott, the FCA's Director of Enforcement, noted the FCA's resolve to continue with the policy of 'credible deterrence' adopted by the FSA: 'Let me reassure you that the FCA is just as committed to achieving credible deterrence as the FSA was. We will continue to build on the enforcement successes we have achieved to date, and will use our expertise to support the FCA in achieving its overall objective of ensuring markets work well'.[359] **9.272**

The FSA also emphasised the importance of systems and controls, and training within firms, and the importance of suspicious transactions reports and in addition has emphasised the need for a collaborative approach involving dialogue on important matters and understanding new risk areas in order to agree priority areas of focus, and encouraging learning from good practice, whether identified by the industry or by FSA thematic work. According to the FSA: **9.273**

> if the senior management of firms meet our expectations and can demonstrate that their firms have good systems and controls and are complying with them, we will not take enforcement action against the firm, but only against the individual, if an individual within a firm commits market abuse.[360]

The FSA's determination can be illustrated by steps it has taken in various enforcement cases. For example, in the *Jabre* reference to the FSMT (*Philippe Jabre v FSA*, FSMT Case 35, 10 July 2006—Decision on Jurisdiction), the FSA, acting through its Enforcement Department, sought to persuade the FSMT that its own decision, reached by its own decision-making body (the RDC), was too lenient and could ask the FSMT to direct a more severe sanction. Similarly, the FSA successfully argued before the Upper Tribunal in the Chaligné, Sejean, and Dallio reference[361] that Mr Sejean's fine should be increased on the basis that, contrary to the RDC's finding, he had committed market abuse on two separate days, rather than just one. In the Hobbs case (see paragraph 9.209), the FCA sought to appeal the fact that, notwithstanding the finding that Mr Hobbs had not committed market abuse, the Upper Tribunal had failed to consider whether Mr Hobbs was not a fit and proper person (and that a prohibition order should accordingly be issued). Note also the differing views taken by the Upper Tribunal to the RDC in the *Geddis* case discussed at paragraph 9.212. **9.274**

Overview of effectiveness of the market abuse regime and trends in enforcement

The FCA has acknowledged that the tougher approach is likely to mean that the sanctioning process is more drawn out as civil cases seeking significant financial penalties or other sanctions against individuals are hard fought, and are rarely concluded in less than two years. The **9.275**

[359] Speech at the Thompson Reuters Compliance & Risk Summit, 18 June 2013
[360] FSA *Market Watch* Issue 26, April 2008.
[361] *Chaligné, Sejean and Dallio v FSA*, Upper Tribunal, Cases FS 2001/0001, 0002, and 0003.

timetable for criminal prosecutions is similar—it is likely to take well over a year from laying an information (or 'charging') to a trial.

9.276 It is also worth looking at other recent, and proposed, developments in the regulator's approach in this context. Behind the scenes it would appear that the FCA has been laying the ground work to obtain a higher conversion rate: the enforcement division has overhauled its staff, and at the same time, has recruited criminal barristers and other lawyers to bolster its criminal firepower; the FCA's enhanced IT system should significantly enhance monitoring of unusual market activity; the FCA has used bolder approaches to capture evidence. For example, despite objections, the FCA has persisted with its policy of cold-calling traders and front desks and asking them to explain what they perceive as unusual trading. To preserve the admissibility of anything said on those calls for use in any future criminal trial, the calls are accompanied by a criminal caution. The FSA has stated that it 'found this to be a useful way of getting an individual's version of events on record at an early stage before recollections have dimmed';[362] suspicious transaction reporting has helped improve the quality of the FCA's information from the market; in 2011, call-taping requirements in the FSA handbook intended to preserve evidence were extended to mobile telephones.[363]

9.277 A perceived major impediment to previous prosecutions has been addressed, by giving accomplices the incentive to give evidence. Following a consultation in May 2008, a new factor was added to those in the Enforcement Guide which the FCA will take into account when deciding whether to commence a prosecution for market misconduct rather than impose a sanction for civil market abuse, which is that where the misconduct in question was carried out by two or more individuals acting together, where one of the individuals provides information and gives full assistance in the FCA's prosecution of the other(s), the FCA will take this cooperation into account when deciding whether to prosecute the assisting individual or bring market abuse proceedings against him.[364] In practical terms, therefore, the FCA may wish to go for alternatives to criminal prosecution for those suspects who are prepared to come forward with evidence against other, more culpable, parties. Depending on the facts, the FCA might also agree a lower penalty, but as a minimum the expectation is that a cooperating witness is to be stripped of the profits of his or her wrongdoing.

9.278 To take an example of how this has operated in practice, when the FSA prosecuted Malcolm Calvert for insider dealing in 2010, it took only civil action against Bertie Hatcher, in return for his evidence in the prosecution and the fine levied amounted only to his profit of the market abuse, after tax (see paragraph 9.260). Since 6 April 2010 the FCA has also had powers under sections 71 to 74 Serious Organised Crime and Police Act 2005 to give a cooperating offender immunity from prosecution or an undertaking that certain information will not be used against him in any criminal proceedings. The FCA can also enter into an agreement with a cooperating offender to receive a reduction in sentence provided he enters into a guilty plea.

Enforcement of market abuse actions

9.279 Overview of effectiveness to date. As mentioned in paragraph 9.02 earlier, the market abuse regime was introduced as a result of perceived failures in obtaining prosecutions under the

[362] FSA *Market Watch*, Issue 26, April 2008.

[363] FSA publishes new rules on telephone recording, FSA/PN/017/2008, 3 March 2008; see <http://www.fsa.gov.uk/pages/Library/Communication/PR/2008/017.shtml>.

[364] Enforcement Guide, para 12.8(12A).

criminal regime. It is therefore interesting to consider whether the new regime has indeed achieved this objective, what lessons have been learned in terms of enforcement, and what can be expected going forward.

Looking at this in the round, in the 12-year period from 1986 to 1997, there had been only 30 criminal market abuse prosecutions—and only 13, just over one a year, were successful. By way of contrast, in the four or so years following the introduction of the civil provisions (1 December 2001), the FSA successfully concluded 27 disciplinary actions for market abuse/misconduct and imposed total financial sanctions of £40 million. This figure probably put the position at its highest, including listing rule sanctions, findings under Principle 5 of the FSA Principles, and findings against both firms and individuals. For 'pure' market abuse, the figure is more like 15 actions. **9.280**

Between 2005 and 2007 the FSA started to experience difficulties in enforcement under the new civil regime, mainly because of the FSMT's expectations in terms of cogency of evidence as discussed in paragraph 9.30 earlier.[365] At the same time, the FSA's own processes and procedures were subject to criticism by the FSMT in *Legal and General*, leading to a subsequent review and overhaul. **9.281**

In terms of volume, fines and censures from publicly available decision notices have since risen from a fairly low level between 2007 and 2008 (none in 2007 and six in each of 2007/8), to 18 in 2010, and 13 in 2012, with eight in the intervening year (2011). The penalties imposed in 2011, however, at £18,381,525, exceeded those in 2010 and 2012 (at £9,416,000 and £ 10,658,795 respectively). **9.282**

Most notably, there has been a marked increase since 2009 in the use of criminal cases, with 23 convictions, with sentences ranging from 8 months to 48 months. Operation Tabernula, involving dawn raids on various City institutions and residential addresses in March 2010 has been described as the 'biggest ever' insider dealing investigation in the UK. These are discussed further in Chapter 10. **9.283**

European Developments—The Proposed Market Abuse Regulation and Criminal Sanctions Directive

Overview of work undertaken by the EU institutions

Following preparatory work, notably its Call for Evidence and public consultation (published on 20 April 2009 and 28 June 2010 respectively), on 20 October 2011, the European Commission (the Commission) adopted legislative proposals for the CSD (a proposed directive on criminal sanctions for the market abuse offences of insider dealing and market manipulation) and the proposed Market Abuse Regulation (relating to insider dealing and market manipulation). In July 2012, the Commission adopted amendments to each of the **9.284**

[365] See, eg, the *Davidson and Tatham* case and the *Baldwin* case. In the latter case, the FSMT overturned a decision by the FSA to fine Baldwin and WRT, an investment vehicle controlled by Baldwin, for market abuse. The FSA had imposed fines on Baldwin (of £25,000) and WRT (of £24,000) in relation to purchases of shares, following the alleged passing of inside information from the chief executive officer of the company in question to Baldwin by telephone conversation. The FSMT found in favour of Baldwin and WRT, concluding it found no evidence that the relevant telephone call had taken place. The FSMT was satisfied that WRT's trading had been innocently conducted.

proposals to take into account additional measures considered necessary as a result of the LIBOR and EURIBOR scandal.[366]

9.285 Compared with the original MAD, the Commission's proposed CSD and Market Abuse Regulation together provide for a more extensive market abuse regime which would:

- increase the scope of the existing MAD regime by including OTC traded financial instruments which might have an effect on the underlying market;
- create the new offence of 'attempted market manipulation' (to cover the situation where an activity which is intended to manipulate the market is commenced but not completed, for example, because the instruction to trade is not acted on);
- enhance and harmonise the enforcement and sanction powers of competent authorities to tackle and investigate market abuse;
- enhance the level of coordination among EU regulators, with the objective of creating a 'single rulebook'; and
- more closely align the market abuse regime's application to commodities markets and commodity derivatives trading with that of securities markets.

Status

9.286 In the case of the Market Abuse Regulation, political agreement on wording for a level 1 text was reached between the European Parliament (the 'EP'), the Council of the European Union (the 'Council') and the Commission on 20 June 2013.[367] This text, however, is provisional upon, and will be subject to technical alignment in light of, the final version of the proposed recast Markets in Financial Instruments Directive ('MiFID') and the proposed Markets in Financial Instruments Regulation ('MiFIR')[368]—in particular, a number of definitions which appear in both the Market Abuse Regulation and the recast MiFID and MiFIR remain to be finalised by the European institutions. At the time of writing, the EP, Council, and Commission were commencing a series of negotiations (or 'trialogues') to seek agreement on a text for the recast MiFID and MiFIR. Consequently, it appears unlikely that the Market Abuse Regulation will be formally adopted by the EP until Q4 2013 at the earliest.

9.287 In the case of CSD, rather less progress has been made. The EP and Council have, however, each separately agreed the amendments that they would wish to see made to the Commission's proposal and 'trialogue' negotiations are now underway, involving all three EU institutions. Although only one such meeting was held in the first half of 2013, in due course, it was expected that these negotiations would lead to an agreed final level 1 text. Again, this was to be some degree dependent upon the agreed texts which emerge from negotiations on the recast MiFID and MiFIR, since, as with the Market Abuse Regulation, certain definitions are common to both legislative initiatives.

9.288 By virtue of Protocol 21 of the Treaty on the Functioning of the European Union, the UK is not automatically bound by EU legislative proposals in respect of matters relating to freedom, security, and justice but may, instead, decide whether or not to opt in to any such measures on a case-by-case basis. CSD falls within this category of legislative proposal.

[366] See Chapter 1, paras 1.42 and 1.43.

[367] The agreed Market abuse Regulation text can be found at: <http://register.consilium.europa.eu/pdf/en/13/st11/st11384.en13.pdf>.

[368] See Chapter 3.

On 2 February 2012, the UK Government announced (in a ministerial statement) that it had decided not to opt in to the proposed CSD now, particularly given that the UK already covers all of the offences in its criminal law. The UK Government will, however, participate fully in negotiations with a view to opting in later once the proposals are better progressed.

The EP's plenary meeting on 9 December 2013 was been scheduled as the date for the first reading, at which the level 1 text of CSD would be adopted. It should be noted, however, that this date is no more than indicative and the vote may well be postponed (or - though this is less probable - brought forward). **9.289**

Once the framework level 1 texts for the Market Abuse Regulation and CSD are formally adopted and published in the Official Journal of the European Union (the OJ), attention will turn to adding further detail by way of level 2 and level 3 measures. These will be developed by the Commission with the assistance of ESMA and will comprise a variety of delegated acts and technical standards (both regulatory and implementing), including, for example, the power to: **9.290**

- adopt measures which specify the procedures by which actual or potential breaches of the Market Abuse Regulation may be reported to regulators;
- set the criteria, procedure and requirements for establishing accepted market practices;
- specify the circumstances under which an issuer may permit trading during a closed period;
- specify the form of notification to a regulator of each financial instrument the first time that is admitted to trading, has been traded or for which there has been a request for admission to trading on a trading venue;
- specify the conditions to be met by buy-back programmes and stabilisation measures; and
- develop guidelines on the legitimate interests of the issuer and on situations where omitted disclosure is likely to mislead the public.

Timing

The Market Abuse Regulation will apply 24 months after it formally enters into force (that is to say 20 days after its publication in the OJ)—however, the powers conferred upon the Commission and ESMA to develop draft technical standards will have immediate effect upon entry into force. **9.291**

The Market Abuse Regulation will have direct application and effect in all Member States. As a directive, on the other hand, Member States will be required to transpose the CSD into national law within 24 months after its entry into force The date of entry into force will be twenty days after publication in the OJ. Implementation of the CSD will be contemporaneous with application of the Market Abuse Regulation. Given the level 2 and level 3 measures to be developed, as referred to earlier, it is unlikely that the provisions of either CSD or the Market Abuse Regulation will be implemented before 2016. **9.292**

Territorial scope

The provisions of the Market Abuse Regulation are intended to have extra territorial effect, in that actions prohibited under the Market Abuse Regulation will be expressed to be caught whether they are carried on within or outside the EU. **9.293**

Scope of markets covered

9.294 When the Market Abuse Regulation becomes effective, the EU-wide market abuse regime will cover not just financial instruments admitted to trading on EU-regulated markets as is currently the case, but also to those admitted to trading on an EU-regulated 'multilateral trading facility' ('MTF') (as defined in MiFID) and EU-regulated 'organised trading facility' ('OTF') (provided OTFs are introduced as part of the revision of MiFID).

Scope of instruments covered

9.295 Under CSD and the Market Abuse Regulation, the instruments to be covered under the new regime will be extended to align with the definition of financial instruments in MiFID.

9.296 As before, related instruments are included in relation to the MAD information offences, being those whose price or value depends on a financial instrument that is admitted to trading on a relevant market. The Market Abuse Regulation specifically includes guidance that such instruments would include credit default swaps and contracts for differences.

9.297 In the UK, the FCA and its predecessor, the FSA, have already given their view that credit default swaps are within scope as a related investment.

Definition of inside information

9.298 Broadly, the current definitions within MAD are retained in the new regime. In respect of information relating to financial instruments or issuers of such instruments, the three step test under MAD states that the information in question must be (in summary):

- information of a precise nature relating, directly or indirectly, to one or more issuers of financial instruments or to one or more financial instruments
- information which has not been made public, and
- information which, if public, would be likely to have a significant effect on price.

9.299 In respect of commodity derivatives, on the other hand, MAD defines inside information as being information of a precise nature which has not been made public, relating, directly or indirectly to one or more such derivatives and which users of markets on which such derivatives are traded would expect to receive in accordance with accepted market practices on those markets. Users are deemed to expect to receive information which is routinely made available to them, or required to be disclosed in accordance with legal or regulatory provisions, market rules, contracts, or customs on the relevant underlying commodity market or commodity derivatives market.

9.300 There is currently no requirement that information must have a significant effect on relevant prices. This will change under the Market Abuse Regulation since, as well as extending the definition to related spot commodity contracts, as a 'significant effect' test will be introduced, although this is followed by a statement that this applies to various information which is required to be disclosed (or reasonably expected to be disclosed) in accordance with legal or regulatory provisions, market rules, contracts, practices, or customs on the relevant underlying commodity derivatives or spot market.

9.301 The single biggest change proposed in the Commission's proposal, however, was the extension of the definition of inside information (via a 'sweep up' provision) to include information 'relating to one or more issuers of financial instruments or to one or more financial instruments, which is not generally available to the public, but which, if it were available to a reasonable investor, who regularly deals on the market and in the financial instrument or related spot commodity contract concerned, would be regarded by that person as relevant when deciding the terms on which transactions in the financial instrument or a related spot commodity contract should be effected'.

This was an attempt to incorporate within the EU-wide regime an aspect of the UK's domestic regime, which includes the concept of 'relevant information not generally available' ('RINGA'), and its inclusion in the Market Abuse Regulation was lobbied for by the UK regulators who regarded the existing MAD definition of 'inside information' as being too narrow. Crucially, however, the UK regime incorporates a further limb which requires the use of the information to be regarded by the regular user as 'a failure on the part of the person concerned to observe the standard of behaviour reasonably expected of a person in his position in relation to the market'. **9.302**

Problematically, the Commission's proposal contained no such qualifier and, consequently, would have left as potential inside information any non-public information which a reasonable investor would be likely to regard as relevant, without any materiality qualifier. **9.303**

After much lobbying from industry, the EP and Council agreed, in the final level 1 text, to delete this new element (proposed Article 6(1)(e)) in its entirety, while amending other aspects of the definition of inside information to incorporate a form of RINGA test which is generally regarded as being workable in practice. **9.304**

Dealing or behaviour

Previously, in relation to insider dealing, and market manipulation, the offence under MAD required a dealing to take place. Borrowing again from the UK's regime, the Market Abuse Regulation extends this, in the case of the insider dealing offences to include use of the information to cancel or amend an order already placed before a person came into possession of the information. **9.305**

Similarly, the market manipulation offence provided for by Article 8 of the Market Abuse Regulation has been extended (beyond what was transposed into the section 118 regime or as effecting transactions or orders) to entering into transactions; placing an order to trade 'or any other behaviour' (the concept of behaviour already being used in the context of the UK legacy offences). Attempting to manipulate the market will now fall within the Market Abuse Regulation. **9.306**

Market manipulation

The scope of the market manipulation offence under MAD is retained within the new regime but with further extensions in relation to the commodities markets, such that related spot commodity contracts are now within its scope. **9.307**

Also noteworthy, continuing a theme focused on in the recast MiFID, is guidance given in the Market Abuse Regulation on the potential for market manipulation in the context of 'algorithmic trading', using the definition to be contained in the recast MiFID, where such trading is for the purpose of disrupting the functioning of a trading venue or creating a false or misleading impression as to supply or demand. While this guidance is topical, and reflects concerns on the part of the EP, in particular, over high-frequency trading generally, it does not seem to create any new scope offence for algorithmic traders per se. There was, however, concerted resistance on the part of industry to the specific references within the Market **9.308**

Abuse Regulation to algorithmic and high-frequency trading as strategies likely (in the eyes of some) to constitute market manipulation on the basis—many market practitioners were concerned that such references would tend to stigmatise entirely legitimate trades which happened to be executed through the use of an algorithm.

9.309 A further alignment with the recast MiFID is the imposition of additional obligations on market operators to have arrangements and procedures aimed at preventing and detecting market abuse. Details as to what such arrangements should comprise will be set out in technical standards in due course.

Issuer announcements

9.310 The other side of the insider dealing 'coin' is the timely release of accurate information by issuers. An issuer is required to announce inside information as soon as possible, with the ability to delay if its legitimate interests would be prejudiced. A common complaint is that issuers do not announce information in a timely manner and interpretation has been inconsistent across Member States as to what are legitimate grounds for an issuer to delay announcement. While the FCA and its predecessor, the FSA, have traditionally been active in requiring issuers to announce inside information in a timely manner, there remained a perception that other regulators had, perhaps, been less focused on this issue.

9.311 The Market Abuse Regulation aims to introduce more rigour. An issuer will have to inform its competent authority that it intends to delay disclosure of inside information for legitimate reasons and provide evidence that the conditions permitting such delay are met, including that the information is of systemic importance and delay is in the public interest. ESMA has been invited to develop technical standards to determine the means for delaying the public disclosure of inside information.

Safe harbours and clarifications

9.312 The insider dealing offence requires not just dealing in possession of inside information, but also 'use' of that information. There has been increased uncertainty since the ECJ *Spector Photo* case[369] as to when a person would be treated as having 'used' information in his dealing. The Spector Photo case creates a rebuttable presumption that a person in possession of inside information would be deemed to be using the information. Spector Photo focuses on whether a person is seeking to profit from the use of the information having regard to the spirit and purpose of the market abuse rules, which makes for some lack of clarity. Despite requests during the MAD review process to clarify this issue, the Commission did not include any such clarification in its proposed Market Abuse Regulation. However, there was limited success following lobbying on this point and the final agreed level 1 text contains a number of helpful provisions, albeit contained in the recitals rather than in the operative articles within the text, which follow Spector Photo in creating a rebuttable presumption that the person possessing inside information used it when entering into a subsequent transaction.

9.313 Another notable omission within the Commission's proposal which was ameliorated to a greater or lesser extent in the trilogue negotiations, was that MAD contained, in its recitals, certain safe harbours including for market makers, for use of inside information acquired in

369 (C-45/08) *Spector Photo Group NV, Chris Van Raemdonck v Commissie voor het Bank-, Financie-en Assurantiewezen* (*CBFA*).

the context of a takeover bid, and for dealing in the knowledge of one's own prior decision to deal. A number of these safe harbours (including for market makers; for research and estimates developed from publicly available information; for legitimate interests; and for legitimate behaviours) were eventually included within the final text and provide some form of comfort to market practitioners, which is to be welcomed since such aspects are commonly regarded as being essential components in making the market abuse regime workable in practice (particularly given the broadening of the scope of inside information as it applies to commodity derivatives). It should be noted that, domestically, the FCA has embedded such safe harbours into the UK regime, including clarifying that knowledge of future activist intentions is included within the 'knowledge of own intention to deal' safe harbour.

A number of potentially problematic provisions, which had been contained in the EP's amendments to the Commission's proposal at the outset of trialogues, did not find their way into the final text—these included an article dealing with abusive order entry and also a requirement (which many practitioners were concerned would be impossible to comply with in practical terms) that a firm must notify its national competent authority of any 'material' change to an algorithm which it uses. **9.314**

Although the level 1 text of the Market Abuse Regulation which emerged from the trialogues was, in many regards, a significant improvement over the Commission's original proposal, the resultant text still contains several areas which may turn out to be problematic in practice. One of these is the onerous obligation that a market participant which has disclosed information to a person in the course of a market sounding must subsequently inform that person when the information has ceased to be inside information. **9.315**

Criminal offences

The proposed CSD which accompanies the Market Abuse Regulation is designed to ensure a more level playing field in terms of sanctions across Member States. This follows a 2007 CESR review,[370] cited in the 2010 Commission consultation paper on the review of MAD,[371] which found a divergence in sanctions regimes across the EU. It is proposed that, where any market abuse offences are committed with intent, then Member States should ensure that this constitutes a criminal offence. **9.316**

Complete harmonisation will not occur, however, because it is open to Member States to set their own penalties, including whether the penalty is a fine or custodial sentence. **9.317**

The UK already has a wide range of criminal penalties in its armoury, both for insider dealing and market manipulation. It would be required, however, to extend criminal penalties to cover the proposed use of RINGA offence described earlier, currently only a civil offence in the UK regime. **9.318**

One new extension would be the proposal that all criminal offences of market misconduct could be committed by a non-natural person. Currently the UK insider dealing regime is limited to crimes committed by criminal individuals (although non-natural persons can commit other market manipulation offences). The CSD proposes that, where the offence **9.319**

[370] CESR 'Report on Administrative Measures and Sanctions available in Member States under the MAD', 22 November 2007.

[371] European Commission, 'Public Consultation on a Revision of the Market Abuse Directive (MAD)', 25 June 2010, 10.

has been committed by a person with a leading position in the organisation for its benefit, the organisation itself should also face criminal liability. This is similar to existing UK law on corporate liability for criminal offences in other areas.

9.320 The proposed CSD would require the Commission to report after four years on the application of the CSD, in particular looking at whether any common minimum rules should be introduced on types and levels of criminal sanctions. Presumably if it felt that the disparity of approaches across Member States meant that the sanctions were not having a sufficient deterrent effect.

Electricity and gas markets

9.321 As a final note, following consultation as to the most appropriate way to address market abuse and transparency issues, a European regulation, the Regulation on Wholesale Energy Market Integrity, and Transparency, or 'REMIT', was adopted on 25 October 2011 to deal with the specifics of the wholesale electricity and gas markets.

10

INSIDER DEALING AND MISLEADING STATEMENTS AND IMPRESSIONS

Introduction

Having considered in Chapter 9 the civil market abuse offences brought in under FSMA,[1] and revised following the implementation of MAD,[2] this chapter will consider the criminal offences of insider dealing under the Criminal Justice Act 1993 ('CJA') and misleading statements and impressions under Part 7 of the Financial Services Act 2012 ('FSA 2012'), as well as considering briefly regulatory requirements relating to market misconduct. It will then outline the roles of the various regulatory and prosecuting authorities with power to take action in respect of market misconduct and how these bodies interact.[3] With effect from 1 April 2013 the Financial Conduct Authority ('FCA') took over responsibility for prosecuting offences under the CJA and FSA 2012 from the previous Financial Services Authority ('FSA'). **10.01**

CJA Insider Dealing

The criminal law—insider dealing

Insider dealing first became a criminal offence in the UK in 1980.[4] Following a revision of the Companies Act in 1985, the statutory basis for the offence was replaced by the Companies Securities (Insider Dealing) Act 1985. The introduction of new legislation in 1993 was prompted by the passage of the EU Directive on Insider Dealing,[5] and the current legislative provisions are contained in Part V of the CJA. **10.02**

Criminal Justice Act 1993, Part V

Section 52 of the CJA lays down the general prohibition of insider dealing, and this can be separated out into three distinct offences, namely the dealing offence,[6] the encouraging **10.03**

[1] The Financial Services and Markets Act 2000 as amended.

[2] Directive 2003/6/EC on insider dealing and market manipulation (market abuse).

[3] This chapter does not deal with other offences, such as common law offences or offences under the Fraud Act 2006.

[4] Companies Act 1980, ss 68–73.

[5] Council Directive EEC/89/592 of 13 November 1989 coordinating regulations on insider dealing (no longer in force).

[6] CJA, s 52(1).

offence,[7] and the disclosure offence.[8] Section 53 sets out a number of general defences as well as providing for a number of special defences,[9] to which section 52 is subject. The remainder of Part V contains relatively lengthy provisions dedicated to the interpretation of the basic offences.

Territorial Scope

10.04 In terms of territorial scope, section 62 requires that there is a link between the activities in question and the UK.[10] Accordingly, an individual will not be guilty of the 'dealing offence' unless he was within the UK when he did any act constituting or forming part of the dealing, or the dealing took place on a market regulated by the UK, or the professional intermediary concerned was within the UK when he did any act constituting or forming part of the dealing. An individual will not be guilty of either the encouraging offence or the disclosure offence unless he was within the UK at the time of the disclosure/encouragement or the recipient of the disclosure/encouragement was within the UK.

The Offences

10.05 The following sections consider each of the three discrete offences established under section 52 of the CJA.

The dealing offence—section 52(1)

10.06 An individual[11] who has 'information as an insider' will be guilty of the dealing offence where he deals in securities that are 'price-affected'[12] in relation to that information, either by acquisition or disposal of those securities on a regulated market, or through reliance on a 'professional intermediary', or by acting himself as an intermediary.[13] To break this offence down into the constituent elements of a criminal offence, the *actus reus* can be identified as dealing in the manner described earlier. The *mens rea* of the offence is that the person dealing as an insider knows that he is in possession of inside information and knows that he has it from an inside source[14]—there is no requirement of intention or recklessness.[15]

---

[7] ibid, s 52(2)(a).
[8] ibid, s 52(2)(b).
[9] ibid, s 52(4) and Sch 1.
[10] For a discussion of the territorial scope of insider dealing under the market abuse regime, see Chapter 9, para 9.79.
[11] It should be noted that the CJA offences relate only to individuals, cf the FSMA market abuse regime which also applies to legal persons.
[12] 'Price affected securities' are those which are affected by price-sensitive information (ie information which would, if it were to be made public, be likely to have a significant effect on the price of securities). For further discussion, see para 10.25.
[13] CJA, s 52(3).
[14] See CJA, s 57(1). See also Johnstone and Jones, *Investigations and Enforcements* (2001): guilt 'will depend on the view held by the person in possession of the information as to its 'insiderness' (para 1.89); and Jain, 'Significance of mens rea in insider trading', (2004) *Comp Law* 25(5), 132–40, at 136: 'if the accused does not have the requisite knowledge that the information is either inside information or that it is from an inside source, even if he deals in securities based on that information, he will not be held guilty of insider trading'.
[15] Traditionally, serious crimes require that the defendant intended to commit the relevant acts or was subjectively reckless as to their commission, although certain other offences require that the defendant 'knowingly'

'Securities'

For the purposes of the CJA, 'securities' means any security which is listed in Schedule 2 of the CJA and which satisfies the conditions laid down by Articles 4 to 8 of the Insider Dealing (Securities and Regulated Markets) Order 1994 ('IDO'). Schedule 2 lists the relevant securities as shares; debt securities; warrants; depositary receipts; options; futures; and contracts for differences ('CFDs'). [16] Articles 4 to 8 of the IDO require that the security (or relevant right subsisting under a warrant, debt security, or depositary receipt) be officially listed in a State within the European Economic Area ('EEA') or be admitted to dealing on, or have its price quoted on or under, the rules of a regulated market. A 'regulated market' for the purposes of the CJA is any market established under the rules of one of the investment exchanges listed in the Schedule to the IDO, and the former OFEX market (now ISDX).[17] The Schedule to the IDO lists a large number of European investment exchanges and also includes NASDAQ,[18] bringing this United States market within the scope of the CJA regime whereas it is not within the scope of the FSMA market abuse regime. **10.07**

'Dealing in securities'

Section 55 states that 'dealing' includes the acquisition or disposal of securities, either as principal or agent,[19] or the direct or indirect procurement[20] of an acquisition or disposal of securities by any other person (who is his agent, nominee, or any other person acting at his direction).[21] It goes on to establish that this includes any agreement to acquire[22] or dispose[23] of a security, or the entering into[24] or conclusion of[25] any contract which itself creates a security. The definition of dealing does not include abstaining from dealing, and therefore where a person decides not to deal on the basis of inside information, where he was previously intending to deal, this will not be caught by the CJA.[26] **10.08**

or 'dishonestly' carried out a particular commission. For example, the 'arrangements' offence under s 328(1) of the Proceeds of Crime Act 2002 ('PoCA 2002') which states that: 'A person commits an offence if he enters into or becomes concerned in an arrangement which he knows or suspects facilitates (by whatever means) the acquisition, retention, use or control of criminal property by or on behalf of another person'. See also, for example, the offence of handling stolen goods under s 22(1) of the Theft Act 1968 which states that: 'A person handles stolen goods if (otherwise than in the course of the stealing) knowing or believing them to be stolen goods he dishonestly receives the goods, or dishonestly undertakes or assists in their retention, removal, disposal or realisation by or for the benefit of another person, or if he arranges to do so'.

16 CJA, Sch 2 para 1 to 9.

17 IDO, art 9. Contrast the definition of regulated market for CJA purposes with the definition under the post-MAD version of FSMA (as discussed at Chapter 9, para 9.76). Under FSMA, 'regulated market' means those listed by EEA regulators in accordance with the Markets in Financial Instruments Directive. The IDO at the time of writing still refers to OFEX, but that has since become ICAP Securities & Derivatives Exchange (ISDX).

18 ibid, art 9 and Sch. See M Blair, G Walker, and S Wiley, *Financial Markets and Exchanges Law* (2nd edn OUP 2012) Chs 1 and 2.

19 CJA, s 55(1)(a).

20 ibid, s 55(1)(b).

21 ibid, s 55(4). This list is not exhaustive as to the circumstances in which one person may be regarded as procuring an acquisition or disposal of securities by another.

22 ibid, s 55(2)(a).

23 ibid, s 55(3)(a).

24 ibid, s 55(2)(b).

25 ibid, s 55(3)(b).

26 E Lomnicka, 'The New Insider Dealing Provisions: Criminal Justice Act 1993', Part V, (1994) *JBL MAR*, 173–88, at 177. For a discussion of the position under the FSMA market abuse regime, see Chapter 9 at para 9.95.

'Professional intermediary'

10.09 The inclusion of the 'professional intermediary' provision within both the dealing offence and the encouraging offence is to ensure that those dealing otherwise than on the market itself are caught by the statutory provisions. A person is acting as a 'professional intermediary' where he carries on a business of acquiring or disposing of securities,[27] or he acts as an intermediary between persons dealing in securities,[28] and he holds himself out to the public or any section of the public as willing to engage in any such business.[29] This business activity must not be merely incidental/occasional.[30] He will also be considered to be a professional intermediary where he is employed by such a person to carry out any such activity.[31]

The encouraging offence—section 52(2)(a)

10.10 An individual who has information as an insider will be guilty of the 'encouraging offence'[32] where he encourages another person to deal in price-affected securities, knowing or having reasonable cause to know that the dealing would take place in the manner described in paragraph 10.06.[33] The *actus reus* of this offence is encouraging another person to deal in price-affected securities in relation to that information. The *mens rea* of this offence is (similarly to the 'dealing' offence) the defendant's knowledge that he has information as an insider, and knowledge or reasonable cause to believe that dealing will take place as just described. It is important to note that the individual will be guilty of the offence whether or not the person encouraged realises that the securities are price-affected securities. It is also immaterial whether or not dealing actually takes place; the mere act of encouragement to deal is sufficient to amount to a criminal offence.

10.11 Although the CJA offences relate to the actions of individuals, the person encouraged does not need to be an individual. Thus where an individual has information as an insider, and encourages a company to deal in price-affected securities in relation to that information, he will be guilty of the offence under section 52(2)(a).[34]

10.12 The CJA does not provide any interpretative guidance as to the meaning of the term 'encourage', and therefore it is left to the courts to decide on the facts of each individual case whether or not an activity amounts to encouraging.[35]

The 'disclosure' offence—section 52(2)(b)

10.13 An individual who has information as an insider will be guilty of the disclosure offence where he discloses that information to another person otherwise than in the proper performance of the functions of his employment, office, or profession.[36] Similarly to the other two insider

---

[27] CJA, s 59(2)(a).
[28] ibid, s 59(2)(b).
[29] ibid, s 59(1)(a).
[30] ibid, s 59(3).
[31] ibid, s 59(1)(b).
[32] ibid, s 52(2)(a).
[33] ibid, s 52(3).
[34] Band, 'Trustees and Insider Dealing: Part I', (2000) *PCB* 5, 293–303, at 301.
[35] Analogous guidance is given in MAR 1.2.23G(2) on the meaning of encouraging in the 'requiring or encouraging' provision under the FSMA market abuse regime: 'a person recommends or advises a friend to engage in behaviour…'. The pre-MAD version of MAR 1.8 provided extensive guidance on the meaning of requiring or encouraging, but that guidance has now been deleted.
[36] CJA, s 52(2)(b).

dealing offences, the elements of the offence can be divided into the *actus reus* of disclosing this information otherwise than in the proper performance of the functions of an insider's employment, office, or profession. The *mens rea* is that the defendant knows that the information in his possession is inside information and that he has it from an inside source.

Having 'Inside Information' as an 'Insider'

For the purposes of the section 52 offences, an individual will only be guilty of insider dealing where he has information as an insider. A person will only be considered to have information as an insider if it is, and he knows that it is, inside information, and he has it, and knows that he has it, from an inside source.[37] It is therefore necessary to explore what is meant by the term 'inside information', and respectively, when a person will be considered to have received this information from an 'inside source'. **10.14**

'Inside information'

Scope

Section 56(1) provides that 'inside information' means information which: **10.15**

(i) relates to particular securities or to a particular issuer, or particular issuers, of securities (and not to securities generally or to issuers of securities generally);
(ii) is specific or precise;
(iii) has not been made public; and
(iv) if it were made public would be likely to have a significant effect on the price[38] of any securities.[39]

The use of the term 'any' securities makes it clear that the disclosure does not need to affect the price of the particular securities about which the information is held—it is enough that the price of some other security is affected.

---

[37] ibid, s 57. This can be distinguished from the civil insider dealing behaviour under FSMA where only one of the five categories of 'insider' requires that that person knows, or could reasonably be expected to know, that information is 'inside information'. According to MAR 1.2.8E(1), one of the 'factors' to be taken into account in considering the question of reasonable expectation of knowledge (and an indication of it) is if a normal and reasonable person in the position of the person who has inside information would know or should have known that the person from whom he received it is an 'insider'. Note that in MAR 1.5.6E(1), for the purposes of market abuse (misuse of information), the extent to which information is reliable, including how near the person providing the information is, or appears to be, to the original source of that information is a 'factor' in determining whether a regular user would regard information as relevant, and are indications that he would.

[38] ibid, s 56(3) states that 'price includes value'.

[39] This test is similar to the definition of inside information (other than for commodity derivatives, and ignoring the elaboration in respect of pending orders) set out in the FSMA regime. That definition applies to information in relation to qualifying investments or related investments which is of a precise nature and which (a) is not generally available; (b) relates, directly or indirectly, to one or more issuers of the qualifying investments or to one or more of the qualifying investments; and (c) would, if generally available, be likely to have a significant effect on the price of the qualifying investments or on the price of related investments. For these purposes, information is precise if it indicates circumstances that exist or may reasonably be expected to come into existence or an event that has occurred (or may reasonably be expected to occur) and is specific enough to enable a conclusion to be drawn as to the possible effect of those circumstances or that event on the price of qualifying investments or related investments. Information would, under the FSMA regime, be likely to have a significant effect on price if and only if it is information of a kind which a reasonable investor would be likely to use as part of the basis of his investment decisions. See discussion in Chapter 9 at para 9.118.

'Particular securities' and 'particular issuers of securities'

10.16 Further guidance is offered by section 60(4) which states that information is to be treated as relating to 'an issuer of securities' not only where it relates to the issuer company itself, but also where it may affect the company's business prospects. For example, an announcement which might affect business prospects within a particular sector would potentially be inside information without relating to any one company. It would also follow that information relating to one specific company which will have a significant effect on the market price of a different company would be caught.

10.17 The information itself can relate to more than one issuer, or the securities of more than one issuer. This again would presuppose that information relating to a particular sector or group of companies could be caught. However, there is a limit on the type of information which will be caught, in that information relating to securities generally, or issuers generally, is excluded from the definition. For example, on this basis, information forecasting a general decline in the stock markets would not be considered to be inside information. It may be difficult in some circumstances to know where the line should be drawn between information which is to be considered general, and that which is specific to particular securities or their issuers, and this needs to be considered on a case-by-case basis.

'Specific' or 'precise'

10.18 The requirement that information be 'specific' or 'precise' would appear intended to prevent generic information or rumour from being caught by the CJA provisions. However, it casts a wider net than was necessitated by the original Directive.[40] The CJA itself provides no interpretative guidance in relation to these terms, although it is possible to gain some insight as to their intended meaning from the parliamentary discussions which took place prior to its enactment. According to the then Economic Secretary and Minister of State at HM Treasury, Mr Anthony Nelson, MP:

> if somebody were to say... during a lunch, 'Our results will be much better than the market expects or knows,' that would not be precise. The person would not have disclosed what the results of the company were to be. However, it would certainly be specific, because he would be saying something about the company's results and making it pretty obvious that the information had not been made public... It would be inside information because it would be specific.[41]

Again, the courts are left to consider whether or not this criterion has been satisfied by making an objective decision based on the evidence in each case. In *R v Cross*[42] it was held that knowledge that there was to be a placing of shares was sufficiently specific, even though the defendant was not aware of the exact details of the placing.[43]

[40] Council Directive 89/592/EEC of 13 November 1989 coordinating regulations on insider dealing (no longer in force), Art 1 provides that information must be of a 'precise' nature.
[41] As cited by A Alcock, 'Insider Dealing—How did we get here', (1994) *Comp Law* 15(3), 67–72, at 70.
[42] (1990) 91 Cr App R 115.
[43] The discussion as to whether information is precise is, however, made clearer in the context of the discussion under the FSMA market abuse regime. According to FSMA, s 118C(5), information is precise if it (a) indicates circumstances that may exist or may reasonably be expected to come into existence or an event that has occurred or may reasonably be expected to occur; and (b) is specific enough to enable a conclusion to be drawn as to the possible effect of those circumstances or that event on the price of qualifying investments or related instruments. There is also further discussion in the FCA Handbook Market Conduct Sourcebook ('MAR') 1.2.10–1.2.16.

'Made public'

10.19 Guidance on determining when information can be regarded as having been 'made public' is outlined in section 58 of the CJA. This gives four non-exhaustive examples of circumstances in which information *will* be regarded as having been made public, and five examples of circumstances in which information *may* be regarded as having been made public. Section 58(2) states that information is made public if:

(i) it is published in accordance with the rules of a regulated market for the purpose of informing investors and their professional advisers;
(ii) it is contained in records which are open to inspection by the public;
(iii) it can be readily acquired by those likely to deal in any securities to which the information relates, or of an issuer to which the information relates; or
(iv) it is derived from information which has been made public.

It would appear, in principle at least, that the use of the term 'published' in section 58(2)(a) may create an opportunity for those in possession of inside information to deal on the basis of that information as soon as the publication is made official, without strictly falling foul of the CJA legislation. Commentators have observed that, as the market effect of the information published will never be immediate, this potentially detracts from the purpose of the legislation in providing a level playing field for investors.[44]

Section 58 goes on to provide that information may be made public even though:

(i) it can be acquired only by persons exercising diligence or expertise;
(ii) it is communicated to a section of the public and not to the public at large;
(iii) it can be acquired only by observation;
(iv) it is communicated only on payment of a fee; or
(v) it is published only outside the UK.

Star analysts

10.20 In Chapter 9, consideration was given to whether a recommendation from a 'star analyst', which could in itself be enough to cause a significant movement in the price of the securities in question, could constitute market abuse under the FSMA market abuse regime. In terms of the CJA, the first question, therefore, and one which prompted debate both during the parliamentary processes that preceded the CJA and in the academic discussion surrounding it, is whether the analyst's report itself could fall within the scope of CJA insider dealing, to which the answer would seem to be 'no'.[45] Assuming the report itself has been derived wholly from publicly

[44] For further commentary on this argument, see M Ashe, 'Insiders at the Starting Blocks', (1993) *Comp Law* 14(8), 153–4. See also the example given in the Treasury consultation on the sunset clauses in the context of the civil market abuse regime Chapter 9, para 9.59 *et seq*., although note that a number of the examples given have been criticised in practice.

[45] This reflects parliamentary discussion at the time. See also Rider, Abrams, and M Ashe, *Guide to Financial Services Regulation*, (3rd edn, Croner CCH Group 1997) at para 609: 'This provision [s 58(2)(d)] was added to placate analysts, who considered that despite the assurances of the Government that this was already implicit in the notion of public information, there was still some degree of uncertainty. Thus, the superior insight of an insider will not be counted against him, if he uses it to derive insight from information which is generally available'. Similarly, see M Stallworthy, 'The United Kingdom's new regime for the control of insider dealing', (1993) ICCLR 4(12), 448–53. In a broad discussion paper on the regulation of investment analysts, the FSA itself concluded that: 'To the extent that the research is derived from information made public, the research will not be inside information (CJA, section 58)'. See FSA DP15, Investment research: Conflicts and other issues (July 2002) at 5.24.

available sources, information will be considered to be 'made public' (and therefore not inside information).[46] The fact that some of the information used by the analyst was derived from sources that make the information available only for a fee should not necessarily affect this. Section 58(3)(d) makes it clear that such information may still be treated as having been made public even though a fee is payable. Similarly, a star analyst's expertise in producing the report should not affect this conclusion as section 58(3)(a) states that information may be treated as made public even where it is acquired only by persons 'exercising diligence or experience'.

10.21 However, an interesting issue is whether a distinction can be drawn between the report itself (which would not be inside information on the basis of the preceding analysis) and knowledge in the hands, say, of a fellow employee that a particular recommendation that might have a significant effect on the share price was about to be issued. It would seem that in this instance the knowledge of an impending recommendation could be inside information—it would relate to a specific issuer, be specific and precise, and not have been made public (the information that the recommendation was impending would not in itself be derived from public information); the fellow employee would presumably be an insider[47] in that he would know the impending recommendation would be inside information, and in the example given would have received the knowledge directly or indirectly from a person who had access to information by virtue of his employment.[48]

As an 'insider'

10.22 For the purposes of the section 52 offences, information must be held as an 'insider'.

'Insider'

10.23 According to section 57(1) a person has information as an insider if and only if it is, and he knows that it is, inside information, and he has it, and knows that he has it, from an inside source. In order to determine whether someone is an insider the courts must apply a subjective test. The individual must have himself known both that the information was inside information and that the information came from an inside source. It is not enough that he ought to have known, or that a reasonable person would have known. However, Neha Jain argues that if a person deliberately closes his mind to the obvious, or fails to ask questions in circumstances where those questions are prompted, knowledge may be imputed.[49] Put another way, according to academic discussion, the test would appear to be whether the individual has consciously failed to question the unusual.[50]

'From an inside source'

10.24 Section 57(2) deals with the interpretation of the term 'from an inside source'. A person will have inside information from an inside source if he has it through being a director, employee, or shareholder of an issuer of securities, or having access to the information by virtue of his employment, office, or profession. He will also have information from an inside source if the direct or indirect source of his information is one of these persons. This catches two categories of 'insider': those who come into contact with the information directly through their work (often referred to as 'primary insiders'); and those who come into contact with

[46] CJA, s 58(2)(d).
[47] See discussion at para 10.23 *et seq.*
[48] See also discussion in Chapter 9 at para 9.120.
[49] N Jain, 'Significance of Mens Rea in Insider Trading' (2004) *Comp Law* 25(5), 132–40, at 136.
[50] Band, 'Trustees and Insider Dealing: Part 1' (2000) *PCB* 5, 293–303, at 293.

the information through a primary insider (often referred to as 'tippees' or 'secondary insiders'). The latter category is particularly wide ranging, as a person could be a secondary insider irrespective of how long the chain of communication is and how he acquired the information, as long as the original source was a 'primary insider'.[51] There is no requirement that the individual seeks out the information. This is made clear by the wording of section 57(2) which simply talks of a person 'having' information.

Price-affected securities—the dealing offence and the encouraging offence

Both the dealing offence and the encouraging offence relate to dealing in 'price-affected securities'. 'Price-affected securities' are those which are affected by price-sensitive information, and 'price-sensitive information' is defined as information which would, if it were to be made public, be likely to have a significant effect on the price of securities.[52] The CJA provides no clarification of what is meant by the use of the word 'significant',[53] and in providing guidance to issuers on the dissemination of price-sensitive information the London Stock Exchange, the UK listing authority at the time, commented that: **10.25**

> It is not feasible to define any theoretical percentage movement in a share price which will make a piece of information price-sensitive. Attempts at a precise definition of 'price-sensitive' are not possible, since it is generally necessary to take into account a number of factors specific to the particular case...[54]

Defences

Section 52(4) provides that the offence has effect subject to the defences outlined in section 53. The CJA provides both 'general' and 'special' defences. **10.26**

General defences—section 53

No expectation of profit[55]

It is a defence to all three of the offences under section 52 for the defendant to show that he did not at the time expect the insider dealing to result in profit (or the avoidance of loss)[56] attributable to the fact that the information in question was price-sensitive information.[57] **10.27**

---

51 E Lomnicka, 'The New Insider Dealing Provisions: Criminal Justice Act 1993, Part V' (1994) *JBL Mar*, 173–88, at 176. Note, however, commentary in the Treasury consultation on the sunset clauses in the civil market regime Chapter 9, para 9.59 *et seq.*which discusses practical problems in proving information comes from an inside source where there are multiple levels of information transfer.

52 CJA, s 56(2).

53 Compare this to the FSMA market abuse regime where s 118C(4) stipulates that information would be likely to have a significant effect on price if and only if it is information of a kind which a reasonable investor would be likely to use as part of the basis of his investment decision. The FCA guidance in the Disclosure Rules as to when an issuer of shares should consider that information would have a significant effect on the price of financial instruments expresses this slightly differently. In that guidance, the FCA recommends that an issuer should 'assess whether the information in question would be likely to be used by a reasonable investor as part of the basis of his investment decisions and would therefore be likely to have a significant effect on the price of the issuer's financial instruments'. For further discussion see para 10.79 *et seq.*

54 'Guidance on the Dissemination of Price Sensitive Information' (July 1996) para 4; <http://www.fsa.gov.uk/Pages/Library/Other_publications/UKLA/1996/index.shtml>. This guidance has now, for the most part, been replaced by the DTRs.

55 CJA, ss 53(1)(a), 53(2)(a), and 53(3)(b).

56 ibid, s 53(6).

57 See W Blair, A Allison, G Morton, P Richards-Carpenter, G Walker, and N Walmsley, *Banking and Financial Services Regulation* (3rd edn, Butterworths 2002), para 9.23: 'This [defence] would apply, for example, if the dealing was 'against' the information'.

Wide disclosure[58]

10.28 It is a defence to both the dealing offence and the encouraging offence for the defendant to show that he believed on reasonable grounds that 'the information had been or would be disclosed widely enough to ensure that none of those taking part in the dealing would be prejudiced by not having the information'. This defence has been explained in a number of ways but it is possible to identify two broad strands in its interpretation, one which requires 'equivalence of information' in the disclosure, and the other which focuses more on finding a lack of prejudice in the scope of the disclosure.

10.29 The first of these strands of interpretation suggests that the requisite lack of prejudice is satisfied through the principle of 'equivalence of information'.[59] This turns on the idea that it does not matter if a person deals on the basis of inside information provided that all of the counterparties to the dealing are fully aware of the information. It has been suggested that:

> [t]he most obvious example of this defence is where the person with the information discloses it to another person and then enters into a dealing with that other person. For this reason, the defence is often referred to as the 'equality of information' defence.[60]

However, an alternative view is that the defence does not require all parties to the transaction to be in possession of the same information, as the statute merely stipulates that the defendant's belief must have been that the information was disclosed widely enough to ensure that no party to the transaction was prejudiced by their level of knowledge (it does not require every party to have the same degree of disclosure). A regularly cited example of this is an underwriting transaction. It is the nature of such transactions that different participants may have different levels of knowledge (for example, the issuer may know far more than a sub-underwriter about the underwriting) without the parties with less knowledge being prejudiced by their lack of knowledge.[61] There is no equivalent of this 'equivalence of information' defence in the civil FSMA insider dealing regime, and so a dealing relying on this defence could still amount to civil market abuse.

Immaterial information

10.30 It is also a defence to both the dealing offence and the encouraging offence for the defendant to show that he would have acted as he did even if he did not have the information.[62] As a result of the broad scope of the section 52 offences, this defence is required to carve out a protection for those acting in good faith and in the ordinary course of their dealings. An example often cited is a liquidator who may be in possession of inside information, but will be required to dispose of securities regardless of whether this information, if released, would have a significantly negative impact on the price of those securities. To take another example, a professional investor may have thoroughly researched a particular stock and made

[58] ibid, s 53(1)(b) and s 53(2)(b).

[59] M Stamp, 'Insider Dealing', in *Practical Company Law and Corporate Transactions* (3rd edn, Thompson Reuters 2011) 421–444, at 437, and see also Blair et al. (n 62) at para 10.28.

[60] Blair et al. (n 62).

[61] See, eg, Lomnicka (n 31), and Alcock (n 46). Lomnicka at 185 cites the defence as applying in an underwriting transaction where 'the issuer possessed information about the securities which was neither public nor known to all the underwriters'.

[62] The equivalent discussion under the FSMA market abuse regime relates principally to whether the behaviour for market abuse (insider dealing) and market abuse (misuse of information) is 'on the basis of' the information under discussion, as to which, see Chapter 9, para 9.131 *et seq.*

a decision to invest in that stock, on the basis of its own research analysis, when a piece of information is inadvertently disclosed to it by the management of the issuer in question.

No expectation of dealing

10.31 It is a defence to the disclosure offence if the defendant can show that he did not at the time expect anyone to deal in the price-affected securities because of the disclosure. This is to be judged subjectively, and therefore an honest but unreasonable belief that no dealing would take place would be sufficient to amount to a defence on the basis that the person making the disclosure genuinely did not believe that persons would deal on the basis of this disclosure.[63]

Special defences—Schedule 1

10.32 Section 53(4) also provides for a number of 'special defences'. These are set out in Schedule 1 to the CJA. These defences apply only in relation to the dealing offence and the encouraging offence. These defences are largely aimed at ensuring the proper functioning of professional market making, intermediary, and corporate finance activities.[64]

Market makers

10.33 A 'market maker' is provided with a special defence under Schedule 1 where he can show that he was acting in good faith in the course of his business as such, or in the course of employment in such a business.[65] A market maker is someone who holds himself out as acting in compliance with the rules of a regulated market, or an approved organisation, as willing to acquire or dispose of securities, and is recognised as doing so under those rules.[66] For the purposes of this definition, the only body that presently has 'approved organisation' status from the Treasury is the International Capital Market Association ('ICMA').[67]

Market information

10.34 It is a defence for the defendant to show that the information he possessed was market information, and that it was reasonable for an individual in his position to have acted as he did despite having that information as an insider.[68] (Market information[69] is information

63 There is no equivalent to this defence under the market abuse (improper disclosure) offence discussed in Chapter 9 at para 9.159 *et seq.*

64 For a discussion of the safe harbours in the FSMA market abuse regime relating to 'dutiful execution of clients' orders' and 'legitimate market making etc', see Chapter 9, para 9.146 *et seq.*

65 CJA, Sch 1, para 1(1).

66 ibid, s 1(2).

67 According to s 1(3) of Sch 1, an 'approved organisation' means an international securities self-regulating organisation ('ISSRO') approved by the Treasury under any relevant order under s 22 FSMA. Article 35 of the Financial Services and Markets Act 2000 (Regulated Activities) Order 2001 (SI 2001/554) (the 'RAO'), made under s 22, makes provision for the Treasury to recognise ISSROs. ICMA was created in May 2005 out of the merger of the International Securities Market Association and the International Primary Market Association and is the self-regulatory organisation which represents both banks and investment firms that issue and deal in capital markets instruments.

68 CJA, Sch 1, para 2(1).

69 ibid, Sch 1, para 4 offers a full definition of the term 'market information', namely information consisting of one or more of the following facts: (a) that securities of a particular kind have been or are to be acquired or disposed of, or that their acquisition or disposal is under consideration or the subject of negotiation; (b) that securities of a particular kind have not been or are not to be acquired or disposed of; (c) the number of securities acquired or disposed of or to be acquired or disposed of or whose acquisition or disposal is under consideration or the subject of negotiation; (d) the price (or range of prices) at which the securities have been or are to be acquired or disposed of or the price (or range of prices) at which the securities whose acquisition or disposal is under consideration or the subject of negotiation may be acquired or disposed of; (e) the identity of the persons involved or likely to be involved in any capacity in an acquisition or disposal.

relating to the acquisition or disposal of particular securities which a person may acquire through the course of his involvement in those dealings.) The CJA does not give direct guidance on what behaviour should be considered to be reasonable, but it does stipulate that in determining reasonableness, particular factors should be considered. These relate to the content of information, the circumstances in which the information was gained, and the capacity in which the person in question acted and now acts. It is likely that the courts would look at typical market practice as a means of guiding their judgement as to reasonableness.[70] It is also a defence for the defendant to show that he acted to facilitate an acquisition or disposal which was under consideration or negotiation, and that the information which he had as an insider was market information arising directly out of his involvement in the acquisition or disposal.[71]

Price stabilisation

10.35 It is a defence for the defendant to show that he acted in conformity with either the price stabilisation rules[72] as set out in the FCA Handbook[73] or the relevant provisions of Commission Regulation (EC) No 2273/2003 detailing exemptions for buy-back programmes and stabilisation of financial instruments.[74] These are the same rules as those that apply to the market abuse regime under section 118 FSMA.

Penalties and Prosecution

10.36 On summary conviction for an offence under section 52 of the CJA, the courts may impose a fine not exceeding the statutory maximum, or imprisonment for a term not exceeding six months, or both.[75] On conviction on indictment, the courts have the power to impose a fine of any amount deemed appropriate, or to a term of imprisonment not exceeding seven years, or both.[76]

10.37 In addition to these sentencing powers, the FCA may also use its powers to apply to the court for an injunction or a restitution order[77] relating to offences under Part V of the CJA. Pursuant to section 380 FSMA, an injunction may be granted where there is a reasonable likelihood that any person will contravene a relevant requirement or that a contravention which has occurred will be continued or repeated. The court also has power to require a

[70] For a discussion as to the 'trading information' safe harbour under the pre-MAD market abuse regime, and the safe harbour relating to the legitimate business of market makers/dealers and the dutiful execution of client orders under the current market abuse regime, see Chapter 9, para 9.145.

[71] CJA, Sch 1, s 3. For a discussion of takeover/corporate finance related provisions under the FSMA market abuse regime, see Chapter 9, para 9.148.

[72] FSMA, s 137Q.

[73] MAR sets out the price stabilisation rules in Chapter 2.

[74] Commission Regulation (EC) No 2273/2003 of 22 December 2003 implementing Directive 2003/6/EC of the European Parliament and of the Council as regards exemptions for buy-back programmes and stabilisation of financial instruments. See also Chapter 9, para 9.234, for the equivalent provisions in the market abuse regime.

[75] CJA, s 61(1)(a).

[76] ibid, s 61(1)(b).

[77] FSMA, ss 380 (injunctions) and 382 (restitution orders) which apply in respect of contraventions of a relevant requirement. See Chapter 9, para 9.266 for a further discussion on this matter and in particular the meaning of 'relevant requirement'. The insider dealing regime under Part V CJA is a 'relevant requirement' for these purposes pursuant to s 380(6)(a)(ii) FSMA.

person who has contravened a relevant requirement, or who has been knowingly concerned in the contravention, to take steps to remedy the contravention or to restrain him from dealing with his assets. Pursuant to section 382 FSMA, the court may, on the application of the FCA, the PRA, or the Treasury, make a restitution order if it is satisfied that a person has contravened a relevant requirement and either that profits have accrued to him as a result, or that one or more persons have suffered loss or have been otherwise adversely affected as a result of the contravention.[78] This power also applies in respect of persons knowingly concerned in the contravention. The amount of the restitution order will be such as appears to the court to be just having regard to the profits made or loss or adverse effect suffered (or both).

Key Steps in Proving CJA Insider Dealing

As discussed in the previous chapter at paragraph 9.04, the perception used to be that the CJA offence was inappropriate to or ineffective in capturing the complicated fact patterns of dealings in the financial markets. This in part related to the difficulties faced by prosecutors in satisfying the higher burden of proof that will apply in respect of criminal proceedings,[79] and partly as a result of the multiple layers of facts or knowledge that need to be proved under the CJA offence. However, since 2009 the FCA (previously, the FSA) has prosecuted 12 insider dealing cases criminally which resulted in guilty pleas or convictions of some or all of the defendants in each of those cases. **10.38**

Cases

The policy of the FCA in respect of criminal prosecutions is outlined in Chapter 9 at paragraph 9.257. The first successful conviction for insider dealing under the CJA since the market abuse regime was brought in was the *Asif Butt* case,[80] brought by the Crown Prosecution Service. Butt was a compliance officer at an investment bank and passed confidential information obtained through this position to a number of associates, who placed highly profitable spread bets on the basis of the information. Butt and four of his associates were found guilty of conspiracy to insider dealing by a jury in December 2004. **10.39**

Chapter 9 contains a discussion of the FCA's approach in deciding whether to pursue criminal or civil sanction as part of its 'credible deterrence' strategy. The practical manifestation of this is the number of criminal prosecutions for insider dealing by individuals which have been launched since 2009 amid considerable publicity.[81] **10.40**

---

[78] See also discussion of compensation/confiscation orders in the *AIT* case at para 10.68 *et seq*. Although either the FCA or the PRA may apply to the court for an injunction under s 380 FSMA or a restitution order under s 382, only the FCA may apply to the court for an injunction in a market abuse case under s 381.

[79] Although see commentary in Chapter 9, para 9.27 relating to the standard of proof required under the civil market abuse offences as a matter of practice.

[80] Unreported.

[81] Under s 402 FSMA the FCA may institute proceedings for an offence under Part V of the CJA, except in Scotland. S 61(2) of the CJA provides that proceedings for offences under Part V shall not be instituted in England and Wales except by or with the consent of the Secretary of State or the Director of Public Prosecutions. In *R (on the application of Uberoi) v Westminster Magistrates' Court* [2009] 1 WLR 1905, the defendant to a prosecution brought by the FSA argued that the FSA required this consent in order to institute proceedings. The Divisional Court held that the structure and context of FSMA amply demonstrated that it must have been Parliament's intention that the FSA could institute proceedings without obtaining consent from outside.

10.41 In March 2009, Christopher McQuoid and James Melbourne were each convicted of one count of insider dealing. McQuoid was the general counsel of TTP Communications plc. The prosecution's case was that he disclosed information as to a forthcoming takeover offer for the company to his father-in-law, Melbourne, who then traded ahead of the announcement of that offer. Both defendants were sentenced to eight months' imprisonment, with Melbourne's sentence being suspended. McQuoid subsequently appealed against his sentence. In *R v McQuoid* [2010] 1 Cr App R (S) 43 the Court of Appeal upheld McQuoid's sentence. In his ruling Lord Judge CJ agreed with the trial judge's observation that insider dealing was not to be treated as a victimless crime. The Lord Chief Justice observed:

> Those who involve themselves in insider dealing are criminals: no more and no less. The principles of confidentiality and trust, which are essential to the operations of the commercial world, are betrayed by insider dealing and public confidence in the integrity of the system which is essential to its proper function is undermined by market abuse... If there ever was a feeling that insider dealing was a matter to be covered by regulation, that impression should be rapidly dissipated. The message must be clear: when it is done deliberately, insider dealing is a species of fraud; it is cheating. Prosecution in open and public court will often, and perhaps much more so now than in the past, be appropriate. Although those who perpetrate the offence may hope, if caught, to escape with regulatory proceedings, they can have no legitimate expectation of avoiding prosecution and sentence.

10.42 The Court of Appeal also laid down sentencing guidelines in cases of insider dealing. The following considerations are relevant:

(1) the nature of the defendant's employment or retainer, or involvement in the arrangements which enabled him to participate in the insider dealing of which he is guilty;
(2) the circumstances in which he came into possession of confidential information and the use he made of it;
(3) whether he behaved recklessly or acted deliberately, and almost inevitably therefore, dishonestly;
(4) the level of planning and sophistication involved in his activity, as well as the period of trading and the number of individual trades;
(5) whether he acted alone or with others and, if so, his relative culpability;
(6) the amount of anticipated or intended financial benefit or (as sometimes happens) loss avoided, as well as the actual benefit (or loss avoided);[82]
(7) although the absence of any identified victim is not normally a matter giving rise to mitigation, the impact (if any), where proved, on any individual victim; and

[82] In *R v Rollins* [2012] 1 Cr App R (S) 64, the Court of Appeal was invited in an appeal on sentencing to draw a distinction in terms of culpability between cases in which the motivation for the insider dealing was to make a profit as opposed to those where it was to avoid a loss but declined to do so. Owen J said (at para 22): 'We recognise that the motivation for committing such offences will vary from case to case, and that a shareholder's motivation in buying or selling in insider dealing is likely to be a factor for the court to consider. But we are not persuaded that, as a point of general application, there is any distinction to be drawn between cases in which there is an intention to make a profit, and those in which the intention is to avoid a loss. Whilst the degree of culpability may be greater in cases in which the motivating factor is the desire to make a profit from inside knowledge, that will not necessarily be the case. All will depend on the facts of the individual case'. Prior to conviction, the defendant in this case had also appealed to the Supreme Court on the issue of whether the FSA had power to prosecute offences of money laundering contrary to PoCA 2002 in addition to insider dealing charges. The Supreme Court ruled that it did: *R v Rollins* [2011] 1 Cr App R 4.

(8) the impact of the offence on overall public confidence in the integrity of the market—because of its impact on public confidence it is likely than an offence committed jointly by more than one person trusted with confidential information will be more damaging to public confidence than an offence committed in isolation by one person acting on his own.

Age and a guilty plea will always be relevant. So, too, will good character. In assessing sentence full weight must be given to the impact on the defendant and his family, as well as the destruction of his professional reputation.

There have been a further 11 cases since *McQuoid* in which the FSA prosecuted cases of insider dealing resulting in convictions or guilty pleas.[83] The FCA's strategy clearly now appears to be that where it comes across suspected misconduct amounting to insider dealing it prefers to prosecute that conduct criminally rather than pursuing regulatory proceedings under the FSMA market abuse regime. **10.43**

Flow Chart

A flow chart illustrating the key components of the CJA insider dealing offence is set out at Figure 10.1 for ease of reference. **10.44**

Part 7 Financial Services Act 2012: Offences in Relation to Financial Services

Part 7 of the FSA 2012 contains three offences in relation to financial services. These are the 'misleading statements' offence in section 89, the 'misleading impressions' offence in section 90, and the 'misleading statements etc in relation to benchmarks' offence in section 91. The first two of these largely re-enact the previous section 397 FSMA offence. The third is entirely novel and was adopted following the LIBOR scandal. Unlike CJA insider dealing, the offences under Part 7 FSA 2012 can be committed by legal persons, not just by individuals. **10.45**

Until its repeal with effect from 1 April 2013, section 397 FSMA contained two criminal offences in relation to false and misleading statements and practices. These provisions re-enacted the repealed section 47 of the Financial Services Act 1986 ('FSA 1986'), with a few drafting amendments. As noted in Chapter 9, at paragraph 9.03, it was perceived by both academics and practitioners that the section 47 (and subsequently section 397 FSMA) offences in themselves had proved unsuccessful at capturing misconduct occurring on the market. These failings led to the introduction of the civil market abuse regime, the coverage of which also includes various types of false or misleading statements and practices. This regime is discussed in further detail in Chapter 9. **10.46**

[83] Matthew Uberoi and Neel Uberoi (November 2009), Malcolm Calvert (March 2010), Anjam Ahmad (June 2010), Neil Rollins (November 2010), Christian Littlewood, Angie Littlewood, and Helmy Omar Sa'aid (February 2011), Rupinder Sidhu (December 2011), James Sanders, Miranda Sanders, and James Swallow (May 2012), Ali Mustafa, Pardip Saini, Paresh Shah, Neten Shah, Bijal Shah, and Truptesh Patel (July 2012), Thomas Ammann (December 2012), Paul Milsom (March 2013), and Richard Joseph (March 2013).

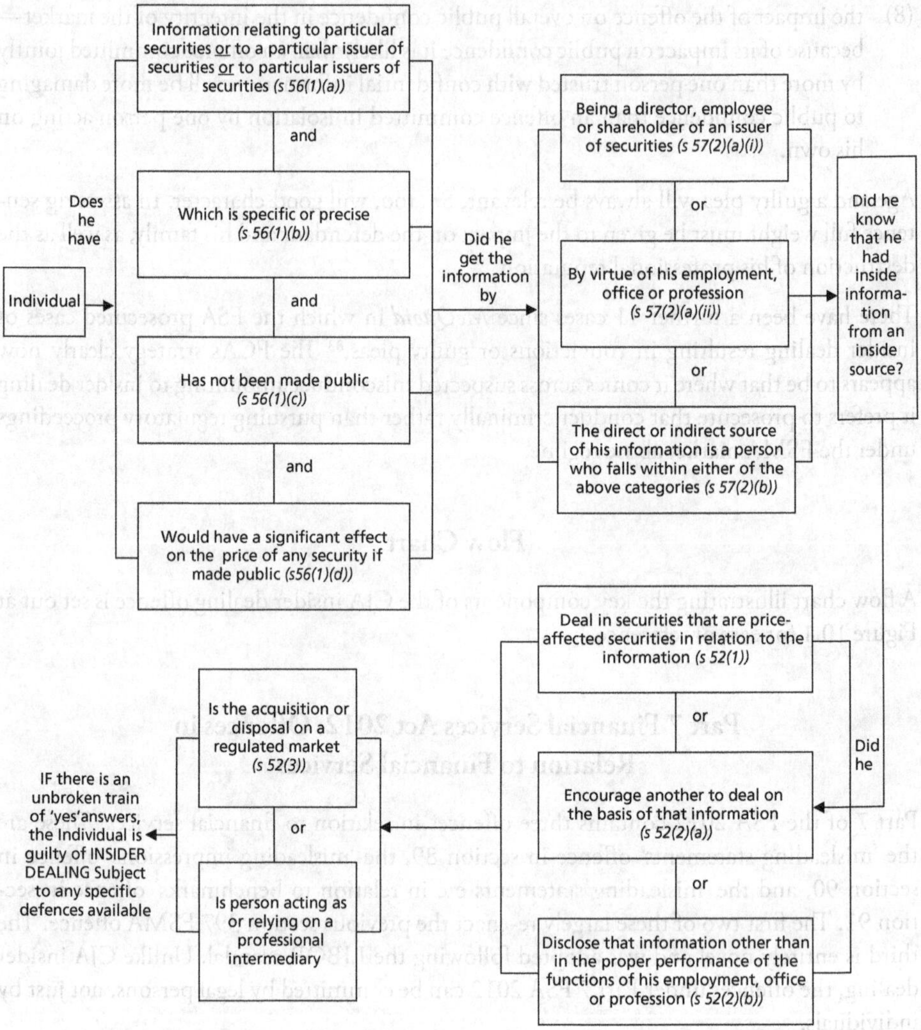

Figure 10.1 Insider dealing, Criminal Justice Act 1993, Part V Misleading Statements and Impressions

10.47 Section 401 FSMA gives the FCA the power to institute prosecutions for offences under Part 7 FSA 2012.[84] The Secretary of State has concurrent jurisdiction with the FCA to prosecute this offence, and this interaction is discussed at paragraph 10.91 *et seq.*

Misleading Statements

10.48 Secion 89 FSA 2012 provides the misleading statements offence. There are a number of elements to this. First, for the offence to apply, a person must make a statement which he knows to be false or misleading in a material respect, or dishonestly conceal any material facts

[84] By reason of s 403(3B) FSMA the FCA is the 'appropriate regulator' for these purposes. Proceedings may also be instituted by or with the consent of the Director of Public Prosecutions.

(whether in connection with a statement made by him or otherwise). Further, a person who is reckless as to whether the statement made by him is false or misleading in a material respect also falls within the scope of section 89.[85] The second element requires the person making the statement or concealing the facts to have done so either *with the intention* of inducing another person (whether or not the person to whom the statement is made) to do or refrain from doing certain acts, or to have been *reckless* as to whether the statement or concealment may have that effect. The acts to which the inducement must relate are entering or offering to enter into, or refraining from entering or offering to enter into, a relevant agreement, or exercising or refraining from exercising any rights conferred by a relevant investment.[86]

Defence

Section 89(3) FSA 2012 provides a defence to the misleading statements offence if the relevant person can show that the statement was made in conformity with price stabilising rules, control of information rules,[87] or the relevant provisions of Commission Regulation (EC) No 2273/2003 regarding exemptions for share buy-back programmes and stabilisation of financial instruments. The 'price stabilising rules' are those made under section 137Q FSMA (contained in the Code of Market Conduct (MAR) sourcebook within the FCA Handbook) and the provisions of the Regulation are those in place to implement aspects of MAD concerning price stabilisation. **10.49**

Territorial scope

For the misleading statements offence to be committed, either: **10.50**

(i) the statement must be made in or from the UK, or the facts must be concealed in or from the UK, or such statement or concealment is arranged in or from the UK;
(ii) the person on whom the inducement is intended to, or may, have effect is in the UK; or
(iii) the agreement is or would be entered into or the rights are or would be exercised in the UK.[88]

Misleading Impressions

Section 90 FSA 2012 provides the misleading impressions offence. There are a number of elements to this. First, for the offence to apply, the person must do an act or engage in a course of conduct which creates a false or misleading impression as to the market in or the price or value of any relevant investments. Secondly, the person must *intend* to create the impression. Thirdly, the person must either (i) *intend*, by creating the impression, to induce another person to acquire, dispose of, subscribe for, or underwrite the investments or to refrain from doing so or to exercise, or refrain from exercising, any rights conferred by the **10.51**

[85] A distinction was drawn in *R v Page, Holden, Dunning and Bradshaw* [1996] Crim LR 821 between (a) conspiracy to commit an offence under FSA 1986, s 47, for which no dishonesty is required as the reckless statement may be made dishonestly or otherwise; and (b) the offence of conspiracy to defraud for which dishonesty is required.

[86] As to the meaning of relevant investment and relevant agreement, see para 10.56.

[87] That is to say, rules made by the FCA or PRA in respect of the disclosure and use of information by an authorised person pursuant to the powers conferred by s 137P FSMA. See, eg, the Senior Management Arrangements Systems and Controls SYSC 10.2 for the rules regarding keeping information behind a Chinese Wall, as discussed at Chapter 9, para 9.234.

[88] FSA 2012, s 89(4).

investments, or (ii) *know* that the impression is false or misleading, or *be reckless* as to whether it is, and *intend* by creating the impression to bring about the making of a gain for himself or another, or the causing of a loss to another or the exposing of another to the risk of loss,[89] or *be aware* that creating the impression is likely to produce any of those results.

Defences

10.52 It is a defence to the misleading impressions offence under section 90(9) FSA 2012 if the relevant person can show that, to the extent that the offence results from his intending, by creating the impression, to induce another person to acquire, dispose of, subscribe for, or underwrite the investments or to refrain from doing so or to exercise, or refrain from exercising, any rights conferred by the investments, he reasonably believed that his conduct would not create an impression that was false or misleading as to the market in or price or value of any relevant investments.[90] It is also a defence that he acted or engaged in the conduct for the purposes of stabilising the price of investments and in conformity with price stabilising rules, or in conformity with the same control of information rules and EU Regulation relating to share buy-back programmes and stabilisation of financial instruments[91] referred to in paragraph 10.49.[92]

Territorial Scope

10.53 For the misleading impressions offence to be committed, the relevant act or course of conduct must be done, or engaged in, in the UK, or the false or misleading impression must be created there.[93]

Sanctions

10.54 The maximum penalty for either offence is seven years' imprisonment or a fine, or both. The sentencing policy of the court was considered in the Court of Appeal case of *R v Feld*.[94] In that case, the Court of Appeal held that, in addition to the factors set out in *R v Barrick*[95] the following non-exhaustive list would be relevant considerations for the sentencing judge: the amount involved and the manner in which the fraud is carried out; the period over which the fraud is carried out and the degree of persistence with which it is carried out; the position of the defendant within the company and his measure of control over it; any abuse of

89 Per s 90(5)–(8) FSA 2012, 'gain' and 'loss' extend only to gain or loss in money or other property of any kind and include such gain or loss whether temporary or permanent. 'Gain' includes a gain by keeping what one has, as well as a gain by getting what one does not have, and 'loss' includes a loss by not getting what one might get, as well as a loss by parting with what one has.

90 FSA 2012, s 90(9)(a).

91 Regulation 2273/2003.

92 FSA 2012, s 90(9)(b)–(d).

93 ibid, s 90(10).

94 *R v Feld* [1999] 1 Cr App R (S) 1. This relates to FSA 1986, s 47, the precursor to FSA 2012, ss 89 and 90.

95 (1985) 7 Cr App R (S) 142. The factors stated in *Barrick* are: (a) the quality and degree of trust placed in the defendant; (b) the period over which the crimes were perpetrated; (c) the use to which the money dishonestly taken was put; (d) the effect upon the victim; (e) the impact of the offences on the public and public confidence; (f) the effect on fellow employees or partners; (g) the effect on the offender himself; (h) his own history; (i) those matters of mitigation special to himself such as illness, strain, and cooperation with the police.

trust which is revealed; the consequences of the fraud; the effect on public confidence in the City and the integrity of commercial life; the loss to small investors, which will aggravate the fraud; the personal benefit derived by a defendant; the plea; and finally the age and character of the defendant.

As to injunctions and restitution, section 397 FSMA was a 'relevant requirement', the contravention of which founded the FCA's powers of injunction and restitution under sections 380 and 382 FSMA.[96] However, the amendments to FSMA as a result of the repeal of section 397 do not appear to have captured breach of the Part 7 FSA 2012 provisions as 'relevant requirements' for these purposes. This appears likely to be an error in the statutory drafting.[97] By way of illustration of the use of the equivalent powers under the FSA 1986,[98] in *Grant*,[99] both injunctive relief and a compensation order were granted against the defendants in connection with an unauthorised investment scheme under sections 6 and 61 of FSA 1986 and consequent misleading statements to the public contrary to section 47 FSA 1986 in advertisements.[100] **10.55**

Relevant Investments and Relevant Agreements

Both the misleading statements offence and the misleading impressions offence apply in relation to 'relevant investments'. The inducement specified in the misleading statements offence refers in turn to 'relevant agreements'. 'Relevant investment' is defined[101] as an investment of a specified kind, which includes:[102] deposits; rights under contracts of insurance; shares in a company; debentures; loan stock; bonds; certificates of deposit; rights under an alternative finance investment bond; government and public securities; warrants or other securities which give an entitlement to investments; certificates representing securities; units in a collective investment scheme; rights under a stakeholder pension scheme; options; futures; CFDs; participation in Lloyd's syndicates; loans secured on land and rights in investments, amongst others. 'Relevant agreement' is defined[103] as an agreement (i) the entering into or performance of which by either party constitutes an activity of a specified kind; and (ii) which relates to a relevant investment (as defined earlier). For these purposes, an activity of a **10.56**

96 See para 10.37 in the context of insider dealing and n 77. As noted earlier, the PRA also has powers of injunction and restitution under these provisions.

97 Under s 380(6) FSMA a 'relevant requirement' means one imposed 'by or under this Act' or 'by or under any other Act and whose contravention constitutes an offence mentioned in section 402(1)'. Section 402(1) includes offences under Part V CJA (insider dealing), but does not mention Part 7 FSA 2012. Therefore, whereas the previous s 397 FSMA was a 'relevant requirement' because it was imposed 'by or under this Act', on the face of it, Part 7 FSA 2012 offences are not.

98 FSA 1986, s 61(1).

99 *Secretary of State for Trade and Industry v Grant* [2000] WL 33122486 (Ch D) 15 September 2000.

100 See also *Securities and Investments Board v Pantell SA (No 2)* [1991] 3 WLR 857 involving injunctive relief pursuant to s 61(1) of FSA 1986 relating to persons knowingly concerned in contraventions of s 47 of FSA 1986. Section 61(1) is broadly equivalent to s 380 FSMA but related to specified provision rather than using the 'relevant requirement' definition.

101 FSA 2012, s 93(5).

102 The Financial Services Act 2012 (Misleading Statements and Impressions) Order 2013, SI 2013/637 is the relevant Order, art 4 of which specifies the kinds of investment by reference to Part 2 of Sch 1 to the Financial Services and Markets Act 2000 (Financial Promotion) Order 2005, SI 2005/1529.

103 FSA 2012, s 93(3).

specified kind includes: accepting deposits; effecting and carrying out contracts of insurance; dealing in securities; arranging deals in investments; operating a multilateral trading facility; managing investments; safeguarding and administering investments; advising on investments; advising on syndicate participation at Lloyd's; sending dematerialised instructions; and establishing a collective investment scheme or stakeholder pension scheme, amongst others.[104]

No Civil Law Right of Action Under Sections 89 and 90 FSA 2012

10.57 The sections 89 and 90 FSA 2012 offences do not give rise to a civil law right of action for damages for breach of statutory duty actionable by those affected by the practices in question. The point was argued in the *Norwich Union* case[105] but rejected both at first instance and on appeal.

Effectiveness of the Offences

Type of actions brought under FSA 1986, section 47

10.58 As discussed earlier in this chapter, it was the perceived failure of the existing common law and statutory offences (which included FSA 1986, section 47) to deal with particular types of market misconduct that led to the introduction of the civil market abuse regime in FSMA. Indeed, the significant burden of proving beyond reasonable doubt the criminal offences relating to misleading statements and practices,[106] and the tests that have to be satisfied (for example, in the case of misleading statements, it is necessary to show knowledge, dishonest concealment, or recklessness as well as showing that the defendant had the necessary purpose or was reckless as to the effect) is illustrated by the small number of prosecutions reported. The cases successfully prosecuted under FSA 1986, section 47 have tended for the most part to be fairly clear-cut.

10.59 For example, in *Chauhan*,[107] two defendants, the principal shareholder and managing director of a company and the finance director of the company, pleaded guilty to engaging in a course of conduct which created a false or misleading impression of the market in or the price or value of investments. Their action, which included backdating sales contracts, the creation of non-existing debts in the company's accounts, and inflating the value of the company's stock by removing plates to make machinery appear newer than it in fact was, had been undertaken in order to allow the company to proceed to flotation. The defendants received prison sentences of 18 months and five years (later reduced to four years on appeal) respectively.

[104] As per the Financial Services Act 2012 (Misleading Statements and Impressions) Order 2013, SI 2013/637, by reference to Part 1 of Sch 1 to the Financial Services and Markets Act 2000 (Financial Promotion) Order 2005, SI 2005/1529.

[105] *Aldrich and others v Norwich Union Life Insurance Co Ltd; Norwich Union Life Insurance Society v Qureshi and others* [2000] Lloyd's Rep IR 1 under s 47, FSA 1986.

[106] s 47, FSA 1986 referred to misleading statements and practices, whereas ss 89 and 90, FSA 2012 now refer to misleading statements and impressions.

[107] *R v Chauhan and another* [2000] 2 Cr App R (S) 230.

In *Feld*,[108] the managing director of a company was found guilty of making misleading statements contrary to section 47. The company in question had issued a prospectus for a rights issue which contained statements intended to give a misleadingly favourable impression of the company's financial health. Forged documents were also supplied to the company's accountants and in support of a false profit announcement. The defendant was sentenced to six years' imprisonment for each of these counts of making a misleading statement, to run concurrently.[109] **10.60**

In *Page*,[110] both of the defendants, Page and Holden, were convicted of three offences of recklessly making a misleading statement to induce entry into an investment agreement contrary to section 47(1)(b) of FSA 1986. The relevant statement was included in a brochure intended to be read by prospective investors in a fund and stated that 'funds placed with [the fund] are secured and guaranteed to the full amount designated overleaf, against mortgages on UK properties'. In fact, investments in the fund were shown to be not so secured. Page and Holden were sentenced to 30 months' imprisonment (reduced to nine months on appeal). **10.61**

The case of *R v Stevens*[111] illustrates the difficulty in bringing successful prosecutions under these provisions. In this case, the Court of Appeal ordered a retrial of Stevens' conviction under section 47 of FSA 1986 due to inadequacies of the trial judge's summing up causing the defendant to have an unfair trial. The court held that: **10.62**

> [t]he summing up is unclear in that it did not focus the jury's attention on the real issues the jury had to decide. It did not identify the false or misleading statement or statements. The result is that this court cannot be satisfied that all members of the jury, in reaching a verdict of guilty, were identifying the same statement or statements as being false or misleading.

The final case brought under section 47 FSA 1986, and which achieved a certain amount of notoriety, is the so-called 'City Slickers' case.[112] James Hipwell and a colleague, Anil Bhoyrul, were journalists who tipped various shares in the 'City Slickers' column in the *Daily Mirror* newspaper. They allegedly bought relevant investments which were to be tipped in the column and then sold them afterwards to make a profit. Hipwell, Bhoyrul, and another were found guilty of conspiring to create a misleading impression of the value of the shares, in breach of section 47(2), FSA 1986. The judge at first instance ruled that if the position of a tipper is not disclosed at the time the tip is given, this was relevant to the evaluation and could mistakenly create an impression, irrespective of whether anyone was actually misled. The judge held that the misleading impression in this case did not rely on the mere non-disclosure of the tipper's position but the non-disclosure in the context of the pattern of trading, tone, and content. James Hipwell's application to appeal was rejected by the Court of Appeal. **10.63**

Interrelation with other offences and processes

A number of cases of FSA 1986, section 47 offences have also involved other alleged offences. In *R v Feld*,[113] a case which involved giving a misleadingly favourable impression of the **10.64**

---

108 *R v Feld* [1999] 1 Cr App R (S) 1.

109 The case was appealed on the basis of the length of the sentences. On appeal the concurrent sentences of six years for the s 47 offence were upheld, but the sentences for obtaining money by deception were reduced as the Court of Appeal decided on the facts that they should run concurrently, not consecutively.

110 *R v Page, Holden, Dunning and Bradshaw* [1996] Crim LR 821.

111 *R v Stevens*, transcript available at [2000] WL 1544599 (CA (Crim Div)) 12 October 2000.

112 See the Court of Appeal decision, *R v Hipwell* [2007] All ER (D) 361 (Feb).

113 n 108.

financial health of a company undertaking a rights issue, as well as the production of forged documents which were given to the company's auditors, a prosecution was also brought under section 3 of the Forgery and Counterfeiting Act 1981. In *R v Page*,[114] one of the defendants was separately convicted of conspiracy to defraud.

10.65 Section 47 prosecutions have also been used to assist with other processes. In *FSA v Lukka*,[115] a motion for judgment was granted in the absence of the defendant who had left the country. He was accused of persuading investors to give him large amounts of money on the basis of false promises as to the profit they would make on the foreign exchange transactions in which he would invest the money on their behalf. Once this money had been transferred, he provided post-dated cheques as proof of the return the investors would receive. These cheques were not met. The evidence in relation to the alleged breach of section 47 of FSA 1986 was very strong, and the judge noted that the declaratory relief would be granted in order:

(i) to assist domestic regulators in determining whether the defendant was a fit and proper person to be carrying on investment business;
(ii) to be of assistance in a subsequent consideration of any disqualification order;
(iii) to assist any individual investors considering making a claim for compensation; and
(iv) to assist overseas regulators in determining whether the defendant should be authorised to provide services in their jurisdiction.

AIT—the first prosecution under section 397

10.66 The first prosecution by the FSA under section 397 FSMA was *R v Rigby, Bailey and Rowley*[116] (known as the *AIT* case).[117] The three defendants, all former directors of AIT, were accused of both making a statement, promise, or forecast which they knew to be misleading, false, or deceptive (contrary to section 397(1)(a)) and recklessly making a statement, promise, or forecast which was misleading, false, or deceptive in a material particular (contrary to section 397(1)(c)).[118] Rigby and Bailey were both convicted of the section 397(1)(c) offence and Rowley was acquitted on both counts. The conviction of Rigby and Bailey resulted from a statement issued by them in May 2002 that AIT's profits would meet the forecasts of £6.7 million for that year. This forecast depended on the existence of a number of contracts, which the jury accepted did not exist at the time the statement was made by Rigby and Bailey. The conclusion was therefore reached by the jury that the statement was 'misleading, false or deceptive in a material particular' because the contracts did not exist, and Rigby and Bailey were guilty of the section 397(1)(c) offence by virtue of their recklessness in affirming the profit forecast in those circumstances. It is noted, however, that the jury did not accept the FSA's case that any of the three defendants was guilty of the section 397(1)(a) offence. The FSA therefore failed to convince the jury that the defendants made a statement which they 'knew' to be misleading, false, or deceptive in a material particular.

10.67 Rigby and Bailey were found guilty only of recklessness (not knowledge) in making the statement. Rigby was sentenced to three and a half years' imprisonment and was disqualified from acting as a company director for six years, and Bailey received a sentence of two years' imprisonment

[114] n 110.
[115] *Financial Services Authority v Lukka* (Ch D, 23 April 1999).
[116] August 2005.
[117] FSA/PN/091/2005, 18 August 2005.
[118] Now replaced by the s 89 FSA 2012 offence.

and was disqualified from being a company director for four years. Given that both were acquitted of the more serious offence under section 397(1)(a), the sentences were widely perceived to be harsher than anticipated. Following a hearing at the Court of Appeal, Rigby's sentence was reduced to 18 months and Bailey's sentence was reduced to nine months.[119]

Following the convictions, private and institutional investors who lost money after purchasing AIT shares on the basis of misleading information were invited by the FSA to apply to the court for compensation. Private investors applied for compensation totalling £18,716, while institutional investors (including pension funds) applied for compensation totalling £1,262,736.[120] The court ordered that they should be paid in full, with one exception where the court ruled that the investment decision was not based on the misleading statements. **10.68**

On 11 November 2005, Rigby was ordered to pay £208,796 in compensation to investors, £381,273.97 by way of confiscation of assets, and £250,000 towards litigation costs incurred by the FSA. For Bailey, the judge ordered confiscation of £106,572.53 and compensation of £141,686. Rigby and Bailey both appealed against the confiscation orders, and Bailey appealed contingently against the compensation order. **10.69**

With respect to the first ground of appeal, that the temporary and unrealised increase in the value of Rigby's shares should not be taken into account as a benefit from the offences, the Court of Appeal held that there was 'no proper sense in which Rigby obtained a benefit or derived a pecuniary advantage'[121] (he had not sold any shares during the time when they had an inflated price—it was during a period when, by Stock Exchange rules, he was unable to sell his shares). With respect to the second ground of appeal, that the appellants' salaries and other emoluments earned after 2 May 2002 should not be taken into account as a benefit from the offence,[122] the Court of Appeal did not find a sufficient cause or link in the offences of which they were convicted and their continued employment.[123] The Court of Appeal allowed the appeals and quashed the confiscation orders. **10.70**

The FSA brought only one other prosecution under section 397 FSMA against four former directors of iSoft plc. Three of the defendants were tried twice. The jury at the first trial failed to reach a verdict in August 2012. The jury at the second trial was discharged in July 2013 midway through the trial 'following legal argument about an exhibit handling issue that arose late in the trial' and the FCA subsequently announced that it would not pursue a further retrial.[124] **10.71**

Misleading Statement etc. in Relation to Benchmarks

The third offence in Part 7 FSA 2012 relates to benchmark manipulation and is entirely new. In proceedings before the Parliamentary Commission on Banking Standards in relation to LIBOR,[125] the FSA's position was that it did not have criminal jurisdiction to take action **10.72**

[119] FSA, 'Carl Rigby and Gareth Bailey—update'; <http://www.fsa.gov.uk/pages/Library/Communication/Statements/2005/rigby_bailey.shtml>; *R v Bailey (Gareth Scott)* [2006] 2 Cr App R (S) 36.

[120] FSA, 'Former AIT directors ordered to compensate investors', 11 November 2005, FSA/PN/120/2005.

[121] *R v Rigby and another* [2006] 1 WLR 3067, para 17.

[122] The appellants continued to be employed after the statements, and indeed were retained during a transitional period while refinancing/restructuring was undertaken and a new board brought in.

[123] *R v Rigby and another* [2006] 1 WLR 3067, para 21.

[124] FCA press release FCA/PN/069/2013 dated 22 July 2013. The FCA also announced that it would not be pursuing the prosecution of the fourth director.

[125] The London Inter-Bank Offer Rate. On LIBOR, see Chapter 1, paras 1.42–1.43, and paras 1.81 and 1.84.

against persons seeking to manipulate the benchmark under the existing FSMA framework. Section 91 FSA 2012 was introduced to fill this lacuna.

10.73 Section 91 creates two new criminal offences. The first is where a person makes a false or misleading statement to another person (i) in the course of arrangements for the setting of a relevant benchmark, (ii) he intends that the statement should be used by the other person for the purpose of setting the relevant benchmark, and (iii) he knows that the statement is false or misleading or is reckless as to whether it is.[126] The second is where a person (i) does any act or engages in any course of conduct which creates a false or misleading impression as to the price or value of any investment or as to the interest rate applicable to any transaction, (ii) he intends to create the impression, (iii) the impression may affect the setting of a relevant benchmark, (iv) he knows that the impression is false or misleading or is reckless as to whether it is, and (v) he knows that the impression may affect the setting of a relevant benchmark.[127]

10.74 There are defences to both benchmark offences if the defendant shows that the statement was made, or the action or course of conduct engaged in, in conformity with price stabilising rules, control of information rules or the relevant provisions of Commission Regulation 2273/2003.[128]

10.75 The first benchmark offence applies only where the statement is made in or from the UK or to a person who is in the UK. The second benchmark offence applies only where the act is done, or the course of conduct engaged in, in the UK or the false or misleading impression is created there.

10.76 As at July 2013, LIBOR is the only 'relevant benchmark' to have been specified by the Treasury for the purposes of section 91.[129]

Other Regulatory Provisions Relating to Undesirable Market Conduct

Introduction

10.77 There are a number of other regulatory requirements relevant in the context of undesirable market misconduct. Although not the primary focus of Chapters 9 and 10, these are outlined below for the sake of completeness.[130]

Other Requirements

FCA and exchange rules

10.78 Market misconduct may also fall within the ambit of other regulatory requirements. For example, misconduct by FCA regulated firms and approved persons, and by members of exchanges may be subject to sanctions under relevant FCA rules (including principles) and

[126] FSA 2012, s 91(1).
[127] ibid, s 91(2).
[128] ibid, s 91(3) and (4). See also para 10.49 as to price stabilising rules, etc.
[129] ibid, s 93(4) and art 3 of the Financial Services Act 2012 (Misleading Statements and Impressions) Order 2013, SI 2013/637.
[130] As mentioned earlier, Chapters 9 and 10 do not however deal with common law or other criminal offences, eg relating to the Fraud Act 2006.

exchange rules respectively. This is discussed further in Chapter 9 at paragraph 9.236. As to the scope of the FCA's Conduct of Business Sourcebook and related principles and statement of principle, see Chapters 12 and 13.

Listing Rules, Prospectus Rules, and the Disclosure and Transparency Rules

As mentioned in Chapter 9 at paragraph 9.13 *et seq.*, there are provisions in the Disclosure Rules (which comprise chapters of the Disclosure Rules and Transparency Rules ('DTR'))[131] which oblige 'issuers'[132] to comply with an additional layer of rules concerning the use, control, and disclosure of inside information.[133] **10.79**

Sanctions for non-compliance with the Disclosure Rules

In terms of sanctions, the FCA may require the suspension of trading of a financial instrument. Such suspension does not relieve the issuer (or any persons discharging managerial responsibilities on behalf of the issuer, or any connected person of such person) from compliance with the Disclosure Rules. Once the matter causing suspension has been resolved, the FCA may nevertheless impose such conditions on the procedure for lifting the suspension as it considers appropriate.[134] In addition to the suspension of trading sanction, if the FCA considers that an issuer (or a person discharging managerial responsibilities, or a connected person) has breached any of the disclosure rules[135] it may, subject to the provisions of FSMA, impose on that person a financial penalty or publish a statement censuring that person.[136] The FCA's powers to impose penalties in this instance are a facet of its powers to impose penalties as competent authority under the listing regime.[137] In this context, it should be noted that the FCA may also bring enforcement proceedings against an issuer if it fails to take reasonable steps to establish and maintain adequate procedures, systems, and controls to enable it to comply with its obligations under the DTRs.[138] This includes the rules relating to the disclosure of inside information.[139] **10.80**

The basic rule on the disclosure of inside information

The basic requirement is that an issuer must disclose inside information to a Regulatory Information Service ('RIS') as soon as possible,[140] subject to the 'delaying disclosure' exception set out at paragraph 10.85. An issuer will be deemed to have complied with the basic **10.81**

---

[131] DTR 2.

[132] An issuer is any company or other legal person or undertaking (including a public sector issuer), any class of whose financial instruments: (a) have been admitted to trading on a regulated market; or (b) are the subject of an application for admission to trading on a regulated market; other than issuers who have not requested or approved admission of their financial instruments to trading on a regulated market—see the FCA Glossary.

[133] DTR 2.1.1G specifically acknowledges that the provisions of the Disclosure Rules overlap with s 118 FSMA, Part 7 FSA 2012, and with Part V CJA. As far as s 118(1) FSMA is concerned, if an issuer complies with the provisions of the Disclosure Rules, either by making disclosure of inside information as soon as possible (as required by the basic rule) or by delaying disclosure in accordance with the 'legitimate interests' exception, then such behaviour is a safe harbour from potential accusations that the disclosure constitutes market abuse under s 118(1) FSMA.

[134] DTR 1.4.1R–DTR 1.4.3R.

[135] DTR 1.5.3G(1).

[136] For a discussion of actions taken for breaches of the Listing Rules in the pre-MAD regime, see Chapter 9 at para 9.270.

[137] FSMA, s 91(1)–(2).

[138] LR 7.1.

[139] ibid, 7.2.2(2).

[140] DTR 2.2.1R. Issuers operating an Internet site are obliged also to publish the inside information on such a website and it must remain there for a year—see the Rules at DTR 2.3. For the purposes of DTR 2.2.1R,

rule if an event comes into existence but is not yet formalised and the issuer notifies an RIS as soon as is possible.[141] Additional guidance from the FCA allows issuers a short delay when faced with an unexpected or significant event, subject to the requirement to make an interim 'holding announcement' in some circumstances.[142] An issuer that has financial instruments admitted to trading or financial instruments listed on an overseas stock exchange in other jurisdictions must ensure that the disclosure of inside information to the public is synchronised as closely as possible in all jurisdictions.[143]

10.82 In June 2008, the FSA fined Woolworths Group plc[144] £350,000 for breaches of Disclosure Rule 2.2.1 and Listing Principle 4 and also considered a number of issues raised in submission, including when information could be said to have a 'significant effect' on price for the purposes of the definition of 'inside information'. In that case, Woolworths contested, amongst other things, that the information in question (which it had not announced) would not have a 'significant effect' on the price of Woolworths' shares.

10.83 The facts as found were that Woolworths became aware of a variation to the terms of a major supply contract of one of its subsidiaries, which would reduce Woolworths' profits for the following year 2006/07 by an estimated £8 million. This was considered by the Regulatory Decisions Committee of the FSA to be inside information as it was likely to have a significant effect on Woolworths' share price and should therefore have been disclosed to the market as soon as possible.

10.84 The FSA was satisfied that 'likely to have a significant effect on price' had to be assessed against the test in section 118C(6) only, namely that information would be likely to have a significant effect on price if and only if it was information of a kind which a reasonable investor would be likely to use as part of the basis of his investment decisions, and that section 118C was not merely a set of factors to take into account, as had been contested. The FSA considered that while an analysis of actual price movement and the matters contributing to it could be relevant for certain purposes (eg the penalty) it was, in the FSA's view, the wrong approach to seek to analyse, as had been suggested, the amount of an actual fall that might be attributed to a particular piece of information in order to determine whether it was 'inside

inside information has the same meaning as in s 118C of FSMA (discussed at Chapter 9, para 9.106 *et seq.*, p 9, although DTR 2.2 considers various criteria that issuers may use in identifying inside information. DTR 2.2.4, eg, states that in determining the likely price significance of information an issuer should assess whether the information in question would be likely to be used by a reasonable investor as part of the basis of his investment decision 'and would therefore be likely to have a significant effect on the price of the issuer's financial instruments' (the reasonable investor test) and in this respect see n 58. Further, there is an elaboration of the reasonable investor test (there is no equivalent in the COMC to these elaborations). For example, the DTRs indicate that there is no set figure (percentage change or otherwise) in determining what constitutes a significant effect—this will vary from issuer to issuer— and that a variety of factors such as the issuer's size, recent developments, market sentiment and the sector in which the issuer operates will come into play in ascertaining the significance of the information. While not generally speaking prescriptive in terms of how the reasonable investor test will apply in this context, the DTRs do indicate that any assessment would need to take account of the anticipated impact of the information in light of the totality of the issuer's activities, the reliability of the source of the information, and other market variables likely to affect the relevant financial instruments. DTR 2.2.6 goes on to set out a non-exhaustive list of information which is likely to be considered relevant to a reasonable investor's decision. Note also DTR 2.2.2R (n 135).

[141] ibid, 2.2.2R, implementing the requirement of art 2.

[142] ibid, 2.2.9G(2).

[143] ibid, 2.4 for the full Rules.

[144] FSA Final Notice to Woolworths Group plc dated 11 June 2008 [RDC hearing].

information'. This was, according to the FSA, entirely consistent with the guidance in the Disclosure Rules to the effect that there was no set percentage or other figure to determine whether there was a 'significant effect on price'. On the facts, the FSA was satisfied that the variation in question resulted in a profit reduction of more than 10 per cent and that that was, on any view, information of a type that a reasonable investor would be likely to use as a part of his investment decision. In this regard the decision would seem to indicate a reduced emphasis on the likely effect of the relevant information on the company's share price per se in the analysis of whether an announcement is required.

Exception from the basic rule allowing an issuer to delay disclosure

There is an exception to the basic disclosure rule, which allows an issuer to delay disclosure of **10.85** inside information to an RIS in order not to 'prejudice its legitimate interests', provided that:

(i) such omission would not be likely to mislead the public;
(ii) any person receiving the information owes the issuer a duty of confidentiality, regardless of whether such duty is based on law, regulations, articles of association, or contract; and
(iii) the issuer is able to ensure the confidentiality of that information.[145]

Two non-exhaustive examples of not prejudicing legitimate interests are then given by the FCA, such that non-disclosure is permissible first where negotiations concerning the future financial viability of the issuer would be threatened by disclosure (eg in a potential insolvency situation). The second example given is where the organisational structure of the issuer means that decisions need to be taken by more than one body within that issuer.[146] However, the issuer's ability to delay making disclosure to the RIS does not mean that the issuer is permitted to make disclosure to other persons. On the contrary, it is specifically stated in the Disclosure Rules that where an issuer makes selective disclosure of inside information to a third party, it must make immediate disclosure to an RIS.[147]

The requirements relating to the EU-based requirements to disclose 'inside information', the **10.86** definitions used, and the circumstances in which disclosure can be delayed are also discussed in Chapter 9, paragraph 9.13.

Provisions relating to the control of insiders and inside information

As noted in Chapter 9 at paragraph 9.14, in addition to the basic disclosure rule and excep- **10.87** tions to that rule, the Disclosure Rules also impose rules on issuers relating to the control of insiders and inside information. For example, issuers are required to establish effective arrangements to deny access to inside information to persons other than those who require it for the exercise of their functions within the issuer,[148] and to have in place measures which enable public disclosure to be made via an RIS as soon as possible in case the issuer is not able to ensure the confidentiality of the relevant inside information.[149] Further, issuers are required to draw up and maintain lists of persons who have access to inside information.[150] There is also a set of rules which controls the notification by issuers to an RIS of transactions

145 DTR 2.5.1R, implementing art 6(2) of MAD.
146 ibid, 2.5.3R, implementing art 3(1) of the MAD Implementing Directive 2003/124/EC.
147 ibid, 2.5.6R, although guidance at DTR 2.5.7G permits disclosures to persons who owe the issuer a duty of confidentiality (eg its professional advisers).
148 ibid, 2.6.1R.
149 ibid, 2.6.2R.
150 ibid, 2.8, implementing art 6(3) of MAD. See also discussion in Chapter 9 at para 9.15.

by certain officers of that issuer in financial instruments of the issuer. Persons discharging managerial responsibilities and their connected persons must notify the issuer in writing of the occurrence of all transactions conducted on their own account in the shares of the issuer, or derivatives, or any other financial instruments relating to those shares within four business days of the day on which the transaction occurred.[151] The issuer must in turn inform the RIS of any disclosure by such a person.[152] As discussed in Chapter 9 at paragraph 9.13, issuers must also comply with 'listing principles', which include the principle that listed companies take reasonable steps to put in place systems and controls for complying with these obligations. The sanctions for a breach of these requirements would be the same as discussed earlier in this chapter.

10.88 The FSA set out in *MarketWatch* 27 Principles of Good Practice for the Handling of Inside Information. This was produced by an industry working group comprised of market practitioners and relevant representative bodies. This followed up on the FSA's desire to consider ways to share good practice points with firms it did not regulate.

10.89 While the FSA fully supported the document, it is not FSA guidance and the FSA said it will not be assessing firms' compliance against it. The main aim is that the work contributes to an overall heightened awareness of the ways to protect sensitive information.

The City Code on Takeovers and Mergers

10.90 The City Code on Takeovers and Mergers (the 'City Code') is a statutory set of rules which obliges market participants to act in accordance with certain rules on the procedure of making a takeover offer for a listed company. The Panel on Takeovers and Mergers (the Panel) is the UK regulatory body that issues and enforces the City Code on Takeovers and Mergers and oversees its daily application.[153] The Panel is able to investigate and punish breaches of the City Code (in the sense that the Panel may issue public censures or require other listed companies not to deal with 'blacklisted' firms).

Regulatory and Prosecuting Bodies

Interaction between the various regulatory and prosecuting bodies with powers relating to market misconduct

10.91 Under the UK financial services regime, a number of bodies have the power to investigate and take proceedings in respect of market misconduct. Again, the lack of clear and effective demarcation lines between the powers of these various bodies had historically given rise to considerable criticism. This section outlines the primary regulatory and prosecuting bodies and their various powers. It then considers the interaction between the prosecuting powers of these bodies and the FCA, as set out in the FCA's Guidelines on the interaction between prosecuting bodies[154] (the 'Prosecuting Guidelines'), and the arrangements that are now in

[151] ibid, 3.1.2R.

[152] ibid, 3.1.4R(1)(a). The Rules are set out in full at DTR 3.1 and implement art 6(4) of MAD. See also discussion in Chapter 9 at para 9.16.

[153] The Panel on Takeovers and Mergers was granted formal statutory powers pursuant to the implementation of the Takeover Directive (2004/25/EC), which was implemented in the UK by Part 28 of the Companies Act 2006 on 20 May 2006.

[154] FCA Enforcement Guide ('EG') Annex 2G sets out the guidelines on investigation of cases of interest or concern to the FCA and other prosecuting and investigating agencies. See also EG 12.11 which states that

place between the FCA and other regulatory bodies relating to the operation of regulatory investigations ('Operating Arrangements').[155]

Overview of the UK's Prosecuting Bodies

The following bodies all have responsibility for investigating or prosecuting matters of market misconduct. **10.92**

The FCA

The FCA has the power to commence investigations and commence prosecutions or regulatory action in any part of the UK regarding possible market abuse under section 118 FSMA; the offences under Part 7 FSA 2012 (offences relating to financial services), and, except in Scotland, Part V of the CJA 1993 (insider dealing).[156] **10.93**

In addition to this the FCA has a number of investigative and disciplinary powers relating to misconduct by firms and individuals regulated by it. **10.94**

With reference to breach of DTRs as discussed at paragraph 10.79 *et seq.*, powers in respect of enforcement are also vested in the FCA. **10.95**

The Department for Business, Innovation and Skills [157]

The Secretary of State of the Department for Business, Innovation and Skills ('BIS') shares with the FCA a concurrent jurisdiction to investigate a number of market misconduct matters by reason of section 401(2) FSMA (a jurisdiction shared with the FSA, and now the FCA, since 2001). In practice, the BIS's role is primarily an investigatory one, through the appointment of 'inspectors' or 'investigators'.[158] However, the investigations may lead to prosecution by the BIS. For example, Timothy Power was prosecuted by the BIS for insider **10.96**

guidelines have established a framework for cooperation in cases where one or more of these bodies also has an interest in prosecuting a matter that the FCA is considering for investigation. The Prosecuting Guidelines were previously set out in the FSA Handbook Enforcement manual Chapter 2 Annex 1G until 27 August 2007. The Enforcement manual ('ENF') and the Decision Making manual ('DEC') were deleted and replaced by the Decision Procedure and Penalties manual ('DEPP') and a regulatory guide, the EG, as part of the FSA's work on simplifying the Handbook and promoting better regulation. The EG does not form part of the Handbook and comprises neither FCA rules nor guidance on the FCA rules but it is 'general guidance' as defined in section 139B of FSMA.

[155] The FCA entered into new Operating Guidelines with the Takeover Panel on 1 April 2013.

[156] The FCA's power to prosecute offences under part 7 FSA 2012 is stated in s 401 FSMA. The power to initiate prosecutions for criminal insider dealing under the CJA is contained in s 402(1)(a) FSMA, which specifically excludes Scotland from the ambit of the FCA's prosecuting powers for CJA insider dealing. See also Chapter 9 at para 9.257.

[157] The Department for Business, Innovation & Skills ('BIS') was previously the Department for Trade and Industry.

[158] The Secretary of State has the power to appoint an inspector where requested to do so by a prescribed proportion of the members of a company, or where it appears that appointment is necessary where circumstances suggest the company's affairs have been conducted for a fraudulent or unlawful purpose—ss 431–2 of the Companies Act 1985 (now amended by Companies Act 2006) (it was these powers under which Ernest Saunders was investigated, see Chapter 9, para 9.10). An investigator may be appointed by the Secretary of State to require the company to produce documents or provide information, or to enter premises to investigate a company, under s 447 of the Companies Act 1985, (as amended by the Companies (Audit, Investigations and Community Enterprise) Act 2004) and s 448 (as amended by the Companies Act 2006). The DTI had published guidance on the amended provisions—DTI, 'A guide to the investigations provisions introduced by the Act', January 2005.

dealing and convicted in February 2009. However, it would be more common for the BIS to disclose information to the FCA or other prosecutors to allow them to take appropriate action.[159] Any enforcement action taken by the BIS would ordinarily relate to corporate matters, for example orders for the winding up of a company, or the disqualification of directors.[160]

The Serious Fraud Office

10.97 The Serious Fraud Office ('SFO') is charged with the investigation of matters of serious or complex fraud. Its remit overlaps with that of the FCA where the market misconduct could constitute serious fraud, with the SFO taking into account factors such as the financial value of any crime, the national interest, specialist knowledge required for the investigation, and any international dimension when determining whether to take action in a particular fraud case.[161]

Public prosecution bodies

10.98 The Crown Prosecution Service ('CPS') is the prosecuting body in England and Wales in those cases of suspected misconduct where a criminal investigation has been initiated by the police (in Scotland prosecutions are initiated by the Crown Office and Procurator Fiscal Service ('COPFS') and in Northern Ireland by the Public Prosecution Services ('PPS') for Northern Ireland).[162] There is a possibility of overlap with the FCA, especially in the area of fraud.[163]

Other Powers of Review, Enquiry, and Discipline

10.99 While not prosecuting powers as such, the following are also relevant in the context of market misconduct or market failings:

Exchanges

10.100 As noted at paragraph 10.78, exchanges in the UK will have various investigative and disciplinary powers relating to misconduct by members or affecting the relevant exchange. The question of when misconduct should be considered by the FCA, and when by the exchanges, is discussed further at paragraph 10.105.

The Takeover Panel

10.101 As noted at paragraph 10.90, the Panel can investigate and take action in respect of breaches of the City Code. There are a set of operating guidelines between the FCA and the Panel.[164]

The police

10.102 The police are responsible for the arrest of persons suspected of arrestable offences and in certain situations they will assist the FCA with the investigation of market misconduct matters.

---

[159] Disclosure is permitted under s 449(2) of the Companies Act 1985, as amended by the Companies Act 2006, to such agencies and persons as are stated in Sch 15C, which includes the Director of Public Prosecutions, a police constable, and the FCA.

[160] Prosecuting Guidelines, Appendix, para 2.2.

[161] ibid, Appendix, para 3.3.

[162] The CPS, headed by the DPP, is the Government department responsible for prosecuting criminal offences investigated by the police.

[163] Prosecuting Guidelines, Appendix, para 4.1.

[164] See n 153.

There is a memorandum of understanding ('MOU') in place between the FCA and the police to assign responsibility in such instances.[165]

Interaction Between the FCA and Other Prosecuting Bodies

It is apparent from the foregoing discussion that there is potentially a significant overlap in the investigatory and prosecuting functions of a number of bodies which has historically given rise to criticism. To address this, in addition to the centralisation of certain powers in the FSA which took place under FSMA, Prosecuting Guidelines were introduced in 2007 to enable the various agencies to determine which is responsible for pursuing a particular incident of market misconduct.[166] **10.103**

The Prosecuting Guidelines

The Prosecuting Guidelines list first a number of situations which would 'tend' towards enforcement by the FCA being considered appropriate, and then set out a number of factors which would tend towards action by another prosecuting body being appropriate. There is no prescribed number of these factors which must be satisfied in order to conclude which is the appropriate body to take action. Rather it is presupposed that this will be apparent after a comparison of these factors. **10.104**

Interaction between the FCA and other bodies with regulatory powers

The FCA has entered into a number of operating arrangements with certain other bodies which have a role in regulating the financial markets or taking regulatory action against suspected market misconduct. At present, there are such guidelines in place between the FCA and the Panel and arrangements with various recognised investment exchanges. The purpose of these operating arrangements is to determine those situations in which it would be appropriate for either the FCA or the other party to the operating arrangements to pursue suspected misconduct, where a particular matter may otherwise fall within both of their jurisdictions. In general, the recognised investment exchange will deal with misconduct that is limited to the exchange, where the perpetrators are all members, and where the exchange's powers are sufficient to deal with the matter, and the FCA will focus on cross-market abuse, abuse by persons who are not members of an exchange, and criminal activity. **10.105**

Memorandum of Understanding with the Police

As mentioned at paragraph 10.102, there is an MOU in place between the FCA and Association of Chief Police Officers of England & Wales ('ACPO'). The purpose of the MOU is to set out the agreed best practice for cooperation between the police and the FCA with regard to: **10.106**

(i) the arrest of suspects where the FCA and the police have reasonable grounds to suspect that an individual has committed an arrestable offence,[167] and the FCA seeks the assistance of the police in questioning the suspect; or

[165] MOU between the FCA and the Association of Chief Police Officers of England & Wales ('ACPO'), available at <http://www.fsa.gov.uk/pubs/mou/fsacolp.pdf>; brought into force in August 2005 to replace the former memorandum in place with the City of London Police.

[166] EG Annex 2, paras 3–7. The parties to the Prosecuting Guidelines, the current version of which are annexed to EG, are FCA, SFO, BIS, CPS (and therefore DPP), ACPO, Crown Office (for Scotland), PPS (for Northern Ireland), ACPO(S) (Scotland).

[167] At the time of the MOU this was defined as an offence which has a punishment on conviction on indictment of a term of imprisonment of five years or greater.

(ii) a warrant obtained by the FCA where the FCA seeks the assistance of the police in connection with the execution of the warrant.[168]

The MOU sets out in considerable detail the procedures for this agreed cooperation to be implemented in practice (paragraphs 4 to 13 of the MOU).

Interaction with overseas regulators under MAD

10.107 As discussed in Chapter 9,[169] directives such as MAD forming part of the EU Financial Services Action Plan are predicated on the enhancement of cross-border business by the creation of harmonised standards. In the case of MAD, for example, this is illustrated by the territorial scope[170] of the offences envisaged by the directive. Thus offensive conduct undertaken in London relating to qualifying investments listed on a regulated market in Germany would in principle fall within the MAD determined market abuse regimes in both the UK and Germany. MAD addresses this by stating that it ought to be the authority of the State in which the abusive acts took place or, where acts affect securities listed on an exchange, the State in which the exchange is located.[171] The risk of double jeopardy (that is to say, in the example just given, that action will be taken both in the UK and in Germany) is reduced to an extent by giving foreign regulators the right to refuse to take action if a 'final judgment' has already been delivered (Article 16(2)).

10.108 As a general proposition, MAD also sets out detailed provisions for the cooperation expected between Member State regulators. The guiding principle in Article 16(1) is that these regulators 'shall co-operate with each other whenever necessary for the purpose of carrying out their duties'. The detail of the expected behaviour is set out in the remainder of Article 16, including information sharing, and making and responding to requests for an investigation to be carried out in another Member State.

[168] Para 3 of the MOU. The MOU also replaces the MOU that was in place between the FSA and the City of London Police.

[169] See Chapter 9, para 9.11.

[170] Discussed further at Chapter 9, para 9.79.

[171] Art 16(3), although this does not seem to resolve the debate in particular. DEPP 6.2.21G states that where it is appropriate for both the FCA and an overseas or domestic regulatory authority or enforcement agency to take action, the FCA will work with the relevant authority to ensure that cases are dealt with efficiently and fairly, under operating arrangements in place (if any) between the FCA and the relevant authority.

11

MONEY LAUNDERING AND FINANCIAL CRIME[1]

What is Money Laundering?

The October 2004 UK anti-money laundering policy document[2] adopted a practical description of what constitutes money laundering. It is: 11.01

> a term generally used to describe the ways in which criminals process illegal or 'dirty' money derived from the proceeds of any illegal activity (eg the proceeds of drug-dealing, human trafficking, fraud, theft or tax evasion) through a succession of transfers and deals until the source of illegally acquired funds is obscured and the money takes on the appearance of legitimate or 'clean' funds or assets.

In the UK, the legal definition of money laundering is provided by the Terrorism Act 2000 and the Proceeds of Crime Act 2002 ('PoCA'). The definition in those Acts is relied on by both the Money Laundering Regulations 2007[3] ('MLR 2007') and the Financial Conduct Authority's ('FCA') Handbook.[4] In summary, the PoCA definition provides that a person commits the offence of money laundering if he: 11.02

(a) conceals, disguises, converts, transfers, or removes (from the UK) criminal property;
(b) enters into or becomes concerned in an arrangement which he knows or suspects, facilitates (by whatever means) the acquisition, retention, use, or control of criminal property by or on behalf of another person; or
(c) acquires, uses or has possession of criminal property.

The process of money laundering is considered to consist of three stages: 11.03

(a) placement;
(b) layering; and
(c) integration.

Placement

In the initial stage of money laundering, the launderer places the cash generated from his criminal activity into the financial system or uses it to buy goods. This may be done by breaking up large amounts of cash into less conspicuous smaller sums and depositing them in a 11.04

1 The contributors to Chapter 11 were assisted by Mark Chalmers, Norton Rose Fulbright LLP.
2 HM Treasury, Anti-Money Laundering Strategy (October 2004).
3 The Money Laundering Regulations 2007, SI 2007/2157.
4 SYSC s 6.3 (Financial crime).

bank account or by purchasing negotiable financial instruments such as money orders or cheques. This process is sometimes referred to as 'smurfing', with the launderers employing a number of low-level criminals to make deposits at different branches of the same institution. It is at this stage of the laundering process that the 'dirty' funds are most easily identifiable. Given the fact that the laundered funds are most often held in cash form, launderers are generally considered to be most likely to target deposit-takers such as banks and building societies and suppliers of high value goods such as antique dealers.

Layering

11.05 Once the funds have entered the system, the second stage—layering—takes place. This is the stage where the dirty money is distanced from the original source. This is done by the launderer engaging in a series of transactions. These transactions will involve conversions or movements of the funds. As well as simple transfers between different accounts, the funds may be channelled through the purchase or sale of investments. Sometimes the layering stage is conducted cross-border, with the launderer making use of accounts held in jurisdictions where anti-money laundering standards are low. The launderer may also disguise the transfers as payments for goods or services, thus giving them a legitimate appearance.

Integration

11.06 Once the original source of the funds has been obscured, the launderer moves on to the third and final stage: integration. Having successfully processed his criminal funds through placement and layering, the launderer is able to reintroduce them to the economy so they appear to be legitimate by converting them into legal business earnings through normal financial and commercial operations.

United Kingdom Policy Drivers

11.07 The Government Strategy Document[5] and the subsequent 'Financial Challenge to Crime and Terrorism' document[6] both made clear the UK Government's intention to combat money laundering. Fighting money laundering is not just seen as an end in itself, rather limiting the ability of criminals to launder the proceeds of criminal activity is seen as a vital part of the wider fight against criminal activity generally. Illegal arms sales, smuggling, and the activities of organised crime, such as drug trafficking and prostitution rings, can generate huge sums of money and lax financial markets and anti-money laundering standards will tend to attract criminal elements with consequences for law and order generally. The Government's overriding goal is to protect its citizens and reduce the harm caused by crime and terrorism. Whilst finance is the lifeblood of criminal and terrorist networks, it is also one of their greatest vulnerabilities.

11.08 The Government's objectives are to use financial measures to:

(a) deter crime and terrorism in the first place;
(b) detect the criminal or terrorist abuse of the financial system; and
(c) disrupt criminal and terrorist activity.

---

[5] HM Treasury, Anti-Money Laundering Strategy (October 2004).
[6] HM Treasury (February 2007).

Given the pre-eminence of its financial markets, and their international nature, the UK is an obvious target for money launderers. In recent years, Government policy has set great emphasis on restricting the ability of criminals, both domestic and international, to use the UK to launder funds. The importance of the financial markets to the wider UK economy cannot be overstated and, as a consequence, protecting and developing the reputation and standing of the UK as a financial centre is a major policy goal of all UK Governments, regardless of their political complexion. Whilst domestic criminal policy is largely driven by the Home Office and latterly by the Ministry of Justice, HM Treasury plays a major part in the development of anti-money laundering policy generally and leads Government negotiation of EU legislation in this area as well as developing and implementing specific domestic anti-money laundering legislation such as the MLR 2007. **11.09**

HM Treasury was responsible for coordinating the implementation of the Financial Services and Markets Act 2000 ('FSMA'). The importance of the fight against crime and the need to reduce the use by criminals of the UK's financial markets is expressly provided for in FSMA. The Act contains three FCA operational objectives which includes the integrity objective at section 1B (3). The integrity objective is further described at section 1D which provides: **11.10**

(1) The integrity objective is: protecting and enhancing the integrity of the UK financial system.
(2) The 'integrity' of the UK financial system includes:
  (a) its soundness, stability, and resilience,
  (b) it not being used for a purpose connected with financial crime,
  (c) it not being affected by behaviour that amounts to market abuse,
  (d) the orderly operation of the financial markets, and
  (e) the transparency of the price formation process in those markets.

Additional interpretive provisions are provided at section 1H, including:
(3) 'Financial crime' includes any offence involving:
  (a) fraud or dishonesty,
  (b) misconduct in, or misuse of information relating to, a financial market,
  (c) handling the proceeds of crime, or
  (d) the financing of terrorism.
(4) 'Offence' includes an act or omission which would be an offence if it had taken place in the UK.

FSMA originally gave the Financial Services Authority ('FSA') the power to make rules[7] and also the power to institute proceedings under Part V of the Criminal Justice Act 1993 (insider dealing) or regulations relating to money laundering.[8] The significance of the FSA's role in the fight against money laundering was underlined by the provision in FSMA of a specific power to the FSA to create money laundering rules at section 146. **11.11**

On 1 April 2013, the Financial Services Act 2012 ('FSA 2012') amended certain provisions of FSMA and transferred many of the functions of the FSA to the FCA and the Prudential Regulatory Authority ('PRA'). Under the new regulatory regime, the FCA assumes all of the FSA's financial crime responsibilities, including the ability to institute proceedings under the **11.12**

[7] FSMA, s 138.
[8] ibid, s 402.

Criminal Justice Act 1993 and money laundering regulations, as well as the power to make money laundering rules under the new section 137A(1) FSMA.

11.13 Prior to being amended by the FSA 2012, section 6 of FSMA made explicit reference to the reduction of financial crime as a stand-alone regulatory objective. The fact that financial crime has now been subsumed within the wider integrity objective does not mean that the commitment of the UK to fight financial crime has been diluted. Instead, it represents a new, holistic view of financial crime which is inextricably tied to the integrity of the financial system as a whole rather than as an isolated phenomenon.[9]

The UK's Fight Against Money Laundering: The Policy Backdrop

11.14 Although the fight against money laundering has assumed greater prominence since the implementation of FSMA and the establishment of the FSA, anti-money laundering legislation has been in place for some time. The Money Laundering Regulations 1993[10] ('MLR 1993') which covered financial institutions implemented the First Money Laundering Directive ('1MLD'),[11] and came into effect in 1994. The MLR 1993 were developed as Government policy sought to extend the scope of regulation to other activities, such as money services businesses (including bureaux de change). However, the criminal offence of money laundering pre-dates the MLR 1993 (see, for example, the Criminal Justice Act 1988 and the Drug Trafficking Offences Act 1986).

11.15 Increasing concerns that those behind high-profile terrorist acts had been heavily involved in money laundering in order to support their activities led to specific legislation to deal with money laundering in the context of terrorism, (see, in particular, the Terrorism Act 2000 (as amended by the Anti-Terrorism, Crime and Security Act 2001)).

International Nature of the Fight against Money Laundering

11.16 The international nature of the activities of money launderers has led to action against the problem at supra-national level. The European Union ('EU') has implemented various pieces of legislation in an attempt to coordinate anti-money laundering activity within the EU.[12]

11.17 Concern about money laundering has been on the European policy agenda for many years with the 1MLD reaching the European statute books in 1991. The policy background to the perceived need for EU-level action on money laundering was restated in the European Commission Communication on Organised Crime and the Financial Sector dated April 2004[13] (the 'Communication on Organised Financial Crime'). The Communication on

[9] Please see Chapter 4 (European Financial Services) at paras 4.157–4.165 for further discussion on Insider Dealing and Market Abuse at the EU level.

[10] The Money Laundering Regulations 1993 (now repealed and substituted by the Money Laundering Regulations 2007, SI 2007/2157).

[11] Council Directive (EC) 91/308 on prevention of the use of the financial system for the purpose of money laundering [1991] OJ L166, P 0077–0083. Council Directive of 10 June on prevention of the use of the financial system for the purpose of money laundering (91/308/EEC) [1991] OJ L166, P 0077–0083.

[12] This legislation is discussed in detail at paras 11.38–11.84.

[13] Communication from the Commission to the Council and the European Parliament on the Organised Crime in the Financial Sector COM (2004) 262 Final, Brussels, 16.4.2004.

Organised Financial Crime notes that the fight against money laundering 'has been a top political priority of the European Union for a number of years, based on the need to protect the financial system from contamination and misuse, and to support efforts to combat organised crime in the financial sector'.

The importance of the fight against money laundering to the integrity of the internal market was emphasised in a statement by Internal Market and Services Commissioner Michel Barnier. Commissioner Barnier explained: **11.18**

> The Union is at the forefront of international efforts to combat the laundering of the proceeds of crime. Flows of dirty money can damage the stability and reputation of the financial sector, while terrorism shakes the very foundations of our society. In addition to the criminal law approach, a preventive effort via the financial system can help to stop money-laundering. Our aim is to propose clear rules that reinforce the vigilance by banks, lawyers, accountants and all other professional concerned.[14]

European legislators consider that the need to protect the financial system from misuse and the desire to avoid Member States employing 'radically different measures' against money laundering, which could prejudice the proper functioning of the internal market, justify action at EU level. The recitals to 1MLD make it clear that one of the key drivers behind that and subsequent money laundering directives was the desire to avoid Member States taking individual measures that could be inconsistent with the completion of a single European market.[15] **11.19**

The Financial Action Task Force

The international fight against money laundering has not been limited to the European stage. In response to growing concerns regarding the development of money laundering, the Financial Action Task Force on Money Laundering[16] ('FATF') was set up by the G-7 summit in Paris in 1989. FATF was established expressly to develop an international response to what had become an international problem. **11.20**

FATF is an intergovernmental body and its members include countries that are home to the world's major financial centres. FATF states its purpose as being 'the development and promotion of policies, both at national and international levels, to combat money laundering and terrorist financing'. It considers itself to be a ' "policy-making body" which works to generate the necessary political will to bring about national legislative and regulatory reforms in these areas'. **11.21**

Whilst FATF has been in existence since 1989, it reviews its mission at regular intervals. The latest revised mandate for 2012–2020, having been agreed in April 2012 by ministers from FATF Member States, will only continue as long as it is considered to have a viable role. **11.22**

The founding members of FATF gave it the responsibility of examining money laundering techniques and trends, reviewing the action which had already been taken at a national or international level, and setting out the measures that still needed to be taken to combat money laundering. **11.23**

[14] <http://europa.eu/rapid/press-release_IP-13-87_en.htm>.

[15] Please see Chapter 4 (European Financial Services) at paras 4.168–4.172 for further discussion on Money Laundering Directives at the EU level.

[16] The FATF website can be accessed at <http://www.fatf-gafi.org>.

11.24 FATF, since its establishment, has focused its work on three main activities:

(a) standard-setting;
(b) ensuring effective compliance with the standards; and
(c) identifying money laundering and terrorist financing threats.

11.25 These activities remain at the core of the new mandate and FATF will build on this work and respond to new and emerging threats, such as proliferation financing and vulnerabilities in new technologies which could destabilise the international financial system.

11.26 The initial membership of FATF numbered 16 States but this has steadily expanded. As of Spring 2013, there were 34 Member States and two regional organisations: the Gulf Cooperation Council and the EU.

The 40 Recommendations

11.27 FATF has developed 40 Recommendations which set out minimum measures that national governments should take to implement effective anti-money laundering programmes. Since their initial drafting, the 40 Recommendations have been updated several times to reflect the evolution of anti-money laundering policies and best practice. The FATF website describes the 40 Recommendations as having been:

> recognised, endorsed or adopted by many international bodies. The Recommendations are neither complex nor difficult, nor do they compromise the freedom to engage in legitimate transactions or threaten economic development. They set out the principles for action and allow countries a measure of flexibility in implementing these principles according to their particular circumstances and constitutional frameworks. Though not a binding international convention, many countries in the world have made a political commitment to combat money laundering by implementing the 40 Recommendations.

11.28 The 40 Recommendations have a broad scope and are detailed. The full text of the 40 Recommendations and the accompanying interpretive notes can be accessed on the FATF website. The original form 40 Recommendations were given force at EU level by 1MLD and have been revised to take account of the changes in money laundering trends and to anticipate future threats. The FATF completed thorough reviews and updates of the Recommendations in 1996, 2003 and again in early 2012. The Recommendations continue to be the cornerstone of the current 3MLD and will serve as the basis for the 4MLD which is discussed in more detail later in this chapter.[17]

Terrorist financing

11.29 The international community's concern with regard to terrorism has been reflected in the development by FATF of nine Special Recommendations on Terrorist Financing. These Special Recommendations were published by FATF on 31 October 2001 and recognised that terrorists were increasingly relying on the international financial system both to fund terrorist activity and to launder funds obtained by terrorist organisations. FATF considers that the combination of the Special Recommendations and the 40 Recommendations has so far provided the right balance between giving the required stability to the FATF standards, whilst allowing for the necessary flexibility to respond to the changing nature of the threats

[17] Please see Chapter 4 (European Financial Services) at paras 4.170–4.172 for further discussion on 3MLD and 4MLD.

faced. Maintaining this balance between stability and flexibility allows for more predictability and consistent implementation globally.

Identifying and responding to new threats

Globalisation has created potential new risks as criminals and terrorists seek to penetrate the global financial system. The FATF intends to remain at the centre of international efforts to protect the integrity of the financial system and will respond to the significant new threats emerging which are related to, but may fall outside its core activities. **11.30**

Proliferation financing is a current example of an area where the FATF can add value to the wider efforts of the international community. **11.31**

FATF and the UK

The UK has been, and continues to be, an active member of FATF and held the Presidency in 2007/8. The Financial Challenge to Crime and Terrorism document[18] emphasises the UK's commitment to FATF, and the Government's desire to continue to play a leading role in the work of FATF. **11.32**

Non-cooperative countries and territories

FATF has also identified a number of jurisdictions which it considers have failed to establish and maintain proper anti-money laundering regulation. These jurisdictions are generally referred to as Non-Cooperative Countries and Territories ('NCCTs'). The list of NCCTs is updated regularly and can be accessed on the FATF website. **11.33**

As well as the activities of FATF, other public international bodies have sought to develop guidelines and principles for national supervisors of financial services firms to follow. Such initiatives include the Basel CDD paper,[19] IAIS Guidance Paper 5,[20] the Egmont Group, and the Wolfsberg Group.[21] IOSCO has also been active in the area of anti-money laundering generally.[22] **11.34**

Law and Regulation

Most of the anti-money laundering legislation that impacts on the UK financial services sector finds its basis in EU legislation. To date, most of this legislation has taken the form of directives, although the EU has implemented FATF Special Recommendation 7 (information on the payer accompanying transfers of funds) by means of a European Regulation.[23] **11.35**

---

[18] HM Treasury, 'The Financial Challenge to Crime and Terrorism' (February 2007).

[19] Basel Committee on Banking Supervision's report on Customer Due Diligence for Banks issued in October 2001.

[20] Guidance Paper 5 'Anti-money Laundering and Combating the Financing of Terrorism' October 2004 is published by the International Association of Insurance Supervisors and can be accessed at: <http://www.iaisweb.org/index.cfm?pageID=41>.

[21] The Wolfsberg Principles—Global Anti-Money Laundering Guidelines for Private Banking, Revised 1 May 2002.

[22] See IOSCO website at: <http://www.iosco.org/>.

[23] Regulation (EC) No 1781/2006 of the European Parliament and of the Council of 15 November 2006 on information on the payer accompanying transfers of funds.

Other Developments Driving EU Legislation

11.36 The Communication on Organised Financial Crime explored the need for future EU level policy initiatives. While some of these take the form of policy initiatives to encourage Member States to develop domestic capacity to combat identified money laundering risks, experience tends to indicate that such initiatives often lead to EU legislative action.

11.37 Some of the policy areas not now covered by the EU money laundering directives are:

(a) Database of currency transactions
The Communication on Organised Financial Crime discussed the feasibility of Member States establishing an electronic database of currency exchange transactions above a certain amount. The database would be available to the police and judicial authorities.

(b) Financial havens
Consideration is being given to the adoption by the EU of legislation covering on-shore and off-shore financial centres and tax havens operating in Member States and their dependencies and a common EU policy towards financial centres and tax havens lying outside the EU.

(c) Underground banking
The European Commission is concerned about the operation of underground banking and 'alternative remittance systems', which it considers are frequently used by criminals and terrorists for the international transfer of illegal funds. To combat the risks posed by such arrangements, the European Commission is participating in the establishment of an early warning system to promote information exchange and joint action to disrupt the unlawful international transfer of funds.

(d) Asset recovery bodies
The Commission proposes the establishment of asset recovery bodies at national level and supports Europol's 'Asset seizure knowledge centre' to facilitate the identification of criminal assets in the course of major criminal investigations conducted by Member States.

(e) FIU-NET project
This is designed to establish a fully operational computer network linking all Member States' financial intelligence units for the processing and exchange of financial information, including intelligence suspected to be associated with terror financing.

The First and Second Money Laundering Directives

11.38 FATF initially identified certain areas, which were vulnerable in the money laundering process and could, if monitored, assist in the fight against the money launderer. These were the entry of cash into the financial system, transfers to and from the financial system, and cross-border payments.

11.39 1MLD, which was based on the 1989 Banking Directive, originally concentrated on combating the laundering of the proceeds of drugs through the traditional financial sector and was published in the Official Journal in June 1991. It set out to ensure that money laundering was prohibited by requiring that financial institutions identify their customers when entering into a business relationship or when carrying out a one-off transaction above a certain value. Peripheral activities such as bureaux de change and money transmission agencies were excluded as well as the bulk of client accounts of lawyers and accountants.

Other features were the requirement for banks and financial institutions to report suspicious transactions to the authorities and the prohibition on 'tipping off', where a customer is advised that a report has been made. Banks were also required to provide training for their staff and establish internal systems and controls to prevent money laundering. **11.40**

The limited scope of 1MLD was soon recognised as a weakness by European legislators and one of the key changes introduced by the Second Money Laundering Directive[24] ('2MLD') was the expansion of the range of criminal offences covered to 'serious crimes'. These included offences which may generate substantial proceeds and which are punishable by 'a severe sentence of imprisonment'. **11.41**

2MLD also expanded the scope of persons captured from credit and financial institutions to persons carrying on other activities such as certain types of professional adviser, estate agents, and casinos. Article 6 provided that Member States are required to ensure that credit and financial institutions and their directors and employees 'cooperate fully with the authorities responsible for combating money laundering'. This captured a number of persons not previously subject to regulation and Article 6 was amended in part to reflect some of the consequences of this expansion of scope. For example, Article 6(3) expressly protected legal professional privilege. **11.42**

Reporting obligations and the 'tipping off' provision were the subjects of much debate and, due to the differing structures of the professions between Member States, further legislation was required to clarify the position. **11.43**

Implementation of 2MLD was uneven due to the accession of new Member States in May of 2004 and the failure of Greece and Italy to meet the June 2003 deadline. **11.44**

Identification procedures under the two directives were broadly similar and were implemented in the UK by secondary legislation (originally the MLR 1993 and MLR 2003 and now by the MLR 2007). These requirements are examined later in this chapter. **11.45**

2MLD introduced an important concession. 1MLD provided that where the customer was a credit or financial institution that was itself regulated by the directive there was no need to identify it for anti-money laundering purposes. 2MLD extended this concession to cover credit or financial institutions 'situated in a third country which imposes, in the opinion of the relevant Member [State], equivalent requirements to those laid down by [the directive]'.[25] **11.46**

The Third Money Laundering Directive

The Third Money Laundering Directive[26] ('3MLD') was adopted on 26 October 2005. It reflected the belief among EU legislators that the substantial changes to the FATF 40+9 **11.47**

[24] Directive (EC) 2001/97 of the European Parliament and the Council amending Council Directive (EC) 91/308 on prevention of the use of the financial system for the purpose of money laundering [2001] OJ L344, P 0076–0082.

[25] Please see Chapter 4 (European Financial Services) at paras 4.168–4.169 for further discussion on 1MLD and 2MLD.

[26] Directive 2005/60/EC of the European Parliament and of the Council dated 26 October 1995 on the prevention of the use of the financial system for the purpose of money laundering and terrorist financing.

Recommendations, agreed in June 2003, should be implemented in a coordinated way at EU level and replaced the existing amended directive (ie 1MLD and 2MLD), to help ensure clarity. The directive confirms in Article 5 that it is a so-called 'minimum harmonisation' directive as it expressly permits Member States to implement super-equivalent anti-money laundering provisions.

11.48 In its original explanatory memorandum[27] the European Commission set out the detailed policy aims of 3MLD and confirmed its view that the scope of the new directive should further widen the scope of anti-money laundering activity. For example, it suggested that the definition of money laundering should include terrorism to reflect the amended FATF 40 Recommendations. The definition of criminal activity was widened although this has no impact in the UK as Government policy has been to make any criminal activity a predicate to a money laundering offence. Other significant changes included the extension of the scope of regulation in 3MLD to capture life/investment insurance intermediaries and trust company service providers.

Customer due diligence

11.49 Articles 7 to 19 of 3MLD deal with customer due diligence ('CDD') procedures. The provisions contained in these articles are more detailed than those in the previous money laundering directives. The directive introduces the concept of a risk-based approach at EU level for the first time, which, the European Commission notes in its commentary on the directive, reflects the requirement in the FATF 40+9 Recommendations.

11.50 Article 7 of 3MLD requires Member States to ensure that firms complete the due diligence procedures before the establishment of a business relationship or the execution of a transaction. In other words, the directive acknowledges expressly that on occasion it may not be possible for a person falling within the scope of the directive to identify his customer before the relationship has started. The *quid pro quo* for this concession is that, where satisfactory information cannot be obtained, the relationship between the firm and its customer must be terminated.

11.51 Article 8 requires firms to apply due diligence procedures not only when taking on new customers, but also to conduct 'ongoing monitoring of the business relationship including scrutiny of transactions undertaken throughout the course of that relationship'. This policy approach is familiar to UK firms which were subject to regulation by the FSA, as it is broadly similar to its 'monitoring customer activity' initiative.

Beneficial owner

11.52 Article 3(6) of 3MLD introduces a definition of 'beneficial owner'. This definition is far more detailed than anything that has been seen in previous money laundering directives and captures a 'natural person who ultimately owns or controls a legal entity through direct or indirect ownership or control over a sufficient percentage of shares or voting rights in that legal entity'. A percentage of 25 per cent plus one share is deemed sufficient to meet this criterion. Beneficial ownership is relevant not just for natural persons, but also for legal entities, trusts, and unincorporated associations. In each case the persons controlling the accounts need to be identified.

11.53 Where a legal entity is a holding company for the assets of another, it is important to know the beneficial owner of the assets and where the money came from to purchase them.

[27] Document reference COM (2004) 448 Final 2004/0137 Brussels, 30.06.2004.

In the case of trusts, the situation is slightly different as the beneficial owner will probably be the person in whose favour the trust was created and it is the settlor that would need to be identified. **11.54**

The approach of both the MLR 2007 and the FSA has been that, where an applicant for business/customer appears to be acting on behalf of another person, the firm should take reasonable steps to identify that other person as well. The Joint Money Laundering Steering Group Guidance Notes ('JMLSG Guidance')[28] stress that firms need to look behind an applicant for business/customer, especially if it is a corporate. However, the JMLSG Guidance suggests that generally identification evidence will only need to be obtained from shareholders that have an interest of 25 per cent. Although further proposed amendments to the JMLSG Guidance dated 1 July 2013[29] highlights if no individual owns or controls more than 25 per cent of the shares or voting rights, firms should use judgment in determining whether an individual owning or controlling a lower percentage exercises effective control. **11.55**

Simplified due diligence

The UK successfully argued the case that 3MLD should allow firms to reduce customer due diligence checks in certain circumstances and also to rely on a third party for undertaking the customer due diligence measures. Article 11 allows institutions covered by the directive not to apply customer due diligence where the risk of money laundering is low. **11.56**

The examples provided by Article 11 are where a firm deals with: credit or financial institutions from Member States; third countries that are subject to similar regulatory requirements; listed companies; beneficial owners of pooled accounts held by notaries and other independent legal professionals from the Member States or third countries subject to supervision of international requirements; and where the product offered has a low risk profile (such as life assurance with an annual premium of €1,000). **11.57**

It is however still necessary to conduct ongoing monitoring of the business relationship and the relaxation of the identification requirement is not applicable where it is suspected that a transaction involves terrorism or money laundering. **11.58**

Enhanced due diligence

In contrast to Article 11, Article 13 of 3MLD requires Member States to ensure that firms carry out enhanced due diligence in situations where the risk of money laundering is perceived to be higher. Article 13 provides a non-exhaustive list of three such higher risk propositions: distance contracts; cross-frontier correspondent banking relationships; and where a firm is dealing with a politically exposed person ('PEP'). **11.59**

Article 13(6) of the directive requires Member States to ensure that persons covered by the directive: **11.60**

(a) pay special attention to any money laundering or terrorist financing threat that may arise from products or transactions that might favour anonymity, and take measures, if needed, to prevent their use in money laundering or terrorist financing purposes.

[28] Joint Money Laundering Steering Group revised Guidance Notes 2007. Please see section on Joint Money Laundering Steering Group guidance notes at 10.240.

[29] Proposed Amendments to JMLSG Guidance (1 July 2013) can be accessed at: <http://www.jmlsg.org.uk/industry-guidance/article/summary-of-proposed-guidance-amendments>.

11.61 The European Commission has the power (in Article 40(1)(c)) to establish detailed rules for identifying situations which represent a high risk of money laundering, assisted by the Committee on the Prevention of Money Laundering.

11.62 The risk-based provisions in Article 13 are broadly consistent with the UK policy approach. The Treasury noted in its Consultation Document[30] that the UK already had provisions in the MLR 2003 that required firms to take account of the higher risk of money laundering, however the risk-based approach established by the 3MLD includes examples of instances that are considered high-risk. Further guidance on the risk-based approach can be found in the FATF Guidance on the Risk-Based Approach to Combating Money Laundering and Terrorist Financing[31] and the JMLSG Guidance.

Politically exposed persons

11.63 3MLD sets out the enhanced due diligence that is required when entering into transactions or business relationships with a PEP residing in another Member State or in a third country. Institutions and persons covered by the directive should:

(a) have appropriate risk-based procedures to determine whether the customer is a PEP;
(b) have senior management approval for establishing business relationships with such customers;
(c) take adequate measures to establish the source of wealth and source of funds that are involved in the business relationship or transaction;
(d) conduct enhanced ongoing monitoring of the business relationship.

11.64 Article 3(8) of the directive defines a PEP as:

(a) a natural person who is or has been entrusted with prominent public functions and immediate family members or persons known to be close associates of such persons.

11.65 The term is very general and is open to interpretation. The Swiss Federal Banking Commission defines a PEP as 'persons occupying an important public function' whilst the US inter-agency guidance defines these as a 'senior foreign political figure'.

11.66 Schedule 2(4) to the MLR 2007 sets out the examples of a PEP used in the UK, which are very wide and include members of supreme courts, or high-level judicial bodies, members of the board of central banks and members of supervisory bodies of state-owned enterprises. Generally, a PEP is a person whose current or former position can attract publicity beyond the borders of the country concerned and whose financial circumstances may be the subject of additional public interest.[32]

11.67 In the UK the objectives for identifying and performing enhanced due diligence were set out in a Treasury consultation document[33] which included to help and protect national economies and to prevent the misappropriation of UK and international aid.

11.68 JMLSG Guidance[34] recommends that firms have appropriate risk-based procedures for establishing whether a customer is a PEP and obtain appropriate senior management approval

---

[30] HM Treasury, Informal consultation on the Third EC Money Laundering Directive (May 2004).
[31] High-Level Principles and procedures (June 2007).
[32] Wolfsberg group FAQ 2007: 'How to define "Politically Exposed Persons"'.
[33] HM Treasury, 'Implementing the Third Money Laundering Directive' (January 2007).
[34] JMLSG Guidance, s 5.5.26–5.5.29.

for establishing and maintaining business relationships with such customers. Reasonable measures should be taken to establish the source of funds and enhanced ongoing monitoring of the relationship should be conducted. It is also seen as important that specific training is given to staff in this area.

Performance by third parties

Article 14 of 3MLD provides that persons covered by the directive may rely on third parties to perform the due diligence requirements in Article 8. However, this provision makes it clear that ultimate responsibility for the proper completion of the due diligence requirements of Article 8 rests with the person covered by the directive. In other words, it is possible to delegate the task of due diligence but not the legal responsibility. Article 15 provides that where a Member State permits that certain persons can be relied on in their own jurisdictions, they must also permit reliance on similar persons located in other Member States, with the exception of currency exchange offices and money transmission or remittance offices. **11.69**

Article 15(1) and (2) taken together have the effect of permitting reliance on 'third parties' located in countries outside the EU where anti-money laundering requirements meet certain specified criteria. Articles 16 and 18 list the requirements that must be met for reliance on the third party due diligence and provide that information requested by the third party in accordance with the Article 8 due diligence procedures, should be made available to the person to which the customer is being referred. **11.70**

Article 19 provides that Articles 14 to 18 (inclusive) do not apply to an outsourcing or agency relationship, where the effect of the arrangements between the outsourced service provider or agent and the principal are such that they are, in effect, to be regarded as part of the principal. **11.71**

Reporting obligations

Section 1 of Chapter III of 3MLD covers reporting obligations. These provisions have had little effect on the UK anti-money laundering regime, as the UK already has a financial intelligence unit ('FIU') established in the form of the National Crime Agency ('NCA') (previously National Criminal Intelligence Service ('NCIS')). However, there has been much litigation in this area in the UK.[35] The MLR 2003 allowed professional legal advisers to be excused from reporting obligations if the information came to him in privileged circumstances. This was later extended to cover other relevant professional advisers.[36] **11.72**

Article 23 allows regulated persons to designate their regulatory body as the first instance for reporting suspicious transactions and the regulatory body shall be responsible for forwarding the information to the FIU promptly and unfiltered. **11.73**

Article 23 provides an exemption to the reporting requirements when notaries, independent legal professionals, auditors, external accountants, and tax advisors receive information in privileged circumstances. **11.74**

[35] This is discussed further at paras 11.139–11.146.

[36] By ss 2 and 3 of the Proceeds of Crime Act 2002 and Money Laundering Regulations 2003 (Amendment) Order 2006.

11.75 Article 24 of 3MLD provides that persons covered by the directive should not carry out a transaction where they know or suspect that the transaction is related to money laundering. However, the second paragraph of Article 24 provides:

> where such a transaction is suspected of giving rise to money laundering or terrorist financing and where to refrain in such manner is impossible or is likely to frustrate efforts to pursue the beneficiaries of a suspected money laundering or terrorist financing operation, the institutions and persons concerned shall apprise the FIU immediately afterwards.

11.76 This provision can be contrasted with the defences in sections 327 to 329 PoCA, which permits a person to continue with a transaction if he has 'appropriate consent' within the meaning of section 335 of PoCA. As noted earlier, 3MLD is a minimum standards directive, and as long as it does not breach the principles of EU law, the UK Government can retain the current super-equivalent provisions of section 335 of PoCA.

11.77 Section 2 of Chapter III of 3MLD covers the prohibition of disclosure of information. Article 28 creates a 'tipping off' provision, which has had little impact on financial services firms.

Record keeping

11.78 Chapter IV of 3MLD covers record keeping and statistical data. The basic requirement to keep records for five years does not differ from the previous directives. However, there are certain points to note. Article 31 of 3MLD obliges firms to instigate customer due diligence record keeping procedures in branches and majority owned subsidiaries located in third countries that are 'at least equivalent to those set out in this directive'. In practice, many UK institutions previously employed this approach as a matter of good practice but it has had an impact on some firms. Moreover, if local laws prevent the firm applying the relevant EU standards, there is an obligation on firms to report this fact to the regulatory body in their home Member State.

11.79 There is also a requirement, in Article 32, that credit and financial institutions put in place systems to enable them to cooperate with the national FIU and other authorities as to whether they maintain or have maintained a business relationship with a specified natural or legal person within the previous five years and details of that relationship.

11.80 Article 33 places an obligation on Member States to assess the effectiveness of systems to combat money laundering and terrorist financing by producing a report containing the following statistics:

(a) the number of suspicious transaction reports made to its FIU;
(b) the number of cases investigated;
(c) the number of persons prosecuted for money laundering or terrorist financing offences; and
(d) value of assets frozen, seized, or confiscated.

Enforcement and implementing measures

11.81 Articles 34 to 39 (inclusive) of 3MLD cover matters such as firms' internal procedures, training, and enforcement.

11.82 Article 34 requires that institutions and persons covered by 3MLD should establish policies and procedures of customer due diligence, reporting, internal control, risk assessment, risk management, compliance management, and communication. This built in the extra policies and procedures to cover the new risk-based approach to money laundering and terrorist financing and also meant that those covered by 3MLD have had to set up procedures to monitor their customers and transactions to maintain the required level of management information.

Article 40 of 3MLD provides the European Commission with a new power to 'ensure uniform implementation of [the] directive'. Using the procedure provided by Article 38(2) the European Commission may adopt measures for the: **11.83**

(a) clarification of the technical aspects of the definitions in Article (3)(2)(a) and (d), (6), (7), (8), (9), and (10);
(b) establishment of technical criteria for assessing whether situations represent a low risk of money laundering or terrorist financing as referred to in Article 11(2) and (5);
(c) establishment of technical criteria for assessing whether situations represent a high risk of money laundering or terrorist financing as referred to in Article 13;
(d) establishment of technical criteria for assessing whether, in accordance with Article 2(2), it is justified not to apply this directive to certain legal or natural persons carrying out financial activity on an occasional or very limited basis.

Although the directive is intended to be implemented uniformly throughout the EU, it is only at a high level that this uniformity can be achieved as each Member State will have its own FIU and detailed guidance on implementation. In fact, in June 2008 the Commission decided to take action against 15 Member States for failure to implement 3MLD into national law.[37] **11.84**

The European Regulation on FATF Special Recommendation 7

FATF Special Recommendation 7 provides: **11.85**

> Countries should take measures to require financial institutions, including money remitters, to include accurate and meaningful originator information (name, address and account number) on funds transfers and related messages that are sent, and the information should remain with the transfer or related message through the payment chain. Countries should take measures to ensure that financial institutions, including money remitters, conduct enhanced scrutiny of and monitor for suspicious activity funds transfers which do not contain complete originator information (name, address and account number).

FATF countries agreed to implement Special Recommendation 7 by December 2006. This was implemented in Europe by Regulation EC 1781/2006 on 15 November 2006, which laid down rules on payer information accompanying transfers of funds. The Regulation applies to transfers of funds in any currency, which are sent or received by a payment service provider in a Member State. **11.86**

There are some exclusions, payments made by credit or debit card (for instance, where the transaction has a unique identifier and can be traced back to the payer); payments made by mobile phone or any other digital or IT device, where funds are withdrawn from the payer's own account; or payments to public authorities for taxes, fines, or other levies. **11.87**

Information on the payer is required, consisting of his name, address, and account number; where the payer does not have an account number the payment service provider must substitute a unique payment identifier to allow the payment to be traced back to the payer. **11.88**

[37] Please see Chapter 4 (European Financial Services) at paras 4.170–4.171 for further discussion on 3MLD.

11.89 As with the MLR 2007 records of information on the payer must be kept for five years.

11.90 In the UK the Regulation was implemented by The Transfer of Funds (Information on the Payer) Regulations 2007,[38] and the offences are listed as failure to comply with the various articles of the EU Payments Regulation.

UK Legislation

Proceeds of Crime Act 2002

11.91 The Proceeds of Crime Act 2002 ('PoCA') replaces previous UK anti-money laundering legislation.

11.92 Section 1 of PoCA established the Assets Recovery Agency ('ARA') which became operational in February 2003 and with effect from 1 April 2008 was merged with NCA.[39] PoCA provides the NCA with wide powers to investigate and recover assets. It provides five investigative tools for law enforcement agencies, all of these powers have the potential to be significant for financial services firms.

11.93 The powers are:

(a) Production Order under section 345;
(b) Search and Seizure Warrant under section 352;
(c) Disclosure Warrant under section 357;
(d) Customer Information Order under section 363; and
(e) Account Monitoring Order under section 370.

11.94 Part 7 of PoCA covers money laundering and makes it a criminal offence to:

(a) conceal, disguise, convert, transfer, or remove criminal property from the UK (Section 327);
(b) enter into or become concerned in an arrangement which [a person] knows or suspects facilitates the acquisition, retention, use or control of criminal property by or on behalf of another person (Section 328); or
(c) acquire, use or have possession of criminal property (Section 329).

11.95 Section 340(11) of PoCA extends the offence of money laundering to include acts which constitute an attempt, conspiracy, or incitement to conceal, enter into, or acquire as well as acts that constitute aiding, abetting, counselling, or procuring the commission of such activity. PoCA also makes it an offence to do such an act outside the UK.

Criminal property/criminal conduct

11.96 The potential impact of these offences is wide as a consequence of the definition of criminal property and its relationship with the definition of criminal conduct.[40]

11.97 Property is criminal property if it:

(a) constitutes a person's benefit in whole or in part (including pecuniary and proprietary benefit) from criminal conduct; or

38 SI 2007/3298 effective 15 December 2007.
39 Serious Crime Act 2007, s 74.
40 PoCA, s 340(3).

(b) represents such a benefit directly or indirectly, in whole or in part; and
(c) the alleged offender knows or suspects that it constitutes or represents such a benefit.

Criminal property[41] includes, but is not limited to: **11.98**

(a) the proceeds of tax evasion;
(b) a benefit obtained through bribery and corruption (including both the receipt of a bribe and the income received from a contract obtained through bribery or the promise of a bribe);
(c) benefits obtained, or income received, through the operation of a criminal cartel; and
(d) benefits (in the form of saved costs) arising from a failure to comply with a regulatory requirement, where that failure is a criminal offence.

The original definition of criminal conduct in PoCA was very wide. Conduct fell within the definition if it constituted an offence in any part of the UK or would have constituted an offence in any part of the UK if it had occurred there. In the much cited Spanish bull fighter example, it was suggested that a UK bank accepting a deposit from a Spanish citizen from his legitimate earnings (in Spain) as a bull fighter would be committing the offence of money laundering since bull fighting is illegal in the UK. **11.99**

The scope of this definition was heavily criticised and despite initial scepticism the Government was persuaded to amend the principal money laundering offences in sections 327 to 329 of PoCA and the offences of failure to disclose under sections 330 to 332 by section 102 of the Serious Organised Crime and Police Act 2005 ('SOCPA'). **11.100**

Section 102 of SOCPA introduces a new defence, which is available where: **11.101**

(a) it is known or believed on reasonable grounds that the conduct occurred outside the UK;
(b) the conduct was not criminal in the country where it took place; and
(c) it is not of a description prescribed by the Secretary of State by Order.

It is of no consequence who carried out the conduct, who benefited from it, or when the conduct occurred. PoCA considers a person to have benefited from the conduct if he obtains property as a result of, or in connection with, the conduct concerned. **11.102**

The UK definition of criminal conduct is wider than that set out in Article 3(4) of 3MLD which includes any kind of criminal involvement in the commission of a serious crime. Section 340(2) of PoCA defines conduct as 'that which would have been an offence in any part of the UK', and has not been limited to serious offences but is applied to all crimes. Article 5 of 3MLD allows Member States to adopt or retain super-equivalent provisions to prevent money laundering and terrorist financing. In this area, the UK legislation is said to be 'gold-plated' as it extends beyond the requirements of 3MLD. **11.103**

The 'all crimes' approach allows UK money laundering legislation to be more flexible and dynamic and the initial crime is often referred to as the 'predicate offence'. **11.104**

Reporting as a defence to a money laundering offence

Sections 327 (concealing, etc.), 328 (arrangements), and 329 (acquisition, use, and possession) of PoCA provide that a person does not commit an offence if he makes a section **11.105**

[41] ibid, s 340(3).

338 'authorised disclosure'; had intended to make such a disclosure but had a reasonable excuse for not doing so; or the act concerned was done in relation to a function relating to the enforcement of relevant criminal law.

11.106 Section 338 of PoCA provides that a disclosure is authorised if it is made to a constable, a customs officer, or to a person nominated by a person's employer to receive such disclosures. In the case of most financial services firms, the person so nominated will be the firm's money laundering reporting officer ('MLRO'). This section is subject to two conditions, one of which must be satisfied. The first condition is that the disclosure must be made prior to the person carrying out the act (ie concealing, entering into, acquiring, etc.). The second condition is that the disclosure was made after the act, but there is a good reason for failing to make disclosure prior to the act and the disclosure, when made, was made at the initiative of the person disclosing and as soon as it was practicable for him to make it.

11.107 Where a disclosure has been made a person may still commit a money laundering offence unless he has received 'appropriate consent'. Section 335 defines appropriate consent as:

(a) the consent of a nominated officer;
(b) the consent of a constable; or
(c) the consent of a customs officer.

11.108 A person will be treated as having been given appropriate consent if he has made an authorised disclosure and seven working days have elapsed and he has not received notice from a constable or customs officer that consent has been refused.

11.109 Where consent has been refused before the period of seven working days has elapsed, a person is treated as having received appropriate consent where a 31-day moratorium period has elapsed starting from the day on which the person received the refusal.

The regulated sector

11.110 Section 330 of PoCA provides a separate offence of failure to disclose by a person in the regulated sector.

11.111 A person commits the offence of failure to disclose (sections 330 to 332) if three conditions are satisfied:

(a) if a person knows or suspects, or has reasonable grounds to know or suspect, that another is engaged in money laundering;
(b) if the information came to him in the course of business in the regulated sector; and
(c) if he does not make disclosure as soon as is practicable after the information came to him.

11.112 In deciding whether an offence has been committed, a court is required to consider any guidance issued by a supervisory authority or other body which has been approved by HM Treasury. The most recent version of the JMLSG Guidance was approved by HM Treasury on 18 December 2007 with certain amendments approved in January 2011. Further amendments to the JMLSG Guidance published in December 2011 are awaiting approval by HM Treasury and JMLSG published further proposed amendments to the JMLSG Guidance dated 1 July 2013.

11.113 Section 331 of PoCA provides a separate offence of failure to report by a nominated officer in the regulated sector. This offence is subject to conditions that are similar to those that apply in section 330.

Part 1 of Schedule 9 to PoCA (as amended)[42] sets out the scope of the regulated sector. Not all activities regulated by the FCA and PRA are captured by PoCA (or the MLR 2007). **11.114**

The activities which are caught are: **11.115**

(a) accepting deposits;
(b) effecting or carrying out contracts of long-term insurance when carried on by a person who has received official authorisation pursuant to Article 4 or Article 51 of the Life Assurance Consolidation Directive;
(c) dealing in investments as principal or as agent;
(d) arranging deals in investments;
(e) managing investments;
(f) safeguarding and administering investments;
(g) sending dematerialised instructions;
(h) establishing (and taking other steps in relation to) collective investment schemes;
(i) advising on investments; and
(j) issuing electronic money.

A business is not in the regulated sector to the extent that it engages in any of the following activities: **11.116**

(a) the issue of withdrawable share capital within the limit set by section 6 of the Industrial and Provident Societies Act 1965 (c 12) by a society registered under that Act;
(b) the acceptance of deposits from the public within the limit set by section 7(3) of that Act by such a society;
(c) the issue of withdrawable share capital within the limit set by section 6 of the Industrial and Provident Societies Act (Northern Ireland) 1969 (c 24 (NI)) by a society registered under that Act;
(d) the acceptance of deposits from the public within the limit set by section 7(3) of that Act by such a society;
(e) activities carried on by the Bank of England;
(f) any activity in respect of which an exemption order under section 38 of FSMA (c 8) has effect if it is carried on by a person who is for the time being specified in the order or falls within a class of persons so specified;
(g) the regulated activities of arranging deals in investments or advising on investments, in so far as the investment consists of rights under a regulated mortgage contract; or
(h) the regulated activities of dealing in investments as agent, arranging deals in investments, managing investments or advising on investments, in so far as the investment consists of rights under, or any right to or interest in, a contract of insurance which is not a qualifying contract of insurance.

Objective test

Both sections 330 and 331 of PoCA apply an objective test of reasonable suspicion. This is in contrast to offences under section 328 (arrangements) which apply a subjective test. The implications for financial services staff and MLROs in the regulated sector are significant, as **11.117**

[42] The Proceeds of Crime Act 2002 (Business in the Regulated Sector and Supervisory Authorities) Order 2003 which came into force on 1 March 2004 aligns the definition of 'regulated sector' with that of 'relevant business' in the 2003 Regulations.

it means that they will be judged according to the standard of the reasonable person carrying on their particular task. For MLROs in particular, this is likely to be quite a high standard.

Reporting by firms

11.118 Firms should make their money laundering disclosures to the NCA. NCA has published guidance notes on the practical aspects of making a disclosure in accordance with the requirements of PoCA.[43]

Where consent is urgently needed

11.119 NCA also operates a fast-track reporting procedure where firms need appropriate consent to complete a transaction at short notice. This procedure generally requires a firm to complete a disclosure using the SAR Online[44] facility or where the firm has no access to these online facilities a fax can be used to submit a disclosure report to NCA indicating that it requires it to be treated as a first track enquiry. Anecdotal evidence suggests that the procedure has functioned reasonably well to-date.

Tipping off

11.120 Section 333A of PoCA provides that a person commits an offence if:

(a) he discloses that he or another person has made a disclosure under Part 7—Money Laundering of information that came to him in the course of business in the regulated sector; and
(b) the disclosure is likely to prejudice an investigation that might be conducted following the disclosure; or
(c) the person discloses that an investigation into allegations that an offence under Part 7 is being contemplated or carried out; and
(d) the disclosure is likely to prejudice that investigation; and
(e) the information on which the disclosure is based came to the person in the course of a business in the regulated sector.

11.121 A person convicted of an offence under this section can be subject to a fine or imprisonment of up to two years or both.

11.122 Defences to this offence can be found in sections 333B, 333C, and 333D[45] and allow disclosures to be made within an undertaking or group, between certain institutions, or in certain other situations where disclosures are permitted.

11.123 Section 333B allows for disclosures within an undertaking or group and an offence is not committed if:

(a) an employee, officer, or partner of an undertaking makes a disclosure to another employee, officer, or partner of the same undertaking.
(b) a person makes a disclosure in respect of a credit or financial institution if:
  (i) the disclosure is to a credit or financial institution,
  (ii) the institution to whom the disclosure is made is situated in the EEA State or in a country or territory imposing equivalent money laundering requirements, and

[43] The NCA website can be accessed at: <http://www.nationalcrimeagency.gov.uk/>.
[44] <http://www.ukciu.gov.uk/saronline.aspx>.
[45] These new sections have been added by the Terrorism Act 2000 and Proceeds of Crime Act 2002 (Amendment) Regulations 2007.

(iii) both the institution making the disclosure and the institution to whom it is made belong to the same group.

(c) A professional legal adviser or a relevant professional adviser makes a disclosure to another professional legal adviser or a relevant professional adviser and both parties carry on business in an EEA State or country or territory imposing equivalent money laundering requirements, and those persons perform their professional activities within different undertakings that share common ownership, management or control.

Section 333D allows disclosures between institutions, for example between credit institutions, financial institutions, professional legal advisers, and other relevant professional advisers. An offence is not committed if the disclosure relates to: **11.124**

(a) a client or former client of the institution or adviser making the disclosure and the institution or adviser to whom it is made;
(b) a transaction involving them both; or
(c) the provision of a service involving them both; or
(d) the purpose only of preventing an offence under Part 7 of PoCA, the institution to whom the disclosure is made is situated in an EEA State or country or territory imposing equivalent money laundering requirements and the institutions or advisers are subject to equivalent duties of professional confidentiality and the protection of personal data.

Section 333D sets out other situations where a person does not commit an offence under section 333A if the disclosure is to a supervisory authority by virtue of the MLR 2007 or for the purpose of detection, investigation, or prosecution of a criminal offence or an investigation or enforcement of a court order under PoCA. **11.125**

A professional legal adviser or other relevant professional adviser does not commit an offence if the disclosure is to the adviser's client and is made for the purposes of dissuading the client from engaging in conduct amounting to an offence. **11.126**

A person will also not commit an offence if he does not know or suspect that the disclosure is likely to have the effect of prejudicing an investigation. **11.127**

Protected disclosures

Section 337 of PoCA provides that disclosures made under PoCA do not amount to a breach of any restriction on the disclosure of information, subject to three conditions being met: **11.128**

(a) the information or matter being disclosed must have come to the person in the course of his trade, profession, business, or employment;
(b) the information must either have caused the discloser to know or suspect, or to have reasonable grounds for knowing or suspecting, that another person is engaged in money laundering; and
(c) the disclosure must have been made to a constable, a customs officer or a nominated officer as soon as is practicable after the information or matter came to the discloser.

Penalties for breach of PoCA

The maximum penalty for an offence of money laundering under PoCA is 14 years' imprisonment and/or an unlimited fine. The maximum penalty for a person in the regulated sector who fails to make the required money laundering report, who commits a 'tipping off' offence, or who destroys or disposes of relevant documents is five years and/or an unlimited fine. **11.129**

The Terrorism Act 2000 ('TA') (as amended by the Anti-terrorism, Crime and Security Act 2001)

11.130 Property, including money, is considered to be terrorist property[46] if it is likely to be used for the purposes of terrorism, or if it is the proceeds (directly or indirectly, wholly or partly) of the commission of an act of terrorism or of acts carried out for the purposes of terrorism. The important point to note is that whereas under PoCA only illegitimate funds (ie the proceeds of crime) are at issue it is quite possible for money which falls within the definition of terrorist property to have been obtained legitimately. For example, when an individual makes a payment from his salary to another who uses it for the purposes of terrorism that payment becomes terrorist property.

11.131 Section 15 of the TA outlaws fundraising for the purposes of terrorism. Section 15(2) provides that a person commits an offence if 'he receives money or other property and intends that it should be used, or has reasonable cause to suspect that it may be used, for the purposes of terrorism'.

11.132 Section 16 provides that a person commits an offence if he uses money or other property for the purposes of terrorism. A person commits an offence if he possesses money or other property and intends that it should be used, or has reasonable cause to suspect that it may be used, for the purposes of terrorism.

11.133 Section 17 of the TA provides that an offence is committed if a person enters into or becomes concerned in an arrangement as a result of which money or other property is made available or is to be made available to another and he knows or has reasonable cause to suspect that it will or may be used for the purposes of terrorism.

11.134 Section 18 of the TA provides that a person is engaged in money laundering if he enters into or becomes concerned in an arrangement which facilitates the retention or control by, or on behalf of, another person of terrorist property by: concealment; removal from the jurisdiction; transfer to nominees; or in any other way. A person charged under section 18 has a defence if he can prove that he did not know and had no reasonable cause to suspect that the arrangement relates to terrorist property.

11.135 The TA contains similar reporting obligations as PoCA. The Anti-terrorism, Crime and Security Act 2001 introduced a new section 21A of the TA whereby a person commits a criminal offence if he does not report the existence of criminal property where there are reasonable grounds for knowing or suspecting its existence.

---

[46] Section 14(1) of the TA defines terrorist property as:

(a) money or other property which is likely to be used for the purposes of terrorism (including any resources of a proscribed organisation),
(b) proceeds of the commission of acts of terrorism, and
(c) proceeds of acts carried out for the purposes of terrorism.

(2) In subsection (1):

(a) a reference to proceeds of an act includes a reference to any property which wholly or partly, and directly or indirectly, represents the proceeds of the act (including payments or other rewards in connection with its commission), and
(b) the reference to an organisation's resources includes a reference to any money or other property which is applied or made available, or is to be applied or made available, for the use of the organisation.

Changes to PoCA introduced by SOCPA

As mentioned earlier, SOCPA introduced a defence to the principal money laundering offences where overseas conduct is legal under local law. **11.136**

From 1 July 2005, SOCPA also implemented a *de minimis* threshold for deposit-takers. The secondary legislation[47] implementing these changes created a new section 339A in PoCA, which sets the threshold amount at GBP250. **11.137**

Section 104 of SOCPA amends the failure to disclose provisions in sections 330 to 332 of PoCA, by inserting an additional condition that needs to be satisfied if the offences in those sections are to be committed. Under the amendment there is no need to report to NCA where the identity of the culprit or the whereabouts of the property are unknown and there is no information that could assist in identifying the person or where the property is. **11.138**

Case law and PoCA

To date there have been few significant judgments on the meaning of PoCA. However, there were a number under the previous legislation.[48] *Bowman v Fels*[49] reached the Court of Appeal as a result of county court litigation between two former cohabitees. As a result of information received by them prior to the county court hearing solicitors to one of the parties involved made an authorised disclosure (see section 338, PoCA) to NCIS in accordance with the requirements of PoCA. The reporting solicitors sought to adjourn the hearing as they considered that they were unlikely to receive appropriate consent from NCIS. **11.139**

In a judgment given by Brooke LJ, the Court of Appeal held that the proper interpretation of section 328 of PoCA was that it was not intended to cover or affect the ordinary conduct of litigation by legal professionals, which included any step taken by them in litigation from the issue of proceedings and the securing of injunctive relief or a freezing order up to its final disposal by judgment. Neither the European nor the UK legislature could have envisaged that any of these ordinary activities could fall within the scope of section 328. Such legal duties could not be considered to result in a person 'becoming concerned in an arrangement which . . . facilitates the acquisition, retention, use or control of criminal property'.[50] **11.140**

Legal proceedings are a State-provided mechanism for the resolution of issues in accordance with the law. Every person has the right to a fair and public trial in the determination of his civil rights and duties, which was secured by Article 6 of the Convention for the Protection of Human Rights and Fundamental Freedoms. Parliament could not have intended that proceedings or steps taken by legal advisers with a view to determining or securing legal rights and remedies for their clients should involve them in the type of 'arrangements' envisaged by section 328 of PoCA. **11.141**

Under the Proceeds of Crime Act 2002 and the Money Laundering Regulations (Amendment) Order 2006[51] the defence for failure to disclose offences under section 330 PoCA available to professional legal advisors was widened to include 'relevant professional advisors' where information or other matters came to them in privileged circumstances. **11.142**

---

47 Serious Organised Crime and Police Act 2005 (Commencement No 1, Transitional and Transitory Provisions) Order 2005.

48 Namely the Criminal Justice Act 1988, s 93D cases which included *Bank of Scotland v A Ltd* [2001] EWCA Civ 52 and *P v P (Ancillary Relief: Proceeds of Crime)* [2003] EWHC 2260 (Fam).

49 ibid, *Bowman v Fels* [2005] EWCA Civ 226 (CA).

50 ibid, [100].

51 SI 308/2006.

11.143 Whilst in strict terms *Bowman v Fels* is primarily relevant to the legal profession,[52] the case may have some application to financial services firms that are involved in court action where there are grounds to know or suspect (or reasonably suspect) that a party is involved in money laundering.

11.144 In *Shah v HSBC Private Bank (UK) Ltd*,[53] the claimant sought over $300 million in damages against HSBC for breach of contract. Mr Shah argued that he had suffered loss due to HSBC's failure to execute four payment transfers from his account promptly and subsequent refusal to provide reasons for the delays. The transfers were delayed because HSBC, suspecting that the funds were criminal property, made a number of suspicious activity reports and were waiting for consent from NCA before proceeding with the transactions.

11.145 In dismissing the claim, the High Court implied two terms into the contract between HSBC and Mr Shah. The first was that HSBC was entitled to refuse to execute instructions in the absence of appropriate consent from NCA where there was a suspicion of money laundering. The second term was that HSBC did not have to provide information regarding the delays to the client if there is a risk that providing such information may constitute the offence of 'tipping off'.

11.146 The ruling in *Shah* was welcomed by banks and other financial services firms. From a practical perspective, placing a duty on banks to tell their customers about disclosures made in relation to their accounts would have a chilling effect on the willingness of employees to report suspicious activities which, in turn, would defeat the purpose of the money laundering reporting regime. The ruling is also significant for having set out a number of examples of best practices which banks and other financial institutions should adopt in relation to the operation of their anti-money laundering procedures.

The Money Laundering Regulations 2003

11.147 The MLR 2003[54] consolidated and expanded on existing anti-money laundering secondary legislation[55] and came into force on 1 April 2004. The MLR 2003 were the primary legislative tool for the UK's implementation of 1MLD and 2MLD. The activities captured by the MLR 2003 were wider than those originally caught by the MLR 1993 and reflected the increased scope of 2MLD.

11.148 The aim of the MLR 2003 was to ensure that all relevant businesses had systems and procedures in place to identify and prevent money laundering, which was achieved by the recognition and reporting of suspicious transactions and the facilitation of the tracing of the proceeds of money laundering activities. Failure to comply was a criminal offence and prosecutions could be made by the Crown Prosecution Service or, where appropriate, the FSA.

11.149 All persons carrying on a 'relevant business' were required to have appropriate measures in place to forestall and prevent money laundering. Specifically these procedures were to cover staff training, client identification, record keeping, and internal reporting.

---

[52] The significance of which is underlined by the fact that both the Law Society and the Bar Council intervened in the case.

[53] *Shah v HSBC Private Bank (UK) Limited* [2012] EWHC 1283 (QB).

[54] The Money Laundering Regulations 2003, SI 2003/3075.

[55] In particular, the Money Laundering Regulations 1993 SI 1993/1933.

The Money Laundering Regulations 2007

The Money Laundering Regulations 2007 ('MLR 2007') were introduced on 15 December 2007 to implement 3MLD and replaced the MLR 2003 which were revoked. **11.150**

Application of the MLR 2007

Regulation 3 sets out those persons captured by the MLR 2007; these are referred to throughout the MLR 2007 as 'relevant persons'. **11.151**

Financial services that fall within the definition of relevant persons are the same in scope as those captured by PoCA[56] and include the activities in the Annex to the Consolidated Banking Directive.[57] **11.152**

[56] Regulation 3 provides that 'relevant persons' means:
(a) credit institutions;
(b) financial institutions;
(c) auditors, insolvency practitioners, external accountants, and tax advisers;
(d) independent legal professionals;
(e) trust or company service providers;
(f) estate agents;
(g) high value dealers;
(h) casinos.

Where a 'credit institution' means:
(a) a credit institution as defined in Article 4(1)(a) of the banking consolidation directive; or
(b) a branch (within the meaning of Article 4(3) of that directive) located in an EEA State of an institution falling within sub-paragraph (a) (or an equivalent institution whose head office is located in a non-EEA State) wherever its head office is located,

when it accepts deposits or other repayable funds from the public or grants credits for its own account (within the meaning of the banking consolidation directive).

And a 'financial institution' means:
(a) an undertaking, including a money service business, when it carries out one or more of the activities listed in points 2 to 12 and 14 of Annex 1 to the banking consolidation directive (the relevant text of which is set out in Schedule 1 to these Regulations), other than—
  (i) a credit institution;
  (ii) an undertaking whose only listed activity is trading for own account in one or more of the products listed in point 7 of Annex 1 to the banking consolidation directive where the undertaking does not have a customer,

and, for this purpose, 'customer' means a third party which is not a member of the same group as the undertaking;
(b) an insurance company duly authorised in accordance with the life assurance consolidation directive, when it carries out activities covered by that directive;
(c) a person whose regular occupation or business is the provision to other persons of an investment service or the performance of an investment activity on a professional basis, when providing or performing investment services or activities (within the meaning of the markets in financial instruments directive, other than a person falling within Article 2 of that directive;
(d) a collective investment undertaking, when marketing or otherwise offering its units or shares;
(e) an insurance intermediary as defined in Article 2(5) of Directive 2002/92/EC of the European Parliament and of the Council of 9th December 2002 on insurance mediation, with the exception of a tied insurance intermediary as mentioned in Article 2(7) of that Directive, when it acts in respect of contracts of long-term insurance within the meaning given by article 3(1) of, and Part II of Schedule 1 to, the Financial Services and Markets Act 2000 (Regulated Activities) Order 2001;
(f) a branch located in an EEA State of a person referred to in sub-paragraphs (a) to (e) (or an equivalent person whose head office is located in a non-EEA State), wherever its head office is located, when carrying out any activity mentioned in sub-paragraphs (a) to (e);
(g) the National Savings Bank;
(h) the Director of Savings, when money is raised under the auspices of the Director under the National Loans Act 1968.

[57] Listed in Sch 1, MLR 2007 and include:
2. Lending including, inter alia: consumer credit, mortgage credit, factoring, with or without recourse, financing of commercial transactions (including forfeiting).

Criminal offence

11.153 A person who is found guilty of contravening the regulations is liable to a fine and/or imprisonment for up to two years. However, in deciding whether a person has committed an offence the court handling the case is obliged to consider whether the person concerned followed any relevant guidance:

(a) issued by a supervisory authority or other appropriate body;
(b) approved by HM Treasury; and
(c) published in a manner approved by HM Treasury.

11.154 An 'appropriate body' as described earlier is any body which regulates or is representative of any trade, profession, business, or employment carried on by the alleged offender. In the context of financial services the JMLSG is a relevant body and the Treasury has approved their 2007 guidance.

11.155 A person accused of an offence under the MLR 2007 will have a defence if he can show that he took all reasonable steps and exercised all due diligence to avoid committing the offence.

Duty to identify

11.156 The duty to identify a customer has been the central obligation of anti-money laundering legislation since the introduction of the MLR 1993. The limitations of heavy reliance on identification material are now well accepted and have led to the development of wider CDD obligations and the requirement to monitor transactions and the operation of customer accounts. Notwithstanding these developments, the requirement to identify continues to form a major element, perhaps the major element, of anti-money laundering obligations.

11.157 A relevant person is required to identify a person in four situations:

(a) establishment of a business relationship; where a business relationship is defined as a business, professional, or commercial relationship between a relevant person and a

3. Financial leasing.
4. Money transmission services.
5. Issuing and administering means of payment (eg credit cards, travellers' cheques and bankers' drafts).
6. Guarantees and commitments.
7. Trading for own account or for account of customers in:
   (a) money market instruments (cheques, bills, certificates of deposit, etc.);
   (b) foreign exchange;
   (c) financial futures and options;
   (d) exchange and interest-rate instruments; or
   (e) transferable securities.
8. Participation in securities issues and the provision of services related to such issues.
9. Advice to undertakings on capital structure, industrial strategy, and related questions and advice as well as services relating to mergers and the purchase of undertakings.
10. Money broking.
11. Portfolio management and advice.
12. Safekeeping and administration of securities.
14. Safe custody services.

customer, which is expected by the relevant person at the time when the contact is established, to have an element of duration;

(b) carrying out of an occasional transaction; where occasional transaction means a transaction (carried out other than as part of a business relationship) amounting to £15,000 or more, whether the transaction is carried out in a single operation or several operations which appear to be linked;

(c) suspicion of money laundering or terrorist financing; or

(d) where the relevant person has doubts of the veracity or adequacy of the documents, data, or information previously obtained for the purposes of identification or verification.

Offences committed by a body corporate

Regulation 47 has the effect of drawing individual officers of a body corporate into the criminal law regulatory net. If a firm commits an offence under the regulations and it can be shown that the offence was either committed with 'the consent or the connivance of an officer' or 'attributable to any neglect on his part', that individual officer will also be guilty of an offence. **11.158**

In addition, partners in a partnership, officers in an unincorporated association, and members of a body corporate, who manage that body, are also liable to prosecution where the connivance or attribution tests have been met. **11.159**

Identification procedures

Regulation 5 sets out the meaning of the CDD measures that a firm must follow. However, the detail regarding the form of the documentation that is required for identification and verification is set out in the JMLSG Guidance. **11.160**

Customer due diligence measures means; **11.161**

(a) identifying the customer and verifying the customer's identity on the basis of documents, data or information obtained from a reliable and independent source;

(b) identifying, where there is a beneficial owner who is not the customer, the beneficial owner and taking adequate measures, on a risk-sensitive basis, to verify his identity so that the relevant person is satisfied that he knows who the beneficial owner is, including in the case of a legal person, trust, or similar legal arrangement, measures to understand the ownership and control structure of the person, trust, or arrangement; and

(c) obtaining information on the purpose and intended nature of the business relationship.

Regulation 9 sets out the timing of the customer due diligence measures. A relevant person must verify the identity of the customer (and any beneficial owner) before the establishment of a business relationship or carrying out an occasional transaction. However, verification may be completed during the establishment of a business relationship if it is necessary to avoid interruption of the normal conduct of business and there is very little risk of money laundering. In these circumstances verification must be completed as soon as is practicable after contact is first established. **11.162**

Identification in practical terms

In reality, the identification requirements provided in Regulation 5 are drafted at a very high level. Regulation 5 does not attempt to distinguish between clients, other than those who are obtained by distance means. In reality, firms will deal with many different types of client depending on the nature of their business. The UK anti-money laundering regime deals **11.163** with this issue by passing the burden of setting out the detail of the identification process to the JMLSG Guidance. Chapter 5 of the JMLSG Guidance provides detailed guidance on identification requirements including the type of evidence that a firm should gather to verify the identity of its client.

Identification procedures should be risk-based

11.164 Regulation 7(3) requires the relevant person to determine the extent of CDD measures on a risk-sensitive basis, depending on the type of customer, business relationship, product, or transaction.

11.165 The JMLSG Guidance emphasises the importance of employing a risk-based approach to the identification of clients. Firms are required to carry out a risk assessment of their customers. A customer may present a higher money laundering risk for a number of reasons. Such reasons include the nature of the product, the nature of the client, the location of the client, and the level of contact that the firm has with the client. Firms should expect to be able to demonstrate that they have completed a risk assessment of their business and the types of clients with whom they deal.

Customer due diligence

11.166 Chapter 5 of the JMLSG Guidance refers to firms employing CDD procedures. There is an important and subtle distinction between simple identification of a client at the start of a business relationship and CDD procedures. CDD is a wider obligation: it requires firms to get to know their customer and carry out ongoing monitoring of the business relationship.

11.167 The term 'ongoing monitoring' has been defined in Regulation 8 to ensure that the obligations on the firm are clear and section 5.7 of the JMLSG Guidance sets out detailed guidance on what monitoring is and how it can be carried out. The depth of this obligation will depend on the nature of the business, the relationship with the client, and the client itself. For example, a firm dealing on an ongoing basis with a corporate client may be expected to understand in detail the nature of the corporate's business, whereas a firm offering a simple savings product to a private customer, where the money laundering risk has been adjudged to be low, will in most cases need to understand less about its client.

Exceptions to the duty to identify

11.168 Regulation 4 introduces a number of exclusions to the MLR 2007 when persons are carrying out certain activities. However, none of these exclusions apply if a firm knows or suspects that a transaction involves money laundering. Also, as with all money laundering requirements, firms need to review the level of money laundering risk in their business on a risk-based analysis.

11.169 Regulation 13(2) provides that CDD measures set out in Regulation 7 do not apply where the customer is:

(a) a credit or financial institution which is subject to the requirements of the money laundering directive;

(b) a credit or financial institution (or equivalent institution) which:
  (i) is situated in a non EEA State which imposes requirements equivalent to those laid down in the money laundering directive; and
  (ii) is supervised for compliance with those requirements;

(c) a company whose securities are listed on a regulated market subject to specified disclosure obligations;
(d) an independent legal professional and the product is in an account into which monies are pooled; or
(e) a public authority in the UK or one which fulfils certain criteria set out in the MLR 2007.

Long-term insurance

It is not necessary to identify where a person enters into a long-term insurance contract in connection with that person's contract of employment or occupation. To benefit from this exemption, the insurance contract concerned must not contain a surrender clause and should not be of a type that can be used as collateral for a loan. To qualify for the exemption, a single premium policy must be for a premium in excess of £2,500. If premiums are to be paid periodically, the total payable in any calendar year must not exceed £1,000. **11.170**

Record-keeping, procedures, and training

Part 3 of the MLR 2007 covers record-keeping, procedures, and training. This section has been greatly expanded compared with the MLR 2003 and sets out detailed requirements. **11.171**

Regulation 19 covers record-keeping and requires that copies of the customer's identity are retained for a period of five years following the end of the business relationship or if an occasional transaction, five years from the completion of that transaction. Supporting records such as ongoing information and additional due diligence measures also need to be kept for the same five-year period. **11.172**

Regulation 20 covers policies and procedures and sets out the risk-based policies and procedures that should be adopted to cover: **11.173**

(a) customer due diligence and ongoing monitoring;
(b) reporting;
(c) record-keeping;
(d) internal control;
(e) risk assessment and management; and
(f) the monitoring and management of compliance with, and the internal communication of, such policies and procedures,

in order to prevent activities related to money laundering and terrorist financing.

These policies should include monitoring of complex or unusually large transactions and unusual patterns as well as determining whether a client is a PEP. The systems should enable a credit or financial institution to respond quickly and fully to requests and queries from the FCA or NCA. **11.174**

Regulation 21 provides that every relevant person must take appropriate measures so that all relevant employees are: **11.175**

(a) made aware of the law relating to money laundering and terrorist financing; and
(b) regularly given training in how to recognise and deal with transactions and other activities which may be related to money laundering or terrorist financing.

Chapter 7 of the JMLSG Guidance explores and develops the details of Part 3 of the MLR 2007. **11.176**

Appointed representatives

11.177 Where the firm is an appointed representative within the meaning of section 39(2) of FSMA, it is the duty of its principal to ensure that the firm complies with the record-keeping requirements. If the appointed representative's principal fails to do this, he will be treated as having committed an offence under Regulation 20 of the MLR 2007 (failure to have systems, etc., to prevent money laundering).

Internal reporting procedures

11.178 Regulation 20 sets out the requirements applicable to a firm for internal reporting procedures. A firm is required to nominate a person from within its organisation to receive money laundering disclosures from within the firm. The MLR 2007 refer to this individual as the nominated officer. In practice most firms use the term 'MLRO'.

11.179 A firm must establish and maintain procedures so that any individual to whom information or other matter comes in the course of relevant business and which leads that individual to know or suspect, or have reasonable grounds for knowing or suspecting, that someone is engaged in money laundering, discloses such information or matter to the MLRO, or to a person authorised by the Director General of NCA, as soon as practicable after it becomes known to him.

11.180 The firm must also ensure that once an individual makes a disclosure to the MLRO, he must consider the disclosure in the light of any available information that is available to the firm. In practice, this means that the MLRO has to be given wide access to information maintained by a firm. The firm is also obliged to ensure that the MLRO determines whether the disclosure and his further investigations, give rise to knowledge or suspicion, or reasonable grounds for knowledge or suspicion, that someone is engaged in money laundering.

11.181 Where the MLRO does so determine, the firm must ensure that he makes a report to NCA or any other person authorised to receive disclosures by the Director General of NCA.

11.182 Unsurprisingly, the requirement to have internal reporting procedures does not apply to sole traders who do not employ any staff or who do not act in association with any other person.

The FCA Anti-money Laundering Regime

11.183 FSMA established the basic framework of financial regulation in the UK and the FSA took over some of the work of the previous Self Regulating Organisations which were abolished under FSMA. As noted earlier, the FCA and PRA have now replaced the FSA and assumed many of its regulatory responsibilities with the FCA specifically acting in connection with financial crime and money laundering.

11.184 The FCA has its regulatory objectives set out by statute[58] and one of those objectives is to ensure the integrity of the UK financial system through the reduction of financial crime.

11.185 FSMA grants the FCA powers to make rules necessary 'for the purpose of advancing one or more of its operational objectives'[59]—from the FSA 2012, which inserted a new

---

[58] See FSMA 2000, s 1B(2) & (3).
[59] See FSMA 2000, s 137A (1).

section 137A into FSMA providing a general rule-making power—which would include rules for prevention and detection of money laundering, whilst section 402(1)(b) of FSMA provides the FCA with a specific power to prosecute money laundering offences which apply to offences under prescribed regulations relating to money laundering.[60]

There have been various consultation and discussion papers which have set out the FSA's, **11.186**
and now the FCA's, approach to money laundering, the latest of which issued in October 2012,[61] sets out how the FCA will approach its regulatory objectives, including the reduction of financial crime.

Risk-based regulation

The FSA's risk-based approach towards money laundering was consistent with its general **11.187**
risk-based approach to financial services regulation, the principles of which were set out at the FSA's inception.[62] Initially, there was some uncertainty as to how a risk-based approach should be applied to money laundering regulation.

The FSA described a risk-based approach as: **11.188**

> a management tool for developing and managing a firm's systems and controls. The risk-based system displays the following features that are essential for a regulatory regime that seeks to deliver value for money whilst at the same time disrupting those who seek to use the financial system for criminal purposes.

The FSA did not maintain a zero failure regime, as it considered that this would be dispropor- **11.189**
tionate, and instead wanted to see firms taking reasonable steps to identify and strengthen weaknesses in their systems and controls. Spending should be targeted at the weakest points in the system so that it makes it harder for criminals to use firms to launder money.

The risk-based approach recognises that much of the expertise in assessing risk lies within the **11.190**
firms themselves, as it is they who have the best knowledge and experience of their customers and products. Criminals themselves operate in a risk-based manner, constantly updating and changing their tactics to avoid detection. Firms need to be flexible and dynamic to keep up with the changing face of money laundering.

There will always be a requirement for firms to monitor their customer's activities, but specif- **11.191**
ics depend on the size and nature of the firm.

Identification and CDD should also be carried out on a risk-sensitive basis, for example, an **11.192**
elderly person opening a basic bank account is unlikely to require extensive procedures to identify him and the nature of the account usage, as long as sufficient monitoring procedures are in place.

Staff training is also an area where the requirements will vary depending on the size and **11.193**
nature of the firm. Customer contact staff for instance, will need training in spotting forged identity documents, whereas their managers will be looking at the overall anti-money laundering requirements and procedures that are necessary to address the risks they face.

60 Not in Scotland.
61 'Journey to the Financial Conduct Authority' (October 2012), can be accessed at: <http://www.fsa.gov.uk/static/pubs/other/journey-to-the-fca-standard.pdf>.
62 See, eg, 'Building the new regulator'—progress report 1 December 2000, Financial Services Authority.

11.194 The risk-based approach requires firms to be proactive in their approach in seeking out information regarding money laundering trends and threats from external sources as well as relying on their own experience.

11.195 The FCA will continue to follow the risk-based approach to money laundering established by its predecessor. This was made clear in an October 2012 policy document which states:

> Stopping firms being used to facilitate financial crime will continue to be a priority. We [the FCA] will focus on the types of firms that are most vulnerable to abuse by criminals (whether because of their size, customer base, product lines or corporate culture).[63]

Registered businesses

11.196 The registration of high-value dealers and money service businesses was introduced under the MLR 2003, but the MLR 2007 added trust or company service providers to the list of persons required to be registered.

11.197 There are several bodies that are responsible for supervision including the FCA, which is the supervisory authority for:

(a) credit and financial institutions which are authorised persons;
(b) trust or company service providers that are authorised persons;
(c) annex I financial institutions (which excludes consumer credit financial institutions, money service businesses, and authorised persons);

11.198 and the Commissioners for HM Revenue and Customs ('the Commissioners'), which are the supervisory authority for:

(a) high-value dealers;
(b) money service businesses that are not supervised by the FSA; trust or company service providers which are not supervised by the FSA, or one of the professional bodies listed in Schedule 3 to the MLR 2007;
(c) auditors, external accountants, and tax advisors that are not supervised by one of the bodies in Schedule 3 to the MLR 2007.

11.199 A 'money service business' means an undertaking which by way of business operates a currency exchange office, transmits money (or any representations of monetary value) by any means, or cashes cheques which are made payable to customers.

11.200 Other supervisory authorities include the Office of Fair Trading ('OFT'), the Gambling Commission, the Department for Enterprise, Trade and Investment in Northern Ireland, and the professional bodies listed in Schedule 3 to the MLR 2007.

11.201 The supervisory authority is responsible for monitoring the relevant persons for whom it is the supervisory authority and must take the necessary measures to ensure that such persons comply with the MLR 2007.

11.202 Regulation 25 provides that the Commissioners must maintain registers of persons who are required to be registered with them.

---

[63] 'Journey to the Financial Conduct Authority' (October 2012), ibid.

Under Regulation 27 an applicant for registration must provide such information as the Commissioners may specify. Such information may be: **11.203**

(a) the applicant's name and (if different) the name of the business;
(b) the nature of the business;
(c) the name of the nominated officer (if any);
(d) in relation to a money service business or trust or company service provider;
  (i) the name of any person who effectively directs or will direct the business and any beneficial owner of the business; and
  (ii) information needed by the Commissioners to decide whether they must refuse the application pursuant to Regulation 28 (fit and proper test).

The Commissioners may request additional information from applicants as they reasonably consider necessary to enable them to determine the application. Where such additional information is requested, the applicant for registration must provide it within 21 days. **11.204**

Where an applicant has provided information to the Commissioners in connection with an application for registration and there has been a change affecting any matter contained in the information or it becomes apparent to the applicant that any aspect of the information is inaccurate, the applicant must, within 30 days, provide details of the change or correct the inaccuracy. **11.205**

The Commissioners must refuse to register an applicant as a money service business or trust or company service provider if they are satisfied that the applicant, any person covered by Regulation 27(1)(d)(i), any beneficial owner, or nominated officer is not a fit and proper person. This fit and proper test requirement has been introduced by the MLR 2007 and is designed to look at the persons owning and running the business, in much the same way as the approved persons in financial services firms are reviewed. **11.206**

The fit and proper person test is set out in Regulation 28 and states that a person is not a fit and proper person if he: **11.207**

(a) has been convicted of:
  (i) an offence under the Terrorism Act 2000;
  (ii) an offence under paragraph 7(2) or (3) of Schedule 3 to the Anti-Terrorism, Crime and Security Act 2001 (offences);
  (iii) an offence under the Terrorism Act 2006;
  (iv) an offence under Part 7 (money laundering) of, or listed in Schedule 2 (lifestyle offences: England and Wales),[64] 4 (lifestyle offences: Scotland), or 5 (lifestyle offences: Northern Ireland) to, the Proceeds of Crime Act 2002;
  (v) an offence under the Fraud Act 2006 or, in Scotland, the common law offence of fraud;
  (vi) an offence under section 72(1), (3), or (8) of the Value Added Tax Act 1994 (offences); or
  (vii) the common law offence of cheating the public revenue;

(b) has been adjudged bankrupt or sequestration of his estate has been awarded and (in either case) he has not been discharged;

[64] These include offences such as drug trafficking, money laundering, directing terrorism, arms trafficking, counterfeiting, etc.

(c) is subject to a disqualification order under the Company Directors Disqualification Act 1986;
(d) is or has been subject to a confiscation order under the Proceeds of Crime Act 2002;
(e) has consistently failed to comply with the requirements of these Regulations, the Money Laundering Regulations 2003 or the Money Laundering Regulations 2001;
(f) has consistently failed to comply with the requirements of regulation 2006/1781/EC of the European Parliament and of the Council of 15 November 2006 on information on the payer accompanying the transfer of funds;
(g) has effectively directed a business which falls within sub-paragraph (e) or (f);
(h) is otherwise not a fit and proper person with regard to the risk of money laundering or terrorist financing.

11.208 The Commissioners may also refuse to register an applicant if any requirement as to registration (Regulation 27) or payment of fees (Regulation 35) has not been complied with or if any information supplied to them is false or misleading. The Commissioners have 45 days in which to accept or refuse a registration.

11.209 Regulation 30 provides that the Commissioners must cancel the registration of a money service business or trust or company service provider if they are satisfied that the person mentioned in Regulation 28 is not a fit and proper person. The Commissioners may also cancel a registration at any time if it appears to them that they would have grounds to refuse an application. Where the Commissioners cancel a registration, they must give notice of their decision. The person has a right to know the reasons for the decision and the fact that they have a right to require a review of the decision under Regulation 43 and a right of appeal under Regulation 44.

11.210 The MLR 2007 provides the Commissioners with certain powers including a power to enter premises and inspect information or currency found on the premises. Regulation 38(2) provides that the Commissioners may obtain an order requiring a relevant person to give them access to recorded information, to copy it, or to remove it from premises, subject in the latter case to certain specified procedures.

11.211 Registered firms differ from FCA-authorised firms as they will only have their anti-money laundering systems and controls supervised by the FCA, whilst authorised firms are subject to regulation that covers many more aspects of their business. Registered businesses, unlike authorised firms, do not have the need for a 'fit and proper' check on owners and managers.

11.212 Registered businesses will also not be members of the Financial Services Compensation Scheme and customers will not be eligible for compensation if the business becomes insolvent. Customers who find themselves in dispute with a registered business will also not be able to approach the Financial Ombudsman Service to help seek a resolution.

11.213 Failure to register is an offence that potentially carries either a civil or criminal sanction; however where a business performs an activity that would otherwise be required to be registered, on an occasional or very limited basis, then it will not need to register.

11.214 Part 4 of the MLR 2007 provides detail as to how a business is supervised and registered. Regulation 23 lists the businesses which fall under the FCA's supervision and Regulations 32 to 35 set out the power to maintain registers, the requirement to be registered, applications for and cancellations of registration, and the costs of supervision.

Supervision

The FCA's risk based approach to supervision means that it concentrates the greatest resources where it perceives the risk to be greatest. The FCA expects firms to follow the same principle when designing their anti-money laundering systems and controls. **11.215**

The FCA has said it will continue to use thematic reviews and targeted visits to identify money laundering vulnerabilities within the financial services sector. In order to ensure that the largest retail and investment banks are complying with their legal and regulatory obligations, the FCA will rely on its 'Systemic Anti-Money Laundering Programme'[65] which involves a series of in-depth reviews of anti-money laundering and sanctions systems and controls. **11.216**

Enforcement

The FSA also used a risk-based approach when enforcing the MLR 2007. The seriousness and nature of any breach is considered before a decision is made as to the appropriate action to take. Failures in anti-money laundering controls will not automatically result in disciplinary sanctions, although enforcement action is more likely where a firm has not put in place systems and controls to identify and mitigate risks. **11.217**

The tools that are used for investigation and enforcement are the issuing of written notices, the requirement of persons to attend interviews, and the use of search warrants to allow the police to enter premises, search, and take possession of documents. **11.218**

The MLR 2007 allow a designated authority to impose 'appropriate' penalties on relevant persons who fail to comply with any requirement set out in them, where appropriate means effective, proportionate, and dissuasive. The FCA is one of the authorities that has been defined as a designated authority[66] and as such has been given wide-ranging powers. Officers of the FCA, including members of staff or its agents, have the power set out in Regulations 37 to 39 to: **11.219**

(a) require information from, and the attendance of, relevant and connected persons;
(b) enter, inspect without a warrant, etc.; and
(c) enter premises under warrant.

Power to impose civil penalties

Regulation 42 of MLR 2007 gives the FCA as a designated authority the power to impose civil penalties in such amounts as it considers appropriate on a relevant person who fails to comply with the Regulations. The FCA must not impose a penalty where there are reasonable grounds for it to be satisfied that the person took all reasonable steps and exercised all due diligence to ensure that the requirements would be complied with. **11.220**

When deciding whether a person has failed to comply with the Regulations the relevant authority must consider whether any relevant industry guidance has been followed. **11.221**

---

[65] See p 39 of 'Journey to the Financial Conduct Authority' (October 2012), which can be accessed at: <http://www.fsa.gov.uk/static/pubs/other/journey-to-the-fca-standard.pdf>.
[66] MLR 2007, reg 36.

11.222 The burden of proof for the civil offence is lower than that of a criminal offence, being on 'balance of probabilities' rather than 'beyond reasonable doubt'. Where the FCA decide to impose a penalty it must give the person notice of:

(a) their decision to impose a penalty and the amount;
(b) the reasons for imposing the penalty;
(c) the right to make representations to it within a specified period (not less than 28 days).

11.223 Appeals to a decision made by the FCA are directed to the Upper Tribunal. However, the scope of the Upper Tribunal's power to substitute its opinion for that of the FCA is far more limited than under the previous regime. In cases involving individuals or firms that have been banned and in cases involving refusal of regulatory approval the Upper Tribunal can only refer decisions back to the FCA for reconsideration.[67]

11.224 Detailed guidance of the FCA's powers under the MLR 2007 is set out in the FCA's Enforcement Guide at sections 19.71 to 19.84.[68]

11.225 It lists the powers given to the FCA under the MLR 2007 and confirms that the remit is extended to cover not only relevant authorised firms but also certain non-authorised firms described in the Regulations as 'Annex I financial institutions'.

11.226 The FCA has confirmed that where both the MLR 2007 and FSMA apply it will discipline authorised firms using FSMA powers. Use of investigation powers will be limited to those cases where the FCA expects to take action under the MLR 2007, which will generally be to investigate civil breaches of the MLR 2007.

Criminal offences

11.227 Criminal offences are dealt with under Regulations 45 to 47 of the MLR 2007 which state that where a person fails to comply with the requirements of the MLR 2007, he is guilty of an offence and can be liable to a fine or imprisonment up to a term not exceeding two years. As with the civil offences, the court must take into account whether any industry guidance has been followed and a person is not guilty of an offence if he has taken all reasonable steps and exercised all due diligence to avoid committing the offence.

11.228 Where an offence has been committed by a body corporate under Regulation 45, and it can be shown that the offence has been committed with the consent or connivance of an officer of the body corporate or is attributable to any neglect on his part, the officer as well as the body corporate is guilty of an offence and liable to be punished accordingly.

Taking Money Laundering Seriously

11.229 The FCA, as the FSA before it, takes its anti-money laundering role seriously and is active in developing policy initiatives. Prior to the creation of the FCA, the FSA produced a number of publications reviewing and commenting on the regulatory response to the problem of money laundering in financial services.

---

67 See the newly inserted s 133 of FSMA 2000.

68 The FCA Enforcement Guide is available at: <http://media.fshandbook.info/Handbook/EG_FCA_20130401.pdf>.

In line with a public commitment given by the FSA, the Financial Crime Operations Team launched a major project aimed at establishing the extent to which a wide range of firms across the industry had adapted to the FSA Handbook rules found in the Senior Management Arrangements, Systems and Controls Handbook ('SYSC') and the JMLSG Guidance. 11.230

The results were published in a review dated March 2008 which covered the following areas: 11.231

(a) money laundering risk assessment;
(b) senior management responsibility;
(c) changes to anti-money laundering policies and procedures;
(d) customer due diligence;
(e) enhanced due diligence;
(f) correspondent banking;
(g) monitoring customer activity; and
(h) staff awareness and training.

The report summarises key findings and includes observations of good practice adopted by firms, as well as some examples of poor practice. It recognises that smaller firms generally represent a lower risk without having fewer resources to devote to money laundering risk assessment and mitigation measures. One of the important points raised was the need for adequate staff training and not to treat reviewing anti-money laundering policies and procedures as a one-off exercise. 11.232

Subsequent reports examined the financial crime systems and controls employed by small firms and how banks and building societies addressed money laundering in high-risk situations. Some of the failings which the FSA identified in these reports included inadequate due diligence procedures when dealing with high-risk customers such as PEPs; the use of anti-money laundering policies and procedures not tailored to a firm's particular business; and poor management of correspondent banking relationships. The results of these reports have served as the basis for a number of enforcement actions.[69] 11.233

Following its review of how banks manage situations where there is a high risk of money laundering, the FSA published guidance setting out its expectations for firms' systems and controls for dealing with financial crime and managing high-risk situations.[70] The FSA also provided helpful guidance to firms by regularly publishing a financial crime newsletter which highlighted areas of regulatory concern, enforcement actions and examples of good and poor practices in relation to anti-money laundering systems and controls. 11.234

The FSA, and now the FCA, have shown a continuing commitment to combat money laundering and other forms of financial crime through the use of themed visits to brokers, banks and, more recently, investment management firms. Themed visits are an important method by which the FCA gathers information in order to identify and assess the specific risks posed by certain sectors of the financial services industry. The FSA had used themed visits with greater frequency in recent years and it is likely that this trend will continue under the FCA. 11.235

[69] This is discussed at paras 11.242–11.245.

[70] Financial Crime: a guide for firms, is available at: <http://fshandbook.info/FS/html/handbook/FC/link/PDF>.

FCA Rules Relating to Anti-money Laundering

11.236 The starting point for FCA regulated firms is the Principles for Businesses. Principles 1 (Integrity), 2 (Skill, care and diligence), and 3 (Management and control) have particular relevance. Firms should also pay due regard to their responsibilities under Principle 11 (Relations with regulators).

11.237 One of the themes of FSA policy was the key role of senior management in ensuring that firms are not used for the purposes of money laundering. The FCA has recently stated that it will increase the focus on the conduct of senior management at regulated firms, noting the key role they play in setting the culture of their organisations.[71]

11.238 SYSC 3 looks at areas covered by systems and controls, and SYSC 3.2.6 looks at money laundering specifically. SYSC 6 deals with the areas of compliance, internal audit, and financial crime, and SYSC 6.3 deals with financial crime.

11.239 Rule 3.2.6 of SYSC requires firms to take reasonable care to establish and maintain effective systems and controls for compliance with the applicable requirements and standards under the regulatory system and for countering the risk that a firm might be used to further financial crime.

11.240 Guidance at SYSC 3.2.6 D provides:

(a) A firm may also have separate obligations to comply with relevant legal requirements, including the Terrorism Act 2000, the Proceeds of Crime Act 2002 and the Money Laundering Regulations.

11.241 In other words, failure to comply with the requirements of PoCA or the MLR 2007 would result in a breach of FCA rules.

FSA Enforcement

11.242 The FSA has, in the past, been active in enforcing its systems and controls in relation to compliance, financial crime, and money laundering. The FSA sought to underline its clear policy goal that firms should take money laundering seriously. Assessment of firms' anti-money laundering arrangements has been a major element of the FSA's ARROW visits to firms. More significantly, the FSA has taken enforcement action against a number of firms whose anti-money laundering arrangements have fallen below an acceptable standard. These actions have involved significant fines. In its Final Notice dated 9 December 2003, the FSA imposed a fine of £2 million on Abbey National plc for failures in its anti-money laundering arrangements.

11.243 The FSA has also shown itself willing to take action against firms that are incorporated and authorised in other EEA States. On 5 April 2004, the FSA imposed a fine of £150,000 on the London branch of Raiffeisen Zentralbank Österreich, for not updating its anti-money laundering and compliance manual promptly to reflect the introduction of new rules. Similarly, Investment Services (UK) Limited was subject to a fine of £175,000 because it did not

[71] 'Journey to the Financial Conduct Authority' (October 2012), ibid.

conduct its business with due care, skill, and diligence and for failing to control its business effectively in relation to anti-money laundering systems and controls.

On 23 March 2012, the FSA fined Coutts & Company £8.75 million for breach of Principle 3 as well as SYSC 6.1.1R and SYSC 6.3.1R. The FSA stated that Coutts failed to establish effective systems and controls relating to customers that posed a greater money laundering risk, such as PEPs. In particular, the FSA identified deficiencies in 71 per cent of high-risk customer files that it reviewed. The severity of the resulting fine reflects the fact that the inadequacies of Coutts' anti-money laundering procedures were serious, systemic and persisted over a number of years. 11.244

The FSA had also shown a willingness to hold MLROs personally liable for the anti-money laundering deficiencies of their firms. On 4 May 2012 it published final notices against Habib Bank AG Zurich for beaches of Principle 3 and provisions of SYSC, and against its MLRO for failings in the performance of the money laundering reporting controlled function. A fine of £17,500 was imposed on the MLRO for, amongst other things, failing to take reasonable steps to ensure that Habib Bank complied with its obligations under the FSA Handbook. 11.245

Themes from FSA Final Notices

Whilst there are hints in at least one of the cases that the FSA may have suspected that money laundering had in fact taken place,[72] it is a notable feature of the actions taken by the FSA that they were not taken as a result of the identification of money laundering activity. Rather, the FSA decided to act pre-emptively because it had identified failings in the firms' anti-money laundering arrangements. 11.246

Also of significance in some of the cases[73] is that the firm itself had identified the failings in its anti-money laundering arrangements and reported the matter to the FSA. Whilst this may, presumably, have reduced the level of the fine imposed, it did not persuade the FSA that it did not need to act. 11.247

More than one of the FSA Final Notices refers to the role of senior management in anti-money laundering arrangements. The increase in emphasis on the role of senior management in anti-money laundering arrangements is a theme of recent FSA policy and was one of the drivers behind the redrafting of the JMLSG Guidance. As outlined earlier in Habib Bank, along with the increased focus on the role of senior management there has been a trend in recent years toward holding MLROs personally liable for the failings of their firm's anti-money laundering arrangements. 11.248

The implementation of robust systems and controls is also important to FSA action. Each of the Final Notices in Abbey National plc, Coutts & Company and Habib Bank AG Zurich refer to breaches of one or a combination of rules 3.2.6, 6.1.1, and 6.3.1 of SYSC. This 11.249

[72] In the case of Abbey National plc at least part of the firm's failings related to lengthy reporting times for suspicious transactions to NCIS.

[73] For example, the Abbey National plc case referred to in para 11.242.

emphasis on systems and controls is consistent with the development of the FSA's policy on money laundering prevention generally.

11.250 Finally, it seems clear from all the Final Notices issued by the FSA that the single biggest failing it has identified is the failure by the firms concerned to demonstrate that they took money laundering seriously.

The Joint Money Laundering Steering Group Guidance Notes

11.251 Both the MLR 2007 and the FCA Handbook cross-refer to the JMLSG Guidance. The JMLSG has been publishing guidance since 1990. Initially, the guidance was part of a self-regulatory arrangement which involved the Bank of England. However, following the introduction of the MLR 1993, the JMLSG was used to provide guidance on that secondary legislation. In its most recent version the JMLSG Guidance[74] was updated to provide guidance on the MLR 2007.

The status of the JMLSG Guidance

11.252 Whilst the JMLSG Guidance is not formally part of the UK's anti-money laundering legislation, it is important in legal terms. Section 330(8) of PoCA and Regulation 42(3) of the MLR 2007 provide that a court must consider whether a person followed any relevant guidance issued by a supervisory body or other appropriate body that has been approved by HM Treasury and published in a manner most likely to bring it to the attention of those affected by it. Further, guidance in SYSC 3.2.6 provides that in assessing whether a breach of its rules on systems and controls against money laundering has occurred, the FCA will have regard to whether the firm has followed the relevant provisions of the JMLSG Guidance.

The revised JMLSG Guidance

11.253 Following the extensive review of the JMLSG Guidance in 2006 and the introduction of the MLR 2007 the revised new format of JMLSG Guidance was launched in December 2007 and, in general, has been well received. Particular effort was made to improve the clarity of the guidance and provide a substantial amount of guidance and information that is relevant to non-retail providers of financial services. The JMLSG Guidance overlapped with, and effectively replaced, the earlier FSA Money Laundering Sourcebook—itself consequently deleted.

11.254 The JMLSG Guidance sets out the detail of a business's obligations under the MLR 2007 and is split into two parts. Part 1 contains generic guidance that applies to the UK financial services industry generally. Part 2 provides supplementary guidance for a number of specific sectors such as trade and asset finance and private equity.

11.255 One of the key features of the new JMLSG Guidance is that it has been drafted to accommodate the regulatory emphasis on risk-based anti-money laundering regulation.

[74] Prevention of Money Laundering—Guidance for the UK Financial Sector, 2007 edition, Joint Money Laundering Steering Group, Pinners Hall, 105–108 Old Broad Street, London EC2N 1EX.

JMLSG Guidance—risk-based regulation

Chapter 4 of the JMLSG Guidance examines risk-based anti money laundering regulation and looks at core obligations and actions required to be kept under regular review. **11.256**

The JMLSG Guidance sets out steps to assess the most cost effective and proportionate way to manage and mitigate money laundering and terrorist financing threats faced by firms. These are: **11.257**

(a) identifying money laundering and terrorist financing risks that are relevant to the firm;
(b) assessing the risks posed by the firm's particular:
(c) customers;
(d) products;
(e) delivery channels;
(f) identifying geographical areas of operation;
(g) designing and implementing controls to manage and mitigate these assessed risks;
(h) monitoring and improving the effective operation of these controls; and
(i) recording appropriately what has been done and why.

The JMLSG Guidance recognises that no system will be infallible, but the risk-based approach will balance the burden of the cost of these measures with a realistic assessment of where the greatest dangers are that a firm will be used in connection with money laundering or terrorist financing. It focuses effort where it is needed and will have most impact. **11.258**

A risk-based approach assists with the overall objective to prevent money laundering and terrorist financing in the following ways: **11.259**

(a) recognises that the money laundering/terrorist financing threat to firms varies depending on customers, jurisdictions, products, and delivery channels;
(b) allows management to differentiate between their customers in a way that matches the risk to the particular business undertaken;
(c) allows senior management to apply its own approach to the firm's procedures, systems, and arrangements in particular circumstances; and
(d) helps to produce a more cost effective system.

Identifying and assessing the risks

Given the planning that is required to develop and implement risk-based anti-money laundering policies it is essential that senior management are fully committed to the process. As noted earlier, the FSA criticised what it considers to be the failings of senior management in relation to money laundering. Not only must senior management be committed to the development of anti-money laundering policies, but they must communicate such commitment to all levels of their business. Senior management must decide on the appropriate approach in the light of their firm's structure. **11.260**

The risk assessment process begins with identification and assessment of the risks involved in the business; a number of factors influencing these may be: **11.261**

(a) customer product and activity profiles;
(b) distribution channels;
(c) complexity and volume of transactions;
(d) processes and systems; and
(e) operating environment.

11.262 In assessing the ability of their firm to be used for terrorist financing or money laundering, senior management should also ask themselves a number of questions, including, for example:

(a) What are the risks posed by the firm's customers, eg PEPs, complex business structures, and businesses involving large amounts of cash?;
(b) What risk is posed by the customer's behaviour, eg no commercial rationale for the purchase of a product or service, requests for unusually large or complex transaction which has no apparent economic or legal purpose, unwillingness to divulge information regarding the transaction, and requests for undue levels of secrecy?;
(c) How does the way the customer comes to the firm affect the risk, eg occasional transactions, introduced business, or non face-to-face transactions?; and
(d) What risk is posed by the products/services, eg can the product be used for money laundering or terrorist financing; do the products allow payments to third parties; do customers migrating from one product to another within the firm carry a risk?

11.263 Firms should not judge the level of risk solely on the nature of the customer, product, delivery channel, or location. Where one of these categories carries a higher level of risk, then the combination of the whole customer/product relationship should be viewed accordingly. Allowing a high-risk customer to acquire a low risk product using standard verification appropriate to that product may lead to a requirement for further verification, particularly where the product is subsequently changed or the transactions have significantly changed in nature.

Design and implementation of controls

11.264 Once the firm has identified and assessed the potential risks to its business, senior management must implement adequate controls to manage and mitigate those risks. In order to decide on the most appropriate and effective controls for the firm senior managers must ask themselves what the best procedures are to manage and mitigate these threats and risks in the most cost-effective way.

11.265 Some examples of control processes can include:

(a) introduction of a customer identification programme that varies procedures in a way that is appropriate to their assessed risk;
(b) requiring that the quality of verification evidence should be of a certain standard;
(c) obtaining, where appropriate, additional customer information; and
(d) monitoring customer transactions/activities.

11.266 To allow the firm to be able to identify suspicious transactions, some form of monitoring of all transactions is necessary; procedures need to be set out as to the course of action to be taken when such transactions are identified.

Monitor and improve operation of control

11.267 The policies and procedures of the firm need to be kept under constant review. An example picked up in the FSA's March 2008 Review of Firms' Implementation of a Risk-based Approach to Anti-Money Laundering is the need to update anti-money laundering policies and procedures.

11.268 In this paper, the FSA found that large firms were well used to assessing the money laundering risks in their business and responding appropriately. Medium-sized firms had carried out a gap analysis of existing policies against those outlined in the JMLSG Guidance and had made appropriate changes in client take-on, client monitoring, anti-money laundering staff awareness and training, and senior management reporting. It was unclear whether this process was a one-off event or would be continuous. Small firms had reviewed the JMLSG Guidance and had made changes where appropriate, although not all said that they would carry out further reviews to ensure that they were still suitable for their business.

The JMLSG Guidance recommends that policies and procedures are kept under regular review. Aspects that firms should consider include: **11.269**

(a) appropriate procedures to identify changes in customer characteristics, which come to light in the normal course of business;
(b) reviewing ways in which different products and services may be used for money laundering/terrorist financing purposes and how these ways may change, supported by typologies/law enforcement feedback, etc.;
(c) adequacy of staff training and awareness;
(d) monitoring of compliance arrangements (such as internal audit/quality assurance processes or external review);
(e) the balance between technology-based and people-based systems;
(f) capturing appropriate management information;
(g) upward reporting and accountability;
(h) effectiveness of liaison with other parts of the firm; and
(i) effectiveness of the liaison with regulatory and law enforcement agencies.

Responses to these and similar issues will enable the firm to tailor its policies and procedures on the prevention of money laundering and terrorist financing. Responses should be documented to allow the firm to demonstrate how it assesses its risks, implements systems and procedures, how it monitors and improves the effectiveness of systems and procedures, and the arrangements for reporting to senior management. **11.270**

The risk-based approach to anti-money laundering is not a 'soft option'. Whilst it does enable firms to develop policies that are suited to the nature of the business that they undertake, the process of developing, implementing, and monitoring such policies is likely to make greater demands on a firm than the so-called 'box-ticking' approach of anti-money laundering regulation. **11.271**

Firms should also be aware that the regulatory regime is not an absolute risk-based regime. Although the implementation of 3MLD led to some relaxation of mandatory requirements, the basic anti-money laundering obligations are still retained. For example, the requirements on firms to identify customers and take and retain records of identification material remain in place. The risk-based regime is therefore characterised as a 'minimum standards plus' regime rather than a regime which permits firms to set their own minimum standards. **11.272**

Judging firms against their own standards

Firms also need to be aware that where they have developed risk-based policies that exceed the requirements of the legislation and FCA regulatory regime, it will be against these standards that the FCA will be likely to assess the effectiveness of their anti-money laundering procedures. A firm that fails to meet its own internal anti-money laundering standards may be censured by the FCA even where the firm has complied with the relevant legislation. **11.273**

JMLSG Guidance—CDD

11.274 The MLR 2007 specify the CDD measures that must be carried out, and their timing, as well as what actions must be taken if CDD measures are not carried out. The JMLSG Guidance looks in detail at the application of these measures and what is required to verify the identity of different types of customers.

11.275 The firm identifies its customer by obtaining certain information about that customer and then verifying that information by comparing it to other documents, data, or information from an independent reliable source. Evidence of identity may take a number of forms and in respect of individuals the most common form of verification are so-called identity documents such as passports, identity cards, and photocard driving licences. Paragraphs 5.3.68 to 5.3.114 of the JMLSG Guidance describe the documents that are standard identification documents and what can be done if customers cannot provide these standard documents. It also looks at mitigation of risk of impersonation as identity theft is a growing problem in the UK and worldwide.

11.276 Paragraph 5.4 of the JMLSG Guidance describes where simplified due diligence may be applicable and Paragraph 5.5 looks at the instances where enhanced due diligence is appropriate. Non-face-to-face identification and verification are instances where enhanced due diligence procedures need to be applied. Transactions are increasingly being undertaken remotely, eg by online and telephone banking (including smartphone applications), as well as online share dealing. Although these transactions do not appear to pose any greater risk than other non-face-to-face transactions, such as applications submitted by post, there are other factors which, when taken together, increase the risks to businesses.

11.277 These other factors which increase the risks to business are:

(a) ease of access to the facility, regardless of time and location;
(b) ease of making multiple fictitious applications without incurring extra cost or the risk of detection;
(c) absence of physical documents; and
(d) the speed of electronic transactions.

11.278 Where the customer has not been physically present, extra measures need to be taken to verify the customer's identity. For example, ensuring additional documentary evidence is provided or requiring that the first payment of the operation is carried out through a bank account in the customer's name. Detailed guidance is provided in Part II of the JMLSG Guidance which deals with each industry sector.

11.279 The extent of the extra information required will depend on the nature and characteristics of the product or service provided and the assessed money laundering risk presented by the customer.

11.280 Enhanced due diligence procedures must be carried out on PEPs and firms should also carry out checks to see whether individuals are listed on reports and databases on corruption risk published by specialised national, international, non-governmental, and commercial organisations. One such database is the Transparency International Corruption Perceptions Index, which in 2012 ranked 176 countries and territories according to their perceived level of corruption.

Any business relationship with PEP should be approved by senior management and ongoing monitoring of the relationship performed. Firms should remember that new and existing customers may not initially meet the definition of a PEP but may subsequently become one. In this instance it is vital that firms keep up to date with public information regarding the possible change in status of its customers. As soon as an existing customer is identified as a PEP enhanced due diligence must be performed on that customer. **11.281**

Paragraph 5.7 of the JMLSG Guidance looks at monitoring customer activity and describes the essentials of any system of monitoring. These are: **11.282**

(a) flags to highlight transactions and/or activities for further examination;
(b) reports to be reviewed promptly by the right person(s); and
(c) the appropriate action to be taken on the findings of any further examination.

In designing monitoring arrangements it is important to take into account the frequency, volume, and size of transactions with customers, in the context of the assessed customer and product risk. The effectiveness of the monitoring system, automated or manual, will depend on the following: **11.283**

(a) the quality of the parameters built into it which determine what alerts it makes; and
(b) the ability of the staff to assess and act appropriately.

The needs of each firm will be different and each system will vary according to the scale, nature, and complexity of its business. **11.284**

JMLSG Guidance—suspicious activities, reporting, and data protection

Under sections 330 and 331 of PoCA and section 21A of TA persons in the regulated sector are required to make a report in respect of information that comes to them within the course of a business in the regulated sector: **11.285**

(a) where they know;
(b) where they suspect; or
(c) where they have reasonable grounds for knowing or suspecting that a person is engaged in money laundering or terrorist financing. The JMLSG Guidance refers to this as 'grounds for knowledge or suspicion'.

Knowledge means actually knowing something is true. In a criminal court, it must be proved that the individual in fact knew that a person was engaged in money laundering. Knowledge can also be inferred, so a failure to ask obvious questions may be relied upon by a jury to imply knowledge as in *R v Duff*[75] where the defendant 'wilfully and deliberately shut [his] eyes to the truth and has refrained from making proper enquiry' or, as in *R v Griffiths*:[76] 'closed your eyes to what would otherwise have been the clearest of evidence staring you in the face'. **11.286**

Suspicion is more subjective and falls short of proof based on firm evidence. Suspicion has been defined by the courts in *R v Da Silva*[77] as being the dictionary definition: 'an act of **11.287**

[75] [2002] EWCA Crim 2117.
[76] [2006] EWCA Crim 2155.
[77] [2006] EWCA Crim 1654.

suspecting, the imagining of something without evidence or on slender evidence, inkling, mistrust…' and also as being 'beyond mere speculation and based on some foundation'.

11.288 A transaction that is unusual is not necessarily suspicious. Even customers with stable and predictable transactions will have transactions which are unusual for them. Further enquiry may give a perfectly reasonable explanation for the transaction.

11.289 Where a member of staff of a firm knows facts or circumstances that, if known to a reasonable person in a business subject to the MLR 2007, would have inferred knowledge or formed the suspicion that another person was engaged in money laundering then that member of staff should have reason to know or suspect money laundering. If he does not know or suspect money laundering then he fails the objective test and may be liable to prosecution. To defend against failure to meet this objective test, firms need to ensure that they can demonstrate that they took reasonable steps to identify the customer and understand the rationale behind the transaction in question.

JMLSG—record-keeping, procedures, and training

11.290 The JMLSG Guidance explores and develops the details of Part 3 of the MLR 2007 which deal with record-keeping, procedures, and training.

11.291 Chapter 7 of the JMLSG Guidance covers staff awareness, training, and alertness and sets out core obligations to relevant persons.

11.292 These core obligations state that:

(a) relevant employees should be:
(b) made aware of the risks of money laundering and terrorist financing, the relevant legislation, and their obligations under that legislation;
(c) made aware of the identity and responsibilities of the firm's nominated officer and MLRO;
(d) trained in the firm's procedures on how to recognise and deal with potential money laundering or terrorist financing transactions or activity;
(e) staff training should be given at regular intervals, and details recorded;
(f) the MLRO is responsible for oversight of the firm's compliance with its requirements in respect of staff training; and
(g) the relevant director or senior manager has overall responsibility for the establishment and maintenance of effective training arrangements.

11.293 A firm's employees are one of the most important tools in the fight against money laundering. Staff who are alert to the risks of money laundering/terrorist financing and are well trained in the identification of unusual activities or transactions are essential, as even the best designed systems are ineffective if staff do not recognise what the data means or what to do with it.

11.294 The FCA sets outs in its Training and Competence Sourcebook ('TC') that the firm's commitments are that:

(a) its employees are competent;
(b) its employees remain competent for the work they do;
(c) its employees are appropriately supervised;
(d) its employees' competence is regularly reviewed; and
(e) the level of competence is appropriate to the nature of the business.

Staff should be trained on the firm's procedures and specifically how its products and services can be used as a vehicle for money laundering or terrorist financing, and the firms' procedures for managing this risk. Relevant persons should be trained in what they need to know in order to carry out their particular role.[78] **11.295**

Chapter 2 of the JMLSG Guidance sets out the legal and regulatory obligations with respect to internal controls. Firms are required to establish and maintain adequate and appropriate policies and procedures to forestall and prevent money laundering. They are also required to introduce appropriate controls to take account of the risks faced by the firm's business and maintain control and oversight over outsourced activities. **11.296**

Chapter 8 of JMLSG looks at record-keeping and gives the details of what records need to be kept and in what format they need to be stored. Usually the firm's records need to cover: **11.297**

(a) customer information;
(b) transactions;
(c) internal and external suspicion reports;
(d) MLRO annual (and other) reports;
(e) information not acted upon;
(f) training and compliance monitoring; and
(g) information about the effectiveness of training.

As these documents need to be kept under review and may need to be produced to the Police quickly, they can be kept in different formats for ease of reference and storage. Original documentary evidence may be stored off site, but electronic, scanned, or microfiche copies must be easily accessible. Notwithstanding how the records are held the retention periods set out in MLR 2007 are the same. **11.298**

Where there are ongoing investigations, records should be retained until the case is closed. However, if a firm is not advised of an ongoing investigation following the reporting of a suspicious transaction, there is no requirement for it to retain its records for longer than the firm's record management policy specifies. **11.299**

Looking Forward: 4MLD

In February 2013 the European Commission published a legislative proposal to amend 3MLD known as the Fourth Money Laundering Directive ('4MLD').[79] The proposal comes after the Commission's own review of 3MLD as well as in response to FATF's revised Recommendations published in February 2012. When implemented, 4MLD will introduce a number of significant changes to the current EU level anti-money laundering framework. **11.300**

The main modifications include: extending the scope of the anti-money laundering regime to include 'providers of gambling services' rather than only casinos; increased reliance on the risk-based approach by requiring firms to identify, understand, and mitigate their risks, and to document and update their risk assessments; recognition that resources can be concentrated on areas where the risks of money laundering and terrorist financing are greater; **11.301**

[78] Paras 7.25–7.33 set out how staff should be alert in specific situations.

[79] The 4MLD is available at: <http://eur-lex.europa.eu/LexUriServ/LexUriServ.do?uri=COM:2013:0045:FIN:EN:PDF>.

clarifying that simplified due diligence is not a full exemption from carrying out client due diligence; strengthening the enhanced due diligence rules to include domestic PEPs; lowering the 25 per cent threshold of the current beneficial ownership test; and amending the rules on third country equivalence to recognise that customer due diligence is becoming more risk-based making the use of exemptions on the basis of geographical factors less relevant.

11.302 Under 3MLD, regulatory authorities in Member States have considerable freedom to design their own risk-based approaches which firms are expected to apply. As noted earlier, the FSA and JMLSG have produced extensive guidance on the application of the risk-based approach in the UK. However, variation of approaches among Member States can impede effective cross-border compliance. Moreover, in its study on the application of 3MLD, Deloitte identified the lack of practical guidance at the EU level on the application of the risk-based approach as a further complication.[80]

11.303 4MLD aims to standardise the requirements of the risk-based approach across Member States. This will be achieved in part by producing a single set of guidelines specifying the degree of customer due diligence that firms are expected to apply. In its proposal for 4MLD the Commission stated that the European Supervisory Authorities (or 'ESAs') will play an important role in drafting guidance for firms and regulatory technical standards. However, the development of a harmonised, EU-level approach to anti-money laundering guidance raises questions about the future relevance of the JMLSG and its anti-money laundering guidance in the UK.

11.304 The Commission is seeking to have 4MLD adopted by the European Parliament and Council by the end of 2013 to enable Member States to transpose and implement 4MLD by 2014/15.[81]

Conclusions

11.305 The UK has been a significant architect in the development of international standards and underlining its policy aims to reduce the harm caused by crime and terrorism at home by the implementation of a package of measures which combine:

(a) solid legal foundations that outlaw the financing of terrorism and money laundering;
(b) financial safeguards applied by industry—backed up by law; supervision and guidance that help identify and trace illicit funds;
(c) measures to maximise the investigative and intelligence value of the financial information generated by criminals as they move through the financial system; and
(d) an armoury of measures to disrupt the flow of criminal or terrorist assets and hold those responsible to account.

11.306 The 'all crimes approach' of PoCA provides for a single set of money laundering offences which apply to the proceeds of all crimes, unlike the previous legislation which tended to

80 'European Commission DG Internal Market and Services—Budget Final Study on the Application of the Anti- Money Laundering Directive' is available at: <http://ec.europa.eu/internal_market/company/docs/financial-crime/20110124_study_amld_en.pdf>.

81 Please see Chapter 4 (European Financial Services) at para 4.172 for further discussion on 4MLD.

focus on targeting money derived from drugs trafficking. It also targets assets gained from the proceeds of a criminal lifestyle which can be recovered to break up criminal networks.

The role of the financial sector is to act as 'gatekeeper' preventing criminals from moving illicit money through the financial system. The verification of identity of customers and the reporting of suspicious activities are fundamental to this process. However, there is increasing emphasis on monitoring transactions and the increasing sophistication of money launderers has placed greater demands on firms and their staff. This in turn has led to higher expectations in terms of staff training. The FCA enforces the high-level regulatory requirements in a risk-based way and expects firms under its supervision to have appropriate systems and controls in place to prevent money laundering. **11.307**

Practical and enforceable guidance issued by the JMLSG (and approved by HM Treasury) has been updated to reflect the new money laundering legislation and is now set out in two very detailed sections. The first section covers the general money laundering procedures in great detail giving examples where appropriate for customer due diligence, senior management responsibility, and suspicious activities and reporting. The second section is detailed sector-specific guidance to be read in addition to the general guidance. **11.308**

APPENDIX I

Financial Conduct Authority Handbook (Extracts)

Senior Management Arrangements, Systems And Controls 1 Annex 1

Who?

1.1 R…

(3) for an *incoming Treaty firm* which has *permission* only for *cross border services* and which does not carry on *regulated activities* in the *United Kingdom*, *SYSC* 3.2.6AR to *SYSC* 3.2.6JG do not apply;

(4) for a *sole trader*:
  (a) *SYSC* 2 applies but only if he employs any person who is required to be approved under section 59 of the Act (Approval for particular arrangements);
  (b) *SYSC* 3.2.6IR does not apply if he has no *employees*; and

(5) *SYSC 2* and *SYSC 3* do not apply to an incoming ECA provider acting as such.

What?

1.3 R *SYSC* 2 and *SYSC* 3 apply with respect to the carrying on of:

(1) *regulated activities*;

(2) activities that constitute *dealing in investments as principal*, disregarding the exclusion in article 15 of the *Regulated Activities Order* (Absence of holding out, etc.); and

(3) *ancillary activities* in relation to *designated investment business*, *home finance activity* and *insurance mediation activity*; except that *SYSC* 3.2.6AR to *SYSC* 3.2.6JG do not apply as described in *SYSC* 1 Annex 1.1.4R.

1.4 R *SYSC* 3.2.6AR to *SYSC* 3.2.6JG do not apply:

(1) with respect to the activities described in *SYSC* 1 Annex 1.1.3R(2) and *SYSC* 1 Annex 1.1.3R(3); or

(2) in relation to the following *regulated activities*:
  (a) general insurance business;
  (b) insurance mediation activity in relation to a general insurance contract or pure protection contract;
  (c) *long-term insurance business* which is outside the *Consolidated Life Directive* (unless it is otherwise one of the *regulated activities* specified in this *rule*);
  (d) business relating to contracts which are within the *Regulated Activities Order* only because they fall within paragraph (e) of the definition of 'contract of insurance' in article 3 of that *Order*;
  (e)
    (i) arranging, by *the Society*, of deals in *general insurance contracts* written at Lloyd's; and
    (ii) *managing the underwriting capacity of a Lloyd's syndicate as a managing agent at Lloyd's;*
  (f) *home finance mediation activity* and *administering a home finance transaction;* and
  (g) reversion activity.

1.5 R *SYSC* 2 and *SYSC* 3, except *SYSC* 3.2.6AR to *SYSC* 3.2.6JG, also apply with respect to the *communication* and *approval* of *financial promotions* which:

(1) if communicated by an unauthorised person without approval would contravene section 21(1) of the Act (Restrictions on financial promotion); and

(2) may be communicated by a firm without contravening section 238(1) of the Act (Restrictions on promotion of collective investment schemes).

1.6 R *SYSC* 2 and *SYSC* 3, except *SYSC* 3.2.6AR to *SYSC* 3.2.6JG, also:

(1) apply with respect to the carrying on of *unregulated activities* in a *prudential context*; and

(2) take into account any activity of other members of a *group* of which the *firm* is a member.

Where?

1.8 R *SYSC* 2 and *SYSC* 3 apply with respect to activities carried on from an establishment maintained by the *firm* (or its *appointed representative* or, where applicable, its *tied agent*) in the *United Kingdom* unless another applicable rule which is relevant to the activity has a wider territorial scope, in which case *SYSC* 2 and *SYSC* 3 apply with that wider scope in relation to the activity described in that *rule*.

1.11 G

(1) In considering whether to take regulatory action under *SYSC* 2 or *SYSC* 3 in relation to activities carried on outside the *United Kingdom*, the *appropriate regulator* will take into account the standards expected in the market in which the *firm* is operating.
(2) Most of the *rules* in *SYSC* 3 are linked to other requirements and standards under the regulatory system which have their own territorial limitations so that those *SYSC rules* are similarly limited in scope.

Senior Management Arrangements, Systems And Controls 3

Systems and controls in relation to compliance, financial crime and money laundering.

3.2.6 R A *firm* must take reasonable care to establish and maintain effective systems and controls for compliance with applicable requirements and standards under the *regulatory system* and for countering the risk that the *firm* might be used to further *financial crime*.

3.2.6A R A *firm* must ensure that these systems and controls:

(1) enable it to identify, assess, monitor, and manage *money laundering* risk; and
(2) are comprehensive and proportionate to the nature, scale and complexity of its activities.

3.2.6B G '*Money laundering* risk' is the risk that a *firm* may be used to further *money laundering*. Failure by a *firm* to manage this risk effectively will increase the risk to society of crime and terrorism.

3.2.6C R A *firm* must carry out regular assessments of the adequacy of these systems and controls to ensure that it continues to comply with *SYSC* 3.2.6AR.

3.2.6D G A *firm* may also have separate obligations to comply with relevant legal requirements, including the Terrorism Act 2000, the Proceeds of Crime Act 2002 and the *Money Laundering Regulations*. *SYSC* 3.2.6R to *SYSC* 3.2.6JG are not relevant for the purposes of regulation 42(3) or 45(2) of the *Money Laundering Regulations*, section 330(8) of the Proceeds of Crime Act 2002 or section 21A(6) of the Terrorism Act 2000.

3.2.6E G The *FCA*, when considering whether a breach of its *rules* on systems and controls against *money laundering* has occurred, will have regard to whether a *firm* has followed relevant provisions in guidance for the *UK* financial sector issued by the Joint Money Laundering Steering Group.

3.2.6F G In identifying its *money laundering* risk and in establishing the nature of these systems and controls, a *firm* should consider a range of factors, including:

(1) its customer, product, and activity profiles;
(2) its distribution channels;
(3) the complexity and volume of its transactions;
(4) its processes and systems; and
(5) its operating environment.

3.2.6G G A *firm* should ensure that these systems and controls include:

(1) appropriate training for its employees in relation to *money laundering*;
(2) appropriate provision of information to its *governing body* and senior management, including a report at least annually by that *firm's money laundering reporting officer (MLRO)* on the operation and effectiveness of those systems and controls;
(3) appropriate documentation of its risk management policies and risk profile in relation to *money laundering*, including documentation of its application of those policies (see *SYSC* 3.2.20R to *SYSC* 3.2.22G);
(4) appropriate measures to ensure that *money laundering* risk is taken into account in its day-to-day operation, including in relation to:

(a) the development of new products;
(b) the taking-on of new customers; and
(c) changes in its business profile; and

(5) appropriate measures to ensure that procedures for identification of new customers do not unreasonably deny access to its services to potential customers who cannot reasonably be expected to produce detailed evidence of identity.

3.2.6H R A *firm* must allocate to a *director* or *senior manager* (who may also be the *money laundering reporting officer*) overall responsibility within the *firm* for the establishment and maintenance of effective anti-*money laundering* systems and controls.

The money laundering reporting officer

3.2.6I R A *firm* must:

(1) appoint an individual as *MLRO*, with responsibility for oversight of its compliance with the *FCA's rules* on systems and controls against *money laundering*; and
(2) ensure that its *MLRO* has a level of authority and independence within the *firm* and access to resources and information sufficient to enable him to carry out that responsibility.

3.2.6J G The job of the *MLRO* within a *firm* is to act as the focal point for all activity within the *firm* relating to anti-*money laundering*. The *FCA* expects that a *firm's MLRO* will be based in the *United Kingdom*.

The compliance function

3.2.7 G (1) Depending on the nature, scale and complexity of its business, it may be appropriate for a *firm* to have a separate compliance function. The organisation and responsibilities of a compliance function should be documented. A compliance function should be staffed by an appropriate number of competent staff who are sufficiently independent to perform their duties objectively. It should be adequately resourced and should have unrestricted access to the *firm's* relevant records as well as ultimate recourse to its *governing body*.

APPENDIX II

Summary of UK Legislation

Proceeds of Crime Act 2002 (as amended)

1 The Proceeds of Crime Act 2002 ('PoCA') consolidates and extends the existing UK legislation regarding money laundering. The legislation covers all crimes and any dealing in criminal property, with no exceptions and no *de minimis*. PoCA:

(a) establishes the Assets Recovery Agency ('ARA'), to conduct an investigation to discover whether a person holds criminal assets and to recover the assets in question.

(b) creates five investigative powers for the law enforcement agencies:

(i) a production order

(ii) a search and seizure warrant

(iii) a disclosure order

(iv) a customer information order

(v) an account monitoring order

(vi) establishes the following criminal offences:

(A) a criminal offence to acquire, use, possess, conceal, disguise, convert, transfer, or remove criminal property from the jurisdiction, or to enter into or become concerned in an arrangement to facilitate the acquisition, retention, use, or control of criminal property by another person.

(B) a criminal offence for persons working in the regulated sector of failing to make a report where they have knowledge or suspicion of money laundering, or reasonable grounds for having knowledge or suspicion, that another person is laundering the proceeds of any criminal conduct, as soon as is reasonably practicable after the information came to their attention in the course of their regulated business activities.

(C) a criminal offence for anyone to take any action likely to prejudice an investigation by informing (eg, tipping off) the person who is the subject of a suspicion report, or anybody else, that a disclosure has been made to a nominated officer or to NCA, or that the police or customs authorities are carrying out or intending to carry out a money laundering investigation.

(D) a criminal offence of destroying or disposing of documents which are relevant to an investigation.

(E) a criminal offence by a firm of failing to comply with a requirement imposed on it under a customer information order, or in knowingly or recklessly making a statement in purported compliance with a customer information order that is false or misleading in a material particular.

sets out maximum penalties:

(vii) for the offence of money laundering of 14 years' imprisonment and/or an unlimited fine.

Note: An offence is not committed if a person reports the property involved to the National Crime Agency ('NCA') or under approved internal arrangements, either before the prohibited act is carried out, or as soon afterwards as is reasonably practicable.

(viii) for failing to make a report of suspected money laundering, or for 'tipping off', of five years' imprisonment and/or an unlimited fine.

(ix) for destroying or disposing of relevant documents of five years' imprisonment and/or an unlimited fine.

Terrorism Act 2000, and the Anti-terrorism, Crime and Security Act 2001

2 The Terrorism Act establishes a series of offences related to involvement in arrangements for facilitating, raising or using funds for terrorism purposes. The Act:

(a) makes it a criminal offence for any person not to report the existence of terrorist property where there are reasonable grounds for knowing or suspecting the existence of terrorist property.

(b) makes it a criminal offence for anyone to take any action likely to prejudice an investigation by informing (ie, tipping off) the person who is the subject of a suspicion report, or anybody else, that a disclosure has been made to a nominated officer or to NCA, or that the police or customs authorities are carrying out or intending to carry out a terrorist financing investigation.

(c) grants a power to the law enforcement agencies to make an account monitoring order, similar in scope to that introduced under PoCA.

(d) sets out the following penalties:

 (i) the maximum penalty for failure to report under the circumstances set out earlier is five years' imprisonment, and/or a fine.

 (ii) the maximum penalty for the offence of actual money laundering is 14 years' imprisonment, and/or a fine.

3 A number of organisations have been proscribed under the Terrorism Act. The definition of terrorist property, involvement with which is an offence, includes resources of a proscribed organisation.

4 The Anti-terrorism, Crime and Security Act 2001 gives the authorities power to seize terrorist cash, to freeze terrorist assets and to direct firms in the regulated sector to provide the authorities with specified information on customers and their (terrorism-related) activities.

Money Laundering Regulations 2007

5 The Money Laundering Regulations 2007[82] specify arrangements which must be in place within firms within the scope of the Regulations, in order to prevent operations relating to money laundering or terrorist financing.

6 The MLR 2007 apply,[83] inter alia, to:

(a) The regulated activities of all financial sector firms, that is:

 (i) banks, building societies, and other credit institutions;

 (ii) individuals and firms engaging in regulated investment activities under FSMA;

 (iii) issuers of electronic money;

 (iv) insurance companies undertaking long-term life business, including the life business of Lloyd's of London;

 (v) bureaux de change, cheque encashment centres, and money transmission services (money service businesses);

 (vi) trust and company service providers;

 (vii) casinos;

 (viii) dealers in high-value goods (including auctioneers) who accept payment in cash of £15,000 or more (either single or linked transactions);

 (ix) lawyers and accountants, when undertaking relevant business.

7 Persons within the scope of the MLR 2007 are required to establish adequate and appropriate policies and procedures[84] in order to prevent operations relating to money laundering or terrorist financing, covering:

(a) customer due diligence;

(b) reporting;

(c) record-keeping;

(d) internal control;

(e) risk assessment and management;

(f) compliance management; and

(g) communication.

8 The FCA may institute proceedings (other than in Scotland) for offences under prescribed regulations relating to money laundering. This power is not limited to firms or persons regulated by the FCA. Whether a breach of the MLR 2007 has occurred is not dependent on whether money laundering has taken place: firms may be sanctioned for not having adequate anti-money laundering/CTF systems. Failure to comply with any of the requirements of the MLR 2007 constitutes an offence punishable by a maximum of two years' imprisonment, or a fine, or both.

---

[82] The Money Laundering Regulations 2007, SI 2007/2157.

[83] See art 3 of MLR 2007.

[84] See art 20 of MLR 2007.

FCA-Regulated Firms—the FCA Handbook

9 FSMA gives the FCA a statutory objective to maintain the integrity of the UK financial system by reducing financial crime. In considering this objective, the FCA is required to have regard to the importance of taking action intended to minimise the extent to which it is possible for a business carried on by an authorised person or recognised investment exchange or, in contravention of the general prohibition, to be used for a purpose connected with financial crime.

10 Firms may only engage in a regulated activity in the UK if it is an authorised or exempt person. A person can become an authorised person as a result of: (a) being given a 'permission' by the FCA under Part IV of FSMA (known as a 'Part IV permission'); or (b) by qualifying for authorisation under FSMA itself. As an example of the latter, an EEA firm establishing a branch in, or providing cross-border services into, the UK can qualify for authorisation under FSMA, Schedule 3 and, as a result, be given a permission; although such firms are, generally, authorised by their home state regulator, they are regulated by the FCA in connection with the regulated activities carried on in the UK.

11 A firm may only carry on regulated business in accordance with its permission. A firm with a Part IV permission may apply to the FCA to vary its permission, add or remove regulated activities, to limit these activities (for example, the types of client with or for whom the firm may carry on an activity) or to vary the requirements on the firm itself. Before giving or varying a Part IV permission, the FCA must ensure that the person/firm will satisfy and continue to satisfy the threshold conditions in relation to all of the regulated activities for which he has or will have permission. If a firm is failing, or is likely to fail, to satisfy the threshold conditions, the FCA may vary or cancel a firm's permission.

12 Threshold condition 5 (Suitability) requires the firm to satisfy the FCA that it is 'fit and proper' to have Part IV permission having regard to all the circumstances, including its connection with other persons, the range and nature of its proposed (or current) regulated activities, and the overall need to be satisfied that its affairs are and will continue to be conducted soundly and prudently. Hence, the FCA will consider whether 'the *firm* has made arrangements to put in place an adequate system on internal control to comply with the requirements and standards for which the FCA is responsible under the *regulatory system*'. The FCA will also have regard to all relevant matters, whether arising in the UK or elsewhere. In particular, the FCA will consider whether a firm 'has in place appropriate systems and controls against financial crime, including, for example, *money laundering*'. (COND 2.5.6G.)

13 The FCA Handbook of rules and guidance contains high-level standards that apply, with some exceptions, to all FCA-regulated firms, (for example, the FCA Principles for Businesses, COND and SYSC) and to all approved persons (for example, the Statements of Principle and Code of Practice for Approved Persons). SYSC sets out particular rules relating to senior management responsibilities, and for systems and controls processes. Some of these rules focus on the management and control of risk, and specifically require appropriate systems and controls over the management of money laundering risk.

14 In addition to prosecution powers under the Regulations, the FCA has a wide range of enforcement powers against authorised persons and approved persons for breaches of its Rules.

12

REGULATION AND FINANCIAL DISPUTES IN THE CIVIL COURTS

Introduction

The Financial Services and Markets Act 2000 ('FSMA') provides consumers[1] with enhanced protections, both in terms of dispute resolution through the Financial Ombudsman Scheme, and (in the case of dealings with firms that have become insolvent or are in financial difficulty) through the Financial Services Compensation Scheme.[2] FSMA also provides a number of mechanisms to facilitate investor redress, some of which are available to any class of person, and others are more restricted. In the context of an authorised firm, these include a statutory claim in tort for breach of some of the rules made by the regulatory authorities,[3] and a statutory claim against firms acting beyond the scope of authorisation under the Act.[4] In addition, those affected by the activities of firms acting in breach of the general prohibition, have a statutory claim to recover sums invested as well as compensation for losses.[5] **12.01**

The availability of remedies through the civil courts for breaches of contract or other duties is, of course, not something newly introduced under FSMA. However, as Professor Gower noted in his 1984 'Review of Investor Protection',[6] seeking redress through the civil courts was not historically straightforward, and was not regarded by him as providing as effective a mechanism for enforcing compliance: **12.02**

> Only drastic changes in the basic organisation of legal services could make civil litigation by individuals an attractive and effective remedy in most cases. Nevertheless it is an enforcement mechanism which should be more readily available for use in the few cases where it might be sought.[7]

The Financial Services Act 1986, enacted to implement the reforms advocated by Professor Gower, included a provision[8] (the equivalent is now found in section 138D FSMA) to make some breaches of regulatory requirements actionable by private individuals in tort, **12.03**

---

[1] The term 'consumer' is used in various different ways in the FSMA regime. In the context of the Ombudsman and the Compensation Scheme the protections are focused on natural persons not acting in the course of a business, trade or profession, although some small businesses may also be eligible (see Dispute resolution sourcebook, DISP 4.7 and Compensation sourcebook, COMP 4.2, in the FSA Handbook). Certain of the rights of action provided by the FSMA are open to other users of the financial services sector, as described later in this chapter.

[2] See Chapter 8.

[3] s 150 FSMA when first enacted—now s 138D.

[4] s 20 FSMA.

[5] s 26 FSMA.

[6] 'Review of Investor Protection' (January 1984), Cmnd 9125.

[7] ibid, para 10.29.

[8] s 62 Financial Services Act 1986.

as breaches of statutory duty. As Sir Leon Brittan (then Secretary of State for Trade and Industry) said in the second reading debate:

> If the rules are broken, an investor who suffers loss as a result will be able to make a claim against the business; but, to help him avoid having to go to the courts, the agency will have the power to set up an ombudsman or arbitration scheme to resolve disputes.[9]

12.04 Despite the introduction of this additional potential cause of action for investors suffering a loss as a result of rule breaches, there are few reported cases in which investors relied on the private right of action under the 1986 Act, although the 1986 Act did have other impacts on civil actions, for example, the enforceability of contracts for differences which had previously been regarded as unenforceable because they were classed as gaming contracts.[10]

12.05 Since the introduction of the FSMA in 2001, including the re-enactment of the right to bring civil claims by 'private persons' based on breaches of regulatory rules, there has been an increase in litigation in the civil courts in which regulatory obligations have featured. This increase has become even more marked since the beginning of the financial crisis in 2007/8, as clients of financial services firms have more frequently resorted to the courts to seek relief from transactions entered into in more bullish market conditions. A number of these are discussed in more detail later in this chapter, but it is worth noting that many such claims have been made when the Financial Ombudsman Service has not been available as a mechanism to seek relief—in particular for small businesses.

12.06 Of the claims that have resulted in reported decisions, the most common issue is whether there is an advisory relationship at all (inevitably intertwined with issues of whether the advice alleged to have been given met the appropriate standard of care).[11] Other issues that have been handled by the courts include claims to protection under the client money trust imposed by the FSA's rules[12] (now rules made by the FCA), and the relationship between the FSA rules and enforceability of credit.[13] It is, perhaps, not surprising that these have been the focus, as they involve the most explicit and substantive of the positive duties imposed (along with the parallel suitability obligation for discretionary managers) by the regulator's rules. Regulatory requirements, such as record keeping obligations, that focus on a firm's internal administration will inevitably be a less obvious basis for a private claim because of difficulty in establishing sufficient nexus in causation.[14] Many of the rules imposed by the regulators relate to documenting policies and providing information about the firm and its terms of business, so are less likely to form a basis for establishing a loss caused by their breach.[15]

---

[9] Hansard, HC Deb 14 January 1986 vol 89 cc938–1024.

[10] s 63 of the Financial Services Act 1986 disapplied the (now defunct) Gaming Acts provisions that had previously rendered contracts for differences void and unenforceable. See *City Index v Leslie* [1992] QB 98, Court of Appeal.

[11] See, eg, *Springwell Navigation.*

[12] See, eg, *Re Lehman* [2012] UKSC 6, *Re MF Global (UK) Limited* [2013] EWHC 92 (Ch), *Re Global Trader* 2009 EWHC 602 (Ch).

[13] For example, *Zaki v Credit Suisse (UK) Ltd* [2013] EWCA Civ 14, *Harrison v Black Horse Ltd* [2011] EWCA Civ 1128, *Spreadex Limited v Battu* [2005] EWCA Civ 855.

[14] See, eg, the claim in *Winnetka Trading Corp v Julius Baer International Ltd* [2011] EWHC 2030 (Ch), in which the court declined to find liability for losses when funds were paid out on instruction from the client but the shares being bought were not received.

[15] An attempt to found a claim (or partially found a claim) on a failure to comply with the regulatory requirements for classifying clients as retail or otherwise was tried in *Wilson v MF Global UK Limited* [2011] EWHC 138 (QB). However, the court was dismissive of the attempt given that the classification carried out by the firm relied on information provided by the claimant, who was seeking to persuade the court that the firm did

Causes of Action Available to Investors

An investor suffering loss has a range of potential causes of action to rely on in seeking redress through the civil court system. FSMA itself provides several possibilities, including: **12.07**

- Section 138D rights of action for breaches of some of the rules made by the FCA or PRA.[16]
- Section 241, applying section 138D rights of action to breaches of restrictions in sections 238 and 240 which restrict promotions of unregulated collective investment schemes.
- Section 20 rights of action against authorised firms conducting business for which they do not have permission.
- Section 71 rights of action against authorised firms that fail (a) to take reasonable care to ensure that a prohibition order is complied with;[17] or (b) to take reasonable care not to engage a person who is subject to a prohibition order to perform a controlled function; or (c) to ensure that controlled functions are not performed except by persons who have been approved to do so by the relevant regulator.
- Sections 26 and 27 which render some contracts, effected in breach of the general prohibition, unenforceable and enabling affected customers to be reimbursed and compensated.[18]
- Section 30 which has a similar effect on agreements resulting from financial promotions which contravene the restriction in section 21.
- Sections 90, 90A, and 90B, rights of action against issuers for (a) untrue or misleading statements in prospectuses, listing particulars and certain published information; (b) breaches of requirements to include information in a prospectus or listing particulars; (c) dishonest omissions from certain information; and (d) dishonest delay in publishing certain information.[19]

Each of these provisions explicitly contemplates that affected investors are in a position to bring an action. By contrast, the imposition of obligations and prohibitions punishable by criminal sanctions, does not in itself give rise to civil law rights to damages—notably the offences now in Part 7 of the Financial Services Act 2012 relating to misleading statements and impressions.[20] **12.08**

---

not have the information necessary to classify him as anything other than a retail client even though the lack of information resulted from his failure to provide it (and in circumstances in which he was telling the court that information he had provided was inaccurate). It is difficult to see how losses proceed from misclassification—the line of argument described in the judgment was that the failure to classify as retail resulted in a failure to comply with other rules, which in turn resulted in loss (see paras 81–87).

[16] Re-enacting with consequential changes the provisions previously in s 150, and before that in s 62 Financial Services Act 1986.

[17] See s 56(6).

[18] These sections do not apply to deposit taking, in relation to which there is a separate right in s 29 to seek a court order for the immediate return of the money deposited—but this makes no provision for compensation for losses.

[19] In the context of these provisions, the information concerned is prescribed by Sch 10A, FSMA, and is (in essence) information published by an issuer through a recognised information service (such as the RNS service operated by the London Stock Exchange).

[20] See *Norwich Union Life Insurance Co Ltd v Qureshi & Others* (1999), Times Law Reports, 13 August 1999, ruling in relation to the version of these offences in s 47 of the Financial Services Act 1986.

Breach of Statutory Duty

Section 138D

12.09 While litigation founded on FSMA rights of action has not been confined to claims based on the breach of rules, these have been the most commonly reported. Section 138D makes contravention of the relevant rules

> actionable at the suit of a private person who suffers loss as a result of the contravention, subject to the defences and other incidents applying to actions for breach of statutory duty.

12.10 Not all rules made by the PRA or FCA are actionable under section 138D if breached. PRA rules are included within the scope of section 138D only if the PRA so provides[21]—there is therefore, in effect, an expectation that its rules are not actionable under section 138D. FCA rules, by contrast, are within the scope of section 138D unless the FCA provides that they are not.[22] Rules, for the purpose of section 138D, do not include:

a. Part 6 rules (relating to listing, prospectuses, and disclosure obligations on issuers of publicly traded securities);
b. the threshold condition code;
c. rules requiring parent undertakings to provide information; and
d. rules requiring financial resources to be held or maintained.[23]

This approach acknowledges that the PRA's role as an exclusively prudential regulator means that many of its rules will be about the maintenance of sufficient financial resources, whereas the FCA (in addition to its prudential role) has a more obvious and more direct consumer protection role, in which its rules play an important part.

12.11 The scope of the duty imposed under the FCA's conduct rules is likely to be reasonably clear from the rules themselves (as informed by the statutory objectives of the regulator). As Lord Hoffmann pointed out in *SAAMCO*:[24]

> ...in a case of statutory duty the question as to scope of duty is to be answered by reference to the statute itself, and in such a context the position in negligence and contract will fall in behind the statutorily discerned purpose....
>
> ...[I]t seems reasonably clear that the statutory purpose of the COB regime pursuant to FSMA is to afford a measure of carefully balanced consumer protection to the 'private person'.... These basic principles and purposes are reflected in the imposition under the COB rules of onerous duties (albeit in a well conducted operation these should not be difficult to achieve and they are couched for the most part in terms of 'reasonable care') designed to ensure that the investment adviser understands his client and his client understands risk.[25]

12.12 The concept of the 'private person' is important when considering the availability of a right of action under section 138D. A 'private person' is defined[26] as:

> (a) any individual, unless he suffers the loss in question in the course of carrying on—

[21] s138D(1).
[22] s 138D(2) and (3).
[23] s 138D(5).
[24] *South Australia Asset Management Corp v York Montague Ltd* [1996] UKHL 10, at para 15.
[25] *Rubenstein v HSBC Bank PLC* [2012] EWCA Civ 1184, at paras 114 – 115.
[26] Financial Services and Markets Act 2000 (Rights of Action) Regulations 2001 (SI 2001/2256) now having effect under s 138D(6).

(i) any regulated activity; or
(ii) any activity which would be a regulated activity apart from [exclusions under the Regulated Activities Order for overseas persons or information society services]; and
(b) any person who is not an individual, unless he suffers the loss in question in the course of carrying on business of any kind.[27]

In addition governments, local authorities (in the United Kingdom or elsewhere) and international organisations are not 'private persons'.

On the face of the definition, individuals are in a better position than companies or other incorporated bodies. This is true even to the extent of sole traders being able to sue under section 138D when an incorporated business in otherwise identical circumstances cannot. As Steel J noted in *Titan Steel Wheels Limited v The Royal Bank of Scotland*,[28] the difference between the two exceptions 'strongly suggests that the scope of the exception in Reg 3(1)(b) embraces a corporation which carries on business of any kind even if it does not constitute a regulated activity or something akin to it'. He went on to conclude that a wide interpretation of that provision was required, even though corporate entities who sustain losses as a result of purchasing financial products will usually be in business of some kind.[29] Consequently, in practice, section 138D is likely to be of value only to individuals (possibly also to charitable organisations, although even these may be carrying on a business).[30] **12.13**

Section 138D provides a cause of action for breach of statutory duty and is subject to the 'defences and other incidents' of such a claim. As a result, a claim under the section requires that the claimant can show that he is within the class of those intended to be protected by the rule in question. In practice this is likely to be clear from the rule itself—in particular conduct of business rules (on which claims have most often relied) typically make clear that the firm's duty is toward its clients (or a subset of them). **12.14**

A section 138D claim is also subject to the usual limitation periods for tort claims,[31] as well as the requirement to establish causation and foreseeability of loss (section 138D provides a claim for losses suffered as a result of the contravention)—see further paragraphs 12.17–12.24 following. A section 138D claim is also susceptible to questions of whether the client suffers damage partly as a result of his own fault,[32] and to the possibility of a firm seeking contribution from another party involved in providing an investment product or service.[33] **12.15**

27 Rights of Action Regulations, regulation 3(1).
28 [2010] EWHC 211 (Comm), at para 51.
29 See *Titan Steel Wheels* paras 68–70. See also *Camerata Property Inc v Credit Suisse Securities (Europe) Ltd* [2012] EWHC 7 (Comm), and *Grant Estates Limited (in liquidation) and others v The Royal Bank of Scotland and others* [2012] CSOH 133.
30 See also *Re Grant Estates Ltd* [2012] CSOH 133, in which the court concluded that this distinction did not infringe a duty under EU law in implementing the Markets in Financial Instruments Directive, Directive 2004/39/EC.
31 See, eg, the comment in *Green and Rowley v The Royal Bank of Scotland* [2012] EWHC 3661 (QB) at para 2. Contrast the position in relation to complaints before the FOS, where the limitation defence may be disapplied if that results in a fair and reasonable outcome (*R (IFG Financial Services Ltd) v FOS and Jenkins* [2005] EWHC 1153 (Admin)).
32 See, eg, the comments at paras 322–324 of *Wachner*.
33 See, eg, *Seymour v Ockwell* [2005] EWHC 1137.

Liability for representatives

12.16 The ordinary common law principles applicable to the authority of agents, and to liability for agents and employees apply as much in the financial services context as in others. In the case of appointed representatives (and tied agents) this is reinforced by a statutory requirement that the principal must accept responsibility for the representative.[34] As illustrated in *Martin*[35] this responsibility is not confined to the strict elements of a particular recommendation or transaction, but covers the ancillary matters such as assessing a client's position and assessing a range of products before making a recommendation. Nor is the responsibility confined to matters of negligence or similar lapses in duty. A firm may also be liable for what its appointed representative, agent or employee does fraudulently, if he is carrying on in a way that a client, would perceive as within the scope of his role.[36]

Causation and foreseeability

12.17 The ordinary common law rules about causation and foreseeability apply in the context of claims based on breaches of FCA or PRA rules (see, in particular, the discussion in *Rubenstein*).[37] The scope of the duty assumed by a firm will, as noted earlier, be important in ascertaining whether responsibility for losses falls to the defendant firm. In *SAAMCO*[38] Lord Hoffmann said:

> The scope of the duty, in the sense of the consequences for which the valuer is responsible, is that which the law regards as best giving effect to the express obligations assumed by the valuer: neither cutting them down so that the lender obtains less than he was reasonably entitled to expect, nor extending them so as to impose on the valuer a liability greater than he could reasonably have thought he was undertaking.[39]

12.18 *Rubenstein* involved an individual who, in 2005, was seeking an environment in which the proceeds of the sale of the matrimonial home could be invested pending the acquisition of a new home. He was concerned not to put the capital at risk, but did want (so far as possible) to achieve a better return than the deposit products he had identified for himself. The bank advised investment into a particular fund operated by AIG through a life policy, the nature of which was not understood by Mr Rubenstein, who was under the impression from the adviser's comments that it was akin to a deposit. In 2008, the investment still existed, and shortly before the Lehman insolvency in September that year, Mr Rubenstein applied to take his money out. He was unable to do so immediately because AIG restricted withdrawals from the fund. Ultimately, he did cash in the investment but suffered a substantial loss in the capital invested. He therefore brought a claim for negligent advice, and was successful.

12.19 As the Court of Appeal noted in *Rubenstein*, the importance of this way of assessing the scope of the duty, and the example of a mountaineer consulting a doctor used by Lord Hoffmann,[40]

---

[34] ss 39 and 39A FSMA.

[35] See paras 2.2.12–2.2.14 of the judgment.

[36] See, eg, *Parabola Investments Limited and another v Browallia Cal Limited and others* [2009] EWHC 901 (Comm).

[37] *Rubenstein v HSBC Bank PLC* [2012] EWCA Civ 1184—see further later in this chapter.

[38] [1997] AC 191.

[39] At 212E, cited in *Rubenstein v HSBC*, para 101.

[40] At 213, Lord Hoffmann's example was:

'A mountaineer about to undertake a difficult climb is concerned about the fitness of his knee. He goes to a doctor who negligently makes a superficial examination and pronounces the knee fit. The climber goes on the

is 'that it illustrates the manner in which we think naturally of causation and responsibility'.[41] *Rubenstein* confirms, in the context of investment advice, that wholly extraneous influences on an investment decision will not result in liability, but the assessment of whether this is so will be for analysis in a particular case:

> An investment adviser, with his statutory duties of various kinds, owed to a consumer as a result of the latter's statutory status as a private person, who as adviser recommends a particular investment, which he must take care to be suitable for his client and, if a packaged investment, to be the 'most suitable' on the adviser's menu, may well be responsible if some flaw in the investment turns out materially to contribute to some investment loss. The doctor did not advise, let alone recommend, his patient to go mountaineering: he merely told him that his knee was in good shape. Mr Marsden, however, not only advised Mr Rubenstein on the investment of his capital, he recommended a particular investment. He, so to speak, put him in it. If such an investment goes wrong, there will nearly always be other causes (bad management, bad markets, fraud, political change etc): but it will be an exercise in legal judgment to decide whether some change in markets is so extraneous to the validity of the investment advice as to absolve the adviser for failing to carry out his duty or duties on the basis that the result was not within the scope of those duties.[42]

Liability, in financial services cases (particularly in an alleged advisory relationship), is likely to be influenced markedly by the investor's attitude to risk (which played a key part in the *Camarata* decisions),[43] and on what risks are being advised about: **12.20**

> Where the obligation of a defendant is not merely to avoid injuring his claimant but to protect him from the very kind of misfortune which has come about, it is not helpful to make fine distinctions between foreseeable events which are unusual, most unusual, or of negligible account....

Consequently when an investor can demonstrate that market risk was something he was seeking advice to avoid, it will not assist a negligent adviser that the degree of market risk was far beyond the extent that might ordinarily be expected—hence the result in *Rubenstein*. Even so, even negligent advice may not result in liability for substantial damages, if the court forms the view, as in *Wachner*, that the client would have carried on regardless of the advice.[44] **12.21**

Limitation

As noted later in this chapter, claims under section 138D (and its predecessors) have often been brought in parallel with other causes of action. One reason for adopting this course is the potential different application of limitation periods. As confirmed in *Martin and Martin v Britannia Life Limited*[45] the Limitation Act 1980[46] imposes a limitation period of six years **12.22**

expedition, which he would not have undertaken if the doctor had told him the true state of his knee. He suffers an injury which is an entirely foreseeable consequence of mountaineering but has nothing to do with his knee.... the doctor is not liable. The injury has not been caused by the doctor's bad advice because it would have occurred even if the advice had been correct'.

[41] *Rubenstein* at para 102.

[42] *Rubenstein* para 103.

[43] *Camerata Property Inc v Credit Suisse Securities (Europe) Limited* [2011] EWHC 479 (Comm), *(No. 2)* [2012] EWHC 7 (Comm), and *(No. 3)* [2013] EWHC 29 (Comm), in which there was no negligence in not giving more pessimistic advice about the creditworthiness of Lehman than was given.

[44] See *Wachner* paragraphs 313-321.

[45] Ch D, December 1999. The claimants in *Green and Rowley v The Royal Bank of Scotland* (supra) admitted that their claim under s 150 was time barred, and so pursued claims in terms of breach of duty and misstatement.

[46] Not applicable to Scotland—where the prescription period is five years—see s 6 and para 1(d), Sch 1, of the Prescription & Limitation (Scotland) Act 1973.

for claims for sums recoverable under any enactment, beginning from the date on which the cause of action accrues.[47] In cases brought under section 138D, this will generally be when loss is suffered as a result of the breach of the rules concerned—in turn this is likely to be the point when the investor acts to his detriment on the basis of negligent advice, for example by taking out the insurance policy recommended.[48] This can, plainly, be at an early stage—before an investor actually appreciates that he has acted to his detriment.

12.23 Section 14A of the Limitation Act provides that the limitation period for negligence expires after either six years, or (if later) three years from the earliest date on which the claimant had the knowledge needed to bring an action and a right to bring an action. However, the latter formulation of the limitation period is specifically only applicable to claims for negligence, and consequently does not apply to claims for breach of statutory duty.[49]

12.24 There is potential for the limitation period to be extended under Section 32 of the Limitation Act 1980, in cases where 'any fact relevant to the plaintiff's right of action has been deliberately concealed from him by the defendant' Although this ground for an extension of the limitation period was applied to a breach of section 62 of the Financial Services Act 1986 (a statutory predecessor of section 138D) in *Loosemore v Financial Concepts*,[50] this was on a reading of section 32(2) which was subsequently held to be incorrect by the House of Lords in *Cave v Robinson*.[51] In the light of that ruling, the section 32 extension seems unlikely to assist in any claim based on breaches of rules involving failure to take care.[52]

Advice and mis-selling

12.25 As noted earlier, probably the most common issue considered by the courts in the context of regulated investor–firm relationships is whether a particular relationship was truly to be considered to be, or to include, an advisory relationship, even when the contractual documentation states that it is not. A number of the reported cases reveal claims that assert, in effect, that firms were providing services beyond those (or varied in practice from those) specified in the contractual terms (notably in *Wilson*[53] and *Springwell Navigation*).[54] In the absence of clear contractual terms establishing that there is an advisory relationship,[55] this question is likely to be fact sensitive. Even so, as Proudman J noted[56] in *Balducci*:

> That does not however mean that the contractual position is irrelevant; it is the background against which the alleged advice falls to be construed and understood.

---

47 s 9, Limitation Act 1980.

48 *Martin* at paras 9.2 and 9.16–9.17.

49 See *Martin and Martin v Britannia Life Limited.*

50 [2001] Lloyd's Rep PN 235, QBD (Merc).

51 *Cave v Robinson Jarvis & Rolf* [2002] UKHL 18.

52 The wording in s 6(4) of the Prescription & Limitation (Scotland) Act 1973, which is applied 'in relation to any obligation for the purposes of this section', is in similar terms to s 32.

53 *Wilson v MF Global* [2011] EWHC 138.

54 *Springwell Navigation Corp v JP Morgan Chase Bank and others* [2010] EWCA Civ 1221.

55 The firm in each of *Balducci* and *Wilson* did not, in fact, have permission under their FSMA authorisations to give advice, but this did not feature in the analysis of whether advice was actually given. In *Wilson* there was a parallel claim under s 20 FSMA, but the judge did not treat it as needing a different analysis.

56 Having cited *Geniki Investments International v Ellis Stockbrokers* [2008] 1 BCLC 662, on the need to have regard to the reality of the trading relationship rather than the formal position in the contract alone (see *Balducci* para 39).

Inevitably, in relationships which are covered by contract, the courts, while not shy of doing so,[57] have not readily read into a business relationship an assumption by firms of responsibility to provide advice.[58] Both in *Balducci* and *Wilson*, the court viewed the interactions between the firm and the client said to amount to advice in the light of the contractual provisions stating that there was no advisory relationship. In *Wilson*[59] the court viewed the context of particular discussions as key to understanding whether or not they amounted to 'personal recommendations', ie advice as contemplated under the rules: **12.26**

> How would a reasonable person in either of the parties' shoes interpret [the broker's] observations? It is not simply a question of taking passages from the transcripts in isolation, regardless of those individuals' past relationship, and asking whether it should be construed to contain a personal recommendation. Their communications took place against a particular factual background. This included an 'execution only' account, specifically designed to enable [the client] to implement his own strategy and personal day-to-day judgments about the market and the opportunities it presented. That strategy was always the backdrop against which their discussions took place. It was not something on which [the broker] was called upon to advise or on which he ever did so. That would be contrary to their established modus operandi (reflecting, of course, what was set out in the contracts).
>
> One can see, regularly in the course of their recorded telephone conversations, a situation in which [the client] shares his thoughts with [the broker] on how, in the immediate future, he was contemplating particular steps by way of forwarding his strategy. [The broker] may react and make suggestions, but they could not be construed as 'personal recommendations' because of that very context.
>
> A significant part of the strategy [the client] had selected for himself... involved frequent day-trading in a very active and aggressive way.... This strategy can be seen reflected in his modus operandi before coming into contact with [the broker] and may be a factor of [the client's] character and personality. One can see it also in his communications with other traders... At all events, it was certainly not a modus operandi adopted on the advice of the Defendants.... While he might make off the cuff comments to [the broker] about whether he should take long or short positions, in the light of possible movements in the market, it would be quite unrealistic to suppose that [the broker] was, on any given occasion, making a 'personal recommendation' one way or the other.

Wilson was an instance of an individual with his own strong ideas about his trading,[60] and one in which the claimant traded extensively (frequently intra-day) over a lengthy period. Even though many trades took place after discussion with the firm, Mr Wilson could not persuade the court that there was a pattern in which he followed 'advice' given in those discussions. The lengthy period during which the trading took place on a frequent basis does not seem to be highlighted as such in the judgment, but may be a strong differentiator from cases in which an advisory relationship was considered to have arisen. **12.27**

In *Walker* the court followed the approach in *Martin*, and noted that: **12.28**

> the giving of investment advice [is not] the giving of purely factual information. However, it can often be difficult to say where the dividing line falls.... Thus the provision of purely factual

[57] See, eg, *Walker v Inter-Alliance Group PLC* [2007] EWHC 1858 (Ch).

[58] See, eg, *Springwell Navigation*, *Wilson* and *Balducci*; also *Grant Estates Limited (in liquidation) and others v The Royal Bank of Scotland and others* [2012] CSOH 133.

[59] Supra at paras 102–104.

[60] See also *Basma Al Sulaiman v Credit Suisse Securities (Europe) Limited and Another* [2013] EWHC 400 (Comm).

information about a transfer value, the differences between with-profits and unit-linked policies, the shareholdings of a fund, or the investment strategy of a fund would all be acceptable; but on the other hand advice whether to effect a transfer, whether with-profits or unit-linked would be better for an investor, whether to switch to a particular fund, or whether a fund is low or high risk would all constitute investment advice.... [A]ny element of comparison or evaluation or persuasion is likely to cross the dividing line. However, the provision of purely factual information does not become objectionable merely because it feeds into the client's own decision-making process and is taken into account by him. It is obvious that any informed decision making requires the provision of accurate information and will be based upon it.[61]

12.29 Given the particular background, which (as one can see from this extract) was founded on a particular ad hoc requirement from a client for assistance with a particular question, Henderson J concluded[62] that:

I have no doubt that [the adviser's] repeated statements of what he would do if he were in [the client's] position constituted the giving of investment advice. The same is true, in my opinion, of his statements comparing and evaluating the benefits available to [the client] under the Taylor Woodrow scheme on the one hand and under a phased retirement drawdown arrangement on the other hand, and of his promotion of the concept of drawdown as embodied in [the particular] product which I am satisfied went far beyond the mere provision of factual information in a neutral way. In short, [the adviser gave] investment advice when he should not have done. Nor was this an isolated lapse. On the basis of the evidence I have heard, I am satisfied that [the adviser] took the lead at both meetings in discussing the relevant merits of the Taylor Woodrow scheme and drawdown, and in seeking to persuade [the client] to make the change.

12.30 This focus in *Walker* on whether advice was given in the context of a relationship concerned with the client considering and taking out a particular investment, is in marked contrast to *Wilson*. That was a case about whether an advisory relationship arose in the course of what was, otherwise, a trading relationship based on an execution-only contract.[63] The two are not mutually exclusive, of course. For example, different business units within a single firm may provide different services for different product lines—potentially providing execution-only dealing facilities for equities but also a discretionary management service for a particular portfolio. This can lead to a more complex analysis of the underlying facts to establish whether or not a firm was acting in an advisory capacity or not in the particular context being considered by the court.[64] This will be particularly true where an intermediary passes on market-related information in the course of conversations with clients who are seeking to place particular trades—the courts have been willing to distinguish between this kind of conversation and the provision of advice.[65]

12.31 That approach to identifying advice (and thus the potential extent of the duty underpinning the claim for breach of statutory duty) was also adopted in *Martin v Britannia*, albeit in the context of advice under the 1986 Act:

In my judgment, advice as to the 'merits' of buying or surrendering an 'investment' cannot be sensibly treated as confined to a consideration of the advantages or disadvantages of a particular 'investment' as a product, without reference to the wider financial context in which the

61 *Walker* at para 30.

62 *Walker* at para 96.

63 See also, eg, *Springwell Navigation*; also some aspects of *Bank Leumi (UK) Plc v Wachner* [2011] EWHC 656 (Comm).

64 See, eg, *Redmayne Bentley Stockbrokers v Isaacs and others* [2010] EWHC 1504 (Comm) paras 79–82.

65 See *Springwell Navigation, Bank Leumi, Wilson* and others, in which the potential issue of misrepresentation seems to have been intricately bound up with that of whether there was advice.

advice is tendered. . . . In my judgment it is neither appropriate in the context of the 1986 Act, nor for that matter would it be realistic, to seek to limit the concept of 'investment advice' by reference to the extent to which the advice relates to the 'merits' (ie to the advantages or disadvantages) of a particular 'investment' as defined; and if that be accepted, it seems to me that it must follow that the concept of 'investment advice' will comprehend all financial advice given to a prospective client with a view to or in connection with the purchase, sale or surrender of an 'investment', including advice as to any associated or ancillary transaction notwithstanding that such transaction may not fall within the definition of 'investment business' for the purposes of the 1986 Act.[66]

Even if an advisory relationship is identified, there is still an important distinction between some general, ongoing, duty to advise, and more specific claims. As the court noted in *Springwell Navigation*,[67] the court's task is to assess the breadth of the advisory activity held out as being undertaken, given the spectrum of possibilities, from an ad hoc piece of advice in response to a specific question to advising on general portfolio composition and on an ongoing basis.[68] The client in *Springwell*, despite being experienced and sophisticated, asserted an advisory relationship of a wide nature—in effect asserting that the firm had assumed a responsibility to maintain a watching brief over the investments sourced through it and proactively advise accordingly. Gloster J decided that the nature of the communications in that case was such as to found a relationship in which investment advice was given,[69] but not the general proactive advisory role asserted by the claimant.[70] **12.32**

Other duties and alleged duties considered by the courts

Cases brought to court have not been restricted to advice and mis-selling. The court has considered questions of losses brought about by failures to operate the client money rules correctly—although these have typically been in the context of the court assisting insolvency practitioners to determine who is entitled to receive what funds there are.[71] The courts have also considered the relationship between consumer credit protection and the FSMA regulatory regime. In particular in *Harrison v Black Horse*,[72] the Court of Appeal ruled that non-disclosure of the particular commission in a payment protection insurance sale, even commission that formed 87 per cent of the premium paid, did not breach ICOBS (there being no obligation in that case to disclose receipt of commission under ICOBS, even though the FSA had considered the ICOBS obligations in the context of payment protection mis-selling complaints), and did not in itself give rise to an unfair relationship so as to trigger relief to the borrower under sections 140A and 140B of the Consumer Credit Act 1974. **12.33**

The issue of margin calls, and whether firms may close out client positions in derivatives, has also been considered several times. As a matter of common practice, the contractual relationship between a client and a firm is likely to include an express provision giving the firm wide discretion to close trading positions if the client fails to meet a call for margin.[73] When doing **12.34**

[66] Para 5.2.5 of the judgment in *Britannia*.

[67] *JP Morgan Chase v Springwell Navigation* [2008] EWHC 1186 (Comm).

[68] See *Springwell* paras 44 and 57.

[69] See *Springwell* paras 101 and 107.

[70] See *Springwell* paras 108–110, 112, and 132.

[71] For example, *Re Lehman* [2012] UKSC 6, *Re MF Global (UK) Limited* [2013] EWHC 92 (Ch), *Re Global Trader* 2009 EWHC 602 (Ch).

[72] [2011] EWCA Civ 1128.

[73] Assuming that the margin call is, itself, lawful under the relevant contractual provisions—see *Spreadex v Battu* [2005] EWCA Civ 855.

so, the firm will not be subject to the general duty under COBS 2.1.1 (requiring a firm to act in the best interests of a client).[74] Nor, generally speaking, is the firm likely to be under any duty of care towards the client—the obligation being merely to act honestly and rationally.[75]

Breach of contract, negligence, and misrepresentation

12.35 As noted earlier, the contract underpinning the relationship between client and firm is important in assessing the duties owed and whether any duty has been breached. Inevitably many claims plead other breaches of duty in parallel with claims for breach of statutory duty. The claims for statutory duty have largely been based on breaches of duty to take reasonable care in advising under the suitability obligations in the FCA Handbook. Accordingly, the parallel claims are likely to be argued in very similar form and substance to the regulatory obligations. However, it is likely that the court will decline to find tortious or contractual liability where none arises under the regulatory regime.[76] (The hurdle will be higher still if the contractual documentation is worded so as to preclude an advisory relationship.)[77] This is, perhaps, to be expected. As Cooke J noted in *Basma Al Sulaiman*:[78]

> Although a duty of care was pleaded in contract and tort, it is common ground that it adds little or nothing to the claim for breach of statutory duty, since it was alleged that there was a duty of care in advising BAS with regard to the purchase of Notes, to explain the risks associated with such purchases including the risk of leverage and to ensure that BAS understood those risks, and to ensure that the investments were suitable for her. The reasonable steps required under COB and COBS[79] correlate with the exercise of reasonable care required in contract and tort to achieve the same ends.

12.36 However, the overlap between the duties imposed by the regulatory rules and those in tort and contract becomes important where the claimant is not able to claim under section 138D because it is not a 'private person.' In those circumstances the courts' consideration of the COBS and other rules will remain highly relevant to the assessment of standard of care required. Direct incorporation of the regulatory provisions as specific (although implied) contractual terms is probably now unlikely, but not impossible, in the light of judicial comments that there is no need to imply such terms into contracts on the basis of business

[74] See, eg, *ED&F Man v Fluxo-Cane Overseas Ltd* [2010] EWHC 212 (Comm), and *Sucden Financial Limited v Fluxo-Cane Overseas Ltd* [2010] EWHC 2133 (Comm). The position was potentially different under the pre-MiFID rules of the FSA, which contained a specific provision requiring a firm to close out positions if a margin call remained unmet for more than five working days—see *Spreadex v Sekhon* [2008] EWHC 1136 (Ch), in which the firm was found liable for the additional adverse impact suffered by a client between the date on which this requirement should have operated, and the date on which it would no longer have applied to the relationship (the liability for losses were also reduced by the finding of contributory negligence on the part of the client).

[75] See *Euroption Strategic Fund Limited v Skandinaviska Enskilda Banken AB* [2012] EWHC 584 (Comm) relying on *Socimer International Bank v Standard Bank London* [2008] 1 Lloyds Rep 558; also *IG Markets v Crinion* [2012] EWHC B4 (Merc).

[76] See, eg, *Re Grant Estates.*

[77] See, eg, *Springwell Navigation* and *IG Markets v Crinion* (the latter also noting that there was a contractual estoppel precluding a claim that the claimant did not have a proper opportunity to read the terms of business before agreeing to be bound, citing *Peekay International Ltd v ANZ Banking Group Ltd* [2006] 2 Lloyd's Rep 511).

[78] *Basma Al Sulaiman v Credit Suisse Securities (Europe) Limited and Another* [2013] EWHC 400 (Comm), at para 18.

[79] The original Conduct of business sourcebook (being part of the FSA's Handbook of rules and guidance), was known as 'COB'. In late 2007, with implementation of the Markets in Financial Instruments Directive (Directive 2004/39/EC) it was replaced by a new version of the sourcebook, known as 'COBS'.

efficacy nor on the 'officious bystander' test, in particular because the obligations apply to the relationship anyway under the regulatory regime.[80] For example, in *Wilson*:[81]

> One is inevitably wary, of course, of any attempt to introduce into 'execution only' contracts terms which would have the effect of simply undermining and controverting that fundamental basis of doing business or of unbalancing the statutory regime put in place by the legislature.... There is, of course, no need to imply an obligation to comply with [COB], since it is imposed by statute – and can be enforced by statutory remedies... For good measure... [the firm's] terms of business... point up the distinction between the regulatory and the contractual obligations.... It would thus simply be contradictory to drag in the statutory obligations and given them a contractual status by implication.

Those rules which are specified as being outside the scope of section 138D,[82] are equally unlikely to be regarded as implied into the contract, given the rejection by Rimer J of an argument that the Principles for Business (in the form originally made under the 1986 Act) were implied into the contract in *Clarion v National Provident Institution*[83] in terms similar to those expressed in *Wilson*. However, as between an appointed representative and his principal the court may be more ready to treat regulatory obligations as implied terms, for example, a requirement to have and maintain professional indemnity insurance.[84] **12.37**

The overlap between regulatory and common law duties is not always complete, even where there is an advisory relationship. For example, if product literature produced by an insurer is inaccurate, a financial adviser may not have breached his own duty to take care. There may still be a claim available to the investor against the insurer in that case, as in *Petrie v Standard Life*.[85] That case related to a fund, the stated purpose of which was to provide a temporary home for cash, but which actually invested a substantial proportion in asset backed securities. The fund literature did not alert the reader to the fact that over 44 per cent of the fund was so invested. The judge was unimpressed with Standard Life's reference to industry classifications as if that overrode any other comments about the fund, and with its arguments that the adviser was at fault[86] because he should have worked out that there was substantial investment in asset backed securities irrespective of anything else said about the objective, historical investment, or marketing of the fund, and awarded the investor compensation from Standard Life. In particular he commented: **12.38**

> Bearing in mind the underlying stated purpose of the fund, I think it is expecting far too much to expect an adviser to read into what was overall very uninformative documentation that a substantial part of the fund was actually made up of [asset backed securities].... The adviser, and the investor, were and are entitled to consider the documentation *as a whole*, and to consider *all* of the representations made by Standard Life, not just those which in retrospect support Standard Life's position.

[80] The court did imply conduct of business requirements into a contract under the 1986 Act in *Larussa-Chigi v CS First Boston Ltd* [1998] CLC 277, and in *Brandeis (Brokers) Limited v Black and Others* (Commercial Court, 2001).

[81] *Wilson*, at paras 13–15.

[82] See para 12.10 supra. Note also that the FCA specifies that s 138D does not apply to certain rules, including the Principles for Businesses.

[83] [2000] 1 WLR 1888.

[84] See, eg, *Professional Financial Services v Fiona Dick* [2010] CSOH 131.

[85] [2009] EW Misc 9 (EWCC).

[86] The adviser, who happened to be the claimant's son, was not a defendant in the action.

12.39 In *Seymour v Ockwell*[87] a product provider misrepresented features of the relevant product and failed to pass on material information about the product's risks after the product provider had identified the relevant issues for itself. The product provider was, however, found not to be liable directly to the underlying investor. Responsibility to the investor was regarded by the court as solely that of the financial adviser. Even though the adviser was given misleading information, she was still found to be at fault for 'failing to see the wood for the trees', and missing material that was available to her that pointed to the riskiness of the product in question.

12.40 The direct liability of Standard Life in *Petrie* is reconcilable with the absence of direct liability for the product provider in *Seymour v Ockwell*, on the basis that Mr Petrie ended up with a direct relationship with the issuer of the offending materials, and the Seymours did not. The information and advice provided to Mr Petrie resulted in his having an insurance policy (invested in the fund concerned) with Standard Life, the information provider. The Seymours' policy was with an offshore insurer not the information provider (the fund concerned being provided by yet another entity).

Relationship with Ombudsman Awards

12.41 The Financial Ombudsman Service is established under FSMA to provide a mechanism to resolve disputes between firms and their customers 'quickly and with minimum formality'[88] However, its ability to make monetary awards in favour of complainants is restricted, currently to a maximum of £150,000.[89] The Ombudsman may add non-binding recommendations, and may, as an alternative to a monetary award, order a firm to take practical steps which could result in costs to the firm of more than £150,000.[90] In the majority of cases handled under the Ombudsman scheme, this is likely to be sufficient. From time to time, however, complaints have been taken through the Ombudsman scheme even though they involve losses that exceed the limit. FSMA itself contemplates that this might occur—section 229(5) permits an ombudsman 'if he considers that fair compensation requires payment of a larger amount, [to] recommend that the respondent pay the complainant the balance'. FSMA does not go further to explain the impact of an award on the ability of a complainant to obtain redress beyond the limit of the award. It does permit a complainant to decide whether to rely on the ombudsman award after the process has essentially been completed, since the award only becomes binding if the complainant decides to accept the award (the complainant is not obliged to accept it, whereas the firm is bound by the complainant's decision).[91] But that still leaves the question of whether an investor can accept an ombudsman award and seek, in effect, to top it up through court proceedings.

12.42 The approach of the courts in answering that question is to consider whether the award and any cause of action (under section 138D, for negligence or otherwise) are merged so that the award extinguishes other claims.[92] If, in principle, the merger doctrine can apply to an FOS award, the key question about the viability of a later court action in respect of the same loss

[87] [2005] EWHC 1137.
[88] FSMA, s 225(1).
[89] See FSMA, s 229, and the rule in the FCA Handbook's Dispute resolution module, DISP 3.7.4 R.
[90] Although this power may not be used to attempt to circumvent the monetary limit through a purported direction to make a further payment—see *Bunney v Burns Anderson* [2007] EWHC 1240 (Ch).
[91] s 228(5), FSMA.
[92] See *Clark and Clark v In Focus Asset Management & Tax Solutions Ltd* [2012] EWHC 3669 (QB).

becomes 'the question of whether the cause of action the subject of these proceedings is in law the same as the subject matter of the complaint to FOS'.[93]

Andrews v SBJ Benefit Consultants

Crucial to that analysis has been the question of whether an FOS award is to be regarded as a final judgment from a judicial tribunal of competent jurisdiction. In *Andrews v SBJ Benefit Consultants* the court concluded that the FOS was to be regarded as fulfilling the requirements of a relevant tribunal—the analysis appears to rely heavily on the distinction between a 'judicial tribunal' and a 'mere administrative decision'. The judge reached his conclusion as to the status of the FOS for a number of reasons: **12.43**

- To conclude that the FOS is not a judicial tribunal would be inconsistent with the Court of Appeal decision in *Heather Moor & Edgecomb* that the FOS was a tribunal to which Article 6 of the European Convention on Human Rights applied.
- The FOS procedure set out in the DISP rules satisfies the requirements of, and bears all the hallmarks of, a court or tribunal. Informality of procedure, the obligation to resolve issues by reference to what is fair and reasonable, and the ability of the FOS to depart from the strict principles of English law, are not features that undermine a view that the FOS is a tribunal.
- Even though a claimant may reject an award, which operates to render the award a nullity, this does not mean that an accepted award (which is binding on both parties) should not be treated as a judgment. The same is true of the fact that the award is not immediately binding on being rendered. Likewise the power of the ombudsman to recommend payments beyond the financial limit has no bearing—a complainant has a month to decide whether or not to accept the award and make it binding, and in the meantime can seek agreement from the respondent to comply.
- There is nothing in the FSMA mechanism that implies that a claimant can both accept an award and commence court proceedings. The principle that access to the courts is not to be excluded except by clear statutory wording is not offended if the Ombudsman scheme is optional for the claimant.
- Considering the Ombudsman scheme as a whole, the key provision (section 225(1)) specifies a scheme 'under which certain disputes may be *resolved*...'—the emphasis was added in the judgment. The judge regarded an approach that did not result in a binding award (if accepted by the claimant) as being alien to that provision.
- Two judges,[94] who had previously considered the scheme, expressed themselves in terms which the judge viewed as consistent only with the conclusion that the FOS is a relevant tribunal. In particular the judge quoted from *R (IFG Financial Services Ltd) v Financial Ombudsman Service:*

> The scheme is one which is compulsory so far as the financial adviser is concerned, but the result of a determination is not binding on a complainant... They have an option to accept or to reject the determination. If they reject it they may, if they think fit, take legal proceedings in respect of their complaint. Nonetheless, the scheme as a whole is intended to provide, as required by section 225(1), a quick resolution of disputes within its scope with a minimum of formality by an independent person.[95]

[93] *Andrews v SBJ Benefit Consultants* [2010] EWHC 2875 (Ch), para 30.

[94] *R (IFG Financial Services Ltd) v Financial Ombudsman Service* [2005] EWHC 1153 (Admin), and *Bunney v Burns Anderson plc & Financial Ombudsman Service* [2007] EWHC 1240 (Ch).

[95] *R (IFG)* at para 12.

- The fact that an Ombudsman award precludes recovery of the whole of a complainant's losses does not undermine the applicability of the merger doctrine. The judge considered that any non-binding recommendations made by the Ombudsman (and the willingness of a firm to abide by them) were correctly to be regarded as factors in a decision whether or not to accept the award.

12.44 Although not entirely clear, the judgment in *Andrews* appears to rely, in part at least, on the fact that the Ombudsman process permits the parties an opportunity to present evidence and argument, and a contrast with administrative bodies that do not.[96] The judge does not seem to have been asked to consider other scenarios in which evidence is considered but no judicial function is contemplated. Within the FSMA itself there is the example of the obligations on the FCA to consider representations made in response to a warning notice[97]—the statutory regime in that context does, however, go further by making it clear that there is an independent tribunal that reconsiders the matter,[98] which is not a feature of the ombudsman scheme.

Clark and Clark v In Focus Asset Management

12.45 By contrast, in *Clark and Clark v In Focus Asset Management & Tax Solutions Ltd*, Cranston J considered the *Andrews* case to have been wrong in regarding the doctrine of merger as applying to FOS awards.[99] In particular, noting that the statutory scheme is neutral on the question of merger, 'the term "final" simply means the end of the Ombudsman's process'.[100]

12.46 Cranston J disagreed with each of the conclusions in *Andrews*. He considered that *Andrews* did not address the relevance of Rix LJ's statement in *Heather Moor & Edgecomb* that 'the Ombudsman deals with complaints, not causes of action', a statement that Cranston J regarded as important:

> The doctrine of merger turns on a cause of action being extinguished – it is merged in the judgment. If the Ombudsman considers complaints, not causes of action, as Rix LJ said, the doctrine of merger has no purchase in this context.[101]

12.47 In addition, Cranston J regarded the analysis of whether the FOS is a tribunal for the purposes of applying the principle of merger, as unpersuasive and clearly viewed it as being somewhat simplistic:

> Just because the complainant in *Heather Moor* conceded that the Ombudsman was to be treated as a tribunal under the European Convention on Human Rights...does not mean that it is necessarily to be treated as a tribunal for the purposes of the doctrine of merger.[102]

In the judge's view, on a detailed analysis of the functions of the FOS, *Andrews* was wrong to decide that the FOS scheme is analogous to a magistrates' court and an employment tribunal, noting that the FOS' functions are different to those of a typical tribunal.[103]

---

96 See *Andrews* para 35.
97 See, eg, s 387 FSMA.
98 s 133, FSMA.
99 *Clark and Clark*, para 30.
100 Para 29.
101 Para 25.
102 Para 26.
103 Para 27.

Cranston J was equally critical of the approach to statutory construction in *Andrews*: 12.48

> In my view the correct approach is to consider the Ombudsman scheme as a whole. The statutory aims, as outlined earlier, are to provide a scheme for the summary and informal resolution of disputes. As was confirmed in *Heather Moor* the Ombudsman need not apply the law in reaching a fair and reasonable disposal of a complaint. The Ombudsman's procedure is designed to be expeditious. Complainants may accept or reject the Ombudsman's determination, but if they take the former course the award is binding on the parties and final. It is widely accepted that the scheme has been remarkably successful in resolving the complaints of clients against those offering financial services. If the Ombudsman's award, even though accepted, does not lead to the end of proceedings in any one case, that would not undermine the statutory aims. The scheme would still yield a final outcome in cases where there was no prospect of the complainant receiving more than £100,000 in compensation. There would be no point in a complainant contemplating legal action in that situation. With amounts beyond that the Ombudsman's non-binding recommendation for the respondent to under section 229(5) might well encourage the parties to compromise without recourse to the courts. It seems to me that for a complainant to use an award of £100,000 to finance the legal costs of bringing court proceedings for a greater amount is not inconsistent with the statutory aims.[104]

The judge therefore concluded that the doctrine of merger had no application, so that the Clarks could pursue the respondent to the FOS complaint through the courts for additional compensation to top up the award.[105] 12.49

Given a statutory scheme plainly aimed at consumer protection, the decision in *Clark* serves to avoid undue legalisation of process. The approach in *Clark* gives an Ombudsman's recommendation to pay more than an award a real role in the dispute resolution process, and it reflects the role of a recommendation as a key difference from the financial limits in the County Court jurisdiction cited in *Andrews*. As recognised by the judge in *Clark*, allowing claimants to sue (in the relatively few cases in which the issue arises) for the excess above the cap could hardly (as appears to have been the view in *Andrews*) render the FOS statutory scheme pointless. Where complainants have no prospect of compensation above the cap there will be a final outcome because there would be no point in court proceedings. In any event, the decision in *Clark* has been appealed, and a resolution of these conflicting first-instance decisions is awaited. 12.50

Disputes about the Consequences of Unauthorised Business

FSMA provides a range of rights of action in respect of regulated activities carried out in breach of the general prohibition (ie without authorisation), or outside the scope of an authorised firm's permission under the Act. 12.51

Sections 26 and 27—breaches of the general prohibition

As noted earlier, a breach of the prohibition can result in the unenforceability of agreements and compensation for losses. Section 26 provides:[106] 12.52

104 Para 29.

105 One potential point of difference between the two cases—the fact that the Clarks sought explicitly to reserve their rights to pursue additional damages when accepting the FOS award, was regarded by the judge as having no effect—see para 35.

106 s 27(1A) and (2) provide the same result when agreements are made in consequence of something said or done in the course of a third party's breach of the general prohibition. In addition, the FCA and PRA have power to seek restitution through the courts for the benefit of affected investors, under Part XXV FSMA.

(1) An agreement made by a person in the course of carrying on a regulated activity in contravention of the general prohibition is unenforceable against the other party.

(2) The other party is entitled to recover—

(a) any money or other property paid or transferred by him under the agreement; and

(b) compensation for any loss sustained by him as a result of having parted with it.

12.53 However, the consequences of these provisions can be relieved by the court. Section 28, which applies to agreements rendered unenforceable under sections 26 and 27, specifies:

(3) If the court is satisfied that it is just and equitable in the circumstances of the case, it may allow—

(a) the agreement to be enforced; or

(b) money and property paid or transferred under the agreement to be retained.

(4) In considering whether to allow the agreement to be enforced or (as the case may be) the money or property paid or transferred under the agreement to be retained the court must—

(a) if the case arises as a result of section 26, have regard to the issue mentioned in subsection (5); …

(5) The issue is whether the person carrying on the regulated activity concerned reasonably believed that he was not contravening the general prohibition by making the agreement.

…

(7) If the person against whom the agreement is unenforceable—

(a) elects not to perform the agreement, or

(b) as a result of this section, recovers money paid or other property transferred by him under the agreement, he must repay any money and return any other property received by him under the agreement….

12.54 In *Helden v Strathmore Limited*[107] the court concluded that, although residential mortgage loans had been advanced in breach of the general prohibition, it was just and equitable to allow enforcement of the charge. The factors identified by Newey J at first instance, and approved by the Court of Appeal, as justifying relief from unenforceability were:

v) Mr Helden has had the use of the property which Strathmore's loan enabled him to buy… since 2006 without making any rent or interest payments;

vi) The property has increased substantially in value. Whereas it was bought for £1 million, agents last year suggested that it should be marketed at £1.8m…. The loan from Strathmore has thus enabled Mr Helden to achieve a large profit;

vii) …I accept that… Strathmore would not have been willing to make the loan on an unsecured basis;

viii) … Strathmore could be expected to have generated a return on the £1 million by investing it elsewhere had it not been lent to Mr Helden. They have lost that potential profit as a result of lending the money to Mr Helden;

ix) There is no question of Mr Helden having been taken advantage of. He had considerable experience in property matters, including as a mortgage broker. Further, the rates of interest charged were agreed with Mr Helden and were not exorbitant;

x) Mr Helden preferred not to pursue alternative funding because of his concern that he should be able to make lump sum repayments without penalty…;

xi) Mr Helden has not identified respects in which he would have been better placed if Strathmore had been an 'authorised person' for FSMA purposes….[108]

[107] [2011] EWCA Civ 542.

[108] Quoted by the Court of Appeal at para 45.

Thus the considerable commercial benefits enjoyed by the 'customer', Mr Helden, coupled with the fact that the judge considered that he had not been taken advantage of, were regarded as compelling both at first instance and in the Court of Appeal. **12.55**

The Court of Appeal had more difficulty with the proposition that section 28(5) might apply. In particular, the Court of Appeal was troubled by the argument that ignorance of the general prohibition could properly be the basis of reasonable belief that the general prohibition was not being breached, although the court declined to resolve the point.[109] The judgments do, however, reinforce the conclusion that relief from unenforceability will be a highly fact-specific issue. **12.56**

Section 20—business outside the scope of an authorised person's permission

The FCA's conduct rules are often expressed by reference to what an authorised person is actually doing, and are not typically expressed to apply to firms with a particular scope of permission. In addition, section 20, as with section 138D, is only available to a private person (or someone acting for one, when the private person could not).[110] As a result, it is not altogether clear what section 20 would add, by way of remedy, to a claim under section 138D. Unlike the position under sections 26 and 27, unenforceability of investments and contracts is not an issue. As noted in *City Index Ltd v Balducci*:[111] **12.57**

> Both sections only afford rights of action to persons who suffer loss of (as the case may be) a breach of the rule or the [unauthorised activity]. In both cases, again, the claim is one of breach of statutory duty and the defences and incidents of such a claim apply.

So far at least, the courts have not often been asked to consider the potential for a difference. *Balducci* was an instance of an investor seeking to recover losses on the basis of a claimed advisory relationship, when advice was beyond the scope of permission of the authorised person concerned. Ultimately, the court found that advice had not been given, whether or not within the scope of permission, and the court considered in some detail various conduct rules that would have applied to advice, had it been given. But it did note, as mentioned earlier, the potential difficulty in identifying additional rights under this section. **12.58**

[109] See paras 46–52.

[110] Regulation 4, Financial Services and Markets Act 2000 (Rights of Action) Regulations 2001 (SI 2001/2256).

[111] [2011] EWHC 2562 (Ch), at para 36.

Part III

FINANCIAL SECTORS AND ACTIVITIES

13

BANKS AND BANKING

Introduction

Banks are subject to the new integrated regulatory regime set up under FSMA as amended by the most recent institutional changes brought into effect under the FSA 2012. These specifically provide for the establishment of the PRA as a subsidiary of the Bank of England with the other non-systemic functions of the FSA being transferred to the FCA.[1] While much of the substantive and operational systems set up under FSMA reflected the earlier supervisory practice applied by the Bank of England under the Banking Acts 1979 and 1987, the system had inevitably become more formal and rules based. A number of changes were adopted by the FSA to attempt to replace a more formalistic approach which included the development of a more principles based system of oversight and direction. One of the most significant objectives of the new institutional structure set up with the PRA and FCA is to attempt to restore more of the personal judgement and discretion that applied before, which is reflected in the new operating systems and supervisory approaches adopted by both the PRA and FCA. **13.01**

Banks operating in the UK are required to be authorised (FSMA, section 19(1)) and hold permission to carry on deposit taking business (FSMA, section 21(1) and Schedule 2). Responsibility for banking supervision was transferred from the Bank of England to the FSA under the Bank of England Act 1998 (section 21(a)) in summer 1998 which was referred to as N1) and then to the PRA under the FSA 2012. The FSA had assumed responsibility for building societies and other financial institutions under FSMA with effect from 1 December 2001 (referred to as N2). Both banking and building society business fall within the definition of deposit-taking which is included as a regulated activity for the purposes of FSMA (FSMA, section 22 and Schedule 2). The effect of this had been to extend the earlier definition of investment business as set out in Schedule 1 to the Financial Services Act 1986 to include deposit taking (as well as insurance business and Lloyd's of London syndicates) as regulated activities for the purposes of FSMA. Under the new regime set up under the FSA 2012, the PRA is responsible for the prudential regulation of around 1,400 financial entities including 900 banks, building societies, and credit unions, and 500 insurance businesses including general insurers, life insurance companies, wholesale firms on the London market, and mutual insurers including friendly societies, with their conduct being subject to FCA oversight and control. The FCA regulates around 23,000 other firms directly including asset managers, insurance brokers and advisers, hedge funds, and stock markets and exchanges. **13.02**

[1] Chapters 1 and 5.

13.03 The statutory regime for the regulation of banks and banking business had been introduced under the Banking Act 1979 which gave effect to the requirement in the European First Banking Directive for all Member countries to establish a formal system of authorisation and supervision for banking business. The original provisions set out in the 1979 Act were subsequently amended in 1987 following a government White Paper into the conduct of banking supervision by the Bank of England. The regime was further amended during the early 1990s following the collapse of BCCI and then Barings. This resulted in the production of a new consolidated Guide to Supervisory Policy which restated all of the earlier Bank of England non-statutory papers that applied to banking activity and bank supervision. Following the conferral of full operational and policy autonomy with regard to the conduct of monetary policy on the Bank of England in 1997, it was decided to transfer bank supervision to the FSA. This was considered necessary to avoid any future crises, such as in connection with BCCI and Barings, which could potentially undermine the ability or credibility of the Bank in the conduct of its monetary activities. It was only following the decision to transfer bank supervision to the FSA that the new integrated regulatory regime was extended to include all other key financial sectors and markets within the UK in addition to banking and investment services. Following the global and UK financial crisis beginning in Autumn 2007, the UK has created a new central bank-based macro-prudential model around the Bank of England with prudential regulation being managed by the PRA and financial conduct by the FCA.

13.04 Building societies are regulated in a parallel manner due to the common deposit taking function involved.[2] Building society supervision was initially conducted by the Building Societies Commission under the Building Societies Act 1986. This provided for a parallel regime to that set up under the Banking Act 1987, although adjusted to reflect the property secured nature of the main lending conducted. The provisions set out in the Building Societies Commission rule book were continued on an interim basis following N2 under the FSA's Interim Prudential Sourcebook for building societies ('IPRU(BSOC)') with most of these provisions being replaced by new integrated general provisions in GENPRU and prudential requirements for deposit-taking institutions (banks and building societies) and investment firms in BIPRU.[3] The earlier constitutional provisions contained in IPRU(BSOC) have been moved to a new Building Societies Regulatory Guide ('BSOG') which is contained in the PRA and FCA Handbooks. A separate Building Societies Sourcebook ('BSOCS') has been produced covering inter alia lending, Treasury investments and liquidity, funding, financial risk management, and business model diversification, which is included within the PRA Handbook. The earlier liquidity provisions on mismatch liquidity ('LM') and sterling stock liquidity ('LS') contained in volume 2 of IPRU(BANK) were continued on an interim basis before the coming into effect of the strengthened of liquidity regime set up under BIPRU12.

13.05 As regulated entities, banks (and building societies) have to comply with all relevant provi sions set out in the regulatory Handbooks. The earlier provisions contained in the FSA Handbook have since been split between the PRA and FCA Handbooks with a Combined version also available. These include the general provisions set out in the High Level standards Block including, in particular, the Principles for Businesses ('PRIN'), the Senior Management Arrangements, Systems and Controls ('SYCS'), the Threshold Conditions

[2] Chapter 17.

[3] Paras 13.204–13.210 and 13.211–13.241, and Chapter 14.

('COND'), the Statements of Principle for Approved Persons ('FIT'), and the Code of Conduct for Approved Persons ('APER'), General provisions ('GEN'), as well as the more recent provisions on Financial Stability and Market Confidence ('FINMAR') and the Fees Manual ('FEES').[4] They previously had to comply with the interim prudential measures for banks ('IPRU(BANK)' and building societies 'IPRU(BSOC)') although these have now been replaced by the new rules contained in the restructured Prudential Standards Block of the Handbook including General Application and Group Risk requirements ('GENPRU') and the Banks, Building Societies and Investment Firms prudential sourcebook ('BIPRU').[5] They were subject to the requirements on money laundering which were set out in a separate sourcebook ('ML') and the three sets of process provisions previously contained in Authorisation ('AUTH'), Supervision ('SUP'), and Enforcement ('ENF'). Authorisation is now dealt with under the revised procedures adopted by the PRA.[6] SUP and COMP have been retained within both the PRA and FCA Handbooks with the Decision Procedure and Penalties Manual in the FCA Regulatory Block. Money laundering has since been removed with a shortened Financial Crime Guide ('FC') in the FCA Handbook and with ENF being superseded by the Enforcement Guide ('EG') within the FCA Handbook.[7] Banks were subject to the new Supervisory Enhancement Programme ('SEP') set up by the FSA following the Northern Rock crisis and now the new regulatory approaches adopted by the PRA and FCA.[8] The integrated redress provisions have been split with Compensation ('COMP') retained within both Handbooks and Dispute Resolution: Complaints ('DISP') and Consumer Redress Schemes sourcebook ('CONRED') within the FCA Handbook and a new Complaints Scheme established under Part 6 of the FSA 2012.[9] Banks may also be subject to some of the other more particular sourcebooks to the extent relevant such as administering collective investment schemes ('COLL' which replaced 'CIS') with the Collective Investment Scheme Information Guide ('COLLG').

While the FSA had been intended to bring the new single Prudential Sourcebook ('PRU') into effect during 2005, this was not possible due to the extended consultation required on the revised capital standards produced by the Basel Committee on Banking Supervision under its new Capital Accord (Basel II) and parallel European measures under the Capital Requirements Directive ('CRD') as amended.[10] These replaced the earlier rules set out in the 1988 Capital Accord (Basel I) and European Own Funds Directive and Solvency Ratio Directive for banks and Capital Adequacy Directive for securities firms.[11] Basel II and the CRD created a new framework for calculating credit risk capital cover based on the three pillars of revised minimum standards, supervisory review, and enhanced market discipline. The European measures were to be implemented in the UK under the final provisions set out in the PRU although the PRU has since been replaced by a number of separate sub-sourcebooks which include in the banking area GENPRU and BIPRU.[12] Basel II has since **13.06**

[4] Paras 13.96–13.105 and Chapter 5.

[5] Paras 13.161–13.170, 13.191–13.203, 13.204–13.210, and 13.211–13.241.

[6] Paras 13.91–13.94. See also: <http://www.bankofengland.co.uk/pra/Pages/authorisations/newfirm/banking.aspx>.

[7] Paras 13.45 and 13.106–13.160, and Chapter 6.

[8] Paras 13.114–13.123.

[9] ss 84-88 FSA 2012. See also Bank of England, PRA and FCA, *Complaints against the regulators* (April 2013); available at: <http://www.bankofengland.co.uk/financialstability/Documents/fmi/complaints.pdf>.

[10] Para 13.53 and nn 84, 85, and 86, and paras 13.160–13.167.

[11] Paras 13.165–13.179 and 13.180–13.290.

[12] Paras 13.204–13.210 and 13.211–13.241.

being revised under the Basel III amendments put into effect following the global financial crisis with corresponding amendments to be made under the proposed European CRD IV.

13.07 The extended regime for banks and building societies also includes measures adopted with regard to mortgage advice and general insurance sales.[13] These were not transferred to the FSA initially but were added subsequently to protect the interests of consumers. The Government had announced that the FSA would be required to adopt measures in connection with the provision of mortgage advice and general insurance sales and that these will fall within the scope of the new regime set up under FSMA. The necessary requirements would be included within a new Conduct of Business Sourcebook and additional special Handbook Guides.[14] These new regimes came into effect in October 2004 and January 2005 (referred to as N3). The responsibilities of the FSA were further extended to cover personal pension schemes including self-invested personal pensions ('SIPPS') from April 2007 and connected travel insurance ('CTI') which is sold with holiday or other related travel firms and holiday providers from 1 January 2009. The Mortgages and Home Finance: Conduct of Business sourcebook ('MCOB') has been retained within the FCA Handbook and a Prudential sourcebook for Mortgage and Home Finance Firms and Insurance Intermediaries ('MIPRU') added to the PRA Handbook.[15]

13.08 The purpose of this chapter is to consider the background to and development of UK banking supervision. The traditional nature of bank supervision and the role and function of the Bank of England are reviewed. Earlier and more recent crises in UK banking markets, including with regard to Northern Rock, are noted and the circumstances surrounding the transfer of responsibility for bank supervision initially from the Bank to the FSA and then from the FSA to the PRA are referred to. The main provisions contained in the Bank of England Act 1998 are outlined and later amendments under the BA 2009 and FSA 2012. The relevant sections of FSMA are then considered in further detail with the principal parts of the PRA and FCA Handbooks of Rules and Guidance that are relevant to banks. This includes, in particular, the Supervision manual ('SUP') and earlier Interim Prudential Sourcebook for banks ('IPRU(BANK)') as well as the final measures contained in General Application and Group Risk requirements ('GENPRU') and Banking and Investment Firms ('BIPRU'). Relevant supporting international and European bank measures are also referred to. The most recent changes announced with regard to Ring-fencing, Recovery planning, and Resolution are also discussed.

UK Banking Supervision

13.09 UK bank supervision has traditionally been conducted on an informal basis. Historically, bank supervision refers to the general oversight of the banking and financial markets in the UK as conducted by the Bank of England as one part of its more general central bank functions. Supervision can be distinguished from regulation which refers to the imposition of specific legal, secondary, or administrative obligations on financial institutions.[16] Formal

---

[13] Chapters 15 and 17.

[14] These consisted of the Mortgages and Home Finance Conduct of Business Sourcebook ('MCOB') in Block 3 and Handbook Guides in Block 8 on Small Mortgage and Insurance Intermediaries General Rules (('MIGI'), Mortgage Intermediaries ('MOGI'), and Insurance Intermediaries ('GIGI')). See generally Chapter 17.

[15] Chapter 17.

[16] GA Walker, *International Banking Regulation—Law, Policy and Practice* (2001) Introduction (n 1).

statutory regulation was only introduced in the UK under the Banking Act 1979 following the UK's accession to the then European Economic Community (EEC) and the coming into effect of the 1977 First Banking Directive in 1979.

Bank of England

A formal statutory framework for the regulation of the banking markets was only created in 1979. Until then, the Bank of England had monitored the efficiency and stability of the banking and financial markets in the UK on an informal basis.[17] Bank supervision was, in particular, regarded as a necessary part of the lender of last resort support role within the financial system.[18] The Bank would manage the amount of liquidity in the banking system on a daily basis especially through its operations in the primary money market (or discount market) and provide emergency assistance to particular institutions in the event that credit or other financial difficulties arose. **13.10**

This lender of last resort role is regarded as being particularly necessary in the banking sector due to the inherently unstable nature of the financial risks involved with banks funding medium to long-term loans through sight or demand deposits. This creates an essential maturity mismatch or maturity transformation within the banking system. Banks maintain a necessary reserve of approximately one third of their deposit base in a liquid form to cover possible withdrawal demands. In the event that this is exhausted due to unexpected withdrawals or a run on the bank, it will have to obtain funds from other financial institutions failing which it will approach the central bank for emergency assistance. The Bank of England's lender of last resort role was confirmed at the end of the nineteenth century following the first Barings crisis in 1890. **13.11**

While the Bank of England has informally monitored the daily operations of the markets, this process had become more structured as its ability to collect statistical and reporting information from banks has evolved during the twentieth century. The collection of increasingly detailed data in connection with all of the main activities of banks allowed the Bank to monitor market activity on an increasingly more sophisticated and accurate basis. The collection of market information was then supplemented through formal and informal meetings and contact with senior bank staff, with the Bank being able to advise institutions on an individual basis of any concerns that arose and to issuance guidance or recommendations as appropriate. This process of informal direction given by the Bank to particular institutions came to be known to as 'moral suasion'.[19] This, in particular, referred to the market or moral authority of the Bank which historically commanded sufficient weight that individual institutions would always act on any recommendations or directions made. The supporting **13.12**

[17] H Thornton, *An Enquiry into the Nature and Effects of the Paper Credit of Great Britain* (1802); and W Bagehot, *Lomdard Street* (1873). On the history of the Bank of England, see, W Marston Acres, *The Bank of England from Within* (1931); Sir John Clapham, *The Bank of England 1797–1914* (1944); RS Sayers, *The Bank of England 1891–1944* (1976); and J Fforde, *The Bank of England and Public Policy 1941–1958* (1992). See generally, Guy Morton and Andrew Marsh, 'UK Central Banking and the Financial Stability' in M Blair, G Walker, and S Wiley, *Financial Markets and Exchanges Law* (2nd edn, OUP 2012), Chapter 3. See Chapter 1, paras 1.90–1.157.

[18] GA Walker (n 16), ch 3 (n 51).

[19] JJ Norton, 'The Bank of England's Lament: the Struggle to Maintain the Traditional Supervisory Practices of "Moral Suasion"' in Norton (ed), *Bank Regulation and Supervision in the 1990s* (1991), ch 2; and G Penn and Wadstone, *Banking Supervision* (2000), ch 1.

or implied threat was always that daily liquidity assistance or emergency support may be withheld in the event that a bank failed to comply with the directions given.

Overseas banks and secondary banking crisis

13.13 The non-statutory based nature of the system of bank supervision that emerged was characterised by the personal contact, flexibility, and judgement or discretion-based nature of the oversight exercised and with the most minimum and then only implied threat of sanction. This system proved sufficiently effective to allow the Bank of England to monitor and control the London and UK markets until the early 1970s.

13.14 The informal and individual contact nature of this system began to break down with the large influx of overseas banks into London during the end of the 1960s and early 1970s. By 1973 and 1974, the Bank was forced to reconsider the nature of its traditional supervisory function and activities. Following a crisis in the secondary banking markets in 1972 and 1973 and over-exposure by a number of smaller banks to property prices, the Bank had to organise a 'lifeboat' operation to support institutions threatened with closure.

13.15 Following this, the Bank set up the first formal Banking Supervision Department rather than continue with this function being carried on by the Discount Office. A formal prudential (rather than purely statistical) return was introduced to allow Bank staff to assess individual banks' capital and financial positions more accurately. While bank supervision was already becoming a more formal process within the Bank, the need to establish a formal licensing or authorisation system only became necessary with the coming into effect of the European First Banking Directive in 1979 which required that a formal licensing system was set up. The Banking Act 1979 was accordingly enacted to establish a statutory framework for bank supervision within the UK, although much of the traditional nature of the earlier informal practices developed by the Bank of England was continued in connection with the daily operation of the supervision conducted.

Banking Act 1979

13.16 The Banking Act 1979 introduced a formal definition of deposit taking business and imposed a general prohibition on the conduct of such activities unless licensed to do so under the Act. A general distinction was drawn between recognised banks and licensed deposit-takers. This reflected the perceived market or reputational distinction that existed between the larger more established banks and new lending institutions that had grown up during the late 1960s and 1970s. The Bank was given legal power to issue and to restrict bank licences and to issue directions as well as to require information to be provided by banks and to conduct investigations as required. Controls were introduced on the use of banking names and descriptions. A formal appeals procedure was created and provision included for the establishment of a deposit protection support scheme. Statutory restrictions were placed on the exchange of confidential information between banks and the authorities except under prescribed channels (or gateways).

13.17 As part of this new more formal supervisory process and in response to the changes that were taking place within the banking markets, the Bank of England issued a number of supervisory papers during the late 1970s and 1980s on such matters as foreign exchange currency management, capital adequacy, and liquidity. The objective was to attempt to identify relevant best market practice in each of these areas at that time and to set this out in the form of recommended guidelines with which banks would be expected to comply. There was no legal obligation imposed on banks to comply with these measures as such, although the Bank had power to restrict or revoke a licence where they failed to continue to satisfy the threshold conditions set out in Schedule 2 to the Banking Act (then Schedule 3 to the 1987 Act and now Schedule 6 to FSMA).

Johnson Matthey and the Banking Act 1987

13.18 Despite the improvements adopted in the conduct of supervisory practice, the Bank's intervention in the markets was questioned especially following the Johnson Matthey crisis in autumn 1984. The Bank was again compelled to rescue a major financial institution through the provision of a £150 million guarantee to Johnson Matthey. The shares in Johnson Matthey were also purchased which effectively nationalised the institution. The Bank of England had insisted that the intervention was necessary to avoid a potential threat to the stability of the markets as Johnson Matthey was involved in the daily fixing of the price of gold within the London gold market.

13.19 Following a further government White Paper, the Banking Act 1987 was enacted.[20] This abolished the earlier two-tier system of recognition for banks and licensed deposit-takers and strengthened the authorisation criteria set out in Schedule 3 to the Act. The powers of the Bank to revoke or restrict licences and issue directions were revised and a new Board of Banking Supervision established. The role of auditors was strengthened to investigate and confirm the accuracy and validity of prudential information provided and systems and controls maintained within banks, as well as to report suspicious transactions to the Bank.

BCCI and Barings

13.20 Further steps were again taken to improve the conduct of UK bank supervision following the collapse of the Bank of Credit and Commerce International ('BCCI') in July 1991.[21] BCCI had been closed in a coordinated response arranged between all of the major supervisory authorities in the countries within which it operated. The closure was led by the Bank of England following the confirmation of fraud in the UK. Although no statutory changes to bank supervision were given effect to, a number of internal corrections were adopted at the time by the Bank.

13.21 The nature of the supervision effected was further reconsidered following the collapse of Barings in February 1995.[22] Barings had to be purchased by ING after it had suffered £650 million of trading losses through the activities of a financial derivatives subsidiary in Singapore under the management of Nick Leeson. Following the scandal, a report was commissioned by the Bank of England from Arthur Andersen which made a number of recommendations that were given full effect to by the Bank.[23] These included the adoption of a new supervision by risk framework referred to as 'RATE' (Risk Assessment, Tools of

[20] 'Banking Supervision' (Cmnd 9695) of 17 December 1985. See also 'Report of the Committee Set up to Consider the Question of Banking Supervision' (Cmnd 9550, 1985).

[21] Lord Justice Bingham, 'Inquiry into the Supervision of the Bank of Credit and Commerce International' (22 October 1992).

[22] Board of Banking Supervision, 'Inquiry into the circumstances of the Collapse of Barings', HC (1994–95) 673.

[23] Arthur Andersen, 'Findings and Recommendations of the review of Supervision and Surveillance' (July 1996).

Supervision, Evaluation).[24] All of the Bank's earlier supervisory papers were restated in a consolidated Guide to Supervisory Policy which was issued in two volumes in 1998. The function and structure of the Bank of England more generally was considered by a Treasury and Civil Service Select Committee report in 1993/1994. The internal organisation of the Bank was subsequently then divided into a separate Monetary Stability wing and Financial Stability wing in July 1994.[25]

13.22 Responsibility for bank supervision was then formally transferred from the Bank of England to the FSA under the Bank of England Act 1998. This was considered necessary partly to insulate the conduct of monetary policy by the Bank from potential difficulties arising in the conduct of bank supervision and, in particular, the possibility of further crises such as with BCCI or more recently Barings. While the Bank of England had historically always claimed that it considered it necessary to maintain an essential link between bank supervision and the provision of lender of last resort support to the financial system, this policy was reversed following the conferral of full policy and operational autonomy in respect of the conduct of monetary policy on the Bank. Bank supervision was then to be conducted by the FSA under the Banking Act 1987 between the coming into effect of the Bank of England Act 1998 in summer 1998 ('N1') and the coming into effect of FSMA in December 2001 ('N2'). Since then, deposit taking has been included as a regulated activity for the purposes of FSMA and banking, included within the new integrated regulatory regime created under the Act.

Financial Crisis

13.23 The relative stability of the new integrated system of financial regulation set up under FSMA was most substantially tested with the liquidity crisis in the inter-bank market beginning in August 2007 and the funding difficulties that this caused at Northern Rock in September 2007 which led to its later acquisition by the Treasury in February 2008.[26] Following the credit tightening that had occurred in many of the principal inter-bank markets across the world in August 2007, Northern Rock was forced to ask for liquidity support from the Bank of England which was agreed on 14 September 2007. The Government had initially confirmed that it would prefer a private market solution to the problems at Northern Rock and various private sector bids were considered for its acquisition during autumn 2007. Following the Treasury's rejection of the remaining bids by the Virgin Group and a

[24] Bank of England, 'A Risk Based Approach to Supervision (the RATE framework)' (March 1997); 'A Risk Based Approach to the Supervision of Non-EEA Banks (the SCALE framework)' (July 1997); and 'A Risk Based Approach to Supervising Foreign Exchange and Other Market Risks' (July 1997). See 'Bank of England, A Risk Based Approach to Bank Supervision (the RATE Framework)' (May 1998).

[25] Treasury and Civil Service Select Committee Report: 'The Role of the Bank of England', HC (1993–94) 98; and 'Reorganisation of the Bank of England' Press Notice, July 1994.

[26] Chapter 1, paras 1.22–1.27; and GA Walker, 'Financial Markets and Exchanges Law' in Blair, Walker, and Wiley, *Financial Markets and Exchanges Law* (n 17) Chapter 1, paras 1.122–1.34. See also GA Walker, 'Northern Rock Falls' (2008) *Bankers' Law* Vol 2, No 2, 4–12. See also GA Walker, 'The Deconstruction of Financial Risk' (2008) *Palgrave Journal of Banking Regulation* (October) 1, 2; and GA Walker, 'Credit Crisis—Regulatory and Financial Systems Reform' (2007) *Butterworths JIBL* (November) 567–72; and GA Walker, 'Sub-prime Loans, Inter-Bank Markets and Financial Support' (2007) *The Company Lawyer* (November) 22–25. See also GA Walker, 'Credit Contraction, Financial Collapse and Global Recession' *Butterworths JIBL* (January 2009) 5–10; and GA Walker, 'Credit Crisis, Bretton Woods II and A New Global Response' *Butterworths JIBL* (February 2009). See also Chapter 1, paras 1.151–1.180.

private management team in February 2008, the Government announced that it would take Northern Rock 'into public ownership' on Sunday 17 February 2008. While Northern Rock had only limited direct exposure to the US sub-prime crisis that had caused the larger credit crisis in global markets during summer 2007, its low deposit base and wholesale funding business model had meant that it was unable to borrow sufficient continuing funds in the market with the credit tightening that had occurred.

Credit crisis

The credit crisis began with concerns of default in the US sub-prime mortgage market with almost two-thirds of a $12 trillion market being reported to have been used to support securitised instruments sold in the asset-backed securities sector. These included collateralised debt obligations ('CDOs') which were used to trade separate tranches of underlying securitised sub-prime debt with many of these being purchased by structured investment vehicles ('SIVs') or bank 'conduits' that had been set up on an off-balance sheet basis to invest in high-yield products such as CDOs and other structured instruments including credit linked notes ('CLNs').[27] These instruments had been created as part of a larger process of the securitisation and 'deconstruction' of financial risk with the transfer of debt and credit from loan to securities markets and then with the further breaking up and separate trading of the individual risk components created within this new debt.[28] **13.24**

Difficulties in the US sub-prime mortgage market had arisen as this had been unregulated at the federal level with up to one-quarter of the loans granted being expected to go into default and with a huge number of early fixed rate mortgages having to be reset with new adjustable rate policies. This was blamed on the sales practices of aggressive unregulated brokers and the use of self-certification by many borrowers as well as the questionable provision of credit by banks and other financial institutions to fund these commitments. The problems within the US sub-prime markets spread elsewhere as two-thirds of this sub-prime debt had been securitised. This securitised debt had been incorporated into larger structured products including principally CDOs which were sold across the globe to major financial institutions including through their SIVs and conduits as well as to hedge funds and other investors. The debt was attractive as the returns were generous, with the quality of the debt having been overrated by the rating agencies involved who had been paid by the debt issuing companies concerned. **13.25**

The value of this debt began to collapse in summer 2007 with evidence of underlying default in the sub-prime sector and with many major banking and securities groups having to write off substantial losses.[29] This led to an immediate drying up of credit in the main domestic and international inter-bank markets as banks decided to hoard cash and became increasingly reluctant to deal with counterparties with unknown structured product losses. Total losses in connection with the sub-prime crisis were initially estimated to be in excess of £100 billion and then increased to £500 billion. This also led to separate difficulties in related markets such as the mono-line insurance market in the US which was valued at $2.3 trillion and with **13.26**

27 GA Walker, 'Sub-prime loans, inter-bank markets and financial support' (n 6); and GA Walker, 'Credit crisis: regulatory and financial systems reform' (n 26) 568.

28 GA Walker, 'The deconstruction of financial risk' (n 26) 1–2.

29 Initial figures announced included: UBS $13.5bn, City Group $11bn, Morgan Stanley $9.4bn, Merrill Lynch $8bn, HSBC $3.4bn, Bear Stearns $3.2bn, Deutschebank $3.2bn, Bank of America $3bn, Barclays $2.6bn, and Royal Bank of Scotland $2.6bn.

other losses being suffered at individual institutions such as Société Générale which lost $7.2 billion (£3.1 billion or €4.9 billion) through its trader Jerôme Kerviel. Evan Dolley lost $141 billion in unauthorised wheat trades at one of the largest global commodity brokerages, MN Global. Bear Stearns also had to write off $3.2 billion in CDO-related losses which led to its subsequent acquisition by JP Morgan Chase in March 2008 under a support facility organised through the Federal Reserve Board.

13.27 The Federal Reserve Board and European Central Bank ('ECB') had attempted to support the markets by injecting liquidity following the drying up of inter-bank credits on 9 August 2007. The ECB made available €95 billion ($131 billion) on 9 August (more than after the terrorist attacks on 11 September 2001) and a further €61 billion on 10 August. The Federal Reserve injected $24 billion and then $38 billion with the central banks in Canada, Japan, and Australia following. The US discount rate was cut by 0.5 per cent on 17 August and then again on 31 October and 11 December 2007.

13.28 The major world central banks agreed to a further coordinated injection of $100 billion in the short-term inter-bank markets on 13 December 2007. The Federal Reserve intervened on 7 March and 11 March 2008 under its Term Auction Facility ('TAF') which had been set up the previous December. A new Term Securities Lending Facility ('TSLF') was also created on 11 March 2008 to allow primary dealers (rather than banks) to borrow up to $200 billion of Treasury securities for 28 days against lesser quality bond collateral. While the Bank of England had initially been more cautious than other central banks, it announced a series of auctions on 19 September 2007 although none of the funds available was taken up due to the perceived stigma attached.

Northern Rock

13.29 The major UK casualty from the credit tightening was Northern Rock which was forced to accept emergency funding from the Bank of England on 14 September 2007. The Northern Rock Building Society had originally been set up in 1965 following the merger of the Northern Counties Permanent Building Society (established in 1850) and the Rock Building Society (set up in 1865). The society was demutualised and converted into a bank in 1997, with a Northern Rock Foundation having been set up in 1986 to carry out local community and charity work. Northern Rock became one of the five top mortgage lenders in the UK although it was heavily dependent on wholesale mortgage securitisation with only 22.4 per cent of its lending being covered by retail deposits. The bank accordingly became unable to borrow following the contraction of credit on the inter-bank markets in August 2007 with a further proposed securitisation that autumn having to be postponed. Northern Rock had minimal direct exposure to the US sub-prime market and US CDO market although it was caught out on the drying up of wholesale inter-bank funding due to its high wholesale funding-based business model.

13.30 Emergency liquidity support was agreed with the Bank of England on 14 September 2007 although a run on the bank's deposits persisted through 15 and 16 September. A statement was issued by the Treasury on 17 September confirming that all of the bank's then existing deposits would be covered. This was extended on 20 September to cover all existing accounts, new money into existing accounts and reopened accounts, as well as unsecured wholesale borrowing. All new retail deposits were also covered under a further announcement on 9 October. These Treasury support announcements represented a considerable extension of traditional lender of last resort ('LLR') funding in the UK.[30] A new financing package was then announced on 21 January 2008 under which the Bank of England's loan of £25 million would in effect be securitised with a Treasury guarantee.

The difficulties at Northern Rock nevertheless only represented one part of the larger damage caused by the credit crisis in global markets following the original sub-prime mortgage scandal in the US.[31] The initial credit contraction in the money markets beginning in August 2007 then erupted into a full financial crisis during September 2008. This followed the announced losses at the giant US mortgage providers Federal National Mortgage Association ('Fannie Mae') and Federal Home Loan Mortgage Corporation ('Freddie Mac') and the decision by the US Treasury to provide over US$85bn in support for the troubled lenders as well as to bail out the largest insurance company American International General ('AIG'). The Treasury had nevertheless decided not to support the third largest Wall Street investment bank, Lehman Brothers, which was forced into Chapter 11 insolvency protection in September 2008. This led to the collapse in the share price of many financial institutions in the US and the UK and elsewhere as earlier concerns with market liquidity shifted to solvency. Following successive collapses in the share prices of Halifax Bank of Scotland (HBOS) and the Royal Bank of Scotland Group (RBS) in the UK, the Government announced a three-part rescue package based on a £50m recapitalisation of the major banks and an increase in the amount of the Special Lending Scheme ('SLS') made available by the Bank of England from £100 million to £200 million with a separate guarantee facility on money market lending for up to three years at commercial rates. This was intended to stabilise the financial system and to reactivate the money markets. The UK model was subsequently adopted in a number of other countries following earlier EU resistance with parts of the recapitalisation package also being incorporated into the $700 billion US Troubled Asset Recovery Programme ('TARP'). 13.31

UK regulatory response

The circumstances surrounding the crisis at Northern Rock were considered by the House of Commons Treasury Committee in an initial report on 'The Run on the Rock' on 26 January 2008 (HC56-1). An exploratory discussion paper on *Banking Reform: Protecting Depositors* was issued by the Bank of England, FSA, and Treasury as the 'Tripartite Authorities' in October 2007. This was followed by a more formal consultation document on *Financial Stability and Depositor Protection: Strengthening the Framework* on 30 January 2008.[32] Under this paper, regulatory reform would be based on the five key objectives of strengthening the financial system, reducing the likelihood of banks failing, limiting the impact of collapse, developing effective compensation arrangements, and strengthening the Bank of England and securing improved coordination between the authorities.[33] 13.32

30 GA Walker, 'Credit Crisis—Regulatory and Financial Systems Reform' (n 26); and GA Walker, 'Sub-prime Loans, Inter-Bank Markets and Financial Support' (n 26).

31 Chapter 1, paras 1.25–1.28; Walker, 'Financial Markets and Exchanges Law' (n 17).

32 HM Treasury, Bank of England, and FSA, 'Banking Reform—Protecting Depositors: a Discussion Paper' (October 2007); and HM Treasury, Bank of England, and FSA, 'Financial Stability and Depositor Protection: Strengthening the Framework' (January 2008) Cm 7308. See also Bank of England, HM Treasury, and FSA, 'Financial Stability and Depositor Protection: Further Consultation' (July 2008) Cm 7436; Bank of England, HM Treasury, and FSA, 'Financial Stability and Depositor Protection: Special Resolution Regime' (July 2008); and HM Treasury, 'Financial Stability and Depositor Protection: Cross-Border Challenges' (September 2008).

33 For comment, GA Walker, 'Northern Rock Falls' (n 26) 5–6.

13.33 The FSA had commissioned a separate internal audit which published its results on 26 March 2008. This confirmed that there had been a lack of sufficient supervisory engagement with the bank with the supervisory team having, in particular, not followed up rigorously enough with management on increased business model vulnerability arising through changing market conditions. There had been a lack of adequate oversight and review by FSA line management on the quality, intensity, and rigour of the bank's supervision. There had been inadequate specific resources assigned to supervising the bank and a lack of intensity by the FSA in ensuring that all available risk information was properly utilised to inform its supervisory actions.

13.34 A number of high-level recommendations were made. The engagement of FSA senior management would be increased in high impact firms. There would be increased rigour in day-to-day supervision with an increased focus on prudential supervision (including liquidity and stress testing) as well as improvements in the use of information and intelligence in supervision. There would be corresponding improvements in the quality and resourcing of financial and sectoral analysis, a strengthening of supervisory resources, and an increased level of firm supervision oversight. The principal result was to create a new Supervisory Enhancement Programme ('SEP') to strengthen the overall supervisory process which also incorporated other changes that were already being given effect to. Seven general high-level recommendations were made with 10 specific Recommended Actions. FSA Chief Executive, Hector Sants, agreed to implement the improvements in an FSA response statement which included further specific enhancements with regard to culture and people, organisation, process, and technology.

Treasury acquisition

13.35 It was separately announced on 17 February 2008 that Northern Rock would be taken into public ownership after the private bids tendered were rejected by the Treasury on the advice of Goldman Sachs. The deadline for private offer bids had been 16 November 2007 with the preferred bid having been made by the Virgin Group and two others from Olivant and a private management group. Virgin had offered £1.3 billion of equity with £11 billion of the Bank of England loan to have been repaid immediately and the balance cancelled by 2010. Virgin had been pressed to pay more for the government guarantee and to issue equity warrants although it considered that it could only offer £300 million in total and £500 million in the event of Northern Rock's recovery.[34]

13.36 Legilsation to facilitate the acquisition of Northern Rock had already been prepared and was introduced to the House of Commons on 19 February 2008 within two days of the acquisition announcement. This received Royal Assent as the Banking (Special Provisions) Act on 21 February 2008. This allowed the Treasury to make an order in specified circumstances relating to the transfer of securities issued by an authorised deposit-taking institution (including a building society) as well as with regard to the property, rights, and liabilities of such an institution. The Act applies to 'authorised deposit-takers' which covers any UK undertaking that holds permission to accept deposits under Part 4 of FSMA 2000 (s 1(1)). This will include banks and building societies.

[34] For comment, GA Walker, 'Northern Rock Falls' (n 26) 7.

The Treasury was given power to transfer securities or property, rights, and liabilities where this was considered desirable for one of two stated purposes (s 2(1)(a) and (b)). This applied with regard to (a) maintaining the stability of the UK financial system in circumstances where the Treasury considers that there would otherwise be a serious threat to its stability, or (b) protecting the public interest where financial assistance has already been provided by the Treasury to the institution for the purpose of maintaining the stability of the UK financial system (s 2(2)(a) and (b)). Financial assistance covers both funding provided by the Bank of England or guarantee arrangements by the Treasury either with or without the involvement of the Bank (s 2(3)(a) and (b)). Treasury orders only last for one year although the powers confirmed may be re-exercised within the year (s 2(8) and (9)) with relevant orders being provided for under Schedules 1 and 2. **13.37**

The Treasury may transfer securities and property (under ss 3 and 6) with securities being transferred either to the Bank of England, a nominee of the Treasury, a company wholly owned by the Bank or the Treasury or another body corporate (s 3(1)(a)–(d)). Any subscription rights in the institution or any subsidiary undertakings may be cancelled (s 4(2)) with the Treasury being required to determine how compensation will be payable to shareholders or other persons holding relevant rights (s 5(1) and (2)). Compensation is to be valued without reference to the financial assistance provided (s 5(4)). Similar provisions apply with regard to the transfer of property, rights, and liabilities of any authorised deposit-taker. The Banking (Special Provisions) Act 2008 was used to manage the restructuring of Northern Rock in February 2008, the Bradford and Bingley in September 2008, and Heritable Bank (Landsbanki) and Kaupthing Edge (Kaupthing, Singer and Friedlander) in October 2008.[35] **13.38**

The mechanisms contained in the Banking (Special Provisions) act were made permanent under the Banking Act 2009 (BA 2009) which received Royal Assent on 12 February 2009. This included specific provision to set up the new special resolution regime ('SRR'), including private sector bank purchase, bridge bank and temporary public ownership (nationalisation), as well as a special bank insolvency procedure ('BIP') and bank administration procedure ('BAP').[36] Dunfermline Building Society was restructured in March 2009 using the provisions adopted under the BA 2009. The Act also made revisions to the operation of the Financial Services Compensation Scheme ('FSCS') and new measures in Inter-Bank Payment Systems and Scottish and Northern Irish Banknotes with other miscellaneous provisions. **13.39**

Further legislation with the FSA 2010 received Royal Assent on 8 April 2010 immediately before the General Election in May 2010. This amended the statutory objectives of the FSA to include an express financial stability objective with consumer education being transferred to a new Consumer Financial Education Body ('CFEB') which was subsequently relaunched as the Money Advice Service.[37] The FSA 2010 also contained new measures on executive remuneration,[38] recovery and resolution plans,[39] short selling,[40] strengthened FSA disciplinary powers,[41] new consumer redress schemes and additional consumer protection,[42] **13.40**

[35] Chapter 1, para 1.33 and n 54.
[36] Chapter 1, paras 1.57–1.58, and Chapter 13, paras 13.258–13.267.
[37] <http://www.moneyadviceservice.org.uk>.
[38] ss 4-6 FSA 2010.
[39] s 7 FSA 2010.
[40] s 8 FSA 2010.
[41] ss 9-13 FSA 2010.
[42] ss 14-15 FSA 2010.

amendments to the FSCS[43] and additional power to require information,[44] with further amendments to the BA 2009 and miscellaneous and general provisions.[45]

13.41 A number of further regulatory reforms were adopted by the incoming Conservative and Liberal Democrat Coalition Government following the General Election in 2010. This followed an initial announcement by the Chancellor of the Exchequer in June 2010 at the Mansion House that the institutional structure of UK financial regulation would be fundamentally reformed with the creation of the PRA as a subsidiary of the Bank to assume regulatory responsibility for banks, insurance companies, and major investment firms, and with all other activities of the FSA being transferred to the new FCA.

Bank of England

13.42 The new regulatory regime has been constructed around the Bank of England with the creation of a central bank macro-prudential model in the UK.[46] The Bank was originally established in 1694 and given monopoly rights over banknote issuance under the Bank Charter Act 1844 subject to the reserve powers of Scottish and Northern Irish banks. It was nationalised under the Bank of England Act 1944 and its structure and operations amended under the Bank of England Act 1998 (BEA 1998). These provisions were further amended under the BA 2009 and FSA 2012.

13.43 The BEA 1998 revised the constitution and duties of the Court of Directors of the Bank of England and contains new provisions with regard to the funding, accounts, and profits of the Bank. The Act confirmed the establishment of the Monetary Policy Committee and a formal statutory basis conferred for the conduct of monetary policy. Responsibility for bank supervision under the Banking Act 1987 was transferred to the FSA as well as the Bank's functions under the Banking Coordination (Second Council Directive) Regulations 1992 and the Building Societies Act, as well as section 43 of the Financial Services Act 1986 and the Investment Services Regulations 1985 (section 171 of the Companies Act 1989). The gilt registration function of the National Savings Stock Register was transferred to the Bank to create a brokerage service for gilt registration with the amendment of section 27 of the Companies Act 1989 with regard to bearer securities. Further amendments were proposed to the institutional structure and statutory function of the Bank following the Northern Rock crisis.[47]

13.44 The Bank was given an additional financial stability objective under the BA 2009 to contribute to protecting and enhancing the stability of the financial systems in the UK.[48] A new Financial Stability Committee ('FSC') was created within the Bank to consider and advise on financial stability matters.[49] The number of directors in the Court was reduced from 16 to nine.[50] Court meetings were reduced from once a month to seven times a year.[51] The chair

[43] ss 16-17 FSA 2010.

[44] ss 18-19 FSA 2010.

[45] ss 20-27 FSA 2010.

[46] Chapter 1, paras 1.90–1.96. See generally, Morton and Marsh, 'UK Central Banking and the Financial Stability' in Blair, Walker, and Wiley, *Financial Markets and Exchanges Law* (n 17). Chapter 3.

[47] Chapter 1, paras 1.23–1.24, and paras 13.23 and 13.29–13.30.

[48] s 2 A BEA 1998.

[49] s 2 B BEA 1998.

[50] s 239 BEA 1998.

[51] s 240 BA 2009.

of the Court was appointed by the Chancellor.[52] The tenure of the Governor and Deputy Governor was limited to two appointments.[53] The Bank was given immunity in acting as a monetary authority.[54] The weekly return required under section 6 of the Bank Charter Act 1844 was abolished.[55]

Further amendments were made under the FSA 2012. The Court was amended to include the Governor, Deputy Governors for Financial Stability, Monetary Policy, and Prudential Regulation as well as nine other non-executive directors.[56] The financial stability objective was amended to more directly refer to protect and enhance the stability of the UK financial system in the singular.[57] Further provisions were included on the financial stability strategy of the Bank with a new Financial Policy Committee ('FPC') being created to replace the earlier FSC.[58] The Governor and Chancellor had to meet as soon as practicable after the publication of the FPC financial stability report with new statutory coordination and crisis management procedures being adopted.[59] The Bank is given a power of direction to obtain information from the FCA and PRA.[60] A new Oversight Committee was established within the Bank.[61] **13.45**

Constitution and regulation

The Court of Directors of the Bank has been continued with three Deputy Governors for Financial Stability, Monetary Policy, and Prudential Regulation. Schedule 1 BEA 1998 contains provision with regard to the offices of the Governor, Deputy Governors, and Directors, and the procedures and proceedings of the Court. These replaced the provisions previously set out in the Bank of England's Charter of 1696. The functions of the Court are stated to be to manage the Bank's affairs including determining the objectives and strategy required to ensure the effective discharge of its functions and the most efficient use of its resources. Certain functions may be delegated to a non-executive sub-committee of the court with an annual report being produced which is to include the role of the sub-committee, financial information, and directors' remuneration rates. The Report is to be laid before Parliament and published. Additional provisions are included with regard to the custody and use of the Bank's seal. **13.46**

Financial arrangements

The BEA 1998 contained further provisions concerning the maintenance of cash ratio deposits which did not formally operate on a statutory basis before (Schedule 2). A written notice is to be issued to banks specifying the amounts to be deposited calculated having regard to the liability base of the institution concerned. Sterling and foreign currency liabilities may be specified by the Treasury by order with the requirements being subject to a penalty payment in lieu of deposit. The Bank is required to keep proper accounts and records **13.47**

52 s 241 BA 2009.
53 s 243 BA 2009.
54 s 244 BA 2009.
55 s 245 BA 2009.
56 s 1 FSA 2012.
57 s 2 FSA 2012.
58 ss 9 A-W BEA 1998. See Chapter 1, paras 1.02 and 1.118-1.124.
59 ss 58-67 FSA 2012.
60 ss 9 X-Z BEA 1998.
61 s 3 FSA 2012. See also Chapter 1, paras 1.108-1.110.

including an annual statement of accounts consisting of its balance sheet and profit and loss accounts. The Bank is to pay the Treasury an amount equal to 25 per cent of the Banks' net profits from its previous financial year or such other sum as the Treasury and Bank may agree. Failing agreement, payment is to be made in two instalments equal to 50 per cent of the Bank's post-tax profits from the previous year. These replace the earlier provisions set out in the Bank of England Act 1946.

Transfer of functions

13.48 The Bank's functions with regard to the supervision of banks were transferred from the Bank to the FSA under section 21(a) BEA 1998 although these have since been returned under the FSA 2012. The Bank's functions in connection with listing settlement arrangements under section 171 of the Companies Act 1989 were transferred under section 21(b) and (c) BEA 1998. Schedule 4 contained supplementary provisions with regard to the transfer of functions. These included guaranteeing the legal validity of all previous activities and transactions.

Additional provisions

13.49 Miscellaneous and general provisions were set out in Part IV BEA 1998. These include exempting transactions between listed money market institutions and the Treasury, empowering the Treasury to close the National Savings Stock Register with regard to gilts, issuance of regulations in respect of the purchase and sale of government stock and bonds through the Bank, extending the Treasury's power to make regulations in respect of the dematerialisation of securities applicable to bearer securities, and amendments to the restrictions on the disclosure of information contained in the Banking Act 1987. The schedules contain further provisions concerning the Court of Directors, cash ratio deposits and bank supervision fees, the Monetary Policy Committee, and supplementary and consequential amendments related to the transfer of function as well as revised restrictions on the disclosure of information. The Bank's constitutional arrangements and operations have been further amended under the FSA 2012 and following the Northern Rock and other global and UK financial crises.[62]

Financial Services and Markets

13.50 The statutory basis for UK bank supervision is FSMA 2000. Banks are subject to the general prohibition set out in FSMA, section 19(1) which requires that they are either authorised or exempt under the Act. They must also hold the relevant permission under section 20(1) and comply with the restrictions on the issuance of financial promotions under section 21(1) and (2) of FSMA. Deposit-taking and deposits are included as regulated activities and investments under Schedule 2 of FSMA and the Financial Services (Regulated Activities) Order (as amended) and fall within the scope of authority of the PRA.[63]

62 Part 1 and Sch 2 FSA 2012.

63 Para 5(2)(a) Financial Services and Markets Act 2000 (PRA-regulated Activities) Order 2013, SI 2013/556. See also Financial Services and Markets Act 2000 (Regulated Activities) Order 2001, SI 2001/544 as amended. See, in particular, The Financial Services and Markets Act 2000 (Regulated Activities) (Amendment) Order 2012, SI 2012/1906; and Financial Services and Markets Act 2000 (Regulated Activities) (Amendment) Order 2013, SI 2013/655.

Banks were subject to the Handbook of Rules and Guidance issued by the FSA (under sections 138 and 157 of FSMA) in the conduct of their activities. The FSA Handbook has been split between the PRA and the FCA. In light of the high degree of overlap and function, a number of provisions are applied on a common basis with the text of the specific Handbook sections being revised to refer to the regulators collectively rather than the FSA specifically. The structure and content of the substantive regulatory regime set up under FSMA is fundamentally retained. Banks are subject to the provisions contained in the PRA Handbook for prudential purposes and the FCA Handbook with regard to conduct matters. **13.51**

Banks have to comply with all of the general provisions in the High Level Standards Block of the PRA Handbook, the more speficic measures in the Prudential Standards Block 2 applicable to banks ('GENPRU' and 'BIPRU') and the Supervision Manual ('SUP') within Regulatory Processes Block. Authorisation was dealt with under AUTH although this is now managed by the PRA separately.[64] The earlier Enforcement manual ('ENF') was replaced by the Enforcement Guide ('EG'), although this is only retained with the FCA Handbook with the Decision Procedure and Penalties Manual ('DEPP'). Banks are also subject to the Compensation sourcebook ('COMP') in the Redress Block in the PRA Handbook and Dispute Resolution: Complaints ('DISP') in the FCA Handbook. Banks have separately to comply with the Banking: Conduct of Busines Sourcebook ('BCOBS') within the Business Standards Block in the FCA Handbook. Additional provisions will apply where they carry out other permitted activites. **13.52**

The main obligations with regard to capital and financial requirements as well as internal systems and controls are set out in GENPRU and BIPRU which replaced the earlier interim measures in IPRU(BANK) apart from liquidity. The final prudential provisions have come into effect in stages with the revised capital adequacy standards produced by the Basel Committee on Banking Supervision on Basel II[65] which were given effect to in the EU under the Capital Requirements Directive ('CRD').[66] The CRD was amended under CRD II[67] and CRD III.[68] These provisions will be further revised with the coming effect of the Basel III measures on capital, liquidity and leverage,[69] and EU CRD IV.[70] **13.53**

---

64 <http://www.bankofengland.co.uk/pra/Pages/authorisations/newfirm/banking.aspx>.

65 Paras 13.145–13.159.

66 Paras 13.160–13.170.

67 This included specific measues on large exposures, capital quality, liquidity risk management, and securitised products as well as supervisory colleges. Directive 2009/111/EC of the European Parliament and of the Council of 16 September 2009 amending Directives 2006/48/EC, 2006/49/EC and 2007/64/EC, Official Journal L 302, 17/11/2009 P. 0097–0119.

68 This included further provisions concerning trading book capital, re-securitisations, and the supervisory review of remuneration. Directive 2010/76/EU of the European Parliament and of the Council of 24 November 2010 amending Directives 2006/48/EC and 2006/49/EC, Official Journal L 329, 14/12/2010 P. 0003–0035.

69 Basel Committee on Banking Supervision, *Basel III: A global regulatory framework for more resilient banks and banking systems* (December 2010 and revised June 2011); and Basel Committee, *Basel III: International framework for liquidity risk measurement, standards and monitoring* (December 201) and Basel Committee, *Basel III: The Liquidity Coverage Ratio and liquidity risk monitoring tools* (January 2013).

70 Commission Proposal for a Directive on the access to the activity of credit institutions and the prudential supervision of credit institutions and investment funds and amending Directive 2002/87/EC on the supplementary supervision of credit institutions, insurance undertakings and investment funds in a financial conglomerate COM (2011) 453 final, Brussells 20 July 2011. See also European Commission proposal for a Regulation on prudential requirements for credit institutions and investment firms COM 2011 0452. On UK implementation, see <http://www.bankofengland.co.uk/pra/Pages/crdiv/default.aspx>.

General prohibition

13.54 A person cannot carry on a regulated activity in the UK (or purport to do so) unless it is an authorised or exempt person under the general prohibition (section 19(1) and (2) of FSMA). A person who contravenes the general prohibition commits an authorisation offence (section 23(2)) and is liable for up to six months in prison (on summary conviction) or two years (on indictment) or a fine or both (section 23(1)(a) and (b)). It is a defence to show that the person took all reasonable precautions and exercised all due diligence to avoid committing the offence (section 23(3)).

13.55 An agreement made by or through an unauthorised person is unenforceable against the other party who is entitled to recover the property or money transferred and compensation for any loss sustained (sections 26(1) and (2) and 27(1) and (2)). The amount of compensation is as agreed between the parties or as determined by the court (section 28(2)). Where money has been received by a person without authorisation or exemption and the depositor is not entitled under the agreement to recover the amount deposited without delay, he may apply to the court for an order directing repayment (section 29). The order will be made unless the court is satisfied that it would not be just and equitable for the money deposited to be returned having regard to whether the deposit taker reasonably believed that he was not in contravention of the general prohibition (section 29(3) and (4)).

13.56 An activity is a regulated activity for the purposes of FSMA if it is of a specified kind carried on by way of business and relates to investments of a specified kind or is of a specified kind and relates to property of any kind (section 22(1)(a) and (b)). Specified means by order of the Treasury with the detailed definitions of investments and regulated activities and investments being set out in the RAO (as amended). The Treasury is to specify by order the regulated activities that are PRA-regulated activities for the purposes of the FSMA.[71]

13.57 The RAO follows the earlier deposit taking definitions included within sections 5 and 6 of the Banking Act 1987. Accepting deposits is an activity of a specified kind if money received by way of deposit is lent to others or any other activity of the acceptor is financed wholly or to a material extent out of the capital of or interest on money received by way of deposit (RAO, article 5(1)(a) and (b)). Deposit means a sum of money paid on terms under which it is to be repaid, with or without interest or premium, and either on demand or at a time or in circumstances agreed by or on behalf of the person making the payment and the person receiving it, and which is not referable to the provision of property (other than currency) or services or the giving of security (article 5(2)(a) and (b)).

13.58 Money is paid on terms which are referable to the provision of property or services or the giving of security if (and only if) it is paid by way of advance or part payment under a contract for the sale, hire, or other provision of property or services and is repayable only in the event

[71] Section 22A. See The Financial Services and Markets Act 2000 (Regulated Activities) Order, SI 2001/544 as amended; and The Financial Services and Markets Act 2000 (PRA-regulated Activities) Order 2013, SI 2013/ 556. Deposit taking and insurance are referred to in art 2(a), (b), and (c) and Lloyd's of London related activities by art 2(e), (f), and (g) of the PRA RAO. The PRA may designate a person dealing in investments as principal to be subject to PRA regulation under arts 2(d) and 3(1). The PRA RAO includes supplementary provisions on the exercise of the power, review of designations, withdrawal and cessation (arts 4, 5, 6, and 7) with the PRA to produce a statement of policy under art 9. The Bank of England and FSA produced a draft policy statement in October 2012. See Bank of England and FSA, *Designation of investment firms for prudential supervision by the PRA: consultation on a draft policy statement* (October 2012). See Chapter 1, para 1.246.

that the property or services is or are not in fact sold, hired, or otherwise provided (article 3(a)). This includes money paid by way of security for the performance of a contract or by way of security in respect of loss that may result from the non-performance of the contract or is otherwise paid by way of security for the delivery up or return of any property whether in a particular state of repair or otherwise (article 5(3)(a) and (b)).

Deposits are included as specified investments for the purposes of FSMA (RAO, article 74). Certain payments are nevertheless excluded. These include sums paid by exempt or other persons such as the Bank of England, the central bank of an EEA State or the European Central Bank, another bank or insurance company, a local authority, and the main international financial institutions (article 6(1)(a)). Businesses consisting wholly or to a significant extent of the lending of money are excluded and payments between group companies or close relatives (article 6(1)(b),(c), and (d)). Sums received by solicitors and persons authorised to deal in investments and payments in consideration of the issue of debt securities are excluded (articles 7, 8, and 9). **13.59**

Regulated activities must also be carried on by way of business in the UK (section 20(1)). Under the Carrying on of Regulated Activities by Way of Business Order 2001,[72] a person accepting deposits is not to be regarded as doing so by way of business unless he holds himself out as accepting the deposits on a day-to-day basis and provided that he does not only accept them on particular occasions whether or not involving the issue of any securities (article 2(1)(a) and (b)). In determining whether deposits are accepted only on particular occasions, regard is to be had to the frequency of those occasions and to any characteristics distinguishing them from each other (article 2(2)). This follows the earlier extended definition of deposit taking under sections 5 and 6 of the Banking Act 1987. **13.60**

A number of institutions are separately exempt from the general prohibition under the Financial Services Exemptions Order 2001.[73] Exempt persons include the Bank of England, the central bank of any EEA State, and the main international financial institutions as well as municipal banks, local authorities, charities, industrial and provident societies, and student loan companies. This replaces the earlier regulations issued under the Banking Act 1987. **13.61**

Permission

FSMA creates a dual authorisation and permission regime. An authorised person can only carry on a regulated activity (or purport to do so) in accordance with the permission given to him by the FSA under Part 4A or any other provision of the Act (section 20(1)(a) and (b)). If a PRA-authorised firm acts wthout proper permission, it is treated as having contravened both an FCA and a PRA requirement (section 20(1A)). Breach of the permission requirement is liable to administrative penalty such as a fine or censure, or restriction or withdrawal of permission. Contravention does not constitute an offence and transactions are not void or unenforceable (section 20(2)(a) and (b)). No separate right of action for breach of statutory duty arises except in prescribed cases (section 22(2)(c) and (3)). The significance of the permission requirement is that banks must be both authorised (under section 31(1)) and **13.62**

[72] Financial Services and Markets Act 2000 (Carrying On Regulated Activities by Way of Business) Order 2001, SI 2001/1177 as amended. See, in particular, Financial Services and Markets Act 2000 (Carrying On Regulated Activities by Way of Business) (Amendment) Order 2001, SI 2011/2304.

[73] Financial Services and Markets Act 2000 (Exemption) Order 2001, SI 2001/1201, as amended. See, in particular, Financial Services and Markets Act 2000 (Exemption) (Amendment No 2) Order 2011, SI 2011/2716; Financial Services and Markets Act 2000 (Exemption) (Amendment) Order 2012, SI 2012/763.

hold the relevant permission to carry on the particular regulated activity (including deposit-taking) intended to be engaged in the UK.

13.63 Banks do not apply for authorisation directly. They are automatically authorised once they obtain a Part 4A permission (section 31(1)(a)). Institutions will then generally apply for permission to carry on deposit-taking activity (under section 55A of FSMA) after which they will become authorised for the purposes of section 19(1) (under section 31(1)). Banks apply to the PRA for permission (section 55A(2)(a)) with the PRA collaborating with the FCA on the assessment of the application (section 55F) as the bank will become a dual regulated firm and be regulated by the PRA for prudential purposes and the FCA for conduct purposes. Accepting deposits may only be carried on by a body corporate or partnership.

13.64 The regulators will grant permission to carry on one or more regulated activities where they are satisfied that the institution complies with and will continue to comply with the threshold conditions set out in Schedule 6 to FSMA (section 55B(2)). Schedule 6 generally requires that institutions have appropriate legal status, a head or registered office in the UK, and have no close links that may prevent the effective supervision of the institution. They must have adequate resources and be judged fit and proper to carry on the activities concerned (paragraphs 1 to 5, Schedule 6 to FSMA). These restate the earlier Schedule 3 conditions set out in the Banking Act 1987 although restricted only to include the main market entry components. The more specific continuing requirements with regard to ongoing prudential obligations are now given effect to under the PRA's Handbook of Rules and Guidance and, in particular, GENPRU and BIPRU supported by the Supervision (SUP) process manual.

13.65 The PRA may grant the permission applied for subject to such requirements as may be considered appropriate (sections 55M). Permission may be varied by adding or removing a regulated activity or amending the description of the activity on request (section 55I or on the regulators' initiative (section 55J)). The PRA may vary a requirement by adding, removing or cancelling a requirement following consultation with the FCA (section 55M(3) and (4)). A requirement may be imposed or varied following the acquisition of control of a UK authorised person (section 55(O)). Asset requirements may be imposed which prohibit the disposal of an institution's assets or require that the assets are to be held in trust (section 55P). An own-initiative power may be exercised in response to an overseas regulator's request (section 55Q). Connected relationships are to be considered in granting, varying, or cancelling a Part 4A permission or requirement (section 55R). Additional procedural requirements are included within FSMA (sections 55U to 55Z) with applicants having a right to refer any decisions to the Tribunal (section 55Z1(1)). Authorised persons aggrieved by the regulators' exercise of its powers to vary permission or impose or vary a requirement may also refer the case to the Tribunal (section 55 Z1 (2)).

Authorisation

13.66 Authorisation is automatically conferred under FSMA where a person holds a Part 4A permission to carry on one or more regulated activities (section 31(1)(a)). EEA firms holding passport rights under any of the main European financial directives and exercising rights under the European Community Treaty are pre-authorised (section 31(1)(b) and (c) and Schedules 3 and 4 to FSMA).[74] A person is also authorised where this is otherwise provided for under the Act (section 31(1)(d)).

[74] Treaty refers to European Community Treaty, FSMA, s 417(1).

European firms may either exercise passport rights under Schedule 3 or Treaty rights under Schedule 4 FSMA. Passport rights apply with regard to actitvities within the scope of the 'single market directives' which include the First and Second Banking Directive (now the Banking Consolidation Directive), the insurance directives, reinsurance directive, and insurance mediation directive as well as the Investment Services Directive (now the Markets in Financial Instruments Directive) and UCITS directive.[75] An EEA right means the entitlement to establish a branch or provide services in another EEA State in accordance with the European Community Treaty and subject to the conditions set out in the relevant single market directive.[76] **13.67**

EEA firms exercising passport rights are required to satisfy the establishment or service conditions to become authorised.[77] The establishment conditions reflect the requirements set out in the main financial directives that have to be complied with by firms wishing to exercise branching rights in another Member State under the particular measure. These include the provision of notice to the regulators from the home country competent authority (referred to as a consent notice) with the firm being advised of any applicable conditions that it has to comply with within two months of receipt of the notice.[78] Where the PRA receives a consent notice it must provide the FCA with a copy. **13.68**

The service conditions only require that notice is given to the home State regulator (a notice of intention) and that the regulators is provided with a notice (a regulator's notice) from the home authority containing such information as may be prescribed.[79] The regulators must prepare for the firm's supervision and notify it of any applicable provisions within two months of receipt of the notice. Permission is then automatically conferred on European firms that have qualified for authorisation under paragraph 12 of Schedule 3 to FSMA equivalent to the terms set out in the consent notice, regulator's notice, or notice of intention.[80] Where the PRA receives a regulator's notice it must provide the FCA with a copy. **13.69**

UK firms wishing to exercise passport rights in other EEA countries are required to notify the regulators which will send a consent notice to the host State regulator. The firm will have to comply with any notified conditions.[81] The regulators may nevertheless refuse to issue a consent notice provided that the firm concerned is served with a warning notice and then a decision notice with the firm having the right to refer the matter to the Tribunal.[82] A notice of intention must also be served on the regulators where a UK firm wishes to provide services in another EEA State.[83] A UK firm may be fined where it breaches these procedural requirements.[84] Regulations may be issued by the Treasury in connection with the exercise of EEA rights.[85] The PRA and FCA are required to make arrangements as to how they will consult and cooperate with regard to these procedures. **13.70**

---

75 FSMA, Sch 3, para 1.
76 ibid, Sch 3, para 7.
77 ibid, Sch 3, para 12(1) and (2).
78 ibid, Sch 3, para 13(1)(a), (b), and (c).
79 ibid, Sch 3, para 14(1)(a) and (b).
80 FSMA, Sch 3, paras 12 and 15(1) and (2).
81 ibid, Sch 3, para 19(1), (2), (4), and (6).
82 ibid, Sch 3, para 19(8) and (12).
83 ibid, Sch 3, para 20(1).
84 ibid, Sch 3, para 21(1) and (2).
85 ibid, Sch 3, para 22(1). Financial Services (EEA Passport Rights) Regulations SI 2001/1376 and SI 2001/2510 as amended.

13.71 European firms may qualify separately for Treaty rights where their head office is situated in an EEA State other than the UK (its home State), and they are recognised as a national of that State and satisfy certain authorisation conditions.[86] The firm must have been authorised in its home State to carry on a particular permitted activity and the laws of the home State provide for equivalent protection or satisfy relevant Community requirements relating to the carrying on of the activity. The firm must also have no EEA right under Schedule 3 and the home State regulator must have informed the regulators in writing.[87] Provisions are considered to be equivalent where they afford consumers protection which is, at least, equivalent to that provided by or under FSMA with regard to the particular activity considered. Permission is again automatically conferred on Treaty firms where they qualify for authorisation under Schedule 4.[88]

13.72 The effect of section 31 and Schedules 3 and 4 of FSMA is to treat European firms exercising either passport or Treaty rights as being automatically authorised and holding equivalent permission for the particular activity (or activities) for which they are already licensed to carry on and which also constitute regulated activities for the purposes of FSMA. Such firms will then not have to comply with the Part IV application procedures although they will be subject to the separate notification conditions provided for under Schedules 3 and 4. The regulators is nevertheless entitled to inform European firms of the relevant UK requirements that will apply with regard to the conduct of the activity concerned. This will generally involve most of the ongoing regulatory obligations imposed under the Handbook of Rules and Guidance apart from initial authorisation and ongoing capital and related systems and controls obligations. Each Member State within the Community may impose equivalent continuing regulatory obligations on banks where this can be justified as being in the general good under the banking and other financial directives.

Promotions

13.73 Banks issuing financial promotions have to comply with the separate requirements set out in section 21 of FSMA. This prohibits the communication of an invitation or inducement to engage in an investment activity unless this is issued by an authorised person or the content of the communication has been approved by an authorised person (section 21(1) and (2)). Engaging in an investment activity means entering (or offering to enter) into an agreement involving a controlled activity or exercising any rights conferred by a controlled investment to acquire, dispose of, underwrite, or convert a controlled investment. A controlled activity is an activity of a specified kind and which relates to an investment of a specified kind with a controlled investment also being as specified. A controlled investment generally corresponds with the specified investments set out in FSMA, Schedule 2.

13.74 Exemptions to the restriction on the issuance of financial promotions are included within the Financial Promotions Order and in the Conduct of Business Sourcebook (COBS) within the FCA Handbook. Exemptions within the FPO include generic promotions, promotions to investment professionals, overseas recipients, one-off communications, promotions to certified high net worth individuals, certified sophisticated investors, and high net worth

[86] FSMA, Sch 4, paras 1, 2, and 3.
[87] ibid, Sch 4, para 3(1).
[88] ibid, Sch 4, para 4(1).

companies. Additional exemptions are provided for within the COBS 3 of the Handbook although only from the rules themselves.

Breach of the restriction on promotions constitutes an offence liable to six months in prison (on summary conviction) and to two years in prison (on indictment) or a fine or both (section 20(1)(a) and (b)). It is a defence to show that the person believed on reasonable grounds that the content of the communication had been prepared or approved by an authorised person or that all reasonable precautions had been taken or the person had exercised all due diligence to avoid committing the offence (section 25(2)(a) and (b)). **13.75**

Approved persons

In addition to being authorised and holding the relevant permission, banks must ensure that they comply with the approval requirements imposed under FSMA with regard to key management and personnel. Every authorised person is required to take reasonable care to ensure that no person carries on a controlled function unless the performance of the function by that person has been approved by the PRA (section 59(1) of FSMA). A controlled function means as specified in the PRA or FCA rules (section 59(3)) and generally includes customer-dealing functions and significant influence functions (section 59(5), (6), (7), (7A) and (7B)).[89] **13.76**

Applications for approval are to be in such manner as the regulator may direct and contain such information as may reasonably be required (section 60(2)). The regulator must be satisfied that the candidate is a fit and proper person to perform the function (or functions) to which the application relates (section 61(1)). Approval may be withdrawn by the PRA where the person fails to continue to satisfy the fit and proper standard (section 63(1A)). Notice must be given where the regulator proposes or decides to refuse an application to the applicant and all other interested parties (section 62(2), (3), and (5)). Decisions to refuse an application or withdraw approval are referable to the Tribunal (sections 62(4) and 63(5)). **13.77**

Approved functions

The list of controlled functions is set out in the PRA and FCA Handbooks.[90] The FSMA as amended refers to the FCA and PRA being able to specify contolled functions in their rules with the FCA functions covering customer dealing function and significant influence functions, and the PRA significant influence functions (section 59(4), (5), and (6)). This basic classification was developed under the original FSA Supervision Manual (SUP 10) to include, inter alia, allocation and apportionment functions, compliance functions, money laundering reporting functions, EEA investment business oversight functions (if applicable), and appointed actuary functions (where applicable).[91] These have since been relisted for FCA-regulated firms in SUP 10A.10.4R and PRA firms in SUP 10B.10.4R. **13.78**

Controlled functions

The list of controlled functions has been revised over time with a number of earlier FSA funtions having been removed although the original FSA numbering has been retained. These have then been split between the PRA and FCA Handbooks. PRA functions consist of **13.79**

89 Chapter 6 and Chapter 13, paras 13.78–13.82 and paras 13.143–13.145.
90 SUP 10B PRA Handbook and SUP 10A FCA Handbook.
91 On the earlier FSA functions, see Blair, Walker, and Wiley (n 17) paras 14.54–14.60. The list of PRA controlled functions is set out in PRA SUP 10B.4.3 R.

governing functions, required functions and systems and control functions. PRA governing body functions include the director of a company or a holding company (1), non-executive director (2), chief executive officer (3), and partner or limited partner (4), as well as director of an unincorporated incorporation (5), and small friendly society (6). PRA required functions consist of the actuarial function (12), with-profits actuary function (12A) and Lloyd's actuary function (12B). PRA systems and control functions consist of the systems and control function (2B).

13.80 FCA functions consist of governing functions, required functions and systems and control functions (28), with additional significant management functions (29), and customer-dealing functions (30). Governing functions again include the director (1), non-executive director (2), chief executive officer (3), and partner functions (4), as well as director of an unincorporated incorporation (5), and small friendly society (6). FCA required functions consist of the apportionment and oversight function (8), compliance function (10), CASS operational oversight function (10A), money laundering reporting officer ('MLRO'). Benchmark submission (40) and Benchmark administration (50) have also been added following the LIBOR scandal. FCA controlled functions for PRA-authorised persons are shortened to FCA required functions, significant management functions (29) and customer-dealing functions (30), with governing functions and systems and control functions (28) being covered under the PRA Handbook. The FCA has specified all functions apart from customer-dealing functions (30) as significant influence functions.

Customer-dealing functions

13.81 The FCA has listed customer functions as the sole customer-dealing function which is expanded in SUP 10A.10.7R. The customer-dealing function includes investment advice (other than non-investment insurance contracts), corporate finance advice, pension transfer advisers, dealing as principal, acting as an investment manager, and acting as an auction bidder's representative.

Property functions

13.82 Property functions were provided for in the FSA Handbook which included persons dealing or arranging deals on behalf of customers and discretionary fund management although this is no longer listed.

Code of conduct

13.83 The PRA and FCA may issue statements of principle with respect to the conduct expected of approved persons (section 64(1) and (1A)). Where the regulators issue statements of principle, they must also issue a code of practice to assist in determining whether or not a person's conduct complies with the principles issued (section 64(2)). The PRA and FCA are required to consult on the production of the code of conduct of approved persons (section 65(1)). These principles are set out in the APER section within the High Level Standards Block of the Handbooks.

13.84 The first four principles apply to all controlled functions with the last three to significant influence functions although the third is no longer applied by the PRA:

(a) an approved person must act with integrity in carrying out an accountable function;
(b) an approved person must act with due skill, care, and diligence in carrying out an accountable function;

(c) an approved person must observe proper standards of market conduct in carrying out an accountable function;

(d) an approved person must deal with the regulators and other regulatory authorities in an open and cooperative manner and disclose appropriately any information that would reasonably be expected;

(e) an approved person performing a significant influence function must take reasonable steps to ensure that the business of the firm for which he is responsible is organised so that it can be controlled effectively;

(f) an approved person performing an accountable function must exercise due skill, care, and diligence in managing the business of the firm for which he is responsible in the accountable function; and

(g) an approved person performing a significant influence function must take reasonable steps to ensure that the business of the firm for which he is responsible complies with the regulatory requirements and standards imposed on that business (APER 2.1 (FCA) and 2.1B(PRA)).

The regulators may take action against an approved person who is considered guilty of misconduct and it is appropriate to proceed (section 66(1)). Misconduct includes failing to comply with any of the statements of principle specified or the person has been knowingly concerned in a contravention by an authorised person of any requirement imposed under FSMA or a directly applicable EU regulation (section 66(2) and (2A)). The regulators may impose a financial penalty, suspend approval, or impose restricitons for a period of up to two years, or publish a statement of misconduct (section 66(3) and (3A)). A copy of any statement of misconduct must be sent to the person concerned (section 68). Disciplinary action is subject to the issuance of warning and decision notices with final decisions being referable to the Tribunal (section 67). **13.85**

The regulators are required to issue a separate statement of policy with regard to the imposition of fines against approved persons subject to appropriate consultation (sections 69(1) and 70(1)). The regulators may additionally impose a prohibition order on any individual not considered to be fit and proper to perform functions in relation to a regulated activity carried on by an authorised person (section 56(1) and (1A)). Private parties who suffer loss as a result of breach of the approved persons requirement or a prohibition order may proceed in action for breach of statutory duty (section 71(1)). This remedy may also be available to non-private persons in certain prescribed circumstances (section 71(2)). This parallels the more general action from damages available under section 138D of FSMA for breach of statutory duty.[92] **13.86**

Handbook of Rules and Guidance

The obligations with which banks have to comply on a continuing basis are set out in the regulators's Handbooks of Rules and Guidance issued under sections 137A–F, 137G–K, 137O–R, and 139A and 157 of FSMA. The FCA and PRA are given rule-making powers under the amended FSMA. The effect of the PRA and FCA Handbooks is to create a rules-based regulatory regime rather than one with the detailed regulatory provisions being set out **13.87**

[92] Chapters 7 and 12.

in a statutory form. The advantage of this is flexibility and speed of amendment in response to changes in market structure and practice. Although the corresponding disadvantages are possibly of accessibility and complexity, the regulators have attempted to ensure maximum transparency within its consultation processes in preparing all of the separate sections that make up the Handbook. Final rules and guidance were made available in hardcopy, CD ROM, and Handbook online formats to ensure that all interested parties have full, timely, and cost effective access to all relevant provisions.

13.88 The regulators have separately tried to ensure that the Handbooks are as easy to follow as possible. Certain stylistic formats have been adopted including marking in the margins to the text rules as 'R', guidance with 'G', and other evidential provisions with the letter 'E'. Regular contents listings are included as well as a supporting glossary of terms. Earlier preparatory and consultation documents are also made available in the archive sections on the website. The FSA was nevertheless remained sensitive to concerns with regard to complexity and continues to attempt to simplify Handbook provisions whenever possible.

13.89 Banks and other deposits-takers will generally have to comply with the authorisation requirements set out in the application pack section of the website (previously the Authorisation Manual ('AUTH')) and then the High-Level Standards set out in Block 1 and continuing prudential obligations with regard to capital and controls contained in the Integrated Prudential Sourcebook applicable to banks (GENPRU and BIPRU) in Block 2. They are also subject to oversight and reporting requirements contained in the Supervision Manual ('SUP') and will have to comply with any investigation or verification requests and sanctions imposed under the Enforcement Guide ('EG'). Each of these provisions are considered in further detail in the following sections.

13.90 The PRA Handbook now consists of the High Level Standards (PRIN, SYSC, APER, FIT, FINMAR, GEN, and FEES), Prudential Standards (GENPRU, BIPRU, INSPRU, MIPRU, IPRU-FSOC, IPRU-INS, and IPRU-INV), Business Standards (COBS), Regulatory Processes (SUP), Redress (COMP), Specialist Sourcebooks (BSOCS and CREDS), and Regulatory Guides (BSOG).[93]

Bank authorisation

13.91 Banks are regulated by the PRA for prudential purposes with their conduct being subject to FCA oversight. Banks must initially be authorised to carry on their activities (under section 19(1) of FSMA). Deposits and deposit taking are included within the definitions of investments and regulated activities referred to in Schedule 2 and in the RAO.[94] Rather than apply for authorisation directly, banks will submit an application for Part IV permission to conduct deposit taking business (section 40(1)) and will then automatically become authorised for the purposes of the Act (section 30(1)(a)).[95]

13.92 An application for permission will be granted if the financial institution satisfies the threshold conditions set out in Schedule 6 of FSMA. These are generally concerned with legal status, location, close links, adequate resources, and suitability. Relevant procedural requirements were set out in AUTH within the Regulatory Processes Block section of the FSA

[93] See Chapter 1, paras 1.16–1.19; and Chapter 5.
[94] Paras 13.54–13.61.
[95] Paras 13.62–13.65 and 13.66–13.72.

Handbook which essentially consisted of guidance rather than rules to which the relevant application forms are attached. As a large number of different types of firms have to apply for relevant permission under FSMA, the FSA had created a special 'application pack' section on its website, firms can 'build their own' applications using up to six portals depending upon the type of business involved.[96] Applications from prospective new banks are managed by the PRA directly.[97]

Banks were generally required to complete and submit a corporate application to obtain permission to conduct regulated activities and a series of individual applications for approved persons and controllers. The purpose of the application documentation is to provide all necessary information in connection with the applicant's business plans, management and organisational structure, outsourcing arrangements, financial budgets and projections, systems, compliance procedures and documentation, senior management and staffing numbers, and controls and close links. **13.93**

The revised application pack generally included a Core Details Form (with a business-specific supplement), a Regulatory Business Plan (with a business-specific supplement), Personnel details, and Compliance arrangements with separate individual forms, Owners and Influencers, and supporting documents as well as a Change of Legal Status application pack for firms that wish to amend their permission.[98] The relevant application fee would also be paid. Decisions were taken in accordance with the procedures set out in DEPP with applicants having the right to make representations. **13.94**

Part IV permission

Where an application has been accepted, the firm would be advised of the activities that it may carry on including any specified limitations or requirements where applicable. The grant of the Part IV permission would take effect from the specified date, although this may differ from the business commencement date set out in the applicant's regulatory business plan. The regulator may vary or revoke the permission where the applicant has not carried on a regulated activity for which it has a Part IV permission for 12 months including commencing to do so. Any significant changes in particulars must be notified to the regulator subsequently. **13.95**

High-level standards

All regulated persons are subject to general provisions set out in the High Level Standards Block of the PRA and FCA Handbooks of Rules and Guidance. These set out the general principles and standards with which all regulated firms are expected to comply in the conduct of their regulated activities. These accordingly constitute a set of absolute minimum standards of good practice expected by the regulators from all financial institutions and across all sectors. These apply to firms, senior management, and other approved persons, and include such matters as integrity, skill, care, and diligence, financial, and market and client interests. Many enforcement decisions including the imposition of financial penalties are most often based on breach of the high-level standards rather particular regulatory rules or obligations. **13.96**

96 Chapter 6.
97 <http://www.bankofengland.co.uk/pra/Pages/authorisations/newfirm/banking.aspx>.
98 Chapter 6.

Principles for Businesses ('PRIN')

13.97 The Principles for Businesses ('PRIN') contain a statement of 11 fundamental obligations with which all regulated institutions are expected to comply. These develop the main aspects of the fit and proper standard referred to in the threshold condition 5 (suitability). Firms are expected to comply with the Principles at all times. This is considered critical in applications for permission under Part IV of FSMA and any breach will involve the possible withdrawal or restriction of permission on the basis that the firm is no longer fit and proper. It has been held that breach of the Principles set out in PRIN are directly actionable without the need to establish infraction of any separate implementing rule.[99]

Senior Management Arrangements, Systems, and Controls ('SYSC')

13.98 Senior Management Arrangements, Systems, and Controls ('SYSC') sets out the main requirements governing senior management responsibility and control systems. The purpose is to encourage banks' directors and senior managers to take appropriate responsibility for the banks' arrangements on matters likely to be of interest to the regulators and to encourage banks to assign responsibility for effective and responsible organisation to specific directors and senior managers.

13.99 The money laundering provisions previously contained in the Money Laundering Sourcebook have since been restated as general principles within SYSC and the sourcebook cancelled.[100] A new common platform regime was created for firms subject to the EU CRD and MiFID[101] with both directives containing provisions concerning management and internal systems and controls standards. Seven new chapters were to be added to SYSC to create the new common platform regime which would take effect from 1 November 2007 following implementation of MiFID. The following new measures apply to common platform firms:

(a) Chapter 4: General Organisational Requirements (including business continuity);
(b) Chapter 5: Employees, Agents and other Relevant Persons (including senior management requirements);
(c) Chapter 6: Compliance (including internal audit);
(d) Chapter 7: Risk Controls (including certain CRD risk-specific material);
(e) Chapter 8: Outsourcing;
(f) Chapter 9: Record-keeping; and
(g) Chapter 10: Conflicts of Interest.

Various other modules have been added to SYSC subsequently.

(h) Chapter 12: Group risk systems and controls requirement;
(i) Chapter 13: Operational risk: systems and controls for insurers;
(j) Chapter 14: Risk management and associated systems and controls for insurers;
(k) Chapter 18: Guidance on Public Interest Disclosure Act: Whistle blowing;
(l) Chapter 19a: Remuneration Code;
(m) Chapter 20: Reverse stress testing;
(n) Chapter 21: Risk control—additional guidance.

---

99 *British Bankers Association v Financial Services Authority and Financial Ombudsman Service* [2011] EWHC 999.

100 Chapter 10. See also GA Walker, 'Money Laundering' in *Encyclopaedia of Banking Law* (Butterworths, 6 Volume Looseleaf) Division A.

101 Chapter 3.

Threshold Conditions ('COND')

Threshold Conditions ('COND') develops the threshold conditions set out in Schedule 6 of FSMA with which firms have to comply to be granted Part IV permission (section 41(2) of FSMA) and to continue to comply with to retain that permission (section 45(1)(a)). The threshold conditions generally relate to legal status, location of offices, close links, adequate resources, and suitability. The meaning and content of each of these conditions is expanded in COND. COND is only retained within the FCA Handbook. 13.100

Statements of Principle and Code of Practice for Approved Person ('APER')

The regulators' requirements with regard to approved persons are developed in the Statements of Principle and Code of Practice (both contained in APER) and in the fit and proper tests for approved persons ('FIT'). APER is issued under section 64 of FSMA which allows the regulators to issue statements of principle with regard to the conduct expected of approved persons within financial firms with such statements being supported by a code of practice for the purpose of assisting to determine whether a person's conduct complies with the principles set. 13.101

The Statements of Principle for Approved Persons are set out in section 2 of APER. General and specific guidance is provided under the Code of Practice sections 3 and 4. Further direction is provided with regard to record keeping requirements (Schedule 1), notification requirements (Schedule 2), fees and other required payments (Schedule 3), powers exercised (Schedule 4), rights of action for damages (Schedule 2), and waiver (Schedule 6). 13.102

Fit and Proper Test for Approved Persons ('FIT')

The criteria to be taken into account in assessing whether an individual is fit and proper to conduct a particular controlled function is set out in the FIT. This applies to applicants and approved persons. The FSA will generally have regard to honesty, integrity and reputation, competence and capability, and financial soundness. In making assessments with regard to honesty, integrity, and reputation, the regulators will have regard to a number of matters including convictions, civil settlements, previous investigations or disciplinary proceedings, regulatory action, complaints, insolvency, professional discipline, censure or suspension, fiduciary infractions, director disqualifications, and previous honesty and cooperation with regulatory authorities. In examining competence and capability, the regulators will have regard to whether the person satisfies the relevant requirements of the Training and Competence Sourcebook ('TC') with regard to the specific controlled function concerned and whether the person has demonstrated by experience and training that he or she is able to perform the control function. 13.103

General Provisions ('GEN')

Matters that apply across the Handbook as a whole are set out in the General Provisions ('GEN'). These are considered by their nature not to be suitable to be set out in any particular manual or sourcebook. These include necessary or useful material relevant to all modules such as transitional arrangements, provisions that apply to all authorised persons, guidance on interpreting the Handbook, and fees. 13.104

Financial Stability and Market Confidence Sourcebook ('FINMAR')

FINMAR contains provisions on gathering financial stability information and short selling. FINMAR has been split with financial stability information being retained within the PRA 13.105

Handbook[102] and short selling within the FCA Handbook.[103] This is relevant to authorised and unauthorised persons whose activities may be relevant to the stability of the financial system. FINMAR1 provides a statement of PRA policy on the exercise of its financial stability information power and oversees financial stability information power.[104] The PRA may require a person to provide specified information or documents or information or documents of a specified description that it considers relevant to the stability of the UK financial system. Notice is generally to be provided in advance unless the request is necessary without delay. Addressees of requests may make representations. A financial stability information requirement will be imposed following review of the material and consideration of the representations made having regard to the nature and extent of the risks to financial stability involved.

Banking Supervision

13.106 Bank supervision is generally concerned with ensuring that banks conduct themselves in accordance with agreed or established standards of best market practice. For this purpose, they have initially to be authorised (or licensed) to enter the market. They must then carry on their activities in compliance with a series of prescribed regulatory obligations or best market practices governing such matters as liquidity and capital, internal control systems, and management suitability and oversight. They may be subject to sanction or discipline in the event that they breach any relevant requirements which may include the imposition of financial penalties or restrictions on the scope of the licence to carry on banking activities. One of the general objectives of the new regulatory regime set up under the FSA 2012 has been to attempt to restore a more judgement and discretionary element which reflects the earlier moral suasion approach adopted by the Bank of England previously.

13.107 The core functions of licensing, continuing oversight, and sanction were governed by the three process manuals set out in Block 3 of the FSA Handbook of Rules and Guidance. Market entry was dealt with under AUTH and now the application procedures subject to the general threshold conditions set out in Schedule 6 to FSMA (and COND). Oversight is governed by SUP which sets out the continuing information and reporting obligations that banks and other financial firms have to comply. Sanctions are applied under the FCA Enforcement Guide ('EG' previously 'ENF') which clarifies the range of powers available to the authorities under FSMA. The core supervisory obligations imposed under SUP were revised to give effect to the new Supervisory Enhancement Programme ('SEP') set up following the crisis at Northern Rock and again under the regulatory approaches adopted by the PRA and FCA.[105]

13.108 The particular regulatory obligations that banks have to satisfy with regard to such matters as capital, liquidity, and internal controls are set out in the Integrated Prudential Sourcebook sections applicable to banks (GENPRU and BIPRU) although their application and compliance is supported by the Authorisation, Supervision, and Enforcement Manuals.

102 <http://fshandbook.info/FS/html/PRA/FINMAR>.
103 <http://www.fshandbook.info/FS/html/FCA/FINMAR>.
104 ss 165A and 169A FSMA.
105 Chapter 1, paras 1.23–1.24, 1.51 and 1.54. See also paras 13.114- and 13.123.

UK bank supervision was previously conducted by the Bank of England under the Banking Acts 1979 and 1987 until responsibility in this regard was transferred to the FSA under the Bank of England Act 1998.[106] The FSA initially carried out its bank supervision under the transferred powers conferred under the 1998 Act until the coming into effect of FSMA on 1 December 2001 (N2). **13.109**

UK bank supervision has generally been conducted on the basis of five general processes or practices. Banks are initially required to provide continuing information through the submission of regular prudential returns in respect of both their individual (solo) and group (consolidated) activities. This is in addition to the general information provided under annual accounts or company law returns. The information produced is discussed in meetings between the senior management within the bank and relevant supervisory staff. The purpose of these meetings is to clarify and expand the paper submissions made. These can either be conducted on a bilateral basis or trilateral basis with the bank's accountants or auditors also in attendance. **13.110**

The supervisory authorities may conduct on-site visits to confirm or verify particular matters and have a general power to require documents or other information to be provided. Separate reports may be commissioned from special parties such as the bank's accountants or auditors in connection with such matters as the quality of internal systems and controls. These more informal possesses are supported by a range of enforcement powers which may include the conduct of formal investigations if necessary or to access premises or to call for documents to be provided or persons interviewed. This will, in turn, be supported by a range of formal sanctions including the imposition of penalties, prohibitions, or other actions against individuals (including bankruptcy), restriction or withdrawal of permission, and ultimately the winding up of institutions. **13.111**

The manner in which these Information and other confirmatory powers are exercised in practice is now set out in the Supervision Manual ('SUP'). This contains provisions concerning all of the separate processes referred to including information reporting and requests, meetings, on-site visits, reports and investigations, and formal disciplinary action. All of this is expanded in the individual chapters within SUP. The FSA's general approach to supervision was set out in SUP 1 although this has since been deleted. The PRA's general approach to supervision was set out in its 2013 policy statement.[107] The FSA approach was risk-based and used impact and probability factors with lead regulation. The new PRA model generally contrasts Gross Risk with Mitigating Factors. Gross risk is made up of Potential Impact and Risk Context which includes External Context and Business Risk. Mitigating factors consist of Operational Mitigation (including Management and Governance and Risk Management and Controls), Financial Mitigation (Capital and Liquidity), and Structural Mitigation (Resolvability). Information gathering is dealt with under SUP 2 with special provisions concerning auditors (SUP 3), actuaries (SUP 4), and reports commissioned by skilled persons (SUP 5). Applications to vary or cancel Part IV permission are provided for (SUP 6) with waiver and modification of rules (SUP 8). PRA-approved persons are now dealt with under SUP 10B. **13.112**

---

106 Paras 13.16–13.22.

107 Prudential Regulation Authority, *The Prudential Regulation Authority's approach to banking supervision* (n 120).

13.113 Provisions are also included with regard to particular categories of persons. These include approved persons (SUP 10), controllers and close links (SUP 11), and passport rights by UK firms and incoming EU firms (SUP 13 and 14). Notifications are considered (SUP 15) with reporting requirements (SUP 16). Additional guidance is provided with regard to business transfers (SUP 18) with further provisions included within the FCA Handbook.

Supervisory approach (SUP 1A)

13.114 Distinct approaches to supervision have been developed by the PRA and FCA. The PRA approach has been set out in separate guidance papers[108] with the FCA policy outlined in a new SUP 1A which replaces the FSA's earlier SUP 1 in its Handbook. While these frameworks nominally appear to be different and distinct from the earlier FSA approach, each of these contains a number of common elements. The FSA policy was risk-based with the PRA being judgement-based and forward-looking and the FCA described as pre-emptive and forward-looking.

13.115 The FSA generally adopted a risk-based approach the purpose of which was to focus resources on the mitigation of risks to its regulatory objectives and to use its resources in the most efficient and economic way (SUP 1.3.1G). The FSA approach to risk assessment was based on the extent to which firms created risks to the FSA's regulatory objectives having regard to the impact and probability of such exposures arising.[109]

13.116 The FSA had been developing a new regulatory approach and supporting operating framework since its creation in 1997.[110] This was, in particular, based on applying a standard risk assessment process across all activities which involved assessing the risks posed by a firm against a number of impact and probability factors on both an initial and a continuing basis. The impact of a firm was assessed by reference to a range of factors derived from the FSA's regulatory objectives. These included the degree to which the exposures related to the firm could damage market confidence, the extent to which the firm may undermine public understanding, the extent to which consumers may be adversely affected, and the possible incidence and materiality of any criminal activity with which the firm may be involved (SUP 1.3.3G).

13.117 The FSA framework consisted of five main steps in its risk assessment process which consisted of a preliminary assessment of the firm's potential impact on the regulatory objectives, a probability assessment, use of a validation panel for peer review of risk grading and resource allocation, informing the firm of the risk assessment selected and any remedial action required, and subsequent continuing review of the risk assessment made as necessary (SUP 1.3.8G).

13.118 The FSA developed a supervision by risk framework which referred to the threat to the FSA's statutory objectives. The term can also be used to refer to the particular type of risk involved (such as credit risk, market risk, or interest rate risk). This is the manner in which it was

[108] Prudential Regulation Authority, *The Prudential Regulation Authority's approach to banking supervision* (April 2013). See also Bank of England and FSA, *The PRA's approach to banking supervision* (October 2012); and'The Prudential Regulation Authority' Bank of England *Quarterly Bulletin* [2012] 1–9.

[109] Blair, Walker, and Purves (n 17) paras 14.94–14.103.

[110] Para 13.22. See FSA, 'A new regulator for the new millennium' (January 2000); FSA: 'Building the New Regulator—Progress Report' (December 2001); and FSA, 'Building the New Regulator—Progress Report 2' (February 2002); and FSA, 'The FSA's Risk-Based Approach' (November 2006).

originally used as part of the Bank of England's RATE framework which was adopted in the mid-1990s following the Arthur Andersen Report.[111] The adoption of a cumulative or aggregation approach with regard to each of the main financial exposures was later referred to as 'risk-by-risk' supervision which was followed under the Integrated Prudential Sourcebook ('PRU') and then BIPRU.

The PRA policy documents generally restate its key objective of promoting the safety and soundness of firms. PRA approach to supervision is referred to as being judgement based and forward looking.[112] Supervisory judgement is based on evidence and analysis with the PRA engaging with boards and senior management and with decision taking being rigorous, well documented, and consistent with public law.[113] The PRA focuses on issues and firms that create the greatest risk to the stability of the UK financial system and assesses safety and soundness against credit risks and future risks.[114] **13.119**

The PRA risk framework generally contrasts 'Gross Risk' with relevant 'Mitigating Factors'. Gross risk is made up of Potential Impact and Risk Context which includes External Context and Business Risk. Mitigating factors consist of Operational Mitigation (including Management and Governance and Risk Management and Controls), Financial Mitigation (Capital and Liquidity) and Structural Mitigation (Resolvability).[115] The PRA divides authorised institutions into five impact categories[116] with a separate five stage Pro-active Intervention Framework ('PIF') being constructed.[117] The PIF model examines recovery and resolution options with regard to low and moderate risk viability firms (stages 1 and 2), risk to viability without firm action (stage 3), imminent risk to viability (stage 4), and active resolution (stage 5). The PRA will attempt to use its powers to secure remedial action by firms on an ex ante basis with other disciplinary powers being used where firms fail to comply with PRA requirements.[118] The PRA will generally apply the same prudential standards to all types of domestic and cross-border operations working with other agencies as necessary.[119] **13.120**

The FCA generally adopts a pre-emptive and forward-looking approach based on its judgements of burdens of business models, product strategy, and business operations (SUP 1A.3.1G).The FCA's overall approach is stated to be based on 10 key principles.[120] The FCA will be forward-looking and interventionist, focused on judgement and not process, 'consumer-centric', focused on 'big issues and causes of problems', interface with executive management and board, be 'robust when things go wrong', focus on business models and culture as well as products superprovision, consider 'pure behaviour' having regard to consumer impact, audience programs to do 'the right thing'and be 'externally focused, engaged and listening to all sources of information' (SUP 1A.3.2G). **13.121**

---

[111] Paras 13.20–13.21 and (n 24).

[112] Prudential Regulation Authority, *The Prudential Regulation Authority's approach to banking supervision* (April 2013) 5 and paras 10-15.

[113] P 6 and para 41.

[114] Paras 38 and 39.

[115] Para 44 and Figure 1, p 12.

[116] Para 50.

[117] Paras 182–187 and Table A, p 32.

[118] Paras 199–200.

[119] P 34, Box 5,

[120] FCA, *FCA Factsheet*; available at: <http://www.fca.org.uk/static/fca/documents/factsheet.pdf>.

13.122 The FCA's supervision model is based on three pillars consisting of a Firm Systematic Framework (FSF), event-driven work, and issues and products including thematic work (SUP 1A.3.4G). The FCA will communicate the outcomes of its pillars of supervision to each firm within an appropriate time frame with any remedial programme of action required with firms not generally disclosing their FCA risk assessment to third parties (SUP 1A.3.6G). Supervisory issues will generally be dealt with through the FCA Contact Centre rather than through supervisory staff directly (SUP 1A.3.7G). The FCA will cooperate closely with the PRA (SUP 1A.3.7G).

13.123 The FCA follows the earlier FSA approach. The FCA may rely on one or more of a number of tools of supervision to correct identified risks to its regulatory objectives. The FCA distinguishes between diagnostic, monitoring, preventative, and remedial tools (SUP 1A.4.2G). Diagnostic measures are designed to identify, assess, and measure risks. Monitoring options follow the development of identified risks wherever these may arise. Preventative responses limit or reduce perceived risks and prevent crystallisation or aggravation. Remedial measures respond to risks following occurrence. Particular tools may serve more than one purpose and may or may not involve a direct relationship with the particular firm concerned. The main supervisory tools include desk-based reviews, liaison with other agencies or regulators, management meetings or representative meetings, on-site inspections, reviews and analysis of periodic returns and notifications, past business reviews, transaction monitoring, and use of auditors and skilled persons (SUP 1A.4.5G). Specific risks may also be dealt with through a number of additional tools including making recommendations for preventative or remedial action, providing individual guidance, imposing requirements, or varying a firm's permission (SUP 1A.4.6G).

Information (SUP 2)

13.124 SUP 2 contains rules and guidance concerning the collection of information from firms for supervisory purposes. Cooperation between firms and the regulators is necessary to allow it to discharge its responsibility to monitor compliance. SUP 2 was originally issued under the regualtors' statutory obligation to ensure compliance and the obligation to cooperate with other regulators. Firms are required to deal with regulators in an open and cooperative manner and to disclose anything of which the regulators would reasonably expect notice (PRIN 11 and SUP 2.2 and 2.3). Firms may be required to provide information to the regulators (section 165 FSMA) with the PRA having specific power to obtain information for financial stability purposes (section 165A FSMA).

13.125 Under SUP, the regulators may conduct visits, hold meetings with staff at the regulators' offices or elsewhere, and request information or documents including by telephone, during meetings or in writing and by electronic communication (SUP 2.3.1G). Meetings or access can only be requested during reasonable business hours and on reasonable notice. The regulators expects firms to make themselves readily available and provide reasonable access to all records, files, tapes, or computer systems or facilities as may be reasonably requested (SUP 2.3.3(1) and (2)G). Firms may be required to produce any specified material as reasonably asked for, print information in the firm's possession or control, permit the copying of documents or other material, and answer truthfully, fully, and promptly all reasonable questions or inquiries (SUP 2.3.3(3), (4), (5), and (6)G).

13.126 The regulators and their agents must be allowed access during reasonable business hours to any of a firm's premises which obligation is extended to its agents, suppliers under material outsourcing arrangements, and appointed representatives (SUP R 2.3.5(1) and (2)). Outsourcers must deal with the regulators in an open and cooperative manner (SUP R 2.3.7). While the regulators will generally only seek information from firms directly, it may approach outsourcers as appropriate (SUP 2.3.10G). Firms may be required to provide information on behalf of another regulator including the Takeover Panel or an overseas authority (SUP 23.3.11). Information may be disclosed subject to banking confidentiality and legal privilege.

Firms are liable to sanction for breach of SUP or PRIN 11. This includes any disciplinary measures under Part XIV of FSMA although breach is not a criminal offence nor contempt (section 177 of FSMA). The regulators will not generally seek to obtain information using the methods set out in SUP 2.3 where they could not have obtained it under the powers in Part XI FSMA (SUP 2.2.3 and 3A). Confidential information must be kept confidential (SUP 2.2.4 and 4A). Supervisory information is subject to bank confidentiality (section 175(5) of FSMA) and may not be disclosed unless a relevant exception applies or consent is available.[121] Information obtained by the regulators using the methods described in SUP 2.3 is admissible in evidence in any proceedings, so long as it complies with any requirements governing the admissibility of evidence in the circumstances in question (SUP 2.2.5 and 5AG). **13.127**

Auditors (SUP 3)

The role and function of auditors is developed in SUP 3. This includes appointment rules (SUP 3.3), minimum qualifications (SUP 3.4), and the rights and duties of auditors (SUP 3.5–10). The statutory basis for these provisions is sections 340 to 346 of FSMA. **13.128**

Firms may be required to appoint an auditor if they are not already under an obligation to do so and the regulators may issue rules requiring authorised persons to produce periodic financial reports and have them reported on by an auditor (section 340(1) and (2) of FSMA). Auditors may be made subject to such duties as the regulators may specify. Further directions may be given with regard to the manner and time of appointment, notification requirements, remuneration and terms of office, removal, and resignation (section 340(4) of FSMA). It is an offence to provide false or misleading information to an auditor (section 346) and auditors may be disqualified where they have failed to comply with any duty imposed under the Act (section 345(1)). **13.129**

Auditors have a statutory right of access to books, accounts and vouchers, and to ask for any information or explanation as may be required (section 341(1)). Auditors are immune from an action in damages where they have disclosed to the regulators any matter or opinion in good faith and reasonably believed to be relevant to the regulators' functions (section 342(3)). The circumstances in which auditors may communicate matters with the regulators are developed in Treasury regulations (issued under section 342(5)). The regulators are to be **13.130**

[121] FSMA, s 349(1) and the Financial Services and Markets Act 2000 (Disclosure of Confidential Information) Regulations 2001, SI 2001/2188. See also Financial Services and Markets Act 2000 (Disclosure of Confidential Information) (Amendment) Regulations 2001, SI 2001/3437 and Financial Services and Markets Act 2000 (Disclosure of Confidential Information) (Amendment (No 2)) Regulations 2001, SI 2001/3624 as amended. See also The Financial Services and Markets Act 2000 (Disclosure of Confidential Information) (Amendment) Regulations 2012, SI 2012/3019.

separately notified where an auditor has been removed from office, resigns before the expiry of term, or is not reappointed (section 344).

13.131 Bank auditors are subject to the provisions set out in SUP. This includes application (SUP 3.1), purpose (SUP 3.2), appointment (SUP 3.3), qualifications (SUP 3.4), independence (SUP 3.5), firm's cooperation with auditors (SUP 3.6), notifications (SUP 3.7), and rights and duties (SUP 3.8). Auditors are expressly required to cooperate with the regulators in the discharge of its functions, provide any skilled person with all assistance as may be reasonably required, act in an independent manner, take reasonable steps to satisfy themselves that they are free from any conflicts of interest, notify the regulators without delay of removal, resignation, or loss of reappointment, and notify the regulators of any matter that ought to be drawn to its attention or that there is no such matter, including termination of office (SUP R 3.8.2–12).

Actuaries (SUP 4)

13.132 The statutory provisions with regard to actuaries are developed in SUP 4. These are based on Part XXII of FSMA and generally only apply to insurers or friendly societies that carry on long-term insurance business. These are generally inapplicable to banks.

Skilled persons report (SUP 5)

13.133 The requirements with regard to the appointment of skilled persons are set out under Part XI FSMA as developed in SUP 5. These replace the earlier section 39 reports provided for under the Banking Act 1987. The regulators are given statutory power to require reports to be prepared for any authorised person, member of a firm's group, a partnership of which it is a member, or any such person provided that it was carrying on business at the relevant time (section 166(2)). Reports may be requested on any matter as may reasonably be required in connection with the exercise of the regulators' functions under the Act (section 166(1)). The report may be in such form as may be specified and is to be conducted by persons nominated or approved by the regulators with the necessary relevant skills (section 166(3)).

13.134 The provisions set out in SUP 5 apply to every firm (SUP R 5.1.1). Reports may be commissioned for diagnostic or reporting and preventative or remedial purposes (SUP 5.3.1G). Reports are generally to be requested for information purposes, as part of a risk mitigation programme, in response to a specific event, or for the provision of expert advice. Appointment and reporting procedures are specified (SUP 5 5.4) with additional provisions concerning the duties of skilled persons and confidentiality and legal privilege (SUP 5.5 and 5.6).

Part 4A permission, variation, or cancellation (SUP 6)

13.135 Applicable procedures for the variation or cancellation of a Part 4A permission are dealt with under SUP 6. SUP 6 contains specific provisions with regard to applications (SUP 6.1), statutory basis (SUP 6.2), variation (SUP 6.3), cancellation (SUP 6.4), and ending authorisation (SUP 6.5). Relevant procedures were summarised in SUP 6 Annexes 1, 2, and 3 with additional guidance on firm's winding down their business in SUP Annex 4. Variation and cancellation application forms are provided in Annexes 5 and 6.

13.136 Applications are generally considered on an individual basis having regard to all relevant information in the specific case (sections 55E and F). Applications for the variation of an existing permission are made under section 55H-I(1) and cancellations under section 55K

(SUP 6.3 and 6.4). Applications are generally made online under the Online Notifications and Applications ('ONA') system to the relevant regulator.

Individual requirements (SUP 7)

Requirements may be imposed on a firm's permission to carry on a regulated activity under section 55L–P of FSMA although SUP 7 and SUP 9 are only included within the FCA Handbook. Specific requirements may be considered where a firm is not in full compliance with all threshold conditions such as with regard to relevant systems and controls. Firms may, for example, be required to maintain higher capital ratios or be subject to certain geographic or product restrictions. Relevant criteria are set out in SUP 7.3. **13.137**

Waiver and modification of rules (SUP 8)

The waiver or modification of the application of particular rules is provided for under section 138A of FSMA. This is developed in SUP 8. Rules may also be waived with regard to collective investment schemes under section 250. **13.138**

Applications for waiver must be in writing (SUP 8.3.3G and Annex 2). Decisions are generally made within 20 business days of receipt with reasons for refusal being given (SUP 8.3.5 and 7G). Additional provisions are included with regard to reliance (SUP 8.4), notification or changes in circumstances (SUP 8.5), publication (SUP 8.6), variations (SUP 8.7), revocation (SUP 8.8), and decision-making (SUP 8.9). **13.139**

Individual guidance (SUP 9)

Individual guidance may be provided with regard to the activities of specific firms (section 139A(2), FSMA). General guidance may also be issued under the Act and guidance provided with regard to a particular class of regulated persons (section 139(1) and (3)). Compliance is required with the relevant consultation requirements set out in section 138J (section 139(3)). SUP 9 is only included within the FCA Handbook. **13.140**

Firms may apply to the FCA for individual guidance as to how rules and general guidance set out in the Handbook apply to their activities (SUP 9.1.3G). Applications may be made in writing or orally (SUP 9.2.1G). Guidance may, for example, be requested with regard to the amount of financial resources including individual financial resources (SUP 9.3.2(5)G). Firms are considered to have complied with the relevant rules where they act in accordance with the guidance provided (SUP 9.4.1G). Further guidance may be requested where circumstances have changed (SUP 9.4.3G). **13.141**

The FCA may publish its guidance (section 139(6)(a)). It may offer copies of its guidance for sale at a reasonable price and make a reasonable charge in response to requests for individual guidance (section 139(6)(b) and (c)). **13.142**

Approved persons (SUP 10A and B)

Additional rules and guidance are provided with regard to approved persons under SUP 10A for FCA firms and SUP 10B for PRA firms. Regulated entities are required to apply for prior approval from the FSA in connection with any person carrying on a controlled function (section 69(1) of FSMA).[122] An earlier registration system had operated under the **13.143**

122 Paras 13.76–13.86.

self-regulatory regime set up under the FSA 1986 although this has since been extended under the provisions contained in Part V, FSMA on the performance of regulated actitvies and the Handbooks. The effect of this is to create a parallel assessment and approvals system for individuals carrying on regulated functions as well as firms themselves.

13.144 SUP 10B contains specific provision with regard to application (SUP 10B.1), purpose (SUP 10B.2), basic rules (SUP 10B.3), specified functions (SUP 10B.4), temporary vacancies (SUP 10B.5), governing functions (SUP 10B.6), other functions (SUP 10B.7), require functions (SUP 10B.8), and systems and controls functions (SUP 10B.9) (SUP 10B.5–10). Additional provisions are included with regard to procedures and forms (SUP 10B.11), applications (SUP 10B.12), changes to an approved person's details (SUP 10B.13), and how to apply for approval (SUP 10B.14).

13.145 The relevant forms attached to SUP include Application to perform controlled functions under the approved persons regime (SUP 10B Annex 2), Notice to withdraw an application to perform controlled functions (SUP 10B Annex 5), Notice to cease to perform controlled functions (SUP 10B Annex 6), Notification of changes in personal information or application details (SUP 10 Annex 7), and internal transfer of an approved person (SUP 10 Annex 8).

Controllers and close links (SUP 11)

13.146 Guidance with regard to the exercise of the PRA's powers with regard to controllers and close links is outlined in SUP 11. Any person proposing to acquire, increase, or reduce a controlling interest in an authorised person must notify the regulators under section 178(1) of FSMA. A person acquires control where they own or can exercise or control the exercise of 10 per cent or more of the shares in the company or exercise a significant influence over the management of the company or its parent (section 181). The acquirer refers to the acquirer or any of its associates or the acquirer and any of its associates. Increases or reductions in control refer to any alteration in holdings up to 10 per cent, from 10 per cent to below 20 per cent, from 20 per cent to below 33 per cent, from 33 per cent to below 50 per cent and 50 per cent or more (sections 182(2) and 183(2)). The regulators must be notified of the change in control in writing and is required either to approve it or serve a warning notice within 60 working days (sections 178(1) and 189(1)). Notice is to be in such form as the regulators may specify with receipt being acknowledged within two days (sections 179(1) and 180(1)). The PRA and FCA are to consult with each other and EC competent authorities on the assessment of notices (sections 187A and B and 188). Approvals may be subject only to such conditions as may be considered appropriate (sections 187(1) and 187C).

13.147 Acquisition may only be objected to on the basis of the assessment criteria set out in section 186 or where incomplete information has been provided (section 185(3)). Relevant criteria include reputation and financial soundness of the notice provider or the reputation and experience of the person who will direct the business (section 186(2) and (3)). Offences are dealt with under section 191F with the Treasury having power to issue regulations under section 192.

13.148 The statutory provisions are developed in SUP 11. This includes application (SUP 11.1) and guidance on objectives (SUP 11.2), relevant requirements (SUP 11.3 and 4), notification forms (SUP 11.5), and subsequent notification requirements (SUP 11.6). The approval procedures for acquisition or increase in control are provided for (SUP 11.7) with changes in circumstances of existing controllers (SUP 11.8) and changes in close links (SUP 11.9). Relevant procedures are summarised in SUP 11 Annex 1.

Appointed representatives (SUP 12)

SUP 12 contains guidance on the application of section 39 of FSMA under which appointed representatives may be exempt from the general prohibition under section 19(1). SUP 12 is only included within the FCA Handbook. Specific provision is included with regard to firm responsibility (SUP 12.3), appointment requirements (SUP 12.4), required terms of contracts (SUP 12.5), continuing obligations (SUP 12.6), notification requirements (SUP 12.7), termination of appointment (SUP 12.8), and record keeping (SUP 12.9). Assessments of the financial position of appointed representatives and their fitness and proprietary are included within Annexes 1 and 2. **13.149**

The rules governing the operation of the appointed representatives regime were relaxed with the introduction of the polarisation regime in 2005. Financial advisers had to act act as either tied appointed representatives, fully independent financial advisers, or multi-tied agents. Sales practices and disclosure of services and charges were considered again as part of the FSA's Retail Distribution Review ('RDR') which came into effect at the end of 2012. This will not apply with regard to pure banking activities although it may be relevant where banks provide financial advice or wealth management services or sell insurance and other financial products.[123] **13.150**

Passport rights (SUP 13)

The exercise of passport rights by UK firms is dealt with under SUP 13 and incoming EEA firms under SUP 13A and SUP 14. SUP 13 applies with regard to the establishment of a first branch or the provision of services in another EEA country or revising existing arrangements (SUP 13.1.5 and 13.1.6G). The provisions apply to UK firms that are authorised persons under FSMA as well as to wholly owned subsidiaries of credit institutions capable of exercising the right of establishment or services under the Banking Consolidation Directive (SUP 13.2.1G). **13.151**

Guidance is provided with regard to the establishment of a branch in another EEA State (SUP 13.3), the provision of cross-border services (SUP 13.4), notices of intention (SUP 13.5), changes to branches (SUP 13.6), changes to cross-border services (SUP 13.7), changes of details (SUP 13.8), application (SUP 13.9), applicable provisions (SUP 13.10), record keeping (SUP 13.11), and further information (SUP 13.12). Details of the relevant forms to be used for different types of activity under specific directives, including banking, insurance, and MiFID as well as emissions trading are provided in Annexes 1 to 7. Additional provisions on qualifying for authorisation have been included within SUP 13A. **13.152**

Incoming firms (SUP 13A and 14)

Incoming EEA firms are authorised under section 31(1) of FSMA to exercise passport rights under the main European financial directives or Treaty rights directly. While the authorisation issued was previously dealt with under AUTH, relevant notification procedures for EEA firms are set out in SUP 13 for outgoing firms and SUP 13A and SUP 14 for incoming firms. SUP 13A applies to incoming EEA firms that wish to establish a branch or provide services on a cross-border basis and SUP 14 to firms that have already established a branch or are already providing cross-border services into the UK. **13.153**

123 Chapters 15, 16, and 17.

13.154 SUP 13A contains guidance on EEA and Treaty firms (SUP 13A.2), qualifications for authorisation under FSMA (SUP 13A.3), establishing a branch (SUP 13A.4), and providing services on a cross-border basis (SUP 13A.5), applicable rules (SUP 13A.6), top-up permission (SUP 13A.7), and further information (SUP 13A.8). SUP 14 provides guidance for firms that wish to change the details of a branch or the services provided or cancel their qualification for authorisation (SUP 14.1.1). Additional guidance is provided with regard to changes in branch details (SUP 14.2) and cross-border services (SUP 14.3), notices (SUP 14.4), variation of top-up permission (SUP 14.5), cancellation of authorisation (SUP 14.6), and top-up permission (SUP 14.7) and further guidance (SUP 14.8).

Notifications (SUP 15)

13.155 Supervisory information provision under the Handbook is generally dealt with in SUP 15 and 16. Additional provisions on applications and notifcations under the European Markets Infrastructure Regulation No 648/2012 (EMIR) are set out in SUP 15A. General notifications are made under SUP 15 with reporting requirements in SUP 16. The transaction reporting requirements for specific firms in SUP 17 have only been retained in the FCA Handbook. Firms are generally required to cooperate with regulators and provide any information relating to their activities which the regulators would reasonably expect to be provided with (PRIN 11). This applies to regulated and unregulated activities including group activities. This will include such matters as proposed restructurings, reorganisation or business expansions, and any significant failure of a firm's systems and controls or any action that would result in a material change in its capital adequacy or solvency position (SUP 15.3.8G).

13.156 A number of rules are included within SUP 15 concerning notification. These include any matters having a serious regulatory impact(SUP R 15.3.1), breaches of rules or any other regulatory requirements, and civil, criminal, or disciplinary proceedings against the firm (SUP R 15.3.11 and 15) or fraud, errors, or other irregularities (SUP R 15.3.17) and any insolvency, bankruptcy, or winding up (SUP R 15.3.21). Reasonable advance notice of certain other matters must also be provided including change of name, change of address, change in legal status, and any changes with regard to supervisory authority (SUP R 15.5.1–8). Overseas firms are required to notify any change of position of global chief executive, any person with purely strategic responsibility for UK operations, and any two or more persons that effectively direct a bank's business (SUP R 15.4.1). This is necessary as such persons would otherwise fall outside the regulators' reporting requirements. Firms must also take all reasonable steps to ensure that the information provided is factually accurate and complete (SUP R 15.6.1).

13.157 The regulators must be notified immediately if any false, misleading, or incomplete or inaccurate information has been provided or information has changed in a material respect. Updated information must be provided as soon as reasonably practicable (SUP R 15.6.4 and 5). Additional guidance is provided with regard to the form and method of notification (SUP 15.7), notification in respect of particular products or services (SUP 15.8), financial conglomerates (SUP 15.9) and adjustments for incoming EEA or Treaty firms that have top-up permission (SUP 15 Annex 1).

Reporting requirements (SUP 16)

13.158 SUP 16 sets out the general reporting requirements with which firms have to comply on a continuing basis. This includes general reporting conditions (SUP 16.3), annual reports on controllers (SUP 16.4), annual close links reports (SUP 16.5), as well as compliance reports (SUP 16.6). Banks must generally submit a list of all overseas regulators for each legal entity in the firm's group and an organigram which sets out all authorised entities within the group within six months after the firm's accounting reference date (SUP R 16.6.4 and 5). A number of additional provisions have since been added on appointed representatives, verifcations, integrated regulatory reporting, European Payment Services Regulation, Electronic Money Regulations and Alternative Investment Fund Managers reporting, client money and asset returns, prudent valuation reporting, and remuneration reporting (SUP 16.9–18).

Transaction reporting (SUP 17)

SUP 17 contains rules and guidance concerning the submission of transaction reports in connection with particular securities and related derivatives activities. This is only been retained in the FCA Handbook. Such reports were required under Article 20 of the European Investment Services Directive ('ISD') and given effect to in the UK under the earlier rule books of the SFA, PIA, and IMRO. **13.159**

Transaction reporting is now required under the MiFID Directive. SUP 17 contains specific provisions governing application (SUP 17.1), making transaction reports (SUP 17.2), reporting channels (SUP 17.3), information in transaction reports(SUP 17.4), and the minimum content of a transaction reporting (SUP 17 Annex 1). **13.160**

Integrated Prudential Regulation

The earlier regulatory requirements imposed under the Interim Prudential Sourcebook IPRU(BANK) were to be replaced by a single set of integrated prudential provisions. One of the underlying objectives within the new regulatory regime was to create a common set of prudential requirements for all financial firms. This would require that they maintain adequate financial resources as well as proper systems and controls at all times irrespective of the particular type and range of activities carried on although within a single overall regulatory and supervisory framework. **13.161**

The core difficulty that arises is that distinct underlying financial risks are involved in each of the main sectors which require differentiated treatment. It was for this reason that the original supervision by risk policy adopted by the FSA was extended to include a 'risk-by-risk' approach in the new Prudential Sourcebook. This was to be dealt with by a separate chapter being included on each of the main sources of exposure identified, although still within a single common approach or methodology and integrated set of rules. The six key risks initially identified for this purpose were credit risk, market risk, insurance risk, liquidity risk, operational risk, and group risk. Financial firms would then be required to comply with the separate chapters to the extent that their activities involved any of the particular types of exposure covered. **13.162**

This process of designing and building the new single Integrated Prudential Sourcebook was originally referred to as the 'PSB'. It was subsequently confirmed that the new sourcebook to be included within the Handbook would be designated the 'PRU'. The FSA then confirmed that separate sub-sourcebooks would be issued in each of the main sector areas covered. This was considered necessary, in particular, to reflect the structure and content of the main recent European directives that had been adopted in each sector area and that had to be separately **13.163** implemented in the UK. The timetable for the PRU and each of the sub-sourcebooks coming into effect had also had to be extended to correspond with the dates agreed for the coming into effect of the relevant European and supporting international Basel II standards on which they are based.[124]

13.164 A number of separate sub-sourcebooks have since been produced within the new Prudential Standards Block 2 of the Handbook with a revised set of common provisions applicable to all firms (GENPRU) and dedicated requirements for banks, building societies, and investment firms (BIPRU). Additional specialised sourcebooks have then been issued in respect of insurers (INSPRU), and mortgage and insurance mediation firms (MIPRU) with the earlier interim rules continued in respect of insurers, friendly societies, and investment firms (IPRU-INS, IPRU-FSOC, and IPRU-INV) The sourcebook for unit trust managers and UCITS firms (UPRU) has been moved to the FCA Handbook.

Basel II and Basel III

13.165 The capital rules incorporated within the PRU were necessary to give effect to the revised framework agreed by the Basel Committee on Banking Supervision under its new Basel II Accord.[125] These revised capital measures were prepared between June 1999 and June 2004. The Committee had issued an initial consultation document on capital revision in June 1999 which was supplemented by the publication of a number of separate component papers in January 2001. Following the comments received, a further consultation document was issued with a number of further calibration exercises being conducted through industry-based quantitative impact studies ('QIS'). The revised capital rules were then produced in June 2004 subject to some final adjustments under a QIS 5 to be conducted during 2005/2006. The new framework was to come into full effect between 2007 and 2009 in all participating countries. Basel II has been revised following the global financial crisis.[126]

13.166 The Basel II framework is stated to be based on three pillars. These consist of a revised set of minimum capital requirements (Pillar 1), a new supervisory review process (Pillar 2), and enhanced market discipline through mandatory market disclosure (Pillar 3). Pillar 1 includes a revised set of minimum capital requirements in respect of credit risk, an amended market risk charge, and a new operational risk charge. Basel III refers to the proposed further amendment of the Basel II provisions.[127]

13.167 The current minimum charge introduced under the 1988 Capital Accord has been retained within the revised standardised approach, although this been made more risk sensitive through the use of external credit rating agency scores rather than the earlier simple risk bands or buckets. Bank loans are generally classified depending upon whether they are with OECD government or central banks borrowing in their own currencies, OECD government

[124] See FSA CP2005/3, 'Strengthening capital standards' (2005); FSA CP189, 'Report and First Consultation on the Implementation of the New Basel and EU Capital Adequacy Standards'; and FSA DP13, 'UK implementation of the New Basel and the New Capital Adequacy Standards'.

[125] Walker (n 16), 'Capital Supplement'.

[126] The Basel Committee, *Basel III: A Global Regulatory Framework for More Resilient Banks and Banking Systems* (December 2010 and revised June 2011); and Basel Committee, *Basel III: International Framework for Liquidity Risk Measurement, Standards and Monitoring* (December 2010). See also Basel Committee, *Strengthening the Resilience of the Banking Sector* (December 2009); and Basel Committee, *The Basel Committee's Response to the Financial Crisis: Report to the G20* (October 2010).

[127] Para 13.178.

or central bank borrowing in other currencies, secured borrowers, or other commercial borrowers. Each is then assigned a risk grading which approximates with the underlying credit risk involved (the possibility of non-payment of interest during term or repayment of principal on maturity). The main risk factors used are 0 per cent (cash or OECD debt) or 10 per cent or 20 per cent (domestic public sector entities), 20 per cent (non-OECD or development banks), 50 per cent (secured borrowing), and 100 per cent (commercial and private sector claims).

Off-balance sheet items (such as guarantees and other credit substitutes as well as performance and bid bonds and sale and repurchase agreements (repos)) are multiplied by specified conversion factors (either 20 per cent, 50 per cent, or 100 per cent) to create on-balance sheet credit equivalent amounts. The same general credit risk factors are then applied depending on the nature of the borrower. The total exposure in each risk category is multiplied by the amount of the loans outstanding at any time and then aggregated to produce a total risk adjusted asset figure for the loan book of the bank. This must be covered by, at least, 8 per cent of available capital as defined. Tier 1 capital (4 per cent) is essentially made up of paid-up share capital or disclosed reserves, and Tier 2 (the other 4 per cent), undisclosed reserves, asset revaluation reserves, general provisions, hybrid instruments or five-year subordinated debt (but only up to one-quarter (2 per cent) of the total 8 per cent). **13.168**

Under Basel II, the earlier simple bucket system (0 per cent, 20 per cent, 50 per cent, or 100 per cent) is to be replaced by a series of more sophisticated gradings based on external credit rating agency figures for the individual borrowers involved. This should allow the process to be considerably more accurate provided that necessary external rating information is available. The rating agencies themselves have to be approved as eligible having regard to a set of assessment criteria provided (which include objectivity, independence, international access and transparency, disclosure, resources, and credibility). **13.169**

Security related risks continue to be dealt with under the terms of the Basel Committee's January 1996 Market Risk Amendment. This provides for the use of a number of options to be made available in respect of the calculation of general and specific risk on interest rate debt (bond) and equity positions. Separate charges are imposed in respect of settlement delays, foreign exchange, and commodities with a system of allowances being available against underwriting exposures. This cumulative (building block) approach generally follows that developed under the European Capital Adequacy Directive ('CAD'). **13.170**

With regard to market exposures, interest rate risk-specific risk is either assigned a 0, 0.25 per cent, 1 per cent, 1.60 per cent, or 8 per cent charge depending upon whether it is government, qualifying, or other general interest rate risk. General risk may be calculated on either a maturity basis (10 per cent to 150 per cent of weighted matched positions) or a duration-based approach (or 2 per cent to 150 per cent of matched duration). Specific equity position is essentially 4 per cent of the gross amount subject to a 2 per cent concession if it is well diversified and liquid. General equity position risk is 8 per cent of the net position. The foreign exchange charge is 8 per cent of the total net foreign exchange position in excess of 2 per cent of capital. Commodity related risks may be calculated on a simplified, maturity ladder, or models basis. **13.171**

The main market risk charges may alternatively be calculated on an internal models basis subject to certain qualitative and quantitative standards. Qualitative standards include **13.172** independent risk control, regular back testing, full involvement of the board of directors and senior management, integrated internal risk measurement models, internal trading and exposure limits, routine and rigorous stress testing, a compliance documented set of internal policies, and regular independent review. Quantitative requirements include use of a daily value-at-risk ('VAR') calculation, a 99 per cent (1 tailed) confidence interval, a 10-day holding interval, a one-year historical observation period, updated data sets every three years and a supervisory safety multiplier of three. The particular risk model selected must also be subject to stress testing and external validation procedures. These options have been continued under Basel II.

13.173 The new capital framework includes a new charge in respect of operational risk. This is designed to cover losses arising as a result of fraud, personnel, or other systems or controls failures. Although not calculated in the same manner as other financial risks having regard to the particular exposures concerned (such as credit, market, or liquidity risk), larger banks have been setting aside amounts of capital against operational risk failures for some time. The Basel Committee accordingly decided to extend this to create an additional general charge included within the new minimum requirements imposed under Pillar 1.

13.174 With Basel II, the operational risk charge may either be calculated on a basic indicator approach (a fixed percentage of the factor selected of gross income), a standardised approach (using distinct business units and lines with a beta factor being applied), and an advanced measurement approach (using a separate exposure indicator ('EI'), probability of loss event ('PE'), and expected loss ('EL')). The new basic operational risk charge is estimated to be equivalent to approximately 20 per cent of total capital. While bank charges should fall under the more sensitive credit risk approach followed under the rest of Pillar 1, in practice this will generally be more than offset by the new operational risk charge imposed with no overall reduction in capital levels or costs.

13.175 Two further internal ratings-based approaches ('IRB') were also to be made available in respect of credit risk under Pillar 1 of Basel II. This can operate on either a foundation or an advanced basis which uses a number of additional factors including probability of default ('PD'), loss given default ('LGD'), and exposure at default (the 'EAD'). Effective maturity ('M') and expected loss ('EL') are also used in connection with retail exposures. Banks are generally to be allowed to use their own internal measures of PD in estimating credit risk under the foundation approach. This will be extended under the advanced approach to include the LGD and EAD. The factors which banks do not supply themselves are subject to supervisory estimates. These IRB approaches do not, however, allow for the use of full credit risk modelling at this stage (as under the Market Risk Amendment or CRD in respect of trading book charges) although this may be reconsidered over time under the further Basel III revisions as models become more sophisticated and more reliable historical data becomes available.

13.176 Pillar 2 of Basel II consists of a new supervisory review process. This imposes an express obligation on national supervisory authorities to confirm the adequacy of banks' internal control systems to measure and manage their capital exposures. This is based on four general components including maintaining an effective capital assessment process, a new supervisory obligation to review systems and strategies, use of supplementary capital amounts (such as the trigger and target ratios used in the UK), and supervisory intervention or correction in appropriate cases.

This Pillar 2 supervisory review is further strengthened under Pillar 3 enhanced market discipline. This operates on the basis of the mandatory disclosure of information concerning banks' capital policies and practices. These are divided into core and supplementary disclosures with the information to be provided set out in a series of templates included within the Basel II framework documents. The objective is to facilitate the additional or parallel supervision of bank activities by the markets themselves with banks becoming subject to market discipline, in particular, either through increases in lending premia or share price falls. **13.177**

Basel III refers to the ongoing revision and update work that has been undertaken since Basel II. The same process occurred with Basel I as the authorities knew at the time of agreement and adoption in 1988 that a number of residual issues remained (such as with regard to the underlying simplicity of the model and the absence of any market risk controls under Basel I) with further work being carried out immediately. This, in particular, led to the adoption of the Basel Market Risk Amendment in 1996 and with the later Basel II amendments which reflect the continuing nature of these processes and successes. The principal capital revisions under Basel III consist of increasing Core Tier 1 capital (paid up share capital and retained earnings) from 2 per cent to 4.5 per cent with a further 2.5 per cent Conservation Buffer which increases Core Tier 1 capital to 7 per cent. A discretionary 0.2.5 per cent countercyclical buffer is also to be applied with a further systemic risk buffer of 2–3 per cent for larger banks and complex groups. Two new liquidity ratios are applied with a liquidity cover ratio ('LCR') and net stable funding ratio ('NSFR').[128] A 3 per cent Tier 1 leverage ratio has also been imposed for the first time. The Basel Committee has also adopted a number of other sets of papers in important areas including bank remuneration, bank governance, college supervision, cross border bank resolution, and macro prudential oversight.[129] **13.178**

Further changes were then expected under Basel III with regard to such matters as agreement on new measurement approaches to credit risk, the treatment of diversification effects,the assessment of complex counterparty credit risks, the treatment of interest rate risk, and firm approaches to validation of internal capital assessments. The key revisions will to a large extent be based on the increased use of internal risk management data and systems within banks including credit (as opposed to market) risk modelling as at present and new focus on interest and other risks in addition to core credit, market, and operational risk under Basel II. The underlying objective is to achieve a closer approximation of internal economic and regulatory capital within banks which should, in turn, make them more efficient at the same time as better risk managed and more stable. Much of this work on capital regulation will now be further reviewed before the final implementation date of 2019 for the Basel III amendments and any other meaures adopted in response to the global financial credit crisis. **13.179**

Capital Requirements Directive

The Basel Committee capital standards have been adopted within Europe subject to certain revision and amendment under the European Capital Requirements Directive ('CRD').[130] **13.180**

[128] On liquidity, see, eg, Basel Committee on Banking Supervision, 'Liquidity Risk: Management and Supervisory Challenges' (February 2008); and Basel Committee, 'Principles for Sound Liquidity Risk Management and Supervision' (September 2008).

[129] See GA Walker, 'Financial Markets and Exchanges' in M Blair, G Walker, and S Wiley, *Financial Markets and Exchanges Law* (n 17) paras 1.135–1.136.

[130] Capital Requirements Directive COM (2004) 486 final of 14 July 2004 ('CRD'). The Directive was approved by the European Parliament in September 2005 and by the Council in October 2005.

The Commission has produced a further proposed directive to create a CRD IV and Capital Requirements Regulation ('CRR') which will implement Basel III within the EU as well as implement other regulatory changes including on corporate governance, sanctions, rating agencies, and pro-cyclicality considered necessary following the crisis.[131] Pillars 1 and 3 amendments will generally be effective under the CRR, which will be directly applicable, with Pillar 2 revisions imposed under the CRD. The CRD package was agreed by the European Parliament on 16 April 2013 with Official Journal publication expected 1 July 2013 and implementation by 1 January 2014.[132] Two public consultations were to be undertaken by the PRA on UK implementation.

13.181 The objective of the CRD was to ensure the common application across Europe of the new international capital standards agreed by the Basel Committee under its Basel II framework. This should more closely align financial risks with capital support and enhance consumer protection, reinforce financial stability, and increase the competitiveness of the European financial industry. The CRD replaces the earlier Own Funds Directive ('OFD') (EC) 89/299 of 17 April 1989 and the Solvency Ratio Directive ('SRD') (EC) 89/647 of 18 December 1989 as consolidated under the Banking Directive (EC) 2000/12 of 20 March 2000 in respect of banks and the Capital Adequacy Directive (EC) 93/6 of 15 March 1993 in respect of investment funds.

13.182 The earlier capital regime was considered to be inadequate with the crude estimates of credit risk provided, the scope for capital avoidance or arbitrage, lack of recognition of effective risk mitigation, gaps in the risks covered (including specifically operational risk), absence of any obligation on the part of supervisors to assess the risk profile or capability of financial institutions, lack of any supervisory cooperation, and requirements for proper market disclosures as well as inflexibility in the overall regulatory framework imposed. Capital requirements and financial risks would then continue to be misaligned resulting in limited effectiveness of the prudential rules and increased risk to consumers of financial instability. A number of risks would be omitted while the most recent and most effective risk management techniques would not have been properly encouraged and recognised with firms conducting overseas business being significantly disadvantaged as against other institutions due to the disproportionate regulatory burdens imposed.

13.183 Following agreement on the Basel II rules, it was considered necessary to agree a corresponding package of measures that could be given effect to across Europe although sufficiently differentiated to create an effective new capital regime for the whole of the single marketplace and for all institutions operating within it. An appropriate degree of variation had to be included for less complex institutions, although without resulting in an inferior or 'second class' perception or condition. A number of significant modifications had to be incorporated to allow the new measures to apply to both credit institutions and investment

[131] European Commission, Proposal for a Directive on the access to the activity of credit institutions and the prudential supervision of credit institutions and investment firms and amending Directive 2002/87/EC of the European Parliament and of the Council on the supplementary supervision of credit institutions, insurance undertakings and investment firms in a financial conglomerate (Brussels 20.7.2011) COM (2011) 453 final; and European Commission, Proposal for a Regulation of the European Parliament and of the Council on prudential requirements for credit institutions and investment firms (July 2011) COM 2011 0452. Para 14.53 and (nn 84, 85, and 86).

[132] Para 13.53 and nn 66, 67, 68, and 70.

services providers. Sufficient flexibility had to be provided to ensure that the new framework could respond to changes in market and supervisory innovation. The Commission has also tried to make the text more user friendly with increased simplification and less prescription while nevertheless retaining the existing options and alternative approaches available as firms proceed from simpler to more complex calculation systems.

The legal basis for the directive was Article 47(2) of the EC Treaty which allows for measures to be adopted supporting the achievement of the Internal Market in financial services. A directive (rather than a regulation or decision) was considered to be the most appropriate instrument, although a 're-casting technique' is adopted under the Institutional Agreement 2002/C 77/01. This allows substantive amendments to be made to existing legislation without the need for any new self-standing amending directive. This is considered more appropriate in reducing complexity and increasing accessibility and comprehensibility. Some non-substantive amendments may nevertheless be made to improve the structure, layout, and drafting of relevant provisions. The general content of the new measures are set out in the explanatory memoranda attached to the CRD. A correspondence table was provided in the earlier consultation document produced on 1 July 2003. **13.184**

Some new definitions were incorporated within the CRD to clarify the meaning and relevance of certain concepts (Article 4). The obligation of credit institutions to maintain effective internal risk management systems were strengthened (Article 22). Some amendments were incorporated to the existing definition of own funds especially in connection with the modified approach to expected loss although these are stated not to be substantial (Articles 56 to 677). Credit institutions were to continue to hold adequate own funds on an ongoing basis but expressly required to state the minimum level of those funds (Articles 68 to 75). The existing solvency regime requirements for credit risk were replaced by the new standardised approach (Articles 78 to 83) and internal ratings-based approaches (Articles 84 to 89). New provisions were included on risk mitigation (Articles 90 to 93) with harmonised rules for securitisation activities and investments (Articles 94 to 101). Supporting technical provisions were set out in Annex VI. **13.185**

The Basel II proposals on operational risk were incorporated (Articles 102 to 105). This allows for the three different methodologies to be used consisting of either the basic indicator (Article 103), the standardised (Article 104), or the advanced measurement approaches (Article 105). The existing large exposures rules were amended in response to the extended recognition of credit risk mitigation provided for (Articles 106 to 119). Second Pillar supervisory review was provided for (under Articles 123 to 124) with improved coordination and cooperation between national supervisor agencies (Articles 125 to 143). Minimum disclosure requirements were imposed (Article 144) to enhance convergence of implementation and transparency with the new full Pillar 3 disclosure requirements being included (Articles 145 to 149). Additional technical provisions were provided for under Annex XII. The CRD also extends the technical areas that may be amended under the flexible revision procedure provided for under Directive (EC) 2000/12, in particular, with the distinction between core and technical rules with many of the more detailed provisions being included in the annexes to allow for their separate quick revision (Article 150). **13.186**

Equivalent revisions were made to the Directive (EEC) 93/6 (CAD) in respect of the capital adequacy obligations of investment firms and credit institutions in relation to their securities activities. These included provisions dealing with scope (Article 2), definitions (Article 3), **13.187** trading book capital (Article 11), and minimal market risk requirement (Articles 18 and 20). Further amendments are made with regard to large exposures (Article 28), valuation of positions for reporting purposes (Article 33), consolidation (Article 22), risk management and capital assessment (Article 34), supervision (Article 37), and amendment (Article 42).

13.188 The Basel II Pillar 2 requirements were dealt with under the new 'supervisory review process' rules in the CRD. This is intended to ensure that firms hold adequate capital consistent with their risk profile and strategy subject to external supervisory review and assessment. This was given effect to in the UK through an Internal Capital Adequacy Assessment Process ('ICAAP') supported by an external Supervisory Review and Evaluation Process ('SREP'). High-level guidance was developed by Committee of European Banking Supervisors ('CEBS') which has since been replaced by the European Banking Authority ('EBA') which came into operation in January 2011.[133]

13.189 The FSA conducted a number of exercises to determine to how to apply the ICAAP and SREP in practice. The FSA confirmed that Pillar 2 would not be automatically additive with the effect that higher charges will not arise in all cases. Firms would nevertheless be expected to operate above the minimum Pillar 1 requirements set and to hold sufficient additional capital to cover all risks involved with their activities at all times. Firms were expected to be responsible for assessing their own internal capital needs which will form part of the evaluation process conducted by supervisors. Senior management had to be fully involved in the Pillar 2 process. While some larger firms had already been looking towards developing an economic capital model, the FSA accepted that this would not be appropriate for all firms. Smaller firms may be able to rely on their basic Pillar 1 methodology provided that this covers all relevant risks.[134]

13.190 The Pillar 3 disclosures would generally be given effect to through revisions to many banks' existing disclosure practices as provided for under SUP and BIPRU. Firms would be expected to integrate Pillars 1, 2, and 3 with Pillar 3 being based on the firm's Pillar 1 compliance.

Prudential Sourcebook

13.191 IPRU(BANK) was originally to be replaced by the provisions set out in the Integrated Prudential Sourcebook. The FSA originally consulted on the proposed Interim Prudential Sourcebook in Consultation Paper 27 in June 2001. Provisional draft rules and guidance were set out in Annex C to CP97 with separate commentary on the main sections in Part II. A number of further papers were subsequently issued with more expected to follow on such issues as implementation of the European CRD and MiFID in the UK.

13.192 In designing the final sourcebook, the FSA had to include appropriate provisions to deal with the different exposures that arise in each of the separate financial sectors. For this purpose, a risk-by-risk approach was adopted which amplifies and extends the more general supervision by risk system adopted within the new regime constructed by the FSA. As a number of distinct financial risks can be identified within any financial system, the FSA has decided that

[133] Regulation (EU) No 1093/2010 of the European Parliament and of the Council of 24 November 2010 establishing a European Supervisory Authority (European Banking Authority), amending Decision No 716/2009/EC and repealing Commission Decision 2009/78/EC. See <http://www.eba.europa.eu/>.

[134] K Hale, 'The FSA's strategic view of regulation of the banking sector' address before the British Bankers Association, 16 February 2005.

the core exposures involved are credit risk, market risk, and insurance risk as well as liquidity risk, operational risk and group risk. A six-part framework was accordingly adopted.

The proposed Integrated Sourcebook was originally to be divided into eight separate modules with two general sections on application and general requirements (PRAG) and capital (PRCA).[135] Six further chapters were to be included on credit risk (PRCR), market risk (PRMR), liquidity risk (PRLR), operational risk (PROR), insurance risk (PRIR), and group risk (PRGR). Each module would have been divided into a number of separate chapters with a glossary of definitions also being provided. The credit risk (PRCR) would have included separate chapters on credit risk systems and controls, credit risk in the trading book, counterparty risk in the trading book, provisioning, concentration risk, collateral (credit and counterparty risk), netting (credit and counterparty risk), securitisation, credit derivatives risk, and credit risk in insurance funds. The market risk module ('PRMR') was to include market risk systems and controls, interest rate risk capital component, equity risk capital component, commodity risk capital component, securities underwriting, foreign-exchange risk, options risk, collective investment schemes, and traded endowment policies as well as use of CAD 1 models, value-at-risk models, market risk in insurance funds, and derivatives in insurance funds. Operational risk ('PROR') was to include operational risk systems and controls, outsourcing, and professional indemnity insurance. **13.193**

The original approach was subsequently revised to refer to the Integrated Prudential Sourcebook as the PRU. This was then to be divided into eight and then nine chapters. These consisted of application and general requirements (PRU 1), capital (PRU 2), credit risk (PRU 3), market risk (PRU 4), liquidity (PRU 5), operational risk (PRU 6), insurance risk (PRU 7), and group risk (PRU 8) with a further Integrated Prudential Sourcebook chapter being added (PRU 9). Relevant transitional provisions were set out in PRU TP 1 with six further schedules. Almost final text was released in October 2003.[136] **13.194**

The FSA announced during 2004 that a further restructuring was to be considered in light of the implementation obligations imposed under the European CRD of 14 July 2004 which would substantially amend the Banking Consolidation Directive (EC) 2000/12 and the CAD (EC) 93/6. The prudential and systems and controls material in the Handbook would be revised to make them more accessible to specialised firms and to improve navigability although the idea of grouping material by risk would be retained. This was also considered desirable to align more closely the structure of the PRU with the FSA's 'copy-out' approach to European implementation and avoid unnecessary 'super-equivalence' or complex drafting in non-scope areas. With its copy-out approach to implementation, the FSA will restate relevant EU measures with more additional (super-equivalent) obligations only being added where this is considered necessary to secure its statutory objectives or to clarify the operation **13.195**

[135] FSA, Integrated Prudential Sourcebook (June 2001), Consultation Paper 97; and FSA, Integrated Prudential Sourcebook, Annex C: Draft Rules and Guidance (June 2001), Consultation Paper 97a. See also FSA, Integrated Prudential Sourcebook—timetable for implementation (November 2001), Consultation Paper 115. Two subsequent consultation papers were then released in 2002 with a Policy Statement in October 2003. FSA, 'Liquidity Risk in the Integrated Prudential Sourcebook—Systems and controls chapter' (March 2002) Consultation Paper 128; and FSA, 'Operational risk systems and controls' (June 2002) Consultation Paper 142; and FSA, 'Integrated Prudential Sourcebook—Near-final text on prudential risks systems and controls' (October 2003). On early policy approach, see FSA, 'The FSA's approach to setting prudential standards' (1999), CP31.

[136] FSA, 'Integrated Prudential Sourcebook—Near-final text on prudential risks systems and controls' (October 2003).

or application of relevant rules. A more general correspondence and comparability of relevant requirements should also be achieved between UK and European measures.

13.196 The FSA issued a further policy statement on Strengthening Capital Standards 2 in July 2006 (CP06/3).[137] This followed two earlier consultation papers on restructuring the Handbook and common platform firms (CP06/10 and CP06/09) and a following feedback statement in July 2006 (PS06/6).[138] The core provisions on the revision of the capital regime were set out in PS06/6 which included specific chapters on each of the main capital tranches in CP06/3. This dealt with the clarity and accessibility of copy-out rules, key policy decisions and updates, status of the material produced by the CEBS, individual guidance, international implementation, and outstanding issues. The FSA was committed to the adoption of a copy-out approach to UK implementation with only limited super-equivalence and sufficient flexibility where necessary. The clarity and accessibility of the text would be dealt with through extended guidance and navigational tables and worked examples with personal handbooks being provided containing dedicated sets of relevant provisions. Personal handbooks would be issued in response to ten specific questions concerning firms' business activities.

13.197 Certain difficulties remained with regard to the operation of provisions based on effective home host relations and, in particular, with regard to firms adopting an advanced approach under Pillar 1 in more than one jurisdiction and the operation of Pillar 2 with regard to international groups. Guidelines had been produced by the CEBS with further recommendations being issued by the Basel Accord Implementation Group ('AIG') for non-EEA countries. A series of 'regulatory colleges' had also been set up to allow authorities to work together effectively and to limit duplication of activity.

13.198 A number of industry groups had been set up to assist the FSA in implementing the new capital provisions within the UK and, in particular, preparing relevant measures. A Basel/CRD Implementation Advisory Group ('BIAG') was established with representatives from the FSA, the Treasury and Bank of England as well as trade associations and regulated firms to discuss strategic objectives, implementation review, and exchange of information and timetable issues. A number of other groups were also set up including the Banks and Investment Firms Commodity Standing Group ('BIFCOM'), the Capital and Groups Standing Group ('CGSG'), the Commodity Standing Group ('COMSG'), the Covered Bond Standing Group ('CBSG'), the Credit Risk Mitigation Standing Group ('CRMSG'), the Credit Risk Standing Group ('CRSG'), the Market Risk and Trading Books Standing Group ('MRTSG'), the Operational Risk Standing Group ('ORSG'), the Pillar Two Standing Group ('PTSG'), and the Securitisation Standing Group ('SSG').

13.199 Following this work, the final Integrated Prudential Sourcebook has since been divided into a number of separate sub-sourcebooks. This consists of a revised set of common provisions applicable to all firms ('GENPRU') with separate requirements for banks and investment firms ('BIPRU') and insurance and Lloyd's managing agents ('INSPRU') as well as unit trust managers and UCITS firms ('UPRU') and mortgage and insurance mediation firms

[137] FSA CP06/3, 'Strengthening Capital Standards 2' (July 2006).

[138] FSA CP06/10, 'Strengthening Capital Standards—Restructuring the Handbook' (May 2006); FSA CP06/09, 'Organisational Systems and Controls—Common Platform for Firms' (May 2006); and FSA PS06/6, 'Strengthening Capital Standards Figures 2—Feedback on CP06/3' (July 2006).

('MIPRU'). Investment firms not subject to the CRD were to be dealt with under INVPRU with other residual friendly societies in FPRU. The provisions on financial groups (originally contained in PRU 8.4) have been moved to GENPRU 3.1).

Banks and investment firms are now subject to the provisions contained in GENPRU, **13.200** BIPRU, and the revised post-MiFID SYSC. Advanced capital measures came into effect on 1 January 2008 although firms had the option of complying with IPRU(Bank) during 2007 or adopting the revised standard provisions contained in BIPRU subject to certain exceptions. The liquidity provisions within IPRU(Bank) were continued on a provisional basis until revised measures could be agreed at the international and European levels with the issue being further reconsidered following the Northern Rock crisis. This applies with regard to the provisions on mismatch liquidity ('LM') and sterling stock liquidity ('LS') in volume 2 of IPRU(Bank). Revised liquidity requirements have since been included as BIPRU 12.

Building societies are also subject to GENPRU, BIPRU, and the revised SYSC although the **13.201** constitutional provisions within volume 2 of IPRU(BSOC) have been retained and reissued in the form of a separate Regulatory Guide. The Building Society sourcebook (BSOCS) is now contained in the PRA Handbook and the Buidling Society Regulatory Guide (BSOG) in the FCA Handbook. A new common platform regime was created for firms subject to both the EU CRD and MiFID with effect from 1 November 2007 on implementation of MiFID. Seven new chapters have been inserted within SYSC for common platform firms which expand the general management and internal systems and controls requirements set out in PRIN 3. (Firms must take reasonable care to organise and control their affairs responsibly and effectively with adequate risk management systems.) IPRU(INV) would continue in effect for firms not subject to BIPRU.

These are important provisions which assisted the construction of a more coordinated but **13.202** still not fully integrated Handbook of Rules and Guidance in the UK. A single set of relevant prudential obligations was to have been provided for all types of financial firms. A common risk-based methodology had to be adjusted to reflect the separate and distinct underlying exposures involved. The principal compromise that was been made to the use of the original risk-by-risk approach was to divide the sourcebook into a number of separate sub-sourcebooks to reflect the individual categories of financial institutions used under the European financial directives rather than operate on a purely risk basis. This was, in turn, necessary to give effect to the copy-out implementation approach adopted and to simplify transparency and accessibility of relevant measures within the UK. This integrated prudential model has then been split between the PRA and FCA for different types of regulated entities.

The residual gap that remained for some time was with regard to liquidity rather than capi- **13.203** tal controls. The fallout from the credit crisis in 2007 and 2008 revealed the importance of liquidity and funding risk and the dependence of banks and other financial institutions on stable and effective inter-bank markets. Substantially tightened requirements were initially proposed by the FSA with the Basel Committee also being able to incorporate liquidity ratios within its Basel III amendments which was the first time that this was possible at the international level, with liquidity traditionally being left for domestic control. Parallel progress will be needed in these areas before any complete new regime will have been created.

General Prudential Sourcebook ('GENPRU')

13.204 The general provisions applicable to banks, building societies, BIPRU investment firms, insurers, and groups containing such firms are now set out in GENPRU which came into effect on 1 January 2007. This restates many of the earlier provisions contained in the Integrated Prudential Sourcebook (PRU) including financial resources, risk identification and assessment, minimum capital resources, and the definition of capital including relevant deductions and other risks.

13.205 GENPRU 1 is concerned with the identification and assessment of risks that may undermine the ability of firms to cover their liabilities as they fall due, how those risks are dealt with, and the amount and nature of the financial resources considered necessary to do so. Adequate financial resources and systems and controls are stated to be necessary for the effective management of prudential risk (GENPRU 1.2.12G). Firms must maintain at all times overall financial resources (including capital and liquidity resources) that are adequate both as to amount and quality to ensure that there is no significant risk that their liabilities cannot be met as they fall due (GENPRU 1.2.26R).

13.206 Firms must have sound, effective, and complete processes, strategies, and systems to assess and maintain on an ongoing basis the amounts, types, and distribution of financial resources, capital resources, and internal capital required to cover all relevant risk including credit risk, market risk, liquidity risk, operational risk, insurance risk, concentration risk, residual risk, securitisation risk, business risk, interest rate risk, pension obligation and group risk to the extent relevant (GENPRU 1.2.30R). Pillar 2 processes, strategies, and systems must be comprehensive and proportionate to the nature, scale, and complexity of a firm's activities (GENPRU 1.2.35R). Firms must also carry out stress tests and scenario analysis appropriate to the nature of each major source of risk (GENPRU 1.2.42R).

13.207 GENPRU 2.2. contains the revised provisions on the definition and measurement of capital. Firms must maintain at all times capital resources equal to or in excess of their variable capital requirement (GENPRU 2.1.40R). This is the aggregate of the credit risk capital requirement, market risk capital requirement, and operational risk market requirement for banks and building societies and full scope BIPRU investment firms (GENPRU 2.1.45R). Firms must also maintain on an initial and continuing basis capital resources equal to or in excess of their Base Capital Resources Requirement (GENPRU 2.1.41 and 42R). This includes Tier 1 capital, upper and lower Tier 2 capital, Tier 3 capital for investment firms, non-standard capital instruments and capital deductions, as well as limits and applications (GENPRU 2.2.9G–2.2.276).

13.208 Core Tier 1 capital includes permanent share capital, profit and loss account and other reserves, share premium account, externally verified interim net profits, eligible partnership capital, eligible LLP members' capital, and sole trader capital with other Tier 1 capital consisting of perpetual non-cumulative preference shares. Upper Tier 2 capital consists of perpetual cumulative preference shares, perpetual subordinated debt, perpetual subordinated securities, revaluation reserves, general/collective provisions and surplus provisions with lower Tier 2 being made up of fixed term preference shares, long-term (five-year) subordinated debt, and fixed term subordinated securities. Upper Tier 3 capital consists of short-term (two-year) subordinated debt for investment firms and lower Tier 3 capital net interim trading book profits. Innovative Tier 1 capital has also been included for building societies and investment firms.

Required deductions from Tier 1 capital are investments in own shares, intangible assets, excess drawings over profits for partnerships and limited liability partnerships, and net losses on equities held in the for sale asset category. Deductions from total Tier 1 and Tier 2 include qualifying holdings, material holdings, expected loss amounts and other negative amounts, securitisation positions, reciprocal cross-holdings, investments in subsidiary undertakings, and participations not already deducted as well as connected lending of a capital nature. Excess trading book position and free deliveries are to be deducted from total capital. Summary tables are provided in the Annexes to GENPRU 2 and, in particular, Annex 2 for banks. **13.209**

BIPRU firms are also required to comply with the provisions on individual capital adequacy (BIPRU 2.2), common provisions (BIPRU 4.3), group risk and consolidation (BIPRU 8), concentration risk requirements (BIPRU 10), and settlement and counter party risk (BIPRU 14). Financial conglomerates are dealt with under GENPRU 3. **13.210**

Prudential Sourcebook ('BIPRU')

The revised capital and financial provisions for banks, building societies, and investment firms are set out in BIPRU. BIPRU is made up of 14 sections with additional transitional provisions and schedules. These consist of application (BIPRU 1), capital (BIPRU 2), standardised credit risk (BIPRU 3), the IRB approach (BIPRU 4), credit risk mitigation (BIPRU 5), operational risk (BIPRU 6), market risk (BIPRU 7), group risk consolidation (BIPRU 8), securitisation (BIPRU 9), large exposure risk requirements (BIPRU 10), disclosure under Pillar 3 (BIPRU 11), liquidity risk (BIPRU 12), counterparty risk exposure for financial derivatives, securities financing and loan settlement transactions (BIPRU 13), and settlement and counterparty risk (BIPRU 14). Complex transitional provisions applied with regard to the application of GENPRU and BIPRU. BIPRU will be further amended on implementation of the EU CRD IV with the Capital Requirements Regulation (CRR) having direct effect. Implementation was expected in January 2014. **13.211**

Application—BIPRU 1

BIPRU applies to banks, building societies, BIPRU investment firms, and groups containing such firms. Each chapter of BIPRU is separately applied. BIPRU applies to a firm in relation to the whole of its business except where a particular provision otherwise provides. BIPRU 1 includes provisions concerning the definition of the trading book (BIPRU 1.2), special provisions on advanced approaches and waivers (1.3) and the disapplication of a right of action for breach under section 150 of FSMA (1.4). **13.212**

Capital—BIPRU 2

BIPRU contains rules and guidance concerning solo consolidation (2.1), internal capital adequacy standards (2.2), and interest rate risk in the non-trading book (2.3). Firms must incorporate in the calculation of their main Pillar 1 rules (and large exposures requirement under BIPRU 10) each subsidiary undertaking to which any solo consolidation waiver applies except with regard to the base capital resources requirement. Firms must treat themselves and each such subsidiary as a single undertaking. **13.213**

BIPRU 2.2 provides for the operation of the internal capital adequacy assessment process (ICAAP) and the supervisory review and evaluation process or SREP (BIPRU 2.2.4G). **13.214**

Firms must carry out regular assessments of the amounts, types, and distribution of financial resources, capital resources, and internal capital considered adequate to cover the nature and level of the risks to which they are exposed under the ICAAP. Where a firm is a member of a group, it should base its ICAAP on the consolidated financial position of the group. The firm should ensure that its ICAAP is the responsibility of its governing body, reported to the governing body, and forms an integral part of its management process and decision-making culture. The regulators will review the firm's ICAAP (and any IRB stress tests) as part of its SREP.

13.215 The purpose of the SREP is to allow the regulators to review the arrangements, strategies, and processes and mechanisms implemented by the firm to comply with GENPRU, BIPRU, and SYSC and any other requirements imposed under the regulatory system. It will also determine whether such arrangements ensure a sound management and coverage of the risks concerned and require the firm where necessary to take any additional actions or steps to address any failures identified. The regulators may give firms individual capital guidance including a statement of the amount and quality of capital the regulators consider that the firm requires to comply with its overall financial adequacy requirement. BIPRU 2.2 contains further guidance on the risks covered within the ICAAP.

13.216 Separate provisions are included concerning interest rate risk in the non-trading book. This may apply with regard to risks relating to the mismatch or repricing of assets and liabilities and off-balance sheet short and long positions, risks arising from hedging exposures under different conditions, risks relating to transaction uncertainties and risks from consumers redeeming fixed rate products as market rates change. Firms must carry out an evaluation of their exposures to interest rates arising from their non-trading activities. This must include the effect of a sudden and unexpected parallel change in the interest rates of 200 basis points in both directions with the regulators being notified where the economic value of the firm may decline by more than 20 per cent of its capital resources in the event of such an event. Additional conditions apply with regard to more complex firms with firms being required to maintain written records of their assessments. The regulators will periodically review whether the level of shock referred to is appropriate in light of changing circumstances and the general level of interest rates and volatility.

Standardised Credit Risk Approach—BIPRU 3

13.217 BIPRU contains the revised provisions concerning the minimum capital requirements to be held under the standardised approach to credit risk contained in Basel II Pillar 1 and the CRD. This generally applies the earlier minimum 8 per cent capital adequacy regime subject to amendment to make this more risk-sensitive and responsive. The minimum 8 per cent of total risk weighted exposure amounts is retained as the core credit risk capital component. Greater risk sensitivity is nevertheless created through the use of external credit ratings. Firms are required to assign their credit exposures across 16 classes and apply more risk-sensitive weightings to each ranging from 0 per cent to 150 per cent depending upon the perceived credit quality of the counterparty.

13.218 Separate provisions apply with regard to central governments and central banks, regional governments and local authorities, administrative bodies and non- commercial undertakings, multilateral development banks, international organisations, financial institutions, corporate bodies, retail exposures, real estate property, past-due items, regulatory high-risk categories, covered bonds, securitisation positions, short-term claims on institutions and corporates, collective investment undertakings and other items. Relevant risk weights are set out in BIPRU 3.4. Firms that only have incidental credit risk exposures may use the 'simplified standardised approach' which does not use external credit risk weightings. Firms can also apply a single risk weight to all exposures in each class as under the previous regime. Rating agency assessments are dealt with under BIPRU 3.6 and off-balance sheets items in BIPRU 3.7.

IRB Approach—BIPRU 4

The Basel/CRD internal ratings-based ('IRB') approach is implemented under BIPRU 4. Capital requirements are based on a firm's internal estimates of certain parameters which are as specified in the BCD. Exposures are divided into a number of distinct classes (with special rules for purchased receivables). The foundation IRB approach is available for sovereign, institution, and corporate exposure classes using a firm's own estimates of probability of default ('PD'). Advanced IRB approaches allow firms to use their own estimates of loss given default ('LGD') and supporting conversion factors. Firms use own estimates of PD (LGD) and conversion factors for retail exposures. Two approaches based on market-based measures or own estimates of PD only can be used in connection with equity exposures. A separate sub-class of specialised lending exposures applies in connection with corporate exposures. BIPRU 4 contains specific provisions with regard to high-level material (4.2), common provisions (4.3), corporates, institutions, and sovereigns (4.4), standardised lending exposures (4.5), retail exposures (4.6), equity exposures (4.7), purchased receivables (4.8), securitisation (4.9), and credit risk mitigation (4.10). **13.219**

Credit Risk Mitigation—BIPRU 5

BIPRU 5 implements the provisions concerning the recognition of techniques used to reduce the credit risk associated with a particular exposure. The credit risk mitigation ('CRM') rules allow firms to hold lower capital under either the standardised or IRB approaches. CRM can be achieved either through the use of funded or unfunded protection. Funded protection applies with regard to the taking of rights over assets or reducing liabilities in the event that the borrower does not pay (such as under a mortgage) with unfunded protection being provided by third parties (such as under a guarantee or insurance policy). CRM techniques include netting, collateral, guarantees, and credit derivatives. BIPRU 5 generally applies to firms relying on the standardised approach with BIPRU 4.10 being used for IRB approaches. **13.220**

Certain high-level principles have to be considered to ensure that a particular type of CRM can provide sufficiently effective protection against credit risk. The main principles of credit risk mitigation are set out in BIPRU 5.2. BIPRU contains additional provisions concerning on-balance sheet netting (5.3), financial collateral (5.4), other funded credit risk mitigation including deposits and life insurance policies or other purchased instruments and credit linked notes (5.5), master netting agreements (5.6), unfunded credit protection (5.7), maturity mismatches (5.8), and CRM combinations (5.9). **13.221**

Operational Risk—BIPRU 6

The new operational risk regime created under Basel II is applied under BIPRU 6. Firms are required to hold capital to cover operational risk losses and maintain appropriate systems and controls to manage operational risk and explain how the operational risk capital requirement ('ORCR') is calculated. Firms can generally either use a basic indicator approach, standardised approach, or advanced measurement approach ('AMA'). The ORCR under the basic indicator approach is stated to be equal to 15 per cent of the relevant indicator **13.222** as defined. Firms must divide their activities into a number of business lines under the standardised approach (including corporate finance, trading and sales, retail brokerage, commercial banking, retail banking, payment and settlement, agency services, and asset management). Firms must satisfy certain general risk management standards imposed under SYSC as well as additional qualitative and quantitative standards to be able to make use of the AMA approach to operational risk. The AMA must produce a practical and appropriate 99.9 per cent confidence level, produce sufficiently robust overall model outputs, and be reviewed on an ongoing basis.

Market Risk—BIPRU 7

13.223 BIPRU 7 reapplies the market risk rules originally developed in the Basel Committee 1996 Market Risk Amendment and EU CAD. These were previously contained in IPRU(BANK) and IPRU(INV) Chapter 10. The earlier provisions are generally restated with additional measures on collective investment undertakings ('CIUs'), interest rate specific risk treatments and the modelling of default risk under value-at-risk ('VAR') models.

13.224 The rules generally impose capital requirements on interest rate related instruments (bonds and debentures), equities, and CIUs in the trading book and foreign exchange risk and commodities risk across the firm. Firms are required to mark-to-market ('MTM') their positions daily. Firms can either adopt a standard 'building block' or internal models-based approach to the calculation of their minimum capital requirements. Under the standard rules, identical or similar long and short positions are netted with a percentage capital haircut or position risk addition ('PRA') being calculated on a percentage basis. The haircut varies with the risks involved. Interest rate and equity exposures are divided into general risk (market factors) and specific risk (individual issuer) components. Specific rules are imposed with regard to interest rate risk (BIPRU 7.2), equities (7.3), commodities (7.4), foreign exchange (7.5), options (7.6), CIUs (7.7), and credit derivatives (7.11). Firms can also use more sophisticated 'CAD 1 models' including interest rate pre-processing models (to net positions within certain maturity bands before applying the standard rules for general interest rate risk) and options aggregation models (to recognise hedging within options portfolios). The CAD 1 rules and guidance are contained in BIPRU 7.9.

13.225 Firms can separately apply for waivers to use VAR models. The firms have to comply with specific quantitative and qualitative minimum criteria (BIPRU 7.10). Separate provisions apply with regard to underwriting commitments (BIPRU 7.8). Valuation is dealt with in GENPRU 1.3 and trading book positions in BIPRU 1.2.

Group Risk—BIPRU 8

13.226 Group capital resources and resource requirements are imposed with regard to larger financial groups. The detailed rules and guidance on consolidated capital requirements for BIPRU firms and groups are contained in BIPRU 8. This applies with regard to UK consolidation groups, non-EEA sub-groups and parent financial holding companies. These implement the relevant provisions contained in the BCD and CAD. This replaces IPRU(BANK) consolidated supervision and IPRU(INV) Chapter 14. Firms not subject to consolidated supervision under BIPRU 8 may still be subject to IPRU(INV) Chapter 14 such as commodities firms under an Article 48(2) CRD exemption. Diagrams (decision trees) are provided to identify relevant groups.

13.227 Some new elements are included within the rules. The CRD provisions apply consolidation at each Member State level rather than only to the ultimate parent firm within the EEA.

A non-EEA sub-group exists where a subsidiary BIPRU firm or its parent (where it is a financial holding company (FHC)) has a subsidiary or participation in an institution, financial institution, or asset management company established outside the EEA. Groups that contain only limited licence or limited activity investment firms are exempt subject to minimum conditions. Groups that do not contain credit institutions or investment firms dealing on own account are not subject to consolidated operational risk requirements. Firms can include requirements calculated using non-EEA regulations provided that they are deemed to be equivalent to the CRD rules. A list of equivalent measures is provided in BIPRU 8 Annex 6R. This includes those used in the USA, Australia, Canada, Switzerland, Japan, South Africa, Hong Kong, Singapore, India, and Korea measures governing market risk, credit risk, and operational risk.

The application of the consolidation provisions is dealt with under GENPRU 1.3. Financial conglomerates are covered in GENPRU 3.1 with banking and investment services groups headed by a non-EEA parent undertaking in GENPRU 3.2. Embedded waivers (including groups) are dealt with under BIPRU 1.3 and consolidated Pillar 3 requirements under BIPRU 11. **13.228**

Securitisation—BIPRU 9

New securitisation measures are provided for under BIPRU 9. This replaces the securitisation and asset transfer provisions in IPRU(BANK) Chapter SE and IPRU(BSOC). This includes specific rules dealing with exposures to tranched positions arising under a securitisation. **13.229**

Firms must calculate the risk weight exposure amounts for securitisation positions under BIPRU 9. Firms must apply the securitisation framework to determine regulatory capital requirements on exposures arising from traditional and synthetic securitisations or similar structures that contain equivalent features. Traditional securitisation involves the economic transfer of exposures to a special purpose entity ('SPE') which issues new securities following a full transfer of ownership with securities not representing payment obligations of the originator. Synthetic securitisations provide for the tranching of risk through the use of credit derivatives or guarantees with the exposure pool not being removed from the balance sheet of the originator. Firms must look to the economic substance of a transaction to determine whether the securitisation framework is applicable for the purposes of determining regulatory capital. **13.230**

The securitisation rules apply both with regard to whether the capital position of the originator can be reduced in some way as well as that of firms holding relevant securitisation positions. Different results may apply in each case. Securitisation positions include loans, liquidity facilities, and counterparty exposures under derivative positions. **13.231**

Specific provisions apply with regard to originators. The originator is either the originator of the underlying exposures that are securitised or the securitisation. A sponsor of an asset-backed commercial paper ('ABCP') conduit is generally not considered an originator unless the sponsor is economically the same. The provisions impose three operational requirements with regard to effective risk transfer, significant risk transfer, and the absence of implicit support. **13.232**

Securitisation recognition may be achieved under either a standardised or internal ratings base (IRB) approach. This is dependent on the Pillar 1 minimum capital requirement applied with regard to the underlying portfolio of securitised exposures. Under the standardised **13.233** method, the risk weighted asset amount of a securitised exposure is calculated by multiplying the amount of the position by a specified risk weight (varying from 20 per cent, 50 per cent, 100 per cent, 350 per cent, and 1,250 per cent). Special rules apply with regard to unrated securitisation positions. The IRB approach uses three potential calculations with a ratings-based approach ('RBA'), internal assessment approach ('IAA'), and supervisory formula method (SF). Ratings are similar to the standardised approach although the tables are more sophisticated and include a granularity element. IAA only applies to ABCP programme exposures and is generally concerned with liquidity facilities and credit enhancement. A firm's internal assessment process is mapped against an external credit assessment institution ('ECAI'). SF applies with regard to non-rated exposures with five inputs being used. Special rules apply with regard to securitisations containing early amortisation provisions.

Large Exposures—BIPRU 10

13.234 BIPRU 10 formerly applied with regard to large exposures and concentration risk capital component ('CNCOM'). New large exposure requirements were adopted following the FSA Large Exposures Instrument in 2010.[139] A large exposure is any total exposure to a counterparty, or group of connected counterparties, in a firm's trading book or non-trading book which exceeds 10 per cent of the firm's capital resources. Large exposures may threaten the financial position of a firm through increased counterparty risk. Various limits are imposed following relevant EU requirements. These include a 25 per cent ceiling on exposures to the same counterparty and an 800 per cent total limit with regard to non-trading book items. A 500 per cent limit is imposed on exposures to the same counterparty for up to 10 business days on trading book items. A 600 per cent limit applies with regard to exposures held for over 10 days. Special rules apply with regard to the application of these provisions to integrated groups ('UKIGs') and wider integrated groups ('WIGs'). The IG rules are relevant to parents or subsidiary companies within a larger financial group with one or more exposures to each other. The measures apply on a solo and consolidated basis.

Disclosure—BIPRU 11

13.235 New disclosure requirements are imposed under BIPRU 11 which give effect to the Basel Committee and CRD Pillar 3 obligations. The disclosure provisions apply with regard to individual firms, EEA parent institutions, significant subsidiaries of EEA parent institutions or firms controlled by an EEA parent financial holding company, and a significant subsidiary of an EEA parent financial holding company. Specific measures apply with regard to information to be disclosed, frequency and verification, technical criteria on disclosure and content (including risk management objectives and policies, capital resources, credit risk and dilution risk, credit and market risk disclosures, interest rate risk, and securitisation), and IRB and credit risk mitigation disclosure.

Liquidity—BIPRU 12

13.236 Liquidity is dealt with under BIPRU12. The FSA had undertaken a detailed examination of liquidity regulation in the period immediately following the UK financial crisis. The FSA conducted a substantial review with a view to overhauling the UK liquidity regime. Consultation papers were published in December 2008, April 2009, and June 2009 with

[139] FSA, *Capital Requirements Directive (Large Exposures) Instrument 2010* (FSA 2010/41). The CEBS had published, *Guidelines on the implementation of the revised large exposures regime* (December 2011).

a substantial Policy Statement on *Strengthening liquidity standards* in October 2009.[140] The FSA had also been working with the then Committee of European Banking Supervisors and the Liquidity Working Group within the Basel Committee and with UK stakeholder involvement being carried out through its Liquidity Advisory Group.

BIPRU applies to BIPRU firms, incoming EEA firms and third-country BIPRU firms. Firms must maintain liquidity resources at all times that are adequate as to amount and quality to ensure that there is no significant risk that their liabilities cannot be met as they fall due (BIPRU 12.2.1R). This is referred to as the overall liquidity adequacy rule. Firms must ensure that their liquidity resources include an adequate buffer of high-quality unencumbered assets and that they maintain a prudent funding profile (BIPRU 12.2.8R). Firms generally have to undergo an Individual Liquidity Adequacy Assessment ('ILAA') for standard firms or an Individual Liquidity Systems Assessment ('ILSA') for simplified firms as well as a Supervisory Liquidity Review Process ('SLRP') (BIPRU 12.2.14G). Additional provisions apply with regard to liquidity risk management, stress testing and contingency funding, Individual Liquidity Adequacy Standards ('ILAS') and Simplified ILAS, liquidity assets buffer, cross-border and intra-group liquidity management, and individual liquidity guidance and regulatory intervention (BIPRU 12.3–9). **13.237**

Counterparty Risk—BIPRU 13

Counterparty risk is concerned with default before final settlement on a transaction. Trading book exposures are covered by the counterparty rules with non-trading book transactions being dealt with under the credit risk provisions. While traditional credit risk can be assessed at the time the transaction is entered into, the potential exposure under a financial derivative or securities financing transaction ('SFT') may vary over the life of the transaction. An assessment is accordingly made of both the mark-to-market ('MTM') value and potential future exposure ('PFE'). Counterparty exposures are calculated on a position-by-position basis unless a legally enforceable netting agreement applies. Firms may use either an MTM method, standardised method, or internal model method. Only the MTM option was previously available. BIPRU 13 applies to the calculation of counterparty risk exposure values for financial derivatives, securities financing transactions, and long settlement transactions. CCR may be calculated on a mark-to-market, standardised, or internal model basis with specific provisions on contractual netting and securities financing transactions. **13.238**

Under the MTM option, the exposure is calculated as the MTM plus the PFE with the PFE being determined as a percentage of the notional value of the contract which varies having regard to product and maturity. The standardised method is more risk-sensitive with exposures being classified (or bucketed). An effective expected positive exposure (effective EPE) is calculated under the internal model approach. Specified quantitative and qualitative minimum criteria again apply before waivers are granted to use internal models and SFTs. **13.239**

Unsettled transactions and free deliveries—BIPRU 14

BIPRU 14 deals with settlement and counterparty risk including calculation on settled transactions and free deliveries. BIPRU 14 contains the capital requirements with regard to unsettled **13.240**

[140] FSA, *Strengthening liquidity standards* (December 2008) CP08/22; FSA, *Strengthening liquidity standards 2: Liquidity reporting* (April 2009) CP09/13; FSA, *Strengthening liquidity standards 3: Liquidity transitional measures* (June 2009) CP09/14; and FSA, *Strengthening liquidity standards including feedback on CP08/22, CP09/13, CP09/14* (October 2009).

transactions and free deliveries. Unsettled transactions are those dealt with through a delivery versus payment DVP system providing for the simultaneous exchange of securities for cash with the specific transaction not settling. The loss is the difference between the transaction value at the agreed settlement price and current market price. Free deliveries arise where one party has paid for securities before receiving them or delivered securities before receiving payment. The potential loss is the full amount of the cash paid or securities delivered. The rules then apply with regard to transactions that have been confirmed but not settled. The rules do not apply with regard to repos, securities and commodities borrowing or lending, long settlement transactions, or one-way cash payments due under OTC derivative transactions.

13.241 The provisions with regard to unsettled transactions are generally the same as under the earlier rules with some minor amendments. Firms have a five-day grace period where no charge applies with capital being calculated on the basis of a percentage of the difference between the agreed settlement price and current market value up to 48 days after which the full difference applies. Under the free delivery rules, firms must deduct the full value of the transaction from their capital resources after five days following the due settlement date although greater flexibility is applied with the use of either a standardised or IRB approach.

Ring-Fencing

13.242 The Banking Reform Bill was introduced to Parliament in February 2013 with an amended copy being produced in April 2013 as amended in Public Bill Committee.[141] The final Financial Services (Banking Reform) Act received Royal Assent on 18 December 2013. The Act contains specific provision governing ring-fencing,[142] depositor preference, and FSCS matters,[143] revision of the bail-in stabilisation option,[144] new provisions on approval of persons working in the financial services sector,[145] the establishment of a Payment System Regulator,[146] the administration of infrastructure system operators,[147] and miscellaneous and final provisions.[148]

13.243 The Act provides for amendment to the objectives of the PRA and FCA. The PRA is required to exercise its functions to protect the continuity of core services in acting in relation to ring-fenced matters.[149] The FCA is assigned a new Continuity Objective where a core activity is not regulated by the PRA.[150] The Continuity Objective is defined as protecting the

---

141 Financial Services (Banking Reform) Bill 130 2012-2013; and Financial Services (Banking Reform) Bill 159 2012-2013. See also Financial Services (Banking Reform) Bill Explanatory Notes Bill 130 EN 2012-2013. Amended Bills HC 159 2012-2013 and 002 and 142 2013-2014 and HL 038, 54, 62 and 67 2013-2014 were subsequently produced following Parliamentary debate and government revision with Bill 62 2013-2014 including inter alia additional provisions on Bail-in stabilisation option (Part 3 Bill), Conduct of persons working in financial services sector (Part 4), Regulation of payment systems (Part 5) and Special administration for operators of certain infrastructure systems (Part 6). On the work of the Independent Commission on Banking (ICB) and Parliamentary Commission on Banking Standards (PCBS), Chapter 1 paras 1.79-80 and 1.81.

142 ss 1-7 and 8-12 FS(BR)A 2013.

143 ss 13 and 14-16 FS(BR)A 2013.

144 s 17 FS(BR)A 2013.

145 ss 18-38 FS(BR)A 2013.

146 ss 39-110 FS(BR)A 2013.

147 ss 111-128 FS(BR)A 2013.

148 ss 129-141 and 142-148 FS(BR)A 2013.

149 s 2B(3) FSMA.

150 s 1IA FSMA.

continuity of the provision of core services in the UK.[151] The conditions for the exercise of the PRA of its powers of FCA direction are amended to include potential threats to the continuity of core services in the UK.[152] A new Part 9B is to be incorporated within the FSMA to deal with ring-fencing.[153] This follows the revised Part 9A on FCA and PRA rules and guidance.[154] A ring-fenced body means a UK institution that carries on one or more core activities which refers to accepting deposits except in circumstances specified by the Treasury by order.[155]

Core services and excluded activities are separately defined.[156] Core services involve the accepting of deposits or other payments into accounts involving a core activity, facilities for withdrawing money or making payments from such an account or account overdraft facilities including any other services specified by the Treasury by order. Excluded activities relate to dealing in investments as principal unless subject to Treasury exemption and any other activities specified by Treasury by order. The Treasury may impose separate prohibitions on the entering into transactions of a specified kind or with persons of a specified class, establishing or maintaining a branch in a specified country or territory, and holding shares or voting power in companies of a specified description.[157] **13.244**

Regulations may authorise or require the PRA or FCA to make relevant rules or instruments or refer to specified publications.[158] Ring-fenced bodies cannot carry on an excluded activity or act in contravention with a prohibition.[159] Contravention does not constitute an offence, make the transaction void or unenforceable, or give rise to an action for breach of statutory duty.[160] Rules must specifically ensure the effective provision of services or facilities to the ring-fenced body to allow it to carry on the core activity and make suitable provision for group ring-fencing purposes.[161] The PRA, and if necessary, the FCA are to keep their ring-fencing rules under review.[162] Additional provision is included with regard to pension provision, loss-absorbency, and Parliamentary approval through affirmative procedure.[163] **13.245**

FSMA was to be separately amended to require that the directors of ring-fenced bodies were approved persons although further provisions were subsequently added on professional standards and with a new offence of causing a financial institution to fail being created.[164] The PRA is to include ring-fencing in its annual report.[165] Special provision is included with regard to ring-fencing transfer schemes.[166] The Treasury may extend the application of the ring-fencing requirements to building societies by separate regulation.[167] **13.246**

---

151 s 1EA FSMA.
152 s 3I(4)(c) FSMA.
153 s 4 FS(BR)A 2013.
154 s 24 FSA 2012.
155 s 142A(1) and 142B(2) FSMA as amended.
156 ss 142C and 142D FSMA as amended.
157 s 142E FSMA as amended.
158 s 142F FSMA as amended.
159 s 142G(1) FSMA as amended.
160 s 142G(2) FSMA as amended.
161 s 142H(1) FSMA as amended.
162 s 142 J FSMA as amended.
163 ss 142 K–N FSMA as amended.
164 cl 5 Bill 130 and Part 4 Bill 62. This is now provided for under s 36 FS(BR)A 2013.
165 s 5 FS(BR)A 2013.
166 s 6 FS(BR)A 2013.
167 s 7 FS(BR)A 2013. Further amendments were included on building societies in Bill 62 Schedule 9.

13.247 The Insolvency Act 1986 is amended to make deposits covered by the FSCS preferential debts.[168] Preferential debts are unsecured debts that have to be paid in priority to other claims which will allow the FSCS to recover ahead of other creditors including unsecured depositors.[169] The FSCS scheme manager is to consider the need for efficiency and effectiveness in the manner in which it discharges its functions.[170] The manager may be required to provide specified information to the Treasury.[171] The manager must have a chief executive who is a member of the board.[172]

13.248 The Treasury is given power to issue regulations to require the FCA, PRA, or Bank of England to impose fees on authorised persons or recognised clearing houses to cover relevant expenses.[173] These apply with regard to the cost of UK membership of international organisations provided that the expenses represent a contribution to the resources of the organisation and are connected with its work in relation to financial stability or financial services. The concessions applicable to the Bank of England in disregarding certain equivalent requirements imposed under the Companies Act 2006 on its accounts are amended with the effect that the Bank may only disregard a requirement where this is necessary having regard to its financial stability objective under the BEA 1998.[174]

Recovery and Resolution Plans

13.249 Banks and other major financial institutions are to be required to prepare and maintain Recovery and Resolution Plans (RRPs) following the recent financial crises. This follows the work being carried out by the FSB at the international level, in particular with regard to Global Systemically Important Financial Institutions ('GSIFIs') and the Basel Committee on Global Systemically Important Banks ('GSIBs'). A number of papers were issued by the FSA before being taken over by the PRA an FCA with a draft Directive on recovery and resolution and Staff Working Document being produced by the European Commission.

Financial Stability Board

13.250 The FSB had identified 29 GSIFIs in November 2011 which was reduced to 28 in November 2012.[175] The FSB issued a report on reducing the moral hazard created by SIFIs and a first progress report on SIFI supervision in November 2010.[176] Further progress reports were issued in

---

168 s 13 FS(BR)A 2013. Equivalent provisions were to apply under the Bankruptcy (Scotland) Act 1985; cl 9 Bill 130.

169 Commentators have argued that this is unfair and will create instability. See, eg, Memorandum submitted by Neil Jeffares on the Financial Services (Banking Reform) Bill (fs02) 16 April 2013; available at: <http://www.publications.parliament.uk/pa/cm201213/cmpublic/financialservices/memo/fs2.htm>.

170 cl 9 Bill 62 and s 224ZA FSMA as amended.

171 cl 12 Bill 62 and s 218B FSMA as amended.

172 cl 13 Bill 62 and s 212 FSMA as amended.

173 cl 125 Bill 62 and s 410A as amended.

174 cl 127 Bill 62 and s 7A BEA 1998 as amended.

175 FSB, 'Policy Measures to Address Systemically Important Financial Institutions' (4 November 2011) Annex; and FSB, 'Update of group of global systemically important banks (G-SIBs)' (1 November 2012). This used a template prepared by the Basel Committee. Basel Committee on Banking Supervision, *Global systemically important banks: Assessment methodology and the additional loss absorbency requirement* (November 2011).

176 FSB, *Reducing the moral hazard posed by systemically importantly financial institutions* (20 October 2010); and FSB, *Intensity and Effectiveness of SIFI Supervision* (2 November 2010).

November 2011 and 2012.[177] A Consultative Document on *Effective Resolution of Systemically Important Financial Institutions* was produced in July 2011[178] with *Key Attributes of Effective Resolution Regimes* in October 2011.[179] A further progress report on SIFI resolution[180] and operational guidance was issued in November 2012[181] and peer review results in 2013.[182]

The FSB October 2011 *Key Attributes* contained specific provision on 12 essential aspects of effective resolution. These covered scope, resolution authority, resolution powers, set-off (netting, collateralisation, and client asset segregation), safeguards, funding firms in resolution, cross-border cooperation legal framework, Crisis Management Groups ('CMGs'), institution specific Cross-Border Cooperation Agreements ('COAGs'), resolvability assessments, recovery and resolution plans ('RRPs'), and information access and sharing. Additional guidance was provided on COAGs, resolvability assessments, RRPs, and temporary stays on early termination rights.[183] **13.251**

A specific paper on RRP planning was issued in November 2012.[184] This consisted of a number of substantial annexes on guidance for recovery triggers and stress scenarios, developing resolution strategies and operational resolution plans and identification of critical functions and shared services.[185] Responses to the consultation were published on the FSB website with a further Peer Review report on resolution regimes in April 2013.[186] **13.252**

UK RRPs

The FSA issued a consultation paper and discussion paper on RRPs in August 2011 in the UK.[187] A Feedback Statement was published in May 2012 with Draft Core Rules and a substantial Information Pack.[188] The Information Pack consists of six Modules covering Executive summary, Recovery plans, Group structure and key legal entity information, Economic function identification matrix, UK critical Function Contingency Analysis (CFCA), and Debt and Equity in issue information and Plans to overcome barriers to resolution. **13.253**

The main provisions governing RRPs are to be incorporated in FINMAR with additional amendments to Supervision ('SUP') and the Client Assets Sourcebook ('CASS'). Specific provision is included with regard to application and purpose (FINMAR 4.1). The purpose is to set out rules and guidance relating to recovery plans and resolution packs to assist in the exercise of powers conferred under the BA 2009 (FINMAR 4.1.5). Firms must have and keep up-to-date an effective Recovery Plan which is made available to the regulators on request (FINMAR 4.2.1R and 4.2.3G). The Recovery Plan must set out the actions that **13.254**

[177] FSB, *Intensity and Effectiveness of SIFI Supervision* (27 October 2012); and FSB, *Increasing the Intensity and Effectiveness of SIFI Supervision* (1 November 2012).

[178] FSB, *Consultative Document—Effective Resolution of Systemically Important Financial Institutions* (July 2011) and see also FSB, 'Effective Resolution of Systemically Important Financial Institutions—Overview of responses to the public consultation' (4 November 2011).

[179] FSB, *Key Attributes of Effective Resolution Regimes for Financial Institutions* (October 21).

[180] FSB, *Resolution of Systemically Important Financial Institutions* (November 2012).

[181] FSB, *Recovery and Resolution Planning: Making the Key Attributes Requirements Operational* (November 2012).

[182] FSB, *Thematic Review on Resolution Regimes* (11 April 2013).

[183] Annexes I–IV.

[184] FSB, *Recovery and Resolution Planning: Making the Key Attributes Requirements Operational* (November 2012).

[185] Annexes I–III.

[186] FSB, *Peer Review report on resolution regimes* (April 2013).

[187] FSA, *Recovery and resolution plans* (August 2011) CP11/16.

[188] FSA, *Recovery and resolution plans* (May 2012) fs12/1; and FSA, *RRP Information Pack* (May 2012).

could be taken to secure that the business of the firm, or any part of its business, is capable of being carried on and returned to a stable and sustainable condition if circumstances arise that adversely affect the carrying on of its business (FINMAR 4.2.4R). It must also contain a comprehensive range of options setting out the actions available including with regard to capital and liquidity levels and applicable governance arrangements, triggers, and procedures and timelines (FINMAR 4.2.5R). Firms are to notify the authorities as soon as they become aware of the occurrence or expected occurrence of certain regulatory events that indicate a potential instability (FINMAR 4.2.6R and 4.2.8R).

13.255 Firms must maintain and keep up-to-date a separate Resolution Pack and make this available on request (FINMAR 4.3.1R and 4.3.3G). This must include sufficient information and analysis to facilitate planning by the Treasury or Bank of England on the exercise of any powers under the stabilisation options, BIP or BAP within the BA 2009 (FINMAR 4.3.5R). Recovery Plans and Resolution Packs are subject to annual review (FINMAR 4.4) with firms establishing appropriate internal governance arrangements having regard to the nature, scale, and complexity of their business (FINMAR 4.5).

EU BRR

13.256 The UK RRP requirements will be further revised following the adoption of the European draft Directive for recovery and resolution of credit institutions and investment firms (BRR) published in June 2012.[189] This was accompanied by a comprehensive Staff Working Document which dealt with procedural issues and consultation, policy context, definition and subsidiarity, policy options, analysis and impact and overall impact of the preferred options identified with continuing monitoring and evaluation.[190] The paper notes that 37 per cent of EU GDP (€4.5 trillion) was approved in terms of public support between October 2008 and October 2011 with 13 per cent of GDP (€1.6 trillion) being drawn-down in 2008–2010 and 9.8 per cent of GDP (€1.2 trillion) made available in guarantees and liquidity and 3.3 per cent GDP (€409 billion) in recapitalisation and impaired assets. The EU economy had contracted by 4.2 per cent of GDP (€700 billion) in 2009. The general objectives of the new framework are to maintain financial stability and confidence in banks and to avoid contagion with losses to society being minimised and moral hazard reduced.

13.257 The BRR consists of 11 Titles and 117 Articles with an Annex and legislative financial statement. The BRR deals with legal basis, subsidiarity and proportionality. Specific provision is included dealing with subject matter and scope (Article 1), resolution authorities (Article 3), recovery and resolution plans (Articles 5–13), impediments to resolvability (Articles 14–16), intra-group financial support (Articles 17–23), early intervention and special management (Articles 23–26), resolution conditions (Art 27), general principles and 'no creditor worse off' (Article 29), valuation (Art 30), resolution tools and powers (Articles 31–64), bail-in tool (Articles 37–51), restrictions on termination and safeguards for counterparties (Articles 68–73), restriction on judicial proceedings (Articles 77–78), cross-border resolution (Articles 80–83), relations with third countries (Articles 84–89), and resolution funding (Articles 90–99) with additional compliance, amendments, and ancillary measures.

---

[189] European Commission, Proposal for a Directive establishing a framework for the recovery and resolution of credit institutions and investment firms and amending Council Directives (6 June 2012) COM/2012/0280 final.

[190] European Commission Staff Working Document, *Proposal for a Directive establishing a framework for the recovery and resolution of credit institutions and investment firms* (Brussels 6 June 2012) SWD(2012)166 final.

Resolution

Resolution applies once it is clear that a financial institution is not able to restructure itself effectively. Firms will attempt to avoid any instability through their Recovery Plan failing which the Resolution Pack will assist the authorities intervene formally. Recovery then operates on an internal and pre-crisis basis and resolution on a post-crisis and external basis. Key Attributes of effective resolution regimes were set out in the FSB October 2011 paper.[191] This followed its earlier consultative document in July 2011 and the comments received which were published in September 2011 with guidance on RRPs in November 2012[192] and *Peer Review* report on resolution regimes in April 2013.[193] New UK resolution procedures were introduced under the Banking (Special Provisions) Act 2008 and continued under the BA 2009. **13.258**

Banking (Special Provisions) Act 2008

The Banking (Special Provisions) Act 2008 was brought into effect to facilitate the public acquisition of Northern Rock after the failure to find a suitable private purchaser. The Act provided for the transfer of the securities or property, rights, and liabilities of authorised UK deposit-takers to maintain the stability of the UK financial system or protect the public interest. The Act contained 17 sections dealing with definitions, transfer of securities, transfer of property, further transfers, supplementary, building societies, and general measures with two schedules on transfer of securities orders and transfer of property orders. The Act came into effect immediately on 21 February 2008 and was to last for one year. This was used to assist with a number of restructurings.[194] **13.259**

Banking Act 2009

The 2008 Act was replaced by the permanent provisions contained in the Banking Act 2009 which received Royal Assent on 12 February 2009. The BA 2009 was to come into effect on the dates specified by the Treasury with four commencement orders being issued.[195] The BA 2009 consists of eight Parts and 265 sections. It establishes the Special Resolution Regime ('SRR'), Bank Insolvency Procedure ('BIP'), and Bank Administration Procedure ('BAP') with amendments to the FSCS and a new regime for Inter-Bank Payment Systems and Scottish and Northern Irish Banknotes and other miscellaneous and general provisions.[196] **13.260**

The BA 2009 establishes the SRR to provide special resolution options to deal with banks in difficulty. The SRR procedures also apply with regard to building societies with amendment[197] **13.261**

---

[191] FSB, *Key Attributes of Effective Resolution Regimes for Financial Institutions* (n 179).

[192] FSB, *Effective Resolution of Systemically Important Financial Institutions* (n 178); and FSB, 'Effective Resolution of Systemically Important Financial Institutions—Overview of responses to the public consultation' (n 178); and FSB, *Recovery and Resolution Planning: Making the Key Attributes Requirements Operational* (n 181).

[193] FSB, *Thematic Review on Resolution Regimes* (n 182).

[194] The Banking (Special Provisions) Act 2008 was used to acquire or transfer the assets or liabilities of Northern Rock in February 2008, the Bradford and Bingley in September 2008, and Heritable Bank (Landsbanki) and Kaupthing Edge (Kaupthing, Singer and Friedlander) in October 2008.

[195] s 263 BA 2009. See The Banking Act 2009 (Commencement No 1, 2, 3, and 4) Orders 2009 No 296, 2009 No 1296, 2009 No 2038, and 2009 No 3000.

[196] s 4 (4)–(8) BA 2009.

[197] ss 84–88 BA 2009. Dunfermline Building Society was restructured in March 2009 using the provisions adopted under the BA 2009.

and the Treasury may apply these with regard to credit unions by order and Parts 2 and 3 to building societies and credit unions by order.[198] Insolvency provisions were included in Part XXIV of the FSMA 2000 which included administration powers[199] although it was considered that these did not provide sufficient flexibility to manage a bank insolvency and specifically preserve the provision of critical functions.

Resolution powers and objectives

13.262 The BA 2009 sets out three sets of special resolution powers with three stabilisation powers and special BIP and BAP. Five special resolution objectives are specified covering the protection and enhancement of the stability of the UK financial systems and public confidence in the banking systems as well as depositor protection and public fund protection at the same time as avoid interfering with property rights protected under the Human Rights Act 1998.[200] Two further objectives of protecting client assets and minimising adverse effects on institutions were added by the FSA 2012.[201] The Treasury has issued a Code of Practice on the stabilisation powers, BIP, and BAP.[202] This provides an overview of the Code and restates the special resolution objectives with further provisions on the roles of the authorities, general and specific conditions for selecting SRR tools, ensuring that resolutions are effective, partial transfers and safeguards, governance arrangements for bridge banks and institutions in temporary public ownership, and the operation of the FSCS and compensation.[203] A Banking Liaison Panel ('BLP') is set up under the Act to advise the Treasury about the effects of a special resolution regime on banks, persons doing business with banks, and financial markets.[204]

Stabilisation

13.263 The three stabilisation powers consist of private sector purchaser, bridge bank, or temporary public ownership (nationalisation).[205] A series of special and specific conditions are imposed on the exercise of the powers. A stabilisation power may only be exercised if the regulator is satisfied that a bank is failing, or likely to fail, the threshold conditions, or it is not reasonably likely that action will be taken to allow the bank to satisfy the threshold conditions having regard to relevant circumstances and timing.[206] Once the general conditions have been satisfied, the Bank may only use the private sector purchaser or bridge bank option if this is necessary in the public interest to protect the stability of the UK financial systems, maintain public confidence in the UK banking systems or protect depositors.[207] The Bank may only act following a recommendation from the Treasury that this is necessary in the public interest where the Treasury has already provided financial assistance to a bank.[208]

198 ss 89, 130 131, and 158–159 BA 2009.
199 ss 359–362A FSMA.
200 s 4(4)–(8) BA 2009.
201 s 96 FSA 2012.
202 s 5 BA 2009; and HM Treasury, *Banking Act 2009. Special resolution regime: Code of Practice* (November 2010).
203 Chapters 2–11.
204 s 10 BA 2009.
205 ss 11, 12, and 13 BA 2009.
206 s 7(1)–(3) BA 2009.
207 s 8(1)–(2) BA 2009.
208 s 8 (5) BA 2009.

Temporary public ownership is exercised by the Treasury in the event that this is necessary to resolve or reduce a serious threat to the stability of the UK financial systems or that this is necessary to protect the public interest where financial assistance has already been provided.[209] Specific provisions are included on the transfer of securities and property[210] and compensation and incidental functions.[211] These include general and special continuity obligations in respect of property and share transfers as well as special provisions on pensions, enforcement, disputes, tax, and legal amendment. **13.264**

Insolvency and administration

The BIP amends existing liquidation provisions to allow for the orderly winding up of a failed bank and to allow timely payments by the FSCS to eligible claimants or the transfer of accounts to another financial institution.[212] The BAP is designed for use following a partial transfer of business from a failing bank with a bank administrator being appointed to administer the affairs of the residual bank created.[213] Amendments are made to Part 15 FSMA to improve the operation of the FSCS compensation arrangement. Specific provisions are included to allow for pre-funding, the use of the FSCS to contribute to the cost of exercising special resolution options, and to allow loans to be made to the FSCS by the National Loans Fund.[214] **13.265**

The BA 2009 includes additional provisions for extending the resolution options to apply to building societies with the Treasury consulting separately on the application of these arrangements to investment firms.[215] This would include extending the resolution regime to apply to investment firms and parent undertakings, CCPs (central counterparties) and non-CCPs' financial market infrastructures.[216] **13.266**

Financial Stability

The objective of all of these provisions is to allow for the managed resolution of any major financial institution or financial group. Firms in difficulty will have pre-planned restructuring and recovery facilities in place including capital, liquidity, and disposal options all of which will have been reviewed by the regulatory authorities and stress tested. In the event that these are insufficient, the authorities will have a range of special resolution options to manage an organised restructuring or transfer using statutory powers. **13.267**

The additional capital and liquidity obligations imposed on banks will substantially assist to prevent them experiencing difficulty with the new RRP and resolution structures facilitating managed reorganisations or disposals with full protection for critical services and at minimum public cost. A number of other significant reforms were also adopted by the FSA in the immediate aftermath to the financial crisis including on more principles based regulation, **13.268**

---

[209] s 9 (1)–(3) BA 2009.
[210] ss 14–32 and 33–48 BA 2009.
[211] ss 49–62 and 63–75 BA 2009.
[212] Part 2 BA 2009.
[213] Part 3 BA 2009.
[214] Part 4 BA 2009.
[215] HM Treasury, *Financial sector resolution: broadening the regime* (August 2012) Cm 8419.
[216] ss 100–102 FSA 2012.

strengthened supervision, enhanced enforcement, remuneration, product regulation, and treating customers fairly more generally. These represent substantial advances on the earlier regime in place before the global financial crisis and could arguably secure sufficient protection by themselves against future crises.

13.269 A sophisticated new macro-prudential regime has also been created within the UK and at the European level with the establishment of the European Systemic Risk Board ('ESRB') in January 2011. These developments parallel the creation of the Financial Stability Oversight Counsel (FSOC) in the UK under the Dodd Frank Wall Street Reform and Consumer Protection Act 2010.[217] Macro-prudential oversight was initially introduced in the UK with the Financial Stability Committee ('FSC') set up within the Bank of England under the BA 2009[218] and the proposed creation of the Council for Financial Stability ('CFS') which was to have been given a statutory basis under the FSA 2010.[219] The FSC has since been replaced, the FSC set up under the FSA 2012,[220] and the CFS by the new institutional relations and statutory collaboration arrangements established under the FSA 2012.[221] The earlier MoU including on Financial Stability has since been replaced by a MoU on Crisis Management and a series of other parallel MoU.[222]

13.270 The more recent institutional changes and structural reforms, including ring-fencing and higher capital requirements, brought into effect since 2010 will add additional levels and layers of protection which will certainly increase financial stability further. All of this will nevertheless impose substantial additional obligations and costs on financial institutions which will ultimately be passed back onto businesses and household customers in the form of lower credit volumes and higher rates and charges while overall international UK competitiveness is reduced. The Bank of England, as central bank, and the Government will also always have to support the UK financial system in the event of an unexpected, extreme future event. This contingent liability can never be wholly removed although its occurrence and magnitude can be reduced by more effective regulation and improved supervision. The ultimate question to be determined is simply one of balance between regulatory obligation and cost effective service provision and between short term market control and longer term financial market innovation, profitability and sustainability.

[217] ss 111–123 Dodd Frank Wall Street Reform and Consumer Protection Act 2010 (Pub L 111-203, HR 4173).

[218] s 2B BEA 1998 inserted under s 238(1) BA 2009. See Chapter 1, paras 1.102, 1.106, and 1.118–1.124.

[219] ss 1-4 Financial Services Bill 6-EN of 19 November 2009. See Chapter 1, paras 1.106, 1.50, and 1.62–1.63.

[220] s 9B BEA inserted under s 4(1) FSA 2012.

[221] ss 58-67 FSA 2012.

[222] HM Treasury, Bank of England and PRA, 'Memorandum of Understanding on financial crisis management'; available at: <http://www.bankofengland.co.uk/about/Documents/mous/moufincrisis.pdf>. Chapter, 1 paras 1.158–1.170.

14

INSURANCE REGULATION

Introduction

14.01 This chapter looks at insurance regulation; it covers the regulation of insurers and of intermediaries which deal with insurance products. This introduction is followed by five sections—History and Background;[1] EU Law;[2] UK Law and Regulation;[3] UK Law and Regulation—the regulatory Handbooks;[4] and UK Law and Regulation—FOS and FSCS.[5] There is extensive EU legislation concerning insurers and insurance intermediaries. EU legislation dictates the structure and much of the detail of the UK regime and domestic law and regulation often has to be interpreted in the light of EU requirements.

Terminology and categorisation

14.02 Insurance is categorised in a variety of different ways under EU legislation and UK regulation. It is important to have an overview of how this terminology is used. Some of the key terms are therefore considered later in this chapter.

14.03 European legislation for insurers deals separately with non-life insurance and life insurance.[6] These correspond to 'general insurance' and 'long-term insurance' in the UK regime. Most insurers are authorised for one but not the other. Those which underwrite both are referred to as composite insurers. Life/long-term and non-life/general are each broken down into 'classes of insurance'.[7]

14.04 UK regulation of sales and mediation is based on a variety of defined categories of insurance set out in the Regulated Activities Order[8] (as amended to reflect the changes introduced by the Financial Services Act 2012 ('FSA 2012')) and in the regulatory Glossary and Handbooks. A 'qualifying contract of insurance' is defined in Article 3(1) of the RAO;[9] broadly, it is a long-term insurance which is neither reinsurance nor a pure protection

---

[1] See para 14.7 *et seq.*
[2] See para 14.24 *et seq.*
[3] See para 14.82 *et seq.*
[4] See para 14.160 *et seq.*
[5] See para 14.367 *et seq.*
[6] See para 14.29 *et seq.*
[7] See paras 14.40 and 14.41.
[8] Financial Services and Markets Act 2000 (Regulated Activities), Order 2001, SI 2001/544 (as amended) (the 'RAO'). The Financial Services Act 2012 required the RAO to be amended to reflect the changes to the supervisory authorities. These changes have been made primarily through the Financial Services and Markets Act 2000 (Regulated Activities) (Amendment) Order 2013, SI 2013/655, and the Financial Services and Markets Act (PRA-regulated Acitivities) Order 2013, SI 2013/556.
[9] A 'qualifying contract of insurance' (as defined at art 3, RAO) means a contract of long-term insurance which is not (a) a reinsurance contract; nor (b) a contract in respect of which the following conditions are

policy.[10] It includes insurance with an 'investment element' such as 'with-profits' insurance or unit linked contracts and annuities. A pure protection policy (a defined term in the Glossary) includes certain term life and permanent health contracts. Under the RAO, rights under a qualifying contract of insurance constitute 'contractually based investments' and rights under any contract of insurance constitute 'relevant investments'. 'Designated investments' (defined in the Glossary) include contractually based investments which are 'life policies' (a separately defined term with a different meaning to the EU term 'life insurance') and long-term care insurance contracts[11] which are pure protection contracts (long-term care insurance sales are regulated under the FCA's Conduct of Business Rules ('COBS'), ie as an investment product). 'Non-investment insurance' is other kinds of insurance, ie all general insurance and pure protection (long-term) insurance other than long-term care insurance.

14.05 A further distinction in EU legislation (also used in the UK regime) is between insurance of 'mass risks' and 'large risks'. Mass risks are all risks other than large risks. Large risks are defined as contracts of insurance covering the following risks:

(a) railway rolling stock, aircraft, ships (sea, lake, river, and canal vessels), goods in transit, aircraft liability, and liability of ships (sea, lake, river, and canal vessels);
(b) credit and suretyship where the policyholder is engaged professionally in an industrial or commercial activity or in one of the liberal professions and the risks relate to such activity; and
(c) land vehicles (other than railway, rolling stock), fire and natural forces, other damage to property, motor vehicle liability, general liability, and miscellaneous financial loss, insofar as the policyholder exceeds the limits of at least two of the following three criteria:
    (i) balance sheet total: €6.2 million;
    (ii) net turnover: €12.8 million;
    (iii) average number of employees during the financial year: 250.[12]

---

met: (i) the benefits under the contract are payable only on death or in respect of incapacity due to injury, sickness, or infirmity; (ii) the contract has no surrender value, or the consideration consists of a single premium and the surrender value does not exceed that premium; and (iii) the contract makes no provision for its conversion or extension in a manner which would result in it ceasing to comply with any of the above conditions. This definition was amended in 2007 to remove a further condition that 'the contract provides that benefits are payable on death (other than death due to an accident) only where the death occurs within 10 years of the date on which the life of the person in question was first insured under the contract, or where the death occurs before that person attains a specified age not exceeding 70 years'. This definition was amended in order to remove some contracts of long-term insurance (such as whole of life policies) from the definition of a qualifying contract of insurance so that they would fall under the less stringent regulation of ICOBS.

[10] A 'pure protection policy' is one falling under (b) in n 9.

[11] Long-term care insurance contract is defined in the Glossary as a long-term insurance contract which: (a) provides (or would at the policyholder's option) or is sold or held out as providing, benefits that are payable or provided if the policyholder's health deteriorates to the extent that he cannot live independently without assistance, and that is not expected to change; and (b) the benefits under the contract are capable of being paid for periodically for all or part of the period that the policyholder cannot live without assistance; where 'benefits' are services, accommodation, or goods necessary or desirable for the continuing care of the policyholder because he cannot live independently without assistance.

[12] The Glossary definition of 'contracts of large risks'. Also defined in the Second Council Directive (EEC) 88/357 on the coordination of laws, regulations and administrative provisions relating to direct insurance other than life assurance and laying down provisions to facilitate the effective exercise of freedom to provide services and amending Directive (EEC) 73/239[1988] OJ L172/1 (the 'Second Non-life Directive').

The expression 'direct insurance' is used in EU legislation to distinguish insurance (of the original risk) from reinsurance and retrocession (taken out by an insurer or reinsurer). 'Direct selling', on the other hand, is used to describe the situation where an insurer sells directly to the policyholder without an intermediary being involved. **14.06**

History and Background

Insurers

Prior to the Financial Services and Markets Act 2000 ('FSMA'), UK insurers (general and long-term)[13] were subject to authorisation under the Insurance Companies Act 1982 ('ICA'). This legislation reflected the initial EU directives and developed as further EU insurance legislation was adopted. The ICA was focused on prudential regulation, particularly the solvency regime. The Department of Trade and Industry ('DTI') (ie a government department) was responsible for authorising and regulating insurers under the ICA. The detailed requirements were set out in statutory instruments which were supplemented by circular letters and notices from the DTI. **14.07**

Financial Services Act 1986

Concerns about the UK investment market led to the Gower Report[14] and to the Financial Services Act 1986 ('FSA 1986'). This established the Securities and Investments Board ('SIB')[15] and a number of self-regulating organisations ('SROs')[16] and recognised professional bodies ('RPBs').[17] Intermediaries dealing with investment insurance[18] (or other investment products) had to be a member of an SRO/RPB, be directly regulated by SIB or appointed as an appointed representative (of an authorised firm which took responsibility for their representative). Insurers providing these insurance products were also subject to the FSA 1986 and were effectively dual regulated under this act as well as the ICA.[19] They were prudentially regulated by the DTI, while their sales of relevant products were regulated under the FSA 1986 and under the rules of SIB/LAUTRO/PIA. **14.08**

Intermediaries and Brokers

A statutory regime for the regulation of 'insurance brokers' operated in the UK for over 20 years.[20] The effect of the Insurance Brokers (Registration) Act 1977 ('IBRA')[21] was that insurance intermediaries could only use the title 'broker' if they were registered under that Act with the Insurance Brokers Registration Council ('IBRC').[22] This was described as regulation 'by title'; an intermediary could avoid registration and the related requirements simply **14.09**

13 See the explanation of 'general' and 'long-term' at paras 14.03–14.04.

14 Review of Investor Protection Report by LCB Gower: Presented to Parliament by Secretary for Trade and Industry (January 1984).

15 FSA 1986, Sch 9, para 8.

16 ibid, s 8(1).

17 ibid, s 16(1) and 17(1).

18 ie qualifying contracts of insurance.

19 Part 1, Sch 1, paras 10 and 28(1)(d) of the FSA 1986; s 2(1) and 3(2) of the ICA.

20 Insurance Brokers (Registration) Act 1977, ss 1 and 2.

21 IBRA was introduced as a Private Members Bill.

22 IBRA, s 1.

by avoiding the use of 'broker' and describing himself as an advisor or consultant. Those that did register were subject to a Code of Conduct and other requirements established in statutory instruments including a disciplinary regime.[23] The effect of the legislation was to divide general insurance mediation between, on the one hand, regulated brokers and, on the other hand, intermediaries or agents which operated outside statutory regulation. A broker was regulated on the basis that he acted as the agent of the insured, independent of insurers, and offering access to a sufficiently wide range of insurers. This was broadly similar to the concept of an insurance broker in EU legislation (including the terminology used in the VAT Directives) and in other Member States, many of which, like the UK, regulated brokers but not insurers' agents. It was a requirement that all 'Lloyd's brokers' (ie those able to place insurance at Lloyd's) be registered with the IBRC. These brokers were subject to dual regulation by Lloyd's, for example, under the Lloyd's Brokers Bye-law, and by IBRC under the IBRA and related requirements.[24]

14.10 As already noted, the FSA 1986 introduced an authorisation requirement for intermediaries selling investment insurance. This prohibited a firm from selling, arranging sales, or advising on such products unless the intermediary was directly authorised by SIB or a member of an SRO/RPB (such as LAUTRO, FIMBRA, and PIA). The regime included SIB's 10 Principles[25] and included detailed Conduct of Business Rules in common with other investment products, as well as rules covering discipline, complaints and dispute resolution, client money, investment advertisements, and an Investors Compensation Scheme. Within the insurance industry, the modern compliance function first evolved in this sector. One particular feature of the regime was 'polarisation'. Prompted by a variety of concerns, including a lack of transparency about the role of intermediaries, SIB's rules (and those of the SROs) split intermediaries selling investment insurance to the public into two 'polarised' sectors. An intermediary had either to be 'independent' acting for and advising the customer, offering a choice of products drawn from all providers generally (like a 'broker' under IBRA) or it was restricted to acting as a tied agent selling only the products of the particular company or group which it represented.[26] This has been a contentious and much discussed feature of the UK investment market. It was a classic example of restrictive regulation (it prohibited multi-tying and prevented intermediaries offering products from a limited range of providers) and attracted the critical attention of the Office of Fair Trading ('OFT') acting under its competition powers.[27] The polarisation regime survived the migration to Financial Services Authority ('FSA') regulation, but was abolished in 2004. More recently the FSA's Retail Distribution Review ('RDR'), has revisited the issues around independent advice and requires advisors to disclose whether they provide 'independent advice' or 'restricted advice'. Independent advisors must make recommendations based on the full range of products and providers in the market taking into account the client's needs.[28] Restricted advice is based on a more limited range of products and providers. The rules, which came into force on 31

[23] ibid, ss 10, 11, 13, and 14–19.

[24] ibid, ss 2 and 3; ss 2 and 3(3) of Lloyd's Brokers Byelaw No 5 of 1988 revoked on 6 December 2000 by Byelaw No 17 of 2000 and revoked on 1 December 2004 by Lloyd's Brokers Byelaw No 7 of 2004.

[25] Volume I SIB Rules and Regulations: Statements of Principle.

[26] Volume I, Chapter III SIB Rules and Regulations: Conduct of Business Rule 4.

[27] 'The Rules on the Polarisation of Investment Advice' A report by the Director General of Fair Trading August 1999 (OFT 264).

[28] FSA Policy Statement 10/6 Distribution of retail investments: Delivering the RDR—feedback to CP09/18 and final rules, March 2010.

December 2012, aim to ensure that advice given to retail customers is either clearly independent or restricted in the scope of products on the markets which are offered.

The IBRA and FSA left a considerable gap in the regulation of insurance intermediaries. Intermediaries selling general and other non-investment insurance[29] fell outside regulation if they avoided describing themselves as a 'broker'. The Association of British Insurers ('ABI') had been formed in 1985 as the principal UK trade body for insurers. It published two codes for general and for long-term insurance.[30] **14.11**

A particular feature of the ABI codes was the distinction between independent intermediaries on the one hand (which acted for the insured like an insurance 'broker') and agents which were restricted to offering the products of a limited number of insurers. Independent intermediaries were required to maintain professional indemnity insurance. **14.12**

In July 1998, the Government announced the repeal of IBRA, having concluded that a system of statutory regulation which applied only to those general insurance intermediaries using the title 'broker' was no longer appropriate.[31] This paved the way for the industry to establish a new body, the General Insurance Standards Council ('GISC') which commenced regulation in July 2000. GISC was established outside any statutory authority but with the apparent support of the Government. It was established as a 'voluntary' regulator of general insurance sales by both insurers and intermediaries. Lloyd's dismantled most of its regime for the regulation of Lloyd's brokers which all became members of GISC. The regime was also intended to replace the ABI code on general insurance. Many insurers and intermediaries joined, but plans to achieve full industry coverage were thwarted, initially by the new competition law procedures[32] and more finally by adoption of the Insurance Mediation Directive ('IMD')[33] and the Government's decision not to make GISC a competent authority under it. **14.13**

The GISC rulebook was based on two codes of conduct, one for private customers (an individual acting for non-business purposes) and another for commercial customers. When the FSA was given responsibility for the regulation of general insurance intermediaries on 14 January 2005, GISC ceased its operations. **14.14**

Financial Services and Markets Act 2000[34]

Both the ICA and FSA 1986 were repealed and replaced by the regulatory regime introduced by FSMA which came into effect on 1 December 2001 (a date known as N2). (The responsibilities of the DTI under the ICA had already passed to HM Treasury and day-to-day operations were taken over by the FSA before FSMA came into full effect.) The FSA was therefore responsible for the authorisation of all insurers (general and long-term) and for the detailed regulation of designated investment insurance sales (ie sales of long-term insurance which constituted designated investments). The insurance regime introduced by FSMA, however, **14.15**

[29] See explanation of 'general' and 'non-investment insurance' at paras 14.03–14.04.

[30] ABI Codes of Practice on 'General Insurance Sales' and 'Long Term Insurance Sales'.

[31] IBRA was repealed on 30 April 2001 by ss 416(1)(c), 432(3), and Sch 22 of FSMA.

[32] The OFT clearance of the GISC rulebook and its proposed rule F42 to prevent insurers dealing with non-GISC intermediaries was the subject of appeals to the Competition Commission Appeals Tribunal which overturned the OFT's decision and referred the rulebook for consideration under the procedure for exemption of anti-competitive agreements.

[33] Directive 2002/92/EC of the European Parliament and of the Council on insurance mediation [2005], OJ L009/03.

[34] Referred to as 'FSMA'.

was considerably wider than previous regimes; in particular it included a new regime for the regulation of the Lloyd's insurance market, ie the Society of Lloyd's, its members, the managing agents which underwrite insurance on their behalf, as well as members' agents and advisors. The new Financial Promotions Regime under FSMA (which extended the investment advertisement regime under the 1986 Act) covered all forms of insurance including general insurance.

14.16 At that stage the regulation of the sales and administration of general and pure protection insurance products[35] was limited, broadly, to the financial promotions regime and limited provisions applicable to insurers, such as those reflecting the requirements in the First,[36] Second,[37] and Third[38] Life Directives (which were later consolidated),[39] and the First,[40] Second,[41] and Third[42] Non-life Directives.[43] The application of the FSA's Principles for Businesses ('PRIN') to general insurers was limited to reflect the definition of regulated activities which did not include the sale and administration of general or pure protection insurance products[44] by authorised insurers (or intermediaries).

14.17 For four years (from 2000 to 2004) many general insurers were members of GISC and followed the GISC rulebook. In January 2005, after the IMD was adopted GISC ceased its operations and its insurer members became subject to broader FSA regulation covering the sale and administration of non-investment insurance products.

14.18 At the time the IMD was adopted, the Government announced that the FSA would be the sole authority for the registration of insurance intermediaries. The FSA regime under FSMA was extended by amending the secondary legislation and the FSA Handbook. This involved:

- extending the perimeter of the section 19 prohibition to bring mediation of general and protection products (non-investment insurance) into regulation;

[35] See the explanation of 'general' and 'pure protection insurance products' in paras 14.03–14.04.

[36] First Council Directive (EEC) 79/267 on coordination of laws, regulations and administrative provisions relating to the taking-up and pursuit of the business of direct life assurance (as amended) [1979] OJ L63/1 (the 'First Life Directive').

[37] Council Directive (EEC) 90/619 on coordination of laws, regulations, and administrative provisions relating to direct life assurance, laying down provisions to facilitate the effective exercise of freedom to provide services and amending Directive (EEC) 79/267 [1990] OJ L330/50 (the 'Second Life Directive').

[38] Council Directive (EEC) 92/96 on coordination of laws, regulations, and administrative provisions relating to direct life assurance and amending Directives (EEC) 79/267 and 90/619 (as amended) [1992] OJ L311/1 (the 'Third Life Directive').

[39] Council Directive (EC) 2002/83 concerning life assurance [2002] OJ L345/1 (known as the Consolidated Life Directive, 'CLD').

[40] First Council Directive (EEC) 73/239 on the coordination of laws, regulations, and administrative provisions relating to the taking up and pursuit of the business of direct insurance other than life insurance [1973] OJ L228/3 (the 'First Non-life Directive').

[41] Second Council Directive (EEC) 88/357 of 22 June 1988 on the coordination of laws, regulations and administrative provisions relating to direct insurance other than life assurance and laying down provisions to facilitate the effective exercise of freedom to provide services and amending Directive (EEC) 73/239 [1988] OJ L172/1 (the 'Second Non-life Directive').

[42] Council Directive (EEC) 92/49 on the coordination of laws, regulations, and administrative provisions relating to direct insurance other than life assurance and amending Directives (EEC) 73/239 and 88/357 [1992] OJ L228/1 (the 'Third Non-life Directive').

[43] The three non-life directives are collectively referred to as '3NLD'.

[44] ibid.

- new FSA rulebooks (or chapters) for non-investment insurance business such as the Insurance: Conduct of Business Sourcebook (ICOB, now 'ICOBS'),[45] chapter 5 of the Client Assets Sourcebook ('CASS'), and chapter 9 of the Integrated Prudential Sourcebook;[46] and
- a large number of amendments to other secondary legislation and to existing rulebooks of the FSA Handbook.

The changes went well beyond the requirements of the IMD (which only related to intermediaries), reflecting the decision to introduce more comprehensive regulation of the sale and administration of all insurance products for both insurers and intermediaries. As a result: **14.19**

- the new regulated activities for non-investment insurance applied to insurers (as well as intermediaries). Authorised insurers had to apply for new mediation permissions, and the ICOB rulebook regulated insurers as product providers and as sellers of insurance; and
- intermediaries were subject to various aspects of the FSA regime which went beyond the IMD such as the FSA's high-level standards and its various initiatives based on PRIN (see paragraph 14.170 *et seq*.) and the approved persons regime.

The extension to regulation took effect on 14 January 2005 (a date known as NGI). A large number of intermediaries and brokers had to apply for FSA authorisation (a much greater number than all the authorised firms before NGI). Most applied before the 14 July 2004 deadline, but late in the day a system of interim authorisation was adopted to allow firms to apply at any time before NGI. **14.20**

At the time the FSA took over the regulation of insurers under FSMA, it submitted a report to HM Treasury on the future regulation of insurance.[47] This report, promoted by the problems of Equitable Life, was followed by a further progress report in October 2002 from John Tiner (then managing director of Consumer, Investment and Insurance at the FSA).[48] The Tiner Project made the reform of insurance regulation a key priority for the FSA. The reports had three policy objectives—'securing a fair deal for consumers', 'firms that are soundly managed and have adequate financial resources', and 'smarter regulation of insurance'.[49] **14.21**

The reform of policy which followed the Tiner Project was much broader than the original issues arising from Equitable Life and with-profits policies. It led to (amongst other things) the reform of financial regulation of insurers as described at paragraph 14.274 *et seq*. **14.22**

Following the financial crisis that began in 2007, the single regulatory regime was dismantled in favour of 'twin peaks' regulation whereby prudential supervision and conduct of business matters are dealt with by two separate regulatory authorities—the Prudential Regulatory Authority ('PRA') with responsibility for prudential matters and the Financial Conduct Authority ('FCA') for all supervision of conduct. Accordingly, following the FSA 2012 coming into force on 1 April 2013, insurers (in addition to managing agents and the Society of **14.23**

[45] In January 2008, ICOB was changed to ICOBS following substantial amendments.

[46] Chapter 9 of the Integrated Prudential Sourcebook ('IPRU') is now contained in the Prudential Sourcebook for Mortgage and Home Finance, and Insurance Intermediaries ('MIPRU').

[47] 'The future regulation of insurance'. Report submitted by the Board of the Financial Services Authority to the Economic Secretary to the Treasury (November 2001) in response to 'The regulation of Equitable Life: an independent report' Ronnie Baird (September 2001).

[48] 'The future regulation of insurance: a progress report' (October 2002) which responded to 'The Equitable Life Inquiry' Lord Penrose (2002).

[49] 'The future regulation of insurance'. Report submitted by the Board of the Financial Services Authority to the Economic Secretary to the Treasury (November 2001).

Lloyd's) are now subject to dual regulation by both the PRA and FCA in accordance with their statutory objectives under FSMA. Insurance intermediaries are solely regulated by the FCA for both prudential and conduct of business matters.

European Union Law

14.24 EU law in the insurance field is critical to the domestic regulatory regime. In addition to the single passport system for cross-border business, it provides the framework for insurer and intermediary regulation and detailed requirements in many key areas such as solvency. There is now EU legislation in almost all areas of insurance regulation. An understanding of EU insurance law is critical because so much of the domestic regime implements or reflects EU requirements and concepts. Although one refers to EU legislation, the insurance and single market directives apply to the 30 States of the EEA,[50] including the new accession States.[51]

14.25 Switzerland is not a member of the EEA, but there are bilateral arrangements for mutual recognition of insurers in relation to direct insurance other than life (ie, general)[52] between the EU and Switzerland.[53] The Channel Islands and the Isle of Man are not part of the EU or EEA for these purposes. There are special arrangements dealing with insurers established and authorised in Gibraltar.[54]

14.26 EU legislation deals separately with insurers and intermediaries. Intermediary regulation is dealt with under the IMD, while the main legislation covering direct insurers is dealt with under:

- the Consolidated Life Directive ('CLD') (which replaced and consolidated the First, Second, and Third Life Directives);[55] and
- the three Non-Life Directives ('3NLD') (ie the First, Second, and Third Non-life Directives).[56]

14.27 The CLD and the 3NLD only apply to insurers who undertake direct business; they do not apply to specialist or 'pure' reinsurers. However, with the adoption of the Reinsurance Directive ('RID')[57] the authorisation and single licence regime was extended to pure reinsurers.[58]

---

50 EEA States: Iceland, Liechtenstein, Norway, and the 27 EU States, namely Austria, Belgium, Bulgaria, Cyprus, the Czech Republic, Denmark, Estonia, Finland, France, Germany, Greece, Hungary, Ireland, Italy, Latvia, Lithuania, Luxembourg, Malta, the Netherlands, Poland, Portugal, Romania, Slovakia, Slovenia, Spain, Sweden, and the United Kingdom.

51 Accession States which joined on 1 May 2004: Cyprus, Czech Republic, Estonia, Hungary, Latvia, Lithuania, Malta, Poland, Slovakia, and Slovenia. Accession States which joined the EU on 1 January 2007: Bulgaria and Romania.

52 See the explanation of 'life' and 'general' in paras 14.03–14.04.

53 Council Regulation (EEC) 91/2155 Provisions of the Agreement between the EEC and the Swiss Confederation [1991] OJ L205/1; Council Decision (EEC) 91/370 Conclusion of the Agreement between the EEC and the Swiss Confederation [1991] OJ L205/2; Council Directive (EEC) 91/371 Implementation of the Agreement between the EEC and the Swiss Confederation [1991] OJ L205/40; Council Decision (EC) 01/776 Switzerland Joint Committee Decision No 1/2001 amending annexes and protocols [2001] OJ L205/37.

54 For further detail, please see the Financial Services and Markets Act 2000 (Gibraltar) Order 2001, SI 2001/3084. For EU purposes, Gibraltar forms part of the UK, but there are domestic arrangements under UK and Gibraltar law to enable 'passporting' between Gibraltar and the UK.

55 See n 36–39.

56 See n 40–43.

57 Council Directive (EC) 05/68/EC on reinsurance and amending Council Directives (EEC) 73/239, 92/49 as well as Directives (EC)98/78 and 02/83 [2005] OJ L323/1.

58 See para 14.52 *et seq.*

A revised EU capital adequacy regime has been created for insurance under the Solvency II framework which will consolidate the insurance directives into a single directive.[59] **14.28**

Insurers and Reinsurers

Direct insurers—CLD and 3NLD

Unlike investment services, the single licence regime for insurers has emerged in stages. The CLD and the 3NLD apply to insurers that undertake 'direct' business (before the implementation of the RID),[60] there was no EU requirement for a specialist or 'pure' reinsurer to be authorised. In the UK, however, 'pure' reinsurers were required to be authorised and were subject to solvency and capital requirements, but some Member States either had no authorisation requirement at all or had only a light regulatory regime for reinsurers. **14.29**

The First Life Directive and the First Non-life Directive established a common authorisation requirement for insurers. The directives introduced common basic authorisation procedures and requirements including harmonised solvency margins (so that the home Member State regulator was solely responsible for the insurer's solvency in respect of its entire business). Insurers had a right to establish branches in other Member States but this was subject to local or host State authorisation and local regulation of technical reserves. **14.30**

Following the European Court of Justice decision in the German Co-Insurance case,[61] freedom of services for insurers was introduced in the Second Life and Non-life Directives (see the explanation of 'services' business at paragraph 16.43 *et seq.* under the heading 'Passporting and cross-border business'). This reflected the findings in the German Co-Insurance decision that (i) a requirement for a foreign insurer from another Member State to be established (ie to have a local branch) in the host State contravened the Treaty, (ii) that a requirement for local authorisation for services business was, in principle, contrary to the Treaty, and (iii) that a requirement for local authorisation, for certain types of policyholder, was not justified even without further harmonisation. The second generation of Directives therefore introduced limited freedom of services enabling insurers to conduct cross-border business without a separate authorisation in the host State. For non-life (general), this freedom was restricted to 'large' risks;[62] for life, it only applied to group and employment related life policies and those taken out (with the foreign insurer) on the consumer's own initiative. **14.31**

The third generation of Directives introduced the full single licence system or European 'passport'. This removed dual authorisation completely; an insurer's home State authorisation covered all services business and any branches established in other States. Critical to this development was the harmonisation of technical reserves (to enable home State authorities to regulate the reserves for business written by branches in other States); the Insurance Accounts Directive,[63] adopted at the same time as the Third Non-life Directive, was an important part of this harmonisation. **14.32**

59 See para 14.327 *et seq.*
60 See para 14.52.
61 Case 205/84 *Commission v Federal Republic of Germany* [1987].
62 An explanation of large risks can be found in para 14.5.
63 Council Directive (EEC) 91/674 on the annual accounts and consolidated accounts of insurance undertakings [1991] OJ L374/7.

Key aspects of the CLD and 3NLD regimes

14.33 The Directives require all direct insurers to be authorised and set out common standards and procedures for the authorisation process and for prudential supervision, particularly in relation to solvency, including the solvency margin, technical reserves, and admissible capital.

Solvency requirements and the minimum guarantee fund

14.34 Over and above technical reserves, the insurers must have what the directives describe as a 'supplementary reserve' or 'solvency margin'. This is the amount by which an insurer's assets exceed foreseeable liabilities and are free to provide against business fluctuations. There must be an adequate solvency margin in respect of the insurer's entire business.

14.35 For non-life business, the solvency margin requirement is the greater of two sums calculated by reference to premiums on the one hand and claims on the other. Regardless of the amount set by the solvency margin calculation (which may be small during the initial stages of establishment), the margin cannot fall below the minimum guarantee fund requirements.

14.36 The original solvency regime for insurers was updated by the Solvency I Directives.[64] This made some relatively minor amendments and was an interim measure pending a more fundamental review of the solvency regime for insurers known as Solvency II (see paragraph 14.327 *et seq.*).

Special characteristics of authorised insurers

14.37 The CLD and the 3NLD both require insurers to limit their 'objects to the business of insurance and operations arising directly therefrom to the exclusion of all other commercial business'.[65] This is incorporated into UK regulation though rule 1.5.13 of the Prudential Sourcebook for insurers ('INSPRU').[66] Unlike a firm conducting mediation or providing investment services, an insurer must be a specialist insurance entity. It is not possible to conduct the business of an insurer as a secondary activity. A company cannot therefore apply for authorisation to write insurance as an ancillary activity nor can authorised insurers conduct unrelated business (although a subsidiary or group company may be able to do so).

14.38 Under the Directives, the only types of private sector entity which can be authorised in the UK as an insurer are a body corporate (other than a limited liability partnership), a registered friendly society, or a member of Lloyd's.[67]

14.39 The Directives do not define insurance or the essential elements of a contract of insurance nor do they harmonise insurance contract law. The idea of a harmonised EU contract law has, however, been considered in order to further the aims of the single market. In 2011, the European Commission proposed a Common European Sales Law ('CESL') which would operate as an optional 28th legal regime in the EU.[68] As the CESL excludes insurance

---

[64] Council Directive (EC) 02/12 amending Council Directive (EEC) 79/267 as regards the solvency margin requirements for life assurance undertakings [2002] OJ L77/11; Council Directive (EC) 02/13 amending Council Directive (EEC) 73/239 as regards the solvency margin requirements for non-life insurance undertakings [2002] OJ L77/17 (the 'Solvency I Directives').

[65] CLD, Art 6.1(b); the Third Non-life Directive, Art 8.1(b).

[66] Previously in the Interim Prudential Sourcebook for Insurers (IPRU(INS)) 1.3.(1)R and (in a slightly different form) at s 16 of the ICA.

[67] Art 8(1) of the First Non-life Directive; Art 8(1) of the First Life Directive as repealed by Art 6(1) of CLD.

[68] Proposal for a regulation on Common European Sales Law (COM(2011) 635 final.

contracts the Commission is currently considering whether there is a need for an additional insurance contract regime to improve cross-border sales.[69]

The Directives divide life and non-life insurance into different classes; an insurer must be authorised in respect of each class it underwrites (subject to certain provisions on ancillary risks). The classes are reflected in Schedule 1 to the RAO[70] (albeit in slightly different terms). The classes of non-life (general) insurance are: **14.40**

(i) Accident (section 1)
(ii) Sickness (section 2)
(iii) Land vehicles (section 3)
(iv) Railway rolling stock (section 4)
(v) Aircraft (section 5)
(vi) Ships (section 6)
(vii) Goods in transit (section 7)
(viii) Fire and natural forces (section 8)
(ix) Other damage to property (section 9)
(x) Motor vehicle liability (section 10)
(xi) Aircraft liability (section 11)
(xii) Liability for/of ships (section 12)
(xiii) General liability (section 13)
(xiv) Credit (section 14)
(xv) Suretyship (in the RAO this includes fidelity, performance, administration, bail and custom bonds and similar contracts of guarantee if the provider is not carrying on a banking business; it is not merely incidental to some other business carried on by the person effecting it; and it is effected in return for the payment of one or more premiums (section 15))
(xvi) Miscellaneous financial loss (section 16)
(xvii) Legal expenses (section 17)
(xviii) Assistance (section 18).

For life (long-term) insurance, the classes are. **14.41**

I Life and annuity
II Marriage and birth
III Limited long term
IV Permanent health (which is excluded for non-life)
V Tontines
VI Capital redemption contracts
VII Pension fund management (by insurers)
VIII Collective insurance
IX Social insurance.

Class VII is peculiar in that it relates to an activity unrelated to a contract of insurance; it reflects the extension of a life office's permitted/authorised business to include the management of group pension funds. **14.42**

[69] See further at para 14.91 *et seq.*
[70] RAO, Sch 1, Part 1 paras 1–18 and Part 2 paras I–IX.

Passporting and cross-border business

14.43 As is the case with other single market directives, the single licence means that insurers and reinsurers are effectively authorised to write insurance business across the EEA. However, there are mandatory procedural requirements before an insurer can start, for the first time, to write business in a Member State (a host State) other than the State of its registration and authorisation (home State) (see paragraph 14.353 *et seq.*).

14.44 The CLD and the 3NLD provide rules to determine where insurance business is to be regarded as being conducted for passporting purposes.[71] For life business it is the Member State where the policyholder has his/her habitual residence or, in the case of a company insured, the location of the relevant office/branch (the State of commitment). For non-life business this depends on the location of the risk which is (in summary):

- property insurance—location of property;
- vehicle insurance—place of registration;
- place of purchase for short-term travel policy;
- other policies—habitual residence/company branch (as for State of commitment cited earlier).

14.45 As well as determining the State of the risk or commitment, it is also necessary to determine the location of the insurer's establishment which is underwriting the insurance. If the risk is located in the home State, there is no 'passporting' involved. If the establishment is in the home State and the risk in another, a service notification to the host State must have been completed. If the State of the establishment is not the home State, a branch notification for that State must have been completed. If that branch underwrites risks in another State, a service notification for that State is also required. The European Commission has published its view of when the use or involvement of a local intermediary or agent will be regarded as constituting a local branch of the insurer.[72]

14.46 The process for exercise of the passport to establish a branch of an insurer in another Member State is much more onerous than for services business or for the branch of an intermediary (see paragraphs 14.353 to 14.366 following).

General good and the review of policy terms/premium rates

14.47 The CLD and the 3NLD expressly forbid any prior or systematic substantive control of insurance policies and documents.[73] Member States should already have abandoned the previously widespread practice of controlling policy terms and premium scales/rates in this way. There are some limited exceptions, for example it is permissible for regulators to require the terms of compulsory insurance to be notified.

14.48 More broadly, the CLD and the 3NLD permit various host State regulation subject to the general good—for example in relation to the operations of a local branch of an insurer or in relation to laws on insurance policies or advertising. The case law on the 'general good' in the context of insurance is considered in some detail by the Commission in its interpretative

[71] CLD, art 1(g)–(h); the Third Non-life Directive, art 1(e).

[72] Commission Interpretative Communication (EC) 43/03: Freedom to provide services and the general good in the insurance sector [2000] OJ C043/5.

[73] CLD, art 45; Third Non-life Directive, arts 29 and 39.

Communication.[74] Under the concept of the general good an undertaking operating in the EU under a single passport must comply with those host State rules adopted in the interest of the general good. The concept derives from the case law of the Court of Justice of the European Union ('CJEU'). The CJEU requires that such national provisions must meet specified criteria if they are to limit the general principles of freedom of establishment and freedom to provide services. These criteria are that provisions must: fall within a field which has not been subject to EU harmonisation, must pursue an objective of the general good, must be non-discriminatory, be objectively necessary, be proportionate to the objective pursued, and must not be safeguarded by rules imposed by the home Member State.

Applicable law

The CLD and the 3NLD contain provisions dealing with the ability of Member States to require that their law is the applicable law for an insurance contract[75] (see paragraph 14.95 *et seq.* which refer to the applicable regime from a UK perspective—the UK allows a greater freedom of choice than some Member States). **14.49**

Information for policyholders

The Directives set out certain information requirements for policyholders; these are implemented in the UK through the FCA's Conduct of Business Rules (contained in COBS and ICOBS).[76] **14.50**

The CLD and the 3NLD also deal with: **14.51**

- transfer of policies 'en bloc' under insurance business transfers (in the UK, these are Part VII transfers or transfers relating to Lloyd's business under section 323 of FSMA);[77]
- cancellation rights in relation to life (long-term) policies;[78]
- transparency in group structures to ensure effective supervision[79] (the post-BCCI directive amendments).

Reinsurers—The Reinsurance Directive[80]

Background

The 1964 Directive on the abolition of restrictions on the freedom of establishment and freedom to provide services in respect of reinsurance and retrocession (the reinsurance of reinsurance)[81] was one of the first pieces of EU insurance legislation. It prohibited the discrimination against incoming reinsurers, but it did not require Member States to authorise or regulate **14.52**

[74] Commission Interpretative Communication (EC) 43/03: Freedom to provide services and the general good in the insurance sector [2000] OJ C043/5.

[75] CLD, art 32; Third Non-life Directive, art 31.

[76] See para 14.205 *et seq.*

[77] CLD, arts 14 and 53; Third Non-life Directive, arts 12 and 53.

[78] CLD, art 35.

[79] Council Directive (EC) 95/26 amending Directives (EEC) 77/780 and 89/646 in the field of credit institutions, Directives (EEC) 73/239 and 92/49 in the field of non-life insurance, Council Directives 79/267/EEC and 92/96/EEC in the field of life assurance, Council Directive (EEC) 93/22 in the field of investment firms, and Directive (EEC) 85/611 in the field of undertakings for collective investment in transferable securities ('UCITS'), with a view to reinforcing prudential supervision [1995] OJ L168/7.

[80] See n 57.

[81] Council Directive (EEC) 64/225 on the abolition of restrictions on freedom of establishment and freedom to provide services in respect of reinsurance and retrocession [1964] OJ 56/878.

'pure' reinsurers (ie insurers which only underwrite reinsurance and retrocession, and which do not underwrite any 'direct' insurance and which therefore fall outside the CLD and the 3NLD). Member States were therefore free either to regulate pure reinsurers or not, as they saw fit. Some States did not regulate pure reinsurers at all or adopted a very light touch regime, whereas others (such as the UK) regulated them in much the same way as direct insurers.

14.53 The lack of harmonisation and a 'single passport' for pure reinsurers was not initially a major concern, partly because reinsurance was already an international business, and direct insurers faced greater cross-border barriers.

14.54 The RID was adopted in December 2005, and was implemented in December 2007. The legislation:

(i) harmonised the authorisation and regulation (principally prudential regulation such as solvency) of pure reinsurers; and
(ii) introduced the single passport system for pure reinsurers.

14.55 It aimed to improve consumer protection (because EU direct insurers would be better protected by their reinsurance arrangements with EU pure reinsurers and this would indirectly benefit the policyholders of the direct insurer), cross-border operation, and hence competition. It was also envisaged that a harmonised EU regime might assist in trade negotiations with the US, particularly in the context of onerous US collateral requirements in relation to foreign reinsurers.

Authorisation and solvency

14.56 Like direct insurers, the Directive requires authorisation of pure reinsurers and imposes conditions such as the form of reinsurance undertakings, close links and controllers, and a scheme of operations. There is a limitation on activities, but this is a little broader than that for direct or primary insurers.[82]

14.57 The single passport system and home State authorisation for the entire EEA apply for both cross-border services business and for branches in other EEA States. The RID does not mirror the procedural requirements for cross-border notifications in the regime for direct insurers. As with direct insurers, pure reinsurers incorporated outside the EEA are subject to separate authorisation in each EEA State.

14.58 The RID introduces a harmonised solvency regime based on the Solvency I regime for direct non-life insurers. When in force, Solvency II will govern the treatment of pure reinsurers, replacing the RID.

Collateralisation

14.59 The RID improved the position of EU pure reinsurers by amending the CLD and the 3NLD to restrict some collateral requirements imposed on direct insurers in relation to their reinsurance.

Other provisions

14.60 The RID also:

(i) defines 'finite' reinsurance and permits Member States to regulate it;[83]

[82] See para 14.168.
[83] RID, art 2.1(q) and art 45.

(ii) introduces Insurance Special Purpose Vehicles ('ISPVs'),[84] which are defined as SPVs that accept risks from insurers/reinsurers and are funded by debt issuance (or other financing) subordinated to the SPVs' reinsurance obligations. ISPVs can be authorised, if a Member State so permits, without compliance with RID requirements (but under appropriate domestic procedures and requirements);

(iii) completes the system for EU wide portfolio transfers.[85]

Other EU insurance legislation

There is further EU legislation adopted or proposed in the following areas: 14.61

- Motor insurance (there have been five generations of directives dealing with compulsory motor insurance, now consolidated into a sixth directive).[86]
- Insurers Winding-Up Directive,[87] which came into force on 15 April 2003.
- Supervision—establishing the European Insurance and Occupational Pensions Committee ('EIOPC'); and creating the European Insurance and Occupational Pension Authority ('EIOPA') as the European Supervisory Authority with responsibility for insurance supervision.[88] EIOPA was established as one of the three supervisory authorities of the financial sector following reforms to the structure of financial supervision in the EU. EIOPA replaced the Committee of European Insurance and Occupational Pensions Supervisors ('CEIOPS').
- Co-insurance,[89] legal expenses insurance,[90] accounting,[91] and exchange of information with third countries.[92]
- Mergers and Acquisitions in the financial services sector.[93]
- Solvency and financial supervision.[94]
- Amendments to the Third Non-life Directive concerning tourist assistance, credit insurance, and suretyship insurance.[95]

---

[84] ibid, art 2.1(p) and art 46.

[85] ibid, art 18.

[86] Directive 2009/103/EC of 16 September 2009 relating to insurance against civil liability in respect of the use of motor vehicles, and the enforcement of the obligation to insure against such liability [2009] OJ L263/11.

[87] Council Directive (EC) 2001/17 on the reorganisation and winding-up of insurance undertakings [2001] OJ L110/28.

[88] Commission Decision (EC) 04/9 of 5 November 2003 establishing the European Insurance and Occupational Pensions Committee [2004] OJ L003/34, as amended by Regulation (EC) No 1882/2003, Directive 2005/1/EC and Directive (EC) 2008/21; Regulation (EU) No 1094/2010 of the European Parliament and of the Council of 24 November 2010 establishing a European Supervisory Authority (European Insurance and Occupational Pensions Authority), amending Decision No 716/2009/EC and repealing Commission Decision 2009/79/EC [2010] OJ L331/48.

[89] Council Directive (EEC) 78/473 on the coordination of laws, regulations and administrative provisions relating to Community co-insurance [1978] OJ L151/25.

[90] Council Directive (EEC) 87/344 on the coordination of laws, regulations, and administrative provisions relating to legal expenses insurance [1987] OJ L185/77.

[91] Council Directive (EEC) 91/674 on annual and consolidated accounts of insurance undertakings [1991] OJ L374/7; Council Directive (EEC) 78/660 on annual accounts of certain types of companies [1978] OJ L222/11; Directive (EEC) 83/349 Seventh Council Directive—Consolidated accounts [1983] OJ L193/1.

[92] Council Directive (EC) 00/64 amending Council Directives (EEC) 85/611, 92/49, 92/96, 93/22 as regards exchange of information with third countries [2000] OJ L290/27.

[93] Council Directive (EC) 2007/44 amending Council Directive (EEC) 92/49 and Directives (EC) 2002/83, 2004/39, 2005/68 and 2006/48 as regards procedural rules and evaluation criteria for the prudential assessment of acquisitions and increase of holdings in the financial sector [2007] OJ L247/1.

[94] See para 14.274 *et seq.*

[95] Council Directive (EEC) 84/641 amending, particularly as regards tourist assistance, the First Directive (EEC) 73/239 on the coordination of laws, regulations, and administrative provisions relating to the taking-up and pursuit of the business of direct insurance other than life assurance [1984] OJ L339/21.

- Insurance Guarantee Schemes—unlike credit institutions and investment services, there is currently no EU legislation requiring or regulating compensation schemes to protect policyholders when insurers become insolvent. In response to calls for harmonised rules on guarantee schemes across the EU, the European Commission has consulted on whether to harmonise insurance schemes.[96] A proposed directive is anticipated but is unpublished at the time of writing.
- Money Laundering Directives—three directives which include identification requirements for certain life business.[97]
- Distance Marketing Directive ('DMD')[98]—this applies to insurance contracts and insurance mediation contracts with consumers and is implemented in the UK, in relation to insurance, through COBS and ICOBS, and the Financial Services (Distance Marketing) Regulations 2004, SI 2004/2095. It prohibits unsolicited services and requires, for distance contracts, the provision of information to consumers (normally in good time prior to the conclusion of the contract) and gives cancellation rights (long-term insurance contracts—including face-to-face sales—were already subject to cancellation under the 3NLD).
- E-Commerce Directive ('ECD')[99]—the ECD is designed to remove potential restrictions on e-commerce across the EU. The ECD applies to the provision of services (to businesses and consumers) by means of electronic equipment (and therefore has a wide application which includes some areas of insurance business). The ECD removes restrictions on the cross-border provision of services by electronic means, introducing a 'country of origin' approach to regulation.[100] Member States must therefore impose their requirements on the outward provision of such services and lift them from inward providers. Insurance is one of the few areas where 'derogations' are available to allow host States to apply their advertising rules in the 'general good' under CLD and 3NLD.[101]
- Anti-discrimination—the Gender Directive[102] prohibits both direct and indirect discrimination in the provision of goods and services. A derogation allowing insurers to price risks according to the gender of the insured was successfully challenged in the *Test-Achats*[103] case in the CJEU. Following the decision of the CJEU, all contracts concluded after 21 December 2012 must not price risk with reference to the gender of the insured.

[96] White Paper on Insurance Guarantee Schemes COM(2010) 370 (see also Chapter 4, paras 4.127–4.128 on banking and investment protection).

[97] Directive 2005/60/EC of the European Parliament and of the Council of 26 October 2005 on the prevention of the use of the financial system for the purpose of money laundering and terrorist financing [2005] L309/15.

[98] Council Directive (EC) 02/65 concerning the distance marketing of consumer financial services and amending Council Directive (EEC) 90/619 and Directives (EC) 97/7 and 98/27 [2002] OJ L271/16. See also Chapter 4 paras 4.133–4.135.

[99] Council Directive (EC) 00/31 on certain legal aspects of information society services, in particular electronic commerce, in the Internal Market [2000] OJ L178/1 (the 'ECD'). See also Chapter 4 paras 4.136–4.137.

[100] This approach means that Member States must impose their requirements on the outward provision of the relevant services, but must not impose them for inward service providers.

[101] Member States which have adopted the derogations may continue to impose their existing requirements on the inward provision of services, but in accordance with the ECD, they will not be able to impose their domestic requirements on the outward provision of services falling with the scope of the ECD. Instead, the country of destination's requirements (if any) will apply. See ICOBS 1 Annex 1 8.4 for further information.

[102] Council Directive 2004/113/EC of 13 December 2004 implementing the principle of equal treatment between men and women in the access to and supply of goods and services [2004] OJ 373/37.

[103] Case C-236/09 *Association Belge des Consommateurs Test-Achats ASBL and Others v Conseil des ministers* [2011].

Insurance Intermediaries

Pre-IMD measures

Prior to the IMD, there were two EU measures dealing with insurance intermediaries. These were the Insurance Agents and Brokers Directive of 1976[104] and the subsequent Commission Recommendation of 1991 (the 'Recommendation').[105] The Directive was intended as a transitional measure pending mutual recognition of qualifications and was very limited in scope. It required those Member States which imposed qualification or experience requirements to recognise experience in other Member States. The Recommendation was not binding on Member States and envisaged the introduction of a more comprehensive system of compulsory registration and professional competence requirements. Both measures focused on the activities of professionals rather than firms and distinguished between independent brokers (as registered in the UK under the IBRA—see paragraph 14.9 *et seq.*) and agents of insurers. **14.62**

The IMD

The IMD was adopted in 2002. This was a binding directive which replaced the two previous measures and introduced an EEA wide registration requirement for intermediaries with the single or 'European' passport. **14.63**

The IMD definition of intermediary is not limited to the concepts, in the earlier legislation, of brokers and insurers' agents. It can apply to a company (as well as to self-employed individuals). It is based on five mediation activities[106] where these relate to direct insurance contracts or reinsurance or retrocession contracts. It does not apply to the mediation of risks located outside the EEA nor to authorised EEA insurers or their employees. **14.64**

There is no requirement for an insurance intermediary to be a specialist company (as with insurers); insurance mediation is often conducted as a secondary or ancillary activity. Indeed, a firm may be authorised as a credit institution under the Banking Consolidation Directive[107] (or as an investment firm under the Markets in Financial Instruments Directive)[108] and, at the same time, it can be registered as an insurance intermediary under the IMD; such a firm can 'passport' under both directives. **14.65**

The IMD introduced a 'registration' requirement (unlike the insurance, banking, and investment firms legislation, the IMD refers to 'registration' rather than 'authorisation'). In the UK, insurance intermediaries are 'registered' with the FCA through authorisation under FSMA or, in the case of appointed representatives, by registration with the FCA following their appointment.[109] There are exclusions for certain introducers and those dealing with 'connected contracts'.[110] **14.66**

---

[104] Council Directive (EEC) 77/92 on measures to facilitate the effective exercise of freedom of establishment and freedom to provide services in respect of the activities of insurance agents and brokers [1977] OJ L26/14.

[105] Commission Recommendation (EEC) 92/48 on insurance intermediaries [1991] OJ L019/32.

[106] See para 14.127.

[107] Council Directive (EC) 06/48 relating to the taking up and pursuit of the business of credit institutions [2006] OJ L177/1 (the 'BCD').

[108] Council Directive (EC) 04/39 on Markets in Financial Instruments, amending Council Directives (EEC) 85/611 and 93/6 and Directive (EC) 2000/12, and repealing Council Directive (EEC) 93/22 [2004] OJ L245/1 ('MiFID').

[109] See paras 14.150–14.155.

[110] See paras 14.142 in relation to art 72B and 72C of the RAO, and para 16.207 *et seq.* in relation to the relevant ICOBS requirements.

14.67 There are minimum professional requirements for intermediaries concerning knowledge and ability and good repute, professional indemnity insurance, and the protection of customers (against the failure of intermediaries to transfer premiums to insurers or to pay claims or premium refunds to customers). In this last area, Member States are given the choice of four measures under Article 4(4):

(a) provisions (in law or contract) whereby payment by the customer to the intermediary is treated as payment to the insurer (and payment by the insurer to the intermediary is not treated as payment to the customer);
(b) capital requirements with a minimum of 4 per cent of annual premiums received or €15,000, if greater;
(c) segregated client accounts; and
(d) a guarantee fund.

14.68 The UK has adopted measures in all four areas but for Directive compliance it relies on a mixture of the rules under Article 4(4)(a) and (c). The IMD is unusual in allowing Member States a choice of measures within a single licence/mutual recognition system. It appears that there is some scope for conflict, although the intention is that home State rules will apply.

14.69 The passporting process is relatively simple even in the case of a branch with a maximum two-month waiting period from notification. The Directive makes special provision for Member States to waive the right to receive notifications in respect of incoming firms.

14.70 There are requirements for intermediaries to provide their customers with information about their regulatory status and the service they provide as well as a demands and needs statement (these do not apply to large risks[111] or reinsurance mediation). These requirements are reflected within the FCA's conduct of business rules in COBS and ICOBS.[112]

14.71 As the IMD does not apply to authorised EEA insurers, the demands and needs requirement does not apply to direct sales. However, insurers must be prohibited, under home State regulation, from using the mediation services of unregistered intermediaries—a provision incorporated in MIPRU 5.2 (see paragraphs 14.351 to 14.352).

14.72 Unlike the CLD and the 3NLD, IMD does not define what amounts to 'cross border' or 'services' business (which requires a notification and potentially brings 'host' State's general good rules into play). Mediation by, say, a UK intermediary, may involve a variety of different contacts or potential links with other Member States—such as the location of the risk, the location of the policyholder, the location of the insurer, the location of a producing broker in relation to the placing broker and vice versa, or the location at which mediation or placing activities take place. The predecessor Committee in place before EIOPA, considered these issues and advocated a combined test, namely that an intermediary would be carrying on business on a freedom of services basis if it intends to supply a policyholder established in a Member State different from the one where the intermediary is established, with an insurance contract relating to a risk situated in a Member State different from the one where the intermediary is established. This test is currently contained in the Luxembourg Protocol—which provides the framework for the cooperation of Member State supervisory authorities

111 See the explanation of 'large risks' in para 14.5.
112 See para 14.207 *et seq.*

in dealing with issues under the IMD—but it is anticipated that, when adopted IMD2 may include clarification on the provision of services across borders.[113]

Shortly after the implementation of the IMD in 2005 the European Commission conducted a review to gauge the effectiveness of the new regime. The review found that, although the IMD had introduced a level of consumer protection for sales of insurance products, the minimum harmonisation nature of the Directive had resulted in a patchwork of national regulations—with some governments 'gold-plating' implementation measures while others introduced the bare minimum required to be compliant. As a result, there are numerous gaps and inconsistencies in the single market for insurance resulting in limited sales across borders. The Commission review found there to be insufficient consumer knowledge of the risks, costs, and features of insurance products and a lack of transparency around remuneration meant that there were too many commission-driven conflicts of interest in the market.[114] 14.73

The draft IMD2[115] tackles the issues of scope of regulation, conflicts of interests and remuneration transparency, quality of advice and information for customers in addition to recognition of professional standards. The draft proposes bringing direct writers (insurers and reinsurers selling to customers without the use of intermediaries) and sales of insurance through aggregator websites within scope and proposes the mandatory disclosure of both the amount and basis of any remuneration received for selling policies. The draft also creates a distinction between investment products and other products for the application of certain requirements, for example a requirement to identify, prevent, manage, and disclose conflicts of interest when selling insurance investment products. 14.74

Competition Issues

Block exemption for the insurance sector

In the competition law field, there is some specific sectoral legislation dealing with insurance. The general prohibition on anti-competitive agreements and practices is applicable to insurance but there is a block exemption for certain agreements and practices relating to insurance (a new exemption[116] came into force in April 2010; this replaced the previous block exemption introduced in 2003).[117] The block exemption exempts a number of agreements from the application of normal competition rules where certain conditions are met. 14.75

[113] Protocol Relating to the Cooperation of the Competent Authorities of the Member States of the European Union in Particular Concerning the Application of Directive 2002/92/EC of the European Parliament and of the Council of 9 December 2002 on Insurance Mediation April 2006 (CEIOPS). The Protocol takes into consideration the intention of the intermediary provided in art 6 of the IMD. This definition creates no artificial barriers for existing mediation activities and it minimises the administrative burden; the protection of the consumer is guaranteed since it is based on the decision of the consumer to request the services of an intermediary operating in another Member State.

[114] Proposal for a directive of the European Parliament and of the Council on insurance mediation COM(2012) 360/2.

[115] ibid.

[116] Commission Regulation (EU) 267/2010 on the application of art 101(3) of the Treaty on the Functioning of the European Union to certain categories of agreements, decisions and concerted practices in the insurance sector [2010] OJ L83/1.

[117] Commission Regulation (EC) 358/2003 on the application of art 81(3) of the Treaty to certain categories of agreements, decisions and concerted practices in the insurance sector [2003] OJ L53/8.

14.76 The regulation is unusual in providing an exemption on a sectoral basis. It deals with the following types of agreement:

- joint calculations of risks and joint studies on future risks; and
- the establishment and management of insurance pools.

14.77 The block exemption provides an automatic exemption for those agreements that come within its scope. If an agreement falls outside of the block exemption this does not necessarily mean that the agreement will infringe the EU rules on competition. The agreement may not infringe competition rules or it may satisfy the generic criteria for exemption. The exemption is also important in the context of the Competition Act 1998 as compliance with an EU block exemption provides a 'parallel' exemption under the 1998 Act.

14.78 Prior to the existing block exemption, the establishment of non-binding standard policy conditions and agreements as to standards for security devices were also exempted. However, following a consultation the European Commission decided to renew only two types of agreements. Under the current exemption, insurers are able to collaborate in compiling information which enables the calculation of the average cost of covering a specific risk, and to have joint case studies assessing the likely impact of an extraneous event on the frequency or scale of claims. However, these activities are only exempted to the extent that it is necessary to achieve these aims and only a minimal amount of information should therefore be shared. For insurance pools the Commission has retained the exemption for new risks and for other pools where the participants meet certain market share thresholds (based on the turnover of the pool). The current Block Exemption Regulation will expire on 31 March 2017.

Regulation and competition law overlap—the Commission's sectoral inquiry into business insurance

14.79 There is a considerable overlap and inter-play between insurance regulation and competition, or anti-trust, issues. This could be seen at an EU level in the Commission's 2007 report on business insurance.[118] Despite being a competition inquiry conducted by the Directorate General for Competition, the Commission's report looked at conflicts of interest in the insurance sector, particularly insurer bias deriving from intermediary remuneration structures and, for SME clients, the lack of commission disclosure. These are all also regulatory issues which concern insurance regulators. The FCA's approach is considered at paragraph 14.160 *et seq*. The Commission's proposal for IMD2 seeks to address some of the concerns raised in the report by introducing much more stringent rules on commission disclosure and the management of conflicts of interest. In addition, the Commission's report raised a number of other concerns about competition and considered various aspects of subscription insurance markets such as the London Market; these included the traditional arrangements for, and respective roles of, a 'lead' underwriter and 'following' underwriters and the use of standard insurance policy wordings or clauses.

14.80 In February 2013, a study was published by the European Commission who had invited Ernst & Young LLP to undertake research into the operation of co-insurance pools and co-insurance agreements (including reinsurance) in the subscription market across the EU.[119]

[118] Sector Inquiry under art 17 of Regulation (EC) No 1/2003 on business insurance (Final Report) (SEC (2007) 1231).

[119] European Commission study on co(re)insurance pools and on ad hoc co(re)insurance agreements on the subscription market (2013).

The study indicates that there may be compliance issues in relation to how these markets meet competition restrictions. The research is part of the Commission's continued monitoring of competition issues in the insurance sector.

Another overlap of competition and insurance regulation can be seen in the approach taken to the mis-selling of payment protection insurance ('PPI'), where both the Competition Commission and FSA considered concurrently what the issues were with the sales of these products.[120] **14.81**

UK Law and Regulation

In the next sections we look at how the legislation and regulatory Handbooks, described in outline in earlier chapters, apply to insurers and insurance intermediaries. Paragraph 14.82 *et seq*. deal mainly with the relevant legislation, contracts of insurance and regulated activities, financial promotions, appointed representatives, and other issues; and paragraph 14.160 *et seq*. with parts of the regulatory Handbook (namely COND,[121] PRIN,[122] SYSC,[123] ICOBS, CASS, GENPRU,[124] INSPRU,[125] MIPRU,[126] TC[127]). In the final section, we look at the Financial Ombudsman Scheme ('FOS') under DISP[128] and the Financial Services Compensation Scheme ('FSCS') under COMP.[129] **14.82**

Contracts of insurance

There is no comprehensive statutory definition (in EU or UK legislation) to determine whether a contract amounts to a contract of insurance. (The issue had received surprisingly little attention in a regulatory context until the FSA decided to consult on draft guidance, although the courts have had to determine the issue in relation to various specific contracts which were the subject of litigation.) The question is important in a variety of contexts including tax and regulation. **14.83**

The definition of insurance in the context of the regulatory perimeter and regulated activities under the RAO is considered at paragraph 14.103 *et seq*.; there are particular aspects which are dealt with in the statutory provisions but the fundamental issue of what does or does not constitute a contract of insurance is considered in the FCA's guidance and is based on case law. **14.84**

FCA Guidance: what constitutes a contract of insurance

The FCA's Perimeter Guidance Manual ('PERG') outlines principles to be used in the identification of insurance contracts. **14.85**

---

[120] See Chapter 1 para 1.46.
[121] FCA Handbook: Threshold Conditions.
[122] The Principles For Businesses found in both the PRA and FCA Handbooks.
[123] Senior Management Arrangements, Systems and Controls sourcebooks in both the PRA and FCA Handbooks.
[124] General Prudential sourcebook in both the PRA and FCA Handbooks.
[125] Prudential Sourcebook for Insurers in the PRA Handbook.
[126] Prudential Sourcebook for Mortgage and Home Finance Firms, and Insurance Intermediaries in the FCA Handbook.
[127] Training and Competence sourcebook in the FCA Handbook.
[128] Dispute Resolution: Complaints sourcebook in the FCA Handbook.
[129] Dispute Resolution: Compensation in both the PRA and FCA Handbooks.

14.86 The guidance stresses that each case will be considered on its own merits.[130] The principles outlined are to be used as guidance only and whether a contract is one of insurance or not can only be decided by the courts.[131] In line with case law, the FCA view is that the substance of the contract prevails over its form.[132] The agreed starting point is the definition in *Prudential v Commissioners of Inland Revenue*,[133] but there has been other more recent case law which is also considered by the FCA.[134] If case law is unclear the FCA will interpret and apply the law in a way that is consistent with the purpose of its statutory objectives.[135]

14.87 The FCA summarises the description of an insurance contract as an enforceable contract under which a 'provider' undertakes:

- in consideration of one or more payments;
- to pay money or provide a corresponding benefit (including in some cases services to be paid for by the provider) to a 'recipient';
- in response to a defined event the occurrence of which is uncertain (either as to when it will occur or as to whether it will occur at all) and adverse to the interests of the recipient.[136]

14.88 Additionally the FCA use the following guidelines:

- Substance over form. The FCA regards the substance of the contract, in particular the substance of the provider's obligation, to be more important than its form in determining whether it is a contract of insurance.[137]
- One cannot rely on the contract having a dominant purpose other than insurance, or the relatively small element of insurance within it, to conclude that it is not a contract of insurance. The FCA simply requires the presence of an insurance obligation undertaken by the provider—it need not be substantial, nor does it need to form a significant part of the provider's business.[138]
- Providers must be obliged to provide a benefit. Contracts where a provider has an absolute discretion as to whether any benefit is provided are not contracts of insurance, even if the provider has never exercised this discretion to deny the benefit.[139]
- There must be an 'assumption' or 'transfer of risk', this is considered an important descriptive feature of contracts of insurance and the FCA has derived its meaning largely from case law.[140] The 'assumption of risk' or 'transfer of risk' can be seen as an 'enforceable obligation to respond to the occurrence of some uncertain event'. Transfer of risk is not viewed as the same thing as the insurer's risk of profit or loss from insurance business.[141]
- Contracts that constitute a simple payment for services (where the payment is related to cost) are not insurance contracts. Factors considered are the amount and timing of the

---

[130] PERG 6.4.3G.

[131] PERG 6.4.1G.

[132] PERG 6.5.4(1)G citing *Fuji Finance Inc v Aetna Life Insurance Co Ltd* [1997] Ch 173 (CA).

[133] PERG 6.5.1G.

[134] *Department of Trade and Industry v St Christopher's Motorist Association Ltd* [1974] 1 WLR 99, [1974] 1 All ER 395; *Medical Defence Union v Department of Trade* [1980] Ch 82, [1979] 2 WLR 686.

[135] PERG 6.5.3G.

[136] PERG 6.3.4G.

[137] PERG 6.5.4(2)G.

[138] PERG 6.6.7(2)(3)G.

[139] PERG 6.6.1G.

[140] PERG 6.6.2G.

[141] PERG 6.6.2G.

payments made by the insured.[142] Where the provider simply undertakes to provide periodic maintenance of goods/facilities irrespective of any events occurring,[143] or where in consideration for an initial payment a provider undertakes to provide services on the condition that they are to be paid at the commercial rate,[144] a contract of insurance is unlikely to be involved.

- Consideration in a contract of insurance does not need to be a distinct or discrete premium. Consideration may either be part of some other payment or be provided in a non-monetary form.[145]

Other factors influencing the FCA's determination of whether a contract of insurance exists include: how the amount payable by the recipient is calculated,[146] whether the risk is 'pure' or 'speculative',[147] whether the contract is actually described as insurance,[148] and in some cases the existence of terms inconsistent with obligations of good faith.[149] The FCA refers to the general position that a contract of insurance[150] need not be in writing although there are exceptions such as marine insurance[151] and guarantee insurance.[152] **14.89**

'Finite' or financial reinsurance

In an FSA consultation[153] in 2002 financial engineering was described as 'an umbrella term for certain types of arrangements used by insurance firms for financing or regulatory reporting purposes, or both. These arrangements are used to improve, or sometimes to smooth, reported profits or to improve the reported balance sheet position'.[154] Financial engineering was recognised as a valid method of strengthening an insurer's solvency and of recognising and reporting economic reality. However, it should be properly constructed and applied and must involve genuine and material risk transfer to an unconnected third party. If used inappropriately financial engineering can obscure the financial condition of an insurer, thereby misleading consumers, investors, and regulators, which will breach several regulatory requirements. The PRA Handbook now has specific provisions designed to ensure sufficient transparency in financial returns regarding financial reinsurance agreements.[155] The RID[156] specifically allows Member States to regulate finite reinsurance[157] (including the use of mandatory contractual provisions, accounting and risk management controls, and solvency requirements). **14.90**

142 PERG 6.6.3G.
143 PERG 6.6.4G.
144 PERG 6.6.5G.
145 PERG 6.6.6G.
146 PERG 6.6.8(1)G.
147 PERG 6.6.8(2)G.
148 PERG 6.6.8(3)G.
149 PERG 6.6.8(4)G.
150 PERG 6.5.4(4).
151 Marine Insurance Act 1906, s 22.
152 Statute of Frauds 1677, s 4.
153 FSA CP144: 'A new regulatory approach to insurance firms' use of financial engineering'.
154 ibid, s 3.
155 SYSC 17.1.34A and IPRU (INS) 9.32A and 9.32B in the PRA Handbook.
156 See n 57.
157 Art 2(1)(q) defines finite reinsurance as 'Reinsurance under which the explicit maximum economic risk transferred, arising both from a significant underwriting risk and from a timing risk transfer, exceeds the premium over the lifetime of the contract, by a limited but significant amount, together with at least one of the following two features: (i) explicit and material consideration of the time value of money; (ii) contractual provisions to moderate the balance of economic experience between the parties over time to achieve the target risk transfer'.

Insurance contract law and regulation

14.91 There is currently no harmonised law of insurance contracts at European level and the lack of an optional 'European' contract law has been considered to be one of the factors restricting a single market in financial services. Following a European Commission Green Paper on policy options for progress towards a European contract law for consumers and businesses,[158] an expert group has been set up to consider whether differences between Member State laws create barriers to cross-border trade.[159] There are, however, existing European rules relating to applicable law, jurisdiction, and unfair terms which are relevant to insurance contracts. In addition, we consider later in this chapter the domestic legislation concerning third party rights which is also relevant to insurance contracts.

Unfair Terms in Consumer Contracts Regulations 1999

14.92 The Unfair Terms in Consumer Contract Regulations 1999[160] ('UTCC Regulations') apply to contracts of insurance where the contracting insured is a 'consumer'.[161] Those terms in insurance contracts defining risk, including exclusions, relate to the 'definition of the main subject matter of the contract' and fall outside the 'fairness obligation' if they are written in plain intelligible language;[162] this also applies to exclusions that define the cover provided. The FCA will interpret the exclusion narrowly however, and firms should take a cautious approach to exclusions—if the terms are not considered to be intelligible, the UTCC Regulations will allow the FCA to identify the term as unfair.[163] Other provisions in an insurance contract, which do not define risk, or any term not in plain intelligible language, are subject to the full regulations. A term will be considered unfair if 'contrary to the requirement of good faith it causes a significant imbalance in the parties' rights and obligations arising under the contract, to the detriment of the consumer'.[164] A term which is unfair cannot be enforced or relied upon against the consumer.[165]

14.93 Under the UTCC Regulations the FCA (as well as the OFT) is a qualifying body which may apply for injunctions against unfair terms.[166] The FCA's approach to the use of its powers in relation to the Regulations is captured in the FCA Unfair Contract Terms Regulatory Guide ('UNFCOG'). The FCA may consider the fairness of a contract following a complaint from a consumer or on its own initiative.[167] If the FCA after first expressing its concern and inviting comments from the firm in question remains of the view that a term is unfair it will normally ask the firm to undertake to stop including the term in new contracts and stop relying on it in contracts which have been concluded.[168] This may have a major impact if the term is

158 Green paper from the Commission on policy options for progress towards a European Contract Law for consumers and businesses COM(2010) 348.

159 Commission Decision 2013/C 16/03 of 17 January 2013 on setting up the Commission Expert Group on a European Insurance Contract Law [2013] C16/6.

160 Unfair Terms in Consumer Contract Regulations 1999, SI 1999/2083, replacing SI 1994/ 3159 and implementing Council Directive (EEC) 93/13 on Unfair Terms in Consumer Contracts [1993] OJ L95/29.

161 Unlike the Unfair Contract Terms Act 1977, which did not apply to 'contracts of insurance'.

162 Reg 6(2) of the UTCC Regulations.

163 See FSA undertaking Legal & General Insurance Limited, 9 December 2011.

164 Reg 5(1) of the UTCC Regulations.

165 Reg 8(1) of the UTCC Regulations.

166 The Unfair Terms in Consumer Contracts Regulations 1999, Regulation 12; the FCA became a Qualifying Body for the purposes of unfair contract terms under the Financial Services Act 2012 (Consequential Amendments and Transitional Provisions) Order 2013/472, having taken over responsibility for supervision of conduct from the FSA.

167 UNFCOG .4.1.

168 UNFCOG 1.3.4.

important and has been used in a large number of consumer contracts. Undertakings given by firms to change contractual terms which have been found to be unfair are published on the FCA website.

Contracts (Rights of Third Parties) Act 1999

This Act removed the difficulties arising from the English law of 'privity of contract'. It assists third party insureds to claim under a contract of insurance to which they were not a party (subject to the requirement to hold an insurable interest in the subject matter of the policy). Under the Act a third party may in his own right enforce a contract term provided (a) the contract expressly so provides or (b) the term purports to confer a benefit on the third party.[169] The Act also gives the third party similar rights to those of the contracting party, for example the right not to have contract terms varied without its consent. However, parties to a contract are able to exclude the operation of this Act in part or completely. For this reason insurers often insert an exclusion of the Act in a wide range of insurance contracts.[170] Separate legislation deals with the rights of certain victims where the responsible person is insured but becomes insolvent.[171] **14.94**

Applicable law

The determination of the correct applicable law of an insurance contract is an important feature of the insurance; it also has regulatory importance. The relevant European law is to be found in: **14.95**

- The Rome I Regulation,[172] which applies the rules on applicable law in the Second Non-Life Directive and CLD implemented into UK law by the Financial Services and Markets Act (Law Applicable to Contracts of Insurance) Regulations 2001, to contracts concluded before 17 December 2009 (reinsurance contracts remain out of scope); and,
- The Rome Convention,[173] which applies to all non-EEA risks and to EEA contracts concluded before 17 December 2009; in addition to reinsurance contracts, whether written in the EEA or not.

Before the implementation of Rome I, choice of law was determined by the Second Non-Life Directive and CLD which were implemented into UK law by the Financial Services and Markets Act (Law Applicable to Contracts of Insurance) Regulations 2001. **14.96**

[169] ss (1)(1) (b) and (2) of the Contracts (Rights of Third Parties) Act 1999.

[170] This act does not apply in Scotland. Policies written under Scots law will be subject to the doctrine of *jus quaesitum tertio* which provides that third-party rights cannot be excluded. Such rights are enforceable subject to certain conditions being met. The Third Parties (Rights against Insurers) Act 1930 does apply in Scotland.

[171] The Third Parties (Rights Against Insurers) Act 1930 confers on third parties rights against insurers of third-party risks in the event of the insured becoming insolvent (and in certain other events). The act was put in place to deal with situations where an insured had caused damage or personal injury and then becomes bankrupt. In such circumstances, the insured's right to claim on his insurance is transferred by the act to the victim, allowing him to claim directly on the insured's insurance and obtain the proceeds of that insurance. A revised act passed in 2010 allows a person with a claim against an insolvent person to proceed against the insolvent's insurer directly, without first establishing the liability of the insolvent person. The Third Parties (Rights Against Insurers) Act 2010 has yet to be implemented.

[172] Regulation (EC) No 593/2008 of the European Parliament and of the Council of 17 June 2008 on the law applicable to contractual obligations (Rome I).

[173] Council convention 80/934/EEC on the law applicable to contractual obligations [1980] OJ 266/1.

14.97 Rome I does not substantially change the rules set out in the Second Non-Life Directive and CLD which contain detailed rules to determine, in a variety of situations, which Member State's law applies and whether there is any choice of law and, if so what choice is available to the parties.

14.98 The UK signed up to the Rome I Regulation to take effect in 2009. Rome I preserves the freedom to choose the applicable law for parties to a contract covering large risks regardless of whether the risk is situated within the EU or in an outside territory. Where no express choice of law is given, the law for large risks will be determined by the habitual residence of the insurer. Other insurance contracts have a more limited choice of law depending upon where the risk is deemed to be located.

14.99 The basic position is that the applicable law for an individual policyholder will be the EEA state in which the policyholder was 'habitually resident' when entering into the contract. Where the policyholder is not an individual but has an establishment in the EEA, the risk will be situated in the Member State where that establishment is located. For motor insurance, the risk will be located in the Member State where the vehicle was registered; for buildings and contents, where the building is located. Travel policies taken out for less than four months will be located in the State within which the policy was taken out. For life policies the risk will be situated in the location where the policyholder has their habitual residence.

14.100 There are disclosure requirements relating to choice of law in both directives and these are reflected in ICOBS chapter 6 and COBS 13.

14.101 For reinsurance of all risks and for direct insurance of non-EEA risks, the Rome Convention applies; this is implemented in the UK in the Contracts (Applicable Law) Act 1990.

Jurisdiction

14.102 EC Council Regulation No 44/2001 which supersedes the Brussels Convention, provides the rules for determining allocation and for the enforcement of judgments between all Member States except Denmark.[174] Regulation 44/2001 sets out the basis for jurisdiction[175] (including domicile) and includes special rules with regard to jurisdiction for insurance matters.[176] For example, it is not possible for an EEA insurer of a mass risk[177] to exclude the right of an EEA policyholder or insured to sue the insurer in the courts of the Member State where the policyholder is domiciled.

174 Council Regulation (EC) 01/44 on jurisdiction and the recognition and enforcement of judgments in civil and commercial matters [2001] OJ L307; these regulations do not apply to Denmark, but the Commission extended the provisions of these regulations by parallel agreements between Denmark and the Member States. The parallel agreements, which entered into force on 1 July 2007, contains various provisions to ensure uniform interpretation by the courts of the Member States and Denmark, and acceptance by Denmark of any future amendments to these regulations.

175 Council Regulation (EC) 01/44 on jurisdiction and the recognition and enforcement of judgments in civil and commercial matters [2001] OJ L307, arts 2, 3, 5, 6.

176 Council Regulation (EC) 01/44 on jurisdiction and the recognition and enforcement of judgments in civil and commercial matters [2001] OJ L307, s 3, arts 8–13.

177 See para 14.05.

Regulated Activities[178]

The definition, or 'perimeter', of regulated activities is important in various contexts. In particular, it defines the key elements in determining, for activities relating to insurance contracts, whether the prohibition under section 19, FSMA applies and whether authorisation (or exemption) is required. Regulated activities are defined in the RAO; additional elements relevant to the section 19 prohibition are set out as follows: 14.103

- the 'By Way of Business' order under section 22 of FSMA;
- section 418 of FSMA (relevant to territorial scope);
- the definition of policyholder in Article 3 of the Financial Services and Markets Act 2000 (Meaning of 'Policy' and 'Policyholder') Order 2001, SI 2001/2361.

The definition of regulated activities is also important to authorised firms (and their appointed representatives): 14.104

- in relation to the Part 4A permission they hold; a firm can only conduct those regulated activities for which it holds a permission;
- the scope of requirements in the regulatory Handbooks relating to regulated activities (although some requirements have broader application).

The scope of the financial promotion regime is, however, based on a separate definition of controlled investments, activities, and exemptions in the FPO.[179] There are differences between the scope of the FPO regime and the section 19 'perimeter' that are relevant to insurance. 14.105

By way of business and remuneration

Under section 22 of FSMA, an activity will not be a regulated activity unless it is carried on 'By Way of Business'. For the main activity of insurers (effecting and carrying out contracts of insurance under Article 10 of the RAO), there is no further statutory amendment or definition of the requirement in section 22. The narrower test (for investment business—see Article 3 of the By Way of Business Order)[180] of carrying on 'the business of engaging in' regulated activities does not apply. In most cases it will be clear that a commercial entity conducting an Article 10 activity will be doing so 'by way of business' and will require authorisation. 14.106

For insurance mediation activities, the activities must be conducted by way of business (section 22) and also must be taken up or pursued 'for remuneration'. (Again the 'engaging' test for investment business does not apply.) The second limb reflects the definition of an insurance intermediary in the IMD and was introduced at NGI. 14.107

Some intermediaries could fall outside the section 19 perimeter if they receive no remuneration for their mediation activities. However, the concept of remuneration is interpreted 14.108

[178] The RAO; PERG 2; HM Treasury consultation document: 'Financial Services and Markets Act Regulated Activities—Second Consultation Document' (October 2002).

[179] See paras 14.146–14.149.

[180] The Financial Services and Markets Act 2000 (Carrying on Regulated Activities by Way of Business) Order 2001, SI 2002/1177 as amended.

very broadly by the FCA[181] and includes direct or indirect remuneration which may be a benefit other than commission from the insurer or fees paid by the customer. For example, it may include remuneration earned through enhanced sales of another product sold with the insurance.

14.109 The adoption of the 'remuneration' element of the IMD can be used by the FCA, in some contexts, to focus on the recitals to the IMD which refer to providing mediation services to third parties for remuneration. In the context of companies which arrange or purchase insurance for other companies in the group, the FCA's position is that the activity may fall outside the IMD and the section 19 perimeter, on the basis that the other group companies do not constitute third parties (even though the expression is not adopted in the UK legislation and only appears in a recital to the IMD).

In the United Kingdom

14.110 The question of whether or not an activity is conducted in the UK (and may therefore require authorisation under FSMA) is not comprehensively defined in FSMA or related statutory instruments. There are, however, various situations where an activity is deemed to be carried on in the UK under section 418 of FSMA.

14.111 For example, an activity carried on from a UK establishment maintained by a foreign firm is carried on in the UK. The activities of an EEA branch of a UK insurer or insurance intermediary are deemed to be conducted in the UK. This extends the section 19 prohibition and UK regulation to the activities of the overseas branch.

14.112 For non-EEA insurers not authorised in the UK (essentially those established and operating outside the EEA), it is possible to underwrite risks located in the UK without breaching the section 19 prohibition. Unlike other countries, there is no prohibition on insuring risks located in the UK (and in contrast to the use of the 'location of risks' rules for the EU insurance passport regime—see following). However, all Article 10 activities, both effecting/concluding and carrying out the contract of insurance (such as paying claims), must take place entirely outside the UK/EEA. Where an intermediary or agent in the UK is involved, this may result in an Article 10 activity being conducted in the UK with the result that the insurer breaches the section 19 prohibition. Great care is required if an unauthorised foreign insurer is to underwrite a UK risk with a UK insured. There is an absolute prohibition on the marketing of certain life policies of foreign insurers.[182]

Location rules for UK and EEA authorised firms

14.113 The location test for determining whether non-EEA intermediaries require UK authorisation depends on the activity they are conducting. The FCA's guidance distinguishes between, for example, advice (where the location of the customer or client is critical) and arranging (the location where the arrangement takes place is critical) and dealing (which depends on the contractual mechanics and place of acceptance). However, the position will often depend on the application of the overseas persons exclusion in Article 72 of the RAO (but this is not available for insurers in relation to the Article 10 activities). This may be available where the intermediary does not have a permanent place of business in the UK and it deals only with or through authorised (or exempt) firms such as UK authorised insurers (including the Lloyd's

[181] PERG 5.4.8G.
[182] See para 14.149.

market) or brokers. A further part of the exclusion can cover services (eg advice) provided to UK customers where the business resulted from a legitimate approach (ie where there was no breach of the financial promotion's regime—see paragraphs 14.146 to 14.149).

Finally, while Article 10 applies irrespective of the location of the risk, mediation of non-EEA 'large' risks[183] (even within the UK) is not regulated. 14.114

UK and other EEA insurers and intermediaries are authorised for the entire EEA but location is still important in determining whether passport notifications are required and which Member State's rules apply. In this context, the location of the risk is the critical test for determining in which Member State an Article 10 activity is being conducted under the single passport system as it applies to general insurance[184] in relation to the distinction between branch and services business. 14.115

The test for mediation activities is different. For EEA intermediaries there are no strict rules (as there are for EEA insurers) to determine in which Member State an activity is taking place under the single passport system. As explained at paragraph 14.72, under the IMD there is no definition of what constitutes carrying on mediation in another Member State, although the Luxembourg Protocol, agreed by EIOPA members in 2006, provides a definition. 14.116

The regulated activities relating to insurance

The structure of the RAO is explained in Chapters 1 and 2. There are 10 activities relating to insurance (three of which are specific to the Lloyd's Market) defined by a complex series of definitions of activities, investments, and exclusions (specific to an activity or general). 14.117

Under the RAO the mediation activities apply to 'relevant investments' which include 'rights under a contract of insurance' rather than merely 'a contract of insurance' (the expression used in the IMD). This means, for example, that mediating in relation to rights under an existing insurance contract is a regulated activity; this covers fresh investments under a life policy or additional coverage added during the term of an existing general insurance policy. Regulated mediation therefore arises not only in relation to a new policy (eg at renewal) but also during the term of the policy. For investment/qualifying contracts of insurance, but not for general/pure protection/non-investment insurance, there is an additional specified investment of 'rights to, or interests in'. This extends the scope of regulated mediation for this type of insurance (see further following).[185] 14.118

In addition, the RAO expressly includes various contracts as contracts of insurance, reflecting the provisions of CLD and 3NLD and the different classes of insurance (see paragraph 14.40 *et seq.*). These include tontines and, in certain circumstances, fidelity, performance, administration, bail and custom bonds and similar contracts of guarantee (see 'suretyship' at paragraph 14.40). 14.119

Effecting and carrying out

Article 10 of the RAO sets out the regulated activity for insurance underwriting as an insurer (and replaced the 'carrying on of insurance business' test in the ICA). It covers 'direct' insurance, reinsurance, and retrocession. There are two separate activities—'effecting' and 'carrying out' contracts of insurance. The former covers entering into insurance contracts and the 14.120

[183] Art 72D of the RAO. See the explanation of 'large risks' in para 14.5.

[184] See paras 14.44 *et seq.*

[185] See the explanation of 'life policy', 'investment/qualifying contracts of insurance', 'general/pure protection/non-investment insurance' in paras 16.03–16.04.

latter covers the performance of the contract, such as paying claims. In both cases there is a qualification in that this must be 'as principal'; so neither an underwriting agent nor a claims agent falls within this definition. If an insurer is in run-off, it is still conducting an Article 10 activity as it is carrying out (although not effecting) contracts of insurance.

14.121 For this purpose the RAO lists the classes of insurance, reflecting the classes in the CLD and the 3NLD[186] (see paragraphs 14.40 to 14.42). An insurer's Part 4A permission specifies the different classes it is permitted to underwrite; it must therefore apply to amend its permission if it wishes to underwrite a different class of business.

14.122 Two activities, which otherwise constitute the effecting or carrying out of contracts of insurance, are expressly excluded:

- in circumstances specified in Article 11 of the RAO, the activities of an EEA firm where participating in a community co-insurance operation other than as leading insurer; and
- in circumstances specified in Article 12 of the RAO, activities that are carried out in connection with the provision of on-the-spot accident or breakdown assistance for cars and other vehicles.

14.123 The special provisions relating to underwriting in the Lloyd's market are considered later in this chapter (see paragraph 14.144). An Article 10 activity is conducted by 'members' (and not by the Society or by members' agents or managing agents) but currently there is no requirement for members to apply for authorisation.

Dealing as principal

14.124 There is a further regulated activity which concerns dealing as principal. Article 14 of the RAO covers buying, selling, or underwriting contractually based investments which include rights under, or rights to or interests in, qualifying contracts of insurance.[187] This covers various activities of life offices and of those who buy or sell indirect rights and interests in qualifying insurance contracts, eg those buying and selling the entitlement to payments under an endowment policy (sometimes referred to as 'traded' endowments).

Mediation activities[188]

14.125 Prior to the IMD, while the RAO covered the underwriting of all forms of insurance under Article 10, mediation activities were only regulated in relation to qualifying contracts of insurance. To implement the IMD the RAO needed to be extended to bring the mediation of general insurance and pure protection long-term insurance within the perimeter of regulated activities. Certain changes were also required to the scope of pre-NGI mediation activities relating to qualifying insurance contracts.[189]

---

[186] The 18 classes of general insurance and nine classes of long-term insurance in Sch 1 of the RAO are supplemented by additional definitions in art 3(1) including fidelity, performance, and other bonds and similar contracts of insurance where these are not effected by a banking business, are not incidental to another business, and a premium is paid.

[187] See the explanation of 'qualifying contracts of insurance' in para 14.04.

[188] The Financial Services and Markets Act 2000 (Regulated Activities) (Amendment) (No 2) Order 2003, SI 2003/1476; PERG, FSA PS04/1, 'Insurance selling and administration and other miscellaneous amendments—Feedback on CP187 and made text'; FSA CP187, 'Insurance selling and administration and other miscellaneous amendments'; FSA CP160, 'Insurance selling and administration—the FSA's high-level approach to regulation'; HM Treasury Consultation Document: Regulating Insurance Mediation (21 October 2002) and Summary of consultation feedback and HM Treasury decisions.

[189] See the explanation of 'qualifying contracts of insurance', 'general insurance', 'pure protection', 'non-investment insurance' in paras 14.03–14.04.

The RAO amendments for NGI did not adopt the IMD definitions directly. Instead it used the existing breakdown of dealing as agent, arranging, and advising (an activity not directly referred to in the IMD definition) but added the new IMD activity of 'assisting'. Existing exclusions had to be amended, for example where they did not mirror the IMD. For this reason a number of RAO exclusions[190] are now not available or are limited in relation to insurance. **14.126**

The mediation activities are: **14.127**

(a) dealing in investments as agent (Article 21);
(b) arranging (bringing about) deals in investments (Article 25(1));
(c) making arrangements with a view to transactions in investments (Article 25(2));
(d) assisting in the administration and performance of a contract of insurance (Article 39A);
(e) advising on investments (Article 53);
(f) agreeing to carry on a regulated activity in (a) to (e) (article 64).

The additional activities relating to the Lloyd's market are considered later in this chapter. **14.128**

Activities and exclusions

The RAO was also amended to apply the regulated mediation activities to insurers in relation to their 'mediation' of their own general and pure protection insurance contracts. This was not required by the IMD (and was 'super-equivalent'); it underpinned the broader policy objective of regulating the sale and administration of these products by insurers (as well as intermediaries) as reflected, for example, in the application of ICOBS.[191] **14.129**

Under the RAO, the noun to which mediation activities apply is 'rights under a contract of insurance'. As already noted, this extends regulation to include the mediation of additional coverage added during the term of an existing policy. In relation to qualifying contracts of insurance it extends to indirect rights and beneficial interests (eg in relation to the trading of interests in an endowment policy in the second hand market). The RAO therefore extends mediation regulation beyond the scope of the IMD. **14.130**

The activities. The three activities of dealing as agent, arranging, and advising relate to 'buying' and 'selling' which are broadly defined to include acquiring insurance rights (or interests where relevant) for valuable consideration and surrendering, assigning, and converting—in each case for valuable consideration. This is wider than the IMD. **14.131**

Dealing as agent. This covers the contractual activity of buying or selling as agent and covers, for example, intermediaries which hold a binding authority to conclude contracts of insurance (or otherwise sell rights under such contracts) as agent of the insurer. It also applies where the intermediary, such as a broker, concludes a contract of insurance as agent of the insured. **14.132**

Arranging. This covers two separate activities; in essence, making general arrangements for someone to buy or sell insurance, or making arrangements which bring about a specific insurance transaction. The first activity may apply to introducing customers to an intermediary or **14.133**

[190] These exclusions include art 22 (dealing as agent with or through authorised persons), art 29 (arranging deals with or through authorised persons), art 68 (in connection with the sale of goods and supply of services), art 69 (groups and joint enterprises), and art 70 (in connection with the sale of a body corporate) of the RAO.
[191] See para 14.207 *et seq.*

insurer (although a distinction can be drawn between introducing and some purely passive display of insurance marketing materials). The second limb covers activities closer to the conclusion of the insurance contract, for example negotiating or assisting the insured to complete the application and deliver it to the insurer. For insurance, this activity is relevant even where the arranger will be a party to the insurance contract (or will conclude it as agent); so it covers insurers in relation to their own products. The party contracting with the insurer will also be arranging except where it is, or will be, the sole policyholder. So the purchase/conclusion of insurance by the policyholder can involve 'arranging' if other parties have rights under the policy, for example as 'insureds'.

14.134 The definition of policyholder for this purpose is 'the person who for the time being is the legal holder of the policy, including any person to whom, under the policy, a sum is due, a periodic payment is payable or any other benefit is to be provided or to whom such a sum, payment, or benefit is contingently due, payable or to be provided'.[192]

14.135 A policyholder can therefore be 'arranging' in relation to the rights of other insureds. In some cases this activity, on its own, may fail the 'by way of business/remuneration test' but it may apply in other cases, for example where one lender takes out insurance covering other lenders under a syndicated loan.

14.136 Article 72C implements an IMD exclusion for introducing or the 'provision of information on an incidental basis'.[193] It only covers the provision of information incidental and complementary to a business which does not otherwise involve regulated activities. (It does not cover activities such as assisting in the completion of application forms or forwarding them to insurers; it only covers the flow of information down the chain.) The classic example is a vet, who does no more than passively display marketing materials for pet insurance, for example by drawing a client's attention to the product and handing out or mailing the insurer's marketing material (but where no advice is given and where the pet owner is left to complete the application form and return it to the insurer). The introducer, in this case, the vet, can be remunerated for introductions made and still remain within this exclusion.

14.137 There are other exclusions including those relating to very limited activities which simply enable parties to communicate (Article 27) and for money lenders arranging transactions in connection with lending on the security of insurance contracts (Article 30) but only where the person is not carrying on insurance or reinsurance mediation (but see paragraphs 14.142 to 14.143).

14.138 The FCA's view is that the Article 33 exemption for introducing is unlikely to apply to introductions for general insurance.[194]

14.139 **Advising.** The Article 53 activity relates to advice on the merits of buying and selling insurance. It does not cover generic advice about the need to disclose material information to insurers or about the benefits of insurance or about the strength of an insurer or the merits of a broker, if the advice in all cases is unrelated to, and not given in the context of, a particular product. It is also possible to construct a decision tree for insurance sales whereby

[192] The Financial Services and Markets Act 2000 (Meaning of 'Policy' and 'Policyholder') Order 2001, SI 2001/2361.

[193] IMD, art 2(3) (see n 33).

[194] PERG 5.6.19G.

information is solicited from the customer in order to select a particular product to offer but without the process amounting to the regulated activity of advising. The FCA gives detailed guidance on this issue,[195] which is important in the context of whether suitability obligations will apply. Subtle distinctions often have to be drawn between the mere provision of information and the provision of information in circumstances which will constitute advice.

There are a number of exclusions relating to the periodical publications, broadcasts, and websites (Article 54 of the RAO)—see FCA's guidance in PERG 7 which explains the arrangements for applying to the FCA for a certificate that this exclusion applies. **14.140**

Assisting in the administration and performance of a contract of insurance. This activity, in Article 39A, reflects the IMD wording and was a new activity added at NGI. It brings claims handling for insureds/policyholders into regulation but it does not apply to agents appointed to handle claims for certain insurers (or expert appraisal or loss adjusting for insurers)—see Article 39B. The scope of the activity is uncertain. The FCA offers certain guidance without reaching any firm conclusions on the precise 'perimeter'.[196] **14.141**

General exclusions. There are various exclusions that can apply to more than one activity. Certain exclusions (including Article 30 referred to earlier) are subject to an IMD override,[197] ie if directive mediation is being conducted the domestic exclusion does not apply. Article 72B reflects the IMD exclusion for connected contracts modified to reflect the UK Government's decision to regulate connected contracts in the motor trade. This is relevant to those selling non-motor goods who sell certain complimentary insurances against breakdown, loss, or damage to the goods. There are a number of detailed conditions which must be satisfied. Following NGI, this was also relevant to travel agents and tour operators selling certain travel policies linked to travel booked with them. The IMD requires the sale of general insurance (including stand-alone travel insurance) by intermediaries to be regulated. Prior to 1 January 2009, the sale of connected travel insurance ('CTI') (ie travel insurance sold alongside a holiday or other related travel by, for example, travel firms) was exempt. When the UK implemented the IMD, it adopted a CTI exclusion. However, following concerns about mis-selling of CTI by travel agents and tour operators it was decided to bring this area into FSMA regulation.[198] With effect from 1 January 2009, tour operators and travel agents are no longer able to rely upon the CTI exclusion in IMD. In order to sell, advise, or conduct other regulated activities in relation to CTI, they will have to be authorised or appointed as an appointed representative and will have to follow FCA's rules and requirements (see paragraph 14.210 *et seq.*). **14.142**

The IMD does not cover the mediation of non-EEA risks (eg a London broker placing insurance at Lloyd's for a UK owner of property in the United States—see location of risk rules in section 14.98 *et seq.*). However, in the RAO, the exclusion at Article 72D only applies to large (non-EEA) risks[199]—so the mediation of mass non-EEA risks is regulated under the RAO (although this falls outside the IMD). **14.143**

195 PERG 5.8.15G.

196 PERG 2.8.7AG and 5.7.7G.

197 Art 4(4A) of the RAO (as amended) applicable to arts 30, 66, and 67.

198 For further information, please see FSA CP07/22 and PS08/04 ('Regulating Connected Travel Insurance') and the Financial Services and Markets Act 2000 (Regulated Activities) (Amendment) (No. 2) Order 2007, SI 2007/3510.

199 See the explanation of 'large risks' in para 14.05.

The Lloyd's market activities

14.144 The specific Lloyd's related activities in the RAO are:

(i) arranging (bringing about) deals in the underwriting capacity of a Lloyd's syndicate or membership of a Lloyd's syndicate (Article 25(1));[200]

(ii) making arrangements with a view to transactions in the underwriting capacity of a Lloyd's syndicate or membership of a Lloyd's syndicate (Article 25(2));[201]

(iii) advising on syndicate participation at Lloyd's, that is advising a person to become, or continue, or cease to be, a member of a particular syndicate (Article 56)[202]—this activity is undertaken by members' agents;

(iv) managing the underwriting capacity of a Lloyd's syndicate as a managing agent at Lloyd's (Article 57)[203]—this activity is unique to managing agents;

(v) arranging deals in contracts of insurance written at Lloyd's, that is arranging by the Society of Lloyd's of deals in contracts of insurance written at Lloyd's (Article 58)—this activity is unique to the Society of Lloyd's.

14.145 The regulation of the Lloyd's market is considered further in paragraph 14.358 *et seq*.

Other Aspects of Insurance Legislation

Financial promotions

14.146 At N2, section 21 of FSMA (which imposes a restriction on the communication of financial promotions unless an authorised person makes the communication or an authorised person has approved the content of the financial promotion) and the Financial Services and Markets Act 2000 (Financial Promotions) Order[204] came into force. The regime deals with real time and non-real time promotions. The section 21 'perimeter' is different to the section 19 regulated activities perimeter; it is defined by reference to controlled activities and investments in the FPO. Detailed guidance on the scope of the financial promotions regime is set out in PERG 8 in the FCA Handbook. Although not appreciated by everyone at the time, promotions concerning all types of insurance were subject to the section 21 prohibition from N2. In the case of non-investment insurance[205] (general and pure protection), for which mediation fell outside the section 19 perimeter until NGI, there are several important exceptions which cover the following:

- a generic promotion which does not identify the insurer (or any person carrying on a controlled activity); the promotion can identify the intermediary as non-investment insurance mediation is not a controlled activity (Article 17 of the FPO);

200 This regulated activity may be carried on in connection with the following specified investments: underwriting capacity of a Lloyd's syndicate (art 86(1)), membership of a Lloyd's syndicate (art 86(2)), rights to or interests in investments (art 89) in so far as they relate to underwriting capacity of a Lloyd's syndicate, or membership of a Lloyd's syndicate.

201 ibid.

202 This regulated activity may be carried on in connection with membership of a Lloyd's syndicate (art 86(2)).

203 This regulated activity may be carried on in connection with underwriting capacity of a Lloyd's syndicate (art 86(1)).

204 Financial Services and Markets Act 2000 (Financial Promotion) Order 2001, SI 2001/1335, since replaced by the Financial Services and Markets Act 2000 (Financial Promotion) Order 2005, SI 2005/1529 (the 'FPO').

205 See the explanation of 'non-investment insurance' in para 14.04.

- a non-real time communication concerning relevant insurance (ie broadly, non-investment insurance) which contains the following information (Article 24):

  (i) the full name of the insurance undertaking;
  (ii) the country or territory in which the insurance undertaking is incorporated (described as such);
  (iii) if different from the above, the country or territory in which the insurance undertaking's principal place of business is situated (described as such);
  (iv) whether or not the insurance undertaking is regulated in respect of its insurance business;
  (v) if the insurance undertaking is regulated, the name of the regulator in its principal place of business or, if there is more than one regulator, the name of the prudential regulator;
  (vi) whether any transaction to which the non-investment financial promotion relates would be covered by a dispute resolution scheme or compensation scheme, if so identifying each such scheme;

- reinsurance and large risks[206] (Article 25); and
- real time communications (Article 26).

These exemptions were not removed at NGI, reflecting the Government's decision not to extend the section 21 regime to promotions concerning mediation services for non-investment insurance. **14.147**

The FSMA gives the FCA separate powers to make rules on financial promotions; these are set out in COBS 3 and ICOBS 3. The rules in ICOBS relating to financial promotions and communications to customers are explained at paragraph 14.220 *et seq*. In addition, there are also high-level requirements in the regulatory Principles for Businesses, including Principle 6 (firms must pay due regard to the interests of its customers and treat them fairly) and Principle 7 (communications to the customer must be clear, fair, and not misleading)—see further at paragraph 14.170. **14.148**

The prohibition on the promotion of foreign life policies

The effect of Article 10 of the FPO and COBS 4.9.3 is to prohibit absolutely (even by an authorised intermediary) the promotion of life policies except, broadly, those of UK and EEA authorised insurers and those of life offices authorised in Jersey, Guernsey, the Isle of Man, or the states of Pennsylvania and Iowa. **14.149**

Appointed representatives

The appointed representative regime applies to the mediation of investment and non-investment insurance. An appointed representative conducting insurance mediation cannot commence its mediation activities until its name is entered on the record of insurance intermediaries (ie registered on the Financial Services Register) and if it ceases to be so registered, it can no longer carry on such activities (this reflects the IMD requirement for an insurance intermediary to be registered); a provision to this effect must be included in the agreement appointing the appointed representative. **14.150**

[206] See the explanation of 'large risks' in para 14.05.

14.151 An appointed representative cannot conduct various regulated activities including the following insurance activities:

- Article 10 (effecting and carrying out contracts of insurance);
- Article 14 (dealing as principal);
- Article 21 (dealing as agent in relation to qualifying contracts of insurance or long-term care insurance);
- Article 25 (arranging transactions in the underwriting capacity of a Lloyd's syndicate or in the membership of a Lloyd's syndicate);
- Article 56 (advice on syndicate participation at Lloyd's), Article 57 (managing the underwriting capacity of a Lloyd's syndicate, Article 58 (arranging by the Society of Lloyd's).

14.152 Either an authorised insurer or an authorised insurance intermediary can appoint an appointed representative to conduct insurance mediation (but only within the scope of the principal's Part 4A permission).

14.153 The requirements of section 39 of FSMA, the Appointed Representative Regulations[207] and the FCA Handbook apply including:

- the appointed representative must have a contract with an authorised person (the 'principal') permitting the appointed representative to carry on business of a prescribed description;[208]
- the principal must have accepted responsibility in writing for those prescribed activities of the appointed representative;
- the appointed representative is exempt (from authorisation) only in relation to the carrying on of those regulated activities for which the principal has accepted responsibility (and cannot therefore carry on any other regulated activities unless under another appointed representative appointment);
- the principal of the appointed representative is responsible, to the same extent as if he had expressly permitted it, for anything done or omitted by the appointed representative in carrying on the business for which he has accepted responsibility.

14.154 A firm which is authorised under FSMA cannot be an appointed representative. This applies where the firm is directly authorised by either regulator for any activities, even for activities unrelated to insurance. The FCA's Supervision Sourcebook ('SUP') Chapter 12 contains rules and guidance relating to the appointed representative agreement/relationship. Some of the restrictions on appointed representatives that are worth noting are as follows. All firms carrying on insurance mediation activity, including principals of appointed representatives, must establish in relation to any appointed representative that a reasonable proportion of the persons within its management structure and all other persons directly responsible for insurance mediation activity demonstrate the knowledge and ability necessary for the performance of their duties and are of good repute—see paragraph 14.347 *et seq.*[209] Appointed representatives are generally restricted to one principal (although a firm can have multiple

207 The Financial Services and Markets Act 2000 (Appointed Representative) Regulations 2001, SI 2001/1217 (as amended).

208 The Financial Services and Markets Act 2000 (Appointed Representative) Regulations 2001, SI 2001/1217 (as amended) stipulate the type of business which appointed representatives may carry out (if permitted to do so by their principals).

209 MIPRU 2.3.1R; MIPRU 2.3.3R; SUP 12.4.8R.

principals from the same group in respect of some types of investment products).[210] There are no restrictions on the number of principals an appointed representative may have in relation to non-investment insurance contracts. If an appointed representative has more than one principal for investment insurance contracts, a multiple principal agreement between the principals will be required.[211]

An introducer appointed representative is an appointed representative appointed by a firm whose scope of appointment is limited to effecting introductions and distributing non-real time financial promotions. An introducer appointed representative must enter into an agreement with its principal (similar to an appointed representative agreement) and broadly similar rules apply to an introducer appointed representative as to an appointed representative. One exception is that an introducer appointed representative does not need to have any approved persons registered with the FCA.[212] 14.155

Misleading statements and impressions

Section 397 of FSMA was repealed by the FSA 2012 and replaced by Part 7 of the Act. The regulators can prosecute offences in relation to misleading statements, misleading impressions, and misleading statements in relation to benchmarks.[213] 14.156

An offence will be committed where an individual or a firm, in the course of an insurance contract: 14.157

- makes misleading statements in the course of selling insurance;
- material facts are dishonestly concealed;
- a false or misleading impression is given as to the market in, or price of, insurance.

Part VII Transfers[214]

Part VII of FSMA, reflecting the EU legislation, provides for the approval of insurance business transfer schemes. There are special provisions for transfers involving Lloyd's.[215] Subject 14.158

[210] SUP 12.4.5BG; SUP 12.5.6AR; SUP 12.5.6BG.

[211] SUP 12.4.5BR to SUP 12.4.5GG. As part of its initial consultation on the implementation of the IMD, the FSA proposed that an appointed representative should be able to have one principal for 'substitutable product categories' but in the end decided that there would be no restriction on the number of principals and no rule preventing the sale of substitutable products for different insurers in the non-investment insurance market. It concluded that the risks of consumer detriment in this market could be appropriately addressed through multiple principal agreements and the FSA's wider rules on the sale and administration of non-investment insurance products.

[212] See SUP 10.1.16R and SUP12.

[213] ss 89-91 of the FSA 2012.

[214] Schemes of Arrangement: Insolvent and solvent insurers can also enter into schemes of arrangement under Part 26 of the Companies Act 2006. The essence of the procedure is a three stage approval process; first an application is made to the court by the company or its members or creditors for the court to give directions for a meeting or meetings of members or creditors (or any class of members or creditors) to be convened; at the second stage the members or creditors must approve the proposal by the requisite majority, namely a majority in number representing not less than 75 per cent in value of those who attend and vote, in person or by proxy; at the third stage the court must sanction the scheme. Although schemes of arrangement for insurance companies are nothing new (many of the early cases on schemes relate to insurance companies, particularly insolvent life insurance companies) they enjoyed a renaissance in the 1990s as a legal framework to enable insolvent non-life insurance companies to effect an orderly run-off of the remaining business, permitting them to continue as nearly as possible in the same way, subject only to agreed claims being paid in part only, rather than paid in full.

[215] The definition of an insurance business transfer scheme at s 105 of FSMA includes transfers from members of Lloyd's to reflect the effect of the Financial Services and Markets Act 2000 (Control of Transfers of Business Done at Lloyd's) Order 2001, SI 2001/3626.

to court approval, it is possible to transfer obligations under insurance contracts from one insurer to another which means that primary liability under the insurance policies (forming part of the business transferred) is transferred to the transferee and, for practical purposes, the policyholders are thereafter treated as if their contracts had always been with the transferee. Schemes must be approved by the court under section 111. The Financial Services and Markets Act 2000 (Control of Business Transfers)(Requirements on Applicants) Regulations 2001 also apply and detailed guidance is set out in the regulatory Handbooks in SUP 18. These provisions now take into account the RID.

14.159 The PRA will lead the Part VII process but will consult with the FCA before approving the independent expert or approving notices to be published in the press or to be sent to policyholders as required by FSMA. Both the PRA and the FCA are entitled to be heard in court proceedings.[216]

UK Regulation—the Regulatory Handbooks

Introduction

14.160 Authorised insurers and insurance intermediaries (and their appointed representatives) are subject to many of the rulebooks and other sourcebooks/manuals which make up the regulatory Handbooks (see also Chapter 6).

14.161 Both the PRA and FCA each have Handbooks which have replaced the FSA Handbook. A combined Handbook sharing both PRA and FCA rules is currently available through the FCA website. For now the regulatory Handbooks include legacy rules inherited from the FSA, divided up between the two authorities. Over time new rules will amend the Handbooks so that they begin to take on distinct characteristics. PRA-authorised firms such as insurers must comply with rules in both the PRA and FCA Handbooks; intermediaries need only comply with the FCA Handbook. Where a rule appears in both the PRA and FCA Handbook it should be interpreted in the light of the relevant regulator's objectives. It is not possible to review all the rules which might be applicable to firms but this section highlights some of the ways in which regulatory rules will impact insurance; it deals in particular, with the rules for non-investment insurance and some of the approaches taken by the regulators to issues in the market.

Insurance chains

14.162 The sale of non-investment insurance often involves, in addition to the insurer, 'chains' of intermediaries introducing, selling, placing insurance, and in the claims process. It is important to have a clear understanding of how the different FCA rules apply to each of the chain participants. For example, ICOBS imposes obligations on the insurer, as the product provider; it places separate obligations on the firm which deals with the customer (ie the purchasing policyholder) which may also be the insurer in the case of a direct sale where no intermediary is involved. ICOBS does not apply to a 'wholesale' intermediary (such as a placing broker). However, 'wholesale' mediation is a regulated activity and it is subject to the FCA's high-level standards as is other mediation falling outside of ICOBS such as the broking of reinsurance. CASS 5 (client money) is concerned with clients (rather than the customers/policyholders), so it does apply to wholesale broking (and may or may not apply to the broking of reinsurance depending on the elections made by the individual firm).

216 SUP 18.2.1A(2).

Threshold Conditions for authorisation (COND)

To become, and to retain, the status of a person authorised by either the PRA or FCA an applicant must satisfy, and continue to satisfy, the Threshold Conditions required by each authority (set out in Schedule 6 of FSMA). The FSA 2012 replaced the single set of Threshold Conditions required by the FSA with separate requirements depending on the type of firm seeking authorisation. **14.163**

Firms regulated only by the FCA must meet conditions found in Schedule 6, paragraphs 2B–2F. Guidance on these conditions is found in the FCA Threshold Conditions sourcebook (COND). PRA-authorised firms must meet FCA conditions found in Schedule 6, paragraphs 3B–3E and also PRA conditions found in Schedule 6, paragraphs 4A–4F. There is no PRA Handbook guidance on these conditions but the FCA Handbook contains guidance on its conditions in COND. **14.164**

FCA-authorised firms, such as insurance intermediaries, must satisfy conditions that relate to: **14.165**

- Location of offices;
- Being able to be effectively supervised by the FCA with regard to the nature of the regulated activities being carried on and the complexity of the products provided, the way in which the business is organised, whether membership of a group may hinder supervision, whether the business is subject to consolidated supervision under an EU directive and the influence of any close links;
- Appropriate resources (both financial and non-financial) including resources appropriate to the nature, scale, and complexity of the business;
- Suitability in terms of being fit and proper to be authorised taking into account any connections, the nature of the business being regulated, the interests of consumers and the integrity of the financial system, whether the applicant complies with FCA requirements in the exercise of their functions, whether those managing the business have adequate skills and experience and can be expected to act with probity, whether the business is being managed in such a way as to ensure it will be conducted in a sound and prudent manner and the extent to which the business might be connected with any financial crime;
- The suitability of the business model for the activities that will be undertaken.

PRA-authorised firms, such as insurers or Lloyd's managing agents, must satisfy FCA conditions that relate to: **14.166**

- Being able to be effectively supervised by the FCA (as cited previously);
- Appropriate non-financial resources including resources appropriate to the nature, scale, and complexity of the business;
- Suitability in terms of being fit and proper to be authorised (as per earlier);
- The suitability of the business model for the activities that will be carried on (as per earlier);
- The appointment of a claims representative.

In addition, however, PRA-authorised firms must also satisfy conditions specified by the PRA in FSMA that relate to: **14.167**

- Legal status limiting authorisation to a body corporate, registered friendly society or a member of Lloyd's;

- Location of offices;
- Whether the business is to be conducted in a prudent manner requiring appropriate financial and non-financial resources including being willing and able to value assets and liabilities appropriately and to be able to measure and monitor risks to the safety and soundness of the business and enable compliance with relevant PRA requirements;
- Suitability in terms of being fit and proper to comply with PRA requirements and whether those managing the business have adequate skills and experience to act with probity;
- Being able to be effectively supervised by the PRA with regard to the nature of the regulated activities being carried on and the complexity of the products provided, the way in which the business is organised, whether membership of a group may hinder supervision, whether the business is subject to consolidated supervision under an EU directive and the influence of any close links.

14.168 For an insurer to be authorised in the UK, it must have its head office and registered office in the UK. As noted in the section on EU Law (paragraph 14.24 *et seq.*), this reflects CLD and 3NLD. INSPRU 1.5.13[217] prohibits an insurer (other than a pure reinsurer) from carrying out activities 'other than insurance business and activities directly arising from that business'. A pure reinsurer must not carry on any business other than the business of reinsurance and related operations. The regime for the prior approval of controllers is described in Chapter 6. For insurers the initial threshold for a controller is 10 per cent.

14.169 For insurance intermediaries there is no prescribed legal form; the applicant may be a company, limited liability partnership, individual, sole trader, or partnership. For insurance intermediaries formed in the UK the registered office or, if it has no registered office, the head office must be in the UK.[218] The controller threshold, which is higher than for insurers, is 20 per cent. As already noted, intermediaries may conduct insurance mediation as a secondary activity (for example a bank) or a tertiary activity (for example a retailer acting as a creditor broker and promoting payment protection insurance).

Principles for Businesses and the regulatory approach to sector issues

14.170 The Principles for Businesses ('PRIN') provide high-level obligations that govern all authorised firms. The Principles reflect the statutory objectives of the PRA and FCA and provide firms with a concise statement of their regulatory obligations. Following the demise of the FSA, the Principles are applied by both the PRA and FCA and appear in both Handbooks.

14.171 In summary, the Principles require an insurer or intermediary to:

- Conduct its business with integrity and with due skill, care, and diligence;
- Take reasonable care to organise and control its affairs responsibly and effectively, with adequate risk management systems;
- Maintain adequate financial resources;
- Observe proper standards of market conduct;

---

217 This rule replaced PRU 7.6.13 which had replaced IPRU(INS) 1.3(1) which had replaced s 16 of the Insurance Companies Act 1982.

218 COND 2.2.1A.

- Pay due regard to the interests of customers and treat them fairly;
- Communicate with clients in a way which is clear, fair, and not misleading;
- Manage conflicts of interest fairly;
- Take reasonable care to ensure suitability of advice and discretionary decisions;
- Arrange adequate protection for clients' assets when it is responsible for them; and
- Deal with its regulators in an open and cooperative way and keep them informed.

Principles-based regulation

Regulatory enforcement actions are almost invariably founded on breaches of Principles, rather than merely on breaches of detailed rules. The decision in *R (on the application of British Bankers Association) v Financial Services Authority*[219] confirmed the ability of the regulator to take action against a firm for breach of a Principle alone. During its tenure, the FSA shifted its approach further away from a prescriptive rules-based system of regulation towards a more principles-based approach or 'MPBR' (see Chapter 5). Rather than adding rules, the FSA moved towards providing firms with guidance, such as statements of good and poor practice and case studies illustrating ways in which firms could successfully meet regulatory expectations. The aim of this approach was to allow firms greater scope to focus on the outcomes identified in PRIN rather than on complying with the letter (but perhaps not the spirit) of Handbook rules. **14.172**

In theory, MPBR allows firms greater flexibility to interpret the Principles in a way that will best reflect the particular risks and challenges for their business and avoids the need for the regulator to create rules to meet every eventuality. With the advent of the financial crisis enthusiasm for MPBR and 'light touch' regulation dampened. The current approach, 'outcomes-focused' regulation, maintains the importance of PRIN as the benchmark for authorised firms but has shown a greater appetite for rules to address specific risks and more intrusive supervision in the day-to-day management of the business.[220] For example, the FSA, and subsequently the FCA, have proposed a single set of rules and guidance on product governance, including turning some of the guidance into rules.[221] **14.173**

Treating customers fairly

Principle 6 states 'A firm must pay due regard to the interests of its customers and treat them fairly'. Based on this Principle, the FSA developed an approach to regulation which focused on how firms could reach the outcomes envisaged in PRIN. Treating customers fairly or 'TCF' was central to the FSA's approach to ensuring that consumers got a fair deal from financial services. In the first publication on TCF in 2001 the FSA identified areas where customers were being let down.[222] These areas were: poor consumer understanding of products, a failure to keep customers informed after the point of sale, a failure for products to meet consumer expectations, a lack of ability to switch between either products or providers, and poor complaints handling. These issues remain at the heart of the regulatory approach to conduct of business now undertaken by the FCA. **14.174**

219 *R (on the application of British Bankers Association) v Financial Services Authority* [2011] EWHC 999.
220 Hector Sants' speech 'UK Financial Regulation: After the crisis' (delivered on 12 March 2010) provides insight into the shift from MPRB towards 'outcomes-focused' regulation.
221 FSA FS11/3: Product intervention—Feedback on DP11/1 (June 2011).
222 FSA DP7: Treating Customers fairly after the point of sale (January 2001).

14.175 In 2006 the FSA set out six outcomes which firms should achieve to ensure customers are being treated fairly:[223]

- Outcome 1—Consumers can be confident that they are dealing with firms where the fair treatments of customers is central to the corporate culture.
- Outcome 2—Products and services marketed and sold in the retail market are designed to meet the needs of identified consumer groups and are targeted accordingly.
- Outcome 3—Consumers are provided with clear information and are kept appropriately informed before, during, and after the point of sale.
- Outcome 4—Where consumers receive advice, the advice is suitable and takes account of their circumstances.
- Outcome 5—Consumers are provided with products that perform as firms have led them to expect, and the associated service is both of an accepted standard and as they have been led to expect.
- Outcome 6—Consumers do not face unreasonable post-sale barriers imposed by firms to change product, switch provider, submit a claim, or make a complaint.

14.176 These outcomes, which operate as a benchmark, are supported by six cultural indicators which should demonstrate the extent to which TCF has been embedded into the firm's internal processes and culture: leadership, strategy, decision making, systems and controls, recruitment and training, and reward. Senior management in firms will be required to demonstrate that they understand TCF and are receiving appropriate information to monitor whether there are TCF risks in the business.

14.177 Of particular concern, following the PPI mis-selling scandal, the FCA has turned its attention to TCF issues in product design. Financial products must be developed and sold with the consumer at the centre. Boards must be motivated by good consumer outcomes and ensure that they are kept fully abreast of the consumer experience of their products and services, addressing any problems that come to light. In particular, the FCA has emphasised the need for insurers and intermediaries to address TCF at each stage of the product life-cycle including:

- Product/distributor interface;
- Product design and information;
- Identifying target markets;
- Marketing and promoting the product;
- Claims handling;
- Sales and advice;
- The remuneration of sales forces and advisers;
- After sales information;
- Complaints handling; and
- Linked sales.[224]

14.178 The FCA aims to focus its supervision on those firms with the greatest potential to cause the most harm. Accordingly, insurers with a large amount of retail products will face greater

[223] FSA: Treating Customers Fairly—towards fair outcomes for consumers (July 2006).
[224] See FSA: Journey to the FCA (October 2012), FSA DP11/1: Product intervention (January 2011), FSA FS11/3: Product intervention (June 2011).

scrutiny than small intermediaries. The FCA will review firm governance and culture to determine whether products and services meet customer needs. The review will include both sales and after-sales processes to ensure there are sufficient systems and controls in place to enable TCF outcomes to be met. In particular, firms will be expected to have procedures in place to assess their target market and products should undergo stress testing before they are sold to the public. In a marked change to the approach of the FSA, the FCA will examine products to consider whether they provide value for money. Charging structures must therefore stand up to TCF scrutiny. Policy terms and conditions may be reviewed for fairness by the FCA in those lines of business where the regulator believes there are significant customer risks.

Early intervention in the product life-cycle will enable the FCA to prevent harm to customers. One of the new powers granted under the FSA 2012 allows the FCA to ban temporarily products that pose an unacceptable risk to consumers.[225] Examples of when such bans can be imposed are: **14.179**

- The widespread selling of products outside their target market;
- Products that are made unacceptable by the inclusion of terms and conditions that make them inappropriate for a significant number of customers;
- Products where incentives encourage inappropriate sales;
- Cases where a product is considered inherently flawed due to its poor value or disadvantageous features.

Product providers and distributors

As part of the TCF initiative, the FSA looked at the responsibilities of providers and distributors for the fair treatment of customers. In September 2006, the FSA published a discussion paper,[226] which set out the FSA's view of the respective regulatory responsibilities of providers and distributors in relation to TCF, and included an overarching statement of responsibilities for providers and distributors and sector-specific case studies. This led to a 'Regulatory Guide' which was published to assist firms to meet their TCF obligations (now contained in the FCA Handbook).[227] **14.180**

The regulatory action taken by the FSA following widespread mis-selling of PPI policies is an example of how TCF was applied in practice to address problems associated with a particular product. The FSA relied largely upon PRIN as the basis for enforcement action against firms for mis-selling. In many cases firms complied with the detailed requirements of ICOBS, but nonetheless failed to satisfy the overarching Principles—in particular Principles 3 and 6 and 7. **14.181**

Conflicts of interest[228]

Legal principles and FCA rules

Principle 8 provides that a firm must manage conflicts of interest fairly, both between itself and its customers and between a customer and another client.[229] The effective management **14.182**

---

[225] ss 137D, 137E, 138M, 138N, and 138O FSMA.
[226] See FSA DP06/4.
[227] The Responsibilities of Providers and Distributors for the Fair Treatment of Customers ('RPPD').
[228] On conflicts of interest more generally see FSA Principle 8.
[229] In addition, FSA Principle 6 provides that a firm must pay due regard to the interests of its customers and treat them fairly.

of conflicts of interest within the insurance industry has been of long-standing concern to UK regulators and to the European Commission.[230]

14.183 Firms must have effective systems to identify conflicts, to manage them fairly, and to ensure the firm is not in breach of the general law applicable to agents and fiduciaries.[231]

Conflicts in the insurance sector

14.184 This is an important issue for insurance intermediaries and brokers. Unlike many other service relationships in the financial sector insurance brokers fall within the common law scope of fiduciary relationships. Brokers have fiduciary obligations which often conflict with their own interests or duties owed to another client or customer. Insurance brokers frequently provide services to both insurers and insureds which may lead to conflicts of interest. Examples of such conflicts include:

- an intermediary holding a binding authority from a particular insurer to conclude contracts of insurance and yet also advising clients on policies from a range of insurers;
- an intermediary assisting insureds in making claims and yet also assisting the insurer, even to the point of having authority to settle claims;
- an intermediary providing services to insurers relating to the insurance policies of its insured clients, such as administration and line slip services;
- a broker placing insurance and related reinsurance;
- a broker negotiates its commission with an insurer or obtains payments from an insurer which increase by reference to the volume of business the broker places with that insurer.

The remuneration of insurance brokers, conflicts, and commission disclosure

14.185 Shortly after it took over the regulation of insurance intermediaries, the FSA raised particular concerns in relation to the remuneration of brokers, as remuneration structures may pose conflicts between the broker and its client (see above), and may involve a breach of the duties under the general law relating to fiduciary and agents.

14.186 **Fiduciaries and agents.** The general law on agents and fiduciaries applies to many insurance intermediaries such as brokers which cannot make a 'secret profit' and should not put themselves in a position where their own interests conflict with the duties they owe to their principals. They will be liable to account to their principal for any secret profits. In certain circumstances and by way of exception, insurance brokers who are not remunerated by fees paid by their client are entitled to agree with insurers and to retain a commission within market rates. In other cases it may be necessary for an intermediary to obtain its client's consent in order to retain a commission or another form of remuneration paid to it by insurers.

14.187 Case law has clarified that if the intermediary is to be entitled to retain commission, in the context of a client who has paid a fee, there must be informed consent from the client, and not merely knowledge of the possibility that the profit may be made.[232] In all cases an agent or fiduciary is obliged on request to disclose the remuneration and other benefits received

[230] See FSA FS08/7: Transparency, disclosure and conflicts of interest in the commercial insurance market; FSA *Annual Report 2004/0*; Communication from the Commission to the European Parliament, the Council, the European Economic and Social Committee of the Regions—Sector inquiry under art 17 of Regulation EC No 1/2003 on business insurance (Final Report).

[231] See, eg, the FSA's 'Dear CEO Letter' on conflict of interest dated 18 November 2005.

[232] *Hurstanger Ltd v Wilson* [2007] EWCA Civ 299.

as a result of his acting on the principal's behalf. This covers all remuneration: commissions, fees, profit shares, etc.[233]

Spitzer invesitigations. High profile investigations by former New York Attorney General Eliot Spitzer[234] in the US focused attention on the conflicts of interests posed by various forms of remuneration paid by insurers to brokers and other intermediaries, notably contingent commissions, volume overriders, and profit commissions. **14.188**

The Competition Commission insurance sector inquiry. Following the Spitzer investigations in the US, the European Competition Commission undertook a sector inquiry into business insurance that sought to identify potential anti-competitive practices and distortions of competition.[235] When considering the distribution of business insurance through intermediaries, the Commission identified the tendency for brokers to act as advisors to their clients and as distribution channels to insurers as a potential source of conflict. In particular, fair competition was undermined by various practices aimed at inciting brokers to place business with particular insurers, often without complete, clear, or understandable disclosure to the client. The Commission found that the potential for conflicts of interest is highest where a broker is acting under a delegated authority for an insurer regarding their own insurance clients. **14.189**

Current position in the UK

The FSA expressed concern not only about the lack of transparency in commission information (both regarding the client-facing intermediary and others further down the chain), but also about the fact that clients are not always aware of the extent to which an intermediary searches the market when acting on their behalf, nor the extent to which an intermediary acts on behalf of the client as opposed to the insurer. In a 2008 discussion paper on transparency and conflicts of interest in the insurance sector, the FSA considered that this information should be clear and accurate, easily accessible, and presented in a way that facilitates comparisons across the market and over time.[236] In response to concerns about transparency and bias in sales of investment products, the RDR sought to remove commission bias from the sale of investment products including life policies, to retail customers. The RDR has banned commission from advised sales of invesments and has accordingly reduced issues relating to conflicts of interest for such products; there remain however concerns relating to conflicts for non-advised sales of investments (see paragraph 14.193 *et seq.*). **14.190**

ICOBS Rules. There are specific rules in ICOBS dealing with remuneration which gives rise to a conflict and to conflicts in claims handling. While prior disclosure of fees is mandatory under ICOBS 4.3.1R, there are no requirements for own-initiative prior disclosure of commission. ICOBS 4.4 (commission disclosure to customers) gives commercial customers enhanced rights to require commission disclosure. This is an unusual rule in that it gives commercial consumers rights that were not given to consumers. The effect of ICOBS 4.4.1 is to give commercial customers enhanced rights to require disclosure (i) even where the intermediary is not acting on their behalf (as an agent or fiduciary) and (ii) including remuneration **14.191**

[233] ibid.

[234] 'Spitzer Complaint'; *People of the State of New York v Marsh & McLennan Companies, Inc, and Marsh, Inc* No 04403342 (Sup Ct New York County, 14 Oct 2004).

[235] Sector Inquiry under art 17 of Regulation (EC) No 1/2003 on business insurance (Final Report) (SEC (2007) 1231).

[236] FSA DP08/02, 'Transparency, disclosure and conflicts of interest in the commercial insurance market'.

received by the intermediary's associates. Disclosure is required in 'cash terms'. The rule does not address the disclosure of commission retained throughout the insurance chain.

14.192 **Rules on Inducements.** The FCA gives guidance under ICOBS 2.3.1G on the accepting and offering of inducements.[237] It requires a firm to take reasonable steps to ensure that it does not offer or accept inducements or direct business to any person if it is likely to conflict to a material extent with any duty that the firm or the recipient owes to its customers in connection with insurance mediation activities. This rule can apply to remuneration, commission, or benefits in kind paid to individual sales staff and from one company to another. The guidance may be breached both by an insurer who pays, and a broker who receives, an inappropriate form of remuneration.

The Retail Distribution Review

14.193 Given the existence of various insurance market practices which can cause conflicts of interest to arise (see earlier), regulatory authorities have shown an increasing interest in finding ways to increase remuneration transparency to reduce the risk that commission prevents policies being sold in the best interests of the customer.

14.194 In June 2007, the FSA launched the RDR.[238] One of its aims was to remove commission bias from the sale of investment products including life policies to retail clients. The RDR rules came into effect at the beginning of 2013. Following the ban of payments of commission, advisor charges must be paid by the client. The adviser firm can set the amount of its charges, provided that they are agreed up front with the client. A client can still be obliged to pay the charge, even if they decide not to accept any of the adviser firm's recommendations.

14.195 The ban on the payment of commission applies to advised sales (those involving a personal recommendation) of a retail investment product to a retail customer (which will include consumers and small businesses). The rules cover sales of all life insurance aside from pure protection contracts. It therefore remains possible to pay/receive commission in relation to pure protection products, whether sold under COBS or ICOBS. Commission can also continue for retail investment products (other than certain group pensions products) sold without advice and for legacy business (ie business issued prior to the implementation of the RDR). Other consequential effects are that rebates from product providers, factoring or indemnity payments, and soft commission are banned.

14.196 In determining the level of adviser and consultancy charges, a firm should have regard to the best interests of the client. The FCA rules require adviser charges for similar products to be the same, and any ongoing adviser charges must relate to services provided or to regular premiums paid under the policy—although there will be an exemption for ongoing trail commission on products sold prior to the RDR rules coming into force. The rules also provide that there should be no product bias in favour of products with ongoing charges, unless these products are in the client's best interest.[239]

14.197 **IMD2.** In 2012 the European Commission published a draft of the directive which will replace the IMD.[240] The IMD2 proposal makes a number of significant changes to the

---

[237] See para 14.223 *et seq.*

[238] FSA DP07/1: A Review of retail distribution (2007).

[239] Chapter 6 of COBS.

[240] Proposal for a directive of the European Parliament and of the Council on insurance mediation (recast) COM(2012) 360/2.

regulation of sales of insurance products within the EU. One of the areas which IMD2 seeks to address is remuneration transparency and conflicts of interest. The draft directive proposes the introduction of mandatory disclosure of remuneration for life insurance products and a five-year on-request disclosure regime for non-life products. After the five-year transitional period, disclosure of the amount or basis of any remuneration paid to intermediaries will become mandatory for all sales of insurance. In addition, the proposal seeks to create a distinction between insurance investment products and other products for the application of certain requirements, for example a requirement to identify, prevent, manage, and disclose conflicts of interest when selling investment products; a measure which reflects the requirements contained in MiFID.[241] At the time of writing, these proposals are in draft and it remains to be seen whether the final text of IMD2 will go so far as to make all disclosure of commission mandatory.

Systems and Controls in relation to conflicts

Firms conducting insurance activities are subject to requirements in the regulatory Handbook rules[242] to: **14.198**

(1) Apportion significant responsibilities among senior executives, including for monitoring and managing conflicts;
(2) Have appropriate systems and controls, especially where conflicts exist, and establish an effective compliance system to help manage those conflicts; and
(3) Have an appropriate flow of management information, including information about the incidence and management of conflicts.

Senior Management Arrangements and Systems and Controls ('SYSC')

The regulatory Senior Management Arrangements, Systems and Controls Sourcebook ('SYSC') and the related regime for the prior approval and individual regulation of approved persons under APER is covered in Chapter 6. The underlying regulatory themes behind these Handbooks are to ensure that firms have adequate systems and controls in place, and to hold senior management responsible for ensuring that all business operations are conducted within the regulatory framework.[243] These obligations derive from Principle 3 in PRIN and are reflected in the extensive SYSC requirements that apply to firms. An increasing number of enforcement actions find that where rules have been breached or there is a TCF failure, there has also been a failure to take reasonable care to organise and control affairs responsibly and effectively and a lack of adequate risk management. **14.199**

There are extensive systems requirements for insurers in GENPRU, INSPRU,[244] and in SYSC. **14.200**

Some applicable SYSC requirements are general high-level requirements which apply to all firms including insurance intermediaries, some are specific requirements for insurers. The applicable SYSC requirements for insurers are: **14.201**

(i) 2 (Senior management arrangements);
(ii) 3 (Systems and controls);

241 For further detail on MiFID rules on conflicts of interest see Chapter 3.
242 See SYSC 2, PRIN, and the FSA's CEO letter on Conflicts of Interest dated 18 November 2005.
243 Principle 3, SYSC 2.1.1R and 3.1.1R.
244 See para 14.274 *et seq.*

(iii) 11 (Liquidity risk systems and controls);
(iv) 12 (Group risk systems and controls requirements);
(v) 13 (Operational risk systems and controls);
(vi) 14 (Prudential risk management and associated systems and controls);
(vii) 15 (Credit risk management systems and controls);
(viii) 16 (Market risk management systems and controls);
(ix) 17 (Insurance risk systems and controls);
(x) 18 (Guidance on Public Interest Disclosure Act: Whistle blowing); and
(xi) 21 (Risk control: additional guidance).

14.202 These requirements include, for example, the establishment and maintenance of systems and controls, in relation to the management of operational risk—ie the risk of loss, resulting from inadequate or failed internal processes, people and systems, or from external events. They also include requirements relating to insurance risk (ie the risk as an underwriter of insurance policies that the quantum, timing, or frequency of claims will not be as expected) including, for example, the aggregation of risk and the need for a written policy setting out an insurer's risk appetite and how it identifies, measures, monitors, and controls that risk.

Systems and controls and the possible extension of the common platform requirements

14.203 The common platform (ie those rules contained within SYSC 4-10) includes rules specifically dealing with conflicts[245] such as:

(i) The requirement for a written conflicts policy;[246]
(ii) The requirement to take all reasonable steps to identify conflicts and prevent them;[247] and
(iii) The requirement to clearly disclose the general nature and/or sources of conflicts of interest to a client before undertaking business for that client.[248]

14.204 The common platform does not apply to insurers but is applied to insurance intermediaries as guidance.

Business Standards

Conduct of Business Rules—insurance investment products ('COBS')

14.205 Broadly speaking, COBS applies to regulated activities which fall within the definition of designated investment business[249] and long-term care insurance contracts.[250]

14.206 COBS is considered in more detail in chapter 16. The COBS chapters specifically dealing with insurance include: chapter 7 (Insurance mediation), chapter 20 (With-profits), chapter 17 (Claims handling for long-term care insurance), and chapter 21 (Permitted links).

Conduct of Business Rules—non-investment insurance ('ICOBS')

14.207 It is not possible to cover all the detailed rules in ICOBS; the following paragraphs highlight, in broad terms, some of the more important provisions.

245 SYSC 10.
246 SYSC 10.1.10R.
247 SYSC 10.1.3R.
248 SYSC 10.1.8R.
249 COBS 1.1. See the explanation of the 'designated investment' in para 14.04.
250 See the explanation of 'long-term care insurance contracts' in para 14.04.

The application and scope rules for ICOBS (principally in chapter 1 of ICOBS) are complex, sometimes more so than the obligations themselves. This is partly to cope with the difficulty of implementing provisions contained in a number of EU Directives[251] and the different cross-border regimes which they establish. 14.208

Scope and EU implementation

ICOBS applies to the sale and administration of non-investment insurance; these are general insurance and pure protection contracts (other than long-term care contracts). Pure protection contracts are those long-term contracts which do not fall within the definition of qualifying contracts of insurance (and therefore of relevant investments) under the RAO. ICOBS does not therefore apply to insurance products regulated under COBS or where an election for COBS regulation of a pure protection product has been made by the firm in question. Certain long-term life products (such as some whole of life contracts) were switched to regulation under ICOBS (instead of COBS) in 2007.[252] 14.209

With effect from 1 January 2009, ICOBS was extended to cover sales of connected travel insurance ('CTI'). Like standalone insurance, CTI is not subject to the additional requirements for higher risk or protection products (see paragraph 14.218 *et seq.*); indeed certain other ICOBS requirements that apply to standalone travel insurance do not apply to CTI. This disapplication is possible in relation to ICOBS provisions implementing IMD because CTI falls outside the scope of that directive.[253] 14.210

ICOBS does not apply to reinsurance of any kind. It has limited application to 'large risks' (although it recites the broader application of Principle 7); generally the mediation rules do not apply to large risks unless the risk is located in the EEA and the customer is a consumer. 14.211

ICOBS applies to business conducted from a UK establishment but it contains an EEA territorial scope rule which modifies this principle (see paragraph 14.216). 14.212

ICOBS does not apply to a 'wholesale' intermediary (such as a placing broker) which is not in contact with the end customer. 14.213

ICOBS rules (on the production of product information and claims handling) apply to insurers as product providers; insurers which sell direct without an intermediary are also subject to some (but not all) of the selling rules (such as the obligation to provide the product information to the customer). 14.214

ICOBS rules implement various requirements in different EU directives; these include the IMD, distance marketing, E-commerce, Consolidated Life and Non-life directives. These 14.215

[251] The IMD (see n 33), in respect of non-investment insurance contracts; the DMD (Council Directive (EC) 02/65 on distance marketing of consumer financial services [2002] OJ L271/16), in respect of non-investment insurance contracts and distance non-investment mediation contracts; the CLD (see n 39) in respect of cancellation rights and information requirements relating to non-investment insurance contracts which are pure protection contracts; the Third Non Life Directive (see n 42); and the Fourth Motor Insurance Directive (Council Directive (EC) 00/26 on the approximation of the laws of the Member States relating to insurance against civil liability in respect of the use of motor vehicles and amending Council Directives (EEC) 73/239 and 88/357 [2000] OJ L181/65), in respect of claims made by an EEA resident arising from a motor accident in the EEA but outside his country of residence.

[252] See n 9.

[253] See FSA CP07/22 and PS08/04 ('Regulating Connected Travel Insurance') and the Financial Services and Markets Act 2000 (Regulated Activities) (Amendment) (No 2) Order 2007, SI 2007/3510.

rules (and domestic requirements in these areas) are subject to different cross-border regimes which determine whether, for example, home or host State rules apply.

14.216 The scope rules are therefore extremely complex. An 'EEA territorial scope rule' states that the scope provisions in ICOBS are deemed to be overridden to the extent required by EU law (which is left unspecified and as to which the FCA may be uncertain); this leaves the reader to interpret EU law and apply or disapply ICOBS provisions accordingly! The benefit from the FCA's point of view is that its rules cannot be criticised for incorrect implementation of EU requirements.

Differential requirements and the changes from ICOB

14.217 ICOBS is considerably shorter than the previous rulebook, ICOB, which was considered to be overly prescriptive and burdensome for firms. Following criticism that the UK had 'gold-plated' IMD provisions the FSA cut back the application of selling rules (such as status disclosure and demands and needs statements) to insurers (which was possible because the European requirements of IMD did not apply to insurers).

14.218 ICOBS imposes additional obligations in relation to 'pure protection contracts' and 'payment protection contracts' in recognition of the greater risks posed by such products to consumers.

14.219 ICOBS is concerned with policyholders, ie those entitled to make a claim under a policy. In the context of insurance sales, many of the rules apply only to the person buying the insurance. These are split into 'consumers' and non-consumers referred to as 'commercial customers' (which includes those who are acting in both capacities).

Communications, financial promotions, and distance communications (ICOBS 2.2 and 3)

14.220 There are high-level requirements (clear, fair, and not misleading) for all promotions and for all communications to a customer or other policyholder. There are some further limited provisions (for example, in relation to pricing claims) for promotions which are not covered by one of the various exemptions in the FPO.

14.221 For distance marketing to consumers (within the DMD), a variety of directive requirements are applicable under ICOBS 3. These include the regulation of oral and written marketing, the provision of prescribed pre- and post-contract information and documents, requirements for telephone sales, and a prohibition in relation to unsolicited services.

14.222 There are separate rules concerning insurance business conducted from the UK under the E-Commerce Directive.[254]

Inducements and information about the firm, its services, and remuneration (ICOBS 2.3 and 4)[255]

14.223 ICOBS 4.1 implements IMD provisions; it requires intermediaries (but not direct selling insurers) to give 'status disclosure' comprising certain specified information about the firm and information about the type of service it will provide (whether advised or non-advised service, whether a full market service is provided or a limited range, and whether the intermediary is tied by an exclusivity obligation to an insurer). This must be given before the sale

254 Council Directive (EC) 00/31 on certain legal aspects of information society services, in particular electronic commerce, in the Internal Market [2000] OJ L178/1.

255 See para 14.192 for further discussion of ICOBS 2.3.1 concerning inducements and para 14.191 for further discussion of ICOBS 4.

and may be required at renewal or amendment of a policy. Guidance is given on the use of 'panels' in order to provide a service which can be described as 'whole of market'.

The information must be given in a durable medium unless the customer requests it orally or cover is required immediately. Telephone sales are governed by the distance marketing rules. There are also requirements for the prior disclosure of all fees (ie charges other than premiums) and for commission disclosure on request to commercial customers.[256] A standard form 'initial disclosure document' can be used for status and fee disclosure. **14.224**

There are additional requirements for the sale of payment protection and pure protection contracts to consumers. Intermediaries have to provide additional information about the limits of the service they will be providing which will include, in the case of a non-advised sale, explaining orally to the customer that he is responsible for determining whether the policy meets his demands and needs. Insurers (when selling direct) must give status information and confirm whether they will be giving a personal recommendation. **14.225**

Identifying client needs and advising (ICOBS 5)

The distinction that existed in the ICOB rules between advised and non-advised sales has been watered down to some extent in ICOBS. The rules however contain additional obligations in relation to non-advised sales. The suitability requirement applies to advice which is given by a firm to a customer who is entitled to rely upon its judgement; there are additional obligations for payment protection and pure protection contracts and in relation to policies included in a bundle as part of a bank account. **14.226**

The IMD requirement for demands and needs statements apply to both advised and non-advised sales by an intermediary and are extended to direct sales by insurers of payment protection and pure protection contracts to consumers. For non-advised sales there is helpful guidance as to the different ways in which these statements can be given during the sales process; for example it might be included in product documentation, an application form, or a key features document. **14.227**

In addition, there are general obligations applicable to non-advised sales by insurers and intermediaries; for example they are required to take reasonable steps to ensure that the customer only buys a policy under which he is eligible to claim benefits. There are additional requirements in relation to sales of payment protection insurance. **14.228**

Preparation and provision of product information (ICOBS 6)

The rules draw a distinction between the responsibility for producing product information, which normally falls on the insurer, and for the provision of the information which normally falls on the intermediary arranging the sale or, in the case of a direct sale, on the insurer. There are a variety of situations (including various cross-border scenarios) where the responsibilities may differ. **14.229**

There are specific information requirements for pre-contract information for general insurance (from the Third Non-life Directive and also relating to cancellation) and pre-contact and post-contract information (ie mid-term changes) for pure protection and payment protection contracts (the former includes the requirements of the CLD). The additional requirements include obligations in relation to oral sales, the provision of a policy summary, and significant regulation of the way in which price information for payment protection policies is provided (with a distinction between policies for revolving and non-revolving credit). **14.230**

[256] See further at para 14.185 *et seq.* and 14.191 in particular.

14.231 The general requirements applicable to all polices do not require the use of a policy summary but these, and a key features document, can be used to meet the general requirements. The basic rule requires reasonable steps to ensure a customer is given appropriate information (including price information) about a policy in good time and in a comprehensible form so that the customer can make an informed decision; these obligations extend post sale to mid-term changes and to renewals. Guidance under Principle 7 requires evidence of cover to be provided promptly after inception and that in the case of group policies information should be provided for the customer to pass on to each policyholder.

Cancellation (ICOBS 7)

14.232 A consumer has the right to cancel pure protection and payment protection contracts within 30 days and the right to cancel any other contract of insurance within 14 days. This implements the requirements of the CLD and the DMD but extends cancellation to all general insurance sales including those made face to face. There are a variety of exceptions which either reflect directive exceptions or relate to sales outside those directives.

14.233 The rule also stipulates the start of the cancellation period, how the right is exercised, and the effects of cancellation.

Claims handling (ICOBS 8)

14.234 The final chapter of ICOBS deals with claims handling. There are rules which impose general requirements on insurers in relation to all claims and extend to claims by a policyholder who was not the original customer on the sale of the policy. These requirements, originally taken from ABI codes, restrict the ability of the insurer to reject claims from a consumer where the insurer would be entitled to do so under the general law on account of certain non-disclosures.

14.235 There are additional requirements in relation to the handling of claims under motor vehicle liability policies including Consolidated Motor Insurance Directive requirements for a claims representative in each Member State.

14.236 There is guidance under Principle 8 on the conflicts of interest which may arise for insurance intermediaries (or insurers handling claims on another insurer's policy). In some situations, an intermediary will be unable to act for both an insurer and the policyholder.

14.237 Since April 2012, ICOBS 8.4 has required all insurers who have actual or potential liability under commercial lines employers' liability policies, entered into or renewed after April 2011, to include details about these policies on a public register. The purpose of these rules is to assist individuals with claims arising out of the course of their employment to identify the insurer with liability for those claims. The rules for those firms obliged to publish details on the register are quite prescriptive in contrast to other ICOBS provisions and reflect a change to more onerous rules to cover those risks which may pose particular harm to consumers.

Client money[257]

14.238 CASS sets out the rules for dealing with client money. It is divided into five chapters dealing with application and general provisions ('CASS 1'); firm classification and operational oversight ('CASS 1A'); collateral ('CASS 3'); client money: insurance mediation activity ('CASS 5');

[257] FSA CP174, 'Prudential and other requirements for mortgage firms and insurance intermediaries'; FSA PS174, 'Prudential and other requirements for mortgage firms and insurance intermediaries: feedback on CP174 and "near final text"'; FSA CP04/13, 'Quarterly consultation (No 1)'; FSA Handbook notice 29;

custody rules ('CASS 6'); client money rules ('CASS 7'); client money distribution ('CASS 7A'); mandates ('CASS 8'); prime brokerage ('CASS 9'); and resolution pack ('CASS 10').

In this section we look at some of the key elements of CASS 5. This contains the rules introduced at NGI for non-investment insurance mediation and which are part of UK compliance with Article 4(4) of the IMD. During the consultations on how to regulate client money, two key issues emerged for insurers: 14.239

(i) the practice of the London Market of paying premiums (or claims) out of a broker's insurance bank account ('IBA') before the client had paid the premium to them (and the payment of claims out of the IBA before the insurer had paid). This necessitated the development of non-statutory client bank accounts referred to later in this chapter;
(ii) the handling of insurer monies—the lack of clear documentation and clarity concerning the basis on which premium/claims monies were held by intermediaries in their IBAs (ie whether the monies were held for clients/insureds or for insurers), the implication of intermediaries acting as agents under a binding authority in relation to related premium and claims monies and the IMD/FSMA requirements that client money bank accounts protect monies held for customers, whereas IBAs were used to 'co-mingle' insurer monies and client money.

Scope of CASS 5

Which firms does it apply to? As stated earlier, CASS 5 applies to an intermediary (not an insurer acting as such) which receives or holds money in the course of or in connection with insurance mediation activity.[258] Insurance intermediaries can also elect to treat monies relating to reinsurance under the client money rules. The election must be in respect of all the firm's reinsurance business.[259] It can also elect to treat monies relating to large risks[260] situated outside the EEA in the same way; again it must apply to all such business. Absent an election, these monies fall outside CASS 5. A firm which mediates in relation to both investment and non-investment insurance may elect to operate entirely under the CASS 7 rules for designated investment business.[261] The CASS 5 rules are intended to apply to UK registered firms on a home State basis across the EEA. 14.240

Who is a client? A client is any person with or for whom the intermediary conducts or intends to conduct insurance mediation activities. A client includes: 14.241

- a potential client;
- a client of an appointed representative of an intermediary with or for whom the appointed representative acts or intends to act in the course of business for which the intermediary has accepted responsibility.[262]

FSA Handbook notice 38; Insurance Mediation and Mortgage Mediation, Lending and Administration (Prudential Provisions) Instrument 2004 (2004/1): Client Assets Sourcebook (Amendment No 2) Instrument 2004 (2004/92); Guide to the FSA Handbook for Small Mortgage and Insurance Intermediaries Part III; FSA Frequently Asked Questions; FSA letter to CEOs of all general insurance intermediaries supervised within the FSA's wholesale unit, dated 20 July 2005.

258 CASS 5.1.1R.
259 CASS 5.1.1R(3).
260 See the explanation of 'large risks' in para 14.05.
261 See the explanation of 'non-investment insurance' and 'designated investment business' in paras 14.04–14.05.
262 Regulatory Glossary.

14.242 A policyholder/insured may be a client. An insurer will be a client,[263] if it agrees to become one.[264] An insurance intermediary can be the client of another insurance intermediary, for example in the following chain the retail producing broker is the client of the wholesale placing broker:

Policy holder → 'Retail' producing broker → 'Wholesale' placing broker → Insurer

Statutory and non-statutory accounts

14.243 According to CASS 5 an intermediary must hold client money in a segregated bank account on a statutory or non-statutory trust basis.[265] Statutory and non-statutory trust client bank accounts can be operated side by side.[266]

14.244 A statutory account is a bank account with individual client ledgers, but with no cross-lending between each client ledger.[267] These accounts (like those under CASS 7) are governed by the statutory trust established under section 139(1) of FSMA.

14.245 A non-statutory account is a bank account where one client's money may be used to pay the premium/claim of another client, ie to allow an intermediary to pay a premium which has not yet been received from the client out of the client bank account (to the insurer) and to pay premium refunds/claims monies which have not yet been received from the insurer.[268] Under a non-statutory trust an intermediary can also make use of a 'letter of credit' (see paragraph 14.270).[269]

14.246 Non-statutory trusts are subject to more detailed rules on systems and controls. An intermediary must also execute a formal trust deed (or the equivalent in Scotland) in line with CASS 5 requirements to establish the trust and set out its terms.[270] It must also obtain the informed consent of the client.[271]

Operating segregated accounts

14.247 Paying client money into the client bank account. The main obligation is to segregate client money.

14.248 If an intermediary is liable to pay money to a client, it must as soon as possible, and no later than one business day after the money is due and payable:

- pay it into a client bank account as soon as practicable. The FCA expects that in most circumstances this will be the next business day after receipt;[272] or
- pay it to, or to the order of, the client.

263 CASS 5.1.1R.
264 See para 14.261 *et seq.*
265 ibid.
266 CASS 5.4.2R.
267 CASS 5.3.
268 CASS 5.4.1G.
269 CASS 5.4.8R(2).
270 CASS 5.4.7R.
271 CASS 5.4.4R(5).
272 CASS 5.5.5R and 5.5.6G.

Mixed remittance. Mixed remittance can be paid into client bank accounts provided the money which is not client money or has ceased to be client money is withdrawn from the client bank account as soon as is reasonably practicable (and no later than 25 business days) after remittance is cleared in the account (or, if earlier, when the firm performs the client money calculation in accordance with CASS 5.5.63(1)).[273] **14.249**

For intermediaries unable to identify remittance transactions, if there is any doubt the money should be treated as client money while the intermediary takes steps to match the remittance as soon as practicable.[274] **14.250**

Interest. There are specific requirements for retail customers, relating to interest on client money (eg, there is a requirement for an explanation of and, where necessary, the client's informed consent to treatment of interest).[275] Where a client is entitled to interest, it must be treated as client money. **14.251**

Withdrawal of commission. CASS prohibits an intermediary from removing commission from the client bank account until the client or premium finance provider firm has paid the premium to it (ie the bank account must be operated on a 'commission received' basis and not on a 'commission earned' basis). The commission may only be withdrawn from the client bank account at the point at which it is due to the firm for its own account. Until then the commission will remain client money.[276] **14.252**

Where an intermediary's terms of business with its client *and* its terms of business with the insurer set out when the commission element will become due, the withdrawal of commission must be consistent with this. Commission can be withdrawn before the intermediary pays the premium to the insurance company if the intermediary has received the premium from the client or premium finance firm and the insurance company's terms of business allow this. **14.253**

If the commission becomes due immediately upon receipt of the premium from the client, the premium must be treated as mixed remittance (see paragraph 14.249). **14.254**

If the insurance company's terms of business do not specify a time for withdrawal of commission, then the intermediary may assume that commission is due on receipt of the premium from the client.[277] **14.255**

When a client pays premiums to an intermediary in instalments, then in most cases, the commission must also be withdrawn from the client bank account in instalments. The withdrawal must also comply with the intermediary's terms of business with both client and insurer.[278] **14.256**

Paying money out of the client bank account to an insurer. If it is a statutory account the intermediary cannot meet the client's premium obligation to the insurer unless it is funded, ie that the client has already paid the monies to the intermediary.[279] If it is a non-statutory **14.257**

273 CASS 5.5.16R(2).
274 CASS 5.5.17G(4).
275 CASS 5.5.30R.
276 CASS 5.5.16R.
277 Guide to the FSA Handbook for Small Mortgage and Insurance Intermediaries, Part III, para 2.4.7.
278 CASS 5.5.17G(3).
279 CASS 5.3.3G(2).

account a client's premium obligation can be met from the pool of client money held for the intermediary's other clients before the client pays the premium to the intermediary.

14.258 Paying money out of the client bank account to another intermediary. An intermediary may allow another person, such as another broker, to hold or control client money, but only if:

- the intermediary transfers the client money for the purpose of a transaction for a client through or with that person; and
- in the case of a retail customer that customer has been notified (whether through a client agreement, terms of business, or otherwise in writing) that the client money may be transferred to another person.[280]

14.259 When a firm transfers a premium to a third party, it will not automatically discharge its duties to its client as trustee. Therefore, if the intermediary pays a premium to a third party firm, the premium will remain client money of the intermediary until it is paid to the insurer. The premium will also be client money of the third party firm, held on behalf of the intermediary, until it is paid to the insurer. However, if the money is held at any time by a firm which is an agent of the insurer, the premium then becomes the insurer's money.

14.260 Where the money remains client money of the intermediary, the intermediary must use appropriate skill, care, and judgement when transferring monies to third parties[281] and track the payments in the chain for the purposes of performing its own client money calculation and reconciliation which will include monies held by third parties.

Insurer monies—acting as agent of insurers, client money, and subordination

14.261 Under CASS 5, the intermediary may have one of three relationships with an insurer. These may vary between individual risks.

14.262 Providing the intermediary is not operating a binding authority for the relevant business, the intermediary may receive and hold the money as agent of its client and not for the insurer. In this situation, the money received/held by the intermediary is held for the client and is, therefore, client money which must be held in a client bank account. Payments of premium by the client to the intermediary do not discharge the debt due to the insurer—this occurs when the intermediary pays the insurer (or its agent). Money paid by the insurer to the intermediary constitutes payment by the insurer to the client or ultimate policyholder.

14.263 The intermediary may act as agent of the insurer to receive/hold premiums and to hold premiums refund/claims monies.[282] This is compulsory if the intermediary has a binding authority agreement with the insurer in relation to the relevant business.[283] In this situation, premiums paid by the client to the intermediary are a payment to the insurer (through its agent). This is sometimes referred to as a risk transfer because in this situation it is the insurer which bears the risk of the intermediary becoming insolvent. Money paid to the intermediary by its client or by the insurer (within this agency) is insurer money and, unless the necessary agreements for co-mingling are in place, cannot be paid/held in the client bank

[280] CASS 5.5.34R.
[281] CASS 5.5.81G.
[282] CASS 5.2.
[283] CASS 5.2.3R.

account, ie it must be held in other bank accounts of the intermediary (either office accounts or non-FCA/specific insurer accounts).

There are specific requirements for an agency agreement between intermediary and insurer in these circumstances, and requirements to inform relevant clients of the arrangement.[284] (These requirements reflect Article 4.4(a) of the IMD as distinct from the provisions requiring segregated client accounts for customer's money under Article 4.4(c) of the IMD.) 14.264

When the intermediary acts as an agent of an insurer in receiving/holding monies, the insurer may agree with the intermediary that the insurer's money may be co-mingled in the intermediary's client bank account.[285] This situation is then as described earlier except that money received/held as agent of the insurer may be held in the client bank account as if the insurer were a client of the intermediary. 14.265

To co-mingle, an intermediary must obtain the insurer's written agreement that the monies may be treated as client money and its written consent and acceptance that its interest under the trust is subordinated to the intermediary's 'true' clients.[286] 14.266

Appointed representatives

An appointed representative cannot operate its own client bank account. It may, however, receive money as agent of the insurer (see paragraph 14.261 *et seq.*). Alternatively it can accept client money under one of three procedures in accordance with the relevant CASS requirements. The options are (i) the money is paid directly into the principal's client bank account,[287] (ii) 'immediate segregation' which involves forwarding the funds to the principal to arrive within three business days,[288] or (iii) 'periodic segregation' under which the principal maintains a balance in its client bank account equivalent to the estimated amount of client money held by the appointed representative (subject to reconciliation against the actual amount held on a periodic basis).[289] 14.267

Reconciliation, insurance debtors, and letters of credit

Under CASS 5, intermediaries are required to carry out a client money calculation and reconciliation.[290] 14.268

The client money calculation requires an intermediary to calculate—at least every 25 business days—the amount of money which ought to be segregated in its client bank account(s) (and at third parties) to meet its obligations to its clients.[291] This is done by comparing the client money resource with the client money requirement. Any shortfall or surplus should be rectified by the end of the day on which the calculation is performed.[292] 14.269

There are two methods permitted for the client money calculation—a cash-based method and an accruals method.[293] Under the accruals method (which includes insurance creditors 14.270

284 ibid.
285 CASS 5.1.5AR.
286 ibid.
287 CASS 5.5.19R.
288 ibid.
289 CASS 5.5.23R.
290 CASS 5.5.62G–5.5.77R.
291 CASS 5.5.63R.
292 ibid.
293 CASS 5.5.66R and 5.5.68R.

and debtors), the intermediary is required to value debts on a prudent and consistent basis.[294] If the client bank account is a non-statutory trust, the intermediary can make use of a 'letter of credit'[295] provided by an approved bank to satisfy a shortfall in the intermediary's client money resource when compared to its client money requirement.[296]

Review of the Client Assets Sourcebook

14.271 Amid growing concerns that client money has not being adequately protected, the FSA consulted upon proposals to revise the rules in CASS 5.[297] In keeping with the tougher regulatory approach to client money following the collapse of Lehman Brothers, insurance intermediaries will face more stringent requirements on how they deal with client money and assets.

14.272 A series of firm visits undertaken by the FSA in 2010 revealed that firms' practices in protecting client money were frequently inadequate and there was a general lack of understanding about obligations under CASS 5.

14.273 The proposals to revise the insurance client money rules focus on simplifying the distribution and transfer of client money, enhancing record keeping and reconciliations, and improving segregation, risk transfer, and the diversification of client money. Methods of dealing with unallocated funds and some specific provisions in relation to credit write-backs are also addressed. It is expected that revised rules will be introduced during 2014.

Prudential Standards—Insurers[298]

14.274 The Prudential requirements in the PRA Handbook are concerned with financial resources, capital solvency, and related systems requirements, particularly for risk mitigation. Broader requirements relating to systems and controls are set out in SYSC[299] (within 'High-level' standards). This section looks briefly at the current financial regime for insurers in the PRA Handbook and the Solvency II initiative and then at the financial regime for insurance intermediaries.

Background to the current UK regime

14.275 The current EU minimum requirements are set out in the CLD, the 3NLD, and the RID; these were subject to relatively minor amendments under the Solvency I Directives, which came into effect in 2004.[300] For many years UK solvency requirements were based on the EU regime, although insurers were frequently required by the FJA to maintain higher levels of capital or a higher 'solvency ratio'. This reflected the view that the EU requirements were generally set too low; there is also general recognition that the whole structure of the solvency ratio regime was out of date and needed to be replaced.

294 CASS 5.5.65R(3)(a).
295 CASS 5.4.8R(2).
296 ibid.
297 FSA CP 12/20: Review of the client money rules for insurance intermediaries (August 2012).
298 This section looks mainly at the position of 'Directive' insurers authorised under the CLD or 3NLD. It does not address the variations and different prudential requirements for other risk carriers such as reinsurers, captives, ISPVs, mutuals, composites, non-directive insurers, and the Lloyd's market.
299 See para 14.199 *et seq.*
300 Council Directive (EC) 2002/12/EC amending Council Directive (EEC) 79/267 as regards the solvency margin requirements for life assurance undertakings [2002] OJ L77/11; and Council Directive (EC) 2002/13 amending Council Directive (EEC) 73/239 as regards the solvency margin requirements for non-life insurance undertakings [2002] OJ L77/17.

It was clear that the project, named Solvency II, of developing a modern financial regime for insurers, and securing political agreement across Europe, would take many years. In the UK the Tiner Project[301] had identified reform as a priority and the PRA therefore decided not to wait for EU agreement on Solvency II and to develop and implement its own updated regime. This would meet the historic EU minimum requirements as updated under Solvency I (which still applied) but would include a more modern, sophisticated, and demanding regime which anticipated, in very broad terms, many of the approaches which would emerge in Solvency II. **14.276**

This new regime was initially introduced in the Integrated Prudential Sourcebook ('PRU') section of the Handbook but is now found in the General Prudential Sourcebook ('GENPRU') and the Prudential Sourcebook for Insurers ('INSPRU'). **14.277**

The UK regime—GENPRU and INSPRU[302]

The three pillars

In broad terms, the UK regime for insurers and the emerging Solvency II regime are risk-based and reflect some aspects of the modern financial regime for banks, particularly under the Basel II accord (see Chapter 4). This is based on the three pillars of: **14.278**

(1) Minimum capital requirements.
(2) Supervisory review.
(3) Public transparency and market discipline.

GENPRU contains requirements both for banks and investment firms (subject to the Capital Requirements Directive) and insurers;[303] it reflects the move towards common elements across the sectors, for example, with a similar approach to 'tiered' capital. (This is a different technique to the current insurance directives, which are based on deducting foreseeable liabilities from total assets but the same result can be reached using the alternative approach.) **14.279**

GENPRU 2 sets out the calculation of an insurer's capital resources requirements ('CRR') and its admissible forms of capital and how the amounts or values of capital, assets, and liabilities are to be determined. These reflect the minimum requirements of the CLD, the RID, and the 3NLD; in addition the firm is required to make its own assessment of its capital needs and this assessment and the process and systems by which it is made, and reviewed by the PRA, are explained later in this chapter in relation to 'Individual capital assessment'. **14.280**

Pillar 1—minimum capital rule

An insurer must maintain at all times capital resources ('CR') equal to or in excess of its CRR.[304] The CRR represents a required cushion of free capital over and above all liabilities (after technical provisions for all liabilities which will arise on insurance underwritten and allowances for other risks). **14.281**

---

[301] See para 14.22.
[302] The General Prudential Sourcebook for Banks, Building Societies, Insurers and Investment Firms, and the Prudential Sourcebook for Insurers.
[303] GENPRU 1.1.2G.
[304] GENPRU 2.1.13R.

14.282 **Capital Resources.** CR is the sum of the 'Total Capital' and, if a waiver has been granted, of 'other capital resources'. CR is the sum of various capital components calculated according to various tiers/types (ie components) of capital as follows:

(i) Tier 1 capital—
Core Tier 1 capital components (eg permanent share capital, share premium account and externally verified interim net profits);
Perpetual non-cumulative preference shares; and
Innovative Tier 1 capital.

(ii) Tier 2 capital—
Upper Tier 2 (permanent cumulative preference shares, perpetual subordinated debt, and perpetual subordinated securities); and
Lower Tier 2 (fixed term preference shares, long-term subordinated debt, and fixed term subordinated debt).

(iii) Other capital resources (unpaid share capital and implicit items).

14.283 Various requirements and limitations apply to different capital components. Deductions are made from each component and deductions and positive adjustments made to the totals and sub-totals as follows:

(a) From Tier 1 capital—investments in own shares, intangible assets, and negative valuation differences.
(b) Positive adjustment to the total for related undertakings which are regulated.
(c) Deductions from the total for inadmissible assets;[305] and assets in excess of market risk and counterparty limits in INSPRU 2.1.22 R (see paragraph 14.311).

14.284 The full capital resources calculation is as follows:[306]

Table 14.1

Type of capital	Stage
Core Tier 1 capital	**(A)**
Permanent share capital	
Profit and loss account and other reserves (taking into account interim net losses)	
Share premium account	
Externally verified interim net profits	
Positive valuation differences	
Fund for future appropriations	
Perpetual non-cumulative preference shares	**(B)**
Perpetual non-cumulative preference shares	
Innovative Tier 1 capital	**(C)**

305 Inadmissible assets—any asset (except where held to cover property linked or index linked liabilities) other than the list of admissible assets (investments (eg shares, loans, debt securities, land and approved derivatives, quasi-derivative, and stock lending transactions that satisfy certain conditions), debts and claims (eg debts owed by reinsurers including reinsurers shares of technical provisions), deposits and debts owed by ceding undertakings, debts owed by policyholders and intermediaries) and other assets (eg tangible fixed assets and cash). FSA can grant waivers for the inclusion within limits of Implicit items under the CLD (which are economic reserves within long-term insurance provisions relating to future profits, zillmerisation, and hidden reserves).

306 This is taken from GENPRU 2 Annex 1.

Type of capital	Stage
Innovative Tier 1 instruments	
Total Tier 1 capital before deductions = A + B + C	(D)
Deductions from Tier 1 capital	(E)
Investments in own shares	
Intangible assets	
Amounts deducted from technical provisions for discounting and other negative valuations differences	
Total Tier 1 capital after deduction = D – E	(F)
Upper Tier 2 capital	(G)
Perpetual cumulative preference shares	
Perpetual subordinated debt	
Perpetual subordinated securities	
Lower Tier 2 capital	(H)
Fixed term preference shares	
Long-term subordinated debt	
Fixed term subordinated securities	
Total Tier 2 capital = G + H	(I)
Positive adjustments for relating undertakings	(J)
Related undertakings that are regulated related undertakings (other than insurance undertakings)	
Total capital after positive adjustments for insurance undertakings but before deductions = F + I + J	(K)
Deduction from total capital	(L)
Inadmissible assets	
Assets in excess of market risk and counterparty limits	
Related undertakings that are ancillary services undertakings	
Negative adjustments for related undertakings that are regulated related undertakings (other than insurance undertakings)	
Total capital after deductions = K + L	(M)
Other capital resources*	(N)
Unpaid share capital or, in the case of a mutual, unpaid initial funds and calls for supplementary contributions	
Implicit items	
Total capital resources after deductions = M + N	(O)

*Items in section (N) of the table can be included in capital resources if subject to a waiver under s 148 FSMA.

There are various limits on the use of different forms of capital. These include the requirement that Tier 1 capital must represent at least half, and innovative Tier 1 capital must represent no more than 15 per cent, of total Tier 1 capital after deductions (GENPRU 2.2.29 and 2.2.30). **14.285**

Capital Resources Requirement. The CRR of an insurer is the MCR (Minimum Capital Requirement) or, if the insurer is a realistic basis life firm (ie a firm which has with-profits liabilities above a threshold), the higher of the MCR and the Enhanced Capital Requirement for long-term business ('ECRLT').[307] **14.286**

[307] GENPRU 2.1.18R.

14.287 MCR[308] is the higher of:

- the base capital resources requirement ('BCRR') for general/long-term insurance; and
- the general/long-term insurance capital requirement plus, for long-term insurers which are regulatory basis only life firms (ie those which are not realistic basis life firms and which are not subject to an ECRLT), the resilience capital requirement[309] (calculated in accordance with INSPRU 3.1.9G to 3.1.26R) ('RCR').
  - (a) The BCRR is €2·2 million for general business and €3·2 million for long-term business (or other amounts depending on the type of insurer).[310]
  - (b) The general insurance capital requirement ('GICR')[311] is the highest of:
- the premiums amount[312] which is 18 per cent of gross adjusted premiums (which is the higher of the gross written and gross earned premiums as calculated and adjusted under INSPRU 1.1.56) less 2 per cent of the excess over €53·1 million multiplied by the reinsurance ratio (which is based on the ratio of net claims to gross claims over three years);
- the claims amount[313] which is 26 per cent of the gross adjusted claims (as calculated and adjusted under INSPRU 1.1.57) amount less 3 per cent of the excess over €37·2 million multiplied by the reinsurance ratio; and
- the brought forward amount.[314]
  - (c) The long-term insurance capital requirement ('LTICR')[315] is the sum of the:
- insurance death risk capital component;
- insurance health risk and life protection reinsurance capital component;
- insurance expense risk capital component; and
- insurance market risk capital component (based on adjusted mathematical reserves).
  - (d) The ECRLT is the sum of the LTCIR and the with-profits insurance capital requirement (calculated in accordance with the extensive and detailed rules and guidance at INSPRU 1.3).

Overall financial adequacy rule

14.288 The 'overall financial adequacy rule' ('OFAR') requires an insurer, at all times, to maintain overall financial resources, including capital resources and liquidity resources, which are adequate, both as to amount and quality, to ensure there is no significant risk that its liabilities will not be met as they fall due.[316] This is supported by the 'Overall Pillar 2 rule'.

Overall Pillar 2 rule[317]

14.289 The Overall Pillar 2 rule requires systems to assess and ensure sufficient resources are maintained based on a risk assessment. Key aspects of this rule are:

(a) It covers financial, capital, and internal capital.
(b) The assessment covers the amount, type, and distribution of those resources.

---

308 GENPRU 2.1.24R.
309 GENPRU 2.1.25R.
310 GENPRU 2.1.30R.
311 GENPRU 2.1.34R.
312 INSPRU 1.1.45R.
313 INSPRU 1.1.47R.
314 INSPRU 1.1.51R.
315 GENPRU 2.1.36R.
316 GENPRU 1.2.26R.
317 GENPRU 1.2.30R.

(c) The risk to be assessed is the risk of a failure to comply with:
  (i) OFAR and
  (ii) CRR.
(d) Risks to be identified and managed include credit, market, liquidity, operational, insurance, and other risks.
(e) Both the assessment and the process/systems used must be reviewed regularly.

Scenario and stress testing. As part of the Overall Pillar 2 rule, the general scenario and stress testing rule requires an insurer, for each of the major risks, to carry out stress tests and scenario analysis.[318] There is related additional guidance which explains the use of these forward looking analysis techniques to anticipate possible losses that might occur, if an identifiable risk crystallises, in order to test the adequacy of overall financial resources. Such analyses can provide a better understanding of the vulnerabilities that an insurer faces under extreme conditions for three purposes:[319] **14.290**

- quantification of capital required on a 'what if' basis;
- review of risk model outputs particularly for non-linear effects of risk aggregation; and
- to explore sensitivities in longer-term business plans and how capital needs may change over time.

There is further guidance on the use of stress tests and scenario analysis in relation to individual capital assessment (which involves higher confidence levels than the once-in-25-years start point in this rule) and SYSC 11 relating to liquidity risk systems and controls. **14.291**

Individual capital adequacy and assessment[320]

This is an additional regime which insurers must follow as part of the GENPRU 1.2 requirements relating to the assessment of risks to OFAR (it is therefore separate from the assessment of risk to CRR which is another part of Overall Pillar 2 rule—see earlier). Key aspects are: **14.292**

(a) Individual capital assessment ('ICA') is a risk-based assessment reflecting the higher-level requirements of OFAR.
(b) The ICA is focused on the capital elements of the OFAR; so a firm must first consider whether capital is an appropriate mitigant for risks identified and then consider the quality and amount of the capital it holds.
(c) INSPRU 7.1 sets out detailed requirements for an insurer to follow when conducting an ICA.
(d) The PRA assess whether the CRR—ie the minimum requirements of Pillar 1 derived from the CRR calculations above eg the claims and premium-based calculations of the GICR—are sufficient for the individual firm in question. In doing so, PRA considers/reviews—
  (i) the firm's own assessment of its capital needs ('ICA');[321]
  (ii) the process and systems used in the ICA;[322] and
  (iii) where relevant, the ECRGI[323] will be a key part of the review.

318 GENPRU 1.2.42R.
319 GENPRU 1.2.66G.
320 Contained in INSPRU chapter 7.
321 INSPRU 7.1.
322 ibid.
323 See para 14.296.

14.293 Assessments that assets exceed liabilities over different time periods and confidence levels[324]—

(i) benchmark of confidence level of 99.5 per cent over one year;

(ii) assessment according to firm's own model but detailed guidance given and subject to PRA review.

14.294 After review of a firm's ICA, related information and other factors, such as the firm's wider risk management, the PRA gives feedback and provides the firm individual capital guidance ('ICG') with reasons why any capital add-ons identified were applicable. If an insurer does not accept this guidance, it must inform the PRA and the issues will normally be resolved through analysis and discussion leading to an undertaking to hold a particular level of capital. If not agreed the PRA can vary an insurer's permission to require the additional capital.[325]

14.295 The ICA may also be important in any application for a waiver from CRR elements that are not directive requirements.

14.296 Enhanced capital requirement for general insurance ('ECRGI'). There is a rule requirement to calculate (but no absolute rule to meet) the ECRGI calculated in accordance with INSPRU 1.1.72AG *et seq*. Key aspects of this requirement are:

(a) ECRGI is an indicative measure of the capital resources that an insurer may need to hold based on risk-sensitive calculations applied to its business profile and is used by the PRA as a benchmark for its consideration of the appropriateness of the firm's own capital assessment.

   (i) ECRGI is the sum of the asset-related capital requirement (in accordance with INSPRU 2.2.10R *et seq*. which involves applying a stipulated ECR asset-related capital charge factor (percentage of value) to specified assets and producing the total figure); insurance-related capital requirement ('IRCR'); and the firm's equalisation provisions.

   (ii) IRCR addresses risk of adverse movements in a firm's liabilities, ie volatility in claims and technical provisions resulting from a wide range of sources both in relation to assets and insurance liabilities and of premiums from particular business not being sufficient to fund liabilities arising. It is calculated by multiplying the value of net written premiums and technical provisions in respect of each class of business by prescribed capital charge factors and adding these together.

   (iii) Additional market risk provisions relating to the assumed rate of interest used in calculating the present value of general insurance liabilities are contained in the insurance accounts rules and are outlined at INSPRU 3.1.27G.

(b) ECRGI assumes that the firm's business is well diversified and well managed, with good matching and controls and stable with no large, unusual, or high-risk transactions; if this is not the case the ICA is likely to produce a higher capital requirement.

Reserves (technical provisions) and matching[326]

14.297 Technical provisions are on balance sheet provisions for liabilities under insurance contracts (and are therefore deducted from a firm's resources before CR, etc. is calculated).[327]

324 INSPRU 7.1.42R *et seq.*
325 INSPRU 7.1.98G *et seq.*
326 See INSPRU chapter 1.
327 INSPRU 1.1.

For general insurance, these are established according to the general accounting rules applied by GENPRU[328] and take into account the expected ultimate outcome of claims including those not yet incurred and related expenses. It includes provisions for: **14.298**

- outstanding claims,
- unearned premiums,
- unexpired risk, and
- equalisation provision (for which there are specific rules in INSPRU 1.4 for credit and non-credit equalisation provisions)—an allowance for smoothing claims for volatile claims (in business such as property, marine and aviation, nuclear, credit insurance and certain non-proportional reinsurance treaty business).

There are restrictions on discounting (ie discounting for the time value of money) in order to protect against uncertainty in the timing of claims.[329] **14.299**

For long-term insurance, in addition to provisions for liabilities that have fallen due under general accounting standards, there are mathematical reserves calculated in accordance with the rules and guidance of INSPRU 1.2 and with due regard to generally accepted accounting practice— **14.300**

(a) These are the main components of technical provisions for long-term business. They are a minimum and so alternative methods and assumptions may be used, subject to certain requirements and that these produce reserves equal to or greater than the INSPRU methodology.
(b) INSPRU 1.2 deals with—
 (i) the best valuation method;
 (ii) methods and assumptions;
 (iii) margins for adverse deviation;
 (iv) valuation of individual contracts;
 (v) negative mathematical reserves;
 (vi) avoidance of future valuation strain;
 (vii) cash flows to be valued; and
 (viii) valuation assumptions—detailed rules and guidance—on valuation rates of interest, future premiums, expenses, mortality and morbidity options, persistency assumptions, and reinsurance.

There are additional rules and guidance on the methodology to be used in relation to long-term insurance liabilities at INSPRU 3.1.28R to 3.1.48G. **14.301**

Credit for reinsurance. INSPRU 1.1.19AR only allows credit for reinsurance based on genuine risk transfer which is effective in all circumstances. This extends to analogous non-reinsurance financing arrangements and reinsurance with an ISPV (insurance special purpose vehicle). Guidance is given on the factors which will determine the effectiveness of risk transfer for these purposes (eg the legal enforceability in all relevant jurisdictions of the agreements and the potential impact of termination rights). **14.302**

Credit make be taken in various different ways: **14.303**

(a) Treating the reinsurer's share of technical provisions as an admissible asset.

328 See para 14.307.
329 INSPRU 1.1.14G.

(b) Reducing the solvency requirement in accordance with the deduction for reinsurance allowed in the calculation of the GICR.
(c) Bringing into account receivables under the contract when valuing cash flows under prospective valuation of mathematical reserves.
(d) See also credit risk in relation to reinsurance.[330]

14.304 **Admissible assets**[331] must be held to a value of at least—

(i) technical provisions; and
(ii) other general/long-term insurance liabilities.
 (a) For long-term business, the rules apply at a fund level for each with-profits fund. There are additional requirements for a realistic basis life firm in this context.
 (b) Long-term assets must be held in a separate fund under INSPRU 1.5 (internal contagion risk) and are effectively ring-fenced in calculating capital resources.

14.305 Admissible assets must be localised ie generally held in an EEA State and must match liabilities in terms of[332]—

(a) safety, yield, and marketability;
(b) diversification and adequate spread;
(c) being of sufficient amount, appropriate currency, and term to ensure cash inflows from those assets will meet expected cash flows from the firm's insurance liabilities as they fall due. This permits some currency mismatching if sufficient excess assets are held. The level of mismatching is further restricted by INSPRU 3.1.52 *et seq*. which is based on an 80 per cent matching.

14.306 There is a prohibition on writing long-term business unless the firm is able to establish the necessary technical provisions, hold the admissible assets required, and meet the OFAR.

Accounting and valuation

14.307 The rules and guidance on how, when applying GENPRU and INSPRU, insurers should recognise and value assets, liabilities, exposures, and other items, are set out in GENPRU 1.3.

14.308 These include compliance with applicable requirements such as the insurance accounts rules, Financial Reporting Standards and Statements of Recommended Accounting Practice and international accounting standards, and the Companies Acts.

Credit risk and related limits[333]

14.309 **Overall limitation of credit risk.**[334] An insurer must restrict its counterparty exposures (including reinsurer exposures) and asset exposures to prudent levels and ensure that those exposures are adequately diversified. It can only take account of loss mitigation techniques (rights on default—set-off, collateral, charges—and third-party rights, ie guarantees and credit insurance/derivatives—and reinsurance-related rights—eg back-up reinsurance such

330 See para 14.309 *et seq.*
331 INSPRU 1.1.20R *et seq.*
332 INSPRU 1.1.34R *et seq.*
333 INSPRU 2.1.
334 INSPRU 2.1.8R.

as 'top and drop' reinsurance), if it has good reason to believe they will be effective, which may require legal opinions.

Large exposure limits.[335] An insurer must limit counter-party or asset exposure (but excluding reinsurance exposures and assets held to back unit linked liabilities) to a single counterparty/group or an assets/class, so that if a total default occurs, it will not become unable to meet its liabilities as they fall due. **14.310**

Market risk and counterparty limits. Where a firm has assets in excess of market risk and counterparty limits, as specified in INSPRU 2.1.22(3), a firm must deduct the excess from its assets as valued under GENPRU—this is a deduction from capital when calculating the CR (see paragraph 14.283(c)). **14.311**

Large exposure calculation for reinsurance exposures.[336] Various obligations arise if a reinsurance exposure to a reinsurer or group of closely related reinsurers is reasonably likely to exceed 100 per cent of the insurer's CR; these include notification to the PRA and the need to demonstrate how the reinsurance exposure is being safely managed. In addition, there is an evidential provision restricting reinsurance concentration and credit risk—gross earned premiums paid to a reinsurer or reinsurer group are restricted to the higher of £4 million or 20 per cent of the firm's projected gross earned premiums for that financial year. **14.312**

Market risk[337]

This is addressed in various ways, including: **14.313**

(i) the CRR—see paragraph 14.281;
(ii) currency risk requirements—matching requirements described earlier and the requirements for cover to be held for a contract for the purchase or sale of foreign currency; and
(iii) requirements, for long-term business, to hold assets for coverage of property-linked liabilities and index-linked liabilities.

Derivatives in insurance. A derivative or quasi-derivative is approved (and so no deduction is required as an inadmissible asset and also it is allowed as a permitted asset of a unit-linked fund, 'permitted link') if it is based on an admissible asset or permitted link and: **14.314**

(a) held for efficient portfolio management;
(b) covered; and
(c) on/under the rules of a regulated market or is off-market with an approved counterparty and on approved terms and capable of valuation.

Detailed rules and guidance are set out in INSPRU 3.2. **14.315**

Other risk management—liquidity and operational risk

INSPRU contains additional detailed requirements for insurers for the management of liquidity ('INSPRU 4') and operational risk ('INSPRU 5'). **14.316**

In addition to the already cited provisions in GENPRU and INSPRU, there are extensive systems and controls requirements in SYSC (see paragraph 14.199). **14.317**

[335] INSPRU 2.1.20R.
[336] INSPRU 2.1.23R *et seq.*
[337] See INSPRU chapter 3.

Internal contagion risk

14.318 The requirements in INSPRU 1.5 address internal contagion risks including risks from a firm carrying on:

(a) insurance and non-insurance risks;
(b) two or more different types of insurance;
(c) insurance activities of non-EEA insurers from offices or branches both within and outside the UK.

14.319 Insurers are prohibited from carrying on any commercial activity other than insurance business and activities directly arising from that business (see paragraph 14.137). It must also limit, manage, and control its non-insurance activities so that there is no significant risk arising that it may be unable to meet its liabilities as they fall due. Financial penalties imposed by the PRA cannot be paid from the long-term fund. There are specific requirements for property-linked funds.

14.320 Composites cannot use long-term insurance assets to meet general insurance liabilities (and these assets must be separately identified and maintained) and those assets are separated from shareholders' funds.

14.321 The PRA cannot grant permission for a newly authorised composite or an existing insurer to become a composite (subject to certain limited exceptions).

14.322 There are requirements for certain non-EEA insurers relating to their worldwide financial resources and a UK (or EEA) MCR; there are also requirements for the localisation of assets and the deposit of assets as security.

Groups

14.323 **Insurance groups.** INSPRU 6 implements the Insurance Groups Directive ('IGD') as amended by the Financial Groups Directive (and the RID). It contains the sectoral rules for insurance groups, insurance conglomerates, and insurers with participating interests in other insurers.

14.324 The requirements include:

(a) INSPRU 6.1.8—The calculation of the group capital resources ('GCR') and the group capital resources requirement ('GCRR') for the ultimate insurance parent undertaking and (if different) the ultimate EEA insurance parent undertaking and for an insurer itself if, for example, it has a subsidiary which is an insurer or the insurer has a participation in another insurer. The GCRR is the sum of the individual CRRs of the relevant group companies. The GCRR must be covered by appropriate capital resources in respect of the EEA insurance parent undertaking and its group or sub-group.
(b) INSPRU 6.1.9—An insurer, as mentioned earlier, must maintain Tier 1 capital resources and Tier 2 capital resources, so that the insurer's GCR are equal to or exceed its GCRR (this is an adjusted solo calculation—it addresses potential double gearing).
(c) INSPRU 6.1.15—An insurer's CR are of such an amount that the GCR of its ultimate EEA insurance parent undertaking is equal to or exceeds the GCRR for that undertaking. This is a 'hard' requirement for an insurer to hold sufficient capital resources so that the group capital resources, are at least equal to the group capital resources requirement, which goes beyond the soft IGD (ie calculation) requirement in (a) above. In addition, the adequacy of group capital resources is assessed by the insurer and by PRA. The

insurer will carry out an assessment of the adequacy of their financial resources under the OFAR, the Overall Pillar 2 rule and GENPRU 1.2.39R. This will be reviewed by the PRA and it may provide individual guidance on the amount and quality of capital resources and as to the appropriateness of the group capital resources requirement and group capital resources. The PRA may give individual guidance on the capital resources a firm should hold in this context.

Cross sector/financial conglomerate groups. There are separate requirements for financial conglomerates and mixed financial holding companies. Chapter 3 of GENPRU on cross-sector groups implements the Financial Groups Directive. **14.325**

Financial reporting

Most of the old Interim Prudential Sourcebook for insurers ('IPRU(INS)') has been replaced by INSPRU and GENPRU but there are still extensive requirements in IPRU(INS) relating to financial reporting by insurers. **14.326**

Solvency II

The two main objectives of the new legislation are: **14.327**

- to consolidate EU legislation on insurance; and
- to introduce modern prudential regulation of insurers across the EU.

Current status

Solvency II is a framework Lamfalussy-style directive[338] which aims to create a harmonised system for risk-based prudential regulation. The Level 1 framework directive was adopted on 25 November 2009.[339] The Level 1 directive consolidates, with minor amendments, most of the existing insurance and reinsurance directives. The directive is expected to be implemented in 2016. **14.328**

The provisions in the Level 1 directive will be supplemented by more detailed Level 2 implementation measures drawn up in accordance with the Lamfalussy process. CEIOPS which was composed of authorities from Member States including the FSA, drafted advice on Level 2 and conducted a number of quantitative impact studies ('QIS') to investigate whether the proposed detailed requirements are necessary and appropriate. CEIOPS' final advice was sent to EIOPC and the European Commission. CEIOPS has been replaced by EIOPA.[340] **14.329**

What follows is a brief overview of the legislation and proposed changes. A number of the issues in the Level 1 text and details proposed by EIOPA have given rise to further discussions and proposed amendments to the Level 1 text. These amendments are expected to be adopted by a further directive known as Omnibus 2. Until that is adopted much of the detail and importantly the implementation date will not be known. **14.330**

Scope and consolidation

The framework directive will apply to all life and non-life insurance undertakings and to reinsurance undertakings. It will consolidate and replace the main insurance directives—the **14.331**

[338] See Chapter 3 para 3.33 *et seq.*

[339] European Parliament and Council Directive (2009/13/EC) on the taking up and pursuit of the business of Insurance and Reinsurance (Solvency II).

[340] See para 14.61.

CLD, the 3NLD, and the RID and related directives (14 in total including those relating to insurance groups, winding up of insurance undertakings, legal expenses, tourist assistance, and co-insurance). It does not consolidate the motor vehicle directives nor does it change the regime applicable to financial conglomerates. Although the text of the existing directives has been amended by a large number of amendments and deletions, these are not intended to be of a substantive nature, except for those relating to the new solvency regime.

14.332 The new solvency provisions are principles-based and adopt the Lamfalussy structure; the main framework directive gives implementing powers to the Commission, which is assisted by EIOPC; the supervisory authority EIOPA, has a major role including responding to mandates from the Commission and for producing technical standards.

The new solvency regime

14.333 As already mentioned, Solvency II is based on the three pillars of:

- Pillar 1—minimum capital requirements (harmonised standards for the valuation of assets and liabilities, and the calculation of capital requirements);
- Pillar 2—supervisory review process (to help ensure that insurers have good monitoring and management of risks, and adequate capital); and
- Pillar 3—market discipline and disclosure (requirements that allow capital adequacy to be compared across institutions).

14.334 Under the existing EU regime, insurers are subject to requirements relating to technical provisions and a regulatory capital requirement. The main solvency requirement is the Required Minimum Margin ('RMM') although this is subject to an absolute minimum—the Minimum Guarantee Fund ('MGF').

14.335 As explained earlier, the UK has already anticipated some of the broad approaches in Solvency II with the introduction of requirements over and above the current EU requirements in the insurance directives and Solvency I;[341] these include tiered approach to capital resources in common with the Basel rules for banks, Pillar 2 requirements, individual capital assessment (including a 'soft' Enhanced Capital Requirement calculation for general insurers), the PRA review of ICAs, and ICG from the PRA.

14.336 Solvency II capital requirements will be based on:

- a Minimum Capital Requirement (MCR)—the minimum level of regulatory capital;
- a Solvency Capital Requirement (SCR)—a risk-based level of regulatory capital;
- adjusted SCR—SCR including any supplemental capital requirements ('add ons') determined through the Pillar 2 supervisory review.

14.337 The SCR is a more flexible and risk-sensitive analysis that the MCR; an insurer will either use a standard formula to determine its SCR or it can use its own full or partial internal model. The use of an internal model will have to be approved by the regulator according to criteria. Failure to maintain the SCR (which will be higher than the MCR) represents the first regulatory intervention point.

---

[341] The latest material from UK authorities at the time of writing includes: FSA FS08/4, 'Review of the interaction of our solo and group capital requirements—Feedback on DP07/5'; and HMT's 'Solvency II: a partial Impact Assessment' (June 2008).

Insurers will be subject to broad Pillar 2 requirements in relation to risk management including an Own Risk and Solvency Assessment ('ORSA'). This will include a Supervisory Review Process ('SRP') which may result in supplementary capital requirements within an adjusted SCR. Adjusted SCRs are expected to be less common than ICG under the current UK regime. **14.338**

Pillar 3 requirements provide for an enhanced regime for the publication and disclosure of information about the insurer's regulatory capital position. In time this will extend to the amount of the SCR (and any enhanced SCR or capital add ons) and any non-compliance with it; currently in the UK the ICG/ECR is not published and there are concerns about the publication of the SCR information because it may then effectively replace the MCR as the absolute minimum level of capital. **14.339**

One of the most important and controversial areas relates to the supervision of groups. The original idea was that the SCR would only have to be met at the group level, so other insurers in the group in other States would only have to meet the MCR on a solo basis under the rules of that State. This would mean that the insurance group could deal with its group regulator (and not have to deal with various regulators in different countries with split responsibilities) in relation to SCR, internal model approvals, and any Adjusted SCR. Agreement was not reached on this Group Support concept and the Level 1 text therefore provides for all solo requirements to be met in each member state. However, the directive does provide for a review to consider the introduction of group support at a later point in time. The group regulator will also have an enhanced role, for example in relation to internal model approval under the new regime. **14.340**

Under Solvency II, capital will be divided into three tiers (reflecting the Basel approach for banks) with further sub-divisions. For example, ancillary elements (as distinct from basic elements) in Tiers 2 and 3 can only be used with regulatory approval. Letters of credit will be included for the first time. Technical provisions (ie the reserves for insurance liabilities which must be held before capital is measured) will be based on a current exit value (the expected payment to secure an immediate transfer to another insurer) and will include a risk margin in addition to this estimate of liabilities. **14.341**

Prudential Standards—Insurance Intermediaries

Capital resources

The capital requirements for insurance intermediaries are set out in MIPRU 4.2. These apply to an FCA-authorised firm which carries on insurance mediation activities. They do not apply to various firms, including a Lloyd's managing agent, a bank, building society, a solo consolidated subsidiary of a bank or building society, an insurer or a friendly society, or a firm which carries on designated investment business only. For firms carrying on designated investment business the higher of MIPRU 4.2 or IPRU(INV) applies.[342] (MIPRU 4.2 does not reflect the capital requirements for insurance intermediaries in the IMD because the UK chose other means to implement Article 4.4 of the IMD on the basis that the IMD capital **14.342**

[342] MIPRU 4.2.5.

requirements were unnecessarily high.)[343] The capital resources requirements ('CRR') for insurance intermediaries are as follows:

- For a firm which does not hold client money or other client assets in relation to insurance mediation activity it is the higher of £5,000 and 2.5 per cent of the annual income from its insurance mediation activity.
- For a firm which holds client money or other client assets in relation to insurance mediation activity it is the higher of £10,000 and 5 per cent of the annual income from its insurance mediation activity.

14.343 The CRR is calculated by reference to insurance income; so a 'secondary' intermediary with large non-insurance income and small insurance income would have a relatively small CRR. However, the firm's capital resources are calculated by reference to the intermediary's entire business and assets. Losses of the non-insurance business may therefore lead to a breach of the FCA's requirements and a need for additional capital to maintain capital resources in excess of the CRR.

Professional indemnity insurance[344]

14.344 The professional indemnity requirements in MIPRU 3 apply to insurance and reinsurance intermediaries only and not to insurers or managing agents.[345] MIPRU 3.2 requires FCA authorised insurance intermediaries to take out and maintain professional indemnity insurance which covers its insurance mediation activity from the date of authorisation and which:[346]

(i) provides a minimum level of cover of €1 million for each single claim and €1.5 million or, if higher, 10 per cent of annual income in aggregate (up to €30 million);
(ii) (for firms with the ability to hold client money) provides an excess which is less than the higher of £5,000 and 3 per cent of annual income (subject to a higher excess where additional capital is held up to a maximum of £200,000);
(iii) covers claims for which the firm may be liable as a result of its own conduct or the conduct of its employees and/or its appointed representatives (acting within the scope of their appointment as the firm's appointed representatives in performing insurance mediation activity);
(iv) covers Financial Ombudsman awards made against the firm in connection with its insurance mediation activity; and
(v) covers costs of legal assistance in relation to clauses (iii) and (iv) above.

14.345 'Annual income' is the annual income given in the firm's most recent annual financial statement from insurance mediation activities, ie all brokerage, fees, commissions, and other related income due to the firm in respect of or in relation to those activities. Annual income

[343] IMD, art 4(4)(b). As noted at para 14.67, it is unusual to give Member States a choice of this kind.
[344] For original consultation in this regard please see FSA PS174, 'Prudential and other requirements for mortgage firms and insurance intermediaries—Feedback on FSA CP174 and 'near final' text'; FSA CP174, 'Prudential and other requirements for mortgage firms and insurance intermediaries'.
[345] MIPRU 3 does not apply to an insurer, a managing agent, a firm to which IPRU(INV) 13.1.4(1) applies or an exempt CAD firm to which IPRU(INV) 9.2.5 applies (MIPRU 3.1.1(5)).
[346] MIPRU 3.2.4R; MIPRU 3.2.12R.

includes amounts due to appointed representatives in respect of insurance mediation activities for which the firm has accepted responsibility.

In relation to insurance mediation activity, the professional indemnity insurance described earlier is not required by a firm if it can obtain a 'comparable guarantee'[347] from another authorised person with net tangible assets of more than £10 million. Where there is another authorised person with net tangible assets of more than £10 million within the group of the relevant firm, then the guarantee must come from that person. **14.346**

Other requirements

Competence—MIPRU 2.3 and TC

In this section we look at the application of Training and Competence ('TC'), as well as the application of rules in the Prudential Sourcebook for Mortgage and Home Finance Firms, and Insurance Intermediaries ('MIPRU') to insurers and insurance intermediaries. **14.347**

MIPRU 2.3.1 R (which implements Article 4(2) of the IMD and applies to intermediaries) imposes general requirements relating to knowledge and ability and good repute to the firm's management and staff involved in insurance. This requirement extends to insurance intermediaries' appointed representatives.[348] **14.348**

In addition, the FCA/PRA's approved persons regime requires persons performing controlled functions such as senior managers and directors (including non-executive directors) and certain advisers to be individually registered as 'approved persons'. For insurers and insurance intermediaries carrying on insurance mediation activities in relation to non-investment insurance contracts the relevant controlled functions are governing functions, required functions (the apportionment and oversight function is the only relevant applicable function), systems and controls functions, and significant management functions, as appropriate. For secondary insurance intermediaries the only relevant function is the apportionment and oversight function (so only one approved person is required). MIPRU 2.2.1 provides that an insurance intermediary must allocate the responsibility for the firm's insurance mediation activity to a director or senior manager. All firms therefore have to have at least one individual who is individually regulated by the FCA and subject to the FCA's Statements of Principle and Code of Practice for Approved Persons ('APER'). For all other authorised firms there is a customer function (eg investment adviser function). The customer function has no application to non-investment insurance business but does apply to designated investment business. SUP 4 requires a number of firms, including all long-term insurers, to appoint an actuary (known as the actuarial function holder) who must be an approved person. With-profit insurers also need to appoint a with-profits actuary. **14.349**

TC 1 imposes general, high-level commitments[349] to training and competence which apply to every firm—including insurers and insurance intermediaries. TC 2 contains detailed rules **14.350**

---

[347] MIPRU 3.1.1R.

[348] In determining a person's knowledge and ability, the firm should have regard to whether the person has demonstrated by experience and training that he is or will be able to perform duties related to the firm's insurance mediation activity and satisfies the FCA's training and competence requirements. In considering a person's 'good repute' a firm must ensure that the person has not been convicted of any serious criminal offences linked to crimes against property or other crimes related to financial activities (other than spent convictions under the Rehabilitation of Offenders Act 1974 or any other national equivalent), and has not been adjudged bankrupt unless the bankruptcy has been discharged.

[349] FCA Training and Competence Sourcebook ('TC') Chapter 1.

and guidance applicable to certain activities carried out by regulated firms.[350] The application of TC 1 and TC 2 to designated investment is explained in Chapter 12.

Use of unregistered intermediaries—MIPRU 5

14.351 The purpose of MIPRU 5 is to implement Article 3.6 of the IMD in relation to insurance undertakings.

14.352 MIPRU 5.2.1–5.2.2[351] requires insurers to ensure that, in relation to a person whose insurance mediation services they are using, that person has either permission to carry on such activities (ie a Part 4A permission from the FCA) or is exempt—(such as an appointed representative) or is a registered insurance intermediary in another EEA State or does not carry on these activities in the EEA. This can be confirmed, for example, by checking the Financial Services register if the person is a UK incorporated entity or is resident in the UK or by checking the relevant register of that person's home State regulator, if it is a non-UK based person.

Cross-border Business

EEA insurers and intermediaries

14.353 Overseas firms may become authorised in the UK under FSMA by:

- exercising single market directive rights;
- exercising treaty rights; or
- applying to the UK regulators for authorisation.

14.354 The different procedural requirements for insurers and intermediaries are set out in Schedule 3 to FSMA and in the regulatory Handbooks in SUP Chapter 13A (which includes provisions relevant to both dual regulated firms such as insurers and to intermediaries). Notifications are made by the firm wishing to use passporting rights to their home State regulator who then passes on details of the notice to the PRA or FCA. Notifications under the RID, CLD, or 3NLD will be given to the PRA which mirrors its responsibility for authorising UK insurers. Notices under the IMD (for intermediaries wishing to passport into the UK) will go to the FCA. As conduct is regulated under the 'general good' provisions,[352] FSMA requires the PRA to give a copy of any notice received to the FCA without delay.[353]

[350] TC 2.

[351] For original consultation in this regard see FSA CP174: 'Prudential and other requirements for mortgage firms and insurance intermediaries'; FSA PS174: 'Prudential and other requirements for mortgage firms and insurance intermediaries—Feedback on CP174 and 'near final' text'.

[352] For an overview of the general good concept see para 14.48.

[353] General requirements set out in Sch 3 paras 19 and 20 of FSMA. In order to qualify for rights to establish a branch or provide services into the UK the insurer must be an 'EEA firm' set out in Sch 3 para 5 to FSMA and SUP 13A.2.1; SUP 13A.3.1. General conditions for establishing a branch: Sch 3, paras 12–13 to FSMA: SUP 13A.4.1. General conditions for provision of services: Sch 3, paras 12–14 to FSMA: SUP 13A.5.3. Consent notice requirements for establishing a branch: given in CLD and First Non-life Directive. Consent notice requirements for provision of services: reg 3(3) of the Financial Services and Markets Act 2000 (EEA Passport Rights) Regulations 2001, SI 2001/2511.

An EEA firm which is not covered by a single market directive[354] or which is conducting an activity outside the scope of a directive may have treaty rights based on its home State authorisation and home State regulatory regime where it affords equivalent protection to the UK regime. The procedure for exercising treaty rights is set out in Schedule 4 of FSMA and in SUP Chapter 13A.[355] 14.355

UK insurers and intermediaries

A firm applying for authorisation as an insurer or intermediary will effectively exercise passport rights (services and branch) as part of its application to either the PRA or FCA. Thereafter it will need to follow the procedure in Schedule 3 of FSMA and SUP 13 before undertaking (for the first time) services business or establishing a branch in a Member State. These procedures and the timetables reflect the directive requirements. Notifications of an intention to passport are made to the appropriate regulator: the PRA for insurers; the FCA for intermediaries. The notification for the establishment of a branch of an insurer requires much more information;[356] minimal information is required for intermediary notifications, even for establishing a branch.[357] 14.356

Appointed representatives

An appointed representative undertaking insurance mediation is regarded as a registered intermediary under the IMD (see paragraph 14.150). It is therefore able to exercise the IMD passport (on a services or branch basis). Under SUP 13, the representative cannot give the requisite notification directly to the appropriate regulator; the notification must be made by the principal (ie the authorised insurer or intermediary) which has appointed the representative.[358] It is not entirely clear how appointed representative status operates in all the other Member States; appointed representatives cannot 'passport' under any of the other single market directives. 14.357

The regulation of the Lloyd's insurance market

The structure of the Lloyd's market is unusual; regulation of Lloyd's has evolved since the difficulties which it experienced and the subsequent market reforms in the 1990s. EU legislation recognises 'the Association of Underwriters known as Lloyd's' as a form of permissible insurance undertaking but does not generally make specific provision for the unusual structure of Lloyd's. It is therefore the responsibility of the UK to ensure that the regulation of Lloyd's satisfies the requirements of the EU insurance directives (and there have been challenges in the past as to whether the UK has correctly implemented the European legislation as it applies to Lloyd's). 14.358

[354] Before the implementation of the RID, treaty rights were potentially relevant to 'pure' reinsurers which then fell outside the single market directives. Where the home State already required such reinsurers to be authorised and equivalence could be demonstrated, treaty rights could be exercised. Pure reinsurers however, can now 'passport' under the RID and do not need to rely on treaty rights.

[355] Sch 4, para 3(1) to FSMA: SUP 13A.3.4; SUP 13A.3.5; SUP 13A.3.6; SUP 13A.3.7.

[356] Notification requirements for insurers (but not pure reinsurers)—EEA Firms passporting in: SUP 13A 4.1G; SUP 13A.4.2; SUP 13A.4.4G; SUP13A.4.4AG; SUP 13A.5.3G; SUP 13A.5.4G; UK Firms passporting out: SUP 13.3.2AG; SUP 13.3.5(1)(c)G; SUP 13.4.2(3)G; SUP 13.4.4(2)(a)G.

[357] Notification requirements for intermediaries—EEA Firms passporting in: SUP 13A.4.2G; SUP 13A.4.4G; SUP 13A.5.3; SUP 13A.5.4; UK Firms passporting out: SUP 13.3.2A; SUP 13.3.5(2)(d); SUP 13.4.2(3); SUP 13.4.4(2A)G.

[358] SUP 13.3.2B; SUP 13.4.2A.

14.359 A full review of the complex structure of Lloyd's and the regulatory regime that applies to it under FSMA and the Lloyd's Acts falls outside the scope of this book. This section however gives a brief overview.

14.360 The key participants or entities are:

- the Society of Lloyd's;
- members of Lloyd's—individual members and corporate members which accept risks and contract as insurers via a syndicate;
- managing agents (which effectively act as agents for syndicates of members);
- members' advisers—corporate advisers and managing agents (who advise members);
- Lloyd's brokers;
- the Council of Lloyd's (which is the governing body of the Society and which has various roles under the Lloyd's legislation); and
- the franchise board (to which certain functions have been delegated, and which impose requirements on individual Lloyd's market participants in the interests of the 'franchise' as a whole).

14.361 The most unusual feature of Lloyd's is its hybrid role—part insurance undertaking and part insurance market (with competing underwriters within it insuring different risks). The EU legislation treats the Society of Lloyd's (or the Association of Underwriters) as an insurance undertaking; indeed, the Society is authorised under FSMA. All policies underwritten at Lloyd's are supported by the 'Central Fund' which all members are liable to pay into and which will be available to pay claims on a policy if a member which underwrote that policy becomes insolvent. This is very different from the so-called 'company market' in London where insurance companies do not guarantee each other's solvency. In many respects, however, Lloyd's operates as a market (rather than a single underwriter) with underwriters competing for business. Individual risks are not underwritten by the Society; they are underwritten by a member or particular members (grouped together in a syndicate). There are other unusual aspects to Lloyd's; for example, mediating on the transfer of underwriting capacity at Lloyd's is a regulated activity under FSMA.[359] Another complexity was that previously, Lloyd's operated its accounting on a three-year rather than an annual basis.

14.362 The structure of Lloyd's has therefore represented something of a challenge in terms of regulation. The different mechanics by which regulation (both EU and domestic) is applied to market participants is somewhat complex.

14.363 Lloyd's brokers, managing agents, members' advisers, and the Society of Lloyd's itself conduct regulated activities under FSMA and are authorised by the PRA; the members themselves do not need to be authorised to underwrite business at Lloyd's. Section 316 of FSMA provides that the general prohibition or a 'core provision'[360] only applies to the carrying on of an insurance market activity by a member of the Society, if either regulator so directs. Neither regulator (nor the FSA beforehand) has directed that members need to be authorised.

[359] See para 14.144 *et seq.*

[360] The core provisions are FSMA Parts V, 9A, XI, XII, XIV, XV, XVI, XXII, and XXIV, ss 384–386 and Part XXVI (s 317, FSMA).

The FSA did, however, direct that certain core provisions apply (for example the compulsory jurisdiction of the FOS under section 266 of FSMA), and, in relation to financial requirements, directions have been given concerning the central fund and the application of GENPRU in order to require members to maintain adequate financial resources (directions are given under section 318 and are marked in the margin of the Handbooks with the letter 'D'). Regulatory requirements are applied to the Lloyd's market in various other ways. For example, Chapter 8 of INSPRU (see paragraph 14.274 *et seq.*) contains general provisions applying INSPRU and GENPRU to Lloyd's.[361] In relation to certain requirements applied to insurers, the Society is required to manage members' funds, central assets, and to supervise the insurance business carried on by each member, so as to achieve the same effect as the requirements have as applied to an authorised firm. Some requirements are applied to managing agents in the same way in relation to their management of syndicate assets and of the insurance business carried on by the members of the syndicate through that syndicate. There are also special requirements relating to Lloyd's, including requirements for the capacity transfer market, the Central Fund, future underwriting members, risk management, reinsurance to close and trust funds. Managing agents are also treated as a proxy for the insurer under ICOBS (see paragraph 14.207 *et seq.*) and therefore generally have to comply with the ICOBS rules applicable to insurers. **14.364**

For Conduct of Business Rules, Lloyd's brokers are regulated directly by the FCA and are subject to exactly the same requirements and rules as non-Lloyd's brokers.[362] **14.365**

The Legislative Reform (Lloyd's) Order 2008[363] amended the Lloyd's Act 1982 to remove a prohibition on certain links between managing agents and Lloyd's brokers and to enable any FCA-authorised insurance intermediary to undertake broking activities at Lloyd's. Lloyd's has not, however, dispensed with the registration of 'Lloyd's brokers' who must meet certain standards required by the Society. **14.366**

UK Regulation—FOS and the FSCS

The Financial Ombudsman Service

The Financial Ombudsman Service ('FOS') is covered in Chapter 7. The work of the FOS is divided into different areas, one of which deals with complaints (by eligible complainants) involving insurance. (The Insurance Ombudsman Bureau ('IOB'), along with several other financial services ombudsman schemes, was incorporated to form the FOS at N2.) The jurisdiction of the FOS is divided into compulsory[364] and voluntary[365] jurisdictions. Voluntary jurisdiction covers firms which are not covered by the compulsory jurisdiction, but choose to participate in the FOS scheme by contractual agreement with the FOS.[366] **14.367**

361 There was previously a separate sourcebook: 'Lloyd's (LLD)' but this was replaced at the end of 2006.
362 See para 14.62 *et seq.*
363 Legislative Reform (Lloyd's) Order 2008, SI 2008/3001.
364 FSMA, s 226.
365 ibid, s 227.
366 DISP 4.

14.368 UK-authorised insurers and insurance intermediaries and UK branches of EEA insurers and intermediaries are subject to the FOS's compulsory jurisdiction (which includes responsibility for complaints concerning their appointed representatives).

14.369 An important feature of the FOS regime is that it allows eligible complainants to pursue a complaint at no cost to themselves. In addition, the FOS will determine a complaint by reference to what is, in its opinion, fair and reasonable in all the circumstances of the case. Importantly, the FOS is not bound by the law; it is required only to take account of the law and will determine what, in its opinion, were the applicable standards at the time. The FOS may make awards for policyholders against either insurers or intermediaries, and its jurisdiction can pre-date its statutory remit under FSMA. For example, where an intermediary was a member of the old GISC regime prior to 14 January 2005, the FOS can make an award against that firm in relation to a sale which took place before FSA regulation of the sale of general insurance began.

14.370 The FOS is in a position to see industry or product-specific issues arising from the complaints it receives across a number of firms. As a result, the FOS may decide to refer an issue to the 'wider implications process' where it considers there to be a new issue which affects a large number of customers or firms, the financial integrity of a firm, the interpretation of FCA rules or guidance, or a common industry practice. (The FOS may also consider the implications in any one case to be of sufficient importance that the FCA's attention should be drawn to it.)

14.371 The significance of the wider implications process is that the FCA becomes involved (as conduct regulator) and, if it considers it appropriate to do so, the FCA may ask the Treasury to authorise an industry-wide review under section 404 of FSMA. Under section 404 of FSMA, the FCA can establish a consumer redress scheme for reviewing past business if it is satisfied that there is evidence suggesting that there has been widespread or regular failure on the part of authorised firms to comply with the rules relating to a particular kind of activity and, as a result, private persons have suffered loss in respect of which authorised firms are liable to make payments. Firms are required to comply with such a scheme in order to establish the nature and extent of the failure, the liability of the firms, and the amounts payable by way of compensation.

The Financial Services Compensation Scheme

14.372 The Financial Services Compensation Scheme[367] ('FSCS') was established under FSMA and provides compensation to eligible claimants where authorised persons (or appointed representatives, but not necessarily EEA firms)[368] fail[369] (see further at Chapter 7). The FSCS replaced the previous regime under the Policyholders Protection Acts 1975 and 1997. As well as paying compensation, the FSCS also has the power to replace long-term insurance cover.

14.373 The rules governing the operation of the FSCS are set out in the Compensation sourcebook ('COMP'). The FSCS currently protects policyholders where the insurer is in default for 90 per cent of any claim under a general or life insurance policy with no upper limit. As mentioned at paragraph 14.61, there is currently no EU legislation requiring or regulating

[367] FSMA, s 213.
[368] ibid, s 213(1).
[369] ibid, s 213.

compensation schemes to protect policyholders when insurers become insolvent (whereas for credit institutions and investment firms there is EU legislation which is implemented in the UK through COMP).[370]

14.374 In the wake of the financial crisis, and as part of ongoing efforts to improve consumer protection, the European Commission announced plans to review the adequacy of existing insurance guarantee schemes. In July 2012, the Commission published a White Paper[371] proposing the introduction of a directive to ensure the existence of guarantee schemes across the EU. All such schemes would be required to comply with a minimum set of design requirements.

370 Working paper MARKT/2534/05.

371 See paras 14.61 and n 96.

15

WHOLESALE INVESTMENT FIRMS

Evolution

The evolution of investment firms' regulation has been, as is the case with most modern forms of regulatory regime, an event-led process. This branch of financial services regulation is fascinating for a number of reasons, primarily because of the way in which securities products and trading methodologies have evolved through the years. Contemporary investment firms embrace technological developments in ways which pose constant challenges for regulators and for the firms themselves. 15.01

Increased global competition and the commoditisation of investment and other products have contributed to a fast changing landscape which is perhaps at its most dynamic in the investment firms sector of financial services. Regulators are constantly challenged and have to constantly revise their rules, methods, and procedures. This has been markedly demonstrated by the failings exhibited by a large number of firms during the global financial crisis and the ongoing struggles of the financial industry in the years since the failing of Lehman Brothers in 2008. At the same time, regulators in the UK, as elsewhere, have always been, and will no doubt continue to be, under-resourced in comparison with the leading investment firms. This partly explains the relatively recent shift by the UK regulatory authorities to so-called 'risk-based regulation', which, in plain English, means concentrating regulatory efforts on those firms or sectors which are most likely to cause market destabilisation or to put at risk the objectives which the regulator is mandated to achieve. The Financial Services Authority ('FSA') focused in recent times on honing its approach to 'principles-based regulation'. Whilst this concept has obvious inherent attraction both for regulators and for regulated firms, its appeal has certainly lost some of its shine in light of the monumental losses incurred by certain investment firms pursuant to the sub-prime mortgage crisis and the associated lack of discipline that some firms seem to have suffered from. 15.02

In addition to this, the European Union ('EU') has been making every effort to consolidate regulation in the EU's financial markets, in particular with the aim of creating a single rulebook and a banking union.[1] Part of this process involves the introduction of a large number of directives which have changed the face of investment firms' regulation across the European Economic Area ('EEA'), which comprises the EU Member States, Norway, Iceland, and Liechtenstein. For investment firms, the most significant of these measures (in the non-prudential context) has been the Markets in Financial Instruments Directive ('MiFID')[2] with its implementing measures, the proposed update in the form of a new 15.03

[1] See Chapter 3.
[2] Council Directive (EC) 04/39 on markets in financial instruments [2004] OJ L145/1.

directive and a regulation (MiFID II and the Markets in Financial Instruments Regulation ('MiFIR')),[3] as well as the regulation of over-the-counter ('OTC') derivatives under the Regulation on OTC derivatives, central counterparties and trade repositories (known as the European markets infrastructure regulation or 'EMIR').[4]

15.04 As a prelude to a detailed review of the current position, there follows a brief historical overview of the evolution of investment firms' regulation so that readers are able to put the rest of this chapter in context.

The Anderson Report

15.05 On 9 March 1936, the Board of Trade appointed a committee chaired by Sir Alan Anderson to 'enquire into Fixed Trusts in all their aspects and to report what action, if any, is desirable . . .'. The committee reported in July 1936.[5] The terms of reference in fact extended not only to those collective investment schemes where the investments would be fixed for the life of the scheme, but also to collective investment schemes—as we know them today—which give investment managers scope for switching between different securities as they see fit or in accordance with a defined mandate.

15.06 The reason for the appointment of the committee was the occurrence of numerous cases of misleading advertisements and mis-selling of unit trusts to members of the public. Promoters of unit trusts, unlike those of companies, were at that time subject to no regulation at all. In a typical fashion, the committee advised against direct regulation of unit trusts in favour of reliance on self-regulation by then existing industry bodies. However, the committee did recommend that statutory provisions be introduced to regulate the marketing of units in such trusts by prescribing what information must be included in any public offering document.

15.07 The committee also proposed the registration of unit trusts' managers at Companies House (including the filing of specified documentation in connection with the trust), and recommended that managers of unit trusts should deposit a substantial amount of money with the Paymaster General (to be earmarked for the protection of unit-holders in the event of an adverse event). A further recommendation was that managers of unit trusts should be liable to pay compensation for any loss sustained by investors as a result of false statements in advertisements.

The Bodkin Report

15.08 Shortly after the report of the Anderson Committee, the Board of Trade appointed a committee chaired by Sir Archibald Bodkin 'to consider the operations commonly known as share-pushing and share-hawking and other similar activities . . . and report what, if any, action is desirable'. The committee reported in July 1937.[6] The reason behind the appointment was the occurrence of an alarming number of fraud cases involving securities where, for example, members of the public were offered worthless securities or paid for securities they were offered only to find that the dealer absconded with the purchase price.

---

[3] See paras 15.41–15.44.

[4] Regulation (EU) No 648/2012 on OTC derivatives, central counterparties and trade repositories [2012] OJ L201/1. See Chapter 3.

[5] Fixed Trusts: Report of the Departmental Committee appointed by the Board of Trade (Cmd 5259, 1936).

[6] Share Pushing: Report of the Departmental Committee appointed by the Board of Trade (Cmd 5539, 1937).

The committee was very reluctant to recommend the imposition of regulatory requirements for fear of 'serious interference with [investment firms'] legitimate and useful activities'—but managed to overcome its reluctance. As a result, the committee's report became the first instance of a UK body expressing the rather obvious concern that there should be some type of mechanism to ensure that only persons of good character and with relevant expertise should be permitted to deal in securities. The committee recommended that anyone, other than a member of one of the then existing stock exchanges, who proposed to enter into the business of dealing in securities should be registered with a public authority, subject to satisfaction of certain conditions as to good repute and, significantly, should comply with prescribed conditions as to the conduct of that business. This was the first time rules of conduct for investment firms were referred to in official UK literature. 15.09

Prevention of Fraud (Investments) Acts 1939/1958

The recommendations of the Anderson Committee and the Bodkin Committee formed the basis for the enactment of the Prevention of Fraud (Investments) Act 1939 ('PFA'), whose name alone tells us that it was never intended to be a comprehensive legislative measure to regulate investment firms. The PFA was a somewhat rushed attempt to get rid of a number of loopholes which facilitated the operation of dishonest firms to the detriment of mainly retail customers. 15.10

The PFA required, for the first time in the UK, that persons 'dealing in securities' (as principal or agent) must obtain a licence prior to engaging in such activities. This requirement applied both to firms and to individuals operating within firms. Breach of this requirement constituted a criminal offence. Members of the various Stock Exchanges (and persons acting on their behalf) were excluded from this requirement as it was deemed that their self-regulatory status was sufficient to ensure protection for investors. As a result of this limitation, the licence and conduct of business requirements made under the PFA applied to only a minority of the investment firms operating at the time. 15.11

Furthermore, with regard to transactions in securities with licensed or exempt persons the Board of Trade was empowered by the PFA to make 'rules for regulating the conduct of business by holders of licences'.[7] These rules covered, amongst other areas, classification of customers, forms of contracts to be used, and record-keeping requirements. Section 12 of the PFA provided the first explicit statutory provision directed at preventing fraudulent conduct intended to induce persons to invest in securities, a provision which forms the basis of what is now section 397 of the Financial Services and Markets Act 2000 ('FSMA'). (The enactment of the Prevention of Fraud (Investments) Act 1958 added little to the regime established by the PFA save for its conferring on the Board of Trade the power to appoint an inspector to investigate the affairs of unit trust schemes.) 15.12

Review of investor protection—the Gower Report

It was not until the late 1970s that the shortcomings of the PFA were exposed. The lifting of exchange control in 1979 and the increasingly international nature of the securities industry meant that the then rather patchy regulatory regime came under an enormous amount of pressure. At the same time there was a marked increase in the sophistication of investment firms and the products which they devised for their customers; products such as, 15.13

[7] PFA, s 7(1).

for example, commodity derivatives were definitely not within the contemplation of those responsible for the drafting of the PFA. Also, while the PFA regulated dealers in securities, there was no explicit regulatory regime to cover investment advisers and investment managers, whose roles grew in prominence as the benefits of investing in securities though mutual funds became well known and appreciated by investors.

15.14 As is often the case with regulatory reform, the final triggers for changes to the PFA regime were specific problems in the market place, in this instance the rather spectacular collapse of Norton Warburg in February 1981 and the investigation into the affairs of senior executives of Halliday Simpson between 1978 and 1983.

15.15 In 1981, Professor Jim Gower was entrusted, by the then Secretary of State for Trade, with the mammoth task of considering both the need for statutory protection of private and business investors in securities and other property, and the need for statutory control of dealers in securities, investment consultants, and investment managers.

15.16 Professor Gower reported to Parliament in January 1984[8] with his recommendations. He had encountered unanimous dissatisfaction with the regime created under the PFA and this resulted in the most far-reaching proposals ever made for reform of the regulation of investment firms in the UK. The principles emanating from this report (the Gower Report) still form the fundamental pillars of financial services regulation to this day.

15.17 The Gower Report's recommendations advocated the establishment of a comprehensive and self-contained statutory framework for regulation which was to be based, so far as possible, on self-regulation subject to governmental supervision. Self-regulation alone was found to be inadequate as a means of achieving the objectives of financial services regulation. The Gower Report concluded that self-regulation would only work with adequate and well-balanced supervision from the Government. The Gower Report further recommended that the new statutory regime, the scope of which, as proposed, could, where necessary, be extended with ease by the Department of Trade and Industry, should regulate a far wider range of activities and investments (including contracts for commodity or financial futures or options) than had previously been the case.

15.18 Furthermore, all investment firms would require a licence. For members of self-regulatory agencies (which in turn comply with strict regulatory criteria) a licence would be granted by virtue of membership. Alternatively, a licence could be obtained directly from the relevant statutory body (which later became the Securities and Investments Board).

15.19 The Gower Report also continued the trend of empowering the relevant statutory body to make rules for the conduct of business; investment firms, regulated by a self-regulatory agency, would be bound by the rules to that effect issued by that agency. One of the basic requirements for a self regulatory agency would be its ability to demonstrate that rules adopted by it for the regulation of conduct of business would provide a minimum level of protection to investors 'in relation to such matters as conflict of interest, disclosure of all sources of remuneration, recommendations unsupported by evidence or belief, information to be supplied to clients, custody of clients' money and investments . . .'.[9]

---

[8] LCB Gower, 'Review of Investor Protection Report Part 1' (Cmnd 9125, HMSO, London, 1984–85) ('The Gower Report').

[9] The Gower Report, para 6.29.

One of the matters discussed at some length in the Gower Report was the need for rules addressing conflicts of interest.[10] It was clear to Professor Gower, as it is clear today,[11] that the tendency of investment firms to conduct a wide spectrum of activities and to contain multidisciplinary sections significantly increases the risk of conflicts of interest arising without being accounted for. This issue continues to trouble investment firms, as can be seen from the various FSA revisions of the rules relating to the publication of investment research (now incorporating the requirements of MiFID), and the issue of securities. **15.20**

The recommendations contained in the Gower Report were implemented by the Financial Services Act 1986 ('the FSA 1986'), which was the first piece of legislation in the UK to create a comprehensive regulatory framework for the regulation of all investment firms. This Act gave effect to (and took further) the recommendation of Professor Gower to rely, to a material extent, on self-regulating organisations and provided that they would be regulated by a statutory body, the Securities and Investments Board. **15.21**

Investment Services Directive 1993

The coming into force, on 31 December 1995, of the Investment Services Directive 1993[12] ('ISD') marked a very significant step towards the removal, within the EEA, of trade barriers in the financial services field. The ISD facilitated the establishment by an EEA firm of branches in EEA Member States other than the one in which it was licensed, and the provision of cross-border services without the need to obtain a separate licence in each and every EEA Member State in which a firm might wish to set up a branch or into which it might wish to provide services (the principle of home Member State-led regulation). **15.22**

Whilst the core idea behind the ISD was revolutionary by any standards, its practical operation proved to be less than satisfactory. First, the ISD was a minimum harmonisation measure. This means that Member States were left free to impose (potentially onerous) local requirements over and above those specified in the ISD. This was the result of a political compromise and is naturally counter-productive in the context of facilitating a truly level playing field across the EEA. **15.23**

Secondly, the activities set out in the ISD as identifying what constitutes an 'investment firm' ('core activities') did not correspond to the 'regulated activities' under the FSMA. The result was an inevitable uncertainty in determining whether or not a firm which clearly engages or proposes to engage in a 'regulated activity' under the FSMA is also an investment firm under the ISD. Such a determination is critical because ISD firms are more rigorously regulated with regard to, amongst other things, capital requirements. **15.24**

Thirdly, because the ISD had been rushed through the legislative process, the activity of investment advice was not included as a core service and commodity derivatives were not included as financial instruments. One effect of this was that firms operating in the EEA and providing exclusively investment advisory services would not be subject to regulation under the ISD. These deficiencies, with the exception of the continued mismatch between regulated activities and core activities, have been remedied by the replacement of the ISD with **15.25**

---

[10] The Gower Report, para 6.30.

[11] See paras 15.58 (Principle 8), and 15.155–15.158.

[12] Council Directive (EEC) 93/22 on investment services in the securities field [1993] OJ L141/27.

the implementation of the MiFID[13] (art 4(4) of the Financial Services and Markets Act 2000 (Regulated Activities) Order 2001, SI 2001/544 ('RAO') provides for an 'override' of certain exclusions from the requirements to obtain authorisation for regulated activities where the relevant person is engaged in core investment services under MiFID).

15.26 Fourthly, there was very little detail in the ISD concerning the type of conduct of business rules to which investment firms must be made subject. As a result, different EEA Member States had very different conduct of business rules for investment firms. This, for a large, internationally active investment firm, was very inconvenient. It required each of the national offices of such a firm to have different compliance strategies to deal with different rules and different regulators. This aspect of the ISD gave rise to many practical difficulties and justifiably featured regularly in trade associations' discussions with the EU Commission ('Commission') with regard to revision of the ISD.

15.27 In addition to this, Articles 17 and 18 of the ISD—which were the operative Articles insofar as the freedom to provide cross-border services and to set up branches in other EEA Member States are concerned—were rather flimsily drafted (to accommodate a political compromise) to state that host Member States in relation to both the provision of cross-border services and the establishment of branches may stipulate 'rules of conduct, under which, in the interest of the general good, that business must be carried on [or with which providers of the investment service in question must comply] in the Host Member State'. The concept of 'general good' was not defined in the ISD. However, the Court of Justice of the European Union ('ECJ') has created substantial jurisprudence[14] concerning the interpretation of this concept, particularly in the context of insurance business.

15.28 Accordingly, rules imposed in the interest of the general good must 'pursue an objective of the general good'. The ECJ has acknowledged, on an incremental basis, that the following areas (amongst others) fall within the scope of the general good: consumer protection; preservation of the good reputation of the national financial sector; prevention of fraud; and fairness of commercial transactions. Additionally, any measure imposed in the interest of the 'general good' must be objectively necessary and proportionate to the objective pursued. Consequently, regulatory authorities in Member States acquired the power to impose conduct of business rules, the content of which may be completely unfamiliar to a firm from another State seeking to provide services into or setting up a branch within the relevant Member State. This trend is now in the process of being reversed and the host Member State now has far less scope for imposing rules on firms which they do not principally regulate or more generally, which are inconsistent with the requirements of the common market directives.[15]

15.29 It would be surprising if that state of affairs did not result in cases where firms, no doubt inadvertently in many instances, failed to understand and thus to comply with the rules imposed by host Member States and where such non-compliance either went undetected or was tolerated by the home Member State regulator lest its own regulated firms' non-compliance was not tolerated in return when they offer their services or establish branches in other Member States.

13 See paras 15.41–15.44.

14 See, eg, *Gebhard* [I-1995] ECR I-4165. See also 'Freedom to provide services and the general good in the insurance sector', Commission Interpretative Communication (2000/C 43/03).

15 See para 15.63.

Financial Services and Markets Act 2000

In May 1997, the Government announced its intention to overhaul the regulatory framework for financial services firms in the UK. The move was mainly a reaction to the well-established perception—unaffected by the coming into force of the Financial Services Act 1986—that the self-regulatory system had failed its intended beneficiaries. It was also clear that many firms with multi-disciplinary practices were regulated by numerous regulatory authorities with regard to different aspects of their financial services business. This was seen as inefficient and unduly burdensome on the firms concerned. **15.30**

In July 1998, HM Treasury published a consultation document[16] in which it set out the case for reforming the regulation of financial services in the UK by consolidating a fragmented regulatory regime into the hands of a single, statutory 'super-regulator' which would regulate the insurance, banking, and investment sectors. The new regime was intended to simplify the authorisation process for financial services firms in the UK and the supervision and enforcement process for the FSA. In addition to the rationalisation of the powers and objectives of the FSA, the proposals included two new concepts. **15.31**

First, the rather dated distinction between the restrictions on the issue of investment advertisements and the making of unsolicited calls was scrapped in favour of a more modern restriction on communicating financial promotions, a restriction which was intended to be media-neutral in order to cope with the ever-changing methods through which financial services solicitations were being delivered. Second, the proposals contemplated a new market misconduct restriction to tackle market abuse. This civil regime was deemed appropriate in order to maintain orderly and efficient markets and tackle conduct which could also give rise to criminal offences (such as that of insider dealing)[17] but which proved difficult to prosecute. The FSMA, the implementing statute, came into force on 1 December 2001. **15.32**

The reception given to the FSA was, at best, lukewarm. Initially, the large investment firms greeted with some degree of scepticism the ability of the FSA to consolidate efficiently and effectively a somewhat disparate group of regulatory organisations and deliver a more rational result. Subsequently, certain financial debacles, such as those concerning the decline of Equitable Life and of the Split-Capital Investment Trusts sector, the failure of Northern Rock and forced support of the Royal Bank of Scotland (RBS) and HBOS, as well as the mis-selling of payment protection insurance, have done little to inspire public confidence. **15.33**

Additionally, the FSA was criticised by the Financial Services and Markets Tribunal (subsequently replaced by the Upper Tribunal in April 2010)—in the course of dealing with an application by Legal & General—of lacking rigour and objectivity in its decision-making process with regard to pursuing enforcement actions. Subsequently, the then Prime Minister stated—in a speech to the Institute for Public Policy Research on 26 May 2005—that 'the Financial Services Authority . . . is seen as hugely inhibiting of efficient business by perfectly respectable companies that have never defrauded anyone'.[18] **15.34**

Observations such as these must have dismayed the FSA as a regulator who undoubtedly faced immense challenges. The objectives of protecting consumers and clients while not **15.35**

[16] Financial Services and Markets Bill: A Consultation Document (July 1998).

[17] Part V, Criminal Justice Act 1993.

[18] Only available online: <http://www.theguardian.com/politics/2005/may/26/speeches.media>.

imposing a disproportionate burden on the industry were in an inevitable and constant conflict with each other. Add to this a constant raft of EU directives under the EU Financial Services Action Plan ('FSAP')[19] to implement and the ever-increasing scope of regulation,[20] and the FSA's task seemed increasingly difficult.

15.36 Nonetheless, isolated events and sporadic criticism must be viewed in the context of the FSA's general operations. The FSA regulated thousands of firms conducting a wide range of differing businesses and did so on a very tight budget. Given the size of this task it may have been unrealistic to expect a zero-failure environment not only for regulated firms but for the FSA itself.

The Financial Services Act 2012

15.37 Following the fallout from the global and UK financial crisis, the Government decided to reform the regulatory and supervisory structure in the UK and to remove the FSA in the process. Confidence in the FSA's ability to fulfil its functions was seen as irreparably damaged after its failing to predict or prevent the failure of a number of UK banks and its inability to protect consumers from the mis-selling of financial products such as payment protection insurance.

15.38 In the hope of creating a more effective regulatory structure, the UK Government created a system in which the Bank of England has been accorded responsibility for macro-prudential oversight through the Financial Policy Committee ('FPC') and micro-prudential regulation of banks, insurance companies, and large investment firms under the Prudential Regulation Authority ('PRA'). As part of these reforms, the PRA was set up as an operationally independent subsidiary of the Bank, with the Financial Conduct Authority ('FCA') being established as an independent consumer protection and market authority with effect from 1 April 2013.[21]

15.39 The PRA is responsible for day-to-day prudential supervision of financial services firms managing significant balance-sheet risk (deposit takers, insurance companies, and large investment firms). The FCA was created as a proactive conduct of business regulator to protect consumers, promote competition, and ensure integrity in markets. The FCA supervises all regulated firms to ensure that business across the financial services and markets is conducted in a way that advances the interests of all users and participants.

15.40 Whether the FCA and PRA can live up to the promises of more effective regulators with better abilities to regulate firms and to fulfil their mandates remains to be seen.

Markets in Financial Instruments Directive

15.41 On 15 November 2000, the Commission issued a communication to the European Parliament and the Council of Europe setting out the case for reforming and upgrading the ISD. The reasons for the initiative behind MiFID had been visible to all participants in the EEA securities markets for some time.[22]

[19] This is the legislative framework for the reform and consolidation of EU financial services regulation which was agreed upon by the European Council in March 2000.

[20] The FCA also regulates mortgage and general insurance intermediaries and will, in 2014, regulate credit providers under consumer credit legislation.

[21] See Chapter 1.

[22] See paras 15.22–15.29.

The MiFID, which forms a fundamental pillar in the FSAP, seeks to address these concerns. It has introduced, for the first time, a truly comprehensive investment 'passport' enabling investment firms to offer their services across the EEA in compliance with a single set of rules. The provision of investment advice now constitutes a regulated activity across the EEA as is transacting business in commodity derivatives. The MiFID also deals with the regulation of all securities trading venues including investment firms that either match clients' orders or operate as a securities trading venue on an own account basis.[23] **15.42**

The finalisation of the MiFID was not free from controversy. In particular, there had been stiff resistance (particularly from the UK) to the introduction of pre-trade transparency obligations—the requirement to display a bid/offer spread which must be adhered to—on investment firms which systematically deal on their own account in the course of executing client orders outside regulated securities markets. **15.43**

MiFID was implemented successfully in the UK on 30 November 2007, with the majority of provisions relevant to client-facing activities implemented via the FSA's Conduct of Business Rules ('COBS'). The scope of the MiFID is broad and encompasses all key aspects of business conduct. These necessitated substantively amended (or entirely new) provisions on client classification, inducements, best execution, suitability, appropriateness, and client solicitation/communication amongst others. **15.44**

However, drawing lessons from the financial crisis, the G20 agreed at the 2009 Pittsburgh summit on the need to improve transparency and oversight of less regulated markets further and to address the issue of excessive price volatility in commodity derivatives markets. Following its review of MiFID, the EU concluded that while MiFID promoted competition and brought more choice and lower prices for investors, these changes had not been far-reaching enough to avoid market failings of the type which occurred during the financial crisis.[24] **15.45**

The EU proposed a new directive and a new regulation replacing the MiFID with the aim to make financial markets more efficient, resilient, and transparent, and to strengthen the protection of investors by enhancing pre-trade transparency for fixed income and derivative markets and by bringing OTC derivatives markets deeper into scope. **15.46**

However, the process for agreeing the new directive and regulation has been much slower than the EU originally anticipated and it remains unclear when the new rules will become effective. **15.47**

Derivatives Regulation

Another outcome of the financial crisis and the G20 commitments made subsequently is the European Markets Infrastructure Regulation ('EMIR'),[25] which is coming into force incrementally, although a number of obligations under it remain yet to be finalised. EMIR imposes requirements to clear certain OTC derivatives and to mitigate risks arising for non-cleared derivatives by confirming trades promptly, exchanging collateral, and reconciling and compressing derivative portfolios regularly. All derivative trades, cleared and uncleared, **15.48**

---

[23] See also para 15.179.

[24] The EU Commission's MiFID review documents are available at: <http://ec.europa.eu/internal_market/securities/isd/mifid/index_en.htm>. See also Chapter 1.

[25] See n 2.

will also need to be reported to trade repositories, who will share the information they collect with the regulatory authorities.

15.49 While this regulation is not specific to investment firms and affects all parties trading derivatives within the EEA, as well as a number of institutions established outside of the EEA, it will impact on the business of investment firms by imposing additional costs and compliance responsibilities on derivative trades through the clearing, collateralisation, and other risk mitigation requirements. As the obligations under EMIR are not yet fully in force, it is not possible to put a precise value on such increased costs, but in addition to increased costs, there is also a chance that in combination with the US derivative regulation included in the Dodd–Frank Wall Street Reform and Consumer Protection Act, it will reduce the depth of the OTC derivative market. This will, in turn, affect the profitability and returns of investment firms and their business models.

Rules of conduct

15.50 It is appropriate, before analysing the specific issues which arise, to attempt to clarify what is meant by an 'investment firm'. The term 'investment firm' is defined in the PRA and FCA Glossaries. This definition identifies the type of firms which are the subject of this chapter, namely investment managers, investment banks, stockbrokers, and custodians operating in the wholesale markets. The MiFID has intensified the divide between 'buy' (eg investment managers) and 'sell' (eg investment banks) firms, principally through enhancement of the client order protections and liberation of securities trading venues (through abolition of the concentration rule). This chapter is concerned with the former aspect of regulation as it applies to 'sell' firms, but will clearly be of use to 'buy' firms as well.

15.51 These are firms which used to be regulated by the Securities and Futures Authority ('SFA') and the Investment Management Regulatory Organisation ('IMRO') prior to December 2001, at which time the FSMA came into force.

15.52 The rules of conduct are of great importance as far as investment firms' day-to-day activities are concerned. They may dictate or alter business practices and they therefore have a significant and direct impact on the way in which investment firms do business. The rules of conduct also indirectly affect the way in which firms receive remuneration for the services they provide and, therefore, their business models.

15.53 The concept of rules to regulate the conduct of investment firms was first introduced in the Prevention of Fraud (Investments) Act 1939.[26] Many of the fundamental principles established by that Act remain with us to this day, including the types of customers with whom an investment firm may deal, forms of contracts which investment firms must use, and so on.

15.54 The current FCA Handbook's COBS is the result of an amalgamation of what used to be three separate rule books prior to the coming into force of the FSMA, heavily revised and supplemented to implement the MiFID.

15.55 The analysis which follows deals with a selection of important and topical issues but it is not a comprehensive description of COBS nor intended to be a substitute for COBS.

[26] See paras 15.10–15.12.

Principles for Businesses

There is value in setting out the PRA and FCA Principles for Businesses ('PRIN' or 'the Principles') at this stage for two reasons. First, the Principles provide the fundamental pillars of the regulatory regime established by COBS. Secondly, COBS is substantially based on the Principles; in most cases, a rule within COBS (henceforth Rule or Rules) will constitute an elaboration of the application of a particular Principle to a particular set of circumstances. Consideration of the Principles is even more important as the FCA continues to pursue Principles-led regulation, particularly on enforcement.[27] 15.56

There will be many instances where advice is sought from an investment firm as to a proposed course of conduct in relation to which there is no specific Rule. In such case, resort must first be had to the Principles so as to assess whether or not the conduct in question is likely to contravene one of the Principles. Many market participants find the difficulty with this approach is that there is no helpful definition of the material which is relevant in determining the precise scope of a particular Principle or its practical application. Accordingly, there is an element of substantial uncertainty on what constitutes valid evidence for compliance with the spirit or the letter of specific Principles. 15.57

These are the Principles. 15.58

1. A firm must conduct its business with integrity.
2. A firm must conduct its business with due skill, care and diligence.
3. A firm must take reasonable care to organise and control its affairs responsibly and effectively, with adequate risk management systems.
4. A firm must maintain adequate financial resources.
5. A firm must observe proper standards of market conduct.
6. A firm must pay due regard to the interests of its customers and treat them fairly.
7. A firm must pay due regard to the information needs of its clients, and communicate information to them in a way which is clear, fair, and not misleading.
8. A firm must manage conflicts of interest fairly, both between itself and its customers and between a customer and another client.
9. A firm must take reasonable care to ensure the suitability of its advice and discretionary decisions for any customer who is entitled to rely upon its judgement.
10. A firm must arrange adequate protection for clients' assets when it is responsible for them.
11. A firm must deal with its regulators in an open and cooperative way, and must disclose to the FSA appropriately anything relating to the firm of which the FSA would reasonably expect notice.

Some important points need to be made with regard to the application of the Principles to the activities of investment firms. The Principles distinguish between a 'client' and a 'customer'. A client is a reference to all and any persons to whom the firm provides its services. A 'customer' on the other hand denotes all of the firm's clients apart from those which are classified as 'eligible counterparties'. This important distinction, and the fine tuning of the distinction described in paragraph 15.74, is pervasive and needs to be kept in mind whenever the effect of the Principles is in issue.[28] 15.59

---

[27] See Chapters 1 and 5.

[28] See, eg, Principles 8, 9, and 10 in para 15.58.

15.60 The Principles do not solely apply to the UK activities of an investment firm. Principles 1, 2, 3, and 8 apply to international activities of investment firms but only to the extent that a firm's financial resources or its ability to continue to be a 'fit and proper person' to conduct regulated activities (which is by no means an easy determination!) may be affected. Principle 5 applies to international activities of investment firms to the extent that a firm's conduct may impact on 'confidence in the financial system operating in the United Kingdom'. Principle 11 applies equally to firms' domestic and international activities.

15.61 Breaching a Principle exposes an investment firm to the risk of disciplinary action by the FCA which may, depending on the circumstances (including the magnitude of the breach), impose a financial penalty, publicly censure the firm, or, in more extreme cases, vary or cancel the scope of a firm's permission to conduct regulated activities (effectively barring a firm from one or more business lines). There is now a substantial body of regulatory enforcement cases where firms have been disciplined by the FSA on the basis of them breaching the Principles.

15.62 The regulation of investment firms across the EEA has been substantially harmonised by the MiFID. Investment firms across the EEA, upon transposition of MiFID into domestic law,[29] now have a uniform set of conduct of business rules by which they must abide. Whilst there remain super-equivalent provisions for individual EEA States (for example, the UK rules on use of dealing commission, or the Solicitation Rules in France go beyond the remit of the MiFID), a minimum set of requirements has been established.

Scope of regulation

15.63 COBS applies to, amongst others, most firms which engage in designated investment business. Generally, the FCA regulates conduct for all firms, although large investment firms are also subject to prudential regulation by the PRA. In this context, it is important to note that non-UK investment firms which are regulated by the FCA pursuant to the EU single market directives[30] and operate through the passport regime[31]—whilst conducting business through a branch in London—need, in general terms,[32] only comply with the conduct of business regime as applied by the host State (UK). Prudential regulation (including organisational requirements) is, with very few exceptions, the exclusive territory of the 'home State' regulator. The FCA's ability to impose rules of conduct on firms for whom it is a 'host State' regulator was significantly limited when the MiFID was fully implemented in the UK. Broadly speaking, the rules of conduct apply to investment firms' activities which are conducted from an office in the UK (and therefore not to EEA firms providing cross-border services into the UK). The main exceptions concern (a) dealings concluded through branches of UK firms with persons from outside the territory of the branch (this is an unfortunate feature of the MiFID which is subject to a protocol procedure established by CESR in October 2007);[33] and (b) dealings with a UK client classified as either a 'retail client' or a 'professional client'[34] from an office based outside the UK, in which circumstances the rules of conduct are subject

[29] The MiFID Implementing Regulation (1287/2006) is directly applicable without the need for further action.

[30] Which in connection with investment firms mean primarily the MiFID.

[31] The regime entitling a firm established and authorised in one EEA Member State to provide cross-border services and establish branches in other EEA Member States.

[32] As regards services provided in the jurisdiction of the branch (ie in this case in the UK).

[33] CESR/07-672.

[34] See para 15.74.

to certain modifications in areas affected by the Distance Marketing Directive[35] and the Electronic Commerce Directive.[36]

Clients and Commissions

One of the cornerstones of any financial services regulatory system is that different types of clients should attract varying degrees of protection. This is, of course, to reflect the fact that certain clients are more sophisticated than others. Indeed, in the wholesale market certain clients may be more sophisticated than the provider of the service to them. **15.64**

The rules of conduct are thus selective in their application depending on the type of client that the investment firm is serving. Client classification is essentially a mechanical process by which each client is placed by the investment firm concerned into one of three predetermined classes. These are, in ascending order of sophistication, 'retail clients', 'professional clients', and 'eligible counterparties'. **15.65**

MiFID has brought substantial changes to the client classification rules. It has broadened the scope of the category of 'retail clients' (which, under the old regime, was the narrower conception of 'private customer'). Professional clients (which would have been classified as 'intermediate customers' before the MiFID implementation) attract a greater level of regulatory protection than previously, by means of communications, best execution, appropriateness, suitability, and the requirement to provide further information concerning specific risk warnings (non-exhaustive list). **15.66**

Eligible counterparty business

Traditionally, the UK regulatory regime has always favoured self-regulation where effective self-regulation can be achieved. This approach is reflected in a special 'light-touch' conduct of business regime[37] which applies to investment firms conducting eligible counterparty business. While 'light-touch' regulation has fallen out of favour in recent years, it currently remains available for eligible counterparty business. The definition of the term 'eligible counterparty business' contains a number of elements. First, the regulated services and activities (and related ancillary activities)[38] must (in connection with the MiFID business) concern dealing in investments on own account, the execution of orders on behalf of clients or the reception and transmission of orders. Second, the service or activity must be undertaken with or for a client classified as an 'eligible counterparty'. **15.67**

The term 'eligible counterparty business' does not include, amongst others, the following activities: **15.68**

- approval by an investment firm of a financial promotion;[39]
- corporate finance business;
- safeguarding and administering investments (custody);
- investment management.

[35] Council Directive (EC) 02/65 concerning the distance marketing of consumer financial services [2002] OJ L271/16.

[36] Council Directive (EC) 00/31 on electronic commerce [2000] OJ L11/48.

[37] See para 15.80.

[38] Non-regulated activities which are closely related to the conduct of regulated activities.

[39] As defined in FSMA, s 21.

The consequences of a determination that part of an investment firm's business constitutes 'eligible counterparty business' is that only very few Rules apply to the conduct of such business.

Special conduct regimes

15.69 It is also to be noted that the application of the Rules is modified—in fact tailor-made versions apply—in the context of professional firms, energy market participants, and oil market participants, among others. These are available in the Handbook Guides and Specialist sourcebook sections of the FCA Handbook.

Senior management responsibilities

15.70 It can be agreed that the increased emphasis on senior management responsibilities and accountability following the implementation of the FSMA has been (and continues to be) one of the most radical changes to have been made in the past to the UK financial services regulatory regime. This aspect of the regime operated by the FCA was created following catastrophic events that occurred to UK regulated firms (eg Barings Bank) in which senior management pleaded lack of direct supervisory control over the unit responsible for the calamitous activity.

15.71 The PRA and FCA's Senior Management Arrangements Systems and Controls Sourcebook ('SYSC') requires that an investment firm takes 'reasonable care to maintain a clear and appropriate apportionment of significant responsibilities among its directors and senior managers' and must appoint a person to manage its compliance with SYSC. The appointee (who must be either a director or a senior manager and for whom the regulators' prior approval is required) must assume the designated 'Controlled Function 8' of Apportionment and Oversight. It should be noted that this function is separate and distinct from a firm's compliance function. This escalation in the seniority of the personnel within an investment firm who can be made directly responsible for inadequate allocation of responsibilities and indirectly for problems which arise from such a failure led to some anxiety within investment firms. Nevertheless, this seemingly effective regulatory tool is now accepted as being responsible for some positive changes in the way investment firms' risk management structures have evolved.

15.72 The principle of senior management responsibility has been supplemented by requirements to operate effective systems and controls which specifically (but not exclusively) include effective and safe delegation of managerial tasks, provision of timely and comprehensive information to management, and provisions for risk assessment and business continuity. The effectiveness of this aspect of the regime obviously depends on the extent to which, in practice, the PRA and FCA hold senior managers within investment firms accountable for their firm's conduct.[40]

Client classification

15.73 The significance of this topic must not be overlooked. Although mechanical, the task of classifying an investment firm's new clients is fundamentally important.[41] Investment firms

[40] See, eg, FSA Final Notice dated 10 April 2007 concerning Mr David Whistance, and FSA Final Notice dated 15 January 2013 concerning Mr Harbinder Panesar.

[41] See COBS 3.

frequently have their focus on a particular sector or sub-sector of clients. Thus, where a firm's strategy is to provide services to clients other than those classified under COBS as retail clients, its compliance policy and systems and controls will be framed accordingly. In such circumstances, it would be unsafe for the firm to accept retail clients as clients or, more generally, to take on new clients for which the firm does not have policies and systems which will ensure compliance with its regulatory obligations.

There are three categories of client under COBS (pursuant to the MiFID): **15.74**

(a) retail client—in plain English this equates to 'the man in the street';
(b) professional client—a reference to a more sophisticated person;
(c) eligible counterparty—as its name implies, a client which is likely to be proficient in matters of investments (eg another investment firm).

The requirement to classify clients is to be satisfied by an investment firm *before* it conducts any investment business with or for them because otherwise it would not be able to establish what would constitute compliant conduct in relation to a particular client—as mentioned earlier,[42] the rules of conduct vary depending on what type of client the firm is dealing with. COBS requires a firm to notify a client of its status. **15.75**

COBS, with regard to client classification, deals with a few cases in which it is not obvious whom an investment firm needs to classify (and indeed treat) as its client. **15.76**

Agent as client

One such case is where the potential client acts as an agent and wishes to engage the services of an investment firm in that capacity. The general rule is that only the agent should be regarded as the firm's client provided that the arrangement involving the agency relationship is not intended to prevent the firm from having an obligation towards the agent's principal and complies with the Rule on agents as clients within COBS 2.4.3R. Nonetheless, this general rule can be overridden by the parties' agreement that the firm concerned would treat the principal as its only (or additional) 'client'. **15.77**

In a pragmatic compromise, the client classification rules permit an investment firm to satisfy most of its obligations to communicate with its clients by communicating with the agent, with exceptions for certain required risk warnings, transaction confirmations, and the provision of periodic statements.[43] **15.78**

There are a number of additional points which arise from the regulatory classification of an agent. First, the classification does not affect the general legal position in relation to an investment firm's duties to the principal. Secondly, investment firms are under anti-money laundering obligations (both under the rules of conduct and under the general law) to verify the identity of both the principal ('beneficial owner' as it is framed under the provisions of the Money Laundering Regulations 2007) and the agent. Thirdly, the FSA has provided guidance to the effect that the determination of who is an investment firm's client for regulatory classification purposes should not affect the reality of the situation in so far as capital adequacy rules are concerned (in that the true identity of a firm's counterparty must be taken into account to reflect the true credit risk posed). **15.79**

42 See para 15.65.
43 COBS 2.4.3.

15.80 It is possible for an investment firm to classify one or more of its clients differently for different purposes. This facilitates the application of a light-touch regime[44] where it is merited.

Terms of business

15.81 COBS requires that an investment firm must provide a retail client with its terms of business in good time before it provides services.[45]

15.82 COBS does not specify the minimum contents of a terms of business agreement which is largely dictated by an array of various mandatory disclosure and information requirements.[46] A firm's terms of business may take various forms so that 'low impact' customers do not need to bother with a long list of items which may not be relevant to their relationship with the firm. Thus, it is common for investment firms to have separate terms of business to cover investment management, custody, derivative transactions, and so on.

15.83 It must be noted in this context that although the FCA's requirements in relation to terms of business are not extensive, investment firms dedicate significant time and resources to ensure that their terms of business documents (for all categories of clients) are regularly updated and reflect the commercial reality of their relationships with their customers. Despite this, it is not uncommon in practice to encounter documentation prepared by firms, large and small, which is either legally incorrect or incompatible with other documents prepared by the firm or with the latest regulatory requirements. Given the pace of development in financial services regulation, an investment firm's terms of business need to be regularly reviewed, perhaps as frequently as monthly.

Inducements and dealing commission arrangements

15.84 The Rules concerning inducements and dealing commission are an elaboration of the FCA's Principles for Businesses on fair treatment of customers and the avoidance of conflicts of interest.

15.85 The regime on inducements, as set out in the MiFID, is wider than any preceding regime and captures a very broad range of arrangements, some of which would certainly not have fallen within the ordinary conception of the term inducement. The substantial broadening of the regime was endorsed by the Committee of European Securities Regulators ('CESR', now replaced by the European Securities and Markets Authority, 'ESMA') in its recommendations paper of May 2007.[47] The key changes brought about by the MiFID included the need for and format of disclosure and an absolute prohibition on certain inducements (such as trail commissions and commission overrides). These are expanded upon later in this chapter.

Inducements

15.86 The MiFID[48] contains a wide-ranging prohibition on the receipt or payment by investment firms of inducements in connection with the provision of investment and/or ancillary services to clients (other than eligible counterparties). In order to be allowed under the regime,

44 See para 15.67.
45 COBS 8.1.1.
46 See COBS 6.
47 CESR/07-228b.
48 The MiFID art 19(1); art 26 and Recital 39 of the MiFID Implementing Directive, as implemented into the UK domestic regime through the FCA Handbook.

inducements paid to or received from third parties must be fully disclosed and designed to enhance the quality of service to the client.

The ISD did not contain specific rules on inducements. Article 11 provided principles underlying conduct of business rules to be drawn up by EEA Member States. These included that investment firms should act honestly and fairly in conducting their business activities in the best interests of their clients, and that investment firms should try to avoid conflicts of interest and, where they cannot be avoided, to ensure that their clients are treated fairly. 15.87

PRA and FCA Principle for Businesses 1 requires a firm to conduct its business with integrity. Principle 6 requires a firm to pay due regard to the interest of its customers and to treat them fairly. Previous FSA rules contained a prohibition on inducements. These prohibited a firm, or any person acting on its behalf, from offering, giving, soliciting or accepting an inducement, or directing or referring any actual or potential item of designated investment business to another person on its own initiative or on the instructions of an associate if it was likely to conflict to a material extent with any duty that the firm owes its customers in connection with designated investment business, or any duty which such a recipient firm owes to its customers. This requirement was supplemented by evidential provisions relating to 'packaged products'. Specific additional requirements applied to firms relating to the use of dealing commission, which continue to apply to firms as a super-equivalent provision notified to the Commission under Article 4(4) of the MiFID Implementing Directive. 15.88

Article 26 of the MiFID Implementing Directive provides that the provision or receipt of inducements breaches Article 19(1) unless the conditions set out in Article 26 are satisfied.[49] 15.89

Article 26 applies to payment of any fee or commission or provision of any non-monetary benefit in relation to the provision of an investment and/or ancillary service to a client. Provision or receipt of a fee, commission, or non-monetary benefit (collectively a benefit) is prohibited unless it is one or more of the following: 15.90

(a) a benefit paid or provided to or by the client (or a person acting on behalf of the client);
(b) a benefit paid or provided to or by a third party (or a person acting on behalf of a third party), in relation to which the following conditions are satisfied:
  (i) the existence, nature, and amount of the benefit or, where the amount cannot be ascertained, the method of calculating that amount, has been clearly disclosed to the client in a manner that is comprehensive, accurate, and understandable, prior to the provision of the relevant investment or ancillary services; and
  (ii) the payment or provision of the benefit is designed to enhance the quality of the relevant service to the client and does not impair compliance with the firm's duty to act in the best interests of the client; or
(c) a 'proper fee' which enables or is necessary for the provision of investment services, such as custody costs, settlement and exchange fees, regulatory levies, or legal fees, and which, by its nature, cannot give rise to conflicts with the firm's duties to act honestly, fairly, and professionally in accordance with the best interests of its clients.

Instead of disclosing benefits paid to or received from a third party in accordance with Article 26(b)(i), firms may disclose the essential terms of the arrangements relating to the benefit, 15.91

[49] Where, here and in later paragraphs reference is made to provisions in the MiFID as if they apply directly to firms and individuals, the reader is asked to accept that the provisions have been transposed into UK law.

provided that they undertake to disclose further details at the request of the client and honour that undertaking.

15.92 Guidance on Article 26(b)(ii), states that where a firm provides investment advice or personal recommendations which are not biased as a result of the receipt of commission, then the advice or recommendation should be considered to enhance the quality of the investment advice to the client. The inducements requirements have been the subject of CESR recommendations.[50] These clarify certain issues raised through consultation:

- Article 26 applies to all benefits (including standard commissions or fees), not just those which may influence the actions of a firm. It also applies to benefits paid to or received by an entity in the same group as the firm;
- in considering whether a benefit is designed to enhance the quality of the relevant service for the purpose of Article 26(b)(ii), the following factors should be taken into account:
  - the type of service provided and any specific duties owed to the client in addition to those under Article 26;
  - the expected benefit to the client (which may be assessed at the level of the service, rather than on a client by client basis) and any expected benefit to the firm;
  - whether there will be any incentive for the firm to act other than in the best interests of the client and whether the incentive is likely to change the firm's behaviour;
  - the relationship between the firm and the third party paying or receiving the benefit; and
  - the nature of the item, the circumstances in which it is paid or provided and whether any conditions attach to it;
- Recital 39, which relates solely to investment advice, does not prohibit payment or receipt of benefits to or from third parties in respect of non-advice based distribution models. This is because non-advice-based distribution models benefits can be seen as being designed to enhance the quality of service by allowing an investment service to be provided over a wider range of financial instruments;
- disclosure under Article 26 of the 'essential terms' must provide adequate information to enable the investor to relate the disclosure to the particular service or product to which it relates and enable him to make an informed decision whether to proceed with the relevant service and whether to ask for full information—a purely generic disclosure is insufficient for these purposes;
- the list of types of fees set out in Article 26(c) is non-exhaustive as other items may also fall within the category of proper fees. In determining whether such other items fall within that category, it is particularly important to ascertain whether the item by its nature cannot give rise to conflicts with the firm's duties to the client;
- where a number of investment firms are involved in the distribution channel, each firm is obliged to comply with its obligation of disclosure to its clients.

15.93 Establishing that benefits are designed to enhance the quality of service to a client is likely to prove particularly difficult in the case of distribution structures (other than those involving investment advice, which are effectively carved out from this requirement by virtue of Recital 39). It seems clear that commission overrides or other structures which cause the

[50] CESR/07-228b.

interests of the firm to be misaligned from those of the client are intended to be prohibited under Article 26.

Whilst CESR has provided some helpful commentary in connection with this determination (principally that the assessment may be conducted at the level of a class of customers) there are ample prevailing practices where it is very difficult to ascertain that the relevant fee or benefit has been 'designed' to provide any added value to the service provided by the firm. Trade associations continue to explore this topic with little success mainly due to the inconsistency that has emerged in firms' treatment of inducements. This state of affairs is not helped by the fact that certain EEA regulators have issued pronouncements on this topic which are feared to have created precedents limiting the available courses of actions for firms. **15.94**

Dealing commission

The regulation of dealing commission (which is a subset of the MiFID inducement regime) is an example of the MiFID super-equivalence in the UK (which has been duly notified to the Commission by the UK). **15.95**

In July 2005, the FSA completed a consultation process[51] with regard to proposals to reform the regime in connection with bundled brokerage[52] and soft commission arrangements.[53] The FSA review was triggered by a report commissioned by HM Treasury and conducted by Paul Myners on institutional investment in the UK. The Myners Report—Institutional Investment in the United Kingdom: A Review—identified certain weaknesses in the currently popular practices of bundled brokerage and soft commission arrangements, in that they may give rise to potential conflicts of interest for investment managers. The report also focused on the fact that whilst management fees are very much a focal point for institutional investors, bundled brokerage and soft commission arrangements allow fund managers to impose on their clients, in an indirect (and non-transparent) way, a charge for which it is difficult to ascertain a direct and exclusive benefit to the investor concerned. In fact, the report suggested, these practices enable fund managers to cut their operating expenses and in effect increase their management fees in an indirect way. The report recommended that fund managers should absorb the costs of dealing in securities in their entirety and charge an amount they deem appropriate to their clients. **15.96**

Two fundamental problem areas were identified by the FSA in its own review at the time. The first of these is that bundled brokerage and soft commission practices are, at best, a mystery to investor clients. The opaque nature of these arrangements—as well as evidence from market research commissioned by the FSA—strongly suggests that fund managers have no incentive to be efficient or provide value for money to investors when negotiating terms of trading with securities brokers. These factors may also act as an obstacle for investment managers to comply fully with their 'best execution' obligation.[54] **15.97**

---

[51] The first Consultation Paper was published in April 2003 (CP176: 'Bundled Brokerage and Soft Commission Arrangements') and the final paper was published in March 2005 (CP05/5: 'Bundled Brokerage and Soft Commission Arrangements').

[52] The provision of services by securities brokers to investment managers which are additional to mere execution (such as investment research) and which are essentially paid for from the trading commission paid by investment managers.

[53] An arrangement involving securities brokers paying third party providers of services (other than execution services, eg computer terminal, hardware, and software, dedicated telephone lines, etc.) from the trading commission paid by investment managers; PS05/9: 'Bundled brokerage and soft commission arrangements'.

[54] Which currently focuses on the achievement of the best price for the security concerned by reference to a benchmark.

15.98 The second area of concern is that the way in which some of these arrangements are structured is such that the higher the volume of trading, the greater is the potential benefit for the fund manager concerned. This clearly gives rise to a conflict of interest; fund managers have an incentive to achieve a certain trading volume and potentially may over-trade. Furthermore, an investment manager's focus on achieving the best possible soft commission or bundled deal may clearly hinder its scrutiny of the quality and price of execution offered by securities brokers.

15.99 The first consultation paper (CP176—see note 33) concluded that the regulatory regime which was applicable to soft commission and bundled brokerage arrangements was inadequate and proposed changes on two counts. First, the services that can be bought under such arrangements should be limited to the purchase of execution[55] and research[56] services. Secondly, there should be imposed on fund managers a requirement to determine the cost of any services additional to trade execution which they buy with their customers' commission and to increase its customers' funds with a rebate of an equivalent amount.

15.100 These new rules applied to both soft commission and bundled brokerage arrangements, (which are in many ways one and the same thing), and were expected to add a competitive edge to the market for services traditionally provided under such arrangements by forcing fund managers to look more closely at the value of such services.

15.101 The FSA proposals in CP176 attracted unprecedented industry feedback. This is understandable given that the proposed changes would require the commitment of substantial resources and thus need to be clearly justifiable in the light of the objective cost–benefit analysis to which the FSA was statutorily committed.[57] Industry participants also suggested that implementation of the FSA proposals would put them at a serious competitive disadvantage in the international arena.[58]

15.102 The latter suggestion prompted the FSA to commission an independent report from Deloitte which concluded, in general terms, that the FSA proposals were unlikely to have a significant impact on the competitive position of the UK fund management business. The report also supported earlier indications from the FSA that the potential savings to investment customers as a result of the proposals far outweigh the likely cost of implementation.

15.103 From the final FSA proposals on bundled brokerage and soft commissions (CP05/5—see note 33), it appears that the FSA was persuaded in the course of the consultation that an industry-led solution could work as an effective alternative to the rebate proposal.

The current dealing commission regime

15.104 In order to implement the new rules, a new section was inserted into what are now the FCA Rules.[59] As originally proposed, the scope of the rules' application was to be limited to shares and investments related to shares (eg they were not applicable to bond trading

[55] Services directly linked to arranging and finalising a transaction which arise from the point in time in which a decision to deal is taken by the fund manager until the transaction is finalised.

[56] Original material which involves analysis or manipulation of data and enabling the fund manager to reach a meaningful conclusion.

[57] FSMA, s 2(3)(c).

[58] The FSA was and the FCA is also statutorily committed to maintaining the competitive position of the UK's financial services industry—FSMA, s 1B(3)(c).

[59] COBS 11.6.

arrangements), but applied to UK investment management firms regardless of the client's location.

Additionally, the Rules require firms to provide their customers with periodic disclosure at least once a year[60] (unless the customer resides outside the UK and has waived this right or the firm reasonably concludes that a particular customer does not wish to receive this information). The disclosure should cover the percentage of soft commission out of the total commission paid by or at the direction of the firm, the value of goods or services received by the firm under soft commission arrangements as a percentage of the total commission paid by the firm, a summary of the goods or services received, a list of the brokers with whom the firm has soft commission arrangements, and an explanation of the firm's policy on soft commissions for the coming year. **15.105**

Further rules regarding commissions came into force on 31 December 2012 with the Retail Distribution Review ('RDR').[61] This requires firms who provide advice to retail clients to stop using a commission-based remuneration structure and instead charge clients for advice. The advice provided must be labelled as and meet the requirements of either independent advice on the whole market covering all types of investments or restricted advice limited to a particular product provider. Finally, employees advising retail clients must pass new qualifications, with the aim of increasing the standard of advice. **15.106**

Financial Promotions and Client Communications

One of the most notable changes introduced by the FSMA was the consolidation of the previously applicable restrictions on the issue of investment advertisements and the making of unsolicited calls into a single restriction. This restriction is applicable to all media and carries a criminal sanction for contravention. The scope of this regime, created by section 21 of FSMA, is very much determined—as is frequently the case—by reference to exemptions which offer relief from compliance to the persons who may avail themselves of them. **15.107**

Section 21 states that a financial promotion is a '[communication] in the course of business [which is] an invitation or inducement to engage in investment activity…and which is capable of having an effect in the United Kingdom'. Two terms merit further analysis. First, an invitation or inducement to 'engage in investment activity' covers, broadly speaking, invitations or inducement to acquire, dispose of, or underwrite certain investments, or exercise rights conferred by such an investment for such purpose or for the purpose of converting it or receive or undertake an investment service such as managing certain investments. **15.108**

Secondly, the phrase 'capable of having an effect in the United Kingdom', the meaning of which has been clarified to only a limited extent in FCA Guidance, covers a potentially wide range of communications which include, but are not limited to, communications originating abroad with persons present in the UK. This is clearly unsatisfactory as the boundaries of what is a serious criminal offence remain uncertain. When the FSMA came into force some **15.109**

---

[60] COBS 11.6.18.

[61] The main documents on the RDR as implemented are the FSA's Consultation Paper: Distribution of retail investments: Delivering the RDR (available at: <http://www.fsa.gov.uk/pubs/cp/cp09_18.pdf>), and the FSA's Policy Statement: Distribution of retail investments: Delivering the RDR—feedback to CP09/18 and final rules (available at: <http://www.fsa.gov.uk/pubs/policy/ps10_06.pdf>).

concerns were expressed about the financial promotion regime applying to a wide range of unintended situations, for example, a promotion which is ordinarily exempt as being made to an overseas person but which would result in that individual dealing through a foreign firm which would then execute the order on a UK investment exchange (this being the effect in the UK). As fanciful as this may sound, it is arguable that the financial promotion regime would apply in such circumstances.

The financial promotions restriction

15.110 Prior to the implementation of the MiFID, the financial promotions restriction contained in section 21 of FSMA often did not apply to firms' promotional activities. The restriction in section 21 of FSMA did not apply where the relevant promotion was communicated (or formally approved) by a person who was authorised under the FSMA. The MiFID has had a big impact on the scope of the financial promotions regime (in addition to extending the ambit of regulation to any client communications). Certain of the carve-outs within the FSMA[62] are no longer compatible with the MiFID, and consequently a division has emerged between financial promotions which are caught by the MiFID and financial promotions which fall outside the MiFID (the latter category falling back upon the financial promotions regime under the FSMA). The result is an unwieldy regime which—in equal measures—begs for reform and is very difficult to interpret and apply in practice.

15.111 Where conducting the MiFID service or activity, communications with clients[63] (including financial promotions) are regulated by COBS,[64] whereas if the service or activity is non-MiFID, the financial promotions regime under the FSMA takes effect. The essence of the exercise is to ensure that investment firms are sufficiently diligent in ensuring that their communications with clients—principally in the UK—are clear, fair, and not misleading.

15.112 Under COBS 4, communications with clients in the course of the MiFID business, including financial promotions, are regulated on a mandatory basis. However, a number of exceptions apply, for example prospectuses drawn up and published in accordance with the EU Prospectus Directive[65] (for which the firm is not responsible) by a third party are excluded from the remit of COBS 4.

15.113 There are other wider issues which investment firms must focus on when determining the desirability of selling securities comprised in a new issue directly to such individuals. Among the key concerns is the extent to which the investment firm (which typically acts as underwriter and is the initial purchaser of the securities) exposes itself to additional prospectus liability under English law. Increasing the circle of investors in the way described earlier may well increase the chances of a successful claim against an underwriter in the event of an omission or a mis-statement in the prospectus, particularly in negligence where the extent of the duty of care may vary depending on the characteristics of the allegedly injured party.

15.114 There is ongoing uncertainty as to the extent to which a single communication can constitute a financial promotion and at the same time cause the relevant firm/employee to be engaged in the regulated activity of giving investment advice. The MiFID has clarified this

---

[62] See FSMA (Financial Promotion) Order 2005, SI 2005/1529.
[63] A term not including corporate finance and venture capital contacts.
[64] Conduct of Business Sourcebook, as found in the FCA Handbook.
[65] European Parliament and Council Directive (EC) 2003/71, as amended.

issue by refining the definition of a personal recommendation and applying the onerous suitability requirement only to such recommendations. The safe position to adopt is that when a communication contains a positive recommendation to acquire an investment it should be viewed as both a financial promotion and investment advice—but not necessarily a personal recommendation (and, potentially, a research recommendation).

Communication rules

The following rules of conduct apply to investment firms when they communicate with clients. **15.115**

(a) **Form and content.** Specific rules, which vary depending on the nature of the promotion, regulate the required content of a communication. In this context, the principal types of promotion are: an ordinary written communication; a written communication which identifies and promotes a particular investment or service (in which case the rules are very detailed); a direct offer financial promotion (which takes the form of offering an investment or a service to anyone responding to it and which specifies the manner of response, such as including a tear-off slip); and an oral promotion. The topics covered include presentation of comparisons, disclosure of risks, and past performance (a particularly sensitive topic).

(b) **Record keeping.** Written promotions (together with confirmation that the promotions comply with the communication rules) must be kept by firms and be readily accessible for inspection by the FCA. Such records must be kept for at least three years and in some cases (including promotions involving certain retail products), indefinitely.

(c) **Oral promotions.** There are special rules that apply where a promotion takes the form of an interactive dialogue (eg a telephone conversation). Amongst other things, these rules cover manner and timing of the calls and the proper identification of the firm and the service or investment offered.

(d) **Direct offer financial promotions.** This category of financial promotion is deemed the most worthy of regulatory scrutiny as it may result in the purchase of an investment or investment services without further action by the promoting firm. The rules contain a detailed list of matters to be referred to in the promotion, including numerous forms of risk warnings and statements concerning taxation and charges.

(e) **Unregulated collective investment schemes.** Securities legislation in the UK has historically[66] taken a strict approach to the regulation of collective investment schemes and particularly to the promotion of such schemes which are not authorised by the FCA and therefore enjoy complete freedom to invest in any asset in any manner (subject, where either the manager or the promoter is regulated by the FCA, to the Principles for Businesses).[67]

The restriction concerning promotion by authorised persons of unregulated collective investment schemes[68] is twofold. Section 238 of FSMA provides that authorised persons (eg investment

[66] One of the cornerstones of this approach can be traced to the Anderson Report (see paras 15.5–15.7).

[67] See paras 15.56–15.62.

[68] A term which includes any collective investment scheme other than: a UK authorised unit trust (FSMA, s 242); a UK authorised Investment Company with Variable Capital (FSMA, s 262); an EEA UCITS scheme (FSMA, s 264); or a scheme recognised under special dispensation rules (FSMA, ss 270 and 272). For the purposes of promotion only, an FCA Qualified Investor Scheme, essentially an authorised scheme intended for certain non-retail investors, is regarded as an unregulated collective investment scheme.

firms) must not communicate[69] an invitation or inducement to participate in an unregulated collective investment scheme, but a statutory instrument (the Exemption Order) made under the FSMA contains various exemptions from this restriction.[70] The most notable of these exemptions include those relating to investment professionals (Article 14), to existing participants in an unregulated scheme (Article 18) and to certified sophisticated investors (Article 23).[71]

15.116 The FSMA provides for additional FCA rule-making powers in connection with permissible promotions (and approval of promotions) of unregulated collective investment schemes. These are contained in the financial promotions rules of conduct. A distinction must be drawn, however, with regard to promotions by investment firms of unregulated collective investment schemes pursuant to these two separate sets of exemptions. Where a proposed promotion is exempt under the Exemption Order, the relevant firm is, if engaging in the MiFID service or activity in the course of the promotion, subject to general rules of COBS 4 and the Principles for Businesses.

Appropriateness

15.117 Investment firms which are subject to the MiFID but which do not provide investment advice or discretionary investment management services are required to assess the appropriateness of services and products which they provide to retail and professional clients. Investment firms may provide execution-only services without assessing appropriateness in relation to 'non-complex' financial instruments if certain conditions are met.

15.118 The relevant rules are contained in COBS 10 and further helpful materials can be found in the FSA-confirmed industry guidance, the MiFID Connect Guideline on Suitability and Appropriateness, and further FSA guidance.

15.119 The ISD requirements in this area were relatively unspecific. The ISD provided that Member States were required to draw up a list of rules implementing the principles set out in the ISD, which included the principle that an investment firm must 'seek from its clients information regarding their financial situations, investment experience and objectives as regards the services requested' and must act 'in the best interests of its clients'. Before the MiFID, there was no obligation for an FCA-regulated investment firm to assess the appropriateness of a product or service in relation to any client where the firm was acting on an execution-only basis (ie where no investment advice was given or investment management undertaken).

15.120 An investment firm is required to assess the appropriateness of a product or service (as described later in the chapter) if:

- The transaction falls within the scope of the MiFID (ie it relates to a financial instrument which is within the scope of the MiFID, excluding, for example, a spot foreign exchange transaction unless it is an integral part of a transaction that falls within the MiFID).[72]

---

[69] FSMA, s 240 prohibits investment firms from approving a financial promotion which they would be unable to communicate pursuant to the restriction set out in FSMA, s 238.

[70] The Financial Services and Markets Act 2000 (Promotion of Collective Investment Schemes) (Exemptions) Order 2001, SI 2001/1060.

[71] The exemption contained in art 23 is rarely used because a promoting firm cannot itself certify that a person to whom it wishes to issue a financial promotion is a sophisticated investor and because firms are in any event reluctant to provide such a certification because of the consequential risk of liability to such an investor when an investment performs badly.

[72] COBS 10.1.1.

- The service does not include the provision of investment advice or portfolio management (if the service does include either of these, the relevant obligation is to assess 'suitability', rather than 'appropriateness', as to which see following).
- The service consists of receiving or transmitting orders, executing orders on behalf of clients dealing on own account, underwriting, or placing.
- The service is provided to a retail client or professional client.
- The firm is unable to or has not taken advantage of the carve-out in relation to non-complex financial instruments (discussed later in the chapter).

The FSA has also applied the MiFID appropriateness test to certain non-MiFID business so that for the MiFID firms the test also applies in respect of arranging or dealing in relation to a non-MiFID derivative or warrant with, or for, a retail client where the firm is aware or ought reasonably to be aware that the application or order is in response to a direct offer financial promotion. **15.121**

Investment firms required to assess the appropriateness of a product or service are required to ask their clients to provide information regarding their knowledge and experience in the relevant investment field so as to enable the investment firm to assess whether the investment service or product envisaged is appropriate for the client.[73] Investment firms should determine, using this information, whether the relevant client (or potential client) 'has the necessary experience and knowledge in order to understand the risks involved in relation to the specific type of product or service offered or demanded'.[74] This is referred to as 'the appropriateness test'. **15.122**

To meet the appropriateness test a firm must (to the extent appropriate to the nature of the client and the nature and extent of the service/product to be provided) obtain information on: **15.123**

- The types of service, transaction, and investment with which the client is familiar.
- The nature, volume, and frequency of the client's transactions in investments and the period over which they have been carried out.
- The level of the client's education, profession, or relevant former profession.[75]

There is no need for investment firms to verify this information, unless they are aware (or ought to be aware) that the information is manifestly out of date, inaccurate, or incomplete. If, having carried out the appropriateness test, the investment firm determines that the product or service is not appropriate for the client, it must warn the client of this fact. If a client refuses to provide the information required to enable an investment firm to satisfy the appropriateness test, or provides insufficient information to enable it to do so, the investment firm will be able to provide the product/service without undertaking the appropriateness test, provided it has warned the client that it is therefore unable to determine whether the product or service to be provided is appropriate for it. However, the investment firm should ensure that the provision of required information by a client is encouraged. **15.124**

If the client in question is classified as a professional client, the investment firm can assume that it has the necessary experience and knowledge to understand products or services in **15.125**

[73] COBS 10.2.1.
[74] COBS 10.2.1(2)(a).
[75] COBS 10.2.2.

relation to which it is so classified.[76] The FSA has indicated that provided that a firm has categorised a professional client in line with the relevant requirements, it does not envisage it generally needing to obtain additional information from the client (or maintain additional records) for the purposes of the appropriateness test.

15.126 A firm which provides services consisting solely of the execution and/or reception and transmission of client orders (with or without ancillary services) relating to 'non-complex' financial instruments (see following) can provide such services without carrying out the appropriateness test if:

- The service is provided at the initiative of the client. The recitals to the MiFID provide that this will be the case unless the client has asked for the service in response to a personalised communication to him containing an invitation or which is otherwise intended to influence the client in respect of that specific service/transaction. In other words, services provided in response to general marketing material will be 'provided at the initiative of the client'.
- The client has been clearly informed that in the provision of this service the firm is not required to undertake the appropriateness test, and the corresponding protections in the relevant conduct of business rules will not apply (this warning may be provided in a standardised format).
- The firm has complied with the applicable rules relating to conflicts of interest.[77]

15.127 MiFID specifies a number of instruments which are 'non-complex' for the purposes of the 'appropriateness test'. These are shares admitted to trading on a regulated market or equivalent third-country market (a list of which is maintained by the Commission on its website); money market instruments; bonds or other forms of securitised debt (excluding those which embed a derivative); and UCITS (undertakings for collective investment in transferable securities). The MiFID Implementing Directive[78] sets out criteria for determining which other types of financial instrument should be considered non-complex. These criteria include the ability to realise the instrument at market price, the availability of comprehensive and understandable information about the instrument's characteristics, and the lack of exposure to potential liability exceeding the cost of acquiring the instrument. Derivatives are expressly excluded from the category of non-complex financial instrument.

15.128 The effect of this carve-out is that only in relation to non-complex financial instruments can firms provide execution only services without having carried out the appropriateness test.

15.129 The appropriateness test is less wide-ranging than the suitability test, which applies to firms providing investment advice or discretionary investment management services. The appropriateness test requires firms to assess whether the client has the knowledge and experience necessary to understand the risks in relation to the specific type of product or service in question, whereas the suitability test also requires a firm to collect information about the client's financial situation and investment objectives. The regulatory consequences of the two tests are also different: while an investment firm is not allowed to provide an 'unsuitable'

[76] COBS 10.2.1.
[77] COBS 10.4.1.
[78] Commission Directive (EC) 2006/73 of 10 August 2006.

recommendation, it may provide a service which it considers as not 'appropriate', as long as the client is given the required warning.

Covered warrants, options, and contracts for differences are among the investments traded by retail clients that as complex financial instruments trigger appropriateness obligations. It should be noted, however, that all UCITS will be considered 'non-complex', irrespective of their underlying investment strategies, with the result that retail clients may be provided execution-only services relating to products with derivative exposures. In the case of non-UCITS collective investment schemes and funds, it is necessary to consider the extent to which the fund satisfies the specified criteria. The fact that a fund invests in derivatives, however, will not automatically make the fund itself 'complex' for the purposes of the appropriateness test. **15.130**

The FSA has taken the view that bonds or other forms of securitised debt that embed a derivative are per se complex financial instruments. In relation to notes structured to return capital in full with regular 'interest' payments linked to the performance of an index, the FSA's understanding is that such notes are 'complex' instruments under MiFID because, although they may be structured as a bond and regarded as a form of debt security, they also involve features of a financial contract for differences (the MiFID derivative). The FSA acknowledged that each note will have to be considered separately to identify the derivative element and consider, among other things, its impact on risk profile and pricing.[79] **15.131**

The Commission recognised that in many EEA Member States 'execution-only' markets were established in relation to financial instruments which do not qualify as non-complex under the MiFID. For this reason, Recital 59 to the MiFID Implementing Directive provides that where a client has engaged in a course of dealings involving a specific type of product or service before the MiFID came into effect, the investment firm can assume that such client has the necessary experience and knowledge to understand the risks involved in relation to such products or services. The recital also provides that the appropriateness test does not need to be applied in relation to each separate transaction in a course of dealings, provided that the assessment is made before the course of dealings commences. **15.132**

As regards the information which must be sought to support the appropriateness test, firms can rely on information previously provided by clients, unless they are aware or ought to be aware that the information is manifestly out of date, inaccurate, or incomplete. **15.133**

Advising customers

The activities of advising on securities (which may concern buying, selling, subscribing for, or underwriting a security or exercising any right conferred by such security to buy, sell, subscribe for, or underwrite a security)[80] and selling securities are core activities for most investment firms. Although there has been a proliferation of so-called 'execution-only' brokers,[81] most investment firms provide advisory as well as execution services in securities. It should be emphasised that the rules that relate to advising and selling now seek to protect retail and professional customers (although outside of eligible counterparty business, they apply to **15.134**

[79] The boundary between complex or non-complex instruments is subject to further consideration in Europe as part of the MiFID II and MiFIR proposals.

[80] Art 53 of the FSMA (Regulated Activities) Order 2001, SI 2001/544.

[81] As to which see the appropriateness requirement set out in para 15.117 *et seq*.

eligible counterparties as well). This is a marked change following the implementation of the MiFID as the previous position used to be that the bulk of the regulatory obligations either automatically did not apply to business with any client other than a retail client or were capable of being disapplied to such client base.

Suitability

15.135 The rules of conduct require that before an investment firm makes a personal recommendation to a client or acts as a discretionary investment manager for such a client it must take appropriate steps to familiarise itself with the customer's personal characteristics, including his or her knowledge, risk appetite, and financial resources, so as to ensure that any recommendation which is made is suitable for the customer.

15.136 The MiFID contains 'know your customer' ('KYC') and suitability requirements which apply when an investment firm provides investment advice or discretionary portfolio management. These requirements apply to both retail and (in more limited form) professional clients. The obligation will in practice extend to 'eligible counterparties' for whom investment advice or portfolio management services are provided as eligible counterparty status is only available in relation to dealing activities.

15.137 Article 11 of the ISD required Member States to have rules which implemented specified principles. These principles did not include a suitability provision but provided that a firm should act honestly and fairly and with due skill, care, and diligence in the best interests of clients and should seek from clients information about their financial situations, investment experience, and objectives. FCA Principle for Businesses 9 (Customers: relationships of trust) requires a firm to take reasonable care to ensure the suitability of its advice and discretionary decisions. This principle was amplified by conduct of business rules imposing KYC and suitability obligations. Prior to the implementation of the MiFID, these obligations only applied in relation to private customers. Specific additional suitability obligations applied in relation to 'packaged products' such as regulated funds, pensions advice, and broker funds and these have been maintained post-MiFID.

15.138 The suitability obligation applies in relation to the provision of investment advice and portfolio management. These are both core services under the MiFID. Investment advice is defined as the 'provision of personal recommendations to a client, either upon its request or at the initiative of the investment firm, in respect of one or more transactions relating to financial instruments'. The MiFID Implementing Directive provides that the recommendation must be made to a person in his capacity as an investor or potential investor, or as an agent of an investor or potential investor.[82] This means that certain advice given in connection with primary market transactions, corporate reorganisations, and other corporate finance transactions will not be caught.

15.139 In addition, the recommendation must be presented as suitable for the recipient or be based on a consideration of his circumstances and be to buy, sell, subscribe for, exchange, redeem, underwrite, or hold a particular financial instrument or exercise a right to buy, sell, etc., a financial instrument. A recommendation is not a personal recommendation if it is issued exclusively through distribution channels or to the public.[83]

---

[82] Art 52 of the MiFID Implementing Directive.
[83] 'Distribution Channel' is defined in Directive (EC) 2003/125.

The recitals to the MiFID Implementing Directive seek to draw a distinction between personal recommendations—which trigger suitability obligations—and general recommendations which do not. This means that published research and marketing material are not subject to suitability (and an obligation to have performed KYC in relation to the recipients) but are subject to contents and presentation requirements. Furthermore, recipients who deal in response to a general promotion addressed to the public or a larger group or category of clients do not trigger the appropriateness obligation in relation to non-complex products. **15.140**

The FSA has noted in consultation that it is therefore possible for a firm to provide information or opinions about markets, prices, and instruments to a professional client without going as far as to provide a 'personal' recommendation to the client. It accepts that, in such a situation, the position of the firm will be reinforced if it makes it clear to the client that in providing the information it is not providing a recommendation. However, the FSA has cautioned that if it is clear from the circumstances that the firm is making a personal recommendation, a 'disclaimer' (eg to the effect that a recommendation is not being provided), whether in the terms of business, a notification, or otherwise, will have no effect. The FSA considers that a firm cannot contract out of the requirements applying to the provision of personal recommendations if that is what it has given but raises the question as to whether a 'disclaimer' statement can change the nature of the communication. It concludes that all the circumstances will have to be considered and that the proximity, prominence, and timeliness of such statements may have a bearing on this.[84] **15.141**

The recitals to the MiFID Implementing Directive also provide that generic advice about a type of financial instrument is not investment advice and thus does not trigger the suitability obligation. However, if an investment firm presents such generic advice as suitable or based on a consideration of the client's circumstances and that is not the case, the firm is likely to be in breach of the MiFID, Article 19(1) which requires investment firms to act honestly, fairly, and professionally, or the MiFID, Article 19(2) which requires all information, including marketing communications, to be fair, clear, and not misleading. **15.142**

Portfolio management means managing portfolios in accordance with mandates given by clients on a discretionary client-by-client basis where the portfolios include one or more financial instruments. For the purposes of the suitability provisions, a transaction entered into in the course of providing a portfolio management service amounts to a 'recommendation'. The MiFID Implementing Directive includes a recital to the effect that a request or advice/recommendation to alter the portfolio management mandate defining the manager's discretion should also be treated as a recommendation. The MiFID, Article 19(4) requires an investment firm, when providing investment advice or portfolio management to a client, to obtain the necessary information regarding a client's: **15.143**

- knowledge and experience in the investment field relevant to the specific type of product or service; and
- financial situation and investment objectives,

to enable the firm to make a suitable recommendation.

This test is more onerous than the appropriateness test which requires a firm to assess knowledge and experience but not financial situation and objectives. Article 35 of the MiFID **15.144**

[84] See FSA CP06/19.

Implementing Directive provides criteria to be satisfied in relation to the 'necessary' information for the firm to be able to meet the suitability test. The information obtained must be that necessary for the firm to:

- understand the essential facts about the client;
- have a reasonable basis for believing that the recommendation/transaction meets the client's investment objectives;
- is such that the client is able financially to bear any related investment risks; and
- is such that the client has the necessary experience and knowledge in order to understand the risks involved.

15.145 In the case of a professional client, the MiFID Implementing Directive provides that the investment firm may assume that the client has the necessary experience and knowledge in relation to the products, transactions, and services for which he is so classified. In addition, where an investment firm provides investment advice to a per se professional client, the firm can assume that the client is able to bear any related investment risks consistent with his investment objectives.

15.146 The MiFID Implementing Directive gives examples of the information which should be obtained from a client in relation to his financial situation, investment objectives, knowledge, and experience. However, the MiFID is clear that this should only be collected 'to the extent appropriate to the nature of the client, the nature and extent of the service to be provided and the type of product or transaction envisaged, including their complexity and the risks involved'. The FSA considers that there is an irreducible minimum level of information without which it is not possible to provide a personal recommendation. However, it accepts that as long as it is consistent with the client's objectives and best interests, and understood by the parties, it is possible for a firm to focus the scope of its advice to suit the information the client wishes to disclose. For example, advice could be given in relation to just part of a client's portfolio if that is what the client wants or agrees to, and if sufficient level of information has been provided for suitability to be assessed in relation to that part of the portfolio (see FSA PS07/6).

15.147 A firm is entitled to rely on the information provided by a client unless it is aware or ought to be aware that the information is manifestly out of date, inaccurate, or incomplete. If a firm does not obtain the relevant information it may not make a recommendation to the client. The FSA has provided guidance to the effect that this does not preclude the firm responding to the client's request for another service, for example, arranging a deal or dealing as agent, but that the firm should ensure that it receives written confirmation of the client's instructions.[85]

15.148 The MiFID addresses the situation where a firm (A) receives an instruction on behalf of a client through the medium of another investment firm (B). In these circumstances, A can rely on information about the client provided by B (who will be responsible for its completeness and accuracy). In addition, B will remain responsible for the appropriateness for the client of any recommendations or advice provided.

15.149 A firm must retain records relating to suitability for a minimum of five years. The FSA has noted that records of the client information a firm obtains to assess suitability can include a firm's use

[85] See FSA PS07/2.

of information it has already obtained for a different purpose, and that this may be particularly relevant for professional clients. The FSA recognises that, where possible, firms which provide personal recommendations to professional clients will wish to avoid having to re-establish (and record again) such a client's investment objectives in relation to each routine trading recommendation the firm makes concerning a plain vanilla instrument, if the client's commercial objectives are clear and the particular transaction does not raise additional considerations.[86]

It would be best practice for an investment firm which is subject to this regime to produce, on an annual basis, a form which requires a confirmation from each client concerning, at least, his or her financial standing, investment objectives, and risk appetite. This is likely to provide the firm with at least the starting point for a defence against regulatory claims of mis-selling and against potential civil claims. **15.150**

Disclosure of charges, remuneration, and commission

There are specific rules of conduct within COBS requiring an investment firm to disclose (in a comprehensible form) to retail clients the basis or amount of all the firm's charges and of any other income which is receivable by the firm or its associates and is in any way attributable to business conducted for such clients. This disclosure is usually made in a firm's standard terms of business, but it is nevertheless very important for a firm's client-facing personnel to be reminded that if there is a transaction where the firm's remuneration does not correspond with the terms of business, then any discrepancies must be reported to the relevant client before the execution of the transaction or the provision of services. There are many more detailed and prescriptive rules relating to the disclosure to retail clients of commissions in respect of packaged products. **15.151**

Misconduct in securities offerings

In February 2003, the FSA published a Consultation Paper[87] in which it reviewed, among other matters, the extent to which UK investment firms had engaged in malpractices associated with the management of issues of securities. The FSA's efforts were in response to large-scale US investigations which concluded that certain investment firms had engaged in two particular types of misconduct. **15.152**

The first type of misconduct[88] involved investment firms acting as underwriters in an Initial Public Offering ('IPO') of securities seeking to recapture profits made by their investor clients through charging unusually high commissions on unrelated transactions. The main concern in such circumstances is that the underwriting firm has a strong incentive to achieve a significant increase in the price of the security upon commencement of trading so that the profit of its investor clients is sufficient to cause them to agree to pay the high commissions. **15.153**

The second type of misconduct[89] involved investment firms which were acting as underwriters in an IPO allocating the (highly desirable) securities to senior executive officers of potential or existing clients in return for past or future loyalty to the investment firm concerned. **15.154**

These practices constituted a serious failure on the part of the relevant investment firms to manage their conflicts of interest effectively. In an IPO transaction, as in many other **15.155**

[86] See FSA PS07/6.
[87] Consultation Paper 171: 'Conflicts of Interest: Investment Research and Issues of Securities'.
[88] Referred to as 'laddering'.
[89] Referred to as 'spinning'.

transactions involving the issue of securities, the investment firm's duty is first and foremost to the issuer. The practical problem within a multi-disciplinary investment firm is that in the context of an IPO there is a constant tension between the firm's duties to its primary client (ie the issuer) and its desire to achieve the best possible outcome for its investor clients who essentially create the much sought-after demand for the securities which the firm promotes. It can be easily seen that such firms need very robust internal systems and controls to address potential conflicts of interest.

FSA guidance

15.156 Following a limited survey of a number of selected investment firms, the FSA concluded that 'internal procedures and systems and controls to address the conflicts involved vary quite markedly between firms'. This implies, as the FSA stated elsewhere in the document, that no clear evidence of abusive practices was unveiled. Nevertheless, the FSA came to the view that it would be beneficial to set out, in guidance, some principles in relation to three specific areas: supervision and management of issues of securities, allocation of securities, and the determination of pricing.

15.157 The FSA guidance emphasises the fact that when dealing with issues of securities on behalf of the issuer, an investment firm's primary duty is owed to the issuer client. Furthermore, the guidance states that firms must have in place appropriate systems, controls, and procedures concerning policies for allocation of securities in IPOs, and the determination of pricing and for securing the absence from this process of personnel from that part of the firm which serves investment clients.

15.158 Particular emphasis is placed on ensuring that investment firms have robust internal arrangements to ensure that the process of allocating securities is made by persons who exclusively serve the issuer client and take into account the issuer client's views. To preclude abuse involving an investment client's executives, investment firms are now required to delegate responsibility for allocating securities to the firm's retail clients to senior managers. Firms are further reminded that allocations to a client should not be undertaken with a view to increasing the level of the firm's business with that client, the objective being to ensure that the allocation process is more transparent and unlikely to yield results which conflict with the interests of the issuer client.

15.159 The FSA clarified in its guidance that the following practices would be deemed to constitute a breach of its Principles for Businesses (as to which see paras 15.57 to 15.63):

- allocation of securities made as an inducement for the payment of excessive remuneration for unrelated services;
- allocation of securities to senior executives or officers of an existing or potential corporate finance client in exchange for future or past transaction mandates;
- allocation of securities which is expressly or implicitly conditional on receipt of orders for transactions in securities or the purchase of any other investment services.

Dealing in Securities

15.160 Reference is made in paragraph 15.20 to the importance for investment firms of adequately addressing any real or potential conflicts of interest that may arise in their businesses. As Professor Gower stated in his report, this area is one where '[the regulatory] aims . . . cannot be achieved in the absence of specific rules'. This is as true today as it was in 1984, and although the rules of conduct in the area of conflicts have traditionally been widely drafted with a view to allowing firms as many alternative ways as possible to deal with conflicts and potential conflicts of interest, this approach is now gradually being tightened up.

The rules on the management of conflicts of interest generally apply whenever an investment firm engages in investment services or activities (with or for all categories of clients). **15.161**

Conflicts of interest

SYSC 10 sets out the principles which prohibit investment firms from engaging in a course of action which is likely to harm the interests of its clients including in the following circumstances that is if it: **15.162**

- is likely to make a financial gain, or avoid a financial loss, at the expense of the client;
- has an interest in the outcome of a service provided to the client or of a transaction carried out on behalf of the client, which is distinct from the client's interest in that outcome;
- has a financial or other incentive to favour the interest of another client or group of clients over the interests of the client;
- carries on the same business as the client; or
- receives or will receive from a person other than the client an inducement in relation to a service provided to the client, in the form of monies, goods, or services, other than the standard commission or fee for that service.

SYSC 10 allows investment firms to conduct business in such circumstances only if they take one or more mitigating steps, such as identifying any conflicts (SYSC 10.1.3), keeping adequate records of any conflicts (SYSC 10.1.6), managing and disclosing conflicts (SYSC 10.1.7–10.1.9, maintaining a conflicts management policy (SYSC 10.1.10–10.1.12), and establishing appropriate internal systems and procedures (such as Chinese Walls—see SYSC 10.2 for detailed requirements).[90] Disclosure of a conflict is, under MiFID, a mitigating measure of last resort.[91] Fundamentally, the purpose of disclosure to clients must be to inform them of the general policy of the firm on dealing with conflicts of interest and to inform them on a case–by–case basis of the existence of a conflict. In practice, most investment firms seek to bypass this approach by including a widely drafted clause in their terms of business to allow them to act in all possible situations despite an actual or potential conflict. This approach will not suffice to comply with the relevant rules. Disclosure will only be deemed acceptable where the circumstances dictate that no other mitigation method is relevant and the client is sufficiently sophisticated. **15.163**

It is becoming increasingly clear that there will be situations where the relative bargaining powers of the parties, or the subject matter of the conflict, means that disclosure alone is not sufficient to ensure that the interests of customers are adequately protected (such as when an investment firm communicates investment research to its customers). **15.164**

[90] There are separate conflict rules for corporate finance business, research statements, collective portfolio management and alternative investment fund managers (SYSC 10.1.13–10.1.27).

[91] Please see SYSC 10.1.8 R for the detailed rules regarding disclosure of conflicts in situations where a firm's arrangements to manage conflicts are not sufficient.

Other restrictions

15.165 Investment firms are also subject to the following restrictions when they engage in investment activities with customers.

(a) **Churning and switching.**[92] Encouraging a customer to deal frequently in or switch an investment or an investment portfolio carries financial incentives for investment firms' securities dealers because they are commonly remunerated on an executed transaction basis. A series of transactions that are each suitable when viewed in isolation may be unsuitable if the recommendation or the decisions to trade are made with a frequency that is not in the best interests of the client. A firm should have regard to the client's agreed investment strategy in determining the frequency of transactions.

(b) **Customer order priority.** Where a securities dealer receives an execution order for a securities transactions from a customer the dealer might be tempted (especially where the order is a substantial one) to 'front-run' the customer, that is to place an order for the firm's own account before executing the customer's order so as to benefit from an anticipated increase/decrease in the price of the securities. The rules of conduct now specify that customers' orders must be executed fairly and in due turn. This Rule relates to both orders of customers and the firm and as between the orders of customers themselves.

(c) **Timely execution.** For reasons which are self-explanatory, it is fundamentally important that securities brokers execute their customers' orders in a timely fashion so as to avoid any potential adverse impact from movements in the market. Thus, once an investment firm has received an order and agreed to execute it or has decided to execute an order in the exercise of a discretion, it must carry out the relevant order 'as soon as reasonably practicable'. There will be occasions, however, when it is in the customer's best interest for the firm to postpone execution of a securities transaction (eg where improved trading volumes in the security concerned is expected to better the terms on which the deal can be made). Timeliness is considered one of the execution factors, as delineated in COBS 11.2.

(d) **Aggregation and allocation.** It is common for securities dealers to aggregate clients' orders and own account orders. Here COBS 11.3.7 specifies that securities dealers adopt a detailed policy (which they must disclose to their customers) on the allocation of securities following aggregation. Allocation of securities following aggregate trading (whether or not the order has been completely filled) must be fair (which essentially means that as a general rule priority must be given to satisfying customers' orders first). Securities dealers are only permitted to aggregate clients' orders if to do so will not result in adverse consequences for the customers concerned.

(e) **Personal account dealing.**[93] These rules restrict the ability of investment firms' employees to engage in personal transactions in circumstances which may compromise the interests of the firms' customers—a rule which in practice applies to all clients. It is mandatory for investment firms to obtain a strict undertaking from their employees (which is incorporated into their contracts of employment), prior to the commencement of their employment, to comply with the firm's personal account dealing restrictions. The rules also require a firm to monitor—in practice, firms approve all such

---

[92] See COBS 9.3.1.

[93] COBS 11.7.

dealings—any personal transactions by employees and also by parties to whom the firm outsources the conduct of certain activities related to dealings or which provides exposure to confidential information. There are also specific restrictions placed by rules covering investment analysts who conduct personal transactions.

Best execution

Under the MiFID,[94] investment firms which execute client orders (whether as principal or as agent) in relation to financial instruments need to comply with detailed best execution requirements. In addition, firms which undertake portfolio management or receive and transmit orders on behalf of clients in relation to financial instruments will be subject to analogous requirements. Firms subject to the MiFID requirements (brokers, dealers, and asset managers) need to: **15.166**

- put arrangements in place to comply with the best execution framework;
- produce and implement a best execution policy consistent with the new framework;
- provide appropriate information on the best execution policy to clients and obtain their consent to this policy; and
- undertake continuous monitoring of compliance with the policy and update and notify clients of amendments to the policy.

Best execution is a key plank of investor protection under the MiFID. When providing investment services to their clients, investment firms are subject to a general obligation to act honestly, fairly, and professionally in accordance with the best interests of their clients.[95] Best execution elaborates on this obligation by focusing on the way client orders should be executed by an investment firm. This area is singled out due to the information asymmetry arising between the investment firm and the client—because clients generally have little access to (or ability to evaluate) pricing information, there is a danger that investment firms could take advantage of this information asymmetry and consequently treat customers unfairly. **15.167**

A further driver of the best execution requirements under the MiFID is the loss of the so-called concentration rule under the ISD, whereby EEA Member States may require retail order flow to be put through a regulated market. The loss of the concentration rule enables competition between trading venues and, in principle, lowers the cost of transacting financial instruments, but also gives rise to fragmentation concerns—in particular, the possibility that firms could fail to deal through a range of execution venues in a product, thereby depriving investors of access to the best price. The best execution requirement seeks to deal with this concern by mandating transparency on the part of firms as to the execution venues which they use. **15.168**

The ISD did not specifically address best execution. Article 11 set out a series of general principles which Member States were required to implement in domestic legislation and to apply in such a way as to take account of the professional nature of the client for whom the service is provided. These included principles that an investment firm should act honestly **15.169**

[94] The MiFID, arts 14(3), 21, and 24(1) and Recital 33. The MiFID Implementing Directive, arts 44, 45, and 46 and Recitals 66–76. Level 3: Best Execution under the MiFID Questions & Answers (CESR/07-320) (which includes the European Commission response to CESR questions on scope as an appendix); Best Execution under The MiFID Questions & Answers—Feedback Statement (CESR/07–321).

[95] MiFID, art 19(1).

and fairly in conducting its business activities, and act with due skill, care, and diligence, in each case in the best interest of its clients and the integrity of the market.

15.170 The previous set of FSA rules required a firm executing a customer order in a designated investment to provide best execution, subject to certain exceptions. For the purposes of the previous requirements, a 'customer order' was an order to execute a transaction as agent (including a decision to execute a transaction in the exercise of discretion) for a customer, or any other order to a firm from a customer to execute a transaction in circumstances giving rise to duties similar to those arising on an order to execute a transaction as agent. The obligation did not apply with respect to orders executed with or for clients which were classified as market counterparties.

15.171 In providing best execution, a firm was required to take reasonable care to ascertain the price which is the best available for the customer order in the relevant market at the time for transactions of the kind and size concerned, and execute the customer order at a price which is no less advantageous, unless the firm had taken reasonable steps to ensure that it would be in the customer's best interests not to do so. Execution of transactions traded on SETS (the London Stock Exchange order book for the most liquid equities) was generally deemed to constitute best execution for the purpose of the previous rules.

15.172 In providing best execution, a firm was required to disregard any charges or commissions made by it or its agents which are disclosed to the customer.

15.173 Firms were able to contract out of the obligation to provide best execution with clients classified under the previous regime as intermediate customers (other than certain pension funds). In practice, many firms did so. Accordingly, firms could (and frequently did) avoid providing best execution in the wholesale market.

15.174 Where a firm passed a customer order to a third party for execution, the firm could rely on the third party to provide best execution if it took reasonable care to ensure that the third party would do so. Portfolio managers simply relied on a contractual best execution obligation on the part of the brokers with which they dealt to discharge their best execution obligation.

15.175 By contrast the best execution obligation under the MiFID applies to three investment services undertaken with respect to financial instruments: execution of client orders, reception and transmission of orders on behalf of investors, and portfolio management. The expanded range of financial instruments caught by the MiFID means that the best execution obligation applies not only to securities market transactions but also with respect to commodity, credit, and other derivatives newly brought within the European regulatory regime.

15.176 There is a core obligation on investment firms to 'take all reasonable steps to obtain... the best possible result for their clients taking into account price, costs, speed, likelihood of execution and settlement, size, nature or any other consideration relevant to the execution of the order'.[96] Price, costs, speed, likelihood of execution and settlement, size, nature, and any other consideration are referred to as the factors.

15.177 The term 'best possible result' is not conclusively defined by the MiFID. However, where the client is a retail client the best possible result is to be determined in terms of the total

[96] The MiFID Implementing Directive, art 21.

consideration, representing the price of the financial instrument and the costs related to execution, including all expenses incurred by the client directly related to the execution of the order.[97] These include execution venue fees, clearing and settlement fees, and any other fees paid to third parties involved in execution of the order. For the purpose of the best execution regime, the term 'execution venue' means a regulated market, an MTF, a systematic internaliser, or a market maker or other liquidity provider, or an entity that performs a similar function in a non-EEA jurisdiction. The firm's own commissions and costs are to be taken into account when assessing best execution as between different execution venues.[98] Investment firms are also required not to structure their commissions in such a way as to discriminate unfairly between execution venues.

The requirement to include assessment of the firm's own commission when providing best execution represents a significant change from the previous FSA rules, which did not require the firm's own commissions to be taken into account, as long as they are disclosed. **15.178**

In respect of retail clients, total consideration (the price of the financial instrument less costs associated with execution on the relevant execution venue) is paramount—accordingly, speed, likelihood of execution and settlement, size, nature of the transaction, market impact, and implicit transaction costs should be given precedence over the immediate price and cost consideration 'only insofar as they are instrumental in delivering the best possible result in terms of the total consideration to the retail client'.[99] **15.179**

Accordingly, for retail orders it may be expected that the factors which are not related directly to costs will need to be subordinate to those which are. There is no such guidance in relation to execution for professional clients. **15.180**

The MiFID does not otherwise specify the relative importance of the factors to be taken into account for non-retail clients. Rather, it provides four sets of characteristics to be taken into account in determining the importance of the factors (referred to following as the characteristics). These are: **15.181**

- the client;
- the order;
- the financial instruments that are subject of the order; and
- the execution venues to which the order may be directed.

The importance of the factors will vary depending on the nature of the financial instrument—for example, likelihood of settlement will be a more significant factor in respect of an OTC derivative carrying ongoing counterparty risk than in respect of a cash equity transaction. This lack of uniformity is recognised and it is considered that the obligation should be applied in a manner which takes into account the different circumstances associated with the execution of orders related to different types of instruments.[100] It will be for firms to determine how the factors are to be weighted across their different product lines. **15.182**

The MiFID does not mandate the number of execution venues to be used by a firm in discharging its best execution obligations. However, Article 21(3), which sets out the **15.183**

[97] The MiFID Implementing Directive, art 44.
[98] The MiFID Implementing Directive, art 44(3).
[99] The MiFID Implementing Directive, Recital 67.
[100] The MiFID Implementing Directive, Recital 70.

requirement for an execution policy, states that a firm must deal on venues that enable it to obtain on a consistent basis the best possible result for the execution of client orders. Firms therefore need to engage their execution venues based on their determination of what constitutes the best possible result (including the weighting of the factors) in light of their client base and order flow in respect of any given product. The firm's resources are likely to be a relevant determination in this regard.

15.184 Article 45 of the MiFID Implementing Directive sets out the obligations of investment firms when undertaking portfolio management and reception and transmission of orders (RTO) on behalf of clients. Article 45(4) contains the same obligation—to take all reasonable steps to obtain the best possible results for their clients (and refers to the same factors and criteria as those detailed earlier). However, it is clear that the MiFID is not intended to duplicate effort between the firm undertaking reception and transmission of orders or portfolio management on the one hand, and the firm executing on the other hand.[101]

15.185 In addition, the focus of the best execution policy required under Article 45 is the choice of entities with which orders are placed or to which they are transferred for execution. A portfolio manager/RTO should determine that the entities it uses will enable it to comply with the overriding best execution requirement when placing an order with, or transmitting an order to, another entity for execution. A portfolio manager/RTO should review the execution arrangements of the entities it wishes to use to determine whether they will allow it to comply with its best execution requirements. This may include considering whether the entity is itself subject to Article 21 of the MiFID or will undertake by contract to comply with the MiFID best execution requirements.

15.186 However, when portfolio managers/RTOs execute their own decisions to deal/orders directly with an execution venue, they are subject to Article 21 of MiFID (rather than Article 45 of the MiFID Implementing Directive). A portfolio manager/RTO may produce a single best execution policy which covers both its order execution and portfolio management best execution obligations.

15.187 Article 21 excludes from the best execution obligation specific instructions from a client. There is some doubt as to how far it will be feasible to argue that instructions from a client to transact are 'specific instructions' disapplying the obligation—see further discussion following.

15.188 Article 14(3) disapplies the obligation as between participants dealing on a regulated market or MTF (although this does not affect any best execution obligations the participants may have to their clients for whom they trade on the regulated market or MTF).

15.189 Accordingly, the flexibility which used to be inherent in the ISD in enabling EEA Member States to lift best execution obligations taking account of the professional nature of clients has been replaced by a harmonised and more prescriptive regime conferring best execution rights on all but a limited subset of institutional clients.

15.190 From a UK perspective, the ability to contract out of best execution has been substantially removed. In addition, investment firms which solely receive and transmit orders or pass

[101] The MiFID Implementing Directive, Recital 75.

orders to third parties for execution are, for the first time, subject to the best execution requirement.

Investment firms subject to the best execution requirement must establish and implement effective arrangements to ensure compliance with their obligations.[102] A written order execution policy must be established and implemented. The order execution policy must include, by class of instrument: **15.191**

- the execution venues used to execute client orders (this must include at least those venues that deliver the best possible result on a consistent basis); and
- the factors affecting the choice of venue.[103]

The policy should set out the firm's strategy for determining best execution. It should include an account of the relative importance, or process for determining the relative importance, placed on the factors when executing client orders and how the factors affect the choice of execution venues.[104] A single execution venue may be justified if a firm can show that it is able to obtain the best possible result on a consistent basis. A portfolio manager may include a single entity in its policy if this allows it to satisfy its overarching best execution obligation. **15.192**

The policy must be reviewed annually and whenever a material change occurs which affects the ability of the firm to comply with the best execution requirement on a consistent basis using the venues set out in the policy.[105] In addition, the effectiveness of the policy must be monitored, including regular assessment of whether the execution venues included in the policy provide for the best possible result for the client or whether changes need to be made. **15.193**

Investment firms which provide best execution are required to provide appropriate information to their clients on their order execution policy, and to obtain the prior consent of the client to it.[106] The policy must: **15.194**

- specifically draw attention (and prior express consent must be obtained from the client) to the possibility of execution away from a regulated market or MTF (consent may be in the form of a general agreement);
- (for retail clients only) include an account of the relative importance the firm assigns to the factors, or the process by which the firm does so;
- list the execution venues on which the firm places specific reliance in meeting its best execution obligation; and
- include a warning that specific instructions from a client may prevent the firm from taking the steps that it has designed and implemented in its policy to give best execution.

Material changes to the policy must be notified to clients. **15.195**

CESR acknowledges that 'prior consent' may, at least in some jurisdictions, be tacit and result from behaviour of the client such as the sending of an order to the firm after having received information on the firm's execution policy. **15.196**

---

[102] COBS 11.2.14.
[103] COBS 11.2.15.
[104] COBS 11.2.23.
[105] COBS 11.2.28.
[106] COBS 11.2.25.

15.197 CESR[107] considers that 'prior express consent' for OTC order execution entails an actual demonstration of consent by the client (by written signature or equivalent means (electronic signature), by a click on a web page, or orally by telephone or in person, with appropriate record keeping). The express consent requirement is not regarded as applying in relation to financial instruments which are not admitted to trading on a regulated market or MTF.

15.198 Investment firms which execute client orders must be able to demonstrate to their clients, at their request, that they have executed orders in accordance with their policy. This requirement does not apply to portfolio management or reception and transmission of orders.

15.199 Best execution has been one of the most controversial areas of the MiFID. There remain a number of areas of uncertainty around the scope of the regime. These largely relate to conceptual difficulties in applying best execution to principal (own account) dealing arrangements or to highly bespoke products.

15.200 There remains some difficulty in determining when the best execution requirement is intended to apply to principal dealers (ie firms which put their own capital at risk to trade). The MiFID contains countervailing indications in this respect: Recital 33 states that the best execution obligation 'should apply to the firm that owes contractual or agency duties to the client'. In circumstances where a firm makes prices (and risks its own capital), it may be argued that it may owe no such duties.

15.201 A related argument centres on the question of whether a principal dealer receives 'client orders', on grounds that a request to trade in response to an offer to deal on risk by a firm does not constitute an order. As against each of these arguments, however, Recital 69 of the MiFID Implementing Directive states that dealing on own account with clients should be considered as the execution of client orders.

15.202 The Commission has now agreed an interpretation of the MiFID rejecting the previously cited approaches and focusing on the words 'on behalf of'. Under this interpretation, firms which deal other than where they act on behalf of their clients do not have a best execution obligation. Whether a firm acts on behalf of a client when dealing as principal will be largely a question of fact. Generally, riskless principal dealings and orders worked by a firm will be executed on the client's behalf. The key issue will be whether the client legitimately relies on the firm to protect its interests.

15.203 As indicated earlier, a possible route to avoid the application of the best execution obligation is to argue that particular instructions received are 'specific instructions' from the client which the firm is following in executing the order. However, there is a prohibition on investment firms inducing or inviting specific instructions from clients when the firm ought reasonably to know that an instruction to that effect is likely to prevent it from obtaining the best possible result for the client.[108] It also clarifies that when an investment firm executes an order following specific instructions from the client, it should be treated as having satisfied its best execution obligations only in respect of the part or aspect of the order to which the client instructions relate.

15.204 The Commission has sought to provide some clarification on the application of the specific instruction provision in relation to customised products. It acknowledges that where the

[107] CESR/07-321.

[108] The MiFID Implementing Directive, Recital 68.

investment firm proposes to a client the elements of an OTC derivatives contract that would respond to the client's needs, it is more appropriate to characterise this as investment advice (triggering a suitability obligation) rather than best execution. However, it considers that the fact that the client specifies what he needs in terms of exposure and protection does not necessarily exclude the application of best execution. Where best execution applies because an order is executed on behalf of the customer, the identity of the instruments sought will be a matter of the information contained in the order rather than a question of specific instructions.

In the case of complex products, the Commission notes that best execution (when applicable) applies to the product as a whole and may be obtained even if best execution for each component, when considered in isolation, is not obtained. **15.205**

CESR issued a consultation paper in February 2007[109] on best execution under the MiFID covering the following areas: **15.206**

- the contents of the execution policy and arrangements;
- disclosure to clients;
- client consent;
- relationships between firms in chains of execution;
- review and monitoring; and
- quality of data.

In May 2007, CESR produced a feedback statement[110] summarising the most significant issues raised during the consultation and a Best Execution Q&A (to which the Commission interpretation referred to earlier is appended). Key issues addressed by the Q&A include the different obligations of investment firms executing orders directly with execution venues and portfolio managers and other firms which transmit or place orders with other entities for execution; the content of the best execution policy; the information about the policy which should be provided to clients; obtaining consent to the policy; and the distinction between reviewing and monitoring best execution arrangements. **15.207**

The CESR Q&A is intended to explain CESR's views on how firms can comply with the MiFID which members of CESR can use on a voluntary basis in day-to-day supervision. It does not constitute European legislation and does not require national legislature action. **15.208**

Investment Research

The provision of investment research[111] has been the subject of much debate in regulatory circles since the US authorities unveiled irregularities in the way in which investment research **15.209**

[109] CESR/07-321.

[110] ibid.

[111] The term 'investment research' is defined in the FCA Glossary (as derived from the MiFID) as research or other information recommending or suggesting an investment strategy, explicitly or implicitly, concerning one or several financial instruments or the issuers of financial instruments, including any opinion as to the present or future value or price of such instruments, intended for distribution channels or for the public, and in relation to which the following conditions are met:

(a) it is labelled or described as investment research or in similar terms, or is otherwise presented as an objective or independent explanation of the matters contained in the recommendation; and
(b) if the recommendation in question were to be made by an investment firm to a client, it would not constitute the provision of a personal recommendation.

was used to facilitate favourable results for certain investment firms (and their corporate finance clients) to the detriment of their investment clients. Investment analysts were heavily involved in marketing efforts in order to gain corporate finance mandates. This meant that their objectivity was compromised as they would be inclined to issue research (presented as being objective) which would favour the company concerned. Additionally, internal reporting structures within investment firms and investment analysts' remuneration structures were linked with the activities of corporate finance personnel which provided a further indication of the existence of a conflict of interest.

FSA consultation

15.210 In July 2002, the FSA issued a Discussion Paper concerning the state of investment research in the UK.[112] The summary conclusions were not encouraging. The paper produced evidence[113] which was difficult to reconcile with the premise that investment research was objective.

15.211 The paper identified as the main source of conflict for investment firms the practice of requiring research analysts to share their skills and knowledge in corporate finance deals as well as fulfilling their traditional role of providing research recommendations to the brokerage section of their firm. The result has been impaired integrity of investment research due to the desire to produce favourable results for corporate finance clients.

15.212 It was clear that the modern phenomenon of bringing research analysts closer to corporate finance clients was also liable to produce a negative effect on the willingness of analysts concerned to publish adverse research notes on their corporate clients. Corporate finance clients have shown throughout the years that they are willing to impose severe sanctions on investment firms and their analysts if they are not pleased with a particular research recommendation. These commercial issues are at the heart of the regulatory concerns as to the objectivity and integrity of investment research.

15.213 The paper also highlighted the significant impact that investment research was having on the price of the securities covered by the research. Some highly rated research analysts prove time and time again that their recommendations can mean doom or boom for the share price of the companies concerned. This gave regulators a wide mandate to address any actual and potential problems in this area due to its potential adverse effect on the integrity and orderly nature of the securities markets.

15.214 In July 2003, the FSA published Consultation Paper 171.[114] In the paper, the FSA advocated the strengthening of its regime to counteract any potential for abuse. The actual regime includes prescriptive guidance on how internal control structures are expected to operate within investment firms in connection with investment research and on acceptable standards of analysts' conduct.

[112] The publication of this Discussion Paper coincided with negotiations of the EU Market Abuse Directive which contains certain elements regulating the issue of research recommendations in relation to securities which are admitted to trading on an EEA Regulated Market or in respect of which an application for admission has been made.

[113] In the FSA's own words 'there is evidence that in certain cases analysts have compromised their integrity by issuing recommendations contrary to their own views'.

[114] 'Conflicts of Interest: Investment research and issues of securities'.

FSA guidance

Following further consultation,[115] the FSA published in March 2004 its rules and guidance in Policy Statement 04/6, which came into force on 1 July 2004. These were incorporated into COBS 12. The following is a summary of the main provisions. 15.215

- Investment firms are required to establish a policy[116] for managing conflicts of interest (see SYSC 10.1.11) in the context of the publication of impartially presented investment research. The policy, which must be recorded and made available to clients, must identify conflicts of interest which might affect the impartiality of its investment research and must at least deal with the following matters: (a) supervision and management of investment analysts; (b) remuneration structure for investment analysts; (c) rules governing investment analysts' activities other than the production of investment research (eg involvement in corporate finance transactions); (d) identification of persons who may comment on the content of investment research and the weight and force of such comments; (e) the timing and manner in which investment research should be communicated; and (f) disclosures for inclusion in investment research.
- It would generally not be appropriate for an individual with corporate finance responsibilities to be supervising or controlling investment analysts, making decisions on the subject matter or content of investment research, or deciding investment analysts' remuneration.[117]
- Whilst it is legitimate for investment firms to utilise the knowledge and information of investment analysts in corporate finance business, the participation of investment analysts in a marketing capacity (eg presentations to solicit corporate finance business) is likely to be inappropriate as it would give the impression of lack of impartiality in their investment research. Furthermore, the appearance of investment analysts in securities 'roadshows' (to promote interest in new issues of securities) is also noted as inappropriate.
- Investment firms must not give editorial control of investment research materials to persons within the firm whose role involves the representation of interests that could conflict with those of the target audience of the research and must not allow anyone other than the analyst concerned to provide final approval of the content of the investment research.[118]
- Investment firms are no longer allowed to engage in own account transactions in securities (and related securities) which are the subject matter of investment research (intended for circulation to the firm's clients) ahead of the publication of the research.[119] Such own account transactions are only permitted when the firm's clients have had 'a reasonable opportunity to act upon the research'. It is suggested that firms allow at least three working days from the time of the communication of the research before any own account transactions can be undertaken.
- Investment firms must prohibit analysts from undertaking personal account transactions in securities which are the subject matter of their investment research unless the transaction is in line with any current recommendation for which they are responsible or to enable them to meet prior obligations with the permission of the firm. FSA Guidance further

[115] Consultation Paper 205: 'Conflicts of interest: Investment research and issues of securities' (October 2003).
[116] COBS 12.2.3.
[117] COBS 12.2.4.
[118] COBS 12.2.9.
[119] COBS 12.2.5.

provide that investment firms will be well advised to impose a voluntary restriction on their investment analysts requiring them not to engage in personal account transactions at all or not to engage in personal account transactions in the sector which they cover.[120]

Market Abuse Directive

15.216 The EU Market Abuse Directive[121] introduced various requirements (mainly of disclosure) for investment firms which prepare or publish research recommendations. The term 'research recommendation' is defined more narrowly than the FCA Handbook term of 'investment research' mainly in that it only covers instruments which are listed on one or more EEA regulated markets or where an application for admission to trading of the relevant instrument is pending. In order for investment research to constitute a 'research recommendation' it must:

- recommend or suggest an investment strategy;
- express a particular investment recommendation; or
- express an opinion as to the present or future value or price of a security.

15.217 A short term investment recommendation originating from the sales or trading departments of an investment firm and which is not intended for wide circulation is excluded from the definition of 'research recommendation'. This is an important carve-out for more informal and frequent (sometimes daily) communications to a select group of clients (usually institutional clients).

15.218 The following is a summary of the obligations, as set out in COBS 12.4, of an investment firm under the Market Abuse Directive as they would apply to investment firms involved in the preparation of research recommendations.[122]

- Disclose interests or conflicts of interest concerning securities which are the subject matter of a research recommendation.[123] In particular, disclose any relationship and circumstances which could impair the objectivity of the recommendation. This includes: a major (exceeding 5 per cent) shareholding existing between the firm concerned (or its affiliates) and the relevant issuer; any other financial interests of the firm (or its affiliates) in the relevant issuer, where relevant; details of the firm's (or its affiliates') acting as lead manager or co-lead manager during the previous 12 months in respect of the relevant issuer's securities or related derivatives, where relevant; and details of any agreements with the relevant issuer to provide investment banking services (insofar as this would not give rise to disclosure of confidential commercial information).
- Adhere to prescribed rules concerning the need for clear distinctions to be made between facts and estimates, interpretations, opinions, and the like.[124]
- Ensure that the substance of recommendations can be substantiated as reasonable upon request by the FCA.[125]

---

[120] COBS 12.2.5A.

[121] Council Directive (EC) 03/6 on insider dealing and market manipulation (market abuse) [2003] OJ L96/16. The market abuse rules are currently being updated at the EU level.

[122] Where certain disclosure obligations are disproportionate to the length of a specific research recommendation, investment firms may include a reference in the body of the research to an easily accessible source providing such information (eg a link to a website).

[123] COBS 12.4.4.

[124] COBS 12.4.6(1)(a).

[125] COBS 12.4.6(1)(d).

- Indicate whether the issuer of the securities concerned has had an opportunity to review the recommendation and comment on it (if relevant).[126]
- Include any basis of valuation or methodology used to evaluate the issuer or the securities.[127]
- Where the substance of the recommendation differs to a material extent from a recommendation of the firm relating to the same security or issuer in the previous 12 months, this must be set out in a prominent manner.[128]
- Disclose the firm's internal systems and controls aimed at the prevention and avoidance of conflicts of interest in connection with research recommendations (including any 'Chinese Walls' arrangements).
- Additionally, investment firms must disclose in their research recommendations, on a quarterly basis, information concerning the proportion of all recommendations published during the relevant quarter that are 'buy', 'hold', or 'sell' and the proportion of securities in each of these categories issued by issuers which have been investment banking clients during the previous 12 months.

Dissemination of third party recommendations, whether altered or not, are generally treated as the relevant firm's own work for disclosure purposes and investment firms must treat such recommendations as if they had produced them themselves. **15.219**

The market abuse regime is in the process of being updated at the European level, which will include criminal sanctions for market abuse and outlaw the manipulation of benchmarks such as LIBOR.[129] This later change is a response to the LIBOR manipulation which came to light in the course of 2012. These requirements were implemented under Part 7 FSA 2012.[130] So far, proposals for a new regulation on insider dealing and market manipulation as well as a directive on criminal sanctions have been published by the EU. **15.220**

Clients' Assets

Investment firms are subject to strict rules—set out in a module of the FCA Handbook entitled 'Clients Assets' ('CASS')—concerning the way in which they hold assets (including cash) belonging to clients. The rules are intended to create an environment in which it is difficult for an investment firm to mix or mistake client assets with or for its own and to ensure that in the event of the firm's insolvency, the clients of the firm are in the best possible position as against any other creditors of the investment firm. It is clear, however, that whilst the rules seek to minimise any risk of loss to investment firms' clients they by no means guarantee that clients will not ultimately suffer loss. **15.221**

MiFID had little impact on CASS. However, a number of amendments have been made following the client asset failings at Lehman Brothers' UK subsidiary. The aim of these amendments is to ensure a speedier return of client assets and client money in the case of a firm's insolvency and include: **15.222**

- limiting the ability for custodians to place liens on custody assets to assets in the same account;
- setting out requirements for prime brokerage agreements;

[126] COBS 12.4.7(1)(a).
[127] COBS 12.4.7(1)(b).
[128] COBS 12.4.7(1)(f).
[129] See Chapter 3.
[130] See Chapter 10.

- resolution processes for client asset and client money holdings,
- a new way to pool an insolvent firm's client money holdings before returning it to clients.

15.223 An additional important change post-MiFID was the removal of the ability of professional clients to opt out of the client money regime and all professional clients will be covered by the client money regime (unless the relevant firm can make use of the extensive carve-outs from the definition of client money on which the FSA has provided liberal guidance).[131]

15.224 One of the main features of the rules is the requirement to inform clients (particularly vulnerable clients, eg retail clients) of the potential risk that they face as a result of the firm taking a particular course of action in relation to their assets. The clients' assets rules are divided into three parts: custody rules; collateral; client money.

Custody rules

15.225 The custody rules[132] apply to the regulated activity of safeguarding and administering investments.[133] Firms need to be aware that they are subject to the custody rules where they use a dedicated custodian unless the custodian is authorised as such under the FSMA or exempt for this purpose and has undertaken to the relevant clients to be responsible for the assets. The custody rules apply to any assets entrusted to the firm as long as they consist of regulated investments.

Segregation and internal controls

15.226 The custody rules are designed to ensure that in the event of the insolvency of the firm concerned, assets belonging to the firm's clients do not form any part of the pool of assets which are available for distribution to the firm's general (including secured and unsecured) creditors. There is a large body of authorities concerning which assets constitute part of an insolvent company's estate.[134] These authorities establish that in order to exclude assets from an insolvent entity's estate, client assets must be segregated from those belonging to the firm and this must be effectively recorded. As well as this, firms are also required to send to clients' custody statements indicating the assets which are held, at least on an annual basis, and to conduct a periodical reconciliation of custody investments which are not held by the firm.

15.227 The custody rules contain specific provisions in relation to the registration and recording of legal title to clients' investments which require firms to use one or more of a number of alternative legal entities for this purpose, as appropriate, eg a nominee company or a custodian (and to provide, in certain circumstances, risk warnings to affected clients).[135] Whilst it would be ideal for clients to have legal title to their regulated investments, in practice this rarely happens. The reason for this is that modern custody methods involve the use of nominee companies, omnibus accounts, and specialised custodians (which may mean that a large financial institution will delegate custody to an affiliate).

---

131 CASS 7.2 and CP38, CP06/14 and CP08/6 for guidance. CASS has been updated following the insolvencies of the financial crisis, but these elements have not changed.

132 A comprehensive analysis of the law and practice relating to custody of financial assets is outside the scope of this chapter which contains only a brief outline of the basic principles.

133 (Regulated Activities) Order 2001, SI 2001/544, art 40.

134 See, eg, *Re Kayford Ltd* [1975] 1 WLR 279.

135 CASS 6.2.3.

In addition, there are specific rules concerning retention of documents of title to regulated investments and the steps required before a custodian is appointed to hold regulated investments of the firm's clients.[136] **15.228**

Terms of business

COBS 6.1.7 contains a list of information which must be provided to a retail client as regards custody (which should be read in light of the requirements in COBS 8 regarding client agreements). The custody terms may form part of the firm's general terms of business or may be provided in a separate document as soon as the firm expects to be providing custody services to the client. The objective is to inform clients of the manner in which their assets will be held by the firm and, if relevant, any third parties which may have a role in the custody of those assets. **15.229**

The terms must include comprehensive risk disclosure provisions, particularly in respect of regulated investments held with third party custodians, and depositaries outside the UK which are subject to different legal and regulatory systems. Such arrangements frequently present complex questions of insolvency law and conflict of laws as to the level of protection afforded in the event of the third party's insolvency or the occurrence of other supervening events. **15.230**

Custody

There are conflicting authorities[137] (and therefore the law is far from being settled) on the question of whether or not fungible securities held by a custodian are capable of forming the subject matter of a trust (the issue being lack of certainty as to the subject matter at any given time). Recognising this, the custody rules require an investment firm to have prior written consent from the client before it uses custody investments for its own account (whether for stock lending transactions or otherwise). **15.231**

Stock lending

Where an investment firm engages in a stock lending transaction involving securities owned by clients, it must ensure that the borrower provides adequate collateral at the outset and is obliged to top up the collateral on a regular basis (otherwise the firm must provide for any shortfall). **15.232**

Collateral

The term 'collateral' in this context denotes securities which are provided by clients effectively as security for their contingent obligations and which the firm may use (including by way of hypothecation) for the purposes of its business. Unless otherwise agreed, investment firms must monitor the collateral they hold for their clients and maintain appropriate records. **15.233**

Client money

Investment firms' conduct in relation to monies placed by, or which are due to, their clients is subject, in the absence of an exemption, to a system of prescriptive rules concerning segregation and internal systems of controls (these rules being subsequently referred to as 'CMR'). **15.234**

[136] CASS 6.2.7.

[137] *Re Goldcorp Exchange Ltd* [1994] 2 All ER 806; *Hunter v Moss* [1994] 3 All ER 215, CA; *Re Harvard Securities (in liquidation)* [1997] 2 BCLC 369; *Re CA Pacific Finance Ltd (in liquidation)* [2000] 1 BCLC 494.

Monies which qualify as 'client money' are (unless there is an exemption) subject to a statutory trust for the benefit of the relevant clients.[138]

15.235 By far the most significant exemption[139] from the application of the CMR is that relating to 'approved banks'. This reference includes all UK deposit-takers and means, in practical terms, that a UK bank may treat all monies which it receives in the course of conducting securities transactions with or for clients as deposits placed with the bank in the ordinary course of its business.

15.236 Given that the relationship between a banker and a depositor is that of a debtor and a creditor,[140] the depositor ranks together with all other general creditors in the event of the bank's insolvency. Although it may be possible to negotiate with a particular bank to apply the CMR, as this would clearly be for the benefit of the client, most banks would not have the required administrative machinery to operate the CMR and would no doubt take a dim view of the client's perspective on their solvency!

Operational issues

15.237 A firm which is subject to the CMR must segregate the firm's own monies from those of its clients and hold client monies in designated bank accounts. Monies should be paid into the designated client account without delay and in the case of an automated transfer system, directly into that account.

15.238 There are further onerous requirements relating to dealing with mixed remittances, monitoring of client entitlements to monies, and the payment of interest. Investment firms should, in their terms of business for retail clients, set out the rate of interest payable on client monies because in the absence of such provisions they must pay retail clients all interest earned in respect of such monies.

15.239 There are further restrictions on the type of banks with which the designated client accounts may be held. The starting position is that designated client accounts must only be opened with an 'approved bank'. For a UK-based bank account this means the Bank of England and any other OECD central bank, a UK deposit-taker, a UK building society, or an OECD supervised deposit-taker. For a bank account established anywhere else, an approved bank would mean any of the banks specified earlier, a bank which is regulated in the Isle of Man or the Channel Islands, a bank supervised by the South African Reserve Bank, or a regulated bank which is required to produce audited accounts, has minimum net assets of £5 million, and surplus revenue over expenditure over the last two financial years and whose annual audit report is not qualified.

15.240 However, a firm (other than a trustee firm) may open designated client accounts with a bank which is not an approved bank where the securities transactions concerned are subject to laws and regulations of a country outside the UK and if due to legal and regulatory requirements, it is impossible to hold client monies with an approved bank. In such case the firm must notify its clients (and obtain the consent of any retail clients) that client money will not be held with an approved bank, that different legal and insolvency systems would apply from that of the UK in the event of the bank's failure, and, if such is the case, that the bank insists

[138] CASS 7.7.
[139] CASS 7.1.8.
[140] *Carr v Carr* (1811) 1 Mer 541n; 35 ER 799.

on retaining a right of set-off in relation to the account. This requirement is best dealt with by a provision in a firm's standard terms of business.

When an investment firm opens designated client accounts with a bank (whether or not an approved bank) it must require the bank to acknowledge the special trust relationship which the firm has with its clients in relation to the monies deposited in the accounts. This is designed to ensure that all parties in the chain are aware of the firm's obligations as a trustee and (subject to what is said in the previous paragraph) that the funds may not be subject to set-off or counterclaims as they are not the property of the firm. Transfer of client monies to a third party (eg by way of transaction margin) does not discharge the firm from its general obligations under the CMR. **15.241**

Trustees

Because of the nature of trustee firms, the CMR have limited application to such firms so as to avoid a conflict with the terms of the trust document. Consequently, the main obligation on trustee firms is to hold client money in accordance with the terms of the trust instrument and in any event separate from their own monies.[141] **15.242**

Takeovers and Listing Rules

In the course of their business, investment firms may well become subject to the voluntary and regulatory regimes which apply to takeovers, to certain issues of equity securities, and to members of the London Stock Exchange. **15.243**

Takeovers

The City Code on Takeovers and Mergers (the Code) is a code of conduct which is designed to afford fair and equal treatment to shareholders in the context of a takeover. The Code is upheld and enforced by the Panel on Takeovers and Mergers (the Panel). Breaches of the Code may attract public censure and sanctions by the Panel and/or sanctions by the FCA (which formally endorses the Code and may, at the request of the Panel, take an enforcement action against a firm or any person within the firm who is approved by the FCA). The EU Directive on Takeover Bids[142] has introduced, for the first time, a statutory framework for the regulation of takeover activity in the UK. Under this framework, the Panel has additional powers to enforce compliance with the Code (including by ordering a person to pay compensation). Part 28 of the Companies Act 2006 implements the provisions of the Directive in the UK. Whilst the Code is primarily of interest to investment firms involved in corporate finance and investment management, it also has significant provisions which may affect, and should be familiar to, securities traders. **15.244**

The Code applies to offers for public companies resident in the UK, Channel Islands, and Isle of Man and a small proportion of private companies residing in such territories (most notably, a 'delisted' company which was listed within 10 years prior to the announcement of the offer). In the context of this chapter it is appropriate to mention only those provisions (rules) of the Code that directly affect investment firms. **15.245**

[141] CASS 7.7.
[142] Council Directive (EC) 04/25 on takeover bids (text with EEA relevance) [2004] 25 OJ L142/12.

Independence

15.246 Rule 3.1 of the Code requires that 'The board of the offeree company must obtain competent independent advice on any offer and the substance of such advice must be made known to its shareholders'. The Code emphasises the importance of obtaining advice at an early stage of the engagement where the takeover involves offers that are initiated or backed by existing shareholders so as to ensure that independent advice is separate to any information made available by, or migrating from, the shareholders backing the takeover.

15.247 Rule 3.2 of the Code requires that 'the board of an offeror must obtain competent independent advice on any offer when the offer being made is a reverse takeover (where the offer might necessitate an increase of more than 100 per cent of the offeror's issued voting share capital) or when the directors are faced with a conflict of interest. The substance of such advice must be made known to its shareholders.' An example of a conflict of interest for a director is where the director is a board member in both the offeree and the offeror companies.

15.248 The task for the advising firms is to operate effective systems and procedures in order to ensure that they are in fact independent for the purposes of advising in such circumstances. This must involve a rigorous review of all the aspects of the relationship that the relevant firm has with the parties involved in the transaction. For example, advisers may not be regarded as independent in relation to a party (and consequently may be precluded from advising such party) in circumstances where they have previously advised the opposite party (ie the offeree or offeror).

Prohibited dealings

15.249 The following rules are intended to prevent persons who take part in a takeover transaction from benefiting unfairly from their knowledge and are complementary to the general restrictions on insider dealing and market abuse.

15.250 Rule 4.1 of the Code requires that no person other than the offeror deals (or recommends others to deal) in securities of the offeree (including related derivatives) whilst in possession of price-sensitive information concerning an offer or a contemplated offer. This prohibition ends either upon termination of discussions concerning a possible offer or when the approach of the offeree or the offer itself is announced by the offeror.

15.251 Rule 4.2 of the Code imposes a restriction on the offeror and persons acting in concert with it[143] from selling any of the offeree's securities during an offer period except with the prior consent of the Panel and following a public notice that such sales would be made.

15.252 Rule 4.4 of the Code prohibits financial advisers and stockbrokers (other than exempt principal traders[144] and exempt fund managers)[145] to the offeree from doing the following:

---

[143] Briefly, persons who, pursuant to an agreement or understanding (formal or informal), actively cooperate, through the acquisition by any of them of shares in a company, to obtain or consolidate control of that company.

[144] A firm which is registered as a market-maker with the London Stock Exchange, or is accepted by the Panel as a market-maker, or is a London Stock Exchange member firm dealing as principal in order book securities, which is recognised by the Panel as an exempt principal trader for the purposes of the Code.

[145] A firm whose business involves discretionary investment management and is recognised by the Panel as an exempt fund manager for the purpose of the Code.

- carrying out own-account or discretionary transactions in shares and related derivatives of the offeree;
- providing a non-arm's length loan to assist a person to purchase such shares or derivatives;
- entering into an agreement requiring any person to retain, deal, or refrain from dealings in the offeree's 'relevant securities'.[146]

Disclosure of dealings

Disclosure of dealings in the offeror's relevant securities is only required if the offer involves the offeror's securities as part of the consideration. **15.253**

Rule 8.1 of the Code requires public disclosure of dealings in relevant securities by the offeror, the offeree, and any of their associates[147] (such as the parties' financial advisers) during the offer period. **15.254**

There are specific rules relating to the offeror, offeree, and associated parties where they act as discretionary fund managers and may engage in restricted transactions as part of that role. The guiding principle is that any such transaction must be disclosed to the public, but where an associate connected with the offeree or the offeror is an exempt fund manager (see note 145) such transactions, as a general rule, need only be privately disclosed to the Panel. Public disclosure is required, however, where the fund manager concerned owns or controls 5 per cent or more of the shares of either the offeror or the offeree. **15.255**

As regards non-discretionary management by an exempt fund manager which is an associate of the offeree or the offeror, disclosure of relevant dealings is to be made privately to the Panel. **15.256**

Dealings by 1 per cent shareholders

Rule 8.3 of the Code states that any person who owns or controls 1 per cent or more of any class of relevant securities of an offeror or of the offeree company (or who will do so as a result of further purchases) must publicly disclose any dealings in such securities during the offer period. In the context of derivative securities, disclosure of dealings is required where the person dealing owns or controls 1 per cent or more of the class of securities which is the subject of the option or to whose price the derivative is referenced. **15.257**

Investment management firms are treated for the purpose of this disclosure rule as the controllers of securities held for and on behalf of their clients for whom they undertake discretionary management. Furthermore, securities holdings should be consolidated within the group to calculate the level of control. **15.258**

Exempt principal traders are not generally required to disclose information under Rules 8.1 and 8.3 of the Code with regard to their holdings of relevant securities as such disclosure is regarded as a disruption to their legitimate activities. **15.259**

In note 10 to Rule 8 of the Code it is stated that securities dealers and banks dealing in relevant securities are expected to cooperate with the Panel and supply information regarding dealings and positions to the Panel, including client identities and full contact details. **15.260**

[146] Generally, securities of the offeree company being offered for or which carry voting rights, shares of the offeror, and any convertible and other securities having substantially the same rights (including options and other derivatives).

[147] Which covers all persons (whether or not acting in concert) who directly or indirectly own or deal in the shares of an offeror or offeree company and who have an interest or a potential interest in the outcome of the offer.

15.261 In 2005, the Code Committee of the Panel extended the scope of required disclosure to instances where a person has a derivative position such as a call option or a long derivative interest. The disclosure obligation arises where a person holds interest in relation to 1 per cent or more in any class of a relevant security of the offeree company (or, in the case of an exchange offer, of the offeror) or where a person would hold such a position as a result of a particular transaction. Thus, the Committee treats a person who has, or may have, a long economic exposure[148] to changes in the price of securities as interested in those securities.

Telephone campaigns

15.262 Campaigns conducted by financial advisers to solicit acceptance from shareholders must be handled by staff conversant with the requirements of the Code. Telephone campaigns can only be undertaken after an offer has been announced; there are strict rules regarding the secrecy of any offer prior to an announcement of a firm intention to make it. Information which is relayed to shareholders must conform to that which has already been published and continue to be accurate and up-to-date. Shareholders should not be put under undue pressure and must be encouraged to consult their professional advisers before making up their minds.

Dealings by exempt principal traders

15.263 Rule 38 of the Code prohibits an exempt principal trader who is connected with one of the parties, whether offeror or offeree, from transacting with the purpose of assisting that party. Additionally, an offeror (and any person acting in concert with it) must not deal as principal with a connected exempt principal trader in relevant securities of the offeree company during the offer period. The Code requires the offeror's financial advisers to ensure that their client complies with this requirement.

15.264 Dealings in relevant securities by an exempt principal trader connected with an offeror or the offeree company should be aggregated and disclosed to an FCA designated Regulatory Information Service and the Panel following the date of the transaction.

Listing rules (sponsors)

15.265 The FCA (acting as the United Kingdom Listing Authority) sponsor regime applies to certain London-listed issues of equity securities (eg initial public offerings and rights issues). Where the sponsor regime applies, the issuer must appoint an approved investment firm (the sponsor) to act as a key liaison point between the issuer and the FCA.[149]

15.266 The sponsor's primary role is to provide assurances to the FCA that the issuer has met (and is well-placed to meet on a continuing basis) its obligations under the listing rules and assist the issuer in understanding and complying with the listing rules.

15.267 Investment firms seeking to be approved by the FCA as sponsors for the first time must submit a formal application which includes details about the firm's capability and, more importantly, the competence and experience of its relevant employees.

[148] For example, the person will benefit economically if the price of that security goes up or has a right or option to acquire it or to call for its delivery.

[149] See Chapter 8 on Listing and Public Offers.

FCA approval

In order to be approved as a sponsor by the FCA, an investment firm must demonstrate that it is competent to perform the services envisaged by the listing rules and has adequate systems and controls to ensure that it can carry out such a role. The FSA has confirmed, informally, that firms with less than two experienced employees are unlikely to meet the required threshold of competence. The rules are prescriptive as to the type of an employee's experience that can be taken into account for this purpose.[150] **15.268**

For the purposes of satisfying the systems and controls threshold, investment firms must establish effective reporting lines, adequately supervise employees engaging in transactions where they act as sponsors, effectively manage conflicts of interest, and maintain records of all matters in connection with their role as sponsor for the required period of six years. **15.269**

It is possible, as was the case under the previous sponsor regime, for more than one investment firm to act as joint sponsor. In such case the obligations of each sponsor are absolute as if each sponsor were acting on a sole basis. However, one sponsor must be designated as taking the prime responsibility for communicating with the FCA. **15.270**

Sponsor's obligations

An investment firm acting as a sponsor under the listing rules must ensure that it conducts a thorough risk analysis of the role and a compliance schedule to ensure that its obligations under the listing rules are fully complied with. An issue which tends to figure prominently is the extent to which sponsors expose themselves to suit by investors in cases where they fall short of their duties under the listing rules. A sponsor's general obligations are to: **15.271**

- provide assurances, when required to do so by the FCA, that the responsibilities of the issuer under the listing rules have been met;
- guide the issuer in understanding and complying with the listing rules;
- deal with the FCA in an open and cooperative way;
- disclose to the FCA, in a timely manner, any material information relating to the sponsor's or the issuer's non-compliance with the listing rules (including the disclosure rules).

More specifically, in connection with a new applicant issuer, the sponsor is required to conduct a due diligence exercise (for which it may use external experts such as accountants and lawyers) before it submits documents for and on behalf of the issuer. The objective is to ensure that the documents (particularly the prospectus) comply with the listing rules, that the directors of the issuer have established procedures to comply with the listing rules (and with the disclosure rules) on an ongoing basis, to judge the financial position and prospects of the issuer, and to establish that the directors have a reasonable basis on which to make the required working capital statement under the listing rules. **15.272**

The sponsor is also required to lodge a declaration with the FCA, once it lodges the final version of the prospectus, that the prospectus and other related disclosure to the FCA contain all matters that in the sponsor's reasonable opinion should be taken into account in considering the application for listing. **15.273**

[150] Experience should normally be demonstrated by the provision of relevant advice or services at least three times in the preceding 36 months and at least once in the preceding 12 months.

16

RETAIL INVESTMENT FIRMS

Introduction

Traditionally the wares and labours of investment firms would have only been of interest to, and affordable by, the richest in society. Such individuals or families might engage the services of a stockbroker or investment manager in respect of their portfolio of shares, corporate and government bonds.[1] However, in the twenty-first century many of the most significant purchases by the typical, middle-income citizen are financial products. Such an individual may have a large proportion of his or her wealth tied up in securities, life insurance, collective investment schemes and other contracts for the purpose of saving, investment, property acquisition or pension provision. **16.01**

Over the last four decades there has been a major expansion of the retail investment industry in the United Kingdom. It was the avowed intention of the Conservative administrations of the 1980s and 1990s to create and promote a property-owning, and in particular a share-owning, democracy. **16.02**

Three factors have contributed to greater retail participation in investments. First, the wider prevalence of employee share schemes. Secondly, the privatisation of formerly nationalised industries. Thirdly, the introduction of Personal Equity Plans ('PEPs') as a tax-free shelter for shares, in order to encourage saving, and investment. In 1998, PEPs were replaced by Individual Savings Accounts ('ISAs') as a tax-exempt vehicle for saving and investments. **16.03**

At the end of 2006 private individuals in the UK owned shares worth £239 billion. Other significant holdings by insurance companies (£273 billion) and pension funds (£236 billion) represented ways in which individuals indirectly participate in the market for shares.[2] **16.04**

The legal and regulatory environment has struggled to keep pace. Whilst the common law, in the general principles of private law, has the basic toolkit to determine many issues which arise out of consumer financial services cases, it is only in a comparatively small number of cases in which the judiciary have had to grapple with the issues thrown up by the modern **16.05**

---

[1] See S Banner, *Anglo-American Securities Regulation—Cultural and Political Roots, 1690–1860* (CUP 1998) 24, discussing the rise of a securities market in late seventeenth-century England: 'As the secondary market in government debt and shares of businesses grew, the portion of the nation's total wealth consisting of land and other tangible things gradually declined, replaced more and more by mobile pieces of paper, representations of intangible fractions of a future stream of income. Within a generation, contemporaries came to realise that an entirely new form of property had come into existence.'

[2] W Clarke, *How the City of London Works—An Introduction to its Financial Markets* (7th edn, Sweet & Maxwell 2008), although this represented only 14 per cent of the total market capitalisation, having fallen from 20 per cent in 1994. Foreign investors accounted for £742 billion of shares.

mass market in retail investment products and services. The detailed conduct of business rules laid down by successive regulators has proved increasingly prominent in recent litigation in the wake of the financial crisis of 2007–2008, although investors' claims tend to mix existing causes of action for breach of contract, negligence, breach of fiduciary duty, and misrepresentation with statutory duties based on regulatory rules.[3] In 2008, Rix LJ in the Court of Appeal observed:

> It is a feature of our commercial law, robust, pragmatic and internationally respected as it may be, that it grew up in an age of commerce between merchants, when what we now think of as financial consumer contracts must have been relatively few in number, limited in their scope, and entered into by a small range of professional, mercantile and land-owning people. I speak of contracts outside ordinary sale of goods. Nowadays, however, huge numbers of consumers have pensions, make investments, and enter into contracts of all kinds.[4]

His Lordship went on to observe that, for example, the principles of insurance law, were developing (and were being developed by the Financial Ombudsman Service, following in the footsteps of its predecessor, the Insurance Ombudsman) to meet this rise in consumer transactions. However, the task of setting the standards for financial professionals dealing with ordinary consumers has largely fallen on the shoulders of the legislature, the European institutions, and the regulators and ombudsmen to whom the tasks of standard-setting and supervision has been entrusted. Despite this (and that may be a charitable judgment) the experience of the last thirty years has been far from happy.

Retail financial scandals

16.06 Between 1988 to 1994 it was estimated that between one million and two million ordinary investors were sold the wrong type of pension. They were persuaded to opt out of, or not join, occupational pension schemes (with defined benefits) and instead take out an investment product-based pension. The latter involved greater exposure to risk, and fewer benefits than the occupational schemes. Such investors potentially faced a highly significant financial loss. The scale of the pension mis-selling scandal and its financial extent was, at the time, unprecedented.[5] The total cost of redress for the industry was £11.8 billion. The pension mis-selling scandal was one of the principal reasons cited for the financial regulatory reforms undertaken by the Labour Government elected in May 1997. What were the causes of mis-selling? Payment of salespersons by commission is a cause emphasised by many commentators and which has now been addressed as part of the Retail Distribution Review.[6] However, the emphasis on remuneration may be an over-simplification. In the House of Lords in *Lloyds TSB General Insurance Holdings v Lloyds Bank Group Insurance Co Ltd*[7] Lord Hoffmann succinctly recorded the key factors (putting payment by commission into perspective): 'The

[3] On financial redress see Chapter 7. On financial services disputes see Chapter 12.

[4] *R (on the application of Heather Moor & Edgecomb Ltd) v Financial Ombudsman Service* [2008] EWCA Civ 642, para [87].

[5] For detailed discussion of the saga see G McMeel, 'The Consumer Dimension of Financial Services Law: Lessons from the Pension Mis-selling Scandal' [1999] *Company, Financial and Insolvency Law Review* 29; J Black and R Nobles, 'Personal Pensions Misselling: The Causes and Lessons of Regulatory Failure' (1998) 61 MLR 789; and G McMeel, 'Liability of Financial Advisers in the Wake of the Pension Mis-selling Scandal' (1997) 13 *Professional Negligence* 97.

[6] See para 16.124.

[7] [2003] UKHL 48.

underlying reasons for mis-selling were partly the method by which salesmen were paid but largely the inadequacy of the training and monitoring by the companies employing them.'[8]

Other significant scandals affecting the retail investment sector included a more limited review of past business in respect of Free Standing Additional Voluntary Contributions ('FSAVCs') in respect of occupational schemes.[9] **16.07**

In respect of the almost equally time-consuming and costly (from the firms' perspective) mortgage endowment saga the regulators took a different tack, and rather than employ a general review of past business the Personal Investment Authority ('PIA'), and subsequently the Financial Services Authority ('FSA'), required firms to write to consumers to warn them of the risk of under-performance of endowments used to finance house-purchase, and (in effect) invite complaints of mis-selling.[10] The total cost of redress for the industry was £3 billion. The recent past has also seen the mis-selling of home income plans to vulnerable elderly consumers.

In 2000, in the wake of Equitable Life's near-collapse, with profits life insurance products fell under a cloud, and the issue of compensation for policyholders has rumbled on for more than a decade. In the investment sector, split capital investment trusts, 'precipice bonds' (dubbed 'Structured Capital at Risk Products' or SCARPs by the FSA), and, most recently, sales of Unregulated Collective Investment Schemes ('UCIS') to retail investors have also attracted the soubriquet 'scandal'. Beyond the investment sector the payment protection insurance ('PPI') mis-selling scandal which embraces banks, credit card companies, and other credit providers, has resulted in £5.9 billion being paid out in compensation between January 2011 and July 2012, with the final bill yet to be ascertained.[11] **16.08**

In 2011, the FSA estimated that the total bill for compensating consumers for all of these financial scandals was some £15 billion (with the bulk of PPI compensation yet to come).[12] Lord Turner, then Chairman of the FSA, writing in January 2011, accepted that the regulator's sales-focused philosophy 'has not been effective in preventing waves of consumer detriment'.[13] Since then further concerns have arisen from what the FSA has determined are serious failings in the sale of interest rate hedging products by banks to small and **16.09**

[8] Para [5].

[9] FSA and PIA, CP27, *Free-standing Additional Voluntary Contributions* (August 1999); FSA and PIA, *FSAVC Review—Model Guidance* (May 2000); FSA and PIA, *FSAVC Review—Model Guidance Update (March 2001); FSA and PIA, FSAVC Review—Model Guidance Update* (May 2001).

[10] FSA, *Progress Report on Mortgage Endowments* (October 2000); FSA CP75, *Endowment Mortgage Complaints* (November 2000); FSA PS, *Endowment Mortgage Complaints: Feedback on CP75 and 'Final Text'* (May 2001).

[11] The FSA published a monthly update on PPI refunds and compensation payments. On a smaller scale the FSA's consumer redress scheme scheme for 15,000 to 20,000 investors in Arch cru funds—two FSA authorised Open-Ended Investment Companies: FSA CP12/9, 'Consumer redress scheme in respect of unsuitable advice to invest in Arch cru funds' (April 2012). The FSA describes these investments as high risk (at para 3.8) and does not believe that a reasonably competent independent financial adviser could have properly assessed them as low or medium risk (at para 3.11). For the final redress scheme, which it is anticipated may deliver £20 million–£40 million of redress, made under FSMA 2000 section 404 see FSA PS12/24, 'Consumer redress scheme in respect of unsuitable advice to invest in Arch cru funds' (December 2012) and Appendix 1: The Arch cru Funds Consumer Redress Scheme Instrument 2012. See Chapter 1, para 1.46.

[12] FSA, 'The Financial Conduct Authority: Approach to Regulation'. (June 2011), para 1.1.

[13] FSA DP11/1, 'Product Intervention' (January 2011), Foreword by the Chairman, 3. See also paras 2.3, 2.4, and 5.14 of the Discussion Paper, and FSA SP, Adair Turner, British Bankers' Association Conference (13 July 2010).

medium-sized businesses, with banks undertaking to review sales and provide redress where appropriate.[14]

The changing regulatory scene for investment business

16.10 As a result of the numerous scandals, stability of the regulatory environment has not been a feature of the landscape. Prior to the reforms associated with the Big Bang in the second half of the 1980s there was a rudimentary regime represented by the unambitiously-named Prevention of Fraud (Investments) Acts 1939 and 1958. Since the implementation of the Financial Services Act 1986 ('the 1986 Act') there have been five major phases of the regulatory regime in respect of investor protection in the retail financial sector. First, under the 1986 Act, from its implementation on 29 April 1988 to 1 May 1994 there was the initial regime, under the overall supervision of the Securities and Investments Board ('SIB') comprising the regulatory rules of various front-line regulatory Self-regulatory Organisations ('SROs'), principally, for the retail sector, the Life Assurance and Unit Trust Regulatory Organisation ('LAUTRO')—broadly speaking the product providers—and the Financial Intermediaries, Managers and Brokers Regulatory Association ('FIMBRA'), representing the client-facing advisers and brokers. Secondly, under the same legislation, from 1994 to 2001, an amalgamated SRO, the PIA superseded LAUTRO and FIMBRA, but to a large extent adopted its predecessors' provisions in its own rulebook. Thirdly, under the Financial Services and Markets Act 2000 ('FSMA 2000') from 1 December 2001 ('N2') to October 2007, the Conduct of Business Sourcebook ('COB')[15] component of the Financial Services Authority (FSA's) *Handbook of Rules and Guidance* consolidated and superseded its various predecessor regulators' rulebooks for the conduct of investment business. After N2 COB was further amended on a number of fronts, including the depolarisation initiative and the reaction to the 'precipice bonds' or SCARPs scandal. In mid-2005, the FSA proposed fundamental changes to COB.[16] The main impetus came from the need to implement new European law—the Markets in Financial Instruments Directive ('MiFID')—with effect from 1 November 2007 and resulted in the new COBS component of the Handbook.[17] Lastly, the adoption of 'twin peaks' regulation under the Financial Services Act 2012 ('FSA 2012'), and the establishment of the new Financial Conduct Authority ('FCA') to concentrate on conduct of business regulation, appears intended to herald a more interventionist and product regulation oriented future,[18] which includes the first prohibition or restriction on the provision of particular investment products—namely Unregulated Collective Investment Schemes ('UCIS')—which was introduced on 1 January 2014.[19] Accordingly, in just over

[14] FSA Update, 'Interest rate hedging products—Information about our work and findings' (June 2012). See Chapter 1, para 1.47.

[15] For discussion of the original version of COB see G McMeel and J Virgo, *Financial Advice and Financial Products—Law and Liability* (OUP 2001), chapter 14.

[16] FSA CP05/10, *Reviewing the FSA Handbook—Money Laundering, Approved Persons, Training and Competence and Conduct of Business* (July 2005), chs 1 and 5; and Annex 5 which contained the proposed new structure for COBS.

[17] Directive 2006/31/EC: extending the time limit for the implementation of MiFID.

[18] The FSA had earlier produced important papers on product regulation: FSA DP11/1, 'Product Intervention' (January 2011); FSA FS11/3, *Product Intervention—Feedback on DP11/1* (June 2011).

[19] FSA 2012 section 24 inserted new powers into FSMA, including section 137D (power to make product intervention rules including rules banning products) and section 137R and 137S (including the power to direct firms to withdraw or refrain from approving misleading financial promotions). For the restrictions on UCIS sales and advice see FSA CP12/19, *Restrictions on the retail distribution of unregulated collective investment schemes and close substitutes* (August 2012) and FCA PS13/3. *Restrictions on the retail distribution of unregulated collective investment schemes and close substitutes—Feedback to CP12/19 including final rules* (June 2013).

25 years from the beginning of 1988 to 2013 there have been some six significant regulatory phases for investment firms.

General Principles of Conduct for Investment Firms

When Professor Gower published his seminal report, A *Review of Investor Protection*, in 1984[20] he was explicit in setting out the underlying philosophy behind his proposals. A value judgement had to be made as to the balance to be struck between market freedom and investor protection. In Gower's view the optimum degree of regulation 'should be no greater than is necessary to protect reasonable people from being made fools of'.[21] Furthermore, Gower believed it was necessary to rationalise requirements for authorisation of those providing investment services to ordinary investors and to deal with those who operated outside the resulting framework: 'What is needed is a system which will help the public identify the sheep and which will effectively curb the activities of the goats'.[22] **16.11**

The three pillars of the modern standard of behaviour required of a financial intemediary are the obligations to know your client, to make suitable recommendations, and to provide an adequate explanation of risk.[23] These are the main principles underlying the detailed requirements of the 'Conduct of Business' rules. The principles emerged from Gower's review of investor protection undertaken in the early 1980s. Professor Gower, speaking of the proposed requirements of know your customer, suitability and rules for the protection of clients' assets, together with other proposed conduct of business rules, observed: **16.12**

> Together they should go far to ensure the adequate protection of investors. I do not accept the criticism made in some quarters, that they are excessively 'legalistic' and will prove unduly restrictive. On the contrary, they seem to me to be a practical working-out of the gentlemanly ethics, on which the City has traditionally prided itself (even if all its members have not invariably lived up to them) that you should 'do as you would be done by' and not do anything that you would not want found out.[24]

Information or advice?

In some contexts regulators have utilised rules requiring firms to provide adequate information about financial products to ensure that consumers may make informed choices. However, the success or failure of such rules may depend on the extent to which individual **16.13**

[20] LCB Gower, *Review of Investor Protection: Part I*, Cmnd 9125 (1984) ('Gower'). Prior to the report Professor Gower had issued a discussion paper: LCB Gower, *Review of Investor Protection—A Discussion Document* (January 1982). A Government White Paper followed the first part of Professor Gower's report: Department of Trade and Industry, *Financial Services in the United Kingdom—A new framework for investor protection*, Cmnd 9432 (1985) which to a large extent adopted Professor Gower's recommendations in Part I of his Report. Subsequently, the second part of Professor Gower's Report was published: LCB Gower, *Review of Investor Protection—Part II*, Cmnd 9125 (1985). For an account of the background and the main features of the resulting system see L Gower, 'Big Bang and City Regulation' (1988) 51 MLR 1. Note also the view of Ford and Kay, two economists, having observed that the regulatory structure for the financial industry was designed by lawyers, that 'financial service regulation would benefit from the involvement of fewer lawyers and more economists': C Ford and J Kay, 'Why Regulate Financial Services?' in F Oditah (ed), *The Future for the Global Securities Market—Legal and Regulatory Aspects* (Clarendon Press 1996) 145, 146.

[21] Gower, *Review of Investor Protection: Part I*, para 1.16.

[22] Gower, *Review of Investor Protection: Part I*, para 1.10.

[23] For the American securities law origins of these standards see R Cranston, *Principles of Banking Law* (2nd edn, OUP 2002), pp 198–200, 208–9.

[24] LCB Gower, *Review of Investor Protection—Part II*, Cmnd 9125 (1985), para 4.15.

consumers engage with, often lengthy, boilerplate text. Misleading information is obviously actionable under either common law rules on misrepresentation or the Misrepresentation Act 1967. More intervenionist are regulatory rules governing or requiring firms to provide advice about the financial choices, and imposing a requirement of suitability or appropriateness. In the investment sector a mixture of information or disclosure and advice regulation has been deployed. In describing the Pensions Review in the context of a Professional Indemnity policy case—*J Rothschild Assurance plc v Collyear*[25]—Rix J (as he then was) described four elements of compliant advice:

> The assessment of compliance was to be addressed through four essential tests which reflected the regulatory regime: know your customer and suitability, understanding of risk, adequate information, and misleading statements.

It can be observed that Rix J lists both information-giving and advice provision, but a vexed topic is where the line is drawn between the two.

16.14 Whether a representative or intermediary is under a duty only to provide accurate or adequate information or has a duty to advise as to the suitable course of conduct is sometimes said to be one of the scope of duty in the wake of the speech of Lord Hoffmann in the *South Australia Asset Management Corp v York Montague Ltd* or *SAAMCO* case, concerning negligent valuations of commercial property.[26] That does not take things much further forward in the retail investment context, where the line is between advised sales, where a full suitability regime applies, and so-called 'execution only' transactions, where it is only necessary that any information provided is clear, fair and not misleading. Any suggestion of a personal recommendation as to the appropriate course of conduct is likely to push a particular case into the former category.

Know your customer

16.15 Adequate information is the key to complying with the exacting standards required by the modern law for a financial adviser. There are two distinct aspects to this. The first is encapsulated in the 'know your customer' principle. The customer's personal and financial circumstances, needs, and priorities have to be ascertained and assessed. The extent of this investigation will depend on the task assumed. Furthermore, in appropriate cases the customer's attitude to risk may have to be evaluated.

Suitability

16.16 The second dimension to the information requirements on a financial adviser is implicit in suitability: the adviser must investigate and evaluate the products and other financial arrangements available on the market. The range of providers and products may be circumscribed by the scope of business undertaken by a particular intermediary or provider. Obviously it will be much wider in the case of an independent as opposed to a tied or multi-tied intermediary. Nevertheless, an understanding of the available options is a sine qua non of compliant financial advice. The assessment of a suitable transaction or the identification of

[25] [1999] 1 Lloyd's Rep PN 6.

[26] *South Australia Asset Management Corp v York Montague Ltd ('SAAMCO')* [1997] AC 191. Compare the conclusion of the House of Lords in *Aneco Reinsurance Underwriting Ltd v Johnson & Higgins Ltd* [2001] UKHL 51, [2002] 1 Lloyd's Rep 157, [2001] 2 All ER (Comm) 929, [2002] PNLR 8 that in a particular transaction a reinsurance broker owed a duty to advise on whether to undertake a particular transaction, rather than a mere duty to provide information, and its impact on the remedy.

a suitable product is built on the foundations of the information obtained about both the customer and the marketplace.

Best advice

In respect of certain investment products (described as 'packaged products') a separate obligation of 'best advice' was developed. This has its roots in the concept of suitability, but is distinct. Cranston says of 'best advice' that: 'this involves a prior, conscientious search for available services and then, in any particular transaction, recommending the service which is believed to be the best, or at least as good, as any other available, for that customer'.[27] However the 'best advice' appellation was inappropriate in the context of advice proffered by tied advisers of particular product providers or by multi-tied agents, who do not survey the whole of the market. Such advisers are limited to considering the products of one firm or marketing group, or a limited number of providers. In that context the superlative 'best' was necessarily confined to the available products of that particular firm or firms. Perhaps recognising this, the FSA in the implementation of the COB regime preserved the substance of the 'best advice' rules of its predecessor regulators, but no longer described them by that name. Furthermore, the rules were more clearly a subset of the suitability principle. In the wake of the implementation of MiFID the 'best advice' regime was eventually abandoned. **16.17**

Customer's understanding of risk

At bottom the most appropriate advice concerning any proposed financial transaction is that which identifies and explains the risks attending it.[28] The requirement to ensure that the customer has an adequate understanding of the risks involved is a distinct requirement to the firm's investigation into the customer's appetite for, or aversion to, risk pursuant to the 'know your customer' and 'suitability' rules. An appropriate approach to risk might deal with a number of factors which can be separated out: **16.18**

- Risk to capital: is there a risk that the original sum deposited or invested will not be returned in full? If so, what is the extent of that risk? A return of capital is usually the hallmark of a deposit, but endowment policies and some bond products promise the preservation of initial capital.
- Risk in relation to return: how is the return to be generated on the saving or investment? Is this fixed or does it depend upon some person's discretion?
- Insolvency risk: the risk that the product provider or an intermediary may be unable to perform or perform in full.
- Fraud risk: the risk that the product provider or an intermediary may be the perpetrator or the victim of some fraudulent activity which affects their ability to perform.

The first two are usually the focus of financial advice cases. For example, in respect of 'precipice bonds' or 'SCARPS' the concern was often that the risk to capital was not sufficiently highlighted or explained. Similarly, in the wake of the Equitable Life collapse and the subsequent scrutiny of 'with profits' life business, what has been revealed is that the discretionary basis of returns on investment was not always sufficiently highlighted. On occasion the latter two have been important. The Financial Services Compensation Scheme is designed to provide for insolvency risk, which may entail some coverage for fraud risk.

[27] Cranston, (n 23) pp 209–10.
[28] Cranston, (n 23) p 210.

The New Conduct of Business Sourcebook ('COBS')

The hinterland to COBS: previous Conduct of Business regimes

16.19 The introduction of detailed prescriptive rules for the investment sector was a significant element of the reforms launched by the Financial Services Act 1986, and implemented in 1988. Accordingly, 2007 marked the end of the second decade of the investment conduct of business regime. The first phase from 1988 to 1994 was implemented through the rulebooks of the Self-Regulatory Organisations for the retail investment sector, LAUTRO and FIMBRA, albeit the overall regulator was the SIB, the previous incarnation of the FSA, laid down certain minimum standards. From 1994 to 2001 these rulebooks were superseded by that of the merged PIA, but its rules largely replicated those of its predecessors.

16.20 The immediate hinterland of COBS was the FSA's original Conduct of Business Sourcebook ('COB') which applied between 2001 and 2007. COB was more obviously the product of domestic UK concerns, periodically spawning new rules or even chapters to address then current mis-selling crises ('SCARPS') or other regulatory concerns (with profits contracts or stakeholder products). In contrast, COBS is much more obviously the fruit of European-inspired reform (albeit the UK influence on the EU measure is often significant). Where appropriate in discussing COBS, it is helpful to identify points of departure from its predecessor, COB.

What the original FSA COB replaced

16.21 Launched on 1 December 2001, the original FSA Conduct of Business Sourcebook ('COB') replaced miscellaneous provisions, from both legislative and other sources:

(1) the FSA (formerly Securities and Investments Board ('SIB')) rules;
(2) the Investment Management Regulatory Organisation ('IMRO') rules;
(3) the Securities and Futures Authority ('SFA') rules;
(4) the Personal Investment Authority ('PIA') rules (encompassing the adopted rules of PIA's predecessor bodies: the Life Assurance and Unit Trust Regulatory Organisation ('LAUTRO') and the Financial Intermediaries and Brokers Regulatory Association ('FIMBRA'));
(5) the London Code of Conduct—the Bank of England code for principals and broking firms in the wholesale market;
(6) miscellaneous provisions of the Insurance Companies Act 1982, the Banking Act 1987, and the Building Societies Act 1986.[29]

These provisions migrated to COB, and now the equivalent regime is to be found in COBS.

The Markets in Financial Instruments Directive

16.22 The principal motivation of the FSA to revisit and replace COB was to ensure the UK's implementation of the Markets in Financial Instruments Directive ('MiFID').[30] This was one of the most significant measures to emerge from the Financial Services Action Plan

[29] FSA CP 45a, *The Conduct of Business Sourcebook* (February 2000), para 2.11.
[30] FSA CP 05/10, *Reviewing the FSA Handbook—Money Laundering, Approved Persons, Training and Competence and Conduct of Business* (July 2005), chs 1 and 5. See also FSA, *Planning for MiFID* (November 2005).

('FSAP').[31] This directive replaced and extended the Investment Services Directive ('ISD'),[32] implemented in 1995, which was the backdrop to the original COB and its predecessors. Previously Article 11 of the ISD merely required domestic regulators to impose conduct of business rules on incoming firms, but left the detail a matter for domestic implementation. MiFID is far more prescriptive.[33] MiFID had to be implemented by 1 November 2007.[34] European initiatives have not rested there and work is underway on MiFID II.[35]

The EC implementing measures

The principal Markets in Financial Instruments Directive No 2004/39/EC of the European Parliament and Council ('MiFID')[36] is supplemented by 'level 2' implementing measures in accordance with the structure implemented by the FSAP. The secondary measures comprise Commission Regulation (EC) No 1287/2006 ('the MiFID Regulation') and Commission Directive 2006/73/EC ('the MiFID Implementing Directive'). **16.23**

UK implementing legislation

MiFID has required changes to both UK primary and secondary legislation, albeit the changes have all been achieved through the medium of secondary legislation. The main UK domestic legislative measures implementing MiFID are:[37] **16.24**

- the Financial Services and Markets Act 2000 (Regulated Activities) (Amendment No 3) Order 2006;[38]
- the Financial Services and Markets Act 2000 (Markets in Financial Instruments) Regulations 2007;[39]
- the Financial Services and Markets Act 2000 (Markets in Financial Instruments) (Modification of Powers) Regulations 2006;[40]
- the Financial Services and Markets Act 2000 (Appointed Representatives) (Amendment) Regulations 2006;[41]
- the Financial Services and Markets Act 2000 (Exemption) (Amendment) Order 2007.[42]

FSA implementation

The FSA implemented MiFID by extensive revision to its Handbook, most importantly the complete deletion of the original COB and its replacement by COBS. (The additional 'S' is important for accurate citation). These changes came into force on 1 November 2007, implemented by the FSA, The Conduct of Business Sourcebook Instrument 2007.[43] Other changes affect the structure of the remainder of the Handbook and the location of the **16.25**

---

31 See Chapter 3.
32 Directive 93/22/EEC.
33 For an overall cost–benefit analysis see FSA, *The overall impact of MiFID* (November 2006).
34 Directive 2006/31/EC: extending the time limit for the implementation of MiFID.
35 See chapter 3 on European Financial Services, at paras 3.119–3.122.
36 Directive 2004/39/EC.
37 See PERG 13 Annex 4.
38 SI 2006/3384, including amending the RAO to add a new regulated activity of operating a multilateral trading facility (art 25D).
39 SI 2007/126.
40 SI 2006/2975.
41 SI 2006/3414.
42 SI 2007/125. There is also a separate 'Explanatory Memorandum' in relation to SI 2007/126, SI 2006/3384, SI 2006/2975, SI 2006/3414, SI 2007/125, and the other MiFID implementing measures.
43 See also FSA, Glossary (Conduct of Business and Other Sourcebooks) Instrument 2007.

material. For example, the material on conflicts of interest[44] migrated to SYSC.[45] Conversely ECO is no longer a separate handbook, but is integrated in COBS. The Inter-professional Conduct Code (MAR 3) was also deleted from the FSA Handbook in the wake of MiFID.[46] PERG 13 contains detailed guidance on the scope and application of MiFID with regard to firms, services, and products.

The consultation process

16.26 Much ink was spilt on the consultation process leading up to the FSA's implementation of MiFID. An attempt was made to improve both the navigability and overall effectiveness of the regime. The FSA insisted that the predecessor COB rules had improved standards of consumer protection, but conceded that 'mis-selling and mis-buying still happen too often'.[47]

16.27 The main consultation documents were:

- FSA DP06/3, *Implementing MiFID's best execution requirements* (May 2006) ('FSA DP06/3');
- FSA CP06/14, *Implementing MiFID for Firms and Markets* (July 2006) ('FSA CP06/14');[48]
- FSA CP06/19, *Reforming Conduct of Business Regulation (including proposals for implementing relevant provisions of the Markets in Financial Instruments Directive, and related changes in SYSC, DISP, TC, SUP and other Handbook modules)* (October 2006) ('FSA CP06/19');
- FSA CP06/20, *Financial promotion and other communications (Including draft Handbook text for NEWCOB 4 and 5)* (October 2006) ('FSA CP06/20').[49]

16.28 The principal policy statement documents were:

- FSA PS07/2, *Implementing the Markets in Financial Instruments Directive (MiFID)—Feedback on: CP06/14—Implementing MiFID for Firms and Markets (July 2006); CP06/19—Reforming Conduct of Business Regulation (October 2006) [and] Financial promotion and other communications (October 2006)* (January 2007) ('FSA PS07/2');
- FSA PS07/6, *Reforming Conduct of Business Regulation—Feedback on CP06/19—Reforming Conduct of Business Regulation (October 2006) and Financial promotion and other communications (October 2006)* (May 2007) ('FSA PS07/6');
- FSA PS07/14, *Reforming Conduct of Business Regulation—Final feedback on CP06/19* (July 2007) ('FSA PS07/14');
- FSA PS07/15, *Best Execution—Feedback on DP06/3 and CP06/19 (part)* (August 2007) ('FSA PS07/15').[50]

Method of implementation: 'intelligent copy-out'

16.29 Given the need to implement EU requirements accurately the FSA characterised its approach as one based on 'intelligent copy-out' of the text of the relevant directives. This was part of

44 Previously in COB 7.1.

45 SYSC 10.

46 See FSA CP06/19, paras 7.102–7.108; FSA PS07/6, paras 7.9–7.12.

47 FSA CP06/19, para 2.6.

48 See also FSA, *Implementing MiFID's Client Categorisation requirements* (August 2006), which is not strictly a consultation paper.

49 See also FSA CP07/9, *Conduct of Business regime: non-MiFID deferred matters (including proposals for Telephone Recording)* (May 2007).

50 See also for future development: FSA DP07/1, *A Review of Retail Distribution* (June 2007), launching the FSA's Retail Distribution Review ('RDR').

the FSA's approach to financial services directives generally, and it now clearly labels all rules which are derived from EU measures.[51] Some found the modified phrase 'unintelligent cop-out' irresistible, but it is difficult to see what wriggle room the FSA had in many instances, especially in the light of the approach of the European Commission and the Court of Justice to implementation of Directives.

It was also intended that COBS should be a significant step in the FSA's intended move towards more principles-based regulation and higher-level rules. This included less reliance on detailed guidance and, in the opinion of the FSA, the deletion of material it considered to be 'redundant, superfluous or obselete'.[52] **16.30**

Effect of the 'cut-over' from FSA to FCA

In substance the 'legal cutover' from FSA to FCA on 1 April 2013 has had little or no substantive impact on COBS, save that it now forms a component of the FCA Handbook,[53] and is unchanged, unsurprisingly as most of its content is intended to implement the 'maximum harmonisation' MiFID requirements. **16.31**

Status of FCA rules in COBS: rights of action and discipline.

Broadly speaking the FCA Handbook is made up of three main types of provisions: rules (including high-level principles); evidential provisions; and guidance. FCA rules are made under delegated powers in FSMA 2000. Accordingly, they are statutory rules, as is evidenced by the fact that they are potentially actionable by a private person pursuant to section 138D of FSMA 2000 (as substituted by FSA 2012, section 24)[54] or may be the basis for disciplinary action by the FCA against firms under sections 205 or 206, or for other measures under FSMA 2000. **16.32**

Prior to the implementation of COB in 2001 the FSA decided that a right of action should be available to a private person in respect of *any* rule within it.[55] This was despite doubts expressed by some respondents to the consultation exercise about the utility of private claims, given the comparative rarity of actions brought under section 62 of the Financial Services Act 1986.[56] However, despite the claim for breach of statutory duty only appearing in a limited number of reported cases, the existence of the statutory claim was the basis of internal complaints handling and ombudsman redress in millions of cases. **16.33**

The FSA continued the same policy in the wake of MiFID and gave the right to bring an action for breach of statutory duty to private persons for any breach of any of the rules in COBS.[57] **16.34**

FCA rules must (ultimately) be construed by reference to ordinary principles of statutory construction. However, given that many of the rules implement EU measures, and that each **16.35**

[51] FSA CP06/19, paras 1.19 and 2.11.

[52] FSA PS07/6, para 1.9.

[53] Chapters 1, 20, and 21 of COBS also form part of the Prudential Regulation Authority ('PRA') Handbook.

[54] Formerly FSMA, section 150, replacing sections 62 and 62A of the 1986 Act. However, the high-level principles can only form the basis for disciplinary action, and not private causes of action.

[55] For the background see FSA CP45a, *The Conduct of Business Sourcebook* (February 2000) ('FSA CP45a'), para 4.9; and FSA PS45, *Conduct of Business Sourcebook—Feedback on consultation and 'final text' and consultation on supplementary rules* (February 2001) ('FSA PS45'), para 3.46.

[56] FSA PS45, para 3.47.

[57] COBS sch 5. See FSA CP07/9, *Conduct of Business regime: non-MiFID deferred matters (including proposals for Telephone Recording)* (May 2007), ch 18.

rule now explicitly cites the relevant article of the relevant measure, it is likely that the courts may go straight to the relevant Directive should any point of construction arise.

FCA requirements which go beyond MiFID

16.36 The FSA decided to retain a number of existing conduct of business rules which apply to MiFID firms which go beyond the requirements of MiFID. Such additional requirements can only be retained or imposed in 'exceptional cases' where they are 'objectively justified and proportionate to address specific risks to investor protection or to market integrity' which are not addressed by the MiFID regime. Such measures must also satisfy one of two conditions: (a) it addresses specific risks arising out of the market structure of the Member State; or (b) the measure addresses risks which emerge or become evident after MiFID applies, and is not addressed by other EC measures.[58] Such measures must be notified and justified to the European Commission under Article 4 of the MiFID Implementing Directive.[59] Such national additional requirements raise the spectre of 'super-equivalence'[60] (or some call it 'gold-plating' of regulation).

16.37 The measures which the FSA notified to the EU Commission and which the latter body has agreed are consistent with the criteria in Article 4 of the MiFID Implementing Directive included:

- the rules governing the way firms can describe the scope of their advice (in the wake of depolarisation) and the conditions that have to be met before an adviser can describe himself as 'independent';
- the provision of a simplified prospectus or key features document;
- the disclosure of actual commission or equivalent in the sale of packaged products;
- the use of dealing commission.[61]

Other notifications were withdrawn, either because the proposal was abandoned or because it was agreed that notification is not necessary because the measures are only an elaboration of MiFID, and not in addition to it.[62]

The contents of COBS

16.38 In July 2005, the FSA first published its outline plan for the reform of the investment conduct of business regime.[63] The proposed structure was further refined during the consultation process.[64] The final chapter structure which is continued in the FCA Handbook comprises:

1. Application
2. Conduct of business obligations
3. Client categorisation
4. Communicating with clients, including financial promotion
5. Distance communications
6. Information about the firm, its services and remuneration

---

[58] MiFID Implementing Directive, (Commission Directive 2006/73/EC), art 4(1).
[59] MiFID Implementing Directive, (Commission Directive 2006/73/EC), art 4(3).
[60] FSA CP06/19, paras 2.13–2.16.
[61] FSA CP06/19, para 2.14; FSA PS 07/14, paras 1.5–1.13.
[62] FSA PS07/14, paras 1.9.
[63] FSA CP05/10, *Reviewing the FSA Handbook—Money Laundering, Approved Persons, Training and Competence and Conduct of Business* (July 2005), chs 1 and 5; and Annex 5 which contained the proposed new structure for COBS (or NEWCOB as it was often described in the consultation process).
[64] FSA CP06/19, chapter 3 and Table 2: Structure of NEWCOB; FSA PS07/6, para 4.6 and Table: Structure of NEWCOB.

7. Insurance mediation
8. Client agreements
9. Suitability (including basic advice)
10. Appropriateness (for non-advised services)
11. Dealing and managing
12. Investment research
13. Preparing product information
14. Providing product information to clients
15. Cancellation
16. Reporting information to clients
17. Claims handling for long-term care insurance
18. Specialist regimes
19. Pensions: supplementary provisions
20. With-profits
21. Permitted links for long-term insurance business
22. Transitional Provisions and Schedules

Scope and application

Scope

The predecessor rulebook COB *prima facie* applied to all regulated activities and, to some extent to non-regulated activities undertaken by firms. However, in reality most of the provisions were expressly targeted at a subset of regulated activities which fall within the definition of 'designated investment business'. Briefly stated, the Conduct of Business rules were generally not applicable to deposit, mortgage, and general insurance business.[65] **16.39**

In its first consultation on the original COB the FSA announced that it intended that generally 'designated investment business equated with what was previously "investment business" for the purposes of the Financial Services Act 1986'.[66] It therefore aimed to exclude deposit-taking, general insurance, and pure protection policies.[67] 'Designated investment' and 'designated investment business' were defined in detail in the Handbook Glossary by reference to regulated investments and regulated activities in the Financial Services and Markets Act 2000 (Regulated Activities) Order ('RAO 2001') which were carried on by way of business.[68] **16.40**

These definitions continue to be important in the post-MiFID world of COBS, as they still provide the definition for the application of the FCA's conduct of business regime for investment firms, which often has a wider scope than required by MiFID. The scope of MiFID is narrower than the FCA's concept of 'designated investment business'. The Handbook Glossary continues to define 'designated investments' and 'designated investment business' by reference to the RAO. These concepts were the traditional territory of the FSA's COB **16.41**

[65] BCOBS, MCOB, and ICOBS are the components concerned with deposit-taking, mortgages, and general insurance respectively.

[66] FSA CP45a, *The Conduct of Business Rules* (February 2000) ('FSA CP45a'), para 2.10.

[67] For definitions of 'deposit', 'deposit-taking firm', 'general insurance contract', and 'pure protection contract' see the *Handbook* Glossary.

[68] *Handbook* Glossary. For the background see FSA PS45, *Conduct of Business Sourcebook—Feedback on consultation and 'final text' and consultation on supplementary rules* (February 2001) (Interim glossary for COB); FSA CP45a, para 2.9.

regime, and often provide the scope of COBS. In addition, the Handbook Glossary now also defines 'MiFID business', and 'equivalent third country business'.

16.42 'MiFID business' is defined by reference to 'investment services and activities' and 'ancillary services'. The former are defined by reference to MiFID itself: any of the services and activities listed in Section A of Annex I to MiFID relating to any financial instrument, that is:

(a) reception and transmission of orders in relation to one or more financial instruments;
(b) execution of orders on behalf of clients;
(c) dealing on own account;
(d) portfolio management;
(e) the making of a personal recommendation;
(f) underwriting of financial instruments and/or placing of financial instruments on a firm commitment basis;
(g) placing of financial instruments without a firm commitment basis;
(h) operation of multilateral trading facilities.[69]

'Ancillary services' are also defined by reference to the list in the Directive.[70]

16.43 Broadly speaking the FSA generally found it easier to apply the MiFID requirements to 'designated investment business', whether it is MiFID-business or not. However, there are exceptions. Nevertheless, in many cases MiFID-inspired rules are being applied to non-MiFID business.

Application

16.44 COBS 1 contains the rules explaining which rules apply to which firms.[71] The basic rule applies COBS to firms carrying out specified activites from an establishment maintained by it or its appointed representative in the UK. The activities are:

(a) accepting deposits;
(b) designated investment business;
(c) long-term insurance business in relation to life policies.

It also extends to activities connected with them.[72] Therefore, ancillary non-MiFID business may be caught.

16.45 The basic rule is then substantially modified by a detailed table.[73] This limits the scope of certain COBS obligations where the business is MiFID or equivalent third party business with an eligible counterparty.[74] However, the modification does not extend to the suitability regime in COBS 9.[75]

Territorial application

16.46 COBS applies to UK-authorised firms operating in the UK and throughout the EEA in accordance with the principle of home-state regulation. The rule of basic application is

[69] *Handbook* Glossary: MiFID art 4(1) and (2) and the list in Annex I section A.
[70] MiFID Annex I s B.
[71] For the background see FSA CP06/19, ch 5; FSA PS07/6, ch 5.
[72] COBS 1.1.1R.
[73] COBS 1.1.2R and COBS 1 Annex 1 R.
[74] COBS 1 Annex 1 R, Part 1.
[75] This omission is intentional: FSA PS07/6, para 5.10.

further modified so that its territorial scope is compatible with European law.[76] Therefore, the general principle of home-state regulation implemented by MiFID, the Distance Marketing of Consumer Financial Services Directive,[77] Electronic Commerce Directive,[78] and other EU measures is respected, and detailed guidance is provided on this.[79] COBS also applies to the branches of financial services providers from so-called 'third countries', that is non-UK or non-EEA firms, which are operating in the UK.[80]

General conduct of business obligations

COBS 2 contains rules which apply to all designated investment business, comprising general requirements, inducements, and provision of services through another firm.[81] **16.47**

The client's best interests rule

A new MiFID-inspired rule requires that a firm must act 'honestly, fairly and professionally in accordance with the best interests of its client'. This applies to all retail clients and all clients engaged in MiFID or equivalent third country business.[82] Unlike the similar FCA Principle 6 (treating customers fairly), this rule is actionable by private persons in accordance with section 138D of FSMA 2000 (as substituted by FSA 2012, section 24).[83] **16.48**

Exclusion of liability

In the original version of the Handbook, COB 2.5 prevented an authorised person from excluding or limiting any duty or liability it has to customers (private, intermediate, and in relation to distance contracts, retail) which it has under the regulatory system.[84] In relation to private customers, firms were required not to attempt to exclude any other duty or liability 'unless it is reasonable to do so'.[85] In the process of implementing MiFID, initially the FSA proposed removing the rules formerly in COB 2.5,[86] but after consultation the FSA retained a more limited requirement that in relation to designated investment business a firm must not in a communication to a client seek to exclude or restrict any obligation imposed under the regulatory system.[87] Guidance also refers to the general legal restrictions on other duties or liabilities which would otherwise arise.[88] The inability of firms to 'contract out' of the regulatory rules in COBS is an important contrast with the common law rules which judges may be more ready to find are excluded by boilerplate provisions.[89] **16.49**

76 COBS 1 Annex 1 R, Part 2, para 1.1R. This rule overrides every rule in COBS.
77 2002/65/EC.
78 2000/31/EC.
79 COBS 1 Annex 1 R, Part 3. See also PERG 13.
80 FSA CP06/19, para 1.1.5.
81 For the background see FSA CP06/19, ch 6; FSA PS07/6, ch 6; FSA PS07/14, ch 2.
82 COBS 2.1.1R. MiFID art 19(1).
83 Compare FSA PS07/6, para 6.4.
84 COB 2.5.3R.
85 COB 2.5.3R, in effect applying a regime akin to the Unfair Contract Terms Act 1977.
86 FSA CP06/19, paras 6.55–6.67.
87 COBS 2.1.2R. See FSA PS07/6, para 6.7.
88 COBS 2.1.3G, citing the Unfair Terms in Consumer Contracts Regulations 1999.
89 Exemplified by *Springwell Navigation Corp v JP Morgan Chase Bank* [2010] EWCA Civ 1212; affg [2008] EWHC 1186 (Comm); [2008] EWHC 1793 (Comm) (Gloster J). For criticism see G McMeel, 'Documentary fundamentalism in the Senior Courts: the myth of contractual estoppel' [2011] *Lloyd's Maritime and Commercial Law Quarterly* 185.

Inducements

16.50 COBS 2.3 contains a more stringent regime on inducements and indirect benefits than any previous regulatory regime. It is based on an 'intelligent copy-out' of the relevant MiFID provision. The net result is a full disclosure of third-party commission regime. It is also now necessary that any fee, commission, or non-monetary benefit where this is paid or provided to or by a third party 'must be designed to enhance the quality of the relevant service to the client'.[90] In accordance with guidance from the Committee of European Securities Regulators ('CESR') a firm will be able to comply with its obligations on inducements so long as it discloses the essential arrangements relating to any fee, commission, or non-monetary benefit in summary form and undertakes to give further disclosure on request, and honours that undertaking.[91] The regime also extends to packaged products which fall outside the scope of MiFID.[92] In practice these requirements are now superseded by the more stringent requirements following the implementation of the Retail Distribution Review by COBS 6.1A to 6.1D.[93]

Agent as client

16.51 Previously under COB[94] an investment firm which received instructions from another firm on behalf of a client was entitled to treat the firm as the client and therefore not be subject to the (probably more stringent) rules affecting a deal with the underlying client. A corresponding rule, consistent with MiFID, is now to found in COBS.[95]

Client categorisation

16.52 One of the most significant changes from the compliance perspective is COBS 3 which contains the MiFID-based regime for classification of clients,[96] abandoning the FSA's own somewhat complicated three-category regime of COB (private customer, intermediate customer, market counterparty).[97]

16.53 The two principal categories of client under MiFID are retail client and professional client. In addition, in some contexts a third category of 'eligible counterparty' ('ECP') is recognised. The categories are intended to target different levels of regulatory protection. Clients are entitled to 'step up' or 'step down' in order to obtain additional or less stringent protection. Unlike the regime in COB, under MiFID firms must notify clients of this ability and the consequences of so acting.[98] Overall, the FSA anticipated that there would be more persons classified as 'retail clients' under COBS than there were persons labelled 'private customers' under COB.[99]

---

90 MiFID Implementing Directive, art 26(b)(ii), fleshing out MiFID art 19(1).

91 COBS 2.3.1R and 2.3.2R. See FSA PS07/14, ch 2.

92 FSA PS07/14, para 2.6. The remainder of COBS 2.3 contains detailed guidance and evidential provisions in the context of inducements and packaged products.

93 COBS 2.3.6A G. For discussion see para 16.130.

94 COB 4.1.5R.

95 COBS 2.4.3R. See MiFID art 20.

96 For the background see FSA, *Implementing MiFID's Client Categorisation requirements* (August 2006); FSA CP06/19, ch 7; FSA PS07/6, ch 7.

97 Previously COB 4.1.

98 COBS 3.3.1R.

99 FSA, *Implementing MiFID's Client Categorisation requirements* (August 2006), para 1.09.

Rules in COBS 3.2 define who is the client, and deal with issues of trusteeship and agency. A 'retail client' is defined negatively as one who is neither a professional client nor an eligible counterparty.[100] The definition of 'professional client' is elaborate, divides into 'per se professional clients' and 'elective professional clients', and is based on the EU measures. It includes entities required to be authorised in the financial market and other large undertakings.[101] A similarly elaborate definition based on MiFID is provided for 'eligible counterparty'.[102] COBS 3.7 makes provision for 'stepping up' or providing clients with a higher degree of protection than their usual classification. **16.54**

Compare: 'eligible complainants' to the Ombudsman

Given that most retail investment disputes are likely to be resolved by the Financial Ombudsman Service ('FOS') it is useful to compare who is entitled to complain to the FOS. Since 1 December 2001 the FOS has had the power within the scope of its jurisdiction under FSMA 2000 to make awards based on what is 'fair and reasonable in all the circumstances of the case'[103] of up to £150,000 (originally £100,000). In the wake of the implementation of the Payment Services Directive the FSA changed the relevant rules in DISP for all categories of regulated activities so as to embrace European law definitions. Accordingly 'eligible complainants' to the FOS now embrace 'consumers' (previously any 'private individual'), 'micro-enterprises', and small charities with an annual income of less than £1 million.[104] 'Consumer' as defined in the FCA Handbook Glossary means any natural person acting for purposes outside his trade, business or profession, and is accordingly narrower than the previous test of 'private individual'.[105] A 'micro-enterprise' is based on the definition in the European Commission's Recommendation of 2003 defining micro-, small- and medium-sized businesses.[106] It covers persons irrespective of legal form (natural persons, limited companies, partnerships) which both employ fewer than 10 persons and has a turnover or annual balance sheet not exceeding €2 million.[107] **16.55**

Compare: 'private person' under FSMA 2000

It is also necessary to contrast the FCA rules on client categorisation with the definition of a 'private person' under section 138D of FSMA 2000 (as substituted by FSA 2012, section 24) for the purpose of bringing a claim for breach of statutory duty, as amplified by the Financial Services and Markets Act 2000 (Rights of Action) Regulations 2001, SI 2001/2256. Regulation 3(1) provides: **16.56**

> In these Regulations, 'private person' means—(a) any individual, unless he suffers the loss in question in the course of carrying on—(i) any regulated activity; or (ii) any activity which would be a regulated activity apart from any exclusion made by Article 72 of the Regulated Activities Order (overseas persons); and (b) any person who is not an individual, unless he suffers the loss in question in the course of carrying on business of any kind; but does not include a government, a local authority (in the United Kingdom or elsewhere) or an international organisation.

---

100 COBS 3.4.1R.

101 COBS 3.5.1R. MiFID, Annex II.

102 COBS 3.6.1R. MiFID, art 24.

103 FSMA 2000, s 228(2); DISP 3.8.1R(1). For the FOS see Chapter 7.

104 DISP 2.7.3R. See FSA and FOS PS09/4, *Implementation of the Payment Services Directive—changes to the FSA Handbook [-] Feedback on CP08/14 and final rules* (March 2009), para 2.4.

105 *Handbook* Glossary (as from 1 November 2009); PSD art 4(11).

106 2003/361/EC.

107 *Handbook* Glossary (as from 1 November 2009); PSD art 4(26). See also the definition of 'Micro-enterprise recommendation' and art 1 and art 2(1) and (3) of the Annex to that Recommendation: 2003/361/EC.

Accordingly individuals who are not engaged in regulated activities are private persons. In contrast, the courts have proved reluctant to permit corporate bodies entering into investments such as interest rate swap products to bring themselves within the definition of 'private person' under those regulations.[108]

Communication with clients and financial promotion

16.57 COBS 4 contains the rules on client communication and on financial promotion.[109] The chapter applies generally to firms communicating with or communicating or approving a financial promotion in connection with designated investment business with a retail client.[110]

Territorial scope

16.58 The territorial scope of COBS 4 is determined in accordance with the general application rule.[111] In addition, it applies generally to the communication of a financial promotion to a person inside the UK and (subject to some qualifications) the communication of a cold call to a person outside the UK.[112] A 'cold call' according to the *Handbook* Glossary is an unsolicited real-time communication as defined in Article 8 of FPO 2005.

The reference to the 'general application rule' ensures COBS 4 is modified in line with the 'home State' principle of the EU law.

The fair, clear, and not misleading rule

16.59 A very general rule provides a 'firm must ensure that a communication or financial promotion is fair, clear and not misleading'.[113] This differs from the old COB rule on 'clear, fair and not misleading' communications[114] not just in the inversion of the first two adjectives, but also, more importantly, in the move to a strict liability standard, rather than the 'reasonable steps' required by the previous regime. The FSA has acknowledged that this imposes a higher standard and could have an impact on firms in that, whilst FSA Principle 7 could always have been the basis of disciplinary action, it was not actionable by private persons. In contrast, the new strict COBS rule will be actionable in accordance with the policy decision to apply section 138D of FSMA 2000 (formerly section 150 of FSMA 2000, as substituted by FSA 2012) to all rules in COBS.[115]

Financial promotions

16.60 The statutory background to COBS 4 is the basic financial promotion restriction in section 21 of FSMA 2000 and the various exemptions found in the Financial Services and Markets Act 2000 (Financial Promotion) Order 2005 (the 'Financial Promotion Order' or

[108] See *Titan Steel Wheels Ltd v Royal Bank of Scotland* [2010] EWHC 211 (Comm), [2010] 2 Lloyd's Rep 92, paras [44–76] (David Steel J); *Camerata Property Inc v Credit Suisse Securities (Europe) Ltd* [2012] EWHC 7 (Comm), paras [89–98] (Flaux J) and the Scottish case of *Grant Estates Ltd v Royal Bank of Scotland* [2012] CSOH 133, paras [41–62] (Lord Hodge; Outer House, Court of Session).

[109] For the background see FSA CP06/20; FSA PS07/6, ch 26.

[110] COBS 4.1.1R. There are exceptions for qualifying credits, certain home finance schemes, and unregulated collective investment schemes.

[111] The 'general application rule' is defined in the *Handbook* Glossary. COBS 1.1.1R and COBS 1.1.2R.

[112] COBS 4.1.8R.

[113] COBS 4.2.1R. Exclusions include 'non-retail communications' which are directed at recipients who are professional clients or ECPs. See also MiFID art 19(2).

[114] Previously COB 2.1.

[115] FSA, PS07/6, paras 26.9 and 26.10.

'FPO 2005').[116] In this context, where we are concerned with regulated firms dealing with the retail sector the relevant rules to be complied with are to be found in COBS 4. Failure to comply with the regime may expose an authorised firm to private action or disciplinary sanction.

The regulators' approach to financial promotions[117]

The FSA issued various documents on the financial promotion regime for regulated firms and increasingly focused on this issue after N2.[118] Given the perceived role of misleading financial promotions in mis-selling cases and the potential for consumer detriment, the FSA decided in 2004 to increase the resources allocated to financial promotions.[119] Accordingly, it created a specialist Financial Promotions department in April 2004, with about 30 staff.[120] Overall, the FSA's approach to this topic formed part of its overall retail strategy of 'Treating Customers Fairly' ('TCF'), based on FSA Principle 6[121] and FSA Principle 7.[122] The FCA will continue and develop this theme with the benefit of new powers in FSMA (inserted by FSA 2012 section 24), in sections 137R and 137S, including the power to direct firms to withdraw or refrain from approving promotions which do not comply with the financial promotion regime. **16.61**

General COBS Rules on financial promotions

Financial promotions should be clearly identifiable as such.[123] The basic rule in COBS 4.5 for investment firms dealing with retail clients is that: **16.62**

(a) information must include the name of the firm;
(b) information should be accurate, and in particular should not emphasise the benefits of any service or product without giving a fair and prominent indication of relevant risks;
(c) the information is understandable by the average member of the target audience;
(d) the information should not disguise, diminish, or obscure important items, statements, or warnings.[124]

Further rules copy out the MiFID Implementing Directive's rules on comparative information,[125] the requirement that any reference to the fiscal implications of any investment must carry a warning that tax rules may change,[126] and requiring consistency in communications.[127]

[116] Financial Services and Markets Act 2000 (Financial Promotion) Order 2005, SI 2005/1529 ('FPO 2005') came into force on 1 July 2005. It supersedes the original Financial Services and Markets Act 2000 (Financial Promotion) Order 2001, SI 2001/1335 ('FPO 2001'), (as amended by eight prior instruments). FPO revokes and re-enacts FPO 2001, with some further amendments. It preserves the original numbering. For the background to FPO 2001 see HM Treasury, *Financial Promotion: Third Consultation Document*; *Financial Promotion of Collective Investment Schemes—First Consultation* (October 2000).

[117] See FSA, *Financial Promotions: taking stock and moving forward* (February 2005).

[118] FSA, *The FSA's regulatory approach to financial promotions* (April 2002).

[119] FSA, *Business Plan 2004/5* (2004), 23.

[120] FSA, *Financial Promotions: taking stock and moving forward* (February 2005), 5.

[121] ibid, 3. From the second half of 2005 the FSA issued quarterly bulletins for investment firms (subject to COB 3).

[122] FSA, *Financial Promotions: Progress update and future direction* (August 2006), 4.

[123] COBS 4.3.1R, with exceptions including 'image advertising'. MiFID art 19(2), second sentence.

[124] COBS 4.5.2R. MiFID Implementing Directive, art 27(2), developing MiFID, art 19(1).

[125] COBS 4.5.6R. MiFID Implementing Directive, art 27(3), developing MiFID, art 19(1).

[126] COBS 4.5.7R. MiFID Implementing Directive, art 27(7), developing MiFID, art 19(1).

[127] COBS 4.5.8R. MiFID Implementing Directive, art 29(7), developing MiFID, art 19(3).

Past, simulated past, and future performance

16.63 COBS 4.6 contains the rules on past performance, simulated past, and future performance. The basic rule on past performance requires that such information is not the most prominent feature of the communication, is based on five year's previous performance (where available or the whole period if shorter), and must contain a prominent warning, in the familiar terms, that it is not a reliable indicator of future results.[128] Further detailed guidance carries over some old FSA material for particular products.[129] Further rules provide for simulated past[130] and future[131] performance.

Direct offer financial promotions

16.64 Provision is made as to which of the client communication rules must be observed in the case of direct offer financial promotions to retail clients.[132]

Cold calling

16.65 Since the introduction of the Financial Services Act 1986 the practice of unsolicited communications or 'cold-calling' retail customers has been the subject of a general prohibition. The basic provision in COB was that unsolicited real-time financial promotions were prohibited.[133]

16.66 The restrictions on 'cold calling' retail clients and other communications which are not in writing are now to be found in COBS 4.8.[134]

Principal conduct of business rules for retail firms

Distance communications

16.67 COBS 5 now consolidates the conduct of business regime arising out of the Distance Marketing of Consumer Financial Services Directive[135] and the Electronic Commerce Directive,[136] replacing rules previously found in COB and in the separate ECO sourcebook, the latter of which has now been deleted.[137]

Information about the firm, its services, and remuneration

16.68 The detailed disclosure regime concerning provision of information by firms is to be found in COBS 6.[138]

16.69 Article 19(3) of MiFID requires appropriate information to be provided in appropriate form about an investment firm and its services, and its costs and charges. COBS 6.1 contains the MiFID-inspired rules in detail which a firm must provide before conducting business, including rules where the firm undertakes the activity of safeguarding client assets.[139]

---

[128] COBS 4.6.2R. MiFID Implementing Directive, art 27(4), developing MiFID, art 19(1).
[129] COBS 4.6.3G–4.6.5G.
[130] COBS 4.6.6R. MiFID Implementing Directive, art 27(5), developing MiFID, art 19(1).
[131] COBS 4.6.7R. MiFID Implementing Directive, art 27(6), developing MiFID, art 19(1).
[132] COBS 4.7.1R.
[133] COB 3.10.3R.
[134] COBS 4.8.1R and COBS 4.8.3R.
[135] 2002/65/EC. See COBS 5.1.1R–5.1.17R and COBS 5 Annex 1R and Annex 2R.
[136] 2000/31/EC. See COBS 5.2.1R–5.2.9R.
[137] For the background see FSA CP06/20 ch 10; FSA PS07/6, ch 8.
[138] For the background see FSA CP06/20 ch 11; FSA PS07/6, ch 9; FSA PS07/14, ch 3.
[139] COBS 6.1.1R–6.1.17G. MiFID Implementing Directive, arts 29–32, developing MiFID, art 19(3).

Of particular interest in the COBS 6.1 is the rule requiring the firm to disclose to retail clients the total price to be paid by the client in respect of an investment or service, including all related fees, commissions, charges, and expenses.[140] The general rule on the timing of such disclosure is that it must be disclosed in good time before the firm starts to render the service. Only in cases of services effected by distance communication at the request of the client may such information information be delayed until immediately after starting to perform, but only where the firm is unable to comply because of those circumstances.[141] **16.70**

COBS 6.2 contains the rules introduced in the wake of depolarisation, including the continuing requirement for firms to disclose the breadth of the firm's ability to give personal recommendations, whether from the whole of the market, limited to several product providers, or limited to one product provider. This was one of the main points on which the FSA felt it necessary to notify the European Commission under Article 4 of the MiFID Implementing Directive that it was going beyond the scope of EU measures.[142] **16.71**

The rules apply to personal recommendations to retail clients to buy a packaged product.[143] A firm cannot hold itself out as a whole of market adviser unless it provides personal recommendations on all types of personal pension schemes, including SIPPs.[144] A firm cannot hold itself as 'independent' unless it provides personal recommendations to the client on packaged products from the whole of the market *and* offers the client the option of fee-based advice.[145] **16.72**

COBS 6.3 and 6.4 provide further detailed rules for disclosure by firms in relation to its services, fees, and commissions in respect of packaged products. Despite originally proposing to retain the two principal documents implementing its disclosure regime—the 'Menu' and the 'Initial Disclosure Document' ('IDD')—introduced in the wake of depolarisation,[146] the FSA ultimately decided to give firms the option as to how to comply with the MiFID-based information rules. The Menu and the IDD continue in the form of guidance as a safe harbour, so that firms who continue to use them can be sure they have satisfied the MiFID requirements.[147] **16.73**

Excessive charges

The old COB 5.6 conferred on the FSA a power to regulate excessive charging by firms. One consequence of the implementation of MiFID was a reconsideration of whether these rules were necessary, as no corresponding regime exists in the EU measures. Rather the emphasis is on the compulsory disclosure of total cost. Following consultation on not carrying these rules forward in COBS,[148] the FSA decided to delete the excessive charges rules. It had never used them or taken enforcement action in respect of them.[149] **16.74**

[140] COBS 6.1.9R. MiFID Implementing Directive, art 33, developing MiFID, art 19(3). The regime on commission is in practice superseded by the changes introduced under the Retail Distribution Review: see para 16.124.

[141] COBS 6.1.11R.

[142] FSA CP06/19, para 2.14; FSA PS07/14, paras 1.5–1.13.

[143] COBS 6.2.1R.

[144] COBS 6.2.10R.

[145] COBS 6.2.15R. See also COBS 6.2.16R.

[146] See FSA CP06/19, paras 11.1–11.25.

[147] See FSA PS07/14, paras 3.8–3.17. For the guidance see COBS 6.3.3G.

[148] See FSA CP06/19, paras 11.51–11.59.

[149] FSA PS07/6, paras 9.11–9.15.

Insurance mediation

16.75 COBS 7 implements for investment firms in a revised form (based on 'intelligent copy out') the requirements of the separate EU measure on insurance intermediaries, the Insurance Mediation Directive ('IMD'). The rules set out in detail the information which an insurance intermediary must generally provide when doing business with a client.[150]

Client agreements

16.76 The rules formerly found in COB 4.2 are replaced by the rules in COBS 8.[151] Firms must provide to new retail clients both a written basic agreement setting out the essential rights and obligations of the firm and the client (effectively the existing 'Terms of Business' requirement).[152] In addition, firms must in general provide the written terms of that agreement in good time before a retail client becomes bound by any agreement. Only in cases of services effected by distance communication at the request of the client may such information be delayed until immediately after starting to perform, but only where the firm is unable to comply because of those circumstances.[153]

Client assets and client money

16.77 FSA Principle 10 states: 'A *firm* must arrange adequate protection for clients' assets when it is responsible for them'. Section 139 of FSMA 200 provides that rules can be made which ensure client money is held in trust (or in Scotland as agent). The rules concerning client assets and money are found outside of COBS, in a separate component of the Handbook. Prior to the implementation of MiFID, the FSA's Client Assets Rules ('CASS') provided for the handling of client assets[154] and for a statutory trust for client money, creating a fiduciary relationship and priority for the customer on insolvency of the firm.[155] However, professional firms could opt out of the protective rules on client money.[156] These chapters—CASS 2 and 4—still apply to designated investment business which is not MiFID business. In the wake of the implementation of MiFID[157] two new chapter in CASS—chapters 5 and 7—establish rules (with effect from 1 November 2007) in relation to MiFID business for the safeguarding of client assets (the custody rules) and imposing a statutory trust for client money, creating a fiduciary relationship and priority for the customer on insolvency of the firm.[158] There is no professional firm opt out from the client money trust regime, because the FSA considered it to be incompatible with the Directive.

Suitability (including basic advice)

16.78 The important rules on the suitability of advice or portfolio management services are now to be found in COBS 9.[159] Previously the rules on 'know your customer' ('KYC') and

---

150 Directive 2002/92/EC. For the background see FSA CP06/20 ch 12; FSA PS07/6, ch 10.

151 For the background see FSA CP06/20 ch 13; FSA PS07/6, ch 11.

152 COBS 8.1.2R. It applies to 'designated investment business' but excepting 'advising on investments'. MiFID Implementing Directive, art 33.

153 COBS 8.1.3R. MiFID Implementing Directive, art 29.

154 CASS 2.

155 CASS 4.2.3R (non-MiFID). Detailed rules for segregation of client money are provided in CASS 4.3. For consideration see *In the matter of Lehman Brothers International (Europe) (In Administration)* [2012] UKSC 6; [2013] Bus LR 667.

156 CASS 4.1.9R.

157 MiFID, Article 13(7) and (8) and MiFID Implementing Directive, arts 16t–20. For the background to the post-MiFID FSA CASS rules see FSA CP06/14 chapters 9 and 10, and FSA PS07/2 chapter 8.

158 CASS 7.7.2R. For definition of 'client money' see CASS 7.2.

159 For the background see FSA CP06/20 ch 14; FSA PS07/6, ch 12.

suitability were found in COB 5. With the implementation of MiFID the FSA decided to use the EU standards as the basis of its suitability regime in COBS. Accordingly the MiFID standard would be applied to all advisory and discretionary transactions previously covered by COB 5, including products which fall outside of the scope of MiFID, such as life and pensions contracts and other 'packaged products'. Similarly, where dealing with a retail client the standards would be applied to MiFID and non-MiFID firms (which may include IFAs, who do not hold client money).[160] The KYC and suitability requirement are spelt out economically in Article 19(4) of MiFID:

> When providing investment advice or portfolio management the investment firm shall obtain the necessary information regarding the client's or the potential client's knowledge and experience in the investment field relevant to the specific type of product or service, his financial situation and his investment objectives so as to enable the firm to recommend to the client or potential client the investment services or financial instruments that are suitable for him.

That is the basis for all domestic regulation in this field, albeit further prescriptive detail is provided by the MiFID Implementing Directive.[161]

Application. COBS 9 applies to personal recommendations in relation to a designated investment[162] and to firms which manage investments.[163] In respect of non-MiFID business it applies to dealings with retail clients and where the firm is managing the business of an occupational pension scheme, stakeholder pension scheme, or personal pension scheme.[164] **16.79**

'Know your customer'. The new COBS rule on KYC provides: **16.80**

> (1) A firm must obtain from the client such information as is necessary for the firm to understand the essential facts about him and have a reasonable basis for believing, giving due consideration to the nature and extent of the service provided, that the specific transaction to be recommended, or entered into in the course of managing:
> (a) meets his investment objectives;
> (b) is such that he is able financially to bear any related investment risks consistent with his investment objectives; and
> (c) is such that he has the necessary experience and knowledge in order to understand the risks involved in the transaction or in the management of his portfolio.
>
> (2) The information regarding the investment objectives of a client must include, where relevant, information on the length of time for which he wishes to hold the investment, his preferences regarding risk taking, his risk profile, and the purposes of the investment.
>
> (3) The information regarding the financial situation of a client must include, where relevant, information on the source and extent of his regular income, his assets, including liquid assets, investments and real property, and his regular financial commitments.[165]

---

160 See FSA CP06/20, para 14.2–14.11.

161 MiFID Implementing Directive, arts 35, 37, and 52. See also recitals 57 and 58.

162 COBS 9.1.1R. But firms can choose to give basic advice in respect of 'stakeholder products' under the regime in COB 9.6.

163 COBS 9.1.3R.

164 COBS 9.1.4R. A special rule provides for only IMD-required rules to apply to personal recommendations of life policies to professional clients.

165 COBS 9.2.2R. See MiFID Implementing Directive, art 35(1), (3), and (4). For professional clients the firm is entitled to assume the client has the necessary knowledge and experience: COBS 9.2.8R. See MiFID Implementing Directive, art 35(2). There is a discrete rule for small friendly societies: COBS 9.2.9R.

Further provision is made as to the information which must be sought:

> The information regarding a client's knowledge and experience in the investment field includes, to the extent appropriate to the nature of the client, the nature and extent of the service to be provided and the type of product or transaction envisaged, including their complexity and the risks involved, information on:
> (1) the types of service, transaction and designated investment with which the client is familiar;
> (2) the nature, volume, frequency of the client's transactions in designated investments and the period over which they have been carried out;
> (3) the level of education, profession or relevant former profession of the client.[166]

16.81 Echoing a curious requirement of the MiFID Implementing Directive, a rule insists that a firm must not encourage the client *not* to provide this information.[167] A firm must not make a personal recommendation or make a decision to trade if it does obtain the necessary information to assess suitability.[168] This goes somewhat further than the predecessor rules on 'reticent clients'. Nevertheless, a firm is entitled to rely on what its client says, unless it is 'manifestly out of date, inaccurate or incomplete'.[169]

The suitability rule

16.82 The new MiFID inspired 'suitability' rule provides:

> (1) A firm must take reasonable steps to ensure that a personal recommendation, or a decision to trade, is suitable for its client.
> (2) When making the personal recommendation or managing his investments, the firm must obtain the necessary information regarding the client's:
> (a) knowledge and experience in the investment field relevant to the specific type of designated investment or service;
> (b) financial situation; and
> (c) investment objectives;
>
> so as to enable the firm to make the recommendation, or take the decision, which is suitable for him.[170]

16.83 The FSA carried forward as guidance, based on recital 57 of the MiFID Implementing Directive, a provision that unsuitability may arise from the risks of an investment, the type of transaction, the characteristics of the order, or the frequency of the trading.[171] The latter point is reinforced by specific guidance on 'churning and switching'.[172] There is also guidance on the sensitive topics of income withdrawals and short term annuities.[173]

16.84 **Suitability reports.** Article 19(8) of MiFID entitles clients to 'adequate reports on the service provided' by firms, and the costs associated with services and transactions. This has led

---

[166] COBS 9.2.3R. See MiFID Implementing Directive, art 37(1).
[167] COBS 9.2.4R. See MiFID Implementing Directive, art 37(2).
[168] COBS 9.2.6R. See MiFID Implementing Directive, art 35(5). This article refers to the information required under art 19(4) of MiFID itself, rather than the more elaborated version in the MiFID Implementing Directive. See also COBS 9.2.7G.
[169] COBS 9.2.5R. See MiFID Implementing Directive, art 37(3).
[170] COBS 9.2.1R. See MiFID Implementing Directive, art 19(4) and IMD art 12(2).
[171] COBS 9.3.1G.
[172] COBS 9.3.2G. See FSA CP06/20, para 14.11.
[173] COBS 9.3.3G. See FSA PS07/6, para 12.12.

the FSA to modify its traditional requirement of a 'suitability letter'.[174] The new rules appear in COBS 9.4. This is intended by the FSA to be a 'simplified and less prescriptive form' of the previous 'suitability letter' regime,[175] and the change in terminology from 'letter' to 'report' should not be understood as suggesting the contrary. It is inspired by the MiFID language, already quoted. The FSA also withdrew its notification to the EU Commission on the basis that its rules go no further than MiFID requires.[176]

Abandonment of 'most suitable' standard for packaged products. The FSA did not maintain the 'most suitable' standard for recommendations about packaged products from the range on which the adviser can advise. This is the final death-knell for so-called 'best advice'. The FSA believed that other rules, such as the client's best interests rule and the disclosure regime, will achieve the aim of the predecessor rules.[177] **16.85**

Basic advice in respect of stakeholder products. This regime was previously found in COB 5A. MiFID does not recognise the concept of 'basic advice', therefore this initiative is carried forward in a truncated fashion. Only non-MiFID firms can offer basic advice in relation to all stakeholder products and any firm can offer basic advice in relation to stakeholder products which fall outside the scope of MiFID.[178] The detailed rules are now to be found in COBS 9.6.[179] **16.86**

Appropriateness (for non-advised services)

MiFID introduces a new and, for UK practitioners, unfamiliar standard of 'appropriateness' for non-advisory services. The rules are contained in COBS 10.[180] The essential background is MiFID itself. Having concisely defined the 'KYC' and suitability rules for personal recommendations and portfolio management in Article 19(4), the Directive next addresses investment services which fall outside the scope of the preceding sub-article in Article 19(5). Whereas previously UK regulation drew a sharp line between those transactions (advisory and discretionary portfolio management) where a suitability regime applied and 'execution only' transactions, MiFID recognises a distinct 'appropriateness' standard. For those transactions which fall within Article 19(5) the firm must carry out a form of KYC. It must ask: **16.87**

> the client or potential client to provide information regarding his knowledge and experience in the investment field relevant to the specific type of product or service offered or demanded so as to enable the investment firm to assess whether the investment service or product envisaged is appropriate for the client.

If the firm concludes the investment is not appropriate it must warn the (potential) client, albeit it may do so in a standardised format. Where the (potential) client elects to provide no information or inadequate information the firm must warn the client that they are unable to judge the appropriateness of the service or product for him the (potential) client, albeit it may do so in a standardised format. The MiFID Implementing Directive provides that a firm is entitled to assume that a professional client has the necessary knowledge and experience.[181] **16.88**

174 See FSA CP06/20, para 14.16; FSA PS07/6, paras 12.13–12.20; FSA PS07/14, ch 4.
175 See FSA PS07/14, para 4.2.
176 See FSA PS07/14, para 4.4.
177 See FSA CP06/20, para 14.10; FSA PS07/6, para 12.12.
178 See FSA CP06/20, paras 14.27–14.39; FSA PS07/6, paras 12.21–12.28; FSA PS07/14, paras 3.22 and 3.23.
179 COBS 9.6.1–9.6.20R.
180 For the background see FSA CP06/20 ch 15; FSA PS07/6, ch 13.
181 MiFID Implementing Directive, art 36.

16.89 Accordingly, the 'appropriateness' standard is more negative in its approach, in contrast to the positive duty imposed by the suitability regime. Nevertheless, this new standard, with its associated warnings, tilts the balance of responsibility as to the client's interests, requiring more of investment firms than under the predecessor COB regime, where 'execution only' transactions were commonplace, especially in the context of responses to direct offer financial promotions.

16.90 Given its novelty, the FSA only implemented the 'appropriateness' regime for the MiFID business in respect of which it it has no choice, and did not extend it to retail business generally. Nevertheless, its implementation will be a significant new regulatory burden for firms who previously undertook significant 'direct offer' sales business or 'execution only' business in relation to affected products.[182] The basic MiFID rules are copied out in COBS 10.2 and 10.3.

'Execution only' business

16.91 Where a firm claimed to act for a customer on an 'execution only' basis it was on the understanding that it is not required to carry out any investigation into the customer's personal and financial circumstances. Accordingly, the stringent suitablility regime did not apply. However, the FSA was always suspicious of claims that transactions with private customers were 'execution only' and in COB issued guidance that even the provision of 'limited' advice will lift a transaction out of that category.[183] It is often claimed in mis-selling cases that advisers had acted on an execution only basis in deals arranged on behalf of ordinary, often unsophisticated, investors. Such claims were intended to relieve the adviser of the full rigour of the Conduct of Business Rules. However such claims have been treated with scepticism by the FOS and the Courts.[184] It seems similar scepticism exists at European-level, albeit in a more extreme form. One of the most important changes resulting from the introduction of MiFID is a severe reduction of the occasions on which a firm can deal on an execution only basis.[185]

16.92 The last vestiges of 'execution only' business derive from MiFID, Article 19(6) which permits services that 'only consist of execution and/or the reception and transmission of client orders' where all of four conditions are met:

(1) the services relate to 'non-complex financial instruments', which include shares traded on regulated markets, bonds and UCITS;[186]
(2) the service is provided at the initiative of the (potential) client;
(3) the (potential) client is warned (in a standardised format if preferred) that the suitability regime does not apply and the protection of the Conduct of Business Rules is inapplicable;
(4) the firm complies with the conflict of interest rules in MiFID, Article 18.[187]

These provisions are implemented by COBS 10.4,[188] with further provision, based on recital (59) of the MiFID Implementing Directive that the exercise need not be carried out where

[182] See FSA CP06/20, para 15.7; FSA PS07/6, para 13.9. For the scope of COBS 10, see COBS 10.1.1R–COBS 10.1.3R.
[183] See the previous guidance at COB 5.2.2G and COB 5.2.3G.
[184] See, eg, *Loosemore v Financial Concepts* [2001] Lloyd's Rep PN 235.
[185] FSA, *Planning for MiFID* (November 2005), p 13.
[186] The definition is further developed in MiFID Implementing Directive, art 38.
[187] MiFID art 19(6).
[188] COBS 10.4.1R.

a course of dealings is undertaken, save on the first occasion,[189] and that clients who had undertaken such a course of dealing prior to 1 November 2007 can be presumed to have the necessary knowledge and experience.[190] Given the novelty of the regime the FSA provided further guidance on the appropriateness regime in COBS 10.5 and 10.6.

Product information and explanation of risk

Preparing and providing product information to clients comprise respectively COBS 13 and COBS 14. The latter is also the location for the important rules on clients' understanding of risk.[191] These rules supersede the old general rule about customers' understanding of risk in COB 5.4, and the new regime covers products such as SCARPs, albeit any product-specific warnings have been deleted. The new regime is a more general requirement for the disclosure of risks affecting investments, based on an 'intelligent copy-out' of MiFID Implementing Directive, Article 31. **16.93**

COBS 14.3 applies to MiFID business and the following regulated activities when carried on for a retail client: **16.94**

- making a personal recommendation about a designated investment
- managing designated investments;
- arranging (bringing about) or executing a deal in a warrant or a derivative;
- engaging in stock lending activity.[192]

The principal rule provides: **16.95**

> A firm must provide a client with a general description of the nature and risks of designated investments, taking into account, in particular, the client's categorisation as a retail client or a professional client. That description must:
> (1) explain the nature of the specific type of designated investment concerned, as well as the risks particular to that specific type of designated investment, in sufficient detail to enable the client to take investment decisions on an informed basis; and
> (2) include, where relevant to the specific type of designated investment concerned and the status and level of knowledge of the client, the following elements:
> (a) the risks associated with that type of designated investment including an explanation of leverage and its effects and the risk of losing the entire investment;
> (b) the volatility of the price of designated investments and any limitations on the available market for such investments;
> (c) the fact that an investor might assume, as a result of transactions in such designated investments, financial commitments and other additional obligations, including contingent liabilities, additional to the cost of acquiring the designated investments; and
> (d) any margin requirements or similar obligations, applicable to designated investments of that type.[193]

[189] COBS 10.4.2R.
[190] COBS 10.4.3R.
[191] For the background see FSA CP06/19 chs 18 and 19; FSA PS07/6 chs 16 and 17; FSA PS07/14 chs 6 and 7. On understanding of risk see FSA CP06/19 paras 19.21–19.31; FSA PS07/6 ch 17.
[192] COBS 14.3.1R.
[193] COBS 14.3.2R. MiFID Implementing Directive, art 31(1) and (2). See also COBS 14.3.4R (two or more investments) and COBS 14.3.5R (third-party guarantees) implementing the remainder of art 31.

Usually the information must be provided 'in good time' before business is done.[194] Furthermore, clients must be kept up to date with any material change in the information provided.[195]

16.96 COBS 16 provides further rules on reporting information to clients[196]

Cancellation rights

16.97 The rules on the customer's right to cancel (where applicable) are now to be found in COBS 15.[197]

Specialist rules on pensions and with profits

16.98 Special rules are maintained with regard to pensions advice[198] and in relation to with profits policies.[199]

Case law on retail investment business

16.99 Whilst the overwhelming majority of consumer claims arising out of retail investment business have been resolved through the mechanisms of internal complaints-handling by firms or by the FOS and its predecessors, in the wake of the financial crisis of 2007–2008 there are now a significant number of decided cases. Some provide important explorations of the interplay between the regulatory regime and the applicable common law principles. It is noteworthy that some of these cases concern non-linear relationships, where there is either an indirect loss suffered on the consumer side, or there are a number of parties on the industry side, and the respective responsibilities have to be explored.[200] In broad terms the courts have shown themselves sympathetic to ordinary or middle-income investors who have been badly advised in relation to pension matters or advised to invest in more exotic products such as unregulated collective investment schemes. In contrast, and in the wake of the financial crisis of 2007–2008, the English courts have generally proved less sympathetic to corporate investors or high net worth individuals, who while not industry professionals, have experience of investing in more complex products.[201]

---

194 COBS 14.3.9R. MiFID Implementing Directive, art 29(2) and (5).

195 COBS 14.3.10R. MiFID Implementing Directive, art 29(6).

196 For the background see FSA CP06/20 ch 21; FSA PS07/6, ch 19.

197 For the background see FSA CP06/20 ch 20; FSA PS07/6, ch 18.

198 COBS 19. For the background see FSA CP06/20 ch 25; FSA PS07/6, ch 22.

199 COBS 20. For the background see FSA CP06/20 ch 24; FSA PS07/6, ch 23.

200 See also *Investors Compensation Scheme Ltd v West Bromwich Building Society* [1999] Lloyd's Rep PN 496, where a building society was held to be a joint tortfeasor with a firm of independent financial advisers in marketing unsuitable home income plans, and the initial skirmish in *Financial Services Compensation Scheme Ltd v Abbey National Treasury Services Ltd* [2008] EWHC 1897 (Ch), where it was alleged by the FSCS that Abbey collaborated in the development and production of SCARPS products. The case settled before trial.

201 See, eg, *Peekay Intermark Ltd v Australia & New Zealand Banking Group Ltd* [2006] EWCA Civ 386, [2006] 2 Lloyd's Rep 511; revsg [2005] EWHC 830 (Comm); *Springwell Navigation Corp v JP Morgan Chase Bank* [2010] EWCA Civ 1212; affg [2008] EWHC 1186 (Comm); [2008] EWHC 1793 (Comm); *Titan Steel Wheels Ltd v Royal Bank of Scotland plc* [2010] EWHC 211 (Comm), [2010] 2 Lloyd's Rep 92; *Bank Leumi (UK) plc v Wachner* [2011] EWHC 656 (Comm); *Wilson v MF Global UK Ltd* [2011] EWHC 138 (QB); *Standard Chartered Bank v Ceylon Petroleum Corp* [2011] EWHC 1785 (Comm); *Winnetka Trading Corp v Julius Barr International Ltd* [2011] EWHC 2030 (Ch), [2012] BCLC 588; *Camerata Property Inc v Credit Suisse Securities (Europe) Ltd* [2012] EWHC 7 (Comm); *IG Markets Ltd v Crinion* [2012] EWHC B4 (Mercantile); *IG Index Ltd v Ehrentreu* [2013] EWCA Civ 95; *Zaki v Credit Suisse (UK) Ltd* [2013] EWCA Civ 14; *Al Sulaiman v Credit Suisse Securities (Europe) Ltd* [2013] EWHC 400 (Comm); and *Green v Royal Bank of Scotland plc* [2013] EWCA Civ 1197.

Gorham v British Telecommunications

Many financial products confer potential benefits upon persons other than the immediate recipient of the advice. This is especially so in respect of life insurance and pension provision contracts. Accordingly, the question is posed whether a duty is owed directly to the ultimate beneficiaries to take reasonable care in providing information or advice to the customer. Suppose a life company mis-sells a personal pension plan ('PPP') to an employee who was entitled to membership of an occupational pension scheme ('OPS') which was more suitable for his financial needs. The OPS included valuable benefits in the shape of a death-in-service benefit and spouse's pension which were not afforded by the PPP. This was the context of pension mis-selling. **16.100**

In the House of Lords in *Lloyds TSB General Insurance Holdings v Lloyds Bank Group Insurance Co Ltd*[202] Lord Hoffmann observed: **16.101**

> Whether it was in the interests of an employee to leave his employer's occupational scheme and commit his future to a personal scheme was often a difficult question. A fully informed decision required the employee to be aware of the respective risks, costs and benefits of the choices open to him. Much depended upon his personal and family circumstances. The LAUTRO Code of Conduct required a sales representative to make a detailed analysis in order to give the investor what was compendiously called 'best advice' on all relevant aspects of the decision. It imposed a positive duty upon the salesman (who was usually paid commission on the schemes which he sold) to advise the employee against giving up his rights under the occupational scheme unless he honstly thought it was in the employee's best interests to do so.[203]

Suppose further the employee died before it was discovered that the life company had proffered incorrect advice. In principle it seems appropriate that the life company should owe a direct duty to the employee's dependants who were the foreseeable victims if the company broke its duty with respect to the advice provided and that was acted upon by the employee. The analogy with the leading negligence case of *White v Jones*[204] appears irresistible. **16.102**

In *Gorham v British Telecommunications plc*[205] the problem of what is sometimes described as transferred loss arose in the financial services context. An employee of BT was entitled to membership of that company's OPS. He was wrongly advised by Standard Life that he should not join that scheme and instead enter into a PPP. This he did. The OPS provided significantly better benefits in the event of the early death of the employee. Sadly this occurred, raising the question whether the employee's widow and surviving children had any direct claim against the life company? The Court of Appeal unanimously held that a cause of action did vest in the disappointed dependants, applying the principles in *White v Jones* by analogy. In the view of Pill LJ: **16.103**

> the present situation is identical to that in *White* v *Jones*. Mr Gorham intended to create a benefit for his wife and children in the event of his pre-deceasing them. Under the BT scheme they would benefit substantially in that event.[206]

The fact that there was a detailed regulatory scheme did not preclude the court from recognising a duty of care on general principles, given that the regulatory code was silent on the **16.104**

---

202 [2003] UKHL 48.

203 Para [4]. See similarly Lord Hobhouse at para [36].

204 [1995] 2 AC 207 (HL: solicitor liability to disappointed beneficiaries of negligently prepared will).

205 [2000] 1 WLR 2129; noted G McMeel [2001] LMCLQ 321.

206 [2000] 1 WLR 2129, 2140.

rights of beneficiaries. The detailed facts militated strongly in favour of this solution. The adviser had completed a fact find on behalf of both partners, and both signed it. The identified priorities for the couple made pre-eminent 'provision for family'. The possibility of life insurance for Mrs Gorham was canvassed, but not ultimately pursued.

16.105 Sir Murray Stuart-Smith was therefore prepared to go further:

> In a sense the case is even stronger than *White* v *Jones* because Mrs Gorham suffered a real loss; the premiums are paid out of what might be regarded as the family income, and her loss is a reduced pension. The beneficiary in *White* v *Jones* merely lost a windfall.[207]

Alone of the members of the Court of Appeal Sir Murray was concerned about problems posed where there might be a conflict of interest between the customer and his dependants. However he regarded these as borderline factual problems, which should not deter the court from recognising a claim in clear cases such as the instant one.

16.106 In contrast, Schiemann LJ saw no position of conflict: 'the assumption of responsibility to beneficiaries in cases such as the present does not operate to widen the scope of the duty but merely to widen the number of those who can sue in respect of any breach'.[208]

16.107 Some guidance can also be found in *Gorham v British Telecommunications plc*[209] on the relationship between the statutory rules and the common law. The Court of Appeal rejected a submission that the detailed statutory scheme for investor protection created by the Financial Services Act 1986 precluded the court from developing a common law tortious claim that went beyond the statutory code. Whilst primarily concerned with the existence of a duty of care for a third-party beneficiary, some of the observations made by the court also bear on the appropriate standard of liability. Pill LJ observed:

> Had Parliament not intervened, remedies for the abuses which existed in this field would almost certainly have been developed by the courts. The courts now do so in the context, and with the benefit of, rules and codes of practice laid down by those concerned with the maintenance of proper standards. The courts can be expected to attach considerable weight to the content of the codes drafted in these circumstances but are not excluded from making their own assessment of a situation.[210]

16.108 In the particular context of a dependants' claim the court was not bound by the Conduct of Business Rules, as they did not expressly address the question.

Seymour v Ockwell

16.109 The leading case in the financial services context on the duties owed by those other than the immediate adviser, such as product providers or intermediate distributors, is *Seymour v Caroline Ockwell & Co (a firm)*.[211] Mr and Mrs Seymour sold their family farm in Wiltshire yielding net proceeds of about £1.4 million. They were looking for low risk temporary home for their money which could provide an income in the meantime as they intended to reinvest some of the proceeds into a new business within three years in order to benefit from rollover relief from capital gains tax ('CGT'). They approached a friend ('CO') who traded as a sole

[207] [2000] 1 WLR 2129, 2144.
[208] [2000] 1 WLR 2129, 2146.
[209] [2000] 1 WLR 2129.
[210] [2000] 1 WLR 2129, 2141. Contrast *Green v Royal Bank of Scotland plc* [2013] EWCA Civ 1197.
[211] [2005] EWHC 1137 (QB), [2005] PNLR 758 (Bristol Mercantile Court).

practitioner independent financial adviser, and who was also their accountant, for advice. CO in turn approached a representative of Zurich IFA Ltd ('ZIFA', which was part of the Zurich/Allied Dunbar group) for help. ZIFA acted as a marketing wing, providing information to financial advisers about the group's products. Ultimately, an investment of £500,000 was made by the Seymours in an investment comprising (a) a 'wrapper bond' life insurance product provided by an Allied Dunbar subsidiary in the Isle of Man as recommended, and held within that wrapper (b) a fund operated by Imperial Consolidated (a company based in the Bahamas) called the 'Alpha + Fixed Income Fund' ('the Fund'). Imperial Consolidated and the Fund collapsed amid allegations of fraud causing the Seymours (and many other UK and overeas investors) to lose all their money. It is a significant feature of the case that the Seymours were not privy to the communications between the ZIFA representative and CO, and they did not know of these exchanges.[212] At one meeting the ZIFA representative gave to CO a brochure prepared by Imperial Consolidated in relation to the Fund and said that the Fund could be held in the Allied Dunbar wrapper bond. The key features of the Fund was said to be that it offered 100 per cent guaranteed capital with guaranteed annual return of 15 per cent. Two oral representations were held to have been made by the ZIFA representative to CO. First, in response to a specific question by CO as to the status of Imperial Consolidated it was stated that ZIFA or a Zurich group company would have 'gone through their books'. Secondly, that the Fund was being 'marketed by Imperial Consolidated as a low risk fund'. [213] Whilst CO did her own research, including contacting a representative of the Fund, in substance those representations were repeated to the Seymours. At the time that the Seymours were completing their investment, and during a 'cooling off period', doubts were circulating about Imperial Consolidated. An internal Zurich memorandum dated 15 January 2001 stated that there were causes for concern and that no new business should be transacted with Imperial Consolidated.[214] This was never communicated to either CO or the Seymours. The judge held that had CO seen the memorandum she would have taken steps and that had the Seymours seen it they would have reversed their investment.[215] In July 2002 Imperial Consolidated collapsed and the Seymours lost the whole of their investment in the Fund.

First, the Seymours brought claims against the IFA, CO, as First Defendant for negligence **16.110** and breaches of sections 62 and 76 of the Financial Services Act 1986 ('the 1986 Act'). Secondly, the Seymours added a claim against ZIFA as Second Defendant for negligence and also for breach of section 76 of the 1986 Act. Thirdly, CO claimed under CPR Part 20 against ZIFA for an indemnity in the event of her being held liable to the Seymours (or for contribution in the event to their both being liable to the Seymours). In the outcome in the first claim CO was held to be negligent and in breach of sections 62 and 76 of the 1986 Act and therefore liable for the full value of the Seymours' lost investment. The Seymours were unsuccessful in their argument that ZIFA owed them a direct duty of care, and also in the argument based on section 76 of the 1986 Act, which generally prohibited the promotion of unregulated collective investment schemes. In the Part 20 Claim CO was successful in

[212] [2005] EWHC 1137 (QB), para [145].

[213] [2005] EWHC 1137 (QB), para [24]. There was a conflict of evidence. CO understood ZIFA were saying the Fund was low risk. The Judge accepted the ZIFA representative's evidence but added: 'the distinction would in all probability have been lost on Miss Ockwell'.

[214] [2005] EWHC 1137 (QB), paras [51–2].

[215] [2005] EWHC 1137 (QB), para [54].

arguing that ZIFA should indemnify her to the extent of 66 per cent of the lost capital claim by the Seymours.

16.111 HHJ Havelock-Allan QC treated the allegation that ZIFA as in effect 'product provider'[216] owed a duty of care directly to the Seymours as investors as instance of a novel duty of care situation, and refused to take the step of imposing such a duty which would cut across contractual and statutory responsibilities. With regard to the claim by CO against ZIFA, HHJ Havelock-Allan QC held:

> It is unprofitable to consider whether the positive misstatements made Mrs Clarke [the ZIFA representative] constituted advice or information. I am quite satisfied that Mrs Clarke owed a duty of care in making them.... In my judgment the three important statements about risk and investor protection were made negligently and ZIFA is liable to Miss Ockwell for the consequences of that negligence.[217]

16.112 Further there was continuing duty to provide the IFA with information about the investment in certain circumstances:

> ...there are undoubtedly circumstances where a duty to speak does arise and where a failure to do so can and does give rise to liability. The obvious circumstance is where something has been previously said or done which, if not corrected or qualified in the light of subsequent information or events, may appear false or misleading. If the original statement was in the nature of a continuing representation, in the sense of being one which was still likely to be relied upon by the representee, the representor is under a duty to speak and to correct information which will become false or misleading if he remains silent.[218]

16.113 The 'unexplained failure' to communicate the contents of ZIFA's 15 January 2001 memorandum to CO whilst the Seymours were still in the 'cooling off' period was an 'exemplar of circumstances which gave rise to a duty to speak' and there was accordingly a further breach. CO was entitled to know in those circumstances that ZIFA had information that the Fund was no longer regarded as low risk and suitable for inclusion within the Allied Dunbar wrapper bond. Accordingly, on the particular facts of that case the responsibility of provider and adviser was split 66 per cent to 33 per cent.

Walker v Scottish Equitable

16.114 The case of *Seymour v Ockwell* can be usefully contrasted with *Walker v Inter-Alliance Group plc (in administration) and Scottish Equitable plc*.[219] Whilst in the former case there was no allegation that the investors met or had any direct dealings with the product provider's representatives, in the latter a representative of Scottish Equitable ('SE') attended the crucial meetings alongside the IFA and was ultimately held to have provided investment advice direct to the underlying client.

16.115 Mr Walker had been a director and senior manager of a major construction company, and a member of its defined benefits occupational pension scheme ('OPS'), which would have entitled him, after many years' service, to: a pension based on two-thirds of his final salary; an inflation-linked pension; a five-year guarantee in the event of early death; and a 50 per cent widow's pension. Nevertheless, following meetings attended by both his IFA (a representative

[216] [2005] EWHC 1137 (QB), paras [30] and [152].
[217] [2005] EWHC 1137 (QB), para [153].
[218] [2005] EWHC 1137 (QB), para [155].
[219] [2007] EWHC 1858 (Ch).

of the First Defendant) and a representative of SE, Mr Walker executed a pension transfer in the sum of £1.2 million to an SE product, called 'Retirement Control', which was a deferred phased retirement and income drawdown scheme. Whilst the SE scheme was more flexible, it was not guaranteed and it was a money purchase scheme which depended on the future performance of underlying investment funds.

Mr Boakes was the representative of SE who attended the meetings, initially in 1999, and later in January 2001, when Mr Walker actually retired. Mr Boakes was a broker consultant who was described as a 'retirement options specialist'. Nevertheless, at trial it was common ground that Mr Boakes was prohibited both by the regulatory code and by SE's own compliance manual from proffering any investment advice at the meetings which he attended. **16.116**

Subsequently, dissatisfied with the SE product Mr Walker initiated proceedings against the IFA for breach of contract and negligence and against SE for breach of statutory duty (section 62 of the Financial Services Act 1986) and negligence. The IFA went into administration and the trial was solely concerned with the liability of SE, the Second Defendant. Mr Walker complained about maladministration of the SE product and about the performance of the SE investment manager. However his principal contention was that he should never have been advised to effect the pension transfer in the first place. The SE scheme was fundamentally unsuitable for someone with his cautious attitude to risk. In contrast, as Henderson J recorded: 'With the benefit of hindsight the Taylor Woodrow [Mr Walker's employers] scheme represents the gold standard of pension provision that is unlikely to be matched, let alone surpassed, in the foreseeable future'.[220] **16.117**

SE's defence was that no advice was ever proffered by its representative and the decision is largely fact- and evidence-based. There was no dispute in principle that if advice was proffered it would have been a breach by SE's representative of the requirement not to provide investment advice, because it offended the policy of polarisation.[221] SE could, of course, have chosen to give advice on its own products, but had decided not to employ a direct sales force, so accordingly none of its representatives were authorised to provide investment advice.[222] It could be added that the joint representations of IFA and life office representative would have offended the regulatory policy in any event given that a representative of one firm would have been operating in tandem with a supposedly independent adviser. **16.118**

Overall, the Judge preferred the factual evidence of Mr Walker as to what happened in the meetings. He commented that: 'Mr Boakes' attitude to compliance matters was at times rather cavalier'.[223] Henderson J recorded that the issue for him to decide was whether SE through its representative gave investment advice within the meaning of the Financial Services Act 1986, schedule 1 paragraph 15 at the meetings which he attended? The judge decided that Mr Boakes' repeated statements of what he would do in the situation of Mr Walker was investment advice.[224] Furthermore, he was satisfied that the SE representative had in fact taken the lead in the meetings in explaining the relative merits of the OPS and **16.119**

220 [2007] EWHC 1858 (Ch), para [6].

221 [2007] EWHC 1858 (Ch), para [18]: citing PIA Rule 1.2.2(5)(a) requiring members not to exceed the business for which the PIA had granted authorisation. See also para [20]: citing breach of PIA rules 4.2.1 and 4.2.4.

222 [2007] EWHC 1858 (Ch), para [25].

223 [2007] EWHC 1858 (Ch), para [72].

224 [2007] EWHC 1858 (Ch), para [96].

SE's income drawdown scheme. Henderson J rejected a submission that the statements were too vague or ambiguous to constitute investment advice. Henderson J stated:

> It seems to me that the concept of investment advice is broad enough to include any communication with the client which, in the particular context in which it is given, goes beyond the mere provision of information and is objectively likely to influence the client's decision whether or not to undertake the transaction in question. If that, or something like it, is the correct test, I have no doubt that Mr Boakes' statements to Mr Walker constituted investment advice, even if the precise words that he used cannot now be reconstructed.[225]

16.120 On causation, Henderson J was also satisfied that if Mr Boakes had not so advised, Mr Walker would have remained a member of the OPS.[226]

Rubenstein v HSBC Bank Plc

16.121 In *Rubenstein v HSBC Bank Plc*[227] the issue was starkly raised whether the unprecedented consequences of the financial crisis of 2007–2008 should be visited upon the retail investor or the firm which had recommended (in breach of duty) an investment, where some loss was foreseeable, but the extent of that loss was unforeseeable. On ordinary principles if the type of loss is foreseeable (financial loss) it does not matter that the extent of loss was not. On the facts the claimant sought advice from the defendant bank as to a suitable deposit-style investment in which to keep the proceeds of the sale of the family home pending the identification and purchase of a new property. The judge found that the defendant's recommendation to invest the sale proceeds in a Bond issued by AIG Life and more particularly in AIG's Enhanced Variable Rate Fund ('EVRF') was negligent and that the increased risks of investing in that fund rather than a safer alternative (AIG's Standard Variable Rate Fund or 'SVRF') placed the defendant in breach of numerous COB rules. In the events which happened there was a run on the AIG funds in September 2008 as a result of which the EVRF closed with investors who elected to exit the fund losing about 20 per cent of their investment. Investors in the SVRF were not affected. Nonetheless, the trial Judge, HHJ Havelock-Allan QC, awarded only nominal damages stating:

> The run on the fund was triggered by a well-founded rumour in the U.S. financial markets that AIG was going to go bankrupt. It is now known that it might well have done if it had not received support from the U.S. Federal Reserve.… The idea that one of the world's largest insurance companies might go bankrupt was unthinkable in September 2005, just as it was unthinkable then that one of the UK's major clearing banks might find itself unable to repay depositors. But that is what would have happened if the U.K. Treasury and the Bank of England had not stepped in to assist the Royal Bank of Scotland in the autumn of 2008.…What happened to the EVRF on 15 September 2008 and the days following was wholly outside the contemplation of the bank or any competent financial adviser in September 2005.…I find that the loss was not caused by any negligence on the part of Mr Marsden in making the recommendation. I also find that the loss was not reasonably foreseeable by HSBC and is too remote in law to be recoverable as damages for breach of contract or in tort.[228]

---

[225] [2007] EWHC 1858 (Ch), para [97]. That is somewhat broader than the statutory definition of investment advice which is limited to advice on a 'particular investment': Regulated Activities Order 2001, art 53.

[226] [2007] EWHC 1858 (Ch), para [104].

[227] [2012] EWCA Civ 1184; revsg [2011] EWHC 2304 (QB), [2011] 2 CLC 459, [2012] PNLR 7. See also Chapters 6 and 12.

[228] [2011] EWHC 2304 (QB), para [115].

However the Court of Appeal allowed Mr Rubenstein's appeal.[229] Rix LJ rejected the trial judge's approach to causation: **16.122**

> It was the bank's duty to protect Mr Rubenstein from exposure to market forces when he made clear that he wanted an investment which was without any risk (and when the bank told him that his investment was the same as a cash deposit). It is wrong in such a context to say that when the risk from exposure to market forces arises, the bank is free of responsibility because the incidence of market loss was unexpected.[230]

In reality, market movements are eminently foreseeable, and are inherent in the concept of markets. Sometimes such movements are unpredictable and even extreme, but that is merely a difference in the extent of a kind or type of loss which is foreseeable. It should not prevent the sustained loss from being recoverable. The events of 2007–2008 did not constitute a *novus actus interveniens* and break the chain of causation where investors had been mis-advised, and the financial crisis exacerbated the losses which would otherwise have occurred. **16.123**

The Retail Distribution Review

Between 2007 and 2012 the FSA examined in some detail the operation of the retail investment industry and its modes of delivering its products and services to consumers as part of the Retail Distribution Review ('RDR').[231] One initial starting-part for the review was concern over how the regulatory framework placed the responsibility for advice squarely on the shoulders of the direct or immediate adviser. However, it was obvious that there had been repeated failures by small, often small high street, financial advisers to deliver in practice the high standards laid down. Until recently save where a direct sales force or appointed representatives have been employed, product providers, which are often substantial organisations responsible for product design and marketing, have largely been able to absolve themselves from the consequences of the delivery of unsatisfactory products at high street level from an IFA supposedly at arms' length from the provider. In the light of the *Seymour v Caroline Ockwell & Co (a firm)*[232] (discussed earlier) the respective responsibilities of product providers and intermediaries were reviewed by the FSA issues as part of its Treating Customers Fairly (TCF) theme-based work.[233] In a speech in September 2005 by John Tiner, then FSA Chief Executive, stated: **16.124**

> Over the next year we will be carrying out further analysis to clarify the division of responsibilities between product producers and product distributors. In particular, we will consider the implications of the High Court case, *Seymour v Ockwell*, in which it was held that a marketing company must share liability to the end consumer with an adviser. We will review the extent to which product providers can abrogate their responsibility for products, particularly when their performance may be highly susceptible to variability in different market environments. Irrespective of the outcome of this analysis, firms would be well advised to think carefully about different advisers' abilities [to] understand and explain product features. Time taken to consider properly the distribution of products by their manufacturers will go a long way towards mitigating the risk of the products ending up in the hands of consumers for whom they are not suitable.[234]

[229] [2012] EWCA Civ 1184.
[230] [2012] EWCA Civ 1184, para [118].
[231] FSA DP07/1, *A Review of Retail Distribution* (June 2007).
[232] [2005] EWHC 1137 (QB), [2005] PNLR 758 (Bristol Mercantile Court).
[233] See generally FSA, *Treating customers fairly—building on progress* (July 2005).
[234] FSA SP 'Asset management: current challenges and the hedge funds debate' (19 September 2005). See also FSA, *Treating customers fairly—building on progress* (July 2005), para 6.16.

16.125 This led in part to a new Regulatory Guide giving an indication of regulatory expectations in respect of the Responsibilities of Providers and Distributors for the Fair Treatment of Customers, (RPPD), issued as guidance, initially under section 157 of FSMA 2000, and now by the FCA under section 139A of FSMA 2000.

The RDR Discussion Paper

16.126 In June 2007 the principal Discussion Paper on the RDR was published[235] and it was originally intended to provide full feedback in October 2008. However, in August 2008[236] (at the height of the financial crisis) the FSA announced that it would be November 2008 before any full feedback statement would be published, principally in the wake of the appointment of Jon Pain as managing director of retail markets at the FSA. The original Discussion Paper attracted some 888 responses, and obviously prompted some significant further thinking at the FSA, as evidenced by an Interim Report.[237]

The original Discussion Paper pointed out that although the retail investment sector had been regulated for two decades numerous features of the industry—complex charging structures, heavy reliance on commission-based advisers, poor quality advice going undetected for many years, and the limited training of advisers—suggested an inefficient market. It favoured, effectively, a class-based system of 'professional financial planning' for high-income consumers and more basic 'primary advice' for the rest.[238] The latter regime might include a watering-down of the suitability regime.[239] It was not difficult to foresee that both European standards required by MiFID and other Directives, not to say the common law standard of care, might pose obstacles for this project.[240]

RDR Interim Report

16.127 In April 2008, in the Interim Report,[241] perhaps driven by the relatively large consultative response (presumably industry-led), the FSA conceded that there was a consensus among respondents that its original proposals were too complex. The Interim Report was also sympathetic to consultees' calls for a 'simpler landscape' with a clear distinction between 'advice' and 'sales'.[242] It now favoured only one species of adviser, coupled with a 'step-change in the standards required of advisers'.[243] All would be independent, whole of market advisers whose remuneration was set without product provider input. Professional or educational standards would be increased. In contrast, 'sales' would be strictly non-advised, in the form of either execution-only or guided sales in the context of wider government initiatives to promote more saving and investment. Again it was easy to foresee significant obstacles ahead for this proposal, from both European and domestic legal constraints. Furthermore, the long-standing lack of clarity in the consumer financial services context between giving advice and providing information did not look capable of swift resolution,[244] and the widespread incidence of supposedly 'execution only' transactions in the earlier pensions and endowment mis-sales

[235] FSA DP07/1, *A Review of Retail Distribution* (June 2007).
[236] FSA Press Release, 7 August 2008.
[237] FSA, *Retail Distribution Review—Interim Report* (April 2008).
[238] FSA DP07/1, *A Review of Retail Distribution* (June 2007).
[239] FSA DP07/1, *A Review of Retail Distribution* (June 2007), para 22.
[240] FSA DP07/1, *A Review of Retail Distribution* (June 2007), paras 5.32–5.35.
[241] FSA, *Retail Distribution Review—Interim Report* (April 2008).
[242] FSA, *Retail Distribution Review—Interim Report* (April 2008).
[243] FSA, *Retail Distribution Review—Interim Report* (April 2008).
[244] FSA, *Retail Distribution Review—Interim Report* (April 2008), para 4.9.

episodes should not be forgotten. In addition, in this Interim Report, as a first step, the FSA exhorted product providers to drop out of their traditional role of remunerating advisers, and regulated firms generally are prodded in the direction of common professional standards.

The death-knell for commission-driven sales

16.128 In November 2008, the FSA eventually provided its feedback and mapped out the future, in which the RDR spawned the 'Retail Distribution Implementation Programme' ('RDIP'), rolling forward to the end of 2012.[245] A clearer distinction would be drawn between 'independent advice' and 'sales advice'.[246] However, any attempt to draw a clear distinction between sales and advice was dropped following discussions with the European Commission which confirmed that the proposed simpler landscape proposal would be inconsistent with MiFID.[247] Crucially, product providers were to be removed from a role in intermediary remuneration. This was the death-knell of commission driven (mis)sales. In the words of Jon Pain: 'This is the end of the potential for commission bias'.[248] Dan Waters, the FSA's Director of Retail Policy and Conduct Risk, was even more emphatic: 'these rules will bring to an end the current practice in the UK of product providers offering adviser firms amounts of commission for selling their products'.[249]

Implementing the RDR

16.129 At the end of June 2009 the FSA published its consultation paper on delivering the RDR, including draft Handbook text.[250] Despite the proclaimed commitment to greater clarity in the way in which firms describe their services to consumers, the FSA itself—having flirted with suggested distinctions between 'professional financial planning' and 'primary advice', 'advice' and 'sales', and 'independent advice' and 'sales advice'—eventually settled upon 'independent advice' and 'restricted advice'.[251] Long-standing observers of the retail investment industry may detect a hint of 'repolarisation' after 'polarisation' and 'depolarisation'.[252] Crucially, all investment advice firms must set their own charges, with product providers banned from offering commission to secure sales.[253] The intended scope of the new regime embraces not just the traditional 'packaged products' but also unregulated collective investment schemes, all holdings in investment trusts and structured investment products.[254]

COBS after the Retail Distribution Review ('RDR')

16.130 The principal rules implementing the RDR are to be found in COBS 6.1A for all firms providing advice to retail clients, that is intermediaries. In particular COBS 6.1A.4R provides:

> a *firm* must:
>
> (1) only be remunerated for the *personal recommendation* (and any other related services provided by the *firm*) by *adviser charges*; and

---

245 FSA Feedback Statement 08/6, 'Retail Distribution Review—Including feedback on DP07/1 and the Interim Report' (November 2008), with RDIP introduced at para 17.

246 FSA Feedback Statement 08/6, para 3.9.

247 FSA Feedback Statement 08/6, para 13.

248 Jon Pain, 'The Retail Distribution Review—the key to our retail strategy' (SP: 15 January 2009).

249 Dan Waters, 'The Retail Distribution Review—practical challenges for the investment industry' (SP: 16 January 2009).

250 FSA CP09/18, *Distribution of retail investments: Delivering the RDR* (June 2009).

251 FSA CP09/18, chapters 2 and 3.

252 FSA CP09/18, para 45.

253 FSA CP09/18, chapter 4.

254 FSA CP09/18, para 1.5.

(2) not solicit or accept (and ensure that none of its *associates* solicits or accepts) any other commissions, remuneration or benefit of any kind in relation to the *personal recommendation* or any other related service, regardless of whether it intends to refund the payments or pass the benefits on to the *retail client*; and

(3) not solicit or accept (and ensure that none of its *associates* solicits or accepts) *adviser charges* in relation to the *retail client's retail investment product* which are paid out or advanced by another party over a materially different time period, or on a materially different basis, from that in or on which the *adviser charges* are recovered from the *retail client*.[255]

16.131 COBS 6.1B.5R then bans providers and platforms from making such payments:

> a *firm* must not offer or pay (and must ensure that none of its *associates* offers or pays) any commissions, remuneration or benefit of any kind to another *firm*, or to any other third party for the benefit of that *firm*, in relation to a *personal recommendation* (or any related services), except those that facilitate the payment of *adviser charges* from a *retail client's* investments in accordance with this section.[256]

[255] COBS 6.1.A.4R.
[256] COBS 6.1.B.5R.

17

HOME FINANCE TRANSACTIONS

One of the main purchases during an individual's life is residential property. This means that the stability of the home finance sector of the financial services industry is a particularly important challenge for the sector itself and for its regulators. Some years ago, the sector was the more or less exclusive preserve of building societies, but the market has been opened up to wider competition, and a substantial percentage of residential mortgages is now granted by banks. The building society sector has shrunk in size, because of this competition and because some of the larger building societies have converted themselves from a mutual structure and have become, or have merged with, banks. 17.01

This chapter has two purposes. One is to outline the main distinctive elements of the regulation of building societies in their capacity as lenders. The second is to give an account of the regime for the regulation of home finance transactions, which includes lending on mortgage secured on domestic property, home purchase business, and home reversion business. 17.02

Supervision and Regulation of Building Societies

Since building societies are essentially funded from retail or wholesale deposits, they are basically deposit-takers and are regulated in the same manner as banks. This chapter therefore deals only with the aspects of building societies that differ from the regime for banks. 17.03

These differences are attributable to two main causes. First, the historical development of building societies has been different to that for banks. Mutuality, still today one of the distinguishing marks of the movement, is the main feature here. Second, Parliament's decision to create a regime for regulation of mortgage business inevitably meant that the reforms had to apply to building societies themselves, since the grant of a mortgage did not always involve an external intermediary. 17.04

Building societies before FSMA

Building societies are important providers of financial savings and loan services, especially in the residential property market. Building societies are mutual organisations, or incorporated bodies that raise funds principally from shareholders and members. Those funds were, until recently, used exclusively to advance amounts secured on land for residential use. Since the coming into effect of the Building Societies Act 1986 and more particularly the Building Societies Act 1997, building societies have been able to carry on a number of additional financial services. They were also allowed to convert into banks using a simplified transfer procedure, the first major institution to do so being the Abbey National in 1989. 17.05

17.06 The first building society in the UK was set up by Richard Ketley in Birmingham in 1775.[1] This was the first mutual fund set up for this purpose although other alternative forms of financing had been set up earlier. In Scotland, the decision was taken to use an early savings bank model with the first society being the Glasgow and West of Scotland Savings, Investment and Building Society in 1808.

17.07 The original societies were referred to as terminating societies as they would be closed down once all of their original members had been provided with proper accommodation. The first permanent societies were the Chesham in 1845 and the Scarborough in 1846. The permanent societies soon began to focus on lending for the purchase of properties rather than for building them. Early growth was nevertheless limited due to the preference for savings to be placed with friendly societies. Early commercial banks were not commonly used as they required an initial deposit of at least £10 and paid little or no interest (except in Scotland) which restricted their use to the wealthier members of society. The earlier building societies thus tended to be used by skilled or higher paid workers who could afford to purchase their own homes.

17.08 Statutory oversight was introduced in 1836 and provided a friendly societies model for supervision and control. Following a series of complaints including governance difficulties and excessive charging, supervision was transferred to the Chief Registrar of Friendly Societies under the Building Societies Act 1874. This Act established the basic conditions under which building societies would be operated for over 100 years; it confirmed their mutual status and legal personality with members' liability limited to amounts outstanding on their mortgages or otherwise owed. Monies were raised through members' subscriptions and used to advance loans secured on freehold or leasehold property. Mergers were permitted with the consent of three-quarters of members holding two-thirds of the total value of shares issued. Later amending statutes required the provision of more complete information and the auditing and certification of annual accounts.

17.09 The immediate post-war period was characterised by an expansion in the rental market under the new Labour government although private property ownership was subsequently promoted by later Conservative governments. Home ownership rose to 43 per cent by 1961. While the total amount advanced by societies continued to grow, the number of societies and branches contracted as a result of mergers and business transfers. Banks were first allowed to enter the residential mortgage market in the early 1980s closely followed by insurance companies and other financial institutions. Bank penetration in the market initially rose from 26 per cent to 36 per cent but then fell to 25 per cent by 1987.

17.10 Building societies were not immune from the deregulation of the UK financial system, advocated by the Wilson Committee, which took place in the 1980s.[2] The Building Societies Act 1986 enabled societies to retain their mutual status or to convert into bodies corporate through a simplified procedure, and permitted the range of their activities to be considerably extended to include the provision of current accounts and the sale of life assurance and unit trusts to members. The Building Societies Act 1986 created a new statutory framework

[1] Mr Ketley had been the landlord of the Golden Cross Inn, Snow Hill, Birmingham. For the development of the movement, see generally, M Boddy, *The Building Societies* (Macmillan 1980); D McKillop and C Ferguson, *Building Societies: Structure, Performance and Change* (Graham & Trotman 1993), ch 2, and G Davies, *Building Societies and their Branches—A Regional Economic Survey*, (Franey 1981).

[2] See the report by John Spalding to the Council of the Building Societies Association on The Future Constitution and Powers of Building Societies (January 1983) and the Final Report in 1984.

for the supervision and regulation of building societies, including the establishment of the Building Societies Commission, an Ombudsman, and an Investor Protection Board; in this way the legislation in this sector accurately predicted what was to follow in 2000 for the financial services world as a whole.

Further freedom of action was conferred on building societies by legislation at the tail end of the Conservative administration in 1996. **17.11**

Building societies under FSMA

FSMA abolished the Building Societies Commission. As deposit-takers, building societies are (with effect from 1 April 2013, like banks) dual regulated under FSMA by both the FCA and the PRA, the successors to the former FSA following the changes to FSMA made by the Financial Services Act 2012 ('FSA 2012'). Subordinate legislation under FSA 2012 apportions the functions of the FSA under the Building Societies Act 1986 between the FCA and the PRA.[3] The regulatory aspects of the Building Societies Act 1986 were repealed by FSMA with effect from 1 December 2001, but the other provisions of that Act remain in effect. The content and effect of the remaining provisions is explained in the Building Societies Regulatory Guide ('BSOG'), updated with effect from 1 April 2010, the provisions of which have (from 1 April 2013) been designated[4] or adopted as FCA guidance, PRA guidance, or both,[5] and published alongside[6] the FCA and PRA Handbooks. The surviving provisions of the Building Societies Act 1986 are mainly constitutional in nature and include such matters as principal purpose, annual accounts, governance, membership, meetings and voting arrangements, and mergers and transfers. Accordingly, some of the FSMA provisions which apply elsewhere do not have any effect for building societies. An example is accounts,[7] and another is business transfers, where Part VII of FSMA is restricted to banks and insurance companies, and the special arrangements for building societies remain.[8] **17.12**

[3] Financial Services Act 2012 (Mutual Socieites) Order 2013 (SI 2013/496), art 2 and Sch 8 amends the Building Societies Act 1986, s 1 to give the FCA the functions of (i) administering the system of regulation of building societies provided for by or under this Act; and (ii) advising and making recommendations to the Treasury and other government departments on any matter relating to building societies. The same Order inserts Building Societies Act 1986. S 1A, which gives the PRA the functions of (i) securing that the principal purpose of building societies remains that of making loans which are secured on residential property and are funded substantially by their members; (ii) administering the system of regulation of building societies provided by or under this Act, but only insofar as ss 5, 6, 7, 9A, and 9B confer functions on the PRA; and (iii) advising and making recommendations to the Treasury and other government departments on any matter relating to building societies.

[4] See Financial Conduct Authority and Prudential Regulation Authority Handbook Designation Instrument 2013 (FCA 2013/8, PRA 2013/3), Annex 36, and related instruments.

[5] Designation or adoption broadly follows the remit of each regulator.

[6] Not all regulatory guidance forms part of the FCA or PRA Handbooks. See Chapter 5, para 5.83 *et seq*.

[7] See BSOG 1.4.1G: every building society is required (by s 71 of the 1986 Act) to keep accounting records which: (1) explain its transactions; (2) disclose, with reasonable accuracy and promptness, the state of its business at any time; and (3) enable the directors and the society to properly discharge their respective duties under the 1986 Act and art 4 of the Regulation of the European Parliament and of the Council of 19 July 2002 on the application of international accounting standards (1606/2002/EC) ('the IAS Regulations') if applicable.

[8] See BSOG 2 (Merger Procedures) and BSOG 3 (Transfer Procedures): Members' approval by ordinary resolution is required where a society proposes to acquire or transfer a relevant business either directly or through a subsidiary. This is necessary with regard to acquisitions or transfers where the activity does not involve lending on residential property or the acquisition or establishment would cost 15 per cent more of the society's own funds. Mergers or business transfers are permitted subject to special resolution of members and the borrowers of the society. Building societies can be dissolved on a three-quarters vote of all of the members holding two-thirds of the shares. Winding-up is by special resolution of members or by the court on specified grounds.

17.13 Building societies are subject to the general prohibition (FSMA, s 19(1)) and (as dual regulated 'PRA-Authorised persons')[9] the permission requirement in FSMA, s 20(1A). Building societies are required to comply with prudential requirements that are directly effective under EU law and all of the relevant provisions of the separate FCA and PRA Handbooks of Rules and Guidance and the PRA Rulebook. These include the FCA and PRA High-Level Standards, PRA Prudential Standards, and (predominantly FCA) Conduct of Business Standards. The PRA Handbook, PRA Rulebook, and directly effective EU prudential requirements have replaced the earlier rule book of the Building Societies Commission and the FSA Interim Prudential Sourcebook for Building Societies ('IPRU(BSOC)'), which was finally revoked with effect from 1 October 2010. The PRA's prudential requirements are supplemented by PRA guidance in the Building Societies Sourcebook ('BSOCS').[10] This Sourcebook contains guidance explaining how the PRA expects building societies might (given the statutory constraints placed upon them by the Building Societies Act 1986) comply with PRA rules. It does not introduce new requirements, but illustrates how building societies may apply the relevant rules.

The Regulation of Home Finance Transactions

Regulated mortgage business

17.14 The first edition of this work includes[11] an account of the development of the policy thinking by which, from 31 October 2004, the FSA became responsible for the authorisation and supervision of certain activities connected with lending on mortgage. Following the replacement of the FSA by the FCA and the PRA from 1 April 2013, mortgage business is now regulated by the FCA. Regulation rests on FSMA, s 22(1), (regulated activities) supplemented by FSMA, Schedule 2, Part II, paragraphs 23 and 23A. Schedule 2, Part II, describes 'in general terms' the investments that may be specified as regulated investments under section 22. Paragraph 23 (loans and other forms of credit) brings within the scope of regulation, rights under any contract under which one person provides another with credit, whether or not the obligation of the borrower is secured on property of any kind 'Credit' is defined widely, to include any cash loan or other financial accommodation and 'cash' defined to include money in any form.[12] Paragraph 23A (other finance arrangements involving land)[13] brings within the scope of regulation, rights under any arrangement for the provision of finance under which the person providing the finance either (a) acquires a major interest in land from the person to whom the finance is provided, or (b) disposes of a major interest in land to that person, as part of the arrangement. A 'major interest' means in relation to land in England

[9] FSMA, ss 417 and 2B(5) define a 'PRA authorised person' as a person that has permission under FSMA Part 4A to carry on a regulated activity that is designated as a PRA-regulated activity under FSMA, s 22A. The Financial Services and Markets Act 2000 (PRA-regulated Activities) Order 2013 (SI 2013/556), art 2(a) designates deposit taking as such an activity. Authorisation by the PRA subjects a firm to regulation by the PRA in respect of issues relevant to the PRA's statutory objectives, but does not relieve the firm of regulation by the FCA in respect of issues relevant to the FCA's separate statutory objectives. Accordingly, FSMA uses the term 'PRA-authorised person' as shorthand for a firm that is dual regulated by both the PRA and the FCA.

[10] Made by the FSA in 2010 and adopted by the PRA as part of its Handbook from 1 April 2013.

[11] At paras 13.17–13.31.

[12] FSMA, Sch 2, Part 2, para 23(2) and (3).

[13] Inserted by the Regulation of Financial Services (Land Transactions) Act 2005.

or in Wales, an estate in fee simple absolute, or a term of years absolute, whether subsisting at law or in equity.[14] It is immaterial whether either party acquires or disposes of the interest in land directly or indirectly.[15]

The regulated activities described in general terms in FSMA, Schedule 2 are set out in detail the Financial Services and Markets Act 2000 (Regulated Activities) Order 2001 (SI 2001/544) ('the RAO'), as amended. The RAO definition of a 'regulated mortgage contract'[16] follows Schedule 2 in its wide ambit but specifies that what is regulated is borrowing secured by 'a first legal mortgage on land'. The FCA's principal guidance on the scope of the mortgage regime is in Chapter 4 of the FCA's Perimeter Guidance Manual ('PERG 4') (Guidance on regulated activities connected with mortgages). **17.15**

The wide range of transactions caught by this definition can be illustrated by an example: if a bank issues a secured bank guarantee or performance bond in favour of its customer, that is potentially a regulated mortgage contract, because the customer will be indebted to the bank if the bank performs under the guarantee.[17] More obviously, other types of secured loan are also potentially regulated mortgage contracts, including secured overdraft facilities, secured bridging loans, a secured credit card facility, and a 'regulated lifetime mortgage contract' under which the borrower takes out a loan where repayment of the capital (and in some cases the interest) is not required until the property is sold, usually on the death of the borrower.[18] **17.16**

To reduce the width of the definition, all but consumer borrowing in relation to domestic property is excluded from regulation. That is achieved by specifying that in addition to the specific features of a mortgage (borrowing secured on land, as previously mentioned), a regulated mortgage contract must also have three more general features: **17.17**

(a) A regulated mortgage contract is a contract between an individual (or a trustee[19] for an individual beneficiary) and a person (the 'lender') who carries on that activity 'by way of business'.[20]
(b) A regulated mortgage contract must be secured on land[21] in the UK (other than timeshare accommodation).[22]
(c) There is an 'occupancy requirement': the individual borrower (or a related person) must use or intend to use at least 40 per cent of that land as a dwelling, or in connection with a dwelling.[23] A 'related person' is a close relative (grandparent, parent, sibling, child, or grandchild), or partner (spouse, civil partner, partner in fact).[24]

[14] FSMA, Sch 2, Part 11, para 23(2)(a).
[15] ibid, para 23(3).
[16] RAO, art 61(3)(a)(ii).
[17] PERG 4.4.1AG(2).
[18] PERG 4.4.11G.
[19] RAO, art 61(3)(a)(i).
[20] An activity is not a regulated activity unless it is carried on by way of business in the UK.
[21] RAO, art 61(3)(a)(ii).
[22] Overnight accommodation which is the subject of a timeshare contract within the meaning of the Timeshare, Holiday Products, Resale and Exchange Contracts Regulations 2010 (SI 2010/2960).
[23] RAO, art 61(3)(a)(iii).
[24] ibid, art 61(4)(c).

17.18 The combination of these features has the result that, for example, loans to companies secured on company property will not be regulated mortgaged contracts. But loans to individual sole traders or to partners may be, if the loans are secured on residential property.[25]

17.19 If the borrower is a trustee, then the existence of these features is tested by reference to the actions, intentions, and relationships of an individual beneficiary of the trust.[26] All the features must be present at the time the transaction is entered into.[27] If they are all present, the contract is and remains a regulated mortgage contract. If the contract is subsequently amended so that one of the features is no longer present, the contract will still be a regulated mortgage contract. The corollary is also true: a contract cannot become a regulated mortgage contract by subsequent variation.[28] That produces certainty because it means that fine judgments are not required about whether variations might lead to a change in regulatory status. But there may nevertheless, it seems, be difficult questions of degree as to whether a contract has been varied (no change in status) or replaced (status assessed afresh at the time of replacement).[29]

17.20 Because the 'occupancy requirement' imposes an arbitrary 40 per cent threshold it can occasionally produce odd results. But, for the most part it is relatively straightforward in its effect as the following examples show:

(a) The large garden of a residential property will most likely be used 'in connection with' the dwelling.
(b) Loans to purchase farmland that are secured on that land are unlikely to be regulated mortgage contracts. First, because the proportion of the land destined for use as or in connection with a dwelling (the farm house and garden) is probably less than 40 per cent of the total. Second, because the FCA does not regard farmland as 'used in connection with' the farmhouse.[30]
(c) 'Buy to let' mortgages secured on the rental property are generally not regulated mortgage contracts. But they may be in some cases. For example, a mortgage to purchase a property to be leased to a 'connected person' (the flat purchased for the borrower's son or daughter at university), or a mortgage to purchase a property that the borrower intends ultimately to use as a dwelling (the cottage by the sea, purchased in anticipation of retirement, but leased out in the meantime) will both be regulated mortgage contracts.[31]

17.21 A person acting by way of business in the UK might (unless he is otherwise exempt) carry on one of six regulated activities in relation to a regulated mortgage contract:[32]

(a) arranging (bringing about) regulated mortgage contracts;[33]
(b) making arrangements with a view to regulated mortgage contracts;[34]
(c) advising on regulated mortgage contracts;[35]

25 PERG 4.4.2G.
26 RAO, art 61(3)(a)(iii).
27 ibid, art 61(3).
28 PERG 4.4.3G.
29 PERG 4.4.4G.
30 PERG 4.4.7G.
31 PERG 4.4.8G.
32 PERG 4.3.1G.
33 RAO, art 25A(1).
34 ibid, art 25A(2).
35 ibid, art 53A.

(d) entering into a regulated mortgage contract as lender;[36]
(e) administering a regulated mortgage contract, where that contract was entered into by way of business after 31 October 2004;[37] and
(f) agreeing to carry on any of the above.[38]

As always with FCA (and indeed PRA) rules, terminology is important, so it is worth keeping in mind the following definitions and collective nouns extracted from the Glossary to the FCA and PRA Handbooks: **17.22**

(a) A regulated mortgage contract is a subset of '*home finance transaction*'.
(b) Collectively, all the regulated activities in paragraph 17.21 are '*regulated mortgage activities*' and a subset of '*home finance activities*'.
(c) The regulated activities of arranging, making arrangements with a view to, and advising on a regulated mortgage contract are collectively defined as '*mortgage mediation activities*'. A person that has (or ought to have) permission to carry on any of these activities is a '*mortgage intermediary*' and its activities are a subset of '*home finance mediation activity*'. That means the firm is also a '*home finance intermediary*'.
(d) A person that has (or ought to have) permission to arrange or make arrangements with a view to a regulated mortgage contract is a '*mortgage arranger*' and also a mortgage intermediary and a '*home finance arranger*'.
(e) A person that has (or ought to have) permission to advise on regulated mortgage contracts is a '*mortgage adviser*' and also a mortgage intermediary and a '*home finance adviser*'.
(f) A person that has (or ought to have) permission to enter into a regulated mortgage contract is a '*mortgage lender*' and its activities are a subset of '*home finance providing activity*' or '*home financing*'. That means the firm is also a '*home finance provider*'.
(g) A person that has (or ought to have) permission to administer a regulated mortgage contract is a '*mortgage administrator*' and its activities are a subset of '*administering a home finance transaction*'. That means the firm is also a '*home finance administrator*'.

Terminological overload aside, the overall result is that there is a good analogy between the range of regulated activities relating to insurance and to regulated mortgage business. In each case, pre-contract broking or producing activities are regulated (arranging deals or making arrangements for deals in the contract or plan, or advising on it), as is the activity of lending or insuring as principal, and the post-contract activity of administering the contract. **17.23**

Each activity identified in paragraph 17.21 is subject to exemptions, the detail of which can be found in the RAO and on which the FCA has given guidance in PERG 4. For present purposes, however, it is useful to note the following limitations and extensions to the scope of regulated mortgage activities: **17.24**

(a) Mortgage mediation activities are regulated only if the services comprised in those activities are provided to a borrower.[39] Services provided only to a lender are not regulated.

---

[36] ibid, art 61(1).
[37] ibid, art 61(2).
[38] ibid, art 64. The FCA's view (in the context of insurance mediation, at least) is that the art 64 regulated activity concerns 'the entering into of a legally binding agreement to provide the services to which the agreement relates' (see PERG 5.9.1G). Accordingly, a lender or provider should not be carrying on a regulated activity under RAO art 64 merely because it makes an offer to lend or participate in the arrangements.
[39] RAO, art 25A—the regulated activity is arranging (or making arrangements) for a person to enter into a regulated mortgage contract 'as borrower'.

(b) The rider to the definition of mortgage administration (in paragraph 17.21(e)) has the effect that administering a contract is not a regulated activity if the lender was a private lender, not acting by way of business.

(c) A person cannot carry on the regulated activity of arranging or advising unless he does so by way of business. But the 'By Way of Business Order'[40] goes further:

> 'A person is not to be regarded as carrying on by way of business [mortgage mediation activity] unless he carries on the business of engaging in that activity'.[41]

The FCA's interpretation is that 'this is a narrower test than that of carrying on regulated activities by way of business (as required by [FSMA s.] 22…), as it requires the regulated activities to represent the carrying on of a business in their own right.'[42]

Pressure to extend the scope of regulation

17.25 The regime for regulated mortgage activities came under pressure from two developments. First, from the growth of 'equity release transactions' driven by substantial rises in the value of domestic property. These schemes allow a home owner to release some of the capital value in his home by selling some of his interest in it, while retaining the right to occupy the property. Schemes based on 'lifetime mortgages'[43] were already regulated because they included a regulated mortgage contract. But 'home reversion schemes', under which a home owner sells outright an interest in his property, but on condition that he remains entitled to occupy the property, were not caught except to the extent that the transaction included a regulated financial services product, such as a bond or a contract of insurance.[44]

17.26 Second, from the need to accommodate Islamic finance arrangements within the regulatory structure. Some of these are regulated mortgage contracts, for example, Murabaha arrangements, under which an institution buys and re-sells a home to a consumer, accepting payment of the price over a long period. Others were not regulated, including Ijara and Diminishing Musharaka products, under which a provider buys a property and a consumer agrees to purchase it (or an increasing interest in it) over time or at the end of an agreed period, combined with a right (under a lease) to occupy the part of the property that the consumer does not own.[45]

17.27 The process of extending the regulatory regime began in December 2005, when the Regulation of Financial Services (Land Transactions) Act 2005 came into force. That Act (by amendment to FSMA) specified a new class of investment in relation to which a person might carry on a regulated activity:

> …rights under any arrangement for the provision of finance under which the person providing the finance either… acquires a major interest in land from the person to whom the finance is provided, or… disposes of a major interest in land to that person.[46]

---

40 Financial Services and Markets Act 2000 (Carrying on Regulated Activities by Way of Business) Order 2001, SI 2001/1177.

41 ibid, art 3A.

42 PERG 2.3.2G(2).

43 Under which a home owner borrows money on mortgage, but on terms that interest is rolled up and repayable only at the end of the mortgage term.

44 See, eg, *Investors Compensation Scheme Ltd v West Bromwich Building Society* [1998] 1 WLR 896 (HL).

45 HM Treasury, 'Secondary legislation for the regulation of Home Reversion and Home Purchase Plans: A consultation' (March 2006), p 6.

46 FSMA, Sch 2, Part 2 para 23A (Other finance arrangements involving land).

The RAO was then amended[47] to include the detailed specification of two new home finance products, to sit alongside the regulated mortgage contract: the home reversion plan and the home purchase plan. The policy intention was as far as possible to create a level playing field, on which, from 6 April 2007, the existing and new 'home finance transactions'[48] would be treated equally. As a result, the amendments to the RAO closely followed the model used for the regulated mortgage contract. The FCA's principal guidance on the scope of the regime for regulated home purchase plans and regulated home reversion plans is in PERG 14 (Guidance on home reversion and home purchase activities). **17.28**

Home reversion plans, home purchase plans, and regulated sale and rent back agreements

Under a 'regulated home reversion plan'[49] the provider buys a qualifying interest in land (for example, in England a freehold or leasehold estate)[50] from an individual seller, who remains entitled to occupy the land for at least 20 years, or until he enters a care home or dies.[51] **17.29**

Under a 'regulated home purchase plan'[52] the provider buys a qualifying interest in land. An individual purchaser is entitled to occupy the land and agrees to buy the provider's interest over the course of, or at the end of, a specified period. If the provider's interest is an undivided share, it must be held on trust for the provider and the individual purchaser as beneficial tenants in common. **17.30**

Under a 'regulated sale and rent back agreement'[53] the provider buys all or part of a qualifying interest in land from an individual 'agreement seller' who is entitled to occupy at least 40 per cent of the land in question as or in connection with a dwelling, and intends to do so. **17.31**

None of a home reversion plan, a home purchase plan or regulated sale and rent back agreement will be regulated unless in addition to exhibiting these specific characteristics it also exhibits three more general characteristics which limit the scope of regulation to consumer transactions in residential land. These general characteristics are very similar to the general characteristics of a regulated mortgage contract outlined in paragraph 17.15 *et seq.*, but with some variation: **17.32**

(a) Each activity must be performed under an arrangement (comprising one or more instruments or agreements) between an individual (or a trustee[54] for an individual beneficiary) and a person (the 'provider') who carries on that activity 'by way of business'. Except for the reference to 'arrangements'[55] that is the same as for regulated mortgage contracts.

[47] By the Financial Services and Markets Act 2000 (Regulated Activities) (Amendment) (No 2) Order 2006, SI 2006/2383.

[48] The portmanteau term, covering activities relating to regulated mortgage contracts, regulated home reversion plans, and regulated home purchase plans. See para 175.22 and 17.35.

[49] RAO, art 63B(3).

[50] ibid, art 63B(4)(a).

[51] ibid, art 63B(4)(d).

[52] ibid, art 63F(3).

[53] RAO, art 63J.

[54] ibid, art 63B(3)(a)(i) (home reversion plans); art 63F(3)(a)(i) (home purchase plans); and art 63J(3)(a)(i) (sale and rent back agreements).

[55] The same terminology is used elsewhere in the legislation, for example in FSMA, s 235 (Collective investment schemes).

(b) A regulated arrangement, 'plan' or agreement must relate to land or an interest in land[56] in the UK (other than timeshare accommodation).[57] That is essentially the same as for regulated mortgage contracts.

(c) There is an 'occupancy requirement': the individual participant in the plan, arrangement or agreement (or a related person)[58] must be entitled (and intend) to use at least 40 per cent of that land as a dwelling, or in connection with a dwelling.[59] This requirement is the same as for a regulated mortgage contract, except that the individual must in the case of a home reversion plan, home purchase plan or regulated sale and rent back agreement be 'entitled' to occupy the home. 'Related person' is defined as for the borrower under a regulated mortgage contract (see paragraph 17.17(c)). It seems logical that the FCA's guidance on the operation of the occupancy test in relation to regulated mortgage contracts[60] should apply *mutatis mutandis* in this context also, though the guidance does not say so.

17.33 If the participant in the plan, arrangement, or agreement is a trustee, then the existence of these features is tested by reference to the actions, intentions, and relationships of an individual beneficiary of the trust.[61] All the features must be present at the time the transaction is entered into.[62] If they are all present, the plan is and remains a regulated home reversion plan, home purchase plan, or regulated sale and rent back agreement. If the plan, arrangement, or agreement is subsequently amended so that one of the features is no longer present, the plan will still be a regulated home reversion plan, home purchase plan, or regulated sale and rent back agreement. The corollary is also true: a plan cannot become a regulated home reversion plan or home purchase plan by later amendment.[63]

17.34 A person acting by way of business in the UK might (unless he is otherwise exempt) carry on one of six regulated activities in relation to home reversion plans or home purchase plans.[64]

(a) Arranging (bringing about) home reversion plans,[65] home purchase plans,[66] or sale and rent back agreements;[67]

[56] RAO, art 63B(3)(a)(i) (home reversion plans); art 63F(3)(a)(i) (home purchase plans); and art 63J(3)(a)(i) (sale and rent back agreements).

[57] Note that RAO, art 63B(4)(b) (home reversion plans) provides that a 'timeshare' is as defined in the Timeshare Act 1992 and RAO, art 63F(4) (home purchase plans) adopts that definition. However, the Timeshare Act 1992 was repealed by the Timeshare, Holiday Products, Resale and Exchange Contracts Regulations 2010 (SI 2010/2960), Part 9, reg 36. As noted earlier, a revised definition of 'timeshare accomodation' now appears in the Regulations and RAO, art 61(4)(d) adopts the revised definition in relation to regulated mortgage contracts. In addition, RAO, art 63J(4)(b) adopts the revised definition in relation to regulated sale and rent back agreements.

[58] RAO, art 63B(4)(c) (home reversion plans); art 63F(4) (home purchase plans); 63J(4)c) (sale and rent back agreements).

[59] ibid, art 63B(3)(a)(ii) (home reversion plans); art 63F(3)(a)(iv) (home purchase plans); and art 63J(3)(a)(ii) (sale and rent back agreements).

[60] In PERG 4.4.6G to 4.4.9G.

[61] RAO, art 63B(3)(a)(ii) (home reversion plans); art 63F(3)(a)(iv) (home purchase plans); and art 63J(3)(a)(ii) (sale and rent back agreements).

[62] ibid, art 63B(3) (home reversion plans); art 63F(3) (home purchase plans); and art 63J(3)(a) (sale and rent back agreements).

[63] The FCA has not published guidance to this effect, but see HM Treasury, 'Secondary legislation for the regulation of Home Reversion and Home Purchase Plans: A consultation' (March 2006): home reversion plans (para 3.6), and home purchase plans (para 3.21). And see HM Treasury, 'Regulating the sale and rent back market: a consultation', February 2009, para 3.12 (sale and rent back agreements).

[64] PERG 14.2.

[65] RAO art 25B(1).

[66] ibid, art 25C(1).

[67] RAO, art 25E(1).

(b) Making arrangements with a view to home reversion plans,[68] home purchase plans,[69] or sale and rent back agreements;[70]
(c) Advising on home reversion plans,[71] home purchase plans,[72] or sale and rent back agreements;[73]
(d) Entering into home reversion plans,[74] home purchase plans,[75] or sale and rent back agreements[76] as provider;
(e) Administering home reversion plans,[77] home purchase plans,[78] or sale and rent back agreements;[79] and
(f) Agreeing to carry on any of the above.[80]

As indicated in paragraph 17.22, terminology is important: **17.35**

(a) A home reversion plan, home purchase plan, or sale and rent back agreement is subset of '*home finance transaction*'.
(b) Collectively, all the regulated activities in paragraph 17.34 are '*reversion activities*' (when they relate to a home reversion plan), or '*home purchase activities*' (when they relate to a home purchase plan), or '*regulated sale and rent back activities*') when they relate to a sale and rent back agreement. Each of these sets of activities is a subset of '*home finance activities*'.
(c) The regulated activities of arranging, making arrangements with a view to and advising on a home reversion plan, a home purchase plan, or a sale and rent back agreement are collectively defined as '*reversion mediation activity*', '*home purchase mediation activity*', or '*regulated sale and rent back mediation activity*'. A person that has (or ought to have) permission to carry on any of these activities is a '*reversion intermediary*', '*home purchase intermediary*', or '*SRB intermediary*', and its activities are a subset of '*home finance mediation activity*'. That means the firm is also a '*home finance intermediary*'.
(d) A person that has (or ought to have) permission to arrange or make arrangements with a view to a home reversion plan, home purchase plan, or regulated sale and rent back agreement is a '*reversion arranger*' (also a '*reversion intermediary*'), a '*home purchase arranger*', (also a '*home purchase intermediary*'), or an '*SRB arranger*' (also an '*SRB intermediary*'), and a '*home finance arranger*'.
(e) A person that has (or ought to have) permission to advise on a home reversion plan or home purchase plan is a '*reversion adviser*' (also a '*reversion intermediary*'), a '*home purchase adviser*', (also a '*home purchase intermediary*'), or an '*SRB adviser*' (also an '*SRB intermediary*'), and a '*home finance adviser*'.

68 ibid, art 25B(2).
69 ibid, art 25C(2).
70 RAO, art 25E(2).
71 ibid, art 53B.
72 ibid, art 53A.
73 RAO, art 53C.
74 ibid, art 63B.
75 ibid, art 63F.
76 RAO, art 63J(1).
77 ibid, art 63B.
78 ibid, art 63F.
79 RAO, art 63J(2).
80 ibid, art 64. See n 28.

(f) A person that has (or ought to have) permission to enter into a home reversion plan, a home purchase plan, or a regulated sale and rent back agreement is a '*reversion provider*', or a '*home purchase provider*', or an '*SRB agreement provider*' and its activities are a subset of '*home finance providing activity*' or '*home financing*'. That means the firm is also a '*home finance provider*'.

(g) The consumer or trustee participant in the plan, arrangement, or agreement is the '*reversion occupier*',[81] the '*home purchaser*', or the '*SRB agreement seller*'.

(h) A person that has (or ought to have) permission to administer a home reversion plan, home purchase plan, or regulated sale and rent back agreement is a '*reversion administrator*', a '*home purchase administrator*', or an '*SRB administrator*', and its activities are a subset of '*administering a home finance transaction*'. That means the firm is also a '*home finance administrator*'.

(i) Collectively, lifetime mortgages (see paragraph 17.25) and home reversion plans are '*equity release transactions*'.

17.36 The range of regulated activities is, therefore, essentially the same as for regulated mortgage activities, and as in that case, each activity identified in paragraph 17.34 is subject to exemptions, the detail of which can be found in the RAO and on which the FCA has given guidance in PERG 14.

17.37 Unlike the mortgage (and home purchase plan) market, a significant part of the home reversion market is made up of private investors acting as the reversion provider.[82] The same is proabably also true of the regulated sale and rent back agreement market.[83] This is reflected in two ways in the FCA's rules:

(a) Mortgage mediation activities and home purchase mediation activities are only regulated activities if provided to the borrower[84] or to the home purchaser[85] respectively. Similarly, reversion mediation activities and regulated sale and rent back mediation activities are regulated when provided to the reversion occupier and the SRB agreement seller. However, reflecting the number of private investors who act as reversion providers or SRB agreement providers, reversion mediation activities and SRB mediation activities are also regulated when provided to a reversion provider[86] or an SRB agreement provider.[87]

(b) Mortgage administration and home purchase administration are regulated activities only where motgagee or purchaser enters into the mortgage or plan 'by way of business' after the commencement of regulation[88]. However, reversion administration and SRB agreement administration are regulated activities whether or not the provider enters

[81] Referred to in the RAO as the 'reversion seller'.

[82] Explanatory Memorandum to the Financial Services and Markets Act 2000 (Regulated Activities) (Amendment) (No 2) Order 2006, SI 2006/2383, prepared by HM Treasury.

[83] HM Treasury, 'Regulating the sale and rent back market: a consultation', February 2009, para 2.16: 'The sale and rent back market is a relatively new market, and has grown rapidly in recent years. The sector appears to be highly fragmented, comprising a very large number of small firms, including non-professional landlords . . .'.

[84] See para 15.24(a).

[85] RAO, art 25C(1) and 53C(1).

[86] ibid, arts 25B and 53B.

[87] RAO, arts 25(1)(a) and (2); and RAO, art 53D(a).

[88] RAO, art 61(2) (regulated mortgage contracts); RAO, art 63F(2) (home purchase plans).

into the plan or agreement 'by way of business'.[89] The administration of such a plan or agreement on behalf of a private provider is therefore a regulated activity.

A person cannot carry on the regulated activity of advising or arranging unless he does so by way of business. But, as with regulated mortgage contracts (see paragraph 17.24(c)), the 'By Way of Business Order'[90] goes further: **17.38**

> A person is not to be regarded as carrying on by way of business [reversion mediation activity, home purchase mediation activity or SRB agreement mediation activity] unless he carries on the business of engaging in that activity.[91]

The FCA's interpretation is that 'this is a narrower test than that of carrying on regulated activities by way of business (as required by [FSMA s.] 22 ...), as it requires the regulated activities to represent the carrying on of a business in their own right'.[92]

In recognition of the fact that providers of regulated sale and rent back agreements will often be individuals, the By Way of Busines Order deems SRB agreement providers to be acting by way of business (and so, other things being equal, brings them within the scope of regulation), unless the provider of the agreement and the seller are related.[93] **17.39**

Hybrid home finance products

Products that share features of home purchase plans and regulated mortgage contracts are treated as home purchase plans.[94] Products that share features of home reversion plans and regulated sale and rent back agreements are treated as home reversion plans.[95] **17.40**

The Prudential Sourcebook for Mortgage and Home Finance Firms and Insurance Intermediaries ('MIPRU')

The PRA's regulatory remit extends only to (a) firms that are authorised to carry on regulated activities that are designated as 'PRA-regulated activities' in subordinate legislation;[96] and (b) investment firms[97] designated on an ad hoc basis as subject to regulation by the PRA.[98] At the time of writing in 2013, only insurance business and deposit taking have been designated as PRA-regulated activities, and no investment firms have yet been subjected to regulation by the PRA. It follows that despite its title the FCA is in fact responsible for **17.41**

---

89 ibid, art 63B(2) (home reversion plans); and art 63J(2) (regulated sale and rent back agreements).

90 Financial Services and Markets Act 2000 (Carrying on Regulated Activities by way of Business) Order 2001, SI 2001/1177.

91 ibid, art 3B (home reversion plans); art 3C (home purchase plans); and art 3D (regulated sale and rent back agreements).

92 PERG 2.3.2G(2).

93 Financial Services and Markets Act 2000 (Carrying on Regulated Activities by way of Business) Order 2001, SI 2001/1177, art 5. 'Related' in this context means that the buyer and seller are 'related persons' as defined in RAO, art 63J(4)(c).

94 RAO, art 61(3), rider to the definition of a regulated mortgage contract: 'such a [regulated mortgage contract] is not a regulated mortgage contract if it is a regulated home purchase plan'. See also rider to PERG 4.4.1G.

95 RAO, art 63J(3) rider.

96 FSMA, s 22A and the Financial Services and Markets Act 2000 (PRA-regulated Activities) Order 2013 (SI 2013/556).

97 That is, firms with permission to carry on the regulated activity of 'dealing in investments as principal'.

98 Financial Services and Markets Act 2000 (PRA-regulated Activities) Order 2013 (SI 2013/556), art 3 *et seq.*

both the conduct and prudential regulation of firms that are neither banks nor insurers. For present purposes, the result is that the PRA is the prudential regulator and the FCA is the conduct regulator of banks that carry on home finance activities,[99] but the FCA is both the prudential and conduct regulator of home finance firms that are not banks. For these reasons, the Prudential Sourcebook for Mortgage and Home Finance Firms and Insurance Intermediaries ('MIPRU') forms part of both the FCA and the PRA Handbooks and its provisions generally refer to 'the appropriate regulator', meaning the PRA for dual-reglated firms (ie banks) and otherwise the FCA.

The requirement for home finance providers to use authorised intermediaries

17.42 A person that is authorised under FSMA (a 'firm' in the jargon of the FCA and PRA Handbooks) must not use, or propose to use, the services of another person consisting of home finance mediation activity[100] unless that intermediary is itself authorised, or an exempt person, or an exempt professional firm, or is not carrying on his activity in the UK.[101]

17.43 That requirement is contained in MIPRU 5 Guidance indicates that the requirement is intended to have the effect that if there is a chain of intermediaries between the provider and the borrower, reversion occupier or home purchaser, all the UK intermediaries in the chain must be authorised:

> 'To avoid the loss of protection where an intermediary itself uses the services of an unauthorised person this chapter also ensures that each person in the chain of those providing services is authorised'.[102]

17.44 However, it is difficult to see how that result is achieved since the MIPRU 5 applies only to firms which have permission for home financing (that is, providers of home finance transactions, see the hierarchy of glossary definitions in paragraph 17.34) The FCA and the PRA indicate that they each regard a firm as 'using' the services of

in particular, its immediate counterparty (typically the intermediary that passed the business to the firm) and of all other persons who have been granted the right or authority *directly by the firm* to enter into a home finance transaction[103] (emphasis added).

17.45 But that offers little assistance as it is consistent with the application of MIPRU 5 only to immediate counterparties and not to intermediaries lower down the chain.[104]

Prudential requirements for home finance firms

17.46 Most firms regulated by the FCA or PRA must hold capital resources (broadly, net assets of a specified minimum quality) or other financial resources in excess of a capital resources requirement. The precise content of these capital or 'prudential' requirements varies for

99 Restrictions imposed under EC Insurance Directives prevent (with very limited latitude) insurance companies from carrying on business other than insurance.

100 That is, any mortgage mediation activity, home purchase mediation activity, reversion mediation activity or regulated sale and rent back mediation activity.

101 MIPRU 5.2.1R and 5.2.2R.

102 MIPRU 5.1.2G.

103 MIPRU 5.2.1A G.

104 The result would be different if MIPRU 5 applied to firms with permission to carry on 'home finance activities', since that encompasses both home finance providers and home finance intermediaries. Complexity has its perils, for the FCA and the PRA as much as for regulated firms.

different types of firm and for the combination of business that the firm carries on. In outline, MIPRU operates by applying to the firms within its scope a combination of requirements to hold professional indemnity insurance (which apply to home finance intermediaries) and capital requirements (which apply to all firms carrying on home finance activities). The capital requirements and insurance requirements are interlinked (for example because capital requirements rise as the excess applicable to a firm's professional indemnity insurance increases and because both capital and insurance requirements increase as the firm's annual income increases). The capital requirements are proportioned to reflect the volume of the firm's business and are higher if the firm holds client assets or client money.

Professional indemnity insurance requirements for home finance mediation firms

MIPRU 3 requires that (subject to the exceptions in paragraph 17.49), unless a home finance intermediary has net tangible assets of more than a specified minimum amount, it must carry professional indemnity insurance of appropriate quality.[105] **17.47**

That insurance must[106] provide: **17.48**

(a) cover in respect of claims for which a firm may be liable as a result of the conduct of itself, its employees and its appointed representatives (acting within the scope of their appointment);
(b) a specified minimum limit of indemnity per year, usually proportioned to the firm's annual income;
(c) an excess no higher than a specified amount. The permitted excess is higher if the firm holds client money or client assets, reflecting the greater risk to which the firm is exposed. A firm may hold a contract of insurance that imposes a larger excess, but it must then hold a specified amount of additional capital;[107]
(d) appropriate cover in respect of legal defence costs;
(e) continuous cover in respect of claims arising from work carried out from the date on which the firm was given permission to carry on home finance mediation activity; and
(f) cover in respect of Ombudsman awards made against the firm.

A home finance intermediary need not hold professional indemnity insurance in all cases. For example, insurance is not required if the firm has the benefit of a 'comparable guarantee' from another authorised person with a specified minimum level of financial resources. A comparable guarantee is a written agreement on terms at least equal to those in the contract of professional indemnity insurance that would otherwise be required, provided to finance the claims that might arise as a result of a breach by the firm of its duties under the regulatory system or the civil law.[108] **17.49**

Capital requirements

Not all firms that carry on home finance activities have their capital requirements set in MIPRU. A bank, building society, solo consolidated subsidiary of a bank or a building society, insurer, or friendly society that carries on home finance activity is subject to the capital requirements set in the Prudential Sourcebook that applies specifically to firms of that **17.50**

105 MIPRU 3.1.1R.
106 MIPRU 3.2.4R.
107 MIPRU 3.2.14R.
108 MIPRU 3.1.1R(3) and (4).

type.[109] Similarly, MIPRU does not apply to a firm with a permission limited to designated investment business,[110] or authorised professional firms whose home finance activities are incidental to the practice of their profession.[111]

17.51 Credit unions cannot carry on home purchase activities or reversion activities[112] but may carry on mortgage lending activities, mortgage administration activities, or mortgage mediation activities. Small credit unions (assets and number of members below a specified minimum threshold)[113] and credit unions that have permission for mortgage lending activity or mortgage administration activity, but not for insurance or mortgage mediation activity, have their capital requirements set by the FCA and PRA Credit Unions New Sourcebook ('CREDS').[114]

Capital requirements for firms to which MIPRU applies

17.52 MIPRU 4 requires a firm to meet, on a continuing basis, a basic solvency requirement (the firm must at all times ensure that it is able to meet its liabilities as they fall due)[115] and a minimum capital resources requirement (the firm must at all times maintain capital resources equal to or in excess of its relevant capital resources requirement).[116] Unless a rule requires otherwise, the firm must (in determining whether or not it meets these requirements) recognise an asset or liability, and measure its amount, in accordance with the accounting principles that apply to the firm in preparing its annual financial statements.[117] MIPRU 4.3 specifies how a firm's annual income is to be calculated, in order to determine both the limits of the required professional indemnity insurance (if the firm carries on home finance mediation activities) and as a component of the calculation of a firm's capital resource requirement. MIPRU 4.4 contains rules which specify which assets and other items are eligible to contribute to a firm's capital resources, and which items must be deducted.

17.53 The structure underlying MIPRU 4 is that the capital resources requirement for a home finance firm varies according to the particular home finance activity (or combination of home finance activities) that it carries on. MIPRU 4.2.10R sets out the most common combinations in a table, with cross references to the particular rules specifying the capital requirement applicable to that activity or combination of activities. In general the capital resource requirement is the sum of a fixed minimum amount and a percentage of a specified measure of the volume of the firm's activity or its size (commonly annual income). There are also specific additions or deductions to reflect particular risks or features of certain activities combinations of activities.

17.54 There are three deviations from this general approach:

(a) If a firm carries on regulated activities that include designated investment business, the capital resources requirement is the higher of that imposed by MIPRU or the specific FCA and PRA Prudential Sourcebook that applies to its activities.[118]

---

109 MIPRU 4.1.4R.
110 MIPRU 4.1.6R.
111 MIPRU 4.1.10R.
112 MIPRU 4.1.9G.
113 MIPRU 4.1.8R.
114 MIPRU 4.1.8R.
115 MIPRU 4.2.1R.
116 MIPRU 4.2.2R.
117 MIPRU 4.2.3R.
118 MIPRU 4.2.5R.

(b) A credit union to which MIPRU applies (see paragraph 17.51) has its capital requirement set as the higher of the MIPRU requirement in respect of its mediation activities (disregarding its activities that are not mediation), or the requirement imposed by the FCA and PRA Credit Unions New Sourcebook ('CREDS'), or (if it has permission to carry on designated investment business and is approved to provide Child Trust Funds) the requirement imposed under chapter 8 of the Interim Prudential Sourcebook for Investment Firms.[119]

(c) Social housing firms (wholly-owned subsidiaries of local authorities or registered social landlords that carry on non-profit regulated activities in connection with housing) that carry on only home financing (that is, the activity of providing mortgages, home reversion plans, or home purchase plans) or home financing administration activities, have a minimal capital requirement: their net tangible assets must be greater than zero.[120] That concession ceases to apply if the firm takes up mediation activities.[121]

Conduct of Business requirements for home finance firms

The relevant requirements are set out in the Mortgage and Home Finance: Conduct of Business Sourcebook ('MCOB'), which forms part of the FCA's Handbook. MCOB applies to the communication or approval of a financial promotion of qualifying credit,[122] of a home purchase plan, of a home reversion plan and of a regulated sale and rent back agreement[123] and to every phase of the life-cycle of a home finance transaction. **17.55**

Business customers

There is an important adjustment to the way MCOB operates in relation to business loans secured on domestic property. The general position (see paragraphs 17.17 and 17.18) is that loans secured on property used exclusively for business purposes are not regulated mortgage contracts, because the occupancy requirement (at least 40 per cent of the property must be used or intended to be used as a dwelling) is not met. But, of course, loans taken out for business purposes may be secured on domestic property that meets the occupancy requirement. In that case MCOB applies if the loan is for the purposes of a business which has a group annual turnover of less than a specified amount (£1 million at the time of writing). Information in the annual report and accounts of the business, or its business plan, should be a sufficient basis for determining its turnover. A firm may also rely on other information provided by the customer about the annual turnover of the business, unless, taking a 'common sense view', there is reason to doubt it.[124] **17.56**

If the property, the purpose of the loan, and the size of the business are such that MCOB does apply, then the firm has the option of either complying with MCOB in its unmodified **17.57**

119 MIPRU 4.2.6R.

120 MIPRU 4.2.7R.

121 MIPRU 4.2.8G.

122 Credit offered by a person who enters into or administers regulated mortgage contracts and secured on land. Qualifying credit thus includes, but also goes beyond credit provided by way of a regulated mortgage contract.

123 MCOB 3 sets out particular requirements relating to the financial promotion of qualifying credit, home reversion plans, and regulated sale and rent back agreements. MCOB 3.2.-1G (note the use of the minus sign, indicating that this provision appears immediately before MCOB 3.2.1) indicates that (with limited exceptions) the rules in this chapter do not apply to the communication or approval of a financial promotion of a home purchase plan.

124 MCOB 1.2.6G.

form, or of complying with it as modified by a set of 'tailored provisions' for business loans, located throughout MCOB.[125] In general, the effect of the tailored provisions is to reduce the burden on the firm, although some additional requirements apply if the firm opts to rely on the tailored provisions.

17.58 There is guidance to the effect that whether a regulated mortgage contract is for a business purpose is a matter of fact to be determined by a firm depending on the individual circumstances of each case. In the FCA's opinion, a regulated mortgage contract secured, for example, on the borrower's own home, but used to finance the purchase of a single buy-to-let property will not be for a business purpose.[126] That suggests that notions of continuity and regularity that are relevant to determine whether a firm carries on an activity 'by way of business' under FSMA generally,[127] should be relevant also in determining whether a loan is for a business purposes.

Pre-contractual arrangements made by a home finance provider

17.59 Generally, a person who participates in a transaction as a principal does not also carry on the regulated activity of arranging that transaction, or making arrangements with a view to that transaction.[128] That is replicated for home finance transactions by RAO, article 28A. So, for example, when the general position applies, a mortgage lender that carries on the regulated activity of entering into a regulated mortgage contract as lender, does not also carry on a mortgage mediation activity, even if it arranges the loan using its own staff.

17.60 But that is not the position in relation to home finance providers under MCOB. Their activities which would be arranging but for RAO, article 28A are treated as if they were regulated activities.[129] The result is that MCOB applies to those activities.

Responsible lending and responsible financing

17.61 MCOB 11 imposes requirements on mortgage lenders and home purchase providers that sit alongside the more general obligation under FCA Principle for Business 6 to have due regard to customers' interests and treat them fairly. The intention is to ensure that a customer is not exploited by a firm that lends in circumstances where the customer is 'self-evidently unable to repay through income and yet [has] no alternative means of repayment'.[130] In pursuit of that policy a firm is required to be able to demonstrate that, in deciding to make an advance or further advance to the customer, it took into account the customer's ability to repay the loan.[131]

17.62 The firm may rely on the customer's self-certification of income only if appropriate, having regard to the interests of the customer, and where the firm has no reasonable grounds for doubting the information provided.[132] Guidance indicates that it may be appropriate for the firm to accept self-certification for a range of reasons, including an established payment history, where proof of income is not readily available because of the nature of the customer's

125 MCOB 1.2.3R.
126 MCOB 1.2.5G(2).
127 See, eg, PERG 2.3 (The business element).
128 RAO art 28.
129 MCOB 1.2.12R.
130 MCOB 11.2.1G
131 MCOB 11.3.1R.
132 MCOB 11.3.2R.

employment, or where the customer has a deadline for entering into the contract (for example, where a regulated mortgage contract is taken out to fund the purchase of a property at auction), so that there is insufficient time for the firm to complete 'its usual enquiries'.[133] Overall, the tenor of the rules and guidance is that there is a fairly wide margin of discretion available to firms in deciding whether a customer can repay. It will, however, be relatively easy to conclude with hindsight that, for example, a person was 'self-evidently unable to pay'. Robust processes and a well-documented decision are likely to be the best defence against retrospective judgements of that kind.

Two specific requirements apply to mortgage lenders. First, a mortgage lender is required to make and keep an adequate record to show that it took the customer's ability to pay into account.[134] Second, a mortgage lender must put in place, record, and operate in accordance with, a written policy setting out the factors it will take into account in assessing a customer's ability to repay.[135] Guidance indicates that the assumption underlying that policy should normally be that loans will be repaid from the customer's actual or reasonably anticipated income.[136] Although these provisions are expressed to apply to mortgage lenders alone, in practice all firms to which MCOB 11 applies are likely to benefit from formulating and applying a policy and keeping records, as the means of demonstrating that they reached an appropriate decision as to the customer's ability to repay, in the circumstances prevailing at the time and given the information then available. **17.63**

Advising and selling

MCOB 2.4 contains a 'reminder' in the form of guidance that firms are required to have due regard to customers' interests and treat them fairly (FCA Principle for Businesses 6) and to pay due regard to the information needs of their customers and communicate with them in a way that is fair, clear, and not misleading (FCA Principle for Businesses 7). The guidance is framed as a warning to avoid high-pressure selling practices in relation to regulated mortgage contracts and home reversions plans; for example, practices that (a) commit customers (or lead customers to believe that they are committed) to any regulated mortgage contract or home reversion plan before they have been able to consider the illustration and offer document; or (b) give customers a misleading impression that a particular deal is not available after a certain date, unless that really is the case. Similar guidance is given in relation to regulated sale and rent back agreements, enjoining firms to avoid practices that commit customers (or lead customers to believe they are committed) to any such agreement before they have been able to consider pre-sale disclosure information and before the expiry of the required 14 day cooling-off period.[137] **17.64**

MCOB 4 imposes general advising and selling standards for mortgage lenders, mortgage intermediaries, home purchase providers, home purchase intermediaries, reversion providers, reversion intermediaries, SRB agreement providers, and SRB agreement intermediaries.[138] The standards are intended to ensure that the customer is adequately informed of **17.65**

133 MCOB 11.3.3G.
134 MCOB 11.3.1R(2).
135 MCOB 11 3.4R.
136 MCOB 11.3.5G.
137 MCOB 2.4.2G(2).
138 MCOB 4.1.1R and 4.1.2R.

the scope of home finance transactions available to him and that, where advice is given, it is suitable for the customer.

17.66 The application of MCOB 4 to reversion providers and reversion intermediaries is modified[139] by MCOB 8, which imposes advising and selling standards for equity release products. MCOB 2.7 and 2.8 impose additional requirements where sales are made by electronic media, distance communications, or e-commerce (although these are not exhaustive of the requirements relevant to distance selling and e-commerce, which appear throughout MCOB).

Disclosure

17.67 MCOB 5 imposes pre-application disclosure requirements on mortgage lenders, mortgage intermediaries, home purchase providers, home purchase intermediaries, reversion providers, reversion intermediaries, SRB agreement providers, and SRB agreement intermediaries. These are intended to ensure that, before a customer submits an application for a home finance product, he is supplied with information that makes clear the price that he will be required to pay for that product, and (in relation to a regulated mortgage business), the features of the product including any linked deposits and linked borrowing.[140]

17.68 MCOB 6 imposes pre-offer disclosure requirements on mortgage lenders, home purchase providers, reversion providers, and SRB agreement providers. These are intended to ensure that a customer receives a clear offer document to enable him to check the features and price of the home finance transaction before he enters into it.[141]

17.69 MCOB 7 imposes disclosure requirements that bite at the start of the contract and after sale. These apply to mortgage lenders, mortgage intermediaries, mortgage administrators, home purchase providers, home purchase intermediaries, home purchase administrators, reversion providers, reversion intermediaries, reversion administrators, SRB agreement providers, and SRB agreement administrators. They are intended to ensure that:

(a) a customer is supplied with information at the start of a regulated mortgage contract to enable him to check that the regulated mortgage contract has been set up in accordance with his requirements and to notify him of the first and subsequent payments;
(b) when the firm provides subsequent services to the customer, such as a further advance, rate switch, or addition or removal of a party to a regulated mortgage contract, the customer is provided with an illustration to make clear the price and features associated with that variation;
(c) a customer is supplied with information that enables him to check the payments and charges on a home finance transaction, to keep track of the transactions on, and the features of, a home finance transaction and stay informed of material changes.[142]

17.70 The application of MCOB 5, 6, and 7 to mortgage lenders, mortgage intermediaries, mortgage administrators, reversion providers, reversion intermediaries, and reversion administrators is modified by MCOB 9, which imposes product disclosure standards for equity release products.

---

139 MCOB 4.1.5R.
140 MCOB 5.2.1G.
141 MCOB 6.2.1G.
142 MCOB 7.2.1G.

Charges

MCOB 12 imposes requirements on all home finance firms, intended to supplement the disclosure requirements outlined in paragraphs 17.67 to 17.69 (many of which are concerned with disclosure of the price of a home finance product), by preventing firms from imposing unfair and excessive charges. The level of charges under a financial services product is not usually a matter for regulation. Indeed in some cases (as under the Insurance Directives) the regulator is prevented from imposing systematic controls on the price or form of a product. MCOB 12 is intended to address four specific instances in which charges are, in the FCA's view, likely to be unfair: **17.71**

(a) the charges imposed on a customer seeking to terminate a regulated mortgage contract before the end of the term of the contract do not reflect the cost of termination to the firm;
(b) the charges imposed on a customer in payment difficulties are not based upon the costs incurred by the firm;
(c) the charges (including rates of interest) imposed on a customer under a regulated mortgage contract, home reversion plan, or regulated sale and rent back agreement are excessive and contrary to the customer's interests; and
(d) the charges made to a customer in connection with a regulated mortgage contract, home reversion plan, or regulated sale and rent back agreement are excessive.[143]

Arrears and repossessions

MCOB 13 imposes requirements on mortgage lenders, mortgage administrators, home purchase providers, and home purchase administrators in their administration of a home finance transaction and their administration of any unpaid amount due to the home finance provider following the sale of the property after repossession. These requirements set out the information and services that the firm is required to provide to a customer who has payment difficulties or faces a shortfall, or is otherwise in breach of a home purchase plan. The requirements include that the firm must put in place and operate a written policy (approved by its governing body) to ensure that such customers are treated fairly;[144] provide the customer with information about the extent of the arrears, any likely charges, and the possible consequences if the shortfall is not cleared;[145] and refrain from putting pressure on the customer through excessive telephone calls or correspondence or by contact at an unreasonable hour.[146] Where the firm administers a repossessed property, it must ensure that it markets the property as soon as possible and obtains the best price that might reasonably be paid, taking account of factors such as market conditions as well as the continuing increase in the amount owed by the customer.[147] **17.72**

If the firm proposes to recover a sale shortfall it must ensure that the customer is notified of its intention within six years (five in Scotland).[148] **17.73**

---

143 MCOB 12.2.1G.
144 MCOB 13.3.1R.
145 For example, MCOB 13.4.
146 MCOB 13.5.3R.
147 MCOB 13.6.1R.
148 MCOB 13.6.4R.

Post-contract charges and arrears

17.74 A particular feature of the provisions against excessive charges and in relation to arrears and repossessions (in MCOB 12 and 13) is that many of them continue to apply to activities that occur after a regulated mortgage contract or a home purchase plan has come to an end following the sale of a repossessed property, or after a home reversion plan has come to an end for any reason.

18

COLLECTIVE INVESTMENT SCHEMES

Introduction

Investment funds and collective investment schemes

Investment funds,[1] where participants pool financial resources and abdicate management decisions to others, invite particular regulatory treatment. FSMA imposes a special regulatory regime on those funds that fall within its wide definition of 'collective investment scheme' (or CIS).[2] In particular, the Act restricts the promotion of such schemes and regulates various other activities in relation to them.[3] This chapter, therefore, devotes some space to an examination of the definition of a CIS before considering that regime. It will be seen that the definition of CIS covers almost all types of investment funds with the exception of: schemes that take the form of a body corporate other than that of an 'open-ended investment company' ('OEIC'—again as defined in FSMA)[4] or of a limited liability partnership ('LLP').[5] Hence, investment companies,[6] investment trusts,[7] and pooled investment SPVs are not covered, the rationale being that company law and (if the securities are listed) the Listing Rules[8] provide adequate protection in relation to securities issued by such investment vehicles. This exclusion was called into question by the 'Splits' saga,[9] but the response was a tightening of, inter alia, the Listing Rules[10] applicable to them rather than a withdrawal of the exclusion. **18.01**

Although it was the rise of the unit trust in the 1930s that prompted the first regulatory intervention in the UK,[11] the Financial Services Act 1986 first defined 'collective investment **18.02**

---

[1] For a comparison between the position in the UK and US, see T Spangler, *The Law of Private Investment Funds* (2nd edn, OUP 2012).

[2] See para 18.12 *et seq*. But note that when the AIFMD (see para 18.07) is implemented, it will regulate the managers of 'AIFs' (as defined).

[3] See para 18.129 *et seq*.

[4] See para 18.66 *et seq*.

[5] See para 18.57.

[6] Within Companies Act 2006, s 833.

[7] See Income Taxes Act 2007, ss 276–277.

[8] See Chapter 17.

[9] Examined in the FSA's publications: (i) 'Split Capital Closed-Ended Funds' (DP10, Dec 2001) and (ii) 'Split Capital Investment Trusts ("Splits")' (PS, May 2002).

[10] And Conduct of Business Rules applicable to FSA authorised persons, preceded by FSA CP164, 'Investment Companies (including Investment Trusts): Proposed Changes to the Listing Rules and Conduct of Business Rules' (January 2003).

[11] The Prevention of Fraud (Investments) Act 1939, replaced by the 1958 Act of the same name. For a study of the unit trust, see K F Sin, *The Legal Nature of the Unit Trust* (OUP 1997).

scheme'[12] widely and introduced a comprehensive regulatory regime for all such schemes. That approach has been followed in FSMA, which re-adopted that definition almost verbatim.

The European dimension, OEICs, and AIFs

UCITS

18.03 One of the first EC (as it then was) 'single market' initiatives was the attempt to create a single market for open-ended retail investment funds—or rather UCITS, an acronym for 'undertakings for collective investment in transferable securities'. As a result of the first UCITS Directive[13] Member States had to adopt harmonised rules regulating such UCITSs, their management companies, and how units were promoted to the public. In particular, UCITSs must have both a 'depositary' safeguarding the assets and a separate management company with circumscribed powers of investment and borrowing, and investors must have access to detailed information about the scheme. The first UCITS Directive provided the management company with a 'single market passport', enabling it to market the UCITS elsewhere in the EEA, after giving due notice to the home and host regulators, and only needing to comply with the host State's marketing rules and to maintain certain facilities for investors in that State.[14] The UCITS Directive was initially amended ('UCITS II',[15] 'UCITS III'[16]) and has now been 'recast' as 'UCITS IV'.[17] Further amendments ('UCITS V') are proposed.[18] UCITS III permitted UCITSs to invest in a wider range of investments than 'transferable securities' (including certain units in other funds, money market instruments, deposits, and derivatives),[19] and UCITS IV permitted UCITSs to establish 'master–feeder arrangements'.[20] Given the wider investment powers, the term 'UCITS' (in referring to funds investing in 'transferable securities') is no longer entirely apposite to describe these funds—although the name is too well entrenched to be abandoned.

18.04 As will be noted later in this chapter, the UCITS regime is implemented by FSMA and the FCA Handbook. As a result, provision is made for the automatic 'recognition' (after

[12] The definition reflected the US case of *SEC v WJ Howey Co* (1946) 328 US 293; 66 S CT 1100; 90 L Ed 2d 1244 where the definition of 'security' in the (US) Securities Act of 1933, s 2(1) was said to connote four characteristics: (a) the investment of money, (b) in a common enterprise, (c) with an expectation of profits, and (d) solely from the efforts of others. See also Arden LJ in *FSA v Fradley and Woodward* [2005] EWCA Civ 1183, [3]: 'at the heart of the [CIS] concept is the requirement for the sharing of profit or income by participants who do not have day-to-day control over the management of the property'.

[13] Directive 85/611/EEC, [1985] OJ L375/03.

[14] See the Commission Interpretative Communication on the respective powers retained by the Home Member State and the Host Member State in the marketing of UCITS pursuant to Section VIII of the (previous) UCITS Directive (Com (2007) 112).

[15] By Directive 88/220 [1988] OJ L100/31 and Directive 95/26 [1995] OJ L168/07.

[16] By Directive 2001/108 [2002] OJ L41/35 (the 'Product Directive') and Directive 2001/107 [2002] OJ L41/20 (the 'Management Directive'). UCITS III came into force on 13 February 2004. See Rouch and Smith, 'The UCITS Directive and the Single European Funds Market: A Case Review' [2005] JIBLR 251. Note also Commission Directive 2007/16/EC implementing Council Directive 85/611/EEC as regards the clarification of certain definitions.

[17] Directive 2009/65/EC [2009] OJ L302/32. See also the 'Level 2' implementing Commission Directives (Directives 2010/43/EU and 2010/44/EU) and Commission Regulations (Regulation (EU) No 583/2010 and Regulation (EU) No 583/2010). The requisite amendments to UK legislation (esp. FSMA) were made by SI 2011/1613 (in force July 1, 2011 and drafting errors corrected by SI 2012/2015).

[18] See COM(2012) 350 final of 3 July 2012.

[19] But see FSMA, s 283B: managment company must submit annual reports to the FCA in relation to its derivative investments.

[20] See esp. FSMA, Chapter 5A ('Master-feeder structures'), added on 1 July 2011 by SI 2011/1613, reg 2(26) (see n 17).

notification) of UCITSs constituted and regulated in other EEA Member States so that they may be marketed in the same way as domestic authorised funds.[21] And UK schemes that satisfy the UCITS Directive requirements are similarly able to market elsewhere in the EEA.[22]

UK Open-Ended Investment Companies ('OEICs')

The advent of the first UCITS Directive provided the final impetus for the introduction in the UK of open-ended investment companies ('OEICs').[23] The creation of OEICs was not possible under the then existing UK company law, as the capital maintenance doctrine restricted the extent to which registered companies could be 'open-ended' in buying or redeeming their own shares. Nor was there any particular need for such investment vehicles domestically, as the unit trust was available. However, the open-ended corporate vehicle is the usual form taken by retail investment funds elsewhere, especially in Europe[24] where the trust is largely an unknown concept. Hence, the arguments for legislative change to enable a UK form of OEIC to be established became overwhelming in the face of fears that the unfamiliarity of the unit trust would put it at a competitive disadvantage in the single market and beyond. **18.05**

As the introduction of OEICs could be regarded as an aspect of the implementation of the UCITS Directive, the requisite (substantial) legislative changes were initially effected by Regulations made under the European Communities Act 1972.[25] However, this was a short-term expedient because those Regulations could only provide for OEICs (in fact termed 'investment companies with variable capital'—ICVCs—the name still used for a UK OEIC)[26] that satisfied the Directive and hence that could only invest in a narrower category of investments than retail domestic unit trusts. The enactment of FSMA presented the opportunity of placing UK OEICs on the same legislative footing as domestic unit trusts. This was done, not by incorporating the OEIC provisions into the statute itself alongside the unit trust provisions, but by conferring wide powers on the Treasury to issue new OEIC Regulations.[27] Thus the regime for UK OEICs remains in a statutory instrument. **18.06**

Alternative Investment Funds

In the wake of concern about the impact of unregulated investment funds (such as so-called 'hedge funds') on the stability of the financial system as a whole, in June 2011 the EU adopted the Alternative Investment Fund Managers Directive (the 'AIFMD'),[28] a maximum harmonisation Directive, due for implementation on 22 July 2013.[29] **18.07**

---

21 See paras 18.113 and 18.142.

22 See paras 18.93 and 18.102.

23 See Lomnicka, 'Open-ended Investment Companies—A new bottle for old wine' in BAK Rider, *The Corporate Dimension* (1998).

24 For example, the SICAV (société d'investissement à capital variable).

25 s 2(2), see the (now replaced, see n 277) Open-ended Investment Companies (Investment Companies with Variable Capital) Regulations 1996, SI 1996/2827.

26 See para 18.101.

27 See FSMA, s 262 and the Open-ended Investment Company Regulations 2001, SI 2001/1228, as amended, considered in para 18.102. For Northern Ireland, see the Open-ended Investment Company Regulations (Northern Ireland) 2004, SR 2004/335.

28 Directive 2011/61/EU, a Level 1 Directive requiring Commission implementing measures and ESMA binding technical standards. See the Level 2 Commission Delegated Regulation on Alternative Investment Fund Managers, Regulation No 231/2013 [2013] OJ L83/1 (which, being a Regulation, is of course directly applicable). See also ESMA's Guidelines on sound remuneration policies under the AIFMD (February 2013).

29 With the usual transitional provisions.

18.08 An 'alternative investment fund' (AIF) is defined in the AIFMD[30] as a 'collective investment undertaking' (whatever legal form it takes) (a) that raises capital from investors with a view to investing it in accordance with a defined investment policy for the benefit of those investors, but (b) that is not a UCITS.[31] Hence, it covers all forms of collective investment arrangements except those retail schemes that already fall within (and are regulated as a result of) the UCITS Directive. The AIF definition is therefore both narrower than the FSMA definition of a CIS (in excluding UCITSs)[32] and wider in including closed-ended corporate investment funds.[33] Hence, it potentially covers hedge funds, commodity funds, real estate funds, private equity funds, and investment corporations.[34]

18.09 Essentially, the aim of the Directive is to establish an EU-wide harmonised regulatory framework for the managers of AIFs (AIFMs). Thus the focus of regulation is the AIFMs rather than the fund itself (as AIFs are mainly directed at non-retail investors), with organisational and conduct obligations being imposed on them. These include an obligation to appoint an authorised depositary monitoring cash flow and to make detailed reports on their investment activities both to regulators and investors. The usual 'single market passport' for both managing and marketing AIFs is available to AIFMs that are regulated in their home State.[35]

18.10 This chapter to some extent anticipates the consequent amendments to the UK regime (the approach adopted being largely the 'copy-out' of the Directive) but as all the detail was not finalised at the time of writing, only limited reference is made to them. Implementation, requiring the FCA to regulate AIFMs in accordance with the AIFMD, will require amendments to FSMA and secondary legislation made under it (especially the RAO)[36] and amendments to the FCA Handbook.[37]

Basic Definitions

General

18.11 Both FSMA and the FCA Handbook Glossary contain (sometimes very detailed) definitions of the terms used in CIS regulation. The FCA Handbook on the whole adopts the FSMA definitions[38] but often expands them and adds new terminology of its own. This section will consider the FSMA definitions of three basic terms.

30 Art 4. There is ESMA Guidance and there will be FCA Guidance, in the PERG Module of its Handbook: see HMT's Second *Consultation paper on the implementation of the AIFMD* (March 2013): paras 2.17–2.19.

31 ie does not require authorisation under UCITS Directive, art 5. For UCITSs, see para 18.03.

32 See para 18.03.

33 Which are exempted from the CIS definition, see para 18.57.

34 And 'common investment funds' (CIFs) and common deposit funds (CDFs), both used by charities for collective investment and presently regulated under charities legislation.

35 But only for 'full-scope AIFMs' not those that are subject to the *de minimis* regime, being 'sub-threshold' with funds under the Directive's threshold.

36 See the draft regulations appended to the First and Second HMT *Consultation papers on the implementation of the AIFMD* (January 2013 and March 2013). For the RAO, see paras 18.129–18.133.

37 In particular, there will be a new 'FUND' Module, replacing COLL (see paras 18.148–18.150). For the FSA's consultation papers on the implementation of the AIFMD see (i) CP12/32 (November 2012); (ii) CP13/9 (March 2013).

38 But note that although the term 'depositary' is inapplicable to unit trust schemes when used in FSMA (see s 237(2)—'trustee' being the statutory term used in the context of unit trusts), in the FCA Handbook 'depositary' covers the trustee of a unit trust scheme.

Definition of 'Collective Investment Scheme' ('CIS'): FSMA, section 235

The core definition

General The term 'collective investment scheme' (or CIS) is defined in section 235 of FSMA.[39] The core statutory definition is very wide, so provision is made for the Treasury to narrow it by Order ('Treasury CIS Order').[40] Each element of the core definition will be discussed, followed by a consideration of the Treasury CIS Order. The definition has been the subject of judicial comment in a number of cases, in particular the Court of Appeal case: *Financial Services Authority v Fradley*.[41] As that case law demonstrates, there is much uncertainty over the meaning and effect of the definition.[42] **18.12**

'Arrangements' The definition requires there to be 'arrangements' with certain characteristics. The term 'arrangements' is one with wide connotations[43] and, therefore, the scheme may take any form or combination of forms. It may be corporate—although companies other than OEICs and LLPs are excluded from the definition by the Treasury CIS Order.[44] The arrangements may take the form of or include a trust and hence unit trusts are covered. The arrangements may also be contractual and hence partnerships are covered. However, the term has 'a wider ambit than agreement or contract [and] the arrangements in question need not...be legally binding'.[45] In *The Russell-Cooke Trust Company v Elliot*,[46] Laddie J regarded the term 'arrangements' in the CIS definition as covering all the steps undertaken, including the preliminary steps of placing investors' funds in a common account, and considered all the steps as a whole, seeing 'no justification for dividing these arrangements into discrete parts', an approach followed by Hamblen J in *Andrew Brown v Innovatorone Plc*.[47] **18.13**

[39] It replaces, and is in almost identical terms to, the Financial Services Act 1986, s 75 (see para 18.02). The definition (which is widely cross-referenced to, especially in tax legislation) will not be affected by the implementation of the AIFMD (see para 18.07): HMT's First *Consultation paper on the implementation of the AIFMD*, (January 2013), para 5.5.

[40] s 235(5), see para 18.30.

[41] [2005] EWCA 1183, noted by Omoyele (2007) 28 *Company Lawyer* 245. (See also the subsequent proceedings for recovery of monies from the protagonists, for distribution to investors, noted in the FSA's Press Release of 8 August 2008.) The first case was Laddie J's decision in *The Russell-Cooke Trust Company v Elliot* 2001 available on WESTLAW (on the identically worded Financial Services Act 1986, s 75), applied by Lindsay J in *The Russell-Cooke Trust Co v Prentis* [2002] EWHC 2227 (Ch). See also (i) *Andrew Brown v Innovatorone Plc* [2012] EWHC 1321 (Comm), and (ii) the 'land banking' cases: *Re Sky Land Consultants Plc* [2010] EWHC 399 (Ch), David Richards J (a winding up petition by the Secretary of State); *Financial Services Authority v Watkins (t/a Consolidated Land Ltd)* [2011] EWHC 1976 (Ch), Proudman J; *Dhaliwal v Bluebell Land Ltd* [2011] EWHC 2292 (Ch) Newey J; *Financial Services Authority v Asset L.I. Inc (t/a Asset Land Investment Inc)* [2013] EWHC 178 (Ch), Smith J. Note also *Broderick v Centaur Tipping Services Ltd* (2006) 103(34) L.S.G. 32.

[42] A view expressed in 'Operating a Collective Investment Scheme', Financial Markets Law Committee, Issue 86, (July 2008), cited in *Re Sky Land Consultants Plc* [2010] EWHC 399 (Ch) and *Andrew Brown v Innovatorone Plc* [2012] EWHC 1321 (Comm), at [1166]–[1167] and endorsed by Newey J in *Dhaliwal v Bluebell Land Ltd* [2011] EWHC 2292 (Ch) (in refusing to give summary judgement on whether a CIS was established).

[43] See *Re Basic British Slag's Application* [1963] 1 WLR 727 (on 'arrangement' in the Restrictive Trade Practices Act 1956, s 6(3)), applied in *Office of Fair Trading v Lloyds TSB Bank plc* [2006] EWCA 268 in interpreting 'arrangements' in Consumer Credit Act 1974, s 187. In *FSA v Fradley and Woodward* [2005] EWCA Civ 1183, Arden LJ at [33] referred to the discussion of 'arrangements' in the companies legislation in *Re Duckwari plc* [1999] Ch 235, 260, but declined to discuss further the width of the term in the s 235 context.

[44] See para 18.57.

[45] *Re Sky Land Consultants Plc* [2010] EWHC 399 (Ch), per David Richards J at [16], followed by Smith J in *Financial Services Authority v Asset L.I. Inc (t/a Asset Land Investment Inc)* [2013] EWHC 178 (Ch).

[46] Available on WESTLAW (on the identically worded Financial Services Act 1986, s 75).

[47] [2012] EWHC 1321 (Comm) at [1171], so that the scheme was a CIS at the outset and not just when the investors failed to exercise the requisite 'day-to-day control' (as to which, see para 18.21 *et seq*).

18.14 The core definition has no territorial limitation and thus where the 'arrangements' are made is irrelevant. However, the FSMA regulatory regime is territorially limited[48] and therefore only 'regulated activities in the UK' in relation to CISs are caught by it.

18.15 **'With respect to property'** The 'arrangements' must be 'with respect to property of any description, including money'. Thus the underlying property may take any form. In particular, it need not comprise 'specified investments' or even 'investments' as defined by FSMA.[49] This point was confirmed in *The Russell-Cooke Trust Company v Elliot*,[50] where the underlying property was loans secured on land.[51] In the many 'land banking schemes' whereby investors were induced to purchase individual plots of land that formed part of a site (on the understanding that its reclassification for development would generate profits), the 'property' was the land comprising the plots.[52] Normally, the contributions of the participants will be used to acquire the underlying property, but it was confirmed in *Financial Services Authority v Fradley (Fradley)*,[53] that the 'property' may be the contributions themselves.[54]

18.16 However, the type of property involved may be important when it comes to the Treasury CIS Order exemptions, as some only apply in relation to arrangements if the property comprises certain types of assets (often certain 'specified investments').[55]

18.17 **'Purpose or effect'** The 'arrangements' must satisfy a number of conditions. First, they must have a certain 'purpose or effect'. 'Purpose' suggests some subjective motive and looks to the intended effect—although it does not matter whether it is achieved or not. In *Re Sky Land Consultants Plc*[56] David Richards J confirmed that it is the stated 'purpose' of the arrangements themselves that is relevant, not any particular intentions of the investors. The alternative word 'effect' has purely objective connotations and looks to the actual result achieved. Thus the 'arrangements' must be intended to or must achieve a certain objective.

18.18 Second, the 'purpose or effect' of those arrangements must be 'to enable persons taking part in [them] (whether by becoming owners of the property or any part of it or otherwise)' to achieve the requisite objective. Such persons are termed 'participants'.[57] There are no restrictions on the way in which such persons may participate; the definition mentions the possibility that they may become owners of the property, or part of it (as happened in the 'land banking schemes'), but then uses the general phrase 'or otherwise'. Thus the conferment of purely contractual rights on 'participants' will suffice.

---

48 See para 18.129 and n 388.

49 See s 22(4) ('investment'); s 22(1)(a) ('specified investment').

50 Available on WESTLAW (on the identically worded Financial Services Act 1986, s 75).

51 Although rights under certain mortgages are now 'specified investments' (see the RAO, art 88) this was not the case when *The Russell-Cooke Trust Company* was decided and, in any event, the mortgages in that case would not have fallen within the definition of 'specified investments'.

52 *Re Sky Land Consultants Plc* [2010] EWHC 399 (Ch), per David Richards J at [75], followed by Smith J in *Financial Services Authority v Asset L.I. Inc (t/a Asset Land Investment Inc)* [2013] EWHC 178 (Ch).

53 [2005] EWCA 1183.

54 The scheme was a CIS even though the contributions were used to place bets—which (at the time), being void gaming contracts, were held not to be 'property'. There was no appeal on this point from the first instance decision ([2004] EWHC 3008). See also *Broderick v Centaur Tipping Services Ltd* 2006 (2006) 103(34) L.S.G. 32: money contributed to subscription-based services for the 'laying' of horses (the placing of bets on horses to lose) held to be the 'property' within s 235.

55 See, especially, paras 1, 2, 3, 5, and 8 of the Treasury CIS Order, considered at paras 18.31–18.33, 18.37, and 18.40.

56 [2010] EWHC 399 (Ch), at [167] (a winding up petition by the Secretary of State).

57 FSMA, s 235(2). See further, para 18.58.

The use of the plural 'persons' makes it clear that a CIS must have more than one participant. After all, the definition pertains to 'collective' investment. This was confirmed by Laddie J in *The Russell-Cooke Trust Company v Elliot*,[58] although he held that as long as there was some initial commingling of contributions, the fact that funds representing the contribution of one investor were in fact used to invest in one identifiable item of property (a particular mortgage secured on land) did not preclude a CIS arising: the contributions from a number of persons had been pooled for the purpose of communal investment, even though in fact one person's contribution was expended on one, identifiable item.[59] However, as long as the 'purpose or effect' is that there is to be more than one participant, a CIS arises as soon as the first contribution is made.[60] **18.19**

Third, the required 'purpose or effect' is again expressed in wide terms with a number of (somewhat confusing) alternatives.[61] Its essence is the participation in profits or income arising from the underlying property. It may be broken down as follows. It is to enable the participants: either 'to participate in' or '[to] receive' either (a) 'profits or income' or (b) 'sums paid out of profits or income', in both cases those profits or income 'arising from the acquisition, holding, management or disposal of the property'. Thus the arrangements must envisage (or achieve) 'profits or income' (a phrase covering the alternatives of capital appreciation[62] or revenue production), such profit or income arising from at least one of the following activities: the acquisition, holding, management, or disposal of the underlying property. This list is broad enough to cover any activity (and non-activity: 'holding') in relation to the underlying property. Moreover, the 'purpose or effect' of the arrangements must be for the participants either to 'participate in' or 'receive' that profit or income or sums paid out of the profit or income. **18.20**

Section 235(2): No 'day-to-day control' The essence of a CIS—and the reason why it is subject to special regulatory attention—is that participants abdicate control over their contributions to others.[63] Hence, the participants must not have 'day-to-day control' over the 'management' of the property, although they may have 'the right to be consulted or to give directions'.[64] This requirement poses a number of difficulties.[65] **18.21**

First, clearly the line between 'being consulted or giving directions' and having 'day-to-day control' is not always easy to draw. As the intention is to include in the definition of CIS those schemes where the participants have surrendered control over their property to others, it would seem that 'day-to-day' control connotes actual, continuous control over the management of the property or, as Laddie J put it in *The Russell-Cooke Trust Company v* **18.22**

[58] Available on WESTLAW (on the identically worded Financial Services Act 1986, s 75).

[59] But if, from the outset, the intention is that all the contributions be subsequently separated out and expended on one item of property per contributor, then a CIS would probably not arise in that (i) s 235(3), see para 18.27, would be unlikely to be satisfied, and (ii) in any event, the 'common account' exemption in the Treasury CIS Order (SI 2001/1062, art 6, see para 18.38) would be likely to apply.

[60] And see the future tense 'to participate in...', noted in para 18.26.

[61] The wording contains eight 'or's.

[62] As in the 'land banking' schemes: see para 18.15 (and n 52).

[63] But a participant who delegates 'day-to-day' control to an agent that is *independent of the CIS operator* still retains 'day-to-day' control through his agent: confirmed in *FSA v Fradley and Woodward* [2005] EWCA Civ 1183, [46].

[64] FSMA, s 235(2).

[65] 'There was and remains a lack of clarity as to what the 'day-to-day' requirement means': per Hamblen J in *Andrew Brown v Innovatorone Plc* [2012] EWHC 1321 (Comm) at [1166], citing 'Operating a Collective Investment Scheme', Financial Markets Law Committee, Issue 86, (July 2008).

Elliot,[66] 'in colloquial terms, what the subsection is directed at is identifying who is or will be "minding the shop" on a day-to-day basis'. Despite the reference to 'day-to-day', it seems clear that the term 'day-to-day' is not to be taken literally. Thus directions, which are not given daily but merely periodically, may still constitute 'day-to-day' control. On the other hand, some power to 'give directions' (such as shareholders usually have over directors by special resolution) does not take the arrangements out of the definition of CIS; it is only when that power is so extensive as to constitute effective control, that this condition ceases to be satisfied. Hence, in *Broderick v Centaur Tipping Services Ltd*[67] it was held that the possibility of telling the operator of the scheme not to take a particular step (in that case, placing a bet) or querying a step already taken, merely constituted a right to give directions or be consulted (respectively) and not 'day-to-day' control. The issue therefore resolves itself into a difficult question of degree.[68] The FCA gives some guidance on how it interprets this requirement in the context of property investment clubs and schemes.[69]

18.23 Second, a court will look beyond the documentation and consider how the scheme operates in practice. As an Australian judge stated in relation to a similar requirement under Australian legislation, the regulatory regime 'would be easily defeated if the court felt obliged to rely solely upon a strict view of the legal rights and duties created by the documentation and was required to ignore the realities of the scheme as it is designed to operate in practice',[70] an approach that has been cited and applied in a number of UK CIS cases.[71]

18.24 Third, it is enough if *some* of the participants do not have 'day-to-day' control, as the gist of a CIS is the protection of those delegating managerial control to others. Thus this condition is not satisfied only if *all* the participants have 'day-to-day' control, as only then can it be said that 'those persons' (that is, *all* the participants) have 'day-to-day control'.[72] It follows that a limited partnership (under the Limited Partnerships Act 1907) satisfies this condition in that the limited partners leave management to the general partner. It also follows that if there are numerous participants (unless, perhaps, there is some system of majority voting on 'day-to-day' decisions with each participant having the opportunity to control decision-making

[66] Available on WESTLAW (on the identically worded Financial Services Act 1986, s 75), cited in both the FMLC's July 2008 report and by Hamblen J in *Innovatorone* (see previous footnote).

[67] (2006) 103(34) L.S.G. 32. And (following *FSA v Fradley and Woodward* at first instance) the fact that the subscriber could withdraw their contribution did not have any relevance to the question as to who had day-to-day control.

[68] The point was left open in *FSA v Fradley and Woodward* [2005] EWCA Civ 1183 [50]: 'it is not necessary to consider how regularly a client must actually exercise control for his control to constitute "day-to-day control" for the purposes of section 235(2)'. However, it has been discussed since, see *Broderick v Centaur Tipping Services Ltd* 2006 (2006) 103(34) L.S.G. 32; *Re Sky Land Consultants Plc* [2010] EWHC 399 (Ch); *Andrew Brown v Innovatorone Plc* [2012] EWHC 1321 (Comm); *Financial Services Authority v Asset L.I. Inc (t/a Asset Land Investment Inc)* [2013] EWHC 178 (Ch).

[69] See its Handbook, PERG 11, especially FAQ 6–FAQ 11.

[70] *Enviro Systems Renewable Resources Pty Ltd v ASIC* (2001) ACSR 762, per Marin J. The documents gave 'day-to-day' control to investors but in practice they were not expected to and did not exercise these rights. See (to the same effect) the cases cited in next footnote and the FCA Handbook, PERG 11, FAQ 10.

[71] See (i) per David Richards J in *Re Sky Land Consultants Plc* [2010] EWHC 399 (Ch) at [76]; (ii) per Hamblen J in *Andrew Brown v Innovatorone Plc* [2012] EWHC 1321 (Comm), at [1168]; (iii) per Smith J in *Financial Services Authority v Asset L.I. Inc (t/a Asset Land Investment Inc)* [2013] EWHC 178 (Ch) at [169].

[72] See per Laddie J in *The Russell-Cooke Trust Company v Elliot* 2001 available on WESTLAW (on the identically worded Financial Services Act 1986, s 75), confirmed in *FSA v Fradley and Woodward* [2005] EWCA Civ 1183 at [46] and followed by Smith J in *Financial Services Authority v Asset L.I. Inc (t/a Asset Land Investment Inc)* [2013] EWHC 178 (Ch) at [170].

if he can convince the others of his point of view), then this condition (that the participants must not have 'day-to-day control') will necessarily be fulfilled.

Fourth, it will be recalled that the definition of a CIS envisages arrangements, not only involving the 'management' of the property but alternatively the 'acquisition, holding [or] disposal' of property. Normally any arrangements with respect to property will reserve to those holding the property some powers of management, but if the nature of the arrangements is that custodians merely *hold* the property without more, there will be no 'management' and hence no question of any 'day-to-day' control over management. **18.25**

Finally, the condition talks of 'the persons who are to participate' having no 'day-to-day control'. The use of the future tense indicates that the issue must be tested at the outset. As Laddie J said in *The Russell Cooke Trust Company v Elliot*:[73] 'it is relevant to consider not just what happens when the investment is in place but also whether the necessary control function is shouldered by those who *will be* contributing. Therefore the way the investment is promoted is relevant.' **18.26**

Section 235(3): 'Pooling' and/or 'management as a whole' The arrangements must have one or other or both of the characteristics set out in section 235(3): either 'pooling'[74] and/or 'management as a whole'.[75] **18.27**

The 'pooling' alternative requires the participants' contributions *and* 'the profits or income out of which payments are to be made' to be 'pooled'. Thus the contributions of the participants and the resulting profits or income must be aggregated.[76] Subsection (4) provides for the case where there is pooling only in relation to separate parts of the property. Such arrangements are only to be considered as *one* CIS if the participants are entitled to exchange their rights in one part for rights in another part. Otherwise (presumably) the distinct, pooled parts may be separate CISs. **18.28**

The second alternative (or cumulative) characteristic is that the property must be 'managed as a whole' by or on behalf of the 'operator' (a term partially defined in FSMA, in relation only to unit trust schemes and open-ended investment companies).[77] Two of the exemptions in the Treasury CIS Order apply (in certain circumstances) only if this alternative (and not 'pooling') is present.[78] **18.29**

Exemptions

General The section 235 core definition of a 'collective investment scheme' is an all-inclusive one, which catches a wide variety of schemes for collective investment. Not all such schemes merit the regulatory treatment accorded to 'collective investment schemes' and hence the **18.30**

[73] 2001 available on WESTLAW (on the identically worded Financial Services Act 1986, s 75).

[74] FSMA, s 235(3)(a).

[75] ibid, s 235(3)(b).

[76] This condition was held satisfied in *FSA v Fradley and Woodward* [2005] EWCA Civ 1183 where the participants' contributions were paid into a single bank account albeit in circumstances where the money was held on trust and each contribution was identified.

[77] This condition (only) was held satisfied in the land banking cases where the 'management' was taking steps to increase the value of the land: *Re Sky Land Consultants Plc* [2010] EWHC 399 (Ch), at [77]–[79], *Financial Services Authority v Watkins (t/a Consolidated Land Ltd)* [2011] EWHC 1976 (Ch), at [16] and *Financial Services Authority v Asset L.I. Inc (t/a Asset Land Investment Inc)* [2013] EWHC 178 (Ch), see esp. [172]–[173]. See also the discussion by Newey J in *Dhaliwal v Bluebell Land Ltd* [2011] EWHC 2292 (Ch) at [22]–[25].

[78] The Treasury CIS Order, Sch, paras 1 and 2; see paras 18.31 and 18.32.

Treasury is given the power, by Order, to fine-tune the definition by excluding various types of arrangement[79] and arrangements in certain circumstances.[80] The relevant Order is the Financial Services and Markets Act 2000 (Collective Investment Schemes) Order 2001 (the Treasury CIS Order),[81] and its Schedule lists 21 categories of 'arrangements not amounting to' a CIS. These exemptions either relate to schemes which are otherwise adequately regulated,[82] or cover other cases where it was felt unnecessary to extend CIS regulation to the arrangements at issue.[83]

18.31 **Paragraph 1: Individual Investment Management Arrangements** Schemes such as ISAs (Individual Savings Accounts) and their predecessors PEPs (Private Equity Plans) may satisfy the core CIS definition in that investment is undertaken in accordance with an overall policy applicable to all accounts. Hence, although there is no 'pooling', the 'management as a whole' alternative is likely to be satisfied.[84] Paragraph 1 excludes such arrangements if they satisfy three conditions. First, the property must comprise certain 'specified investments' only,[85] for example, shares, debt securities, or units in certain CISs.[86] Second, each participant must be entitled to 'part' of that property and to withdraw it at any time.[87] Third, as far as the 'pooling' and/or 'management as a whole' condition is concerned, there must be no 'pooling' and the 'management as a whole' alternative must only be satisfied because the 'parts' attributable to each participant are not bought and sold separately (except where a person becomes or ceases to be a participant).

18.32 **Paragraph 2: Enterprise Initiative Schemes** In order to encourage investment in new businesses, the Income Taxes Act 2007, Part 5 (previously the Income and Corporation Taxes Act 1988, Part VII, Chapter III) gives income tax relief to individuals when they buy shares in certain new companies (the so-called 'Enterprise Investment Scheme'). To encourage collective investment in such shares, paragraph 2 excludes from the definition of a CIS certain arrangements that constitute a 'complying fund',[88] that term meaning arrangements where the operator will invest in shares that qualify for tax relief (in relation to each participant's individual circumstances) under those tax provisions and where the minimum contribution of each participant is not less than £2,000.[89] For the exemption to apply a number of further conditions are laid down,[90] in particular each participant must be entitled to part of the property and to withdraw it after a certain period.[91]

---

[79] FSMA, s 235(5)(b).

[80] ibid, s 235(5)(a).

[81] SI 2001/1062, as amended by SI 2001/3650, art 2; SI 2005/57; SI 2005/2114, Sch 16(1), para 3; SI 2006/1969, art 8(3); SI 2006/3384, art 36(2); SI 2007/800, art 2(2); SI 2008/1641, art 2; SI 2008/1813, art 2; SI 2010/86, art 3. Although s 235(5) essentially enables the Treasury to decide which situations are regulated by the Act and which are not, the Order is not subject to the affirmative resolution procedure for statutory instruments.

[82] See especially the Treasury CIS Order, Sch, paras 1, 3, 13, 16–21.

[83] See especially the Treasury CIS Order, Sch, paras 2, 4–12, 14–15.

[84] See FSMA, s 235(2), paras 18.27 and 18.29.

[85] ie those specified in FSMA 2000 (Regulated Activities) Order 2001, SI 2001/544, as amended (the RAO), arts 76–80 or contracts of long-term insurance: para 1(a)(i), (iii).

[86] ie units in AUTs (see para 18.93), recognised schemes (see para 18.111), or shares in any OEIC (see para 18.66 *et seq*): para 1(a)(ii).

[87] Presumably this requirement would still be satisfied even if withdrawal requires the payment of a (reasonable) fee and/or entails a short delay to complete formalities.

[88] The Treasury CIS Order Sch, para 2(1)(b).

[89] ibid, para 2(2)(b).

[90] ibid, para 2(1)(a), (c), (d).

[91] ibid, para 2(1)(c). The period depends on the type of shares involved.

Paragraph 3: Pure deposit-based schemes If the whole amount of a participant's contribution is a 'deposit', for the purposes of FSMA,[92] and this is accepted either by an authorised person with permission to accept deposits or by an exempt person (in relation to such an activity), then any arrangements with respect to those deposits which might otherwise fall within the CIS definition are exempted. **18.33**

Paragraph 4: Schemes not operated by way of business The core CIS definition does not have a 'business' element. Thus even family or private arrangements may fall within it. As the FSMA regulatory regime is generally only concerned with activities in the business context,[93] paragraph 4 excludes from the CIS definition arrangements 'operated otherwise than by way of business'. This echoes the wording of FSMA, section 22 which requires regulated activities to be 'carried on by way of business', a narrower concept than 'in the course of business' which is used in relation to financial promotion in section 21.[94] **18.34**

The word 'business' occurs in many legal contexts and has been called an 'etymological chameleon' by Lord Diplock.[95] It is notoriously difficult to decide if activity is done 'by way of business' in that this usually depends on balancing a number of factors (none of which is conclusive), in particular profit motive and regularity.[96] A particularly wide meaning was given to the phrase as it occurred in the predecessor to FSMA, section 412(2)(a)[97] ('entered into... by way of business') by Hobhouse J in *Morgan Grenfell & Co v Welwyn Hatfield DC*.[98] In the context of deciding if the exemption from the gaming laws in that provision applied to swaps contracts, he saw 'no reason to put a narrow meaning on the word "business"' and said 'it should not be given a technical construction but rather one which conformed to what in ordinary parlance would be described as a business transaction as opposed to something personal or casual'. Moreover, he added that a 'one-off' scheme could still be regarded as operated 'by way of business' even though the term 'business' has been construed as requiring some repetition.[99] Thus Hobhouse J added that the 'frequency with which the relevant type of transaction is entered into... can be no more than a guide... it is equally possible that the very first time [a person] enters into such a contact it is doing so by way of business'. Similarly, 'business' does not always connote a profit or commercial motive.[100] **18.35**

[92] RAO, art 5. See further paras 14.36–14.38.

[93] See FSMA, s 21 (financial promotion 'in the course of business') and s 22 (regulated activities 'carried on by way of business'). See further, paras 18.131, 18.136.

[94] The s 22 phrase has been the subject of a clarificatory Treasury Order (FSMA 2000 (Carrying on Regulated Activity by Way of Business) Order 2001, SI 2001/1177, as amended by SI 2003/1475, art 25; SI 2003/1476, art 18; 2005/922; SI 2006/1969, art 9; SI 2006/2383, art 29; SI 2006/3384, art 37; SI 2011/2304, art 2 made under s 419) but this is (in terms) inapplicable.

[95] In *Town Investments Ltd v Department of the Environment* [1978] AC 359 at 383C.

[96] The FCA has given very tentative guidance on the meaning of the phrase in s 22 in its FCA Handbook, PERG 2.3. See further the discussion in E Lomnicka and J Powell, *The Encyclopedia of Financial Services Law*, (2010, Sweet & Maxwell) para 2A–851.

[97] FSA 1986, s 63.

[98] [1995] 1 All ER 1.

[99] See *Smith v Anderson* (1880) 15 Ch D 247, at 277–8, but the phrase there was 'carrying on business'. See *GE Capital Bank Ltd v Rushton* [2005] EWCA Civ 1556: purchase of a number of vehicles as a 'one-off' transaction but as a 'business venture' did constitute the 'carrying on of business' for the purposes of the Hire-Purchase Act 1964, s 29(2).

[100] *Rolls v Miller* (1884) 27 Ch D 71 at 81: business means 'anything which is an occupation as distinguished from a pleasure—anything which is an occupation or duty which requires attention'.

18.36 It would appear that a similarly wide interpretation would be appropriate in the context of paragraph 4, as the regulatory policy seems merely to exclude those private arrangements that do not merit regulation. Thus paragraph 4 would be apt to exclude family arrangements for collective investment and 'private' investment clubs or syndicates operated by groups of friends or colleagues.

18.37 **Paragraph 5: Debt issues** Paragraph 5[101] is a very complex provision that excludes certain arrangements in securitisations under which the rights of the participants are (only) certain debt instruments either issued by a single issuer or arising under swap arrangements (as defined).

18.38 **Paragraph 6: Common accounts** Arrangements under which money is held 'in a common account' on the understanding that it is to be applied either (i) 'in making payments to' the participant, or (ii) 'in satisfaction of sums owed to him', or (iii) 'in the acquisition of property for him or the provision of services to him' are excluded by paragraph 6. The use of the singular 'him' is clearly significant and Hamblen J summarised the exemption in *Andrew Brown v Innovatorone Plc*[102] by saying that it applies where 'money in the account is held on the understanding that an amount representing the contribution of each participant is to be applied only for the benefit of that participant, as opposed to being applied for the collective benefit of more than one participant'. He gave the example of a solicitor's client account. In *Financial Services Authority v Fradley*[103] the money was applied in placing bets for the participants and it was held that this did not fall within any of the three 'uses'.[104]

18.39 **Paragraph 7: Certain funds relating to leasehold property** The Landlord and Tenant Act 1987, section 42(1) requires sums paid into a sinking fund by way of service charges by tenants to be held on trust first to defray the costs and thereafter for the contributors. In this way the tenant-contributors have an equitable claim to the fund that prevails over the payee's creditors should the payee become insolvent. By virtue of paragraph 7[105] such a statutory trust is not a CIS. This exemption has now been extended to a similar 'designated account' of a scheme administrator under a 'tenancy deposit scheme' within the meaning of the Housing Act 2004, section 212(2).

18.40 **Paragraph 8: Certain employee share schemes** Paragraph 8[106] sets out the standard definition of an 'employee share scheme' and exempts such a scheme from being a CIS. For many

[101] As amended by SI 2006/3384, art 36(2) and SI 2010/86 art 3 (to ensure that *Sukuk* (which are potentially CISs) are exempted and regulated in the same way as their non-*Shari'a* equivalents (ie investment bonds): see RAO, art 77A and the Consultation Paper that preceeded the amendment of the legislative framework for the regulation of alternative finance investment bonds (*Sukuk*), issued by HMT and the FSA in December 2008). On Islamic finance, see Chapter 19.

[102] [2012] EWHC 1321 (Comm). He followed *The Russell-Cooke Trust Company v Elliot* 2001 available on WESTLAW (on the identically worded Financial Services Act 1986, s 75) where Laddie J held that the use of the singular in the three alternative uses of the money was deliberate and therefore the exemption did not apply where the money in the common account was paid out on behalf of more than one contributor towards a common investment.

[103] [2005] EWCA 1183.

[104] In particular a bet was neither 'property' nor a provision of 'services' within (iii): see [2004] EWHC 3008 (a point not further considered on appeal: [2005] EWCA 1183).

[105] As substituted by SI 2007/800, art 2(2) to add the reference to the Housing Act 2004. Para 7 was previously amended by SI 2005/57 so as to extend the exemption to trust funds that would be within the 1978 Act, s 42 but for the landlord being exempt under s 58.

[106] As amended by SI 2005/2114, Sch 16(1) para 3.

years it has been government policy to encourage employees to participate in the shareholding of their employer. For example, activities carried on in connection with 'employee share schemes' are excluded from the definition of 'regulated activities' by the RAO,[107] and the promotion of employee share schemes is outside the financial promotion restriction.[108] Paragraph 8 adds to that special treatment and removes a disincentive for employers to establish and operate such schemes by taking them out of CIS regulation.

Paragraph 9: Schemes entered into for commercial purposes wholly or mainly related to existing business[109] This exemption is sometimes referred to as the 'joint venture' or 'existing business' exemption as it operates to exempt certain collective investment 'wholly or mainly for commercial purposes related to' existing (non-investment) businesses. It is a widely used exemption and has been amended on a number of occasions, resulting in a complex provision.[110] **18.41**

Broadly speaking, in order for the exemption to apply, two conditions need to be fulfilled in relation to *each*[111] of the participants. The first is that they each must 'carry on a business other than the business of engaging in' one of the investment business-type of 'specified activities' in the RAO.[112] It is clear that the various exclusions applicable to each of those types of 'specified activities' in the RAO are relevant in deciding if a participant carries on that 'specified activity' for the purposes of this exclusion.[113] Moreover, the non-investment business must be an *existing* business: this first condition is not satisfied where the participant *will* carry on the business by virtue of being a participant in the arrangements.[114] However, that non-investment business need not be the same kind of business in relation to each participant. Moreover, it does not matter if a participant, as well as carrying on a non-investment business, *also* carries on an investment business.[115] **18.42**

The second condition is that each participant must enter 'into the arrangements for commercial purposes wholly or mainly related' to that business. Thus the collective arrangements must be wholly or mainly[116] related to that existing non-investment business. An example **18.43**

[107] ie FSMA 2000 (Regulated Activities) Order 2001, SI 2001/544 (the RAO), as amended, art 71.

[108] FSMA 2000 (Financial Promotion) Order 2005, SI 2005/1529 (the FPO), art 60.

[109] A new para 9 was substituted on 15 July 2008 by SI 2008/1641 and was amended by SI 2008/1813. Previously, a new para 9(1)(a) was substituted on 1 December 2001 by SI 2001/3650. See the similar 'joint enterprise' exclusion (from 'regulated activity') for 'participators in a joint enterprise' where the 'transaction is entered into for the purposes of or in connection with that enterprise' in RAO, art 69.

[110] See the provisions in para 9(1) for arrangements made before the latest version of para 9 came into force (on 15 July 2008). In particular, participants may (unanimously) elect (irrevocably and in writing) to take advantage of the relaxations in the new provision.

[111] See para 9(4).

[112] ie in relation to certain investments: dealing as principal (art 14) or agent (art 21), arranging deals (arts 25 and 25D), managing (art 37), safeguarding and administering (art 40), sending dematerialised instructions (art 45), as well as establishing etc a CIS (art 51), establishing etc., a stakeholder pension (art 52), and advising (art 53). Agreeing to undertake any of these activities (apart from that in art 51) is also covered (art 64).

[113] The various exclusions determine what is and what is not within the relevant articles setting out the 'specified activity' (see RAO, art 4(3)). Thus the activity is not 'specified by' the relevant article if it falls within a relevant exclusion. Elsewhere (eg RAO, art 4(4)(b)) where the exclusions are not to be taken into account, this is made clear explicitly. And see para 14(b) (in relation to exclusions to 'specified investments'), considered at para 18.49. For a contrary view, see E Perry, *The Financial Services and Markets Act: A Practical Legal Guide* (Sweet & Maxwell 2001) para 12.12.

[114] Para 9(5)(i)—a clarification not present (but implicit) in the predecessor to this provision in the FSA 1986.

[115] This has now been made explicit in para 9(5)(a).

[116] A qualification added in the new para 9 inserted by SI 2008/1641.

would be property developers who collectively invest in a further property development or manufacturers who collectively invest in raw materials.

18.44 The latest version of this paragraph has introduced a relaxation in order to facilitate participation by SPVs that (being especially established for the purpose of any arrangements) do not satisfy the 'existing business' requirement. Thus SVPs[117] that only have as their members persons who would satisfy those two conditions[118] do not need to carry on an 'existing business' as long as they do not carry on those investment business type of 'specified activities' mentioned earlier.[119] A further innovation is that if the exemption in paragraph 9 otherwise applies, all[120] the participants may nevertheless agree in writing that the exemption does not apply.[121]

18.45 **Paragraph 10: Group schemes** Arrangements between companies in the same group are exempted. Thus if each of the participants in the 'arrangements' is a body corporate in the same 'group' (as defined in FSMA, section 421)[122] then the arrangements do not constitute a CIS. Consequently, members of the same group may pool resources for investment without the arrangements being regulated as CISs.

18.46 **Paragraph 11: Franchise arrangements** 'Franchise arrangements'—which are defined broadly as arrangements conferring the right to exploit intellectual property (such as a trademark or design) or the goodwill attached to it[123]—are exempted from the definition of a CIS. This is potentially a wide exemption which is likely to be interpreted narrowly so that the right to exploit is the predominant purpose of the arrangements (otherwise they would not be 'franchise arrangements'), so that the mere inclusion of a right of exploitation of (say) a trademark in a scheme with a wider purpose would not bring it within the exemption.

18.47 **Paragraph 12: Trading schemes** Arrangements providing for the payment of incentives for recruitment to schemes may constitute CISs if the funds used to pay those incentives are pooled and/or managed as whole pending their distribution. Paragraph 12 operates to exclude such arrangements where the financial incentives are wholly or mainly funded out of the contributions of other participants.

18.48 **Paragraph 13: Timeshare and long-term holiday schemes**[124] 'Timeshare contracts' and 'long-term holiday product contracts'—as defined by the Timeshare, Holiday Products, Resale and Exchange Contracts Regulations 2010[125]—are now[126] regulated under those

[117] viz.: a body corporate, unincorporated association, partnership, or corporate trustee (para 9(5)(b)).

[118] See paras 18.42 and 18.43.

[119] See n 112.

[120] The election must be unanimous.

[121] Para 9(3), and see para 9(7) (election unaffected by subsequent change in participants or later agreement). There are certain tax advantages to a scheme being a CIS, hence it is sometimes the wish of participants that the exemption does not apply.

[122] Which (as amended by SI 2008/948) in turn refers to Companies Act 2006 (and equivalent Northern Irish legislation) and the Building Societies Act 1986.

[123] Treasury CIS Order, art 2(1).

[124] A new para 13 was substituted on February 23, 2011 by SI 2010/2960, reg 36(3) and Sch 6, para 8(3) and consequential amendments were made to the interpretation provision in Treasury CIS Order, art 2(1). These regulations implemented Directive 2008/122/EC (on the protection of consumers in respect of certain aspects of timeshare, long-term holiday product, resale and exchange contracts), [2009] OJ No L33.

[125] SI 2010/2960. Regulation 7 defines the former, regulation 8 the latter.

[126] Previously, they were regulated under the Timeshare Act 1992, to which the previous version of para 13 made reference.

regulations. Therefore, if arrangements confer rights under such contracts on participants, those arrangements do not constitute a CIS.

Paragraph 14: Other schemes relating to use or enjoyment of property Paragraph 14 broadens the 'timeshare' exclusion to cover arrangements over both real and personal property satisfying two conditions. The first is that their 'predominant purpose' must be to 'enable the participants to share in the use or enjoyment' of property or to make that use or enjoyment available gratuitously to others.[127] Although the terms 'use or enjoy' might imply that only tangible property is covered, the second condition, in excluding certain intangible property, confirms that even intangible property (for example, intellectual property but see the exemption in paragraph 11) can be 'used or enjoyed'. The second condition states that the property must not 'consist of' currency and must not 'consist of or include' any 'investment' specified by the RAO (ignoring any exclusions).[128] Thus collective rights in any property (apart from that excluded by the second condition) where the predominant (not necessarily the 'sole') purpose is that the participants 'use or enjoy' it or allow others to do so without payment, do not constitute a CIS. **18.49**

Paragraph 15: Schemes involving the issue of certificates representing investments The term 'certificates representing securities' is shorthand for one type of 'specified investment' in the RAO: certificates or other instruments (defined to mean a record in any form)[129] conferring rights (contractual or property) over equity or debt securities.[130] Examples are depository receipts. Paragraph 15 exempts from the definition of CIS, arrangements where the rights of the participants are such investments. Although the RAO definition of 'certificates representing securities' is potentially very wide in referring to 'instruments' which confer 'contractual or proprietary rights' over equity or debt securities held by another, it was held in the *The Russell-Cooke Trust Company v Elliot*,[131] that it did not cover mere documentary evidence of rights in a scheme but only covered securities and similar choses in action. Thus the exemption did not apply when participants were issued with a 'Certificate of Mortgage Investment' which (together with other documents) set out their entitlements. This did not fall within the RAO definition because 'if the investor wants to recover his fund he must either sue in contract or under the declaration of trust... he cannot bring an action on the basis of the Certificate of Mortgage'.[132] **18.50**

Paragraph 16: Clearing services This exemption covers clearing services operated either by an authorised person,[133] or a recognised clearing house,[134] or a recognised investment exchange.[135] Such regulatory control as is desirable in these situations can already be exercised by the FCA in its capacity as regulator of authorised persons and recognised investment exchanges and the Bank of England as regulator of recognised clearing houses.[136] **18.51**

---

127 Para 14(a).
128 Para 14(b). This refers to the RAO, Part III, which is the Part that lists the specified investments.
129 RAO, art 3(1).
130 ibid, art 80.
131 2001 available on WESTLAW (on the identically worded Financial Services Act 1986, s 75).
132 ibid, para [32].
133 FSMA, s 31.
134 ibid, s 285.
135 ibid.
136 The Bank took over regulation (from the FSA): see the amendments made to FSMA (esp. the new s 285A(2)) in this regard by the Financial Services Act 2012, ss 29–35 and Sch 8.

18.52 **Paragraph 17: Contracts of insurance** If an arrangement falls within the definition of 'contract of insurance' set out in the RAO,[137] then it is exempted from the definition of a CIS as insurance has its own regulatory treatment under FSMA.

18.53 **Paragraph 18: Funeral Plan Contracts**[138] Providing 'funeral plan contracts', as defined in the RAO[139] is a 'regulated activity' unless the plans are protected by insurance or trust arrangements.[140] Thus such plans are already subject to regulation and no doubt on that basis are excluded from the definition of a CIS.

18.54 **Paragraph 19: Individual pension accounts; Paragraph 20: Occupational and personal pension schemes** These two paragraphs exclude various arrangements for pension provision from the CIS definition as these are already subject to regulation under the pension schemes legislation.

18.55 First, paragraph 19 exempts 'individual pension accounts', which are defined as accounts that satisfy strict conditions,[141] including strict criteria as to investment. Thus they may generally only be invested in 'safe' investments such as units in regulated collective investment schemes.[142] Second, paragraph 20 exempts 'occupational pension schemes' and 'personal pension schemes',[143] both as defined in (and regulated under) the Pension Schemes Act 1993.[144]

18.56 **Paragraph 21: Bodies Corporate**[145] Most bodies corporate fall within the core definition of a CIS in FSMA, section 235.[146] They generally constitute 'arrangements with respect to property' (the share capital raised by the issue of shares and then used in the company's business) which enable participants (the shareholders) to participate in profits arising from the management of the property by the directors of the company. Shareholders generally do not have 'day-to-day' control and the participants' contributions are pooled and the scheme property is managed 'as a whole' by the directors.[147]

18.57 However, paragraph 21 excludes *all* bodies corporate—wherever constituted[148]—from the definition of CIS apart from two categories: OEICs (open-ended investment companies) as defined by FSMA[149] and LLPs (limited liability partnerships).[150] Thus a corporate body can

---

137 See the Treasury CIS Order, art 2(1) cross-referring to RAO, art 3(1). This does not answer the vexed question of what is 'insurance', an issue on which the FCA gives Guidance in its Handbook, PERG 6.

138 A new para 18 was substituted by SI 2001/3650, art 2(3).

139 See the Treasury CIS Order, art 2(1) cross-referring to RAO, art 59.

140 RAO, art 60.

141 Treasury CIS Order, art 2(1) cross-referring to the definition in the Personal Pension Schemes (Restriction on Discretion to Approve) (Permitted Investments) Regulations 2001, SI 2001/117, reg 4.

142 See para 18.89.

143 But not a 'personal pension unit trust' (meaning an AUT of the kind mentioned in the Personal Pension Schemes (Appropriate Schemes) Regulations 1997, SI 1997/470, Sch 1, Part 1: see Treasury CIS Order, art 2(1)) which is or comprises feeder funds.

144 Treasury CIS Order, art 2(1).

145 A new para 21 was substituted on 1 December 2001 by SI 2001/3650, art 2(4).

146 See para 18.12 *et seq.*

147 Moreover, each corporation is potentially a single CIS as its property is one pooled fund and hence s 236(4) (pooling in relation to separate parts of the property) will not be relevant: see FCA Handbook, PERG 9.4.6G.

148 See the definition in FSMA, s 417(1). Thus, for example, Dublin-based Exchange Traded Funds ('ETFs') are not CISs.

149 See para 18.66 *et seq.*

150 These are not defined but may be established in the UK under the Limited Liability Partnerships Act 2000.

only be a CIS if it is either an OEIC or an LLP. In particular, closed-ended corporations, such as UK investment companies and investment trusts[151] that invest in other companies' securities are not CISs.[152]

Other general CIS definitions

Participant The term 'participant' is frequently used in the CIS statutory provisions[153] yet a definition of the term is not listed either in the special CIS definition section (section 237) or in the general FSMA definition section (section 417(1)). However, it is 'defined' in a rather oblique way in section 235(2), which sets out the lack of 'day-to-day control' requirement,[154] by the addition of the bracketed word '("participants")' after the reference to 'persons who are to participate'. Moreover, section 235(3) then refers to the 'contributions of the participants' being pooled. Therefore it is clear that 'participant' has the natural meaning of the contributor to or investor[155] in the scheme, that is, the person who takes part in the arrangements by making contributions to the scheme property.[156] The use of the future tense in section 235(2) ('persons who are to participate') makes it clear that, where relevant, potential investors in the scheme as well as actual investors are covered by the term. 18.58

The FCA Handbook Glossary does define 'participant' for the purposes of that document as 'a person who participates in a' CIS. That definition begins with the words '(in accordance with section 235(2) of the Act)', suggesting that the meaning of the term is the same as in FSMA. However, the FCA Handbook definition uses the present not the future tense and thus, in terms, does not cover future contributors to the scheme. 18.59

The FCA Handbook also contains provision in relation to certain types of participants: 'unitholders' and 'shareholders'. Broadly speaking, a unitholder is the person entered in the register in relation to that unit[157] or if a unit is represented by a Bearer Certificate[158] then the 'unitholder' is the holder of that Certificate. The term 'shareholder' is specific to an ICVC[159] and has a similar meaning, noted in the discussion of ICVCs at paragraph 18.101. 18.60

Unit Although the term 'unit' seems most appropriate to the unit trust context, in both FSMA and the FCA Handbook it is the general term that denotes 'the rights or interests (however described) of the participants in' *any* CIS.[160] Thus, for the purposes of the regulatory provisions, shares in an OEIC and contractual rights in a purely contractual CIS, as well as units in a unit trust scheme, are all 'units' in the CIS. 18.61

Depositary; operator CISs very frequently vest the scheme property in one person for safekeeping and then designate another to manage the property. Indeed, such a division of 18.62

---

151 See para 18.01.
152 But they can be AIFs (see para 18.08).
153 See ss 237, 238, 243, 247, 248, 250, 254, 257, 264, 272, 279, 281, 283, and 284.
154 See para 18.21 *et seq.*
155 The definition of an OEIC in s 236(3) (considered further in para 18.71 *et seq.)* refers to a 'reasonable [potential] investor' where it could have used the term 'participant' but perhaps the former phrase was regarded as more apposite in that (corporate) context.
156 See also s 238(11), which refers to 'participant (within the meaning given by section 235(2))'.
157 See para 18.61.
158 As further defined in the FCA Handbook Glossary.
159 See para 18.101. There is a separate meaning given to 'shareholder' for the purposes of the DTR (Disclosure Rules and Transparency Rules) Module of the Handbook.
160 s 237(2).

responsibility is necessary in order to obtain an authorisation order for the scheme from the FCA.[161]

18.63 FSMA defines 'depositary' as the person to whom the scheme property is 'entrusted for safe-keeping' but expressly states that the definition is inapplicable to unit trust schemes.[162] This is because the more precise term 'trustee' is used in FSMA to denote the corresponding person in a unit trust scheme context. However, as noted later in this chapter,[163] the FCA Handbook uses the term 'depositary' in relation to *all* CISs, including unit trust schemes, and hence the trustee of a unit trust scheme is a 'depositary' for the purposes of the FCA Handbook.

18.64 The term 'operator' is only defined in FSMA in relation to two categories of CISs: unit trust schemes with separate trustees and OEICs.[164] In relation to the former, if there is a separate trustee, it means the manager whilst in relation to the latter, it means the company itself (even if another person manages its property on its behalf). In *Andrew Brown v Innovatorone Plc*,[165] Hamblen J stated that 'operator' meant 'the person (or persons, as there may be more than one) responsible for the management of the property as a whole'. Hence, he held that a solicitor merely holding contributions to a CIS in his client account to the order of an operator of a CIS, was not an 'operator' of that CIS as he performed no discretionary management function.

18.65 The FCA Handbook contains a comprehensive definition (for the purpose of its provisions) of the term 'operator' in relation to *all* CISs. For the purposes of the Enforcement Guide in the FCA Handbook,[166] as far as unit trust schemes and OEICs are concerned, the FCA Handbook definition of 'operator' is broadly consistent with the FSMA definition.[167] For the purposes of the rest of the Handbook the definition of 'operator' varies with the type of CIS at issue but the default definition[168] is 'any person who, under the constitution or founding arrangements of the scheme, is responsible for the management of the property held for or within the scheme'.

Definition of 'Open-Ended Investment Company' ('OEIC'): FSMA, section 236

General

18.66 The term 'open-ended investment company' ('OEIC') is also defined in FSMA (in section 236)[169] and therefore also has a distinct meaning. The statutory definition may be (but has

[161] See paras 18.95 and 18.106. It is a requirement for a UCITS scheme under the UCITS Directive, see para 18.03. It is not an explicit requirement for ss 270 or 272 'recognised schemes' (see paras 18.116 and 18.119).

[162] s 237(2).

[163] Para 18.86.

[164] s 237(2). And see the discussion in 'Operating a Collective Investment Scheme', Financial Markets Law Committee, Issue 86, (July 2008). It is expected that s 237(2) will be amended on the implementation of the AIFMD (see para 18.07) to define an operator of a AIF (as the 'manager').

[165] [2012] EWHC 1321 (Comm) [1188]. The issue was who was 'operating' the CIS for the purposes of the RAO, art 51, see para 18.131. Hamblen J cited text from the 2nd edition of this work at para [1187].

[166] See para 18.151 *et seq.*

[167] See paras 18.81 and 18.88. But if an OEIC within the UCITS Directive (see para 18.03) has appointed a manager, it is that manager.

[168] For an AUT (see para 18.93) it is the 'manager' (as further defined in the Glossary); for an ICVC (see para 18.101) it is that company or 'if applicable' the ACT (for the ACT, see para 18.103); for an OEIC within the UCITS Directive (see para 18.03) that has appointed a manager, it is that manager; for other OEICs it is that company or 'if applicable' whoever has management responsibilities under the constitution; for a unit trust scheme with a separate manager, it is the manager.

[169] A new subs.(4)(a) was substituted on 1 October 2009 by SI 2009/1941, art 2(1) and Sch 1, para 181(3) in consequence of the enactment of the Companies Act 2006.

not yet been) altered by Treasury Order.[170] Unlike the core CIS definition, which is almost a verbatim transcription of the corresponding provision in the Financial Services Act 1986, the FSMA definition of an OEIC differs from the predecessor provision,[171] attempting to clarify some of the difficulties of interpretation that the old definition gave rise to. Nevertheless, the definition is still a difficult one to apply and therefore extensive guidance is provided in the PERG Module of the FCA Handbook.[172] An OEIC is the only type of body corporate (other than an LLP) that can be a CIS[173] and hence it is important to draw the line between OEICs and other corporations. The issue only arises in relation to overseas open-ended investment companies as any such UK company necessarily falls within the definition.[174]

In order to fall within the statutory definition of an 'open-ended investment company', the body corporate must be a 'collective investment scheme' that satisfies two further conditions.[175] Thus before considering those two conditions, the CIS definition must be applied.[176] As noted earlier, most corporations will be CISs unless they fall within one of the exclusions in the Treasury CIS Order.[177] However, the exclusion in paragraph 21 of that Order must clearly be disregarded at this stage, as this excludes all bodies corporate except OEICs (and LLPs) and hence the decision of whether a company is an OEIC needs to be made before paragraph 21 can be applied. **18.67**

The two conditions that a CIS has to fulfil for it to be an OEIC are termed 'the property condition' and 'the investment condition'. Their effect is that, broadly speaking, an OEIC is a corporate vehicle for collective investment whose property is managed so that risk is spread and where most or all of its shares can be realised, typically through redemption or repurchase, on a 'net-asset value' basis within a reasonable period. It will be seen that the status of a corporation—whether it is an OEIC or not—may change from time to time, depending on how the way it operates is perceived by a 'reasonable' potential 'investor' at the relevant time.[178] **18.68**

The property condition: section 236(2)[179]

The so-called 'property condition' requires that the scheme property is both owned beneficially[180] by a body corporate and is managed by (or on behalf of) that body corporate so that investment risk is spread[181] and its shareholders[182] obtain the benefits of that management.[183] As the term 'body corporate' covers both domestic and overseas companies,[184] it is clear that the term 'open-ended investment company' is not confined to domestic schemes.[185] **18.69**

170 s 236(5).
171 FSA 1986, s 75(8).
172 In PERG 9, one of the 'Regulatory Guides' at the end of the Handbook.
173 See para 18.57.
174 See para 18.101. This is because an ICVC is the only form of UK open-ended investment company that may be established and to qualify it must fall within the definition of OEIC in s 236.
175 s 236(1).
176 See para 18.12 *et seq.*
177 See para 18.56 *et seq.*
178 Confirmed in PERG 9.11.1G, FAQ 2 and PERG 9.7.5G.
179 See PERG 9.5G.
180 If it is held by the company on trust, a unit trust may arise, see para 18.83 *et seq.*
181 FSMA, s 236(2)(a).
182 ibid, s 236(2)(b) uses the more general term 'members'.
183 ibid, s 236(2)(b).
184 ibid, s 417(1).
185 Indeed, as noted in para 18.66 and n 174, whether the definition is satisfied is, in practice, only an issue in the case of overseas companies.

According to general principles, whether an arrangement gives rise to a 'body corporate' is a matter for the law of the place where the arrangement takes place.[186] If it does, it will be for the law of the relevant part of the UK in which the question arises to decide if that body corporate is an OEIC within section 236.[187]

18.70 The property condition requires a spread of investment risk and therefore companies that merely hold one or a very narrow category of assets cannot be OEICs. However, nothing is said about the level of risk, merely that the risk (however high or low) is 'spread'.[188] Moreover, this condition requires the active management of those assets. It is therefore not enough that the company merely holds assets in the expectation that they will increase in value. It should be noted that for the purposes of FSMA,[189] the 'operator' of an OEIC is always the company itself, even if it employs a manager to 'operate' the scheme and manage its assets on its behalf.

The investment condition: section 236(3)[190]

18.71 **General** The investment condition has two aspects, both referable to the assessment that a 'reasonable' potential 'investor' would make as regards the scheme. The FCA Guidance, PERG 9, contains a very full discussion of this condition. It makes a number of general points. The first is that, as the condition needs to be satisfied 'in relation to' the company, it is the 'overall impression' that is critical. Therefore the condition 'should not be applied rigidly in relation to specific events such as particular issues of shares or securities or in relation to particular points in time'.[191] The second point is that if shares with different rights are issued, they all need not satisfy the condition as long as 'the overall balance between those that do and those that do not is strongly in favour of those that do'.[192] As regards the 'reasonable investor', the FCA takes the view that the term connotes a person with some knowledge of collective investment and the proposed underlying property.[193] Moreover, as the condition is worded in terms of the assessment that such a person 'would, if he were to participate' make, it is focused on assessments before participation. It follows that if the scheme changes significantly, so that the investment condition becomes, or is no longer, satisfied, the scheme can change throughout its life into an OEIC or into a non-OEIC (and hence not a CIS)[194] and vice versa.[195]

18.72 **Realisation within a reasonable period** The first aspect of the investment condition[196] (called the 'expectation test' in the FCA Guidance)[197] is that the 'reasonable investor' would

---

186 Dicey and Morris on the *Conflict of Laws* (15th edn, Sweet & Maxwell 2012) para 30.001 *et seq.*

187 PERG 9.3.6G. This is also in accordance with the general principle that the words of a UK statute are to be interpreted according to the law of the relevant part of the UK. It is therefore irrelevant whether the overseas applicable law of the place of constitution regards the body corporate as an open-ended investment company or not.

188 PERG 9.5.5G.

189 See the definition of 'operator' in s 237(2), noted in para 18.81. Who the 'operator' is for the purposes of the FCA Handbook depends on the context: see para 18.82.

190 PERG 9.6G–9.9G.

191 PERG 9.6.3G. However, the OEIC's status may change over time: see PERG 9.11.1G FAQ 2.

192 PERG 9.6.4G. See also PERG 9.8.8G and 9.11.1G FAQ 5. But they will all be 'units' in a CIS, even the ones that are irredeemable.

193 PERG 9.7.2G. If an investment is targeted at investors with particular characteristics, the 'reasonable investor' is to be assumed to have those characteristics: ibid.

194 As the only type of corporate CIS possible is an OIEC (or an LLP): see para 21.

195 See n 178.

196 FSMA, s 236(3)(a).

197 PERG 9.6.2G and, generally, PERG 9.8G.

expect that he would be able to realise, within a period appearing to him reasonable, his investment in the scheme represented, at any given time, by the value of the body corporate's shares or securities. In making that assessment a number of factors will be relevant, including the terms on which the securities are issued, the company's constitution, any representations as to policy, and how that policy is implemented in practice.[198]

A number of issues arise. There need not be an actual *entitlement* so to realise the investment; an expectation to be able to do so is enough. So if, in practice, the scheme regularly redeems or repurchases its securities or has a declared policy to that effect, this aspect of the condition is likely to be satisfied[199] at least until that practice or policy changes. Such realisation will usually occur either through redemption or resale to the company—although redemption or resale under certain statutory provisions[200] permitting the reduction of share capital does not amount to realisation for this purpose. Because of the second aspect of the 'investment condition' (which requires realisation on a net-asset value basis) considered below, the possibility of realisation through sale on an exchange, in itself, will not be enough.[201] It seems clear[202] that 'realise' means convert into money and therefore an expectation that the securities will be exchanged for other securities will not suffice—unless those securities themselves can be 'realised', the whole process taking place within a 'reasonable period'. **18.73**

As the requisite expectation is to be able to realise 'within a period appearing to' the 'reasonable investor' to be 'reasonable', there is no need for *immediate* realisation to be available. Thus an expectation that redemption or repurchase will occur periodically suffices as long as a 'reasonable investor' would regard the intervals between the occasions as 'reasonable'. This will depend on the liquidity of the underlying scheme property; the greater the illiquidity, the longer the period that would be likely to be regarded as 'reasonable'.[203] The FCA takes the view that redemption or repurchase every six months 'would generally be too long to be a reasonable period for a liquid securities fund'[204] but that an *initial* period, during which it is not possible to realise the investment would not necessarily preclude the scheme being an OEIC.[205] It seems clear that the participant's *whole* investment needs to be realisable within a reasonable period, although it is enough that it can be realised in stages—as long as realisation of the whole contribution can take place within a 'reasonable period'.[206] **18.74**

Realisation on 'net-asset value' basis The second aspect of the investment condition[207] (called the 'satisfaction test' in the FCA Guidance, PERG 9)[208] is that the 'reasonable investor' must 'be satisfied that his investment would be realised on a basis calculated wholly or **18.75**

198 See PERG 9.8.7G to 9.8.9G.
199 PERG 9.8.5(2)G.
200 Listed in s 236(4) and reflecting (in relation to the UK and other EEA States) the maintenance of capital requirements of Directive (EEC) 77/91 (the Second Company Law Directive). See PERG 9.6.5G. Hence, so-called 'closed-ended' investment trusts which redeem/repurchase their shares under these provisions are not OEICs (confirmed in PERG 9.11.1G FAQ 7).
201 See following, and PERG 9.8.3G; 9.9.4G–9.9.6G.
202 See PERG 9.8.2G.
203 See PERG 9.8.9(7)G.
204 PERG 9.11.1G FAQ 8.
205 PERG 9.11.1G FAQ 9.
206 PERG 9.8.4G.
207 FSMA, s 236(3)(b).
208 PERG 9.6.2G and, generally, PERG 9.9.

mainly by reference' to the net-asset value. The use of the verb 'satisfied'—in contrast to 'expects' in the first aspect of the condition—indicates a higher threshold, requiring him to be convinced that this is the case, rather than merely expect that this will be so. The FCA Guidance states that 'satisfy' connotes 'objectively justifiable grounds on which the reasonable investor could form a view'.[209]

18.76 This aspect of the condition will not be fulfilled if realisation is to occur through a secondary market, as the market price of the securities (determined by the laws of supply and demand) may not exactly reflect the net-asset value of the company's property, unless the company undertakes to take steps (such as intervening in the market) to ensure that the price of its securities is based on the net-asset value.[210] On the other hand, if the company undertakes that it will redeem or repurchase its shares or arranges for some other person to undertake to purchase its shares, on a net-asset value basis, then the condition is likely to be fulfilled.[211] Some flexibility is introduced by the phrase 'wholly or mainly', so that minor departures from the net-asset value basis (for example, by the deduction of redemption charges)[212] are not fatal, as long as the net-asset value is the 'main' basis of realisation.

Other OEIC definitions

18.77 **'Participants' in OEICs** In FSMA and FCA Handbook terminology, the shareholder or other securities holder in an OEIC is the 'participant' in the CIS that is the OEIC.[213] However, for the purposes of the OEIC definition, FSMA uses the alternative terms 'reasonable investor' and (a term appropriate to the corporate context) 'member', rather than referring to 'participant'. Nevertheless, for the purposes of applying the FSMA regime, it is clear that the securities holders are the 'participants'.

18.78 The FCA Handbook, whilst essentially[214] giving the term 'participant' the same meaning as in FSMA, also contains a definition of the term 'shareholder' in relation to ICVCs.[215] If a share is represented by a Bearer Certificate[216] then the 'shareholder' is the holder of that certificate. Otherwise the 'shareholder' is the person entered on the share register in relation to the share.

18.79 **Unit** In both FSMA and the FCA Handbook, the shares or securities in an OEIC are referred to as 'units'—the general term used to denote the rights of the participants in any CIS.[217]

18.80 **Depositary; operator** For the purposes of both FSMA and the FCA Handbook, the 'depositary' in relation to an OEIC is the person to whom the scheme property is 'entrusted for safekeeping'.[218]

---

209 PERG 9.9.3G.
210 PERG 9.9.3(3)G, 9.9.4G–9.9.6G.
211 PERG 9.9.3(2)(a)G.
212 PERG 9.9.7G.
213 See para 18.58.
214 Although, as noted in para 18.58, the present, not future, tense is used.
215 For ICVCs, see para 18.101. There is also a definition of 'shareholder' in the FCA Handbook Glossary in relation to the DTR (Disclosure Rules and Transparency Rules) Module.
216 As further defined in the FCA Handbook Glossary.
217 See para 18.61.
218 FSMA, s 237(2); FCA Handbook Glossary—although in the Glossary, in relation to an ICVC (see para 18.101) such a person must also have been 'appointed for the purpose' in accordance with the OEIC Regulations (see para 18.102).

The 'operator' of an OEIC has a less obvious meaning. FSMA states that it means the company itself.[219] This is even if the OEIC in fact engages another person to manage its property on its behalf. Hence, for the purpose of applying the FSMA provisions,[220] the OEIC is still the 'operator'. **18.81**

The FCA Handbook definition is more qualified and depends on the type of OEIC and which parts of the Handbook are in issue. In the case of an OEIC within the UCITS Directive that has appointed a person to manage 'the scheme', it always means that manager. Otherwise a distinction needs to be drawn between the use of the term 'operator' in the Enforcement Guide (EG)[221] and elsewhere in the Handbook. In EG the 'operator' is the company. Elsewhere it is either the company 'or, if applicable', the ACD in the case of an ICVC[222] and 'any person who, under the constitution or founding arrangements of the scheme, is responsible for the management of the property held for or within the scheme' in the case of other OEICs. **18.82**

'Unit trust scheme'

General

A 'unit trust scheme' is defined in section 237(1) of FSMA as a CIS 'under which the property is held on trust for the participants'. Thus in deciding if a 'unit trust scheme' arises, the first question to ask is whether the arrangements satisfy the definition of a CIS.[223] If so, the second question is whether the scheme property is held 'on trust' for the participants. **18.83**

Other unit trust definitions

Participant In FSMA and FCA Handbook terminology, the unitholder in a unit trust scheme is the 'participant' in the scheme.[224] **18.84**

Unit

The general term used in FSMA and the FCA Handbook to denote a participant's interest in *any* CIS—a 'unit'—has been taken from the unit trust context.[225] Hence, naturally, the beneficial interest of a participant in a unit trust scheme, as declared in the trust deed (his unit, as it is usually known), is a 'unit' for the purposes of the regulatory regime. **18.85**

Trustee/depositary; operator Unsurprisingly, in FSMA the 'trustee' of a unit trust scheme is defined as the person holding the property on trust and the 'operator' in relation to a unit trust scheme with a separate trustee is defined as 'the manager'.[226] **18.86**

The FCA Handbook terminology is less straightforward. It uses the generic term 'depositary' to cover persons to whom the CIS property is 'entrusted for safekeeping' and makes it clear that this covers the trustee of a unit trust scheme.[227] Therefore, as far as the application of the **18.87**

---

[219] FSMA, s 237(2).
[220] For example, FSMA, Sched 5 para 1(1), see further nn 314 and 414.
[221] See 18.151 *et seq*.
[222] See para 18.103.
[223] See para 18.12 *et seq*.
[224] See para 18.58. Note also the FCA Handbook term 'unitholder', which is not confined to unit trusts (as 'unit' refers to participatory rights in *all* CISs).
[225] s 237(2). See para 18.61.
[226] s 237(2). For an argument that the manager of a unit trust is functionally (and so for the purposes of liability) a 'trustee', see A Hudson, *Law of Investment Entities* (2000) p 207. Cf Kam Fan Sin (n 11).
[227] FCA Handbook Glossary, definition of 'depositary', see (b) and (c) thereof.

FCA Handbook is concerned, the provisions applicable to 'depositaries' apply to unit trust scheme trustees. Confusingly, although the term 'depositary' is defined in identical terms in FSMA, that FSMA definition is stated not to apply to a unit trust scheme. Thus in FSMA (and secondary legislation made under it) 'depositary' does not cover the trustee of a unit trust scheme whilst in the FCA Handbook it does.

18.88 The FCA Handbook also uses, and defines, the term 'operator' but in relation to *all* CISs. Curiously, in relation to unit trust schemes, it does not refer to the FSMA definition but starts afresh. However, the Handbook definition does not appear to alter—but merely slightly to expand on—the FSMA definition. Essentially, it defines the operator as the person designated by the trust deed as having management of the property.[228] Thus (unlike the term 'depositary'), the term 'operator' in relation to unit trust schemes essentially has the same meaning in both FSMA and the FCA Handbook.

Regulatory Categorisation of CISs

Introduction: the terminology

18.89 A number of different terms are used to cover different categories of CISs in both FSMA and the FCA Handbook. For the purposes of regulation there are four main categories of CISs:

(1) (UK) authorised unit trust schemes or 'AUTs';
(2) (UK) authorised open-ended investment companies ('OEICs'), (termed 'investment companies with variable capital' or 'ICVCs' in the FCA Handbook);
(3) (Overseas) recognised schemes, of which there are presently[229] three sub-categories:
 (i) section 264 EEA (UCITS) schemes;
 (ii) section 270 schemes authorised in 'designated' countries or territories;
 (iii) section 272 individually recognised overseas schemes;
(4) Other (so-called '*unregulated*') CISs ('UCISs').

18.90 The FCA Handbook, as well as introducing the acronym 'ICVC' to denoted UK-authorised OEICs, uses a number of other terms to cover various categories of CIS. It uses the term '*authorised fund*' to cover the first two categories of UK CISs (that is, both AUTs and ICVCs), the epithet 'authorised' denoting that the FCA has made an 'authorisation order' in respect of the scheme.[230] Authorised funds are subdivided into three categories for promotion purposes: '*UCITS schemes*', '*non-UCITS retail schemes*' (NURSs), and '*qualified investor schemes*' (QISs). As its name suggests, a 'UCITS scheme' is either an AUT or an ICVC that has a 'single market passport' under the UCITS Directive so it may be marketed, without further authorisation requirements, throughout the single market.[231] All other authorised funds are termed 'non-UCITS schemes'. However, these are subdivided into NURs and QISs. A QIS is a type of authorised fund that can only be promoted to the same limited audience

[228] There are separate provisions for AUTs (the operator is the 'manager' who is defined as the firm that is the manager in accordance with the trust deed) and other unit trust schemes (if there is a separate trustee, the operator is the person with responsibility for management under the trust deed).
[229] Note the proposal to repeal s 270 and revise s 272, referred to in n 309.
[230] See paras 18.93 (AUT) and 18.101 (ICVC).
[231] See para 18.03.

as unregulated schemes.[232] A NUR is an authorised fund that does not comply with the UCITS Directive but may be promoted to the general public in the UK (hence 'non-UCITS *retail* scheme').

The FCA Handbook uses the more general term '*regulated collective investment scheme*' to cover the first three categories of scheme listed earlier (that is, (1) AUTs, (2) ICVCs, and (3) 'recognised schemes'), the epithet term 'regulated' denoting that the constitution and operation of these schemes are subject to detailed regulation either by the FCA itself (in relation to the 'authorised funds' within (1) and (2)) or an overseas regulator (in relation to the 'recognised schemes' within (3)). **18.91**

The term '*unregulated collective investment scheme*' ('UCIS') is used in the FCA Handbook to refer to the fourth, residual category which covers all CISs other than regulated schemes, whether UK or overseas. They are 'unregulated' in the sense that the schemes *themselves* do not need to comply with the detailed requirements that 'regulated collective investment schemes' have to satisfy. However, the term 'unregulated' should not be taken to indicate that FSMA has no application to them. As will be explained later in this chapter,[233] the Act generally precludes such CISs being promoted to the public and its regime applies to persons involved in them. **18.92**

(UK) Authorised unit trust schemes ('AUTs')

General

Authorised unit trust schemes or 'AUTs' are defined in FSMA as 'unit trust schemes'[234] that are authorised by virtue of the conferment of an 'authorisation order' by the FCA. FSMA contains the regulatory framework for AUTs, including the conferment of powers on the FCA to impose detailed regulatory requirements,[235] with the COLL Module of the FCA Handbook containing most of that detail.[236] The regulatory requirements reflect the UCITS Directive and hence enable AUTs to become 'UCITS schemes',[237] with the single market passport. However, as noted earlier,[238] AUTs may adopt wider investment and borrowing powers and hence be NURs or even QISs. **18.93**

Requirements for an 'authorisation order'

The basic requirements for obtaining an authorisation order from the FCA are set out in FSMA, section 243 and may be divided into three categories. These are amplified in the COLL Module of the FCA Handbook.[239] **18.94**

First, there are the requirements imposed by the section itself.[240] The manager[241] and trustee, who must both be 'authorised persons' with permission to act as manager and trustee **18.95**

[232] See further, paras 18.142 and 18.149.
[233] See para 18.129 *et seq.*
[234] See para 18.83 *et seq.*
[235] See especially, FSMA Part XVIII, Ch III.
[236] See para 18.148 and note para 18.147. COLL imposes most of these requirements on 'authorised funds' and hence (in so far as possible) treats AUTs and ICVCs together in the same way.
[237] See para 18.03. Section 246 enables the FCA to issue a certificate that the AUT complies with the UCITS Directive.
[238] Para 18.90.
[239] See para 18.148.
[240] s 243(1)(a) and see subss (4)–(11). The FCA must be 'satisfied' that these are fulfilled.
[241] The term 'manager' is not defined in the Act but the term is self-explanatory, FSMA merely stating that the 'manager' of a unit trust scheme is the 'operator' for the purposes of the Act: s 237(2).

respectively,[242] must be independent of each other[243] and must each be a body corporate incorporated either in the UK or another EEA State and have their affairs administered in the country in which they are incorporated, with a place of business in the UK.[244] The scheme's name must not be 'undesirable or misleading':[245] and 'the purposes of the scheme must be reasonably capable of being successfully' effected.[246] Finally, the participants must be able to withdraw their contributions at a price reflecting the net-asset worth of the scheme.[247] The second main requirement is that the scheme must comply with the requirements of the FCA's 'trust scheme rules',[248] noted later in this chapter, which are in the COLL Module.

18.96 The third requirement is a formal one: the FCA must have received (a) a copy of the trust deed, and (b) a solicitor's certificate stating that the scheme complies with the trust deed contents requirements of section 243 and the trust scheme rules.[249]

The AUT regulatory regime

18.97 As noted earlier, FSMA sets out the regulatory framework and, as well as provisions concerning the determination of applications for 'authorisation orders',[250] it confers powers on the FCA to make two types of rules in relation to AUTS: 'trust scheme rules'[251] and 'scheme particular rules'.[252] These may be found in the COLL Module of the FCA Handbook. Provisions in both sets of rules may be waived or modified on request.[253]

18.98 'Trust scheme rules' concern the constitution, management, and operation of AUTs.[254] In particular they regulate the contents of the trust deed itself,[255] deal with the legal position of the various parties. and regulate the powers, duties, rights, and liabilities of both the manager and trustee,[256] as well as the rights and duties of the participants.[257] Thus they

---

242 s 243(7). See further, para 18.130.

243 s 243(4).

244 s 243(5), (5A). However if the manager is incorporated in another EEA State then the scheme must not be one that qualifies for recognition under s 264 (see para 18.113 *et seq*, as EU law—in particular the UCITS Directive (see para 18.03)—requires the 'home' EEA State to authorise and the UK 'host' State to recognise that authorisation without being able to impose any further authorisation requirements itself): subs (6). When the AIFMD is implemented (see para 18.07) it is expected that special provisions will apply to AIFs and therefore subss (5) and (5A) will be disapplied to AIFs.

245 s 243(8).

246 s 243(9).

247 s 243(10). This requirement is regarded as fulfilled if the scheme obliges the manager 'to ensure' (eg, by trading himself) that the participant can sell his units on an investment exchange (not necessarily an exchange recognised under s 285) at such a price.

248 s 243(1)(b). The FCA must be 'satisfied' that these are fulfilled, see para 18.98.

249 s 243(1)(c). Any subsequent proposal to alter the scheme, which involves a change in the trust deed, must also be accompanied by such a solicitor's certificate: s 251(2).

250 ss 244 (determination), 245 (procedure when refusing), 251–252 (alterations to schemes and changes of manager and trustee), 256 (request for revocation of authorisation order). Sections 244 and 251–252 were amended by SI 2011/1613, reg 2(16) (implementing UCITS IV and certain obligations in Commission Directives 2010/43/EU and 2010/4/EU: see n 17).

251 s 247.

252 s 248.

253 s 250: but in only respect of (a) persons to whom they apply or (b) the scheme itself.

254 s 247(1)(a), including their winding up (subs (1)(d)).

255 s 247(3).

256 s 247(1)(b). See also s 253, reflecting arts 24 (depositary), and 34 (management company) of the UCITS IV Directive, which essentially does not permit the exemption of either the management company or depositary from liability for 'unjustifiable failure to perform' duties or their 'improper performance'. Although the FCA trust scheme rules could have included such a prohibition, it was considered desirable to place the prohibition in the Act itself.

257 s 247(1)(c).

regulate the investment and borrowing powers of AUTs[258] and the redemption rights of the participants.[259] The rules are stated to be binding on the parties (the manager, trustee, and participants) 'independently of the contents of the trust deed'[260] and hence in the unlikely case[261] of the deed contradicting the rules, the rules will prevail.

The 'scheme particular rules'[262] require the manager of an AUT to produce and publish an information document resembling a share prospectus ('scheme particulars')[263] and to produce revisions of it when circumstances change.[264] As equivalent requirements are imposed on ICVCs by the OEIC Regulations,[265] where the corresponding document is a true share prospectus (as the 'units' in an OEIC are, of course, 'shares' in the OEIC), and as one set of these requirements (in relation to both AUTs and ICVCs) are imposed by the FCA, the relevant provisions of the COLL Module, refer to the document generically as a 'prospectus'. The rules impose liability to pay compensation for misleading particulars, similar to that which may arise in relation to a misleading share prospectus,[266] and the rules do not affect any common law liability that may otherwise arise—for example in tort (or delict) or contract[267] as a result of misrepresentations in the scheme particulars. As will be noted later in this chapter,[268] FSMA also enables the FCA to make rules corresponding to scheme particular rules in relation to operators of overseas schemes recognised under section 270 (schemes from designated countries), or section 272 (individually recognised schemes), but not operators of section 264 (EEA (UCITSs)) recognised schemes. **18.99**

FSMA also confers extensive powers of investigation (common to all CISs)[269] and powers of intervention (specific to AUTs and ICVCs) in relation to AUTs when things go wrong, for example when there is a breach of the statutory requirements or FCA rules, or where intervention is in the interests of participants. The FCA's less drastic power of intervention is to issue 'directions'[270] requiring that the issue or redemption, or both, of units cease[271] or that the scheme be wound up.[272] Moreover, the FCA may apply to court for an order removing and replacing the manager or trustee, or both, or removing either or both, and for the **18.100**

[258] s 247(2)(d).

[259] s 247(2)(a).

[260] s 247(4). This further provides that, in the case of the participants (only) the rules have effect as if contained in the deed. Thus when a participant wishes to rely on the rules, he may treat them as if they were provisions in the deed itself.

[261] A solicitor will have certified that the deed complies with the trust rules: see s 243(1)(c).

[262] In FCA Handbook COLL 4.

[263] s 248(1). See subs (2) (definition of 'scheme particulars').

[264] s 248(3)–(4).

[265] See para 18.102.

[266] s 248(5).

[267] s 248(7). See Kam Fan Sin (n 11), 81, citing *Graham Australia Pty Ltd v Corporate West Management Pty Ltd* (1990) 1 ACSR 682, 687 holding that the unit trust particulars are the basis of a contract between the unit holders and manager.

[268] See paras 18.115, 18.118, and 18.125.

[269] s 284—except ICVCs as corresponding powers are conferred by the OEIC Regulations 2001, SI 2001/1228 (as amended, see n 277), reg 30.

[270] s 257, as amended by SI 2011/1613, reg 2(16) (implementing UCITS IV and certain obligations in Commission Directives 2010/43/EU and 2010/44/EU: see n 17). See FCA Handbook, EG 14.1–14.5. Contravention of the direction is civilly actionable by persons suffering loss: s 257(5) cross-referring to s 138D. For the procedure, see ss 259–261, as amended by SI 2011/1613, reg 2(16) (implementing UCITS IV and certain obligations in Commission Directives 2010/43/EU and 2010/44/EU: see n 17).

[271] s 257(2)(a): this direction is addressed to the manager.

[272] s 257(2)(b): this direction is addressed to the manager and trustee.

appointment of an authorised person to wind up the scheme.[273] It also may revoke the AUT's authorisation order,[274] but has said[275] it will only do so after the AUT has been wound up and the scheme property has been distributed to the participants.

(UK) Authorised open-ended investment companies ('ICVCs')

General

18.101 The general definition of 'an open-ended investment company' ('OEIC') has been discussed earlier.[276] OEICs are a relatively new phenomenon in the UK and the only OEICs that can be established in the UK are those that obtain an 'authorisation order' from the FCA. Although FSMA calls such schemes 'authorised open-ended investment companies', the FCA Handbook uses the term 'ICVCs' (short for 'investment companies with variable capital').

18.102 Whilst the regulatory framework for AUTs is in FSMA, the corresponding provisions for ICVCs are in the OEIC Regulations 2001,[277] made by the Treasury under FSMA, section 262. Further detailed requirements (imposed under powers conferred by the OIEC Regulations on the FCA for the purposes of regulating ICVCs) are contained, together with the corresponding AUT provisions, in the COLL Sourcebook of the FCA Handbook.[278] ICVCs, like AUTs, may become 'UCITS schemes' or may adopt wider investment and borrowing powers and become NURs or QISs.[279]

18.103 An ICVC is constituted by an 'instrument of incorporation' (corresponding to a trust deed in the case of an AUT) and it must have at least one director. If there is only one director, that director must be a body corporate with permission to act as a director of an ICVC[280] and is termed (by the FCA Handbook) the 'authorised corporate director' (the 'ACD'). Corresponding to the trustee of an AUT, there must also be a 'depositary' to take responsibility for the safekeeping of the scheme property.[281]

18.104 Although, as will be noted later in this chapter, essentially the regulatory regime for AUTs and ICVCs is very similar, there are differences stemming from the fact that an ICVC is a corporation—with a separate legal existence. It acquires its corporate status when the FCA confers an authorisation order.[282] ICVCs have their own 'Corporate Code' which is set out in the OEIC Regulations[283] and ICVCs are entered on a Register kept by the FCA.[284] The Code is a modification of the corresponding provisions in the Companies Act 1985[285] (then) applicable to ordinary registered companies.

[273] s 258. See FCA Handbook, EG 14.1–14.5.
[274] s 254. See FCA Handbook, EG 14.1–14.5.
[275] See FCA Handbook, EG 14.5.
[276] See para 18.66 *et seq.*
[277] SI 2001/1228, as amended by SI 2001/3755, SI 2003/2066, SI 2005/923, SI 2007/1973, SI 2009/553, SI 2011/1613, and SI 2011/3049. For Northern Ireland, see the Open-ended Investment Company Regulations (Northern Ireland) 2004, SR 2004/335.
[278] See para 18.148 *et seq.*
[279] See para 18.90.
[280] OIEC Regulations, reg 15(6), as amended by SI 2003/2066.
[281] ibid, reg 5 and Sch 1. As noted (para 18.63), the FCA Handbook uses the term 'depositary' to cover both the depositary of an ICVC and a trustee of an AUT.
[282] OEIC Regulations, reg 3.
[283] Part III of the Regulations, regs 34–70, as amended by SI 2005/923 and SI 2011/1613, reg 3(7).
[284] Reg 4. See OEIC Regulations Part IV. The FCA performs various 'registrar' functions.
[285] Since replaced by the Companies Act 2006.

Requirements for an 'authorisation order'

The basic requirements for obtaining an authorisation order are set out in the OEIC Regulations[286] and are very similar to those for AUTs but reflect the fact that an OEIC is a separate legal entity, with an ACD[287] instead of an AUT 'manager' and with a 'depositary' instead of an AUT 'trustee'. **18.105**

The ACD and depositary, who must both be 'authorised persons' with permission to act as ACD and depositary respectively,[288] must be independent of each other.[289] The depositary must be a body corporate incorporated either in the UK or another EEA State and have its affairs administered in the country in which it is incorporated, with a place of business in the UK.[290] The ICVC must have its head office in England, Wales, or Scotland[291] and will, of course, be incorporated there (under the OEIC Regulations). The ICVCs name must not be 'undesirable or misleading',[292] and 'the aims of the company must be reasonably capable of being achieved'.[293] Finally, the participants must be able to withdraw their contributions (ie realise their shares) at a price reflecting the net-asset worth of the scheme.[294] **18.106**

The other requirements for an authorisation order are also very similar to those that AUTs have to satisfy. Thus there is the general requirement to comply with the OEIC Regulations and FCA rules[295] (which are mainly in the COLL Module), and the need to provide the FCA with the requisite documents including (a) the instrument of incorporation, and (b) a solicitor's certificate stating that the instrument complies with OEIC Regulations.[296] **18.107**

The ICVC regulatory regime

In setting out the regulatory framework, the OEIC Regulations make provision as to the determination of applications for 'authorisation orders'.[297] In addition, the Regulations extend the FCA's power (under FSMA in relation to AUTs)[298] to make 'trust scheme rules' and 'scheme particular rules' in relation to ICVCs.[299] And provision is made (adapting the **18.108**

286 OIEC Regulations reg 15 and see Part IV.

287 For the 'ACD', see para 18.103.

288 OIEC Regulations, reg 15(6) (ACD) and reg 15(8)(d) (depositary). If the OEIC has more than one director, they must be 'fit and proper' (reg 15(5)) with appropriate combined expertise (reg 15(7)).

289 OIEC Regulations, reg 15(8)(f): the depositary must be independent of both the directors and company.

290 ibid, reg 15(8)(a)–(c).

291 ibid, reg 15(3).

292 ibid, reg 15(9). And see the 'company law' provisions as to names in reg 18 (FCA as Registrar's approval), reg 19 (prohibition of certain names), and reg 20 (Registrar's index of names).

293 ibid, reg 15(10)—the wording is slightly different to the corresponding provision in relation to AUTs (see para 18.95).

294 ibid, reg 15(11) either by redemption or repurchase, or sale on an exchange.

295 ibid, reg 14(1)(a) and (b).

296 ibid, reg 14(1)(c) and (d).

297 See ibid, reg 12 (application), reg 13, as amended by SI 2008/948, art 3(1) and Sch 1 para 221 (particulars of directors), reg 14, as amended by SI 2011/1613 (determination), reg 16, as amended by SI 2003/2066 and SI 2010/22 (procedure when refusing), regs 21–22, as amended by SI 2005/923, SI 2010/22, SI 2011/1613, and 2011/3049 (alterations to schemes and changes of manager and trustee), regs 23–24, as amended by SI 2010/22 (request for revocation of authorisation order).

298 See FSMA, s 247 (trust scheme rules) and s 248 (scheme particular rules), considered at paras 18.98 and 18.99.

299 OIEC Regulations, reg 6. As noted earlier, one set of rules is made for 'authorised funds', ie AUTs and ICVCs.

relevant FSMA sections) for the modification or waiver of these rules on request.[300] For more details of these rules see the discussion on AUTs earlier in this chapter.[301]

18.109 ICVCs are not subject to the extensive powers of investigation in relation to CISs in general, conferred on the FSA by FSMA[302] However, correspondingly wide powers are conferred on the FCA by the OEIC Regulations.[303] Similarly, those Regulations confer corresponding powers of intervention in relation to ICVCs when things go wrong. Thus the FCA may issue 'directions' requiring that the issue or redemption, or both, of shares cease or that the ICVC be wound up.[304] Moreover, the FCA may apply to court for an order removing and replacing any director or the depositary, or both, or removing either or both and for the appointment of an authorised person to wind up the scheme.[305] Finally, the FCA may revoke the ICVC's authorisation order,[306] this time the Regulations making it clear that, before revocation, the FCA must ensure that steps have been taken to secure the winding up of the ICVC.[307]

(Overseas) Recognised CISs

General

18.110 Whilst the term 'authorised' when used in relation to AUTs or OEICs (or rather, ICVCs)[308] connotes a CIS that is established in the UK and that has an 'authorisation order' from the FCA, the term 'recognised' when used in relation to a CIS connotes a CIS constituted *outside* the UK but 'recognised' in the UK by virtue of one of three provisions: section 264 or 270 or 272.[309] Essentially, those provisions apply to those CISs that are regarded as sufficiently regulated in their home jurisdictions to be treated—primarily for the purposes of promotion to the public—as if they were UK AUTs or ICVCs.

18.111 Recognised status is sought for overseas schemes so that they may be promoted to the public in the UK. However, recognition brings with it a degree of regulatory oversight by the FCA, which varies depending on the category of 'recognised scheme'. Common to all recognised schemes is the requirement, imposed by the FCA under powers conferred by FSMA, section 283 and contained in the COLL Module,[310] that they maintain certain 'facilities' at a place of business in the UK[311] so that UK investors may readily obtain information about the

300 OIEC Regulations, reg 7, as amended by SI 2007/1973.

301 Para 18.97 *et seq.*

302 FSMA, s 284—see subs (1)(c), although curiously the FCA Handbook EG 3.11 seems to assume that s 284 applies to all CISs.

303 OIEC Regulations, reg 30.

304 ibid, reg 25. Again (see n 270), contravention is civilly actionable by persons suffering loss: reg 25(6) cross-referring to s 138D. For the procedure, see regs 27–29, as amended by SI 2010/22.

305 OIEC Regulations, reg 26.

306 ibid, reg 23.

307 ibid, reg 23(3). There is no corresponding provision (in relation to AUTs) in s 254, but see FCA Handbook, EG 14.5, noted at n 275.

308 See paras 18.93 and 18.101.

309 The opportunity presented by the implementation of the AIFMD (see para 18.07) is likely to be taken to revise ss 270 and 272, essentially to replace the two sections by a modified s 272 regime: see the weakness in the current approach identified and proposals for reform set out in HMT's *Second Consultation paper on the implementation of the AIFMD*, (March 2013), Chapter 2.

310 COLL 9.4, see further, para 18.148.

311 See COLL 9.4.6R: either the operator's principal place of business in the UK or an alternative 'convenient' address (which, in the case of a s 272 scheme where the operator is not an authorised person, must be the principal place of business of the authorised person who is the representative of the operator).

scheme, be able to redeem their units in it, and complain to it. Moreover, recognised schemes are subject to the FCA's extensive investigation powers over all CISs.[312]

The three categories of recognised scheme will now be considered. The UK is constrained in the extent to which it can exercise regulatory powers over the first category—the EEA (UCITS) recognised schemes—by EU law and this is reflected in the limited regulatory power that the FCA has over them. 18.112

EEA (UCITS) schemes: FSMA, section 264

General The first category of 'recognised' CIS covers those authorised in other EEA Member States and complying with the UCITS Directive.[313] As noted earlier, these have a 'single market passport' enabling them to be marketed, without the need for further authorisation, throughout the EEA single market. FSMA, section 264 makes provision for such CISs, conferring on them 'recognised' CIS status. Moreover, again in compliance with EU obligations, the operator, trustee, or depositary of such a scheme (being authorised in the home Member State) are automatically an 'authorised person' under FSMA[314] insofar as it acts as such.[315] 18.113

In order to be recognised under section 264, a CIS must be 'constituted in another EEA State' and satisfy requirements set out in Treasury Regulations.[316] The requirements in the Regulations[317] are that the CIS falls within the UCITS Directive. The term 'constituted in another EEA State' is defined[318] so that, essentially, the CIS must involve a company incorporated under the law of another EEA Member State: the CIS must either be an OEIC incorporated in that Member State or be managed by a company incorporated in that Member State (in which case it must also be 'constituted'—whether under contract or trust law—under that law). In addition, before the scheme can acquire 'recognised' status under section 264, the home State regulator of its 'operator'[319] must give the FCA notice of how the operator intends to market the scheme in the UK.[320] That notice must comply with EU law and be accompanied by information prescribed by Treasury regulations.[321] Once the scheme 18.114

---

312 See FSMA, s 284(1)(b).

313 See para 18.03.

314 FSMA, s 31(1)(d) and Sch 5, para 1(1),(2). See further, para 18.131. As the 'operator' of an OEIC is always the OEIC itself for the purposes of FSMA provisions (see s 237(2)), if the CIS is an OEIC, it will therefore be an 'authorised person' under these provisions. The FCA Handbook calls such persons 'UCITS qualifiers'.

315 Sch 5, para 2(1).

316 s 264(1)(a).

317 The FSMA 2000 (Collective Investment Schemes Constituted in Other EEA States) Regulations 2001, SI 2001/2383, as amended by SI 2003/2066 (implementing UCITS III, see para 18.03) and as further amended by SI 2011/1613 (implementing UCITS IV and certain obligations in Commission Directives 2010/43/EU and 2010/44EU: see n 17).

318 s 264(5).

319 Partially defined in s 237(2). If the scheme is neither an OEIC nor a unit trust scheme (and hence s 237(2) does not apply), presumably the 'operator' is the manager of the scheme.

320 s 264(1)(b), as substituted by SI 2011/1613 (implementing UCITS IV and certain obligations in Commission Directives 2010/43/EU and 2010/44/EU: see n 17).

321 s 264(1)(c), as substituted by SI 2011/1613 (implementing UCITS IV and certain obligations in Commission Directives 2010/43/EU and 2010/44/EU: see n 17). The information prescribed by Treasury regulation (see n 17) is the UCITS's (a) fund rules or instrument of incorporation, (b) prospectus, and (c) annual report.

is recognised, the operator may, by 'written notice' to the FCA cause the scheme to cease to be recognised.[322]

18.115 **FCA powers** The division of regulatory responsibilities between the home and host regulators under the UCITS Directive[323] is reflected in FSMA, which therefore confers limited powers on the FCA in relation to section 264 recognised schemes. First, all the FCA rules are disapplied in relation to such schemes[324] (as the schemes are subject to corresponding regulatory provisions in their host State), except for the financial promotion rules,[325] and the rules as to facilities and information mentioned earlier.[326] Second, the only sanction the FCA has over such schemes is to issue a direction (of limited duration)[327] suspending the exemption which the scheme enjoys from the general restriction on the promotion of CISs,[328] if the operator breaches the financial promotion rules.[329] As it is the home State regulator that has primary disciplinary responsibility, notice of the direction must be given to it.[330] In addition (as this is consistent with EU law), the provision giving the FCA extensive investigation powers over CISs applies to section 264 recognised schemes in relation to their UK activities.[331]

Schemes authorised in 'designated countries or territories': FSMA, section 270

18.116 **General** FSMA, section 270[332] makes provision for the second category of 'recognised' CIS: certain CISs managed and authorised[333] in a country or territory 'designated' by Treasury Order. The section sets out the circumstances when the Treasury may make such an Order (after consultation with the FCA)[334]—essentially where it is satisfied both that the country's law (and practice) affords UK investors 'at least equivalent' protection to that under UK law in relation to 'comparable' authorised schemes,[335] and that their regulators cooperate with the FCA.[336] This is in contrast to the test under section 272 (see later, in relation to individually recognised schemes), which merely requires 'adequate' protection, presumably because it was thought appropriate to have a more exacting test in the case of the more

[322] s 264(6)–(7). In accordance with EU law (see following) the FCA has no power to terminate such a scheme's recognition of its own accord. But see s 267 (suspension of promotion) also noted later in the chapter.

[323] See para 18.03 and n 17.

[324] s 266.

[325] Made under s 137R and in the FCA Handbook in COBS 4. See the UCITS Directive (n 17), art 91 applying the 'host' State promotion rules.

[326] See para 18.111—made under FSMA, s 283(1). Section 283(2) (notice from FCA requiring information to be included in promotions) also applies to s 264 recognised schemes. See the UCITS Directive (n 17), art 92.

[327] FSMA, s 267(3).

[328] See s 238(3), considered in para 18.142.

[329] s 267. For the procedure, see ss 268–270. For the FCA's policy in invoking this power, see FCA Handbook, EG 14.7

[330] s 268(3)(b). And see FCA Handbook, EG 14.8 where the FCA confirms that it will ask the home State regulators 'to take such action… as will resolve the FCA's concerns' and that as the operator, trustee or depositary are 'authorised persons' (see para 18.131) it may taken regulatory action against them also.

[331] s 284(1)(b).

[332] See n 309 referring to the proposed repeal of s 270 and revision of s 272.

[333] It seems clear from the wording of s 270(1) that the management of the scheme must occur in the same (designated) country in which it is authorised.

[334] The Treasury must ask the FCA for a Report on the criteria for designation (s 270(5)(a)), the FCA must provide such a Report (s 270(5)(b)), and the Treasury must 'have regard' to the Report (s 270(5)(c)).

[335] s 270(2)(a). ie AUTs and/or ICVCs: see s 270(4). Problems arise in maintaining 'equivalence' if there are legislative changes in the UK or the designated territory.

[336] s 270(2)(b).

'blanket recognition' conferred under section 270. The Treasury has made such Orders in respect of:[337] Guernsey, Jersey, the Isle of Man, and Bermuda.

The section also sets out the procedure that must be followed before a CIS from such a 'designated' country or territory becomes a 'recognised scheme'. Thus the 'operator'[338] must give the FCA written notice[339] that he wishes his scheme to be recognised and the FCA has two months to respond.[340] Unless the FCA serves a 'warning notice'[341] that it proposes to refuse recognition within the two months, the scheme becomes recognised unless the FCA has given earlier approval.[342] 18.117

FCA powers The powers of the FCA under section 283 to require all recognised schemes to maintain certain 'facilities' at a place of business in the UK and its extensive investigation powers in relation to all CISs—including 'recognised' schemes[343]—under section 284 have already been noted.[344] In addition, the FCA has further powers over both section 270 (and section 272) schemes. First, it may make rules, corresponding to the 'scheme particular rules' in relation to AUTs[345] and ICVCs,[346] for such recognised schemes.[347] Second, the FCA has powers of intervention if things go wrong. Thus the FCA may revoke recognition[348] and it may also issue 'directions' suspending recognition.[349] Alternatively, the FCA may decide to refer the matter to the relevant home regulator.[350] 18.118

Individually recognised overseas schemes: FSMA, section 272

General FSMA, section 272[351] makes provision for the third category of 'recognised' CIS, enabling the FCA to recognise overseas schemes on an individual basis. This is a residual category in that it only applies to schemes that do not qualify for recognition under either section 264 (schemes from other EEA Member States)[352] or section 270 (schemes from Treasury 'designated' countries or territories).[353] The FCA has a discretion to make an order recognising such a scheme if it 'appears to' the FCA that certain requirements—some formal, some requiring judgement as to their 'adequacy' to be taken—are satisfied. Very few schemes have sought recognition under this head. 18.119

337 See the FSMA 2000 (Transitional Provisions) (Authorised Persons) Order 2001, SI 2001/2636, art 67: scheme recognised under FSA 1986, s 87 (the predecessor to FSMA, s 270) are automatically treated as recognised under s 270. See now the FSMA 2000 (CIS) (Designated Countries and Territories) Order 2003, SI 2003/1181 (covering Guernsey, Jersey, and the Isle of Man).

338 Partially defined in s 237(2). If the scheme is neither an OEIC nor a unit trust scheme (and hence s 237(2) does not apply), presumably the 'operator' is the manager of the scheme.

339 For the contents, see s 270(6) and COLL 9.3.

340 s 270(1)(c),(d).

341 See FSMA, s 387.

342 s 270(1)(d).

343 See especially s 284(1)(b).

344 See para 18.111.

345 Under s 248, see para 18.99.

346 Under OEIC Regulations, reg 6, see para 18.108 and n 299.

347 s 278. See COLL 9.3.2R and 9.3.3R (information in and preparation and maintenance of prospectus).

348 Under s 279 (and see s 280 for the procedure). For the FCA's policy in invoking this power, see FCA Handbook, EG 14.9, and para 18.154.

349 s 281 (and see s 282 for the procedure). See para 18.154.

350 See FCA Handbook, EG 14.10, and para 18.154.

351 See n 309 referring to the proposed revision of s 272 (and repeal of s 270).

352 See para 18.113 *et seq.*

353 See para 18.116 *et seq.*

18.120 Bearing in mind that the main consequence of obtaining 'recognised' status is that the scheme may be promoted in the same way as UK AUTs or ICVCs (and schemes recognised under sections 264, 270, and 272), clearly the essence of these requirements is that such individually recognised schemes are as 'safe' for retail investors as other 'regulated' schemes. Of the requirements, which will be summarised below, the crucial one is that 'adequate' protection is afforded to participants. As noted earlier, this requirement is less exacting than the 'at least equivalent' protection precondition for a country or territory to be designated under section 270. As also suggested earlier, it was probably thought appropriate that the test could be less strict for individual recognition. However, there is no guidance in FSMA on how the FCA is to judge adequacy. In particular, there is no express requirement that the FCA look to 'comparable' UK authorised schemes[354] nor that it look to the law and *practice* of the overseas regulatory regime.[355]

18.121 There are a number of formal requirements. First, the scheme must either be an OEIC[356] or the 'operator'[357] must be a body corporate.[358] Second, the operator and (if any) trustee or depositary must either, if an authorised person under FSMA, have permission to act as such or, if not an authorised person, be a 'fit and proper person' to so act.[359] Third, the participants must be entitled (although not necessarily on demand)[360] to have their units redeemed (or to sell their units on an investment exchange)[361] at a price related to the net-asset value of the scheme.[362]

18.122 There then follow a number of factors requiring the FCA to exercise judgement of their 'adequacy'. In particular, as noted earlier, 'adequate' protection must be afforded to participants in the scheme.[363] The 'arrangements' for the scheme's 'constitution and management' must be 'adequate'.[364] Finally, the 'powers and duties' of the operator and (if any) trustee or depositary must be 'adequate'.[365] In judging adequacy in the last two (but not first) cases, the FCA must 'have regard' to (a) any rule of law, and (b) any matter which is or could be subject to rules applicable to 'comparable' authorised UK schemes.[366]

[354] s 272(5) only makes 'comparable authorised schemes' (as defined in s 272(6)) relevant to other issues (whether the constitution and management are 'adequate' (s 272(3)), and whether powers and duties of operator and (if any) trustee or depositary are 'adequate' (s 272(4))).

[355] Made explicit in s 270, see para 18.116.

[356] As defined in s 236, see para 18.66 *et seq*.

[357] Partially defined in s 237(2). If the scheme is neither an OEIC nor a unit trust scheme (and hence s 237(2) does not apply), presumably the 'operator' is the manager of the scheme.

[358] s 272(7).

[359] s 272(8), (9). Section 273 sets out the matters, which the FCA 'may' take into account in deciding if they are 'fit and proper'. 'Operators' (see n 357) and trustees/depositaries will not need to be 'authorised persons' if they do not carry on 'regulated activities' in the UK: see para 18.131.

[360] s 272(15). But if the CIS is an OEIC, note that s 236(3)(a) (realisation within 'reasonable' period, considered further in para 18.72) will be satisfied.

[361] s 272(14).

[362] s 272(13). Again, if the CIS is an OEIC, note that s 236(3)(b), considered further in para 18.75, will be satisfied.

[363] s 272(2).

[364] s 272(3). And note the formal requirements as to form, status of operator, and (if any) trustee or depositary and redemption of units already noted.

[365] s 272(4).

[366] s 272(5).

Finally, there are three further requirements. Thus the operator and (if any) trustee or depositary must be 'able and willing' to cooperate with the FCA. The name of the scheme must not be 'undesirable or misleading'[367] and the purposes of the schemes must be 'reasonably capable of being successfully carried into effect'.[368] 18.123

FSMA also sets out the procedure, which must be followed by a CIS that wishes to obtain individual recognition under section 272. The 'operator'[369] must make the application[370] and the FCA has six months to respond.[371] Moreover, once recognised, the operator must notify the FCA of alterations of the scheme or of its operator, trustee, or depositary.[372] 18.124

FCA powers The power of the FCA under section 283 to require all recognised schemes to maintain certain 'facilities' at a place of business in the UK and its extensive investigation powers in relation to all CISs—including 'recognised' schemes—under section 284 have already been noted,[373] as have the FCA's further powers over both section 272 (and section 270) schemes.[374] These are the FCA's power to make rules, corresponding to the 'scheme particular rules' in relation to AUTs and ICVCs, for such schemes[375] and its powers of intervention if things go wrong. Thus the FCA may revoke recognition[376] and it may also issue 'directions' suspending recognition.[377] Alternatively, the FCA may decide to refer the matter to the relevant home regulator.[378] 18.125

'Unregulated' CISs

The CISs so far considered, the UK 'authorised funds', and the overseas 'recognised schemes', all have to fulfil detailed requirements as to their constitution and operation. CISs not satisfying these requirements may be established, but they suffer from the disadvantage that generally they cannot be promoted to the general public.[379] Thus 'unregulated collective investment schemes' ('UCISs') are created in order to enable groups of investors to undertake collective investment, unconstrained by FCA regulation as far as constitution and operation is concerned. To that extent they are 'unregulated', although those establishing and operating those schemes in the UK are certainly subject to the FSMA regulatory regime in general. In particular, as well as being unable to promote the scheme to the public, their managers 18.126

367 s 272(11), cf the same requirement for AUTs (s 243(8), para 18.95) and ICVCs (OEIC Regulations, reg 15(9), para 18.106).

368 s 272(9), cf the same requirement for AUTs (s 243(9), para 18.95) and ICVCs (OEIC Regulations, reg 15(10), para 18.106).

369 A term only partially defined in s 237(2), see n 357.

370 Under s 274 which is in similar terms to s 242 (application for AUT authorisation order). See also FCA Handbook, COLL 9.3.

371 s 275—again similar to s 242 in relation to AUTs. See s 276 (procedure when refusing an application).

372 s 272.

373 See para 18.111.

374 See para 18.118.

375 s 278. See COLL 9.3.2R and 9.3.3R (information in and preparation and maintenance of prospectus).

376 Under s 279 (and see s 280 for the procedure). For the FCA's policy in invoking this power, see FCA Handbook, EG 14.9, and para 18.154.

377 s 281 (and see s 282 for the procedure). See para 18.154.

378 See FCA Handbook, EG 14.10 and para 18.154.

379 ss 21 and 238. See the FSA's CP12/19, *Restrictions on the retail distribution of unregulated collective investment schemes and close substitutes*, (August 2012). See also the FSA's publications: (i) *Unregulated collective investment scheme: project findings* (July 2010) and (ii) *Unregulated collective investment scheme: good and poor practice report* (July 2010).

need to be authorised persons[380] and insofar as they (and the depositaries/trustees, if any) are authorised persons, they are subject to the FCA Handbook.[381]

18.127 Some so-called 'hedge funds',[382] funds that invite contributions of a significant size and adopt sophisticated investment strategies, are structured as 'unregulated' CISs, usually entailing contractual arrangements and/or offshore OEICs. Other examples of UCISs are 'private equity' or 'venture capital' funds providing funding for new business. These are often limited partnerships,[383] the general partner being the operator and the limited partners being the other 'participants'. Examples of UCISs set up as unit trusts are Enterprise Zone Property Unit Trusts ('EZPUTs').[384] Moreover, many offshore funds, for example US mutual funds, are also 'unregulated' CISs. *Sukuk*—investment vehicles structured so as to be *Shari'a* compliant—are also potentially 'unregulated' CISs, but they are exempted from that definition and regulated in accordance with their economic substance (as 'alternative finance investment bonds'), rather than legal form.[385]

18.128 However, as noted earlier, *any* arrangement for collective investment is potentially a CIS and hence may constitute an 'unregulated' CIS. In consequence, care should be taken when establishing schemes that involve the pooling of contributions and/or collective management in order to generate profits or income, as a UCIS may, inadvertently, arise. As well as the case law that demonstrates instances where this has occurred,[386] other examples are schemes for producing ostrich meat, overseas forestry and crops schemes, and wine investment schemes.[387] If those involved are not 'authorised persons' then serious consequences may follow, as the next section will now consider.

Application of FSMA to CISs

General

18.129 FSMA uses two key provisions to regulate financial services activities and their promotion. The first is the so-called 'general prohibition' in section 19 which precludes anyone other than an 'authorised person' or 'exempt person' from carrying on 'regulated activity' in the UK.[388] The second is the so-called 'financial promotion restriction' in section 21,

---

380 As they carry on the regulated activity of managing investments (RAO, art 37) and/or advising (RAO, art 53): See 'FSA DP05/4' (n 382), para 2.49.

381 See para 18.146 *et seq.*

382 See the FSA discussion papers (i) DP05/4, '*Hedge Funds: A discussion of risk and regulatory engagement*' (June 2005) ('FSA DP05/4') and the related Feedback Statement (FS06/2), March 2006, (ii) DP05/03, '*Wider range retail investment products: consumer protection in a rapidly changing world*' (June 2005) and the related Feedback Statement (FS06/3), March 2006, and (iii) DP16, '*Hedge Funds and the FSA*' (August 2002) and the related Feedback Statement, March 2003. See also '*Private Equity: A discussion of risk and regulatory engagement*' (November 2006, DP06/6) and the related Feedback Statement (FS07/3), June 2007.

383 Under the Limited Partnership Act 1907.

384 See *Ball v Banner & others* [2000] WL 824097 (CA, Civ Div).

385 See para 18.37 and n 101. For the exemption see SI 2001/1062, Sch, para 5, as amended by SI 2010/86 art 3 and for their regulation see RAO, art 77A.

386 See the case law noted in n 41.

387 See the FSA's CP12/19, *Restrictions on the retail distribution of unregulated collective investment schemes and close substitutes*,(August 2012), passim and Annex 1, para 26.

388 There is limited guidance on the meaning of 'in the UK' in s 418 (as amended). In *Financial Services Authority v Fradley* [2005] EWCA Civ 1183, Arden LJ held that 'it is sufficient if the activities which [take] place in this jurisdiction [are] a significant part of the business activity of running the CIS'. Hence, in that case where

which restricts the promotion of 'investment activity'. Thus the scope of the terms 'regulated activity' and 'investment activity' determines the scope of regulation and is achieved by Treasury Order: the Regulated Activities Order (the 'RAO')[389] and the Financial Promotion Order (the 'FPO'),[390] respectively. These Orders define 'regulated activity' and 'investment activity' respectively. How these terms catch involvement in and the promotion of a CIS is explained below. Breaching section 19 or 21 has serious consequences. Contraventions of the sections are criminal offences,[391] consequent agreements are unenforceable,[392] and the FCA has power to apply to court for injunctive orders[393] and orders requiring the payment of compensation and/or the 'disgorgement' of profits.[394]

It is important at the outset to distinguish the status of an 'authorised *person*' from that of an 'authorised *fund*'. As noted earlier, the latter term refers to an AUT or ICVC, that is, a CIS that has the benefit of an FCA 'authorisation order'.[395] An 'authorised person' is usually (but by no means invariably)[396] a person who has a 'Part 4A permission' from the FCA to undertake one or more categories of regulated activity.[397] **18.130**

Section 19: Regulated activity

The RAO renders each of the three functions of establishing, operating, and winding up a CIS, if done 'by way of business',[398] a 'regulated activity'.[399] Thus only authorised (or exempt) persons[400] are permitted to set up, run, and wind up a CIS by way of business. Moreover, acting in certain specific CIS capacities 'by way of business' is also a regulated activity: acting as trustee of an AUT,[401] acting as the 'depositary' of an OEIC, and as the sole director of an OEIC.[402] **18.131**

(i) the operator had an accommodation address and bank account in the UK and (ii) many participants were UK residents, it did not matter that the operator had moved his operations outside the UK.

389 FSMA 2000 (Regulated Activities) Order 2001, SI 2001/544, as extensively amended.

390 FSMA 2000 (Financial Promotion) Order 2005, SI 2005/1529, as amended, replacing SI 2001/1335, as amended.

391 See FSMA, ss 23 and 25, respectively.

392 See FSMA, ss 26–28 and 30, respectively.

393 See FSMA, s 380. For cases where the FSA applied under this provision, see *Financial Services Authority v Fradley* [2005] EWCA 1183; *Financial Services Authority v Watkins (t/a Consolidated Land Ltd)* [2011] EWHC 1976 (Ch); *Financial Services Authority v Asset L.I. Inc (t/a Asset Land Investment Inc)* [2013] EWHC 178 (Ch).

394 See FSMA, s 382. For cases where the FSA applied under this provision, see *Financial Services Authority v Watkins (t/a Consolidated Land Ltd)* [2011] EWHC 1976 (Ch); *Financial Services Authority v Asset L.I. Inc (t/a Asset Land Investment Inc)* [2013] EWHC 178 (Ch), Smith J.

395 See para 18.89.

396 See FSMA, s 31(b)–(d) for the other categories of 'authorised person' and note Sch 5, para 18.133.

397 As also already noted, in order to obtain an 'authorisation order' the manager/ACD and trustee/depositary of the AUT/ICVC (respectively) need to be 'authorised persons'.

398 The meaning of which is considered in paras 18.34–18.36.

399 RAO, art 51(1)(a). For a consideration of 'establishing' and 'operating', see *Andrew Brown v Innovatorone Plc* [2012] EWHC 1321 (Comm) [1178], [1187]–[1198]. When the AIFMD (see para 18.07) is implemented, art 51 will become art 51ZE and special provision will be made for UCITS managers and depositaries (proposed art 51ZA and art 51ZB) and AIF managers and depositaries (proposed art 51ZC and art 51ZD).

400 As already noted, FSMA, Sch 5 confers automatic 'authorised person' status on (i) the operator, trustee, or depositary of a s 264 (ie an EEA (UCITS)) recognised scheme (see para 18.113), and (ii) on an ICVC (see para 18.133).

401 RAO, art 51(1)(b). Section 243(7) requires a trustee of an AUT to be an 'authorised person': see para 18.93.

402 RAO, art 51(1)(c). OEIC Regulations, reg 15 requires the depositary and ACD of an ICVC to be an 'authorised person': see para 18.106.

18.132 Less obviously, the RAO renders other activities in relation to CISs 'regulated activities'. Participatory rights in CISs— 'units' in FSMA terminology[403]—are one of the so-called 'specified investments' in the RAO[404] with the result that various activities 'by way of business' in relation to such 'units' are also 'regulated activities'. Thus dealing in units as principal[405] or agent,[406] arranging deals in units,[407] managing assets belonging to another which include units,[408] safeguarding and administering such assets (or arranging for others to do so),[409] and advising on the merits of investment in particular units[410] are all 'regulated activities'. Many of these activities will be undertaken by those actually operating the CIS involved, but other persons, for example those merely advising on or arranging investment in the CISs, may be caught by these more general provisions and will require authorised (or exempt) person status in order to undertake them.

18.133 An OEIC is a legal person and therefore if it (as opposed to its manager or depositary)[411] undertakes any 'regulated activity' in the UK it will need to be an 'authorised person'. An ICVC—the only type of OIEC which can be established in the UK—is automatically an 'authorised person',[412] but OEICs from overseas that conduct regulated activities in the UK will need to obtain the requisite permission from the FCA. However, an OEIC from another EEA Member State that is recognised under section 264[413] is (in accordance with UK obligations under the UCITS Directive) automatically an 'authorised person'.[414]

Restrictions on financial promotion

General

18.134 Two provisions of FSMA are relevant to the promotion of CISs: the more general section 21, and the specific (to CISs) section 238. These two provisions have a number of common features.

18.135 First, they are both expressed in terms of restricting the 'communicat[ion of] an invitation or inducement',[415] the word 'communicate' being stated to include 'causing a communication to be made'.[416] Thus they cover every form of making information known ('communicate' or 'causing a communication') as long as there is a promotional element ('invitation or inducement'). Second, they confer power on the Treasury to exempt certain communications from

---

403 See para 18.61.

404 RAO, art 81. They fall within the term 'security' (see RAO, art 3(1)). Moreover, 'any right to or interest in' a unit is itself a 'specified investment' and 'security': RAO, art 89.

405 ibid, art 14, and note the specific exclusion in art 15, and more general exclusions in arts 66(1), 68–72A.

406 ibid, art 21, and note the specific exclusion in art 22, and more general exclusions in arts 67–72E.

407 ibid, art 25, and note the specific exclusions in arts 26–29, 32, 33, and more general exclusions in arts 66(2)–72E. For a consideration of the meaning of 'arranging deals' in CIS units, see *Andrew Brown v Innovatorone Plc* [2012] EWHC 1321 (Comm) [1178], [1199]–[1212].

408 ibid, art 37, and note the specific exclusion in art 38, and more general exclusions in arts 66(3), 68, 69, 72A, 72C, 72E.

409 ibid, art 40, and note the specific exclusions in arts 41–43 and more general exclusions in arts 66–69, 71, 72A, 72C, 72E.

410 ibid, art 53, and note the specific exclusion in art 54 and more general exclusions in arts 66–70, 72–72A, 72B, 72D, 72E.

411 See n 402: acting as depositary or sole director of an OEIC is a 'regulated activity'.

412 FSMA, Sch 5, para 1(3).

413 See para 18.113.

414 See FSMA, Sch 5, para 1(1): the 'operator' of such a scheme is an authorised person and the operator of an OEIC is the OEIC itself (see s 237(2)). See also n 314.

415 ss 21(1), 238(1).

416 ss 21(13), 238(9).

the restriction, by Order.[417] Third, the territorial scope is similar in that there is no statutory territorial limitation apart from a provision that communications originating outside the UK are only caught if they are 'capable of having an effect in the UK'.[418] Thus the restrictions apply to both 'inward' and 'outward' communications, although in practice the relevant Treasury Orders make specific (similar) provision in this respect, for example ensuring that the territorial scope is consistent with the Electronic Commerce Directive.[419]

Section 21: The general financial promotion restriction

Section 21 imposes a general financial promotion restriction. Apart from so-called 'exempt communications', which are set out in the FPO,[420] essentially section 21 requires the involvement of authorised persons in all financial promotions 'in the course of business'.[421] Thus, apart from 'exempt communications', the only financial promotions that are permitted are those communicated *by* authorised persons or those whose contents have been *approved by* authorised persons. The FCA Handbook, in its COBS Module, then regulates the communication and approval of promotions by authorised persons.[422] **18.136**

The way in which the financial promotion restriction, and the FPO made under it, catch the promotion of units in a CIS is rather complex but similar to the way in which the RAO catches the various activities in relation to such units. Section 21 restricts the promotion of 'investment activity' which is defined in terms of 'controlled activity' and 'controlled investments', as specified in the FPO. These two concepts are generally similar to 'specified activity' and 'specified investments' in the RAO, but they are of slightly different scope to reflect the slightly different reach of the general prohibition in section 19 (defined in terms of 'regulated activity') on the one hand and the financial promotion restriction in section 21 (defined in terms of 'investment activity') on the other. In particular, although 'units' in CISs (as well as being 'specified investments' in the RAO) are also 'controlled investments'[423] in the FPO, the activity of establishing, operating, or winding up a CIS (although a 'regulated activity') is not a 'controlled activity' in the FPO.[424] The result is that promoting the buying (or selling) of units is caught.[425] Moreover, as dealing in units as principal or agent,[426] arranging deals in units,[427] managing assets belonging to another which include units,[428] safeguarding and **18.137**

---

417 ss 21(5), (6); 238(6), (7). The Orders made, which contain similar exemptions, are noted later. The FPO (see para 18.129, n 390) is the relevant Order made under s 21.

418 ss 21(3); 238(3). These subsections may be (but have not been) repealed by Treasury Order: s 21(7); s 238(8).

419 Directive No 2000/31/EC, [2000] OJ L178/1—which generally adopts a 'country of origin' approach to the regulation of electronic communications within the EEA.

420 See para 18.129.

421 A wider concept than 'by way of business', the term used in s 22 (and considered in paras 18.34–18.36).

422 In COBS 4, see para 18.156. Note that an authorised person may not approve a 'real time' financial promotion (see n 432): FCA Handbook, COBS 4.10.4R.

423 FPO, Sch 1, para 19. They fall within the term 'security' (see ibid, para 28(c)). Moreover, 'any right to or interest in' a unit is itself a 'specified investment' and 'security': ibid, para 27.

424 As there is no need to control the promotion of these activities themselves (as they are undertaken by professionals), as opposed to the promotion of units (ie participation) in them.

425 By s 21(8)(b): 'exercising any rights conferred by a controlled investment to acquire, dispose of, underwrite or convert a controlled investment'. And see s 21(8)(a) (n 431): as a result of the wide meaning given to 'buying' and 'selling' in FPO, Sch 1 para 28, this would also fall within s 21(8)(a) as the promotion of 'dealing'. For an example of the promotion of units in an (unregulated) CIS, in breach of s 21, see *Andrew Brown v Innovatorone Plc* [2012] EWHC 1321 (Comm).

426 FPO, Sch 1 para 3(1).

427 ibid, Sch 1 para 4.

428 ibid, Sch 1 para 5.

administering such assets (or arranging for others to do so),[429] and advising on the merits of investment in particular units[430] are all 'controlled activities', promoting any of these activities[431] is also caught by the financial promotion restriction.

18.138 The FPO, as well as defining the scope of the financial promotion restriction in section 21, also sets outs which financial promotions are exempt from it. For these purposes, the FPO divides communications first into 'real time' and 'non-real time'[432] communications and then subdivides 'real time' communications into 'solicited' and 'unsolicited'[433] communications. Unsurprisingly, the largest number of exemptions applies to 'non-real time' communications, whilst the least apply to 'unsolicited real time'. This list of 'exempt communications' is very long. As well as covering the more obvious situations, such as non-specific ('generic') communications,[434] communications by 'mere conduits',[435] and communication to 'investment professionals'[436] the FPO also refines the territorial application of the financial promotion restriction.[437] Moreover, there are specific exemptions for 'non-real time' and 'solicited real time' communications by operators of sections 270 and 272 recognised schemes[438] to their participants and by OEICs to certain of their creditors or members.[439] There are also more general exemptions in favour of 'certified high net worth individuals'[440] and 'sophisticated investors'.[441]

Sections 238 and 240: Additional CIS promotion restriction

18.139 **General** Section 238 imposes a further promotion restriction in relation to CISs on authorised persons, with the aim of ensuring that generally only 'regulated schemes' are promoted to the general public.[442] The section is confined, in terms, to authorised persons because persons who are not authorised (or exempt) are caught by the general financial promotion restriction in section 21 discussed earlier.[443] As the promotion restriction in section 21 is inapplicable, not only to communications by authorised persons but also to communications where the contents have been 'approved' by an authorised person, section 240 precludes an authorised person *approving* a CIS communication if they would have been precluded by section 238 from making (or causing the making) of the communication themselves.

[429] ibid, Sch 1 para 6.

[430] ibid, Sch 1 para 7.

[431] To be precise, the promotion of 'entering or offering to enter into an agreement the making or performance of which by either party constitutes a controlled activity' s 21(1), (8)(a).

[432] Defined in FPO, art 7. 'Real time' are those 'made in the course of a personal visit, telephone conversation or other interactive dialogue' whilst 'non-real time' are those which are not 'real time'. Note that an authorised person may not approve a 'real time' financial promotion: FCA Handbook, COBS 4.10.4R.

[433] Defined in FPO, art 8.

[434] FPO, art 17, ie those not identifying a *particular* product.

[435] ibid, art 18, ie by those who have no control over the content but merely transmit the communication.

[436] ibid, art 19, a term which includes authorised persons, exempt persons, governments, local authorities, international organisations. See *Andrew Brown v Innovatorone Plc* [2012] EWHC 1321 (Comm) [1218]: art 19 inapplicable to CIS promotion on facts of that case.

[437] See especially FPO, arts 12, 20B, 30–33.

[438] See paras 18.116 *et seq.* and 18.119 *et seq.*

[439] FPO, arts 40, 44.

[440] FPO, art 48—and see art 49 (high net worth companies, etc.). See *Andrew Brown v Innovatorone Plc* [2012] EWHC 1321 (Comm) [1217]: art 48 inapplicable to CIS promotion on facts of that case.

[441] FPO, art 50, 50A ('self-certified sophisticated investors') and art 51 (associations of high net worth or sophisticated investors).

[442] FSA Handbook, PERG 8.20G contains (limited) guidance on this provision.

[443] See para 18.136 *et seq.*

Contravention by an authorised person of section 238 or 240 constitutes a 'breach of a requirement imposed' by FSMA and thus enables the FCA to exercise its usual powers of discipline[444] and, if necessary, of applying to court for injunctive and/or compensation and/or disgorgement orders.[445] Moreover, section 138D applies[446] to confer a right of action on a private person who suffers loss as a result of the contravention.[447] **18.140**

Section 238 begins with a general blanket prohibition on authorised persons promoting participation in *any* CIS.[448] However, there are a number of exceptions.[449] But it should be noted that in so far as the exceptions apply to permit authorised persons to promote (and approve the promotion) of certain schemes, those persons will be subject to the FCA Handbook,[450] in undertaking that promotion (or approval).[451] **18.141**

Exceptions: section 238(3): 'Safe' collective investment schemes[452] Section 238(3) excludes from the blanket restriction on the promotion of CISs, three categories of schemes: AUTs,[453] ICVCs,[454] and recognised schemes.[455] It will be recalled that the first two categories are FCA-authorised schemes (so-called 'authorised funds' in its Handbook) and the last covers overseas schemes that are similarly heavily regulated by their overseas regulators. It follows that only such 'regulated schemes' (using the FCA term, which covers authorised funds and recognised schemes)[456] may be promoted (or their promotion approved) by authorised persons to the public at large. However, as also noted earlier,[457] there is one type of 'authorised fund', a 'qualified investor scheme' (so-called 'QISs'—intended for particular non-retail investors) that is treated by the FCA Handbook as an unregulated scheme as far as promotion is concerned. **18.142**

Exceptions: section 238(5): Limited promotion under FCA rules The FCA is given the power to make rules permitting the promotion of certain unregulated CISs ('UCISs') 'otherwise than to the general public'.[458] These rules, which also apply to allow the promotion of **18.143**

[444] ie public censure (FSMA, s 205), the imposition of a penalty (FSMA, s 206), suspension of permission (FSMA, s 206A), imposition of requirements (FSMA, s 55L), or even variation or cancellation of permission (FSMA, s 55J).

[445] See ss 380, 382.

[446] s 241, as amended, see (on the similar provision in the Financial Services Act 1986), *Seymour v Ockwell* [2005] EWHC 1137.

[447] See further s 138D (as inserted by the Financial Services Act 2012, s 24) and the FSMA 2000 (Rights of Action) Regulations 2001, SI 2001/2256, defining 'private person' and extending the right of action to certain other persons.

[448] s 238(1). Section 238(11) confirms that 'participate' means becoming a 'participant (within the meaning given by section 235(2)) in the scheme'.

[449] The exemption in relation to 'single property schemes' in s 239 is not considered as the requisite regulations have not been made by the Treasury.

[450] In particular, COBS 4, see para 18.156.

[451] As already noted, authorised persons may not approve a 'real time' financial promotion: FCA Handbook, COBS 4.10.4R.

[452] See the FCA Guidance in its Handbook, PERG 8.20.

[453] See para 18.93 *et seq.*

[454] See para 18.101 *et seq.* Section 238(3)(b) calls these schemes 'constituted by an authorised' OEIC but, as noted (see para 18.91), these are termed 'ICVCs' by the FCA in its Handbook.

[455] See para 18.110 *et seq.*

[456] See para 18.91.

[457] See para 18.90.

[458] The phrase 'promotion otherwise than to the general public' is stated to include promotion designed to reduce 'the risk of participation by persons for whom participation would be unsuitable': s 238(10).

'qualified investor schemes' (QISs),[459] are contained in COBS 4.12 of the FCA Handbook. The rules are primarily in the form of a table, the left-hand column of which categorises the potential recipients of the promotion and the right hand column then sets out what type of CISs may be promoted to such recipients.

18.144 The rules provide that *any* CIS may be promoted by authorised persons to certain categories of recipient, for example an 'eligible counterparty' or 'professional client'[460] (as defined in the FCA Handbook Glossary) or an 'exempt person' (other than an appointed representative)[461] in the context of their exemption.[462] An authorised person may also promote *any* CIS to certain clients[463] if he has taken 'reasonable steps to ensure that investment in the ... scheme is suitable'.[464] A more limited range of CISs may be promoted to other persons. For example, if a person is already a participant in a UCIS or QIS then that scheme or another scheme 'whose underlying property and risk profile are both substantially similar'[465] may be promoted to them.[466]

18.145 **Exceptions: Section 238(6): Exemptions in Treasury Order** Just as the FPO exempts certain communications ('exempt communications') from the general financial promotion restriction in section 21,[467] a corresponding Order has been made by the Treasury[468] exempting communications in similar circumstances from the CIS financial promotion restriction in section 238(1). The result is that (as section 238(1) does not apply in those circumstances) authorised persons are able to promote CISs in similar circumstances as unauthorised persons are able to promote CISs without the approval of an authorised person.

FCA Handbook

Introduction

18.146 Many parts of the FCA Handbook are applicable to CISs and reference has been made to the relevant provisions throughout this chapter. Some parts are of particular relevance to CISs (in particular, their operators and depositaries) whilst others apply more generally by virtue of the relevant persons being 'authorised persons' (or 'firms', using the FCA terminology). OEICs are, of course, separate legal entities and therefore, if they are 'authorised persons', they will be subject to the Handbook and the powers of the FCA over such 'firms'. This is necessarily the case with ICVCs[469] and OEICs from other Member States recognised under section 264,[470] as these are automatically granted 'authorised persons' status. Other overseas

---

[459] See para 18.90.

[460] COBS 4.12.1(4)R, Category 7: 'Any collective investment scheme in relation to which the client is categorised as a professional client or eligible counterparty'.

[461] As defined in FSMA, s 39.

[462] COBS 4.12.1(4)R, Category 6.

[463] 'Established' or 'newly accepted' client, as defined: see COBS 4.12.1R, Notes 2 and 3.

[464] COBS 4.12.1(4)R, Category 2.

[465] See COBS 4.12.1(4)R, Note 1 for an amplification of what this means.

[466] COBS 4.12.1(4)R, Category 1.

[467] See para 18.136.

[468] FSMA 2000 (Promotion of CISs) (Exemptions) Order 2001, SI 2001/1060 as amended by SI 2002/1310, SI 2002/2157, SI 2003/2067, SI 2005/270, SI 2005/1532, SI 2011/1613, made under s 238(6) and (7).

[469] FSMA, Sch 5, para 1(3): see para 18.101 *et seq*. However, see FCA Handbook, COBS 18.9, which modifies the application of parts of COBS to ICVCs.

[470] Sch 5, para 1(1) (the OEIC being the 'operator' under s 237(2): see nn 314 and 414).

OEICs, which carry on regulated activity in the UK[471] and therefore who obtain 'authorised person' status,[472] will similarly be subject to the FCA's regulatory jurisdiction.

One of the Sourcebooks in Block 5 of the Handbook is specifically dedicated to 'regulated collective investment schemes': the COLL module.[473] **18.147**

Regulated collective investment schemes

The COLL Module

The COLL Module[474] is primarily concerned with the regulation of 'authorised funds' (UK AUTs and ICVCs)[475] and their managers[476] and depositaries/trustees. As its focus is the schemes themselves, it also has one chapter on overseas 'recognised schemes' containing the details of the notification procedures which these schemes need to undertake in order to obtain 'recognised scheme' status[477] and the rules as to the facilities which such schemes must provide for UK investors.[478] COLL also contains a chapter on fees payable in connection with the FCA's functions over all these regulated schemes.[479] Thus, essentially, COLL deals with those schemes that may be promoted to the general public by authorised persons.[480] **18.148**

As far as authorised funds are concerned, the regulatory distinctions noted earlier are reflected in how COLL is subdivided. The principal subdivision is between schemes ('retail schemes'—a term not used in COLL)[481] which may be marketed to the general public and 'qualified investor schemes' ('QISs') which can only be marketed to a more limited audience. COLL 2 applies to both categories and deals with applications to become 'authorised funds' and then, depending on whether the fund is a retail scheme or a QIS, COLL 3 to COLL 7[482] or COLL 8 (respectively) contain the product regulation details. Unsurprisingly, the restrictions as to, for example, investment and borrowing powers and the running of the scheme are much greater for retail schemes. The focus of the regulation of QISs in COLL 8 is disclosure.[483] **18.149**

---

471 See para 18.131.

472 See ibid. If they do not obtain authorised person status they will be in breach of the general prohibition, see para 18.129.

473 Before 13 February 2007, there was an older version: the 'CIS' Module. See also the Collective Investment Scheme Information Guide (COLLG)—one of the Guides at the end of the FCA Handbook. As to the future, see next note.

474 As a result of the implementation of the AIFMD (see para 18.07), it is expected that (eventually) COLL will be replaced by a new Module 'FUND' applicable to both AIFMs and managers of UCITSs: see the FSA's two consultation papers on the implementation of the AIFMD of November 2012 and March 2013.

475 See paras 18.89–18.109.

476 The ACD (Capita Financial Managers Ltd) of the ICVC CF Arch Cru was publicly censued (under FSMA, s 205) in November 2012 for breaches of COLL (and PRIN 2 and 3). A consumer redress scheme (a CRS, under FSMA, s 404) to which it contributed £32 million, followed.

477 For recognised schemes, see para 18.110 *et seq.* See COLL 9.2 (for s 264 schemes) and COLL 9.3 (for ss 270 and 272 schemes).

478 COLL 9.4.

479 COLL 10.

480 s 238(1), (3). See para 18.142.

481 But used in COLLG, see n 473. As noted, the term 'non-UCITS retail scheme' (NURS) is defined in the Glossary and used in COLL.

482 The ACD (Capita Financial Managers Ltd) of the ICVC CF Arch Cru was found to be in breach of COLL 6.6.15(3)R and publicly censured: see n 476.

483 See the FSA's CP12/19, *Restrictions on the retail distribution of unregulated collective investment schemes and close substitutes* (August 2012), para 2.9: 'The QIS regime was set up to allow greater investment flexibility to more sophisticated investors and professional investors within a regulated investment framework'.

18.150 Retail schemes are themselves subdivided into 'UCITS schemes' and 'non-UCITS retail schemes' (NURSs).[484] Special provision is made for the latter[485] which, as their name suggests, do not comply with the UCITS Directive[486] as far as investment and borrowing powers are concerned and hence do not benefit from the single passport enabling them to be marketed, without further authorisation, throughout the EEA. However, they may be marketed to the public in the UK by authorised persons.

FCA enforcement powers

18.151 The FCA Handbook, in its final 'Regulatory Guides' Block, contains a special 'Enforcement Guide': EG.[487] EG has a special chapter, EG 14, dealing with the FCA's powers of intervention over 'regulated collective investment schemes': AUTs, ICVCs, and overseas 'recognised schemes'.[488] An earlier, more general, chapter on information gathering and investigation powers, EG 3, also briefly mentions the wide power statutory power the FCA has to investigate *all*[489] CISs under FSMA, section 284. Reflecting the different powers that the FCA has in relation to the three categories of scheme (AUTs, ICVCs, and recognised schemes) separate provision is made for each.

18.152 EG begins with the statutory powers that the FCA has under FSMA over AUTs, which are noted earlier:[490] under section 254 to revoke the authorisation order otherwise than by consent; under section 257 to give directions to the manager and trustee; and under section 258 to apply to court for the removal of the manager and/or trustee and either their replacement or the appointment of a person to wind up the scheme. It explains the FCA's policy in relation to these powers, in particular listing (non-exhaustive) 'relevant factors' it will take into account when deciding whether to invoke the powers.[491] The FCA also explains how it will choose between these powers—and other powers it has against the trustee or manager (as authorised persons).[492] Thus it will only revoke the authorisation order after requiring the winding up of the AUT to ensure that participants receive their entitlements.

18.153 Originally EG 14.6 dealt with the statutory powers that the FSA had (and the FCA now has) under the OEIC Regulations over ICVCs, which are very similar to the powers it has over AUTs[493] and it confirmed that the FSA's policy as to the exercise of its powers over ICVCs was the same as that in relation to AUTs. However, that provision has now been deleted. It should be noted that ICVCs differ from AUTs in that, being legal entities, they are themselves given automatic 'authorised person' status.[494] Hence, an ICVC is subject to the additional disciplinary powers (in particular of public censure[495] and the imposition of financial penalties[496]) that the FCA has over authorised persons.

---

[484] See paras 18.03 and 18.90.
[485] COLL 5.6.
[486] See para 18.03 and n 17.
[487] Replacing the old 'ENF' Module.
[488] See paras 18.89–18.125.
[489] See EG 3.1. This is the only statutory power applicable to *all* (regulated and unregulated) CISs—except ICVCs (over which corresponding powers are given by OEIC Regulations, reg 30). Curiously there is no mention of this corresponding ICVC power.
[490] Para 18.100.
[491] EG 14.1.
[492] In EG 14.2–14.5.
[493] See para 18.109.
[494] See FSMA, Sch 5, para 1(3), noted at para 18.146 and n 469.
[495] FSMA, s 205, see EG 7.
[496] FSMA, s 206, see EG 7.

The rest of EG 14 reflects the different statutory powers the FCA has over EEA (UCITS) recognised schemes[497] and other (sections 270 and 272) recognised schemes,[498] noted earlier.[499] Again, it sets out the different powers and articulates its policy in relation to them. As regards the former, the FCA confirms that it will liaise with the regulators of the relevant EEA Member State as these have the primary responsibility for discipline under the UCITS Directive.[500] **18.154**

As well as these special powers over CISs themselves, the FCA also has its usual disciplinary powers over those involved in CISs who are 'authorised persons' and its usual powers to enforce breaches by non-authorised persons of the general prohibition in section 19 and breaches of the financial promotion restriction in section 21.[501] **18.155**

Collective investment schemes in general

General

As noted earlier,[502] only 'authorised persons' may undertake various activities in relation to *any* CISs and such 'authorised persons' (or 'firms' as the FCA Handbook calls them) will be subject to the FCA Handbook in general. For example, establishing, operating, or winding up *any* CIS can only be done by authorised persons and once these persons have become 'authorised persons', the relevant parts of the rest of the Handbook will apply in the usual way, in particular the PRIN,[503] SYSC, APER, COBS, DEPP, and CASS Modules.[504] The COBS Module is also of particular relevance—the rules on promotion in COBS 4 have been noted earlier[505]—but it is modified in its application to 'operators' and 'depositaries' of CIS, as will now be discussed. **18.156**

COBS Module

Special provision is made in the COBs Sourcebook for 'operators'[506] and 'depositaries'[507] of *all* (both regulated and unregulated) CISs. **18.157**

COBS 18.5 is a special chapter applicable to 'operators' of all CISs. The term 'operator' is defined for the purposes of the FCA Handbook to cover, essentially, the person who **18.158**

---

497 s 267: to suspend promotion: see EG 14.7–14.8.

498 s 279 (revocation of recognition) and s 267 (directions): see EG 14.9–14.10B.

499 Paras 18.116 (s 267), 18.118 (s 279), and 18.125 (s 267).

500 EG 14.8.

501 See para 18.131: the special CIS financial promotion restriction in s 238 is only imposed on authorised persons, see para 18.139.

502 Para 18.131.

503 Esp. Principles 2, 3, 6, and 7: see the FSA's CP12/19, *Restrictions on the retail distribution of unregulated collective investment schemes and close substitutes* (August 2012), Annex 2. See n 476 for an example of the public censure of an ACD for breach of PRIN 2 and 3.

504 See also the 'Regulatory Guide' at the end of the FCA Handbook: The Responsibilities of Providers and Distributors for the Fair Treatment of Customers (RPPD), which is relied on extensively by the FCA (see the FSA's CP12/19, *Restrictions on the retail distribution of unregulated collective investment schemes and close substitutes* (August 2012), Annex 2.

505 See para 18.136.

506 COBS 18.5. This will be modified when the AIFMD (see para 18.07) is implemented: see FSA CP13/9, *Implementation of the AIFMD Pt. 2*, paras 3.9–3.11.

507 COBS 18.7, which lists those limited provisions of COBS that apply to a depositary when not covered by MiFID (see Chapter 3). This will be modified when the AIFMD (see para 18.07) is implemented: see FSA CP13/9, *Implementation of the AIFMD Pt. 2*, paras 3.27–3.29.

manages the scheme property.[508] The chapter has three purposes.[509] The first[510] is to disapply parts of the COBS Module in relation to operators when undertaking 'scheme management activity' (defined[511] to mean managing the scheme property but excluding holding client money, and safeguarding and administering investments), in the light of the other parts of the Handbook that apply to them, in particular the COLL Module for operators of 'regulated schemes' and the rest of COBS 18.5 for operators of 'unregulated collective investment schemes' ('UCISs'). Second,[512] it modifies some of those COBS rules that still apply in such cases. For example, obligations in relation to 'customers' or 'clients' generally apply in relation to the CIS itself.[513] Third,[514] it contains some special rules applicable to operators of UCISs. Operators of 'regulated schemes' are, of course, subject to more onerous requirements in the COLL Module. Thus, in relation to operators of UCISs, the exceptions to the 'best execution' rule in COBS are modified[515] and requirements are imposed as to scheme documents[516] and periodic statements to participants.[517]

[508] In the FCA Glossary definition, see para 18.64. He must be an authorised person: see para 18.131 and as such is, of course, subject to COBS.
[509] As explained in the older (now replaced by COBS) version of the Module in COB 10.1.5G.
[510] COBS 18.5.2R.
[511] In the FCA Handbook Glossary.
[512] See COBS 18.5.2R–18.5.3R.
[513] COBS 18.5.3(1) but see (2) (unregulated scheme).
[514] COBS 18.5.4–18.5.18.
[515] COBS 18.5.4R.
[516] In particular, those that are 'retail customers', see COBS 18.5.5R–18.5.10E.
[517] COBS 18.5.11R–18.5.18E.

19

ISLAMIC FINANCIAL SERVICES

Introduction

Islamic finance firms

Islamic finance firms ('IFFs') are established on the principle that there should be no separation between temporal and religious matters. Compliance with the *Shari'a* is the governing law for all aspects of a practising Muslim's life, including financial and business transactions. Recognising that, under the *Shari'a*, money does not have a time value separate from the value of goods that are exchanged through the use of money, IFFs embrace the principle of sharing profit and loss and reject interest as a cost for accepting and lending money. Within these constraints, IFFs offer various services, including: (a) Islamic commercial banking, where the IFF manages client money using *Shari'a*-compliant accounts, arranges and makes loans to clients using *Shari'a*-compliant contracts, advises on and arranges *Shari'a*-compliant corporate and project finance structures, and offers other banking services such as money transfer services; (b) Islamic wealth and asset management, where the IFF uses investment vehicles, structured in a *Shari'a*-compliant manner, to make *Shari'a*-compliant investments, avoiding investments in, for example, conventional financial institutions or alcohol-related businesses, which are *Haram* or Islamically unacceptable; (c) Islamic insurance, where the IFF uses a *Shari'a*-compliant form of mutual insurance, to offer general or life and family insurance; and (d) social services, where the IFF makes loans, where it only requires the borrower to repay an amount equal to that borrowed, or pays *Zakat*.[1] In practice, a firm will offer Islamic financial services as a full IFF, whereby its entire business is dedicated to offering *Shari'a*-compliant services and products, or offer Islamic financial services through an 'Islamic Window', whereby a part of the firm's business is dedicated to offering *Shari'a*-compliant services and products.[2] In either case, the firm will appoint a *Shari'a* Supervisory Board ('SSB') entrusted with the duty of directing, reviewing, and supervising the firm's activities in order to ensure that they comply with the *Shari'a*.[3] **19.01**

The scope and limits of Islamic finance regulation

The growth in IFFs has resulted in financial services regulators in various jurisdictions, including the United Kingdom, adopting special regimes for the regulation of IFFs, or adapting their existing regimes.[4] **19.02**

---

[1] *Zakat* is a charitable tax. See Ayub, *Understanding Islamic Finance* (Wiley, 2007), p 495 and Ghuddah et al., *Islamic Finance Qualification* (ESA and SII, 2007), p 12.

[2] Islamic Windows are discussed in para 19.64 *et seq.*

[3] SSBs are discussed in para 19.68 *et seq.*

[4] In this chapter, regimes other than that in the United Kingdom are mentioned or discussed. Where the location of any regulatory or legal regime is not mentioned, the reader should assume that the reference is to the regime in the UK.

19.03 Despite the special nature of the services which an IFF offers, it is still a financial services provider that participates in the financial services industry and, generally, poses the same risks as a non-IFF. For this reason, a financial service regulator's primary objective in regulating an IFF remains the same as those for regulating a conventional, ie non-Islamic finance firm.[5] Similarly, like the users of non-*Shari'a*-compliant financial services, the desire for favourable borrowing terms and positive investment returns drives the consumers of *Shari'a*-compliant services. The Islamic nature of a financial service may be a necessary condition for a practising Muslim's decision to use the service. However, it is not a sufficient condition.

19.04 The scope of Islamic finance regulation may also have a bearing on the limits of the role that a financial services regulator plays or should play in the context of Islamic finance; in particular, its role in ensuring that a service or investment, offered by an IFF, is *Shari'a* compliant. The main question in this regard is: 'what role should a secular regulator play in determining standards which are religious in nature?' In this respect, there are two basic models: a *substantive* model and a *formal* model.

19.05 On a substantive model of Islamic finance regulation, a regulator uses its powers to identify or determine the *Shari'a* standards against which an IFF must measure its services and products—if a service or product does not comply with those standards, the IFF may not offer that service or product or hold it out as *Shari'a* compliant. The regulator determines the substance of the *Shari'a*-compliant outcome: the regulator's own scholars, or other scholars identified by the regulator, are responsible for ruling on the standards with which the services or investments offered by an IFF must comply for the IFF to hold them out as *Shari'a* compliant. Aspects of the regulation of *Shari'a*-compliant securities in Malaysia incorporate the substantive model. As part of the Malaysian Islamic Capital Market, the Securities Commission has its own *Shari'a* Advisory Council.[6] The Council was given the mandate to ensure that the running of the Islamic Capital Market complies with *Shari'a* principles.[7] The substantive model has the advantage that the standardisation of particular Islamic finance requirements, which the substantive model seeks to achieve, enhances liquidity by reducing the costs which the originators of investments have to incur on a case-by-case basis to ensure that the investments are *Shari'a* compliant. Enhancing liquidity is hardly at odds with a financial regulator's objectives.[8]

19.06 On a formal model of Islamic finance regulation, a regulator uses its powers to identify the standards, with which an IFF's systems and procedures must comply in order for the IFF to determine the *Shari'a* standards for its services and products services and products—if the process for ensuring that a service or product is *Shari'a* compliant does not comply with

---

[5] In the UK, these include the maintenance of confidence in the financial system and securing an appropriate degree of protection for the consumers of financial services. See FSMA, s 2(2) read together with FSMA, s 3(1) and (2) and FSMA, s 5(1) and (2), respectively. See Chapter 2.

[6] The Commission established the Council in 1996 under s 18 of the Securities Commission Act 1993.

[7] The Council advises the Commission on all matters related to the comprehensive development of the Islamic Capital Market, and functions as a reference centre for issues related to the Islamic Capital Market. The members of the Council consist of Islamic scholars/jurists and Islamic finance experts. The Council advises on and publishes lists of products which, in its view, are *Shari'a* compliant; see <http://www.sc.com>.

[8] Industry bodies may have a role in creating a 'third way' between the formal and substantive models. For example, the joint efforts of the International Swaps and Derivatives Association and the International Islamic Financial Market to develop a *Shari'a*-compliant Master Agreement offer a path to standardisation with the attendant cost reduction benefits; see <http://www.isda.org>.

those standards, the IFF may not offer that service or product or hold it out as *Shari'a* compliant. The regulator determines the form or manner in which an IFF must achieve a *Shari'a*-compliant outcome rather than the substance of that outcome. On this model, the *Shari'a* scholars appointed by an IFF, rather than those appointed by the regulator, are responsible for ruling on the standards with which the service or investment offered by an IFF must comply for the IFF to hold them out as *Shari'a* compliant. In the Dubai International Financial Centre (DIFC), the Dubai Financial Services Authority (DFSA) has adopted specific rules governing the processes which it expects IFFs to implement in order to ensure *Shari'a* compliant outcomes and has summed up its role as a '*Shari'a* Systems Regulator' not a '*Shari'a* Regulator'.[9] The formal model has the advantage for a regulator, charged primarily with the protection of investors' financial welfare rather than their spiritual welfare in that it prevents a regulator from entering an arena, in which it might otherwise feel uncomfortable, and leaves the regulator to regulate systems and controls, something with which the regulator is familiar.[10]

The regulation of IFFs in the United Kingdom

There is currently no dedicated regime in the UK for regulating IFFs. Instead the PRA and FCA are able to regulate IFFs under the general powers, which Parliament has granted them under FSMA, with the PRA being responsible for the prudential regulation and the FCA being responsible for regulating the conduct of those IFFs which are PRA-designated firms and the FCA being responsible for both the prudential and the conduct regulation of those IFFs which have not been so designated.[11] In a 2007 Discussion Paper, *Islamic Finance in the UK: Regulation and Challenges*,[12] the FSA set out the risks and challenges for IFFs and the regulation of IFFs, highlighting the issues for Islamic finance in the retail market and Islamic finance in the wholesale market and the scope for expansion in these markets, mentioning specifically *Takaful*, complex products, hedge funds, EU passporting, and government initiatives.[13] Neither the PRA nor the FCA have issued any general discussion papers or other communications on Islamic finance. However, in the absence of any indication that either the PRA or the FCA would view the issues set out by the FSA in the 2007 Discussion Paper, it remains a useful reference with respect to the approach to the regulation of IFFs in the UK.[14] **19.07**

The approach of the PRA and FCA to regulating IFFs should rest on the principle of non-discrimination or equal treatment which has a bearing, particularly in the context of the **19.08**

[9] *Islamic Finance Regulation in the IFC*, DFSA Leaflet 2, 2008; see <http://www.dfsa.ae>. See also Henderson 'Limiting the Regulation of Islamic Finance: Lessons from Dubai' (2007) LFMR (1) 213.

[10] An important question for a regulator: 'what if an IFF follows a regulator's systems and procedures requirements but achieves an outcome which is not *Shari'a* compliant?' It is submitted that, on a proper application of the formal model, the regulator would not be able to intervene unless it could show that the relevant decision of the *Shari'a* Supervisory Board was so irrational or contrary to the *Shari'a* that no rational SSB adhering properly to the Regulator's could have reached the decision. In this respect, a regulator would be applying a review standard similar to that which a court would use in judicial review proceedings avoiding so-called 'merits review'.

[11] See FSMA, ss 22, 22A, and 55A(2), and the FSMA (PRA-Regulated Activities) Order 2013 (SI 2013/556) and para 19.07 *et seq.* and Chapters 2 and 3. The activities of IFFs have also been subject to the jurisdiction of the courts. For example, in *Riyad Bank and others v Ahli Bank (UK) plc* [2006] EWCA Civ 780, the Court of Appeal held that the defendant's Islamic investment banking unit owed a duty of care in tort to ensure that it properly valued certain leases which comprised part of the investments made by a *Shari'a*-compliant fund established by the claimants.

[12] 'Islamic Finance in the UK', FSA Discussion Paper, November 2007.

[13] ibid, pp 16 *et seq.*

[14] ibid, p 11.

regulatory classification and treatment of the products and services which IFFs offer.[15] In this respect, the approach of the PRA and FCA should not fall within the substantive model discussed earlier:[16] neither the PRA nor the FCA has its own *Shari'a* scholars who might rule on whether a particular product or service is *Shari'a* compliant, and the following statement made by the FSA would apply to the PRA and FCA: 'The FSA is, however, a secular and not a religious regulator. It would not be appropriate, even if it were possible, for the FSA to judge between different interpretations of *Shari'a* law'.[17] However, this approach is unlikely to fall squarely within the formal model, in that neither the PRA nor the FCA prescribe the procedures or expressly identify the standards to which they would expect an IFF to adhere before the IFF could hold out its services or products as *Shari'a* compliant. Instead, the approach of the PRA and FCA could be said to be risk-based whereby they seek to treat IFFs in the same manner as they would conventional firms, taking into consideration the risk which an IFF poses, within a general regulatory framework which is sufficiently flexible to allow the PRA and FCA to regulate IFFs in this manner.

19.09 The FSA regulated IFFs and any IFF continues to be regulated by both the PRA and the FCA, or the FCA only, depending on the types of regulated activity which the IFF carries on to offer wholesale and retail banking services, IFFs that carry on investment business, and IFFs that carry on insurance business, and these IFFs are subject to PRA and FCA oversight and control, as the case may be. The regulation by the PRA and FCA of IFFs must be seen in the context of the UK Government's commitment to entrench London as a leading centre for Islamic finance in the world and to ensure that all British citizens can participate in the financial system, regardless of faith.[18]

The regulation of Islamic capital markets

19.10 The FCA in its capacity as the UK Listing Authority is responsible for the listing of *Shari'a* compliant securities, such as *Sukuk*, in the UK. At present there is no Islamic exchange, per se, in the UK. However, the London Stock Exchange, for example, has listed *Sukuk*.[19] The listing and public offer of *Shari'a* compliant securities in the UK is discussed later in this chapter;[20] the regulation of Islamic securities exchanges, generally, is discussed in Chapter 15 of *Financial Markets and Exchanges Law*, the companion volume to this work.

19.11 The Treasury has also shown an interest in *Shari'a* compliant securities, consulting in November 2007 on the merits of the Government becoming an issuer of *Shari'a*-compliant financial instruments.[21] It published a response to the Consultation in June 2008.[22] The result of the Consultation was, inter alia, proposed amendments to the Finance Bill plus an examination of the application of Stamp Duty Land Tax, Value Added Tax, and the settlement of *Sukuk* within CREST.[23] The regulatory regime for *Sukuk* was also highlighted.

---

[15] This is discussed in para 19.76 *et seq.*

[16] See para 19.05.

[17] 'Islamic Finance in the UK', see n 11.

[18] See HM Treasury, 'Government Sterling Sukuk Issuance: a Response to the Consultation', p 3, which can be found at: <http://www.hm-treasury.gov.uk>.

[19] See <http://www.londonstockexchange.com>.

[20] See para 19.113.

[21] See HM Treasury, '8 Issuance: a Consultation', which can be found at: <http://www.hm- treasury.gov.uk>.

[22] See 'Government Sterling Sukuk Issuance: a Response to the Consultation', n 18.

[23] ibid.

International regulatory bodies

In addition to the establishment of standards for IFFs at a national level, international bodies have been established to set and develop regulatory and *Shari'a* standards for IFFs. The two most significant bodies, insofar as certain national regulators rely on their standards to regulate IFFs, are the Accounting and Auditing Organisation for Islamic Financial Institutions ('AAOIFI'), and the Islamic Financial Services Board ('IFSB'). 19.12

AAOIFI is an Islamic international autonomous not-for-profit corporate body that determines accounting, auditing, governance, ethics, and *Shari'a* standards for Islamic financial institutions and the industry.[24] To date, AAOIFI has issued 25 accounting standards, five auditing standards, seven AAOIFI Governance Standards, two ethics standards, and 41 *Shari'a* Standards, which set out the standards to which the services and products identified in the AAOIFI *Shari'a* Standards have to adhere. 19.13

The IFSB serves as an international standard-setting body of regulatory and supervisory agencies focusing on the soundness and stability of the Islamic financial services industry. The IFSB's work complements that of the Basel Committee on Banking Supervision, International Organisation of Securities Commissions, and the International Association of Insurance Supervisors. At the time of writing, the IFSB has issued guiding principles for risk management for IFFs, capital adequacy standards for IFFs, and guiding principles of corporate governance.[25] 19.14

In addition to AAOIFI and the IFSB, various other international institutions support the Islamic finance industry. These include: the International Islamic Financial Market, established to facilitate international secondary trading of Islamic capital market instruments and enhance cooperation between Islamic financial institutions globally;[26] the General Council for Islamic Banks and Financial Institutions, established to promote Islamic financial institutions and disseminate rules and concepts relevant to Islamic finance; and the International Islamic Rating Agency, established to provide credit ratings for Islamic finance institutions.[27] 19.15

Islamic finance regulation in other jurisdictions

Islamic finance is regulated in other jurisdictions under special regimes for IFFs or as part of the regime for regulating firms, generally. An examination of other jurisdictions is beyond the scope of this work; however, the following Middle East regimes are worth mentioning because their regulatory laws and rules are similar to those in the United Kingdom and the relevant laws and regulations are available in English: 19.16

- Bahrain, where the Central Bank of Bahrain ('CBB') regulates IFFs under the Central Bank of Bahrain and Financial Institutions Law 2006 and has, inter alia, a dedicated Rulebook for Islamic Banks, special rules for *Takaful* and *Retakaful* providers, and those offering *Shari'a*-compliant collective investment schemes.[28]
- The DIFC, where the DFSA regulates IFFs and firms offering *Shari'a*-compliant financial services through an 'Islamic Window' under the Law Regulating Islamic Financial

24 See <http://www.aaoifi.com>.
25 See <http://www.ifsb.org>.
26 See <http://www.iffm.com>.
27 See <http://www.iirating.com>.
28 See <http://www.cbb.gov.bh>.

Business, DIFC Law No 13 of 2004, and has, inter alia, special rules governing IFFS, *Shari'a*-compliant markets and exchanges, and those offering *Shari'a*-compliant collective investment funds.

- The Qatar Financial Centre, where the Qatar Financial Centre Regulatory Authority ('QFCRA') regulates IFFs and firms offering *Shari'a*-compliant financial services through an 'Islamic Window' under the Qatar Financial Centre Law 2005 and has, inter alia, an Islamic Finance Rulebook and special rules that govern *Shari'a*-compliant collective investment funds.[29]

19.17 In addition, Malaysia is a useful comparative source as a Far East jurisdiction both for understanding the regulation of Islamic banks and Islamic capital markets. In Malaysia, the Bank Negrasa Malaysia ('BNM') regulates those institutions offering banking products in Malaysia under the Islamic Banking Act 1983, including the Malaysia International Islamic Financial Centre, and has its own *Shari'a* Advisory Council;[30] and the Securities Commission of Malaysia ('MSC') regulates Islamic capital markets and those offering Islamic securities under the Capital Markets and Services Act 2007, including the Malaysia International Islamic Financial Centre, and has its own *Shari'a* Advisory Council.[31]

The legal effect of international standards

19.18 In the same way that neither the Basel Committee's recommendations nor the EU directives have direct effect on any particular firm, the standards set down by AAOIFI or the IFSB should not have direct effect on any IFI. This is not to say, however, that the PRA or FCA could not implement the AAOIFI and IFSB standards through rules via FSMA, s 138. In this respect, the following examples should be noted:

- In Bahrain, as part of its duty under 'Principle of Business 10—Management, Systems and Controls', the CBB requires an Islamic bank to comply with all AAOIFI issued accounting standards as well as the *Shari'a* pronouncements issued by the *Shari'a* Board of AAOIFI.[32]
- In the DIFC, the DFSA requires a SSB to carry on its internal *Shari'a* review in accordance with AAOFI Governance Standard for Islamic Financial Institutions No 2.[33]

19.19 In the absence of binding legal effect, the various AAOIFI and IFSB standards are useful as a guide which points to best practices for IFFs and serve as examples of the application of regulatory rules in an Islamic finance context. As such, compliance with these standards would not, as a matter of law, serve as a defence to PRA or FCA enforcement action or establish a legitimate expectation for an IFF that the PRA or FCA would not take action against it. They could, however, help an IFF demonstrate that it had not, as a matter of fact, breached a UK rule or standard. For example, an IFF's compliance with the relevant AAOIFI guidelines for SSBs could help it demonstrate that, as a matter of fact, it had complied with its duties under PRIN to take reasonable care to organise and control its affairs responsibly and effectively, with adequate risk management systems.[34]

---

[29] See <http://www.qfcra.com>.
[30] See <http://www.bnm.gov.my> and <http://www.mifc.com>.
[31] See <http://www.sc.com.my>.
[32] CBB Rulebook, Volume 2: *Islamic Banks, The Principles*, Rule PBB-1.1.10.
[33] DFSA Rulebook: *Islamic Finance Module*, Rule 5.2.1.
[34] PRIN 2.1.1 R.

Shari'a Principles

Introduction

19.20 Any examination of the regulation of an IFF would be incomplete without some understanding of the *Shari'a* principles that govern the IFF's business.

19.21 For the purposes of this chapter, the *Shari'a* may be viewed as divine law which embodies all aspects of the Islamic faith, including its beliefs and practices.[35]

Sources and authorities

19.22 The primary source of the *Shari'a* is the Holy *Qur'an*—divine law revealed to the Holy Prophet (PBUH).[36] The *Sunna* of the Holy Prophet (PBUH), supplement the Holy *Qur'an* as a primary source of the *Shari'a*. The *Sunna* can be divided between: the *Hadith* or sayings of the Holy Prophet (PBUH); the acts of the Holy Prophet (PBUH); and the silence or tacit approval of the Holy Prophet (PBUH). The following are secondary sources of *Shari'a*: *Ijma'a*—the consensus of the Islamic community; *Qiyas*—the application of accepted principles by analogy to new cases; and *Ijtihad*—the opinions and interpretations of Islamic jurists on a particular issue.[37]

19.23 There are four *Sunni* Muslim schools of thought on *Shari'a* interpretation: *Hanafi*, *Hanbali*, *Maliki*, and *Shaafi'i*, and the *Shia* Muslim school of thought: *Jaafari*. These five schools all base their *Fatawa*[38] on the Holy *Qur'an* but interpret it and the other *Shari'a* sources differently.[39] In addition, the Islamic *Fiqh* Academy, which is based in the Kingdom of Saudi Arabia and includes members from most Islamic countries, meets periodically to debate contemporary matters and issue resolutions.[40]

The main *Shari'a* principles relevant to Islamic finance

The prohibition on Riba

19.24 *Riba*, means literally, an excess or increase. In the context of Islamic finance, it includes an increase in the principal repayable to the lender in a loan transaction, an increase in a debt, or an increase in value attributed to one part of an exchange transaction, which accrues to the lender/creditor or a party to exchange without an equivalent increase in value or recompense to the other party. There are two types of *Riba*: *Riba Al-Nasiah* and *Riba Al-Fadl*.

- *Riba Al-Nasiah* means an increase due to delay, or due to exchange not being immediate. It includes, for example, lending money on the understanding that the borrower will return to the lender, at the end of the period, the amount originally lent together with an increase on it, in consideration of the lender having granted him time to pay. The charging, paying, and witnessing of interest, in all modern banking transactions, falls under *Riba Al-Nasiah*.

[35] For an overview of Islam and the *Shari'a* see Ruthven, *Islam: a Very Short Introduction* (OUP 1997).

[36] The designation PBUH stands for 'Peace Be Upon Him' and is used whenever reference is made to the Holy Prophet.

[37] See further Ayub, (n 1) pp 21–2 and Ghuddah et al., (n 1) pp 4–6.

[38] The plural of *Fatwa*—a religious decree or edict.

[39] For example, Ayub, (n 1) p 146 reports that while jurists from the *Hanbali* school accept as *Shari'a* compliant the *Arbun* contract, discussed in para 19.49, jurists from the other schools do not because it involves *Gharar*, risk taking and the taking of money without any consideration in return.

[40] See <http://www.fiqhacademy.org.sa>.

- *Riba Al-Fadl* is relevant in the context of an exchange or sale of goods and addresses the situation where there is an exchange of high-quality goods with low-quality goods. It relates to *Ribawi* goods, ie monetary units and items sold by weight and/or by measure such as gold, silver, paper currencies, and edible goods like wheat, rice, barley, dates, and salt.

19.25 The prohibition on *Riba* was the subject of the decision of *Shariat* Appellate Bench of the Supreme Court of Pakistan in 2000 invalidating various banking and financial laws.[41] The Court held at paragraph 245 that:

> Any additional amount over the principal in a contract of loan or debt is the *Riba* prohibited by the Holy *Qur'an* in several verses. The Holy Prophet (PBUH) has also termed the following transactions as *Riba*:
>
> 1. A transaction of money for money of the same denomination where the quantity on both sides is not equal, either in a spot transaction or in a transaction based on deferred payment.
> 2. A barter transaction between two weighable or measurable commodities of the same kind, where the quantity on both sides is not equal, or where the delivery from any one side is deferred.
> 3. A barter transaction between two different weighable or measurable commodities where delivery from one side is deferred.

19.26 The purpose of an obligation to pay interest or the debtor's ability to pay interest made no difference to the analysis. The court held, at paragraph 245 that:

> ... there is no difference between different types of loan, so far as the prohibition of *Riba* is concerned. It also does not make any difference whether the additional amount stipulated over the principal loan or debt is small or large. It is, therefore, held that all the prevailing forms of interest, either in banking transactions or in private transactions do fall within the definition of '*Riba*'. Similarly, any interest stipulated in the government borrowings, acquired from domestic or foreign sources, is *Riba* and clearly prohibited by the Holy *Qur'an*.[42]

The prohibition on Gharar

19.27 *Gharar* means, literally, uncertainty, hazard, or risk. It refers to an element of excessive uncertainty or mere speculative risk in any business or contract. It includes, for example, uncertainty about the subject of a contract or its price. *Gharar* is prohibited because it may lead to undue loss to one party and unjustified enrichment of another. Gambling is a form of *Gharar* because the gambler is ignorant of the result of the gamble. Selling goods without allowing the buyer to properly examine the goods is also a kind of *Gharar*. Further examples of *Gharar* are: selling goods that the seller is unable to deliver; selling known or unknown goods against an unknown price, such as selling the contents of a sealed box without exact information about its contents; selling goods without proper description; selling goods without specifying the price, such as selling at the 'going price'.

19.28 The prohibition on *Gharar* was considered in the context of spot and forward foreign exchange contracts in a case that came before the Court of Cassation in Abu Dhabi, one of the United Arab Emirates, in 1996.[43] The court invalidated the contracts for two reasons.

---

[41] See <http://www.albagh.net/Islamic_economics_riba_judgment.shtml> for the text of the *Riba* case.

[42] For a discussion of the prohibition on *Riba*, see Ayub, n 1, pp 44–57; Ghuddah et al., (n 1) pp 29–30.

[43] Abu Dhabi Court of Cassation Judgment No 158 & 208/18 reported in Price and Tamimi, *United Arab Emirates Court of Cassation Judgments 1989–1997* (Kluwer Law International, 1998) p 23.

First because they amounted to contracts of 'competition' within the meaning of Article 1012 of the United Arab Emirates Civil Code, Federal Law (2) of 1987, which is part of Chapter IV governing 'Contracts of *Gharar*'. Second, because they were contrary to the principles of *Shari'a*. Article 1012 states (in translation) that: 'A competition (for reward) is a contract whereby one person is obliged to pay a sum of money or gives some other thing by way of agreed recompense to a person who succeeds in achieving the object specified in the contract.' The court held that:

> The intention of both parties was to generate profit from the fluctuation of the various currencies. They would not know the result of their speculation until the transactions were closed. When the subject of a transaction is not assessed or known to either party and is based partially on luck, it is very misleading. They become, according to Articles 1012 and 1014 of the Code, illegal bets.[44]

The prohibition on Maisir or Qimar

The words *Maisir* and *Qimar* are used interchangeably to refer to games of chance. *Maisir* refers to easily available wealth or the acquisition of wealth by chance, whether or not at the expense of another. *Qimar* means a game of chance—in which one participant gains at the cost of another. **19.29**

Maisir and *Qimar* appear also to have played a part in the reasoning of the Abu Dhabi Court in the 1996 decision on the compatibility with the *Shari'a* of foreign exchange spot and forward contracts, referred to above.[45] **19.30**

> As regards the appeal filed by the Defendant, the Court of Cassation held that according to Articles 1012 and 1014 of the Code, speculation in foreign currency transactions is illegal as the transactions are normally carried out for a consideration which is never delivered and the only interest both parties have is in the profits generating from the speculation. Such transactions cannot be sanctioned by the UAE Courts.[46]

Islamic business ethics and norms

In addition to the three primary prohibitions above, the *Shari'a* includes a set of principles that provide a basic framework for the conduct of economic activities in general, and financial and commercial transactions in particular. The Holy *Qur'an* and the *Sunna* refer to a number of norms and principles which govern the rights and obligations of parties to a contract. Principles of justice, mutual help, free consent, and honesty on the part of the parties to a contract, avoiding fraud, misrepresentation, and negation of injustice or exploitation provide grounds for valid contracts.[47] **19.31**

Prohibited investments

Islamic investment management and fund management must operate without making investments that may be prohibited or *Haram*. Prohibited investments include investments **19.32**

---

[44] Price and Tamimi, (n 43) p 25. The Abu Dhabi Court of Cassation reached the same conclusion but for different reasons in Judgment No 197/19 dated 21 February 1999 reported in Price and Tamimi, *United Arab Emirates Court of Cassation Judgments 1998–2003* (Brill, 2005), p 27. For a discussion of the prohibition on *Gharar*, see Ayub, (n 1) pp 57–61 and Ghuddah et al., (n 1) pp 31–2.

[45] See para 19.28.

[46] Price and Tamimi, (n 43) p 24. For further discussion of the prohibition on *Maisir*, see Ayub, (n 1) pp 61–4.

[47] For further discussion of Islamic business ethics, see Ayub, (n 1) pp 64–70 and Ghuddah et al., (n 1) pp 26–9.

in the following industries: insurance; banking (including all banks and organisations principally active in conventional finance); alcohol (including producers, distributors, sellers, and businesses deriving substantial income from transactions in alcohol). As a result, supermarkets, airlines, and hotels, also being at risk of exclusion:

- pork—producers, distributors, and meat stores. Businesses that handle pork products, such as restaurants and supermarkets are also at risk of exclusion);
- defence (including businesses which derive substantial income from defence and munitions);
- gambling (including casinos, hotels, and other companies involved with gambling, such as bookmakers); and
- entertainment (including business involved with adult entertainment).[48]

The enforceability of *Shari'a* in the English courts

19.33 In *Shamil Bank of Bahrain EC v Beximco Pharmaceuticals*,[49] the Court of Appeal considered the enforceability of a contract containing the following choice of law clause: 'Subject to the principles of the Glorious *Shariah* [sic], this Agreement shall be governed and construed in accordance with the laws on England'. The defendants denied liability under the contract and associated contracts on the basis that: (a) on a true construction of the governing law clause, the contracts were only enforceable insofar as they were valid and enforceable both in accordance with the English law and the *Shari'a*; and (b) the contracts were unenforceable under the *Shari'a*.

19.34 The Court rejected the defendants' contention holding that English law alone was the proper law of the contract because: (a) the Rome Convention only contemplates the choice of law of a country—it was not applicable to a choice between the law of a country and a non-national system of law; (b) the incorporation of foreign law only applies where the parties have sufficiently identified specific provisions—the general reference to *Shari'a* in this case and not to 'basic rules' was insufficient for this purpose; (c) reference to *Shari'a* was intended merely to reflect the religious principles which the parties held themselves out as doing business, rather than a system of law intended to trump the application of English law to the contracts.

19.35 The *Shamil Bank* judgment appears to leave it open to the parties to a contract to specify the *Shari'a* as the contract's governing law provided that the parties specify the particular *Shari'a* rules that should govern the contract. In this respect, however, there is uncertainty: would it be necessary or sufficient for the relevant clause to identify the particular school of thought on *Shari'a* interpretation?[50] Would it be necessary to specify the particular rules that apply, eg the prohibition on *Riba* and, if so, would this necessarily exclude the other rules not expressly identified, including rules of interpretation? The position remains unclear.

19.36 Nevertheless, Potter LJ's remarks about *Shari'a* in an English court are noteworthy:

> ...so far as the 'principles of... *Shari'a*' are concerned, it was indeed the evidence of both experts that there are indeed areas of considerable controversy and difficulty arising not only from the need to translate into propositions of modern law texts which centuries ago were set out as religious and moral codes, but because of the existence of a variety of schools of thought

[48] See Ghuddah et al., (n 1) pp 158–61.

[49] [2004] EWCA Civ 19.

[50] Cf Abu Dhabi Court of Cassation Judgment No 9/19 reported in Price and Tamimi (n 43), in which the court held that a clause in the United Arab Emirates Penal Code No 3 of 1987 stating that 'Islamic law should

which the Court may have to concern itself with in any given case before reaching a conclusion upon the principle or rule in dispute. The fact that there may be a general consensus on the proscription of *Riba* and the essentials of a valid *Morabaha* [sic] agreement does no more than indicate that, if the *Shariah* [sic], law proviso were sufficient to incorporate the principles of *Shariah* [sic] law into the parties' agreements, the defendants would have been likely to succeed. However, since I would hold that the proviso is plainly inadequate for that purpose, the validity of the contract and the defendants' obligations thereunder fall to be decided according to English law.[51]

His Lordship seems to suggest that an English court would enforce an agreement where the parties had properly agreed that the *Shari'a* would be the sole law governing that agreement. The parties would, however, need to lead expert evidence to prove the contents of the *Shari'a*. **19.37**

Shari'a-compliant Financial Products and Services

Techniques for developing *Shari'a*-compliant products and services

In order to avoid breaching the prohibitions referred to earlier,[52] IFFs have developed various financing techniques for ensuring that the services and products that they offer are *Shari'a* compliant. These may be grouped into the following broad categories: **19.38**

- money acceptance arrangements, used by IFFs for offering *Shari'a*-compliant deposit products;
- deferred payment arrangements, used by IFFs for offering *Shari'a*-compliant asset financing products;
- profit-sharing arrangements, used by IFFs for offering *Shari'a*-compliant equity participation products;
- capital market arrangements, used by IFFs for offering *Shari'a*-compliant products capable of being listed on an exchange; and
- mutual assistance arrangements, used by IFFs for offering *Shari'a*-compliant insurance products.

The arrangements may be used in combination. For example an IFF could: use deferred payment or profit sharing arrangements to create products capable of being listed on an exchange, as in the case of *Sukuk*; or offer a *Shari'a*-compliant investment fund which employs deferred payment arrangements, such as a *Murabaha*, to make investments; use deferred payment arrangements to create a *Shari'a*-compliant risk mitigation product as in the case of a *Shari'a*-compliant currency swap.[53] The arrangements, together with some miscellaneous arrangements and contracts, are discussed in the following.[54]

---

be applied to all crimes specified by Divine Command and to the payment of blood money' did not specify the school of Islamic jurisprudence to be followed. It was, therefore, in the judge's discretion to interpret the clause in accordance with whatever principles were in the best interests of the community.

[51] Para 55 of the *Shamil Bank* judgment.

[52] See paras 19.24–19.32.

[53] *Shari'a*-compliant derivatives are discussed in para 19.99.

[54] Para 19.39 *et seq*. A detailed discussion of the Islamic finance arrangements is beyond the scope of this work. Moreover, the arrangements referred to in para 19.39 *et seq*. are not exhaustive but merely set out those likely to be the most relevant in the context of the regulation of Islamic finance. For further discussion of various Islamic finance arrangements, see Hainsworth 'Islamic Financial Institutions and Islamic Finance' in Blair et al, *Encyclopaedia of Banking Law*, (Lexis Nexis, 2008) para 4.

Money acceptance arrangements[55]

19.39 *Al Wadi'a*—an agreement for an IFF's safe-keeping of *Amana*, deposits held on trust, where the IFF: (a) does not seek profit from the depositor; (b) has no liability to the depositor unless caused by the IFF's breach of duty; and (c) is liable to pay back the full amount deposited with the IFF.[56]

19.40 *Qard*—an agreement whereby a lender transfers ownership in property, including money, to a borrower on the condition that the borrower will pay back the property on demand. In the case of monies deposited with an IFF, the IFF would be the borrower and the depositor the lender. To be *Shari'a* compliant, only the principal is repayable.[57]

Deferred payment arrangements

19.41 *Ijara*—a contract of lease whereby the owner (A) of an asset (the Leased Property) transfers the right to use and enjoy the Leased Property to B for a predetermined period in exchange for a predetermined rental. The Leased Property must be such that B's use of it does not consume it or change its form. In this way, A retains the risk related to the Leased Property in return for the reward in the form of the rental. *Ijara Muntania Bittamleek* is a type of *Ijara*, which ends with transfer of the Leased Property to B.[58]

19.42 *Murabaha*—a contract of sale, in which the seller (A) agrees to sell *Shari'a*-compliant goods to the buyer (B) for a purchase price equal to the cost of the goods plus a profit mark-up. Under a *Murabaha*, A delivers the goods to B on the date of the contract but B pays the purchase price at a future date. There are two types of sale under a *Murabaha*: (a) the IFF purchases the goods from A and makes them available to B without B making any prior promise to buy the goods from the IFF; (b) the IFF purchases the goods from A and makes them available to B who promises to buy the goods from the IFF—a '*Murabaha* for the Purchase Orderer'.[59] A and B might execute the *Murabaha* contract in conjunction with a second or 'Parallel *Murabaha*' contract, whereby B, as buyer under the first *Murabaha* contract, agrees to sell goods with the same specifications as the goods under the first *Murabaha* contract. Under *Shari'a* rules, A, as buyer under the second *Murabaha* contract, cannot buy back from B the same goods which A sold to B under the first *Murabaha* contract.[60] An example of parallel *Murabaha* arrangements arises in the context of a *Shari'a*-compliant profit rate swap where the parties may wish to replicate the cash flows under an interest rate swap in a

[55] IFFs may also use profit-sharing financing arrangements, such as *Mudaraba*, as the primary means for accepting and holding monies. The regulatory treatment of money acceptance arrangements is discussed in para 19.76.

[56] See further Ayub, (n 1) pp 188–91 and Ghuddah et al. (n 1), pp 33–4.

[57] See further Ayub, (n 1) pp 162–3.

[58] See further *AAOIFI Shari'a Standards* (2004), pp 135–58, Ayub, (n 1) pp 279–305 and Ghuddah et al., (n 1) pp 76–8. For capital adequacy purposes, the IFSB Capital Adequacy Standard for Institutions (Other than Insurance Institutions) Offering Only Islamic Financial Services (2005) ('the IFSB CAS') distinguishes between *Ijara* arrangements and *Ijara Muntania Bittamleek* arrangements. The IFSB CAS are discussed later this chapter.

[59] See further *AAOIFI Shari'a Standards* (2004), pp 109–34, Ayub, (n 1) pp 213–39, and Ghuddah et al., (n 1) pp 68–74. Finance Act 2005, s 47 deals with the taxation of *Murabaha* which is described under the heading of 'alternative finance arrangements: purchase and re-sale'. For capital adequacy purposes, the IFSB CAS distinguishes between *Murabaha* arrangements and *Murabaha* for the Purchase Orderer arrangements.

[60] See further *AAOIFI Shari'a Standards* (2004), pp 159–74, Ayub, (n 1) pp 241–63, and Ghuddah et al., (n 1) pp 79–82. For capital adequacy purposes, the IFSB CAS distinguishes between *Salam* arrangements and Parallel *Salam* arrangements.

manner that is *Shari'a* compliant by using a parallel *Murabaha* structure: (a) under the first *Murabaha*, A agrees to purchase a specified commodity from B for a cost price of £1 million plus a mark-up based, inter alia, on a fixed rate; (b) under the second *Murabaha*, B agrees to purchase a specified commodity from A for a cost price of £1 million plus a mark-up based, inter alia, on a floating rate calculated by reference to an index, such as LIBOR. By (a) having the deferred payments under both *Murabaha* arrangements fall on the same date and (b) achieving a net settlement of the offsetting deferred payments, A and B swap a fixed and floating payment flows on a notional of £1 million.

Istisna'a—a forward sale contract where a buyer of *Shari'a* compliant goods (A) asks the seller (B) to manufacture the goods according to the A's specifications using B's materials at a predetermined price for delivery upon completing the manufacture of the goods. An *Istisna'a* contract is often executed in conjunction with a second or 'Parallel *Istisna'a*' contract, whereby A, the buyer of the goods under the first *Istisna'a* contract, agrees to sell goods to B with the same product specifications as the goods specified in the first *Istisna'a* contract. Under *Shari'a* rules, A, as buyer under the second *Istisna'a* contract, cannot buy back from B the same goods which A sold to B under the first *Istisna'a* contract.[61] **19.43**

Salam—a forward sale contract in which a buyer (B) pays seller (A) for specified *Shari'a* compliant goods which A or its agent will deliver to B at a future date. Under a *Salam* contract, B pays the full purchase price for the goods on the date of the contract or within a subsequent period, which the SSB that approves the *Salam* arrangements, deems appropriate. A and B might execute the *Salam* contract in conjunction with a second or 'Parallel *Salam*' contract, whereby B, as buyer under the first *Salam* contract, agrees to sell goods with the same specifications as the goods as that in the first *Salam* contract. Under *Shari'a* rules, A, as buyer under the second *Salam* contract, cannot buy back from B the same goods which A sold to B under the first *Salam* contract.[62] **19.44**

Profit sharing arrangements

Mudaraba[63]—an arrangement whereby investment account holders, the *Rab Al Mal*, provide funds to a manager, the *Mudarib*, who uses its management expertise to manage the funds. The *Rab Al Mal* and the *Mudarib* share in the profits on a pre-agreed basis with the *Rab Al Mal* bearing the risk of any loss and the *Mudarib* being liable for any loss only as a result of its misconduct, negligence, or breach of any conditions governing the *Mudaraba*. The *Mudarib* can offer the *Mudaraba* on a *restricted* basis, where the *Rab Al Mal* allow the *Mudarib* to make investments subject to specified investment restrictions such as type of instrument, sector, or country exposures, or on an *unrestricted* basis, where the *Rab Al Mal* allow the *Mudarib* to invest the funds freely, subject, of course, to the requirement that the funds are not invested in a manner that may be *Haram*.[64] **19.45**

---

[61] See further *AAOIFI Shari'a Standards* (2004), pp 175–95, Ayub, (n 1) pp 263–77, and Ghuddah et al., (n 1) pp 83–5. For capital adequacy purposes, the IFSB CAS distinguish between *Istisna'a* arrangements and Parallel *Istisna'a* arrangements.

[62] See further *AAOIFI Shari'a Standards* (2004), pp 159–74, Ayub, (n 1) pp 241–63, and Ghuddah et al., (n 1) pp 79–82. For capital adequacy purposes, the IFSB CAS distinguishes between *Salam* arrangements and Parallel *Salam* arrangements.

[63] *Mudaraba* are also known as 'Profit Sharing Investment Accounts' ('PSIAs'). The operation of PSIAs is discussed in para 19.83 *et seq*.

[64] See further *AAOIFI Shari'a Standards* (2004), pp 227–45, Ayub, (n 1) pp 320–8 and Ghuddah et al., (n 1) pp 62–4. Finance Act 2005, s 49 deals with the taxation of *Mudaraba* which is described under the heading of 'alternative finance arrangements: deposit'. The regulatory treatment of *Mudaraba* is discussed in para 19.83 *et seq*.

19.46 *Musharaka*—a partnership agreement between two parties A and B, with B usually being an IFF, who both provide capital towards the financing of a project. A and B share any profits on a pre-agreed basis but losses are shared on the basis of equity participation. A and B manage the project. A and B have a right to forgo the right of management/work in favour of each other or another person. There are two main forms of *Musharaka:* Permanent *Musharaka*, whereby the participation shares remain the same, and Diminishing *Musharaka*, whereby one party, usually the IFF, gradually transfers its share until the other becomes owner.[65]

Capital market arrangements

19.47 *Sukuk*[66]—certificates of equal value representing undivided shares in ownership of tangible assets, the right to use and enjoy property, and services.[67] *Sukuk* are capable of being classified in different ways. One system of classification distinguishes between asset-based *Sukuk*, where the underlying assets are governed by *Salam*, *Istisna'a*, or *Ijara* contracts giving predictable returns, and equity-based assets, where the underlying assets are governed by *Musharaka* or *Mudaraba* contracts giving returns based on profit and loss.[68] Another system of classification identifies the following categories: asset-backed *Sukuk* where investors take risk on an identified pool of assets, similar to the position under a conventional, non-*Shari'a*-compliant, securitisation; asset-based *Sukuk* where the *Sukuk* originator enters into a binding promise or purchase undertaking by the *Sukuk* originator where investors take risk on the creditworthiness of the *Sukuk* originator, similar to the position under a conventional bond issue; and 'pass through' *Sukuk* where a separate issuing entity purchases the underlying assets from the originator, packages them as a pool of assets, and acts as issuer of the *Sukuk*.[69]

Mutual assistance arrangements

19.48 *Shari'a* scholars take the view that commercial insurance is unlawful due to the involvement of *Riba*, *Gharar*, *Qimar*, and *Maisir*, and the invalid transfer of risk from the insured to the insurer. Their view is that, as a whole, insurance business contains elements of temptation and cheating and is incompatible with natural and ethical methods of earning money. *Takaful* is an Islamic insurance contract based on the principle of *Ta'awon* or mutual assistance. *Takaful* embodies shared responsibility, common benefit, and mutual solidarity. Every policyholder pays his subscription in order to assist other policyholders who need assistance. *Takaful* incorporates the concept of *Tabarru* or donation. A *Takaful* policyholder agrees to relinquish, as *Tabarru*, the whole or a certain proportion of his *Takaful* contributions that he undertakes to pay, therefore enabling him to fulfil his obligation of mutual help should any of his fellow *Takaful* participants suffer a defined loss. There are two basic types

---

65 See further *AAOIFI Shari'a Standards* (2004), pp 196–226, Ayub, (n 1) pp 312–20, and Ghuddah et al., (n 1) pp 64 8. The Finance Act 2005, s 47A deals with the taxation of Diminishing *Musharaka*, which is described under the heading of 'alternative finance arrangements: diminishing shared ownership'. For capital adequacy purposes, the IFSB CAS distinguishes between *Musharaka* arrangements and Diminishing *Musharaka* arrangements. The regulatory treatment of *Musharaka* is discussed in para 91 further.

66 '*Sukuk*' is the plural of '*Sak*' which is the Arabic translation of 'certificate'.

67 See further *AAOIFI Shari'a Standards* (2004), pp 280–307, Ayub, (n 1) pp 389–415, Ghuddah et al., (n 1) pp 175–94. The Finance Act 2005, s 48A deals with the taxation of *Sukuk*, which are described as 'alternative finance arrangements: alternative finance investment bonds'. The regulatory treatment of *Sukuk* is discussed in para 19.93 *et seq.*

68 See the IFSB CAS, chapter C7.

69 See 'IFSB Capital Adequacy Requirements for Sukuk Securitisations and Real Estate Investment', Exposure Draft, December 2007 (IFSB *Sukuk* CAR), para 9.

of *Takaful*: general *Takaful*—an alternative to general insurance—and family *Takaful*—an alternative to life insurance. In addition, IFFs may offer *Retakaful* as an alternative to reinsurance. A *Takaful* company operates as a trustee or a manager on the basis of *Wakala* or *Mudaraba*. The operator and the participants contribute to the *Takaful* fund. Claims are paid from the fund and the participants share the underwriting surplus or deficit.[70]

Some miscellaneous arrangements

Arbun—a down payment sale with the condition that if the buyer: (a) takes the commodity, which is the subject of the sale, the down payment will become part of the selling price; (b) does not purchase the commodity, the buyer will forfeit the down payment. *Arbun* is similar to a covered call option in that the buyer has the option to confirm or rescind the purchase.[71] **19.49**

Hamish Jiddyya—a refundable security deposit taken by a lender prior to establishing a contract which carries a limited recourse to the extent of the lender's loss if the borrower fails to honour a binding promise to purchase or to lease the asset against which the lender has made a loan.[72] **19.50**

Tawarruq—an adaptation of the *Murabaha* whereby a purchaser buys a commodity on credit and sells it immediately at spot value to a third party with the objective of generating cash.[73] **19.51**

Wa'ad—a unilateral promise whereby the promisor binds himself to do something for the promisee.[74] **19.52**

Wakala—an agency agreement whereby an investor appoints a manager, the *Wakil*, as his agent. The *Wakala* is a means by which an IFF can hold and invest monies on a client's behalf—the *Wakalatul Istitmar*. The *Wakalatul Istitmar* may be contrasted with the *Mudaraba* in that the investor alone shares any profit or loss, with the *Wakil* getting a fixed management fee, whereas, in the case of a *Mudaraba*, both the *Rab Al Mal* and the *Mudarib* share any profits.[75] **19.53**

Waqf—the retention of property for the benefit of a charitable or humanitarian objective whereby the person creating the *Waqf* transfers ownership of property to the *Waqf* in perpetuity. The *Waqf* property cannot be sold but the *Waqf* manager can assign the use and enjoyment of the property to identified beneficiaries. The *Waqf* may be used as the basis for *Takaful*, in the same way as *Mudaraba* or *Wakala*.[76] **19.54**

The Authorisation of IFFs

A non-discriminatory regime

The FSA stated that all financial institutions that it regulated were subject to the same standards and authorisation requirements as other firms.[77] Therefore, an IFF seeking to become **19.55**

[70] See further Ayub, (n 1) pp 418–31 and Ghuddah et al., (n 1) pp 195–212.
[71] See further Ayub, (n 1) p 116.
[72] ibid.
[73] See further Ayub, (n 1) pp 349–51 and Ghuddah et al., (n 1) pp 75–6.
[74] See further Ayub, (n 1) pp 114–16. *Shari'a* scholars do not agree whether the *Wa'ad* creates a legally binding obligation.
[75] See further Ayub, (n 1) pp 347–9, and Ghuddah et al., (n 1) p 45. The Finance Act 2005, s 49 deals with the taxation of *Wakala* which is described under the heading 'alternative finance arrangements: profit share agency'.
[76] See further Ayub, (n 1) pp 423–5.
[77] 'Islamic Finance in the UK', (n 11) pp 11–13.

PRA and/or FCA authorised would need permission to carry on the same regulated activities as a conventional firm and its permission would, generally, relate to the same specified investments as a conventional firm, eg an IFF could carry on the regulated activity of 'arranging deals in investments'[78] albeit that the investments in question would be *Shari'a*-compliant investments.[79] IFFs may nevertheless require special consideration in certain areas: the FSA highlighted the role of the SSB, the regulatory definition of certain products, and financial promotion as special areas that need to be considered.[80]

AAOIFI Standards as Best Practice Guidelines for Establishing an IFF

19.56 Neither the PRA nor the FCA prescribe any special requirements for IFFs. However, as set out earlier, an IFF's compliance with the AAOIFI or IFSB standards could help demonstrate that the IFF had not, as a matter of fact, breached a UK rule or standard.[81] Moreover, an IFF's failure or inability to put in place internal systems and controls that adhere to internationally recognised or developing standards could have damaging commercial consequences, irrespective of any express or implied regulatory duty to follow such standards. In this respect, AAOIFI's *Shari'a* Standard for Conversion of a Conventional Bank to an Islamic Bank[82] sets out useful standards to guide an IFF establishing itself in a manner that would enable it to hold itself out as an IFF.[83] In this respect the following standards are noteworthy:

- *Providing Financial Services in Permissible Ways*—in providing banking services, it is not permissible for [an IFF] to receive interest as compensation for services rendered. It is a requirement that an Islamic alternative be worked out, such as treatment of uncovered documentary credits through *Murabaha* to the purchase orderer [sic], *Musharaka* or *Mudaraba* in accordance with the rules of *Shari'a*. It is not permissible to take a commission for providing a mere facility. However, the commission may be linked to expenses incurred for the execution of the credit facility accordingly.[84]
- *The Mobilisation of Funds*—[An IFF] must confine itself to permissible operations for acquiring the necessary funds to operate or to meet its liabilities. Examples of such operations are:

The shareholders may increase their share capital in order to increase the [IFF's] capital and provide a basis for attracting investment accounts and current accounts.

Issuance of Islamic certificates such as *Mudaraba, Musharaka* or *Ijara* certificates within the parameters of *Shari'a*.

Concluding *Salam* contracts whereby the [IFF] acts in the capacity of a supplier, or *Istisna'a* contracts whereby the [IFF] acts in the capacity of a manufacturer or builder with the condition that the contract price of the *Istisna'a* is paid to the [IFF] in advance, although the deferment of payment of the price in *Istisna'a* is allowed by *Shari'a*.

---

[78] RAO, art 25.

[79] See the definition of 'arranging deals in on *Shari'a* compliant financial instruments' in the CBB Rulebook, Volume 2: *Islamic Banks, Licensing Requirements*, LR-1.3.37, the wording of which is similar to RAO, art 25.

[80] 'Islamic Finance in the UK', (n 11) p 11.

[81] See para 19.19.

[82] AAOIFI *Shari'a* Standard No 6.

[83] Although compliance with this and other AAOIFI standards would not of itself demonstrate to the UK regulators that an IFF should be authorised or would not operate as a 'safe harbour' from enforcement action, compliance with such standards would, to the extent that produces the same outcomes as the relevant UK regulatory standards, help demonstrate compliance with those standards.

[84] *AAOIFI Shari'a Standard No 6*, para 5.

Concluding a sale-and-leaseback deal by selling some of the assets of the [IFF] for liquidity and leasing them back by means of an *Ijara* contract. The transaction must take into account the *Shari'a* standards on *Ijara* and *Ijara Muntania Bittamleek* whereby the contract of sale must be independent from the contract of lease, ie the two contracts must remain separate from each other.[85]

Concluding *Tawarruq* deals in line with *Shari'a* principles by buying a commodity on a deferred payment basis and selling it to a third party, other than the previous seller, for immediate payment.[86]

- *The Disposal of Impermissible Earnings*—Any interest and other non-permissible earnings should be channelled to charity. It is not permissible for the [IFF] to use this money, directly or indirectly, for its own benefit. Examples of charitable channels include, among others, training people other than the staff of the bank, funding research, providing relief equipment, financial and technical assistance for Islamic countries or Islamic scientific, academic institutions, schools, anything to do with spreading Islamic knowledge, and similar channels. The charity money must go to these channels in accordance with the resolutions of the [SSB] of the [IFF].[87]
- *Zakat Obligations*[88]— . . . [IFFs] must take into account that they are obliged to pay *Zakat* even if the revenues and the money earned are impermissible because the shareholders are obliged in the first place to dispose of all accrued interest and impermissible earnings. So, the payment of *Zakat* is part of the obligation to dispose of impermissible earnings and interest.[89]

Prudential standards for IFFs

On the basis that the UK regime is a non-discriminatory regime, the PRA's and the FCA's rules governing capital adequacy and other prudential requirements should apply to IFFs. The Combined Handbook identifies 'an *Ijara* mortgage is an example of an exposure described in BIPRU 3.4.58 R'[90] to which its general risk weighting rules apply.[91] The Combined Handbook does not set out any further guidelines for IFFs, notwithstanding the fact that the special nature of the arrangements which an IFF puts in place, to ensure that it conducts its business in a *Shari'a* compliant manner, may give rise to unique types of risk which the UK prudential regime requires the IFF to address. To assist an IFF in managing such risks, the standards developed by the IFSB are useful but only insofar as they provide non-binding guidance. However, as set out above, compliance with the IFSB standards would not, as a matter of law, serve as a defence to PRA or FCA enforcement action or establish a legitimate expectation for an IFF that the PRA or FCA would not take action against it.[92] **19.57**

The IFSB Capital Adequacy Standard for Institutions (Other than Insurance Institutions) Offering Only Islamic Financial Services, 2005 (IFSB CAS). The IFSB CAS deals with capital adequacy requirements for IFFs.[93] The IFSB describe the IFSB CAS as based primarily **19.58**

[85] See paras 19.40–19.42.
[86] ibid, para 6/2.
[87] ibid, para 10/2.
[88] *Zakat* is a charitable tax. See n 1.
[89] ibid, para 11.
[90] BIPRU 3.4.59 R.
[91] BIPRU 3.4.58 R which governs the risk weighting which a firm should attach to an exposure which it has to a tenant under a property leasing transaction concerning residential property under which the firm is the lessor and the tenant has an option to purchase.
[92] See para 19.19.
[93] In Bahrain, the CBB implemented the IFSB CAS in January 2008. See CBB Rulebook, Volume 2: *Islamic Banks, Capital Adequacy*; <http://www.cbb.gov.bh>.

on Pillar 1 of the Basel II recommendations.[94] The IFSB CAS is intended to apply to non-insurance institutions offering only Islamic financial services however the IFSB indicates that the IFSB CAS may also be applied to conventional firms operating 'Islamic Windows'.[95]

19.59 The IFSB CAS sets out the minimum capital adequacy requirements for both credit risk and market risk exposures arising from an IFF's holding of the following financial instruments: *Murabaha* and *Murabaha* for the Purchase Orderer; *Salam* and Parallel *Salam*; *Istisna* and Parallel *Istisna*; *Ijara* and *Ijara Munatahia Bittamleek*; *Musharaka* and Diminishing *Musharaka*; *Mudaraba*; and *Sukuk* held as investments in the IFF's non-trading book (the *Shari'a* Compliant Instruments Standards).[96] The IFSB CAS also provides guidance on operational risk (the Operational Risk Standards) and sets out capital adequacy requirements for Profit Sharing Invest Accounts.[97]

19.60 The IFSB CAS sets out Capital Adequacy Ratio ('CAR') formulae for IFFs based on the definition of eligible regulatory capital and risk weighted assets (calculated by reference to credit risk and market risk exposures identified in the *Shari'a* Compliant Instruments Standards) and operational risk identified in the Operational Risk Standards.[98] The IFSB CAS identifies the minimum capital adequacy requirements for IFFs as a CAR of not lower than eight per cent for total capital.[99]

19.61 The IFSB CAS identifies credit risk exposures in connection with accounts receivable in *Murabaha* contracts, counterparty risk in *Salam* contracts, accounts receivable and counterparty risk in *Istisna* contracts and lease payments receivable in *Ijara* contracts, capital impairment risk in *Musharaka* and *Mudaraba* contracts, and *Sukuk* held to maturity in the IFF's banking book.[100] The IFSB recommend that an IFF take the following into consideration in assigning risk weightings to the relevant contracts: the credit ratings of a debtor, counterparty, or other obligor or a security based on an external credit assessment; credit risk mitigation arrangements, which may include *Hamish Jiddiyya*, *Arbun* contracts, third party guarantees, assets pledged as collateral in a *Shari'a* compliant manner, or leased assets; and specific provisions made for the overdue portion of accounts receivable or lease payments receivable.[101]

19.62 The IFSB CAS identifies market risk exposures in connection with the risk of losses in on- and off-balance sheet positions arising from movements in market price and includes equity

---

[94] IFSB CAS, paras 3 and 4. The IFSB CAS do not address the requirements covered by Pillar Two (Supervisory Review Process) and Pillar Three (Market Discipline) of Basel II as the IFS plans to deal with these in separate standards. (See IFSB CAS, para 5.)

[95] IFSB CAS, para 6. Islamic Windows are discussed in para 19.64 *et seq*.

[96] IFSB CAS, ss C.1–C.7. In December 2007, the IFSB published the IFSB *Sukuk* CAR, n 114, to address caporal adequacy for requirements for *Sukuk* securitisations and real estate investments, which the IFSB CAS do not currently address.

[97] IFSB CAS, ss B.3 and B.4, respectively. Profit Sharing Investment Accounts are discussed below.

[98] IFSB CAS, paras 13–14 and Appendix A.

[99] IFSB CAS, para 16. In calculating capital adequacy ratios, the IFSB recommends that regulatory capital as the numerator be calculated in relation to the total risk-weighted assets as the denominator. The total of the risk-weighted assets is determined by multiplying the capital requirements for market risk and operational risk by 12.5 to convert into risk-weighted equivalent assets and adding the resulting figures to the sum of the risk weighted assets computed for credit risk. (IFSB CAS, para 17.) This approach is consistent with BIPRU 3.1.5 R.

[100] IFSB CAS, s B.2, generally, and IFSB CAS ss C.1–C.7, which go into detail for each contract. The IFSB are looking to supplement the standards for *Sukuk* with the IFSB.

[101] IFSB CAS, para 20 *et seq*. An IFF would need to test these against the requirements in BIPRU 5.2.

position risks in the IFF's trading book and market risk, which includes specific and general market risk, on trading positions in *Sukuk*; foreign exchange risk; and commodities and inventory risk.[102]

The Disclosures to Promote Transparency and Market Discipline for Institutions Offering Islamic Financial Services, 2007 ('IFSB PTMDS'). The IFSB PTMDS sets out the standards for IFFs in making disclosures and builds on Pillar Three of the Basel II recommendations. It sets out: financial and risk disclosure principles;[103] disclosure requirements for investment account holders, including those for restricted and unrestricted accounts;[104] retail investor-oriented disclosures for investment account holders;[105] risk management, risk exposures, and risk mitigation, including provisions governing credit risk, liquidity risk, market risk, operational risk, rate of return risk, displaced commercial risk, and contract-specific risk;[106] general governance and *Shari'a* governance disclosures;[107] and the treatment of 'Islamic Windows'.[108] **19.63**

The 'Islamic Window' [109]

In jurisdictions, such as the DIFC, regulators allow firms, which are not IFFs, to offer *Shari'a* compliant products and services without the need to apply to become full IFFs.[110] Firms achieve this by operating an 'Islamic Window', ie a part of the firm's business through which the firm can offer *Shari'a* compliant products and services. **19.64**

As it does for IFFs, AAOIFI emphasises the importance of a *Shari'a* Supervisory Board and, where a firm chooses not to have a SSB, the need to disclose the fact:[111] **19.65**

> Institutions offering Islamic financial services shall declare that such services are in compliance with *Shari'a* requirements, and are therefore required to: (a) appoint a [SSB] which shall present a *Shari'a* report; and (b) implement the Governance Standards issued by AAOIFI that relate to the [SSB].
>
> In the exceptional cases where the institution does not appoint a [SSB], which shall be with the approval of the regulatory and supervisory bodies, the institution shall disclose the following: (a) reasons for not appointing a [SSB]; (b) how the institution shall comply with *Shari'a* rules and principles in implementing the financial services it offers; (c) the body that approves the services offered in (b) above.[112]

In addition to the importance of the SSB, AAOIFI highlights the need for a firm to ensure that it keeps its Islamic business separate from its non-Islamic business: **19.66**

(a) Institutions shall disclose whether or not they commingle funds relating to Islamic financial services with funds relating to conventional financial services.

[102] IFSB CAS, s B.3, generally, and IFSB CAS, ss C.1–C.7, which go into detail for each contract.
[103] IFSB PTMDS, s 2.
[104] IFSB PMTDS, s 3.
[105] IFSB PMTDS, s 4.
[106] IFSB PMTDS, s 5.
[107] IFSB PMTDS, s 6.
[108] IFSB PMTDS, s 7. Islamic Windows are discussed in para 19.64 *et seq.*
[109] For further discussion of Islamic Windows, see 'Islamic Financial Institutions and Islamic Finance', (n 54) para 47 *et seq.*
[110] See the Law Regulating Islamic Financial Business, DIFC Law No 13 of 2004, as amended, Arts 9, 11, and 12 and Henderson 'Limiting the Regulation of Islamic Finance', (n 9) p 215.
[111] SSBs are discussed in para 19.68 *et seq.*
[112] ibid, para 6.

(b) Institutions shall disclose, in detail, the sources and applications of funds mobilised and invested by their Islamic financial services and the sources of funds used to cover a deficit if it occurs.
(c) Institutions shall disclose any revenues or expenditures prohibited by *Shari'a* rules and principles related to funds mobilised according to *Shari'a* rules and principles, and the disposition of any such revenues. The latter shall be determined by the [SSB].
(d) Institutions shall disclose any reserves deducted from the funds mobilised according to *Shari'a* rules and principles, the purposes of such reserves and to whom these reserves shall revert in case the activities, in respect of which such reserves were deducted, have ceased.
(e) Institutions shall disclose the percentage amount of the funds relating to Islamic financial services in comparison to the percentage amount of funds relating to conventional financial services.
(f) The disclosure requirements stated in Financial Accounting Standard No. (1) General Presentation and Disclosure in the Financial Statements of Islamic Banks and Financial Institutions should be observed.[113]

19.67 As is the case with IFFs, the FSA does not prescribe any special requirements for a firm wishing to operate an Islamic Window and has stated that it does not expect operations conducted by conventional firms through an Islamic Window to require separate permissions on the assumption that the firm has authorisation; the question will be whether additional permission is required. If a new branch is established to operate as the Islamic Window, the branch will require both authorisation and permission.[114] However, as is the case with an IFF, a firm's failure or inability to put in place internal systems and controls that adhere to internationally recognised or developing standards for the operation of an Islamic Window could have damaging commercial consequences, irrespective of any express or implied regulatory duty to follow such standards. In this regard, AAOIFI has set out a standard for Islamic Financial Services Offered by Conventional Financial Institutions.[115] However, as set out above, compliance with the IFSB standards would not, as a matter of law, serve as a defence to FSA enforcement action or establish a legitimate expectation for an IFF that the FSA would not take action against it.[116]

The *Shari'a* Supervisory Board

Introduction

19.68 The FSA earlier identified the role of the SSB as one that the FSA would consider in examining an IFF's activities.[117] The FSA did not impose any express requirements on IFFs with respect to SSBs but described the key features of SSB scholars as ensuring *Shari'a* compliance

[113] ibid, para 7.
[114] 'Islamic Finance in the UK', (n 11) p 10.
[115] AAOIFI Financial Accounting Standard No 18.
[116] See para 19.19.
[117] 'Islamic Finance in the UK', (n 11) p 13. See also Hainsworth, 'Governance Rules for Islamic Financial Institutions: the New Frontier', (2007) 22 *JIBFL* 515 and Aldohini 'Islamic Banking Challenges Modern Governance: the Dilemma of the *Shari'a* Supervisory Board' (2008) *Company Lawyer* 156.

in all an IFF's products and transactions, examining a new product or transaction and, if satisfied that it is *Shari'a* compliant, issuing its approval.[118]

AAOIFI defines a SSB as follows: **19.69**

> A *Shari'a* Supervisory Board is an independent body of specialised jurists in *Figh Almua'maiat* (Islamic commercial jurisprudence). However, the *Shari'a* supervisory board may include a member other than those specialised in *Figh Almua'maiat*, but who should be an expert in the field of Islamic financial institutions and with knowledge of *Figh Almua'maiat*. The *Shari'a* Supervisory Board is entrusted with the duty of directing, reviewing and supervising the activities of the Islamic financial institution in order to ensure that they are in compliance with Islamic *Shari'a* Rules and Principles. The *Fatawa*, and rulings of the *Shari'a* Supervisory Board shall be binding on the Islamic financial institution.[119]

The regulation of an IFF's SSB

As discussed above, the FSA indicated that, it would not be appropriate to judge between different interpretations of the *Shari'a* made by SSBs.[120] The FSA did not, therefore, seek to regulate the substance of an SSB's activities. The FSA had indicated, however, that it would expect to know, from an operational and a financial perspective, exactly what role an SSB will play in an IFF and, in particular, whether and how the SSB affects the running of the IFF.[121] **19.70**

In its application to become PRA and/or FCA authorised, an IFF would need to indicate to PRA and/or FCA whether the members of the IFF's SSB were intended to play an executive role or an advisory role.[122] **19.71**

Where, the SSB members were intended to play an executive role: **19.72**

- The IFF would need to apply to the PRA or FCA for each member to be an approved person. The candidate SSB member would need to satisfy the requirements set out in the Handbook of rules and guidance relevant to approved persons, including the requirements as to competence and capability.[123] In this regard, the each candidate SSB member would need to have relevant experience.[124]
- An SSB typically plays an active role in an IFF's day-to-day operations. For that reason the role of each member of the SSB in the IFF would be more likely to resemble the role of an executive director than a non-executive director. The IFF would also need to demonstrate that, where a SSB member was also a member of another IFF's SSB, this would not give rise to a conflict of interest.[125]

---

118 'Islamic Finance in the UK', (n 11) p 13.

119 AAOIFI Governance Standard for Islamic Financial Institutions No 1, para 2. The IFSB echoes the final requirement by recommending that IFFs comply with the rulings of the IFF's SSB. (See Guiding Principles on Corporate Governance for Institutions Offering Only Islamic Financial Services, December 2006, Principle 3.2.) It is submitted that this requirement would need to be read subject to the IFF's duty not comply with the rule or ruling of any national regulator to which it was subject.

120 'Islamic Finance in the UK', (n 11) p 13.

121 ibid.

122 ibid.

123 FIT 2.2.

124 'Islamic Finance in the UK', (n 11) p 13.

125 ibid. The FSA indicated that it would be difficult to justify multiple memberships of SSBs of different IFFs because of significant conflicts of interest. The FSA highlighted the fact that this would put further constraints on an industry already facing a shortage of *Shari'a* scholars with suitable skills.

19.73 Where the SSB members are intended to play more of an advisory role, then the IFF would not need to apply for each member to be an approved person.[126] There is no controlled function of 'member of a SSB'. The SSB members' competence should, however, be relevant in assessing whether an IFF is fit and proper to be PRA and/or FCA authorised. Other jurisdictions take a different approach. For example, in Bahrain membership of an SSB is a controlled function.[127]

Compliance with AAOIFI Governance Standards to demonstrate compliance with senior management systems and controls requirements?

19.74 In Bahrain, the CBB takes a similar approach to that in the UK in that it does not seek to regulate the substance of an SSB's activities. The CBB does, however, regulate the manner in which a SSB carries on its activities. Every IFF regulated by the CBB must establish an independent SSB complying with AAOIFI's Governance Standards for Islamic Financial Institutions, No 1 and No 2. That requirement is a component of CBB 'Principle for Businesses 10—Management, Systems and Controls', the text of which is similar to that of Principle for Businesses 3.[128] The CBB also requires every IFF to have a separate *Shari'a* review function to verify the SSB's compliance with the AAOIFI's Governance Standards. The review function must itself comply with AAOIFI's Governance Standards for Islamic Financial Institutions, No 3 and must be part of the IFF's internal audit function.[129] Although the FSA, unlike the CBB, has not imposed any express requirements or sought to determine standards with respect to the manner in which a SSB carries out its functions, such standards could be relevant in the context of regulation by the PRA and/or FCA of an IFF's senior management systems and controls. In this respect, AAOIFI's Governance Standards could serve as a useful guide for an IFF seeking to determine appropriate standards for the functioning of its SSB.

19.75 AAOIFI recommends, amongst other things, that:

- Every IFF should have a SSB appointed by the shareholders in their annual general meeting upon the recommendation of the board of directors; the IFF should properly document the SSB's appointment and fix its remuneration; the SSB should consist of at least three members, none of whom should be directors or significant shareholders of the IFF; any SSB member's dismissal should be subject to the approval of the IFF's shareholders in a general meeting; and the SSB should prepare a written report.[130]
- Every IFF should ensure that its SSB undertakes a '*Shari'a* Review', ie an examination of an IFF's compliance with the *Shari'a*. AAOIFI sets out standards and provides guidance to assist IFF's SSB in performing its *Shari'a* Reviews but emphasises that the *Shari'a* Review

[126] This turns on the issue of whether in issuing their *Futwa*, it could be said that the SSB members were not carrying on the regulated activity of 'advising on investments'.

[127] CBB Rulebook, Volume 2: *Islamic Banks, High Level Controls*, HC-2.1.2.

[128] 'Islamic bank licensees' board of directors and *Shari'a* Boards (where applicable) and management must take reasonable care to ensure that their affairs are managed effectively and responsibly, with appropriate systems and controls in relation to the size and complexity of their operations. Islamic bank licensees' systems and controls, as far as reasonably practical, must be sufficient to manage the level of risk inherent in their business and ensure compliance with the CBB Rulebook. In particular, the CBB requires that banks comply with AAOIFI issued accounting standards as well as *Shari'a* pronouncements issued by the *Shari'a* Board of AAOIFI.' CBB Rulebook, Volume 2: *Islamic Banks, High Level Controls*, HC-1.3.15.

[129] CBB Rulebook, Volume 2: *Islamic Banks, High Level Controls*, HC-1.3.16.

[130] See AAOIFI Governance Standard for Islamic Financial Institutions No 1, para 3 *et seq.*

does not relieve the IFF's management of their duties to ensure that the IFF undertakes all its transactions in accordance with the *Shari'a*. AAOIFI also sets out detailed requirements with respect to: the *Shari'a* Review procedures; quality assurance; and the report which the SSB should prepare upon completion of the *Shari'a Review*.[131]

- Every IFF should ensure that it appoints personnel to undertake an 'Internal *Shari'a* Review' to ensure that the IFF's management discharge their responsibilities in relation to the implementation of the *Shari'a* rules and principles as determined by the IFF's SSB. Unlike the *Shari'a* Review, the SSB does not undertake the Internal *Shari'a* Review. Instead, the IFF must entrust the Internal *Shari'a* Review to IFF personnel who should not have any executive authority or responsibility for the activities which they review and should enjoy a status within the IFF not lower than that of the IFF's internal audit or control department. The IFF Internal *Shari'a* Review should receive IFF management's full and continuous support. AAOIFI also sets out detailed requirements with respect to: the staffing and supervision of the Internal *Shari'a* Review function; a code of ethics for staff; staff knowledge, skills and experience; continuing education and training; due professional care; scope of work; performance of the review, including examining and evaluating Internal *Shari'a* Review information, reporting and follow up; management of the Review process; quality assurance; and the elements of an effective Internal *Shari'a* Review.[132]

The Regulatory Classification of *Shari'a*-compliant Products and Services

CIS regulation and *Shari'a*-compliant arrangements

Although the FSA did not identify Collective Investment Schemes ('CIS') regulation as a general issue in the context of Islamic finance, confining its discussion of the impact of CIS regulation in the context of *Sukuk*,[133] the impact of CIS regulation on the regulatory classification of *Shari'a*-compliant arrangements cannot be overlooked. The issue is particularly acute in light of: (a) the broad definition of CIS in FSMA;[134] (b) the principles of mutual cooperation, one of the general principles of Islamic business ethics and norms;[135] (c) the sharing of profits which underpins arrangements such as *Mudaraba* and *Musharaka*. **19.76**

FSMA defines a CIS as follows: **19.77**

> (1) ... any arrangements with respect to property of any description, including money, the purpose or effect of which is to enable persons taking part in the arrangements (whether by becoming owners of the property or any part of it or otherwise) to participate in or receive profits or income arising from the acquisition, holding, management or disposal of the property or sums paid out of such profits or income.

[131] See AAOIFI Governance Standard for Islamic Financial Institutions No 2.
[132] See AAOIFI Governance Standard for Islamic Financial Institutions No 3. AAOIFI also sets out its recommendations for audit and governance committees responsible for overseeing an IFF's financial reporting. (See AAOIFI Governance Standard for Islamic Financial Institutions No 4.)
[133] 'Islamic Finance in the UK', n 11, p 25. For discussion of collective investment schemes generally, see earlier this chapter.
[134] FSMA, s 235.
[135] See further Ayub, (n 1) p 68.

(2) The arrangements must be such that the persons who are to participate ('participants') do not have day-to-day control over the management of the property, whether or not they have the right to be consulted or to give directions.
(3) The arrangements must also have either or both of the following characteristics:
 (a) the contributions of the participants and the profits or income out of which payments are to be made to them are pooled;
 (b) the property is managed as a whole by or on behalf of the operator of the scheme.
(4) If arrangements provide for such pooling as is mentioned in subsection (3)(a) in relation to separate parts of the property, the arrangements are not to be regarded as constituting a single collective investment scheme unless the participants are entitled to exchange rights in one part for rights in another.[136]

19.78 Acknowledging the definition's breadth, FSMA empowers the Treasury to provide, by order, that arrangements do not amount to a collective investment scheme (a) in specified circumstances; or (b) if the arrangements fall within a specified category of arrangement.[137] The relevant Treasury Order in this regard is the Financial Services and Markets 2000 (Collective Investment Schemes) Order 2001 (the Treasury CIS Order)[138] and its Schedule lists 21 categories of 'arrangement not amounting to' a CIS.[139]

19.79 The classification of an arrangement as a CIS means that those establishing and operating the arrangement would need to be FCA authorised.[140] Moreover, anyone wanting to promote the arrangement to the public would be unable to do so because the arrangement would be an 'unregulated CIS'.[141] Finally, persons appointed to manage the arrangement would need to be FCA authorised.[142]

19.80 As set out further later in this chapter,[143] the regulatory definition of a *Shari'a* compliant product as a specified investment, other than a unit in a CIS, may place it outside the scope of the CIS regime because it falls within a CIS Treasury Order exclusion. Generally, the person looking to avail himself of a relevant CIS Treasury Order exclusion would need to be FSA authorised: in order to carry on business with respect to the specified investment that allowed the person to benefit from the exclusion, the person would need to be FSA authorised with respect to that investment. However, as mentioned above, a product's classification as an unregulated CIS could limit the scope of anyone's marketing efforts with respect to that

---

136 FSMA, s 235.
137 FSMA, s 235(5).
138 SI 2001/1062, as amended.
139 For discussion see earlier this chapter. In addition, there is a risk that, from 22 July 2013 they would also have to take steps to become authorized as alternative investment fund managers within the meaning of the Alternative Investment Fund Managers Directive 2011/61/EU (AIFMD). In this respect, the definition of 'alternative investment fund' in art 1.1(a) requires, inter alia, the raising of capital from a number of investors with a view to investing it in accordance with a defined investment policy for the benefit of those investors. Moreover, the AIFMD would only apply to 'alternative investment funds' in respect of which the activities of 'portfolio management' or 'risk management' are performed. (See art 4.1(w) and Annex 1.1.) The CIS definition potentially creates more concerns however any arrangement would need to be examined also to see whether it is subject to the AIFMD. (See FSA CP12/32 and 13/9 on the implementation of the AIFMD in the United Kingdom. CP13/9 seeks to address the treatment of *Sukuk* under the AIFMD. (See n 186.) For discussion of the AIFMD generally, see Chapter 4.
140 As they carry on the regulated activity of establishing, etc a collective investment scheme (RAO, art 51).
141 See FSMA, s 238 and the discussion in Chapter 19.
142 As they carry on the regulated activity of managing investments (RAO, art 37) or advising (RAO, art 53.) See further, Chapter 19.
143 See para 19.82.

product and the person would find himself subject to parts of the Handbook which it would otherwise prefer to avoid.[144] Moreover, some entities, such as the issuers or originators of *Sukuk*, might want to avoid FCA authorisation altogether. Therefore, the issue of classification as a CIS should be one that anyone offering a *Shari'a* compliant investment based on money acceptance arrangements, profit sharing arrangements, capital market arrangements, mutual assistance arrangements, or some miscellaneous arrangements will need to consider as a threshold issue.[145] In this respect, it is perhaps important to note that, where an IFF seeks to argue that the particular product which it seeks to offer should not require it to seek PRA and FCA authorisation to carry on a particular regulated activity, such as accepting deposits, it could nevertheless find itself becoming regulated as a CIS. The application of the CIS regime to various investments is considered in the discussion of the particular investments in the following.[146]

Money acceptance arrangements as 'deposits'

The RAO[147] defines a 'deposit' as a 'sum of money paid on terms under which it will be repaid, with or without interest or premium, and either on demand or at a time or in circumstances agreed by or on behalf of the person making the payment and the person receiving it; and which are referable to the provision of property (other than currency) or services or the giving of security'.[148] The RAO, therefore, captures money acceptance arrangements designed to avoid the charging of interest, such as the *Al Wadi'a* or *Qard*, structured such that the IFF is the borrower, referred to earlier, or any other interest-free deposit account. On the basis that the IFF sought to mobilise any funds accepted in order to lend the money to others or to finance its own activities, the PRA and FCA would need to authorise an IFF looking to offer clients products or facilities which involved the IFF accepting and holding money on an interest-free basis by way of business. **19.81**

For the purposes of excluding an *Al Wadi'a* or *Qard* from the CIS definition, their definition as a deposit within the meaning of the RAO is important because paragraph 3 of the Schedule to the Treasury CIS Order excludes 'pure deposit-based schemes' from the definition of a CIS.[149] **19.82**

Profit sharing investment accounts as 'deposits'

Unlike, for example, the DIFC, in the UK there is no regulated activity of 'operating a Profit Sharing Investment Account' ('PSIA') and neither the Treasury nor the PRA or FCA has expressly identified a 'PSIA' as a specified investment,[150] although its general characteristics would cause it to fall within the definition of a CIS.[151] The FSA identified the main issue in its authorisation of the Islamic Bank of Britain ('IBB'), the UK's first wholly Islamic retail bank, as the definition of deposit insofar as the IBB originally proposed a *Mudaraba*, a type of PSIA.[152] As set out earlier, under a *Mudaraba*, the *Rab Al Mal*, as the account holders, and the **19.83**

144 For discussion of the sections of the FSA Handbook relevant to a CIS, see Chapter 19.
145 The issue should not generally arise in the context of deferred payment techniques.
146 See para 19.81 *et seq.*
147 FSMA (Regulated Activities) Order 2001 (SI 2001/544) as amended.
148 See RAO, art 5(2).
149 For discussion, see Chapter 17.
150 See DFSA Rulebook: *General Module*, rule 2.2.2 and rule 2.21.
151 This is discussed in para 19.85.
152 'Islamic Finance in the UK', (n 11) p 14.

Mudarib, normally an IFF as manager, share in the profits on a pre-agreed basis with the *Rab Al Mal* bearing the risk of any loss and the *Mudarib* being liable for any loss only as a result of its misconduct, negligence, or breach of any conditions governing the *Mudaraba*. For the FSA, this was inconsistent with the definition of 'deposit' under the RAO, which requires capital certainty because a fundamental characteristic of a *Shari'a*-compliant 'deposit' is that the 'depositor' should take some risk on the underlying asset in which the 'deposit-taker' invests the money deposited with it.[153] The same concern would arise where a PSIA was structured as a *Wakala*.[154]

19.84 The solution adopted by the FSA and IBB whereby, legally, depositors under a *Mudaraba* would be entitled to full payment, thereby satisfying the RAO requirements and enjoying the protection offered with respect to a 'protected deposit' continues to apply.[155] However, account holders would have the right to turn down the deposit protection on religious grounds and choose instead to be repaid under the risk sharing formula under the PSIA.[156] The same approach should be acceptable in the context of a PSIA structured as a *Wakala*.

19.85 The classification of PSIAs as deposits within the meaning of the RAO excludes them from the definition of a CIS on the basis that they are pure deposit-based schemes within the meaning of the paragraph 3 of the Schedule to the Treasury CIS Order.[157] Discussing the authorisation of IBB and the treatment of PSIAs as deposits, the FSA suggested that this may not necessarily be appropriate in other contexts.[158] This suggests that it would not be always be appropriate for the PRA to treat a PSIA or PSIA type product as a 'deposit' for authorisation purposes.[159] Even if this were the case, a PSIA, whether structured as a *Mudaraba* or a *Wakala*, has characteristics which would bring it within the FSMA definition of a CIS.[160] Ultimately, the IFF and the PRA will need to determine which category of specified investment most accurately captures the commercial nature of the product or service that the IFF wishes to offer.[161] In practice, it may be that the IFF applies for PRA and FCA authorisation both to accept deposits and to operate a CIS. Irrespective of how the PRA chooses to classify a PSIA, an IFF's operation of a PSIA may have certain conduct of business consequences for the IFF.[162]

[153] ibid. See also FSA Briefing Note BNO 16/06.

[154] As set out in para 19.53, the *Wakala* may be contrasted with the *Mudaraba* in that the investor alone shares any profit or loss, with the *Waki*, the manager under a *Wakala* getting a fixed management fee, whereas, in the case of a *Mudaraba*, both the *Rab Al Mal* and the *Mudarib* share any profits or losses.

[155] See COMP 5.3.1R and Chapter 8.

[156] 'Islamic Finance in the UK', (n 11) p 14. See also the Finance Act 2005, s 49 which describes *Mudaraba* arrangements as 'alternative finance arrangements: deposits'.

[157] For discussion, see para 17.25.

[158] 'Islamic Finance in the UK', (n 11) p 14.

[159] See para 19.7.

[160] FSMA, s 235. In the DIFC, eg, the DFSA's CIF Rules (CIR), rule 4 excludes a PSIA from the definition of 'collective investment fund' (CIF). The definition of CIF in art 15 of the DIFC Collective Investment Fund Law, DIFC Law No 1 of 2006 is almost identical to the definition of CIS in FSMA, s 235 and the list of exclusions the CIR, rule 4 similar to those in the Treasury CIS Order. Depending on its structure, a PSIA could fall within the 'individual investment management arrangements' in the Treasury CIS Order, para 1. (See para 17.26.)

[161] The FSA suggested this in 'Islamic Finance in the UK', (n 11) p 14.

[162] These are discussed in para 19.111.

Islamic mortgages[163]

In 2007, the Treasury amended the RAO to include two new types of home financing arrangements: the 'home purchase plan' ('HPP') and the 'home reversion plan'.[164] The amendment was designed to capture *Ijara* home financing arrangement under the definition of HPP to 'ensure a level regulatory playing field within the equity release market and within the *Sharia* [sic] compliant home financing market'.[165] *Ijara* arrangements do not fall within the definition of 'regulated mortgage contract'[166] because, as discussed earlier, ownership of the property financed under an *Ijara* remains with the IFF offering finance for the term of the *Ijara* and not with the person selling the property. As set out in the following,[167] the HPP definition brings *Ijara* and other financing services and products, where ownership of the property remains with the IFF, within the RAO's scope. **19.86**

The RAO identifies entering into a regulated HPP as home purchase provider as a specified kind of activity.[168] It defines an HHP as: **19.87**

> An arrangement comprised in one or more instruments or agreements, in relation to which the following conditions are met at the time it is entered into: (i) the arrangement is one under which a person (the 'home purchase provider') buys a qualifying interest or an undivided share of a qualifying interest in land (other than timeshare accommodation) in the United Kingdom; (ii) where an undivided share of a qualifying interest in land is bought, the interest is held on trust for the home purchase provider and the individual or trustees mentioned in... (iii) below as beneficial tenants in common; (iv) the arrangement provides for the obligation of an individual or trustees (the 'home purchaser') to buy the interest bought by the home purchase provider over the course of or at the end of a specified period; and (v) the home purchaser (if he is an individual) or an individual who is a beneficiary of the trust (if the home purchaser is a trustee), or a related person, is entitled under the arrangement to occupy at least 40% of the land in question as or in connection with a dwelling during that period, and intends to do so.[169]

An IFF would need to determine whether a particular *Shari'a*-compliant home financing product had the characteristics of a HPP and if so ensure that the PRA and/or FCA authorised it to carry on the regulated activity of entering into an HPP as home purchase provider or administering an HPP. In this respect, an *Ijara* or Diminishing *Musharaka* arrangement should fall within the definition of an HPP.[170] However, a *Murabaha* arrangement should not because it does not involve a homeowner buying the property from the IFF on deferred payment terms and would be classified as a 'regulated mortgage contract'.[171] To offer a full range of Islamic mortgage services and products, an IFF would, therefore, need to apply to the FCA for authorisation to carry on activities both with respect to HPPs and regulated mortgage contracts. **19.88**

---

[163] See Patient 'Islamic Finance in the UK Consumer Sector' (2008) *JIBLR* 9 and Hainsworth, 'Islamic Financial Institutions and Islamic Finance', (n 54) para 77(iv) and paras 91 *et seq.*

[164] FSMA (Regulated Activities) (Amendment) (No 2) Order 2006, SI 2006/2383.

[165] See 'Secondary Legislation for the Regulation of Home Reversion and Home Purchase Plans: a Consultation', March 2006, para 3.1.

[166] See RAO, art 61, and Chapter 13.

[167] See paras 19.87 *et seq.*

[168] RAO, art 63F(1). 'Administering' an HHP is also a specified activity. (See RAO, art 63F(2) and (3)(b).) See also the FSA guidance on HPPs in PERG 14.4.

[169] RAO, art 63F(3).

[170] See PERG 14.2, Q2.

[171] RAO, art 61(3). See PERG 14.4, Q25.

The regulatory classification of other financing arrangements

19.89 On the face of it, the deferred payment contracts such as *Istisna'a*, which involves a forward sale contract, or *Salam*, which involves immediate payment for goods with deferred delivery fall within the RAO definition of a 'future', defined as 'rights under a contract for the sale of a commodity or property of any other description under which delivery is to be made at a future date and at a price agreed on when the contract is made'.[172] In both cases, however, the parties and their advisers would need to ask whether the contracts were entered into for 'investment purposes' or 'contractual purposes'. If the parties can show that a contract is made for commercial purposes, it will not be a 'future'.[173] In this respect, Article 84 of the RAO states:

(3) A contract is to be regarded as made for investment purposes if it is made or traded on a recognised investment exchange, or is made otherwise than on a recognised investment exchange but is expressed to be as traded on such an exchange or on the same terms as those on which an equivalent contract would be made on such an exchange.

(4) A contract not falling within paragraph (3) is to be regarded as made for commercial purposes if under the terms of the contract delivery is to be made within seven days, unless it can be shown that there existed an understanding that (notwithstanding the express terms of the contract) delivery would not be made within seven days.

(5) The following are indications that a contract not falling within paragraph (3) or (4) is made for commercial purposes and the absence of them is an indication that it is made for investment purposes—

(a) one or more of the parties is a producer of the commodity or other property, or uses it in his business;

(b) the seller delivers or intends to deliver the property or the purchaser takes or intends to take delivery of it.

(6) It is an indication that a contract is made for commercial purposes that the price, the lot, the delivery date or other terms are determined by the parties for the purposes of the particular contract and not by reference (or not solely by reference) to regularly published prices, to standard lots of delivery dates or to standard terms.

19.90 The fact that, for *Istisna'a* and *Salam* arrangements to be valid under the *Shari'a*, the parties must intend to make and take physical delivery of the assets subject to the arrangements, is an indicator that the contracts are made for a commercial purpose.[174] Under an *Istisna'a* arrangement, the fact that one party is the manufacturer of the assets which are delivered upon completion, thereby using it in its business, may also be an indicator that the contracts are made for a commercial purpose.[175] The fact that under both *Istisna'a* and *Salam* arrangements, generally, the contract terms are individually negotiated and the parties determine the price and delivery date, as opposed to determining them by reference to a regularly published price, standard lots or delivery, or to standard terms, will indicate that the contracts are

[172] RAO, art 84(1).

[173] RAO, art 84(2) which states: 'There are excluded from [art 84(1)] rights under any contract which is made for commercial and not investment purposes'.

[174] RAO, art 84(5)(a). The intention to make and take physical delivery is determined at the time that the contract is made. See *CR Sugar Trading Ltd (in administration) v China National Sugar & Alcohol Group* [2003] EWHC 79 (Comm), para 39.

[175] RAO, art 84(5)(b). The parties will have to determine this by reference to the specific facts: an entity that is in the business of purchasing and selling a commodity cannot be said to use that commodity in its business. See *CR Sugar Trading Ltd (in administration) v China National Sugar & Alcohol Group*, (n 174) para 21.

made for a commercial purpose.[176] In practice, it may be that the IFF applies for PRA and/or FCA authorisation to carry on regulated activities with respect to futures where it wishes to offer *Istisna'a* or *Salam* products or services.

As set out earlier, a PSIA could fall within the definition of a CIS. Other profit-sharing arrangements, such as the *Musharaka*, could also fall within the CIS definition depending on how the parties structure them. On its face, a *Musharaka* should satisfy: (a) the 'arrangements', 'property', and 'purpose or effect' conditions in FSMA, section 235(1);[177] and (b) the 'pooling' or 'management as a whole' condition in FSMA, section 235(3).[178] The question of whether any participant in the *Musharaka* relinquishes 'day-to-day control' within the meaning of FSMA, section 235(2) will, however, be one of fact.[179] Where the 'management' of a *Musharaka* or Diminishing *Musharaka* arrangement, for example, in the context of trade financing,[180] may be an activity that is undertaken jointly by the IFF and client, it may be possible for the parties to a *Musharaka* to argue that 'day-to-day control' remains with both parties and, therefore, the arrangement is not a CIS. Alternatively, a particular arrangement could fall within the 'schemes entered into for commercial investment purposes related to existing business' exclusion, depending on its structure.[181] Finally, it is difficult to identify a relevant exclusion in the CIS Treasury Order which would exclude *Musharaka*. Again, in practice, it may be that the IFF applies for FSA authorisation to operate a CIS to give it the most freedom possible to structure and offer *Shari'a*-compliant financing arrangements. **19.91**

Sukuk

Because *Sukuk* originators seek to avoid the interest-bearing structures, *Sukuk* have different legal structures from conventional debt instruments. As set out earlier, *Sukuk* can have different structures capable of being classified in various ways. Potentially, this makes it difficult to classify them in a uniform 'one-size-fits-all', both in the context of any PRA and/or FCA authorisation and for listing purposes. **19.92**

On the face of it, most *Sukuk* arrangements fall within the CIS definition in FSMA, section 235: (a) the *Sukuk* certificate holders participate in or receive profits or income arising from the assets on which the *Sukuk* are based; (b) the *Sukuk* certificate holders do not have day-to-day control of the assets; (c) the *Sukuk* certificate holders' contributions are pooled in order to investment in the property, eg purchase the property; and (d) the property is managed by the operator of the vehicle, which has purchased the property, or is delegated to a third party, possibly the original owner of the property.[182] **19.93**

Therefore, in the absence of a relevant Treasury CIS exemption, the PRA and/or FCA could treat a *Sukuk* vehicle established in the UK as a CIS and require the *Sukuk* manager to be PRA and/or FCA authorised to establish, operate, and wind up a CIS.[183] Moreover, since it **19.94**

[176] RAO, art 84(6).
[177] See para 17.09 *et seq.*
[178] See para 17.22 *et seq.*
[179] See para 17.17 *et seq.*
[180] See Ayub, (n 1) pp 332–43.
[181] See para 17.36.
[182] See Henderson, 'Testing the Water' (2007) ILFR, September: <http//:www.iflr.com>; 'Islamic Finance in the UK', (n 11) p 25; and 'Consultation on the legislative framework for the regulation of sukuk' at p 10 which can be found at: <http://www.hm-treasury.gov.uk> (the '*Sukuk* Consultation').
[183] See, 'Islamic Finance in the UK', (n 11) p 26, and the *Sukuk* consultation, (n 181) p11.

is unlikely that *Sukuk* could be structured as units in an 'authorised fund',[184] the PRA and/or FCA would classify them as units in an 'unregulated CIS' which, as already discussed, has the disadvantage that generally they cannot be promoted to the public.[185]

19.95 *Sukuk* are, however, typically structured to have the same economic characteristics as conventional debt instruments, albeit in a *Shari'a*-compliant manner. Treating *Sukuk* as units in a CIS would mean treating *Sukuk* issuers differently from the issuers of conventional debt instruments, thereby (a) placing them at a competitive disadvantage, and (b) ignoring the economic reality of *Sukuk* where the risks and rewards are equivalent to conventional debt instruments.[186]

19.96 In order to address the issues mentioned, the Treasury CIS Order creates a specific exclusion, alongside the 'Debt Issues' exclusion,[187] for 'alternative finance investment bonds' ('AFIBs'). An AFIB is a specified investment identified in the RAO.[188] It has the following characteristics:

(a) it must provide for a bond holder to pay capital to a bond-issuer;
(b) it must identify assets, or a class of assets, which the bond-issuer will acquire for the purpose of generating income or gains directly or indirectly;
(c) it must specify a period at the end of which it ceases to have effect ('the bond term');
(d) the bond issuer must undertake to repay the capital ('the redemption payment') to the bond holder during or at the end of the bond-term (whether or not in installments), and to pay to the bond holder other payments on one or more occasions during or at the end of the bond term;
(e) the amount of the additional payments must not exceed an amount which would be a reasonable commercial return on a loan of the capital; and
(f) the AFIB must be listed on a recognised investment exchange.[189]

---

[184] See para 17.84 *et seq.*

[185] The classification of *Sukuk* as units may also have an impact in the context of the purchase or offer to purchase *Sukuk* in order to stabilise their price after a primary or secondary offering (Stabilisation). Those performing Stabilisation activities with respect to *Sukuk* may be unable to comply with EU Regulation (EC) 2273/2003 (Buy-back and Stabilisation Regulations) because the Buy-back and Stabilisation Regulations govern 'relevant securities', which the Buy-back and Stabilisation Regulations define as 'transferable securities', within the meaning of Directive (EC) 2001/34 (ISD). Although this includes 'bonds and other forms of securitised debt' (see Title 1, Art 1, (4)), it does not include units. It would not therefore be able to perform Stabilisation in accordance with MAR 2.2.1R which provides a 'safe harbour' from market abuse proceedings (see MAR 2.2.3R). MAR 2.2.5G may offer relief. It states that 'the mere fact that stabilisation does not conform with the provisions in the Buy-back and Stabilisation Regulations or with MAR 2.2.1R(2) will not of itself mean that the behaviour constitutes markets abuse'. This should be read in light of the definition of 'financial instruments' in section C of Directive (EC) 2004/39 (MiFID), which includes 'units in collective investment undertakings' (see para (3)).

[186] See Henderson, 'Testing the Water', (n 183) and 'Government Sterling Sukuk Issuance: a Response to the Consultation', (n 18) p 29. For taxation purposes, the Finance Act 2005, s 48B(5) states expressly that *Sukuk* or 'alternative investment bonds', as *Sukuk* are described, are to be treated differently from, inter alia, a unit trust scheme for the purposes of the Taxation of Chargeable Gains Act 1992.

[187] The 'Debt Issues' exclusion in the CIS Treasury Order is discussed at para 17.32 above. In CP13/9, the consultation on the implementation of the AIFMD, the answer to Question 2.45 in draft PERG 16 indicates that the FCA would not consider the issuer of an AFIB to be an alternative investment fund manager.

[188] RAO, art 77A. An issuer of *Sukuk* should, however, be able to rely on the exclusion in art 18, RAO for a company issuing its own securities.

[189] ibid. See also the Finance Act 2005, s 48A in terms of which an AFIB, which is economically equivalent to a conventional debt security, is treated in the same way as a conventional debt security for both income and corporation tax purposes.

This definition is focused on *Sukuk* which are *asset-based*, where investors take risk on the creditworthiness of the *Sukuk* originator. It does not include *Sukuk* which are *asset-backed*, where investors take risk on an identified pool of assets and would, therefore, not apply to a *Shari'a* compliant securitisation. It is, however, arguable that a *Shari'a* compliant securitisation would generally be closer in structure to conventional securitisation than *Sukuk* would be to conventional debt instruments: the payments under each would, generally, be determined by reference to a fixed asset or pool of fixed assets. *Sukuk* under a *Shari'a* compliant securitisation should, therefore, enjoy the exclusions afforded securities under a conventional securitisation. In any event, the principle of non-discrimination would render it unfair to require the parties to a *Shari'a*-compliant securitisation to become FCA authorised where the parties to a conventional securitisation were not.[190] **19.97**

The consequence of designating *Sukuk* as specified investments for RAO purposes, whether expressly or by necessary implication, is that anyone carrying on a regulated activity with respect to *Sukuk* would require FSA authorisation to avoid breaching the General Prohibition.[191] In the context of an entity looking to carry on activities by way of business with respect to *Sukuk*, this is not an unfair result and, indeed, the principle of non-discrimination would require it. For the issuers and originators of *Sukuk*, the RAO excludes a company's issue of its own AFIBs from the RAO definition of 'dealing in investments as principal'.[192] Without including AFIBs within this exclusion, it would have been unfair to exclude *Sukuk* issuers and originators from the CIS regime only to have them fall within the regime for dealing in investments as principal.[193] **19.98**

Shari'a-compliant derivatives[194]

As set out earlier, the *Shari'a* does not permit conventional derivatives because they may infringe the prohibitions on *Gharar* and *Maisir* or *Quimar*.[195] However, IFFs may offer *Shari'a* compliant products which have a derivative effect. For example, IFFs can create put and call options using *Arbun* contracts,[196] futures or forwards using *Salam* contracts,[197] and **19.99**

190 The distinction between asset-based and asset-backed *Sukuk* is also important in the context of the categorisation for listing purposes, which is discussed in para 20.113.

191 FSMA, s 21.

192 RAO, art 18.

193 See Henderson, 'Testing the Water', (n 183), the *Sukuk* Consultation, (n 182) p 11 and 'Government Sterling Sukuk Issuance: a Response to the Consultation', (n 18) pp 29–30. In the DIFC, the DFSA excludes *Sukuk* from the definition of collective investment fund in art 15 of the Collective Investment Fund Law, DIFC Law No 1 of 2006. DFSA Rulebook: *Offered Collective Investment Rules*, Rule CIR 2.3.9 states: 'Arrangements do not, for the purposes of Article 15 of the Law, amount to a Collective Investment Fund if the arrangements are arrangements under which the rights or interests of the participants are evidenced by *Sukuk* certificates where the holders of the certificates are entitled to rely on the credit worthiness of: (a) the issuer of the *Sukuk* certificates; or (b) any other Person who has assumed obligations under the *Sukuk* certificates, for obtaining their rights and benefits arising under the certificates'. The DFSA's exclusion focuses on *Sukuk* which are *asset-based*, where investors take risk on the creditworthiness of the *Sukuk* originator; it does not include *Sukuk* which are *asset-backed*, where investors take risk on an identified pool of assets. It also acknowledges the fact that in a *Sukuk* structure, the issuer may not also be the originator and, therefore, the creditworthiness on which investors will rely is not necessarily that of the issuer of the *Sukuk*.

194 See further Hainsworth, 'Islamic Financial Institutions and Islamic Finance', n 54, para 35 *et seq.* and Naumowicz and Atkinson, 'Close-out Netting and *Shariah*-compliant Derivatives' (2007) 22 JBIFL 245.

195 See paras 19.28 and 19.30.

196 See para 19.49. There is, however, debate as to the validity of the *Arbun* as a mechanism for creating an option. (See Ayub, (n 1) pp 145 and 116.)

197 See para 19.44.

contracts for differences combining *Murabaha* and *Wa'ad*,[198] whereby the parties enter into purchase undertakings that replicate the two-way cash flows that one would encounter under a conventional contract for differences. In addition, IFFs may offer foreign currency trading services in accordance with 'AAOIFI *Shari'a* Standard No 1—Trading in Currencies'.[199] In all cases, the products and services will be structured so as to include the sale or purchase of physical commodities.[200] Insofar as these *Shari'a*-compliant products and services have a derivative effect, an IFF that wished to offer these services by way of business in the UK would need to be PRA and/or FCA authorised to undertake regulated activities relating to commodity futures, commodity options on commodity futures, contracts for differences, futures, options, rights to or interests in contractually based investments, and rolling spot forex contracts.[201]

Takaful

19.100 The RAO defines a 'contract of insurance' in very broad terms.[202] The FCA summarise the description of an insurance contract as an enforceable contract under which a 'provider' undertakes: (a) in consideration of one or more payments; (b) to pay money or provide a corresponding benefit to a 'recipient'; (c) in response to a defined event the occurrence of which is uncertain and adverse to the interests of the recipient.[203] The characteristics of *Takaful*, as discussed above, suggest that a *Takaful* contract would generally fall within the definition of 'a qualifying contract of insurance': in this respect, the emphasis by the FCA on substance over form is noteworthy.[204] However, the analysis does not stop there: insofar as an IFF used *Mudaraba* or *Wakala* arrangements to offer *Takaful*, it is likely the PRA would require it to be authorised to accept deposits.[205] Therefore, an IFF that wished to offer *Takaful* products, would need to be PRA and FCA authorised,[206] and have permission to effect or carry out contracts as principal, limited to the appropriate classes of insurance set out in the Third Non-life Directive[207] and Schedule 1 to the RAO,[208] or the types of life insurance identified in the Third Life Directive[209] and Schedule 2 to the RAO, as appropriate.[210]

19.101 For the purposes of excluding *Takaful* from the CIS definition, their definition as a qualifying contract of insurance within the meaning of the RAO is important because paragraph 17 of the Schedule to the Treasury CIS Order excludes 'contracts of insurance' from the definition of a CIS.[211]

---

198 See paras 19.42 and 19.52.

199 *AAOIFI Shari'a Standards* (2004–5), p 1 *et seq.* See Ghuddah et al., (n 1) pp 45–9.

200 See the example of a Shari'a compliant swap discussed in the context of *Murabaha* in para 19.42.

201 See, eg, details of the permission for European Islamic Investment Bank Plc (438537) published in the Financial Services Register; <http://www.fsa.gov.uk/register/home.do>.

202 RAO, art 3(1). See Chapter 16.

203 PERG 6.3.4G.

204 See PERG 6.5.4(3)G.

205 See, eg, details of the permission for Principle Insurance Company Limited (467853) published on the Financial Services Register; <http://www. fsa.gov.uk/register/home.do>.

206 See the PRA RAO, art 2(b) and (c) which identify the activities of effecting a contract of insurance as principal and carrying out a contract of insurance as principal, respectively, as PRA regulated activities.

207 Council Directive (EEC) 92/49. See Chapter 16.

208 See, the details of the FSA permission for Principle Insurance Company Limited, (n 204).

209 Council Directive (EEC) 92/96. See Chapter 16.

210 See, the details of the permission for Principle Insurance Company Limited, n 181 above. For discussion of the regulated activities relating to insurance, see para 14.90 *et seq.*

211 For discussion of home finance transactions geneally, see Chapter 17.

Regulating an IFF's Conduct of Business

Introduction

On the basis that the FCA operates a non-discriminatory regime, IFFs will be subject to the same conduct of business requirements as conventional firms according to the type of services which the IFFs offer, eg wholesale or retail investment business, banking business, or insurance business. The mortgage regime under MCOB is currently the only regime with some special provisions for IFFs that offer HPPs and is discussed later in this chapter.[212] However, the FSA had indicated that financial promotion and disclosure requirements for IFFs was an area of particular interest.[213] In addition, the issue of suitability and the extent to which an IFF's duties with respect to its client may extend to ensuring that a product is in fact *Shari'a* compliant is also an area worthy of discussion. Finally, the experience in other jurisdictions with respect to the treatment of PSIAs provides a useful guide to the issues which a PRA and FCA regulated IFF may need to address in order to comply with the FSA Principles for Businesses.[214] **19.102**

Financial promotion and disclosure

The FSA identified two features of *Shari'a*-compliant products and services which reinforce the need for IFFs to ensure that risks are appropriately disclosed in the context of the duty of an IFF under Principle 7 to ensure that its communications are 'clear, fair and not misleading':[215] (a) the novelty of *Shari'a*-compliant products and services and the fact that they differ from conventional products and services;[216] and (b) the relative inexperience of the users of *Shari'a*-compliant products and services.[217] **19.103**

The issue of clear communications may have an important commercial role to play for an IFF that wishes to sell its services or products to customers looking for *Shari'a*-compliant services and products where an IFF would, in practice, need to point to facts to demonstrate that the products and services which it offers are *Shari'a* compliant. In this respect, the disclosures surrounding the systems and controls, which an IFF has put in place to ensure that its products and services are *Shari'a* compliant, assume a central position in an IFF's conduct of its business. Although the FSA did not state it, the need for an IFF to disclose to customers the systems and controls, ie the *Shari'a* scholars, which it has in place to ensure *Shari'a* compliance could be viewed as a necessary component of an IFF's duty to communicate sufficient information about the IFF's products and services to enable a customer to decide whether the products and services satisfy the customer's own *Shari'a* requirements. Without the PRA or FCA's own scholars, or other scholars identified by any regulator, the judgement of whom **19.104**

[212] See para 19.108 *et seq*.

[213] 'Islamic Finance in the UK', (n 11) p 11.

[214] See also the CBB's special requirements for *Takaful* and *Retakaful* firms set out in CBB Rulebook, Volume 3: *Insurance*, Chapter CA-8.

[215] See PRIN 2.2.1.

[216] This implies that investors could confuse a *Shari'a*-compliant product or service for a conventional product or service and assume that the *Shari'a* compliant product or service had the same or similar features and, therefore, same or similar risk profile as the conventional product or service.

[217] This seems to imply that the scarcity of *Shari'a*-compliant products and services, until recently, means that, by definition, the number of inexperienced users of such products or services is far less than the users of conventional products and services. It fails to take into account the possibility that Muslims might use conventional products and services. 'Islamic Finance in the UK', (n 11) p 14.

a customer could assess, the customer must be put in the best position possible to assess the effectiveness and credentials of the IFF's *Shari'a* scholars.

19.105 The full disclosure approach is that taken, for example, in the DIFC where the DFSA sets out a single requirement for an IFF with respect to the marketing and promotion of *Shari'a*-compliant products and services: before an IFF communicates any marketing material to a person, it must ensure that, in addition to the information that a conventional firm must include in any marketing material, the IFF must ensure that the material governing *Shari'a*-compliant products or services state which SSB has reviewed the products or services.[218]

19.106 Another example of such disclosure, albeit more comprehensive, is that under the Saudi Arabia Capital Market Authority Investment Fund Regulations which require the manager of an investment fund established in Saudi Arabia which is 'stated to be operated in accordance with the principles of *Shari'a*' to disclose: '(a) the identity and qualifications of the *Shari'a* committee members; (b) whether those members are compensated for their advice and the nature and source of any compensation provided; and (c) the criteria used to determine the eligibility of investments for the investment fund'.[219]

The suitability of *Shari'a*-compliant investments

19.107 The FCA requires a firm that carries on designated investment business to take reasonable steps to ensure that a 'personal recommendation' or a decision to trade, is suitable for the firm's client.[220] The question for an IFF is whether this duty includes the duty to ensure that a designated investment is *Shari'a* compliant. The FCA defines a 'personal recommendation' by reference to the regulated activity of 'advising on investments', ie advice on the merits of, inter alia, buying a designated investment.[221] In this context, there is an argument to say that, where a person carries on the activity of 'advising on investments' which are *Shari'a* compliant, the regulatory definition assumes or presupposes the *Shari'a*-compliant nature of the investments and does not include it within the scope of the definition of advising.[222] Against this is the requirement on a firm to obtain from its client such information as is necessary for the firm to understand the essential facts about the client and have a reasonable basis for believing, giving due consideration to the nature and extent of the service provided, that the specific transaction to be recommended, or entered into in the course of managing, inter alia, meets the client's investment objectives.[223] Even if an IFF's duties to ensure that a designated investment is suitable extend to the requirement to ensure that the investment is *Shari'a* compliant, that duty should be no greater than the duty that the FCA would impose on it with respect to ensuring *Shari'a* compliance, ie that the IFF or another IFF has subjected the investment to SSB scrutiny and the SSB has issued the appropriate *Fatwa*.[224]

---

[218] See the DFSA Rulebook: *Islamic Finance Module*, Rule 6.1.5 and Henderson 'Limiting the Regulation of Islamic Finance', (n 9) p 217.

[219] Annex 1. The official translation is contained at: <http://www.cma.org.sa>.

[220] COBS 9.2.1R.

[221] See RAO, art 53.

[222] This is the approach which the CBB takes in defining 'advising on *Shari'a* compliant financial instruments', the wording of which is similar to RAO, art 53. (See CBB Rulebook, Volume 2: *Islamic Banks*, Rule LR-1.3.45.)

[223] COBS 9.2.2R.

[224] Ultimately, the issue should be one of contract determined by the precise nature of the service that the IFF, like any other firm, offers. (See, eg, *JP Morgan Chase Bank and others v Springwell Navigation Corp* [2008] EWHC 1186.)

Special considerations for IFFs offering Islamic mortgages[225]

The regime for those firms that offer mortgages under MCOB applies to IFFs that offer HPPs.[226] However, MCOB contains special provisions for IFFs. The FSA described the effect of its regulation of IFFs that offer HPPs as follows: 'It allows us to deliver a level consumer protection playing field with products designed for similar purposes. It also builds on the work that we have already done in the field of Islamic financial services, to improve consumer access to these products.'[227] **19.108**

The special requirements for IFFs under MCOB include the requirement that an IFF ensure that the interests of its customer under an HPP are protected to a reasonable standard.[228] It also requires an IFF to pay due regard to the interests of its customer and treat him fairly when drafting or amending the terms of, or imposing obligations or exercising rights or discretions under an HPP.[229] **19.109**

MCOB prohibits an IFF firm entering into a HPP transaction or agreeing to do so with a customer unless the customer has submitted an application for the particular HPP.[230] MCOB requires the IFF to provide its customer with an appropriate financial information statement for an HPP before the customer submits an application for the HPP and without due delay when the IFF makes a personal recommendation to the customer to enter into an HPP (unless the personal recommendation is made by telephone, in which case an IFF must ensure the financial statement is or has been provided as soon as practicable after the telephone call); the IFF provides written information that is specific to the amount of finance to be provided on a particular plan; or the customer requests written information from the IFF that is specific to the amount of finance to be provided on a particular HPP, unless the IFF does not wish to do business with the customer.[231] MCOB sets out the requirements for the format and content of the financial information statement.[232] An IFF must ensure that its customer has had a reasonable opportunity to consider the financial information statement and risks and features statement before committing the customer to an application.[233] **19.110**

Special considerations for IFFs offering PSIAs

The FSA does not set out any specific requirements for IFFs that offer PSIAs, either by way of *Mudaraba* arrangements or *Wakala* arrangements. The operation of PSIAs, however, offers special challenges for an IFF because the IFF has to balance properly the interests of the PSIA holders against those of the IFF as PSIA manager. In this respect, there is a potential conflict of interest between PSIA and an IFF's shareholders as higher dividend payments to the shareholders may be at the expense of profits that would otherwise accrue to the PSIA holders. In Bahrain, for example, in its 'Principles of Business' for Islamic Banks, the CBB requires an **19.111**

225 See also Patient 'Islamic Finance in the UK Consumer Sector', (n 162) p 9.
226 MCOB 1.2.1R.
227 See FSA/PN041/2006, which accompanied FSA CP06/08 'The Regulation of Home Reversion and Home Purchase Plans'.
228 MCOB 2.6A.1R. For discussion of the protection of customer interests in the context of early redemption, see Hainsworth 'Islamic Financial Institutions and Islamic Finance', (n 54) para 95 *et seq*.
229 MCOB 2.6A.8R.
230 MCOB 5.3.1R.
231 MCOB 5.8.1R.
232 See MCOB 5.8.4R *et seq*.
233 MCOB 5.8.11R.

Islamic bank licensee's management: (a) as part of their duties to observe high standards of integrity and fair dealing under 'Principle 1—Integrity', to 'safeguard not only the interests of the shareholders of the bank but also those of the PSIA holders';[234] and (b) as part of their duties to identify, prevent, or manage conflicts of interest under 'Principle 2—Conflicts of Interest', to 'bear in mind the interests of shareholders and PSIA holders'.[235] There is no reason why the same considerations would not arise for IFFs under the FSA Principles for Businesses governing the same subjects in Principles 1 and 8, respectively, as well as its duty to treat customers fairly under 'Principle 6—Customer's Interests'.[236]

19.112 The CBB also requires Islamic banks to insert minimum terms and conditions in PSIA contracts and a statement of policies and procedures to safeguard the interests of PSIA holders and a policy dealing with the following: (a) the basis for allocation of profit or loss to the PSIA; (b) a policy for making provisions and reserves against assets and equity for PSIAs and to whom these provisions and reserves revert in case of write-back or recovery;[237] (c) a policy on the priority for investment of own funds and those of unrestricted PSIA holders; and (d) the basis for allocating expenses to the PSIA.[238]

The Listing and Public Offer of *Shari'a*-Compliant Securities

The classification of *Sukuk*

19.113 The classification of *Sukuk* under the RAO would not necessarily determine how they would be classified for listing purposes.[239] In practice, the UKLA assesses the *Sukuk* structures in relation to the underlying assets, examining such factors as the on/off balance sheet nature of the assets and the nature of the cash flows that the assets generate. Currently, the Listing Rules and Prospectus Rules would appear to give the UKLA the ability to treat *Sukuk* in a manner consistent with the economic substance and underlying risk without the need for a specific definition of *Sukuk* for listing purposes.[240]

19.114 The UKLA have been able to classify asset-based *Sukuk* where investors take risk on the creditworthiness of the *Sukuk* originator as 'debt securities', ie debentures, debenture stock, loan stock, bonds, certificates of deposit, or any other instrument creating or acknowledging indebtedness, for the purposes of the Listing Rules subject to appropriate additional

[234] CBB Rulebook, Volume 2: *Islamic Banks*, Rule PB-1.1.1.

[235] CBB Rulebook, Volume 2: *Islamic Banks*, Rule PB-1.1.2.

[236] See para s 5.16 *et seq*.76.

[237] IFSB CAS, s B.4 sets out the requirements for PSIAs to make adequate capital adequacy provisions for its PSIAs. Para 76 deals with the concept of 'displaced commercial risk' which it defines as 'the risk arising from assets managed on behalf of [PSIA holders] which are effectively transferred to the [IFF's] own capital because the [IFF] follows the practice of foregoing part or all of its *Mudarib* share of profits on such funds, when it considers this necessary as a result of commercial pressure in order to increase the return that would otherwise be payable to the PSIA holder'. The CBB, DFSA, and QFCRA set out special prudential and capital adequacy requirements for PSIA holders.

[238] CBB Rulebook, Volume 2: *Islamic Banks, Business and Market Conduct Module*, Rule BC-7.1. The CBB must agree the statement.

[239] In this respect, the position in Saudi Arabia is noteworthy. In its Glossary of Defined Terms used in the Regulations and Rules of the Capital Market Authority, the Capital Market Authority states that 'the definition of "share" includes every instrument having the characteristics of equity, including *Sukuk*'. (The official translation is contained at <http://www.cma.org.sa>.) However in practice, *Sukuk* are listed on the debt list of the *Tadawul*, the Saudi Arabia stock exchange. See <http://www.tadawul.com.sa>.

[240] See 'Islamic Finance in the UK', (n 11) p 26.

information requirements.[241] If the performance of the *Sukuk* is directly related to the performance of an underlying asset, ie asset-backed *Sukuk* where investors take risk on an identified pool of assets as opposed to taking risk on the creditworthiness of the *Sukuk* originator, then the UKLA is likely to treat them as 'asset-backed securities'.[242]

Disclosure standards

With respect to disclosure standards, the UKLA does not impose any special requirements. The extent to which it can be said that the details of how an issuer or originator can say that particular *Sukuk* are *Shari'a* compliant should form part of the information which investors and their professional advisers would reasonably require and reasonably expect to find in a prospectus, in order to make any investment decision,[243] is an open question. However, in, for example, the DIFC, the DFSA requires the issuer of securities, which are held out as being *Shari'a* compliant, to disclose details of: (a) the members of the SSB appointed by the issuer who have undertaken a review of the securities; and (b) details of the qualifications and experience of each of the SSB members.[244] Although there is no express requirement under the PR or any other relevant FCA rule for the issuer or originator of *Sukuk* to disclose details of the SSB that approved the *Sukuk*, commercial considerations may, in any event, drive the issuer or originator to do so.[245] **19.115**

Continuing obligations

The UKLA does not impose any special continuing obligations for *Sukuk* issuers in addition to those for the issuers of conventional securities. The continuing obligations relevant to issuers of debt securities or asset-backed securities should also apply to issuers of *Sukuk*.[246] **19.116**

---

[241] ibid. LR 17 and PR Appendix 3 govern the listing requirements and disclosure requirements for debt securities, respectively. See Chapter 9. At the time of writing (September 2008), the UKLA has treated all *Sukuk* listed in the UK as guaranteed debt.

[242] The Prospectus Directive Regulation (No 2004/809/EC) defines 'asset-backed securities' as securities which: (a) represent an interest in assets, including any rights intended to assure servicing, or the receipt or timeliness of receipts by holders of assets of amounts payable thereunder; or (b) are secured by assets and the terms of which provide for payments which relate to payments or reasonable projections of payments calculated by reference to identified or identifiable assets. LR 17 also governs the listing of asset-backed securities but the disclosure requirements under PR Appendix 3 differ. The capital adequacy requirements in BIPRU 9 would apply to an IFF and any other firm with exposures under a *Shari'a* compliant securitisation.

[243] FSMA, s 80(1).

[244] DFSA Rulebook: *Offered Securities Module*, Rule OSR A1.1.1, para 25.

[245] The issues are the same as those discussed in the context of financial promotion and disclosure in para 20.103 *et seq*.

[246] The continuing obligations do not, however, apply to the originator in *Sukuk* tractions. *Sukuk* transactions commonly use a Special Purpose Vehicle ('SPV') to issue the *Sukuk* and the continuing obligations apply to the SPV rather than the originator. The regime is, therefore, less burdensome for the originator of a *Sukuk* as compared to a conventional debt instrument and may be an area for amendment.

information requirements.[241] If the performance of the *Sukuk* is directly related to the performance of an underlying asset, ie asset-backed *Sukuk* where investors take risk on an identified pool of assets as opposed to taking risk on the creditworthiness of the *Sukuk* originator, then the UKLA is likely to treat them as asset-backed securities.[242]

Disclosure standards

19.115 With respect to disclosure standards, the UKLA does not impose any special requirements. The extent to which it can be said that the details of how an issuer or originator can say that particular *Sukuk* are *Shari'a* compliant should form part of the information which investors and their professional advisers would reasonably require, and reasonably expect to find in a prospectus, in order to make any investment decision,[243] is an open question. However, in, for example, the DIFC, the DFSA requires the issuer of securities, which are held out as being *Shari'a* compliant, to disclose details of: (a) the members of the SSB appointed by the issuer who have undertaken a review of the securities; and (b) details of the qualifications and experience of each of the SSB members.[244] Although there is no express requirement under the PR or any other relevant FCA rule for the issuer or originator of *Sukuk* to disclose details of the SSB that approved the *Sukuk*, commercial considerations may, in any event, drive the issuer or originator to do so.[245]

Continuing obligations

19.116 The UKLA does not impose any special continuing obligations for *Sukuk* issuers in addition to those for the issuers of conventional securities. The continuing obligations relevant to issuers of debt securities or asset-backed securities should also apply to issuers of *Sukuk*.[246]

[241] Ibid. LR 17 and PR Appendix 3 govern the listing requirements and disclosure requirements for debt securities, respectively. See Chapter 9. At the time of writing (September 2008), the UKLA has treated all *Sukuk* listed in the UK as guaranteed debt.

[242] The Prospectus Directive Regulation (No 2004/809/EC) defines 'asset backed securities' as securities which: (a) represent an interest in assets, including any rights intended to assure servicing, or the receipt or timeliness of receipts by holders of assets of amounts payable thereunder; or (b) are secured by assets and the terms of which provide for payments which relate to payments or reasonable projections of payments calculated by reference to identified or identifiable assets. LR 17 also governs the listing of asset-backed securities but the disclosure requirements under PR Appendix 3 differ. The capital adequacy requirements in BIPRU 9 would apply to an IPF and any other firm with exposures under a *Shari'a* compliant securitisation.

[243] FSMA, s 80(1).

[244] DFSA Rulebook, *Offered Securities Module*, rule OSR A7.1.1, para 23.

[245] The issues are the same as those discussed in the context of financial promotion and disclosure in para 20.103 *et seq*.

[246] The continuing obligations do not, however, apply to the originator in *Sukuk* transactions. *Sukuk* transactions commonly use a Special Purpose Vehicle (SPV) to issue the *Sukuk* and the continuing obligations apply to the SPV rather than the originator. The structure is therefore less burdensome for the originator of a *Sukuk* as compared to a conventional debt instrument and may be a useful tool for investment.

INDEX